A History of Newfoundland from the English, Colonial and foreign records. ... With ... illustrations and numerous maps.

Daniel W. Prowse

A History of Newfoundland from the English, Colonial and foreign records. ... With ... illustrations and numerous maps.
Prowse, Daniel W.
British Library, Historical Print Editions
British Library
1895
xxiii, 742 p. ; 8°.
9555.f.9.

The BiblioLife Network

This project was made possible in part by the BiblioLife Network (BLN), a project aimed at addressing some of the huge challenges facing book preservationists around the world. The BLN includes libraries, library networks, archives, subject matter experts, online communities and library service providers. We believe every book ever published should be available as a high-quality print reproduction; printed on- demand anywhere in the world. This insures the ongoing accessibility of the content and helps generate sustainable revenue for the libraries and organizations that work to preserve these important materials.

The following book is in the "public domain" and represents an authentic reproduction of the text as printed by the original publisher. While we have attempted to accurately maintain the integrity of the original work, there are sometimes problems with the original book or micro-film from which the books were digitized. This can result in minor errors in reproduction. Possible imperfections include missing and blurred pages, poor pictures, markings and other reproduction issues beyond our control. Because this work is culturally important, we have made it available as part of our commitment to protecting, preserving, and promoting the world's literature.

GUIDE TO FOLD-OUTS, MAPS and OVERSIZED IMAGES

In an online database, page images do not need to conform to the size restrictions found in a printed book. When converting these images back into a printed bound book, the page sizes are standardized in ways that maintain the detail of the original. For large images, such as fold-out maps, the original page image is split into two or more pages.

Guidelines used to determine the split of oversize pages:

- Some images are split vertically; large images require vertical and horizontal splits.
- For horizontal splits, the content is split left to right.
- For vertical splits, the content is split from top to bottom.
- For both vertical and horizontal splits, the image is processed from top left to bottom right.

A

HISTORY OF NEWFOUNDLAND

FROM THE

English, Colonial, and Foreign Records

BY

D. W. PROWSE, Q.C.

Judge of the Central District Court of Newfoundland

WITH A PREFATORY NOTE BY EDMUND GOSSE

*WITH THIRTY-FOUR COLLOTYPES, OVER THREE HUNDRED TEXT
ILLUSTRATIONS, AND NUMEROUS MAPS*

London

MACMILLAN AND CO.

AND NEW YORK

1895

LONDON:
EYRE AND SPOTTISWOODE,
Her Majesty's Printers.

CONTENTS.

	PAGE
SUBJECTS OF CHAPTERS	iii
LIST OF FULL-PAGE ILLUSTRATIONS	viii
PREFATORY NOTE BY EDMUND GOSSE	ix
INTRODUCTION	xiii

CHAPTER I.

THE PRE-COLUMBIAN DISCOVERY OF AMERICA 1

Traditions of early voyages, 1—The Northmen, 1—Their colonisation of Greenland, 1—Discovery of America, 2.

CHAPTER II.

REIGN OF HENRY VII. (1485–1509) 4

The new birth of the world, 5—Cabot's charter, voyages, and landfall, 8—Other early English charters, 13—Cortereal's voyages, 14—England's share in the new fishery, 15—Life on the coast, 19—The Iceland fishery, 24—Ayala's letter to Spain, 29—Sebastian Cabot, 29.

CHAPTER III.

REIGN OF HENRY VIII. (1509–1547) 31

Henry's commercial policy, 32—First Act relating to America, 33—Ships and shipbuilding, 35—Voyages of Verrazano, Rut, Hore, Gomez, Cartier, and Roberval, 37—Commencement of Basque fishing, 43—Early knowledge of the Gulf of St. Lawrence, 46—The Basque fishery, 47—The French Newfoundland fishery, 49.

CHAPTER IV.

REIGNS OF EDWARD VI., MARY, AND ELIZABETH (1547–1603) . . . 51

Acts of Edward and Elizabeth, 53, 55—Character of the Elizabethan Age, 54—Earliest settlements on the coast, 56—A great free trade market, 58—Winter crews, 59—Parkhurst, 60—Hampshire, 61—Whitbourne, 62—Beothics, 63—Whaling, 63—Gilbert's expedition, 66—Raleigh, 75—Peckham's "Brief Discourse," 76—Sir B. Drake's expedition, 79—The Armada, 81—Its effect on the fishery, 83—Charter party, licence to export, and insurance on Newfoundland fish, 84.

1 p. 2729.

CONTENTS.

CHAPTER V.

REIGN OF JAMES I. (1603-1625) 86

The commencement of English colonisation, 87—Spanish opposition, 88—New England, 89—Guy's colony, 91—Piracy on the coast, 102—Mason, 104—His account of the Island, 105—The Six Colonies, 109—Vaughan's plantation, 110—Lord Baltimore's early settlements, 112—Whitbourne's Vice-Admiralty Court, 114—His book, 116—Lord Falkland's proposals, 119—The Act for freer fishing, 121—London and Bristol Co.'s Charter, 122—Guy's and Colston's letters, 125—Wynne's, Powell's, and N. H.'s letters to Baltimore, 128—Charter of Avalon, 131—Lord Baltimore, 132—Beothics, 133.

CHAPTER VI.

REIGN OF CHARLES I. (1625-1649) 134

Vaughan's "Golden Fleece," 135—Hayman's proposals, 137—Star Chamber Rules, 139, 154—Louis XIV.'s Rules, 139—Kirke's charter, 140—Sallee rovers, 145—Kirke's tyranny, 147—French fishermen taxed, 148—Downing made Governor, 150—New England trade, 152—Sir D. Kirke, 155.

CHAPTER VII.

THE COMMONWEALTH (1649-1660) 158

The beneficent policy of Cromwell, 159—Commissioners, 161—Treworgie, the first real Governor, 163—Shipbuilding, 165.

CHAPTER VIII.

REIGN OF CHARLES II. (1660-1685) 170

The Restoration, 172—Attempt to administer justice, 173—Martin's defence of St. John's, 174—William Hinton, 175—The French occupation of Placentia, 176—The Basque fleet, 186—Child's proposals, 183—Parliamentary Report, 190—The attempted expulsion of settlers, 192—Dutch attacks, 197—New Englanders, 197—Irish fishermen, 201—Continued opposition to a settled Government, 201.

CHAPTER IX.

REIGNS OF JAMES II. AND WILLIAM III. (1685-1702) 209

The fishery, 210—Frontenac, 211—Williams attacks Placentia, 212—Holman's defence of Ferryland, 212—Nesmond attacks, and D'Iberville captures and destroys, St. John's, 213—William III.'s Act, 225—The Fishing Admirals, 226—Larkin's report, 228—Rev. J. Jackson, 229.

CONTENTS.

CHAPTER X.

REIGN OF ANNE (1702-1714) 235

Lord Dartmouth's report, 236, 266—Graydon's and Walker's attacks on Placentia, 237—French attacks on Bonavista, 239—M. Gill, 241—Latham's defence of Fort William against Subercase, 244—English attack on the Petit Nord, 246—St. Ovide's capture of St. John's, 248—The effect of the wars upon the fishery, 250—Major Lloyd, 252—Captain Crowe and Sir N. Trevanion's laws, 254, 271—Treaty of Utrecht, 255—Account of the campaign of 1704, 261—The capture of St. John's in 1708, 268.

CHAPTER XI.

REIGN OF GEORGE I. (1714-1727) 274

Result of peace, 274—Placentia, 275—Biscayans, 276—Early English occupation north of Bonavista, 278—Difficulties with the French, 281—English rule at Placentia, 282.

CHAPTER XII.

REIGN OF GEORGE II. (1727-1760) 284

Fishery increasing, 285—Osborne appointed first Governor, 286—Attempts to levy taxes, 287—Difficulties of the new magistrates, 288—The fall of Louisbourg, 289—Lord Rodney, 290—Murder of Keen, 292—Local events, 293—Persecution of Roman Catholics, 293—New English church, 295—Williams's account of the fishery, 296—West Country bye-boat keepers, 297—The seal fishery, 298—Intercourse with New England, 299—The Molasses Act, 300—Justices in 1732, 301.

CHAPTER XIII.

REIGN OF GEORGE III. (1760-1820) 302

Captain Webb, 304—The capture and recapture of St. John's, 305, 412—The Treaty of Paris, 309—Captain Graves, 314—Local events, 315—Captain Cook's survey, 316—Interpretation of the French treaties, 318, 333, 337—The last of the Basques, 320—New England smugglers, 323—Labrador and the Eskimo, 324—Trade and population, 325—Legal abuses, 326—French and Indians, 327—Wesleyanism, 331—Moravian mission, 332—Hon. John Byron, 334—The Beothics, 334, 385—Lord Shuldham, 335—Titles to property, 336—Commodore Duff, 337—The American wars, 338, 388—Social conditions, 341—Palliser's Act, 344—The Bermudians, 345, 416—Governor Edwards, 349—The Treaty of Versailles, 352—Admiral Milbanke, 358—The Supreme Court, 359—Admiral Campbell, 362—Bishop O'Donel, 363—Prince William, 365—The French attack, 367—Lord Radstock, 372—The mutiny on H.M.S. *Latona*, 372—Admiral Gambier, 375—Sir E. Gower, 378—The truck system, 379—The Benevolent Irish Society, 381—James McBraire, 382—Sir J. T. Duckworth, 384—Removal of ships' rooms, 386—Sir R. Keats, 388—Colclough, 390—Titles granted for land, 395—Dr. Carson, 396—Faction fights, 401—The troubles of 1815-18, 403—The Winter of the Rals, 405—Admiral Pickmore, 406—The American Convention, 409—Butler and Lundrigan, 411—The Conspiracy of 1800, 418—The early seal fishery, 419.

CHAPTER XIV.

REIGNS OF GEORGE IV. AND WILLIAM IV. (1820–1837) 421

Act for the better administration of justice, 422—The opening of the Supreme Court, 423—Sir T. Cochrane, 424—Morris's pamphlet, 426—The agitation for a local legislature, 427—The first House of Assembly, 429—The struggle between the Upper and Lower Houses, 433—Contingency Bills, 434—Captain Prescott, 436—The deadlock in the legislature, 438—Appeal to the Privy Council, 438—P. H. Gosse, 439.

CHAPTER XV.

REIGN OF VICTORIA (1837–1857) 442

The Delegates to England, 443—Kielly v. Carson, 445—Sir John Harvey, 449—Hon. James Crowdy, 450—The spring seal fishery, 450—Spanish traders, 453—The Amalgamated House, 456—The Fire of 1846, 457—Sir J. G. Le Marchant, 462—The First Constitution again, 463—Governor Hamilton, 465—Responsible Government in 1855, 466—The French Convention of 1857, 471.

CHAPTER XVI.

REIGN OF VICTORIA (1857–1895) 481

Riots in Conception Bay, 483—Sir A. Bannerman, 484—The Burin contest, 485—Mr. Kent's administration, 485—The coastal steamer contract, 486—The Prince of Wales, 487—The dispute about poor relief and the currency, 488—The St. John's riot, 489—Steamers commence the seal fishery, 493—St. John's waterworks, 493—Confederation, 494—The Anglo-American pre-emption, 497—"Jim Dobbin" Commission, 499—Railway survey, 500—The Halifax Commission, 501—Railway construction, 506—Dry dock, 509—Rope factory, 510—Battle of Fox Trap, 512—The Harbour Grace riot, 513—The Placentia railway, 514—The Bait Act, 515—The Colonial Conference, 519—The Queen's Jubilee, 519—The Trinity Bay disaster, 520—The fire of 8th July, 521—The General Election of 1893, 529—The Blaine-Bond Convention, 533—The election petitions, 535—Black Monday, 536—The future of the Colony, 537.

CHAPTER XVII.

THE PRESENT POSITION OF THE FRENCH FISHERY QUESTION . . . 539

The Bait Act, 539—English and French lobster factories, 540—The French claim to sovereign rights on the Treaty shore, 541—Definition of the French privileges, 542—The proper mode of carrying out the Treaty, 546—French and English naval officers, 547—The "Modus Vivendi" of 1890, 548—The delegation to England, 550—The English resident population, 552—The effect of the "Modus Vivendi," 553—The present position of the French fishery, 554—Captain Campbell's report on the lobster factories on the west coast, 556.

CHAPTER XVIII.

ST. PIERRE AND MIQUELON, THE FRENCH COLONY 564

The early fishery, 566—The English occupation, 566—The Treaty of Paris, 567—The murder of McKeown, 567—Cassini's account of the fishery, 569—

CONTENTS.

PAGE

The Revolution, 572—The Jacobin Club, 573—The Committee of Public Safety, 574—The Acadians, 574—Major Thorne's dinner party, 574—The French smuggling trade with Newfoundland and Canada, 579—The confiscation of the schooner *Mary*, 581—The Admiral Governors, 581—The "Clapboard Revolution," 582—Chateaubriand's description of St. Pierre, 585—Statistics, 586.

CHAPTER XIX.

A HISTORY OF LABRADOR, UNDER THE JURISDICTION OF NEWFOUNDLAND . 587

The discovery of Labrador, 587—The Eskimo, 590—The Moravian Missions, 594—The Montagnais, 595—Brest, 596—The English fishery, 597—New Englanders in Labrador, 597—Cartwright's journal, 598—The expansion of the English fishery, 602—Dr. Grenfell's account of the Deep-sea Mission, 604—Northern Labrador, 605—The winter post to Ungava, 607—The summer mail service, 609—Mr. Bryant's description of the Grand Falls, 611—The Deep-sea Mission Report, 614—The Labrador trade, 616—The Census of 1891, 617—A. P. Low's survey, 618.

CHAPTER XX.

RAILWAY CONSTRUCTION IN THE COLONY 619

The primitive paths and common roads, 619—The Conception Bay Railway, 619—The Halls Bay Line, 620—The results of opening up the country, 620—The projected extension to Port-aux-Basques, 622—The failure of the first promoters, 693—The Reid contract for the Halls Bay Line, 624—The Northern and Western Railway, 626—Its probable effect on the fishery, 630—Opportunities for sport, 632.

CHAPTER XXI.

TELEGRAPHIC COMMUNICATION IN NEWFOUNDLAND 634

Bishop Mullock's letter, 634—F. N. Gisborne's overland line, 635—C. W. Field's ocean cable, 637—The Atlantic Cable and Heart's Content, by F. Perry, 642.

CHAPTER XXII.

THE NEWFOUNDLAND FISHERIES COMMISSION, by Rev. M. Harvey, LL.D. . 647

CHAPTER XXIII.

CHRONOLOGY, JUSTICIARY, AND HOUSE OF ASSEMBLY 652

CHAPTER XXIV.

BIBLIOGRAPHY, MSS., PLANS, RECORDS, AND NEWSPAPERS . . . 666

CHAPTER XXV.

STATISTICS OF TRADE, POPULATION, FINANCE, &c.; CLIMATE, SOIL, TIMBER, MINES AND MINERALS, SPORT AND GAME LAWS 692

INDEX 719

LARGE FOLDING MAP BY STANFORD.

LIST OF FULL-PAGE ILLUSTRATIONS.

	To face page
Views of Quidi Vidi, Logy Bay, and Torbay	10
"Harleyan" and P. Descellier's maps	40
D. Homem and John Dee's maps	58
Views of Clarke's Beach, Brigus, and Harbour Grace	104
,, ,, Topsail Head, Salmon Cove, and The Goulds, near Brigus	136
,, ,, Placentia from the Jersey side, Mount Pleasant, and the Ferry	182
Fitzhugh's map	198
Views of Woodlands, Salmonier, Little Bay, and Colinet Bridge	216
XVIIIth century plan of Bonavista	238
Views of Carbonear and Carbonear Island	244
Plan of Placentia in 1708	248
French fishing rooms at Red Island	256
Plan of St. John's in 1751	292
Military plans of Bois Island, Carbonear Island, St. John's, and Admiral's Beach, Trinity	296
General William Amherst	306
Old views of Long Pond, Conception Bay, and Port de Grave	326
View of St. John's, about 1770	348
Old views of The Narrow's, St. John's, Quidi Vidi, and Quidi Vidi Lake	360
View of St. John's in 1798, showing Fort Townshend	374
,, ,, Portugal Cove	393
,, ,, St. John's in 1848, and Greenspond in 1846	450
The town of St. John's previous to the fire of 1846	458
Landing of the Prince of Wales in 1860	486
Sealing vessels leaving St. John's in 1863, and sealing steamer *Vanguard*	492
St. John's from Riverhead, in 1891	522
St. John's after the fire of 1892	526
French rooms at Fishot Island, St. Julian's, and Cape Rouge Harbour	548
Views of St. Pierre	582
Exterior and interior of a Labrador livier's tilt	598
Labrador liviers at Huntingdon Sound, and Bartlett's crew making fish at Turnavik	604
Views of Whitely's rooms at Bonne Esperance, Labrador green fishers, and Cartwright	608
,, ,, Nichol's Farm, Deer Lake, Shoal Harbour, and Railway Bridge on the N. N. & W. Ry.	622
,, ,, Granite Quarry on the N. N. & W. Ry., Clode Sound, and Botwoodville, Exploits River	624
,, ,, the Humber and Little Rivers	628
,, ,, Bay of Islands, Flat Bay, Bay St. George, and Channel, near Port-aux-Basques	630

PREFATORY NOTE.

My friend, Judge Prowse, has asked me to introduce in a few prefatory words the important colonial history on which he has for so many years been engaged. There is really nothing for me to do but to conduct him down to the footlights, and then to retire with a bow to the audience. His own introduction, a succinct essay on the development of our earliest colony, is a document the importance and the interest of which should, as it seems to me, render any other preamble quite unnecessary. Yet I can but be touched by the kindness of his invitation, which stirs ancient memories in me, and if I accede to it, it is not from personal complacency, but because an old family tie with Newfoundland compels me to a pious interest in the colony. I write these few words because I am sure that, were he alive, my dear father would rejoice to do so.

In the early years of this century, Poole, in Dorsetshire, where my people lived, was almost an offshoot of Newfoundland. It was the English port and emporium of the colony, and each owed to the other a great part of its prosperity. Nothing could be more natural than that the lads of Poole should look to start in life at St. John's or Harbour Grace. Thus, in fact, more than one member of my family did start, and in particular my father, afterwards so widely known as Philip Henry Gosse, F.R.S. One Sunday, sixty-eight years ago, as the bells were ringing people to church in Poole, he was carried away, with a sinking heart, to a counting-house in

PREFATORY NOTE.

Carbonear. I need not repeat the twice-told tale of his innocent adventures there. As will be remembered, it was in Newfoundland that he began his zoological, and particularly his entomological, work, and the colony, as I have reason to know, has not been forgetful of her earliest naturalist.

In 1835 my father left Newfoundland, and soon afterwards the other members of my family also returned. We went no more a-roving on these cold western seas. But down to my own childhood the mystery of Newfoundland was preserved in the English home. Kegs of cranberries and of delicious capelin arrived from Harbour Grace as punctual as the seasons. A great oil painting of the port of Carbonear, more topographical than artistic, perhaps, more conscientious than æsthetic, hung in a sitting-room. Cases of insects, charts, and family stories kept alive the colonial sentiment, and our house in Devonshire was a tiny plantation of Newfoundland. It had been my father's wish and hope to revisit his old haunts, but his crossings of the Atlantic were not to be repeated. In his later years he anxiously collected all that threw light upon the antiquities of Newfoundland, and it is pathetic to me to realise with what ecstasy he and my uncle, Mr. William Gosse, who survived, at a very great age, until 1893, would have welcomed, would have devoured, Judge Prowse's admirable and exhaustive history. It is in their name that I come forward with these brief prefatory phrases.

At a fortunate moment, I think, Judge Prowse has brought out his chronicle of the most ancient and the most unfortunate of our colonies. He has found his material in records which are many of them entirely unpublished, and his book is an original and valuable contribution to early American history. The sorrows of Newfoundland have at last awakened the sympathy of the mother country, and Englishmen were never so ready as they now are to learn more about its inhabitants. To read the ensuing pages is to study a record of extraordinary struggle and vicissitude. Not now for the first or the dozenth time is Newfoundland in a forlorn condition. Frost and fire, the caprices of cod and whale and seal, have reduced her in past years, no doubt, to a far lower ebb than we find her in her present embarrassments. She has suffered much, and her geographical position requires that she should always stand prepared for suffering. But her spirit, we love to think, is indomitable, and if her natural resources are liable to collapse, they are not less liable to sudden and brilliant revival. It may be that before these words see the light, her fortunes will once more be in the rapid ascendant. The perusal of Judge Prowse's book can but increase the number of those who cordially desire that it may be so.

EDMUND GOSSE.

London, March 1895.

INTRODUCTION.

THIS work is an attempt to describe how England's first colony, Newfoundland, was founded and developed; to show the influence of its discovery on the making of England. My plan has been to cite contemporary documents, for the most part hitherto unprinted.

Newfoundland occupies nearly the same position in the new world that Britain does in the old. Stretching far out into the Atlantic, the nearest part of North America to Europe, she became the half-way house, the stepping-stone between the two continents; by her shore passed all the great discoverers and the flowing tide of European emigration which peopled North America. Here England first obtained a foothold in the new world, and laid the foundation of her Colonial Empire. For more than one hundred years Newfoundland was Britain's one and only Colony; her trans-Atlantic fishery the sole link that bound Europe to North America. This large trade was the nursing mother of England's maritime greatness; the long dangerous voyages to the new colony made her a nation of seamen. In this new Island of the West, Englishmen ruled the land only by constant fights with foreign fishermen; here they learnt to measure their strength with the Bretons and the Basques. The cod fishery was the training school for the conquest of the Invincible Armada, a much earlier training ground than the buccaneering and channel roving to which Mr. Froude, in a recent article, attributes our maritime supremacy.

The great English historians ignore altogether the part Newfoundland played in the making of England. Even in the picturesque pages of Froude, the epoch-making adventures of the daring West Country traders and cod fishers, who began the conquest and colonisation of a greater England in the new world, find no place; fortunately we have the testimony of Raleigh, the greatest statesman of his age, that the " Newfoundland fishery was the mainstay and support of the western " counties" (then the great maritime centre of England); " that a

"successful attack on the Newfoundland fleet would be the greatest
"misfortune that could befall England."

Beginning in a small way in 1498, year by year witnessed the rapid growth of this Newfoundland business, the accumulation of wealth, the constant building of larger ships; carried on almost by stealth from the West Country seaports, it is only by brief references in the chronicles and Acts of Parliament that we can trace the development of a great industry, which must necessarily have had immense influence on the maritime prosperity of the lesser England of the Tudor age, when the burthen of the whole Royal Navy was less than the tonnage of a modern first-class cruiser. The most remarkable part of this story is the supremacy and control exercised by these proud beef-eating Englishmen over the great host of foreign fishermen on the Island.

The history of their most ancient Colony should be of interest to Englishmen; not only does it contain the story of the dawn of English colonisation, the foundation of our Colonial Empire, the gradual development of England's naval power, it also throws new light on contemporary annals, and is really an important minor chapter in the history of England. In the policy pursued towards our Island we see reflected, not in a glass darkly, but clearly defined and paralleled, the characteristic moods of the various English sovereigns, and the rule, or rather misrule, of the Home Government. The quaint old chronicle of Weymouth, in which the Mayor has recorded his interview with the King about securing the Newfoundland fleet against the attacks of the Turkish pirates, gives us a vivid picture, a complete *coup d'œil*, of Laud and his sovereign.

To the early American settlers Newfoundland was the parent Colony, a meagre and haggard kind of mother, yet for all that she saved the ancient Colony of Virginia from semi-starvation by a timely cargo of fish. When the New York settlers first tried to establish a fishery at Sandy Hook, it was to this Colony they applied for appliances and men. The same Devonshire adventurers who traded to and colonised Newfoundland were the first to make a similar attempt in New England. The Newfoundland trade was by far the greatest English enterprise in America up to 1630. I have endeavoured to show the close connection between this ancient Colony and the young English settlements on the continent—the story of early struggles and mutual aid between Newfoundland and especially New England.

It must be borne in mind that from 1497 to the permanent settlement in Virginia and the landing of the Pilgrim Fathers in 1620, Newfoundland was the only Colony and the only possession in North America occupied and governed by Englishmen; this period of over a century is completely overlooked by American historians, as, only with reference to the discovery of Cabot, does it concern the early history of the American Colonies. At another period from 1713 to 1763, from the Treaty of Utrecht to the Treaty of Paris, there were virtually only two English Colonies in America, Newfoundland, and the continental Colonies, the nucleus of the present United States: the history of the trade and intercourse between these two British possessions is set forth in these pages. Very little attention has been paid to this subject by American writers; the records show how early in our history the parent Government became jealous of New England, her industries, and her growing trade with Newfoundland.

The history of the Colony is only very partially contained in printed books; it lies buried under great rubbish heaps of unpublished records, English, Municipal, Colonial, and Foreign, in rare pamphlets, old Blue Books, forgotten manuscripts, old English newspapers and magazines, and in the political tracts of the eighteenth century. The accounts of the defence of St. John's against D'Iberville, and the gallant fight of Captain Holman, are from affidavits made before Devonshire justices, the latter to get tardy payment from the Crown for the powder expended in defending the Colony.

I have attempted to reconstruct the true history of Newfoundland from these various documents, to bring to life again the dead and buried memories of the men who made the country, to recount the doughty deeds of the old Devon sailors who, against tremendous odds, retained this island for England without the slightest help from the Crown.

There is no mention, even in the latest works on the Colony, of the Act of Henry VIII., of Peckham, Mason, Vaughan, and Treworgie, John Downing's writings and appeal, the early intercourse with New England, the maps, plans, and views contained in the British Museum, the first Chief Justices, the irruption of the Bermudian planters with their slaves into the Bank fishery. The new information contained in this volume is the principal reason for its publication; my chief difficulty has been to condense the great mass of MSS. I have collected into reasonable compass, and give due proportion to each period and subject.

The history of Newfoundland may be roughly divided into four great epochs of nearly equal duration:—

> The early or chaotic era, from 1497 to 1610, when the Island was a kind of no man's land, without law, religion, or government, frequented alike by English and foreign fishermen, only ruled in a rough way by the reckless valour of Devonshire men, half pirates, half traders.

The Fishing Admiral period, from 1610 to 1711, a dismal time of struggle between the colonists and the western adventurers or ship fishermen from England. This may also be designated the colonisation period.

The Colony under Naval Governors, 1711 to 1825; the advent of the first resident Governor, Sir Thomas Cochrane.

The modern era, the struggle for autonomy.

For the early part of the sixteenth century our sources of information are meagre and often misleading; this is due mainly to the fact that information about the subject of our earliest history, the fishery, was no doubt kept secret by the traders for fear of the Government.

The general view of all writers has consequently been that England had neither lot nor part in the great fishery during the first half of this century. I have endeavoured to show that the evidence contained in the Acts of Henry VIII. and Edward VI., referring to an established fish trade in Newfoundland, the references in Hakluyt of Parkhurst and Hayes to the ancient rule of the English over Spanish, French and Portuguese, the decline of the Icelandic fishery from Bristol and the West of England immediately after the discovery of the New World, and the lower prices realized for cod-fish, all go to prove that English fishermen continuously visited Newfoundland from the very earliest time.

In the reign of Elizabeth the dark curtain which conceals the doings of Englishmen in this wild island of the west is drawn aside for us by the indefatigable Hakluyt and Sir George Peckham; we get a vivid picture of the grand function which heralded the arrival of Sir Humphrey Gilbert, the feudal ceremony of the rod and turf—a ceremony and nothing more; Gilbert's visit had no influence whatever on the future of our island.

The true story of this ill-fated expedition has been most ingeniously misrepresented by all historians. Hayes' narrative shows that Gilbert came to Newfoundland not for discovery—its shores were then as well known as the Devonshire coast; his real object was to obtain supplies from our capital, which was even in those days a great international trading port. The bold foreign policy of Elizabeth showed great results in Newfoundland; the Spanish fishing fleet of two hundred sail, which Peninsular historians declare was manned by six thousand seamen, never visited our shores after the defeat of the Armada.

The second period opened auspiciously; Carlile and others, ably supported by Bacon, pressed Raleigh's policy on King James. Shrewd London and Bristol merchants, after making a hard bargain with the

Scotch monarch, laid the foundation of the first official colony, known as John Guy's, at Cuper's Cove in 1610. Aristocratic adventurers followed: the eccentric Sir Wm. Vaughan, D.C.L., author of "The Newlander's Cure," a strange mixture of religion, poetry, and business, settled at Trepassey; Hayman, a still more fantastic colony-founder, governed Guy's plantation and wrote "Quodlibets," a curious medley, from Harbour Grace. Then came the enlightened Lord Baltimore, the learned Lord Falkland, and the rough old adventurer, Sir David Kirke. The rude colonial life did not suit them; they had all to contend against the fierce hostility of the Devon fishermen. As colonists they were one and all rank failures; the real work was done by poor West Countrymen; no hardships daunted their heroic souls, they clung to their homes, and their sons and daughters grew up to love the wild country of their birth. The first settlements were made by small detached parties of Englishmen known in the island parlance as "winter crews," who remained on the coast to cut wood for building houses, flakes, stages, cook-rooms, and boats for the spring. A shore fishery required their services, and from the records I think it is evident that there were such residents living on the east coast long before the arrival of Guy in 1610.

Our history, as it proceeds, throws a vivid side light on the character of the various English rulers as we see them reflected in their Colonial policy. The most marked contrast is between the honest, intelligent, and statesmanlike administration of Cromwell, when authority was maintained and settlement encouraged by his Governor, John Treworgie, and the corrupt rule of the second Charles. At this period of English history, the first false step was made by the English King selling Placentia to the French to form a settlement, and surrendering the imposition of five per cent. which had been rigorously exacted from foreign fishermen in Newfoundland by former English rulers. Out of this infamous transaction begins the endless, everlasting French Shore question; an irritating, unsolved, international difficulty, which has largely helped to make this poor Colony, in the words of Lord Salisbury, a land of "historic misfortune." One morning in the summer of 1662, to the great astonishment of the English inhabitants, soldiers, guns, men and women were landed from a great French ship in Placentia Harbour, and the town garrisoned and fortified against their only enemy the English; thus, without firing a shot, France took possession of the fairest portion of the island, our bitterest rival was lodged within our gate, ready to destroy us.

In 1676 the Commissioners of Trade and Plantations were bribed by the Devonshire adventurers to issue the order removing settlers from the Colony and destroying their houses and plantations. But for the humanity of the Commodore, the illustrious Sir John Berry, and the vigour and ability with which John Downing prosecuted his appeal to the Privy Council, all the inhabitants would have been ruined. As late as the beginning of this century there were deep lamentations from the West of England merchants over the failure of this ruthless policy of extermination. It was probably the war with France, and the necessity of defending the Colony from attack, that preserved the poor settlers from destruction; the victorious march of D'Iberville with his Abenaquis through the Colony obliged England to send out ships and men to drive away the enemy; admirals and generals on the station declared the Colony could not be defended without permanent settlers, and so the West Country proposals to depopulate the island were eventually defeated. We find, however, that the permanent settlers increased and multiplied, notwithstanding harsh laws and cruel wars, in which they were harried by pirates, spoiled and slain by French and Dutch.

Side by side, as the old colony began to grow, arose in the early days of James I. new colonies in Virginia and New England. The few impoverished fishermen and farmers, who were half starved at Plymouth, soon blossomed into prosperous communities, which spread out and separated into the country which now forms part of the Great Republic. In less than twenty-five years after the landing at Plymouth Rock, there were dealings between Newfoundland and the new settlements. Small trading vessels from Boston and Maine brought cattle and corn; they bartered these for fish and train oil, for gold, wines, olive oils and dried fruits, which the Devonshire fishermen smuggled with their salt from Cadiz, and Spanish fishermen brought from Bilbao. Besides smuggling goods, they smuggled men, headed up in casks. They embarked also in another great industry, the manufacture of New England rum; their greatest customers for this product (and onions, biscuits, and Yankee notions) were Newfoundlanders and Nova Scotians: the chief distilleries were at Nantucket. In the dispute with the Devonshire men, the New Englanders sided with the settlers. The Parliamentary Blue Books of the early Georgian era are full of fierce denunciation for the assistance they gave to our planters, and their sturdy refusal to let Maine be turned into a second and improved edition of Newfoundland. I have endeavoured to trace the early and intimate association between Newfoundland and the continental colonies.

All through this strange, eventful history, Newfoundland settlers of all kinds, from Guy and Baltimore down to the poorest waif from the West of England, had to fight for their lives with the dire hostility of the ship-fishermen or western adventurers from England. In the olden

INTRODUCTION.

time these men had conquered the country, and they looked upon it as their own. Charters were given them by the Crown, conferring on them outrageous rights and privileges. From the days of the second Charles, the Home Government always supported their pretensions. In his evidence before the House of Commons, 26th March 1793, William Knox, one of the Under Secretaries of State in the American Department, thus explained this policy :—

> "The island of Newfoundland has been considered, in all former times, as a great ship moored near the Banks during the fishing season, for the convenience of English fishermen. The Governor was considered as the ship's captain, and those who were concerned in the fishery business as his crew, and subject to naval discipline while there, and expected to return to England when the season was over. The English had then no rivals in the trade but the French, and, though the French fishery exceeded theirs, the English gradually increased, and those who carried it on were generally successful. The Treaty of Paris, by adding Canada and all Nova Scotia and Cape Breton to the British American Dominion, deprived France of the advantages they had for the employment of the inhabitants in the fishery, but at the same time a new rival was raised up to the English traders and fishermen in those and the other Northern British Colonies; as the profit the French inhabitants had made under the French Government by the fishery on their coasts, as well as on the coasts of Newfoundland, naturally turned the attention of the British subjects to the same business, many settlers emigrated to Newfoundland for the purpose, whilst others spread themselves along the shores of Nova Scotia and Cape Breton, so that there appeared evident danger of the trade and fishery being lost to England, and that, instead of it being a *British fishery*, as it had hitherto been, it would become a *Colonial fishery*. To prevent the increase of inhabitants in the Island the most positive instructions were given to the Governors not to make any grants of land, and to reduce the number of those who were already settled there. Their vessels, as well as those belonging to the colonies, were to be denied any priority of right in occupying stations in the bays or harbours, for curing the fish, over the vessels from England, and the Governor was instructed to withhold from them whatever might serve to encourage them to remain in the Island; and, as Lord North expressed it, 'whenever they 'wished to have roasted he was to give them raw, and whenever they wished to 'have the raw he was to give it them roasted,' with a view to secure the return of all the fishermen carried out."

Whilst Nova Scotia and Canada had money lavished on them by the British Government, the policy so cynically expressed by this English official was carried out towards Newfoundland by the British Government down to the very beginning of this century. It is no marvel that Newfoundland did not thrive under such a regime; the real wonder is that the settlers lived at all under such oppressive restrictions. But for their allies in New England, doubtless they would have been obliged to abandon their settlements.

Our treatment by the British Government has been so stupid, cruel, and barbarous that it requires the actual perusal of the State Papers to convince us that such a policy was ever carried out. The Home

Government have sacrificed our interests in every treaty with France. The *expositio contemporanea*, however, of the old admiral governors on the French treaties was very different from the complaisant manner in which the illegal and arrogant aggressions of French naval officers are treated to-day. Palliser held the French should neither trade nor catch anything but cod-fish Duff issued an order prohibiting French men-of-war from visiting our coast. These stout English sailors upheld the rights of England as the sovereign power in Newfoundland in a way that excites our admiration.

The third period of our colonial history commences about 1711. At this date we find some attempt at government in the appointment of Captain Crowe, R.N., who convened an assembly of the principal inhabitants, a crude copy of the New England town meeting, and by mutual consent established a rude code of laws. The British Government had been for over two centuries endeavouring to rule the country without government, and to establish a judiciary without an Act of Parliament. In 1728 the first regular naval governor was appointed in the person of Captain Osborne, R.N. The floating governors, to a certain extent, exercised authority over those judicial monstrosities, the fishing admirals.

Most writers on Newfoundland have been very severe on the naval governors. As a rule the position was held by distinguished officers like Rodney, Graves, Palliser, and, latterly, Lord Radstock. My own opinion is that they filled a very difficult position, on the whole, admirably; of course quarter-deck law was their sole guide, in the rude condition of society then existing it was perhaps the best rule. Later on, as the country became more populous and more civilised, it was simply unbearable. It was only in 1791, after fierce opposition, that the first Act of Parliament was passed giving the Colony a legally appointed court and a chief justice in the person of John Reeves, a most admirable selection. He was law clerk to the Privy Council, and by his advice and assistance the opposition of the West Country merchants to legal reform was defeated.

In 1825 commenced the modern period of our history with the advent of Sir Thos. John Cochrane; no man ever did so much for Newfoundland as this excellent Governor. On the 1st of January 1833 he opened our first Parliament. Since that date, notwithstanding great fluctuations in the fisheries, and disasters like the great fires of 1817, 1846, and the last terrible calamity of the 8th of July 1892, and worst of all the financial crisis of 1894, the Colony has progressed; her resources in minerals and timber are being greatly developed, railways are being extended, steam communication and telegraph lines are promoting civilisation and advancement. The immense resources of the great island have been only, as it were, tapped here and there. Agriculture is slowly progressing. A greater impetus will be given to the Colony when the railway to Port-aux-Basques and a steam ferry across the Gulf brings us into closer connexion with America, and the strong current of progress and prosperity in the Dominion and the United States. Besides our splendid fisheries, timber, and minerals, Newfoundland is without a rival as a sporting country; with increased facilities of communication we should become the playground of America. With her vast resources, her temperate climate, and her unique position,[1] the future of this ill-used and down-trodden Colony should be brighter than it has been of yore.

In the preparation of this work I have to give sincere thanks for assistance received from all quarters. Lord Salisbury allowed my son free access to the vast store of information about the Elizabethan era contained in the noble library at Hatfield. I have had valuable help from American scholars—Justin Winsor, LL.D., John Ward Deane, A.M., Hon. Charles Levi Woodbury, and in a very special manner from James Phinney Baxter, A.M., Vice-President of the Prince Society, and my fellow-countrymen, Mr. Phelan, and Mr. Whittle, of Boston. My thanks are also due to Mr. Noel Sainsbury. From the following friends in Newfoundland I have also had valuable assistance: His Excellency the Governor of Newfoundland, Col. Sir J. T. N. O'Brien, K.C.M.G., the Chief Justice, Sir F. B. T. Carter, K.C.M.G.; in a very special manner from my friend the late Sir R. J. Pinsent, D.C.L., the Newfoundland Government, Sir W. V. Whiteway, K.C.M.G., the Hons. R. Bond and A. W. Harvey, the late R. W. Lilly, Nelson Bailey, of Oderin, and the Hon. Stephen Rendell. I have to thank G. H. Emerson, Q.C., for old Blue Books, the Bishop of Newfoundland, and the Rev. W. Pilot, D.D., for correcting the dates connected with the Church of England in the Colony, the Very Rev. Bishop Howley, who has revised the notices of events in the Roman Catholic Church, and the Rev. F. R. Duffill, who has done the same for the Wesleyan Church. From numerous friends I have received valuable assistance in the preparation of the chronology, especially from J. W. Withers, James Howley, F.G.S., my old friends the late J. J. Howley, Wm. Howley, and T. D. Scanlan, the

---

[1] Newfoundland lies in the North Atlantic, between the parallels of 46° 36′ 50″ and 51° 39′ north latitude, and between the meridians of 52° 37′ and 59° 24′ 50″ west longitude. It is only 12 miles from North America, across the Straits of Belle Isle, and 1,640 from Ireland, about 60 hours steaming for the newest Atlantic steamer. The island forms an important link in the direct route from Europe to Montreal, Chicago, Minneapolis, and the Pacific slope; with fast steamers, and a railway to the Gulf, mails could be delivered in the West much quicker than by New York.

Hon. A. M. Mackay, and D. Ryan. To my eldest son I am indebted for notes, views, and maps, collected chiefly at the British Museum and the Record Office; and I have also to thank especially the authorities of the British Museum, the librarian at Hatfield, Mr. R. T. Gunton, Mr. Sutcliffe, Mr. Reddan, and other friends who have assisted my son in England. The illustrations, except where otherwise stated, are from photographs taken by our excellent photographer, Mr. S. H. Parsons, to whom I am indebted for permission to reproduce them. Our best known writer, the Rev. Dr. M. Harvey, has written a very able paper on the Fishery Commission.

I am painfully conscious, after all the labour, time, and money spent on the work, that it is still a very incomplete history of Newfoundland. To write a full history would require several volumes, and more time and expenditure than I could afford to bestow on it. If, however, I have thrown any fresh light on the tangled story of our Colony, if any of my fellow countrymen are led, by its perusal, to take more interest in this "Newfoundland of Ours," and to understand her history better, I shall feel amply repaid for all the pains I have taken in its preparation.

Many of my readers no doubt feel surprised at the long delay in the publication of this work; it has been caused by various circumstances over which I had no control (public and private business), but principally by the desire to acquire fuller information. My American friends strongly advised me to make haste slowly, and I have followed their advice to some extent, having been six years constantly employed on the work. Some of my Newfoundland readers would probably like to know how this book came into existence. In 1888 I found myself suddenly transformed from a peaceful district judge into a fighting admiral. In carrying out the bait-protection service, in order to while away the tedious time on board ship, I wrote some papers on "The Home of the Herring"; their favourable reception induced me to commence a short "History of the Newfoundland Fishery." After thirty years' experience and extensive reading on the subject, I found that I really knew practically nothing about our island history, and that the real history could only be acquired by much study and research; these investigations resulted in the present work. The labour was so enormous that I have several times dropped it in despair. At one time I intended to end at 1713; however, I suppose West Country obstinacy prevailed, so amid much interruption I completed it, with manifold assistance, which I acknowledge with most sincere gratitude.

I will conclude in the words of a fellow-countryman, who, when asked to give information to a parliamentary committee on the fishery, replied: "Man and boy I have been engaged in the fishery forty years; "I may yet be as ignorant as the novice, but I give my opinion "according to conscience, erudition, and intellect." In the same spirit I dedicate this book to my readers.

To many of my readers, especially my Newfoundland readers, the documents set forth in these pages will be considered the most interesting part of the book—they are chiefly from unpublished records; by others they may be looked on as the very dry bones of history. In order to satisfy my two sets of readers, I have therefore put these old documents in the appendices to the chapters, where the diligent student of our real history may peruse them, and the lighter-minded reader pass them by.

CHAPTER I.

THE PRE-COLUMBIAN DISCOVERY OF AMERICA.

THE history of America is a modern history. Authentic annals of the New World cover only four centuries, and commence from its discovery by Columbus in 1492. Prior to this great and ever-memorable adventure, there are stories of voyages, islands, discoveries; allusions in Aristotle, Plato, and Seneca to a great country dimly seen beyond the western ocean. Nearly every European country had some such obscure tradition; the Spanish Basques, the Bretons, the Italians, with their story of the brothers Zeno, the Irish Saint Brendan, the trip across the Atlantic of a Welsh prince in a ship of glass, with an able crew of twelve harpers,—all these stories are interesting and romantic, some, perhaps, authentic; at present, however, they lie outside the sober domain of history, in the dim regions of myth and fable.

The Atlantic voyages of the Northmen stand on quite a different footing. Mixed up with a shadowy mythology we have a large portion of real history. The discovery of North America by the Icelanders in the tenth and eleventh centuries of our era is now recognised by scholars as being as true and well ascertained as the landing of William the Conqueror in England, 1066. The Icelanders claim to have discovered Greenland[1] in 982. Here they established a number of settlements,

---

[1] In the year 834 the Norwegians were acquainted with a country in the north called Groneland, commonly called *Old Greenland*, to distinguish it from Spitzbergen. In the charter of the Emperor Ludovicus Pius to St. Ansgharius, first Archbishop of Hamburg, dated 834, published by Lindenbrogius in 1706 (p. 125), (which also includes Adam of Bremen's work) we read:—"We make known to the present and future sons of God's Holy Church that, in our days, by the divine grace, a door is opened for preaching the Gospel in the northern regions, viz., Denmark, Sweden, Norway, *Greenland*, Halingalandon [most probably Lapland], Iceland, and Scredevindon [no doubt Finland]."

Pope Gregory varies the names of some of these northern people who were included in this new diocese so much that some can scarcely be recognised now. The Danish Chronicle, it seems, makes Groneland to have been discovered as early as 770; but according to the Iceland Chronicle, not before 982, it being by this last account peopled by a Norwegian who had fled to Iceland. The built churches, forts and houses. Most minute particulars about these are given in the saga of Eric Raude or Red. Dr Rinke in his History of Greenland, says:—

"In a country where no tree can grow, the faintest traces of former buildings can be made out. . . . . Kakortok Church contains three separate entrances; the principal one is covered with very large flat regular stone, measuring about twelve feet in length. In the opposite or eastern wall is a window most skilfully arched, but apparently likewise constructed from rough stones."

About a hundred places have been found scattered along the coast of Greenland, and these localities can be identified by reference to the ancient sagas.

STATUE OF ERIC IN BOSTON, ERECTED BY PROF. HORSFORD.

The daring character of the Northmen is shown by the fact that in their small crazy craft they made Arctic voyages. Four miles beyond Uppernavick, at Kingitoarsuk, a stone has been found with a Runic inscription, stating that it was raised by Erling, the son of Sigvat, and Enride Oddsven, in 1133.

When these adventurous Northmen reached Greenland, the most eastern part of North America, their discovery of Labrador and Newfoundland would certainly follow. The first north-easter would drive their small unweatherly vessels on to the coasts of Labrador. Their finding North America is not only inherently probable, but is proved to us absolutely by the direct testimonies of the ecclesiastical historian Adam of Bremen and of Oderic Vital, and by a brief of Pope

writers of both branches, it is evident, had no knowledge of the centres of the Pope and Emperor. In 1076, Adam of Bremen says that Albert Archbishop of Hamburg sent missionaries to Greenland and to other parts;

his geography is very obscure for Nineteenth-Century students. The Danish and Norwegian Histories give 1348 as the year in which the colony of Greenland was lost.—I am indebted to Mr. Reddan for this note.

THE ICELANDIC COLONISATION.

Nicholas V., dated 1448, addressed to two bishops of Iceland urging them to take measures for the support of the Church in Greenland. Adam of Bremen, who died in 1076, wrote a history of the diocese of Hamburg and Bremen between A.D. 988 and 1072. He mentions the names of Greenland bishops and the discovery of Vinland by the Icelanders.

Gudrid, the widow of Thorfinn Karlsefne, one of the most distinguished of the Icelandic explorers of America, actually visited Rome on a pilgrimage after the death of her husband, about 1028 or 1030.

Beyond stating these brief facts it does not concern our History further to dwell upon the pre-Columbian voyages. In America the colonisation of the Icelanders entirely disappeared—"like the baseless fabric of a vision, left not a rack behind." Their transitory occupation left no result or influence on the New World, of which they were the first European settlers.[1]

MAP OF THE ICELANDER STEPHANUS, 1570.
From Torfaeus' "Groenlandia Antiqua," 1706.

---

[1] In the *Studies on the Vineland Voyages*, by Gustav Storm, *Memoires de la Société Royale des Antiquaires du Nord*, 1888, Newfoundland is recognised as the "Markland" of the Sagas. There is an interesting article by Sir D. Wilson, LL.D., *The Vineland of the Northmen*, in the *Trans. of Royal Society of Canada*, vol. viii., sec. ii., p. 109.

2 The strong resemblance between the Greenland of this map, J. de la Cosa's, and Ruysch's, point to some common source, either Norse or English, prior to, or as the result of, Cabot's voyage; more likely the former. A. "This is where the English have come, and has a name for barrenness, either from sun or cold." B. "This is near where Vinland lies which . . . . . . is called good. Our countrymen (Icelanders) have thought that to the south it ends with the wild sea, and that a sound separates it from America." C. "Land of the giants." For other references see Winsor's *N. & C. H. of America*, I., 130.

CHAPTER II.

REIGN OF HENRY VII.

1485-1509.

1492.—First voyage of Columbus; sailed 3rd August; discovered America 12th October, 1492.

1496.—On the Petition of John Cabot, a patent granted on 5th March by King Henry VII. to him and his sons to discover new lands.

1497.—John Cabot's voyage in the ship *Matthew*, of Bristol; discovered North America and Newfoundland; sailed from Bristol 2nd May, returned 6th August; grant of £10 on 10th August to the discoverer of the new island; letters on 23rd August from Pasqualigo, also on 24th August and 18th December from Soncino, describing the voyage. Same year, Vasco de Gama, Portuguese navigator, doubled Cape of Good Hope, Africa. Pension of £20 per annum to John Cabot on revenues of Bristol on 13th December; passed Great Seal, 28th January 1498.

1498.—Warrant on 3rd February to John Cabot to take up six ships; Cabot sailed along the east coast of North America; arrived home with a cargo of fur and fish, probably in June 1499. Possible exploration of Newfoundland by an independent English expedition anticipating Cabot's arrival on part of the coast. Loans to Carter, Thirkill, and Bradley on 22nd March and 1st April by Henry VII. Letter on 25th July from Puebla and Ayala to the Spanish Sovereigns announcing departure of Cabot's second expedition.

1500.—Gaspar Cortereal, a Portuguese, probably made a voyage to America; his patent is dated 12th May; it refers to former unsuccessful explorations. Juan de la Cosa's map.

1501.—English progress southwards mentioned in Hojeda's charter. 19th March, Charter from Henry VII. to Richard Warde, John Thomas, John Fernandez, &c. for ten years; Portuguese, being aliens, to be charged extra duties. Authentic voyage of Cortereal, sailed on 15th May to the Labrador coast; fifty natives brought home on 8th October; King of Portugal said they were the best slaves he had seen; Cortereal never returned; letters from Lisbon on 17th, 18th, 19th October by Cantino and Pasquiligo about the expedition.

1502.—Grant on 7th January to Bristol men that found "Thisle." Grant on 15th January to Miguel Cortereal, who fitted out an expedition to search for his brother; probably sailed on 10th May; Miguel never returned. Three Indians at the Court of Henry VII. Cantino's map of Cortereal's voyage, 19th November. 9th December. Charter to Ashenhurst, Fernando, Eliot, and Gonzalo for forty years, freedom from duties for five years, &c.; alien clause omitted.

1503.—Further expedition in search of the Cortereals. Grant on 30th September to Bristol merchants who have been in the Newfoundland, and to one who brought hawkes from thence.

1504.—Probable date of the French expedition to Cape Breton. Grant on 8th April to an English priest going to the New Island. A number of French, Breton and Norman, English and Portuguese vessels resorting to the Newfoundland fishery. From this period onward, for a hundred years following, Newfoundland was visited every year by an annually increasing number of English, French, and Portuguese fishermen; subsequently also by Spaniards.

1505.—Popyngais and cats brought from Newfoundland.

1506.—Jean Denys of Harfleur fishing in Newfoundland.

1508.—Ruysch—first engraved map showing America. Aubert, pilot of Dieppe, voyaged to Newfoundland; brought back two Indians. Act severing Fish and Stock-fishmonger's Companies.

The latter part of the fifteenth century forms one of the great epochs of history, the veritable renaissance, the new birth of the world. At this period begins the history of America, the modern history of England, and practically the present history of Europe.

Many remarkable events combined to make this age illustrious, the invention of printing, the general use of gunpowder and artillery in war, and the capture of Constantinople by the Turks. This last event put to flight numerous Greek scholars, who bore their precious manuscripts to Italy and thus inaugurated the new learning—commenced in England by an Oxford scholar, Grocyn, bringing Greek writings to his ancient university.

The advent of Henry Tudor to the Throne, his marriage with the beautiful Elizabeth of York, the destruction or impoverishment of the great feudal houses in the Wars of the Roses, combined with the vigorous manner in which the astute Henry curtailed their power, effaced them for ever as the promoters of domestic war. In place of robber barons and the bloody civil feuds they fomented, for the first time there appears conspicuous upon the stage of our modern history the power of the commoner, the merchant princes of England, and the sure growth of commerce.

HENRY VII.
From an engraving after contemporary portrait.

But of all the causes, great and powerful, working at this wonderful period for the progress of the world, undoubtedly the greatest influence of all was the daring maritime enterprise which simultaneously discovered New Continents in both East and West. The immediate effect was a great expansion of thought, a great stirring up of the imagination, all wonderful things seemed possible to the generation that found a New World. The discovery of America by Columbus, and the doubling of the Cape of Good Hope by Vasco de Gama, gave the Old World new Europes in Asia, Africa, America, and subsequently Australia.

CARAVELS OF COLUMBUS.
After drawings in the Spanish Admiralty Office.

The voyage of Columbus is one of the grandest events in history; it doubled the habitable portion of the globe, and gave Europe new fields for enterprise. Columbus believed the lands he had discovered were a part of Asia, and it took nearly three more centuries to map out the whole configuration of America.

The life of the great Genoese sailor is, and always will be, the grandest romance of history; age cannot wither it, time cannot stale it, nothing can lessen the importance of this splendid achievement. As the brilliancy of a splendid jewel is enhanced by its fine setting, so the picturesque story of the great Italian navigator, devoted son of the Church, the last of the crusaders, has been set in a halo of glory by the most brilliant writers of our age.

The tale is ever fresh and delightful, whether set forth in the graceful pages of Irving, the terse pellucid English of Helps, or the grand sonorous Castilian of Emilio Castelar.

The world has lately been ringing with his praises, the critics have fought over his forty portraits, and the dozen Islands, scene of his veritable landfall.

Alas! for the glory of our Island, for the praise of our discoverer, there are no portraits to discuss, no noble Isabella la Catolica, no devoted friar. No golden haze of romance surrounds our earliest annals. The story of the discovery of Newfoundland and North America, as told by the Cabots, is as dull as the log of a dredge-boat. Every picturesque element is eliminated from it, and the great voyage, so pregnant with moral and material results, is brought down to the low level of a mere trading adventure. But though the tale is dull, and still shrouded in mystery, it must remain one of the greatest events in history; it gave North America to the English by indefeasible right of discovery. How different might have been the future of this great Continent—the home of nearly seventy millions—where, under orderly and settled government, freedom broadens slowly down—where mighty industry and bright intelligence have built up one of the richest, fairest, and freest lands the sun ever shone upon! What might have been our destiny had Columbus, not Cabot with his West of England sailors, discovered Northern America? Heaven only knows what would have been our fate—possibly a great Spanish possession, with chronic revolutions, disordered finances, pronunciamentos, half-breeds, and fusillades.

Until quite recently the history of the discovery of North America by the English could not be written. It is not derived from English records. It can now, however, be told with a fair degree of accuracy, thanks to the labours of Rawdon Brown and other eminent scholars. We derive our main facts from the Calendars of Venice, and that great mine of history, the Archives of Simancas, in Spain. John

Cabot was a Genoese navigator and merchant adventurer, experienced and skilled in all the nautical knowledge of those days. Italy—home of art, science, literature, commerce, and navigation—gave to Spain, France, and England Columbus, Verrazano, and Cabot. Very few facts are known about John Cabot's life: he was made a citizen of Venice in 1476; he had been to Mecca, where he saw the caravans arriving from the far East with spices, &c. The date of his arrival in England is uncertain. Stachey says, in 1496 he was naturalized ("denizened"), and living within Blackfriars, probably only while he was pressing his suit at Court.

PIAZZA DI S. MARCO DI VENEZIA.

VENICE ABOUT 1620.
From an old print.

There was an important colony of Italian merchants and money lenders in London during this reign, who may have helped our explorer with the king; Lombard Street perpetuates their memory. All that we do know positively is that Giovanni Gabotto, or Cabotta, or Gabote (anglicised into John Cabot), some time before 1496, was living in Bristol, then the chief city of the West. At this period Bristol did a large trade with Iceland, exchanging the famous West of England cloth, hats, caps, hosiery, and small wares for Iceland stock-fish. The grand old church, St. Mary's Redcliffe, still bears testimony to the munificence of her princely merchant, William Canynge.

The city[3] had twice given Henry VII. a cordial reception, and the king looked with favourable eyes on her merchants. Some years before the discovery, Cabot was brought under the notice of the sovereign, and employed in negotiating with the King of Denmark about the English trade with Iceland.[4] Doubtless, on his voyages to the island, the shrewd, clever Italian sailor would hear all about

---

[1] It is just possible that Lion's Den, in Bonavista Bay, is the place where Cabot erected the arms of Venice, the winged lion, on his first voyage.

[2] See Appendix, p. 24, THE ICELAND FISHERY.

[3] Henry IV. had given exemptions to Bristol from certain dues, and a separate Admiralty jurisdiction, on account of the many voyages undertaken by her merchants and the great expense they had incurred.

[4] ANSPACH'S *History of Newfoundland*, 1819, p. 25. I have not been able to trace Anspach's authority, but there is no reason to doubt the accuracy of the statement.

the Icelandic expeditions to America. In 1493, when Columbus returned from his famous voyage, "All men at the Court of Henry VII." says Sebastian Cabot, "affirmed it to be a thing more divine than "human to sail by the West to the East." Cabot approached the King with a Petition for discovering new lands:—

"To the king, our sovereigne Lord. Please it your Highnes of your most noble and habundant grace to graunt unto John Cabotto citizen of Venes, Lewes, Sebastyan and Sancto his sonneys your gracious letters patentes under your grete sele in due forme to be made according to the tenour hereafter ensuying (the draft charter is lost) and they shall during their lyves pray God for the prosperous continuance of your most noble and Royal Estate, long to endure."

This is the earliest document definitely connecting England with the New World. William of Wyrcester and Ayala do indeed mention voyages made at the expense of Bristol in 1480, and from 1491 to 1496, but if they bore any results they were kept secret.

The records tell us that the monarch gave him very little encouragement. At last, however, through the influence of the Bristol merchants, he was prevailed on to grant the Genoese a charter, but solely on the condition that he was to have a royal share of the profits, but on no account to bear any of

SEAL OF HENRY VII.

the expenses. It is dated 5th March 1496 (11th year of the reign):—

"Henry by the Grace of God, &c., &c. . . . Be it known to all, that we have given and granted to our well-beloved John Cabot, citizen of Venice, and to Lewis, Sebastian and Sanctus, sons of the said John, and to their heirs and deputies, full authority, &c., &c., . . . to sail to all parts, countries and seas of the East, of the West and of the North, under our banner and ensigns, with five ships, and to set up our banner on any new-found-land, as our vassals and lieutenants . . . upon their own proper costs and charges, to seek out and discover whatsoever isles . . . of the heathen and infidels, which before the time have been unknown to all Christians . . . . to pay to us the fifth part of the capital gain so gotten for every then voyage; and to return to the port of Bristol."

THE FIRST LANDFALL

Cabot, like a wise man, inserted the names of his sons in order to extend the duration of the charter to the full extent of their young lives, but there is no record to show that any of them accompanied him.

On the second of May 1497 John Cabot set sail from Bristol on his famous voyage, accompanied by a Burgundian and sixteen English sailors, in a little West of England vessel, about fifty tons, called the *Matthew*. We read:—

"This year (1497) on St. John the Baptist's Day, the land of America was found by the merchants of Bristowe, in a ship of Bristowe called the *Matthew*, the which said ship departed from the port of Bristowe the 2nd of May, and came home again 6th of August following."[1]

We can picture to ourselves the scene as the brave little ship leaves the Avon, and the wind fills her broad lug sails as she rounds the picturesque coast of North Devon on a fair day in the shining month of May, and steers down the Irish sea, and then on to the great waste of waters and the far unknown ocean. What were the hopes and prospects of the bold Italian navigator and his little crew of sturdy English sailors? Most likely he argued, "My countryman has found land at the south " of this great western sea. The Icelanders found it on the north. It is all " part of Asia. I will strike it somewhere, sailing west." Many writers consider that John Cabot could not have made the voyage out and home in so short a time. I cannot see the force of the argument. Easterly winds generally prevail in the North Atlantic in early May. Given a fair wind, these little vessels, with their flat floors, and broad lug sails, could easily go five to six knots before the wind. Fifty-three days out from Bristol to Newfoundland, and forty-two days home, would not be a record-breaking passage, even for those days. We learn from Soncino, that on this voyage Cabot first sailed around Ireland, then towards the north, and finally steered west. On the 24th June, at early morn, an inscription on the Cabot map says, they first sighted the New World.

There has been much learned discussion regarding this landfall, and after the whole matter has been thoroughly threshed out, there is no absolute certainty as to the exact point first seen. Strong arguments have been put forward in favour of Labrador by Mr. J. P. Howley, F.R.G.S., and others. The inscription on the map of 1544, attributed to Sebastian Cabot,[2] has led many writers to place the landfall at Cape Breton, but

---

[1] *Fust MSS., Hill Court, Gloucestershire.* See *Encl. Brit.*, 9th edit., vol. iv., p. 350. The word America shows it is not a contemporary document, and ...nuineness has been doubted.

[2] The Cabot mappemonde is now in the Paris National Library; it came from Germany. M. Harrisse suggests that S. Cabot placed the English landfall on Cape Breton when the French had begun to colonise

there is no other evidence to support this claim: in fact it is at variance with contemporary accounts of the voyage, and the inferences to be drawn from the earliest maps.

In this colony an unbroken tradition points to Cape Bonavista, Newfoundland, as the first land seen.[1] This tradition is confirmed by an English map of Newfoundland made by John Mason, a distinguished captain in the Royal Navy of England about 1616; opposite to Cape Bonavista he writes these words, probably copying the wording of an older map: "*First found by Cabot*"—"*A Caboto primum reperta.*"[2] On this ground, and for other reasons, as a Newfoundlander, I claim for Cape Bonavista the honour of being the first land seen in North America. In all probability, St. John's was also discovered either on Cabot's first or second voyage.[3]

It is possible that although John Cabot discovered Cape Bonavista, he did not so name it. Some of the Portuguese associated in 1501 with Eliot's company were from the Azores, and may have called the headland after Bonavista in the Cape de Verd Islands; but against this

Canada in order to gain the favour of the English and secure his return, and that his call in 1547 was the result of this piece of duplicity; the map could not have been published much before 1546. Mr. Justin Winsor, the American historian, says: "The map, in its confused nomenclature and antiquated geographical notions throughout, indicates that the draft was made by a 'prentice hand—probably by some Italian map fabricator."

Two things are quite clear, the landfall of Cabot was either on the Labrador or Eastern Newfoundland coast, and this map is not the original one made by John Cabot.

[1] "Bonavista! Oh! good sight!" is the natural exclamation the old Italian might make, as after his long and dangerous voyage he first caught sight of land, bright and green with the springing grass of June. There is no other cape with the same name on the eastern shore of North America.

Cortereal struck this part of the coast on his voyages, and, curiously enough, Cartier made Cape Bonavista on his first voyage (1534). Sailing vessels coming to Newfoundland from Northern Europe nearly always sight Cape Bonavista. Supposing Cabot to be steering towards Labrador, he would meet ice and run south, and be very likely to make in with the land at this point; or even without meeting the ice the Labrador current would drag his vessel south. Tradition, probability, and the certain evidence of Mason's map of Newfoundland, made 278 years ago, demonstrate almost to a certainty Cape Bonavista as the landfall of John Cabot. Cape Race—Capo Rasso, Cape Spear—Cabo Spera or Espera, Bonavista and Bonaventura, are among the earliest names on ancient maps.

The Reverend George Paterson furnishes very valuable information concerning the Portuguese explorations, and their attempted settlement in Cape Breton. I think his enthusiasm carries him rather far when he makes out nearly all the names on our east coast as Portuguese. Conception Bay is so, but *Buonavista* is distinctly Italian (so is *buona Ventura*—good find! lucky hit!). In Spanish it would be *Buena Vista*; in Portuguese *Boa Vista*. *Raso* is also Italian; it means shaved, cut off—an excellent description of our famous headland. The English word razor is from the same source. Cabot made at least two voyages to Newfoundland; he was a skilled seaman and map-maker, and though the originals of his maps have all disappeared, there can be no doubt that he made a running survey of the coast, named the headlands, and marked them on charts. The *King* map, 1502, is the earliest to contain a name that has survived (unless the supposition that the Cape English of J. de la Cosa and modern maps are identical is correct); its Capo Raso is distinctly Italian, although the map was probably made in Portugal, thus showing strong presumptive evidence of its being copied from a Cabotian chart.

[2] See p. 106.

[3] I feel convinced Cabot saw our capital in all its primitive beauty, the bold outlines of the surrounding hills clothed to the water's edge with the dark verdure of the forest; it must have been a beautiful scene; his navigator's eye would specially note its unique value as a land-locked harbour, the most perfect of its kind in the world.

argument is the fact that in most Portuguese maps Bonavista does not appear, whilst in the map of Gaspar Viegas in 1534 it is given as *Boavista*, a translation into Portuguese from the original Italian *Buonavista*. Viegas and others appear to have received the name from sailors on the coast, and not from the geographers.

On his return to England, August 6th, 1497, the old Venetian navigator was received with great rejoicing. On the 23rd of August, seventeen days after his arrival, Pasqualigo, a Venetian in London, writing to his brother in Venice, says:—

" The English run after him like mad. His name is Zuan Cabot, and they call him the great Admiral." [1]

The most interesting account of the voyage is contained in an amusing letter from Raimondo di Soncino, London, to the Duke of Milan, 18th December 1497:—

" The king has gained a great part of Asia without a stroke of the sword. In this kingdom is a popular Venetian called Zoanne Caboto, a man of considerable ability, most skilful in navigation, who having seen the most serene kings, first him of Portugal, then him of Spain, that they had occupied unknown islands, thought to make a similar acquisition for His Majesty [Henry VII.]. And having obtained the royal privileges which gave him the use of the land found by him, provided the right of possession was reserved to the Crown, he departed in a little ship from Bristol with 18 persons, who placed their fortunes with him. Passing Ibernia [Ireland] more to the west, and then ascending towards the north, he began to navigate the eastern part of the ocean, leaving for some days the north to the right hand, and having wandered enough he came at last to firm land, where he planted the royal banners, took possession for his Highness, made certain marks, and returned.

" The said Messer Zoanne, as he is a foreigner and poor, would not be believed if his partners who are all Englishmen, and from Bristol, did not testify to the truth of what he tells. This Messer Zoanne has the description of the world in a chart, and also in a solid globe which he has made, *and he shows where he landed;* and that going toward the east he passed considerably beyond the country of the Tanais. . . . The sea is full of fish which are taken not only with the net but also with a basket in which a stone is put so that the basket may plunge into water . . . And the Englishmen, his partners, say that they can bring so many fish that the kingdom will have no more business with Islanda [Iceland], and that from this country *there will be a very great trade in the fish they call stock fish.*

" They say, now they know where to go, the voyage will not take more than 15 days if fortune favours them after leaving Ibernia. . . . The Admiral, as Messer Zoanne is already styled, has given his companion, a Burgundian, an island, and has also given another to his barber, a Genoese, and they regard themselves as Counts, and my lord the Admiral as a Prince. And I believe that some poor Italian friars will go on the voyage, who have the promise of being Bishops. And I, being a friend of the Admiral, if I wished to go, could have an Archbishoprick." [2]

[1] *Venetian Calendars*, i. 262.
[2] This letter, in the State archives of Milan, was first published in 1865 in the *Annuario Scientifico*.

The king does not seem to have been much moved by the enthusiasm of his subjects. In an entry in the Privy Purse expenses of the monarch, this item is found: "August 10th, 1497. To hym that found the new isle, 10*l*."[1] This may have been paid to the great Admiral, though more probably it was a gratuity to the sailor who first sighted land. However, on the 13th December of the same year, a pension of 20*l*. a year was granted to John Cabot, payable half-yearly. This was sealed on the 28th January following (1498). On the 3rd of February 1498, the following warrant was issued to John Cabot:—

" To all Men to whom theis presenteis shall come gretying: Know ye that We of our Grace especiale and dyvers causes us moving. We have given and granten, and by these presents géve and graunte, to our well beloved John Kabotto, the Venecian, sufficiente auctorite and power that he by him, his Deputie or Deputies, sufficient may take at his pleasure VI Englishe shipes in any Porte or Portes, or other places within this, our Realme of England or Obeisance, so that, and if the said shippes be of the burthen of CC tonnes, or under, with their apparail requisite and necessarie for the safe conduct of the said shippes, and them convey and leade to the *Londe and Isles of late founde by the said John*, in our name and by our commandment. Paying for them and every of them as if we should in or for our own cause pay and none otherwise."

This would enable him to take up six ships on the same terms as if for the use of the Royal Navy, but he has still to pay for them himself, and even the noble pension of 20*l*. is to be taken out of the revenue of Bristol, not from the king's own ample means. In the spring of the next year (1498) John Cabot went on a second voyage. Mindful of the immense quantities of fish seen about our island on the first voyage, other masters also came out this year provided with fishing gear and fishermen; from the following Records we learn that Bristol and London merchants fitted out ships with hats, caps, and hosiery, and the famous West of England blankets and cloth, to barter and trade; also, that some money was received from the king, probably by way of loan:—

"1498.—This year one Sebastian Gaboto, a Genoa's son, born in Bristow, ... caused the king to man and victual a ship at Bristow to search for an island which he knew to be replenished with rich commodities. In the ship divers merchants of London adventured small stocks, and in the company of this ship sailed also out of Bristow three or four small ships fraught with sleight and grosse wares, as coarse cloth, caps, laces, points, and such other."[2]

"April 1st, 1498, a reward of £2 to James Carter, for going to the new isle."

"To Lanslot Thirkill, of London, upon a prest for his shipp going towards the new Ilande, 22nd March, 1498, £20."

"Delivered to Launcelot Tirkill going towards the New Ile in prest £20."

"April 1st, 1498, to Thomas Bradley and Launcelot Thirkill, going to the new Isle, £30."[3]

[1] Bentley's *Excerpta Historica*, 1831, p. 113.
[2] Stowe's *Annales*, 1615, p. 482.
[3] Bentley's *Excerpta Historica*, p. 116.

In 1500 we have unmistakeable evidence from Spanish sources of English discoveries, in the map of Juan de la Cosa.[1] Cape Race, or possibly, Cape English, in St. Mary's Bay, is represented by the "Cavo de Ynglaterra" ("English Cape"); further west on the same map is an inscription, "Mar descubierta por Ingleses" ("Sea discovered by the English"). This map probably shows the results of Cabot's second voyage.[2]

The pension and warrant are the last records of the famous explorer, John Cabot. He utterly disappears from history about this period; whether he died or left England, we cannot tell.[3] He discovered a new continent, and no man knows his grave.

In March 1501 John Cabot's patent seems to have been cancelled, and a new charter granted to three substantial merchants— Thomas Ashehurst, Richard Warde, and John Thomas, and three Portuguese from the Azores— John Gonzalo and John and Francis Fernando. In December of the

CUSTOM HOUSE, BRISTOL.
From Millerd's Map, 1671.

---

[1] JUAN DE LA COSA was a distinguished Biscayan navigator and geographer, native of Santoña. In the list of the crew of Columbus' vessel—the *Santa Maria*—he is mentioned as "Maestre," or "Sailing Master." He was a member of the celebrated Contractation House of Seville for the promotion of navigation and the examination and the licensing of pilots for the Indies.

[2] Pedro de Ayala's letter about this voyage is given at p. 29.

[3] According to the Spanish writers, John Cabot was a kind of second-class Columbus, and had been both to Lisbon and Seville trying to get aid for his scheme of Transatlantic discovery. They admit, however, that there is no very reliable authority for this statement. It is very likely that he may have been in these cities many times in the course of his regular business as a merchant. As the originator, probably, of great-circle sailing, John Cabot showed himself a man of great originality, no mere servile imitator of Columbus; he noticed also the variation of the compass. The knowledge of these two facts seems to have constituted the life-long stock-in-trade of his son Sebastian. It is suggested by Bristol writers that Cathay Street commemorates the voyages of Cabot.

same year another patent was drawn out in favour of Hugh Eliot and Ashehurst, and two Portuguese—John Gonzalo and Francis Fernando. This new charter gave the patentees the very largest powers, and

RUYSCH'S MAP, 1508.[1]

From the Ptolemy published at Rome, 1508.

a monopoly of trade to the new land for forty years. There is a special reservation in favour of the King of Portugal,[2] whose subjects we shall find, later on, were the most friendly and liberal to Gilbert. As far as we can learn, Henry's charters for the new isle were so much waste paper.

In the year 1501 we have an account of the first Portuguese voyage to North America, made by the noble and intrepid navigator, Gaspar Cortereal. He came on this coast with a charter from the King of Portugal to possess the land, and for many years after his death his relatives held the hereditary title of Governor of Terra Nova.[3] The accounts of the first voyages, in which he sailed along the Greenland

---

[1] This is the first engraved map to show Newfoundland. Ruysch says he sailed to the new country in an English ship; he has been thought to be the Burgundian who went in Cabot's first voyage; this map, however, was composed, it is evident, at a somewhat later period.

[2] Possibly the Portuguese granted Englishmen freedom to trade in the Brazils and elsewhere in exchange for the right of fishing in Newfoundland.

[3] Spain and Portugal claimed the new world as their own; they looked upon the English as poachers on their preserves. Pope Alexander VI., in 1493, drew a line of demarcation 100 leagues west from the Azores and

coast and made this island and Labrador, are shadowy. His voyage in 1501 is given by Pasqualigo, the Venetian Ambassador, and Alberto Cantino. Two of his vessels brought home fifty or sixty natives. The king was much pleased with the description of the country, on account of the timber, and he said the captives—probably Montagnais —were the best slaves he had ever seen. The daring Gaspar was lost on the Labrador coast.

The Rev. George Patterson, in his very able and learned paper—"A Lost Chapter in American History"—informs us that:—

"Immediately after Gaspar Cortereal's first voyage—1500 or 1501—fishing companies were formed in Viana, Aveiro, and Terceira, Portugal, for the purpose of founding establishments in Terra Nova. In 1506 the King of Portugal gave orders that all fishermen returning from Newfoundland should pay a tenth part of their profits at the Custom House. At different times Aveiro alone had 60 vessels sailing to Newfoundland, and in 1550 150 fishing vessels. Equal numbers sailing from Oporto and other ports, gave a large increase of revenue."[1]

This is not the only or, to us, the most important of the "lost chapters" of our history. As regards England's share in this great Transatlantic codfishery, most writers have declared that, for the first half of the sixteenth century—from 1500 to 1560—there were no English fishermen or traders in Newfoundland. As I read the testimony of the Records, this is absolutely an incorrect view of history. The silence of historians on such a subject is no evidence whatever. Such a vulgar subject as the fishery and fishermen was quite beneath the dignity of history. The annals of the kingdom were the acts of princes. The destiny of nations was truly, in these times, the sport of kings; consequently, we have every vagary, religious and matrimonial, of Henry the VIIIth, the cut of Elizabeth's ruffs, and the colour of her petticoats, while there is not a word about the daring fishermen who left little obscure western ports to found our Colonial Empire. The public—the common people who formed the British nation—seem to be entirely

---

Cape Verde Islands, measured from a point midway between the two; all west of this line to belong to Spain, all east to Portugal. It is doubtful whether the Pope originally intended to grant the Peninsular Powers territory in America north of Spanish latitudes, especially when we consider that England was still a Roman Catholic country and friendly with Spain; certainly by his charters Henry VII. repudiated any such interpretation; perhaps the divorce of Catherine and Henry's quarrel with the Pope caused the Spanish to claim all America west of the line. I think the Portuguese claimed our island at first under pretence of prior discovery, and not by virtue of the Papal decision. In the earlier maps Newfoundland was placed much too far to the east to come within the Portuguese jurisdiction. Ribero, the Spanish official cartographer, gives Greenland only to the English, whilst our island is marked Tiera Nova de Cortereal, and the United States as Tiera de Esteva Gomez. In the Maiollo map our island is marked Cortereal. In the fine map of Mercator (1569) we have much fuller geographical information, and the Portuguese and Spanish pretensions as owners of the whole new world are no longer maintained.

[1] *Trans. Royal Society of Canada*, vol. viii., sec. ii., p. 145, 1890. *The Portuguese on the north-east coast of America, &c.*, by Rev. G. PATTERSON, D.D.

ignored. Take the very latest English Histories on the Tudor Period, and you will find about three lines on the discovery of North America, and a hundred pages devoted to Anne Boleyn. The true history of the period can only be found in the Records and the grand old Acts of Parliament. It is on the undoubted evidence of these ancient documents that I base my argument that England governed Newfoundland and participated in her fishery continuously from the earliest period. It is certain that Cabot made two, if not three voyages, and that the second was partly for trading. The following entries show that there were English or Anglo-Portuguese trading voyages to the new isle in the first years of the sixteenth century :—

"1502, January 7.—To men of Bristoll that founde Thisle, £5.

"1502, Sep. 30.—To the merchants of Bristoll that have bene in the Newefounde Launde, £20.

"17th Nov. 1503.—To one that brought haukes from the Newfounde Island, £1.

"8th April 1504.—To a Preste that goeth to the New Islande, £2." [1]

"1505, 25 August.—To Clays going to Richmond with wylde catts and popyngays of the Newfound Island for his costs 13/4.

"25 September [?].—To Portzugales that brought popyngais and catts of the mountaigne with other stuf to the kinges grace.[2]

"This year [3] (1502) were brought unto the king three men taken in ye Newfound Islands by Sebastian Gabote before-named, in Anno Domini 1498. These men were clothed in beast skins and eate raw flesh, but spake such a language as no man could understand, of the which three men two of them were seen in the king's court, at Westminster, two yeeres after. They were clothed like Englishmen, and could not be discerned from Englishmen." [4]

We have further proof that the West of England was foremost in these enterprises. Will anyone for a moment believe that these Devonshire fishermen—the most pugnacious and pertinacious race in all the three kingdoms—ever entered upon a most profitable business and then gave it up? This argument, strong as it may appear to anyone acquainted with West Countrymen, is not all or even the strongest proof; the unanswerable argument is contained in the Acts of Henry VIII., 1541, and Edward VI., 1548 (referred to in my next chapter), where the Newfoundland fishery is classed with old-established trades like the Iceland and Orkney fisheries. Then we have the statements of Hayes and Parkhurst about the ancient and established rule of the English in the Colony. How could it be established or ancient if English fishermen were absent from Newfoundland from 1500 to 1500? A late

---

[1] Bentley's *Historia Excerpta*, 1831, pp. 126, 129, 131, 133.

[2] Cf. *M[onte] de Gatto* in the Maiollo map, and the numerous Cat Bays, &c. on our coast. This animal was the Canadian lynx, called in Newfoundland "wild cat"; it was very common in the early days, and Head-Constable O'Reilly informs me they are still abundant on the west coast. Popinjay is from a Portuguese word, "papagayo," for a bright-coloured bird, probably an owl or hawk; these birds are very abundant on the island, and in great variety.

[3] It is generally thought that these natives were brought over in 1502, and that Sebastian Cabot's name was an erroneous interpolation of some later transcriber.

[4] Stowe's *Annales*, 1615, p. 485.

English writer—J. A. Doyle—"The English in America," speaks of the English sailors of this time as "jeopardizing their lives on the dreary "coast of Labrador, and bringing home strange birds and savage men "to amuse the citizens of London." Does Mr. Doyle suppose the Devonshire fishermen let the French and Portuguese reap all the benefits of this splendid and profitable fishery, which Raleigh declared in his day was the mainstay and support of the western countries, and content themselves with catching hawks and capturing Indians? Truly, this would not be the West Country way!

From contemporary records we can now state pretty accurately when the various nations began to fish in Newfoundland. The English in 1498; the records show their continuous operations from that date. The Portuguese appear to have commenced the fishery in 1501. The first account of the French is in 1504. There is a record of a voyage of Jean Denys, of Harfleur, to Newfoundland in 1506;[1] he is said to have made a map of the Island, which has been lost. In the Paris National Library the following record has been found by M. Harrisse:—

"Let a note be made of the mark of my boats and barks which I leave in Newfoundland in the haven of Jean Denys' called Rougnoust."[2]

As we have seen, the first and chief result of the discovery of North America was the immediate establishment of a great fishery. In all ages of the world the fishery has been the mother of commerce, the parent of navigation. The cod fishery, pursued by Englishmen first in Iceland, and afterwards on a larger scale in Newfoundland, made Englishmen sailors, and Britain a great maritime Power. De Witt says:—

"The navy of England became formidable by the discovery of the inexpressible rich fishing bank of Newfoundland."

SEBASTIAN CABOT.

[1] Ramusio's *Delle Navigationi*, 1559, vol. iii., p. 423, &c.
[2] *Paris National Library*; MSS. Francais, 24,269.
[3] From Winsor's *N. & C. Hist. of America*, iii. 5. Mr. Charles Deane (*N. & C. H. of A.*, iii. 31) says the original portrait is mentioned by Purchas; it hung for some time at Whitehall, from whence it disappeared. Mr. Biddle found and purchased it, but unfortunately it was burnt at his house in Pittsburgh, Pa., in 1845, not, however, before two good copies had been made, from one of which, by Chapman, this engraving is made. The portrait represents Cabot after his return to England, when he was a very old man.

[1] p. 2729.

It was this industry that first started the early colonisation of North America; the fishery was the powerful incentive that bound England to the New World for a century. The first attempted settlement of New England by Gosnold and Brereton in 1602 was to prosecute this fishery.

It is amongst the popular fictions of American history that when the Pilgrim Fathers moored their barque on the wild New England shore, their sole object was to worship God in their own way, and to kill Quakers after their own fashion, but sober history tells quite a different tale. In Winslow's "Brief Narration of the True Grounds or Causes of "the first Planting of New England," it is stated that when the Puritans sent agents from Leyden to the High and Mighty Prince James to gain his consent to their going to America, the king at once asked, "What profit might arise?" They answered in one single word—"Fishing." "So God have my soul," said the royal Solon, "'tis an honest trade; 'twas the Apostles' own calling"; and so they obtained leave to go. They sought a place for their settlement convenient for cod fishing and whaling, and in 1624 they sent to England a ship laden with salt-codfish.

The time of the discovery of Newfoundland was a fortunate period for England. Henry's love of money kept him from war, and under his peaceful reign Britain began, as it were, to gird up her loins for the great onward race that was to commence in the succeeding reigns. In order to understand the importance of the discovery of the New World to England, we must first try to realise the contemporary history of the Mother Country.

At this distance of time it is difficult to picture to ourselves how small and unimportant England then was. She had a comparatively small foreign trade, principally in wool. To encourage this manufacture, it was made law that everyone dying should be buried in wool. Even this small commerce was principally in the hands of foreigners. Fancy an age that had neither tea nor coffee, when potatoes and tobacco were unknown. Except for very rich people, who had game, there was no fresh meat to be had all through the winter.[1] Fish, fresh and salted, formed the chief article of winter diet. To our forefathers of that age, therefore, the discovery of the fishing grounds of Newfoundland was a veritable God-send—a piscatorial El Dorado. Codfish was gold in these

---

[1] PRICES OF MEAT AND BEER.—The price of meat in the Tudor age: 1 cwt. of beef, 4s. 8d.; beef and pork, about ½d. per lb.; mutton, 3 farthings per lb.; when the quarter of malt was 2s., ale was one half-penny per gallon; when it rose to 4s., the gallon of ale was one penny. Spaniards were astonished at the English food. "They live in poor houses," said the lordly dons, "but they fare as well as a king." These prices should be multiplied several times to bring them up to modern money value.

DESCRIPTION OF THE EARLY FISHERY.

old days.[1] The History of Newfoundland, especially its earliest annals, is essentially a history of the cod fishery.

It is a strange feature in those turbulent times, amidst wars and rumours of wars, to find fishermen sailing unnoticed from little harbours in Northern Spain, Portugal, France, and the West of England, spring after spring, daring the dangers of the western seas, the fogs, the thick-ribbed ice, and, worse than all, the erring captains—as old Whitbourne called the rovers, pirates, and sanguinary sea-robbers of that wonderful age—to gather a harvest in the new-found-land.

These traders escaped the notice of kings and chroniclers; their humble calling ensured their safety for the first half century. In Newfoundland, besides the fisheries, they carried on a great free trade; oils and wines, and fruits of France, Spain, and Portugal, were exchanged for English cutlery and West of England cordage, cloth-hats, caps, and hosiery.[2] The business was most profitable all round; it built up the West of England. Each year these old mariners came out with the easterly winds in the spring. Of the French and Portuguese, some fished on the banks and brought their fish home green, but the majority met in St. John's every year, spring and autumn. From this harbour they spread themselves out, north and south, to carry on the shore fishery, each nationality going together in small companies of from four to six ships; returning to St. John's as a rendezvous each nation's ships sailed home together in convoy.[3]

Whilst the cod-fisher pursued his calling in some snug harbour—Spaniard's Bay, Portugal Cove, Biscayan Cove, Frenchman's Cove,

---

[1] PRICE OF FISH, 1512 to 1525.—EARL PERCY'S HOUSEHOLD EXPENSES. "Item to be paid to the said Richard Gowge and Thomas Percy to make provision for CXL stock-fish for the expensys of my house for a hole yere after ijd obol the pece by estimacion. And so the hole somme for full contentacion for the said stock-fish for one hole yere is XXXIII jd (33s. 3d.)
  Same account for her-
    rings for a year - £4 10s. 0d.
  Salt fish cod for one
    year - - - 18 4s. 0d.
  Red herrings - - 3 3s. 4d.
  Salt salmon - - 5 0s. 0d."
Newfoundland fish, in the days of Queen Elizabeth, was sold at 10s. per 100 fish—equal to 50s. per qtl. This would be quite up to the old West Countryman's toast in Newfoundland—"the Pope and ten dollars"—a price per quintal often got in Spain early in this century.

[2] Two articles in which the West of England were pre-eminent in the days of Elizabeth (and for which Devon and Dorset are still celebrated in the reign of Victoria) were West of England cloth and Bridport cordage. Even in our time, the Spaniards bought Gundry's lines, twines and cordage in St. John's to take back to Spain.

[3] The names on the east coast of Newfoundland, especially about Conception and Trinity Bay, all prove the early occupation of these localities by the English. There is not a solitary foreign name in Trinity Bay. To escape the exactions of the English, who ruled over all from the very commencement of the fishery, the Portuguese spread themselves south, west, and north. Cartier met Portuguese vessels in the Straits of Belle Isle, and we see from the Basque records (page 48) that the hardy Biscayans fished together in small companies of two and three vessels. The list given of the various ports frequented by them, shows how widely spread were their operations. Their great object was to avoid contact as much as possible with the overbearing English; their poor ragged hireling crews had no chance in a fight with the Devonshire freebooters. In the south of Newfoundland, it is made part of a fisherman's agreement that "a share of a wreck"

B 2

English Harbour—the more daring spirits, chiefly the Biscayans, chased the seal and the walrus in the Gulf, and followed the dangerous trade of the whale fishery. The head-quarters of the latter were the Ramea Islands (the present Magdalen Islands), the Straits of Belle Isle, and the north-east portion of the Gulf of St. Lawrence. They followed their quiet avocations armed to the teeth. Each vessel mounted cannon, and his rude arms always lay alongside the fisherman as he plied his oar and cast his net. But they were merry souls amidst all the dangers of the seas, wars, pirates, and rovers. Each week the Admiral of the port retired, and at every change the new official gave a feast to all. The cheap and generous wines of Europe would then be freely circulated, and the sombre woods of the little port be enlivened, perchance, by the chanson of the French or the rattling of the castanets and lively airs on the Spanish guitar. If it was a Basque port the fun would be fast and furious—there would be the national Gaita (the bag-pipes) and song, dance, and single-stick with broken heads, to enliven the feast.

If there were English there they would be admirals and rulers over all, and woe betide the foreigner who disobeyed the West Countryman's orders, or dared to do anything on Sunday but drink and feast.

We are indebted to a French lawyer, Lescarbot,[1] who was one of the first French explorers of Nova Scotia, for a graphic description of the surroundings of these ancient fishermen. He says one old master, Captain Savalet, of the little French frontier seaport of St. Jean de Luz—

"Received us with all the kindness in the world. The good honest man told me that the same voyage was the forty-second voyage that he had made in those parts, and nevertheless the Newfoundland men do make but one a year. He was marvellously pleased with his fishing, and told me, moreover, that he took, every day, fifty crownes worth of fish, and that his voyage would be worth £1,000. He paid wages to sixteen men and his vessel was of eighty tunnes and would carry 100,000 dry fishes."[2]

Besides this description we have an ancient picture of the mode of fishing, the stage, the water-horse, the splitting-table, the pews, the flakes, the hand barrows; all are exactly like those to be found to this day around our shores. The hook used was very large, and the barb shaped

---

shall form part of his compensation, and in the Elizabethan days the spoils of a Spaniard was considered as regular an incident in the fishery as the share of cod. All foreigners made St. John's their rendezvous for convoy. The end of August was a usual time for sailing, and the presence of so many Portuguese and other foreign vessels in St. John's during Gilbert's visit is thus accounted for. The great Portuguese fishing fleet, which in the Elizabethan age employed several thousand men, is now represented by two banking schooners, and about fifty fishermen.

[1] MARC LESCARBOT—"Avocat en Parlament"—came out to Annapolis (the French Port Royal) with Poutrincourt in 1606. He was a jovial fellow, who enjoyed the rough life with the Indians, fishing, shooting, and camping out. He helped to found the first settlement in Nova Scotia (Acadie). For a promenade in the winter he built a covered verandah to their house. We owe to this whole-souled lawyer "The History of New France."

[2] LESCARBOT'S *Nova Francia*, London, 1609, p. 129.

like a harpoon. The dress of the fisherman is quaint; each worker is represented with a long bib—the barvel—reaching from his neck to his toes, tied in at the waist, long boots, a sort of mop cap, or something like a soft felt with the brim turned down, or else the "borra" copied from the Basque, like the bonnet or Tam-O'Shanter of the Highlander. All wore broad leather belts; braces are quite a modern invention. I have never seen a barvel myself, but an old friend, Mr. John Pike of St. Lawrence, tells me he can remember when all the fishermen used them; they were made of sheep skin, with the wool inside, the outside coated with tar—long aprons, like the dress of the ancient fishermen, fastened with a belt. This was before the invention of oil clothes. Barvels were used by fishermen all along the North American coast.

The shore codfishery, known amongst the French as "*La pêche sedentaire*," was pursued very much in the same manner as it is carried on to-day. The boats went out before dawn, returned with their loads, the fish were thrown up at the stage heads, split, and salted. The splitting table, the trough, known as the water horse (for washing out the fish after salting), the flakes (stages raised on piles and covered with boughs), were all in general use from the very commencement of this great industry.

The bank or deep sea codfishery was carried on very differently from our modern methods. The men all fished from the ship, each in a sort of gangway hung over the side of the vessel, as depicted in the engraving.

In those early days, when bultows were unknown and traps undreamed of, the old-fashioned fishermen, with their primitive hook as big as a small killock, with a huge lump of lead or iron for a sinker, and a rough strong hemp line, caught codfish galore. Some of the early writers stated that the fish were so abundant that the bears used to catch them; I have heard an old planter declare that the cod crowded into the land so in his time that he has seen a dog catch fish; Jukes, in his "Excursions in Newfoundland," mentions a dog of George Harvey's, Isle-aux-Morts, which caught sculpins. Although the early cod catchers fished mostly with hook and line, they had nets in addition, for the capture of herring, and were acquainted with the use of seines, for the taking both of bait and larger fish.

The English was entirely a shore fishery, on the principle of shares, the owners of the vessel receiving two-thirds of the catch, the crew one-third.[1] The Bretons and Normans also divided the proceeds of the voyage. The French and Spanish Basques and the Portuguese all paid

---

[1] This was a custom long before Newfoundland was discovered (cf. PALMER's *Manship*, vol. ii., p. 88).

their men wages. The Portuguese were partly shore fishermen, partly bankers. The Spanish Basques or Biscayans, shore fishermen, whalers, and sealers. The French were mostly bankers, and carried their fish home, as they do now, green, to be afterwards dried and made in France; many, however, were engaged in the shore fishery.

At first the English had very small vessels, their average size being less than fifty tons; by Whitbourne's time they had increased to about eighty tons. From the very earliest period the English had a carrying fleet (sack ships); as the small over-crowded fishing ships were not able to convey the product of their voyage, so larger vessels took the dried fish to the Mediterranean markets. The Bretons and Normans, who were deep-sea fishermen, braved the dangers of the Atlantic in wretched little tubs. Much larger craft were employed by the Basques and Portuguese; we read of Basque vessels of four hundred tons, manned by forty men.

Besides carrying on a shore fishery the fishermen did a barter trade with the Indians for furs, and like good Christians they tried to convert the dusky savages. When one of the chiefs was being taught the Lord's prayer, he came to a full stop when he was told to say, "Give us this day our daily bread"; he asked if he prayed for bread alone, would he get any fish or moose meat? " I am afraid," says Lescarbot, "the sincerity of their conversion is very questionable."

The uncouth West Country name—The New-founde-lande—which has remained the designation of our Island, applied in the sixteenth century not only to this Colony, but also to Nova Scotia, New Brunswick, Cape Breton, Prince Edward's Island, and the islands and coasts of the Gulf of St. Lawrence, even down to the State of Maine. Foreigners called these countries by the generic name of the "Baccalaos"—the land of dried-cod-fish.

By 1509, Henry VII. was gathered to his fathers; he never dreamed of the mighty empire in the West which his subjects were founding— the New England that was to be. Ignoble and inglorious, however, as were the days of his reign, they served as a peaceful preparation for the coming time—the golden age of his descendant, Queen Elizabeth.

APPENDIX TO CHAPTER II.

I. The Iceland Fishery.

The Iceland trade and fishery is frequently mentioned in the Records; I think it embraced, as the Newfoundland fishery did in later times, a much wider area than the name implied. Probably fishermen frequently brought their products to Westmaney, not only from "Gunnbeorn's Skerries" and the east coast of Greenland, but also from Wardhouse, beyond Cape North, and from the Luffoden Islands, the higher prices realised for the cure of the real Iceland fish making it profitable to bring fish from other localities to be re-sold as "Iceland." The extent and ramifications of the trade and exchange formerly carried on in Iceland and the adjacent seas, and England's share in it, are not fully realised by historians. The mention of a "*Bloberhouse*" in the will of John Sparks, of Cromer, in 1483 (RYE'S *Cromer, Past and Present*, p. 51), and the depiction of an English ship whaling in OLAUS MAGNUS' *Carta Marina*, 1539 (see WINSOR'S *N. & C. H. of A.*, i. 123), look as if Englishmen, as well as Biscayners, were engaged in the fifteenth century in whaling. Mr. Palmer says the English merchants went to Wardhouse for herrings, I suppose for bait (PALMER's *Manship*, i. 311).

English fishermen, accustomed to range over the whole north-eastern littoral of the Atlantic, would not be likely to allow the new opening in the west to remain long undeveloped. There seems some ground for supposing that the Labrador section of our fishery, reached by way of Cape Farewell, was at first reckoned as a part of the Iceland voyage, and the catch sold as Iceland fish. (Cf. ZILGLER's map of *Gronlandia* and *Terra Bacallaos*, 1532; we read [from East Greenland], "Inde continuator littori terræ Baccallaos.")

Robert Bacon, a mariner of Cromer, who captured James I. of Scotland in 1405, claims to have been the discoverer of Iceland (RYE's *Cromer, Past and Present*, p. 49); this, probably, only means that he was the first Cromer man who engaged in the trade.

In 1400 England had fishery rights around the Island (*Cotton MSS.*), but even in 1360 it must have been a regular voyage, for one Nicolas of Lynn had been five times there, on one occasion making the voyage in a fortnight. (ZARTMANN's *Nouvelles Annales.*) There is an undated MS. at Hatfield, No. 186/72, about "the priviledge of ancient fishing in Iceland." Kohl, in his *Discovery of Maine* (p. 113), quoting from Magnuesen, says that in one snowstorm in April 1419, as many as 25 English vessels were wrecked, and their crews drowned; the disaster was attributed to the treachery of the islanders, and an armed force was sent from England to take revenge. Kohl also says that Englishmen frequently landed and fortified themselves in Iceland, and acted as if they intended to retain permanent possession of the island. This statement is borne out by a map made about 1520, marked No. 4 in Kuntsmann's atlas, which shows the English standard on the island.

The following records from Rymer's *Fœdera* show to some extent the course of English commerce in the north in the thirteenth, fourteenth, and fifteenth centuries.

FROM RYMER's *Fœdera*.

Letter in 1217, from Henry III. to the King of Norway, saying he will gladly promote commercial intercourse with that realm. Letter from the King of Norway in 1284, asking Edward to protect the Norse merchants from the Germans while in England. In 1309, Edward II. told the King of Norway he would be glad to renew the ancient friendships between the realms. In 1311, compensation was claimed for injuries committed on the sailors of an English ship wrecked in Norway. In 1313 there are two complaints from Edward II. to the King of Norway, that certain English sailors were imprisoned in Norway, and Edward asks the Norwegian king to listen to the petition of the English merchants; and later on, in the same year, he requests the restoration of the goods of the Englishmen. In 1316, compensation was claimed for injuries done to some merchants of Berwick by Norwegians. In 1361, Edward III. demanded restitution to W. de Stokesby and other English merchants whose ship was plundered at Cost, in Norway. In 1408 license was granted to the English merchants in Norway, Sweden, and Denmark, to elect *governors*.

In 1411, Henry IV. informed the council of North Berne [Bergen], that he had forbidden the Hanse merchants to leave England in consequence of the injuries done to English merchants; he also informed them that he had granted licenses to nine merchants at St. Botolph to leave England. In 1412, the merchants of Lenn (Lynn) were illtreated by the Hanse; Henry IV. desired the Lynn and Hanse merchants to investigate the matter. On 28th November 1415, the English king forbade fishermen going to Iceland and the other islands of Norway and Denmark, except in accordance with *ancient customs*. In 1416, a ship was granted to the Danish ambassador to return home. In 1432 there is a resolution to send ambassadors to Denmark.

On 28th January 1438, a license was given to John Bp. of Shalholt in Iceland, to take a ship to Iceland and send it back with merchandise [? fish] for the payment of his creditors. Similar license to John Bp. of Holar. On 26th February a license to John Secheford and John Candeler, to export corn and other victuals to Iceland for the use of the Bp. of Scalhelte, confessor of the King of Denmark. On 12th May 1444, there is a proclamation to the sheriffs of London, Norfolk, and six other places to forbid all persons going to Iceland or other parts prohibited by the King of Denmark. On 4th December 1445, there is a safe-conduct to Godsuin, Bp. of Shalholt, to go to Iceland, and return. In the spring of 1450, all ships were debarred from going to Iceland except two of Canynge's. In 1447, the Dean of Salisbury went as ambassador to Denmark; and in 1449, Sir R. Shottisbroke. On 4th July 1450, there is the exemplification of a safe-conduct until Michaelmas 1451 from the King of Denmark to English merchants, and of a license from the marshall and master of the chamber of the King of Denmark to John Wolffe, of England, to trade to Iceland.

Danish ambassadors were in England in 1464, and a treaty was made in 1465 with Denmark, at Hamburgh. In 1473, Edward IV. promised to keep the treaty for two years, and hold a diet to settle differences. The King of Denmark himself proposed to or did come to England this year, for a safe-conduct was granted to him. In 1476, the treaty was renewed to 1478, and again to 1480, during which time a diet was to be held. A fresh treaty was signed in 1479. On 22nd October 1478, there is a license to John and Thomas Alcok to trade to Iceland, and on April 24th, 1483, a further license to Robert Alcok, of Kingston-on-Hull, to send a ship laden with merchandise to Iceland.

In the course of the negotiations in 1600, Rymer notices the exemplification of a treaty made in 1489-90; this was evidently the basis of all arrangements during the sixteenth century. It must have been in settling this treaty, or in the further discussion which took place about 1492, that Cabot was employed by Henry VII. (cf. ANSPACH's *H. of Newfoundland*, p. 25; no authority given).

In 1531 the Danes complained of injuries done to their subjects, and Henry VIII. made a counter-complaint that 50 Englishmen had been killed that year in Iceland, and Cromwell in 1534 has a "remembrance" of the losses of a Mr. Honyng there (*Records*). The English also had many conflicts with their rivals, the Hanse merchants. This fishery had another special danger; the Scotch used to lay in wait for the ships on their way home and capture them—they did this even late in Elizabeth's reign (*Records*, 1584); for this reason we constantly read of ships being sent to "waft" the Iceland fleet past the Scottish coast (*Records*, 1523). It was the custom at Yarmouth, at a Corporation dinner given on Black Friday (before Palm Sunday), to remind the mayor to write for a convoy for the Iceland fleet (PALMER's *Manship*, ii. 62).

The following interesting Icelandic Annals, which Mr. York Powell has very kindly literally translated for me, give a graphic picture of the early fishing, and show the close social, ecclesiastical, and commercial connexion which existed between the two countries in the fifteenth century. Mr. York Powell says there are several notices of the Iceland fishery in COOPER's *Appendix to the Fœdera*.

ENTRIES IN THE ICELANDIC ANNALS.

"1336. Arne abbot of Lysa beheaded off England and all his ship's crew by the Duggars and all cast overboard.

"1349. At that time a cog sailed out of England with many folk aboard and laid in off Bergen-bay and was but little unladen when all the folk died on board and as soon as the goods came into the town off the ship the townfolk straightway began to die. Then the sickness went all over Norway and laid it so waste that there did not survive one-third part of the people of the land. England's cog sunk with nigh all the goods and the dead and it was not unladen. More ships and busses sunk with their cargo and men yet unladen.

"1412. A ship came from England east of Deerholmsey; they rowed out to them, and they were fishermen out of England; that same fall there were five of the Englishmen that parted from their companions and came ashore east of Horn out of a boat and said they wished to buy food saying that they had starved on the boat many a day. These five Englishmen were here the winter over, for their ship was away when they went back for her and all aboard her.

"1413. A merchant ship came out of England to Iceland the skipper was named Richard New he had the king of Norway's letters to let him sail in his realm with his merchant ship freely . . . many bought wares of him down at the sound [Hafnafiord] but many wise men took it ill. He sailed a short while after, he never came back to Iceland. Vigus Ivarsson took an oath from him that he would be faithful and true to the country. The five Englishmen that had been here over the winter sailed with him.

"Fishermen from England came north off Iceland and took some meat off a yeoman and left money instead thereof. *Item* the English seized in the Eastfirths some sheep in Papey off Elfetfirth. There sailed hither out of England that summer 30 fishing boats or more.

"There came 5 English ships to Iceland and lay inside the Westmanneys. There came out a letter sent from the English king to the Commonalty and the best men in the country to allow leave of trade to his men, especially in the ship that belonged to him. At first they talked about the Bergen tariff but the Englishmen would not take part therein. Afterwards they traded each man as it suited him best.

"Two nights before Allhallowsmass there was a fire at Bergen. The fire broke out first in the *Englishmen's yard*.

"1415. That same summer 6 ships from England lay near Hafnarfirth. Franklin Vigtus Iwarsson sailed out to England, and he had with him 60 lasts of dried fish and a good deal of pure silver.

"1419. On Thursday there came such a bad gale with snow that far and wide round the land English ships were wrecked no fewer than 25, all the men were lost but the goods and pieces of the ships were washed up. The storm came on a little before daymeal and did not last till high day.

"The Icelanders wrote this year to King Eric of Pomerania respecting foreign traders and fishers.

"1420. Thorleif Arnason sailed hence and fought with the English at sea and made Norway safely.

"1425. There were taken on the Westmanneys Baltazar and Sir Hamos and flitted over to England, few thought that a loss.

"1426. Baltazar came out and was greeted as Governor by all. He sailed back to England that same summer, with them that he had come with.

"1427. Bishop John Johnson of Holar came out to Hafnarfirth with the English.

"1428. Many shipwrecks by reason of the great storms at sea 18 ships wrecked at Acreness. Two sexareens were cast up at Musarness far on to the mire, all unhurt.

"1429. The Lord Bishop John Johnson came to Holar from England. [He had gone back to England for a while in 1427.]

"1430. In that same year there came out hither to this country Bishop John Geridisson Bishop of Scalholt he came with his ship to Hafnarfirth Wednesday next after the mass of John the Baptist. The lord bishop came out of England where he had stayed the winter before . . . two priests came out hither with Lord John Bishop of Shalholt one named Matthew the other Nicholas. Priest Nicholas sailed back that same summer later on and with him many lasts of dried fish in the bishop's name, for it was easy for him to get fish and other things for the people of this country favoured the bishop rather.

"1467. The end was that Sir Biorn was slain by the English at Rif . . . and in vengeance thereof afterward in the summer she [the Lady Olaf] had all the English slain and she had twelve of them bound with a rope and all their heads cut off.

"1510. In the days of Bishop Stephen was a fight at the Westmanneys between Englishmen and the men of Side [an Icelandic district]. There fell 14 Englishmen and one priest of the Icelanders Sir John by name and he was called 'butter-nose.' . . . Some years after in 1518, or thereabout, there was a fight between the English and the Hamburgers in Hafnarfirth.

"1530. Erland of Strand and his men fought with the English in Grindwick . . . he also slew two Englishmen guiltless . . . one named John Dalton . . . the other was called Nicholas.

"In the days of Bishop Gredmund the Dutch [Germans] and English fought at Grindwick . . . The Dutch came on them unawares and drunken. There fell 14 Englishmen and their skipper Ricki Bray.

"1520. Sir Martein sailed nine winters with the English. . . he first sailed with Robert that married his sister Gudlang Enias's daughter here. The bridal was at the cut of the English. The English brought a tun of wine out of every ship and there lay 9 ships there. The feast lasted half a month. They sailed thence that same summer and Sir Martein with them, he went to an English school [university]."

Bristol at one time took a leading position in the Iceland trade. In 1436 Henry VI. granted a license to John, the Bishop of Holar, who was then in London from Iceland, in which he authorised him to engage John May [of Bristol], with his ship the *Katherine*, for a voyage to Iceland. May was to act as the bishop's attorney, and to transact his business, as the bishop did not wish to leave England (RYMER's *Fœdera*).

In 1450, all ships were "stayed" from the Iceland and Finmark voyages, exception only being made in favour of two ships of William Canynge, who had lent the king money (cf. SEYER and GALLAWAY). For the next fifty years at least, Bristol, through Canynge's enterprise, was the chief market for dry-cod, and her historians claim the most important port in Europe; from her wharves the products of the Northern fisheries were distributed all over the Latin States. The merchant marine of the Atlantic seaboard was employed largely in carrying for this trade; Columbus in 1477 and, no doubt, Cabot and Cortereal engaged in it; in fact, Cabot must have had great experience in Iceland to be entrusted to conclude an agreement about the fishery with Denmark.

Though the trade up to the discovery of America had been controlled by Bristol merchants, I can only find one occasion recorded in which West Country ships went to Iceland during the sixteenth century (*Records*, 1594). This does not by any means prove that no other ships went, but the marked absence of the names of western ports from the lists of those that sent ships to Iceland is significant.

In 1510 Henry VIII. repealed an Act, 8 Henry VI. cap. ii., 1429, by which it was agreed that all Englishmen going to buy fish were required, upon pain of forfeiture of all goods, to go to the "staple" town of North Bergen, where they would enjoy the same rights as the Hanse; the Act of Henry VI. was to prevent the great disorders then occurring at the fishery. Henry VI. was a nephew of the King of Denmark.

The repeal of this old agreement with Denmark was probably to give relief to the east coast traders, who were already feeling the effect of Newfoundland competition.

In 1517 there were 300 English traders in one port, Hafnar Fiord, but in 1581 the entire fleet apparently numbered only 200, probably all from Suffolk and Norfolk (23 Eliz. cap. vii.). In 1533, for some reason, only 85 ships, all from the east coast, appear to have composed the Iceland fleet; they paid £414 duty on their catch. (*Records*.)

In 1523 we appear to have further evidence that the opening up of our fishery was affecting this trade, for we find Christian II. asking Henry VIII. if he wished to trade to Iceland (*Records*). The frequent changes also in the Charters of the Stockfishmongers would seem to indicate that there was a disturbing element felt in London in the early part of the sixteenth century (cf. HERBERT's *Twelve Livery Co.'s*).

In 1512 the cost of "great dry Hisselonde fish" was 38s. 4d. for every 124; next year it was sold to Government for the army at 53s. 9½d. per 100! (*Records*). This shows indirectly the enormous profits which must have been made in the Newfoundland fishery for the first half of the century. Later, when these high prices could no longer be maintained owing to the Reformation and the increasing supply of Newfoundland fish, we have constant complaints from merchants about false counting, especially of cod fish imported in barrels. (*Lausdowne MSS.*, 1583, &c.; 5 Eliz. V. made it illegal to import cod in barrels). It is interesting to notice a petition in 1568 (when no doubt the market was flooded with Newfoundland fish) which states that badly dried fish was being brought in and sold as "*Iceland*" fish. (*Hatfield MS.*) I think this refers to Labrador fish. The profits of the Eastlanders, who had clung to the Iceland trade, were evidently dwindling away; they could not afford to sell their fish at 10s. per 100.

As the Newfoundland trade monopolized the energies of the West and South coast of England, very little attention was paid to Iceland by the Government; Eastlanders, feeling the effect of low prices, ceased to pay their license fees to the King of Denmark. In 1580 the merchants of Eastland complained of Dr. Rodgers' unjust demands. (*Hatfield MS.*) Rodgers was evidently asking for dues owing to the King of Denmark, as he is the same person who, in 1592, requested the renewal of the Commercial Treaty mentioned below. In 1585, however, the merchants' remonstrance appear to have been attended to, as there is an Order in Council on July 25, "for redressing the wrongs of the English in Iceland" (*Records*).

On the 21st June 1590, the King of Denmark wrote that he had received the charge of C. Perkins, the Queen's ambassador, but must defer replying thereto as his counsellors are absent. (RYMER.)

A further petition was presented by the East Coast traders in 1591:—
"Time out of mind we have proceeded to Iceland for the buying of stock fish and taking of green fish such as codd, ling &c. Now are prevented at Westmaney [Iceland] from pitching booths or buying fish. Used to pay when we had booths 5 marks, if only for fishing one angel and a barrel of salt or a barrel of beare no more." (*Hatfield MS.*)

The loss of revenue was evidently keenly felt in Denmark. We find a warrant in 1586 allowing the king himself, in his own ships, to import a cargo of fish duty free to Harwich, and take away some Wiltshire woollen goods and tin. (*Hatfield MS.*)

Matters reached a climax in 1592, when the agreement allowing the English to fish in Iceland had not been renewed for twelve years, though terminable every seven years, and the King of Denmark was "offended" (*Records*); the reason seems to have been that the trade was carried on at a loss, for Raleigh next year said the Newfoundland was the only profitable fishery, "the Newfoundland voyages are the only ones making any profit." (*Hatfield MS.*)

On the 8th July 1595, the King of Denmark wrote to Elizabeth to say he could permit Englishmen to fish in Iceland except at Westmaney, which is reserved for the Court; he complained of the conduct of English fishermen. (RYMER.)

In 1598 the senate of Denmark advised Sir T. Egerton, Lord Buckhurst, and the Earl of Essex, to use moderation and prudence in settling the differences between the two kingdoms. (RYMER.)

This year Dr. Perkins was sent to Denmark to make fresh arrangements with the Danish king (*Hatfield MS.*), whose "remonstrances" were considered next year by the English Council (*B.M. MS. Vesp. CXIV.*) In 1600 there were apparently some further attempts at a settlement (cf. RYMER's notice of the 1479 treaty in this year). In February 1600, Elizabeth complained that her fishermen had been forbidden by Danish officers to fish in the "deep sea" in the north. (RYMER.) No terms seem to have been arrived at, for in 1602 the King again prohibited fishing in Iceland to all strangers without license. (*Lansdowne MS.*)

In the same year complaint was made of injuries done to Englishmen; Christian IV. justified the seizure of vessels from Hull, and complained of the capture of Danish vessels. On July 15th Elizabeth said she would send commissioners to Bremen by September 25th to treat of commercial matters. The commissioners met in October, but returned home on hearing of the death of the queen. A treaty was ratified in 1621. (RYMER.)

A careful perusal of the Records seems to show that the Iceland voyage was gradually deserted by all but the Norfolk and Suffolk fishermen, who were frequently consulted about the decaying character of the trade. (*Hatfield MS.*, Aug. 7, 1602.)

In 1594 the inhabitants of Beeson and Sherringham are mentioned incidentally as being the chief traders to Iceland. (*Records.*)

The relative insignificance of this fishery in the latter half of the sixteenth century is shown in a petition in 1586 against the importation of foreign fish; the petition speaks of the time "*when the Iceland voyage was most frequented.*" (*Hatfield MS.*) It evidently was not then, nor had been for some time, any longer the dominating factor in the stock-fish market, and the statement of Parkhurst in Hakluyt, made eight years before, which has led many writers astray, that it was still the chief English fishery must be wrong.

It is only fair to state that Mr. Palmer says (*Manship* ii. 89) :—"During the reign of Charles I. the Iceland and North Sea fisheries for cod, &c., which had long been prosecuted with success, attained their greatest prosperity. About 150 vessels were then employed in the North Sea fishery off the coast of Norway and about 20 vessels went annually to Iceland. The half doles from these fisheries alone from 1645-49, averaged £300 per annum, but shortly afterwards they fell off, the fisheries became unsuccessful, and in 1740 only one vessel went to Iceland and doled £47 . . . . In 1607 the half dole only produced £135 on an average." If the £414 paid by 85 ships in 1533 was this same dole, the east coast fishery, or at any rate the Iceland section of it, can hardly be said to have reached its highest point in the seventeenth century. I suggest that the merchants of Norfolk and Suffolk were encouraged to re-embark in this trade on account of an unusual demand for fish caused by the civil war and the consequent cessation of agriculture, &c.

Two special causes helped to increase the Newfoundland fishery to the detriment of the Iceland traders. One was the advantage taken by the West Countrymen of the Act 5 Eliz. cap. V. to embark in a large export trade to make up for the diminishing demand in the home market; "the *poor* inhabitants of Norfolk and Suffolk" petitioned in 1568 against "the *new* evil of the priviledge of exporting fish free of duty." (*Records.*) The Act 23 Eliz. VII. (1580) recites :— "Where[as] the merchauntes of divers places of this realme [? West Countrymen] have for their private gaynes ingrossed unto their hands great quantities of fish taken by alienes, being in goodness farre inferiour to the fysh taken by Englishmen [? Eastlanders] in the Island voyages. . . . . there be of late decayed, not onely the number of two hundred sayle or more of good ships that yearly traded to Island for taking fish usuallye solde in this realme but also the number of maryners." . . . . .

The other cause which militated against treeless Iceland (Englishmen were not allowed to fish in Norway.—PALMER's *Manship*, i. 311) was the abundance of wood in Newfoundland for making stages and barrels. Though the question of barrelled fish, which was so much agitated in the trade from 1560 onwards for many years (cf. 5 Eliz. V. and *Lansdowne MSS.* from 1580 forwards), partly related to Dutch herrings and Cornish pilchards, the demand for licenses by West Countrymen like Downing (*Lansdowne MS.*, 1583) and Sir William Gorges (*Lansdowne MS.*, 1586) to import barrelled fish, and the prohibition in the Act 5 Eliz. cap. V. against importing cod in barrels, show, I think, that the practice of packing Newfoundland fish in this way was in use at this early period, and the facility it gave for easy distribution was no doubt one of the many causes which helped to transfer the English interest from Iceland to Newfoundland. The wording of sec. 7 of 5 Eliz. V., that "forasmuche as ther ys much decceiptful Packing used in Codd brought in Barralles into this Realme," all fish must be brought in "loose in Bulke and by Tale" refers, I venture to think, to dry fish as well as green.

The barrelling of cod fish must not, however, be understood to have originated at this time. In 1482 by 22 Edw. IV. c. 2, and in 1495 by 11 Henry VII. c. 23, most stringent regulations were laid down for barrelled fish, prescribing the size of the barrels, the size of the fish, the manner of splitting, boning, and packing; there were to be no "broken belied" fish; salmon and other fish were to be " xxvij inches from the bone of the fyn to the iij joynte of the taille, the bone to be taken away into the navel, the fyshe splatted [split] down to a handful [within a span] of the taile and not to be packed double in the barrel"; searchers and gangers were to be appointed to see the Act was carried out properly.

This note is simply a compilation of old records. Certain points are mere conjecture. A closer examination of the documents quoted may prove that they will not bear the interpretation put upon them; the history of early English commerce has yet to be written. A study of the Iceland fishery is interesting to Newfoundlanders; it helps to some extent to throw light upon the way in which our own was carried on at first, to fill a blank in our Island history. Englishmen seem to have "commanded all there," to have fearlessly traversed the northern seas to reap a golden harvest which built up the ancient towns of Norfolk and Suffolk.

This fishery is again receiving the attention of Englishmen; fast steam trawlers are now supplying the English markets with fresh fish from Iceland.

II. Pedro de Ayala's letter to Spain.
[*Original in cipher.*]
25 July 1498.

"I well believe that your Highnesses have heard how the King of England has equipped a fleet to discover certain Islands and mainland that certain persons who set out last year for the same have testified that they have found. I have seen the chart which the discoverer has drawn, who is another Genoese like Columbus, and has been in Seville and in Lisbon procuring to find those who would help him in this enterprise . . . . The King determined to despatch an expedition, because he had the certainty that they had found land last year. The fleet consists of five ships provisioned for one year. . . . . The Genoese went on his course. I have seen the course and distance he takes, think that the land they have found or seek is that which your Highnesses possess, for it is the end of that which belongs to your Highnesses by the convention with Portugal. It is hoped that they will return by September . . . . I believe the distance is not 400 leagues. And I told him that I thought they were the Islands discovered by your Highnesses, and I even gave him a reason, but he would not hear it; as I believe your Highnesses now have intelligence of all, as well as the chart or mappe-monde that this Genoese has made, I do not send it now, though I have it here; and to me it seems very false, to give out that they are not the said Islands."

III. Sebastian Cabot.

No history of Newfoundland will be considered complete without allusion to John Cabot's well-known son, although we have absolutely nothing to thank him for, quite the reverse.

Sebastian's friend, Martyr, was forced to admit that the Spaniards denied his claim to be the discoverer of North America.

The members of the Drapers Company in 1521, replying to a request of the king and Wolsey for ships to explore the Newfoundland (a general name then for all North America), said: "We think it were to sore adventure to jopard V shipps with men and goods unto the said Island uppon the singular trust of one man callyed as we understand Sebastyan which Sebastyan as we here say *was never in that land* hymself all if he makes reporte of many things as he hath heard his Father and other men speke in tymes past."

It is stated that he offered his services to the king for a voyage of discovery, but was refused. In 1512 he made a chart for Henry VIII. of the coast of Gascony and Guienne, in France, and in the same year took service with Spain as a reviser of maps and charts. He was specially engaged on account of his supposed exclusive knowledge of our coast. King Ferdinand wrote to Sebastian on 12th September 1512: "Sabeis que en Burgos os hablaron de mi parte Conchillos i el Obp. de Palencia sobre la navegacion á los Baccalos e ofrecistes servirnos." (HARRISSE'S *Disc. of N. America*, p. 20.) In 1518 he was appointed to examine all pilots for America.

In 1524, just before the Congress of Badajos, he came to England on some secret mission to Henry VIII.; 43s. 4d. was paid to J. Goderick for bringing him over. In 1526 he ascended the Paraguay, in South America, in command of an expedition in which Robert Thorne had adventured a large share. In 1547 he was again brought to England, at a cost of £100. In answer to three very urgent demands from Charles V. for his return to Spain—"a very necessary man for the Emperor, whose servant he was, and had a pension of him"—on 21st April 1550 the English Privy Council replied: "He of himself refused to go either to Spain or to the Emperor, and that he being of that mind, and the king's subject, no reason or equity that he should be forced against his will." — (*Harl.*, 523, folio 6.) In 1553 he was an active promoter and governor of the Muscovy Company. He is supposed to have died in 1557.

He claimed amongst the scientific navigators of the age the very highest position as an authority on all geographical questions, but appears to have gradually fallen into discredit.

Unfortunately, he was a great liar; every fresh record that is hunted up fixes him with a fresh falsehood. He told Eden that his father died, leaving him very rich, soon after the discovery of Columbus; his father was alive in 1498, and in the receipt of a pension, and very poor. He told his English friends he was Bristol born; he made Contarini believe he was a Venetian; he declared he could tell the distance at sea by the compass. He lied to Spain, to Italy, and to England. Edward VI. gave him a handsome pension—£166 13s. 4d.—but less than the splendid salary he had in Spain. In Queen Mary's time he had, no doubt at the instance of her husband, Philip II., to divide his pension with Worthington, and, between them, all his maps disappeared. Doubtless he was forced to sell them to the Spanish Government, and this may account for their total loss to the world.

Sebastian Cabot's instructions to Sir Hugh Willoughby show his character. "There is to be no dicing, carding, tabling; morning and evening prayers are to be said." On the other hand, "the natives of strange countries are to be enticed aboard and made drunk with your beer and wine, for then you shall know the secrets of their hearts." They were also to be "cautious about certain creatures with men's heads and the tails of fishes, who swim, with bows and arrows, about the fords and bays, and live on human flesh."

In their insular pride, Englishmen believed Sebastian Cabot, their countryman, was the great explorer who had found the new world. They gloried in his wonderful exploit, and resolutely ignored the real discoverer, his illustrious father.

The works of Biddle, Justin Winsor, Desimoni, and Harrisse contain the fullest documentary records of the Cabots. Recently there have been several new contributions to the history of John and Sebastian Cabot—books by Sr. F. Tarducci, an Italian, and E. Madero of Buenos Ayres—and a review in "La Espana Moderna," by Captain Fernandez Duro of the Royal Spanish Navy. They throw very little fresh light on the lives of the Cabots. Duro brands Sebastian as a traitor to Spain; Tarducci exalts him as a patriot. The name of Sebastian's Spanish wife is given—Catalina Medrano—and his daughter Elizabeth, and a last letter shortly before his death to Charles V. Captain Duro, a very well-informed writer, considers that Sebastian was not in the first voyage, and that he was a great schemer.

The latest work on the Cabots is by Dr. S. E. Dawson, published in "The Transactions of the Royal Society of Canada," 1894; it is very able and exhaustive. Dr. Dawson sets out with the theory that John Cabot's landfall in 1497 was at Cape Breton, which he identifies with the "Cavo descubierta" of Cosa; he cleverly arranges his facts to suit this theory, which forces him to argue that Cabot sailed from west to east along the southern coast of Newfoundland, as far as Cape Race; the author, however, ignores the fact that the old pilots in naming the coast followed the calendar. The position of Cape St. Jorge (April 23rd) and C. St. Lucia (December 13th) *west* of St. Nickolas (December 6th) show conclusively that the navigator whose voyage Cosa's map records sailed from east to west. In addition to the arguments in favour of Cape Bonavista as the landfall of John Cabot, contained at p. 10, there may be added the names near the Cape, of "King's Cove," in the foreign maps Royal Port, showing probably where the Genoese erected the royal arms, and "*Keels*" or Keels strand, where the first boat landed.

CHAPTER III.

REIGN OF HENRY VIII.

1509-1547.

1510.—Repeal of 8 Henry VI. c. II , 1429, about trading to Iceland and Norway.

1511.—Agramonte's voyage to America.

1512.—Rut in command of ships in the Royal Navy. Sebastian Cabot, engaged by the Spanish King on account of his supposed knowledge of Newfoundland, leaves England for Spain. "Great dry Icelande" fish selling for 38s. 4d. per 124.

1513.—Iceland fish sold at 53s. 9½d. per 100 to the Government.

1515.—First printed account of Cabot's voyage in Peter Martyr's *Decades*.

1517.—Three hundred English traders at Hafnae Fiord in Iceland.

1518.—Lescarbot says Baron-de-Lery sailed to America, landed cattle at Canso and Sable Island, and thus made the first attempt at settlement of North America.

1520.—Kuntsman No. 4 map assigning Iceland to the English.

1521.—Portuguese patent to Fagundez, showing a knowledge of our south coast.

1522.—Sabine says there were forty or fifty houses in Newfoundland at this time.

1523.—Verrazano, sent by Francis I., King of France, made land at Carolina, sailed north to Cape Breton. Grant of two fisheries on the U.S. Coast to Ayllon.

1525.—Gomez reports Newfoundland sea full of fish. Paulo Centurione, a Genoese, engaged by Henry VIII. for a voyage of discovery; failed through the death of Centurione.

1526.—Tyson acting as Thorne's agent in the West Indies.

1527.—Robert Thorne's expedition; John Rut wrote his celebrated letter from St. John's to Henry VIII.; found 14 vessels, 11 sail of Norman, one Brittaine, and two Portugal barks, fishing in St. John's Harbour; Rut receives a pension. Maiollo map.

1529.—Acknowledgment by Ribero in his map of discoveries by Bristol men.

1531.—Fifty Englishmen killed in Iceland.

1532.—Ziegler states that the "Baccalaos" country is a continuation of Greenland.

1534.—Jacques Cartier's celebrated voyage; made Newfoundland, and then sailed up St. Lawrence to Bay Chaleur. Gaspar Viegas' map shows Bonavista for the first time on our coast.

1535.—Cartier's second voyage; sailed up to Montreal; founded French Empire in North America.

1536.—Expedition of Master Hoare, of London, and a number of gentlemen and lawyers; disastrous voyage; stole a French ship in Newfoundland, and came home. Stockfish and Saltfishmongers Companies reunite.

1539.—Olaus Magnus' map showing an English ship whaling near Iceland.

1541.—Cartier's third voyage; built a fort near Quebec, called Charlesbourg. 33 Henry VIII. c. II., first Act of Parliament relating to America. Roberval arrived in St. John's; "found 17 ships of fishers"; met Jallobert and Noel there returning to France. Sixty French ships in Newfoundland.

1542.—John Rotz presents a map, showing the New World, to Henry VIII.

1544.—Two French ships left for Newfoundland every day in January and February.

1545.—Probable commencement of Basque fishing in Newfoundland on a large scale. No French ships go to Canada for fear of the Spaniards.

In tracing the course of our Island History during this remarkable reign one of the great debatable grounds of English History, we are fortunately not concerned in any way with the fierce controversial war that wages around this period. Luckily our subject is piscatorial and not polemical.

The enthusiasm aroused by the great discoveries of the last reign had not sensibly abated. Henry was stirred up to make several futile attempts to discover the north-west passage to India. France came late in the field, but, though last, her explorers, Verrazano and Cartier, were not least amongst the world's great navigators and discoverers.

The age produced no great coloniser like Raleigh to arouse and direct the energy of the nation towards founding Greater Britains beyond the sea; the thought of a great Colonial Empire in America never entered the minds of the two first Tudor sovereigns. To Henry VIII., however, belongs the credit of founding the Royal Navy; he fully realised that England should be a great naval power, supreme at sea. Under his fostering care colleges were founded for navigation, hospitals for retired seamen; he passed a law fixing the rate of wages for shipwrights, and gave a bounty of five per cent. for shipbuilding; he employed Italian shipwrights to teach his subjects the art of naval construction. In consequence of these measures, during this period English trade and navigation made wonderful strides; English ships were larger and better built, and large sums were spent on coast defence. England reaped the benefit of these preparations in the Armada year. There were also regular voyages to Spain, the Mediterranean, and the Brazil. Though he regulated shipbuilders' wages, when a new man-of-war was to be laid down the ships' carpenters were corralled like so many cattle, and kept in durance vile until their work was completed; the only difference was that they were paid properly for their work whilst prisoners. Hawkins, in the enlightened age of Elizabeth, carried out the same course of pressing men to work in the dockyards.

According to his lights, the king did his best to make England mistress of the seas. Under his rule, paternal government was carried to the very extreme of absurdity; he not only prescribed his subjects' religion, but he regulated their diet, the price of meat, and their dress; he was specially strenuous in directing all matters about the fishery, and

HENRY VIII.
From an engraving after H. Holbein.

preventing "regrating and forestalling" in the sale of fish,[1] an old-fashioned expression for cornering the market. To this laudable desire on the part of the king we are indebted for a most valuable bit of historical information concerning this Colony; it is contained in an Act which, as a specimen of legislation, is unique. A modern Act of Parliament is as bare and bald as a Blue Book, but these old enactments, "the statutes at large," are the very essence of English History; contained in the quaintest language, their absurd arguments and their extraordinary negation of all our modern notions of political economy make them simply delightful. Amongst these wonderful productions the following is a fairly choice specimen:—

"ACT 33 HENRY VIII. c. XI.

"*The Bill concernynge lying of fisshe upon the see.*

"WHEREAS many and dyvers townes and portes by the see side have in tymes past bene in great welthe and prosperitie well buylded by using and exereysing the crafts and feate of fisshing by the whiche practise it was not onelie great strengthe to this Realme by reason of bringing up and encreasing of Maryners whensoever the King's Grace had nede of them but also a greate welthe to the Realme and habundance of suche wherebie oure sovereigne Lorde the King the Lords Gentilmen and Comons were alwais well served of fisshe in Market townes of a reasonable price and also by reason of the same fisshing many men were made and grewe riche and many poure Men and Women had therebie there convenyent lyving,—to the strengthe encreasing and wellthe of this realme.

"And Whereas many and dyvers of the saide fissherman for their singular lucre and advantage doe leve the saide crafte of fisshing and be confederate w^t Pycardes Flemynghes Norman and Frenchemen and sometyme sayle over into the costes of Pycardie and Flaunders and sometyme doo meote the said Pycardes and Flemynges half the see over.

"Penalty on subjects bying fisshe in Flaunders &c., or at sea to be sold in England £10.

"And be it furder enacted by the auctoritie aforesaide that it shall be lawfull to all and every fissher estraunger to come and to sell.

"Provided furthermore that this Act or any thing therin conteyned shall not extende to any person whiche shall bye eny fisshe in any parties of Iseland Scotlands Orkeney, Shotlande, Irelande, or *Newland*—[Newfoundland]."

---

[1] There are regulations on this subject (Rye's *Cromer, Past and Present*, pp. 45, 46), dating as far back as 1358. At first it was ordered that no fish should be landed until the masters of the ships had settled a price with the merchants, so that the fish should be sold at a reasonable price at the fairs. It was found, however, that the merchants, conniving amongst themselves, refused to buy except at an unprofitable price, and the fish rotted. To remedy this, the fishermen were allowed after six days, if no price was settled, to land their fish, and sell as best they could. Mr. Rye thinks they must have had wells to keep their fish alive.

In Palmer's *Manship* (ii. 81) there is further information on this subject. Mr. Palmer also says:—

"A practice seems to have grown up at an early period for the fishermen to leave the sale of their fish to the 'hosts' or parties with whom they lodged in the town, who thus acted as brokers, paying dues and demands, and being accountable for the price. If we may judge by the numerous ordinances made for their regulation, we must suppose that they attempted to monopolize the trade and to take undue advantage of their position, by appropriating to themselves too large a share of the profits."

1 p. 2729.

REIGN OF HENRY VIII.

Here we have an explanation of the expression "Half seas over"—when the English met the Picardes there would be a big carousal.

The Bill is the first English Act of Parliament relating to America; it seems to have escaped the attention of American and English historical scholars. It is most invaluable for our History, as it completely establishes my argument that the English carried on the Newfoundland fishery continuously from the very discovery of the Island; our fishery, by this Act, is placed on a par with such well-established trades as the Icelandic,

The new founde londe quhar men goeth a fishing

COTZ MAP, 1542.
From B.M. MS. Reg. 20 E. IX.

Irish, and Shetland fisheries. This view of the subject is further confirmed by the Act of Edward VI., and corroborated by Anthony Parkhurst, who had made four voyages to Newfoundland, writing to Hakluyt, in 1578, he said:—

"The English are commonly lords of the harbour where they fish, and use all strange and help in fishing if need require, according to *an old custom of the country*,

---

¹ The map was presented to Henry VIII. by Rose, as I learn from M. Harrisse, the name should be spelt, a French pilot. The map is of a composite character, based upon Cabot's and Cortereal's voyages, and the French expedition to Cape Breton, but not showing the French explorations on our east and north-east coasts. The inscription, "The new founde londe quhar men goeth a fishing," is not the work of the map maker, but has been added by some Englishman.

which thing they do willingly, so that you take nothing from them more than a boat or two of salt in respect of your protection of them against rovers or other violent intruders, who do often put them from good harbours."

In 1583, Hayes, in his narrative, also says:—

"The English merchants that were, and always be, admirals by turns interchangeably over the fleets of fishermen within the same harbour, *for our English merchants command all there.*"

How could they speak of English dominion and usage in the Colony in 1578 as an ancient custom if the English did not participate in the fishery during these past seventy or eighty years? True, History is silent on the subject, but this furnishes no argument; the fishery was quite beyond the scope of history as then understood, and we know, from the records, that no account was kept of the movements of fishing vessels.

The Collector was the dire enemy alike of the Devonshire, the Basque, the Norman, and the Portuguese fishermen; concealment of both their voyages and their prosperity was a settled policy; like the poor fellaheen and the ryots, they hid their treasures from the harpies of the Government. It was only when the English Admiralty officers became too outrageous in their rapacity that complaints were made to the Crown, and an Act passed in 1547 to restrain them.

These adventurous old Devonshire sailors, year by year, left their little ports to reap the harvest of the seas across the Atlantic.

Each autumn the forest resounded to the woodman's axe as he felled the giant oaks to build the fishing-ship; with skill and patient labour the sturdy little craft took form and mould; the obscure West Country haven was busy with riggers, and caulkers, and sailmakers; the hills resounded with the clang of the anvil as they forged the goodly anchor, and made the cable on which hung the lives of men.

Devonshire not only reared true men, but she built good ships; every bit of timber and every nail and treenail that was driven was real honest work done by skilled hands, in the sight of all the village critics; they were not built for "yachting over summer seas," but for encounters with the ice and the hard knocks and rough voyages of the Atlantic.

M. Oppenheim says of the Elizabethan sailor:—

"It speaks well for his seamanship afloat, and the skill and good workmanship of shipwrights ashore, that not one ship was lost by stress of weather, by fire, or by running aground. During those same years, and sometimes during the same gales which the English ships weathered successfully, whole Spanish fleets foundered at sea."[1]

[1] *English Historical Review.*

Year by year, as the wealth from the far-off fishery was poured into the western counties, more ships were made and old ones repaired.

Until 1580 there are but sparse accounts of the English ships that fished in Newfoundland, but we know from contemporary history, and the Act of Henry VIII. and the further Act of Edward VI. that England carried on from Devonshire a considerable fishery in Newfoundland; the west was the great centre of maritime enterprise in England; her seamen the most daring and most numerous; all the great Elizabethan seamen—Drake, Hawkins, Raleigh—were Devonshire men.

They sailed the ships as well as they built them; their models were not our models, nor their ways our ways in the modes of shipbuilding; to use the old sailors' phrase, they built their vessels "for beasts of burthen, not for birds of passage." They had great beam, were low in the waist, high forward and aft, and had great sheer, without fore and aft sails; they were no good on a wind, but sailed fairly well going free; above all they were excellent sea-boats.

PRISMATIC COMPASS.
From Dudley's "Arcano del Mare," 1646.

The type of ship, of course, varied according to the purpose for which she was designed. In a paper by William Borough, in the reign of Elizabeth, three orders are described:—

"1. The shortest, broadest, and deepest order. — To have the length by the keel double the breadth amidships, and the depth in hold half that breadth.

"This order is used in some merchant ships made for most profit.

"2. The mean and best proportion for shipping for merchandise, likewise very serviceable for all purposes. — Length of keel, 2 or 2¼ that of beam. Depth of hold, ⅖ths that of beam.

"3. The largest order for galleons or ships for the wars, made for the most advantageous of sailing. — Length of keel, 3 times the beam. Depth of hold, ⅖ths of beam."

Men-of-war had high poops and deck cabins, which Raleigh condemned as "sluttish dens that breed sickness in peace"; ordinary fishing vessels in the beginning of the sixteenth century had flush decks, three masts, the foremast very far forward, and the mizzen very far aft; the sails were three big lug sails; the ballast carried was always sand, and the cook-room, a solid structure of brick and mortar, was built on the ballast. Hawkins was the inventor of movable top-masts—fishing vessels were rigged low, and their masts were single spars until late in the sixteenth century.

Top-masts or top-gallant sails are not mentioned in official papers till 1618. Studding sails were not those now known by that name. They were called "bonnets" and "drablers"; the bonnet laced on to the foot of the ordinary sail, the drabler on to the foot of the bonnet. The invention of the log line is claimed for an Elizabethan Englishman, named Humphrey Cole, but it appears to have been in use as early as 1521, on board Magellan's ships. Chain pumps, capstans, and other improvements were made only in the reign of Elizabeth. Even in this reign no large vessel had fore and aft canvas.

We have very few records of official voyages to the New World by Englishmen during Henry VIII.'s reign. Ships of the courtiers and gallant gentlemen, like Hore's and Gilbert's, nearly always came to grief, whilst the bluff-bowed, square, extraordinary little tubs, handled by the rough fishermen, who trusted to "latitude, lead, and look-out," made their voyages continuously for forty and fifty years[1] without losing a rope yarn; never a mishap, nor a claim on the Insurance Company, for probably none existed then for fishing ships.[2]

In 1523 four ships were sent out by Francis I. of France, under the command of Giovanni Verrazano, a Florentine navigator; three put back damaged, so Verrazano proceeded in the *Dolphin* alone; he cruised along the whole Atlantic coast from Carolina to Cape Breton, and on the strength of this voyage the

LOG LINE.

From Christopher's Voyages, 1852.

---

[1] The French Basque, Savalet, told Lescabot he had then made forty-two voyages; and Echevete, the Spanish Basque, says he made twenty-eight.
Depositions were taken in 1667 from several seamen at Dartmouth who had been going to Newfoundland for between fifty and fifty-five years.

[2] Marine Insurance was carried on by Lombards and Flemings earlier than this; in Elizabeth's reign it passed into the hands of Englishmen.
See Appendix, p. 84, for an Insurance effected in 1604 on a Newfoundland freight of fish to France.

French claimed a right to the countries visited by him, but the claim had no solid foundation, and was never recognised by England.[1]

The first official voyage that we know of actually made under the direct orders of Henry VIII.—was in 1527; connected with this adventure there are many difficulties arising from the extremely scanty information obtainable on the subject. Hakluyt, our chief authority, wrote many years after the event.

There can be no doubt that the expedition was urged upon the king by Robert Thorne of Bristol, living at Seville, who "exhorteth the "King with very waighty and substantial reasons to set forth a

THORNE'S MAP, 1527.
From Hakluyt's Divers Voyages, 1587.

"discoverie even to the North Pole"; he sent a "little Mappe or Carte of the Worlde" to illustrate his views. It was clearly a royal expedition to find the north-west passage to India. John Rut,[2] the rough

---

[1] Fishermen and traders had penetrated south of Cape Breton before this; Verrazano found the natives quite prepared to trade, and able to drive a good bargain.

[2] Rut, of the Royal Navy, and the master of several ships for Henry VIII., was in the *Gabriell Royall* and *Mary de Loreta*, from 1512 to 1513; he was a yeoman of Ratcliffe; had a pension of £10 per annum, dated Hampton Court, 24 May, 19 Henry VIII.—(*Records.*)

seaman, whose letter gives us the most information about the voyage, was an old master in the navy, and when the expedition failed, through the loss of his consort, he brought home a cargo of fish.

Royal ships often traded in this reign, and were hired for commerce [1] and adventure; there was practically no difference between the armed merchantman of those days and the Tudor Royal Navy; there was no uniform, nothing to mark the distinction between the services.

A difficulty about this voyage arises from Hakluyt's mention of "The Canon of Saint Paul." The diligent chronicler, in his collection of "Diverse Voyages," after speaking of "worthy Master Robert Thorne's "large discourse to the King," tells us "that he was informed by "Masters Hall and Grafton that Henry sent forth two faire ships, well "victualled and manned, on the 20th of May 1527, and after making "enquiries he is told by Sir Francis Frobisher and Richard Allen that "a learned and wealthy canon of Saint Paul's went on the expedition, "that one of the ships was called the *Dominus Vobiscum*, and that "one of the ships was cast away in the Straits of Belle Isle."

It is clear that this refers to the voyage of Rut and his consort; the dates are the same, these ships were sent by the king, and one was wrecked northward, just as the *Sampson* was.

Former writers have jumped to the conclusion that the Albert de Prado [2] who wrote a letter to Cardinal Wolsey, of the same tenour as Rut's, was a Canon of Saint Paul's, London. There may have been a Canon of Saint Paul's on board, but his name was not Albert de Prado, for the Records at St. Paul's contain no such name as De Prado, Field (Prado is Spanish for field), or anything like it. That the expedition was a royal one, and fitted out by Wolsey, is shown by Lord Edward Howard's letter to the Cardinal, saying he "would be "glad to be employed in the expedition to be made to Newfoundland, "and so find his wife and children meat and drink." [3] As a voyage of discovery the expedition was a failure, but Rut's letter is invaluable, as it gives us information about the Island; it was probably not old John's first voyage to Newfoundland, as he seems to be well acquainted with the points of land. Master Grube's two ships from Plymouth appear to have made about the same sort of passage as John Cabot's; evidently these vessels, sailing so late, were not fishing ships, and this is another clear proof of the large English fishery then carried on in Newfoundland; they were sack ships going out to trade and

---

[1] In 1526 we find in the *Records* a proposition to use the idle men-of-war as merchant ships to Iceland, &c.

[2] The *Records* show Prado's debts were paid by the Royal Treasurer, but I can find no other information about him; it seems likely that he was the son of a Spanish-American trader; perhaps he himself had sailed under Gomez.

[3] *Records*.

bring back a cargo of fish, oil, furs, and produce. The regular time of sailing for the fishing would be February or March; some French vessels used to leave even in January.

Sabine, in his history of the fishery,[1] relying apparently upon Oviedo or Herrara, says that in 1517 there were only fifty ships—English, French, Spanish,[2] and Portuguese—fishing in Newfoundland, but according to the Portuguese records this must be an error; as regards the English ships, we can rest assured that Master Grube's two barques and Rut's ships were not the only English vessels there.

Purchas says:—

"King Henry VIII. set forth two ships for discouerie one of which perished in the north parts of Newfoundland the Master of the other John Rut writ this letter to King Henrie in bad English and worse writing over it was this superscription.

"Master Grubes two ships departed from Plymouth the 10th day of June, and arrived in the Newfoundlands the 21 day of July and after we had left the sight of Selle [Scilly Islands] we had never sight of any land till we had sight of Cape de Bas.[3]

JOHN RUT'S LETTER.

"Pleasing your Honourable Grace to heare of your servant John Rut with all his company here in good health thanks be to God and your Graceship—The *Mary of Gilford*,[4] with all her . . . . . thanks be to God—and if it please your honourable Grace we ranne in our course to the Northward, till we came into 53 degrees, there we found many great Islands of ice and deepe water; we found no sounding, and then we durst not go no further to the Northward for feare of more ice [evidently making for a north-west passage], and then we cast about to the Southward, and within foure dayes after we had one hundred and sixtie fathom and then we came into 52 degrees and fell with the mayne land and within ten leagues of the mayne lande we met with a great Island of ice and came hard by her for it was standing in deep water and so went in with Cape de Bas[3] a good Harbour and many small Islands and a great fresh river going up farre into the mayne land and the mayne land all wilderness and mountains and woodes and no naturall ground but all mosse and no inhabitation nor no people in these parts; and in the woods we found footing of divers great beasts but we saw none not in ten leagues—And please your Grace the *Sampson* and wee kept company all the way till within two dayes before we met with all the Ilands of ice; that was the first day of July at night and there arose a great and a marvallous great storme and much foul weather—I trust in the Almightie Jesu to heare good newes of her—and please your Grace we were considering and a writing of all our order, how we would wash us, and what course we would draw and when God doe send foule weather, that with the Cape de Sper shee should go—and he that come first should tarry the space of sixe weeks one for another, and watered at Cape de

---

[1] SABINE's *Report of the principal Fisheries of the American Seas.* Washington, 1853.

[2] See Note 2, p. 43, about Spaniards not being mentioned in Oviedo's narrative.

[3] Cape de Bas—probably Cape de Grace—Cape Bauld, the north-east point of Newfoundland. It may have been the Cape de Raz shown on old maps near Cape Bauld.

[4] "Account of the victuals and wages of *Mary Guildford*, per master and purser, £19 14s. 4d. Lode manage and premage to master and crew at 6d. per ton."

has ten days ordering of your Grace and fishing, and so departed to the Southward to seek our fellowe; the third day of August we entered into a good Harbour called St. John and there we found Eleuen Saile of Normans and one Brittaine [Breton] and two Portugall Barks all a fishing and so we are ready to depart towards Cape de Bas that is 25 leagues as shortly as we have fished and so along the Coast until we may meete with our fellowe and so with all diligence that lyes in me toward parts to that Ilands that we are commanded at our departing [it is evident he had strict instructions to make a vigorous attempt to find a N W. passage; instead of doing so he was making up a cargo of fish], and thus Jesu save and keepe your Honourable Grace and all your Honourable Reuer.

"In the Haven of St. John the third day of August written in haste 1527, by your servant John Rut to his uttermost of his power."[1]

It seems likely that Rut and Albert de Prado wrote their letters hastily to catch one of Master Grube's ships returning to Europe with her freight of fish.

The only outside evidence [2] of any kind which has come down to us about this voyage is the mention by Cartier of a Cape Prato[3] in the Gulf of St. Lawrence, showing that perhaps the *Mary of Guildford* penetrated there; whether the information was given to Cartier by the vessels which were fishing in the Gulf as he passed along, or he got it from a map showing Prado's discoveries, cannot now be ascertained.

The natural curiosity of the human mind, and the spirit of adventure which leads all sorts and conditions of men, even in the present day, to Africa and the wilds of Asia, prompted in the reign of bluff King Hal one of the most extraordinary wild-cap expeditions it has ever been the lot of the historian to describe; it is recorded by the industrious Hakluyt as—

"The voyage of Master Hore and divers other gentlemen to Newfoundland and Cape Briton in the yere 1536.

"Master Hore, of London, a man of goodly stature and of great courage, and given to the study of Cosmographie, in the yere of our Lord 1536, encouraged divers gentlemen and others, being assisted by the king's favour and good countenance, to accompany him in a voyage of discoverie upon the north west parts of America, wherein his persuasions tooke such effect that within a short space many gentlemen of the Inns of Court and of the Chancerie, and divers others of good worship desirous to see the strange things of the world, very willingly entered into the action with him. . . . . The whole number that went in the two tall ships the *Trinitie* and the *Minion* were five score persons, whereof 30 were gentlemen, which all were mustered in warlike manner at Gravesend, and after the receiving of the sacrament they embarked themselves in the ende of April 1536."[4]

---

[1] Purchas' *His Pilgrims*, 1625.

[2] When we remember that Thorne had an agent, Tyson, in the Spanish West Indies, selling armour for him, it seems quite unnecessary to connect (Barrett and Corry) the arrival of an English three-master at Porto Rico with this expedition. English ships were, I believe, frequently in the Brazils, and along the coast of Maine, even as early as this, and the fact that the ship mentioned by Herrara was armed, had come from the Bacallaos, crossed the Gulf Stream, and lost a Piedmont pilot in a fight with the natives, need in no way apply to Rut's expedition.

[3] This may have been, however, only a natural name (Prado—a field) applied to the beautiful grass-covered Magdalen Islands.

They appear to have been so badly victualled that they were guilty of cannibalism; they had no pilot, otherwise they would have gone on the well-known track to Newfoundland. What thirty idle gentlemen and briefless barristers expected to find or do in these unknown regions it is impossible to conjecture. They did not lose the two tall ships, but they were so starved and impoverished that, but for the timely arrival of a French ship in some part of the south-western coast of Newfoundland, probably White Bear Bay, they would all have perished. The only advantage of having so many lawyers aboard appears at this juncture, for, says Hakluyt:—

CASTALDI'S MAP, ABOUT 1550.[1]
From Ramusio's "Le Navigationi."

"When in their dire extremity, and as they were going to cast lots who should be killed, such was the mercie of God, that in the same night there arrived a French ship in that port well furnished with vittaile, and *such was the policie of the English* [acting, no doubt, on the advice of their learned counsel] that they became masters of the same, and, changing ships and vittailing them, they set sail to come into England."

This ill-fated expedition, product of the enthusiasm and ignorance of the age, is one of the many wrecks with which our history is strewn; court gallants and hair-brained lawyers are poor substitutes for practical seamen in dangerous exploring voyages; Gilbert's disastrous expedition is a still more striking example of the utter folly of putting landsmen in charge of ships.

[1] This is the first engraved map specially devoted to Newfoundland.

In the magnificent work of Navarrete, "Colleccion de los Viages &c.," recounting all the discoveries of the Spaniards up to the sixteenth century, he describes the voyage in 1525 of Estevan Gomez, a Spaniard from Corunna, who took with him a crew of hardy Basque fishermen, and explored the American coast, certainly as far north as Cape Race; on the strength of this expedition Diego Ribero marks all the present United States as the land of Stephen Gomez, "Tiera de Estevan Gomez," and therefore belonging to Spain. Navarrete says he found the sea full of fish, and there can be no doubt he was in Newfoundland.

It is clearly proved, as well as any remote historical event can be substantiated, that the English, Portuguese, Bretons, and Normans were the first fishermen in Newfoundland. The Spanish Basques or Biscayans did not engage regularly in the fishery until about 1545; previous to that period they carried on a very extensive fishery in Ireland; gradually this was reduced, and the Biscayans turned their attention to the great Transatlantic fishery; we have abundant evidence that besides the codfishery they carried on a very extensive whale and seal fishery, both in the Gulf of St. Lawrence and to the northward. Their head-quarters were in the gulf and straits known in those ancient times as the Grand Bay. The splendid harbour of Port-Aux-Basques still commemorates their presence on our shores. The Biscayans used to continue their operations until December. From these hardy and daring fishermen England had to obtain harpooners when she first began whaling.

We seem to have proof of the commencement of the Spanish fishery in the Colony in a very complete form. First there is the Spanish permission given in 1511 by Ferdinando el Catolico to Juan de Agramonte to take two ships:—

"Á descobrir cierta tierra nueva en los limites que a nos pertenescen—to discover certain new land within the limits [fixed by the Pope] which belong to us. [The charter goes on to state that the crew must be Spaniards] with the exception of two pilots, who may be Bretons, or of other nation who have been there—á excepcion de dos pilotos, que permitia fueran *Bretones* o de otra nacion que alla hayan estado."[1]

Agramonte sailed to North America, found no gold, but captured some slaves; his voyage was not repeated.[2]

---

[1] Duro, p. 310.

[2] In 1523 Lucas Vasques de Ayllon was granted the title of Adelantado, fifteen leagues square of land, and two codfisheries in the country discovered by him. De Ayllon received a charter in this year to search for a strait north of Florida, but was required to avoid Portuguese possessions (Newfoundland was placed within their limits). I think these fisheries were much further south than our Island.

Oviedo—a Spaniard and contemporary of Gomez—mentions no Spanish vessels in Newfoundland. Herrara, a much later *compiler*, does—apparently about 1527.

REIGN OF HENRY VIII.

Then we have in the English Calendar of State Papers (vol. v., 443), 1535:—[1]

"Sir A. St. Leger said that as many as 200 to 300 sail of Spanish fishermen might sometimes be seen at one time in Valentia Harbour [in Ireland]."

In the Spanish Naval Records edited by Captain C. Fernandez Duro, of the Royal Spanish Navy, there is a—

"Memorial from the son of Matias de Echevete saying that he was the first Spaniard who went to the Newfoundland fishery in a French vessel 1545, and afterwards made 28 voyages up to 1599, being the founder of the Basque fishery there.—Memorial del hijo de Matias de Echevete diciendo que este fuè el primer Espanol que fuè a la pesca de Terra Nova en nao Francesca el ano 1545 y despues hizo 28 viages hasta el de 1599 siendo fundador de la pesca de los Vascongados."[2]

And in 1561 Sir T. Chamberlain said:—

"The Spanish had found a trade to Newfoundland which previously they did not occupy so much."[3]

If the memorial of Echevete is not absolutely true, it represents substantially the truth, for Navarette does not claim a very early participation in our fishery for his countrymen, but considers probably the report of Gomez gave an impetus to the fishery; he mentions the Biscayan lawsuit in 1561, at San Sebastian, when evidence was given by sailors having been forty years in the trade, but Navarette does not lay much stress upon this, and it seems most likely their fishing in Newfoundland did not assume a national character till about 1545; judging from the accounts of the Spanish historians, it is not unlikely that individual ships came upon the coast to trade from the earliest times, possibly bringing salt and returning with fish.[4]

But the question appears to be completely settled by the following account by Captain Duro of this lawsuit, taken from the Records of San Sebastian:—

"In 1561 a dispute arose about the payment to the Church of Two per cent. on the products of the Newfoundland fishery, at which time witnesses were asked if they knew if the Newfoundland fishery had been followed for only a few years. Amongst the declarants were some old men of seventy, who all agreed that this fishery was not more than from seventeen to twenty years established before then. That is to say that they frequented Newfoundland from 1541 to 1545, and on account of the very much gain in these voyages they had abandoned their fishery in Flanders England and other places. Some of the witnesses said that the fishery of Newfoundland had been discovered since the year 1526 and that the Guipuscoans carried it on since 1540."

"En el pleito seguido en San Sebastian el año 1561 con los maestres de Naos, sobre pagar à las iglesias el dos por ciento de los productos de la pesca de Terra Nova en el cual se preguntó a los testigos. *Si saben que la pesqueria de Tierranueva ha seido hallada y usada de pocos años y tiempo à esta parte;* y habiendo entre

---

[1] *Records.* Probably exaggerated.
[2] Duro's *Arca de Noé*, p. 313.
[3] *Records.*
[4] See Harrisse's *Discovery of North America*, 1892.

los declarantes algunos ancianos hasta de setenta años tados estuvieron conformes en que la pesca no contaba mayor antigüedad que de diez y seis a veinte años a la fecha: es decir, que se frecuentaba desde 1541 ó 1545 y que por la mucha ganancia que producian estos viages se habian abandonado los de Flandes, Inglaterra y otros partes, &c.[1]

The celebrated voyages of Jacques Cartier in 1534, 1535, and 1541, gave France the title to Canada. Cartier had probably been an old fisherman on the Newfoundland coast; his native port, St. Malo, every year sent out fishermen to the New World. It is to Cartier that we owe the first description of the noble river St. Lawrence, and a true configuration of our island; although his enterprise was barren of results and his attempts at colonising Canada failed, he greatly enlarged our knowledge of the New World, and laid the foundation of the mighty empire of New France.

Sieur Jean Francis de la Roche, Seigneur de Roberval, who had sailed in August 1541 with three ships with two hundred persons and

JACQUES CARTIER.
After an old portrait.

"divers gentlemen of quality," affords another example like Hore, of the failure of landsmen in naval affairs. On his way to Quebec he met Jallobert and Noel, two of Cartier's captains, in St. John's.[2] His expedition to New France was a series of disasters. In the autumn of 1543 he and all his followers abandoned the Colony. The account of Roberval's voyage is very meagre, and we can only gather from it that our harbour of St. John's, even in that early age, was the capital and head-quarters of the Transatlantic fishery. On his arrival, Roberval tells us that he found seventeen ships of fishers in the harbour; unfortunately he does not give us their nationality. He also had a dispute with some Portuguese fishermen in the Straits of Belle Isle. Clearly these old cod smacks had discovered all around the St. Lawrence long before the court gallants and their grand expeditions. Cartier's patent was strenuously opposed at Court by the Breton merchants, who considered these exploring expeditions would injure their fishing rights in the Gulf, and even when he obtained his grant, they were able to

---

[1] C. F. Duro's *Arca de Noë*, p. 314.
[2] Hakluyt's statement that Roberval met Cartier is disproved by Gosselin. Roberval's arrival at St. John's was most likely in the autumn of 1541; this may account for the small number of vessels he met there.

prevent his getting a crew until the king sent peremptory orders to the authorities at St. Malo. Cartier mentions meeting French fisher-

ST. MALO ABOUT 1620.
From an engraving of Mariette's.

men in the Gulf, probably at Brest—Entre du Golf—from the very earliest times the northern head-quarters of the Gulf fishery.

BREST ABOUT 1620.
From an engraving of Mariette's.

There is little to note concerning our Island history during this reign. Far from the jarring strife of Europe, the fishermen pursued their humble trade in Newfoundland; year by year they built up a great business, which grew and prospered and enriched England.

Both the great Tudor monarchs were statesmen—men of energy and ability—yet both failed to grasp the idea of a Colonial Empire; just as in our days parish politics in the Colonies and narrow views at home obscure from our countrymen the grand idea of Imperial Federation.

APPENDIX TO CHAPTER III.

I. The Basque Fishery.

The words "Biscayan" and "Guipuscoan" occur frequently in the old writers; they refer to two divisions of the Basque provinces in Spain, the third province, "Alava," being inland, is not mentioned.

The Spanish Basques were amongst the most adventurous navigators in Europe, they were the great whalers of ancient days. There are very early notices of their codfishing; a treaty was made between them and Edward III., signed 1st August 1351, which conceded to them the right to fish on the English coast for certain payments during twenty years. NAVARRETE, vol. i., p. 48, says:—

"El padre Las Casas, que poseyó los papeles de Colon, digo que el Admirante, tenia apuntado en su libro de memorias, entre otros indicios de la existencia de tierras al Occidente, que un marinero tuerto, en el puerto de Santa Maria, y otro Gallego, en Murcia, le habian dicho, que un viage que hicieron á Irlanda, desviados de su derrota, navegaron tanto al N.O., que avistaron una tierra que imaginarion ser la Tartaria, y era Terra Nova."

"Father Las Casas, who had possession of Columbus' papers, says that the Admiral had an entry in his note book, amongst other indications of the existence of lands in the West, that a cock-eyed sailor in St.Mary's Port and another, Gallego, in Murcia, had told him that on a voyage which they had made to Ireland, thrown out of their course, they sailed so far to the north-west that they saw land, which they imagined to be Tartary and was Newfoundland."

This is a very doubtful story. If land was seen, it was most probably Greenland, which appeared upon maps before Columbus' voyage, and was undoubtedly visited by traders, most likely Biscayan whalers, before Cabot's discovery. The name Labrador (given apparently to all the land north of Newfoundland at first) has been claimed as that of a Biscayan whaling captain. Scoresby's book contains much information on this whale fishery.

The facts given in the text are strongly against the claim that these men fished in Newfoundland before 1497. Juan de la Cosa, a Biscayan, and the highest authority of his day, does not appear to know our coast, nor do there appear to be any names of a Biscayan source on the earliest maps.

A Spanish writer, Tome Cano, declares, that since the Spaniards lost this fishery 487,500 qtls. have been annually consumed in Spain, costing £600,000.

Bad government has been the curse of Spain, and of all the Spanish colonies; it fell most heavily on these fair Basque provinces. All the industry, both by sea and land, of these hardy toilers, these brave industrious Cantabrians, could make no headway against kings, who, notwithstanding repeated royal promises to respect their rights, laid an embargo on their ships and took their labourers and seamen to man the royal fleets.

There is no more piteous story in European history than the decay and impoverishment of this great Basque nation by Spanish misgovernment. A witty proverb well expresses this chronic cause of national decay. The saintly Alfonso was in such high favour in Heaven that the Holy Virgin could not refuse his prayers; he supplicated that the Spaniards might be the bravest, and their women might be the most lovely, and their country the most fertile; all was granted. "One more favour, Holy Mother," said the king, "give Spain a good government." "No, my son," said the Virgin, "if Spain had a good government I would not be able to keep an angel in Heaven a day longer."

Echevete gives an account of the Spanish fishing and whaling fleet being caught in the autumn of 1577 and frozen up in some port in Newfoundland or Labrador (in the original record the name is left blank), that five hundred and forty men died, and that seventeen of the best sailors of Zarauz were amongst them. We know from Whitbourne and Guy's instructions that the Biscayans remained in Newfoundland until very late in December. With their poor appliances for heating and ragged clothing they may have succumbed to the rigours of an unusually hard winter. By a sudden change of weather, very common in this country, they may have been frozen up. A number of English crews were caught in this way in the winter of 1817 as far south as Renews.

The Basques had fine vessels. In 1586 Bingham mentions the capture of one off Ireland of four hundred tons with a large crew, mostly boys, and very ragged.

We learn from the Spanish Records that, in 1549, a Biscayan Catholic priest ministered to the spiritual wants of his devout countrymen in Newfoundland; the Spanish Basques, like the noble Bretons, being distinguished for their loyalty to the Church. The Basques in our times are celebrated as Catholics,

Conservatives, and Carlists. "Dios, Patria, y Rey," is the provincial war cry.

"1549, Marzo 23. Memorial de Jacobo de Ibaceta Maestro de Nao previendo para la pesca de Terra Nova pidiendo ornamentos para que un clerigo que lleva a bordo puede decir misa en aquella Tierra."—(*Collec. Vargas. Ponce, ley III.*)

The Spanish Records state that during the reign of Philip II. two hundred ships and six thousand men were employed in Newfoundland. The king wished them to have a convoy of ships of war; in 1553 there was a Royal ordinance to this effect. The Biscayans thanked the king for his solicitude about their interests, but they did not wish to have his ships with them; theirs were ready to sail, and they had expended two hundred thousand ducats fitting them out. The order was revoked. The Biscayans argued that they were safer going together in twos and threes than in a fleet.

They were very jealous of their provincial rights, and rebelled against the requisitions made on them by Philip II. for ships and men.

We have preserved the report to the queen of a conversation of Sir T. Chamberlain with the King of Spain, 1561 :—

"In Biscay they had for a long time felled timber for building ships, and planted none, so there was scarcely any now, and that double the price it was 30 years ago. Those of Biscay frankly declared that their ships had been so often stopped for the king's service and so badly paid, that they had to turn to other trades. He [Chamberlain] alleged another reason to prove the country was not destitute of shipping by their trading further off, and that they, the Spanish, have found a trade unto the Newfoundland for fish, which they did not previously occupy so much."

As the result of Sir B. Drake's expedition in 1585, the fishermen did not propose to go to Newfoundland in 1586 (*Advertisements from Spain*), and in fact a general embargo was laid on the whole fleet.

In 1587 (year before the Armada), 24 June, St. Jehan de Luce, Shute wrote to Walsingham :—"In Spain it seems they are in hopes of peace with Her Majesty and along the coasts adjoining France it is much desired insomuch as they are not pressing forward the rigging of ten large ships, he gave Walsingham advice of. And whereas it was prohibited in all the Ports of La Provence and Biscay that none should go forth unto the Newland a fishing, of late it is permitted and they are preparing as they of custom have done hitherto."—(*Hatfield MS.*)

This is confirmed by the Spanish Records. A royal order forbade any ships to sail to Newfoundland without license; the ships were wanted for the Armada, then preparing. It was only on the 15th July that instructions were sent to release them, with a warning to go well armed, and be careful about English pirates from Rochelle.

The scare of the impending conflict virtually destroyed the Biscayan fishery. From this time forward the Newfoundland fishery was principally in English hands. The great Spanish fleet dwindled down in a few years from one hundred and fifty sail to less than ten. For we learn in 1593, from Sylvester Wyat, who made a voyage from Bristol to Newfoundland, that he found only eight Spanish vessels in a fleet of upwards of eighty sail of French and English.

The Spanish fishery not only suffered from the war, but from the excessive duties imposed on their products. It was the most flourishing industry in Spain, but the impecunious Government, instead of encouraging it, helped to destroy it by a load of taxation and severe restrictions, especially the monopoly of salt.

In 1602 seven Basque vessels went to Newfoundland for whaling, and many more for fishing.

In 1631 the Biscayan fishery to Newfoundland was in very low water; in 1632 only six ships went out; in 1638 thirty ships were in the business.

In 1681, however, from the Port of Passage alone, there were 13 vessels of 2,810 tons and 550 men for codfishing in Newfoundland, and nine vessels of 2,060 tons for whaling; they carried from 5 to 20 guns.

In 1681 the French prohibited the Basques from fishing in Newfoundland. I do not think this order was ever really carried out. From the English Records it appears very distinctly that the Biscayans fished with the French, and were on the most friendly terms. The Spanish and French Basques were always most closely allied.

In 1690, according to the Spanish Records, the French again refused to allow them to fish there any more, as it was a French colony.

From a resumé of the sworn testimony taken at St. Sebastian in 1697, given in Captain Duro's book, we have fuller information on the subject of the French excluding the Biscayans from Newfoundland.

The first witness called was Captain Martin De Sapiain. His testimony is as follows :—

"Que en el tiempo de su memoria, que la tiene de cuarenta y ocho años à esta parte, habia visto que los naturales de esta provincia han ido à las islas y costas de Terra Nova à hacer pesca de bacallao en cualquier puerto, como son Traspas, Santa Maria, Cunillas Placencia, Petit Placencia, Petit Paradis, Martiris, Buria Chumea, Buria Andia, San Lorenz Chumea, San Laurenz Andia, San Pierre, Fortuna, Miquele Portu, Chasco Portu, Señoria, Opot Portu, Tres Islas, Portuchoa y Echaide Portu que este ultimo lo descubrio Juan de Echaide."

Having thus stated that, within his memory of forty-eight years, he has seen that Biscayans had gone to the islands and coasts of Newfoundland to fish in any port, such as the following [as above], and at Echaide Portu, which was discovered by Juan Echaide, a native of St. Sebastian, Sapiain says:—

"He knew Echaide, who died forty years ago [1650], being then eighty years old. That in none of these ports had there ever been any embargo or impediment by the subjects of the King of France or of any other kingdom, and that, without distinction or preference, whoever occupied first in the harbour had the preference, according to immemorial custom, whereof the memory of man runneth not to the contrary; and he has seen this until the present year, when they have been interrupted by the French."

With the products of successful whaling, fishing, and sealing in Newfoundland, the Spanish Basques built the stately old houses which are the admiration of travellers, amidst the green hills and lovely vales of Alava, Viscaya, and Guipuscoa, the fairest scenes in all Northern Spain.

Many of the old Biscayan families have a *whale* in their coats of arms, showing that the founders made their fortunes in the fishing and whaling business. Clements R. Markham, C.B., F.R.S., in his paper on the Basque whale fishery, shows that the Basques captured the whale (*Balæna Biscayensis*) from time immemorial in boats; that Baffin and the first English whaling vessels were in the habit of shipping boats' crews of Basques to harpoon the whales; also that the word "harpoon" is derived from the Basque word "*arpoi*," the root being "*ar*," to take quickly; the Basque "*harpoinari*" is a harpooneer.

Viscaya (Biscay) and Guipuscoa and Alava had free institutions long before England.

II. The French Newfoundland Fishery.

The French have always been our great rivals in the Newfoundland fishery, and twice they have overrun the Colony and completely defeated the English.

Their fishermen, the Normans and Bretons, were amongst the first to carry on the great Transatlantic trade in Newfoundland; Parkhurst said these daring old mariners had very small, poorly fitted out vessels, yet they fished on the banks in the most stormy month of the year; Whitbourne mentions meeting them on his way out in the spring.

In 1523 a Captain Coo took several French prizes, amongst them a ship of Rouen, with Newfoundland fish, fisher boats, crays, &c. The Frenchmen seem to have made a stubborn resistance, for it cost £6 18s. to heal sixteen men *burnt* in taking this Newfoundland ship.

I p. 2729.

In 1529, in consequence of robberies by Bristol's barks, no Breton or Portuguese ships dare come to Milford, but in 1537 we find the tables turned and French and Spanish openly plundering English fishing vessels and entering harbours, and as late as 1558 we learn that the trade of Bristol was thoroughly crippled on account of great losses from enemies who had taken their best ships.

In 1542 there is a letter from the Privy Council to the Mayor of Bristol to discharge a French ship laden with fish out of Newfoundland, which was arrested for certain considerations in that port.

In 1531 the *La Barbara*, of "Seynt Bridgeon," John Callaye, master, with fish from Newfoundland *Island*, was stranded at "Rammersgate."

French fishing in Newfoundland was so flourishing in 1540 that the authorities of St. Malo had to stay ships in order to get Cartier a crew. In 1541 and 1542 no less than sixty French ships were fishing in Newfoundland (GOSSELIN). In 1546 we have the report of John Francis of Roan (Rouen) being spoiled by an English pirate of Newland fish. In January and February 1544 from Havre, Rouen, Dieppe, and Harfleur about two ships left every day for the fishery. In 1545 no ship of France left for Canada for fear of the Spaniards.

By the foreign intelligence from France we learn that the English agent found at St. Malo on the 15th April 1560 twenty-five ships waiting for a fair wind for Newfoundland, and at Carcolle five ships ready to start with those of St. Malo.

From the Records in 1561 we know that thirty ships left for Newland from the little towns of Jumieges, Vaterville, and La Bouille, and that the tonnage had risen from seventy to one hundred and fifty tons for these ships, and that many of them were "well appointed." Neither of these statements agree with Parkhurst's description.

Elizabeth's Government seem to have been always eager for information about the French Newfoundland fleet. On April 20 1561 Throckmorton reported to the queen:—

"The Constable of France said that he knew no more about the rigging of a ship than about the day of judgment, nor of army, men, munitions or artillery for these ships; that now was the time their men used to prepare to go to Newfoundland for fishing, and peradventure some would go to *Rome* [a neat bit at the Protestant Walsingham]. That they made three notable voyages in the year, in the spring to Newfoundland fishing, in August to the Bourbage, and in October to Rochelle and Bordeaux for wines."

The French fishing fleet was by far the largest during the early period from 1504 to 1580. Owing probably to the wars and the distracted state of France, the French fishing declined during the reign of Elizabeth, and on

D

the advent of James to the throne, out of 400 vessels engaged in the trade, the English had 250 and later 270; of the remaining 150 vessels there were not probably more than 70 or 80 French. In 1645 the French were the only rivals of the English in Newfoundland; their numbers were then reckoned at 100 sail.

In the following chapters I shall refer to this important subject more at length, in order to show the great change which took place in the relative positions of the great contending parties. During the reign of the Tudors, until the occupation of Placentia by the French, and even for a few years later, they fished, in common with the English, all about the coast, but chiefly on the north part of the Island, called by them "Petit Nord," extending from White Bay to Quirpon, and on the south and west extending from Cape Race to Cape Ray.

CHAPTER IV.
REIGN OF EDWARD VI.
1547-1553.

1547.—2nd & 3rd Edward VI., Act of Parliament punishing officers of the Admiralty for taking bribes from the fishermen of Newfoundland, Iceland, and Ireland.

1549.—A priest accompanies the Basque fleet to Newfoundland.

1550.—Map, B.M. MSS., 17,938b, showing English influence.

REIGN OF MARY.
1553-1558.

1553.—Spanish ordinance that the Basque Newfoundland fleet should be convoyed; order revoked upon protest of the merchants.

REIGN OF ELIZABETH.
1558-1603.

1560.—Twenty-five vessels at St. Malo, waiting for a fair wind for Newfoundland, and five at Carcolle.

1561.—Sir T. Chamberlain's report on Basque shipping. The Constable of France's report upon the movement of French ships; thirty ships go from Jumieges, Vaterville, and La Bonille to Newfoundland; dispute about payment of tithes to the church of St. Sebastian by Basque Newfoundland fishermen.

1562.—Act confirming 2nd & 3rd Edward VI.

1564.—5 Eliz. c. v., Act forbidding cod to be imported in barrels.

1565.—Hawkins, on his way from West Indies, stopping on the banks to fish. Frobisher's voyage of discovery for a north-west passage; names Frobisher's straits.

1568.—Petition against importation of dried fish falsely marked as "Iceland."

1577.—Basque fleet frozen up in Newfoundland or Labrador; five hundred and forty men perished.

1578.—Anthony Parkhurst's voyage and description of the country; fifty English vessels engaged in Newfoundland fishery; France and Spain, one hundred and fifty sail each; Portuguese, fifty. Sir H. Gilbert's first voyage; stayed a short time; lost a ship and a bold captain, Miles Morgan; defeated by Spaniards.

1579.—Whitbourne's first voyage to Newfoundland, in a ship of Master Cotton's, of Southampton; loaded in Trinity.

1580.—Demand of Denmark for payment of usual licence fees in Iceland. Charter-party for Newfoundland fish at 10s. per 100, and oil at £12, freight to Bordeaux 38s.

1581.—Only two hundred traders going to Iceland; 23 Eliz. c. vii., relating to the fishery.

1582.—Voyage of Sir Thomas Hampshire to Newfoundland with five ships; settled the tenure of ships' rooms.

1583.—Sir Humphrey Gilbert's last voyage; came to St. John's to get supplies; took possession of the Colony; made several grants of land; lost on passage home. First important description of the country by Hayes, the captain of the only surviving vessel of the expedition. Peckham's Brief Discourse. Over two hundred sail of Spanish Basques fishing, whaling, and sealing on our coasts and Labrador. Petition of Downing to import barrelled fish; further petition in 1586 of Sir Wm. Gorges on the same subject.

1585.—Sir Walter Raleigh's first colonisation at Roanoke, in Virginia; colony destroyed. Sir Bernard Drake, with a commission from Elizabeth, seized several Spanish and Portuguese vessels in Newfoundland; met Whitbourne in St. John's.

1586.—Indenture of Newfoundland fish for the army in Ireland at 20s. per 100. Basque fleet forbidden to go to Newfoundland. Drake reports "the Passage" full of Newfoundland fish, "new and very good."

1587.—Embargo on Basque fleet not withdrawn this year till 15th July.

1588.—Spanish Invincible Armada defeated by the English; English Newfoundland fleet stayed at home to fight; great fleet of Spanish Basques practically disappears from Newfoundland from this date.

1589.—Only 10,000 Newfoundland fish on the market in the West of England. Merchants of the West prohibited from trading to Brittany (then in the hands of the Leaguers), and ordered to go to Jersey and Guernsey instead.

1591.—Petitions of P. de Hody and Harques for restitution of ships and fish captured by Bristol privateers. Petition about ancient right of English to fish in Iceland, upon payment of merely nominal licences.

1592.—Twenty Spanish ships-of-war off Scilly trying to intercept the English Newfoundland fleet.

1593.—Richard Strange made a voyage to prosecute seal fishery; head-quarters at Ramea, Gulf of St. Lawrence. Sylvester Wyet from Bristol found only eight Spanish ships in a fleet of eighty; statement in the House of Commons by Raleigh, on 19th February, that the Newfoundland fishery was the stay and support of the West of England; there is also a letter of Raleigh's of this year, stating that the Newfoundland "voyages" were the only ones making any profit.

1594.—Captain Rice Jones, of Bristol, made a voyage to Newfoundland, and prosecuted the fishery at St. Pierre. Guernsey destitute of provisions and Newfoundland fish. Newfoundland fleet in danger from three Spanish men-of-war; Raleigh writes to Cecil, that all the Newfoundland fleet of one hundred sail may be taken, "*the greatest calamity which could befall England.*"

1595.—Supplies from Newfoundland for army in Ireland.

1596.—French pirate, Michel de Sancé, captured English vessel commanded by Richard Clark.

1597.—Charles Leigh and Abraham Von Herwic, London merchants, came out to do business in Newfoundland. June 15th to 24th—Sir Anthony Shirley re-victualled in Newfoundland on his way to England. Dutch, Irish, and French ships at Plymouth in September, waiting to buy fish when the English Newfoundland fleet arrived.

1598.—Large cargoes of Newfoundland fish brought to Southampton and Poole; greater part sold by October to go to Spain, by way of France.

1599.—Licence to Bowgan to export 60,000 Newfoundland fish from England.

1600.—Sir Walter Raleigh, Governor of Jersey, inaugurated trade between the Island and Newfoundland; Jersey a free port. Newfoundland fish selling in Bayonne at 14 to 18 royals, "according to goodness."

1601.—Spanish vessels attempting to intercept the Newfoundland fleet.

1602.—Spanish Newfoundland fleet reported to be kept back to take troops to Ireland; seven Basque vessels go to Newfoundland for whaling, and many more for fishing from St. Jean de Luz. Gosnold's voyage to New England.

1603.—Attack on an English ship in Newfoundland by seven French vessels; damage £942.

During the reigns of Edward VI. and Mary—times of great religious and political excitement—commerce and maritime adventure languished. There was, however, already a considerable Brazil trade, and much commerce to the Levant and Spanish America. Sir John Hawkins in

ACT OF EDWARD VI.

1562 began the traffic in negroes between Africa and South America—"the commodious and gainful voyage to the Brazils," as Hakluyt calls this inhuman trade. Up to the end of Mary's reign the trade to Spanish America was partly open to the English; in her time trade between England and Russia also commenced. There are, however, no recorded voyages to this Colony. The Newfoundland fish trade had for some time been a settled business. Not only a large fishery, but a large trade was carried on in Newfoundland, as shown by the presence of merchant ships like Mr Grube's two vessels, noticed in the last chapter. The most important information about the island in this reign is contained in the following Act of Edward VI, proving conclusively the magnitude and continuity of the English fishery transactions and trade to the new land:—

ELIZABETH.
From an engraving after the Newcome picture.

"2nd & 3rd Ed., Cap. VI., A.D. 1548.

"*An Act against the Exacting of Money or other Thing by any Officer for Licence to traffick into Iceland, &c.*

"FORASMUCH as within these few Years now last past there hath been levied, perceived and taken by certain of the officers of the Admiralty, of such Merchants and Fishermen as have used and practised the Adventures and Journeys into *Iceland, Newfoundland, Ireland,* and other Places commodious for Fishing and the getting of Fish, in or upon the Seas or otherwise, by way of Merchandise in those parts, divers great Exactions, as Sums of Money, Doles, or Shares of Fish, and such other like Things, to the great Discouragement and Hindrance of the same Merchants and Fishermen, and to no little damage to the whole Commonweal; And whereof also great Complaints have been made and Informations also yearly to the King's Majesty's most Honourable Council; For Reformation whereof, and to the Intent also that the said Merchants and Fishermen may have Occasion the rather to practise and use the same Trade of Merchandise and Fishing freely without any such Charges or Exactions as is before limited, whereby it is to be thought that more plenty of Fish shall come into this Realm, and thereby to have the same at more reasonable prices:

"Be it therefore enacted by the King our Sovereign Lord, and the Lords and Commons in this present Parliament assembled, and by the Authority of the same, that neither they, nor any Officer or Minister, Officers or Ministers of the Admiralty for the Time being, shall in any wise hereafter exact, receive or take by himself, his Servant, Deputy, Servants or Deputies, of any such Merchant or Fisherman, any Sum or Sums of Money, Doles or Shares of Fish, or any other Reward, Benefit, or Advantage whatsoever it be, for any Licence to pass this Realm to the said Voyages or any of them, nor upon any Respect concerning the said Voyages or any of them; upon Pain to forfeit for the first Offence treble the Sum, or treble the Value of the Reward, Benefit, or Advantage that any such Officer or Minister shall hereafter have to take of any such Merchant or Fishermen, for the which Forfeiture the Party grieved, and every other Person or Persons whatsoever he or they be, shall and may sue for the same by Information, Bill, Plaint or Action of Debt, in any of the King's Courts of Record, the King to have the one Moiety, and the Party complaining the other Moiety: In which suit no Essoin, Protection or Wager of Law shall be allowed: And for the second Offence the Party so offending not only to lose or forfeit his or their Office or Offices in the Admiralty, but also to make fine and Ransom at the King's Will and Pleasure."

During the whole Tudor Period up to the earlier years of Elizabeth's reign, England as an ally of Spain, made no effectual opposition to her exclusive dominion in America. Under a spirited sovereign, however, like Elizabeth, Englishmen could no longer endure the galling yoke and jealous exclusiveness of the Spaniards in South America. In Newfoundland the Devon fishermen learnt how to measure their strength with them, to conquer and to rule the Biscayan and the Basque. Soon the English, following the example of the hardy seamen of Brittany, began to infest the Spanish West Indies. The smuggling piratical trade begun by the French was followed up by Drake, Hawkins, and countless other daring West Country adventurers. English historians do not acknowledge the fact, but it is quite clear that the first lesson in taming the Spaniard was learnt by the courageous Devonshire fishermen in Newfoundland.

"The spacious days of Great Elizabeth" form the most brilliant period of English history. To this golden age our Island story is united by imperishable bands—linked for ever with the Immortals who have made the Elizabethan age the wonder and the glory of all time. The nursing mother of our infant Colony was the Divine Gloriana. The great Bacon was not only a shareholder in Guy's plantation, but with his powerful influence he strongly advocated in a pamphlet the policy of settlement; he speaks of "The Gold Mines " of the Newfoundland Fishery of which there " is none so rich." Spenser—Raleigh's greatest friend—was united with him in his colonisation schemes, and it needs no stretch of the imagination to picture to ourselves the greatest Englishman of action—explorer, warrior, statesman, above all poet expounding with glowing eloquence to Shakespeare his vast schemes of the Plantation in the Newfoundlands and the building up of a greater England beyond the seas.

SIR FRANCIS DRAKE.
From a print in the B.M.

In this age of Elizabeth we seem to breathe a freer and a nobler air. The chains of feudalism have been cast off for ever. Compared with former reigns, Shakespeare's time seems strangely modern. The plays that delighted the subjects of the virgin queen still charm the subjects of Victoria. Cecil, Prime Minister of Elizabeth, has a direct and still more illustrious descendant in Lord Salisbury, Prime Minister of our own time. No other Government in Europe can show such stability and continuity as this. And then the great queen herself is strangely familiar to us, ever in public, graceful, majestic; ready to make a speech on all occasions. The fierce light that beats upon a throne has brought out all her follies and frivolities. Granted that her speech and manner would not suit our modern sensibilities, still she will ever remain a great personality, the most picturesque figure in English history—"the Pilot that weathered the storm"—the great sovereign that ever sought the public weal—"that wrought her people lasting good."

Our own history in this age also opens up more clearly. We are no longer groping in the dark, with obscure records and contradictory testimony. From the illustrious writers of the period we are able now to give "the very age and body of the time his form and pressure."

In the first years of her reign Raleigh was a boy, and neither Elizabeth nor her councillors had any thought of American colonisation; she was, however, most favourable to voyages of discovery. She gave substantial aid to the daring Frobisher in his arctic voyage to discover a north-west passage to India.[1]

She was her father's daughter, and her masculine mind thoroughly realised that England should be mistress of the seas. To this end she encouraged the fisheries as the true foundation on which naval supremacy must rest. One of her first acts (1562) was to confirm the law of Edward VI. protecting the Newfoundland fishermen from the plundering officials of the Admiralty. She further encouraged their business by passing a law to compel everyone to eat fish on Wednesdays and Saturdays:—

ACT 5 ELIZABETH, c. V.

"Touching certain politick constitutions for the maintenance of the Navy."

Sec. XIV. sets out: "And for the increase of the provisions of fish by the more usual and common eating thereof Be it further enacted, by the authority aforesaid, that from the Feast of Saint Michael the Archangel 1564, every Wednesday in every week throughout the whole year which heretofore hath not

---

[1] The idea of a north-west passage to India through some strait north of Labrador was not unnatural. The Elizabethan seamen argued, if there was a passage south, which Magellan had found, there must also be one in a corresponding position north. They never realised the immense northern extension of America. Though the whole three voyages of Frobisher are most fantastic, there can be no question about his daring. Frobisher Straits is a perpetual monument to his memory.

by the laws or customs of the realme been used and observed as a fish day shall be hereafter observed and kept as Saturdays in every week be or ought to be upon pain that every person offending herein shall forfeit three pounds for every time he or they shall offend or else suffer three months' close imprisonment without bail or mainprise.

Sec. XXXIX.: "And because no manner of person shall misjudge of the intent of this estatute limiting orders to eat fish and to forbear eating of flesh but that the same is purposely intended and meant politickly for the increase of fishermen and mariners and repairing of ports towns and navigation and not for any superstition to be maintained in the choice of meats.

Sec. XL.: "Be it enacted, that whosoever shall, by preaching, teaching, writing or open speech notify that any eating of fish or forbearing of flesh mentioned in this estatute is of any necessity for saving the soul of man or that it is the service of God, otherwise than as other politick laws are and be, that then such person shall be punished as the spreaders of false news are and ought to be.

These old Acts are not only quaint and full of a certain dry humour, they contain also the very pith and marrow of English history.

This politic and ingenious device to create a Protestant Lent, and compel Englishmen to eat fish for a hundred days in the year, was a dismal failure. The proud stomachs of our ancestors have always resented interference with their beef and beer; like Falstaff, they would not feast or fast upon compulsion. Fishmongers petitioned Her Majesty that the fish days were not observed; and so, after eighteen years' struggle, like a wise sovereign, she bowed before the inevitable; her legalised fast was left to die out.

By 23 Eliz. Cap. VII. (1581), a most drastic measure, however, was soon passed prohibiting the importation of foreign-caught fish by Englishmen, and imposing a duty on all foreign fish. Sec. VI. enacted:—

"Provided always that this Act or anything therein contained shall not extend or be prejudicial to any providing or bringing of fish in or out of the country of Iceland, Shetland or Newfoundland or any parts or seas thereto adjoining or on the Scottish Seas, nor to any fish that shall be killed taken and salted by the Queen's Natural Subjects, anything in this Act to the contrary notwithstanding."

Newfoundland, as in former statutes, is specially mentioned.

During this remarkable reign English commerce increased by leaps and bounds. Devonshire, however, still remained pre-eminent as the great centre of maritime enterprise—as the Iceland and Irish fish trades declined the Newfoundland enterprise increased. The records show us clearly that the old mariners from Dartmouth and Bideford, and a score more of little West Country coast towns, knew every port and place and headland in Newfoundland; Cape Race, Cape St. Francis, and Baccalieu were as familiar to Devon sailors as Berry Head and the Land's End.

MARTINEZ' MAP, 1589.[1]

B.M. MSS. [?] *Hist.*

Long before Gilbert's famous adventure, the trip to our Island was an everyday voyage, and no longer an expedition of discovery. All around the coast of Newfoundland, the Gulf, and Cape Breton, down to the State of Maine, English and foreign fishermen fished and explored. It is expressly stated by Hayes, the survivor of Gilbert's miserable, ill-fated expedition, that they went by way of our Island to get a supply of victuals, and not on a voyage of discovery, or to take possession of the Island. Sir Anthony Shirley re-victualled in Newfoundland on his way to England in 1597, and Raleigh's fleet called there on his last voyage from Guiana for the same purpose. Hayes says:—

"The last place of our assembly before we left the coast of England was in Cawsand Bay, near unto Plymouth, then resolved to put unto the sea with shipping and provision, such as we had, before our store yet remaining, but chiefly the time and season of the year, were too far spent. Nevertheless it seemed first very doubtful by what way to shape our course and to begin our intended discovery, either from the South northward, or from the North southward. The first—that is beginning South—without all controversy was the likeliest, wherein we were assured to have commodity of the current [the Gulf Stream] which from the

[1] This map is of Spanish-Italian origin, and represents, probably, the ideas of Cartier's explorations in the Gulf of St. Lawrence current in Spain and Italy; it is similar to the map given in Bishop Howley's *Ecclesiastical History*. Newfoundland is split up into islands.

Cape of Florida setteth northward, and would have furthered greatly our navigation, discovering from the aforesaid Cape along towards Cape Breton. . . . . . . These and other like reasons alleged in favour of the southern course first to be taken, to the contrary was inferred that for as much as both our victuals and many other needful provisions were diminished and left insufficient for so long a voyage and the wintering of so many men, we ought to shape a course most likely to minister supply; and that was to take the Newfoundland in our way, ... where being usually at that time of the year until the fine of August a multitude of ships repairing thither for fish, we should be relieved abundantly with many necessaries."

I think I have conclusively proved the continuous dominion and possession of the English in Newfoundland. It appears quite clear that, taking one year with another, twenty years before Gilbert's voyage, at least fifty English vessels engaged in the Transatlantic fishery; as these old ships carried about a man to a ton, they would give from two thousand five hundred to three thousand men engaged in this business. But besides the actual fishing vessels, there were also merchant ships from London, Southampton, and other ports engaged in the trade as freighters. The little fishing vessels, after a good voyage, could not carry all their fish to market, so these freighters, known in the trade as "sack ships," traded and carried; probably the name was derived from sack (sherry), because these vessels often brought salt and a supply of the good wines of Xeres to Devonshire and Newfoundland. That St. John's was a great place for trade—a great mart—is shown by the Irish Government sending out two ships to get fish and *other supplies* in 1595.[1]

It will thus be clearly seen that the prevailing idea about Gilbert's expedition being a voyage of discovery to Newfoundland is entirely erroneous; he came to St. John's because it was a well-known port, where his poor, half-starved company would be sure of an ample supply of food and necessaries.

During nearly all the Tudor Period, England was a close ally of Spain, and the English fishing ships had the run of all the Spanish and Italian ports. The Peninsula has always been our greatest customer. At one time Spain consumed half a million quintals of Newfoundland fish; later in Elizabeth's reign, when she was at war, Devonshire became the great depôt for dried cod, and Dutch and sometimes English ships freighted it to France, and thence to the Mediterranean. In the Appendix will be found a charter-party for freighting a cargo of fish from Chester to France, and a licence to export fish in 1599.[2]

---

[1] In the *Irish State Papers* Sir G. Fenton writes in 1595 to Burghley, that "he has sent out again two ships to Newfoundland for fish and other provisions for the army in Ireland, and the people; and the ships being to touch at Poole or some other part of the West Country, he hopes they will not be detained by some general restraint of shipping."

[2] P. 81.

We cannot fix the precise year in which settlement commenced in Newfoundland; Sabine states that in 1522 there were forty or fifty houses in Newfoundland; but, from scattered information contained in the records, and narratives of voyages, it is clear that, from a very early period, a few crews were left behind every winter to cut timber for building cook-rooms, stages, train vats, wharves, and for the construction of boats. Hayes speaks of the weather observed in December, and of the boats built in Newfoundland.

No doubt it was a daring experiment for the first Devon crew that put up their winter house and did their lumbering and sporting in the lonely isle; but there were no dreaded savages on the eastern coast between Cape St. Francis and Cape Race.

SHOOTING WHITE BEARS.
From De Veer's Waerachtighe, 1605.

After the first successful venture, regular crews would be fitted out with their master carpenters and blacksmiths and boat builders. Game was so prodigiously abundant, good timber close at hand and plentiful, that there never would be wanting volunteers for this work. Whitbourne gives us quite a homily on the necessity of winter crews; and it is obvious to anyone acquainted with our shore fishery that it could not be carried on to any extent successfully without winter men. It is no argument that history does not inform us about these first residents; their presence here would not be mentioned. No lists were kept of fishing vessels or their crews—at any rate from Devonshire—all through the Tudor Period; and no notice would be taken of the doings of those obscure fishermen in the far-off land.

The earliest narrative in the reign of Elizabeth about the ancient Colony is contained in a letter from Anthony Parkhurst, a merchant of Bristol, to Hakluyt, dated November 13th, 1578. He says:—

"He had made four voyages to Newfoundland, and had searched the harbours, creeks, and lands, more than any other Englishman. That there were generally more than 100 sail of Spaniards taking cod, and from 20 to 30 killing whales; 50 sail of Portuguese, 150 sail of French and Bretons, mostly very small; but of English only 50 sail. Nevertheless" he adds "*the English are commonly lords of the harbours where they fish, and do all strangers help in fishing*, if need require, *according to an old custom of the country*; which thing they do willingly, so that you take nothing from them more than a boat or two of salt, in respect of your protection of them against rovers or other violent intruders, who do often put them from good harbours."

KILLING WALRUS.
From D. Peer's Warrerhergh, 1591.

The arrogance of the old West Country buccaneer is amusing—the cool way in which he speaks about plundering the inoffensive foreign fishermen; evidently the Portuguese had better ships and stronger crews, for the bold Antonie abuses them as "Vile Portingals descending of the Jews and Judas kind." After enumerating the various kind of fish in Newfoundland, he says: "The mussels all contain pearls; that he had heard of a Portugal that found one worth 300 ducats."—"That in half a day he could take as many lobsters as would find 300 men with a day's meat." Of the trees, he says: "The trees is most fir, yet plenty of pine-apple trees; few of those two kinds meet to mast a ship of three score and ten tons."

The important expedition of Sir Thomas Hampshire to Newfoundland, in 1582, shows the wise and enlightened policy of the great queen; before Sir Thomas's arrival it had been the custom for the first comer in each harbour to seize any piece of foreshore he might select sufficient to cure and dry his codfish. This custom gave rise to endless disputes. The queen authorised Hampshire to make a new rule: Whatever room

TRINITY HARBOUR.
From a photograph by Mr. White, Trinity.

or space of foreshore a master of a vessel selected, he could retain it so long as he kept up his buildings on it, and employed it for the use of the fishery.

This wise regulation largely increased the Newfoundland fishery, gave the western men a more permanent interest in the country, and augmented the number of wintering crews; permanent fishing establishments, wharves, flakes, stages were built and winter guardians appointed, small plots of land were cultivated, simply gardens; thus settlement and a planter's shore fishery began in the colony. The first of these scattered settlements were between Cape St. Francis and Cape Race, and around Conception Bay.

The people who began as part of a winter crew often became the first permanent settlers. Born hunters, restless roaming spirits, like the Daniel Boones and Kit Carsons of western fame, they produced a race still famous for their woodcraft, their sporting skill, and their daring courage on the ice floes.[1]

[1] Newfoundlanders have been conspicuous from the earliest times for their skill at woodcraft and sealing.
Devonshire, with its wonderful variety of hill and dale and moorland, has always been famous for game and hunting. To the old West Countrymen Newfoundland was a very sportsman's paradise, abounding in fin, fur, and feather. Hayes speaks of the innumerable quantity of game, how their

Two of the most interesting figures in our early history are Gilbert[1] and Whitbourne[2]; both were on the Island together in 1583. Sir Humphrey came as the queen's representative, and Whitbourne, as a common sailor, took part in the function, and watched the ceremonious taking possession of the Colony, in whose affairs he afterwards played such a leading part. One was a gallant gentleman, soldier, courtier, descended of an ancient family; with all respect for the courtly knight, Richard Whitbourne, West Country sailor, our historian, and Newfoundland's steadfast friend, is more to us and dearer to our hearts as colonists than even the brave and most unfortunate Sir Humphrey. Poor Richard, afterwards Sir Richard, had no friends at Court; he rose from the ranks, a sturdy lad made into a smart sailor by the hard usage and rope's-ending, the training by which every Devon mariner rises from the forecastle to the cabin. His first experience in the country was as a hand before the mast, or perhaps as mate "in a worthy ship of the "burthen of 300 tons, set forth by one Master Cotton, of Southampton."

men killed partridges with cudgels. Dr. Vaughan, about 1620, tells of one man killing 300 partridges (willow grouse). Abbé Baudoin (1696) speaks with wonder of the marvellous woodcraft of the Newfoundlanders. These colonial hunters were the lineal descendants of the old Devonian hunters and poachers; keen-eyed, untiring, they took to woodcraft as a duck takes to water.

As a sealer the Newfoundlander has always been without a rival. Nothing astonished the Dundee whalers more when they first came to the Colony than to see our men jump over the side of the ship and skip from pan to pan over the loose ice, locally known as "copying." Sandy thought them "vara wild men," but now he is learning to imitate them. The Scot, however, is a long way behind the genuine native, who has been practising it from a small boy; copying, jigging tomcods, and going in the woods trouting, being the popular amusements of the native boy.

Islanders are proverbially conservative in their habits and customs; the familiar Newfoundland snow shoes—known as pot racquets, the punts, and the long single barrel gun—known as the Poole gun (as shown in DE VEER's picture, p. 59)—are all copies of those used in the old Dorset sea port, and figure as part of a wild fowler's equipment in Colonel Hawker's well-known old book on shooting, published during the last century; from generation to generation the old familiar patterns have remained unchanged.

[1] Sir Humphrey Gilbert was born in 1539; he died in 1583. He was second of three sons of Otto Gilbert, of Greenway, Devon. His mother, a Champernoun, relative of the great family of the Carews, became the third wife of Captain Walter Raleigh, and by him had two sons, the youngest of whom was the great Sir Walter Raleigh. Her three children by Gilbert were all knighted, John, Humphrey, and Adrian. Humphrey was educated at Eton and Oxford, served in Ireland and the Netherlands. In 1576 was published his famous tract, "Discourse of a Discoverie for a new Passage to Cataia." In 1578 he received his large patent from the queen, authorising him "to discover, occupy, and possess such remote heathen lands not actually possessed of any Christian Prince or people as should seem good to him." (This patent and his agreements with Peckham will be found in MR. SAINSBURY's *Colonial Papers Addenda*, 1574–1674.) Gilbert disposed of nearly all his patrimony in fitting out his first expedition, 1578, which was a total failure. June 11th, 1583, began his famous voyage to Newfoundland, in which he perished, with all the crew of his little vessel. Gilbert was an enthusiast, a dreamer, a man with no executive ability, no command of men, of dauntless courage, and undoubtedly pious after the fashion of the age. He did splendid service to England as a pioneer of colonisation. His character has been well portrayed by Kingsley as a weak-headed enthusiast, a totally unfit commander for the rough work of exploring and settlement of new lands. Both expeditions show nothing but disorder, incapacity, and predestined failure.

[2] See pp. 114 to 118 for further account of Whitbourne.

The young sailor, in the beautiful land-locked harbour of Trinity, amidst all the hurry and bustle of the shore fishery, first saw the "natural inhabitants," as he called the Beothics or Red Indians; he says:—

"They are few in number, and as something rude and savage people having neither knowledge of God nor living under any kind of civil government. In their habits, customs, and manners they resemble the Indian of the continent from whence, I suppose, they come," [still they are said to be] "an ingenious and tractable people, being well used," [and as] "ready to assist in the whale fishery for even small reward."

Whaling was successfully prosecuted by the Biscayans, and Cotton's ship was to have been engaged in the same daring enterprise. Whitbourne says:—

"We were bound to the Grand Bay (which lieth on the north side of that land) purporting there to trade then with the savage people (for whom we carried sundry commodities), and to kill whales and to make trayne oil as the Biscaines do there yearly in great abundance. But then our intended voyage was overthrowne by the indiscretion of our captaine and faintheartednesse of some gentlemen of our company, whereupon we set saile from thence and bare with Trinity Harbour in Newfoundland, where we killed great store of fish, deere, beares, beavers, seales, otters, and such like, with abundance of sea-fowle, and so returning to England we arrived safe at Southampton."

Throughout these early narratives there are notices of the aborigines of Newfoundland, the Beothics. Whitbourne speaks of them as tractable if well used. The French everywhere in America seem to have had more friendly relations with the Indians than any other Europeans; in the very beginning of the fishery the French were assisted by the Indians in curing their fish, and a considerable barter trade was carried on with them; the Biscayans also in their whaling operations had help from the Indians. With the other Indian tribes of the continent, Cape Breton, &c., the French kept up the most amicable relations; only with the native Indians of the Colony, called indifferently Beothicks, Beothucks, and Bethicks, was there always dire hostility, brought about by a terrible act of treachery on the part of the Indians, related by Kirke; they first attacked a small party of French who were alone and unarmed, murdered them all, and then dressing up in the Frenchmen's clothes they allured another party of French fishermen and killed twenty-one of them. Like all savages they were inveterate thieves. Whitbourne says:—

"Many of them secretly every yeere come into Trinity Bay and Harbour in the night time purposely to steal sailes, lines, hatchets, hookes, knives, and such like."

On this subject it is unfortunate that we have only the white man's story, and the red man is unheard; the French may have given them great provocation, and revenge is part of the creed of an Indian.

REIGN OF ELIZABETH.

Old Whitbourne himself, much as we love and admire him, admits having shared in a most outrageous spoliation of the poor savages:—

"The Indians have great store of redoaker which they use to colour their bodies, bowes and arrowes, and canowes withal; they use the rinds of spruce trees

HENLEY ISLAND.
From a drawing by the Hon. and Rev. W. Grey.

round and deepe in proportion like a brass kettle to boyle their meat in, which hath been well proved by three mariners of a ship riding at anchor by mee who being robbed in the night by the savages of their apparel and divers provisions, came suddenly upon them where they had set up their tents and were feasting . . . . by shooting off a musket they all ran away naked without any apparel . . . . all their three cannowes, their flesh-knives, volkes of egges, targets, bowers and arrowes, and much fine okar and divers other things were brought away and shared, and they brought to me the best cannowe, bowes and arrowes . . . . which may seem to invite us to find out some other trade with them."

Charles I. issued a proclamation in 1630, prohibiting disorderly trading with Red Indians. The most hopeful effort to establish friendly relations with these poor savages was made in 1612, when Guy and Captain Whittington met the Indians. Purchas says:—

"They met at Randon in Trinity Bay, eat and drank together, and exchanged furs and skins for hatchets and knives, appointed a meeting for next year by a sign

THE IDEA OF COLONISATION.

when the grass should be of such a height to bring down all their furs and skins for traffick with the English. At the time appointed for their meeting, instead of Captain Whittington and other agents, there came a fisherman to this place to make a voyage; seeing Indians and not knowing the reason of their coming, he let fly a shot from aboard; Indians ran off, imagining they were Guy's men, and now will not trade."[1]

Thus, unfortunately, there was an end to the overtures which might have resulted in renewed amity and peace with these poor persecuted savages. With Mic-Mac and Eskimos, Europeans easily established cordial relations, but during the whole period there never seems to have been peace between the English settlers and these unfortunate Boethics. The account of their extinction, and the efforts made to promote intercourse with them, will be given later on. The story of the Red Indian is a sad, dismal tale of wanton cruelty, suspicion, and treachery.

NATIVES OF CANADA.
From Champlains' Voyages, 1632.

To write the complete history of English colonisation in this Island is quite beyond the limits of my work. I can only shortly state a few salient points. It does seem strange to us that for nearly a century England made no official attempt to colonise her new possession. The voyages of Rut and Hoare were distinctly for exploration, to discover a north-west passage; Sir Humphrey Gilbert was full of the same idea, and wrote a tract and made a map to promote an expedition for that purpose.

In the age of Elizabeth, though old conceptions were passing away, credulity, superstition, and the fantastic ideas of bygone days still lingered. All competent authorities now agree that in those days one man alone in England realised the benefits of colonisation. It was the transcendent mind of Raleigh, with the vivid imagination of a poet and the profound wisdom of a statesman, that first expounded to the Elizabethan age the plan of English colonisation, the foundation of greater Englands in the New World; knowing the temper of the time

[1] PURCHAS' *His Pilgrims*, p. 2729.

he had to proceed warily; he held out gold as an inducement for his new projects. Fishermen were urged to capture Indians, to bring home

GILBERT'S MAP, 1578.
From Winsor's N. and C. H. of America.

strange birds and beasts, and products of America. All these things captivated the credulous mind of the public, and, says Raleigh, "helped "forward the Plantation mightily." Whilst he encouraged in every way the working of the gold mine of the Newfoundland fishery, in his emphatic words "the main stay and support" of his own Devon and western counties, his mind was set on gaining the whole vast continent, and on this grand idea he spent a fortune (equal to £200,000 or a million dollars). His half brother, Sir Humphrey Gilbert, a pale reflection of his great relative, assisted in these projects; years before the actual expedition sailed the brothers worked together to expedite their plans. Raleigh's influence at Court procured the charter from Elizabeth; the dread of Spain, then an ally of England, had to be overcome; the Queen agreed to everything, only refusing to allow her favourite courtier to leave England.

The expedition of 1583 was not Gilbert's first attempt; in 1578, with the connivance of the Court, he sailed from England with two ships. His object is disclosed thus:—

"A discourse how Her Majesty may annoy the King of Spain by fitting out a fleet of shippes of war under pretence of a voyage of discovery, and so fall upon the enemies shippes and destroy his trade in Newfoundland and the West Indies, and possess the country."

This paper is still extant;[1] the signature is thought to be Gilbert's; one passage arguing against delay, "for the wings of a man's life are plumed with the arrows of death," shows that, if penned by him, it was conceived and dictated by Raleigh.

"I will," it continues, "undertake to fit out ships well armed for Newfoundland, where they will meet with all the great ships of France, Spain, and Portugal; the best I will bring away and burn the rest; commit us afterwards as Pirates if you will, but I shall ruin their sea force, for they depend on their fishermen for their navies."

Poor Sir Humphrey was a dreamer, an enthusiast; the expedition was a complete failure; he arrived out in Newfoundland, and, probably in a fight with the Spaniards, lost a tall ship and a bold captain, Miles Morgan.

Gilbert was terribly crippled and impoverished, but sooner than forfeit his large patent, which was for six years, and would expire next year, 1584, he sold a large part of his estate, and with the aid of Raleigh (who furnished one ship), Peckham, Hayes, and others, a little fleet of five vessels and two hundred and fifty men were got together.[2] There were of all trades; "hobby horses and morris dancers, and many like conceits

THE NARROWS, ST. JOHN'S.

"were provided to win the savage people by all fair means possible." Gilbert's crew consisted partly of the off scourings of the jails, and the result, as might be anticipated, was most disastrous; one ship took to piracy, and a great portion of his villainous followers deserted. On the 3rd of August 1583, Gilbert arrived at St. John's with two ships and a pinnace—the *Delight*, Admiral's ship, 120 tons, the *Golden Hind*, 40 tons, and the *Squirrel*, 10 tons.

[1] *Records.*
[2] Davy Ingram's account of the country through which he passed seems to have had some influence in gaining Gilbert the support of Peckham and others.

Before the entrance of the harbour they found the little *Swallow*, of 40 tons, at anchor, which the English merchants would not permit to enter:—

"These English merchants that were and always be admirals by turn interchangeably over the fleet of fishermen within the same harbour."

In reading this narrative we are forcibly impressed with the dominion exercised by these extraordinary English merchant adventurers in Newfoundland; they looked upon the whole island as their own dominion, gained by their own valour, without the slightest assistance from the English Government. They therefore resented the entrance of a mere courtier into their domain. They knew full well that they had only their own strong right arms and stout hearts to depend upon; in those days there was no such thing as international justice. If by chance a French vessel captured one of ours, there was no redress, they would be fortunate to escape with their lives from a howling French mob. To be captured by a Spaniard was to fall into the very gate of death; a captured Frenchman had a show of justice in England, but no substantial recompense for injury. There are many cases in the records like the following:—

"April 18, 1591. Petition from Bayonne to the Privy Council that a ship of Peter de Hody of Bayonne from Newfoundland with 108,000 dry fish, 4,000 green. 14 hhds. of Train oil, total value 6,000 crowns, had been taken by a ship of Sir W. Raleigh, and brought to Uphill near Bristol."[1]

Hody spent five hundred crowns, but got no redress from the rich victuallers of Bristol, who had received the proceeds of the merchandise, and kept the ship; so he returned to France.

"Sept. 1591. The *Eliza*, *Beneventure* and *Dudley* took a ship *The Holy Ghost* from M. de Harques of St. Jean de Luz with 15,000 dry fish, 60 hhds. of train, and 48 men whom they stripped to their shirts. De Harques and his two brothers have been suitors in England for past eight months."[1]

The ship was afterwards ordered to be given up, but the owners did not get her—*she ran ashore*—a regular West Country trick.

In our day these daring adventurers would be dubbed "pirates." The only way they exercised dominion was by a reckless dare-devil courage, which made the very name of Englishman a terror to the Spaniards. It was the almost fiendish cruelty to English prisoners that stirred the whole nation against Spain. They have a proverb in the Peninsula expressing the highest tribute to the valour of our ancestors:—

"Con todo el mundo guerra,
Mas paz con Inglatierra."
"War with all the world, but peace with England."

[1] *Records*.

THE IMPORTANCE OF THE FISHERY.

Mr. Oppenheim, in the "English Historical Review," says:—

"It speaks sufficiently for the courage of the Elizabethan sailor that during the whole of the reign but two English men-of-war, the *Jesus of Lubeck* and the *Revenge*, were captured by the Spaniards, and then only after desperate fighting against overwhelming odds."

We realise the power of Elizabeth, when even in remote Newfoundland the moment the merchants knew of her commission they obeyed Gilbert's orders. This narrative will also disabuse our minds of the idea of the Newfoundland trade as carried on by a few poor fishermen. It comes

PISTOLET'S MAP, 1587.[1]
B.M. MSS. Eg. 1513-8.

out clearly in this History that nearly a century before any English colony was founded in North America, England had a great trade and

[1] This map is of French origin, and differs very little from that of Descellier, given at p. 40, John Dee's at p. 59, and Vallard's made at Dieppe. It shows the results of early French explorations in Newfoundland and Labrador, particularly from Notre Dame Bay to the Straits of Belle Isle. The English standard is shown near Hamilton Inlet.

fishery in Newfoundland. In 1594, Sir Walter Raleigh said that if any harm should happen to the Newfoundland fleet it would be the greatest calamity which could befall England.[1]

The entertainers of Sir Humphrey were merchants. St. John's was even then an important free port; a large international trade was carried on, the owners coming out with their masters, and superintending it themselves. It is also expressly told us that they had houses, for the General lived ashore with them for the three weeks he stayed in St. John's.

The character of this business will be easily understood: it was an absolutely free trade; no Custom House officer to trouble the merchant's pocket or his conscience. The principal traffic consisted in selling for cash—or bartering for fish and oil—Mediterranean products, salt, olive oil, fruits, wines, also West of England cordage, cloth hats, caps, hosiery, Sheffield wares, and general English merchandise. The master and his crew fished, the merchant had his store and traded; considering the large number of fishermen of all nations, probably about fifteen thousand, resorting to Newfoundland, it must have been an extensive and, I need not add, a lucrative trade.

There are three narratives of Gilbert's expedition—Hayes', Peckham's, and Clark's. Hayes says:—

"Saturday, 3rd August, we made ready our fights and prepared to enter the harbour, any resistance to the contrary notwithstanding, there being within of all nations to the number of 36 sail.

"But first the General [Gilbert] despatched a boat to give them knowledge of his coming for no ill intent, having commission from Her Majesty for this voyage we had in hand; and immediately we followed with a slack gale, and in the very entrance, which is but narrow, the Admiral fell upon a rock [Cahill's Rock] on the larboard side, by great oversight.

"After the English merchants had been shown our commission they were all satisfied. The merchants with their masters departed. They caused forthwith to be discharged all the great ordinance of their fleet in token of our welcome."

Afterwards arrangements were made to fit out this poor ill-provided expedition with necessary food and supplies. Hayes continues:—

"Commissioners were appointed, part of our own company and part of theirs to go into other harbours adjoining (*for our English merchants command all there*) to levy our provision; whereunto the Portugals (above all other nations) did most willingly and liberally contribute.

"In so much as we were presented (above our allowance) with wines, marmalades, most fine rusk or biscuits, sweet oils, and sundry delicacies; also, we wanted not of fresh salmons, trouts, lobsters, and other fresh fish brought daily unto us.

[1] *Hatfield MS.*

" Moreover as the manner is in fishing every week to choose their Admiral anew, or rather they succeed each in orderly course, and have weekly their Admiral's feast solemnized, even so the General, captains and masters of our fleet were continually invited and feasted.

" Next morning being Sunday, 4th August, the General and his company were brought on land by the English merchants, who showed unto us their accustomed walks into a place they called '*the garden*.'[1] But nothing appeared more than nature itself without art, who confusedly hath brought forth roses abundantly wild, but odoriferous, and to sense very comfortable. Also the like plenty of raspberries, which do grow in every place."

It is quite evident that Gilbert and his companions had a very jovial time in St. John's, then, and now, famous for its hospitality.

It seems, says Hayes, speaking of St. John's—

"A place very populous and much frequented."

And Sir George Peckham says that the English merchants—

"Before endeavouring to fraughte themselves with fish repayred unto Sir Humphrey and assisted him in his designs."

Hayes continues:—

" Upon Monday being the fifth of August the General caused his tent to be set up on the side of an hill[2] in the viewe of all the flete of English men and strangers, which were in number between thirty and forty sail; then, being accompanied by all his Captains, Masters, Gentlemen and Soldiers he caused all, the Masters and principall officers of the shippes as well Englishmen as Spaniards Portugals and all other nations to repayre into his tent and then and there in the presence of them all he did cause his commission under the great seal of England to be openlie and solemnlie reade unto them whereby was graunted unto him his heyres and assignes by the Queen's most excellent Majestie many great and large royalties liberties and priviledges.

" The effect whereof being signified unto the strangers by an interpreter he took possession of the said lande in the right of the Crown of England by digging up a turfe and receiving the same with a hazell wande delivered unto him after the manner of the lawe and custome of England.

" Then he signified unto the company both strangers and others that from thenceforth they were to live in that land as the territories appertayning unto the Crowne of England and to be governed by such lawes as by good advise should be set down which in all points (so neere as might be) should be agreeable to the Lawes of England and for to put the same in execution presentlie he ordained and established three lawes:

" 1. Establishment of the Church of England.

" 2. Any attempt prejudicial to Her Majesty's rights in the territory to be punished as in a case of High Treason.

---

[1] The late Sir R. J. Pinsent and several others have discussed the site of "ye ancient garden." It is difficult to define its exact position, but it was probably somewhere about Cherry Garden, on the banks of Waterford Bridge River, the most picturesque walk about St. John's. A path would go along there into the woods. It is in the direction in which sailors would naturally take a stroll on a Sunday afternoon.

[2] The hill would be, probably, Garrison Hill, the centre of the harbour. In Hatton and Harvey's History the General is described as standing on the beach of St. John's Harbour to perform the ceremony, and the pillar as being set up near the water edge. Peckham's narrative shows that it was on the hill.

"5. Anyone uttering words of dishonour to Her Majesty should lose his ears and have his goods and ship confiscated.

"All men did verie willingly submit themselves to these lawes.

"Then he caused the Queen's Majesties arms to be engraved and set upon a pillar of wood not far from the tent with great solemnity.

"After this divers Englishmen made suit unto Sir Humphrey to have of him by inheritance theyre accustomed stages, standings and drying places in sundry parts of that land for theyre fish as a thing they do make great accompte of. Which he granted unto them in fee farme.

"And by this means he hath possession mayntained for him in many parts of that country.

"To be briefe he dyd lette, sette, give and dispose of many things as absolute Governor there by virtue of Her Majesty's letter patent."[1]

He gave title to a great many English merchants for their fishing places in St. John's and the neighbouring harbours. Some of the St. John's merchants wanted larger grants of land.

"Now," says Hayes, "he became contrarily affected, refusing to make any so large grants, especially of St. John's, which certain English merchants made suit for, offering to employ their money and travail [work] upon the same; yet neither by their own suit nor of other of the company whom he seemed willing to pleasure, it could be obtained."

The merchants evidently contemplated permanent settlement and cultivation, and only wanted to be secure in their tenure; and it tells somewhat against the gallant knight that his "contrariety" helped to retard the progress of the Colony.

The splendid harbour of St. John's and its unique position, midway between Cape Bonavista and Cape Race, where at first all the English fishing operations were carried on, made our capital, from the very beginning, the metropolis and head-quarters of the Newfoundland fish trade, both English and foreign.

It was a grave misfortune for the Colony that the first great

SIR HUMPHREY GILBERT.
From Holland's *Heroologia*.

[1] HAKLUYT.

colonisation scheme fell into the hands of a poor, bankrupt, incapable man like Gilbert; to use Hayes' words—

"He thrust himself into the action for which he was not fit, presuming the cause pretended on God's behalf would carry him to the desired end."[1]

What shall we say of a great patentee like Gilbert, owner of half a continent, refusing the English merchants in St. John's a title to land around the infant capital, on which they were willing to spend their money, time, and labour. Later on, when an official settlement was made under Guy, he was directed by the patentees to go to Conception Bay, not to St. John's. The directors of the company seem to have been well acquainted with the Newfoundland fishery; full directions are given to him about the fish trade, &c.; clearly, long before that time, all the chief and best places in the good harbours of the east coast had been appropriated by merchants and fishermen.

Gilbert had with him a Saxon ore refiner named Daniel; he was so impressed with the mineral wealth of the Colony that he proposed to leave the settlement and discovery of the south to Hayes, for, he said, "I am now become a northern man altogether, and my heart is set on "Newfoundland."

Our Colony undoubtedly possesses great mineral wealth; this has been proved: whether Sir Humphrey and his miner really found anything but the glittering iron pyrites known as "fool's gold" cannot now be ascertained, as ore, papers, and everything else were lost at sea.

The end of this ill-organised expedition was dire disaster; on the 29th of August their Admiral's ship *Delight* was lost off Cape Sable, through utter carelessness and bad seamanship; the little frigate *Squirrel* and the *Golden Hind* escaped; on the 31st of August they bore up for England. Poor Gilbert has been painted for us as so complete an angel that it is a relief to find him at times giving way to human infirmities and acting like an ordinary man. After they had passed Cape Race on their return voyage, Gilbert came aboard the *Hind* to get a wound in his foot dressed; afterwards, on a fair day, he came aboard again "to "make merry, together with the captain, master, and company, and "continued there from morning until evening," no doubt drinking the good wine they had received in St. John's. On the same day, for the loss of some mineral specimens, "he was not able to contain himself, but "beat his boy in a great rage."

Lest I should be charged with misrepresenting the qualities of this most unfortunate adventurer, read his character drawn by Kingsley in the fascinating pages of "Westward Ho": "a philosopher—says Amyas —but not so much of a general, not able to control men."

[1] HAKLUYT.

The death of Sir Humphrey was as sad and tragic an end as ever befell a hero. It seems the Knollys or some of his enemies had questioned his courage on ship board, seamanship he had none; so to prove his mettle he refused to leave the wretched little tub of a *Squirrel* (10 tons). He said :—

"'I will not forsake my little company going homewards with whom I have passed so many storms and perils,' albeit [says Hayes] this was rather rashness than advised resolution, to prefer the wind of a vain report to the weight of his own life."[1]

Unfortunately he was no sailor or he might have known her condition, overweighted on deck with "fight's netting and small artillery," cumbersome for so small a boat to pass through the ocean at that period of the year.

On Monday, 9th September, in the afternoon—

"The frigate *Squirrel* was near cast away oppressed by waves, yet at that time recovered; and giving forth signs of joy, the General [Gilbert] sitting abaft with a book in his hand, cried out to us in the *Hind* (so oft as we did approach within hearing), 'We are as near Heaven by sea as by land,' reiterating the same speech well beseeming a soldier, resolute in Jesus Christ, as I can testify he was.

"Suddenly on Monday night we lost sight of the *Squirrel's* light. Our watch cried out the General was cast away, which was too true; for in that moment the frigate was devoured and swallowed up of the sea."[1]

Poor Gilbert! probably he was so disheartened by failure and losses that he almost courted death. Hayes, a practical sailor, by his skill, and the good seamanship of Master Cox, of Limehouse, arrived safe in England, and to him we are indebted for probably the most interesting narrative contained in the voluminous collection of Hakluyt, the Story of the Unfortunate Expedition to Newfoundland.

Hayes concludes with a fitting tribute to the piety and courage of his unfortunate leader :—

"But such is the infinite bounty of God, who from every evil deriveth good. For besides that fruit may grow in time of our travelling into these north-west lands the crosses, turmoils, and afflictions, both in the preparation and execution of this voyage, did correct the intemperate humours which before we noted to be in this gentleman, and made unsavoury and less delightful his other manifold virtues. Then, as he was refined and made nearer drawing unto the image of God, so it pleased the Divine will to resume him unto himself, whither both his and every other high and noble mind have always aspired."[1]

Almost immediately after the death of Gilbert, the burthen of colonising America, which had been too heavy for his poor weak

[1] HAKLUYT.

shoulders, fell on his illustrious half-brother Raleigh.[1] His plans for founding Virginia were not successful in his lifetime, but with untiring energy and dauntless courage he persisted in his endeavours and spent his substance; he sowed the seed, others reaped the fruit. To Raleigh, above all men in this great age, is due the honour and glory of founding England's Colonial Empire. He was all-powerful in Devon; we find him always mindful of her interests, and urging the Government to buy salt fish for the army and navy.[2]

In the Records the supplying of this fish is very frequently mentioned. It was almost always scarce. The merchants dealt with the Government on sound commercial principles, charging them twenty

SIR WALTER RALEIGH.
From an engraving after an old portrait.

[1] Raleigh was born in 1552, at a small farmhouse called Hayes, near Budleigh, Devon. His father, Walter Raleigh, married for his third wife the widow of Otto Gilbert, of Compton Castle. His mother, a Champernoun, was connected with the illustrious family of the Carews. Young Walter had an experience of life given to few. As a Devonshire boy he had all the usual practice and experience of seamanship, boating, and sailing. At seventeen he left Oxford with his uncle for the wars in France, where he was distinguished for courage and military skill. He next studied law. Next we find him at Court, and a soldier in Ireland. He represented his native county in Parliament. Amongst his compeers his marvellous eloquence is the trait most dwelt upon; but, besides being an orator and a statesman, he was an able general, one of the most accomplished and scientific sailors of his age. He planned the strategy which conquered the Invincible Armada. As a voluminous writer he takes high rank, even in the age of Bacon and Shakespeare. No other Englishman showed genius in so many different capacities as Raleigh. Our own age is astonished at the remarkable conjunction of financier, scholar, debater, and politician exhibited in such marvellous combination by Mr. Gladstone. Our hero possessed all these gifts in equal degree. But whilst our Grand Old Man's chief manual exploit in active life is cutting down trees, Raleigh was soldier, sailor, shipbuilder, and colonizer.

In this age the mists of sectarian prejudice are clearing away. We no longer see Raleigh and Elizabeth through a glass darkly. To us their patriotism shines out clearly, whilst their faults and crimes are not hidden. In the supreme hour of danger Raleigh largely contributed to the salvation of England. In the days of monopolies he was a pronounced free-trader. Every honest Englishman execrates the memory of Henry VIII. for the murder of the noble Catholic Sir Thomas More. Our feelings are still stronger against the drivelling James Stuart for the death of the grandest Englishman of action of all time—Raleigh. His memory has been worthily commemorated by a tablet in Westminster Abbey, erected by Americans to "Raleigh, the Founder of the English Empire in America."

[2] As early as 1338 there is an order from Edward III. to his clerk to provide *stockfish*, presumably for the army in France.—(RYMER'S *Fœdera*.)

shillings per hundred fish when the regular trade price was ten shillings. We find in 1586 :—

"An Indenture of bargain whereby the Commissioner at Chester takes up for Her Majesty's service in Ireland 20,000 Newfoundland fish at 20/- per 100."

In his latter years Raleigh was Governor of Jersey. St. Heliers was a free port, and under his fostering care the trade of the little Norman Isles was vastly increased; he encouraged the islanders to participate in the great Newfoundland fish trade, in which Jersey and her adventurous sons have always played a most prominent part.[1]

In 1583, immediately after the death of Gilbert, Sir George Peckham, a London merchant, who had been chief adventurer with the unfortunate Sir Humphrey, published the first printed book on Newfoundland, entitled :—

"A true report of the late discoveries and possession taken in the right of the Crown of England of the Newfoundlands by that valiant and worthy gentleman Sir Humphrey Gilbert, Knight. Wherein is also briefly set down her highness lawful title thereunto and the great and manifold commodities that are likely to grow thereby to the whole realm in general, and to the adventurers in particular. Together with the easiness and shortness of the voyage written by Sir George Peckham, Knight, the chief adventurer and furtherer of Sir Humphrey Gilbert's voyage to Newfoundland."[2]

TITLE PAGE OF PECKHAM'S BOOK.
From a copy of the first edition in the B.M.

In an age when there were no newspapers and no interviewers, the only chance of obtaining publicity was to write a pamphlet. This work is in the nature of an Elizabethan advertisement, and is worthy of the genius of a modern company promoter. It sets out most truthfully the great internal resources of the new Colony :—

"By establishing a safe harbour and head-quarters, and it is well known to all men of sound judgment that this Newfoundland voyage is of greater importance

---

[1] "Guernsey, April 1594.—Guernsey destitute of provisions for soldiers except 60,000 Newland fish, a barque of herrings, and 40 tuns of cider." Jersey must have had a much larger share at this time in the Newfoundland trade than her smaller sister island.

[2] This is the title of a later edition than the one illustrated.

and will be found more beneficial to our country than all other voyages at this day in use and trade amongst us."

The work is a most sensible, clear-headed, business document, and the author shows himself as a shrewd trader; he offers attractions to everyone—sport for the gentles and nobles; fishing for all; a north-west passage to India from Newfoundland for the scientific and adventurous. The hundred pound subscriber was to have sixteen thousand acres of land with authority to keep Court Leet and Court Baron; to be chosen one of the Council to make laws; to pay one half-penny an acre for the building of forts, towns, churches, &c. The smallest contributions were accepted; even the subscriber of ten shillings had his rights and lands in proportion.

The whole pamphlet is an ingenious attempt to get money from the public and to keep Gilbert's charter alive. Sir John Gilbert maintained his brother's shadowy claim for years after, as I find some Devon fishermen complaining of being prevented by him from going to Newfoundland, probably for claims due under Gilbert's charter. As we proceed with this history we shall see other instances of the extraordinary and fantastic way in which kings and potentates flung away islands and continents to adventurers and Court favourites. All the very early ones came to naught; the later ones caused strife and difficulty everywhere.

This book marks the great advancement of the age; the resources of the island are set forth, perhaps, in too glowing terms, but its immense advantage to England is not in any way exaggerated. The proposal to make St. John's a fortified town was thoroughly practical; it would have secured our capital from the attacks and destruction it afterwards suffered from the French.

Besides the patriotic endeavours of Sir George Peckham to encourage settlement and relieve the distressed poor of England by emigration, the gallant Sydney and Carlile, sons-in-law of Walsingham, wrote and advocated the planting of colonies in Newfoundland and North America. Their only effect was to encourage the prosecution of the fishery, which increased by leaps and bounds.

We have an account in Hakluyt of Strange's prosecution of the seal and whale fishery in the Gulf of St. Lawrence; of Rice Jones's fishing at St. Peter's.

Piracy was prominent; Cecil and Raleigh engaged in it under the guise of privateering. A notable French pirate, De Sancé, behaved very cruelly to one Richard Clark, which is duly recorded as follows, but little is said of the constant raids made by Englishmen on ships of all nations :—

"1596. Report of Richard Clarke and others concerning the piracy committed by three French ships at St. John's, Newfoundland. The Captain of the Admiral Commander of the three ships was named Michel de Sancé; the Master of the Vice-Admiral Martin de Sancé. Having been used with kind entertainment and invited to breakfast on the 25 September, in requital he invited the Frenchman aboard his ship the next day. The captain of the Admiral feigned an excuse and sent for Clarke to visit him in his sickness; upon a sudden the French fell on Clarke and his men, calling out 'rendez vous, rendez vous.' He and nine men were kept prisoners nine days and their ships pillaged. Witnesses: Ric. Clarke, Matt Ryons and Phil. Edwyn, Mate Sam Clarke, Surgeon, and seventeen others."

The most interesting of these voyages is the adventure of Charles Leigh, a London merchant; in Cape Breton he lost one of his ships, the *Chancellor* and came into collision with a big Biscayan ship, whose captain, surrounded by his countrymen, dared to treat him ill. The Englishman wanted to fight, but the Biscayan ran off. Next he captured a Spanish ship in the St. Lawrence. A comrade vessel came to her rescue, so Leigh had to give up his prize and prisoners in order to

SMEATON'S LIGHTHOUSE.   MOUNT EDGCOMBE.
PENLEE POINT   ARMADA MEMORIAL.
DRAKE'S ISLAND.
THE HOE, PLYMOUTH.
From a photograph by A. B. Prowse, Esq., M.D., of Clifton.

rescue his prize crew. Finally, to avenge himself for all these mishaps, he attacked a big French vessel in St. Mary's, captured her after a hard fight, and so returned with two ships and a valuable cargo. The whole story exhibits the daring, reckless character of the English adventurers of the day, and the extraordinary difficulties under which business was carried on.

Though nominally at peace, still for all practical purposes England and Spain were at war between 1584 and 1588. Elizabeth openly aided the Hollanders in their struggles against Philip; Drake plundered the

Spanish main and captured the great treasure ships, his Royal mistress sharing the plunder. When the haughty Mendoza remonstrated with her she sent him packing out of England. Elizabeth and her advisers knew that war with Spain was inevitable; she never shrank from the contest or tried to conciliate the irritated Spanish monarch, on the contrary, she carried the war into the enemy's country. It was a tremendously bold policy for a little country like England, with the present population of London and a revenue of half a million, to attack a colossal power like Spain. In 1585 the most daring blow of all was made on the Spanish fishing fleet in Newfoundland. Whitbourne records the arrival of Sir Bernard Drake in St. John's that year with a commission from the Crown. He also mentions the seizure of several Portuguese vessels by Drake; Portugal at that time formed part of Philip's dominions. Doubtless these vessels were taken in St. John's whilst the Biscayans were away north and south sealing, whaling, and catching cod.

A number of English ships had been seized and confiscated in Spain and their crews treated with great cruelty; one vessel had been capriciously confiscated because an edition of "Cato" was found aboard.

The secret history of this expedition is told in the Records. Mr. Froude says Sir J. Hawkins devised it, arguing, "half the sailors of " the Peninsula went to Newfoundland each year; he proposed to " capture them, and leave their ships to rot in the Harbours." Elizabeth seems to have been opposed to it at first.

On June 20th of this year Walsingham completed the plan (the details are in his handwriting) "for annoying the Spaniard by seizing " their ships in Newfoundland," and on the same date a commission was issued to Sir Bernard Drake "to proceed thither to warn all English " vessels about the seizures in Spain, and prevent them making sale of " their fish there, and to take all Spanish ships and subjects, and to " bring them into some of the western ports of England, without " disposing of any part of the lading until further orders."

The following minute shows he was successful:—

"Oct. 10, 1585. Council to Sir John Gilbert advising of the capture of Spanish ships and sailors at Newfoundland. Returns allowed to 600 Spanish prisoners; allowance reduced from 3s. 4d. per week to 3d. per day per man in consequence of ill-treatment of Englishmen in Spain; to be paid out of the fish taken and the rest distributed in prize money."[1]

The Spaniards were so dismayed by this bold stroke that the next year their fishing fleet did not go to Newfoundland.

All this large quantity of fish, probably fifty to sixty thousand quintals, was smuggled into France and Spain afterwards, as we find

[1] *Records.*

REIGN OF ELIZABETH.

complaints about the Custom House officers having exacted illegal fees upon its export.

It is perfectly marvellous how well Elizabeth knew every movement of her enemies; every intrigue against her was keenly watched by her ubiquitous agents and spies; if Mary Stuart cast an amorous glance at Bothwell it was duly reported; if Philip II. moved a man, or a ship was rigged in Biscay, immediately the queen had word.

Considering the difficulties of communication in those days—the dangers from floods, robbers, pirates—how successfully her intelligence

WHALING.
From Bernard's Record, 1700.

department must have been served. For us, "heirs of all the ages," many secrets of the Courts of Spain and England have now been laid bare. Elizabeth's reputation as a sovereign rests on her success, but an imperishable monument to her memory has been raised in her *Statutes*. The State Papers preserved at Hatfield show her talent as a politician, how cleverly and boldly she played the game against Philip. Posing as a Protestant champion, whilst a Catholic at heart—

simply because they forced her hand—she was all the time planning and preparing for the great struggle with Spain.

Elizabeth's policy in defying and fighting Spain was no rash reckless undertaking, it was a settled policy, based, as I have just said before, on knowledge most varied and intimate of the true position of Spain; besides, it was the only policy the high-spirited English nation would permit; the submission of James Stuart to Spain in the next reign helped to turn the national feeling against him. Out of this great conflict with the colossal power of Philip, England emerged as not only the conqueror, but as Mistress of the Seas—the true genius of the English people had found its occupation.

From the secret history of the reign we get the true state of affairs, we realise the power and activity of the Spanish people, and what they might have done against us if they had been free and well led. There were two to three hundred Spanish vessels on the coast of Ireland in Henry VII. and Henry VIII.'s reigns, and about one hundred and fifty in the early part of Elizabeth's reign, catching bacalao,[1] and whaling in Newfoundland and the Gulf of St. Lawrence. The result of the successful Spanish war was to give England complete control of the Transatlantic cod-fishery; the great Newfoundland Spanish fleet never came again after that terrible defeat, although stray Biscayans, protected by the French, continued to fish in Newfoundland up to a much later date. We shall see subsequently that they claimed the fishery as a right, which Pitt declared he would not acknowledge, even if the enemy were in possession of the Tower of London. From the Armada year until 1630 the English held the Newfoundland fishery practically without a rival; out of the whole number of fishing vessels England had more than double the fleet of her rivals, and all quietly submitted to her control.[2]

1588 is the ever-memorable year of the Invincible Armada; all through this season its coming had been threatened, and many of the Newfoundland fishing ships stayed at home to take part in the battle. Bideford had seven ships in the great fight, and later on the little north of Devon town boasted of having more ships in the northern and

---

[1] This is the general word in Spanish for dried cod, probably derived from the Basque "bacailaba"; the correct Castilian for codfish is "abadejo." "Del abadejo, la cabeza y el pellejo" means the head and the skin are the best of the fish. "Bacalao" was used in Spain long before the discovery of Newfoundland. It is referred to in *Don Quixote* in the queer scene between Maritornes and the arriero.

In the sixteenth century, and later on, "bacalao" was used as a trade word by all the European nations, just as we now use the words "guano" and "tobacco"—both Spanish words which have come into general use.

[2] In April of next year, 1589, Moys writes to Lord Burghley from Plymouth :— "The whole country cannot supply above a hundred thousand Newland fish for the fleet." In ordinary years the stock on hand was twenty times this amount—two million fish, a striking illustration of the destructive influence of war on commerce.

Newfoundland trade than any port in England, save London or Topsham; says Kingsley in "Westward Ho!":—

"It is to the sea life and labour of Bideford and Dartmouth, and Topsham and Plymouth (then a petty place), and many another little western town that England owes the foundation of her naval and commercial glory. It was the men of Devon, the Drakes and Hawkins, Gilberts and Raleighs, Grenvilles and Oxenhams, and a host more of 'forgotten worthies,' whom we shall learn one day to honour as they deserve, to whom she owes her commerce, her colonies, her very existence."

THE ARMADA.
From Pine's engraving, 1739.

Whitbourne was there in his own large ship, and some smaller vessels fitted out entirely at his own expense; Bristol, Bideford, Dartmouth, Plymouth, Topsham, Bridport, Exmouth, Poole, all had their share in the fight.

The Royal fleet, even in Elizabeth's reign, was less than the tonnage of the *Teutonic*, but the English ships were wonderfully strong and well built, thanks to old Hawkins and his father; they were practical seamen as well as shipbuilders. Kingsley states that Young and Prowse, who fired the Spanish fleet in the Calais Roads—"Let their names live long in the land"—were both Devonshire men; the records, however, declare that Young belonged to Chichester. Prowse was undoubtedly from Devonshire, and probably connected with the Newfoundland trade. Like Whitbourne, their valour was their own reward. The action in the fireships was a most gallant exploit, and had the most decisive results. These daring old merchant captains received no honour save the imperishable glory of being recorded in history as the saviours of England.

The defeat of the Armada left England supreme mistress of the seas[1]; the terrible nightmare of Spanish conquest had no longer any terror for the bold islanders; they mocked at all Philip's later attempts to subdue them. The benefits of Elizabeth's bold policy to trade were simply incalculable. Besides the exclusive control of the transatlantic cod-fishery, England now traded everywhere, and mightily increased in wealth, material prosperity, and territory.

Nearly all the great British possessions were gained without the aid of Government. India was won and held for a long time by a trading company, so were America and Australia, and by the same means in our days England will gain a great empire in Africa; such efforts suit the particular genius of Englishmen.

The landing of the Pilgrim Fathers, their dangers and privations, on the wild New England shore, has been an inexhaustible theme for the poets and historians of the United States; but the earlier conquest of North America, the more wonderful exploits of the daring West Country fishermen, who alone and unaided maintained the English sovereignty in Newfoundland and North America against all comers, a century before the *Mayflower*, are still unhonoured and unsung, and really unknown.

In the whole eventful history of English adventure there are no events more remarkable than the doughty deeds of these Devon men, who for a hundred and fifty years kept this colony for England and ruled over the thousands of foreign fishermen who resorted to the island. The consequences of this early dominion were widespread. It has coloured the whole of our history.

Having won the country, the Western adventurers believed they had a right to keep it as a perpetual possession for fishing, and nothing more; for this reason, after the death of Elizabeth, they banded together to resist settlement. Had France or any foreign power over-mastered the Devonshire men and gained Newfoundland, how would New England and Virginia have fared? If once France had possessed the island with her twenty thousand hardy fishermen she would have held the key of North America, and with her sea and land forces the colonies would have ceased to exist as independent communities.

---

[1] About 800 Spanish and Dutch ships were destroyed or captured in the years immediately following 1588.

APPENDIX TO CHAPTER IV.

I. Charter Party and Sale of Newfoundland Fish.

26 Sept. 1580.

"It is agreed this day betwixt Wm. Massie and Thomas Tetlow, merchants of city of Chester, of the one part, and Wm. Dale, master of ye good ship called *ye William of London*, of the other part, and doth bargain and sell 34,000 Newland fish, merchantable at 10s. the 100, current money in England, also foure tonnes traine at £12 per tonne. In consideration the said fish and traine to pay £120 at once, and rest at Ladyday in Lent next ensuing. Provided always that the said shippe shall goe for Rochelle and Bordeaux at 38s. per ton, or for Bordeaux at 42s. per ton, and to stay in one or both places 30 days at the will and pleasure of said merchants or their factors, and for the freight to be paid after the safe arrival and full discharge in Chester water, the one half within three days, and the rest within 20 days after, and be the full payment with the safe arrival of ye said ship, the residue of the fish money within 20 days after the payment of the whole freight."

II. Licence to Export Newfoundland Fish.

"Whereas Her Majestie is pleased at the humble suit of Nicholas Bowgan, that he be licensed to transport out of the Realme three score thousand of Newland fishe, whereof there is at this present good quantitie in the most partes. This is straitly to will and charge you to suffer him to buy and transport from thens the said quantitie of fish, to carry the same to what countrey or place he shall think best for his best market, and therefore you shall not nede to take any bondes of him in that behalf, permitting him also to transport the same in a French bottome or any other straunge bottome whatsoever; not increasing any custome unto him in that behalf. And this I charge you to se accomplished towards him with all favourable and good despatch, for so is Her Majesties pleasure; he paieing such custome only as others Her Majesties subjects are wont to doe. This 17 Sepr. 1599.

"Lord Treasurer, F. Buckhurst.

"To all justices of the peace, maiors, baillifes, and other hed officers. As likewise to all customers, controllers, governors, and surveyors of portes in the counties and portes of Devon and Cornwall."

III. Insurance Policy on Newfoundland Fish in 1604.

AN ASSURANCE.

"In the name of God Amen. Be it known unto all men by theis presentes that A. J. of London Merchaunte and Company doe make assurance and cause themselves and euery of them to be assured Loste or not Loste, knowne or not knowne, from the newe founde Land to Toulone and Marcelleze uppon fishe already Laden or to be Laden in the good shippe called the *Hopewell* of London of the burthen of 120 tonnes or thereaboutes whereof is Master under God in this presente voyage B. G. or whosoeuer els shall goe for Master in the said shippe or by whatsoeuer other name or names the same shippe or the Mr thereof is or shalbe named or called. Begininge the adventure from the day and hower of the lading of the said Fishe aboorde the said shippe in the newe found land aforesaid and so shall continewe and endure untill suche time as the same shippe with the same fishe shalbe ariued at Toulone and Marcelleze and the same their dischardged and laid on Land in good safetye. Touching the adventures and perilles which wee the assurers hereafter named are contented to beare and doe faithfully promise, by theis presentes, to take uppon us in this presente voyage, are of the Seas men of warre, Fier, Enemies, Pirates, Robers, Theeves, Jettesons, Letters of Mark and counter Mark forrestes, Restraintes, and detaynements of kinges and princes and of all other persons, barratrye of the Master and Marriners of all other perilles, Losses and misfortunes whatsoeuer they be, or howsoeuer the same at any time before the date hereof haue chaunced or hereafter shall happen or come to the hurte detriment or damage of the said Fishe or of any parte or parcell thereof. Although newes of any Losse hath alreadie come or by the computacion of one League or three Englishe Miles to one howér might haue come to London before the subscribing hereof, any order, Custome, or usage *heretofore had or made in Lumbard streete* or nowe within the Royall Exchange in London to the contrary in any wise notwithstanding. And that in case of any misfortunes, it shall and may be Laufull to the assured, their factors, servauntes or assignes or to any of them to serve, Labor, and traveil for, in and aboute the defence, safeguard, and recouery of the said fishe or of any parte or parcell thereof without any prejudice to this assurance. To the charges whereof, wee the assurers shall contribute eche one, according to the rate and quantitie of his some herein assured. Yt is to be understood that this presente writing and assurance being made and registred according to the Queenes Majesty's order and appointment, shaibe of asmuch fforce, streingth, and effecte as the best and moste surest pollecy or writinge of assuranch which hath beene euer hertofore used to be made, Loste or not Loste, Knowne or not knowne in the foresaid streete or Royall Exchange in London. And so we the assurers are contented and doe promise and binde ourselves and euery of us, our heires, executors and goodes by theis presentes to the assurede, their Executors, Administrators and assignes for the true performance of the premisses, Submitting ourselves, as well the assurede as the assurers to the order, determinacion and judgment of suche Merchants as nowe be, or heareafter shalbe sworne and aucthorised by the Ld Maior of this Cittie of London for the time being for the deciding and ending of causes of assurances, confessing our selves fully satisfied, contented and paid of and for the consideracion dewe to us for this assurance by theis presentes at the handes of A. J. after the rate of Seaven per Centu. And in testimony of the truth, wee the assurers haue hereonto severally subscribed our names and somes of money assured yeoven in the office of assurance within the Roiall Exchange in London. 3. O. 1604.

"R. C. F. R."

(*From a Petworth MS. by permission of the Right Hon. Lord Leconfield.*)

The above is the oldest known record of English marine insurance, the earliest mentioned by Mr. Martin is in 1613. The Act referred to was passed in 1601 to create a court to settle underwriters' disputes and regulate assurancing, which the Act recites had been "tyme out of mynde an usuage amongste "merchants of this realme and forraine "nacyons."

The rates varied. About 1560 Sir Thomas Gresham paid five per cent. for a cargo of warlike material from Hamburgh to London, insuring to half the value. The above insurance was at seven per cent., but the following entry shows that the rate fell as low as four per cent. under the firm foreign policy of Cromwell :—

Bartholine Laine 16 Oct. 1654 Tho.
fro Newfound-   Griffith   from
land.   Newfoundland to
                Naples in the
                Naples Merchant
                c^h at 4 per c^t. - 4-00-00

(*Rawlinson MS., Bodleian Lib.*)

Whilst the owners of sack ships from London and the larger ports used the above comparatively modern method of paying premiums against loss, it seems likely that the much more primitive form of Bottomry was employed by the West Countrymen in the fishing trade. This system is thought to have been in use amongst the Phœnicians, and is referred to in the Hanseatic articles at Wisby about 1300, and was highly developed at Bruges in the XIV. century. Instead of paying a premium, the ship owner *received* a sum of money by way of mortgage upon the hull or *bottom* of the ship; if she was lost the mortgagor forfeited all his advance, but when she returned safely he received back his capital with an additional bonus. Bottomry is frequently mentioned in connection with our trade during the XVII. century. Insurance frauds were very common even in the fourteenth century. (For fuller information, see Mr. F. MARTIN's *History of Lloyd's.*)

CHAPTER V.

REIGN OF JAMES I.

1603-1625.

1603.—Martin Pring's voyage to New England from Bristol.

1604.—Insurance on a freight of Newfoundland fish at seven per cent.

1605.—Two hundred and fifty English ships in Newfoundland according to Sir J. Child; fish sold at 8s. per 100. Henry Hudson's third voyage.

1608.—Foundation of Guy's Company.

1609.—Sir George Somers and others wrecked at Bermuda.

1610.—Charter to Lord Bacon and others; instructions to Guy; arrival of Guy at Cupids with colonists, &c.; built "Sea Forest" house. Baudoin reports a man being born at Harbour Grace this year who was alive about 1697. The Newfoundland catch at this period valued by Mr. W. Monson at £100,000.

1611.—Guy writes to Slaney in May from Cuper's Cove; proclaimed laws; returns to England.

1612.—Peter Easton, pirate, in Newfoundland. Guy returns to Newfoundland with the Rev. Erasmus Stourton; writes to England in July; attempts to trade with the Beothics. Don Pedro de Cuñega advising King of Spain to destroy English colonies in America.

1613.—Colston's letter, announces birth of a boy on March 27th. Guy abandons Newfoundland, leaving William Colston in charge of the Colony.

1614.—Captain John Smith's voyage to New England. Whitbourne meets the privateer *Sir Henry Mainwaring* with five ships in St. John's. Complaint of French Ambassador to James I. about injuries done to Frenchmen in Canada, &c.

1615.—Whitbourne holds Vice-Admiralty Court. Captain John Mason, R.N., Governor of Guy's Plantation.

1616.—Sir William Vaughan purchases part of Guy's Grant. Letter from Dermer, dated Cuper's Cove, 9th September. Damage to fishermen in Newfoundland by Flemish and English pirates to the extent of £1,700.

1617.—First colonists sent to Vaughan's Colony at Trepassey. Letter from Mason to Scott. Mason's map made.

1618.—Whitbourne sent out to Vaughan's Colony at Trepassey. Colony of Bristol's Hope founded at Harbour Grace. Death of Raleigh. Plunder of Whitbourne's ships by Raleigh's captains on return voyage. Petition of the Western Ports against the Planters, &c. Squantum taken to Cupid's where he meets Dermer. Ordinance for Jersey rectifying the abuse of taking powder for ships sailing to Newfoundland to re-sell there.

1619.—Great fire in Conception Bay; 5,000 acres burnt maliciously by the fishermen.

ENGLISH COLONISATION.

1620.—Great disturbances in St. John's, Petty Harbour, between English and Portuguese. Commission to Mason to take up ships to suppress piracy. Landing of Pilgrim Fathers. Publication of Mason's book on Newfoundland.

1621.—Colony founded by Baltimore; twelve men came out with Capta'n Wynne, Governor. Saw mill and grist mill at Clarke's Beach damaged by fishermen. Mason leaves Newfoundland. Jacobsen's map of Newfoundland. Act for freer fishing in Newfoundland and Virginia thrown out.

1622.—Wynne's and Powell's letters of 28th July to Baltimore; further letters from Wynne and "W. H." to Baltimore in August. Great forest fire near Ferryland noticed by "W. H.," who made a sporting excursion inland. Publication of Whitbourne's book on Newfoundland. Sir William Alexander's Nova Scotia colonists winter in Newfoundland.

1623.—First account of cargo of fish sent from Newfoundland to Virginia. Baltimore's charter. Lord Falkland's advertisement gives 400 French, Biscayans, and Portuguese, and 250 English in Newfoundland; English catch valued at £120,000; fish selling at £4 per 1,000, and oil at £12 per tun; salt costing 20d per bushel. Two men-of-war convoy the English fleet.

The early part of this reign marks the commencement of the colonisation period in English history. All the grand schemes alike of ignorant enthusiasm, of noble aims, and of statesmanlike projects, in Elizabeth's reign had come to nought; neither England, nor France, at the beginning of the Stuart period, possessed a single settlement on the American continent. The Calendar of State Papers at the beginning of this century is full of applications from all sorts and conditions of adventurers, claiming to be the fortunate discoverers of new islands and territories, teeming with gold and valuable commodities; the craze of the seventeenth century was colonisation. The pages of the Records read more like some fantastic mediæval romance than the dull folios of official papers. From this period dates the foundation of our great American colonies; the creation of French dominion in America; the formation of New France and Acadie. In 1607 the London Company made the first settlement in Virginia, at James Town. New England, first known as Northern Virginia, was brought into notice by the successful voyages of Gosnold, Brereton, and Archer 1602; followed by Martin

JAMES I.
From an oil painting after Vandyke.

Pring, 1603; Weymouth, 1605; Popham and Raleigh Gilbert's settlement at the mouth of the Kennebec, 1607; and the celebrated Captain John Smith's adventure in 1614.

The result of all these voyages was the establishment of a large English trade and fishery on the New England coast, carried on by London and Devonshire adventurers in the same manner, but on a much smaller scale than the Newfoundland trade and fishery, which was then entirely in the hands of the English, and employed two hundred and fifty ships and over ten thousand men. It cannot be doubted that it was the great success of the English in Newfoundland that tended to encourage fresh enterprise in the same direction on the North American continent.[1]

CAPTAIN SMITH.
From his History of Virginia, 1626.

These English plantations were watched with jealous eye by the Spaniards. Foreigners, and especially Frenchmen, always endeavour to gain an advantage over England when the country is under a weak sovereign and a vacillating ministry. It was to please the king of Spain that Raleigh was executed, and the plan of his last expedition betrayed. Though humiliated and beaten, Spain still with proud persistence claimed all that had been given to her by the Bull of

---

[1] New Englanders showed great jealousy of Newfoundland. Gosnold says of Cape Cod, which he first named, "Surely I am persuaded that in the months of March, April, and May, there is upon the coast better fishing, and in as great plenty, as in Newfoundland." . . . Brereton predicts, "For as much as merchants are diligent inquisitors after gains, they will soon remove their trade from Newfoundland to New England."

In 1605 James Rosier writes of Waymouth's adventure, "Would warrant (by the help of God) in a short voyage, with a few good fishers, to make a more profitable return from hence [New England] than from Newfoundland, the fish being so much greater, better fed, and abundance with train [large livers for more oil]."

The most spiteful of all our detractors, and the most jealous of Newfoundland's success, is the great eccentric Captain John Smith; he writes:—"If Newfoundland doth yearly freight near 800 sail of ships, with a silly, lean, skinny poor-john and coor fish, and those who adventure there can gain tho' they draw meat, drink, and clothes, and all their necessary gear and outfits, from second, third, fourth, or fifth hand, and from so many parts of the world, ere they come together to be used in the voyage, and if Hollande, Portugall, Spaniard, French, or other, do much better than they, why doubt of success in going to New England, where there is victual to feed us, wood of all sorts to build boats, ships, or barques, the fish at our doors, pitch, tar, masts, and yards." All these fine arguments did not stop the Newfoundland trade.

Donation; Bermuda,[1] Virginia, and Newfoundland she maintained rightly belonged to her. In 1612 we find Don Pedro de Cuñega advising the King of Spain :—

"It will now be an easy matter to remove these people from Virginia (he was well aware of the weak state of the New Colony), and now will be to the purpose to punish them, for they boldly attempt further plantations, having already begun another in Terra Nova."

"[March 10, same year.] Further complaints from Spain about Virginia. The ambassador says may prove of so much inconvenience to the King of Spain."[2]

"1613. Further hot dispute with Spain about England's rights to Bermuda and Virginia."

The landing of the Pilgrim Fathers in New England in 1620 has been so idealised, so woven round with poetry and fancy, that it almost savours of sacrilege to dwell upon its plain prosaic aspect, a fishing adventure combined with a colonisation scheme.

The Puritan element is to-day the backbone of much that works for good in America, both politically and morally. New England was colonised by a pure, unmixed race of Englishmen, mostly from East Anglia; the same stock that carried out the great English revolution, ruled the new Colony. These sober, self-reliant, deeply religious settlers were led and ruled by the same class that charged at Marston Moor, and gave England freedom.

To the Puritan party is mainly due modern English Parliamentary Government. In the new world they achieved almost a greater result;

BERMUDA.
From Smith's Virginia, 1630.

---

[1] In 1609, July 28th, the *Sea Venture*, with Sir Geo. Somers, Sir Thomas Gates, and Captain Newport on their way to Virginia, was wrecked on the Bermudas. They took possession of the Islands for the English Crown. They were divided and settled in an orderly manner, and have a continued and very interesting history from that date. Their early annals do not concern our history save that the object and destination of every runaway from the Plantations both in Virginia and its dependency Bermuda was to reach Newfoundland. These Islands were originally discovered by Bermudez, a Spanish Captain, in his vessel *La Garza*—" The heron". The Spaniards called the Islands "La Garza," the English sometimes "The Somers Islands" after the gallant Sir George, but finally the old euphonious Spanish name of Bermuda became the permanent designation of these beautiful islands.

[2] *Records.*

as clear-headed, practical Englishmen, they inherited the national genius for government. They laid the keel of the constitution of the United States in the compact, written in a crabbed hand aboard the *Mayflower*, with a boldness and cunning worthy of the progenitors of the Yankees; they maintained an absolutely free Republican Government against all the English sovereigns, and developed a great English colonisation, which has outstripped every other attempt of the kind, ancient or modern.

The American historian, especially a New England writer, dwells on this marvellous story with pardonable pride; he expatiates on the spiritual and moral aspect of the Pilgrims and their genius for government, but, like his English prototype, he ignores altogether the plain, simple fact proved by the clearest evidence, that his ancestors, mostly humble, God fearing people, came to New England to earn their living by fishing; and whilst their great political success was chiefly due to the circumstance that the best settlers, gentlemen like Winthrop, governed, their unexampled material prosperity was laid in the fishery. Great commercial nations have everywhere, in the history of the world, risen from the same humble foundation, witness Carthage, Venice, Holland, England; and clearly and directly New England's commerce, and her great maritime prosperity, which, at one time, bid fair to outstrip England, was primarily due to her fishing and whaling.[1]

The history of these great North-Eastern States is closely interwoven with our own; the early intercourse between the two dependencies had immense influence on Newfoundland, and, to clearly

---

[1] In addition to the entries in the Records much information on this subject is to be derived from a number of works on New England, but chiefly from the admirable report of Lorenzo Sabine. Besides the evidence given in Winslow's narrative about the interview with King James I. we have the fact that New England before 1620 was chiefly known as a good fishing country. In Rotz's map, presented to Henry VIII., 1542 (p. 34), the sea south of Newfoundland is called "the Newfoundlande where men go a fishing." Gosnold's and Smith's histories refer principally to this industry. Weston, one of the chief supporters of the Pilgrims, advised them to settle near Cape Cod for fishing. Their crazy bark the *Speedwell* was bought for that purpose.

Captain John Smith says:—"At last, upon these inducements [fishing] some well disposed Brounists [a name for the Pilgrims] as they are termed, with some gentlemen and merchants of Layden and Amsterdam, to save charges, would try their own conclusions, tho' with great loss and much miserie, till time had taught them to see their owne error; for such humorists will never beleeve well till they bee beaten with their owne rod."

In the next chapters he refers to their prosperous condition (1624). "Since they have made a salt worke whereby they preserve all the fish they take, they have fraughted this yeere a ship of 180 tons." The records show their sojourn at Cape Cod. The "Shoal Hope," of Gosnold, was for fishing. After they had held a solemn consultation respecting their final settlement, some were disposed to select Cold Harbour, because it offered some advantages for whale and cod fishing. Others insisted they should proceed to Agwam (now Ipswich), a harbour which was known to fishermen who had been on the coast. In 1625 the Colony despatched two vessels with fish and furs; one was captured by Turkish pirates off the English Coast. In 1628 they were selling fish and corn to the Dutch at New York; by 1643 they were shipping fish to Malaga, and in 1615 their first vessel visited Bay Bulls to fish and trade.

understand our history, it is absolutely necessary to comprehend theirs. The New Englander of to-day is the strongest advocate of temperance and abolition; his Puritan ancestors were just as loud in their claim to export free rum to Newfoundland, to send their refuse fish to the West Indian negroes, to smuggle, and defy the British navigation laws, to trade with this ancient colony, notwithstanding all restrictions, and to steal the Devonshire men's servants. This last point will probably be denied by American historians, but the fact is too clearly proved by official documents, of which space only allows me to quote a few.

The second period of our colonial annals commences with the reign of James I. of England and VI. of Scotland. In studying this period of English history, all feel more or less the glamour of the Stuarts; the beautiful Queen of Scots has to this day votaries from all lands, and ardent and enthusiastic souls are still the champions and defenders of King Charles the Martyr. The subtle, all-pervading influences of art and poetry have shed such a halo of glory around these unfortunate sovereigns, that neither the hard logic of facts, nor time, nor reason, have been able to deaden or destroy the almost universal sympathy for this picturesque dynasty. Even for the slobbering, shuffling, uncouth pedant, with his nameless vices, the first English Stuart, "the most sagacious, high, and mighty Prince James," there is still some sympathy. In his policy to Newfoundland he appears, at first sight, in a favourable light; he was guided, in the early years of his reign, by Elizabeth's minister, Cecil, Lord Salisbury, and his colonial policy was the liberal and enlightened policy of his great predecessor; his advances to Guy's associates were liberal, and in marked contrast to his tyrannical and treacherous dealings with the Virginia Company. James, the pupil of the great scholar, George Buchanan, had undoubtedly a love of learning; his life-long friendship and strong attachment to his great chancellor, Bacon,[1] is one of the redeeming features of his reign. The illustrious English philosopher is known to us by his glorious works, to his contemporaries his chief characteristic was eloquence; this is the theme of "rare Ben Jonson's" discourse on him. How could a vain pedant

---

[1] Lord Chancellor in the reign of James I., the father of English philosophy, whose reputation is world wide, took a deep interest in colonisation schemes; he wrote his celebrated Essay on Plantations to further the settlements in America; he showed special interest in Guy's Plantation by becoming a shareholder and subscriber to the company. On no subject does the genius of Bacon show to greater advantage than in his Essay on Plantations; one passage alone proves how far he was ahead of the age of monopolies in which he lived:—"Let there be freedom from customs till the plantation be of strength, and not only freedom from custom, but freedom to carry their commodities where they may make the best of them, except there be some special cause of caution." Bacon, like Raleigh, preached even then the doctrine of free trade. Bacon strongly advocated settlement in the Colony, and described in his elegant and glowing language the inestimable value of our fisheries to England.

like James resist the adroit flattery, the eloquent adulation, of such a subject as Bacon? It was entirely due to the great chancellor's influence that the king granted the advances and issued the charter to Bacon and his associates in Guy's Newfoundland Colonisation Company.

We shall find that all the other patents granted during this reign for the settlement of colonies were given to the Court party, personal friends of the monarch. Both Sir William Vaughan and his brother, Lord Carberry, were great allies and supporters of the king's political views. The first Lord Falkland was his deputy in Ireland, an honourable and enlightened man, and, strange to relate, a friend of James. Eternal disgrace rests upon our colonisers, Bacon and Baltimore. Bacon—"the greatest, wisest, meanest of mankind," the last English statesman to use the rack and to pervert justice,—to please his master used all his great influence and genius against English liberty and parliamentary government, to further the divine right and absolute authority of the king. Baltimore—in private life an amiable, enlightened man, a sincere and honest Catholic—earned his sovereign's gratitude in the Spanish marriage question, and as a parliamentary tool to bribe, bully, and argue in the House against the great Coke and the noble band of patriots who strove to give England a free Parliament.

Soon after the accession of James the early chaotic period of our history comes to an end. England began at last to give more attention to her ancient Colony. A rude attempt was made to govern and settle the island by means of a Royal chartered company, like the East African schemes of our own day. This was part of the policy of Elizabeth; Bacon, Peckham, Guy, Falkland, and Baltimore were all simply adopting the projects of Raleigh and Gilbert. I have called this period, 1610 to 1711, the fishing admiral period, simply because of the baneful rule of these ignorant tyrants under the sanction of the Home

GUY'S COLONY.

Government; the century might also be called the colonisation period. Through evil report and good report, amidst the fiercest opposition from the Devonshire ship fishermen, small bands of settlers had, for years before Guy's arrival, been settled on the eastern coast, between Cape Race and Cape Bonavista. The first of these colonies were planted in the neighbourhood of St. John's, and gradually extended around Conception Bay, thence north to Cape Bonavista, and south to Cape Race.

The story of the formation of Guy's Colony, called by the founder "Sea forest plantation," is one of the most interesting episodes in our early annals; as there is no detailed information about it in any extant history of Newfoundland, I have set forth all the facts that can now be gathered from the contemporary records. Young Alderman John Guy is a striking personality, shrewd, pushing, energetic, and full of ambition. The company consisted of most of the men of light and leading in James's Court. Bacon was undoubtedly the guiding spirit in the enterprise, whilst Guy and Roberrow were the working members.

We find the same individuals who were in Peckham and Gilbert's company members of Guy's association. They had become so impoverished by the dismal failure of Gilbert's unfortunate adventure and Raleigh's colonisation schemes, that when John Roberrow, John Guy, and others, were appointed a committee to confer with their London associates, they decided that the scheme was quite feasible, and would be profitable and of great value to the kingdom, but a portion of the charges should be borne by the Government. As far as we can ascertain, this took place in 1607. Undoubtedly the company was the outcome of the various projects put forward by Peckham and Algernon Sidney and Carlyle, who were both Walsingham's sons-in-law. It was only by immense Court influence that money was obtained from the Government. The Stuarts as a dynasty were perennially impecunious, and it took three years' pleading and all Bacon's influence to get the desired subsidy; it must have been considerable, as

ARMS OF THE LONDON AND BRISTOL COMPANY FOR COLONISING NEWFOUNDLAND.

94   REIGN OF JAMES I.

Mr. Alderman Guy and his shrewd merchant associates appear to have only put in a nominal sum, less than £100 each, payable in five yearly instalments. In 1610 the charter to Bacon and his associates was issued under the Great Seal.[1] This instrument is very full and comprehensive, it is a far more practical and statesmanlike document than the loose grants of Elizabeth; the extent of territory covered by the charter is defined—from Cape St. Mary's to Cape Bonavista. The public right to the fishery is specially reserved. Guy's instructions show clearly that the charter was a dishonest attempt to give away to Court favourites land occupied and possessed by Englishmen long anterior to the grant.

After obtaining his title deeds, Guy sailed from Bristol, May 1610, with his brother Philip, his brother-in-law Colston, and thirty-nine persons, in three ships. From the records of Bristol and other sources we are able to give a pretty accurate account of their proceedings. They had carefully chosen the site for their new colony. Old Newfoundland traders were evidently connected with the company, and all their arrangements were planned by persons well acquainted with the trade. There remains a MS.[2] containing the—

"INSTRUCTIONS TO JOHN GUY from the Associates of his Company, 1610.

"You shall furnish yourself with at least twelve months victualles with munition nets and with all manner of tooles and implements and you shall make choice of the skill and manuall arts of such as are to go with you that you shall think important for the advancement of the colonie.

"As the benefit and use of domestic creatures without whom not onlie any desolate countrie but also a civilized countrie could not well be inhabited we

SEAL OF JAMES I.

---

[1] See appendix to this chapter.
[2] I was fortunate enough to find this most interesting document—the instructions from Guy's associates about the management of the plantation; the paper has been partially burnt, but the principal part of the contents have been preserved.—*B.M. MSS. Otho E. VIII. 5.*

would have you take with you a small number of evrie kind of them male and female water and other things needful for their transportation not [placing them on the sea shore] but either by islands or necks of lands between Bayes where together with the care of a herdsman they shall escape from wild beasts and so increase and multiplie of which number [we would] not have anyone killed without great and urgent cause.

"When it shall please God to send you and your Companie into the Newfoundland we would have you make choice of some place which you shall find fittest within the limits of the country assigned unto us in order to plant our said colonie. The Baye of Concepsion we prefer before other places for the first attempt.

"Upon your first arrival there the sooner to operate our patent and to prevent ye murmuring of suspicious and jealous persons that perhaps will not [fail] to spread abroad that this enterprize wilbe to the prejudice of ye fishermen as well of our nation as others. We do hould it expedient that you call an assembly of all the fishermen that shall be nere thereabouts and there in their presence openlie and distinctlie cause to be read the graunt under the King's Majesties great seal which you shall have along with you, that by the tenour of it they may be satisfied that there is no intent of depriving them of their former right of fishing which being done you shall declare in the presence of them all that you enter upon that place to take actuall seazin and possession (never by grace and assistance of God to be discontinued) in ye name of the whole country comprehended within the said grant to the use of us and our associates our heirs and assigns to be holden of our sovereign Lord the King by the rents and services secured by the said graunte and that by such your acte the King's Majestie of England is actually invested with the title and supreme dignitie next under God of the said country.

"How you are to spend your time there we need not particularlie [put] you in mind of being in good hope that according to the opinion we do conceive of you all matters shall be carefullie providently and paynefullie ordered and that there shall be no wasting of the victualles nor time misspent in idleness but all industrious courses practised to set forward the enterprize as namelie buildings to be erected for habitation . .

". . (text burnt) . . [With the] returne of the ships after the fishing is ended all fish [which you have] made [and shall] not need for your own use [re]ceive to be transported to England and if it may be [bought?] you may also send some quantity of that wine which you . . . . that trial may be made of it as also of the zansaparilla [to see if it] be good and what else you shall judge fit to be sent.

"If you can buy any train [cod oil] for eight pounds the tonne or [thereabouts] we would have you to deale for it for the use of the Companie and charge us by exchange for the payment of it and to take or send to Bristoll and failing thereof to keep it in your warehouses until we do send for it in the winter time for we doubt not that ships may harbour themselves there in the winter in Januarie or Februarie seeing out of the Grand Bay being 4 degrees to the northward it is a thing yearly experimented that ye Biscainers remain until December. If you can buy there 60,000 of good dry fish reasonable you may likewise do it and charge us home by exchange and place it in our warehouses until we send a bark thither to take it in and to go with it there home to Spain which coming there alone may sell better than that which came first the great glut marring oftentimes that market.

"You shall as soon as may be conveniently done make choice and bring to the sea shore a ships lading of masts sparres and deal boards to be in a readines to reload any ship that shall happen to be sent unto you with salt which you shall unloade and lay it in your warehouses to be readie there for our use to be used in fishing or to be sold to ye fishermen. By employing of shipping of great burden the trade between Bristoll and Newfoundland may be profitable. We are in good hopes that you shall find sufficient cargo there with which the said ship shall be reloaden.

"And if any persons employed in this service shall be found to be seditious mutinous or in any manner unfit you shall by the next returne of any ship from there home send them home to be discharged giving advertisement of their behaviour.

"And for the succession of the principal or head of this enterprize if it should please God to take him away it is thought meete that such person shall succeed him as the said John Guy shall nominate under his hand writing and for default thereof the successor shalbe there unto elected by most of votes of the persons that shall survive and if equal votes the lot to be cast whether of them shalbe preferred.

"And we would have you to assay by all good meanes to [capture] one of the savages of the country and to intreate [him well and] to keepe him and teach him our language that you may after obtayne a safe and free commerce with them which [are] strong there.

"We learne that there is found there and no question [fernes ?] whereby may be gathered that yf workmen experte to [make glass ? were] now sent with you with such forraine simples as the mixture of mettall requireth you might presently rase glase to . . . . . nevertheless for more certaintie we now forbear onlie would have you send home some of the fearne [*i.e.* kelp] dryed and some . . . [that] it may be considered of.

"Every ship that resorteth thither to fishing bringeth with them [sawyers ?] to make or mend their fishing boates which may well be supplied [by you with] pine boards whereof you shall have plentie when ? the saw is set up.

"Such ashes as you make keep and send to Bristoll that we may have tryall of them and that thereby it may be the [better proved] whether such sope ashes as come out of the Sound may [not be sent from] there home.

"And to the end that God may bless this attempt with happy prospects and success you must take order that divine service be publicklie [held] and attentive hearkned unto and that you joine in devout prayers to God that the worship of him may not be neglected that pietie and charitie and sobrietie may dwell amongst us and all swearing and gamming abolished.

"You must not forget to search whether there be any trees thereabouts that will afford timber to make caske and be servicable for hoopes we have heard that pipes have been sometimes made of pine timber and for hoopes young beach will serve. The birch there being large and great as yt is yeeld ? for a neede ? stuffe for caske and seing it is most certaine that oakes are in some places of this country you may peradventure upon search light upon some place where it grow.

"To make experience of the nature of the country for sheep were not amis because there want not warme and firtill places and abundance of poules things most requisite for that kind of husbandrie.

"The cherrie trees and peare trees and filberd trees by removing and graffing may prove as good and as large as ours and for the filberds though they are small yet they are good and being gathered when they are ripe may do you some pleasure we would have you send us home a few of them [for in] flanders they buy barkes lading with hazell nuts to make oyle for which [we] do [think that] these will serve as they.

"[We] require you to have a due regard [to the carrying out] of these our instructions and of all such [as you may in] your discretion judge may any kinde of way to [turn to the use] and benefit of this enterprize committed to your [care]."

These instructions and the letters of Guy, Colston, and Mason indicate a well-considered scheme of colonisation. In this letter of advice there is a curious blending of the practical trader and the enthusiastic theorist; the suggestions to buy cod oil at eight pound per ton and send late cargoes of fish to Spain, are the ideas of good business men, shrewdly intent on making money; whilst those about the manufacture of glass, soap, charcoal, &c. may have come from the experimental philosophy of Bacon. The last project to make oil out of the wild hazel nuts on Southern River can hardly come within the scope of practical projects, it resembles too much the extraction of sunbeams from cucumbers. It is clear, however, from this paper that these recommendations were prepared by keen traders, who knew all about Newfoundland and the business they were embarking in.

At first everything went well with the new Colony; they had a remarkably fine passage out, in twenty-three days they sighted their new home in the deep Bay de Grave (now Port de Grave), Conception

CUPIDS.

Bay. In the bottom of this estuary lies the beautiful little land-locked harbour of Cupids. It was so far embayed that the resident fishermen, who were then sparsely scattered about Harbour Grace, Carbonear, and the bottom of the bay, had passed by this little sequestered nook as unsuitable for the fishery. The selection of the site for the new Colony was a happy one. At the head of the inlet of Bay de Grave, now known as Clarke's Beach, two beautiful rivers discharge their waters into Conception Bay. There are many picturesque scenes in the peninsula of Avalon, but we know of no more charming

1 p. 2729.

vista in all Newfoundland than these beautiful rivers with their lovely wooded banks and smiling fields.

At Cupids, Guy built three houses besides his wharves, stores, and fishing establishment. A fort ninety feet wide by a hundred and twenty feet long was enclosed by a strong stockade, and a battery was mounted with three guns. On Southern River they erected mills, houses, and farm buildings; a considerable quantity of land was cleared and surrounded by stone walls. Early in this century the remains of these buildings were found, together with mill stones, coins, &c.[1] A paper was read on the subject by Admiral Robinson, brother of our late Judge Sir Bryan, before the Royal Geographical Society. There was much discussion on the subject, but no one identified the remains as Guy's. Recently some of the old oak beams were used in the construction of a bridge. Happily we can now have no longer any doubt about the identification of Guy's buildings, as in the Records we find an account in 1620 of damage to the Company's mills reported by Governor

---

[1] There has been considerable misapprehension regarding the site of Guy's settlement; in most Newfoundland histories Mosquito Cove is named as the locality; all doubts about the locality are set at rest by the English *Calendar of State Papers, Colonial Series*. These volumes have been of inestimable value to me in preparing this work; it is a great misfortune that our own records have not been published in the admirable way General Lefroy has written the *Chronicles of Bermuda*. The late Sir R. J. Pinsent, D.C.L., was for some time engaged on this work in Newfoundland. I hope some one may eventually give the public the benefit of all the labour he has bestowed on our Colonial Calendar.

Early in this century a party of settlers proceeding up Southern River observed at a distance of six or seven miles above the bay the appearance of stone walls rising above the surface; on removing the sand and alluvial earth they ascertained these to be the remains of ancient buildings, with oak beams and mill stones sunk in oaken beds; enclosures resembling gardens were also traced out, and plants of various kinds not indigenous to the island were growing around; among the ruins were found different European coins, some of Dutch gold, others of copper. That these were the remains of Guy's buildings is proved by the fact that in 1621 Guy's saw mill and grist mill were partially destroyed by the West Country fishermen, and the damage is estimated at £40.

Mason. Guy and Colston's letters, which will be found appended, are interesting, as showing how little change has taken place in our climate. The Alderman was not the first settler [1] or the first Englishman to discover that Newfoundland, on the whole, was a very pleasant country to live in. The great advantage of Guy's plantation was the bringing of the valuable resources of the island under the immediate notice of the British public.

Soon after the formation of the Colony, hostilities were commenced against the permanent settlers, called planters, by the western adventurers—the ship fishermen from Devonshire. No doubt the proclamation of laws made by the Alderman Governor on the 30th August 1611 roused their indignation.[2] They had been accustomed to look on Newfoundland as peculiarly their own possession. A young upstart of a Governor building a fort and permanent residence, calling his new mansion, after the fashion of English gentlemen, "Sea Forest House"—all this assumption of authority, especially the making of laws, excited the ire of the belligerent West Countrymen. They attempted to destroy the Colony by preparing a petition to the Crown

---

[1] The presence of other settlers is shown by Mason's letters about the carts hauling caplin for manure, the provision of salt for sale to fishermen, and later on, in Baltimore's charter, the reservation of St. John's and Petty Harbours; Baltimore mentions numbers of families in Conception Bay which could not have been Guy's settlers.

There are several other proofs in the Records of the settlement of the Colony anterior to Guy. Baudoin says, in Harbour Grace they told him of a man who had been born there about 1610 or 1611; this must have been the son of an early settler not belonging to the Alderman's colony. There is no record of the official settlement of Bristol's Hope—Harbour Grace until about 1618.

[2] GUY'S LAWS.

Certaine orders for the ffishermen to observe and keepe in the Newfoundlande published the 30th daie of August 1611 by Mr. John Guy the Gov'nor of the Colony ther.

By authority of our Sov. Lord James by grace of God of England Scotland Ffrance Ireland and Newfoundland Kinge. A Plantation and Government is begun to be settled within this Country of Newfoundland and whereas among those persons that use the trade of fishing in these parts many disorders abuses and bad customs are crept in which are continued and yearly practised, more of a corrupt usage then of malicious designs, forasmuch as it concerns not only the fishing but also the public good, if all such grievences should be stopped to the end that all persons should reform themselves in their proceedings, and not plead ignorance that any prohibicion was made, The Governor in the Kings name doth charge and command all persons of what nature soever that shall frequent those parts for ffishing as well strangers as subjects that they offend not in any thing forbidden in the Proclamation, under penalty herein specified and as they will answer to the contrary at their peril.

1. Ballast or anything hurtful to Harbours not to be throwne out but to be carried ashore—Penalty £5 for every offence.

2. No person to destroy, deface, or spoile any stage cooke room flakes &c.—Penalty £10.

3. Every Admiral of each Harbour for time being reserve only so much beach and flake or both as is needful for number of boates—Penalty £10.

4. No person to deface or alter, markes of any boates—Penalty £5.

5. No person to convert to his own use, boates belonging to others without their consent except in case of necessity and then to give notice to Admiral—Penalty £5.

6. No person to set fire in woods—Penalty £10.

7. No person, at end of voyage to destroy stage cooke room or flakes that he hath that year used—Penalty £10.

8. No master of any ship to receive into his ship any person of the Colony, that are already planted by virtue of His Majesty's gracious Patent without speciall warrant under the handwriting of the Governor of the Colony or Colonies in the Newfoundlande aforesaide.

against it.[1] Devon, in this and every succeeding reign, was strong in Court influence. They found out, however, that the Company, with Bacon at its back, was too strongly intrenched in King James's favour to be injured by this kind of attack. Discovering by the King's answer to their petition that the settlers were not to be molested, they seem to have set some evil-doer to wreck the plantation, for according to Mason's account they partially destroyed the Company's grist mill and saw mill.

---

[1] PETITION AGAINST PLANTERS, &c.

ARTICLES OF GRIEVANCES MENTIONED IN THE PETITION OF THE WESTERN PORTES TOUCHING THOSE OF PLANTERS OF NEWFOUNDLAND, DECR. 1618.

1. That those of the Plantacions there have put sundrie of the Peticioners from the chiefest places of ffishinge there and disposed of the same to such as pleased them.

2. That they have taken awaie great quantities of salt, casks, boates stages and other provisions there lefte by the Peticioners and converted the same to their own use.

3. That they have denied and letted the Peticioners from taking birdes upon the Island of Baccaleau, the flesh of which birds the Peticioners have heretofore used for baite until the ordinarie bait come upon that Coaste.

4. That in the chiefest tyme of ffishing those in the said Plantacion have summoned a Courte of Admiraltie and exacted ffees of trayne and ffishe for not apperinge.

5. That those of the said Plantacion have harbored pirats there and dealt with them which hath beane the meanes to induce them to frequent that place to the great prejudice and hinderance of the Peticioners.

ANSWER OF THE COMPANY OF PLANTERS OF NEWFOUNDLAND TO ARTICLES OF GRIEVANCES OF WESTERN PORTES—DECR. 1618.

To 1st Article: That in regard of theire chargeable maintenance of a Colonie on land there all the yeare, it is conceivable to be lawful for them the Inhabitants to make choice of their fishing place, and not to leave the benefit thereof to the uncertayne commers thither; and have not put out anie shippes out of anie harbours being placed there to ffishe accordinge to their ancient customs.

To 2nd Article: They know of no such wrong done to fishermen and suppose none of the Colonie that do inhabit there will presume so to do neither do they approve thereof.

To the 3d Art.: If any of their Colonie have denied the taking of birds for fishermen's baites being a thing altogether unknown to them here — It shall be ordered to the contrary.

To the 4th Art. · That none of their Colonie have attempted any such acts but have heard that some of the western partes have done such things to the hurt of the fishermen which they utterly disclaim.

To the 5th Art.: That they have received very great damage by pirates almost to the overthrow of their Colonie as not being able to resist them they have come and possessed their houses and taken all their provisions at theire pleasure and carried away such men as pleased them and therefore very unlike that they should induce them to come thither, as is alleged. But their coming is to be believed of their friends being some of the western men who are still willing to help them (as it seems to us) with provisions and will make no resistance, tho' they be able to surprize them if they were stronger than they be and therefore we shall humbly desire that some course may be taken for prevention of such mischiefes as by reason of their coming thither may be to further danger of our Colonies. And we are desirous to join with the Western menne in this business and also for keeping good order in the countrie in the contrarie whereof themselves are guilty for we have caused certain orders to be there published in His Majestys name which they have not obeyed.

Signed
JOHN SLANEY, Treasurer.
HUMFREY HANDFORDE.
HUMFREY SLANEY.
ROBART GAIRARD.
WM. PAYNE.
WM. FREEMAN.

REPLY OF THE PETITIONERS OF THE WESTERN PORTES TO THE ANSWER OF GOVERNORS.

No privilege given by the Charter to Planters for fishing before others; if choice of places is admitted, contrary to common usage, the Peticioners contend that they ought rather to have it. Desire that the liberties reserved to them by charter may be confirmed. Disclaim committing any abuses in the country and request that the offender may be examined. The Peticioners knowing better how to manage their fishing than the Planters can direct, declare that they are altogether unwilling to be ordered by the Planters, or to join with them as they desire.

Guy was ambitious of civic honours, his heart hankered after Bristol, he stayed in Newfoundland from 1610 to the end of 1611, as we learn from his letters. In the autumn of this year he returned to England. Next spring, 1612, he came again with more adventurers, "all of civil life"—artizans and farmers—horses, cattle, pigs, poultry, farming implements, &c.; being a sound Churchman, he brought with him, as

CLARKE'S BEACH, SOUTHERN RIVER.
From a photograph by S. H. Parsons.

chaplain of the forces, the afterwards celebrated Evangelical divine, the Rev. Erasmus Stourton.[1]

The Alderman had not only to contend with the opposition from Devonshire. This year, as duly recorded by Whitbourne, the arch-pirate Peter Easton robbed the fishermen, English and foreign, in

---

[1] Erasmus Stourton, the first Church of England clergyman permanently settled in Newfoundland, came out with Guy on his second voyage, 1612; he belonged to the ecclesiastical party in the English Church, which we now call Evangelical or Low Church as distinguished from the Ritualistic party, who in the days of Elizabeth and the Stuarts adhered to nearly all the doctrines of the Roman Catholic Church, except papal supremacy and the worship of the Virgin Mary; he appears to have been a narrow minded sectary, and a troublesome, meddlesome busybody. In Conception Bay he ministered to a considerable congregation, between 150 and 200 permanent settlers, besides migratory fishermen. In 1628 the Reverend Erasmus came into collision with Lord Baltimore; all his militant Protestantism was stirred up by Calvert's Catholic worship, and the Seminary priests in the new settlement of Ferryland. Baltimore banished him from the Colony as an audacious man for his misdeeds. Stourton's offence that he speaks of must have been of a very aggravating character to excite such wrath in the mild and benevolent Calvert, whose character for liberality and enlightenment, rare in that age, is borne out by all contemporary historians. On his arrival in England Stourton hastened to pour into the ears of his Puritan allies the frightful fact that Baltimore had actually had mass celebrated. No one apparently took the least notice of Stourton's complaint.

Newfoundland. We are told that he took a hundred men from Conception Bay. No doubt some of these would be Guy's men. The Governor was a merchant, not a fighting man, and it is not surprising that next year we find him returning home to Bristol. Five years later, 1618, he had the distinguished honour of being appointed Mayor of the ancient city. In this exalted position he greatly distinguished himself as a spirited and independent Chief Magistrate.[1]

William Colston, his deputy governor, seems to have remained only one year, 1613 to 1614. About this time there appears to have been a good deal of disorder in the country. Guy, though nominally Governor, had no force to execute laws, and it was doubtless from Colston's report on the condition of the Colony that, in 1614, Whitbourne went home to obtain some definite authority to repress disorders. The records of this period are full of information about pirates. Raleigh's captains, on the last voyage before his death, turned privateers or pirates. The respected Sir Henry Manering, or Mainwaring, was a titled robber, judging by the account of his actions. The following notice of disorders and pirates only extends from 1612 to 1621. In the year 1625 the English fleet suffered still more serious loss from the attacks of sea rovers. The Colony was practically without law or government; there was no civil or military force to maintain order amongst a floating population of fifteen to twenty thousand turbulent fishermen. No wonder there were disorders and crimes! The marvel is that there were not more. But for the exercise of authority by the English ships no one could have lived here. There must have been some violent scenes in St. John's in those days.

The following Records give us a partial list of the depredations of some of the "erring captains"—Whitbourne's euphonious name for the lawless privateers and pirates of the age :—

"1621.—The names of certaine pirattes with the damage done by them in Newfoundland since the yeare 1612.

"The pirate Eason brought 4 ships from Ile of May with captains and soldiers which he increased to 9 ships, all which he carried away with him besides 100 pieces of ordenance with all manner of victualles and munition to the value of ten thousand four hundred pounds of the goods of the English, besides 500 fishermen of His Majesty's subjects taken from their honest trade of fishing (many being volunteers) but the most enforced to serve them in their courses of piracy. The hurt done by said pirates to subjects of French king by robbing and spoiling 25 ships fishing about coasts of Newfoundland amounts to £6,000. Damage done by them to States of the low countries by taking a great Flemish ship £1,000. By spoiling voyage of 12 Portugal ships £3,000. The total of damage done to all nations by the great Eason and his complices in and about Newfoundland—£20,400.

---

[1] During Guy's year of office he resisted a requisition for £2,500 made upon the city to suppress piracy—contending that £1,000 was enough compared with amounts subscribed by London, &c.

"Anno 1614.— Captain Maneringe with divers other captains arrived in Newfoundland the 4th June having 8 sails of warlike ships one whereof they took at the bank another upon the mayne of Newfoundland, from all the harbours whereof they commanded carpenters maryners victuals munitions and all necessaries from fishing fleet after this rate—of every six maryners they take one, and the one first part of all their victuals; from the Portugal ships they took all their wine and other provisions save their bread; from a French ship in Harbour de Grace they took 10,000 fish; some of the company of many ships did run away unto them. They took a French ship fishing in Carboneir &c. and so after they had continued three months and an half in the country taking their pleasure of the fishing fleet, the 14th Sep. 1614 they departed having with them from the fishing fleet about 400 mariners and fishermen, many volunteers, many compelled.

"Anno 1616.—Captain Jacob a Flemish pirate with one Captain Ellis an English pirate took a French and Portugese ship—damage done to both being at least £1500. They took all the ordinance from a ship of Bristol and a ship of Gurnsey to the value of £200.

"Anno 1618.—Part of the fleet of Sir Walter Raleigh in their return from Orenoqe consisting of two ships and a cartell wherein was chief commander one Capt. Wollaston with divers other captains who took from four French ships their lading of dry fish which they carried away and sold at Ligorne in Italy to value of £3000. More three ships they took and carried with them which they sold at Ligorne to value of £2400. One French ship they left in Newfoundland which was immediately sent home by the Governor of plantation, yet loss of her fishing voyage was £500. On first coming pillaged French fishers 500 pounds. Their taxing of fishermen in all the harbours of Newfoundland for powder shot &c. amounted to £2000, besides one hundred and thirty men they took away.

"Some few instances of certane misdemeanors and injuries comitted by the fishers this last yeare in Newfoundland. 1620.

"Eight stages in several harbours worth at least in labour and cost £180 maliciously burned by certain English fishers, besides many more in the harbours of the country, greatly to prejudice of fishing trade, and not punishable but by good laws to be settled there by His Majestie.

"A man slaine in a controversy for 'halinge of a Seyne.'

"Certain English fishermen entered aboard a Portugal ship in the night in St. John's harbour with swords and axes wherewith they cut many of his ropes and would have cut his cables to the overthrow of the ship had they not been restrained by certain masters of English ships.

"A great combat betweene some insolent English and certain Portugals in Petyte Harbour, and one of the English dangerously hurt with a pike.

"Great damage done by certain English fishers to a saw mill and a grist mill built by the plantacon not to be repaired for forty pounds.

"The woods daily spoiled by fishers in taking the rind and bark of the trees and 5000 acres of wood burned maliciously by the fishers in the bay of Conception anno 1619 with many more thousands of acres burned and destroyed by them within these 20 years.

"Harbours frequented by English near 40 in number, almost spoiled by casting out their balast and presse stones into them.

"Portugals, French and all other nations frequenting that trade are more conformable to good orders than the English fishers."

In 1615 the strongest and ablest ruler of all appeared on the scene—Captain John Mason.[1] The connection of this remarkable man—the future founder, with Sir Ferdinando Gorges, of the State of New Hampshire—with our Colony has been entirely ignored. Mason made himself well acquainted with his new Government, carried on the fish business in Cupids and Harbour Grace prosperously, surveyed part of the coast, and must have been specially energetic in defending the settlers' rights, as it was in his time that the petition was made to the king by the western adventurers.

One very interesting incident occurred during Mason's residence in the Colony, which brings out in a very clear and distinct manner the close connection between the early colonists in Newfoundland and the first settlers in New England, the similarity of the trade and fishery in both colonies. The romantic adventures of the Indian Squantum, his infamous capture by Hunt, and his subsequent slavery in Spain, his visit to Cupids, and his later services as friend and ally of the Pilgrim Fathers, reads more like a scene in a cheap novel than the true story of a poor Redskin.[2]

---

[1] John Mason was born at King's Lynn, Norfolk, England; he was an Oxford man, and a classical scholar; very early in life he entered the Royal Navy; in 1606 he went with Knox, Bishop of the Isles, to reclaim the islanders of the Hebrides. Says an English admiral: "The Christian world could not show a more barbarous, more bloody, or more untamed generation." Mason had command of two ships of war and two pinnaces, and did his work well, but received no payment whatever from James, but probably to requite him in some way for his valuable services he was appointed Governor of the Newfoundland Plantation. Mason came out to Newfoundland with his wife in 1615, and remained six years; he explored the Island, made a map, the first English chart from actual survey which approaches to any degree of accuracy; he also wrote a short treatise *A Brief Discourse of the New-foundland*, published in 1620, and sent to his friend Sir John Scott, of Edinburgh. In 1621, just before Mason's departure from the Island on the petition of divers Scottish adventurers, application was made to the King to send two ships of war to Newfoundland, and to appoint John Mason King's Lieutenant in the Island. This appears to have been granted, and Mason also received at the same time a commission from the Lord High Admiral. Sir Ferdinando Gorges having been appointed one of the Commissioners in England to regulate the Newfoundland fisheries, Mason, on his return to England in 1621, became acquainted with him, and, with Sir William Alexander and his little book on Newfoundland, stirred up the latter, afterwards Earl of Stirling, to obtain a patent for Nova Scotia. In 1622, Mason and Gorges obtained a share of New England which seven years later was named New Hampshire. Mason became afterwards Treasurer of the Army, and Captain of South Sea Castle, and Governor of Portsmouth, England. He died in 1635 and was buried in Westminster Abbey; a monument was erected to his memory in the garrison church of Portsmouth in 1874. I am indebted for all these particulars to the excellent memoir of Mason by Charles Wesley Tuttle, Ph.D., published by the Prince Society of Boston, U.S.

[2] Squantum was seized by Thomas Hunt, one of John Smith's captains in the expedition to New England of 1614, and with nineteen more Indians taken to Malaga and sold as slaves. He was very intelligent, and, probably, being allowed his liberty, wandered about the quay at Malaga. After four years of slavery, he met a captain of a ship belonging to Guy's Colony. He was smuggled aboard, and taken to London, and then out to Cupids. Here he met Mason and Dermer. Dermer knowing of the great interest Sir Ferdinando took in New England, brought him home to Plymouth. From there he went out with Dermer on one of Gorges' expeditions to New England. He was left behind by Dermer in his native land.

When the Pilgrim Fathers arrived, they were astonished at being accosted by an Indian who spoke good English. Squantum was the lifelong friend and ally of the

Mason's tract on Newfoundland is a very quaint and valuable work; it was written between 1618 and 1619, and sent to his friend, Sir John Scott, of Scots Tarvet, Edinburgh, to whom he had also written in 1617.

The map did not appear in print until 1625, in Vaughan's "Golden Fleece." It, however, was made in 1617. The letter is directed:—

"To the Right Worshipfull Mr. John Scott of Scottisterbatt, in Scotland, Director to His Majesty's Court of Chancery there at his house on the Cawsy of Edenborough."[1]

After alluding to the various hindrances to his duty as Governor, he continued:—

"I am now setting my foote into that path where I ended last to discover to the westward of this land; and for two months absence I have fitted myselfe with a small new galley of 15 Tonnes and to row with fourteen oares (having lost one former) we shall visit the naturalls [Indians] of the country with whom I propose to trade and thereafter shall give you a taste of the event, hoping that with all *Terra Nova* will produce *dona nova*, to manifest our gratificacion. Untill which tyme I rest and shall remayne *Tuus, dum suus*. John Mason.

The tract is entitled—

A
BRIEFE DISCOURSE

Of the New-found-land

with the situation, temperature,
and commodities thereof,
Inciting our nation to goe
forward in that hop
-full plantation begunne.

Scire tuum nihil est, nisite scire noc sciat alter.

A. H.
EDINBURGH.
Printed by Andro Hart. 1620.

Colonists. He taught them how to plant Indian corn, and to use fish manure to make it grow well. He was their guide, philosopher, and friend; clothed in an old soldier's uniform, Squantum's heart swelled with importance; he made his fellow countrymen believe that, from close association with the white men, he had gained the control of disease and death; that he could bring them out of sickness, or bury them at will.

This remarkable Indian spoke three languages, and had embraced four religions; first, his native heathenism; secondly, the genial friars in Malaga (in my experience, the kindliest Christians in the world) made him a good Catholic; Mistress Anne Mason converted him into a sound High Churchman; finally, the Brownists captured him; his last request was for Governor Bradford to pray for him that "he might goe to ye Englishman's God in heaven."

The early part of Bradford's history is full of Squantum and his services to the Pilgrims; with his death the Indian trade for the time ceased. When he died, in 1622, he was most sincerely lamented. Governor Bradford says his useful services to the infant settlement entitle him to grateful remembrance.

I am indebted to my friend James Phinney Baxter, B.A., for this note.

[1] The full address:—
"Deliver thers,—
"I desire Moyses Slaney to repaire downe to Whitehall with this letter and to inquire for Sir Willyam Alexander, Master of the Requests for Scotland, and to procure of him conveiance for this letter accordingly." It shows all the trouble that had to be taken to forward a letter in those days.

Mason begins by describing the geographical position of Newfoundland; next the climate. He says:—

"It is fruitfull enough both of sommer and winter corne .... wheate, rye, barlie, oates and pease, which have growen and ripened there as well and as timely as in Yorkshire in England."

This is not in the least exaggerated. Sir Terence O'Brien, K.C.M.G., our Governor, has lately imported some Russian wheat; the return crop, grown by Mr Ross, Grove Farm, showed splendid grain. Barley, rye, and oats are ripened every year in Newfoundland by our farmers. Splendid wheat has been grown over and over again; the price of flour, however, is so low that there is no inducement to grow it. Garden vegetables, peas, beans, cauliflower, &c., are grown to perfection.

MASON'S MAP.[1]

From Vaughan's Golden Fleece, 1625.

His description of the wild fruit is also correct. Of the fishery he says:—

"May hath herings one equall to 2 of ours, cants and cod in good quantity. June hath Capline a fish much resembling smeltes in forme and eating and such abundance dry on shoare as to lade cartes, in some partes pretty store of Salmond, and cods so thicke by the shoare that we nearlie have been able to rowe a boate through them. I have killed of them with a pike; of these three men to sea in a boat with some on shoare to dresse and dry them in 30 dayes will kill commonlie

---

[1] A close examination of this map shows that it was not constructed by Mason, all its features being traceable in much older maps, the only contribution of Mason being "the great Lake or Sea"—Fortune Bay, which he probably saw from some hill in Placentia Bay on one of his exploring expeditions. The map belongs to the Anglo-Dutch group, and is mainly of French origin.

betwixt 25 and 30,000, worth, with the oyle arising from them, 100 or 120 pound. And the fish and traine in one harbour called Saint Johns is yearly in the summer worth 17 or 18 thousand pounds. Julie and so till November hath Macrill in aboundance one thereof as great as two of ours. August hath great large Cods, but not in such aboundance as the smaller, which continueth, with some little decreasing until December.

"I have heard some countries extolled for their two fowld Harvest which heare thou hast tho' in different kinde yet both as profitable. . . . that country say I which in one month's time with reasonable paines wil pay landlord's rent servants wages and all household charges."

He notes the four advantages that Newfoundland possesses:—

"1st. The nearenes to our owne home. In March April and May, which alweyes accommodate faire windes to pass thether in 14 or 20 days seldome in 30 days. Return in June to Novr. in 12, 16, 20 and now and then 30 days.

"2nd. The great intercourse of trade with our nation these three score years and upwards in no small number frequenting the Newfoundland and daylie increasing imploying 3000 seamen also fraiting 300 ships. . . . Revenue to the King by the customes of French Spanish and Straights goods imported from the proceeds of this fish trade at least £10,000 yearly.

"3. The conveniency of transporting planters at the old rate 10 – the man and 20 – for victuals . . . likewise other commodities by shippes that goe sackes at ten shillings per tunne out and thirtie shillings home. Whereas Virginia and Birmooda fraightes are five pounds the man and three pound the tunne . . .

"4. Securitie from Foreign and domesticke enemies. Few savages in the north. None in the south, by whom the planter as yet never suffered damage. Ice a bulwark in winter. In summer we have nine or 10,000 of our own nation with maney good and warlike shippes who must defend the fishing season for their living sake as they have formerly done in the warres with Spaine."

"In the midle of the Month of April many Ships arrive of the *English*, some *French*, and in the midest of May some *Portingalls*. All which as so many Reapers come to the Harvest, gathering in aboundance the wonderfull blessings of the Lord.

"I might heare further discourse of our discoveries, conference with the Salvages by Master *John Gye*, their manner of life. Likewise of the managinge our businesse in our Plantations, with the descriptions of their situations in 2. places 16. miles distant from other, on the northside the bay of Conception; of the manner charge and benefite of our fishings with the severall strange formes, and natures of Fishes, projects for making Yron, Salt, Pitch, Tarre, Tirpontine, Frank-Incense, Furres, Hopes of Trade with Salvages and such like, with many accidents and occurrences in the time of my government there, but these may suffice as *Verbum sapienti*; being of sufficient truth to remove errours of conceiuing the Countrie more pleasant by reason of his naturall sight in the Sphære, then it is indeede, also to convince and take away malicious and scandelous speeches of maligne persons, who out of enuy to GOD and good Actions (instructed by their father the Deuill) haue sought to dispoile it of the dewe, and blamish the good name thereof.

"And lastlie to induce thee, gentle Reader, to the true consideration thereof as a thing of great consequence to our Nation not only at present, but like to bee much more beneficiall when the plaintations there shall increase, which God grant to his owne glorie and the good of our Common-Wealth."

GOVERNOR'S HOUSE, PORTSMOUTH.[1]
From a print in the B.M.

In May 1620 Mason received a commission from the Admiralty to suppress the pirates. We do not know how many he seized in Newfoundland, but we have his own account of the capture of a Sallee Rover, the *Good Fortune*, in Crookhaven in 1625.[2]

[1] Most probably the house where Mason spent his last days.

[2] COMMISSION TO MASON AND BUSHELL.

"Grant of a Commission from George, Duke of Buckingham, Lord Admiral &c &c, to the Treasurer & Company of the Colony of Newfoundland, to take up & press such ships with marriners, Soldiers, gunners, munitions of war, stores &c as may be necessary for the purpose of suppressing pirates and Sea Rovers, who interfere with the sea traffic, & plunder &c the merchant ships. That the sd Treasurer & Company are to set forth in a voyage to Newfoundland the good ship *Peter & Andrew* of London of 320 tons burthen, Capt. John Mason, & Wm. Bushell, master, with men, ordnance &c. for the purpose of taking such pirates or Sea Rovers & their ships, & to bring such ships into any of our ports, Creeks &c. And all Vice Admirals, Justices of the peace, Mayors, Sheriffs, Constables & Gaolers are to aid & assist the sd Capt. John Mason, & Wm. Bushell, & to carefully keep any pirates in prison as may be brought to them, until their trial to answer to Justice, & suffer the pains of the law for their piracies, or be acquitted thereof. And the said Company is authorised to take possession of such ships as may be captured, a moiety of their proceeds to go to the Admiralty & the other moiety to the said Company.

"Given in the High Court of Admiralty 29 May 17 K. James A.D. 1620."
—*Dom. Eliz.* 1790.
Admiralty Eliz. James I. & Charles I. Vol. 237, ss. 30–32.

Mason gallantly captured a Sallee pirate called the *Harts Desire* or *Good Ffortune* at Crookhaven in Ireland. In the report of his claim to the Admiralty about the ship, which was 100 tons, "she was continuallie imployed in pyracyes these 3 or 4 yeares, and therefore Mr. Wyen needs not make any scruple to proceed legallye to a condemnation." It appears the Admiralty case came before the great Sir John Eliot, Vice Admiral of Devon. Eliot distinguished himself by the capture of pirates, especially one Nutt; this corsair had powerful friends at Court, and, at his suit, Eliot was imprisoned.

Mason, like Guy, was young, restless, and ambitious; his little book stirred up a Colonial fever amongst his Scotch friends. On his visit to England in 1621 he found his services in requisition; Buckingham wanted a capable, reliable man as Treasurer for the Navy,[1] and so poor Newfoundland lost a ruler under whose prudent and energetic sway her destinies might have been completely changed. Probably sweet Mistress Anne Mason, a High Churchwoman, influenced the gallant Governor; she found Cupids and the long preaching of Erasmus Stourton rather dull, and longed for a livelier existence in London.[2] Even the pleasant trips and picnics up Southern River did not reconcile her to banishment from England.

Guy's Company appears to have existed up to 1628, at least. In that year we find negotiations going on between Slaney the treasurer, through a Dr. Meadus and Lord and Lady Conway, about a purchase of part of their grant. On June 27th, 1628, Dr. Meadus writes to Lady Conway:—

"Have conferred with Mr. Paine about the Newfoundland business; he will part with his Presidentship if John Slaney, the Governor of the whole land, consents. Hopes of mines of iron and silver in Newfoundland; present profit by fishing, furs and sarsaparilla."

There is another letter on June 30th on the same subject. In 1637 Hamilton and Kirke's grant recites that all the patentees had abandoned Newfoundland. This statement, however, is doubtful.

All writers on Newfoundland history, except Chief Justice Reeves, seem to have gone entirely astray on the subject of the various colonisation companies in the reigns of James and Charles I. A study of the records and various writers would have shown them how these different projects were founded, and how long they existed. Bishop Howley speaks of the Alderman's Colony having been abandoned some ten or twelve years previous to Lord Baltimore's settlement in Ferryland, and the Rev. Dr. M. Harvey says, "We have no authentic account of Guy's settlement." Evidently they were unaware of the existence of the books of Mason, Hayman, and Vaughan on this subject. Reeves gives distinctly the boundaries of Baltimore's grant. The Rev. Dr. M. Harvey says Lord Baltimore obtained a grant of the whole southern peninsula of Newfoundland between Trinity and Placentia Bays;

---

[1] It was in Mason's house Buckingham was stabbed by Felton.

[2] Robert Hayman, a poet of the Quigley and Swanborough type, in 1628 thus addressed her:—

"To all those worthy women who have any desire to live in Newfoundland specially to the modest and discreet gentlewoman Mistress Mason wife to Captaine Mason who lived there divers yeeres:

"Sweet creatures, did you truly understand
The pleasant life you'd live in Newfoundland,
You would with teares desire to be brought thither.
I wish you, when you go, faire wind, faire weather."

Quodlibets (1628), II. Bk. p. 31.

Bishop Howley, more cautious, quotes from Kirke, and says Baltimore's grant "applies to the whole peninsula of Avalon, and this is the common opinion of nearly all historians." Richardson, he quotes as contending that Baltimore obtained the whole Island. Then his Lordship goes on to prove that Baltimore established the Catholic religion in Newfoundland—a pure fiction. His further statements (p. 80), that Guy's Colony "failed through the incursions of the Indians," and that Baltimore bought out the Company in 1621 (p. 82), are entirely opposed to the evidence in the Records.

All the time there was extant and well known, Baltimore's grant and the exact boundaries of his province. Pedley attributes the large proportion of Irishmen and the influence of Roman Catholics in this country to Lord Falkland's Company, a bogus concern that fell flat on the market; its prospectus will be given later on.

Fortunately, we have at hand all the materials to correct these errors. No less than six colonies existed in Newfoundland during the reign of James I. Guy's, the parent Colony; "Bristol's Hope," an offshoot from Guy's at Harbour Grace; a distinct Colony of St. John's, extending south from Cape St. Francis to Petty Harbour, and to the present Holyrood; Vaughan's Colony, with head-quarters at Trepassey; Falkland's comprising part of Trinity Bay, called North Falkland and South Falkland, between Renews and Aquaforte; and lastly, Baltimore's Plantation. The exact division of Baltimore's grant is given, and it will be seen from these minute boundaries, how small a portion of Avalon he really possessed. Though Guy had a large nominal grant, the territory in his actual possession was very limited, and is described in Baltimore's bounds. The sale to Sir William Vaughan in 1616 by Guy's Company was part of the peninsula of Avalon between Petty Harbour and Cape Race, extending across to Placentia Bay.

SKETCH MAP OF THE SIX COLONIES.

Sir William Vaughan, D.C.L.—a brother of Lord Carberry, celebrated as the host of Jeremy Taylor, at Golden Grove, Carmarthenshire—

founded his Welsh colony in Trepassey Harbour, naming it "Cambriol Colchos," and "Golden Grove" after their ancient seat, and "Vaughan's Cove," as we may see it marked on Mason's map of 1617. Vaughan

FERRYLAND, SHOWING BALTIMORE'S HOUSE.
From Fitzhugh's map, 1693.

sent over his first batch of emigrants in this year, and in 1618 Whitbourne, it appears, came out with another detachment.

He informs us :—

"I sayled thither in a shippe of my own which was victualled by that gentleman myself and some others. We likewise did set forth another shippe for a fishing voyage which also carried some victuals for those people which had been formerly sent to inhabit there, but this ship was intercepted by an English erring captaine [a Pirate] that went forth with Sir Walter Rawleigh . . . . whereby the fishing voyage of both our shippes was overthrown and the Plantation hindered."

Poor Sir William Vaughan, after remaining out in Newfoundland some years and spending his time writing his remarkable works, through want of means was first compelled to sell a block of land to Lord Falkland; this piece was six miles wide, extending from Renews to a point between Fermeuse and Aquaforte, and thence extending in two parallel lines west to Placentia Bay. After making this sale, Vaughan disposed of the remaining northern portion of his big territory to Lord Baltimore. They had been friends and fellow students at Oxford and quite in a natural way, as one pawns off a worthless horse on a friend, so Sir William sold a large portion of his grant at a very high price to Lord Baltimore.

Whitbourne gives a sorry description of Vaughan's colonists:—

"For certainly I have already seen and known by experience that the desired plantation can never be made beneficial by such idle fellows as I found there in 1618, when I was there with power by virtue of a grannte from the Patentees, which people had remained there a whole yeere before I came theare or knew any or there and never applied themselves to any commendable thing, no not so much as to make themselves a house to lodge in, but lay in such cold and simple rooms all the winter as the fishermen had formerly built there for their necessary occasions the yeere before those men arrived there."

These wretched emigrants appear to have ruined poor Vaughan; instead of looking after their work and superintending their labours the learned Sir William was busy preparing his fantastic works; friends in England advised him that the best chance for selling his books was to give them curious titles, thus we have his "Newlander's Cure" and his "Golden Fleece," most extraordinary medleys about religion, medicine, and colonisation. King James appears to have been generous and kind to this remarkable exile, a great scholar and most absurd pedant, after the king's own heart. A grant was made to him in his extreme need, and partly at his instance, in 1623, two men of war were sent out to convoy the Newfoundland fleet home.

BALTIMORE ARMS.
From Winsor's N. & C. H. of America.

The names given by Vaughan and Lord Falkland to the southern shore have entirely disappeared; all the other official colonisation schemes, from Bacon to Baltimore and Kirke, failed. They had elaborate charters prepared in the chambers of kings; princes and potentates lent the weight of their names and dignity to these great state documents; they offered court barons, court leet, and territorial aggrandisement to their associates; later on they had those remarkable dignitaries the Nova Scotia Baronets; all these fantastic titles and aristocratic forms, the devices of principalities and powers, faded and died away in the rude free air of the Colonies. None of the great patentees, from Gilbert to Baltimore, exercised the least permanent influence on the history of the Colony, least of all Baltimore; he came and stayed an uneasy discontented stay of two seasons; all his company of forty persons left the colony together, and then his Lordship and his seminary priests[1] and his noble retinue and his Welsh colonists vanish from our annals.

There has been much acrimonious discussion about Calvert's character; on one side he is lauded as a saint, whilst some extreme writers have denounced him as a bigot. With his bastard son he can hardly be set down as a saint, but he was far ahead of his age in enlightenment; his religion was real and sincere; his zeal for the Catholic faith was genuine and honest, it was opposed to all his worldly interests.

The truth is that, though an amiable, gentle and honest man in private life, in public affairs Baltimore was a weak man; in Parliament he prostituted his talents for Court favour; he was undoubtedly brave and an enthusiastic pioneer in colonisation, but the rude life and rough winds of Avalon were morally and physically too strong for him; he was neither an epoch maker nor an empire founder, simply an honest religious Cavalier. The treatment of his son by the Stuarts, whom the father had so loyally and abjectly served, is one of the most treacherous and dishonourable acts of Charles I.

St. John's and the neighbourhood, from Petty Harbour on the south around by Cape St. Francis to Holyrood, Conception Bay, was the first settled part of the Island; from the very earliest times St. John's was the capital, the metropolis and head-quarters of the great fishery and exchange carried on in Newfoundland; the rendezvous for all the convoys, it was connected with the neighbouring settlements by rude paths cut through the woods.

FIRST LORD BALTIMORE.
From Winsor's N. & C. H. of America.

Newfoundland was colonised not by aristocratic and fantastic patentees, but by hard-working humble settlers from the West of England, oppressed by the harsh laws of the Stuarts, and persecuted by the

---

[1] The Southampton Records show that one of Baltimore's priests came home, under an assumed name, in August 1629.—(See *Southampton Municipal Archives*—Book of Examinations, Informations, and Depositions, No. 42, A.D. 1622 to 1643).

I p. 2729.

western adventurers, they clung with sturdy tenacity to the land they had made their home. From the very earliest times they carried on a rude kind of agriculture, raised vegetables, and reared cattle and swine. They lived in the midst of a rude plenty, game and fish being simply in unlimited supply. The settlements were very much scattered, and these hardy pioneers, most skilful in woodcraft, traversed the country in all directions, made visits to each other—"cruizing" it is still called in this country.[1]

Baudoin says:—

"The French deem the country impassable. Not so the English; they know it perfectly, even that part which belongs to France, for they guided us everywhere through the woods and along the coasts, where for more than *one hundred and ninety leagues* they have roads beaten fit for horseback."[2]

Many peculiarities of the Colony can be traced back to our Devonshire forefathers. There are no lakes in the West of England, only ponds, so all our lakes are all called ponds; they had no grouse, so our willow grouse has always been most erroneously called a partridge: our people possess remarkable skill as mechanics, mostly self-taught. The first winter crews left in the Colony, who became permanent settlers, were ship and house carpenters, blacksmiths, &c. Our fishermen's manual dexterity is no doubt partly inherited skill, and partly arises from necessity—the mother of invention.

It was doubtless owing to harsh laws and the hostility of the Devonshire ship-fishermen that the settlers planted their homes in creeks and coves; where ships could not safely lie. In these open roadsteads they were free from molestation. This explains the early settlement of such places as Torbay, Pouch Cove, Grates, and Bonavista, which soon became large settlements. Official returns about the population are misleading; the settlers purposely concealed their numbers from the naval authorities. We notice a great discrepancy between the numbers as given by the French Abbé Baudoin and the official census.

The year 1615 marks the first primitive attempt to create a formal court of justice in Newfoundland; our old friend Sir Richard Whitbourne was sent out to hold courts of Vice-Admiralty in the Colony; it was all carried out at the poor old captain's own expense; he had not so much as a bum-bailiff to serve process, or a room to hold court in, or any power whatever to enforce his decrees. Was there ever such an absurd plan of governing a country, maintaining order, and administering justice, as this cheap device of King James!

---

[1] A lady sent her servant—an outharbour man—to ask a friend to go calling with her. The message delivered was:— "The Mistress wants to know, 'Mam,' if you will go *cruizing* with her this afternoon."

[2] BAUDOIN'S *MS. Diary, Quebec MSS.*

WHITBOURNE'S VICE-ADMIRALTY COURT.

Most extraordinary things have been done in modern times in the Colony; early in this century an ardent liberal medico started on a pan of ice to aid Ypsilanti, the Greek patriot. This project was hardly a wilder scheme than Whitbourne's Vice-Admiralty Court.

Of course it was the duty of the doughty Sir Richard to magnify his duties, and filled with all the dignity of office, and rejoicing in the confidence of his sovereign, he tells us in his own inimitable way the result of his judicial round of lectures to the wild rovers and daring

EXETER.
From Speed's Prospect.

adventurers that then carried on the Newfoundland trade; no doubt they listened to the old mariner with respect, and all promised to behave themselves. During the next two or three years disorders were worse than ever.

Whitbourne tells us :—

"I set forth from the Port of Exceter on the 11th May 1615 in a Barke victualled and manned with 14 men and boyes at my own charges; on the 4th June being Trinity Sunday, I anchored in Trinity Harbour and there in the name of the Holy and Individuall Trinity I called together by virtue of my commission the masters of the English ships there lying and so began to hold the first Court of Admiralty in your Majesty's name that ever was as I believe holden in that

Country to the use of any Christian Prince and proceeded therein according to course of law as the tenour of my commission did warrant me therein; also in other Harbours of the said Coast I did the like."[1]

Having carefully inquired into the disorders committed on the coast, the masters of one hundred and seventy English ships "delivered to the Court, under their hands and seals, their presentments," which in turn Whitbourne transferred to the High Court of Admiralty. These presentments are summarised under twelve heads; the most important were:—

"Non-observance of the Sabbath Day.
"Injury to the Harbours by casting into them large stones.
"Destroying fishing stages and huts.
"Monopoly of convenient space.
"Entering the service of other countries.
"Burning woods.
"And lastly Idleness parent of all evils."[1]

The masters who put their presentments on record declared that these disorders should cease. Thus ended this legal farce. It is to be hoped old Whitbourne got through his cases in what an old bailiff used to call a "summinary" manner, so as to enable him and his crew to get a load of fish when he threw off the burthen of his judicial dignity.

Whitbourne is the Captain John Smith of our colonial history; like his great prototype—the most picturesque figure in the annals of Virginia—he was a devout High Churchman, an utter despiser of Brownists, Puritans, and all other new-fangled religions, a sound high-hearted Englishman, devoted to his country and her ancient Colony; like Smith he was everything by turns—sailor, traveller, author, judge, and colonial governor; in his last years we can fancy the fine old mariner sitting in his pleasant cottage at Exmouth, within sound of the sea he loved so well, writing with his crabbed old hand:—

"A relation of the Newfoundland with a more ample discovery of that Country than euer was yet set foorth to the open viewe, together with the Briefes or such Presentments as were there taken to use of your Majestie, by vertue of a commission vnder the Broad Seale of the Admiraltie directed to me Richard Whitbourne."[1]

He concludes his work with an eloquent appeal to the King:—

"And these excellent benefits distribute themselues, between your Maiestie and your Subiects: your Highnesse part will be the Honour of the Action; the accesse of Territory, increase of strength and power, aduantage against other Princes, augmentation of Reuenew, and ease of your Maiesties Kingdomes, &c. The Subiects part will be the bettering and securing of their Trade; inriching of themselues; reliefe of other Trades; and a meanes of further Discoueries.

[1] WHITBOURNE'S *Discourse*.

But these two haue a relation and dependency, the one on the other, that neither can subsist without the other. I will not therefore diuide your Maiestie from your Subiects; your Highnesse prosperitie being their happinesse; and their wealth, your Maiesties riches.

"The first thing which is to be hoped for, and which hath euer been your Maiesties principall care, is the propagation of the Christian faith: and by that meanes onely, the poore vnbeleeuing Inhabitants of that Countrey may be brought to the knowledge of God, and a ciuill kinde of gouernement: and it is not a thing impossible, but that from those slender beginnings which may bee made in New-found-land, all the regions adioyning (which betweene this place, and the countries actually possessed by the King of Spaine, and to the north of New-found-land, are so spacious as all Europe) may be conuerted to the true worship of God.

"The next is, the vniting of a Countrey so beneficiall already, and so promising vnto your Maiesties Crowne, without bloodshed, charge, or vsurpation, which must needs be a perpetuall Honour to your Maiestie, in all succeeding ages; neither will it be an Honour onely to your Highnesse, but a benefit to the State, by a new accesse of Dominion. And what Prince can enlarge his Territories by a more easie and more iust meanes then this, seeing that of right it appertaineth to your Maiestie, and therefore deserues to be imbraced?

"Now if it please your most excellent Maiestie not onely to lend your care to a Proiect of this nature, but also to approue the matter proiected, and vouchsafe the furtherance therein, the which out of my soules deuotion, and zealous affection to do seruice to your Maiestie and your Kingdomes, I tender on my knees; most humbly beseeching your Highnesse, both to accept of my honest and zealous intent, as also to pardon my boldnesse and presumption therein; for it is, and so hath euer been my resolution, rather to beare the burden of pouerty, than iustly to deserue, or giue cause of reproach; and to subiect all the dayes of my life, and the manifold dangers thereof, thereby to approue my selfe a profitable member, both to your Maiestie, and to my countrey that gaue mee my first breath; for which onely cause I haue adventured to publish this my simple and plaine Discourse, whereunto my very conscience hath a long time, and still doth not forbeare to sollicite me.

"The prosecution and perfection of the worke, I leaue to the pleasure of God, and your Maiesties happy directions, in the discourse and discouery whereof, if I haue either been tedious, or any other way offensiue, it is to be imputed to my want of learning: and so, though perhaps I doe not satisfie some men's curiosities, yet I hope I haue sufficiently informed their iudgements; and beseech God to incline their affections to the furtherance of so pious and so profitable a businesse, as this appeareth to be.

"And so I rest, and euer will remaine, a faithfull and loyall Subiect to your Maiestie, an hearty and true louer of my Countrey, and a zealous wellwisher to this intended plantation.

"RICHARD WHITBOURNE."[1]

With a twinkle in his humorous old eye he tells us of the "mosquitos":—

"Those flies seeme to have a greate power and authority upon all loytering people that come to the Newfoundland; for they have the property, that when they find any such lying lazily, or sleeping in the Woods, they will presently bee

---

[1] WHITBOURNE'S *Discourse*.

more nimble to seize on them, than any Sargeant will bee to arrest a man for debt; neither will they leave stinging or sucking out the blood of such sluggards, untill like a beadle they bring him to his Master, where hee should labour; in which time of loytering those flies will so brand such idle persons in their faces, that they may be known from others as the Turks doe their slaves."[1]

Whitbourne's book, with its quaint conceits, took the fancy of King James, himself a "Royall and noble Author"; he gave him the sole right of printing and selling it for twenty-one years, and orders were sent to the archbishops for its distribution in every parish in the kingdom. Our author seems to have made some profit out of his work, as there were no less than seven editions of the book published between 1621 and 1623.

The last we hear of old Sir Richard is a petition to the Stuarts for a small post under the Crown as inspector of provisions for the merchant ships; he asks—

"To be allowed to superintend the orderly salting and preserving of victuals or the well baking of biskett bread, the tymelie and well breewing of beare, and also the filling of sweet casks for the same. In which kind of employment he has had long experience."

He also prays to be appointed superintendent of one of the western ports, or to get command of a ship; he proposes a method, at no charge to His Majesty or to His Majesty's subjects, for keeping two men of war and pinnaces for the protection of the Newfoundland fishery. Whitbourne's relations belonged to Widdecome, in Devon, where many yeomen of his kith and kin lie buried. There is no monument to mark the last resting place of the poor old battered and decayed Elizabethan hero, our constant ally and friend, Sir Richard Whitbourne.[2]

Lord Falkland, the nominal head of the Dublin Company for colonising Newfoundland, must not be confounded with his son, the

---

[1] WHITBOURNE's *Discourse*.

[2] 1626, November 10, in a Petition to the Duke of Buckingham, in the reign of Charles I. (contained in the Calendar of State Papers), Whitbourne states: "A traveller and adventurer into foreign countries at 15 years of age, he was captain of a good ship of his own in 1588, and rendered good service; has often been greatly wronged by pirates in Newfoundland, where he was subsequently employed, by commission, for the reformation of abuses yearly committed there, and other special affairs on that coast; wrote a large discourse, which was presented to King James, and ordered to be printed and distributed in every parish throughout England, to show the benefits of settling a plantation there. Has been twice to that country to help advance a plantation undertaken by Lord Falkland; encloses a certificate of his good services and losses."

Whitbourne was probably knighted for his "Large Discourse" and his services in the Armada fight, which he states "is to be seen recorded in the book at Whitehall." For this sturdy old sailor every Newfoundlander should feel a deep affection. His love for our island was wonderful; through good report and evil report he always stood by us; his description of the Colony is in the main a true report, and agrees with contemporary accounts of Peckham, Mason, Vaughan, Hayes, &c.; he threw in a few wonderful tales, such as the "Marmaide" and the "Mosquito," to tickle the ears of the groundlings. The Hon. R. Bond did suitable respect to the memory of the old "Worthy of Devon," by naming our first important railway junction "Whitbourne."

distinguished patriot and hero of the Civil War. Falkland's colonisation scheme embraced a settlement between Baltimore's and Vaughan's colony; it extended six miles wide from a straight line drawn half-way between Aquaforte and Fermeuse to Placentia Bay, and a similar line drawn west on the southern boundary.

Henry Cary, the first Lord Falkland, was made Lord Deputy of Ireland by James I.; he was a man of considerable literary ability, and took a deep interest in schemes for colonising America; the organisation of his colony was carried out by his associates; he appears to have taken very little active part in the company. The colonists were like the uncivilized Welsh brought out by Wynne; it was the custom of the age to capture men for all kinds of service, and in all probability Vaughan's settlers and Falkland's colonists were simply corralled like so many cattle, and sent out to the new settlement. There was no practical farmer to teach them how to clear the land; they were green hands, and no use at the fishery; it is no marvel, therefore, to find, after reading Whitbourne's account of their idleness, and Hayman's description of their management, and the dishonesty of agents like Wynne and Powell, that they were failures; these causes, combined with the want of a practical, energetic, experienced man at the head of affairs, fully explains why these aristocratic schemes to colonise Newfoundland did not succeed. We can admire the enthusiasm that set them on foot, the eloquent language with which they were recommended to the public; the colonies were settled by poor hard-working fearless men, not by these courtiers and enthusiastic writers or the poor slaves they sent out to people the New World. Not a vestige of these colonies now remain; all the fantastic names of New Falkland, Cambriol Colchos, Vaughan's Cove, Brittaniola, &c., with the one exception of Baltimore's Avalon, have disappeared from the maps and there is not a Welsh family remaining on the whole southern shore of Newfoundland, except the honoured family of Williams of Bay Bulls.

Lord Falkland's proposals were printed in a book entitled:—

"A short discourse of the New-found-land contayning diverse reasons and inducements for the planting of that countrey.

"Published for the satisfaction of all such as shall be willing to be adventurers in the said Plantation.

"To the Right Hon. Henry Lo. Cary Viscount Falkland Lo. Deputie Generall of Ireland and one of His Majesties most honourable privie Councell in the Realme of England.

"My Lord,

"I present with the view of your judicious censure the short Discourse or rather an abstract of a discourse, intended only as a satisfaction unto such as may be willing to joyne with your Lordship in so noble a designe as is the plantation of the Newfoundland, wherein it is not to be doubted but that many will follow your Lordship's stepps in so honourable a worke especially in the Kingdome where the name of a *Plantation* is so farre from being a stranger as it hath been the originall cause from whence very many have derived their happinesse. I cannot deeme but that the weake handling of this discourse better beseemes the poor demonstration of my zeale to your Lordship's service than any possibility to comprehend the worthinesse of the action within the compasse of a bare relation.

"Reasons for planting—it is for the Honour of God and the King; that Part of the Country is not inhabited; His Majestys undoubted right to the Country; that the London Plantation has been settled 13 years [Guys]; the Bristol Plantation 5 years, and Lord Baltimore the two years last past; the advantages of Trade from Ireland to Newfoundland.

"Conditions are, that any one paying £100 is to have half a Harbour on the north side of Trinity Bay and Stages Room in Fermeuse or Renews, and 1000 acres of land. For £200 a whole Harbour in Trinity Bay, 4000 acres north of Trinity Harbour, and stage room for 2 Rooms at Renews and Fermeuse. Other amounts paid, to obtain benefits proportionably."

The pamphlet is very well written. Sir Francis Tanfield, who figures in Guy's Company, was appointed governor; it appears he never came out to his kingdom, and the whole scheme fell through.

JACODSCZ' MAP, 1621.

In the latter part of James I.'s reign a very important point about fishery rights in the plantations began to be agitated: it raised the whole question as to the absolute authority of the Crown over the colonies, and had a dire effect on the Stuart dynasty.

The Plymouth Company claimed the right to charge the English ship-fishermen who frequented the coast a licence fee equal to eighty-three cents per ton, and to forbid vessels engaged in commerce to enter any port along the entire coast without liability to seizure and confiscation, and such punishment for the captain and crew as the Council thought proper to inflict. Bradford says:—

"About ye later end of June came in a ship with Captaine Francis West who had a Comission to be Admirall of New England to restraine interlopers and such fishing ships as came to fish and trade without a licence from ye Counsell of New England, for which they should pay a rounde sume of money. But he could doe no good of them, for they were to stronge for him and he found ye fisher men to be stuberne fellows."

The West Countrymen brought their grievance before Parliament. A discussion arose, in which Calvert, the Secretary of State, defended the patentees' right to this monstrous monopoly. He argued, "America "is not annexed to the realm, it is a plantation solely governed by the "Crown." The great lawyer Coke[1] made Sir Ferdinando Gorges, the principal patentee, come to the bar of the House. Coke argued:—

"Your Patent contains many particulars contrary to law and the liberty of the subject; it is a monopoly, and the ends of private gain are concealed under color of planting a Colony; to prevent our Fishermen from visiting the Sea Coast for fishing, is to make a monopoly upon the seas which are wont to be free; if you alone are to pack and dry fish you attempt a monopoly of the wind and sun."

On the accession of Charles I., the Commons passed a Bill for the maintenance and increase of shipping and navigation, and for liberty of fishing in Newfoundland, Virginia, and New England. The Bill was thrown out by the Court party in the Lords; on this the Commons refused to grant the king a subsidy. It was one of the first difficulties between Charles and Parliament.

---

[1] Coke posed as a reformer in this matter; the real motive was his bitter hatred of his rival, Bacon. All the same, he rendered great service to England as adviser to those who opposed the tyranny of the Crown. The London Company, who led this attack on Gorges, and the Plymouth patentees had a similar monopoly. For further information on this interesting subject consult *Sir Ferdinando Gorges*, by James Phinney Baxter, B.A.

APPENDIX TO CHAPTER V.

I. London and Bristol Co.'s Charter.

(*Harl* 589, *fol*. 8.)

James by the Grace of god kinge of England Scotland ffrance and Irelande defender of the faith to all people to whome these presents shall come greeting,

Knowe yee whereas divers our lovinge and well disposed subjectes are desirous to make plantacõn to inhabite and establishe a Colony or Colonies in the Southerne and easterne p'tes of the country and Islande commonlie called Newfoundland unto the coast and harbours whereof the subjects of this our Realme of England have for the space of fiftie yeares and upwards yearlie used to resorte in noe small numbers to fishe, intendinge by such plantacõn and inhabitinge both to secure and make safe the trade of fishinge to our subjectes for ever, and also to make some commendable benifitt for the use of man kinde by the land and profitt thereof which hitherto from the beginninge, (as it seemeth manifest) hath remained unprofittable.

And for better performance of such their purpose and intencõns have humblie besoughte our royal authoritie and *assistance*, we beinge well assured that the same country adjoining to the foresaid coastes, where our subjects use to fishe remaineth so destitute and so desolate of inhabitaunte that scarce any one salvage person hath in many yeares beene seene in the moste p'tes thereof. And well knowing that the same lyeing and being soo vacant is as well for the reasons aforesaid as for many other reasons very commodious for us and our dominions and that by the lawe of nature and nations we maie of our royall authoritie possesse ourselves, and make graunte thereof without doeinge wronge, to anie other prince or state, consideringe they cannot justely pretend anie soueraignitie or righte thereunto in respect that the same remaineth soo vacant and not actualie possessed and inhabited by any Christian or any other whomesoever, and therefore thinckeinge it a matter and action well beseeminge a Christian kinge to make use of that w'ch God from the beginning created for mankinde, and thereby intending not onlie to worke and prive the benifitt and good of many of our subjectes, but principallie to ourselves to encrease the knowledge of the omnipotent God and the propagacõn of our Christian faith have graciouslie assented of their intention and suite.

And therefore doe of our speciall grace, certaine knowledge and meere motion for us our heires and successors give graunte and confirme by these p'ts unto our right deare and right wellbeloved cossinne and fellow Henry Earle of Northampton, keeper of our privie seale and to our trustie and right welbeloved Sir Lawrence Tanffield knight cheife barron of our exchequer Sir John Doddridge knighte one of our serjaunts at Lawe Sir ffraunces Bacon knight our Sollicitor generall [here follow forty-two names including] John Slany, John Guy, Philip Guy and Robert Aldworth, theire heires and assignes and to soo many as they shall hereafter admitt to be joyned with them in forme hereafter expressed, whether they goe in their persons to be planters in the plantacõn or whether they goe not but doe adventure theire moneys goods and chattells.

That they shalbe one bodie or communitie perpetuall and shall have perpetuall possession and one common seale and that they and their successors shalbe knowne as the *Tresorer and company of adventurers and planters of the cittie of London and Bristoll for the colony or plantacõn in Newfoundland* and that they and theire successors shalbe from henceforth for ever enabled to purchase by that name (license from us first obtayned) lande and goods within our realme of England and Walles and that they shalbe likewise enabled by that name to pleade and to be impleaded before any our judges in any of our courtes and in any actions.

And under the reservacõns limitacõns and declaracõns hereafter expressed *all that p'te and portion* of the country commonlie called Newfoundland w'ch is situate, *lying and being to the southward of the parallel lyne to be conceaved to passe by the cape commonlie called Bonaviste inclusive w'ch cape is to the Northward of Trinitie Bay and also w'ch is situate to the eastward of the meredian line to pass by the cape St. Maries inclusive w'ch cape is to the eastward of the bay of Placentia* together with the shoare and *islands lying within tenne leagues* of any p'te of the sea coast of the country and *alsoe all those countryes lande and Islands* commonlie called Newfoundland w'ch are situate betweene *forty and sive degrees of Northerlie latitude and two and fiftie degrees of the like latitude* and all the lande soile grounde havens, portes rivers mines aswell royall mines of gold and silver as other mineralls pearles and precious stones woods quarries marshes waters fishing hunnting hawkinge fowkinge commodities and hereditaments whatsoever together w'th all prerogatives jurisdictions royallties, priviledges franchizes and preheminates thereto or thereaboute both by sea and land belonging or appertaininge and w'ch we by our letters pattente canne graunte and in as ample manner as we or any of our noble progenitors have graunted to any adventurers or undertakers of any discoverie plantacōn or traffique into any forraigne p'tes and in as ample manner as if the same weere heerein p'ticularlie mentioned.

Nevertheless that there be saved and reserved unto *all manner of persons of what nation soever and also to all our loving subjectes w'ch doe at this p'nt or hereafter shall trade or voyadge to the partes aforesaid for fishing* all liberties powers easements and all other benifitts *as well concerning their fishing as well all other circumstances and incidents thereunto* in as ample manner as they have heretofore used and enjoyed the same without any impedimente disturbance or oposition any thinge in these p'nts to the contrarie notwithstandinge.

To have and hould all the lands Countryes and territories, with all the premises to the sole and proper use of them, &c. to be holden of us our heires and successors as of our manor of East Greenewich in the county of Kente in free and common socage? and not in capito. Yceldinge to us the fifthe parte of all the stoire of gold and silver gotten and obtayned for all services duties and demands :

And for as much as the good and prosperous successe of the plantacōn cannot but cheifelie depend most under the blessing of god and the support of our royall authoritie upon the provident and good direction of the whole enterprize by a carefull and understandinge counsell, and that it is not convenient, that all the adventurers shalbe soo often drawen to meete and assemble as shalbe requisite for them to have meetings and conference about their affaires.

Therefore that these shalbe perpetuallie one counsell consistinge of twelve p'sons here resident in London w'ch shall governe the plantacōn or any colonies to be established, w'ch counsell shall have a seale, besides the legall seale of the company, each of w'ch shall have our armes engraven on the one side and our portrature on the other and that the legall seale shall have round about on both sides these words : *Sigillum thesauraru et commimitutis terra nova* and that for the counsell : *Sigilum Regis magnæ Britanniæ frauncie et hiberniae* and on the other side : *Pro concilio terrae novae*.

And further that Sir Percivall Willoughbie Knight John Weld Esquire Raphe ffreman, Richard ffisheburne, John Stookely William Turner, William Jones, John Slany, Humfrey Slaney, John Weeld, Thomas Lupon and Thomas Jones shalbe the counsell and John Slany tresurer with authoritie for the warning of the counsell and summoning the companie and the counsell and tresurer shalbe chosen continued displaced changed and supplied as occasions shall require out of the adventurers by the voice of the greater p'te in their assembly for that purpose.

And that the companie maie cause to be made a coine to passe current betweene the people inhabitinge in these territories for the more ease traffique and bargaining between and amongst them of such nature mettle manner and forme as the counsell there shall lymitt and appointe.

And that if the tresurer for the tyme being be sicke or absente from the cittie of London he may constitute one of the counsell to be deputie with power to doe all things which belong to the tresurer.

And further to nominate by such names or styles as shall seeme good to them (and likewise to revoke) all governours, officers and ministers and to make lawes, formes and ceremonies of government and magistratie and revoke and change not onlie within the precincts of the colonie but also upon the seas in going and coming for the good of the adventurers and inhabitors there.

And for divers reasons and considerations that immediately from and after such tyme as any governour soe to be nominated shall arive in Newfoundland and give notice of his commission in that behalfe, all officers governours and ministers formerly appointed shalbe discharged, straightlie commanding them and everie other p'son resident in the Colonie upon their alleageance that they forthwith be obedient to such government as the counsell heere resident shall have named and to all directions w'ch they shall receive from them as well in their p'nt resigneing their authoritie as in all other attendance as shall be by them required.

And that the counsell heere resident in London or any five of them the tresurer being one shall have full power to admit any other person with their companie or freedome.

And further in a generall assemblie of the adventurers with the consent of the greater p'te upon good cause to put any person out of the freedome.

And by direction of the governeur there to digg and to search for gould silver cooz-iron lead tynne and other minerells as well within the precincts as within *any p'te of the maineland not formerlie graunted to any* *other* and to have the gould &c. to the use of the company.

Yeelding thearefrom yearlie unto us as aforesaid without any other manner of profitt or accounte to be given or yeelded.

And to take into that voyage and for and towards the plantacōn all of our loveing subjects or any other straungers that will become our subjects and live under our allegeance as shall willinglie accompanie them with sufficient sopping weepons vittailes and such marchandize or wares as maie be fitting to transport into those partes; and clothing, implements, furniture cattle, horses and mares and all other things necessary and for the use and desoine and trade w'th the people there, yf any be inhabiting in that country or *shall come out of other p'tes*, there to trade with the plantacōn and passing and returning to and froe all such comodities or marchandize as shalbe from thence brought without paying custome for *seaven years*.

Provided that none of the persons be such as shalbe hereafter by speciall name restrained and for their further incouragement that they shalbe free of all customes in Newfoundland for the space of *twenty one years,* and *from all taxes for ever* upon any merchandize at any tyme hereafter either upon importacōn *thether* or exportacōn *from thence into our Realme of England* or into any of our dominions (*except* onelie the five pounds per centum due for custome upon all such goods as shall be brought into our Realme of England according to the ancient trade of merchants), w'ch five pound per centum onelie being paid it shalbe thenceforth free for the said adventurers the same goods to exporte out of our said dominions into forraine p'tes without any custome.

Provided that the said goods be shipped out within thirteen months after the first landing.

And every governours maie for their defence and saftie repell by force and armes by sea and land and by all waies and meanes all persons as without the speciall licence of the tresurer shall attempt to inhabite within the severall precincts and also all persons as shall attempt distruction invasion hurte detriment or annoyance to the Colonie and to take all persons with their shipps and goods and other furniture trafficking in any harbour creeke or place within the limmitts of any colony to be made within any the limmitts aforesaid and not being allowed by the companie to bee adventurers or planters of the Colony untill such time as they being of any realme under our obedience shall paie or agree to pay to the officer deputed over and above such subsidie as the company is to paie five pounds per centum upon all goods so brought in thither *other than such as shalbe brought in for the necessarie use of fishing as hath beene heeretofore accustomed* and also five pounds per centum upon all goods shipped out from thence *other than fishing and other necessaries requisite to fishing* and being straungers and not under our obedience until they have paid over and above such subsidie as the company is to pay tenne pound per centum and the same sommes of money during the space of *one and twentie years shalbe wholly* employed to the *benefitt of the companie* and the one and twenty years *ended* the same shall be taken *to the use of us* by such officers as by us shalbe thereunto appointed.

Alsoe that all persons being our subjects w'ch shall goe and inhabite within any Colony and everie of their children and posteritie that shall to be borne there shall enjoye all liberties of free denizons and naturall subjects within any of our other dominions to all intents and purposes as if they had beene abiding and borne within this our Realme of England &c.

And for as much as it shalbe necessary for all our loving subjects as shall inhabite within any those territories to determine to live together in the feare and true worshipp of allmightie god Christian peace and Civill quietness each with other whereby every one maie with more safetie pleasure and profitt, enjoy that whereunto they shall attaine with great paine and perrill.

Wee graunte that governours officers and ministers according to the nature and limitts of their offices and places respectively shall in Newfoundland or in the waie thither and from thither have absolute power to punish, pardon and rule all subjects of us as shall adventure themselves in any voyage thither or that shall inhabite in the precincts of the land according to such orders as by the counsell shalbe established and in deserte thereof according to the good discretions of the governour as well in cases capitall and criminall as civill both marine and other, soe alwaies as the statutes as neere as convenientlie maie be agreable to the lawes of this our Realme of England.

And that such principall governours shall have full power to axercise Marshall lawe in cases of rebellion or mutinye in as our lieutenaunts in our counties of England have by force of their commissions.

And furthermore if any Adventurers or planters shall transport any moneys or marchandizes out of any of our kingdomes with a pretence to land sell or otherwise dispose them within the limitts of the territories and yet nevertheless being at sea or after he hath landed within the territories shall carry them into any foraigne country there to dispose thereof that the goods together with the shipp wherein such transportacon was made shalbe forfeited to us.

And further that in any difficultie of construction or interpretation of anything contayned in these our letters pattents the same shalbe taken and interpreted in most ample and beneficiall use of the company and every member thereof.

And finally our will is that all persons w'ch shall hereafter adventure any somme of money in and towards the plantacon and shall be admitted as adventurers in forme aforesaid and shall be inrolled in the booke or recorde be accounted and reputed adventurers and enjoye all priviledges as fully as if they had been named in these our letters pattents.

And lastly because the principall effects which we can desire of this action is the conversion of the people in those p'tes if any be there inhabiting unto the true worshipp of god and Christian religion in which respecte we would be loathe that any p'son should be permitted to passe that be suspected to asserte the superstitions of the Church of Rome.

Wee declare that none be permitted to pass to any voyage but such as shall first have taken the oath of supremacie for which purpose we doe give full power to the tresurer and any three of the counsell and to any our Mayors Baylieffes or any other our chiefe officers in any portes where any person shall take shipping to tender the oath to all persons as shall be sent to remaine and plant there.

Provided and we doe hereby declare to all Christians kings princes and States that if any persons which shall be of any Colony or any other by their license or appointment shall robbe by sea or land or doe any acte of unlawfull hostilitie to any the subjectes of us or any kinge being in amitie with us that upon complainte of such prince or their subjects we shall make open proclamacon within the partes of our realme of England commodious for that purpose that the persons having committed any robberie shall within the tyme to be limitted by such proclamacon make full restitution so as the said princes and others soe complayning may hold themselves fullie sattisfied and that if the persons should not make satisfaction accordinglie within such tyme that then it shalbe lawfull to us to put them out of our protection And that it shalbe lawfull for all to pursue with hostilitie the offenders.

In Witness whereof we have caused these our letters to be made pattente **Witnes** our selfe at WESTMINSTER the second day of MAIE in the eighth year of our Raigne of ENGLAND FFRANCE and IRELAND and of SCOTLAND the three and tortieth. *Per breve de privato sigillo.*

II. Letters from Cupids.

(a) Master JOHN GUY, his letter to Master SLANEY, Treasurer, and to the Counsell of the Newfound-land plantation.

RIGHT WORSHIPFUL,—It may please you to understand that it was the tenth day of this month of May before the barke of Northam, called the *Consent*, arriued here in New-found-land; notwithstanding that a ship of Bristoll, called the *Lionesse*, came to this countrey the second of May in a moneth's space: and the *Trial of Dartmouth* arriued here before in sixteene days. By reason of which stay of the aforesaid barke, nothing could be done to take any of the places desired: all being possessed before. So that the ship that commeth, whereof as yet there is no news, is to trust to the place here, which is reserved for her; which I hope will prove a good place. Some yeares as great a voyage hath bin made here, as in any place in this land: God send her hither in safetie. I haue not yet seene any of the country to the southward, or northward of this Bay of Conception since this spring, because I expected daily the arriual of the barke and thought it not fit to be absent here hence until she were arriued, and dispatched: but presently upon her departure, no time, God willing, shall be lost. The care that was taken to require generally the fishermen to assist us, and to supply our wants, if any should be, was most joyfull and comfortable to us which was most willingly accomplished by the most part of those which I have yet seen. Yet, God be praised, such was the state of all things with us as we were in no want of victuals, but had a great remainder, as you shall after understand.

The state of the autumne and winter was in those parts of Newfoundland after this manner. In both the moneths of October and November there were scarce six days wherein it either freezed or snowed, and that so little that presently it was thawed and melted with the strength of the sunne: All the residue of the aforesaid two months being both warmer and drier then in England. In December we had sometimes faire weather, sometimes frost and snow and sometimes open weather and raine, for in the latter end it was rainie, and was open weather. All these three moneths the winde was variable as it would euery fortnight visite all the points of the compasse.

The most part of January and February into the middle of March the frost continued: the winde being for the most part westerly, and now and then northerly; notwithstanding three or four times when the winde was at south it began to thaw and did raine. That which fell in this season was for the most part snow, which with the heate of the sunne would be consumed in the open places within a few dayes. That which abode longest was in February.

During this time many dayes the sunne shone warme and bright from morning to night: notwithstanding the length of this frosty weather, small brookes that did run almost in euell with a slow course, were not the whole winter three nights ouer frozen so thicke as that the ice could bare a dogge to goe ouer it, which I found by good proofe: for euery morning I went to the brooke which runneth by our house to wash. The snow was neuer aboue eighteene inches thicke generally out of the drift; so that the feare of wanting wood or water neuer tooke hold of us: for albeit we made no provision for them, yet at a minute of an houres warning we were furnished where there were lakes of fresh water that stood still and did not run, there it remained frozen able to beare a man almost three moneths, and was not dissolued untill the middle of Aprile. But where the ayre had entrance and issued out of them, there was no frost. When the spring wind in the winter time in England is at the northeast one moneth together, the frost is greater, and the cold more sharpe, then it is here at all. There was no moneth in all the winter that some of our company did not travel in, either by land or by water, and lie abroad and drinke water, in places distant two, three, foure and five leagues from our habitation, and sometimes lay in the woods without fire, and receiued no harme. When April came our spring began, and the first that did bud was the small kesei or the cornith tree. Our company was not letted in working abroad and in the woods and open ayre fifteen days the whole winter. We neuer wanted the company of rauens and small birds: So that the doubt that haue bin made of the extremity of the winter season in these parts of New-found-land are found by our experience causelesse; and that not only men may safely inhabit here without any need of stoue, but navigation may be made to and fro from England to these parts at any time of the yeare.

Concerning the healthfulnesse of these countries, we hauing bin now more than ten moneths upon this voyage, of nine and thirty persons, which was all our number which wintered here, there are wanting only foure; whereof one Thomas Percy, sawyer, died the eleuenth of December of thought, hauing slain a man in Rochester; which was the cause, being unknown unto mee until a day before he died, that he came this voyage. And one other called John Morris Tyler, miscarried the first of February by reason of a bruse. The third, called Marmaduke Whittington, was neuer perfectly well after he had the small poxe, which he brought out of Bristoll with him, who died the fifteenth of February. And the fourth, called William Stone, having at the first only a stiffnesse in one of his knees, kept his bed ten weekes, and would never stirre his body, which lasinesse brought him to his end, who died the thirteenth of April. Of the rest foure or five haue bin sicke, some three moneths, and some four moneths; who now are better than they were, except one. All of them, if they had had as good will to work, as they had good stomackes to their victuals, would long since haue bin recovered. One Richard Fletcher, that is master pilot here and a director of the fishing, reported unto me, that he was one of the company, consisting of forty persons, that went in a drumbler of Ipswich, called the *Amitie*, to the north part of Ireland about eleuen yeeres ago from London in the late Queen's service, under the charge of one Captaine Fleming, and continued there for the space of two yeares: In which time two and thirty died of the Scuruie, and that only eight of them returned home, whereof the said Richard Fletcher was one. So that the accident of death or sicknesse of any persons in these our parts of New-found-land is not to argue any unhealthfulnesse of this country, no more than Ireland is to be discredited by the loss of those two and thirty men; notwithstanding that there were to be had fresh uictuals and many other helpes, which this country as yet hath not, but in good time may haue.

From the first of October until the sixteenth of May our company had bin imployed in making of a store-house to hold our prouisions, and a dwelling house for our habitation, which was finished about the first of December; with a square inclosure of one hundred and twenty feet long and ninetie foot broad, compassing these two houses, and a work house to work dry in; to make boats or any other work out of the raine; and three pieces of ordinance are planted there to command the harboroughs, upon a platform made of great posts, and railes, and great poles sixteene foot long set upright round about, with two plankers to scoure the quarters. A boat, about twelue tons big, with a deck, is almost finished to saile and row about the headlands: six fishing boates and pinnesses: a second saw-pit at the fresh lake of two miles in length and the sixth part of a mile broad standing within twelue score of our habitation, to saw the timber to be had out of the fresh lake, in keeping two pairs of sawyers to saw planks for the said buildings, in ridding of some ground to sow corn and garden seeds: in cutting of wood for the collier, in coling of it: in working at the smith's forge iron workers for all needfull uses: in costing both by land and sea to many places within the Bay of Conception: in making the frame of timber of a farre greater and fairer house, then that which as yet we dwell in which is almost finished, and diuors other things. We haue sowed all sorts of graine this spring, which prosper well hitherto. Our goats haue liued here all this winter; and there is one lustie kiddie, which was yeaned in the dead of winter. Our swine prosper. Pidgens and cowies will endure exceedingly well.

Our poultry haue not onely laid egges plentifully, but there are eighteen young chickens, that are a week old, besides others that are a hatching.

The feare of wilde beasts we haue found to be almost needlesse. Our great ram-goat was missing fifteen days in October, and come home well againe, and is yet well with us. If the industry of men and presence of domesticall cattle were applied to the good of this country of New-found-land, there would shortly arise just cause of contentment to the inhabitants thereof. Many of our masters and sea-faring men seeing our safetie, and hearing what a milde winter we had, and that no ice had bin seen fleeting in any of the bayes of this country all this yeare (notwithstanding that they met one hundred and fifty leagues off in the sea, greate store of islands of ice) doe begin to be in loue with the countrey, and doe talke of comming to take land here to inhabit, falling in the reckoning as well of the commodities that they may make by the banke fishing, as by the husbandry of the land, besides the ordinary fishing. At the Green Bay, where some of our companie where a-fishing in November, they report there is great store of good grounds without woods, and there is a thousand acres together which they say may be mowed this yere. There is great store of deer, whereof they saw some divers times, and twice they came within shot of them; and the greyhound, who is lustie, had a course, but could not get upon them. But nearer unto Cape Razo, Reneuse, and Trepasse there is a great quantitie of open ground and stagges. It is most likely that all the sackes will be departed out of England before the returne of this, our barke, which shall not make any matter, because I am now of opinion that nothing should be sent hither before the returne of the ships from fishing. For as concerning sending of cattle, it will be best that it be deferred untill the next spring. And concerning vituals, in regard to the quantity, we haue of it remaining of old, together with that that it come now, as with the dry fish that here we may be stored with, I am in good hope there will not want any to last till this time twelue moneths. And according to the vituals which shall be found at the end of the fishing, the number of persons that shall remaine here all the next winter shall be fitted, that there shall not want, notwithstanding about Aihollantide, or the beginning of December, a ship may be sent, such a one as our Fleming was with salt from Rochel; for at any time of the winter ships may as well goe and come hither, as when they doe, especially before January. This summer I purpose to see most places between Cape Rase, Placentia, and Bona Vista, and at the returne of the fishing ships to entertaine a fit number of men to maintaine here the winter, and to set over them and to take the care of all things here, with your patience, one master William Colton, a discreete young man, and my brother, Philip Guy, who haue wintered with me, and haue promised me to undertake this charge untill my returne the next spring, or till it shall be otherwise disposed of by you, and then together with such of the company as are willing to goe home, and such others as are not fit longer to be entertained here, I intend to take passage in the fishing ships, and so return home, and then betweene that and the spring to be present, to give you more ample satisfaction in all things, and to take such further resolution as the importance of the enterprise shall require, wherein you shall finde me alwayes as ready as euer I have bin to proceede and goe forward, God willing. And because at my comming home it will be time enough for mee to lay before you mine opinion touching what is to be undertaken the next yeare, I will forbeare now to write of it, because you should be the sooner aduertised of our welfare, and because such of the company as are sent home both for their owne good, and that the unprofitable expense of vituals and wages might cease. I have laden little or nothing backe, that the said company might the better be at ease in the hold. Onely there is sent three hogsheads of charcoels, where numers 1° is, they are of burch, No. 2° is, of pine and spruce, No. 3° is of firre, being the lightest wood, yet it maketh good coles, and is used by our smithe. I send them because you shall see the goodnesse of each kinde of cole. Also I send you an hogshead of the skinnes and furres of such beasts as have been taken here, the particulers whereof appeare in the bill of lading.

While I was writing I had newes of the *Vineyard*, the ship which you send to fishing, to haue bin in company with another ship that is arriued on this side of the Banke and that the master intended to goe to Farillon or Ferland. God send her in safety. So praying God for the prosperity of your Worships and the whole company, with hope that his diuine Maiestie, which hath giuen us so good a beginning, will alwayes blesse our proceedings. My dutie most humbly remembered, I take my leaue.

Dated in Cupers Coue, the 16th of May, 1611.

(b) GUY'S LETTER OF JULY 1612.

RIGHT WORSHIPFULL, by my last of the 17th of June [not preserved] I wrote you of the estate then by the Holland ship, which I hope is long since safely arrived, together with Master Colston who hath (I doubt not) made by word of mouth full relations of all matters. Because the proceedings of one Easton are most fit to be knowne who remained in Harbour de Grace trimming and repairing his shipping and taken munitions &c. together with about a hundred men out of the Bay, he purposes to have five hundred out of the land before he goeth. Two several companies of 180 men each being discontented have stolen away from him in two ships of Barnstable and Plimmoth that they tooke.

As I sailed from hence towards Renoose in a small Barke, I fell into one of their hands and one of my company was hurt with a muskett. There was one of their crew that wintered with me here the first year, by whose meanes, and because I was in the Bark they made shew, that they were sorry that they had meddled with us. And so they departed from us without coming aboard. That which they sought after was men to increase their number." Then Guy mentions that Easton had plundered all along the coast and was then at Feiriland waiting to hear news of his pardon [which was granted but never reached him] which if he did not get he would seek the protection of the Duke of Florence [which he eventually did].

(c) COLSTON'S LETTER IN 1613.

We have not the actual text of this, but Purchas printed it in substance on p. 930 of the 1617 edition and also on p. 1880 of the 1625 edition.

William Colston describes the winter of 1612-13 as being more severe than that 1611-12. They had there Filherds, Fish, Makerels, Foxes, in the Winter: Partridges white in the Winter, in Summer somewhat like ours, but greater; they are much afraid of Rauens: they killed a Wolfe with a Mastiue and a Grey-hound. Nicolas Gure's wife was delivered of a lusty boy March 27. Then he described a voyage made by Guy and thirteen others in the *Indeavour* and five in the *Shallop* in October 1612 to Sauage Harbour, Trinity Bay, where they found houses of Sauages which were nothing but poles set round and meeting in the top, ten foot broad, the fire in the middest, couered with Deeresskins. They are of reasonable stature, beardlesse, and in some conditions like those which Sir M. Frobisher discovered, broad-faced, full-eyed, coloured on their faces and apparell with red Oaker. Their Boates of barke, as in Canada, twentie foote long, four and a halfe broad, not weighing a 100 weight, made in forme of a new Moone, which carry foure men, and are by them carried to all places of their remouings.

A few days later they met with the Natives; Whittington, Tipton, Guy himself, and Master Teage landed and bartered with them. All along the coast they carefully abstained from taking any of the furs evidently left by the natives for trade without leaving some trinket in exchange, thus carrying out the instructions given by the Company to Guy. [*See also* p. 133.]

There wintered 1612 fiftie foure men, six women and two children. They killed there, Beares, Otters, Sables, sowed Wheat, Rye, Turneps, Coleworts. Their Winter till April 1613, was dry and cleere with some frost and snow.

Divers had the Scurvie, whereto their Turneps, there sowne, were an excellent remedie, no lesse then Cartiers Tree. April was worse then the middest of Winter by reason of East windes which came from the Islands of Ice, which the current bringeth at that time from the north.

Purchas continues: The same I have seene confirmed by a letter of Thomas Dermer, one of that Colonie dated at Cupers Cove, the ninth of September last, 1616. In other moneths, hee sayth, the Temperature is as England. He mentions Muske-Cats and Muske-Rats in those parts; the fertilitie of the soyle in producing Pease, Rye, Barly and Oates; probabilities of Metals, with promises of more full Relations hereafter.

III. Letters from Ferryland.

(a) A letter from Captain Edward Wynne, Governor of the Colony of Ferryland, within the Province of Avalon, in Newfoundland, unto the Right Honourable Sir George Calvert, Knight, His Majesty's Principal Secretary, July, 1622.

May it please your Honour,—

Upon the 17 day of May, I received & have your letters of the 19 of February from the hands of Robert Stoning. Upon the 26 of the same, a ship of Master Jennins with your people and provision arrived here in safety; and from the hands of Captain Powell I received then your Honours Letters of 14th March. And upon the last of June Master James came hither, from Renouze and the Salt-maker Master John Hickson; from whose hands I received two Letters more; that by Master James being of the 4th May, & the other by Hickson of the 10th of the same.

All these being received by me, with an humble & a most thankful hand, first, unto God for your Honours health, and next, to your Honour for your continuall favour towards me, beseeching the same Almighty God, long and long to continue your health, to the advancement of his glory, both here, at home and elsewhere: I most humbly pray you to build upon my dutiful care and diligence, in the setting forwards and following of your Honours businesse, even to your best advantage, and advancement of the worke, and also that I shall bee a dutiful observer of your pleasure & commandment.

And so with the like humility, I doe present your Honour with the good tydings of all our healths, safety and good successe in our proceedings (God's holy name be praised for it). It followeth now (as my duty requireth) that I render unto your Honour a due account of what hath been done by us here this yeere, and of all things else, which appertaines unto me to doe.

Therefore it may please your Honour, that as soone as I had delivered my last letters of the 5 of September, I immediately addressed my self onely to our businesse. Notwithstanding our diligent labour & extraordinary paines-taking, it was All hallowtide before our first range of building was fitted for an habitable being. The which being 44 foot of length, & 15 foot of breadth, containing a hall 18 foot long, an entry of 6 foot, & a cellar of 20 foot in length, and of the height betweene the ground floore and that over head about 8 foote, being devided above, that throughout into foure chambers, and four foot high to the roofe or a halfe storie. The roofe over the hall, I covered with Deale boords, and the rest such thatch as I found growing here about the Harbour, as sedge, flagges and rushes, a farre better covering than boards, both for warmth & litenesse. When I had finished the frame, with onely one Chimney of stone worke in the hall, I went forward with our kitchin, of length 18 foot, 12 foot of breadth, and 8 foot high to the eves, and walled up with stone-work, with a large Chimney in the frame. Over the kitchen I fitted another Chamber. All which with a staire case and convenient passages both into the kitchin and the rooms over it, were finished by Christmas Eve. This is all the building with a hen house, that we have been able to accomplish before Christmass.

Many things else were done by us in the interim, as the getting home of timber trees, firewood, the raising up of a face of defence to the waterside ward, with the earth that we digged both for cellar & Kitchin roome (which we found a very laborious worke) also the sowing of some wheat for a triall, and many other businesses besides.

After Christmas, we imployed our selves in the woods especially in hard weather, whence we got home as many boord-stocks, afforded us above two hundred boords and above two hundred timber trees besides. We got home as much or as many trees as served us to palizado into the Plantation about foure Acres of ground, for the keeping off of both man & beast, with post and rayle seven foote high, sharpened in the toppe, the trees being pitched upright and fastened with spikes and nayles. We got also together us much fire wood, as will serve us yet these two moneths. Wee also fitted much garden ground for seede, I meane, Barley, Oates, Pease, and Beanes. For addition of building, we have at this present a Parlour of foureteene foote besides the chimney, and twelve foot broad, of convenient height, and a lodging chamber over it; to each a chimney of stone worke with staires and a staire case, besides a tenement of two rooms, or a storie and a halfe, which serves for a store house till we are otherwise provided. The Forge hath been finished this five weekes: The Salt-worke is now almost ready. Notwithstanding this great taske for so few hands, we have both Wheat, Barley, Oates, Pease, and Beanes about the quantity of two acres. Of Garden roome about halfe an acre: the corne though late sowne is now in earing; the Beanes and the goodliest Pease that I ever saw, have flourished in their bloomes this twenty dayes. We have a plentiful kitchin garden of Lettice, Raddish, Carrets, Coleworts, Turneps and many other things. We have also at this present a flourishing medow of at least three Acres, with many hay-cocks of exceeding good hay and hope to fit a great deale more against another yeere. In the beginning of the last winter, sunke a well of sixteene foote deepe in the ground, the which affords us water in a sufficient measure. The timber that wee have got home first and last, is above five hundred trees of good timber. There have beene about three hundred boords besides the former, sawed since the arrival of Captaine Powell. We have also broken much ground for a Brew-house roome and other Tenements. We have a wharfe in good forwardnesse towards the Low-watermarke. So that our indevour that way affoords a double benefit, the one of ridding and preparing the way to a further worke, the other of winning so much voyd or waste ground to so necessary a purpose as to enlarge this little roome, where on (with your Honours leave and liking) I hope to fortifie; so that within the same, for the comfort of neighbour-hood, another row of building may be so pitched that the whole may be made a prettie streete. For the country and climate; it is better & not so cold England hitherto. My comfort is, that the Lord is with your Honour, & your designes: for wee have prospered to the admiration of all the beholders in what is done. And thus with my humble dutie remembered, I rest,

Your Honour's most humble and faithfull servant,

EDWARD WYNNE.

Ferryland 28. July, 1622.

Post scr.—The ship with the rest of our provision arrived here this morning; and what is omitted by me, shall by Gods help shortly be performed. Your Honour hath greater hopes here, then here to fore I have been able to discerne. All things succeede beyond my expectation.

(b) POWELL'S LETTER TO BALTIMORE.

Right Honourable:

May it please your Honour to understand, that on the 18. of April, my self, and all the company, whose names I sent you in the list, by my last from Plymmouth tooke shipping there and on the 26. of May (God's Holy Name be ever praised for it) wee all arrived safe & in good health in Newfoundland. Our journey proved so long by reason of the contrary winds we continually had,

For at the least three weeks to-gether, wee were forced to traverse the Seas to and againe, and got not forward to the west ward in all that time one hundred leagues. The accidents which happened in our overbound passage were these: The first weeke after our being at sea, three of our Ewe-Goats, by reason of their extreme leane-nesse when they were bought and brought aboord, died, so that now we have but onely one Ewe-Goate and a Buck Goate left: the other Buck dying like wise within few dayes after our landing. On the 16. of May the furnace in our ship tooke fire, and as God would have it, burst forth in the daytime otherwise it had endaungered both ship and us. On the 26. as aforesaid, early in the morning we descryed land in Newfoundland, a little to the north ward of the Bay of Bulls, and before night came to anchor in Capeling Bay within one league of Ferryland. The next morning our ship came about to Ferryland Harbor and there landed all our people, where we found the Governour & all his company in good health, as we all continue in the same, praised be God for it.

The Coast and Harbours which we sailed by, are so bold & good, as I assure my self there can be no better in the world: but the Woods along the Coasts, are so spoyled by the Fishermen, that it is a great pity to behold them, & without redresse, undoubtedly will be the ruine of this good land: For they wastfully barke, fell, and leave more wood behinde them to rot, then they use about their stages, although they imploy a world of wood upon them: and by these their abuses doe so cumber the Woods every where near the shore, that it is not possible for any man to go a mile in a long houre. The Land where on our Governour hath planted, is so good and commodious, that for the quantity, I think there is no better in many parts of England. His house which is strong & well contrived, standeth very warme, at the foote of an easie ascending hill, on the South-east, and defended with a hill, standing on the further side of the Haven on North-west: The Beach on the North and South sides of the Land locke it, and the seas on both sides are so neere and indifferent to it, that one may shoot a Bird-bolt into either Sea. No cold can offend it, although it bee accounted the coldest Harbor in the Land, and the Seas doe mak the Land behind it to the South-East, being neere 1000 Acres of good ground for lay, feeding of Cattell, and plenty of wood, almost an Island, safe to keepe any-thing from ravenous beasts. I have, since my comming, beene a little abroad, and finde much good ground for Medow, Pasture, and arable, about Aquafort, as well neere unto the head of the Harbor, as all the way betweene that & Ferryland. The neerenesse of the place, and the spacious-nesse of those grounds aforesaid, will give comfort and help to the present Plantation, and quickly ease your Honours charge, if a Plantation bee there this next Spring settled. If therefore it will please your Honour to let me be furnished against that time, but with thirteen men, and give mee leave to settle my selfe there, I make no doubt (God blessing my endeavours) but to give your Honour, and the rest of the undertakers such content, that you shall have good incouragement to proceed further therein. So for this time being loth to trouble your Honor any further until the returne of Master Wicot, I humbly take my leave, and ever rest ready to doe your Honour all possible service to the uttermost of my power.

Your Honors humbly at command,
DANIEL POWELL.
Ferryland 28. July 1622.

(c) WYNNE'S LETTER, 17TH AUGUST 1622.

The copy of another letter to Master Secretary Calvert, from Captaine Wynne, of the 17 of August 1622. May it please your Honour;

Upon the 17 day of May, your Honour's Letters of the 17 of February, I received here by the hands of Robert Stoning &c. And so forward as in his former Letter of the 28 July, relating the manner and proportion of the building.

We have Wheate Barly Oates and Beanes both eared and codded, and though the late sowing might occasion the contrary yet it ripens now so fast, that it carries the likelihood of an approaching harvest.

We have also a plentifull Kitchin-Garden and so ranke that I have not seene the like in England. We have a medow of about three Acres.

At the *Bristow Plantction*, there is as goodly Rye now growing as can be in any part of England: they are also well furnished with swine and a large breed of Goates, fairer by far than those that were sent over at first. It may please your honour to understand, that our Saltmaker hath performed his part with a great deale of sufficiency by whom I have sent your honour a barrel of the best salt that ever my eyes beheld. I shall humbly also desire you to remember my last years suite that our delicate Harbours and Woods may not be altogether destroyed. For there hath been rinded this year not so few as 50,000 trees and they heave out ballast in the harbours though I looke on. Asks for men accustomed to labour, six Masons, foure Carpenters two or three Quarry Men, a Slater or two, a Lyme-burner and Lymestones, a good quantity of strong laths, a couple of strong maids, that (besides other work) can brew and bake and wheeles hemp and flax, and a convenient number of West-Countrey laborors to fit the ground for the Plough. Asks for Guns and a gunner and many other things—A compleate Magazine of requirements. I went to Formose and

Renouze upon the fourth of this month and bought salt for the next yeares fishing amounting to 186 hogs-heads, because it is so deare in England.

The last yeere I shewed your Honour of much courtesie receiued from sundry Masters. Many this yeere haue done the like, though some like not our flourishing beginning.

Your Honours &c.

Ferryland 17   EDWARD WYNNE.
August, 1622.

[Then follow, in Whitbourne's 1623 edition, 32 names of those that stay with Wynne that year.] He looked for a Mason and one more out of the Bay of Conception.

(d) N. H.'s LETTER, AUGUST 1622.

The coppy of a letter from N. H. (Nicholas Hoskins?) a gentleman living at Ferryland to a worthy friend W. P. of the 18 of August 1622.

After describing the climate and country he says " in the Whitson-holy daies (I taking with me Master Stoning) did coast some ten miles into the Country, Westward from our Plantation to make some discovery and to kill a Deere and being some 5 miles into the Land where we lodged that night, we found much champion ground of good levels of one two three or four hundred acres together, and at the foot of each hill we alwaise met a faire fresh River which did quench my thirst as well as Beere. We travelled three days but found no Deere save their footings which came to passe by meanes of a great fire that had burned the Woods, a little before, ten miles compasse. It began between Fermouse and Aquafort, it burned a week and then was quenched by a great raine.

" I know not who or what he was that gave fire to it but I think he was a servant hired by the deuill who will pay him for his worke. In the night the Woolves being neer did somewhat affright us but did not hurt us for we had dogs, fire and sword to welcome them." Then follows a further description of various sorts of game and fish. . . . . . "Manny faire Flowers I haue seene heere, which I cannot name, although I had learned Gerrard's Herbal by heart. . . . . . . I wrote in haste to satisfy myselfe, desiring you to looke throught it as thorow a prospective glasse, wherin you may discerne a farre off, what I have seene neere hand &c.

Your servant to be
commanded, N. H."

IV. The Charter of Avalon to Lord Baltimore, 1623.

(*Sloane MSS.*, 170.)

JAMES by the Grace of God King; Whereas our right trusty Counsellor Sir George Calvert being excited with a laudable and pious zeale to enlarge the extent of the Christian world and therewith of our Empire hath heretofore to his great coste purchased a certain region in a country of ours called Newfoundland not yet husbanded or planted though in some parts thereof inhabited by certain barbarous people; And intending now to transport thither a very great colony of the English Nation hath humbly besought us to confirm all the said region with certain priveledges requisite for good government.

BOUNDARIES.

And by the said Pattent of ye said Province contains all ye entere portion of land as aforesaid, beginning southerly from the midde part of a certain neck or promintary situate between the two harbours of Fermose and Aquofort, and from thence following the shore towards ye north unto the middle part or half way over a little harbour called in that regard Petit Port or Petit Harbour, which boundeth upon the south part of the plantacion of St. John's, including the one half of a certain fresh river that floweth into the said porte of Petit Harbour, and so extending along the south border of the said Collony of St. John's, extendeth itself to a certain little bay called Salmon Cove lying on the south side of the Bay of Concepcion, including the one half of the river that falleth into the said cove as also ye one half of ye said cove itself from whence passing along ye shore towards the south, and reaching unto ye bottom thereof where it meets with the land of John Guy, Citizen of Bristolle named Sea Fforest is bounded with a certain river or brooke which there falleth into the Sea, and from the mouth of the said brooke aforesaid unto the furthest spring or head thereof from thence passeth towards the south for six miles together along the borders of the said John Guie's his plantation, and thence crossing over westward in a right line reacheth unto the Bay of Placentia, and the space of one legue within the said Bay from the shoare thereof, thence turning again towards the south passeth along the harbour of Placentia with the like distance from the shoare, and descending unto New Falkland towards the north west part thereof it reacheth itself in a right line eastward, continuing the whole southerly length upon the said New Falkland unto the middle part or point of the Promentary or neck of land aforementioned between the Ports of Ffermose and Aquofort, at which place is described and finished the perambulance or the whole precint, &c. &c.

All the islands within ten leagues of the Eastern shoare of the said region.

POWERS.

The patronage and advowsons of all Churches to be built there. Civil Rights as full as the Bishop of Durham. Region to be held in capite by Knights service, yielding a fifth part of all gold and silver. That the region may be Eminent above all other parts of Newfoundland and graced with larger titles we have thought fitt to erect the same into a Province, to be called the Province of Avalon. Power to make laws, appoint judges; to Pardon, on an emergency to make special laws without the consent of the freeholder; to muster & train men and declare Martial law; to confer titles and incorporate towns. To be free from all customs and power to import and export to England and foreign countries all goods for ten years; afterwards to pay such customs as our subjects are bound to pay and no more. Power to constitute ports of entry at which all ships must unlade and lade, any custom to the contrary notwithstanding.

Saving always and ever reserved unto all our subjects free liberty of fishing as well in the sea as in the ports of the province and the priveledge of drying and salting their fish as heretofore they have reasonably enjoyed which they shall enjoy without doing any injury to Sir George Calvert or to the dwellers and inhabitants and specially in the woodes and be liable for damages. Power to enjoy all customs payable or accruing. And We shall at no time hereafter make any tax upon land tenements or merchandize laden or unladen within the province and this declaration is to be a full discharge to all officers. No interpretation bee admitted whereby Gods holy and true Christian Religion or the allegiance due to us suffer any prejudice— Signed at Westminster the 7 of April in the 21 years of our reign of England.

V. Lord Baltimore.

The first letter relating to his colony is from Ferryland, dated Sep. 5, 1621. Captain Wynne, his Agent, writes that he had arrived with 12 men. In 1622 Captain Daniel Powell arrived with 22 more.

Wynne says the first range of buildings erected about All Hallow Tide was 44 feet long by 15 feet wide containing hall, entry cellar, four chambers, kitchen, staircase, passage, &c. This building was at the foot of the Downs facing the sea. "He raised up a face of defence to the water side ward; sowed wheat for triall and many other businesses besides. After Christmas he built a parlour fourteene foote long and twelve foot broade a lodging chamber, a forge, salt works, a well sixteen foote deepe, a brewe house, a wharfe and a fortification so that the whole may be made a prettie street."

Aug. 17th, 1622. He gives an account of his crops and sends home a barrel of salt as a sample.

Wynne was a Welch man and his emigrants as we learn from his contemporaries were also from Wales.

July 28, 1622. We have a letter from Capn. Daniel Powell evidently a West Country man. He describes the death of "three ewe goats by reason of their extreme leanesse; one ewe and buck goat survived."

Both Powell and Wynne so plundered the unsuspecting Baltimore, that at last he had to visit the Colony to look after his interests. He writes to Lord Stafford in 1627 that "it was necessary for him to go over and settle the Colony in better order or lose the fruit of all his exertions" (*Stafford Corres.*, i. 39.) He originally intended to come out in 1625 (not suspecting the failure of his schemes, for according to Sir Wm. Alexander, Wynne had contrived to make some appearance of profit) but was prevented:—"March 15 1625 : George Calvert to Coke." I intend shortly God willing a journey to Newfoundland to visit a plantation I have begun there some years since. I hired the ship called *Jonathan* now in the River for the transport of myself and such plants as I carry with me. But I understand she is stayed for the King so I must give place. But I am by that means utterly disappointed and you should do me the duty to clear her and her marriners and also the *Peter Bonaventure* for which I contracted for carrying cattle. Whatever favour you do me herein my Lord Duke will not be displeased at it. (*Cowper MSS.*)

In 1627 he made his first visit to Newfoundland to see how bad matters really were but only stayed a few weeks. In 1628 he took with him his wife and all his children, except his eldest son, to permanently reside in his Plantation, his sons-in-law, Sir R. Talbot & William Peasely, accompanied him. At Ferryland they lived in a large substantial stone house, the scene in later years of many an incident connected with the Kirkes, Downings, Treworgie, and others. The house was standing in 1674; Sir Joseph Williamson mentions it as being only a "quoits throw" from the shoare, and it appears to be depicted upon Fitzhugh's map in 1693; a view of it is given. The Baltimore's claim to have spent £30,000 on buildings and breaking up land at Ferryland. The Kirkes also spent some money, but either could not or would not say how much, perhaps it was very little.

In 1625, the last year of James's reign, Calvert, for his services to the Court, had been made Baron Baltimore, Ireland.

Bishop Howley says "If Lord Baltimore had had the good fortune to settle in St. John's, Trepassey &c" but these were outside his grant and his best available Harbour was Ferryland, admirably situated for defence from sea.

Soon after his arrival at Ferryland, Baltimore, in a letter to the King, describes his attack on "a French man of warre one Monsieur De La Rade of Deepe who with three ships and 400 men well armed and appointed came into my harbour of Cape

Broile, where he surprized divers of the fishermen took two of their shippes in the harbour and kept possession of them till I sent two ships of mine with some hundred men being all the force we could make upon the suddayne in this place where I am planted. Upon the approach of which ships near to the Harbour mouth of Cape Broyle one of them being 360 Tons with 24 pieces of ordnance, the French let slip their cables and made to sea as fast as they could leaving behind them both the English ships and 67 of their own crew which I made prisoners. We followed the chase so long as we saw any possibility of coming upp with them but they were much better of saile and we were forced to give over."

De La Rade had done much damage to the northward, so Baltimore went after him, found he had been driven away by a ship of London before he could get there.

"Hereupon being still vexed with these men (and both myselfe and my poore fisherie heere and many others of Your Majesty's subjects much injured this yeere by them) I directed my ship in consort with Captain Fearne's Man of Warre, then in this country, to seek out some of that nation at Trepasse a harbour to the South, where they used to fish. There they found six shippes 5 of Bayonne and one of St. Jean de Luz whom they took with their lading, being fish and trayne, and have sent them to England."

Wherefore Baltimore prays the King to send two Men of War to guard the coast. One of his prize ships the *St. Claude* was sent out under the command of Leonard Calvert Lord Baltimore's natural son. Bishop Howley says two ships were sent, the records show only one:—"Dec. 13, 1628. Sir F. Cottington to Lord Treasurer Weston: has granted *one* of the six Prize ships which Nicholas says are good and warlike." In December of the same year there is a Petition from Will Peasley, on behalf of Lord Baltimore, to the Lords Commissioners of the Admiralty that the *St. Claude* may be substituted for the *Esperance*, and in December a Warrant issued "to deliver *one* of the prize ships [*St. Claude*] to Leonard Calvert son of Lord Baltimore to be lent for Twelve months."

In 1628 there was a dispute between Lord Baltimore and the merchants about the French prizes taken in Newfoundland by their ships, the *Benediction* and the *Victory*. Baltimore claims for his part according to the consort ship, and very cunningly asks to have his letter-of-marque *antedated* to enable him to receive his proportion. We have only Baltimore's version, so we cannot decide the merits of the case.

From Ferryland on Aug. 19, 1629, Baltimore thanks the King upon his knees for the loan of *a fair ship*, complains of the malice and calumny of those who seek to make him appear foul in His Majesty's eyes, and of the slanderous reports raised at Plymouth last winter by an audacious man [Stourton] who was banished for his misdeeds; complains of cold and loss of life by sickness; asks for grant of a precinct of land in Virginia, where he wishes to remove some forty persons with such privileges as King James granted to him in Newfoundland.

Baltimore died in 1632 before his charter of Maryland was completed; it was, however, granted to his distinguished son Cecil, the second Lord, a far more able and energetic man than his father. He showed great ability, courage, and decision in dealing with his opponents in Maryland, and faced and overcame difficulties before which his father would have quailed. The questions between Kirke and Baltimore are fully set forth in the law proceedings between the contending parties; nominally the right to Ferryland was conceded to Baltimore by Charles II., but practically the result was of no benefit to him. The warrant directed to Sir Louis Kirke, Sir David's widow and his sons was issued in the reign of Charles II. [For more information on this subject read the note on Kirke.]

In 1754 the Baltimores renewed their claim to Avalon, but the Government decided their rights had lapsed through want of actual occupation and possession.

VI. Beothics.

Since the above was in print, I have examined a MS. in Lambeth Library which contains a much fuller description of Guy's visit to Trinity Bay than is given in Purchas's condensed account (p. 128). Doubling the Grates they came to Heart's Content, and from thence to Spread Eagle and Bay Bulls arm. Guy describes their pleasant intercourse with the Red Indians. They are, he says, of middle size, broad-chested, and very erect. They go bareheaded, wearing their hair somewhat long; behind they have a great lock of hair plaited with feathers, like a hawk's lure, with a feather on it standing upright by the crown of the head, with a small lock plaited before. They wore a short gown or cassock made of stag skins, the fur innermost, that came down to the middle of the leg, with sleeves to the middle of the arm, and a bearskin about the neck. Their hair was diverse, some black, some brown, some yellow. Some of their wigwams were covered with skins; they had other square-shaped houses covered with canvas obtained from some Christians, probably the Biscayans, who had also given them hooks, and a copper utensil which was kept very bright. Besides paddles, they had some oars shaped like the Biscayan oars. The canoe is also described; it exactly resembles the one at p. 372. Several Indian families must have resided at the bottom of Trinity Bay about this period.

CHAPTER VI.

REIGN OF CHARLES I.

1625-1649.

1625.—Capture of 27 Newfoundland ships and 200 persons by Turkish pirates. Vaughan's "Golden Fleece" published. Mason's capture of the *Good Fortune*, at Crookhaven. Baltimore prevented from visiting Avalon. Bill for maintenance, &c. of shipping thrown out by the Lords.

1626.—Three hundred and fifty families of English settled between Cape Race and Bonavista; 250 English vessels fishing in Newfoundland. Whitbourne's appeal for a Government post as inspector of provisions.

1627.—Lord Baltimore visits Ferryland for a few weeks; brought two priests; found inhabitants and an English clergyman, Stourton, in Conception Bay. Patent to Sir W. Alexander, of Nova Scotia, in 1621, confirmed by the King.

1628.—Baltimore returned to Ferryland with his wife and family. Dr. Meadus negotiating a purchase of part of the plantation from Slany for Lord and Lady Conway. Hayman's "Quodlibets" published. Baltimore drives away a French pirate, named De la Rade; prays for a convoy; one ship granted; dispute between Baltimore and the merchants about French prizes. Baltimore banishes Stourton.

1629.—Baltimore's priests come to England under assumed names; he again prays for a ship to protect his settlements; complains of Stourton, and asks for a grant in Virginia, and permission to move his family and dependants there. Baltimore abandoned Newfoundland; founded Maryland in Virginia.

1630.—Proclamation of Charles I. prohibiting disorderly trading with the Red Indians. Hayman's proposition to the King.

1632.—Death of Baltimore. Quebec, Port Royal, &c. restored to France at the peace of St. Germains.

1633.—Charles I., through the Star Chamber, made his celebrated code of regulations for the government of the Newfoundland fishery, establishing fishing admirals; first skipper arriving from England to be judge or vice admiral for fishing season. Proclamation for the observance of Sunday in Newfoundland.

1634.—Star Chamber issued a charter "to the merchants and traders to Newfoundland." Order in Council passed making the Bishop of London Ordinary of the Plantation.

1635.—Charles I. gave permission to the French to cure and dry fish in Newfoundland on payment of 5 per cent. on the produce; continued for 41 years. This was the first commencement of our difficulties with the French. Death of Mason.

1636.—Mayor of Weymouth visits the king at Woodstock to get a convoy for the Newfoundland fleet.

1637.—Cecil Lord Baltimore's petition against any alienation of his grant of Avalon. Grant to the Duke of Hamilton, Kirke, and others, of all Newfoundland.

1638.—Arrival of Sir D. Kirke at Ferryland.

1639.—Pompone de Bellievre complains of Kirke's collection of taxes from French subjects Bishop of Exeter and others petition against Kirke. Kirke's letter to Laud.

1640.—Further complaints against Kirke. Kirke dismissed, and John Downing, senior, appointed Governor by Patentees. Memorandum about Dutch trading in Newfoundland.
1641.—Cargo of dry fish shipped from Boston to Europe.
1642.—Civil war between Charles and the Parliamentary Party.
1643.—First cargo of fish sent from Boston to Bilbao in Spain.
1645.—First vessel sent from Boston to fish at Bay Bulls seized by a royal cruiser.
1646.—Treworgie married a Miss Spencer, of Newberry, Mass.
1647.—Governor Winthrop records a great storm in Newfoundland.
1649.—Letter from Charles to Kirke about asylum for Lady Hawkins. Kirke offers the king an asylum in Newfoundland. Trial and execution of the king. Commonwealth cruisers sent to defend the fishing ships against Prince Rupert. Kirke only allowed to take to Newfoundland sufficient men to man his ships.

The short and troubled reign of this unfortunate king is, and probably always will be, the battle-ground for a fierce political discussion between Monarchists and Republicans, Cavaliers and Roundheads. Our colonial records throw a vivid side-light on this disastrous period. The treatment of our unfortunate Island by Charles I. was uniformly cruel, tyrannical, and stupid. In every way the interest of the patentees— the courtiers—was preferred to the welfare of the planters. Charles, like his father James I., was influenced entirely by his personal feelings for his immediate adherents; whilst he defended and perpetuated the absurd monopoly of the Plymouth Company in New England against the rights and claims of English merchants and fishermen, he pursued an exactly opposite course in Newfoundland.

The king carried out his policy towards this Colony deliberately. From good, honest men, well acquainted with the Island, settlers, who had lived there, he received the very best advice as to how the Colony should be governed and settlement encouraged. Sir William Vaughan, his intimate friend and a staunch supporter of Royalty, in his "Golden Fleece" says:—[1]

CHARLES I.
From an engraving after Vandyke.

"Many ships from Newfoundland taken by Moorish Pirates. . . . More confusion amongst Fishermen of Newfoundland than any other for want of being sufficiently guarded. . . . King James did about three years past (1622 or 1623)

[1] Part II., p. 102, 1626.

see into the discomforts and directed a commission at the suit of the corporation [Guy's Company] for plan of Newfoundland to provide a couple of good ships in the charge of the fishermen to protect them from Pirates who a few years before had pillaged them the extent of £40,000 besides 100 pieces of ordnance and had taken away 1500 mariners to the hurt of Newfoundland and the Planters."

Vaughan urges that—

"The ships should be retained both in peace and war. That God had reserved Newfoundland for Britain as the next land beyond the sea and not above 9 or 10 days sail that it might be inhabited the sooner by Your Majesty's subjects . . . that the same God overlooks Newfoundland as Europe. . . . I am sorry to find so many hopeless in my country of Wales whereas close by us in Devonshire 150 ships go to Newfoundland transporting from thence those commodities without which Spain and Italy can hardly live. . . . Experience of this fishery sheweth that it yearly maintains 8000 people for six months in Newfoundland . . . products of the colony. tar, pitch &c. codfish, salmon, mackerel, herring &c. &c.

"The benefits of a colony would be to restrain our own fishermen [ship fishers] who seize on one anothers stages; it will serve to restrain their insolence who brag that they are there '*West and by law.*' Organization of a colony would prevent the depredations of the ship fishermen, firing the woods, stealing salt, and fish, casting ballast into the Harbours, &c. &c."

All these practical suggestions were addressed to royal ears that would not hear. The colonies under Charles were as much neglected and misgoverned as his Royal Navy, with its rotten ships and unpaid sailors.

Vaughan says:—

"Capt. Wynne and Welchmen settled Ferryland for Lord Baltimore. One man near Renoos killed 700 Partridges; 3 men catch in 30 days 25,000 to 30,000 fish worth with oil £160; many sail to Newfoundland in 12 to 16 dais about 600 leagues [1800 miles]; 500 to 600 ships yearly resort there; freight 20/- per ton 10/- for a man passenger. Newfoundland a good security for Spain and other foreign enemies as there are constantly between 300 and 400 of our ships there. [This includes fishing ships and cargo vessels.]

"1623. King James sent two ships of war as convoys.

"1626. Discontinued by Charles I. Wooden house best for cold weather. Exercise best to keep off scurvy. Strong liquor prejudicial in cold countries, barley water & spruce beer best. Salt costs England £20,000 annually; may be made in Newfoundland for 3*d.* per bushel. French salt costs 20*d.* per bushel."

It is absolutely necessary for us to see the contemporary records before we can believe that any king or government should decree that this great Colony was not to be inhabited, that any chance settlers remaining should be persecuted, hampered, and impeded in all their labours and industry, that though they were fishermen and had to live by the sea, it was solemnly decreed that none of them should reside within six miles of its shores; all these barbarities were made law in order that West Country fishermen should catch fish on the coast, and a few courtiers make their fortune.

Besides the good, sensible advice contained in Vaughan's book, there is more of the same character in another work written at Harbour Grace, in 1630.

"A proposition of profitt and honour proposed to my dread and gratious sovereigne Lord King Charles by Robert Hayman."

Hayman succeeded John Mason as Governor of Guy's Colony; one part of the Company seems to have separated from the Colony at "Sea Fforest," Cupids, and formed a plantation or colony at Harbour Grace, which they named "Bristolls Hope." We learn from Mason's letter that he had a fishing room or plantation there; and in 1697 the inhabitants told Abbé Baudoin that their harbour was the first place settled in the country by the English; that a man had died there in 1693 or 1694 aged 83. He might, possibly, be the son of one of Guy's settlers, but in all probability he was a descendant of one of the original planters long anterior to Guy's arrival—most likely a Davis, a Thistle, a Pike, a Pynn, a Crawley, or a Parsons—the oldest families in the Bay Metropolis.

Hayman proposes for the king :—

"To build a citie where I have placed your Carolinopole [Harbour Grace] and to privilege that Towne with that fishing. Your Majesty might likewise make it a Mart or free market for fish; has two Harbours three miles apart and would grow populous rich and strong. I would humbly pray this Island may be called Brittaniola.

"The French and Biscays do yearly in great number fish at the Mayne and dispossess us. Proposals about salt; also proposes to take Cape de Verd Island; offers further explanation in person and asks the King to decide in twenty-four hours. Many ship owners are forthcoming to aid the project." [It was an appeal to unwilling ears.]

"He presents a plat [map] of His Majesty's Dominions both possessed pretended and intended &c. but among the several lands God made you Lord over I recommend to Your Majesty's special viewe. a work left for you to finish and furnish with millions of Your subjects viz. Newfoundland.

"In this Island at one time I lived fifteen months together and since I have spent almost every summer in it. I had lots of time, being an overseer and no labour to do. But seeing to my grief the poor support of divers treatises, read over by some, liked by some, derided by others, and neglected by almost all, and these few have either insufficiently begun, or have been deluded and wronged by those they employed or mistaken in good meaning, or have not been able to spread or out of heart with poore lowt, unsupported retournes, or demands of new supplies.

"That unless Your Majesty suddainly assist this costly business is like to vanishe lamentably. . . . As to patents to certain noblemen . . . these noblemen were but only named, or adventured very little. Those gents were soon made weary; those merchants acquainted with most speedy gain first falling out among themselves by reason whereof the principal undertaker [Guy] a man of their qualitie, wise yet inconstant, falling off they concluded to divide the land into severall parts since when some have done a little to no purpose and the most nothing.

"I confess since that time divers noble gents have adventured somewhat, first Sir Percival Willoughbee, then Dr. Vaughan and have been annoyed by dishonest, idle, unfit men, those employed by them and my Lord Falkland, worse; only my Lord Baltimore after much injurie done him [evidently by Wynne & Powell] adventured happily thither himself, where seeing how to mend it and the goodness of the action resolved wisely to see his business done himself and Dr. Vaughan intends to follow his example. But experience of former and these times makes me jealous of their success unless Your Majesty steps in."[1]

He then shows how, in Ireland—

"No good was done until the King began to take the matter in hand, so Newfoundland Colonies will never flourish continuously unless undertaken by the King. If Newfoundland were peopled I dare prove that 1000 good ships only may succeed]. But it may be thought how we stand with France and Spain if a large quantity of fish were sent will have small vent, and I know the Mallowyans [men of St. Malo] have promised their King and the Biskans theirs to furnish them with this commoditie whereupon they have not only proclaimed forfeiture of importation thereof taken by us, but I heare in Spain Hamburghers were this yeare denounced for doing, but Your Majesty might easily amend this, in preventing theirs and making them glad of ours, for without this [fish] they cannot conveniently subsist. Hunger will break down walls. In Queen Elizabeth's time they had it from their enemie the Hollanders."[1]

DE LAET'S MAP, 1630.

Hayman then enumerates the products of the country—pitch, tar, timber, &c.

"Newfoundland is a land worth possessing. There is a rich fishing near this land called the Bank where yearly 400 French ships fish and from whence your subjects have never reaped any."[1]

In 1625 the Commons passed "a Bill for the maintenance and increase of shipping and navigation, and for liberty of fishing in Newfoundland, Virginia, and New England." The Bill was thrown out by Charles's party in the House of Lords. The Commons refused a subsidy, and Parliament was dissolved in anger. The question of free fishery was one of the causes which led to hostility between Charles and Parliament.

In Newfoundland he gave an exclusive monopoly of the Island fishery to the Western adventurers or ship fishermen from Devonshire against the settlers in the Island. Most tyrannical laws were enacted

CHAMPLAIN'S MAP, 1632.

[1] *B.M. MSS., Eg.* 2541.

ANCIENT FRENCH CUSTOMS.

for their governance, from which the English fishermen by express enactment were to be at all times exempted. These laws will be found in the Appendix to this chapter under the head of Star Chamber Rules.[1]

The extraordinary provision in these regulations, making the first rude English skipper who entered the harbour admiral and judge over all for the fishing season, seems to us, in this age, a monstrous anomaly; but it was, as the Rules declare, *an Ancient Custom*, now for the first time legalised. The old arrangement that the first who entered harbour was the admiral, prevailed not only amongst the English but with all the foreign fishermen. The ancient practice, however, was to change about each week. The most curious part of this proceeding is that a highly civilized nation like the French, under France's most able minister

HARBOUR GRACE.

Colbert, adopted precisely the same regulation. By the ordinance of Louis XIV., after prescribing most minute regulations about nets, &c., he gives the following Rules for the Newfoundland fishery:—

" 1. The first who shall arrive at or send his boat to the Harbour called Le Havre du Petit Maitre,[2] shall have the choice, and take the space of ground necessary for his fishery; he shall then put up at the place called the ' Scaffold of the Grapple ' a Bill signed by him stating the day of his arrival and the Harbour which he has chosen.

" 2. All other Masters on their arrival shall go or send to the same place, and write down on the same bill, the day of their arrival, the number of their men, and the name of the Harbour and place, which they have chosen, in proportion to the burthen of their ships and the number of their mariners.

---

[1] NOAKES, the framer of these rules, was Attorney General and the inventor of ship money and other illegal exactions.

[2] See JACOBSZ's map, 1621, p. 120.

"3. The captain that arrives first shall cause the Bill or placard to be guarded by one of his men, who shall remain upon the place till all the Masters shall have made their declaration, which afterwards shall be put into his hands.

"4. No Master or Mariners may settle in any Harbour or station, till they have made their declaration in the form aforesaid; nor shall they disturb any other master in the choice that he may have made under the penalty of 500 livres."

This law applied to all the coasts of New France. The first captain was to keep a correct account of all offences committed against this ordinance, and on his return it was to be delivered to the judge of the Admiralty Court. Ships fishing on the banks were not allowed to set sail at night. All French subjects, of what quality or condition soever, might cause ships to be built or bought, and carry on a trade at sea, by themselves or agents, without its being considered derogatory to their quality, provided they sold nothing by retail. The first French Master who arrived in the harbour was constituted, like his English prototype, Admiral, supreme Ruler, and Judge over all the French fishermen in the port. The fishing admiral still survives in the French prud'homme of the N.E. and West Coast.

STAR CHAMBER.

The Star Chamber Rules were for the benefit of the Duke of Hamilton, Sir David Kirke, and other partisans. When this extraordinary patent was granted, the Newfoundland settlers had been in possession of their homes for a long period. They had built houses and stages, and cleared small patches of ground. All this expenditure of money and labour, all their lawful title to their hard-earned possessions, was ruthlessly swept away, in order to gratify the cupidity of a few courtiers. As far as the king's grant could annul all the rights of former occupants and patentees under King James's charters, this new title to Hamilton and Kirke was intended to do so; there is no saving clause, no reservation; the whole Island is granted to the new patentees. This charter to the Duke of Hamilton, Kirke, and others has such an important bearing on our history that it is set out fully.

Nothing shows more clearly the treachery and ingratitude of Charles than his dealings with Lord Baltimore respecting this new grant. The king was bound by every sentiment of personal feeling and gratitude to treat the Calverts with kindness and consideration. The first Lord Baltimore had been the faithful, abject servant of his father, and his own great personal friend. The records show us how Charles acted in the matter. In February 1637 Cecil Lord Baltimore, in a petition, sets forth his grant and the large sum of money—£20,000—he had expended in the Colony; and that he had left a governor in the Island up to the time of his father's death. He says:—

"It is reported that some persons of quality have a design to demand customs upon all fish taken or sold in Newfoundland, which must needs trench upon his rights; desires that nothing may be done to his prejudice before His Counsel is heard and satisfaction given. If really for the King's service will lay his rights at His Majesty's feet, confident that his great charges will be taken into consideration."

In reply to this petition, in May of the same year, this answer was sent:—

"The King to the Commissioners for Foreign Plantations and all other officers and Ministers; is informed by Lord Baltimore that some grants concerning Foreign Plantations may pass the seals prejudicial to his letters patent for Newfoundland and Maryland. They are therefore commanded not to permit any patent commission or other warrant for plantation or discovery near the Provinces of Avalon and Maryland to pass which may in any way infringe upon the rights or privileges of Lord Baltimore and his heirs for whose better encouragement *the King engages his Royal word never to permit any 'quo warranto' or other proceeding for infringing or overthrowing either of his patents.*"

To show the value of the royal word of Charles I., on the 13th November of the same year, 1637, the charter was granted to Hamilton, Kirke, and others of the whole Island of Newfoundland; and the reason for this grant is set out, that Lord Baltimore, Lord Bacon, and others, to whom grants have been made, have deserted the Island. The contents of this remarkable patent afford a striking illustration of the high-handed tyranny of Charles I.; without the slightest regard for the settlers in the Colony, or the interest of the former patentees, Baltimore, Guy, Falkland, &c., who had expended large sums of money in developing the resources of the Island, he

142   REIGN OF CHARLES I.

gives away to strangers all their valuable possessions held under grants from his father, James I. The influence of Devonshire seems to have been all powerful at Court; all their policy is embodied in this deed. Settlers were not to dwell within six miles of the shores, and practically all their rights were given over to the ship fishermen from the West of England. Special power is given to the patentees to collect taxes from all strangers. Under this charter Sir David Kirke went out to Newfoundland and took possession of all Lord Baltimore's property. On this grant obtained by fraud and Court influence, the Devonshire fishermen always based their claim to exclusive rights of fishing and their right to banish the settlers from the shore. About the 20th February 1634 a charter was issued out of the Star Chamber to the merchants and traders to Newfoundland. This grant has been lost, but it evidently embodied the Star Chamber Rules and the orders in Hamilton's grant. The Crown did all it could do to destroy settlements and to injure the settlers. Fortunately, the king had no force to carry out his tyrannical policy. The charter was a dead letter. The planters continued to live about the harbours, creeks, and coves on the east coast from Cape Race

DUKE OF HAMILTON.
From an engraving after Vandyke.

to Cape Bonavista. The densest population was in the neighbourhood of St. John's. None of the noble patentees exercised any special control in this neighbourhood, at least over the English settlers, or anywhere else, except in the neighbourhood of Ferryland. They owned two rooms in St. John's Harbour, and these remained their sole possession. One was about the present Queen's Wharf and Messrs. March and Harvey & Co.'s premises; the other room was directly east of Messrs. Mudge & Co.'s, on the south side, known as the "Naval Dock and Storehouse," and still owned by the Imperial authorities. The patentee's business and fishing and trading operations were all carried on at Lord Baltimore's premises in Ferryland.

THE GRANT TO THE DUKE OF HAMILTON, SIR DAVID KIRKE, AND OTHERS, OF THE ISLAND OF NEWFOUNDLAND, 13TH NOVEMBER 1637.

After reciting that Lord Baltimore, Lord Bacon, and the London and "divers" other companies to whom grants had been made had deserted the Island, the king grants the whole Island to Hamilton, Kirke, and others between 46° and 53°—

"All being divided from the Continent by an arm of the sea . . . . and all rivers, Harbours, stages, ports, and forts, land and woods, lakes and buildings . . . . . and all and all manner of fish whatsoever in any of the seas or rivers . . . . gold, gems &c. . . . Patronage and advowson of the churches which are or shall hereafter be built and all Rights Jurisdiction &c. . . . which have at any time heretofore been held or enjoyed and they, the said Hamilton &c. to be the true and absolute Lords and Proprietors of the said Continent, Island and region of Newfoundland except only the allegiance due to His Majestye.

"Neither Hamilton &c. nor any Planter or Inhabitant shall fell wood *nor build within six miles of the sea* between Cape Race and Cape Bonavista save only that the Planters shall have liberty to fish there and cut wood for fishing as other our subjects have and enjoy . . . . And also shall have full power and liberty to build any fort or forts for defence of said Country and fishing and shall have timber where it may be spared to the least prejudice of the fishery . . . . Inhabitants shall not take up before the arrival of the fishermen all the best beaches within the capes aforesaid . . nor take away burn &c. any stage or any necessaries which they may leave there . nor shall commit any act or thing to alter change or disturb hinder or interrupt the manner and use of fishing now or at any time hereafter used or accustomed . . . . and all our subjects borne or to be borne within our Kingdom of England or in any of our Kingdoms or Dominions may from time to time and at all times peaceably hold use and enjoy ye freedom of fishing, in any of the seas, lakes, or rivers, of the said Island or in or about or adjoining with full liberty to land, salt, and dry fish. Yielding the one fifth part of all gold &c. to the Crown.

"Power to make laws with the assent of the freeholders or the major part of them. Freeholders to attend when summoned. Power to put the laws in execution and exact the penalty . . . . But the *said laws are not to extend to any fishermen who are to be for ever free from the jurisdiction of the Government of Newfoundland* who are to be subject to and immediately under ye order rule and government of us our heirs &c. as We shall from time to time appoint make and direct and unto the laws made in the 9th year of our reign which laws shall be inviolably kept and observed by the fishermen . . . power to grantees to appoint magistrates . . . . to punish and pardon offenders . . . . to execute justice and to see the said laws be observed if not contrary to the laws of England or prejudicial to the fishery . . . . Proprietors to make laws in case freeholders cannot be called . . . to publish and make them known. Leave to all to congregate there, and build forts, all the Inhabitants and children to be free denizens and to enjoy all English priviledges, to transport their goods without paying Customs provided they get leave in writing from the said Treasurer. Power to make warre and call to their standard all persons whatsoever and wheresoever (except fishermen) and to appoint a General . . . . to declare martial law . . . . to confer honours . . . . to incorporate Towns . . . only to pay customs on goods sent to England as natural born subjects . . Power to build forts . . . . . saving always and reserving to us &c. free and ample liberty of fishing in any of ye seas lakes rivers &c.

"Strangers to pay five per cent. after Christmas day next and the same by all strangers who shall buy fish, and the same for all oyles made there . . . and we will and require the said Proprietors to put this in execution . . . Collectors of Customs to receive the same before they load or depart. Proprietors to be collectors and to account to His Majesty. For their trouble Proprietors to have five per cent. from all strangers making use of any ground and the same five per cent. from all strangers that come there in sack ships and the like out of the oyles . . . These customs to last 51 years. The Crown to have ten per cent. thereof, and giving account of all gold &c. . . . The Proprietors confirmed in all things but the fishing and the sole trade of the country except the fishing. Power to admit partners merchants and others who are to have the same privileges as the others, not to pay any tax. Their ships not to be detained at any port except in case of invasion of England. Every one over Twelve years old to take the oaths upon the Holy Evangelists before Hamilton Kirke or his Deputy to establish the orthodox religion . . . Power to transport necessaries thither . . . All his subjects to aide and assist them."

No county in England contains so many small proprietors as Devonshire; no other county produced so many courtiers during the

FOWEY.

Tudor and Stuart period as this fair southern shire. The influence of this western aristocracy was bound up with the Devonshire adventurers to Newfoundland, and it was entirely to suit their selfish monopoly and greed that laws were enacted. Newfoundland, for more than a century, had been pouring wealth into the western counties. The landed gentry were directly or indirectly interested in this lucrative trade. Through this bus'ness the landlord was often paid his rent. The hard riding, hard drinking squires obtained their potent sherry, and port, and *aguardiente* from the Newfoundland fleet; the housewives' preserves, marmalades, dried fruit, and oil, all came from exchange with the foreigners in Newfoundland. Manufacturers of Bridport cordage and West of England cloth made a large portion of their sales through the Transatlantic fishery and trade. Devonshire was largely interested in the fishery; the western courtiers, powerful at Court, used their influence with the king to carry out the selfish, grasping policy of Devon. For two hundred years following we shall always find the Courtenays, Carews, Northcotes, and other great county families, uniformly assisting to keep Newfoundland simply as a fishing place for their countrymen. The fatal effect of this influence really begins in this reign. It had been attempted before, as we have seen, against Guy, but had failed. Now, however, it burst forth in full vigour, and for two centuries it fell like a blight upon the unfortunate Colony. Paralysing all progress and advancement, it was a fatal barrier alike to agriculture and the peaceful development of the great resources of the island. A Devonian myself, I should be utterly recreant to my duty as a historian if I did not fully set forth the dire effects of West Country influence upon the progress of the Colony.

Whilst nothing can palliate the selfish and persistent attitude of Devonshire traders towards the island, the only possible excuse for their conduct lies in the ignorance of the age, and the claim, or pretended claim, which the West Countrymen set up, that Newfoundland was their own possession, gained by their strong right arms, without aid from the Crown, and defended against all foreign foes by their own dauntless courage. The real blame attaches to the Government, who permitted such a destructive policy to be carried out. In all ages the rule of traders has been selfish and narrow. Bacon had the Devonshire men in his mind when, in his essay on plantations, he said: "Let not the Government of any " plantation depend upon too many counsellors and undertakers in the " country that planteth, but upon a temperate number, and let those be " rather noblemen and gentlemen than merchants, *for they look ever to* " *the present gain.*"

We have seen the constant danger to which both settlers and ship fishermen were exposed from pirates in the preceding period. In the first years of Charles's reign a new peril arose from the Turks. In many instances these so-called Sallee rovers were renegade Englishmen, Frenchmen, and Spaniards, who adopted the Turkish ensign simply as the most convenient flag under which to carry out their depredations on the peaceful commerce of Europe. The following letter from the Mayor of Poole to the Privy Council sets out in graphic terms the danger to which the ship fishermen were exposed from this new enemy, and the disgraceful condition of the Navy under the degenerate rule of the Stuarts. With the exception of two vessels sent out by James I. to protect and convoy the Newfoundland fleet at the instance of Vaughan, and one man-of-war lent to Lord Baltimore, no Royal ships ever visited the Colony during the early part of this reign.

"Letter from Mayor of Poole to Privy Council. Aug. 8th, 1625.

" Right Honourable my very good Lords,

"I have thought it my bounden duty to advertize Your Lordships that the fouerth of this August ther was taken some eyght or nyne leagues off from Plymouth by the Turkish men of warr belonging to Sallye, the *Anne of Poole*. The examination of her Mr. Nicholas Murray have sent Your Lordships here enclosed and with all ye great damage that ye Towne of Poole hath before this lately received having in captivitye diverse men with two shippes of this town taken by this fleete and now we heare that unlesse Your Lordships shall be pleased to take it into your consideration that ye Newfoundland fleete being about two hundred and fiftye sayle of shippes and barques of noe defence haveing some fower or five thousand men belonging to ye Westerne ports expected homewards scattering within this moneth may be provided for by some such provision as shall seeme best to Your Lordships which are not onely threatened to be surprised by this fleet of Sallye but also menacing that within this two years they will not leave his most excellent Majesty Saylors to man his fleetes. Thus leaving the busyneese of soe great consequence unto Your Honourable consideration soe with all humble dutye take my leave." [1]

Also from Mayor of Plymouth, August 12th, 1625:—

"Says there are general fears for the ships from Virginia and Newfoundland. The Turkish pirates [2] had taken in ten dayes 27 ships and 200 persons." [3]

And in the Weymouth Records [4] again of September 1636 :—

"The 300 English ships from Newfoundland will be in great peril from Turkish Pirates. The Mayor of Weymouth followed the King to Woodstock to get help for the [fishing] fleet but was only told the [Royal] fleet should come down with the first fair wind. The Mayor said this would only mitigate not cure the business. The Archbishop [Laud] striking his hand upon his breast said while he had life, he would do his utmost to advance so consequential a business, that within this twelve months, not a Turkish ship should be able to putt out."

This extract gives a vivid picture of the times, a remarkable illustration of the character of Charles I. We can imagine the anxious mayor galloping for his life to save the great fleet of merchantmen on which four fair counties were dependent almost for their existence, on whose safety hung the lives and fortunes of half the seamen from Devon, Dorset, Cornwall, and Somerset. The answer of the king shows his utter incapacity to appreciate the vital interests of his subjects. How

---

[1] *Records.*
[2] Such names as "Turks Gut" and "Turks Cove" in Newfoundland record the memory of these terrible corsairs.
[3] *Records.*
[4] H. J. MOULE, *Descriptive Catalogue of the Charters of Weymouth.*

differently Elizabeth or Cromwell would have acted; all their pride and patriotism would have been roused by this daring attack on Englishmen by outlandish pirates.

How imminent must have been the danger, how terrible the anxiety and fear of the chief magistrate, when it nerved his worship's poor diffident tongue to insist most strenuously, even in the august presence of majesty, on the necessity of sending off the Royal ships. Perhaps the most striking part of the story is the arrogance of Laud—the swelling pride of this little Protestant Wolsey—with his vague threat to annihilate the Turkish pirates. How much more practical it would have been had he used his influence with his Royal master to send immediate help to the endangered Newfoundland fleet.

Besides the ocean pirates, the fishermen suffered grievously from the pressgang; not only were men pressed for the Royal Navy, but even girls were captured to be sent out to the plantations : "October 19, 1613.
" —In Somerset it was reported that forty maidens had fled from their
" homes to obscure places to escape the pressgang."

Sir David Kirke, the active manager of Hamilton's Company, was one of the most remarkable heroes of this age; his gallant capture of Quebec and destruction of the French power in Canada, the most brilliant naval exploit in colonial history. The pusillanimous king threw away, at one blow, all the immense advantages he had gained for the struggling English colonies, and, with true Stuart ingratitude, left Kirke and his associates to bear the enormous expense of the expedition, undertaken under a direct commission from his sovereign.

The policy of scuttle is supposed to be one of the products of modern English statesmanship, but a knowledge of the dealings of the Stuarts with the English dominions in America will convince us that they fairly rivalled the nineteenth century rulers of England in this line. Sir David Kirke and a few gallant adherents had won Nova Scotia for the Crown of England; British sovereigns claimed the country by right of discovery; James I. had made a grant of it to the eccentric Sir William Alexander; Englishmen had it in possession; the young colonies of New England clamoured for its retention as a barrier against their ruthless foes, the French; yet, at the peace of St. Germains, 1632, notwithstanding England was then in possession of the principal French territories in North America—Quebec, Port Royal, St. Croix, and Pentagoet—by the thirteenth article of the treaty, all these places were restored to France.

Cromwell felt the loss of Nova Scotia so keenly that, even though at peace with France, he re-occupied the Colony, and sent out a Governor,

Sir Thomas Temple. In 1662 Charles II. intended to give it back to France, but New England sent such a spirited petition to the House of Commons, that the treacherous hand of the king was stayed for a time; by the treaty of Breda, however, Charles ceded Nova Scotia again to the French; the stout, old Governor Temple stood out; he and his adherents had spent large sums of money on the fortifications, and the country was not finally surrendered to our enemies until 1670. In the policy of scuttle, the Stuarts have a fair claim to pre-eminence.

Bishop Howley and Mr. Henry Kirke's accounts of Sir David are not quite in accord with the testimony of the English records. Kirke and his brothers, Louis and Thomas, were born in Dieppe; David was a member of Sir William Alexander's company; it was probably in some way to recompense him for his losses in the Quebec expedition that the king granted the patent, which was at first in his name alone. He came out to Newfoundland with one hundred men in 1638, accompanied by his wife and family; having taken possession of all Lord Baltimore's property at Ferryland he vigorously set to work to make money in the Colony, charged rent for stage rooms, sold tavern licences, and did a roaring trade in everything. The charter gave him authority to exact dues from foreigners; so he travelled all around the Island, and made every Frenchman and foreigner pay him a commission on their catch; so stringently did the old mariner wring these taxes from the French that on May 16, 1639, Pompone de Bellievre, Seigneur de Grignon, the French Ambassador, complained to King Charles, of Kirke's imposition on French subjects in Newfoundland, in the following letter :—

" L'on m'a aussi donné avis que les nommé Kerq avoient une patente du Roy de la G. B. pour lever quelque chose sur la pesche des morües, ce qu'ils se proposent de prendre non seulement sur les sujets du Roy de la G. B. mais generalment sur tous ceux qui iront pour faire cette pesches, ce qui seroit contraire a tout droit et à la liberté avec laquelle on en a usé jusques icy, ce qui fait que je m'imagine que le Roy de la G. B. ne l'entend pas ainsy et que personne autre que ses sujets ne se resoudra à le souffrir."

" I have also been informed that the said Kerq[s] have a patent from the King of Great Britain to collect something on the cod fishery and that they propose to take this not only from British subjects but also from all who go there to fish. This will be contrary to all justice and to the freedom which has been enjoyed there up to this time. I surmise that the King of Great Britain does not know what has been done and that no one but his own subjects will submit to this."

The king, in reply, referred the Ambassador to the Council Board, who reported :—

"The Lords having been acquainted by Mr. Attorney with the Commission granted to Sir David Kirke the Lord Chamberlain and others, it was decided that a firm but fair answer should be given and the imposition laid by the French on English merchants considered in justification."[1]

For once Charles was firm and decided.

The following ludicrous incident, duly recorded in the Calendar of State Papers, illustrates the extraordinary mode in which merchant

ENGLISH MAN-OF-WAR.
From Dudley's Arcano del Mare, 1646.

vessels were transformed into men-of-war, and the wretched condition of the Royal Navy under Charles I.:—

"Petition of James Marquis of Hamilton and the rest of the Adventurers of Newfoundland To the King. John Kirke Manager of their business in London sold to Nathan Wright and Richard Craudley Merchants of London 6000 qtls. of Newfoundland fish at 10 - per qtl., far under the value, on condition of their setting out the *Confident* as a man of war to attend the Petitioners fleet; but Edward Mabb the Master discovering to the French that *he was no man of war* the French afterwards refused to pay any more ground leave, and Wright and Craudley will not pay for the 1000 qtls. of fish value £1346 previously delivered by the French. Pray that the business may be referred to some honourable persons to determine. Referred to Lord Keeper &c. . . . . . ."[1]

In dealing with both the Tudor and the Stuart period we must always remember that in our sense of the word there was neither organized government, army, nor royal navy then existing, no civil service, or great departments of State, home, foreign, or colonial; there were only the rudiments of such institutions. In many of the writers, even of the Stuart period, we have mention of a "man-of-war of Torbay," a "man of war of London" or "Bristol"; these were simply

[1] *Records.*

armed merchantmen, sometimes with a royal commission, sometimes without, in many cases simply piratical cruisers who made war on Frenchmen and Spaniards, occasionally when no better opportunity offered plundering their own countrymen.

For one more year Kirke went on mulcting the foreigners and rolling up money, leasing out stages, selling liquor, and doing the general Newfoundland business; he acted as monarch of all he surveyed, and his rude strong hands fell heavily on the settlers; even the sturdy West of England fishermen had to submit to this tyrannical old sea captain. During the first year of his reign, as we learn from Kirke's letter to the Earl of Pembroke, 25th January 1639,[1] the West of England had risen in arms; the Bishop of Exeter stood by his diocese and headed the petition against the new Governor; charges were made that Kirke had destroyed cook rooms and stages, had disposed of the principal places to aliens, and had set up taverns, and it is urgently requested that some timely course may be taken for prevention of such abuses.

Sir David manfully replied to these charges:—

"Ffereland 12 September 1640—To the Privy Council he protests before God that all they have alleged against me is most false. Many of the fishermen this year, upon what grounds I know not, have driven in their stages and cooke-roomes so much that ye most civil and wisest men amongst them did complain to me of those outrages. . . . . I confesse he that would interrupt the ffishinge of Newfoundland which is one of the most considerable Business for the Kingdom of His Majesty and benefit of His Subjects and navigation is worthy the name of Traitour, the least thought and imagination whereof I do abhor. . . . . . . Hopes by good proofs to clear himself from causeless clamours against him. Has sent warrants to all Planters and fishermen to see the clauses in the 9th of H.M.'s reign [Star Chamber Rules] duly kept.[1] . . . .

The king ordered a commission to investigate charges against Sir David. After a careful consideration of the facts contained in the records it appears that Kirke's real offence was against his associates: he was evidently unscrupulous, he appears to have followed the old Scotchman's advice to his sons: "Make money honestly if you can, but make money"; he had no hesitation in appropriating Lord Baltimore's property, and he evidently was doing the same with his partners, so in 1640 they dismissed him and sent out John Downing, senior, as Governor, with the following letter of instructions:—[1]

"INSTRUCTIONS for JOHN DOWNING of London Merchant concerning the affairs of the Lords Proprietors Patentees of Newfoundland and others interested and adventurers therein.

"Mr. Downinge, when God shall send you safe arrivall in Newfoundland, we would have you to performe and doe so much as in you lieth for your parte, our

[1] *Records.*

joint instructions deliver'd unto you & Mr. Rigby wherein we would have you to advise together, & assist one another all that you can, soe long as Mr. Rigby remaineth in the country.

"In regard Sr Dav'd Kirke he is to come over hither, we would have you to stay and remain in the house in Ferryland, wherein Sir David Kirke now dwelleth, untill you shall receive advice from us what to do.

"We would have you inform yourself in the best manner you can conferring with Sir David Kirke & otherwise, what course is best to be taken for planting of people in ye countrey & for the reducing the Indians that live in Newfoundland into civility, that soe they may be brot in time to know God.

"We doubt not but you shall find a sufficient quantity of provisions to maintain you, and the Colony all the winter. The next year there shall be further supply, with what further shall be necessary, as we shall receive advice: in case you should want any provision sooner Mr. Rigby will assist you in procuring same, from some ships in the Country or otherwise, but we presume there will be no cause, only thus wee write that you may know what to doe if the Worst should happen.

"Wee would have you give us all needful advice from time to time by all conveyances. And soe we rest.

"Whitehall ye 20th June 1640.   HAMILTON   PEMBROKE
                MONTGOMERY   HOLLAND."

All through the Colonial records in the first half of the seventeenth century there are constant proofs of the importance of this Island as a great centre of trade; nowhere else in America between 1620 and 1640 were so many Englishmen gathered together and employed in one occupation as in Newfoundland. To the poor, ill-treated colonist, who groaned under the tyranny of Argall in Virginia, or the white slavery of Bermuda, Newfoundland was the haven of refuge to which his longing eyes were turned; we have several instances in these early annals of the hair-breadth escapes of men in open boats fleeing to gain their freedom amongst the settlers and fishermen of the ancient Colony.

In 1623, when Virginia was in a terrible state of poverty and want, their hopes of succour from hunger and starvation lay in the timely arrival of a cargo of fish from Newfoundland. When the infant Colony of New York was struggling into existence, the Commissioner Mavericke thus writes home:—

"Tryalls have been made severall times this spring for codfish with very good success, a small ketch sent out by ye Governour hath founde severall good fishing bancks, amongst ye rest one not above two or three leagues from Sandy Hook, on which in a few houres four men took from 1100 to 1200 excellent good codd the last time they were out; and most of ye vessels that goe to and from Virginia take good quantities. A vessel to goe to Newfoundland to get fishermen, lines hooks and other necessaryes for fishing. I doubt not but this coast will afford fish in abundance."[1]

The first authentic account of trade between New England and Newfoundland occurs in 1645; by this time the commerce and shipping of the American Colonies had marvellously increased; everything was

[1] *Records.*

done to promote the great fishing industry. In 1639 an act was passed by the local government exempting fishermen from military duty, and all fishing property from taxation; by 1641 Governor Winthrop records that three hundred thousand dry fish were sent to market, probably first to England. In 1643 the excellent Governor mentions the return of the *Trial*,

"Mr. Thomas Graves, an able and godly man, master from a voyage to Bilbao and Malaga, her outward cargo consisted of dry codfish which she sold at a good rate and she brought as a return wine, fruit, oil, iron and wood which was a great advantage to the country [and which probably the godly man smuggled] it gave great encouragement to trade."

In 1644 a Bristol ship was captured by a cruiser of the Parliamentary party in Boston; the sympathies of the majority were with the Commonwealth, and after some wrangling the Cromwellian vessel carried off her prize. Even in distant Newfoundland the effects of this fierce civil war fell like a blight upon the fishing trade; Winthrop, in 1645, tells of a fishing expedition to Bay Bulls, Newfoundland, sent by merchants of Boston and Charlestown. When the vessels had nearly completed their loading the ship and most of the fish were seized by a Royal cruiser, and retained to the great loss of the merchants.

Newfoundland appears to have been Royalist, or at any rate neutral, and the Devonshire men were under the protection of the king's party. Charles, however, recognised rightly that New England's sympathies were with his opponents. He seems to have had grave doubts about their loyalty, so as an additional precaution passengers going out to the Colony were compelled to take the oath of allegiance.

"Petition of Stephen Goodyeare Merchant. *John* of London about to proceed to Newfoundland and Spain. Leave granted to carry goods and passengers to New England on taking the oath of allegiance at Gravesend. 1640 Jany. 26.

"Similar order about *Charles* of Gloucester freighted for a voyage to the foreign Plantations and thence to Newfoundland. Passage allowed for 100 to New England on taking the oath of allegiance. May 27, 1640.

"Same date similar order for *Amity.* 120 passengers to New England."[1]

The sack ships or freighters, now generally known in Newfoundland as "Foreigners," were constantly employed during these early years transporting freight and passengers to New England, many of the Newfoundland merchants were also concerned in the New England trade and fishery; their ships were sent from Maine and New England to fish about the Newfoundland coast before the New England traders made a regular business of the Newfoundland barter trade. By 1652 there was a steady commerce and connexion between New England and Newfoundland; traders came every year to the Island and bartered their corn and cattle for the Newfoundland fish and oil; even thus early in our history the New Englanders began the practice of stealing away the Devonshire fishermen's servants, in which afterwards they were so extensively engaged.

Hubbard relates in 1652, concerning a petition to the Lords Commissioners of Trade and Plantations with respect to regulations about the fishery, fees for culling, &c., on which disputes had arisen between the Government and the fishing interest, that the petition was only signed by twenty-five:—

"These were for the most part, either young men who came over as Servants and never had over much show of religion in them, or fishermen of Marblehead feared to be profane persons, divers of whom were brought from Newfoundland for the fishing season."[1]

The New Englanders of that age showed all the cuteness and unscrupulous cunning of the Yankee inventor of wooden nutmegs; Charles II. was terribly wroth at the audacity of the colonists in coining shillings with a rude figure of a pine tree; the colonists roundly swore to His Majesty that it was not a pine but an oak, and was intended to show their loyalty and His Royal Majesty's providential escape in the oak tree. The merry monarch was a humorist, and he enjoyed the fine flavour of this impudent falsehood; to further conciliate His Majesty they sent him ten barrels of cranberries and three thousand dried codfish. The earliest account of the New Englanders in the Colony from the Newfoundland records occurs in John Downing's narrative, 1676.[2]

[1] *Records.* [2] *See* p. 205.

APPENDIX TO CHAPTER VI.

I. Star Chamber Rules of Charles I. and additions by Charles II.

Order of Star Chamber 24th Jan'y 1633—On 20th Feb'y foll'g Charter was granted according to tenor of this order unto ye Merchants and Traders of Newfoundland which was since on 24th Jan'y 1660 renewed and confirmed by his Majestie with an additional provision.—(*B. T. Nfld., Vol. 3, p. 5.*)

In renewal of Charter by Charles II. the Patent of Chas I. is recited—

"Whereas our late Royall Father of blessed Memorie by his Lettres Patent under his Greate Seale of Englande beareing date at Westminstre the tenth day of Ffebruary in the nynth yeare of his reigne hereby reciteing that the region or Countrey called Newfoundland had been acquired to the Dominion of his Progenitors, which he held &c &c"

His people had many years resorted to those parts—employed themselves in ffishing whereby great number of his people had been "sett on Worke" & the navigation and mariners of the realm much increased and his subjects resorting thither "one by the other and the natives of these parts were orderly and gently intreated" till of late some of his subjects of realm of England planting themselves in that Countrey "upon conceipt that for wrongs or injuries done there either on the shoares or in the sea adjoining they could not be here impeached" & the rather that he and his progenitors had not given laws to inhabitants—subjects resorting thither injured one another & "used all manner of excesse" to hindrance of voyage and common damage of realme—for preventing of such inconveniences for future he did declare in what manner people of Newfoundland and seas adjoining and Bays and Creeks and fresh rivers there sh'd be guided and governed & did make and order &c "We doe by these presents renew ratify and confirme the laws following in the things after specified"—

1st. If any man kill another or steale to value of forty shillings to be brought to prison to England & the crime made known to Earl Marshall of Eng'd & if proved by two witnesses—delinquent to suffer death.

2. No ballast to be thrown out to prejudice of harbor.

3. That no person deface or spoyle any stage, Cookroome &c.

4. That such ship as first entereth a harbour shall be admiral—wherein for time being he shall reserve only so much beach & flakes as is needful for number of boates as he shall use, with overplus only for one boat, as privilege for his first coming, after content themselves with what he shall have use for with keeping more to prejudice of others next coming—any that possess several places in several harbours with intent to keep all before they can resolve which to choose shall be bound to resolve and send advice to such aftercomers & within 48 howres if the weather so serve, said aftercomers may likewise choose—so none receive prejudice by others delayes.

5. That no person deface or alter the marks of any boats to defraud the owners of them.

6. That no person steale any fish, trayne, or salt or any other provision belonging to fishing ships.

7. That no person set fire to the woodes or rinde the trees except for Cookeroomes.

8. That no man case anchor or ought else hurtful which may breed annoyance or hinder the "haleing of seanes" for baytes in places accustomed thereto.

9. That no person robb the nets of others out of any drift boate.

10. That no person set up any taverne for selling wine, beere, strong waters, cider or tobacco.—by such means fishermen neglect their labours, and spend wages upon which their wives and children depend they are likewise hurtful in many other ways—men make themselves hurtful by purloyning and stealing from owners.

11. On Sunday Divine service to be said by some of the Masters of ships, such prayers as are in Book of Common prayer.

And moreover and further then was ordayned by the laws of our said late ffather and for the encouragement of our subjects in said Newfoundland All owners of ships trading to Newfoundland forbidden to carry any persons not of ships Company or such as are to plant or do intend to settle there, & that speedy punishment may be inflicted on offenders—ordeyned as formerly that " Every of the Maiors of Southton Weymouth and Melcome Regis Lynne Plymouth Dartmouth Eastlowe ffoy and Barnstaple" for time being take cogni'ce of all complaints [on land] and by oath of witness examine, award, amend to parties specified and punish delinquent by fine and imprisonment &c. and Vice-Adml's in Counties of Southton Dorsett Devon and Cornwall proceed against offenders upon the sea—" Also wee will and ordeyne that these laws and ordinances shall stand in forse and be put in due execution untill wee shall otherwise provide and ordeine And we doe require the admirall in every harbour in this next season ensuing calling together such as shall be in that harbour publickly to proclayme these presents and they alsoe proclayme the same on the shoare in Witness &c. Witness ourselfe at Westminster the six and twentieth day of January."

(*Patent Roll*, 12 *Chas. II., part* 17, 30.)

On the 23rd Decr 1670 a Pet'n for regulation of Fishery was presented to His Majestie by Westerne Merchants & Traders & Council of foreign Planters having made report of several rules necessary for support of trade. His Majesty was pleased to order that they sh'd be added to the former Charter viz—

1. That H.M's Subjects may take bayte of fish in Newfoundland provided they submit to established orders.

2. That no alien take bait.

3. That no planter cut down any wood, or plant within six miles of sea shore.

4. That no inhabitant or planter take up best stages before arrival of fishermen.

5. That no master or owner of ships transport seamen or fishermen to Nfd unless belonging to his ship's Company.

6. That no person carry more than 60 persons to a hundred tonnes.

7. That every fifth man be a green man [that is] not a seaman.

8. That masters of ships provide victuals in England according to number of men, for whole voyage, salt only excepted.

9. That no fishing ship part hence for Newfoundland before the month of March.

10. That Masters give bond of £100 to respective Mayors not to carry any persons to Newfoundland as aforesaid & to bring back such as they carry out, or shall employ with fish for market voyages.

11. That no master take up a stage with less than 25 men.

12. That no fisherman or seaman remain behind after fishing is ended.

13. That Adm'l, Vice Adm'l and Rear Adm'l do put these orders in execution and preserve the peace.

14. And bring offenders for any crime into England.

15. That they proclaim on 20th Septr yearly H.M.'s orders.

16. And keep Journals.

17. That Recorders and Justices of the Peace be Joyned in Commission with Mayors.

18. That reasonable fines be imposed on offenders.

19. That a Bill sh'd be prepared for the Greate Seale, for confirm'n of said Charter, with these additional powers.

20. That the clause touching the Marshall sh'd be reviewed by the Atty Gen'l &c who should present to board, someway of Judicature for determining of causes in Newfoundland.

(*B. T. Nfld., Vol.* 3, *p.* 13.)

II. Sir David Kirke.

Kirke to Archbishop Laud.

Oct. 2, 1639.

"Out of 100 persons they took over only one died of sickness. [The temperature and general state of the country is described.] . . . The air of Newfoundland agrees perfectly well with all God's creatures except Jesuits and Schismatics. A great mortality amongst the former tribe so affrighted my Lord of Baltimore that he utterly deserted the country . . . . of the other sect [The Puritans] many frenzies are heard from their next neighbouring Plantation, the greatest His Maj'ty hath in America. Their chiefest safety is a strict observance of the rites and service of the Church of England. Doubts not but the country will be numerously peopled in a short time." (*Endorsed by Laud rec. Jan.* 1640.)

There is considerable difficulty in ascertaining the exact facts about the later history of this celebrated old sea captain. When ordered home by Charles I. he appears to have remained in England some time; he was, however, returned to the Island before 1649. In this year there is a most pathetic letter from the unfortunate Charles to Kirke, written not long before his execution, praying him to find an asylum for his sister Lady Hawkins "in these troublous times."

Under the Commonwealth Kirke's property was taken possession of by the Commissioners, at least all that belonged to the company. Besides Baltimore's mansion at Ferryland, there appear to have been other houses in which George Kirke, Lady Kirke, and the family resided. There was very long delay and putting off of Kirke's case. Sir James Kirke obtained a new Patent in conjunction with Claypole, Cromwell's son-in-law.

In 1651 Kirke is ordered to repair to England. He went out to Newfoundland again in 1652, and was under bonds to return the same year. Either in 1652 or in the following year he died in prison at the suit of Lord Baltimore. Sikes, Pyle, and Treworgie speak of him as dead in 1654; he appears to have died about June 1653.

Witnesses on both sides in the controversy between Kirke and Baltimore seem to give evidence only on behalf of their friends. Amy Wrixon, William Wrixon, and Ann Low swear that "for 7 or 8 years before the arrival of Sir David Kirke Baltimore never had possession or person there upon the property." Cecil Lord Baltimore, on the other hand, testifies that "his father died in 1632; that he, Cecil, had sent out Captain William Hill as his deputy; Captain Hill repaired thither, took possession and gave him a yearly account of his proceedings and the profit, and resided four or five years in Lord Baltimore's house in Ferryland. Not long before the beginning of the late war, Duke Hamilton and others by their power at Court procured a Patent of all Newfoundland, including therein the Province of Avalon, whereupon in 1638 Sir D. Kirke went to Ferryland in Newfoundland, and by force of arms turned Captain Hill out of Lord Baltimore's chief Mansion house (where the said Lord Baltimore had at the time divers things of good value) and took possession of the whole Province and of divers cattle and horses belonging to Lord Baltimore."

Baltimore prays for redress through Parliament, " his property being now in possession of persons sent by the Council of State to dispossess Sir David Kirke."

These Commissioners were Captains Raynor and Pearce; their characters are given in a gossipping letter from Charles Hill, Ferryland, 12 Sep. 1661, to Mr. John Kirke, London :—

HILL TO KIRKE.

Ferryland 12 September 1661.
MR. JOHN KIRKE,

I was advised by Mr. Geo. Kirke of what you was pleased to write to mee at the end of his letter, and could wish I had more pleasing intelligence to write to you than the continuation of the calamity of this Country occasioned not only by the continuance of bad voyages, but to the Inhabitants in a more particular manner by the late Governors arrival here, who have sought themselves so much that I believe they will have but a few Tennants in ye Lord Baltimore's part of Avilon. Upon their arrival here the Inhabitants, as also the masters of ships were summoned, when their patent granted them for ye space or term of 14 years from the now Lord Baltimore was read and then a letter from the Kings Majesty under his hand and privy seal, wherein it was signified that there had beene a tryell between your family and Baltimore about the patent and upon report of His Majestys two Justices of Common Pleas and other Councel it was declared that ye Patent of ye old Lord Baltimore was a good patent and that it was surreptitiously taken away by Sir David Kirke and that therefore His Majesty did require Sir Lewis Kirke &c. to surrender to Lord Baltimore all his houses lands goods &c., and that all Masters and Admirals of ships should be ayding and assisting Lord Baltimore if required.

I pre-advised My Lady and Mr. Geo. Kirke what answer to make unto the Governours, they being absent at ye reading of the Proclamation, when they came with the masters of ships to put them in free possession, who having made a complaymentall demand was suddenly answered that since it was His Majestys pleasure to order ye same they should not in the least dispute but with all readiness surrender it to his use and service, and as for what could be approvedly visible to belong to Lord Baltimore. But as for the houses built by Sir D. Kirke at his own cost My Lady would attornie tenant for the same and pay the acknowledge due to Lord Baltimore for the same.

My Lady and Mr. George have been much threatened to be dispossessed but the fitt is now over for the two Governors do one so thwart the other that they dissent in their judgments. Captain Raynor is a desperado and looks not for right; but Captain Pearce is more a braver soldier and I believe would quit his ingagement upon honourable termes; he hath had very many civil expressions and good affections to your family and said he was resolved for England again, and should be loth to act any thing in Newfoundland that he might not answer in England. He hath heretofore been Sir Davids Leeftenant in ye King's ships and howsoever he was trepaixed into this employment, hath very large respects to your familey. They pretended to have a Commission from the King for full management of all his concerns in the whole Island, which was granted but three days before they came away. I know not how true, you can advise yourself; but thereupon and pretending ye King's letter, Captain Raynor hath received rents and arrears out of the precincts of Avilonia, and hath beene so hard to some that I think few will trust them longer than the next yeare. There hath beene but 150 qtls. [of fish] per boat for the generalitie. Many planters have not made soo much. I know Mr. George hath advised you at full. Tis reported Captain Reynells is returned for England, he is of a good family, who may do something for him. His Bond is £180 [security for return to Lord Baltimore]. If you advise next yeare shall send it if opportunity present to exportation [probably some fish].

I shall further advise you; in the interim shall pray for your welfare with the tender of my humble services remayne,

Your Servant to command,
CHARLES HILL.

(B.M. MSS. Eg. 2395.)

The ingratitude of the Stuarts to their devoted adherents is proverbial; all the Kirkes had fought gallantly for their King, all were deserted and abandoned in their sore hour of need. The curtain closes over the gallant Sir David Kirke's family in misfortune and poverty; all poor Lady Kirke's appeals to her sovereign were entirely unheeded.

In 1673 a Dutch squadron of four ships of 40 guns each entered the Harbour of Ferryland where " they plundered, ruined, fired, and destroyed the commodities, cattle, household goods, and other stores belonging to the inhabitants." The family of Sir David Kirke were then residing there as ordinary Planters, consisting of Lady Kirke, her son George and his wife and four children, David with his wife and one child, and Philip, unmarried—altogether they had 66 men servants, 14 boats, 3 stages, and 3 oil vats. We learn this from a letter of Dudley Lovelace, a prisoner aboard the Dutch fleet at the time; he says, Lady Kirke and her family were the greatest sufferers on this occasion. (Public Records; quoted by Browne in his *History of C. Breton*.)

The following accounts of Sir David Kirke's government may have been sworn to in 1667 to support the opposition to the Newfoundland settlers' petition (18th March 1667, B.M. MSS., Eg. 2395), that his son, George Kirke, should be appointed governor of the district from Petty Harbour to Ferryland. These depositions probably were modelled after those of 1639 to support Exeter and other petitioners against Kirke.

DEPOSITIONS TAKEN AT TOPSHAM, BY VIRTUE OF A COMMISSION DATED AUGUST 28, 1667.

Thomas Cruse of Ashprinton deposes above fifty years last past he went to ye Newfoundland in a ship of Topsham on a ffishing voyage at which time there was noe Governour there, or above two or three poor people inhabited there, and such salt, boates, staiges and other materialls for ye ffishing trade left by ye shippes the fformer year they usually found in ye like condition without hurt or any diminution ye following year.

And about thirty-two years past he went from London to ye Newfoundland and arrived there in ye Harbour of Bay Bulls, where he inhabited eighteen yeares; which was about four yeares before Sir David Kirke the ffirst Governour that came there after ye Lord Baltimore who was there only one winter and then left the countrey saying it was an unfitt place for man or beast to live in.

During all which time of this Deponents aboade there noe nation did ever in ye leaste attempt to molest or trouble ye English there or thare ffishery; neither were thare any ffortifications erected untill the coming there of Sir David Kirke who planted some ffew gunns at Fferriland and two or three other places; and that before Sir David Kirke came there noe one paid any custome or tax concerning the said ffishery or otherwise, butt all was free.

But after Sir David Kirke arrived there (who brought with him about thirty servants) he imposed taxes on all ye inhabitants to pay a great ffine and yearly rents for the houses and ground by ye water side in several Harbours and ffishing places; as this Deponent did ffor a house and some ground graunted to him by ye said Sir David Kirke as by writing made in ye year 1640 ffor which he paid the yearly rent of £3. 6. 8 and a *ffat hog* or 20/ in lew thereof.

And the said Sir David Kirke did summon ye Inhabitants of ye severall harbours to repair at Fferriland and compelled them to take estates in land in severall harbours for erecting of houses and ffishing places by ye water side, and to pay great ffines, tax and rents for the same and in case of reffusall threttned to expel them out of ye land; and alsoe enticed them to take licenses off him ffor ye selling off wine and other liquors and made them pay great rents yearly ffor the same and made this Deponent take and pay for such a license £15 per annum.

And ye said Sir David Kirke himselfe did keepe a Common Taverne in his own House which did drawe and keepe ship masters, ffishermen and others ffrom theire ffishing employments to the great prejudice and hinderance of their voyadges. And Sir David Kirke's constant practice was to engross salt and other necessary provisions brought thither for sale which he sold again to ye shippers at excessive rates. And that during the abode of the Deponent, there was not any Church and if one should be built people too far away to come to Church through the woods, whereas in midst of the harbours there were not above two or three poore families [this means at Bay Bulls].

Similar depositions from Nicholas Luce of Dartmouth, Thomas Pitcher, Richard Parker, Christopher Selman, Thomas Fowler of St. Mary Church, Gabriel Widdomas of Berry Pomeroy; all swear to the same effect, also to Kirke's coming with armed men and turning them out of their stages in June and putting his friends in possession.

(WORTH's *Plymouth Municipal Records*.)

These Depositions, all of one tenour and purpose, are rather suspicious documents; the old West Countrymen swore as boldly, uniformly, and unblushingly as a corporal's guard in a brush with civilians. No doubt Sir David was a tyrant, a bold, determined ruler, who kept everybody—even the West Countrymen—in order. It was not quite in keeping with his gubernatorial dignity for the gallant knight to keep a "grog shop" at Government House; in excuse for him it should be remembered that he had no salary.

CHAPTER VII.

Interregnum. 1649-1653.

CROMWELL, Protector, 1653-1658.

RICHARD CROMWELL, Sept. 1658 to May 1659.

1659-1660, Interregnum.

1649, July 24.—Notification to Colonies of change of Government.

1650.—Warrant served by Matthews against N. Redwood at St. Mary's. Newfoundland at this time probably contained 350 families, or about 2,000 inhabitants, in fifteen settlements, between Cape Race and Cape Bonavista.

1651.—Commission to Treworgie, Sikes, &c. to govern Newfoundland. Kirke ordered to repair to England. Council for the Plantations send for Holdsworth, and supply him with copies of Kirke's defence.

1652.—Kirke in Newfoundland again. Hubbard mentions Newfoundland fishermen being at Marblehead, Mass.

1653.—Treworgie, sole Governor.

1654.—Treworgie arrested by Kirke and imprisoned. Death of Sir D. Kirke in prison, at suit of Lord Baltimore.

1655.—Petition from Plymouth for two men-of-war for convoy to Newfoundland. Charter granted to Claypole and Sir James Kirke. Street's and Sikes' petitions for payment of salary.

1656.—Report of Committee on Newfoundland Trade.—Twelve Articles to be turned (except 11th Article) into instruction to commanders of convoys going thither, and to the Governor there; encouragement of the Newfoundland trade to be respected in the pressing of seamen.

1657.—Convoy provided for several ships bound to Newfoundland.

1659.—Treworgie petitions for payment of six years' salary.

1660.—Mr. Powey's report upon Treworgie's petition.

The stirring events of the great English revolution, the judicial murder of the king, the downfall of the monarchy, and the establishment of the Commonwealth, seem to have had marvellously small effect on the English colonies. One plucky little island, Barbadoes, alone stood in arms for the fallen monarch; it is the proud boast of the Barbadoes negro of to-day:—

"While Bados true to her
England nebber fear."

THE POLICY OF THE PROTECTOR.

Nowhere else amongst the growing British dependencies was there any great commotion or armed resistance to the new government. The orderly course of law and administration in the Colonies went on unimpeded, but Rupert's piratical fleet and the Commonwealth's cruizers seriously interfered with trade; the Newfoundland fish business from the West of England shrank from two hundred and seventy vessels in the reign of James to about 100 sail; New England bullocks which had been worth £25 fell to £10, with a dull sale. The civil war fell like a blight on commerce and industry.

That aristocratic Mr. Facing-both-ways—Cecil, Lord Baltimore—boasted of his prompt conversion to the new republic. Cavalier Virginia made a show of resistance, but surrendered on the first appearance of the Commonwealth's armed force. The Puritans of the old country and New England embraced each other. The American rejoiced that his brethren in the motherland had followed his example in establishing a godly government out of which the shrewd New Englanders got worldly profit and advantage in the shape of various contracts for Jamaica, &c.

The extortions and tyranny of Kirke as a representative of Charles's government had its influence on the western adventurers in Newfoundland; they welcomed the new power that had put an end to Kirke's reign; and though the Devonshire gentry were cavaliers to a man, the merchants and middle class who traded to Newfoundland seem to have all gone over to the Parliamentary party. We find in the records that the new government consulted Mr. Holdsworth,[1] of Dartmouth, a leading man amongst the western adventurers, in making their arrangements for the affairs of the Colony.

The policy of the Protector towards Newfoundland was in marked contrast to the tyrannical oppression of the monarchy. Even in our Island the sagacious statesmanship and firm, strong hand of Cromwell

CROMWELL.
From an engraving after Houbraken.

---

[1] 1654, January 20. "The Council for the Plantations about Newfoundland affairs are directed to send for Mr. Oldsworth or any others who can speak to that business."

On February 11 orders were sent for Holdsworth to have copies of Kirke's defence; he was evidently one of the leading opponents of Kirke.

made itself felt. The rulers appointed for the Colony by the Parliamentary party were designated Commissioners; they were the first real Governors of the Island; all former administrators, although called in

DUDLEY'S MAP, 1647.

our histories Governors of Newfoundland—Gilbert, Guy, Mason, Hayman, Wynne, and Kirke—were in reality only the managers of colonisation companies, and had no direct commission from the Crown; the

THE COMMISSIONERS.

English authorities at home had never given to either or any of these self-styled Governors either a naval or a military force to execute their decrees; under Cromwell's administration all this was changed. The Commissioners, as will be seen from Governor Treworgie's letter of appointment and instruction, were real Governors:—

"You have hereby full power and authority to command such ships and vessels as are upon the coast, to keep together or otherwise to dispose of themselves as may bee most for the comon safety . . . . and all Captaynes of Convoys are hereby required to be assisting to you in the execution thereof and you are to consider in what manner any of the Harbours and Bayes belonging to the Country may bee fortified for preservation both of the Country and fishing . . . . .

"You are by yor'selfe or such fit persons as you shall appoint to collect the imposition of fish due from and payd by strangers and likewise the imposition of oyle for the use of this Commonwealth."[1]

The first act of the Commonwealth regarding Newfoundland is contained in the records of February 23rd, 1649. Sir David Kirke, a staunch Royalist, evidently intended to send over a considerable force to sustain the royal cause in the Colony and to operate in conjunction with Prince Rupert, who was taking some of his ships to plunder the fishing fleet. An order therefore is issued to the Comptrollers of Plymouth, Dartmouth, and Barnstaple:—

"That 400 seamen taken up under pretence of being transported to Newfoundland by Sir David Kirke at great wages and other advantages offered are not to be allowed to go—only sufficient seamen necessary for the service of each ship be permitted to leave."[1]

And in May 27 of the same year, the following notice is sent to the generals at sea:—

"Are informed that it is the intention of Prince Rupert to send some of his revolted ships to Newfoundland to disturb the fishing there. Desire that two ships may be sent thither if they can be spared to defend the fishing vessels."[1]

These wise precautions had the desired effect; Kirke was kept a prisoner under the control of the State, and Rupert's fleet, instead of ruining the Newfoundland fishermen, crippled the English trade in the Mediterranean and the West Indies.

On the 24th of July of the same year there is an order from the Council of State:—

"That letters be written to the English plantations to give them notice of the change of Government, to send the papers necessary for their information, and to require them to continue their obedience as they look for protection."[1]

The first Commissioners appointed (on April 8th, 1651) by the Commonwealth were John Littlebury, John Treworgie, Walter Sikes,

[1] *Records.*

Captain Thomas Thoroughgood, Commander of the *Crescent;* Captain Thomas Jones, Commander of the *Ann and Joyce;* and Captain William Haddock, Commander of the *America*, who, together with other Commissioners—Redwood, Griggs, Pyle, Clotworthy, and Hendy— are to take examinations touching the miscarriages committed by Kirke. The first-named Commissioners are to take charge of the government, and particularly to collect the impositions on fish paid by strangers.

Our history does not concern itself with these various Commissioners.

TOAD'S COVE.
From a drawing by the Hon. and Rev. W. Gray.

Mr. Sikes appears to have been, like Sir David Kirke, troubled a good deal about his accounts with the Commonwealth. The charges against the Governor, after being put off from time to time, were at length finally dropped. His brother, Sir James, having managed to secure Cromwell's son-in-law, Claypole, on his side by the bribe of a share in Lord Baltimore's plantation at Ferryland, a charter seems to have been granted about 1655 to Sir James Kirke, Claypole, and others. It came utterly to naught.

Newfoundland does not appear to have suffered so much commercially from the Civil War as New England. The Puritans of Boston and New Plymouth complained bitterly of the stagnation of trade during this period, when the seas were infested with hostile cruisers, Parliamentary and Royal pirates. The export of fish to the Mediterranean must have been a terribly risky business.

The Newfoundland ships, numerous (though terribly reduced from the grand fleet of the days of Elizabeth), well armed, and escorted by three men-of-war, ran the gauntlet to the Straits of Gibraltar each season; and there appears to be no complaint of captures. The Dutch, from the time of the Armada, had become, like the English at the present day, the great carriers for the world.[1] They bought large quantities of dry cod in Newfoundland, and exported it to Europe and the West Indies.

The most distinguished name in the annals of Newfoundland during the Cromwellian period is John Treworgie, or Treworgay[2]; he was the first real Governor of the Colony. The best illustration we can gather of the character of this able, honest administrator is furnished by his opponents. The West Countrymen found him a far more formidable ruler than Kirke. In the Parliamentary Report published in 1718 they complain of his having encouraged settlement in Newfoundland by transporting passengers and protecting planters. He had been living in Maine, carrying on business for his grandfather, Alexander Shapleigh of Dartmouth. Trained and brought up in the Colonies, he had seen the good effects of orderly settlements and the division of the State into townships, and in Newfoundland he endeavoured to carry out the same enlightened ideas. Even a virulent Tory like Downing admits that good order was maintained during his government, and the poor Newfoundland planters were protected in their possessions. So high was his character that, during the interregnum between the end of the

---

[1] 1640. "Memorandum concerning 'The Bill' to be preferred by the West Countrymen about the Newfoundland fishery."

The paper shows the advantage to British navigation if the Dutch were prohibited from buying fish there, and aliens required to pay the same duties there that are paid in England. It also mentions complaints from Bahamas and Virginia about Dutch traders.

They were universal carriers, and had very fine ships.—(*Calendar of State Papers, Colonial Series.*)

[2] John Treworgie, or Treworgay, appears to have been the son of James Treworgie, who married a daughter of Alexander Shapleigh, of Dartmouth, Devon; all my endeavours to elicit any information from Rev. Baring Gould and others about the Treworgie family in Cornwall have failed. The Shapleighs, however, are an old West Country stock. Four monuments, with coats of arms of the family, are to be found in the Parish Church of Dartmouth, Devon. From some law papers we find that John Treworgie went out to Maine in 1640, when a very young man, as agent for his grandfather Shapleigh. He lived several years at Sturgeon Creek, Kittery, Maine, and figured in law suits about his grandfather's property with John Heard in 1643 and 1646. He was married in January 1646 to a Miss Spenser, of Newberry, Mass. Treworgie and several other merchants in Maine went to Newfoundland for trading and fishing. Governor Treworgie did business with our Island, for on May 27th, 1653, when appointed sole Governor or Commissioner for Newfoundland, it is specially mentioned that he was then residing there.

Commonwealth and the restoration of Charles II., Treworgie was again appointed Governor of the Colony.

The Lord Protector's Government treated Treworgie meanly; they seem to have been just as neglectful as the Stuarts in paying their servants. There is in the records a humble petition from the poor Colonial Governor, praying for the payment of six years' arrears of "sallery," which, as we gather from a similar petition in 1655 from Anne Mansfield, mother of Thomas Street (one of the Commissioners who had been appointed with Sikes in 1652), was only at the rate of £250 per annum, and £61 for disbursements.

Another incident in Treworgie's tenure of office illustrates in a remarkable way the impartial and independent administration of justice under Cromwell's Government. In April 1654 Treworgie complains—

"That in this year Sir James Kirke had him arrested in an action for £600 and kept him close prisoner as a malefactor, thinking by a trick to gain money for his liberty; he prays that Kirke, Hill, and the bailiffs may be ordered to show cause why the Petitioner should not proceed in his Commission [as Governor of Newfoundland] without interruption or arrest, and that he may be secured against them."[1]

By order of Cromwell the petition is referred to Colonel Jones and others, "to consider of a way for the Petitioner's indemnity." Under the Stuarts, such an interference by the courts with a Colonial Governor would have been visited with summary punishment; under the orderly administration of Cromwell the courts of justice, even when they acted perversely against his own officers, were never interfered with. Royalists like Kirke and Baltimore could freely bring their differences before the Protector's courts of law without any fear of such Government action as was the rule under the Stuarts.

Under the fostering care and able management of Treworgie, which extended from 1653 to 1660, the settlement, trade, and fisheries of the Colony were largely increased; no injustice to planters was permitted under his firm control; the cultivation of the land was encouraged; trade between the island and the continental colonies was promoted; the celebrated Trelawney of Richmond Island, Maine, sent ships to Newfoundland. Treworgie himself was connected with the trade of both colonies. New England prospered immensely under the Commonwealth, and so did our island Colony. Amidst the dreary record of wrong and oppression, Treworgie's seven years administration is the one bright spot in our history.

[1] *Records.*

SHIPBUILDING.

The records show that there was a large amount of both ship-building[1] and boat-building going on in the Colony at this period. The English naval officers mention the great superiority of the English-built

SHIPS OF THE TIME OF CHARLES II.
From a drawing by C. H. Moore.

fishing boat as compared with the French, and very stringent orders were given to prevent our rivals obtaining Newfoundland boats from the settlers. Even at this early period there was a smuggling business

---

[1] In the Parliamentary Report of 1718 it is stated that nearly all the Poole vessels engaged in the Newfoundland trade were built in the Colony. Spurriers built barques, brigs, and ships at Oderin, Burin, and St. Lawrence.

going on with the French; it continued after they were removed to Louisbourgh, Cape Breton, and is in full activity up to the present time. The New Englanders were so keen about trade that they actually sold to their enemies the very bricks and boards they afterwards battered down. By the end of the Commonwealth period the New England trade was firmly established in our Colony; it had a general agent in St. John's, with branch agencies in all the principal settlements.

APPENDIX TO CHAPTER VII.

I. Treworgie's Instructions.

(Domestic State Papers, Interregnum. Council of State Order Book. April 29 to July 1, 1653. Vol. 97.)

Friday 3d of June 1653, afternoone.

Majō Genˡˡ Desbrow the Lord Generall, M. Genˡˡ Lambert, Col. Jones, M. Genˡˡ Harrison, Mr. Strickland, Col. Stapley, Col. Tomlinson, Col. Bennet, Mr. Moyer, Sr. Gilb. Pickering.

INSTRUCTIONS to JOHN TREWORGIE Gent. appointed Commisʳ for manageing and ordering the affaires and Interest of this Comonwealth in Newfoundland for this present yeare.

WHEREAS upon consideration had of the present state and condition of affaires in Newfoundland relateing to this Comonwealth, The Councell have thought it expedient to continue you for this sumer upon the place as a Comissioner : for manageing and ordering the affaires there. You are therefore to demeane yoʳselfe in that trust and imploymᵗ according to the powers instructions and authority hereafter mentioned.

1st.—You are hereby required and authorized to take care for the Governmᵗ and well ordering of the said country of Newfoundland and the people there inhabiting, and likewise the fishery according to such lawes and ordinances as are hereto annexed.

2nd. You are by yoʳselfe or such fit persons as you shall appoint to collect the imposition of fish due from and payd by strangers, and likewise the imposition of Oyle for the use of this Comonwealth, and Adventurʳˢ aforesaid, until the Supreame authority shall declare their further pleasure therein.

3rd. You are to use yoʳ best endeavoʳˢ to secure the fishery there against any that shall attempt to disturbe or interrupt it and to that end you have hereby full power and authority to comand such ships and vessells as are upon that coast or in any of the Harborˢ to keepe together or otherwise to dispose of themselves in such manner as may bee most for the comon safety and to use such other meanes for the end aforesaid as you shall judge meet, And all Captaynes of Convoyes are hereby required to bee assisting to you in the execution thereof And you are to consider in what manner any of the Harborˢ and Bayes, belonging to the country may bee fortified for preservation both of the country and fishing.

4.—Whereas securitie is given by Sr. David Kirke such as the Councell doe approve of, for his appearance to the Councell and being responsible as to any matters to be objected against him, Upon which the sequestration or former seisure upon his Estate is to bee taken off, You are therefore to deliver up unto such person or persons as he shall appoint all that remaines of his there that was formerly sequestred or seised, or that belongeth to him, onely of the Ordnance or any other things that doe properly belong to ye Comonwealth you are to take a particular notice and inventory, and unto the person or persons in whose charge you shall leave the same you are to give strict directions that they take care the same bee preserved and forthcoming to the use of the Comonwealth. You are to receive and examine all such complaints as shall bee made unto you as well by strangers as others of any wrong or injury done unto them by any person or persons whatsoever and to certifie their particular cases unto the Councell.

You are upon the close of this sumers fishery to returne back into England and to repaire to the Councell or the Supreame authority of this Comonwealth and to give as well a just and true accompt of all such money and profitts as have come to yoʳ hands due to the Comonwealth or Adventurers, as of all yoʳ proceedings and in what condition you left all things there at yoʳ coming away.

Lawes, Rules, and Ordinances whereby the Affaires and fishery of Newfoundland are to be governed untill the Parlamᵗ shall take further order.

1.—That noe Ballast, Prest stones nor anything else hurtfull to the Harbours bee throwne out to the prejudice of said Harbours, but that it be carryed ashore and layd where it may not doe annoyance.

2.—That noe person whatsoever either fishermen or inhabitants doe destroy or deface or any way worke any spoyle or detriment to any stage, Cookeroome, Flakes, Spikes, Nayles or any thing else that belongeth to the stages whatsoever either at the end of the Voyage when he hath done, and is to depart the country But that he or they content themselves with such stage or stages onely as shall bee needful for them, and that for the repairing of such stages, as he or they take, they shall fetch timber out of the woods, and not to do it with ruining or teareing down of other stages.

3.—That according to the ancient Custome, every ship or fisher that first entereth a

Harbour, in behalfe of the ship, be Admirall of the said Harbour, wherein for the time being he shall onely reserve soe much beach and flakes or both as is needful for the number of boats he shall use with an overplus onely for one boate more than he needeth as a priviledge for his first cominge. And that every ship comeinge after content himselfe with what he shall have necessarye use for without keepeinge or deteyneing any more to ye p'judice of others next comeinge. And that any y[t] are possessed of several places in several Harbo[rs] with intent to keepe them all before they cann resolve upon which to chuse, shalbe bound to resolve and send advice to such after comers in those places as expect his resolution and that within 48 houres if ye weather soe serve that ye said after Comers may likewise choose their place and soe none receive p'judice by others delayes.

4.—That noe person cut out, deface or any way alter or change the marks of any boates or trayne fatts whereby to defraud ye right owners, and that no person convert to his own use ye said boates or trayne fatts soe belonginge to others without their consents nor remove nor take them fr̄o ye places where they be left by ye owners except in case of necessitye, and then to give notice thereof to ye Adm[ll] and others whereby ye owners may knowe what has become of them.

5.—That noe person doe deminish take away perloyne or steale any of ye fish or trayne or salt which is putt in caske Trayne Fatts or Cookeroomes or other houses in any of ye Harbo[rs] or Fishinge places of ye countrye, or any other provisions belonginge to ye fishinge Trade or to ye ships.

6.—That noe person sett fire in any of ye woods of ye countrye or work any detrim[t] or destruction to ye same by rinding of ye trees either for ye seeling of ships houlds or for roomes on shoare or for any other uses except for ye coveringe of ye roofes for Cookeroomes to dresse their meate and these roomes not to extend above 30 foote in length at ye most.

7.—That noe man cast anchor or ought else hurtfull which may breed annoyance or hinder ye halvinge of Saynes for Bayte in places accustomed thereunto.

8.—That noe person robb ye netts of others out of any drifts boate or drover for bayte by night, nor take away any bayte out of their fishing boates by their ships sides nor robb nor steale any of their netts or any part thereof.

9.—That noe person doe sett up any Tavernes for sellinge of wynes beere or strong waters Syder or tobacco to enterteyne ye fishermen because it is found that by such meanes they are debauched, neglecting their labors and poore ill governed men not onely spend most part of their shares before they come home upon which ye life and maynten-ance of their wives and children dependeth but are likewise hurtfull in divers other ways as by neglecting and making themselves unfit for their labor by purloyneing and stealing fr̄o their owners and by making unlawfull shifts to supply their disorders which disorders they frequently followe since these occasions have presented themselves.

10.—That noe planter be permitted to keepe any more stage roome than he hath fishinge men in posson for ye manageing of it and y[t] every planter in each Harbo[r] may take their stages and fishing roome together in one part of ye Harbour and not scattering as they now doe wasting as much roome for one or two boates as may serve 6 or 8 boates.

11.—That noe planter be permitted to build any dwelling house, store house, court-ledge or garden or keepe any Piggs or other cattle upon or near ye ground where fish is saved or dryed.

12.—That all provisions imported for sale necessarye for fishing be free for any person to buy for his own present occasion, soe it be demanded within six dayes after its arrivall, and not to be ingrossed by a few to make benefitt on others thereby.

13.—That upon ye Lords day ye Accompanye assemble in meet place for divine worship.

Signed
JOHN DISBROW Ps[t].

Whitehall 3d.
of June 1653.

II. Petition of John Treworgie.

To the Right Honourable the Council of State.

The humble Petition of John Treworgie Commander of the Colonie of this nation in Newfoundland,

SHEWETH,

That your Petitioner being in the year 1653 commissioned to ye Newfoundland by the Council of State for the managing of the affairs of that Country hath according to his instructions, yearly given them an account of his proceedings therein and for want of a due supply from heare hath been necessitated to return unto England and now takes on him the boldness to inform your Honour with the state of affairs in that Island and also to acquaint your Honour of six years sullary due to your Petitioner. May it therefore please your power to take the matter into consideration and to grant unto your Petitioner a Commission for the advising the affairs there and to appoint two or three frigates (which vessels have been there to assist your Petitioner in collecting the impost surprizing of such Spanish ships as shall be found and to conduct English shipping from heare. . . . . . .

III. Mr. Povey's Report, May 11, 1660.

To the Right Hon. the Committee of the Council for Foreign Plantations.

After reciting the various Patents. . .

. . . . After the death of Duke Hamilton the Council of State did in 1650 give a Commission to John Treworgie merchant who was there upon the place to order affairs there for the best advantage of the State which Commission was also renewed in 1653. Sir David Kirke the only survivor of the former Patentees obtained in 1655 [prob. Sir James Kirke] a Commission from the late Protector Oliver wherein John Claypole Esq. and Col. John Coffin were joined with him but little or nothing was acted thereupon. Upon the whole matter it appeareth by reason of ye severall patents for the settlement . . . . . . the disorders of the late time the interest of State suffers. . . . and it seems very expedient that some suitable person be employed and instructed to hasten thither to manage His Majesty's affaires therefor ye next season of fishing whereby many advantages and profits may arise to His Majesty which must else be wholly neglected and lost of which the person employed is to give an account here in England at ye end of the yeare. For the present it may be expedient that ye aforesaid John Treworgie hath a commission and fit instrument to goe to Newfoundland therefore forthwith he having been a person well used and experienced in those affaires . . . . liberty to return to England and give an account of his Trust.

J. POVEY.

Endorsed :—

By order of Committee of State sitting and taking care of Government in the intervall between ye suppression of ye Rump of ye Parliament and ye return of His Majesty which was not many days before the date of this Report.

CHAPTER VIII.

REIGN OF CHARLES II.

1660-1685.

1660.—Proclamation for stricter observance of Lent. Petition, on June 11th, of Sir L. Kirke and others for better protection of the fishing fleet. Petition, in June, of Lord Baltimore for a renewal of his patent; Sir O. Bridgeman and Col. Finch report, on June 17th, that the patent is good, and still in force; that they cannot calculate the money expended by the Kirkes on the plantation. Warrant granted to Baltimore to take possession from the Kirkes. Gargot probably received commission as Governor of Placentia.

1661.—Captains Raynor and Pearce at Ferryland as Baltimore's commissioners. Charter to Western merchants renewed on 26th January; no persons other than those going to fish or to settle to be permitted to sail; duty on salt remitted. Petition of Lady Kirke that she and her children are starving. Letter from Hill to Kirke in September.

1662.—Placentia founded by French. Immediately after accession of Charles II., who was a vassal of France, Louis XIV. sent out 150 men, guns, and ammunition of war to Placentia. Baltimore obtained renewal of his patent. Mathews, sent by Pearse and Raynor to Placentia, arrested by the French, but escaped.

1663.—Mayors, &c. instructed to enforce an order prohibiting masters of vessels from carrying settlers to Newfoundland; fisheries exempted from tax or toll. The celebrated James Young in Newfoundland as surgeon on the *Reformation*.

1664.—Deposition and complaint made to King Charles II. of French proceedings in Grand Placentia in 1662, when, as sworn to by one Isaac Dethick, soldiers, women, and men landed there from a great French ship, sent to the king by the hands of Mr. Robert Prowse. First agitation against French pretensions in Newfoundland.

1665.—First edition of "Sir J. Child's Discourse." Position of the Newfoundland fishery fully debated with reference to the Dutch war; only one ship of Dartmouth to go out. In June, De Ruyter, Dutch Admiral, plundered and destroyed St. John's and several other harbours. C. Martin endeavoured to defend St. John's.

1666.—H. d'Almy's propositions about the fishery.

1667.—William Hinton in Newfoundland hoping to be made Governor. Petition, on 18th March, to make George Kirke Governor. Petition of Totnes, &c. on 28th August against a Governor. Depositions taken on 28th August, at Topsham, about Sir D. Kirke's misrule, and on 20th November at Totnes. Petition of Bristol and the Merchants Adventurers for a Governor and soldiers, on 6th December, referred to Lord Anglesey. C. Martin again fortifying St. John's. Proclamation of Louis granting bounty to Newfoundlanders settling at Placentia.

1669.—Merchants petition the king against sending out a Governor to Newfoundland, as proposed by Captain Robert Robinson on 15th December; Robinson summoned to London.

1670.—February 4, Order in Council that a chaplain should be sent with the annual convoy to Newfoundland "for keeping people living there in Christianity." Rules issued by the Lords of the Council to regulate fisheries; every fifth man to be a green man; captains to give bond for £100 to bring back every fisherman they took out, &c., &c. James Young, who kept a diary of his journeys, wrote about the fishery. On 23rd December a petition, presented by Western merchants, for the regulation of the fishery.

1671.—Deposition of Mathews sworn on 27th January. Letter from Prowse to Gould on 14th March.

1672.—Order enforcing bonds to prevent men going to New England; ships required to be better armed.

1673.—Dutch squadron of four ships plundered the Kirkes at Ferryland, but beaten off from St. John's by Christopher Martin. The king appointed a Select Committee to take depositions in the West about the fishery.

1674.—Orders made by the Commissioners of Trade and Plantations forbidding planters to inhabit within six miles of the shore, from Cape Race to Cape Bonavista. Sir J. Williamson alludes to Lord Baltimore's house at Ferryland as being still habitable.

1675.—Charles II. gave up duty of 5 per cent. paid by French. On the 12th February both sides were heard about the fishery; on 15th April the Council for Trade reported against a Governor and fortifications; and on 5th May they required the settlers to return to England, or go to other plantations. Letter on 12th September, from Berry to Southwell, about the planters. Troate's report about a murder in St. John's not investigated, though known about by Captain Carter, &c.

1676.—27th January, old charter renewed with additional clauses. Captain Russell compelling several ship fishermen to rebuild stages they had destroyed. Order to Sir John Berry to burn houses, and root out population; owing to the exertions of John Downing, a resident merchant, an order from the king procured to annul it. Mr. John Alyrod's account of Placentia. 24th October, Downing's narrative; first mention of New England traders. Downing's petition of 7th November heard. T. Martin treated by the merchants in St. John's as an alien, and forced to hire a stage. Thompson's report on Placentia. Dutch reported to have destroyed many French fishing vessels.

1677.—Petitions of C. and T. Martin and Troate, of H.M.S. *Swan*; and on 25th January and 23rd March further petitions of Downing. Order sent on March 28th, by the *St. John's Merchant*, directing ship fishermen not to molest the settlers; confirmed on 18th May by Captain Wheler. Petition of St. John's merchants on 10th December brought to England by Sir W. Poole, H.M.S. *Leopard*. T. Oxford's petition reciting damage done to stages.

1679.—Petitions of W. Downing on 10th February and 2nd April; of Oxford on 2nd April, reciting that his family had a warehouse in St. John's for seventy years; of Oxford and Downing, on April 29th, for a Governor, fortifications, and a minister; also petition of Oxford, about his negro servant, on 3rd July; and of Downing on 4th November. T. Weighmouth breaking into Downing's rooms. Captain Wright, H.M.S. *Reverse*, keeping order in St. John's.

1680.—In May, Robinson asking leave to build a fort at St. John's. Petitions of Hinton and Downing. W. Downing probably died on his way to Newfoundland. Account of Downing's family. Captain Robert Robinson and three merchants at Bay Bulls, on 29th September; condemn four fishermen to be ducked for damaging French room at Colinet, &c., and two merchants to pay the damages.

1681.—Destrick and Molin's report of Placentia. Fort in ruins. Twenty-two Basque vessels from Port of Passage fishing and whaling in Newfoundland. French attempting to prevent Basque fishing in their neighbourhood. Captains Talbot and Storys on the coast. Bad fishery.

1682.—Captain D. Jones, H.M.S. *Diamond*, reports about New Englanders, on 12th September, from Bay Bulls. Captain Wren at Bay Bulls in the *Centurion*.

1683.—Petition of Downing on the 11th October.

1684.—Captain Wheler, H.M.S. *Tiger*, reports on French settlements and fishing; no wood to be had within two miles of St. John's; good fishery.

The Commonwealth had only been maintained by the strong hand of Cromwell, soon after his death the English republic came to an end. The general voice of the country was in favour of a limited monarchy and a hereditary sovereign. Under the astute tactics of Monk the Restoration was brought about—unbridled licence in place of Puritan severity.

From the records, reports of naval officers (which began in this reign) and private letters (now for the first time published), we are able to give a pretty accurate description of Newfoundland under the Restoration. It was an unfortunate change for our poor Colony. Charles the father had chastised the settlers with whips, the dissolute son chastised them with scorpions. Lest I should be accused of exaggeration in the matter of the expulsion of the settlers in this reign, I have given in all possible cases the official documents, or, when too long, a *résumé* of their contents. Information about the Colony is much fuller in this period. There was no regular post in England, but we have the rudiments of a newspaper, the short-lived *Publique Intelligencer*, and the still existing *London Gazette*.

CHARLES II.
From an engraving after Lely.

The two most important events in this reign were the irruption of the French into the Colony, the foundation of their capital at Placentia in 1662, and the attempted expulsion of the settlers by an Order in Council from Charles II. in 1675.

On these subjects I have endeavoured to give all the information that can be gathered from the contemporary records. I have been obliged, from want of space, to omit the long discussion before the Council contained in Secretary Williamson's note-book, a very interesting paper from Sir R. Robinson in favour of a Governor, and numbers of naval reports. I have stated the main argument on both sides—all that space would permit; my endeavour has been to give my readers a general view of the actors performing on the Newfoundland scene—to bring to life the dead and forgotten Terra-novian heroes of those days.

One of the first acts of Charles II. in 1660 was the issuing of a long proclamation for the stricter observance of Lent, assigning as one reason "the good it produces in the employment of fishermen." The Puritans

A PRIMITIVE COURT.

of the day refused to fast in Lent or to eat fish; it savoured of prelacy and superstition; they would have none of it. New England's plan of giving a remission of taxation to the citizen who could prove his consumption of fish for one-third of the year, was a more workable way of encouraging the sale of fish.

SMALL CRAFT.
From De Veer's Waerachtighe, 1605.

West Country interest was all-prevailing with the king, so in the same year, 1660, an Act was passed remitting the duty on salt used in the fishery, and exempting other materials required in this industry from all duties. In 1663 the Newfoundland fishery was to be for ever relieved from all taxes and tolls, and the same Act imposed stringent duties on all fish and products of the seas imported into the kingdom by foreigners and aliens. It was a wise and beneficial measure, made entirely for the interest of the West Country adventurers.

There were no court-houses, jails, or regular administration of justice in the Colony in those days. Sir David Kirke, in a patriarchal way, had been wont to administer quarter-deck law from the penthouse of his old house in Ferryland. The captain of the convoy, for the first time in our history, assumes this authority, and we have a very full account of the trial of four prisoners for the destruction of the "cabins" of a Frenchman called Ducarrow, at Colinet Island, where he was the admiral, and of the robbery and destruction of his shalloways and shallops. The case was clearly proved on the admission of the delinquents.

From the evidence it appears to have been a common practice amongst the fishermen to steal French boats in the winter. Both the depredators and the planters who supplied them and shared their plunder richly deserved punishment. Captain Robert Robinson, R.N. (afterwards knighted, and an applicant for the Governorship of Newfoundland), tried them on board the man-of-war. Three merchants sat as nautical assessors, after the Admiralty practice, or as a primitive jury; the whole proceeding was illegal, but it was eminently just, summary, and effective.

The judgment of the Court was:—

"Ducarrow v. Knap and ors.

"Whereas Francis Knapman, John Wallis, William Couch, Samuel Wood, four of the six persons who did the damage at Colinet last winter to the Frenchmen haven been taken and confined aboard this ship:

"We the undersigned have seriously considered to have ye above duck[1] at ye maine yarde of this ship for a public example to all this Island; and they shall be liable for the said damage legally proved and the damage shall be made good by Pollard and Rolson who fitted them out for that fishing voyage. The damage is said to be no more than £50 or £60.

H.M.S. Assistance, Bay Bulls, Sep. 29, 1680.
ROBERT ROBINSON, Captain, R.N.
STEPHEN AKARMAN of Bay Bulls.
JOHN BEVERLEY   do.
AARON BROWNING   do.   and at Trepassey."

We have to recount about this period the ignominous failure of the English Navy in North America and elsewhere; the men, however, were just as brave as ever; the English merchant sailors showed a gallant front to the enemy, whilst Charles's Royal Navy was being thrashed by the Dutch.

An old West Country captain, Christopher Martin, master mariner of Cockington, in Devon, in 1673, the closing year of our war with Holland, beat off the Dutch from St. John's, and defeated four noted pirates, Captain Everson and his comrades.

No doubt there were many such encounters as Martin describes, many mute inglorious Nelsons amongst these Devonian skippers, who fished and traded in Newfoundland; the records give us an account of a still more gallant action fought by Captain Holman, which will be described later on.

Martin was not only a brave mariner, but a sensible, shrewd old fellow; his practical suggestions about a Governor and increase of inhabitants were opposed to the views of all his Devonshire associates.

---

[1] Ducking from the yard-arm, like keel-hauling, was an ancient naval punishment in use probably up to the last century. The culprit was hoisted to the yard-arm, suddenly dropped and hauled up again from one to seven times. In keel-hauling, the sailor was run from yard arm to yard-arm right under the keel of the ship. They were both most barbarous punishments.

I will let this gallant old merchant captain tell his own tale in his own way :—

"Report of Christopher Martin, of Cockington, Devon.

"Has been 17 years Vice-Admiral of St. John's; was once Admiral. If French took Newfoundland and St. John's very hard to get it back again and there would be great danger to ships passing so near the coast to and from America.

"In 1665 and 1667 he landed his guns and built small forts with earth and with his own ammunition defended the harbour. In October 1673, with 6 guns out of the *Elias Andrews* defended St. Johns against Hollanders on their way from New York; he was there with provisions; defended St. Johns against Captain Everson and three other men of warr and with less than 30 men forced them from the Harbour's mouth.

"Considers a Governor and increase of inhabitants absolutely necessary to keep off the French who have three quarters of the Island and Placentia strongly fortified."[1]

In view of the constant danger to which our infant Colony was exposed from pirates, and the still more formidable encounters with the fleets of our enemies, it seems very strange that there were no military or naval preparations to resist this constant, ever menacing danger. Beyond the odd ship or two for convoy of our fishing fleet to the Mediterranean in August and September, England gave us no protection, and no ruler or governor virtually until 1728, and then only a floating ruler for about two months in the year.

Many strenuous efforts were made to obtain a commander-in-chief for the Colony; the attempt was always fiercely resisted by the West Countrymen. In this struggle about the Governorship we catch glimpses of the social condition of the Colony, and of the wealth and position of the leaders of society in the four principal settlements, St. John's, Ferryland, Harbour Grace, and Quidi Vidi.

One of the claimants for the office of Governor appears to have been Captain Robert Robinson, R.N., who made interest with James II., then Duke of York.

Another was William Hinton, an old hanger-on of the Stuart family. His father had been Gentleman of the Chamber, and had spent great sums of money for the king, £700 in Sir George Booth's business raising a troop of horse. The son was several years abroad with His Majesty Charles II. when in exile, and says in his petitions—

"That he never asked the King for anything but the Governorship of Newfoundland which His Majesty had promised to him several times.

"He hath all sorts of household stuff in the country—£2,500 worth—which have layen there a great while and the Inhabitants being sensible of his large expense and endeavours for their welfare; that if the King gives it to any one else he will be ruined; that he hath for a long time studied the advancement of the Colony, and no one His Majesty can send will pretend to know more about the country than he does."[1]

[1] *Board of Trade, Newfoundland.*

This application from an old and faithful retainer received no response; Charles's ministers were bribed and controlled by Child and the West Countrymen.

The only other rival for the Governorship, which was worth £400 per annum, was William Downing. He proposes—

"The just and readiest way the tax upon the boats may be collected is through
George Kirke Esquire at Fermouze,
Mr. John Downing at Que de Vide,
Mr. Thomas Oxford at St. Johns,
Mr. John Pinn at Havre de Grace;[1]
all these persons having correspondence through the whole country would collect the money at no trouble to the Governour."[2]

The Downings were the sons of the former Governor under Hamilton's charter. Mr. Thomas Oxford appears to have been, like Hinton, a man of some position. He kept a negro house-servant—a most aristocratic appendage in those days—whom the West Countrymen forcibly took away.[3]

Many of the Devonians, more sensible and patriotic than their fellows, strongly urged the appointment of a Governor and the fortification of the principal harbours. Weymouth, Bristol, and London were strongly in favour of the appointment. Their efforts were in vain.

The population of Newfoundland during this reign is variously estimated. The various rough calculations are given in the statistics; they appear to understate the number of the resident planters.

By far the most important event in this reign is the occupation of the Island by the French.

It may be argued that the assumption as to the turpitude of Charles in this transaction is based on very slender grounds. I do not think so; the character of Charles is so vile that, to use a Newfoundland expression, we would not "put it past him." He gave up Dunkirk at the very same time.

To fitly describe the epoch in English annals known in our histories as "The happy restoration of Our Sovereign Lord King Charles," one has to borrow the epithet which an American authoress applied to the administration of Indian affairs in the United States—"A century of dishonour:" and truly the sovereignty of Charles II. was a veritable reign of infamy.

Fire and plague decimated the land. To these terrible calamities were added the horrors of war. We were defeated by the Dutch, the

---

[1] The Pynns are one of the oldest English families in this country; the principal branch left about 1842, and emigrated to Wisconsin, where they have helped to build up that rising State.

Sir Henry Pynn, a brave officer, knighted for his gallant conduct on the field of battle, is a descendant of this John Pynn.

[2] *Board of Trade, Newfoundland.*

[3] "Also had his covenant negro servant valued worth £60 taken from him last fishing season, all which he is ready to make out by bill of sale and oath." (*B. T., Nfld.*)

THE SURRENDER OF PLACENTIA.

enemy's guns were heard in London destroying Sheerness and the shipping in the river. Never since the Norman Conquest had England suffered such humiliation. The crowning disgrace of the reign, however, was the secret treaty between Charles and Louis XIV, by which England became the vassal of France, English policy, foreign and domestic, being virtually governed by the French king. Out of this arose the war with our ancient allies, the Dutch.

JEFFERY'S MAP.
From the English Pilot, 1775.

The details of this arrangement are now published, but there were many other questions agreed upon, known only to the two conspirators and their immediate confidants; amongst these was, doubtless, the agreement by which all the southern and western portion of Newfoundland, from Cape Race to Cape Ray, was passed over to France.

No positive evidence, no State documents, can now be produced to prove this surrender of English territory; but the circumstances under which it took place, and the evidence of the contemporary records, leave little doubt that the occupation of Placentia by the French in 1662 was made with the connivance and consent of the English king.

During both the administration of Cromwell and the reign of Charles I. no foreigner had attempted to make any permanent settlement in Newfoundland. Up to 1662 no Frenchman had ever lived a winter on the Island.[1]

I will describe, as well as it can be gathered from the records, the surrounding circumstances of the base surrender by which France, without firing a shot, obtained the largest and fairest portion of our Island colony. By this betrayal of English territory and English rights Charles planted in our midst our most bitter rival; he exposed our infant settlements to those murderous raids afterwards made on the English planters. Not only did the king endanger the safety of this Island, but all the North American Colonies suffered in aftertime from this augmentation of French naval power in America.

The most important evidence on the subject is the testimony of Isaac Dethick, an English resident at Placentia. By this time the British inhabitants had spread themselves not only around the eastern coast, but some small parties had gone beyond Bonavista, fishing and furring as far as Notre Dame Bay, and some, like Dethick, had been attracted by the splendid position of Placentia, and had made it their residence:—

"Deposition of John Raynor late deputy Governor in Newfoundland.

"In 1662 a great French ship full of men and women put into Grand Placentia, where she landed a great number of soldiers and passengers who fortified the Harbour with 18 pieces of ordnance as one Isaac Dethick who was there affirmed.

"Dethick saw the Governor's Commission under the great seal of France for the command of the whole country of Newfoundland, and the following year was forced to remove from his Plantation and settle at the Bay of Ards [Bay de Verds]

---

[1] Answer, in 1614, to the complaints presented to King James I. by the Sieur de Busseaux, French Ambassador at the Court of His Majesty.

The reply to the first point (which concerned Newfoundland) sets forth the title of England "to the fishery there, which is carried on every year with at least two hundred vessels and more than six thousand persons in the English Colony, who have always treated the French well, and protected them in their fishing, and allowed them to leave their vessels until they return to fish the next year.

"The French do not inhabit any part of Newfoundland, but are much further away, in a place called Canada, which they call New France; therefore the accusation against the English is most unjust and far from the truth, seeing they have never been near New France, neither hindered or disturbed the French fishery, nor done any injury.

where deponent found him and took from him an account of the French proceedings which he sent for England by Mr. Robert Prowse to be presented to the King." [1]

Besides this testimony we have the further evidence of John Matthews of Ferryland, who appears to have been a sort of sheriff's officer or bailiff in the employ of the governors of the Ferryland plantation. Raynor and Captain Pearce were deputy-governors and also agents for Lord Baltimore when his patent was revived in 1660. Having to take proceedings against a Mr. Russell, in St. Mary's, about a claim for rent, they heard at the same time that some Canadian Indians, who were allies of the French, were shooting and trapping in the same neighbourhood (then and now the finest game preserve in the Island). They despatched John Matthews to arrest Russell and the leader or chief of the Indians, and bring them to Ferryland to explain their proceedings to the Deputy-Governor. Matthews gives a graphic account of his adventures:—

"These are to certify to whom it may concerne that I John Matthews in ye yeare 1662 being in ye Newfoundland was sent by Captain Pearce and Mr. Raynor the Honble. Deputy-Governors with their warrants to St. Marys to bring one Mr. Russell ye Inhabitant there and ye master of ye Indians (who came to kill beavers and other beasts for ffurres) before them to Fferryland; but instead of having the warrant obeyed, a French Captain seized on me demanding what I came for. I replyed for ye said Mr. Russell and ye Master of ye Indians to go before ye Governours to answer and give an account of their actions for making an attempt upon ye Islande without any authority from His Majesty of Great Brittaine; which he scornfully answered, saying we had no power there nor in any other of ye Southern parts of ye Lande but all did belong to ye Ffrench Kinge whereupon I averring that our King was King thereof and of all for about 30 or 40 leagues around about it, was taken prisoner and so kept for about 2 dayes when ye French carryed me aboard and sett forward untill we came nigh Plaisance Fort which was furnished with 28 gunns from whence a shallop came out from ye Governour with command for our returne to St. Maries in pursuite for ye Indians where by Gods providence I made my escape.

"I also further humbly testify that in the year (50) or (51) I having then a lawe-suit depending there against one Nicholas Redhood did procure a Commission out of ye High Court of Admiraltie directed to Sir David Kirke the then Governour to examine witnesses in that cause which said Commission was speeded and returned hither to ye Admiraltie in due forme of lawe.

"And whensoever any differences arose between ye Planters and Inhabitants these ye said Sir David Kirke did always judge and determine the same; whereby ye said lande was peaceably and quietly governed to ye generall benefitt of ye population and no persons were suffered to carry wood away in shipps, only to cut what was necessary for fishing and all this I do testify upon my certaine knowledge to be true witness my hand this 27th day of January 1670.

"Jo. MATTHEWS." [2]

Lady Hopkings also states, "That the French declared that " King Louis had a grant from the King of England to take as his

[1] *Records.* [2] *B.M. MSS., Eg.* 2395.

" proper right from Cape Race round by the southward and westward
" to Cape Bonavista." [1]

I think we may fairly gather from these statements and from the formal action of the French, their taking possession of a part of the Colony in such an official manner, that King Charles had really surrendered the best part of the Island to the French, leaving only from Cape Race to Bonavista for the English. In further proof of this, in one of his Orders in Council, the English boundary is given as between Cape Race and Cape Bonavista.

Of course such a transaction was kept a profound secret from his subjects both in England and America. Poor dupes like Raynor, Lady Hopkings, and Robert Prowse busied themselves with remonstrances and petitions to the king about the monstrous aggression of the French.

The petitioners presented their addresses and affidavits. In the Court language still in use, "They were laid at the foot of the throne, and his "Majesty was graciously pleased to receive the same." I have heard a Hibernian orator and colonial official expatiate at great length on this expression, as showing the peculiar interest the sovereign takes in the Colony. This stereotyped answer, written by an under-clerk, was the only reply the anxious settlers received from the king.

The French showed excellent judgment in the selection of their colonial capital. The situation of Placentia is extremely beautiful and picturesque; the railway from Whitbourne, instead of descending the north-east valley into the ancient French metropolis, by a curious freak of engineering ascends, and from a lofty height the traveller sees the whole panorama of Plaisance spread out before him; below is the beautiful north-east arm dotted with islands, cottages, and farms,

---

[1] 1660 [? 1670.]
"The information and relation of the Lady Hopkings who came purposely ffrom Newfoundland to make knowne to His Royall Majesty as ffollowes:

"That the lat Sir David Kirke being sent for over by the late usurper and all his estate taken away ffor his faithful service to His late Majesty in Newfoundland and since deceased.

"That Island hath been without a Governour and the Ffrench taking notice thereof have settled a garrison about eight or nine years since at Plesentia and about two years since another at Chapian Rouge 25 leagues distance ffrom the other (which in Sir David Kirke's lifetime they never dirst attempt) and by their yeerly intriguing and threatening of ye English gives them just cause of apprehention of their own saffety and the losse of the Island to ye great prejudice of His Majesty's affaires, if not timely prevented, and the rather the Governour for ye Ffrench keeps ten vessels all ye winter there which carrye 30 or 40 men a pece and are very well fitted to coast; which vessels are sufficient to destroy the English plantation as now it stands. And by sad experience the rutter [?] coming . . there without controlle took gounes [guns] shippes cattle, goods and what he pleased, to ye ruining of His Majesty's subjects in Newfoundland for want of Government.

"The Ffrench this year have given out that the French King hasse a grant ffrom the King of England to take as his proper writ from Cape D race all to the Westward and from Bonavista to ye Norward."

(B.M. MSS., Eg. 2395.)

[The date 1660 is evidently wrong; it has been added by some Board of Trade official.]

beyond is the shining sea, the beach, and the town, with its beautiful Catholic chapel and houses. As the traveller descends a very steep grade to the Jersey side, the other part of the grand panorama unfolds itself: the beautiful south-east arms sweeping past tall fir-crowned bluffs in a winding circuit for eight miles.

It was not, however, for its romantic beauty, but for the sterner reason of defence against the enemy, and for its practical advantage as a trading and fishing port, that the French selected Placentia as their capital and chief port in Newfoundland.

BURIN PLACENTIA BAY.

Whilst French colonisation has been a failure, her military organisation, and especially her skill in works of defence and military engineering, have always been specially prominent. The selection of Placentia was fully justified—it was never captured by the English.

The first fort erected in 1662 was at the entrance of the gut on the Placentia side; the defence was afterwards strengthened by another battery on the Jersey side. The large battery on Castle Hill, Fort Louis, is mistakenly placed by Bishop Howley and Dr. Mullock at the entrance of the gut; the small batteries at Croyeconr and Point Verd are of later date. Placentia was the Gibraltar of North America.

---

¹ This fort Le Hontan describes:—"It stood upon a point of land so close to the narrow entrance of the Harbour [the gut] that ships going in graze so to speak upon the angle of the bastion."

This first fort on the Placentia side of the gut must not be confused with Fort Louis on the hill, built afterwards, or with the second fort erected on the Jersey side, which made Placentia so strong.

Le Hontan was on duty at Placentia for several years; he did not bear a very good character.

It successfully resisted Commodore Williams' attack in 1692, and the still more formidable squadron of Hovenden Walker in 1711. The site was not only admirably situated for military purposes, it was equally well chosen as a metropolis of their fish trade. It was a great oversight on the part of the English not to have secured this desirable harbour: its freedom from field ice in the spring makes it earlier than the eastern bays for fishing operations; its proximity to Cape St. Mary's and its abundant supply of spring herring for bait renders it one of the very best places for the cod fishery.

The gut was then larger and much deeper than it is at present; the beach, with an extension at Little Placentia, an admirable ship harbour in Placentia arm, provided safety for their fleet and drying room for the large French catch.

Strategically, politically, and piscatorially, Placentia was admirably chosen as a capital place of defence and fishing centre. At a later period it became prominent as the only settlement in Newfoundland where there was an important resident French population, chapel, substantial fortress, and garrison.

Our enemies did all in their power to entice the English to settle there. By a proclamation of Louis, about 1667, masters of ships were allowed five livres for every man and three for every woman they carried to Placentia. Newfoundlanders were offered one year free subsistence—afterwards increased to three.

The Colony did not flourish. The first royal governor was an adventurer named Gargot; he had no salary, but was not left without remuneration. He set up a royal store, and obliged all the fishermen to buy from him; one of his occupations was measuring out the beach room for the ships. As she arrived, each vessel took as much water frontage as her foreyard measured; for a consideration Gargot would throw in a few more feet.

All the French fishing admirals were under the Placentia governor; they had to report and be governed by his instructions. Naturally the French are much more subservient to their superiors than the English. Garneau tells us the French Newfoundlanders were a free and hardy race. They chafed under the tyranny of Gargot and his successor De La Poype, and petitioned the king against their harsh rule.[1]

Five times before 1685 English buccaneers raided Placentia, and stripped the inhabitants of all their moveables. The French Government, like the English, soon began to grudge the expense of the

---

[1] Baron Le Hontan says:—"The French Governors look upon their places as a gold mine given them in order to enrich themselves; so that the public good must always march behind private interest."

garrison and fortifications at Placentia. Captain Wheler, Commander of the English convoy in 1684, says:—

"The French leave Placentia in July. They have large ships of 36 guns, about 30 vessels altogether. The French inhabitants are much fewer than ours, they have but one old ruined fort and little ammunition; the Inhabitants are as negligent as ours in the matter of strength.

"Our ships are not denied liberty to fish in the French districts. No forainers fish up the Eastern Coast, but upon the Banks the French frequent much.

"They have a Governor at Placentia. The first Master at each port is Admiral but receives his orders from the French Governor who is of great use to measure out rooms [and thus put an end to the constant fighting that went on about the debateable subject of fishing premises, known in Newfoundland as rooms].

"Seldom any convoy for the French Merchant vessels. At Trepasse but two or three French families where our nation and theirs fish without disagreeing. The French begin to fish about 18 leagues north of Bonavista for 40 leagues [along the N.E. coast] and are at utter variance with the Indians [Red Indians—Beothics, I presume, on account of the terrible massacre mentioned by Kirke] who are numerous and so the French never reside in winter and always have their arms by them. Six years since their trade was great—60 great ships. Any ship of another nation bearing proportion of expense of defence [in those days the attacks were from pirates] might fish. They catch about 200 qtls. per boat with five men and give high wages; the French come in June and stay sometimes until October. Trade decaying extremely. About 52° N. some Biscayners used to fish with no improvement.

"French have advantage of us, as there are plenty of fish at Placentia, and going sooner to market, their fishing ships gain considerably."[1]

This is a plain narration of facts, and agrees with the history of the times.

To understand this weakness of both French and English in Newfoundland, we must bear in mind that from 1665 both countries were at war with the Dutch, then the greatest naval power in Europe. They made two successful attacks on the English in Newfoundland—in 1665 on St. John's, and in 1673 on Ferryland. In 1676, from the *English News Letter* of October 3, we have an account of a successful Dutch raid on the French :—

"The Merchants hear that six Dutch capers have quite destroyed the French fishing fleet in Newfoundland having taken 90 out of 100 sail that were there—They had afterwards landed and taken the Castle of Canida."[2]

It is probable this refers to Placentia, and may be exaggerated, but we may readily believe if the Dutch attacked the English settlements they would not spare their inveterate enemies the French, who had commenced a most unprovoked war against them.

Curiously enough, in studying the early history of the French colonies in America, we find the same causes at work which retarded

[1] *Records.*   [2] *Historical MS. Comn. Report.*

184   REIGN OF CHARLES II.

Newfoundland. The first French settlers in Canada were under the control of "The company of one hundred associates"—they were greedy monopolists; like the West Country adventurers in Newfoundland, fishing and furring were their only occupations, and they did all in their power to prevent colonisation.

PLAN OF PLACENTIA.
From Lt. Henton's Nouveau Voyage, 1708.

The fortifications were neglected, and agriculture so little attended to that, except under the walls of the forts, there was absolutely no cleared land; the country was to be kept for furring and fishing only

All this was changed, however, by the arrival of Frontenac, twice viceroy, the ablest ruler that ever guided the destiny of New France. It was under this gallant Frenchman and his distinguished subordinate, D'Iberville, that the subsequent successful attacks were made on Newfoundland in 1696 and 1697.

In 1676 the French fished at St. Maries, Coroneat (Colinet Island), St. Peter's, Great and Little St. Lawrence, Three Islands, Petit Nord, and several places west, besides Placentia, their chief place. As far as we can learn, the French had really only one permanent settlement—(Placentia), and this was begun in 1662; all the other places mentioned are merely resorted to by the ship fishermen from France for the fishing season, and were abandoned in the autumn.

We have clear proof of this in the evidence given on the inquiry about the damage to Johannis Ducarrow's fishing cabin and premises at Admiral's Beach and Colinet Island.[1] We find from testimony of the servants who confessed to the destruction of the cabin at Colinet Island, and their shelter in the vat at St. Mary's, that all these places were at that date, 1680, uninhabited. Thomson says, in 1676 :—

"Placentia had two Forts thirteen guns fifteen families of which four are English. That there were only two French families at Trepassey."[1]

There were probably guns and some small fortifications at St. Pierre, but at present it seems to me doubtful if there were any winter residents before 1670. Downing says, in 1670 the French had Placentia and St. Peter's fortified. Mr. John Aylrod's description of two hundred and fifty families and 2,000 people, besides the 400 soldiers, is clearly exaggerated; after the treaty of Utrecht in 1713 only one hundred and eighty persons from all the French settlements in Newfoundland left the Island (in war time they would be within the forts), all had to go by the terms of the treaty. The only inhabited places then mentioned as belonging to the French were Placentia and St. Pierre. Baudoin says that the French settlements were small compared with the English. In 1702, when Sir John Leake destroyed St. Peter's, there was only one small fort with six guns. There were French residents in Fortune Bay in 1680, but few in number compared to the Jersey and English settlers.

We get the following description of Placentia in 1681 from two Englishmen residing there, Stephen Destrick and one Molins. They say :—

"The payment of French Fishermen is made by boat [bounty].
"The Fort of 12 guns is in ruins, not above 3 guns now mounted.

[1] *Board of Trade, Newfoundland.*

"The Governor has no allowance from the King nor anything allowed for arms and ammunition but he fishes as other planters do and keeps 8 boats.

"The French have caught this year 300 to 400 qtls. per boat.

"Fish came in sooner upon that coast than on the Eastern shore.

"There are ships of 200 to 400 tons from Bordeaux and St. Jean de Luz, and 15 to 16 Biscainers of 20 and 24 guns.

"Ships of St. Malloes fish at St. Peters. There are 100 ships from St. Mary's to St. Peters and the trade is increasing.

"They let no English live among them except they turn Roman Catholics; and there is a Priest in every ship and they leave some behind to keep the people steadfast in their religion.

"The French have few plantations more than for herbs and roots and a few cattle and do so as we do in winter.

"French generally have a better catch and live cheaper, consequently make more gain.

"A fort at St. Peters is reported.

"There is no trade between the English and French planters.

"The *Biscainers* with ships of great force do fish to the northward of Bonavista and Salvage, and frequently with the French but not with us."

PLACENTIA FARM AND FISHING STAGE.
From Pothorel's History, 1722.

The last of the great Spanish fleet now came only by stealth and under the protection of the French. They were up to this date, 1680, still the great whalers and seal killers on this coast. A shore seal fishery was carried on from the very first settlement by the English, on a small scale, with nets and boats. The product fluctuated very much.

In reading the histories of England and America about this period, the fisheries are almost completely ignored; the truth is that writers love the heroes and despise the economies; the personal, the picturesque, is always attractive, whilst the plain, prosaic aspect of human life, the

---
[1] *Board of Trade, Newfoundland.*

adventures of commerce, the increase of human food, are unnoticed by historians.

Religion and economics are the greatest influences in the world, the two most potent factors in the progress or retardation of the human race. Nothing comes out clearer in our North American history than the preponderating effect of the fishery.

The relative influence and strength of France and England in the New World was entirely controlled by this business. Towards the close of the Stuart period, at the end of the seventeenth century, the French fishery in Newfoundland and the Gulf of St. Lawrence rose to abnormal dimensions; it is variously estimated as employing from sixteen thousand to twenty thousand men; it extended to Nova Scotia, Cape Breton, St. John's Island, now Prince Edward Island, Gaspé, and Newfoundland. The naval power of France rose in proportion; all the

SALMONIER, ST. MARY'S BAY.

English expeditions against New France and Acadié were miserable failures, whilst under Frontenac and D'Iberville the English possessions were raided from Newfoundland to Hudson's Bay. Until the last fall of Louisbourgh and Quebec, France threatened the very existence of the American colonies. She had then undoubtedly the preponderance of sea power in America.

The fishery is the recognised nursery for her navy; the only alleged excuse for the extravagant bounties given to her fishermen at St. Pierre and Iceland is to secure a supply of men for the Marine.

At the profligate Court at St. James's, the Devonshire gentry still held a foremost place; their influence for evil against the Newfoundland settlers was immensely increased by the support of Sir Josiah Child, author of a pamphlet, first published in 1665, "A New Discourse on Trade." He issued a second edition, very much enlarged (from which these extracts are taken) on December 24th, 1694.

His character has been powerfully drawn by Macaulay. An exceedingly able merchant, a vigorous writer, with immense wealth, which he used most unscrupulously to bribe and corrupt. This great monopolist, head of the East India Company, was the evil genius of Newfoundland. He begins his discourse on the various trades by enumerating:—

"Amongst the Trades not yet lost is the Newfoundland fish trade.[1] In the year 1605 the English employed 250 sail of ships great and small in fishing upon that coast and it is now too apparent that we do not so employ from all parts above 80 ships. So that the price of fish has increased from seventeen rials—eight shillings and sixpence—to twenty-four rials or twelve shillings as it now sells in this country.

"This being the case of England in relation to this trade it is certainly worth the enquiry—

"1st. How we came to decay in it? 2ndly. What means may be used to recover our ancient greatness or at least to prevent our further diminution therein?

"The decay I attribute, First and principally to the growing liberty which is every year more and more used in Romish countries, as well as others, of eating flesh in Lent and on Fish days.

"2. To a late abuse crept in that trade of sending over private boat keepers which hath much diminished the number of fishing ships.

"3. To the great increase of the French fishery of Placentia and other ports on the back side of Newfoundland.

"4. To the several wars within these twenty years which have much impoverished the Western Merchants, and reduced them to carry on a great part of that trade at Bottomry taken upon adventure of the ship at 20 % per annum.

"What means may be used to recover it. For this two contrary ways have been propounded.

"Firstly: to send a Governor to reside there, as well for the defence of the country against invasion, as to manage the fishery there by Inhabitants upon the place; this hath often been propounded by the Planters and some merchants in London.

"The second way propounded and which is directly contrary to the former is by West Country Merchants and owners of the fishing ships, and that is to have *no Governour nor Inhabitants permitted to reside at Newfoundland nor any passengers or private boat keepers suffered to fish at Newfoundland. This latter way is most agreeable to my proposition* and if it could be effected *I am persuaded would revive the decayed English fishing trade at Newfoundland and be otherwise greatly for the advantage of this Kingdom* and that for the following reasons:—

"Because most of the provisions the Planters do make use of viz. Bread, Beef, Pork, Butter, Cheese, Clothes, and Irish Bandel Cloth, Linen and Woollen, Irish Stockings, as also nets, hooks, lines &c. they are supplied with from New England and Ireland and with wine oyle and linnen by the salt ships from France

---

[1] Preface.

and Spain; in consequence the labour as well as the clothing and feeding of so many men is lost to England . . .

"If it be the interest of all trading nations principally to encourage navigation especially those trades which employ most shipping . . . . then certainly it is the interest of England to discountenance and abate the number of Planters at Newfoundland for if they should increase it will happen to us as it hath to the fishery of New England which many years since was managed by English ships from the Western Ports but as Plantations there increased fell to the sole employment of the people settled there and nothing of the trade is left the poor old Englishmen but the liberty of carrying now and then by courtesie or purchase a ship-loading of fish to Bilboa when their own New England ships are better employed or not at leasure to do it . . .

"It is manifest before there were boat keepers fish was sold cheaper than it is now by 40 %. Reason: because boat keepers being able fishermen and earlier on the ground beat the ship fishermen but after driving away English ship fishermen from New England and Newfoundland they became lazy."

Then follow the usual West County arguments against a governor. Speaking of the fishing admirals he says :—

"A Government there is already of ancient custom amongst the masters of the ships to which the fishermen are inured and that free from oppression and adapted to the trade insomuch *that though a better might be wished*, I never hope to see it.

"New England is the most prejudicial plantation to this kingdom because of all the American plantations His Majesty has none so apt for building of shipping as New England, nor comparably so qualified for the breeding of seamen not only by reason of the natural industry of that people but principally by reason of their cod and mackerel fisheries and in my poor opinion there is nothing more prejudicial and in prospect more dangerous to any Mother Country than the increase of shipping in her colonies plantations or Provinces."[1]

Well might Bacon expatiate on the narrow selfishness of traders. This shrewd business man could not see that prosperous colonies were England's best customers. In order to rightly appreciate the enormous influence of a monopolist like Child in the corrupt age of Charles II., we must try and picture to ourselves the president of one of the gigantic American trusts of our own time owning all the ministers of State, and the Courts, with unlimited money and unlimited power to bribe, and no questions asked about funds.

Child never rendered an account of the thousands he spent in bribery—£10,000 to Charles, £10,000 to his brother, the Duke of York, diamonds and thousands to the king's mistresses and ministers. Imagine all this if you can, and then you can faintly realise the enormous power of this gigantic bully, this Restoration Jay Gould, on the destinies of Newfoundland.

The main object of Child was to defend the East India Company. It shows how great was his ability and the power of his corrupting

[1] Sir Josiah Child, *A New Discourse on Trade*, 1694, pp. 205-215.

influence, that he maintained himself to the last against all his opponents. The Newfoundland matter was only a trifle to amuse his leisure and help his brother monopolists, the West Countrymen.

This plan so speciously sketched out to exterminate the Newfoundland Colonists, although determined upon, was not immediately carried into effect, even the king and his advisers shrunk from such cold-blooded cruelty. In 1665, when this pamphlet was first published, we were at war with the Dutch, and it was thought advisable that some permanent settlers should be left to defend the Colony.

Various minor attempts, however, were made to carry out this policy piecemeal; a very valuable series of parliamentary papers[1] on Newfoundland affairs set forth the various measures that were taken to destroy the colonial population. Neither the Commissioners for Foreign Trade and Plantation, nor the Western Adventurers, nor least of all Sir Josiah Child, saw anything extraordinary or improper in this decision to destroy a whole population of Englishmen, to condemn them to ruin, extermination, and exile from their cherished homes and all the accumulated wealth of several generations. This paper, which is too long to quote in full, begins by setting forth the state of the fishery in 1644, when, as the Western Adventurers allege:—

SIR JOSIAH CHILD.
From an engraving after Riley.

"There were 270 ships annually employed in the Newfoundland fishery besides those who brought salt and carried the fish to market computing the ships at 80 tons each and for every 100 tons 5 men and 10 boats. There were in all 21,600 tons 10,800 seamen 2,160 boats. To each boat is allowed 5 men. Usual catch 200 to 300 qtls., which was then sold at from 14 to 16 rials—7s. to 8s. per qtl. They attribute the subsequent decline to the civil war and to the settlements encouraged by Treworgie.

"By letters patent 28 Jany. 1660 this additional clause was inserted in the new charter, that no person was to be carried or transported in any of the ships except those of the ships company or such as are to plant and do intend to settle there. In 1663 circular letters were written to the mayors and magistrates of West Country Towns to enforce this order.

[1] I am indebted to George H. Emerson, Q.C., for this work, which formerly belonged to John Hutt Noble, Deputy Naval Officer in Newfoundland.

"In 1669 an order was made to obtain the return of the names of offenders against this rule and in the meantime to stop them proceeding on the voyage to Newfoundland. Then followed a long dispute about the appointment of a Governor which after a protracted debate in the Council was finally rejected in 1670.

"The Western adventurers proposed that the inhabitants should transport themselves to Jamaica, St. Kitts, or some other of His Majesty's plantations. This suggestion the Council refused to adopt.

"In 1674 solicitation was again made for the appointment of a Governor.

"On the 15th April 1675 their Lordships the Committee of the Council for Trade reported: That the French had considerably advanced their fishery in Newfoundland; that the people of New England annually took 60,000 qtls. of fish on their own coast; that the adventurers had lost many of their ships in the late war; that the inhabitants destroyed the woods and whatsoever the adventurers left behind; that they occupied the best places, sold brandy and seduced many to stay behind; that a Governor could not cure any part of these evils because the Planters were scattered in 25 harbours 80 leagues apart; that the Trade could not support the charge of forts and a Governor; and that in winter the colony was defended by ice and in summer by the ship fishermen.

"So that unless there was proper reasons for a colony they could see none for a Governor; and against a Colony there are not only the rigours of the climate and the infertility of the soil but that they, the inhabitants, chiefly consumed the products of New England and other foreign parts. . . . . So that on the whole their Lordships having recourse unto the Rules of 1670 found them all so proper and effectual for the advantage of the Trade as to need only the following additions to make their trade revive and flourish:—

"That all Plantations and inhabiting in that Country be discouraged, and in order thereupon that the Commander of His Majestys Convoy should have a Commission to declare at his going this year His Majestys will and pleasure to all planters *that they come voluntarily away* and in case of disobedience that the charter be put in execution next year, for in this single point consists the validity and good effect of the whole Regulation. That the Convoy help and assist those in their transportation who desire to return home, and do declare that if they choose to betake themselves to any other of His Majesty's Plantations, that the Governors are wrote unto to receive them with all favour.

"On the 5th May following His Majesty in Council thought fit for the several considerations in the said Report mentioned to order the Commander of His Convoy bound to Newfoundland *to admonish the Inhabitants either to return home to England, or to betake themselves to others of his Plantations*, and to direct that letters be prepared unto the severall Governors of the said Plantations, that in case any of the said Inhabitants of Newfoundland should arrive within their respective Governments, that they be received with favour. And that all convenient help and assistance towards their settlement be afforded unto them.

"And on the 27 Jany. 1675 His Majesty after due consideration had of the best ways and means of regulating, securing, and improving the fishing Trade in Newfoundland passed the New Charter which recited and confirmed all the Old Laws, and several others were added for the better Government of the Fishery: which if they had been as steadily supported and executed, as they were carefully concerted, in all probability, the subjects of France and the people of New England had reaped very little benefit by their fisheries, and this valuable branch of the British Trade had been firmly re-established and secured.

"The Additional Regulations to the Charter were as follows:—

"1st. That His Majestys subjects may take bait and fish in Newfoundland, and cut wood for stages &c. provided they submit unto and observe the Rules and Orders that are or shall be established.

"2nd. *That no alien take bait* or fish between Cape Race and Cape Bonavista.

"3rd. *That no Planter cut down any wood or inhabit within six miles of the shore.*

"4th. That no Planter shall take up any of the stages &c. before arrival of the fishermen and that they be all provided for.

"5th. That no Master of a fishing vessel transport any seamen or others to Newfoundland unless they belong to the ships company.

"6th. That no more than 60 persons to the 100 Tons be allowed to sail.

"7th. That every fifth Man carried out of England be a green man and not a seaman; and that the Masters provide in England Victuals and other necessaries for the whole voyage, salt only excepted.

"8th. That no vessel do depart directly for Newfoundland in any year before the 1st of March.

"9th. That the Masters give Bonds in £100 to return all persons to England except those employed in carrying fish to market.

"10th. No Master to take up any stage already built with less than twenty-five men. No fishermen to remain in the country at the end of the voyage.

"11th. Admirals, Rear-Admirals and Vice-Admirals are authorised and required to preserve the peace in the Harbours as well as on shore and to see the rules of the fishery put in execution.

"12th. To secure and bring home offenders to England.

"13th. That they yearly publish on the 20th of Sepr. these orders.

"14th. That they keep journals and deliver Copies to the Council.

"And lastly because there is no Court Martial in Newfoundland at present, that if any man there shall kill another, or steal goods to the value of 40s. he shall be brought a prisoner to England, and his crime made known to one of H.M. Principal Secretaries of State to the end order may be given to punish such offenders according to Law.

"Under these encouragements [says the report] the Western Adventurers immediately returned to the fishery."

The report goes on to say :—

"However the adventurers being encouraged by the Lords of the Committee *to put the laws of the charter in execution, they began in 1676 to restrain the disorders of the Planters* and to prevent the transportation of their servants; but they were restrained upon the Petition of the said Planters in November following and the solicitation of those who were either excited by the hopes of procuring advantage for themselves or influenced by the French whose fishery must have been soon rendered precarious if the Charter had been observed."

This is part of "The Report of the Lords Commissioners for Trade "and Plantations to His Majesty relating to the Newfoundland Trade "and Fishery dated 19 Decr. 1718."

The Western Adventurers, having obtained this most inhuman order to extirpate the inhabitants, went over to Newfoundland flushed with success,[1] and immediately on their arrival began the work of destruction.

---

[1] PETITION OF THOMAS MARTIN, 29 Jany 1677.

"I have been in the trade from a boy and now command a shipp. The Fishermen by their late Patent call all that part where the English cure their fish in St. John's their own. Coming from the West Indies in 1676 I asked the then admiral for roome for my sailing crew to fish and cure. He answered I was *an alien* and not concerned in the Patent and therefore I was forced to hire a stage.

THORNTON'S TRADING PART OF NEWFOUNDLAND, WITH INSET PLANS OF ST. JOHN'S AND TRINITY.
From the English Pilot, 1689.

The king had delivered their enemies the planters into their hands, so they considered they had full liberty to wreak their vengeance. The poor settlers at first were frightened and dismayed; there was terrible havoc and damage; Oxford says "fifteen hundred men would not in three weeks repair the wanton injury and destruction" committed in the first few days by these brutal adventurers.[1]

However, the planters, though taken at first by surprise, banded themselves together under the leadership of the four most prominent settlers in the Colony, Pynn, John Downing,[2] Oxford, and Geo. Kirke. The Pynns, a gallant race, long settled in Harbour Grace, stuck to their rights, and sharply attacked their assailants: Oxford and John Downing headed the defence in St. John's, and George Kirke took command on the southern shore. Immediately Sir John Berry,[3] commander of the convoy, and Captain Davis[4] arrived, they put a stop to further attacks. John Downing, the son of a former governor, was elected by all the

---

[1] THOMAS OXFORD'S PETITION.
"The humble Petition of Thomas Oxford Merchant and late Inhabitant of St. John's.
"That he and his predecessors have been possessed of houses stages &c. in the said Harbour of St. John's for about seventy years but of late they not able to call anything their own by reason of West Country men, who pretend as priveledge not only to take away houses &c., but threatened their persons both by blows and imprisonment which hath caused your Petitioner and family to quit that Country almost to his utter ruine. Such damage was done last year in severall Harbours, that fifteen hundred men in the Harbour of St. John's will hardly make good the damage done there in three weeks, besides the loss of their goods which they violently take away. Petitioner prays for redress. Petitions for a Governor with great guns and ammunition and an Orthodox Minister, who they will maintain at their own cost, so that those removed may be invited to return &c."
(*Board of Trade.*)

[2] EXTRACTS from Reports in which John Downing is mentioned.

"Acc't of ye Inhabitants in St. John's Harbour & Quitevide thereunto belonging with their names and what wives and children they have as also their men and women servants and boats they employ.

In St. John's Harbour.	Wives.	Sons.	Dau'ters.	Women Sert.	MenServants. Winter.	Sum'r.	Boats.
John Downing	01	00	03	02	15	12	05

Rec'd the 11th Oct. 1680.

An Acc't of ye Planters belonging to St. John's Harbour 1682.

Planters' Names.	Men.	Women.	Children.	Boats.	Stages.	Rats.
Jno. Downing	14	03	00	02	01	01

[3] Sir John Berry, whose humane exertions and firmness mainly prevented the expulsion of the settlers, began life as a West Country fisherman in Newfoundland; his brother was also in the fish trade. His career was a very remarkable one. He joined the Royal Navy first as a boatswain in the *Swallow* ketch; for his gallantry under the following circumstances, the Governor of Jamaica made him a lieutenant:—The *Swallow*, Captain Insam, was sent to capture a pirate. They found the enemy at anchor off Hispaniola. Insam had only 40 men and eight guns, whilst the pirate had 20 guns and 60 men. Insam did not want to fight. Berry ordered him into his cabin, took command, and gallantly captured the pirate; he was tried by court martial for coercing his commander, but honourably acquitted. Sir John is described in the *Biographia Nautica* as a great, gallant and good man, who had received the honour of knighthood for his bravery against the Dutch at the battle of Solebay; he had a pension from the king.

[4] Captain Davis, R.N., had been engaged in the Newfoundland trade as a West Country skipper before he was promoted to the Royal Navy.

inhabitants as their representative and delegate to proceed to England and defend their rights.

To appreciate the full measure of this iniquitous order to destroy the property of the Newfoundland planters and to force them out of the country, we must pause for a moment to consider their position. Merchants and planters had been settled in St. John's and around the coast for many years anterior even to Gilbert's arrival. The tilt and the log hut had long disappeared; they lived in substantial, comfortable wooden houses. Everyone acquainted with the Newfoundland trade is aware of the number of buildings that are required, and how large is the expense of a great fishing establishment. Baudoin speaks of the great wealth of the settlers at Carbonear and Harbour Grace. Captain Davis, R.N., a good authority, speaks of one thousand two hundred settlers. A great many of these planters were substantial men; who not only had their houses, stages, &c., and all the paraphernalia of the Newfoundland business; they also possessed cleared land, horses, cattle, sheep, &c. Downing himself was conspicuous as a farmer; he had a small plantation near the present Virginia Lake, known to the old settlers, and called on the old maps "Downing's Pond." By this peremptory order of January 27, 1676, all the Newfoundland settlers were called upon immediately to relinquish their property, to surrender at a moment's notice the patient labour of a lifetime.

Englishmen accustomed to their own highly cultivated land, the labour of many generations, can hardly understand the strong ties of affection which bound the Newfoundlanders to their rugged homes. Their little gardens and fields were rude and rough compared with English culture, but they were the work of their own hands: the apple trees and small bushes brought from the old country, tended with loving care, had developed and blossomed and borne fruit, the admiration and wonder of the little settlement. To be driven from home and the smiling fields and gardens, carved, or as Downing puts it, "cleansed from the wildernesse," was a terrible wrench at their heart strings, a separation that seemed like death.

The poet has sung to us of the sorrows of Evangeline and of the evictions from Grand Pré. The Acadians were not in a more miserable plight than the poor Newfoundland settlers during that long period from 1675 to 1677, whilst the terrible edict hung over their heads. With what anxiety in their lonely homes they awaited during the weary winter months the result of Downing's mission!

The ministry, gagged and bound by the bribes of Child and his colleagues, were for a time deaf to the urgent demands from the colonists for protection against these barbarous attacks. Bye-and-bye, however, the eloquent appeal of Downing and his counsel began to stir public opinion. There were many West Country towns that gave the settlers strong support. John Carter, Mayor of Poole, sent—

"A set of reasons why the Inhabitants should not be removed signed by several Merchants and Masters of Ships which for many years have used the trade of fishing there." [They declare] "the Inhabitants are faithful subjects and that the most eminent of them now resident there, were forced over in the time of the late civil war for their loyalty to His Majesty."[1]

Besides the assistance the settlers received from Poole and Weymouth, there seems to have been a strong party on their side both in Bideford and Barnstaple. All the man-of-war officers were with the settlers. A careful examination of the lengthy documents put forward by both sides shows how well Downing worked up his case. There was a most protracted debate;[2] the decision, long hung in the balance, was at last given in favour of the planters.

Sir John Berry and Captain Davis and several other enlightened West Country men came forward with such arguments on behalf of the planters, that even the Court had to give way. A peremptory order first went forth by the ship *St. John's Merchant*, leaving Dartmouth in March 1677, directing the masters and seamen to forbear all violence to the planters; and in May came the following order:—

"That the Planters in Newfoundland be continued in possession of their Houses and stages according to the usuage of the last years, until further orders."[3]

As the reader will see from the petition of Oxford,[4] they asked for protection for the future. Their children were growing up without

---

[1] *Records.*

[2] The following letter is in the *Plymouth Records*; Prowse was very active on the settlers' side:—

R. PROWSE TO WM. GOULD.
14 March 1670.

"We heare of your bad success at the choice of Mr. Reynell that your boone companion were too hard a party for you. I suppose you hardly return before the terme because tis supposed the House may not sit above 14 days longer therefore I advise you that your Newfoundland business is passed the King in Councill and the Duke of York is by one order to be attended, the Attorney Generall by another, and there is another order that is to come down to strengthen ye business before it passes into a Patent. I am out of purse already &c. &c. and am taken sick.

"Yours,—R. PROWS."

There is also a letter to Wm. Gould about R. Prowse, from which it appears he was trying in a small way, by presents, to counteract the bribes of the other side.

[3] *Records.*

[4] PROPOSALS OF WM. DOWNING AND THOMAS OXFORD ON BEHALF OF THE INHABITANTS.

(Recd. 29 April 1679.)

"To fortify St. John's, naturally very strong, with twenty five guns and two hundred small arms and some small arms to defend the creek Que de Vide to prevent surprise. This Que de Vide is a place where a few skiffs fish, cleared through the rocks by some Inhabitants of St. John's, as well as other conveniences about that harbour to the value of some of thousands of pounds.

"To fortify Carboniere with fifteen great guns and eighty small arms. Salvadge forty leagues from St. John's being about seven years since cleared and possessed only by Inhabitants, never before used by any to fortify it, ten guns and eighty small arms Ferryland seventeen guns and a hundred the ordinances of religion, there was no one to command or organize in case of defence, and there were no fortifications.

They were not allowed, however, to have the Governor, established minister, or forts they prayed for. The residents offered to group themselves in any towns or harbours selected by the Government, to assist about fortifications, and to bear their share of all expenses.

It is only on the assumption of bribery that we can explain the minister's obstinacy in refusing to organize the defences of the Colony. France, their ancient enemy, was at their gate; twice the Dutch had successfully attacked St. John's and Ferryland. De Ruyter declared when he captured St. John's on the 6th of June 1665, that if there had been six guns mounted he would not have ventured in.

The commerce between Newfoundland and the North American Colonies, generally referred to in our Records as "New England," but which at this period embraced New York and Philadelphia, had risen from its modest commencement in 1645 to considerable dimensions; it was largely increased during the time of the Commonwealth.

ADMIRAL DE RUYTER.

The New Englanders, it has been noticed,[1] were mostly traders, not fishermen. They found a lucrative market for inferior fish, first in the English West India Islands, and afterwards amongst the French.

---

small arms. Fformous eighteen guns and sixty small arms. In what other Harbours besides St John's it shall be thought fit for them to settle, it is not desired to give any hindrance to the Fishing ships but they may fish in any of these places, the Inhabitants enjoying such convenient houses and stages as they have formerly built and now enjoy and no more, but as their children grow up they may accordingly enlarge.

"That a Government may be settled to defend them and the Country especially against the French, who are very powerfull there, and against some West Country Merchants whom they have long groaned under.

"For the preservation of navigation they desire to pass their men back and forward by freight or hyer. . . . . Inhabitants will be always willing to protect boats left by fishing ships. . . . .

"The Inhabitants desire (to prevent malicious pretence) that an equal number of Masters be with them to decide all differences.

"Queen Elizabeth was proclaimed Queen of the Whole Country but now the French enjoy two thirds and so far from complaints of them by West Country men that they would not owne any setled there although too much apparent, as appears by the oathes of Oxford T. C. Marton and N. Trout and Masters of Conveys. They humbly beg the Governor may have power over both Inhabitants and fishermen equally, and that they may have a Minister and fortifications and what also Your Honourable Board think fit."
— (Board of Trade, Newfoundland.)

[1] See p. 153.

Dutch, and Spanish possessions; they were not allowed by the French or Spaniards to trade with their Islands, except to barter fish for molasses; they came first to Newfoundland with cattle, corn, lumber, lime, salted beef, pork, pitch, &c. In the course of fifty years the English planters, who had previously obtained all their provisions from England by 1680, received nearly all their supplies from New England.

The planters' best fish, known already in the trade as "prime merchantable codfish," was sold to the English merchants or to traders, who came in the sack ships; the payment was always made by bills on England at 60 or 90 days; these drafts were the usual currency of the Colony. Except for occasional payments in these bills or in gold the trade between British North America and our Island was essentially a barter trade.

The New Englanders, the steadfast friends of the Newfoundlanders, and zealous for their own rights and liberties, gave material aid in the fierce struggle with the West Countrymen. Child and his colleagues were fiercer against them even than against the Newfoundland planters; one witness declares the New Englanders spoke infamously about His Sacred Majesty King Charles II.

There was a constant intercourse between the two countries. West Country servants smuggled away came back in a few seasons as genuine New England men; they cursed, and drank, and swore, in a way to horrify the Puritan divines, but being good sailors and good fishermen their blasphemies were forgiven; "ungodly men and swearers, fishermen chiefly from Newfoundland," is Hubbard's description of them.

Besides their trade in produce and West India fish for the negroes, and the Weatherfield onion business, the Americans soon drove a big trade in rum.[1] Artemus Ward speaks of the New England rum and the measles as equally disagreeable. No doubt the compound was villainous, it was probably worse than the Spanish aguardiente, or the worst French brandy. It had, however, two distinct merits for the fishermen, it was very strong and very cheap. Probably the planter bought it wholesale for not more than 25 cents a gallon; by 1789 it was retailed out to fishermen at $1·20 a gallon, more than double the old-fashioned price.

---

[1] It is said that previous to the commencement of this trade, molasses was thrown away by the planters, and that this article, now so extensively used in commerce, was first saved and put into casks to be brought to New England and distilled into rum.—(SABINE.)

FITZHUGH'S MAP

The American colonists at this period did a trade, mostly contraband, all over the world; besides sending fish to market, they were running negroes from Africa, whaling, smuggling, and frequently selling their fine ships in England. One great business in Newfoundland was stealing servants from the West Countrymen. For his passage the kidnapped fisherman had to serve a long period, as a kind of white bond slave. Probably Massachusett's gave a premium on the introduction of desirable emigrants; but, however that may be, there can be no doubt that the servants were smuggled away. The colonial records are full of statements to that effect, of which the following is an example:—

"REPORT of Captain DANIEL JONES, R.N., H.M.S. *Diamond*.

"Bay Bulls 12th Sepr. 1682.
"Did not arrive until Aug. 23d Admiralty instructions to sail 1st Sepr. with convoy weather permitting. I have sent to your Honour four Bonds for I find none that violate your rules so much as ye Traders from New England spiriting away men. I was an eye witness of one at St. John's coming in with 11 hands and sailing with 20 in addition had not my pinnace brought him to anchor. So I took bonds of the New England men and acquainted Captain Wren of H.M.S. *Centurion*. Bad fishery only 150 qtls. per boat, not as good as reported the French have made. Nothing but confusion and disorder here they require a Governour.

"Bonds of John Sawley of Salem, Mass., of Geo. Snell of Portsmouth or Piscadawery New Hampshire of Thomas Harvey of Portsmouth N.H. and of William Pepperill of Portsmouth N.H., not to take away men from Newfoundland."[1]

Treworgie had combined in his person the anomalous positions of chief factor to the New England merchants in Newfoundland and the governorship of the Colony; he was a perfectly honest man, and seems to have performed both duties to the satisfaction of his employers. At his death the position of chief factor of the American colonies fell to Mr. Gould, who appears on all occasions during this reign as representing New England, and advocating their interests in opposition to the English fishermen.

It is impossible now to give any exact figures about the colonial trade with Newfoundland; it was carried on in an underhand way; its operations were carefully concealed from the captains of the Royal Navy. In their annual reports the only notices to be found of the Americans are accounts of their "spiriting away" the West Countrymen's servants. When Downing writes of eight New England vessels coming to the Island he must have meant St. John's; he had no means of knowing how many other vessels visited the distant outports, and traded off their goods for fish and furs, berries, cod's-tongues and fish-sounds, taking their balances in merchants' bills on England. Early in the eighteenth

[1] *Board of Trade, Newfoundland.*

century at least forty[1] vessels came from the American colonies to Newfoundland; Palliser estimated the trade in 1765 at half a million dollars annually, and by the commencement of the Revolution it had risen to one and a half millions of dollars.

By the end of Charles II.'s reign New England had so marvellously increased and extended her agricultural and commercial operations that she was pretty well able to supply our Island planters with nearly everything they required.[2] The two countries on which the wrath of the West Countryman and Child was poured out are singularly enough Ireland and New England. The monopolists treat both these great English dependencies as foreign countries, and decidedly hostile and opposed to the interests of England.

The fault of poor Erin, her glaring offence in the eyes of the Devonshire men, was her woollen manufactures, which were absurdly cheap and remarkably good; in the plantations they were, like Irish

[1] AMERICAN VESSELS COMING TO NEWFOUNDLAND IN 1698.

[Many of these vessels made several voyages to the Island in each year.]

Where from.	Master's Name.	Tons.	Port of Call in Newfoundland.	Fish bought. (Quintals.)	Inward Cargo.	Destination outwards.
Carolina	Wm. Clay	30	Renowse	250	Provisions	Barbadoes.
New York	Thos. Glave	75	Bay Bulls	1,200	Do.	Bilboa.
Carolina	T. Phelps	50	Carbonear	400	Provisions and rum.	Barbadoes.
Bermoodes	S. Perley	30	Bay Verds	200	Salt and rum	Do.
Boston	T. Barrinzton	60	St. John's	—	Provisions	New England.
Montserrat	N. Hawker	30	Do.	100	Rum and sugar	Montserrat.
Lime (Lima)	Thos. Thomas	80	Brigus	800	Provisions and salt.	Lime (Lima).
Antigoe (Antigua).	William Wood	54	Port de Grave	500	Salt, rum, and molasses.	Oporto.
New England	Michl. Gill	40	St. John's	—	Pork and cyder	New England.
Boston	Jno. Watkins	30	Do.	—	Rum and cyder	Boston.
Do.	N. Easter	50	Do.	—	Rum and molasses.	
New England	Samuel Mould	80	Do.	1,800	Rum and sugar	Jamaica.
Barbadoes	Christopher Munke.	200	Do.	2,000	Do.	Oporto.
Boston	T. Fry	41	Do.	500	Rum, sugar, and bread.	Do.
New England	Wm. Law	50	Do.	—	Provisions	New England.
Boston	John Pitts	30	Do.	—	Salt and molasses.	Boston.
St. John's, New England.	R. Holdsworth	25	Do.	—	Do.	Piscattaway.
Piscattaway	John Card	45	Do	—	Boards	Do.
New England	William Follett	125	Do.	—	Deals	New England.
Bermoodes	Terence Smith	80	Harbour Grace	450	Salt	Virginia, in ballast.
Boston	John Thacker	40	Ferriland	600	Rum and sugar	Barbadoes.

(*Board of Trade, Newfoundland.*)

[2] By about 1690 New England was exporting boots and shoes to Newfoundland. In the manifest of a cargo sent for the use of the St. John's garrison in 1697 are 200 pairs of shoes, 200 pairs of stockings, 26 boxes of medicine, and some garden seeds, "live hoggs and fowles," 19 bushels of turnips, 3 bushels of carrots, 10 hhds. of molasses, and 1 hhd. of "Yorke Tobacco" (*Board of Trade*).

pork and Irish beef and Irish "youngsters,"[1] half the price of the English article, and somehow they got to be the leading staples in the Newfoundland trade. The cheapest goods have always been the ones selected for the planters' and fishermen's use.

It was to buy these Irish woollens, "Frises, Bandel-cloths," "stockins," pork, beef, butter, and to engage Irish servants, that the West Countrymen first touched at Waterford and Cork on their way out to Newfoundland, and thus commenced the Irish Newfoundland trade in "youngsters" and provisions.

The first Irishmen in the Colony were these youngsters, shipped for two summers and a winter; as Baudoin tells us, they were servants to the English, who treated them ill. During the troubled times of 1690, the period of the wars in Ireland and the battle of the Boyne, the peasants were only too glad to flee from the country, so the bye-boat keepers took them out in the West Country vessels in still larger numbers. By this time it had become an established practice for the Devonshire vessels to call at Waterford, Cork, and other harbours on the south coast of Ireland, principally Waterford, to take in a supply of provisions, manufactures, and youngsters. I notice a request of the merchants in 1690 for the convoy to call at Cork for forty-eight hours.

Gradually these brave Irish boys amalgamated with the English settlers, married the planters' daughters, and became an important part of the resident population; compared however with the English, their numbers at first were small. The large Irish population now resident about St. John's and the southern portion of the Island is chiefly the result of the emigration to this country which took place at the end of the eighteenth and the early part of the nineteenth century.

Lest I should be accused of putting the case against the ship fishermen too strongly, the last of their proposals in the reign of Charles II., on the much disputed question of settling the Colony "with a governor, a minister, forts, and great guns," is given. In 1680, the Commissioners for Foreign Plantations, who were merely the mouthpieces of Devonshire, declared :—

"That to entrust the regulating of the fishery in a Governor will tend greatly to the prejudice of the Newfoundland fishery. . . . But if His Majesty should think fit to fortify the Harbor of St. John's and to make a Governor of the Fort and to arm the Governor with a military power to command the people of that country (*on occasion*) for their defence, and with civil power for punishing vice and keeping good order—*without having any power over the Fishery* or infringing the

---

[1] In the ordinary way a youngster in Newfoundland meant an unmarried servant, just as a boy in Ireland is an unmarried man and remains a boy even when he is eighty.

charter—they thought the same might be of good use, and no prejudice to the Trade and His Majesty's Customs."[1]

The same able statesmen a few years later modified their opinion about planters. France had just invaded the Island, and laid all the fishing establishments in ruins. The Commissioners then expressed their opinion, after referring to the necessity for forts and soldiers:—

"That Planters in moderate numbers were at all times convenient for the preparation and preservation of boats, stages, and other things necessary for the fishery *but they should not exceed one thousand.*"[1]

There is one further suggestion, somewhat later, from a military Solomon,—the lieutenant-governor of the Island, Major Elford:—

"That they allow no women to land in the Island and that means should be adopted to remove those that were there."[1]

We can hardly credit rational human beings with the production of these barbarous ordinances for the extirpation of British colonists, and their still more absurd restrictions; they read more like the production of some mischievous demon—the grotesque laws for some Gargantuan island or the territory of the Yahoos—than the sober production of English statesmen.

The eight years succeeding the defeat of the project to expel the settlers are not very eventful ones in the history of Newfoundland; the agitation for a governor was still kept up. By far the ablest argument on this subject is from the pen of Sir Robert Robinson, for many years captain-of-convoy on the coast. He points out very forcibly that, owing to the terrorism of the West Countrymen, many of the planters had gone to live with the French, and—

'the chiefest have gone to New England.[2] That by a settled Government and harbours fortified they will avoid the abuses of the ungoverned seamen, who deal with them as they please. They will be preserved from sea rovers and enemies; have a Minister to christen, instruct, marry, and bury them; and they will have equal justice which will greatly encourage all except those who desire to live under no Government, but in all things to be their own carvers."

But the strongest argument of all was the danger of a French invasion. One per cent. on the fish caught would have borne all the

---

[1] *Records.*

[2] PETITION OF WILLIAM DOWNING.

"That whereas on 11th Oct. last the Lords of Trade made an order about settlement Newfoundland under Government and fortifications:

"That there is now an account given to your petition that (the inhabitants having no security and utterly disparing of redress) the greater part have bought vessels whereby (upon the first alaram of wars) they may remove to other Plantations and the rest are already retireing nearer the French and declare they will put themselves under their protection: All which on oath if required. And that the season again draweth nigh for the ships to go thither. Your petitioner therefore most humbly prays for a speedy conclusion of the settlement &c."

[Not endorsed, prob. 1683.]
(*Board of Trade, Newfoundland*).

moderate expense required for an established government forts,[1] artillery, and a minister:—

"If the French "says Robinson" should take it, whereas they now employ about four hundred sail and eighteen thousand seamen and the English three hundred sail and fifteen thousand seamen, they would employ seven hundred ships and thirty thousand seamen, and the English be shut out of £700,000 yearly; besides which the French would make double that sum. The Newfoundland fishery is the great nursery for seamen. If the French should add, what the English have planted there, to what they possess already in Canada, Nova Scotia and other places thereabouts, they would be bad neighbours to His Majesty's flourishing Plantations of New England, New York, and Virginia."

THORNTON'S MAP, 1685.
From the English Pilot.

Robinson grossly exaggerated numbers, but his argument is unanswerable as regards the danger to all North America from the French encroachments in Newfoundland. West Country obstinacy,

---

[1] PROPOSED BUILDING OF A FORT AT ST. JOHN'S IN 1680.

On April 5, Sir Robt. Robinson asks leave to be allowed to use his crew and such Planters as are willing to raise fortifications, which shall be done with no expense except a little brandy to the crew for labouring. [This was probably the commencement of a fort on the site of Fort William; it is referred to in 1696 and 1697 in the Invasion by D'Iberville and Brouillon.]

however, still opposed all reasonable proposals to defend the Colony from such an obvious danger. A few years later they suffered terribly for their refusal to listen to reason. There was a strong party on Robinson's side; he tried to bring over the Duke of York (afterwards James II.) to his views, but, like his brother, he was the recipient of large bribes from Child and his associates—the Parliament also of that day was utterly corrupt—and so his efforts had no result.

The Colony was left to drift along, a prey to every enemy. Each year the naval officers on the station made reports on the wanton aggression of the ship fishermen,[1] the disorders in the Island, and the need for a settled government; but it was all to no purpose. During the latter

PLAN OF ST. JOHN'S IN 1689.
From Thornton's Map.

years of Charles II.'s reign there were no attacks from the French; both nations quietly fished without disturbing each other. Like ourselves, the French had no military or naval power, their fortresses were in ruins, and there was not a single royal soldier or sailor in any of their settlements.[2] The parent Government was busily employed in Europe; and after the first outburst of energy in 1662, the soldiers were withdrawn, and their defences were entirely neglected; they seldom had even a convoy for their merchant ships.

---

[1] CAPTAIN OF CONVOY'S REPORT, 1684.
Fishermen now using casks instead of flats for their oil.
Hardly a house but sells drink.
If the people do assemble it is not for divine service.
Order 23 March 1677 allows them to live near the shore.
Order 18 May 1677 allows planters to keep their own house, &c.
Order 16 Jany 1677 Masters allowed to bring over passengers.
Order 16 Jany 1677 Bonds not required.

He has had a hundred complaints and Admiral would do nothing at all to redress wrongs.
Charge of fitting out 10 boats and a ship of 80 tons for the West Adventurers service Receive £1350 pay £984—profit £365.
Planters 2 boats take £216 cost £268 loss £52.
[Very full details of both estimates given in the Records.]
(*Records*.)

[2] The Naval Report of 1684 says: "Seldom any convoy for French vessels." —"Forts in ruins."

APPENDIX TO CHAPTER VIII.

I. Downing's Narrative.

A Brief Narrative concerning Newfoundland, by John Downing.

Recd 24th October 1676.

"Recites various patents given—in all which ample privileges were granted for encourag' of all, that w'd inhabit, that the Children there born should be free denizens of England with many other freedoms &c., my father in 1640 was sent over by H.M.'s Commissioners, Duke Hamilton, Earl of Pembroke & Earl of Holland's Instructions to take charge of the Colony; Sir David Kirke being by His M^{atie's} Letter by him sent, called home; my father found under the command of Sir David Kirke, their Gov'r fifty six guns mounted in several forts, as Ferryland, St. John's, Bay Bull, &c, the forts fitted with small arms &c, & manned by inhabitants. The proprietors had given them, even to Duke Hambleton, and the rest six admiralls places for fishing, accounted the best, even St. John's and the rest: alsoe five fishes in six score caught or bought by any shipp having more strangers aboard than free denizens of England; all nations in amity with his M^{atie} might freely buy and catch fish build houses &c as freely as English, provided if demanded he paid his impost.

"By Patent the inhabitants were not within six miles to destroy woods, nor convert rooms for drying fish to other uses, as to plant, plow same, and the rest. Even in Cromwell's time, in the worst of times the inhabitants being accused for traitors to his Government, yett by an order then, wee had liberty to enjoy our houses wee had built &c. Cromwell's Governor Treworgie and his men of war took impost, as proprietors aforementioned had done, even as far as Trespasse.

"There hath been a generatⁿ of men ever since any people settled in Newfoundland, practicing the ruin of inhabit^s. First that no merchants have any fish but from themselves and at their rates and pleasures, next that all men employed in fishing affairs work for and serve for such victualls and pay as they choose to give them. Inhabitants distance from Supreme Rulers Seats, render them liable to false calumnies—that inhabitants burn their train ffats of £60 value which one with other were not worth first year they were built £6 if they were soe wronged they might and would have Reparatⁿ from those that wronged yearly. But I never c'd hear of any man there that c'd complain of any such wrong I having lived there and been every summer these thirty odd yeares.

"The inhabitants burne their stages they complain themselves, as the fishing sailes burne for dressing their victualls & brewing their beare, wood their shipps carry home some to their owners yards give leave to the shipps that take in their fish to take aboard what they will, other shipps wanting wood take leave, some give some to some inhabitants, others howse all their stages and flake stuff for another yeare, by this meanes before all the shipps depart some yeares in St. John's where it is said three hundred boats have been kept, is left of all their stages two or three pieces standing. In 1674: at the goeing out of the last ships was left standing but the Bedd of one of the Admirals Stages which at Spring following the Admiral enjoyed. In 1675: by the care of Sir John Berry their Stages and Roomes were for the most part well left & as well found at their returne as themselves have there & must if called here acknowledge. In 1676, before my coming out, Capt. Russell Command'r of H.M.'s shipp "Reserve" forced several Masters of shipps, even their admiral for one to build up again their trayne houses, themselves had cut down contrary to their order. Trees are rinded, the shipps doing it most, and the comers out of England—done not only for 18 foot Cooke Rommes but to cover whole stages and lodging houses, even last summer it was done. Inhab'ts stages and houses are most covered with New England and the country's boards, so have little occasion of rinding. Woods fired by foreigners and English Shipps Companys going into woods for timber in warme weather & throwing carelessly the fire they light tobacco with.

"From New Eng'd one y'r with other come commonly 8 sail of vessels burthen'd from 16 tons to 60 tons with commodities the produce of which they invest here in Brandy, Cloath'g, apparel for their vessels, pieces of eight, if they can get them some ffrench & Spanish wines, some redd stinking fish for the Negores of Barbadoes. As for men Inhabitants have out of fishing ships we have Masters good will to have them soe have New Eng'd men it sav'g the owners victuals they eat homew'ds & often they carry passengers in their places who pay own'rs for passages.

"Practicers of ruin of Inhabits (if obtained) will produce to themselves this profit of their Labour as formerly the ffrench found before any Governor was sent to Newfoundland by K. Chas Ist—Some English inhabitants w'd burn frenchmen's boats, carry away some, carry away salt, break open their houses and rifle them they being sure to find nothing left nor they who had done it. The English fishing ships leave always either salt or fish or goods for fishing and all their boats, which if their boats be spoiled the voyage is ruined utterly before they can there saw boards or build boats—no merchants will send salt or any other goods to supply any that want or waste salt & provis'ns in his passage over for if it be to be housed no house but Cook rooms allowed of 18 feet & they but for the winter, yet houses unfit for salt neither any man to take charge of it. Some years fishing ships have beene lost forty, sixty leagues from shore being rackt by ice yet in boats some of their men have come to land and been cured of their hurts by cold and hunger, by inhabitants. Almost every year, some of their men sent for possess'n might with cold and hunger starve if not relieved by Inhab'ts; yearly their men are received when sick with scurvy and other sickness into Inhabitants houses and there most times got their cures & become able to do service.

"In case according to some mens desires the inhabitants be forced to quit their houses and employments, they and their man and families and come home they will fall to extreme poverty and want and if they get relief it must come from the landed gentlemen to whom the exteme poverty of distressed families will be neither pleasant nor profitable.

"Of french promiting their interest more and more in Newfoundl'd complainers agst inhabitants take no notice. In y'r 1670 French had Placentia fortified with ordinance a Garrison of Soldires and Chaine also St. Peters fortified with great guns garris'n of Soldrs at both places many inhabitants great stores of Cattle and sheepe. Since this time K. of France hath pub'd in Seaports of France that he will pay passage of any that go and inhabit in Newfld give a gratuity to Mas'r that passeth them other; by Governor they shall be supplied with clothes & necessaries from three years & then pay King in fish fur or board; by these encouragements inhabitants grow more and more numerous, some English live amongst them & are courteously treated, lately more of English Inhabts have been as formerly by French Captains invited to dwell amongst them promising them kindness and protection.

"A Merch't of Waterford in Ireland Mr John Aylrod being in Newfoundland in June 1676 gave foll'g relation concerning Placentia—French inhabitants were there now 250 families which according to our famil's may be more than 2000 men, their garrison of soldiers 400 men paid by King. 300 kintalls for each boat one year with another accounted with them an ordinary voyage; their fishes from Trepass round the Isl'd near to Bonavista many French and Biskenners, the Biskenners subject to King of Spain—French ships supposed to be not less than 200 sail of ships of good force from 30 guns to 12, they have 2 men of war about 50 guns each; to that part of the land where the French forts are as Placentia, St. Peters & the rest, no Indians come but some Canida Indians from forts of Canida in french shallowayes with french fowling pieces all spared them by french of Canida so for them need no chaine, soldiers nor ordinance.

"It is said Newfoundland is guarded after fish'g ships go suffuc'tly by foggs & ice till arrival of English fishermen therefore need no other guard to prevent invasion that it is theirs who are strongest at sea. St. John's & fferryland and other harbours are deemed by some men accustomed to war so strongly fortified by nature that some of them having one fort and necessaries for defence its hard for any ship though never so bravely furnished to enter and if they sh'd pass without burning or sinking or being cast ashore when entered they may stay there perhaps 14 days for a wind to go out the meantime fight rocks and fort. Two or three of these harbours fortified are enough after the manner of french fishing to make use of all the English have for fishing in their pattent from Cape de Race to Cape de Bonavista; except the fortified harbours they may spoyle the rest for ships rideing in the fortified harb'rs their own ships may ride even in war and fish as the French do and go in their boats after the fish from three to eighteen leagues each side their harbours mouth there salt their fish in tilts on shore, after carry and dry it where their shipps ride in guard of forts, when they have taken in their fish a strong westerly wind with night in hand frees them from danger of enemies lying off the shore.

"English fishing ships commonly all gone in September or quickly in October—not to sail out of England till 1st March.

"From England Ireland France & Spain & Portugal & New Eng'd have vessels come to Newfoundland in November & Dec'r & have loaden oyle summer fish & winter fish out of the houses & gone out some of them three days before Christmas & have gone well to their ports desired.

"In beginning of March Ships have arrived from England; French fishing ships have been off St. John's and Ferryland the 2nd Feby and might have come in if they pleased, some of the french harbour, in Feby some in March, their best fish'g being in May. Ice comes on coast commonly in middle of Feb'y, some years in March, some years in April some years none to be seen it is not made here even the ice but breaks up the summer before in some cold straits & so winds and current bring it on this Coast.

Jo. DOWNING.

(*Col. Papers, Newfoundland*, 56.)

II. Downing's Petitions.

(a.) To the King's Most Excellent Matie.

"The Humble Petition of John Downing, Gentleman, Inhabitant of Newfoundland. Sheweth:

"That your Petitioner's Father was sent to Newfoundland, armed with your Royal Father's Commission and authority and instructions from the then Lords Proprietors to plant people there, and reduce the Indians to civility and religion. That to that purpose severall lawes and orders were then made and sent over by your Royal Father to be observed there.... That after some yeares service there, having secured the forts and fishings and brought into some regularity and security the place and imposts payable to your Majesty, Your Petitioner's Father there died, and since his death your Petitioner amongst severall others of your subjects hath settled there and lived for many years under the said lawes and orders given them and by their industry built houses for their habitation and cleansed the wildernesses of the place, whereby to keep some cattle for their sustenance and the support of such of your Majesty's subjects as come to trade there and have by leave of the former Governors and Proprietors erected severall stages and Roomes for their winter and summer fisheries and support.

"They have hitherto lived your Majestys obedient subjects maintaining by their own industry, themselves their wives and their children in peace and comfort. But now some of Your Subjects, pretending Your Majesty's patent and orders for the same, coming over thither, have not only taken the houses goode stages and roomes built and enjoyed by Your Petitioner and his father for many yeares last past, but spoile the boats, keeping, and breake open the houses of the said Inhabitants at their wills and pleasures contrary to the antient lawes and orders of the said place, and also to those of common humanity and the freedome which all other nations which have settled in these parts enjoy.

"For that the said Inhabitants can neither enjoy the effects of their own industry nor have any security from the invasion or spoiles of their neighbours.

May it therefore please Your Majesty that out of Your Royal Favour, you will be pleased to command that for the future no such outrages be committed, but that Your Petitioner may enjoy such houses stages &c. as have been built and enjoyed by his Father and himself according to the said antient lawes and orders of the place and find security for himself, his wife and family from such outrages from time to come.

And Your Petitioner shall ever pray.

At the Court at Whitehall,
November 7, 1676.

"His Majesty is graciously pleased to refer this Petition to the Rt. Honble. The Committee of the Councill for Foraigne Plantacions to consider the contents thereof and take such orders therein as to their Honours shall seeme meete for the reliefe of the Petr.
Thos. Povey.

(b.) Downing's Petition.

"To the Rt Honble ye Lords of his Ma't's most Honble Privy Councell appointed a Committee for Trade and Plantations.

"The Humble Petition of John Downing Gent Inhabitant of Newfoundland Sheweth

"That your Pet'r did on the 6th day of Nov'r last give in a Peticon to his Matie humbly imploring his protection to secure himself and family from ye outrages under which they had suffered, as by ye said Peticon reference being had thereunto doth more at large appeare.

"That his M^{atie} was thereupon graciously pleased on ye 7th Nov'r to refer your Petr to this Honourable Committee to take such order for his releife as they should think fitt. and that your Petr hath ever since attended for what redresse this Honble Board shall judge meet for him.

"That ye season of ye year is now instant wherein shipps bound for Newfld doe set forth and, if he omit ye takeing of his passage now, it may tend to ye utter ruine and undoing of himselfs, his wife and family who are still remaining there.

"Wherefore he most humbly prayes, this Honble Comitee would be pleased to commiserate his condicon and take into their serious consideracon his Mat's said reference, that your Petr may speedily obtain some relief what in your Honor's great wisdom shall be deem'd fitting, and soe may prosecute his voyage, and take care for ye support of his ruinous familly.

And he shall ever pray &c

Endorsed:
Peticon of John Downing Gent of Newfoundland.
Recd 25th January 1676 [o. s.].
(*Colonial Papers, No. 56, p. 104.*)

(c.) Downing's further Petition.

To the King's Most Excellent M^{atie}.

"The further Peticon of John Downing Inhabitant of Newfoundland Sheweth

"That the said Inhabitants till your Maties happy restauracon had a Governor there and fifty-six guns allowed them and fforts for their securities And that the same were maintained by the six admiralties and imposts of the said place.

"That since the practices of the last Patentees, all the same have been neglected and decayed and the said Inhabitants not only oppressed by the Patentees (who now engross the whole trade and profitt and admiralties to themselves) But alsoe are left naked and defenceless to the Invasion of others especially the ffrench their too Potent neighbours To redresse which the said Inhabitants doe humbly offer, that your Matie may be pleased to appoint them a Governor and a minister to live amongst them, and to whom the said inhabitants enjoying their former immunities and Estates will allow a competent maintenance fitt for the support of such employments and having allowed them the said Competent number of guns will erect and manitain fforts necessary for the defence and safety of the s'd place and security of the people, And further to pay and secure to your Matie such imposts and further customes as have been accustomed to be received by such Governour.

Therefore may it please Your Matie to consider the deplorable condiĉon of the said inhabitants and to take such order herein as to you seeme most meete.

And your Petr shall pray &c
Endorsed Petñ of John Downing
Newfoundland
read in Councill March 23rd 1676 [o. s.]
(*Col. Papers, No. 56.*)

III. Report concerning the Fishery & Colony of Newfoundland.
Read in Council March 28th 1677.

"In obedience to H. Matie's order in Councill of 23rd inst &c &c have called before them the Petñ of John Downing appearing on behalf of himself and rest of Colony, as also several Gentlemen of W. Country, & Merchts concerned in the Fishery, but it was alleged by said Gentlemen and Merchants, that by reason of the short warning given them for their appearance, they were in noe manner prepared to make out their pretensions in the validity of their Charter, which they did not doubt to satisfy them in, if space of fifteen days were given them to acquaint their correspondents in the Country and provide themselves with those evidences & demonstrations of right by wh. their patent is supported. Did allow of soe reasonab'e a request, and did assign them the 10th of April next, at which time propose to enter into further examination of whole matter for final settlement. But in meanwhile least Planters at present residing in Newfoundland should be molested by Msrs of Fisg Ships upon pretence of their Charter, offer unto H. Matie that orders bee forthwith sent by a Ship called St. John's Merchant, now at Dartmouth, unto admirals in Newfoundland, whereby Masters and Seamen may be directed to forbear any violence to Planters, upon pretence of said Western Charter and suffer them to inhabit and fish according to usage; provided they do conform to the rules of Charter—and inhabitants do likewise continue good correspondences with Fish'men, until, H. Matie shall proceed to a further resolution."

DANBY, ANGLESEY,
ORMONDE, CARLISLE,
CRAVEN, BRIDGWATER,
FFAUCONBERG

Council Chamber
26 March 1677.

"Which being read in Councill—H.M. was pleased to order, that Council for Trade and Plant'ns cause orders to be sent to admirals according to their Lordships advice in said report."

JOHN NICHOLAS.
(*Col. Papers, No. 56.*)

CHAPTER IX.

REIGN OF JAMES II.
1685–1688.

THE REVOLUTION.

REIGN OF WILLIAM AND MARY.
1688–1694.

1688.—War between France and England.

1689.—Bill of Rights passed. Frontenac Viceroy of New France.

1690.—Battle of the Boyne. Capture of Port Royal. Failure to take Quebec. Garrison of Chedabuctou sent to Placentia.

1692.—De Brouillon appointed Governor of Placentia. Commodore Williams's unsuccessful attack on Placentia.

1694.—Death of Queen Mary.

REIGN OF WILLIAM III. ALONE.
1694–1702.

1694.—Holman's defeat of the French at Ferryland.

1695.—Considerable damage done by eight French privateers to the English settlements.

1696.—Unsuccessful attack on St. John's by Chevalier Nesmond. Capture of St. John's by D'Iberville and De Brouillon in November; destruction of all the settlements except Carbonear and Bonavista.

1697.—Sir John Norris, with fleet and two thousand soldiers, sent out to recover Newfoundland; found it abandoned by the French; he built forts, &c. Treaty of Ryswick left the French in possession of Placentia. Colonel Handyside and three hundred men left to garrison the forts; two hundred and fourteen died. Board of Trade recommended that one thousand persons only might be permitted to remain on the Island to construct boats and stages for drying fish. Rev. J. Jackson, with the sanction of the Bishop of London, settled in St. John's.

1698.—Act of William III. appointing fishing admirals, vice-admirals, and rear-admirals; no alien to fish or take bait; rooms built since 1685 that did not belong to fishing ships made property of residents; colonial produce relieved of duty. Order on 31st March, establishing a permanent garrison in St. John's; Lieutenant Lilburne and sixty soldiers and gunners winter in St. John's. Cock of Bonavista's letter to Colonel Norris about English settlements to the northward.

1699.—Captain Andrews, an engineer, in command at St. John's.

1700.—Captain A. Holdsworth, Admiral of St. John's.
1701.—Large increase of trade with New England; continued complaints against New England transporting fishermen. S.P.G. incorporated. Report of Mr. George Larkin on the affairs of the Colony.

The short period of three years during which James II. reigned over England is only memorable for the treaty made in 1686 between Louis XIV. and the English king for the settlement of their respective territories in America. It was not recognised by James' successor. Like his brother, the new English monarch was the humble dependant and vassal of France. It shows how insecure was the tenure by which our enemies claimed to hold their portion of Newfoundland, that, at the commencement of this reign, Louis XIV. requested permission from James II. to hold Placentia and the other portions of Newfoundland occupied by the French.

I cannot gather from the records that there was any great excitement amongst the fishing folk in our Island over the accession of the Duke of York, and there was certainly no lamentation over his downfall. The Colony was then really more distant from England than the far-off islands of the Pacific. News was conveyed slowly and fitfully. A few of the leading planters, who were Royalists, and some who were Puritans, may have been moved about the great events in the mother country, but to the great bulk of the settlers and the ship fishermen it was of infinitely less importance to them than the price of fish or a good "caplin school," that came early and lasted long. All the old chroniclers declare that on this movement of the bait fishes mainly depended the success of the year's fishing voyage. Though the cod was most abundant, there were then, as now, good and bad seasons—some years abundance to overflowing, in others the fisherman's occupation was almost a complete failure.

The following letter is one out of many illustrations on this subject:—

"Rennouse 29 July 1680.

"At Trepassie first ships have 220 qtls. per boat and 3 h'ds. of Traine, later ships 180 to 190 qtls. and 2½ h'ds. of Traine. The French men that is there have done 250 to 300 from St. Shott's. The Admirals of St. Maries and Collinet were at Trepassie last week, who did inform us, that at Placentia of 36 saile not ten ships would be loaden and St. Mary's fishing doth fail also. . . . I do judge there are severall of our neighbours that will sell their fish, if they can attaine, at a considerable price."[1]

Prior to the accession of William III. in 1688 and the declaration of war there had been a long interval of repose. There were raids by

[1] *Records.*

English and French privateers, but, with one short interval, no open conflict. On neither side were there soldiers or men-of-war to fight and the defences both of St. John's and Placentia had fallen into complete ruin. With the return of the warlike Marquis de Frontenac to the Government of New France in 1689 this peaceful state of affairs quickly came to an end. The defences of Placentia were thoroughly repaired, Fort Louis (now Castle Hill) was built, the trading governor with his fishing boats and Government store was replaced by a smart young officer who had served under the great Luxembourg and campaigned in Flanders; everywhere in North America the old order was changed.

The Marquis was an admirable organiser, a brave soldier; he realised that either France had to destroy the English colonies, or soon New England would rout him out of Canada. He vainly imagined, with his nine thousand Canadians, that he could annihilate the two hundred thousand hardy and prosperous English colonists. At first he had no regular troops nor supplies so he trained militia. In Newfoundland he contented himself with sending French privateers to harry our settlements. In 1690 the garrison of Chedabucton, in Acadie, which had made a glorious defence against Sir William Phipps, was sent to Placentia with their gallant commander De Montorgueil. In 1692 De Brouillon, afterwards the successful invader of the English settlements, was made Governor of Placentia.

WILLIAM III.
From an contemporary portrait.

Owing to the continued attacks of French privateers[1] on the English settlers, England determined to send a powerful fleet to destroy Placentia. The command was given to Commodore Williams, with three sixty-gun ships and two smaller vessels. Brown in his "History of Cape Breton," says:—

"The only defences of the place were Fort Louis, with a garrison of fifty men, situated upon a rock a hundred feet in height, on the eastern side of the narrow

[1] "The French [in 1695] did considerable damage in Newfoundland, where most of the English settlements were destroyed by eight large privateers, and the *Saphire*, a fifth rate, was sunk to prevent her falling into their hands."—S. COLLIER: *Columna Rostrata*, 1728, p. 268.

entrance of the Harbour, and a battery hastily constructed by the Governor, M. de Brouillon, and manned by Sailors from the Privateers and Merchant ships in the Harbour. The Commodore in 1692 after six hours bombardment ignominiously retired having only partially destroyed a portion of the works."

The admiral of the powerful French squadron, Chevalier de Palais, seemed to have been the counterpart of the English commodore; whilst De Brouillon was defending his beleaguered little town, the noble chevalier remained snugly harboured in Sydney.

It is pleasant to turn from these contemptible naval commanders to the exploits of our heroic merchant seamen, who on several occasions gallantly defended Newfoundland from the French. The story of Holman's action at Ferryland in 1694, for which the Lords of the Admiralty gave him a "meddall and chayne," and the defeat of two powerful French frigates of forty and fifty guns, is recounted in the English records. This smart naval action would have been "unhonoured and unsung," but for a very prosaic reason. The following petition and affidavit for payment of powder expended in defending the Colony alone have preserved it from oblivion.¹

NAVAL FIGHT BETWEEN AN ENGLISH AND A FRENCH SHIP.
From La Hontan's *Nouveaux Voyages*, 1703.

¹ Holman's claim was for £495, £150 for spoiled fish, £12 for brandy given to encourage his men in time of fight, &c. On the 24th June, 1697, the Board of Trade recommended the payment of £345, and left the £150 for spoiled fish to be paid if the Treasury thought fit. Holman was probably recompensed by the Government giving him a contract for freighting victuals, &c. for the garrison in Newfoundland this year.

"Account of an action that happened at the Harbour of Ferryland in Newfoundland on August 31st 1694.

"There being eight or nine English ships in the said harbour catching fish, some English Prisoners made their escape from Placentia, came to Ferryland and acquainted Captain William Holman Commander of ye *William and Mary* galley having letters of marque and sixteen guns and the rest of the Masters of ships, that the French had a design to come with five ships of war, one fireship and a Bomb-ketch to destroy the English fishery all along the coast; upon which Captain Holman proposed to build fortifications for defence of the harbour which had been twice before taken by the French. He built four Forts or Fortifications in less than a month and placed in them his and other guns to the number of thirty in all."

Commander Charles Desborow, R.N., who arrived at Ferryland in October 1694, in H.M.S. *Virgin Prize*, tells us:—

"Holman's greatest difficulty was to keep the inhabitants to his assistance, who had got their arms and were making their flight to the mountains; Holman sent after them and let them know that if they at such time did desert him he would certainly make division of their fish amongst the seamen to encourage them to stand by him, and not only so but he would burn and destroy all their houses; upon which seeing the defence Captain Holman was ready to make, they did return, and with his bravery and prudent management, they so battered the French men of war, that they, after five hours fight, ran off leaving their anchors and cables behind them and ye French lost eighty or ninety men as we are informed by some English prisoners who were on board the French; which so discouraged them that they gave over their intended spoile, which might have ruined the whole country there being then no more men of war to defend it." [Affidavits sworn to by Jno. Cleer, Val Carter and Richard Christian.][1]

The Devonshire men, who had been the staunchest adherents of Charles II. and James—patrons and defenders of their monopolies—now became the equally devoted admirers of the Prince of Orange. They hoisted his flag and drank his health in New England rum, with as much noise and enthusiasm as Ulster men of to-day commemorate the same "pious and immortal memory."

Amidst wars and rumours of wars all contentions between planter and ship fishermen were for the time laid aside; they had now to fight for their lives. Many an attack was made on them and repelled with gallantry.

Early in the summer of 1696 the Chevalier Nesmond, Commander of a large French fleet, attacked St. John's. Two small hastily constructed forts, one about Chain Rock, and the other opposite on the south side (Fort Frederick, as it is now called), defended the entrance. The newly erected battlements of Fort William then crowned the hill on the site of the present railway terminus; West Country mariners handled the guns and manned the forts. Nesmond's powerful fleet and

[1] *Records.*

his disciplined sailors and soldiers were completely routed by the inhabitants and the undisciplined West Country crews. Wooden ships in those days had no chance against well-manned forts, especially in the narrow entrance to our harbour.

This first battle of 1696 happened in the early summer. All through the season, news came from Placentia about French preparations, the gathering of stores, the arrival of Canadian Indians, under French officers; still no precautions were taken to put St. John's in a thorough state of defence.

When the Devonshire ships left the coast in August and September, there appear to have been no men-of-war stationed in Newfoundland. The only guard were the people and their Governor Miners—a planter like themselves—a brave, sensible, determined man, elected to the highly honourable and dangerous position for his well-recognised valour.

It never entered their mind that the French would attack by land, preparations were only made to resist shipping. We may infer from the French narrative of Baudoin that De Brouillon had made an attack on St. John's about the end of September 1696, and had been ignominiously repulsed. Doubtless the deluded English settlers thought that two defeats in the same summer would have checked the French. They little knew the daring enemies with whom they had to contend.

To fully understand all the horrors of this war we must revert a little to the early operations of De Frontenac. These desultory attacks of the French privateers on Newfoundland were only preliminary skirmishes in advance of his great design to destroy the English in America. From the date of his second arrival in October 1689, until the Peace of Ryswick in 1697, New England was kept in perpetual terror by the midnight attacks of French and Indians. Shenectady, Haverill, Salmon Falls, are amongst the most memorable scenes of these barbarous massacres.

In the pages of Charlevoix, all the incidents of these affrays are minutely related and gloried in, even to the presentment of the English scalps to the aristocratic Marquis de Frontenac. The horrible cruelties and cowardly attacks on helpless women and children are described by the French historian as if they were so many glorious deeds—splendid and honourable actions. The French Governor boasted of his design to destroy New England, but he prudently avoided a conflict with the powerful colony. The gallantry of France was displayed in minor attacks on fishing villages and unarmed settlers.

Newfoundland soon experienced all the horrors and barbarities of an Indian and French invasion. The leader was the most distinguished Canadian naval officer of his age—the Nelson of the New World—

Captain de Fragate, Pierre Le Moyne D'Iberville.[1] In the spring of 1696 he had received command from De Frontenac to destroy the English settlements in Newfoundland.

The two French men-of-war under his command were the *L'Envieux* and the *Profond*, the latter commanded by M. de Bonaventure. When they arrived in Placentia, on the 12th of September 1696, they found

LE MOYNE D'IBERVILLE.
From Winsor's N. & C. H. of America.

that the Governor, De Brouillon, with his men from St. Malo, had made an attempt on St. John's, but had failed.

D'Iberville, a Canadian, well acquainted with the stealthy Indian warfare, proposed to attack the unguarded English settlements by land.

[1] Le Moine D'Iberville and his brother Bienville, two of the most remarkable Canadians, distinguished themselves in French expeditions to Hudson's Bay and the Mississippi. Le Moine died at Havannah a few years later of fever.

De Brouillon contended for an attack by sea. There were bitter quarrels between the two leaders. Baudoin, the Recollet Father, who was chaplain, tried to reconcile them. The Canadians and Indians would only follow D'Iberville, and he now threatened to go to France. As a final compromise D'Iberville with his Canadians and Indians agreed to proceed against St. John's by land, whilst De Brouillon's Malovians were to make the attack by sea.

From French sources we learn that the Governor had nine privateers belonging to St. Malo, three corvettes and two fireships, and that they all—Canadians and Malovians—embarked for St. John's. Owing to head winds the expedition was a partial failure; they had to return to Placentia for want of provisions, having captured thirty-one vessels (probably boats), and destroyed some fishing establishments. Baudoin does not mention this adventure, and it probably refers to De Brouillon's attempt alone.

On the 1st of November 1696 D'Iberville, with his Frenchmen and Canadian Indians, started to walk on the ice up the south-east arm of Placentia. Amongst the hybrid population, half English, half French, then living there, no doubt they had obtained a guide for the interior. To carry provisions, arms, and ammunition across such a country was a great exploit; white men alone could not have done it.

On the 10th November they arrived in Ferryland, having been for two days short of provisions. The *Profond* was anchored in Renews. All the Ferryland men had run away to Bay Bulls. On the 21st they started for Bay Bulls in boats; there was no defence, and the French captured a vessel of a hundred tons. On the 26th, according to Baudoin's narrative, there was a fight in Petty Harbour with the English settlers, and thirty-six of the inhabitants were slain. On the 28th the French encountered a body of the English from St. John's, numbering eighty-eight, who were posted in a burnt wood, full of rocks, behind which they lay in ambush.

The English account of this battle is that they went out to help the Petty Harbour men, and that about a mile from St. John's they encountered the French on the south side hill. There were four hundred French disciplined troops, and it speaks well for the courage of the planters that they fought against this overwhelming majority for half an hour, and it was only when nearly half their number—thirty-four men—were killed that they retired in good order and reached the fort. The French say nothing about their men-of-war, but they were doubtless brought round to St. John's.

The unfortunate settlers, without ammunition or supplies, with no military force, no military or naval officers to direct the defence, were

THE CAPTURE OF ST. JOHN'S.

in a desperate strait. They held out for three days,[1] and it was only after the brutal threats to scalp all their prisoners, in the same manner as they had fiendishly tortured William Drew, that they capitulated on articles of surrender, which the French commanders dishonourably evaded.

Baudoin[2] says that after the skirmish outside the town the French advanced and captured the two small forts.

"Seeing [he continued] the inhabitants were about to defend themselves [in Fort William] we sent to Bay Boulle for the mortars and bombs and powder. On the night of the 29th and 30th MM. de Mins and de Montigny went with sixty Canadians to burn the houses near the fort. The 30th, the day of St. Andrew, a man came from the fort with a white flag, to speak of surrender. Afterwards the Governour with four of the principal citizens came for an interview. They would not allow us to enter the fort, lest we should see the miserable plight to which they were reduced. It was agreed they should surrender on condition of being allowed to depart for England. The capitulation was brought in writing to the fort, and approved of by the principal citizens and signed by the Governour and M. de Brouillon."[3]

The barbarous treatment of Drew will not surprise anyone who has read the heartrending stories of Haverhill, Seneca Falls, or Shenectady, where the French, after joining in the solemn rites of the church the night before, crept into the villages, murdered the inhabitants, and calmly looked on whilst their Indian allies brained infants and slaughtered children; the French, in fact, encouraged the Indians in their cruelties. A letter was intercepted from Costabelle, Governor of Placentia, to the Minister, dated July 4th, 1711 :—

"Had despatched more officers and people, who knew all the savages, to incite them to defend and take part of a feast which they would have of English flesh at Quebec."[4]

---

[1] "Upon the approach of the French the inhabitants of St. John's fled, but Mr. Miners and Mr. Roberts, with some other stout men, retired to the greatest fortification and kept their ground for 48 hours without any provisions." (*The Post Man*, Jan. 12, 1697.)

[2] BAUDOIN'S *MS. Diary*, Quebec MSS.

[3] ARTICLES OF SURRENDER OF ST. JOHN'S HARBOUR TO DE BROUILLON, 1696.

"These are to certify you who are Inhabitants of the Harbour of St. John's that upon the quiet surrender, that you shall have good quarter and those that will have boats to go in the Bay shall have them to-morrow and those that will go for England shall have two ships to carry them home and they shall have one pound of bread per day for each person for a month and all necessaries convenient for the passage and all those that will stay here and take the oath of allegiance to the King of France shall live as they doe and go off with them and so depart the Fort immediately and every one to go to his own home and no man shall molest them and carry what they have with them given under my hand."

BURALEET.

And those that will go to the Northward to take passage in what ship they can shall have a Passport.
St. Johns the 20th (30) November 1696."
(*Records.*)

[4] Quoted in BROWN'S *History of C. Breton.*

Baudoin gives a very depreciatory account of the settlers, who, he said, were good shots but great cowards, so that one hundred of them would fly before one Frenchman.

"They have not [he says] a single minister of religion in these establishments, though more than twenty of them are larger settlements than Placentia. They do not know what religion they belong to. The greater part of them, born in this country, have never received any instruction, and never make any act of religion, no more than mere savages. Drunkenness and impurity are common and public among them, even among the women. It is impossible to imagine anything more abominable than the life led by the English on these coasts; they are left altogether without the succour of religion and are degenerated into a race almost worst than savages. Crime of the most loathsome nature is quite public among them; they *endeavoured even to entice our men to evil.*"

To anyone acquainted with the morals—especially the military morals—of that age, the idea of French soldiers, the most dissolute set of ruffians in Europe, being led from the path of innocence by our poor honest settlers' wives and daughters is simply incredible.

This bloodthirsty little Recollet Father cursing his enemies and exulting over the slaughter, ruin, and spoliation of the unfortunate Newfoundland settlers is quite in the spirit— the cruel barbarous temper—of the age, which made the New England divines hang Quakers and witnessed the Reverend Cotton Mather on horseback superintending with fiery religious zeal the judicial murder of witches.

PLAN OF THE CAMPAIGNS OF 1698.

The victims of a hundred years of calumny, our self-reliant settlers, constantly petitioning for a settled government and a minister, stand out in contrast to the rough ship fishermen; they constantly succoured[1]

---

[1] See Downing's narrative, p. 205. Downing's statement is confirmed by nearly all the English naval officers.

shipwrecked sailors, and nursed them through sicknesses. There was a baser element among them, as in all communities, subject as they were for many months to the incursion of ten to twenty thousand fishermen, many of them steeped in the wickedness of the great ports of the Old World; in the hurry to be rich during the short season by supplying rum to those unruly crowds, some in the larger settlements, like St. John's, were occasionally wild and lawless.[1]

The long and very interesting diary of Baudoin is an important contribution to our local history;[2] he gives a graphic account of the expedition, a description of all the various English settlements around Conception Bay and on the east coast; he tells us of the comfortable homes of the settlers, their stocks of cattle, horses, &c., the large mercantile establishments in St. John's, Carbonear, and Harbour Grace. Several extracts from this diary will be found in the Notes, it is much too long to quote in full.

A critical examination shows that many of the chaplain's statements are incorrect. We must remember that, in accordance with French usage—of which many amusing instances are given by Parkman—Baudoin was a spy on his superior officers— De Brouillon and D'Iberville. Every official was encouraged to make these kind of reports, so the chaplain recounts, with avidity, to "Sa Grandeur"—evidently the head of his order—the misdeeds of De Brouillon, his quarrels, and his avarice, whilst everything good is said of his own captain— D'Iberville.

FRENCH SOLDIER IN 1705.
From Winsor's N. & C. H. of America.

What makes one doubt the truthfulness of this diary is, first, it is the story of a spy; secondly, the absence of a list of the French killed and wounded. Our settlers were splendid shots; if so many English were killed in these first encounters, the French must have equally suffered, yet all their loss is put down at one man killed. Baudoin's

---

[1] Captain Tavenor, a Newfoundland skipper, reported in 1714 that the English freighters and skippers from Spain and Portugal refused to sell salt to the planters unless they took also a certain quantity of wine and spirits.

[2] The manuscript in French was lent to me by Bishop Howley, and has been carefully translated by my friend, Madame Ribalher des Isles. Charlevoix used it, almost word for word, for his description of this campaign.

explanation about the inferiority of the English guns, and the superior skill of the Canadian Indians in bush fighting, admitting it all to be true, would not account for the tremendous disparity between the losses on both sides. Mr. Christopher Pollard petitioned in 1697 that the planters from Newfoundland should be sent back to take part in the war, because they were such good shots, and accustomed to camping out in the winter. He said the regular soldiers would not be able to fight successfully against the Canadians and Indians.

As to the accusation of cowardice he makes against the Newfoundlanders, his own account of the sally of the brave eighty-eight men to defend their brothers in Petty Harbour is an eloquent reply to this charge. Every movement of the French was watched by our people, the little garrison knew all about the large force of disciplined soldiers they had to contend with, yet these gallant civilians threw themselves into the breach—like the immortal three hundred Greeks—to die in defence of their country. Talk about cowardice! Colonial history has seldom recorded a more heroic action than the battle of this dauntless handful of fishermen against their four hundred foes.

After all, the gasconading chaplain admits that his brave French never made any serious attempt to attack a real fortification like Carbonear. All their heroic exploits were assaults on poor fishermen, helpless women, and children—the burning of their houses, and the plunder and pillage of their goods. One regrets, for the honour of such a distinguished Canadian as D'Iberville, that he acted in bad faith, both at the surrender of St. John's and in the attempted exchange of prisoners at Carbonear Island. The march through the country in winter was a great military feat; but after the capture of St. John's, their exploits during the rest of the campaign were simply acts of barbarity, worthy of the savage Abenaquis; certainly they added no fresh laurels to the great military glories of France.

The French, after their various raids between 1696 and 1713, never remained in possession of any part of the English settlements. They simply swooped down on the peaceful English settlements like birds of prey, harried them, and then flew away to their nests in Placentia.

Their officers and troops were paid out of the booty taken. These expeditions partook more of the nature of a freebooting expedition than a definite scheme of conquest. The rich English settlements, of which, Charlevoix said, the meanest was better than Placentia,[1] offered a tempting bait—a suitable opportunity of employing restless Canadians

---

[1] SHEA's *Charlevoix*.

THE LOSSES OF THE SETTLERS.

and Indian braves during the winter; they always retired before the advent of the English fishing fleet.[1]

During the wars of this reign, especially in the French expedition under D'Iberville, tremendous losses were inflicted on the English in Newfoundland. In a petition to King William the damage to the little Devonshire town of Bideford alone is estimated at £24,700; the planters' loss at Ferryland is put down at £12,000. The greatest sufferers of all were the unfortunate inhabitants of St. John's. Accounts in the reign of Charles II. show the substantial character of the settlers' houses, their wealth, their large stores, shops, and extensive fishing establishments. In this generation we have twice seen our fair city reduced to a heap of ashes. Some of us can remember all the horrors and miseries of that terrible night of June 1846, when thousands of poor forlorn families were huddled together without shelter, food, or clothing. The night of the fire of '46 was a terrible time of calamity, but its miseries were as nothing compared to the sufferings of the inhabitants of St. John's in the bitter winter weather of 1696. By the invasion and destruction of St. John's they were not only made homeless

---

[1] PENHALLOW says:— "Newfoundland has given a melancholy account of the many ravages that have been committed there by the powerful assistance of those savages."

and beggars, they were banished from the land they loved so dearly; many of them had seen their brothers, sons, husbands, and lovers, who had sallied out so boldly on that frosty November morning to assist the men of Petty Harbour, brought back to them dead and mutilated by the savage allies of the French; to crown all the anguish of this terrible time, they were crowded together in one small vessel, two hundred and twenty-four men, women, and children. The horrors of that awful winter passage no pen can describe.[1]

This total destruction of the Newfoundland settlements by the French in 1697 caused great excitement and alarm in New England[2] and Virginia. King William's Government was at length aroused to action. There was tremendous indignation in England against the Ministry for the loss of Newfoundland, and their neglect to send a naval and military force to defend the Island. When it was too late, and the whole English Colony and their possessions had been swept away from the face of the earth, a large squadron, under Admiral Norris, and no less than fifteen hundred soldiers — two regiments, one from Ireland, under Colonel Gibson—were sent out (1697) to recapture Newfoundland.[3] They found St. John's completely abandoned. The French had burnt, pillaged, and destroyed everything movable and immovable in the once flourishing settlement. There was not a solitary building left standing, all the forts were razed to the ground; literally, there was not one stone left upon another.[4]

---

[1] The following entry on the cover of the parish register of the old church of Coffinswell describes these events in simple, but pathetic, language. It was extracted for me by the late Hon. S. Rendell:—

"The 12th November 1696. St. John's in the Newfoundland was taken by the French and ye Indians, and many men were killed. They in the Fort yielded upon articles, and had of the French a ship to bring them home to England. They came out of the ship 224 souls. Elias Bickford came home the 10th of January; the ship came to Dartmouth.

John Bickford, Parish Clerk."

[2] ROYAL LETTER SENT TO THE GOVERNOUR OF MASSACHUSETTS BAY.

24 March 1697.

Relative to the capture of St. John's by the French, the Governour is required to send ships and land forces as may be spared and provisions to join the Royal ships between Cape Race and Cape Bonavista. The letter says more particularly that the Colony of New England is concerned in recovering what has been lost in Newfoundland.

[3] The "Life of Captain Stephen Martin," by Clements R. Markham, contains a full account of this expedition.

[4] There is a very interesting account of the defence of Little Belle Isle in 1696-97.

The first resident on this small island in Conception Bay was John Earle, a West Countryman. He was a very smart, well educated young man; just of age in 1698, when he married in Harbour Grace Fanny Garland, sister of the well-known Justice Garland; a Mr. Pinsent and a Mr. Lilly married other sisters of Mr. Garland. The French attacked Little Belle Isle with two barges full of soldiers. John Earle had cannon upon the cliff; he sank one barge with a shot, and the other then rowed off; he had scarecrows dressed up as men on the top of the cliff to make the enemy believe he had a large force. Earle used to tell of the high prices in those days; Garland, of Trinity, as a favour to a relation, sold him one spring one cwt. and a half of flour for £5 st'g., and one hh'd. of salt for £2. John Earle lived and died and was buried on Little Belle Isle. One of his sons, William, lived in Juggler's Cove, Bay Roberts, and died there of small pox in 1777. The other son, John, lived in Portugal Cove, and is mentioned in the census of 1794-5. There are numerous descendants of both branches. The family bible of the first John Earle's wife is in the St. John's Museum.

FORT WILLIAM REBUILT.

The soldiers were set to work at once, and a new Fort William was erected upon the old site under the direction of a Mr. Richards, an engineer. Not much was done the first year beyond erecting the palisade, but between 1698 and 1708 the ramparts were faced with brick and bomb-proof parapets, and powder-magazines and substantial barracks erected. An additional fort—Fort George—was made below for the townspeople, and connected by a subway with Fort William. All the work about Fort William is the labour of English hands, commenced anew in 1697, with considerable additions made from time to time by English engineers. The French were never in possession of the present fort except from June to September 1762. It appears to have been only partially destroyed in 1708 by St. Ovide, as we find Governor Collins mentioning the fort in 1709 as still in existence. Two substantial batteries were also built between 1697 and 1704 on the site of the earthworks of Captain Martin—the Chain Rock and Fort Frederick batteries of our days. So strong were the sea defences of St. John's that it resisted all the attacks of the French ships. D'Iberville with true military genius was the first to discover that our capital —well-nigh impregnable by sea— could be easily captured in the winter by land.

The movements of the naval and military forces were very much hampered by being under separate commands, and required to call councils of war. Admiral Norris next year had supreme control as Governor for the time being. As a result, there was much indecision. When Nesmond's fleet was reported, in August, to be outside the harbour, instead of going out to engage it, an extra cable was put across the harbour, so that the two imposing expeditions sent out by France and England returned home without having exchanged a blow. Norris's conduct of the war is severely censured by Burnet.

ADMIRAL NORRIS.
From an engraving after Burford.

Lieutenant-Colonel Handyside and three hundred men were left at St. John's for the winter, but the buildings were so badly built, the winter so severe, and provisions so scarce (a ship from

New England having failed to reach them), that two hundred and fourteen died.

On the 31st of March the Privy Council had decided to station a permanent garrison at St. John's, to improve the fortifications, and erect a boom across the harbour. The Board of Ordnance did not carry out this last order; in fact, they objected to do anything for the Colony, claiming that the expense should be borne by the settlers, like the other plantations. Lieutenant Lilburne, with sixty soldiers and gunners, remained through the winter, and in 1699 a Captain Andrews seems to have been in command. Ten recruits sent out from England this year were returned as not being required, so we may conclude that the fortifications were complete, and were considered to be practically impregnable.

The reign of William III., the first real constitutional sovereign of England, has been drawn for us by Macaulay in a history which, despite all its faults and its grievous misstatements, ever will remain an imperishable monument to the character of this illustrious warrior and statesman—the noblest history in the world. William was the hereditary enemy of France. Under his firm rule England threw off the galling yoke of subserviency to the arrogant Louis, which had been borne by Charles and James.

ENGLISH SOLDIERS IN 1710.
From Winsor's N. & C. H. of America.

All the pretensions of the French in the Colony were sternly ignored. The king declared that no alien or stranger shall fish or take bait in Newfoundland, and in his first declaration of war against the French he sets forth :—

"It was not long since the French took license from the Governor of Newfoundland to fish upon the coast and paid a tribute for such licenses as an acknowledgement of the sole right of the Crown of England to that Island; but of late the encroachments of the French on his Majesty's subjects trading and fishing there had been more like the invasions of an enemy than becoming friends, who enjoyed the advantages of that trade only by permission."

AN ACT TO ENCOURAGE TRADE.

This is a plain and clear statement of the English dominion over the island. Unfortunately, William was too much occupied defending Holland to give his brave words effect until the terrible disaster of 1696-7. After the Peace of Ryswick, which left France in possession of all her territory in America, including part of Newfoundland, no great effort was made to drive the French out of Newfoundland.

On the 9th December 1698, in his speech from the throne, King William recommended Parliament "to employ their thoughts about some good Bills for the advancement of trade, they were enjoyned to take the state of the Newfoundland fishery into their consideration"; and in order to restore good government and to prevent contentions and disorders for the future, an Act was passed entitled "*An Act to encourage the Trade to Newfoundland.*" At this distance of time we cannot understand how any intelligent Minister could have propounded such a Bill; but William's Government was notoriously corrupt. It is only through the strong influence of Devonshire and bribery that we can explain the passage of such a measure.

In the first section of the Act the right of England to the Colony was clearly set forth. No alien or stranger whatsoever was to take bait or fish there. It was a re-assertion of our claim to the whole island, but King William's Government never gave it any practical effect.

The only reasonable provision in the Act was the seventh clause, which gave a title "to all persons who have built houses stages &c. since 1685 that did not belong to fishing ships they to occupy and enjoy the same."

The absurdity and monstrosity of the scheme which was arranged for the interest of the West Countrymen lay in the surrender of the entire control of the Colony, including the administration of justice, into the rude hands of a set of ignorant skippers, who were so illiterate, that out of the whole body of these marine justiciaries, only four could be found able to sign their names.

There is one very singular feature about the Act of William III. The statute is entirely declaratory and directory; there is not a single penal clause in it from beginning to end, nor is any compulsory jurisdiction given to any authority acting under it. The framers of the Act had evidently very little confidence in fishing admirals, vice-admirals, and rear-admirals, for they virtually gave them no power to compel anyone to obey their edicts; all the technical words used to constitute a court have been very carefully omitted from this remarkable statute. Charles' Star Chamber Rules contained penalties for certain offences, here there were none—every punishment inflicted by a fishing admiral was, therefore, wholly illegal.

Besides the admirals, there were other functionaries with still more high-sounding titles. We read in the records of the violent acts of Ford, the "Governor of Petty Harbour," and the truculent humours of the "King of Quiddy Vitty."[1]

I will try and describe the fishing admiral, as he appeared to our ancestors, clothed, not in the dignity of office, not in the flowing judicial robes, not in the simple and sober black of the police magistrate, but in his ordinary blue flushing jacket and trousers, economically besmeared with pitch, tar, and fish slime, his head adorned with an old sealskin cap, robbed from an Indian, or bartered for a glass of rum and a stick of tobacco. The sacred temple of law and equity was a fish store, the judicial seat an inverted butter firkin. Justice was freely dispensed to the suitor who paid the most for it. In the absence of a higher bribe, his worship's decision was often favourably affected by the judicious presentation of a few New England apples.

The litigant who commenced his case with the production of a flowing bowl of calabogus[2] captivated the judicial mind most effectually. Sometimes, alas! the dignity of the Bench was diminished by the sudden fall of the Court prostrate on the floor, overcome by the too potent effects of new rum and spruce beer.

The fishing admirals were not satisfied with the powers conferred upon them. The Western adventurers petitioned to allow them to appoint *deputies* to exercise their duties; this was sternly refused. Time would fail to recount all the enormities and barbarities of these ignorant vulgar tyrants. They displaced the rightful owners of room, seizing them either for themselves or their friends; they fined, triangled,[3] and whipped at their pleasure every unfortunate wretch who earned their displeasure, and against whom some trumped-up charge could be made out.

They always put off hearing any cases until August. Invariably they tried their own causes first. Chief Justice Brady, on his first visit to a Western outport, found, to his astonishment, that the agent of the great English house in the place had sat on the Bench and given a number of judgments in favour of his own firm. "How dare you, sir, commit such a perversion of justice?" said the indignant

---

[1] The oldest ship fisherman in each harbour was called the "king."

[2] Calabogus was a favourite drink with the Admirals. It was composed of rum, molasses, and spruce beer. Their principal toast: "The Pope and ten dollars" (meaning ten dollars a quintal for fish).

[3] Mr. Pearce, of Twillingate, who died not long ago, remembered as a boy seeing a man triangled—tied by the outstretched arms—and whipped by order of a fishing admiral.

Chief. "Well," said the agent, quite unabashed, "I must be a pretty sort of a vule of a judge if I could not do justice to myself." This remarkable Justice rejoiced in the name of "the Lord High Hadmiral."

The most celebrated of the fishing admirals—Commander-in-Chief and Generalissimo of the West Country adventurers in 1700—was Captain Arthur Holdsworth, Admiral of the Harbour of St. John's. The old Devonshire family of the Holdsworths of Dartmouth are closely connected with our history. Cromwell consulted a Mr. Holdsworth (or Oldsworth)—probably this Captain Arthur's father—about the affairs of the Colony. A later descendant—also Arthur Holdsworth—was Governor of Dartmouth Castle, probably a grandson of Admiral

AQUAFORTE.
From a drawing by the Hon. and Rev. W. Grey.

Holdsworth. He was the last member of the old family who took any personal share in our trade. He built the large stone house still existing in Ferryland, occupied by Mr. Morey. The late Mr. White an old resident, distinctly remembered the Governor of Dartmouth Castle—a very tall, powerful man. The family is still in existence, and own large property in St. John's (Holdsworth Street, &c.). Both the Brookings and the Studdys are connected with the Holdsworth family. Mr. Brooking, who managed their firm's affairs in Newfoundland in our own time, was called Thomas Holdsworth.

In 1701 the English Government sent out Mr. Larkin, a barrister, to draw up a confidential report on all the English North American colonies. In his report on Newfoundland he shows how the West Country men worked this Act of William III. to their own advantage. In 1701 he says, writing from St. John's :—

" The then admiral of this Harbour, Captain Arthur Holdsworth, brought over from England this fishing season 236 passengers all or great part of which were bye boat keepers and they were brought, under a pretence of being freighters aboard his ship, though it was only for some few provisions for their necessary use. These persons he had put and continued in the most convenient stages in the Harbour which all along since the year 1685 had belonged to fishing ships, insomuch that several masters of fishing vessels had been obliged to hire rooms of the Planters.

"These bye boat keepers," says Mr. Larkin, "were most of them able fishermen and there was not one fresh man or green man amongst them as the Act requires."

Mr. Larkin goes on to state :—

"That Captain Arthur Holdsworth and one or two more who constantly used the fishery, made it their business in the beginning of the year to ride from one market town to another in the West of England on purpose to get passengers, with whom they made an agreement, that in case they should happen to be Admirals of any of the Harbours [The first, second, or third to arrive in the Harbour] they would put and continue Mr. Holdsworth and such persons as he approved of in fishing ships rooms.

"This," says Mr. Larkin, "was very great abuse and discouragement to the other Adventurers ; besides, these bye boat keepers could afford to sell their fish cheaper than the Adventurers, which must lessen the number of fishing ships."

In the last year of King William's reign the great English Missionary Society, which has done and is still doing so much to sustain the Church of England in this Colony, was founded and incorporated as "The Society for the Propagation of the Gospel in Foreign Parts," under a Royal Charter, dated the 16th June 1701. There had been previously several abortive attempts to establish a similar scheme. Laud had proposed one to Charles. Cromwell planned an institution for all Protestant churches that was to rival the great Propaganda of Rome, but up to the beginning of the eighteenth century the Church of England had not properly fulfilled the Divine command to go forth and preach the gospel to all nations. Since then she has nobly redeemed her early neglect of missions. Rome had her enthusiastic missionaries, especially a devoted band of Jesuits, braving all dangers, and bearing the message of the Cross to many lands long before the English Church had a single labourer in the field. There is, however, no record of any Roman Catholic priest living in the English settlements during this or the two succeeding reigns, unless Gowling, mentioned by Roope, was a resident of St. John's.

To the venerable English society, Newfoundland is indebted for the first resident clergyman, the Rev. John Jackson. He had been chaplain of one of the men-of-war that came with Sir John Norris' expedition in 1697, and had resided in St. John's and ministered to a congregation, and a small church had been built close to Fort William, several years before the first grant was made by the S.P.G. In 1703 we find the following entry in the records of the Society :—

"In Newfoundland no public exercise of religion except at St. John's where there is a congregation but unable to subsist a minister. To Mr. Jackson £50 per annum and a benefaction of £30."

Probably this was given to enable him to bring out his wife and family. Jackson seems to have been a good, earnest man. He had a difficult part to play ; to many of the lawless residents the restraints of religious observances of decency and morality were irksome in the extreme. What rendered the poor chaplain's position still more difficult was the direct opposition and bad example of the Commandant and resident Governor.

APPENDIX TO CHAPTER IX.

I. The Campaign of 1696-7.

(a) ENGLISH ACCOUNT OF THE FRENCH ATTACK ON ST. JOHN'S, 1696.

Philip Roberts, Richard Gelman and Samuel May late Inhabitants and fishermen of St. John's in the North part of Newfoundland came this present 10th day of January 1696-7 before me Thomas Hood Esquire Mayor of the Borough of Clifton, Dartmouth Hardness and John Palmer Esquire the last preceding Mayor, two of His Majesty's Justices of the Peace within the same, to swear that on the 16th November last the Inhabitants of St. John's had information that the French to the number of sixteen men had taken Petty Harbour a small fishing place about nine miles distant from St. John's;

Upon which the Inhabitants aforesaid sent out thirty four men, armed to their relief. But the weather proving full of snow they returned the next day, being the 17th November, without effecting anything. On the 18th they sent out another party of men to the number of eighty four armed to the aid and assistance of the Inhabitants of Petty Harbour who had not marched above a mile from St. John's up the South Hill until they met a body of French and Soldiers and Canada Indians, to the number of Four hundred or thereabouts, with whom they engaged half an hour; in which action were killed of the inhabitants thirty four men and several others wounded, the rest retreating back to the Harbour of St. John's, the French pursuing.

About one hundred and eighty men of the Inhabitants besides women and children entered into a fortification called King William's Ffort, which they kept and defended for three days, the French in the meantime burning and destroying all houses boats stages and provisions.

And these Deponents further say that the French took one William Drew, an Inhabitant a Prisoner and cutt all around his sculp and then by the strength of hand stript his skin from the forehead to the crowne and so sent him into the fortification, assuring the Inhabitants that they would serve them all in like manner if they did not surrender; who wanting ammunition and provisions and receiving articles of surrender from the French (of which the annexed is a true copy) were accordingly obliged to doe and with about eighty men of the said Inhabitants went off to the Southward with the French, most of them being forced so to doe contrary to the articles of capitulation.

And Samuell May saith that being present with the Governor of Placentia [De Brouillon] after the said articles of surrender were signed, he heard the said Governor declare by an interpreter, that the English were asleep and fools to suffer their plantation to be thus taken from them; That the French did not doubt of taking all New England next summer except Boston; and that they now intended to inhabit Renews having already fortified that place.

The body of the French and Indians, who attacked them, were commanded by the Governor of Placentia and Canada, who came with the said forces from Placentia in ships and boats to Bay Bulls, and from thence to Petty Harbour and St. John's aforesaid by land and that after the destruction of St. John's a party of the aforesaid forces were detached to march through the woods to commit the like spoyle on all the harbours to the northward.

That on 16th December last these Deponents with about two hundred and twenty men women and children Inhabitants came from St. John's in a small vessel given them by the French to carry them for England, and that at the same time about eighty men more of the Inhabitants were sent in another vessel to France, contrary to the capitulation, and that at the time of these Deponents leaving the Country a party of French were then in possession of St. John's.

(b) BAUDOIN'S DIARY.

THE CAPTURE OF ST. JOHN'S BY THE FRENCH, NOVEMBER 1696.

On the morning of the 28th of November M de Montigny, a brave Canadian [Montigny was at the taking of Schenectady and Pemaquid and served in after years under Subercase and Ovide in Newfoundland], M D'Iberville's lieutenant, was keeping the advanced guard with thirty Canadians marching about one hundred yards in advance. M De Brouillon and M D'Iberville followed with the main body of the troops. M De Brouillon had orders to allow the Canadians to take the lead in case of a sudden attack.

After two hours' march our advance guard came upon the enemy and at about a pistol shot from them; they numbered eighty-eight. They occupied an advantageous position on a rocky hill amongst burnt woods. These hills [South Side Hills] served to protect them. Our advanced guard opened fire upon the enemy who thinking we numbered but twenty four returned fire. These gentlemen

[D'Iberville and De Brouillon] soon joined us, and after having received absolution, every man threw aside the load he had been carrying and rushed upon the enemy. M De Brouillon attacked them first, then M D'Iberville chose the left flank and discovering the enemy amongst the rocks and bushes, he killed a great number; after half an hour's engagement they gave in. [The real number of French in this fight was about 400 men.] M D'Iberville pursued them sword in hand right into St. John's, which was a distance of about three-quarters of a league. He entered St. John's fully a quarter of an hour before the arrival of M De Brouillon with the main body of our troops. M D'Iberville got into St. John's at the same time as the enemy, and immediately took possession of two of the first forts which the enemy had abandoned; he also took thirty-three prisoners, amongst the number some entire families. The others retreated, some into the large Fort and some into a vessel which was then in the Harbour. Fear was so general amongst the enemy [the English] that had M D'Iberville had one hundred men with him he would have taken the larger Fort also, for there were in it but about two hundred men according to the accounts given us by the prisoners, and these but poorly prepared for war.

M De Brouillon having arrived with our main army, M De Mins encamped in the Fort nearest to the enemy with his sixty men, and within cannon shot of them. This Fort was palisaded. The remainder of our troops encamped in the houses. The wind being favourable the Vessel which lay in the Harbour set sail laden with all that was best in St. John's and eighty or a hundred men. The enemy lost fifty men; M De Brouillon's trumpeter was killed whilst standing beside him, three of his men were wounded and two of M D'Iberville's. M De Brouillon acted all through like a brave man; I was quite near him most of the time, and so can judge of his doings.

These people would require one or two campaigns with the Iroquois to learn how to defend themselves against the enemy. Verily the Canadians had much the advantage, having learned how to fight in all their terrible wars with the Iroquois. In these wars, as in this one, it is far better to be killed outright than to be wounded, for there are no remedies to be had, no help, no refreshment for the sick, each man having only just what he can carry on his back, the march being so difficult through this barren island.

We sent a prisoner immediately to the fort, but he was retained there. 29th November, it is snowing heavily, some of our Canadians going into the woods took eight prisoners, and some others came and gave themselves up. These gentlemen [the French commanders] seeing that our enemies are determined to defend themselves, sent to Bay Bulls for the mortars, the bombs, and the powder which M D'Iberville had left there. On the night of the 29th-30th MM. De Mins and De Montigny went with sixty Canadians to burn the houses which were near and beyond the fort; M. D'Iberville stationed himself with thirty of his men to support them, and M. De Brouillon remained at the advanced posts with his men.

The 30th November, St. Andrew's day, a man came out of the fort carrying a white flag and asking for terms. Our commanders agree to an interview. The Governor of the fort came out with forty of the chief inhabitants; they would not allow even one of our people to go within the fort, lest we might see in what a miserable state it was, and to what straits they were reduced. They insisted upon deferring their surrender until the morrow, hoping that the two large vessels [these may have been H.M.S. Dreadnought and Oxford, sent out to relieve them] which they had seen for two days off their Harbour might find a favourable wind to bring them into it. But the commanders would not consent to make any delay. They then decided to surrender, on condition that two ships should be given them to return to England, that those who wished might go to Bonavista, and leave for England from there, and that they should not be searched; which was granted.

The written capitulation was taken to the fort and approved of by the principal inhabitants; it was afterwards brought back to our camp where it was signed by the English Governor [probably Miners or Roberts] and after by M De Brouillon; this latter did not even offer it M D'Iberville for his signature, though he had had at least as much to do with the taking of the place as had M De Brouillon.

I confess, my Lord, that this act shocked me greatly. The Governor then re-entered his fort, from whence he soon afterwards came out accompanied by the whole garrison composed of one hundred and fifty men, some master mariners and some sailors engaged for the fishery, besides women and children. Our enemies had but one man wounded during the time we were reconnoitring the fort. This fort was situated on the hill to the north-west, commanded on one side by two heights both within gunshot of it; it was square in shape, with four bastions, a palisade eight feet high, a covered trench now full of snow, also a drawbridge, with a small tower upon which there were four cannons, the balls for which weighed four pounds, under the tower there was a cellar for keeping gunpowder. There was, however, very little powder in it, and only a couple of dozen of cannon balls. The English not having had time to carry anything to their fort, they only took refuge there when they saw us coming.

They depended solely upon the eighty-eight men whom they had chosen from their entire force to defend them; but these latter were provided with very inferior guns, only suited for fishermen and for those who never had the slightest idea what war really was. The Governor of this fort was simply an inhabitant of the place, and not a captain of one of the English ships; he was without soldiers, and had no commission from the King of England.

Thus one cannot feel surprised at M D'Iberville's venturing an attack upon this place, falling upon St. John's during the night, and taking the inhabitants entirely by surprise. Their forts being without men and their houses quite far one from the other, we should actually have run much less risk than had our advance been discovered.

St. John's has a very fine harbour, which can hold two hundred ships. The entrance lies between two very high mountains, distant one from the other about a gunshot. They are surmounted by a battery of eight guns. The inhabitants of St. John's are very well settled along the north side of the harbour to a distance of about half a league. There were three forts, one on the side towards the roads westward, another in the centre having a native as Governor with sixty men, and a third which gave us a good deal of trouble before capitulating. This latter fort protects the entrance to the harbour; although at a distance from it, it commands the harbour, and a number of the houses—the best part of St. John's—was around this fort and the best houses were built there. Unfortunately these latter were burnt on the night before the capitulation.

On the 2nd of December we took Portugal Cove, which contained three families; also Torbay, which had likewise three families, and Kerividi [Quidi Vidi], which had nine families. We burnt every house in St. John's, and the boats in the harbour. On the 14th of January 1697, we started for Portugal Cove, and arrived there on the 19th. Thence we travelled along the shore of Conception Bay to the bottom, where we found some men sawing wood, who had come from Carbonniere. On the 20th we took Harbor Men [Maine], where there was one house. On the 23rd we left in three boats for Carbonniere. We passed by Brigue, where there were about sixty men, and arrived at Port Grave, which we took. There were one hundred and ten men and seventeen houses there, well armed.

On the 24th we set out for Carbonniere; Le Sr. de Montigny was sent with a detachment to take Musquito. In passing from Harbor Grace to Carbonniere in boats we discovered that the inhabitants of this latter place had entrenched themselves on the Island, and they fired some cannon shots at us. There were about two hundred on the Island, having fled there from Harbor Grace, Musquito, and even St. John's. They had erected barracks and strong forts. Having arrived at Carbonniere, the commander sent to summon the people on the Island, but were met with defiance. We found it impossible to attack it, as it was steep on all sides, with the exception of two places of landing, which were well guarded. On the 29th we received prisoners from Brigue, among whom were eight Irishmen, whom the English treat as slaves.

Several attempts were made by M. D'Iberville to land on the Island, but in vain. On the night of the 31st we went all round the Island in boats. The sentry challenged us and fired. We had ninety men in nine boats, and M. Montigny, when challenged by the sentinel at pistol shot distance off, could almost touch the Island with his hand, he was going to leap ashore first.

On the 3rd we took Bay Ver, where there were some fourteen houses and about ninety men. From there we went to Old Perlican; there were there nineteen houses, several stores, more than thirty head of horned cattle, and a number of sheep and pigs. On the 7th we went to Ance Havre [Hants Harbor]. There were four houses, but the people had all fled. On the morning of the 8th we started for Celicove [Silly Cove], where there were four houses and a great quantity of fish and cattle. Thence we came to New Perlican; there were there nine houses and stores. We left immediately for Harbor Content [Havre Content], where there was a sort of fort or barricade, made of boards, with portholes above and below. This temporary fortress was commanded by an Irishman. They surrendered on being summoned. There were thirty men, besides women and children.

Having left the place in charge of M. Deschaufours with ten men, M. D'Iberville started the following day for Carbonniere. When arrived there he found that the English had taken prisoners one Frenchman and three Irishmen, who had taken part with the French. A detachment under Boisbriand was sent to burn Brigue, Port Grave, &c. Harbor Grace had fourteen houses, Carbonniere, twenty two,—the best built in all Newfoundland. Some of the merchants were men of £100,000 worth of property.

On the 17th we entered into negotiations with the people on the Island for an exchange of prisoners. The English demanded one Englishman in lieu of their French prisoner, and three for each Irishman. The place of exchange was agreed upon, namely, out of gunshot of the Island, about half-way between it and the shore. The English came without their prisoners, and some words ensued. Our officer accused them of breaking their word, and casting ridicule upon the orders of the King. The Commander seized the English officers, and took them prisoners.

On the 28th we burned Carbonniere, and left again for Havre Content. On the 1st of March M. D'Iberville sent MM. de Montigny and de la Peiriere to go with all the prisoners (about two hundred) to Bay Boulle [Bay Bulls Arm], in the bottom of Trinity Bay. He left M. de Boisbriand with a detachment at Havre Content, with orders to keep a strict watch on Carbonniere, and he himself, with nine men, set out across the woods for Plaisance. The road is not quite as good as between Paris and Versailles.

[The list in the Statistical Chapter gives the number of the settlers, fishing establishments, number of fishing boats, and quintals of fish caught as noted by Baudoin.]

II. Act of William III.
10 & 11 Wm. III., Cap. xxv.
An Act
to encourage the trade to Newfoundland.

WHEREAS the trade of and fishing at Newfoundland is a beneficial trade to this kingdom, not only in the employing great numbers of seamen and ships, and exporting and consuming great quantities of provisions and manufactures of this realm, but also in the bringing into this nation by returns of the effects of the said fishery from other countries great quantities of wine, oil, plate, iron, wool, &c., to the increase of revenue, and the encouragement of trade and navigation.

Be it enacted that from henceforth it shall be lawful for all his Majesty's subjects, residing within this realm of England, or its dominions, trading to Newfoundland, to enjoy the free trade of merchandize and fishing to and from Newfoundland; peaceably to take bait and liberty to go on shore on any part of Newfoundland for the curing, salting, drying, and husbanding of their fish and for making oil, and to cut down trees for building stages, shiprooms, tram-fats, hurdles, ships, boats and other necessaries for themselves &c. and all other things which may be useful for their fishing trade, as fully as at any time heretofore; and that no alien shall take bait or use any sort of trade or fishing there.

2. And to preserve the harbours . . . . . . that from the 1st March 1700 no ballast &c. shall be cast out but carried on shore.

3. And . . . . that at their departing no person shall destroy flakes and at their arrival they shall content themselves with such stages as are needful for them, and they shall not repair them by rinding trees or demolishing other stages.

4. And . . . . . . that (according to the ancient custom there used) the master of such ship as shall first enter a harbour shall be Admiral, the second Vice-Admiral, and the third Rear-Admiral and that the master of every ship shall content himself with such beach as he shall have necessary use for, and if possessed of places in other harbours, shall make his election in forty-eight hours of such place as he shall chuse to abide in; and the Admirals shall settle differences and proportion the places to the several ships according to the number of boats which each ship shall keep.

5. And whereas several inhabitants in Newfoundland and other persons have since the year 1685 detained in their own hands, and for their private benefit stages, cookrooms &c. and other places (which before that time belonged to fishing ships) for taking of bait and fishing and curing their fish to the great prejudice of the fishing ships and sometimes to the overthrow of their voyages and to the great discouragement of traders there ; . . . . . . that all persons as since the year 1685 have taken stages &c. shall on the 25th of March next relinquish them to the use of the fishing ships.

6. And to prevent ingrossing in future, ... that no fisherman or inhabitant of Newfoundland shall take any stage &c. which at any time since 1685 belonged to any fishing ship until all such ships shall be provided with stages.

7. Provided always that *all such persons as since the 25th of March 1685 have built houses and stages that did not belong to fishing ships since 1685 shall peaceably enjoy the same without any disturbance from any person whatever.*

8. And . . . . . That all by-boat keepers shall not pretend to meddle with any stage &c. that did belong to the fishing ships since 1685.

9. And . . . . . that every master of a by-boat shall carry out two fresh men in six and that every inhabitant shall be obliged to hire two fresh men like by-boat keepers, and masters of ships one fresh man in five and the masters of by-boats and ships shall take oath before the collector, &c. that they have such fresh men, and the officers are required to give a certificate thereof without any fee.

10. And . . . . . that masters of ships take every fifth man a green man.

11. And . . . . that no person shall deface masts of boats &c.

12. And . . . . . that no person shall rind trees nor set fire to the woods, nor cut timber except for repairing and no person shall cast anchor or do anything to hinder the haling of sayns in the accustomed baiting places, nor steal nets or cut adrift boats.

13. And whereas several persons that have been guilty of thefts, murders and other fellonies, have escaped unpunished because the trial of such offenders hath been ordered before no other court but the Lord High Constable and Earl Marshall of England . . . . . . that all robberies and murders &c. committed there may be tried in any shire of England by virtue of the King's commission of oyer and terminer and gaol delivery according to the laws of this realm.

14. And . . . . . that admirals are required (in the harbours and on shore) to see the rules of this present act duly put in execution and that each shall keep a journal of the ships, boats, stages, transports and of all the seamen imployed in their respective harbours and deliver a true copy to the Privy Council.

15. And . . . . . . in case of dispute between the fishing ships and the inhabitants the Admirals shall determine them and if any party shall think themselves agreived they can appeal to the commanders of His Majestys ships of war appointed as convoys.

16. And to the end all may join their solemn prayers and addresses to Almighty God for his blessing on their persons and endeavours . . . . . that all the inhabitants shall strictly keep every Lords Day and that none keeping taverns shall sell wine &c. on that day.

17. And whereas by an act to grant his Majesty a further subsidy of five per cent. on all merchandize imported (all manner of fish English taken excepted) and whereas some doubt has arisen whether oil, blubber and fins are not liable to the said duty . . . . . . that all oils &c. of English fishing taken in the seas of Newfoundland and imported in English shipping are hereby declared to be free of the said duties.

CHAPTER X.

REIGN OF ANNE.

1702–1714.

1702.—Captain Leake destroyed French fishing stages at Trepassey, St. Mary's, Colinet, St. Lawrence, and dismantled the fort at St. Peter's. French attack on Sillycove and Bonavista.

1703.—Lieutenant Lloyd succeeded Captain Richards in command at Fort William, St. John's. Admiral Graydon's unsuccessful expedition against Placentia. Grant from S.P.G. to Reverend J. Jackson. John Roope sent out to superintend the placing of a boom at St. John's. Further French attacks on Bonavista by way of Trinity and Placentia Bay porterage.

1704.—La Grange repulsed from Bonavista by Captain Gill. Battle of Blenheim. Captain Lloyd suspended by Captain Bridge on petition of the soldiers; Lieutenant Moody succeeded to the command. Reverend J. Jackson returned to England to support his complaints against Lloyd.

1705.—Attack on St. John's by Subercase, Governor of Placentia, and about five hundred troops; successful defence of the forts by Moody and Latham; town destroyed; many inhabitants taken prisoners to Placentia; Montigny and the Abenaquis plundered, during the summer, all the settlements in the northern bays except Carbonear Island, and spoilt the fishing. In November, Captain Moody and the old company replaced by Major Lloyd and ninety-one fresh soldiers. Fishery very much curtailed, only twenty ships from England and seventy-two thousand qtls. of fish exported.

1706.—Attack on the French fishing stations on the northern part of the Island by Captains Underdown and Carleton and Major Lloyd.

1707.—Union of England and Scotland. House of Commons' petition to the Queen about the Newfoundland Trade.

1708.—Destruction of St. John's by St. Ovide de Brouillon; Major Lloyd and the garrison taken prisoners and sent to Placentia, Quebec, and thence to France. Unsuccessful attack on Buoy's Island by a French man-of-war. Militia formed in St. John's.

1709.—Captain Moody again in command at St. John's during the summer. Captains Aldred, Pudner, and Purvis destroyed French fishing stations in the North. Commodore Taylour partially rebuilt Fort William and gave Governor's commissions to Collins for St. John's and the coast as far as Carbonear, to Pynn for Carbonear Island, &c.

1711.—Admiral Hovenden Walker with fifteen ships, nine hundred guns, and four thousand men, decided he was not able to attack Placentia. Preliminaries of peace between France and England. Voluntary assembly made laws, Captain Crowe, R.A., presiding.

1712.—Armistice signed.

1713.—Treaty of Utrecht. The Island was declared to belong of right wholly to Great Britain; French allowed to fish between Bonavista and Point Riche. Survey of the Island ordered to be made by Captain Taverner, R.N., but not carried out for want of funds. One hundred French settlers arrived at Louisburgh from Placentia and St. Pierre.

During the whole of this reign our unfortunate Colony was devastated by war; besides minor attacks from French privateers, twice within this short period of twelve years St. John's and the outlying English settlements were destroyed by the French. Belgium has been designated " the cock-pit of Europe"; we were certainly the cockpit of America.

QUEEN ANNE.
From an engraving after Kneller.

Whilst the British army in Europe was covering itself with glory at Blenheim, Malplaquet, and Ramilies under Marlborough, and the British Navy winning victories under the gallant Rooke and Teake, Benbow and Sir Cloudesley Shovel, North America witnessed the most contemptible British cowardice and inefficiency; anything more ludicrous than the abortive expeditions of Admiral Graydon and Admiral Hovenden Walker against Placentia cannot be conceived.

Amongst the voluminous reports of the Board of Trade at this period is one which brings our history directly in contact with the wits and poets of the classic age of Queen Anne. It purports to be a report of Lord Dartmouth, but it was really written by the genial poet and hard-working official Matthew Prior, whose signature is appended to it.

This interesting document, which is too long to quote in full, is very well written. It denounces the conduct of the fishing admirals, their injustice and incapacity. As one might anticipate from Prior's well-known ability, it is far more moderate, well-reasoned, and sensible than any previous paper on the Colony. It points out very distinctly that Newfoundland can never prosper whilst the French hold Placentia.

In 1703 Graydon was sent out to protect the West Indies after the death of Benbow; he was ordered to attack Placentia; he had a large fleet and a considerable land force. When off Placentia he held a council of war, consisting of Rear-Admiral Whetstone, thirteen captains in the Royal Navy, Colonel Rivers, commander-in-chief of the land forces, six captains, and an engineer. They decided that an attack on Placentia was impracticable, *and might tend to the dishonour of Her Majesty's arms*. For his cowardice Graydon was dismissed from the service. The failure of this expedition no doubt encouraged our enemies to attack the Colony.

Admiral Hovenden Walker's great expedition to capture Quebec and Placentia, in 1711, was a still more ludicrous failure. This nautical Falstaff complained bitterly that "frivolous pamphleteers" had laughed him to scorn as an idiot and a coward; he was terribly indignant because they had held him up to ridicule for not taking Placentia. The frivolous writers declared:—

MATTHEW PRIOR.
From a print in the B.M.

"The taking of the French Newfoundland Capital would have been as easy a task for the admiral as a citizen riding home in his chaise from Hampstead calling at a cake house to regale himself and his wife with a glass of cyder and a cheescake."

And well they might scout and ridicule a British admiral with fifteen ships of war, nine hundred guns, and a land force of four thousand men, actually declaring that it was not practicable to make an attempt on Placentia, whilst they knew from an intercepted despatch of Costabelle's, the French Governor, that the little garrison was in want of supplies of all kinds, that the promised reinforcement of two companies of soldiers had not arrived, and that *La Valeur*, their only armed ship on the station, had been lost.

REIGN OF ANNE.

Anyone who studies the topography of Placentia will see at once that it could have been captured by a flank movement similar to the

OLD FRENCH FORT.   NEW FORT. BREAKWATER. BARRACKS.   HARBOUR. FORT FREDERICK.   BEACH.

CONTOUR OF PLACENTIA.
B.M., K. 199-102.

one adopted against Louisbourg; the attacking force could easily land under cover of night at Little Placentia, and seize the heights commanding Castle Hill. All the defences were seaward; it was open to any vigorous attack on the land side, especially to such overwhelming forces as Graydon and Hovenden Walker commanded. With Castle Hill taken, Placentia was at the mercy of the attacking force.

Between 1697 and 1705 the French directed their whole attention to the unprotected outlying settlements in Conception and Trinity Bays;

TOPSAIL HILL, CONCEPTION BAY.
From a photograph by S. H. Parsons.

detachments of Canadians and Indians came from Placentia either by land or in small boats by the porterage in Trinity Bay. We have an

account of an attack on one settlement, and Mr. Campbell mentions losses sustained by him at Bonavista in 1702 and 1703 :—

"To Mr. Samuel Merrett. Sept. 21, 1702 from Pool.

"This serves to advice you that yesterday Mr. Thos. Wadham in the *Hopewell* of this place arrived here in three weeks from Trinity Harbour; he brings the bad news that about a week before he left 40 or 50 armed Frenchmen came over by land from Placentia to Sillicove, surprised the inhabitants killing 3 or 4 and took Mr. John Masters out of his bed rifled his house, and carried him and his goods aboard a Jersey ship laden with fish and sailed northward with the ship and 1,000 qtls. of fish but took no fish from the rocks; they much doubt their being gone to Bonavista where is only Captain Weston. A French man of war hath been off St. John's all the summer and hath taken seven ships in sight of that harbour. The Convoys were not arrived when he came away."

Charlevoix mentions a further attack on Bonavista in 1704 made by La Grange, who had served in Hudson's Bay under d'Ibberville :—

"Equipping two barks with a hundred Canadians, he came to Bonavista in the hope of surprising the ships there. On arriving within twelve leagues of that port, he left his bark to escape observation and kept on in two gigs entered the port at night, boarded a 24 gun frigate loaded with codfish captured it, burned two store-ships of two or three hundred tons each, sank another small frigate and sailed off with his prize and a great number of prisoners. There were six hundred English in Fort Bonavista, who appeared under arms next morning but it was too late, our gallant fellows were already under sail."

The following very graphic letter, which agrees with Penhallow's description, exposes the skilful evasions of the French writer :—

"*The Flying Post.*—March 10th, 1705.

"St. John's in Newfoundland. Sep. 21.

"On the 18th of August last, about 144 French and Canada Indians came about two o'clock in the morning in two sloops and canoes to Bonavista Harbour, about 30 leagues to the Northward of this place and surprised the *Pembroke* galley of London of 250 tuns, 44 men and 20 guns, John Noll, Commander laden with dry fish. And the *Society* of Pool of 140 tons, 14 guns and 24 men, Captain Auten, Commander. And also the *William* of about 115 tuns, 10 men but no guns, having 30 tuns of lamp oil on board. They also attempted to surprize Captain Michael Gill of Charles-Town in New England, of 14 guns and 24 men, who discovering their boat to be French, fired briskly upon them, killed and wounded some of them so that they returned to the Prizes they had taken and brought the great guns of both ships to bear upon Captain Gill and continued firing upon him with both great and small arms for the space of 6 hours, till his ship was much shattered. He, on the other hand, playing his great guns and small arms all the time on them.

"During the action, he veered his ship somewhat to the shoar. About 8 o'clock, when they found he could not be taken, they set fire to the *Society* and cut her loose in a flame to drive upon him, but by the great diligence of Captain

Gill, he got clear of her and she burnt to the keel. Finding that would not do, they set fire to the ship *William* and set her before the wind, furiously burning to that degree, that the lamp-oil burning in a flame on the water, was like to have set him on fire, but that both he and his men laboured in the fire, and turned her clear of them. The buoy-rope of the *William's* anchor got between the rudder and the stern and kept her clear of them.—*Peuhallow.*] And when the inhabitants who had fled into the woods and rocks, saw Captain Gill's courage, they came down and appeared in a body in arms, which when the French saw, they immediately weighed and set sail and carried the Masters and men with them. And about forty leagues off [on the N.E. coast], they gave the Masters and some of the men a boat, who soon after returned, to whom the French declared, that had they taken Captain Gill they would not have left house, stage or goods in the harbour; all which is owing under God to the courage and conduct of Captain Gill. He had but one man killed and three wounded; but the enemy had several killed and wounded."

To understand rightly Gill's success we must remember that New England, from the very first, had a trained militia. The American soldiers were the admiration of the British officers who came to America. They were fine marksmen and scientific artillerists; we need not then wonder at Gill being such a splendid gunner. It requires no effort of the imagination to picture to ourselves the scene on that memorable morning of the 18th of August, 1704; the fish vessels lying at anchor in calm placid waters of Bonavista; the stealthy approach of the French

BONAVISTA.

From a photograph by S. H. Parsons.

with the war-vessels, and the Indians in their canoes; the sudden attack, surprise, and surrender of the West Country vessels; the fright of the inhabitants. Newfoundlanders dreaded the murderous savages—the Abenaquis—more than the foreign foe. Above all this panic and din and craven fear rises the master spirit of the bold New England skipper, Michael Gill; in a moment he is on the alert, the deck is cleared for action, his guns are loaded, his men at their post ready to give the French a warm reception.

Capt. Michael Gill, of Charles Town, in New England, first appears in our history in the list of shipping for 1698. Capt. Michael's vessel was a very small one at this time, only 40 tons, and she brought rather a mixed cargo: salt, pork, and New England cider.

By the year 1704 our old friend Capt. Michael, a shrewd trader—brave as a lion—had profited by the Newfoundland business. His little hooker of 1698 had been exchanged for a fine ship of 150 tons, carrying 24 men, and armed with 14 guns. There had been considerable trade between New England and Newfoundland from 1698 to 1704. Fort William was being rebuilt in St. John's; there was a garrison, and large supplies were required. The English commandant complains bitterly of the way he was fleeced by provincials. Gill's name does not appear as one of the army suppliers, but there is mention of a shrewd Bostonian, Captain Gladstane. Gill found more profit in the out-ports, and he appears to have traded chiefly with Bonavista.

Gill's[1] gallant conduct saved Bonavista, but when Montigny appeared there next spring, George Sciffington, who was in command, being a Quaker and "the spirit not moving him," capitulated at once and paid a ransom. But more serious attempts were soon to be made upon the English settlements. On the 7th of September Lieutenant Lloyd was suspended by Commodore Bridge upon a petition of his own soldiers, and when the fleet departed Lieutenant Moody was left in command at St. John's. Moody, though a remarkably brave man, had not sufficient control over his subordinates; his authority was soon disputed by Roope, an engineer, and by the next in command, Lieutenant Latham, a master mason.

Latham disliked the position assigned to him as commander of the "south side castle," a substantial stone fort with a wooden block-house; besides, his commission as lieutenant does not appear to have been quite in order, and no doubt at the south side he had not as full scope to trade on his own account as he had had under Captain Lloyd.

Roope, who was engaged at "Maggott's Cove, near Mr. Latham's house," in constructing the boom, wishing to have a little authority, advised the planters not to keep watch in the north battery, a terribly trying duty, or obey Mr. Moody's regulations. The planters, not having been paid for former services of this kind or for scouting, though the

---

[1] Michael Gill seems to have resided in New England; about 1748 or 1750 his son Michael came to this colony. He soon rose to an eminent position; was the first colonel of militia. His brother Nicholas was naval officer and afterwards chief magistrate in St. John's. The son of this Nicholas Gill, also called Nicholas, and whom some of us can remember as a very old man, carried on a large West India business. The only survivor of his children is old Mr. Frederick Gill (Torbay Road), great grandson of the hero of Bonavista, 1704. His sister, Miss Gill, died recently, leaving $7,000 to the Church of England, and $500 to the Belvidere Orphanage.

I p. 2729.

money had been sent from England, were easily persuaded. Another actor on the scene was Colin Campbell, the prize agent.

Campbell and Roope were accused of treachery in furnishing the French with information; the charges and countercharges do not seem to have been at all justified. Most certainly the French had spies in St. John's at this time, in consequence, nearly everyone except Moody and Latham were accused; it was a time of painful suspicion, every man mistrusted his neighbour. The truth seems to have been, that when in the power of the French and exposed to the strong arguments of the Indians, Roope, Campbell, and others turned cowards and time-servers, and became subservient to the crafty French tactics. The fishing admirals took the side of Roope and afterwards of Major Lloyd.

PETTY HARBOUR.
From a photograph by S. H. Parsons.

In November three men were murdered at Renewse by the Indians, but it was not till the middle of January that Subercase, with about two hundred and fifty inhabitants of Placentia and Canada, ninety regulars, and a hundred Indians, passed through Bay Bulls and Petty Harbour and camped a short distance from St. John's. The snow was falling heavily. Rising before daybreak, benumbed, and doubtless without food, the French, in their cruel rage, attacked the slumbering inhabitants near the fort, and killed many in cold blood. With a strange lack of generalship they failed to promptly attack the fort, which it appears might easily have been taken. The garrison once aroused, their opportunity was lost. Securing the men as prisoners in the church, they sent the women and children into the fort in the hope of starving the garrison out. These brave women were afterwards of great help to

Lieutenant Moody in strengthening the defences. At first the French were sheltered by houses built dangerously near the fort, but they were gradually driven from these by the heavy firing and burning them. They retreated under cover of the smoke to a safer position.

The garrison were taken at a great disadvantage. On Friday there had been a very heavy fall of snow, and on Sunday, the morning of the attack, the guns were still buried deep in snow. The soldiers, wretchedly clothed, and many without boots or stockings, set to work with a will to clear them. They suffered also in another way; the guns were mounted on the ramparts without any shields to protect the gunners from the galling fire of the enemy, directed from various points of vantage near the fort; working night and day with the help of the women, and even, in defiance of military custom, during the four days' armistice, this was partially remedied. Fortunately they had no lack of provisions and ammunition.

The French had no heart to take the fort by storm, so they tried to effect it by intimidation, by flattery, by bribery, by playing Moody against Latham. Moody says:—

"About eight o'clock on the morning of the attack the French sent one of the inhabitants with a flag of truce with a young child in his arms with its throat cut, threatening if I killed one of their men they would put all persons (without distinction of age or sex) to the sword—and hang me at the Fort Gate."

CANADIAN SOLDIER ON RACQUETS.
From Potherie's History, 1722.

Perceiving after a fortnight's siege that he could neither force nor bribe the English commanders to surrender, Subercase sent them the following letters:—

"M. SUBERCASE TO LIEUT. MOODY.

"SIR,

"I would not until now let you know my business here (it was not convenient) I now say it is my intention to possess myself of all ye English settlements which by God's help I have done with an intention to intirely ruin the trade, hoping in a little time to become master of ye Forts that you command and I believe you yourself see the impossibility that you can long defend yourself against the attacks that I can make, I do not at all doubt of it; but to save blood am willing to grant a reasonable capitulation provided it be done in a few days otherwise I shall not be able to hinder the fury of ye Indians which with the rest of our troops do importune me vigorously to prosecute my design; its your business to consider ye fate of ye number of prisoners I have in my hands and also ye plantations and settlements.

"I will send you one of ye prisoners that you shall think fit if you think of entering into a treaty [Prisoners sent in because Moody could not understand French.]

"If I can do you any particular service as to your owne affairs you may command me who am

"Your most humble servant,
"February 1705. SUBERCASS."

"MR. JOHN ROOPE to MR. ROBERT LATHAM [written under SUBERCASE'S dictation].
"Feby. 4, 1705.

"My misfortune hath made me a prisoner but I hope in good hands, ye Governor having hitherto been very kind. He was much enraged against you because there were three musketts fired at his flag of truce but I told him it must be done without your knowledge in which he seemed satisfied. He declared he knew nothing of the burning of your house but to the contrary he is for making anything good to an officer. There is a treaty on foot between Mr. Moody and him. I think it is about a surrender, he would not at first hear that you should be concerned in ye treaty but now is satisfied, so desire you to take ye best measures that you can think of for ye good of all and the preservation of whole country which is threatened with fire and sword; ye properest measures you know better than I can inform you so commit you to ye protection and direction of Allmighty God.

"Your humble servant,
"JOHN ROOPE."

Moody procrastinated, and asked for four days' truce, employing the time in strengthening the fort. After several conferences with Campbell and Pemberton, two of the principal inhabitants, Moody refused to surrender. Subercase sent him a brace of partridges, and proposed a personal interview, but Moody said it would be of no use.

The French, after burning nearly all the houses on the north side, directed all their attention to the castle. They first tried to induce Lieutenant Latham, by means of a letter from Moody, taken by Campbell, to cross over to consult with Moody, intending to kill him on the way, but Latham stubbornly refused to quit his post, and the Indians could scarcely be restrained from murdering Campbell in their rage at his failure. They then bombarded the castle with two guns, found on the south side, which they loaded with powder they had accidentally discovered in the "Queen's warehouse at the waterside." They had spoilt most of their powder in fording rivers on their march. The guns having no effect they tried fire-arrows, but they were badly made, and fell harmless.

Their provisions and powder exhausted, the planters from Placentia more anxious to carry off their spoil than to risk their lives, and their expected supplies of ammunition not arriving, the French retired to Ferryland after a five weeks' siege. They took to Placentia, where

VIEW FROM THE BEACH, CAPLONE.

VIEW OF CAPLONE, SHOWING THE PIER.

Subercase now returned, the best of the fishermen to carry their plunder and assist in their fishery. Some eventually were sent to Canada and France, some escaped to St. John's, and the rest, chiefly Irish, entered the French service. The coolness, judgment, and bravery shown by Moody and Latham in the face of overwhelming numbers and French diplomacy is worthy of the highest praise. On the other hand, the French showed great want of courage, and again availed themselves of the barbarities committed upon the helpless planters by Montigny and the Abenaquis. In the words of their own chronicler, "The very name of Montigny made the arms fall from the hands of the most resolute." The English loss in the forts was very small, but the French suffered very heavily, though probably the English estimate of two hundred is exaggerated.

From Ferryland, Montigny and the Indians marched through Holyrood to Harbour Grace, murdering and destroying as they went. Carbonear Island, gallantly defended by Davis and Pynne, again resisted their attack, much to Montigny's mortification.

CANADIAN SOLDIER.
From Winsor's N. & C. H. America.

"LETTER from CARBONERE, 29 March 1705.

"Montigny £500 out of pocket on his Indians and resolved to have it of us and have our lives, and will wait all the summer to take vengeance on us for keeping the Island, for which he says he will lose his Commission."

Montigny then proceeded to Bonavista, where the inhabitants had retired to Green Island, under command of Geo. Sciffington, but he surrendered at once upon terms of ransom.

Moody says in his narrative :—

"The French surprised Bonavista but about 80 or 90 of the inhabitants got on Green Island where they fortified themselves and might have made good their defence but their courage failing and unwarily admitting the enemy to come among them, they heaved their guns (being nine in number) over the cliffs into the sea and afterwards the inhabitants capitulated and ransomed their houses for 450 pounds payable to Montigny."

In July 1706, Montigny was reinforced by more Indians from Placentia. Lurking in the woods, they kept the whole of Trinity and Conception Bay in terror, and spoilt the year's fishing. They carried their spoil away by the porterage at Bay Bulls arm, in Trinity Bay, to Placentia.

246 REIGN OF ANNE.

Captain Moody and his company, who appear to have been resident in St. John's since 1698, were in November succeeded by Major Lloyd and ninety-one new soldiers, volunteers from various English regiments. Major Lloyd, who was in England, had skilfully used Moody's disgrace to secure his own re-appointment; he came out armed with a power of holding court-martial. During the winter of 1705–6 Lloyd behaved with great vigour, personally leading out detachments of troops to protect Ferryland, Harbour Grace, and other points threatened by the French and Indians.

Captain Moody, upon his return to England, explained his conduct to the satisfaction of the Board of Trade, who strongly recommended him for promotion. In a few years Nemesis overtook the tyrant Lloyd, and his rival Moody was again in command at St. John's.

The loss incurred by the planters in 1705 was very great; it shows the recuperative power of the people that they were able to survive it:—

"Sworn value of destruction made to Captain Moody.

St. John's and Quidividi	45,000
Ferryland and Bay Bulls	25,000
Harbour Grace &c.	38,000
Carbonere, Bay de Verds &c.	46,000
Parlican, Trinity &c.	34,000
	£188,000 Stg."

Beyond the destruction of the French fishing stages at Trepassey, St. Mary's, Colonet, St. Lawrence, and the dismantling of the fort at St. Peter's, by Captain Leake in 1702, and the abortive attempt of Graydon on Placentia, all the English operations had been directed to the capture of the French fishing fleets on their way out from France and back, and in this they had been very successful; we have noticed the presence of a special prize agent at St. John's. Now, however, acting upon the suggestion of Roope and others, the Government determined to destroy the French fishery in the Petit Nord. Anspach thus describes these operations :—

"In the following year, viz. on the 25th July, 1706, a report was brought to

ADMIRAL LEAKE.
From an engraving by Cook.

[1] For about the same time [1702] Captain John Leake (afterwards Sir John), sailing with a small squadron to Newfoundland, took or destroyed no less than fifty-one ships and ruined all the French settlements on the islands."—S. Cockburn, *Columna Rostrata*, 1727, p. 292.

St. John's, that the enemy had a considerable number of ships employed in the fishery in several harbours to the northward, and other parts of the island. Captain John Underdown, commander of the Queen's ship the *Falkland*, was then in St. John's harbour with the *Nonsuch*, commanded by Captain Carleton. Having been petitioned by the merchants, masters of vessels, and inhabitants of that place, to protect the British trade in those parts, he accordingly set sail from St. John's, on the 26th of July, accompanied by Major Lloyd, who desired to be employed in this expedition, with twenty of his company, on board the *Falkland*, and as many on board the *Nonsuch*. The next day they came before Bonavista, and finding there no appearance of an enemy, the Commodore ordered Captain Hughes, commander of the *Medway* on that station, to join him with a French ship of war, which the latter had taken a few days before.

"On the 2nd of August they stood into Blanche Bay till they arrived off Fleur-de-Lys Harbour, when Major Lloyd in the Commodore's pinnace, and the first lieutenant of the *Falkland* in the pinnace belonging to the *Nonsuch*, were immediately sent into the harbour. They found there several stages and other necessaries for the fishery, which they destroyed, and afterwards returned to their ships. At six o'clock next morning they doubled the Cape, and saw a ship which struck upon the brisk exchange of a few shot; this was found to be *Le Duc d'Orleans*, from Saint Maloes, of about three hundred and sixty tons, thirty guns, and one hundred and ten men.

"In another arm of the same bay, called Eguillete, they saw another large ship; but the place being rocky, and the water so shallow that none of the English men of war could come near her, the *Medway's* prize was ordered to go in as close as she could with safety, whilst Captain Carleton, Major Lloyd, and the first lieutenant of the *Falkland*, in boats well manned and armed, were directed to land upon the island under which that ship lay. This was executed so promptly and ably that the French ship struck, after having fired several broadsides, her crew being no longer able to keep the deck against the small shot from the shore. This ship also belonged to Saint Maloes, carrying twenty guns and eighty men.

"Having here received information that about three leagues farther north, in a place called La Conche, or Conche Harbour there were two ships of thirty-two and twenty-six guns, both of Saint Maloes, the commodore directed Captain Hughes to burn the last prize, and afterwards to join him at that place, whither he proceeded himself with the *Falkland* and the *Nonsuch*. On the afternoon of the fifth, they arrived at Conche Harbour, where they found two ships ready for sailing. After exchanging several broadsides, the French set their ships on fire, and went over to the next harbour, called Carouge. The commodore being informed that there were four French ships in that place, immediately stood for it, meeting in his way, at about eight o'clock in the evening, the *Medway's* prize; but there being very little wind, and that at south-west, it was near six o'clock the next morning before he could get off the harbour's mouth. He then sent in his boat, and found that the French ships had escaped, taking advantage of their great number of men and boats by cutting and towing out.

"The English ships then proceeded to the northward, and about five o'clock in the afternoon came off the harbour of Saint Julian, where they discovered a large French ship; standing in for that harbour, they came to an anchor in twenty-six fathom water. The place where that ship had been hauled in being very narrow and shoaly, the *Medway's* prize was ordered to go as near her as possible. The French ship then fired two guns; but it being late in the evening, and the enemy appearing determined to make a spirited resistance, it was not thought advisable to commence the attack before the following morning.

"On the sixth of August, at four o'clock in the forenoon, Captain Carleton, Major Lloyd, and Lieut. Eagle went towards her with all their boats, well manned and armed; and having effected their landing, attacked, and at last drove the enemy from a strong post which they occupied on the shore. They then boarded the French ship, where they found several trains of powder laid, for the purpose of blowing her up. By this timely discovery the ship was preserved, and, by noon, towed out to sea.

"The British pilots being unacquainted with the coast, the commodore resolved not to proceed any farther north, but to sail back to Carouge and there await the arrival of the *Duke of Orleans* prize, which had been left at Grand Canarie with a lieutenant and sixty men. They looked into Petit Maitre, where they destroyed a considerable number of stages and boats, and found vast quantities of fish and oil; and at about seven o'clock in the afternoon they came to an anchor, and moored in Carouge Harbour. On the 12th and 13th it blew a hard gale at south-west; on the 14th, having been joined by the *Duke of Orleans* prize, they weighed at four o'clock in the morning, stood out to sea with her, and came into Saint John's Harbour, where the *Falkland* and the *Nonsuch* arrived with the two prizes on the 17th, the *Medway's* prize having before been ordered to proceed to Trinity.

"From this expedition, which deserves to be recorded on account of the activity and judgment displayed by Captain Underdown and his associates, equal to the good fortune that attended their operations, it appears that, while the English had on that station only the *Falkland* and *Nonsuch* in St. John's, and the *Medway* at Bonavista, the French had in the northern parts of the island no less than ten armed ships, mounting from twenty to thirty-two guns. The loss which the latter suffered by the capture or destruction of six of them and the ruin of their fisheries, must have been a severe blow to their trade. So large a force shows the degree of importance which they then attached to the Newfoundland trade."[1]

The French, after a period of inactivity, caused doubtless by the better organisation for defence of the different settlements, again attacked St. John's in 1708, and this time with success. They must have been acquainted through their spies in St. John's of the want of vigilance shown by the once-energetic Major Lloyd. The first exaggerated reports brought to England accused him of treachery, but there appears to have been no real foundation whatever for this charge; it would seem more likely, from the account of Keen and the serjeant, that he had become quite incapable, perhaps through intemperance.

The French guides, either through design or mistake, brought St. Ovide de Brouillon and his troops too late to St. John's to effect a complete surprise; they were seen advancing in the clear moonlight by

[1] ANSPACH'S *H. of Newfoundland*, pp. 124-129.

the sentry on the new fort, but, in spite of his alarm, the French were soon in possession of Fort William, and, through a blunder, the Colonial Militia were unable to enter the fort by the subterranean passage specially provided for such a contingency. The capture of Fort William was effected in half an hour. The new fort, which was overlooked by Fort William, surrendered upon terms of quarter which were not fully kept. The "south side" castle surrendered next day.

St. Ovide, anxious to secure all the advantage to himself of his fortunate adventure, sent word direct to France, and immediately two hundred soldiers were dispatched with a commission appointing him Governor of St. John's; but they arrived too late. Costabelle, partly jealous of St. Ovide's success, and presuming that the home Government were too much occupied in Europe to spare troops for the retention of St. John's, had ordered St. Ovide to destroy the fortifications and return immediately to Placentia, which he was reluctantly obliged to do, leaving St. John's on March 31st.

During his stay in St. John's, St. Ovide sent Captain Larond to take Ferryland, but the inhabitants were too strongly fortified; it is significant to note they even refused to admit a flag of truce.

Major Lloyd was first taken to Placentia and Quebec, and afterwards to France. Captain Moody succeeded him in command, but returned to England for the winter to report upon the condition of affairs. One of his proposals was to remove the garrison to Ferryland, and not rebuild the fortifications at St. John's, but it met with no favour.

The only other French movement during this year was an unsuccessful attack on Buoy's Island, Ferryland, by a French man-of-war. The settlers were by this time too well organised to be surprised. Commodore Taylour employed his men in 1709 in rebuilding Fort William,[1] which had been entirely demolished except the earthworks, upon an improved plan, mounted eight guns, and erected huts in the fort for the inhabitants for the winter. The fort and the coast from Ferryland to Carbonear were placed under John Collins; Pynn was in command at Carbonear, and others at Trinity and Bonavista, with local commissioned officers under them. The French claimed a ransom for St. John's and neighbourhood of over £7,000 which appears to have been promptly paid to the Placentia Governor Costabelle. This was one of the last episodes in the dreary guerilla warfare carried on by the

---

[1] There is a rough plan of the new fort in the Record Office, *Bd. of Trade, Newfoundland,* No. 6, K 21.

French from Placentia against our settlements; from 1708 the land had rest for over fifty years.

FRIEND'S MAP OF 1713.
B.M.—S. 9(8) 36.

Turning from these stirring scenes of fights and pillage to the more peaceful subject of the fishery, we realise in the terribly shrunken state of the trade the immense destruction, loss, and waste produced by the incessant warfare waged by the two countries in this unfortunate Colony.

THE EFFECT OF WAR ON THE FISHERY.

These poor meagre figures in the war times of 1705 are in striking contrast to the great results of former affluent seasons of peace :—

"An account of the trade and fishery of Newfoundland for the year 1705 :—

Number of fishing ships	20
Number of sack ships	20
Number of ships from America	20
	60
Burthen of fishing ships	2,400 tuns.
Number of fishing ships' boats	60
Number of by-boats	40
Number of inhabitants' boats	160
	260
Quantity of fish made by ships	18,000
Quantity of fish made by boats	12,000
Quantity of fish made by inhabitants' boats	4,800
	78,000 qtls.
Quantity of fish carreyed to market	72,000 qtls.
Quantity of train-oil made by ships	105
Quantity of train-oil made by boats	70
Quantity of train-oil made by inhabitants	280
	455 tuns.
Number of stages	80
"Number of inhabitants :—	
Men	800
Women	130
Children	200
	1,130

Besides 6,000 Qtls. of fish left on land; A further quantity was spoyld by bad weather computed at 2,000 Qtls.

STATISTICS OF THE NEWFOUNDLAND FISHERY.
1700 to 1713.
From the Reports of the Naval Officers.

Years.	Fishing Ships.	Boats.	Inhabitants' Boats.
1700	171	800	764
1701	75	338	—
1702	16	35	380
1703	23	44	214
1704	23	—	—
1705	20	60	200
1706	46	136	232
1707	70	196	257
1708	49	170	356
1709	35	130	258
1710	49	153	365
1711	62	168	439
1712	66	198	370
1713	46	162	483

In the former reign mention was made of the Reverend John Jackson, the first resident clergyman appointed by the Society for the Propagation of the Gospel in Newfoundland, and his difficulties with the military commandant and governor of the Colony, Major Lloyd. The records give us a very full account of these proceedings.

Major Lloyd was appointed commandant of the forces in Newfoundland in 1703, succeeding Major Richards, as being the "eldest lieutenant"; he came to Newfoundland in 1700 as paymaster. It is hard to imagine anything more scandalous than the conduct of this unprincipled and tryannical officer. He seems to have taken a mischievous delight in annoying and insulting Parson Jackson. The naval chaplain, however, was not one to fear the face of man. Lloyd's character is typical of the military roué of that day—unprincipled, reckless, dissipated, yet withal as valiant a soldier as ever sought "the bubble reputation at the cannon's mouth." Anspach has given us some account of his exploits in 1706. The condensed account of the charges made against him by the Reverend John Jackson, all of which are substantiated by the evidence of the various witnesses, is graphic and grotesque.

Mr. Jackson spent many weary months in London, tormented with sickness, petitioning the Government and the Church. He and his large family were recommended to the attention of charitable people; eventually he was appointed to a living in England by Queen Anne. Lloyd was killed in France, probably in a duel with some fire-eating Frenchman whom he had insulted. Thackeray's immortal Irish hero, Barry Lyndon, strongly resembles this brave, unprincipled swashbuckler.

"1705.—Complaints against the then Lt. Thomas Lloyd. In letter from Mr. John Jackson Minister at St. John's to the Lords Commissioners for trade and plantations :—

- 1st.—Lt. Thos. Lloyd came to command in chief at Fort William in St. John's harbour, Sept. 24th 1703. He put in practice all sinister ways and base means he could devise to get money. £660 of Queen's money to pay soldiers he converted into trade. Supplanted inhabitants by falling price of fish, buying liquors at low rates &c.
- 2ndly.—Ruined families by his tyranny; beat one Adams a planter, so that poor man is incapable of getting bread for his numerous family.
- 3rdly.—Caused Mr. James Benger to be imprisoned for not paying debt of £50 another man owed him, and though Benger paid it, got him kept in prison till season was past in order to ruin him. Benger dealt that year for about 2000 qtls. of fish and said Lloyd worsted him £300 that year.
- 4thly.—His debtors would run from their flakes and business in fishing season as from an Indian when they saw him coming, which he often did with his sword and caine in his hand and threatning, if not beating, those he lighted on. When ships arrived in harbour he would forestall inhabitants in choosing goods and when Masters of ships demanded pay cavilled with and beat them as Capt. Hatch, Capt. Davy, Capt. Pickering, &c. for demanding reasonable rates.

5thly.—In taking farewell demanded hands of inhabitants to testimony of good behaviour &c; refusers he threatens to murther and beat; drew his sword upon some and pulled them out of their beds.

6thly.—His return to the country amasing to most; old traders left the country fearing he should treat them as formerly.

7thly.—If speedy care be not taken, trade of country must fall to ruin. He has declared as it cost him dear to reassume command, is resolved to repay himself by trade.

8thly.—So greedy of getting money he neglected seriously the garrison and soldiers.

9thly.—Took to live with him a woman of disreputable character, who caused the soldiers to be whipped and abused at her pleasure.

10thly.—A constant breaker of the Sabbath, threatening and cursing those who would attend service, going about the harbour with his fiddle to divert the people and spending remainder of the day in most disgraceful rioting &c.

11thly.—Took care no account should reach home and intercepted letters relating to his conduct.

12thly.—Suspended by Commodore; command devolved on Lieut. John Moody."

The following complaints were made againt Major Lloyd during his second term of office, from 1705 to 1708, and may be appropriately mentioned here. He told the planters it had cost him a large sum to obtain his re-appointment, and he meant to have it out of them. Many settlers left the country on his account:—

"Mr. Minshew's Affidavit.

.1707-8.

"(a.) His tyranny in generall; (b.) his dispossessing Mr. Benger, for not signing a paper against Moody; (c.) his wounding an inhabitant; (d.) his barbarity to the surgeon; (e.) his cruelty to his maid servant; (f.) his small allowance to the soldiers letting them out to hire and taking three parts in four of their wages; (g.) his plundering in the north; (h.) his feasting Monsr. Bellater; (i) his extorting three qtls. out of every fishing boat; (k.) his oppression causing the inhabitants to remove; (l.) his contriving certificates and compelling them to subscribe them; (m.) his agent's cruelty to Adams; (n.) his barbarity to Burt; (o.) his injustice to Minshew's wife; (p.) his menacing Minshew for asking his money; (q.) his abuse to Commodore Underdowne; (r.) Minshew durst not return to his family.

"Seven affidavits with other papers to prove the allegations in Mr. Campbel's memorial relating to the unwarrantable proceedings of Major Lloyd in Newfoundland."

One most beneficial effect flowed from these extraordinary proceedings of Major Lloyd. As the result of the inquiry into these scandals, the position of Governor was taken from the Commander of Fort William and conferred upon the commodore, and remained vested in the superior naval officer on the Newfoundland station from 1708 until 1825. It appears from the records that from 1697 to 1703 the commodore had been governor; in the latter year the appointment was conferred on Lloyd as commandant.

The command in Newfoundland became afterwards one of the great prizes of the service; it was held by some of the most distinguished officers in the navy. Sir John Leake, Rodney, Duckworth, Graves, Lord Radstock, &c., are amongst the honoured names of Newfoundland's floating governors.

Much abuse has been bestowed on our naval rulers; never was censure less deserved. No doubt they were often severe, sometimes narrow in their views. We must remember they were always hampered by instructions to repress settlement. On the whole, I think they filled their very difficult positions admirably. In order to protect the settlers, they encroached on the prerogatives of the fishing admirals, and after a few years virtually superseded them. Of course, quarter-deck law was their sole guide; in the rude state of society then existing amongst the fishermen it was probably the best. As the Colony became more populous and civilised, naval government became simply intolerable; it was, however, decidedly a great improvement on the fishing admirals' law.

"In the year 1711, I find," says Mr. Reeves, in his history of Newfoundland, "a record of several laws and orders made at St. John's. " It is worth while considering whether such a local legislature which " the people seem in this instance to have created for themselves might " not be legally lodged somewhere for making bye-laws and regulations " as occasion should require." The Commander, Captain Crowe, presided at this voluntary assembly. His successor, it seems, followed his example, and held a meeting of the same sort. These assemblies were somewhat anomalous, a kind of legislative, judicial, and executive all blended together.

It is very easy to discover the original idea from whence Captain Crowe and Sir Nicholas Trevanion's voluntary assemblies were taken. These gatherings of the inhabitants were literal copies of the New England town meetings. All the citizens of the township assemble in general meeting once a year or oftener, levy taxes, decide on improvements, and appoint the necessary executive officers to carry out their arrangements during the ensuing twelve months. All men meet on an equality, every citizen is entitled to free speech and free vote. As the New England towns become more populous they pass out of the stage of town meetings into representative government.

Unfortunately for the development of home rule in this Colony, we stopped short at the callow stage of the town meeting. What one admires most in this assembly is the political ability of the New Englander who engineered the proceedings; we have had clever wire-pullers in the Colony, but we doubt if any of our party managers were ever skilful enough to blend together into one harmonious meeting such antagonistic elements as the fishing admirals, the Devonshire adventurers, and the planters. The great principle of politics is compromise; these laws show us how adroitly the American satisfied the Devonshire party by declaring certain rooms used by the bye-boat keepers were ship's rooms, and turned out the all-grasping Holdsworth. The inhabitants were gratified by the arrangements for their defence and the support of their minister.

Under this astute settlement, everything seems to have worked harmoniously; doubtless the war and their common danger from the French made the discordant elements for the time at least united. We notice the poor pay received by the Rev. Jacob Rice; it was, perhaps, the insufficient salary which had driven away his predecessor, J. Jackson.

From the re-appointment of our old friend Governor Collins, it appears that the Home Government had again withdrawn the military, otherwise a civilian would not have been left in charge of the forts.

At this time preliminaries for peace began: for two years the negotiations dragged their slow length along. From 1710 the merchants kept making representations to the Board of Trade that in any treaty of peace with the French, Newfoundland might be reserved wholly to the English. This idea was adopted by the Board, who pressed it strongly on the Ministry. The treacherous way in which the peace of Utrecht was concluded is well known, how England abandoned her allies. The literature of the day is full of the subject; one of Dick Steele's most trenchant articles is an attack on

HARLEY, EARL OF OXFORD.
From an engraving after Recant.

---

[1] Harley was impeached for his conduct in negotiating the Treaty of Utrecht.

this peace. No condition was more disgraceful than the surrender of the Newfoundland fishery to the French.

English statesmen in Queen Anne's reign were violent partisans,[1] many of them corrupt and venal, but the most prejudiced and ignorant amongst them understood that in the struggle with France victory rested with the nation that possessed the strongest sea power; they were also well aware that France was almost solely dependent on her great North American fishery for the manning of her navy; they knew also that her restless aggressive policy was a constant menace to English power, both in Europe and America.

In 1713 France was at England's feet; never since Crecy and Agincourt had the French armies received such overwhelming defeats.

FRENCH FISHING STAGES AT ST. JULIAN.

France has always valued her trans-Atlantic fishery not for the sake of peaceful commerce, but as an engine of war. The enormous bounties paid to her fishermen in Newfoundland are not to sustain the paltry trade of St. Pierre, but, as it has been declared over and over again by French Ministers, to recruit her navy.

It may be argued that, compared with the European interests involved in the Utrecht negotiations, the North American fishery was of quite minor importance. But this is not the case. For England, the

[1] Contemporary writers quoted by Hallam say that "The desire for French wine and the dearness of it alienated many from the Duke of Marlborough. The hard drinkers complained that they were poisoned by port; all the boon companions, many physicians, a great many of the lawyers, the inferior clergy, and the loose women, were united in a faction against the Duke."

North American fishery was of paramount importance; it involved the question of British supremacy at sea, and the English dominion in North America.

The vast naval force of France had grown up and was sustained by her fishery in Newfoundland and the St. Lawrence, yet with the full knowledge of all that happened in the past, England, with her enemy at her mercy, gave back to her rival both Cape Breton and the fishery in Newfoundland.

In the negotiations about the treaty of Utrecht the French knew that they must lose Newfoundland. English public feeling at the time was indignant at the frequent French raids made on the Island, and insisted on its entire possession. France offered to surrender our Island and the fisheries and St. Martin and St. Bartholomew in the West Indies for Acadie (Nova Scotia). The English Government were firm in their refusal to give up Nova Scotia, and insisted on fishing rights in Cape Breton, and that it should not be fortified. But in all these demands, except the retention of Nova Scotia and Newfoundland, they were outwitted by their opponents.

The French argument about Cape Breton was that the English and French could not fish together there—that it would be impossible to preserve peace amongst them. Yet in the face of this unanswerable argument, England consented that there should be a concurrent fishery in Newfoundland, involving perpetual quarrels between the subjects of both nations. The surrender of the Newfoundland fishery was a wilful blunder on the part of the English Ministry.

The entire exclusion of the French from Newfoundland and from all participation in the fishery was strongly urged on the Government by the Board of Trade, by the whole body of British merchants, by the united voice of the North American colonies, and by the urgent entreaty of the Newfoundland settlers. The appeal was made to unwilling ears. Prior, one of the chief negotiators, had expressed in his report in 1706 the absolute necessity of excluding the French from the Island, every naval commander had reiterated the same opinion, but it was all to no purpose—there has hardly ever been a more senseless surrender; the consequences have been lasting and widespread—for the English Colonies an exhausting war. Unfortunately to-day we suffer for the base treachery of Queen Anne's Ministry.

This great treaty, over which the fierce intellectual giant, Swift, and the well-beloved Joseph Addison fought their great literary battles, is to-day the rule under which the French fisherman builds his temporary hut and erects his stage on the treaty shore of Newfoundland.

It remains a dangerous cause of quarrel between two great nations, a perpetual irritating sore, a bar to the progress and prosperity of the Colony.

By Article XIII. of the Treaty of Utrecht, 1713, it was agreed that—

"The island called Newfoundland, with the adjacent islands, shall, from this time forward, *belong of right wholly to Britain*, and to that end the town and fortress of Placentia, and whatever other places in the said Island are in the possession of the French, shall be yielded and given up within seven months from the exchange of the ratifications of this treaty, or sooner, if possible, by the Most Christian King to those who have a commission from the Queen of Great Britain for that purpose. Nor shall the Most Christian King, his heirs and successors, or any of their subjects, at any time hereafter *lay claim to any right to the said island* and islands, or to any part of it or them. *Moreover, it shall not be lawful for the subjects of France to fish in any place in the said island of Newfoundland, or to erect any buildings there, besides stages made of boards, and huts necessary and useful for drying of fish, or to resort to the said island beyond the time necessary for fishing and drying of fish. But it shall be allowed to the subjects of France, to catch fish and to*

French Fishing Rooms at Cape Rouge Harbour.
From Black and White.

dry them on land in that part only, and in no other besides that, of the said Island of Newfoundland, which stretches from the place called Cape Bonavista to the northern point of the said island, and from thence running down by the western side, reaches as far as the place called Point Riche. But the island called Cape Breton, as also all others, both in the mouth of the River St. Lawrence and in the gulf of the same name, shall hereafter belong of right to the French, and the Most Christian King shall have all manner of liberty to fortify any place or places there."

The language of this treaty is very clear and explicit, the sovereignty of Great Britain over the Island of Newfoundland is made absolute,

The French are confined to a temporary user of the shore for one purpose only, the *fishing and drying of fish*; no other rights are granted to them. It will be seen that their preposterous claim to build factories and tin lobsters is entirely opposed to the plain language of this treaty, which is still in force. No other fishery but the cod fishery was in existence at that time, and no other fishery was contemplated by the treaty; which view is further confirmed by the Treaty of Versailles, 1783:—

"The XIII. Article of the Treaty of Utrecht and the method of carrying on the fishery, which has at all times been acknowledged [a ship cod fishery], shall be the plan upon which the fishery shall be carried on there; it shall not be deviated from by either party; the French fishermen building only their scaffolds, confining themselves to the repair of their fishing vessels, and not wintering there; the subjects of His Britannic Majesty on their part not molesting in any manner the French fishermen during their fishing nor injuring their scaffolds during their absence."

In the original draft proposal of the French the word used was *codfish*, not fish, but the purists who drew the treaty considered codfish too vulgar a word, and inserted in place of it *fish*. The meaning, however, is exactly the same, as the codfishery was the only fishery then carried on as a ship-fishery by both nations, the only fishery in which stages and *flakes* (scaffolds) are used.

By the terms of the Treaty of Utrecht, Placentia was to be given up to the English immediately. Brown writes:—

"M. De Costabelle, the Governor, therefore lost no time in sending off the garrison and inhabitants to Cape Breton so that the latter might not lose their summer's fishing. Some of the people objected to leaving Plaisance [probably the English and Irish] and would willingly have remained under English domination, but Costabelle urged all to go except idlers and vagabonds, whom he discreetly left as a legacy to his successor.

"In the first instance the garrison and inhabitants went to Havre à L'Anglois (Louisbourg), which was known to be favourably situated for carrying on the fishery. In the course of the summer about one hundred and eighty persons, chiefly fishermen and their families, arrived from Plaisance and the Isle of St. Pierre. Some of these settled at Balcine, Scatari and the out harbours, but the majority took up their abode at Havre à L'Anglois. All were supplied with provisions by the French Government for some time after their arrival."[1]

This is the last episode in the history of the French Colony in Newfoundland. The settlement existed there over half a century, but during all that time it never increased, it was essentially military; after fifty years of occupation the whole permanent French population of Newfoundland numbered less than two hundred souls. As colonisers the

[1] Brown's *History of Cape Breton.*

French have been failures, always and everywhere. In one respect they were superior to their English rivals. "No other Europeans," says Merivale, in his lecture on colonies and colonisation, "have ever "displayed equal talents for conciliating savages, and, it must be added, "for approximating to their usages and modes of life as the French."

The French in Cape Breton were just as bad neighbours to Nova Scotia as they had been to Newfoundland; they secretly encouraged the Indians to make raids on the English settlers; they were always planning the re-conquest of Acadie.

French writers differ somewhat in their views of the Treaty of Utrecht. Charlevoix says:—

"France was amply compensated for the loss of Newfoundland by the acquisition of Cape Breton, where the inhabitants of Plaisance found themselves more agreeably and more advantageously situated than they had ever been in Newfoundland, whilst the English were now absolute masters of the country, where before they could not assure themselves of anything so long as they had us for their neighbours."

Abbé Raynal laments bitterly over the loss of Newfoundland and Acadie. Garneau says:—

"The Treaty of Utrecht snatched from the feeble hands of Louis the portals of Canada, Acadie, and Newfoundland. From this treaty dates the decline of the monarchy and the coming of the revolution."

APPENDIX TO CHAPTER X.

I. Campaign of 1704-5.

[No event in the whole of our history is so fully recorded as this siege of Fort William; we can trace the course of events from day to day, after a lapse of almost two hundred years.]

(a.) Charlevoix's Account.

M. de Subercase set out on the 15th of January with 450 well armed men, soldiers, Canadians, privateersmen and Indians, all determined men accustomed to walk in snow shoes. Each man had provisions for twenty days, his arms, his blanket and a tent to each mess in turn.

The severest part of the march was caused by four of the rivers not being frozen over. Arriving at Rebou [Bay Bulls] on the 26th at noon the people begged for quarter. Here the army found considerable provisions. They proceeded after 48 hours rest three leagues to Petty Harbour. They entered it the next day and leaving forty men to guard the prisoners taken at Rebou, marched forward. The English at St. John's were ignorant of the proximity of the French and perhaps of their departure from Placentia, but the want of order preserved in leaving Petty Harbour and the neglect to reconnoitre St. John's well, deprived the army of all advantage of surprising it.

There were then at St. John's two forts, one much larger than the other. They began at the former, which was well defended, the English keeping upon the besiegers a constant fire of bombs and cannon balls which the French stood with all possible intrepidity. Nevertheless we had only fifteen killed or wounded, the Chevalier de Lo, ensign among them. Want of ammunition at last forced our men to raise the siege, a part of the powder brought from Placentia having been wet in crossing the rivers ; but they did not draw off till they had laid in ashes every house around the harbour.

On the 5th of March the army decamped and marched to Forillon, where the inhabitants at first made a show of defence but soon surrendered. The town was burned, after which Martigny, who had brought his faithful Nescambiouit, was detached with the Indians and a part of the Canadians to Carbonniere and Bonavista with orders to burn and destroy all the coast, which he executed without losing a single man, so great was the terror among the English.

His very name made the arms fall from the hands of the most resolute and gave him a number of prisoners whom he had only the trouble of binding. But he had to reserve Carbonniere Island for another time. It held three hundred, and was, as I have said, inaccessible in winter.

Every other place was carried or submitted; MM. de Linctot, de Villedonné and de Beletre thoroughly supported Montigny, and Nescambiouit, as usual, distinguished himself. In fine, this campaign completely ruined the English trade in Newfoundland.

(Shea's *Charlevoix*.)

(b.) Penhallow's Description.

The descent that the enemy again made on Newfoundland was more terrible and surprising than the former; for on January 21st, at break of day, M. Supercase fell on St John's, where in the space of two hours all were become prisoners of war except those in the castle and fort. The night before the enterprise, they were obliged to lie on a bed of snow, six feet deep, for fear of being discovered, which caused such numbness in the joints of several, that the General vowed revenge, and accordingly executed his resentment, for that he destroyed all before him, and gave no quarter for some time, till M. Boocore, who was a gentleman of more humanity, did interpose and abate his fury. The number that they took alive was one hundred and forty, whom they sent into the garrison, not out of pity to the prisoners but with a design to starve the whole [confirmed by Lieut. Moody]. After that they laid siege to the garrison and fort, which continued thirty days without relief; (excepting three who made their escape to the former and seventeen to the latter). In the fort were only forty men under the command of Captain Moody and twelve in the castle under Captain Latham, who behaved themselves with such bravery that they slighted all manner of tenders that were made them of surrender, with the highest contempt imaginable. Upon this, the enemy committed many barbarities and sent several threatenings; but they had no influence on either officers or soldiers, for they plied their bombs and mortar pieces to so good effect, that they killed several, and lost but three in the whole engagement.

After this the French steered to Consumption Bay, having first demolished all the English settlements in Trinity and Bonavista, where they burnt their stages and boats and laid a contribution besides upon the inhabitants. From thence they went to Carboneer, where they met with some repulse, and finding their provisions fell short, they sent a further number [of the inhabitants] into the fort [William], reserving the most skilful and able fishermen for themselves until the succeeding spring. [The latter part of the account is slightly confused.] [S. PENHALLOW, *Indian Wars*, 1723.]

(c.) CAMPBELL'S ACCOUNT.

Account on June 15th 1705 of Colin Campbell merchant of the attack on St. John's written from memory—the despatches from Lt. Moody &c. having been thrown overboard to prevent their falling into the hands of a French privateer:—

That on the 21st Jany 1705 the French forces under M. Subercass to the number of 600 men (Indians and Canadians about 150 included) marched from Placentia to Bay Bulls and Petty Harbour, reaching St. John's at 3 o'clock in the morning, took it by surprise and after having barbarously murdered many of the inhabitants and made the best prisoners, they laid siege to the fort and castle commanded in chief by Lt. John Moody and Mr. Robert Latham with seventy men, whereof about twenty inhabitants; they continued in the harbour till the 23 February in which time the French had many men killed and wounded amongst whom were severall officers of note particularly the Governour's own nephew; the fort and castle were bravely defended without the loss of any more than one serjeant and two or three private men; during the time the French burnt and distroyed all the houses storehouses goods &c. whatsoever in St. John's and marched South as far as Fair Ellen's [Ferryland] carrying away as prisoners all the inhabitants and myself (a few sick men excepted) and left behind the Canadians and Indians to make good their retreat, who joined them soon after committing the like barbarity as they had done at St. John's all along as they went as Kitty Vitty, Petty Harbour, Bay of Bulls, and Fair Ellen &c., where I obtained my liberty by humble sollicitations. At Fair Ellen M. Subercass ordered the Canadians and Indians [about one hundred and fifty men] under M. Montigny to march Northward which next day they did by Holyrood burning and destroying in like manner the harbours of Harbourmaine, Breckhouse [Brigus] Portegrave, Island Cove, Harbour Grace, Carbineer, Bay of Vardes &c. and when I came away on the 4th May they were not gone away from Trinity Bay; M. Subercass with the rest of the forces returned to Placentia by Trepasse and St. Mary's with 200 English prisoners and is there safely arrived.

He says further: The packet also contained depositions from Lt. Moody against one Mr. John Roop of St. John's importing that the said Roop had indeavoured to persuade the inhabitants during the winter from contributing any assistance by watching at the forts and harbour and while the French were there discovered to them whatever he knew of the weakness of the Fort and Castle and that the enemy acknowledged to have received considerable services from him and after three or four days he was at perfect liberty during all the time the French continued at St. John's. I believe the fortifications require to be repaired especially Fort William and the outworks.

(*Records.*)

(d.) CAMPBELL'S FURTHER ACCOUNT.

Collen Campbell maketh oath that M Supercass' men during the time they were at St John's, they in a most barbarous manner did murder in and about St John's to the number of thirty and failing to reduce the forts burnt all the houses, 2 or 3 excepted, and when they departed the Governor said in his bearing: That at another time they would destroy what they now left, and carried away as prisoners the greater part of the harbour; as far as he can remember the losses sustained by them from the French on this occasion did amount according to the oaths of the principal inhabitants taken by Lt Moody to between one hundred and forty and one hundred and fifty thousand pounds stg.

COLN CAMPBELL.

(*Records.*)

(e.) RICHARD SAMPSON'S ACCOUNT.

He says two companies of French soldiers each between 40 and 50 commanded by M Supercass, 90 Indians and between two and three hundred inhabitants of Placentia arrived at St John's on the 21st January half an hour before day and surprised the harbour (they not having kept this winter any guards and killed nine of ye inhabitants viz.: [names given] and some of the soldiers who were permitted to lie in the harbour.

There being no guard kept in ye North Battery they took ye Cannon there being 13 with which they annoyed ye South Battery having found two barrells of powder which belonged to ye fort or ye *Queens storehouse by the water side*. The first day they attacked the South Battery which was commanded by Lt. Robert Latham who had 12 soldiers and 15 inhabitants; ye French fired on them out of ye woods very much with two great guns which they found on ye South point.

In ye main garrison we had two men killed J. Bargery a serjt. and John Tieldad inhabitant. The French sent very often small parties between 10 and 20 to amuse the garrison which were generally commanded by a Serjt but to the south side they always sent a commissioned officer. They allowed the people at Kitty Vitty having a hundred men fit to bear arms to live in their own houses but they never offered to go to the help of the garrison and told the enemy of one Richard King proposing going to ye fort and they had him presently killed. Several inhabitants were suspected of being in correspondence with the French.

They destroyed all the town except four houses and took all the inhabitants with them to Petty Harbour four men being killed on the road from whence the inhabitants were at liberty except 60 or 70 whom they carried to Placentia several of which have since escaped.

The said Campbell and one Pemberton was sent from ye French several times with a flag of truce and of that the French having found some papers with John Roope have taken him to Placentia and intend to send him to France and the sd Roope is afraid they will never release him.

RICHARD SAMPSON.

18 June 1705.

(*Records.*)

(*f.*) ROOPE'S ACCOUNT.

M. Supercass surprized the town all but ye garrison and neare ye fort for some little time gave no quarter but soone contradicted that order; all ye men which were about 222 were put in ye Church for a prison which is an open place and itt being bitter sharp frost and much snow often falling severall died of ye cold and several had their feet frozen. Some days after he sent some Indians to Torbay who killed two men several hours after they had given them quarter; and after those in ye Church had been there a month he sent 80 of them under guard of a French party without Indians (each prisoner having a burden of 80 lbs. on his back) to carry to Petit harbour their plunder but five being faint and not able to carry their burdens and for no other reason were barbarously murdered.

The Indians for some months after went in parties and everywhere disturbed ye fishery and in Trinity Bay and Bonavista committed several barbarous murders as 'tis said 10 men and 2 little children after quarter.

M. Supercass when departed burned and destroyed all ye boates, houses &c. and carried with him 150 of the ablest men and forced them by ill usage to work on their fishery; some officers did pay them others did not and ye inhabitants gave them nothing, and att ye end of the season he sent severall to Canada, some to France and some still at Placentia who are said to have entered the French service all ye Irish are certainly entred.

(*Records.*)

(*g.*) ROOPE'S FURTHER ACCOUNT.

About daybreak M. Subercass came and in two bodies fell in uppon ye harbour viz one of them by ye fort who killed and tooke all ye people yt were in ye houses under ye glacis neare an hour before it was known in ye fort and it was known by means of one Archebald Taylour a soldier about suns ryseing lowered ye little drawbridge and went out with a bottle of rum to drink with some of his consorts but when he came to ye uttmost part of ye glacis he saw ye enemy who fyered on him which made him turne and runn to ye bridge and pull it up and allarmed ye garrisons who came some cloathed and some not and then about five or six of the enemy crep up to the top of the glacis and fired and killed one of our people, one of them was killed, ye rest retireed to their body which was under shelter of some houses about 80 paces from there and then our people went to clear away ye snow from ye gunns which there was all ye times ye enemy was neare ye forts. And immediately after they sate fire to one of ye houses and retired in ye smoake thereof; about 14 days after M. Subercass sent a truce with a letter, a copy of which I herewith offer [see p. 243] ye purport whereof was to have a parlee, which was held for four days and then broke off; on ye 2d day M. Subercass forced me to write the letter to Mr. Latham then commanded ye Southside Castle and that is the letter yr Lordships were informed was treasonable which letter I herewith present [see p. 244]. M. Subercass not giuning his point, having found two barrels of powder gott two facre guns on a hill about 300 yards from ye Southside Castle began to cannonade ye woodwork thereof and fired on ye first day about 50 shot but seeing he did little or no damage, he fired but now and then and seeing ye sloope he had ordered to come with 200 shells and an 11 inch mortar did not appear nor their fire-arrows that they threw into ye Southside Castle did not take (for they were not well made) he prepared to go off.

I have before described how they burnt ye houses and treated ye prisoners, I only forgot that one Gouling a missionary Jesuit allways kept close to ye Indians until they came to Ferriland. In eight days he arrived at Ferriland where they destroyed all, for on going forth they had burned none and whilst in St. John's they declared that if they could take the fort they would destroy nothing, that M. Costabelle ye Leut du Roy was to be Governour and a Capucian Friar come to be chaplain, that which friar came from Quebec and is still at Placentia and tis said there that there was an order from ye Court of France for ye expedition; 'tis agreed by all there that as soon as ye *Charente* which is a Kings ship arrived att Placentia, *La Vespe* was with all speed fitted out for Quebec and brought back about 100 Indians and Canad'ans of ye race of ye French.

Three days after they came to Ferriland they departed and then sent away M Montigny and most of the Canadians who went first to Conception Bay and plundered and destroyed all there (Carbonear Island excepted), from thence to Trinity Bay; from thence to Buena Vista where Lt Moody (as 'tis said) had constituted one George Sciffinton Chiefe who is a Quaker and ye spirit not moving him, he capitulated as soon as summoned and agreed to pay a certain sum, 250 li of wch was to be paid by bill of exchange in Boston to M Montigny but when he capitulated he was on an Island and had 120 men with 8 guns and severall stores and arms of ye Queens which he had had from Lt Moody; had notice of ye enemy and well on ye watch as 'tis said.

They carried all ye plunder of Conception and Trinity Bay over ye ishmus of Bay Bulls in Trinity Bay where ye land carriage is butt 2 little miles on plaine ground and where they launch over boats of three or four tun and it is that way they infest our northern parts.

About ye beginning of July there came to Placentia about 150 Indians of another nation and brought their wives and children and went immediately to disturb our fishery and ye Governor did declare that our fishery should always be disturbed and that he expected a greater force and then would again attempt St Johns.

JOHN ROOPE.

(*Records.*)

(*h.*) ANOTHER FRENCH ACCOUNT.

[Bishop Howley, who translated this MS. and published it in the *Evening Telegram* of December 13, 1893, says:— "This account is taken from the *Collection de Documents Relatifs à l'Histoire de la Nouvelle France*, published under the auspices of the Legislature of Quebec in 1883. The original of the present MS. is in French. The name of the author is unknown, but it is supposed to be either *Chaussegros de Lery* or *Gedeon de Catalogne*."]

Monsieur de Subercasse was named Governor of Placentia in 1702. In 1704, M. Subercasse sent to Quebec to M. the Marquess of Vaudreuil, Governor-General and Commander-in-Chief of Canada, the King's ship *Le Vespe*, commanded by Monsieur Delepiney, to demand a detachment of troops to go and destroy the colonies (or settlements) of the English on the coasts of Newfoundland. * * * We left Quebec on the 2nd of November (*le lendemain de la Toussaint*) to the number of 40 French, and 40 Abenaquis (Indians), and arrived at Placentia the 15th. Preparations were at once made; rackets and slides got ready to go direct to St. John's. But as the winter was very mild, and it did not freeze up to the 13th of January, we began to despair of carrying out the project, although everything was ready.

On the 14th it froze hard, and on the 15th we began the march. Each one carried his outfit and grub (*vivres*) on his back, as there was no snow down to enable us to use the slides, which were left behind, and the greater part also threw away their rackets; but when we were at a short distance from Beboulle, an English settlement, snow fell to a depth of two feet. So we were delayed for two days. Among 400 men we had only 60 pairs of rackets. It was pitiable to see those who had none sinking to the thighs in the snow.

At length we arrived at Beboulle, where we surprised the inhabitants, and we refreshed ourselves for two days and left a garrison there. We then scaled the mountain, which is very steep, high, and wooded; then follow a sort of marshes or barrens (*plaines*) for four leagues, with little drokes of woods here and there. The snow was very deep, and the men without rackets were very much fatigued. M. de Costabelle was of this number, and, not being able to reach the camp, he remained in a small wood, where he had spread a sail to serve as a tent, and, being seated beneath it, one of his men, in cutting a tree to make a fire, let it fall upon the tent, so that M. de Costabelle was caught like a marten-cat in a trap! It was necessary to cut the tree in order to get him out, during which time he was very much inconvenienced. We did not know anything of this accident until the following day. M. Subercasse sent me with four strong Canadians to his assistance. I found him lying down, and unable to walk. I made a litter and had him carried by two men, and in many places we had to cut a road through the bushes to get him along. That evening we made a tilt for him (*cabane*); the troops took Petty Harbour without any resistance. The following day we left him in charge of 8 Abenaquis, to whom we promised eight dollars (*huict escus*). So we left him there with a good escort.

The following day, 31st March, we gained the depth of the wood to round the bottom of the bay of the harbour of St. John's, where we arrived before sunset. Altho' it was intensely cold we were not allowed to make a fire. Each one sought a bed beneath the firs, which are very thick, and we placed our moccasins under us, to thaw them, so that we would be able to put them on next day. Before nightfall we ascended with M. Subercasse a height from which one could see all the harbour without being able to distinguish the fort. Having returned, M. de Subercasse told me that M. De Costabelle and the other Messieurs (*qu. officers*) were not for attacking the fort until after all the merchants and inhabitants should have been taken. I said that that was a sure way not to succeed. They relied upon the fact that they had despatched, from Placentia, a brigantine, with orders to join us at St. John's. She was armed with a mortar and a number of bombs. However, he gave orders to M. De Beaucourt to go straight to the fort, to surprise and enter it, saying to him that appetite comes with eating. M. de Montigny commanded another detachment of Canadians and Indians, and M. L'Hermitte marched at the head of the Placentia men, who, for want of rackets, could not follow the racketers, who waited for them till broad daylight.

He (L'Hermitte) had taken the beaten path by which the English bring their wood, so that it was necessary to run at full speed to invest all the houses, and the inhabitants were taken in their night shirts (*tous nuds en chemise*, the MS. is not very clear here.—M. F. H.)

At the fort :—M. de Beaucourt contented himself with walking along the glacis of the fort, without a soul stirring; and the Indians took three or four families outside, or beyond the fort. For all that the garrison did not wake up, and it was about 8 o'clock when I arrived at the foot of the glacis, where I found M. L'Hermitte, who was awaiting orders. I proposed to him to go direct to the fort. The ditches were filled with snow; he said he had not orders to do that. At last an Englishman appeared on the parapet, who admired us running on rackets upon the snow, and when we aimed at him he ran to give word to the guard, who, with shovels, cleared the cannons of snow and commenced to cannonade us, and forced us to retire, and killed two of our men.

All the inhabitants and merchants, to the number of 317, were placed in the *temple* (sic), and four merchants who were left on parole among our people. As there were about 60 women, who would have caused disorder, I advised M. Subercasse to send them to the fort, which was done. The fort was enclosed with stakes to a certain height in form of a terrace, which gave it the depth of a ditch, which palissade was also terraced behind, and almost bristling with cannon. Over the fosse (or ditch) there is a drawbridge, and the glacis on the water side and towards the houses is sloping at a moderate incline (*en pente entre la douce et la rapid*). *Vis-à-vis* on the other side of the harbour was the castle, enclosed by good and strong walls, partly wet at high tide, to attack vessels either entering or going out (*qu.* Chain Rock Battery— M. F. H.) There were two other batteries, one above the other, the first well vaulted and ranging at water level (*battant a fleur de l'eau*), with cannon of 36 (*qu.* lbs.). The one above of 12; the batteries made in form of horse-shoe (*qu.* Waldegrave and Queen's batteries).

As the stores and houses of the inhabitants were situated all along the harbour for about half a league, the French troops took up their lodgings as they chose, but out of range of the cannon, and they established a service of guards at the foot of the glacis.

Some days passed without any action being taken, although the garrison made several discharges of cannon every morning upon the houses from which they saw smoke issuing. One ball carried away the pillow from under the heads of MM. Monsengs and Davigrand, who were sleeping together, without wounding them.

At about a league from the fort there is a small harbour, called Quidimity, where there were 72 English fishing. M. De Montigny, with some Canadians and Indians, went to take them, and there was there a Reformer of the Tremblers, a Quaker (*un Religionnaire de la Tremblade un Quakre*), who was their commander. They asked to be allowed their parole. It was granted on condition that if anyone deserted to go to the fort, all the rest would be put to the sword, to which they consented. Some of our Indians went there occasionally to count them. As soon as the Indian came they all put themselves in a row. It happened that one day one of them wished to desert; the others followed and arrested him, and gave notice of it to the French, and without further trial or procedure he had his head broken on the spot where he was taken.

After three or four days of refreshment M. Subercasse sent M. de Beaucourt and an interpreter to summon the governor, whose name was John Maudy, to surrender the fort. He replied that first he would like to consult with Mr. Cambell, the Commissary, and two of the principal merchants, who were prisoners. He asked M. Subercasse to send them to him under parole; an irreparable mistake, for, instead of intimidating him they only reassured him, and in reply he requested M. Subercasse to send and find out the sentiments of the commander of the castle, which he did; but at the approach of the flag, the commander fired upon them and would not enter into any discussion.

As this castle is at the foot of the mountain which commands it, almost perpendicularly (*meme en plongeant*), we hoisted up with capstans four pieces of cannon, of those which we had taken from the detached platforms. We fired a few shots with but little effect. However, we formed a guard to harass them night and day. They kept themselves always on guard for the 33 days that we besieged them. The steep brow of the hill prevented the cannon from the fort from doing much harm, as they could not reach the houses. So they erected a scaffolding in the fort and placed cannon on it, by which means they could command the houses. One shot struck a chimney, and some of the bricks or stones flying from it broke the leg of a Spaniard whom they (the French) had as a prisoner; also of M. Delean, nephew of M. de Subercasse. The former died the next day, the latter the third day after.

Seeing that the brigantine did not come, and as the season was advancing, they determined to decamp. They took three loads (*charrors*) of goods from the stores and houses, estimated at the value of about 40,000 pounds (*livres, qu. francs*). M. de Montiguy escorted them by night-time past the castle.

The night before the departure it froze hard, and the whole harbour was caught strong enough to bear a horse, which forced them to burn the boats and almost all the merchandise, not being able to bring them by land. In the meantime the inhabitants of Quimidity, who had twelve shaloupes ready, offered to carry our loads to Beboulle. Their offer was accepted; but we only gave them provisions to carry. And we left on the 5th of March, after having set fire to all the vessels, and broken up a ship, and a great number of boats.

Note that M. Montigny had been to Conception Bay, where he found all the inhabitants retired to the Isle of Carbonniere, which is inaccessible. When we got to Petit Harbour, where we had left M. de Costabelle, as we had made almost all our prisoners follow, we resolved to send on some of them; so we fitted out three shaloupes. M. de Costabelle embarked on one of them; M. Durant, commissary, on another, and we coasted along, destroying all the English settlements.

When we arrived at Forillon the enemy were entrenched with cannon. M. Subercasse sent to summon them to surrender, which they refused to do; so he determined to give battle. As soon as the enemy saw this movement, they abandoned their posts, opened the door to us, and surrendered at discretion.

As we had no further enemies to fear, M. de Montigny demanded a detachment of Canadians and Indians to go and try to take the island of Carbonniere. They made some prisoners there, and some plunder, and returned to Placentia, where we had arrived about a month previously. M. de Montigny was scarcely arrived, when he asked for a party to go along the English coasts, which was granted. He left, and took the route of the Bay of Carmel, made the portage of Trinity Bay, where he captured the inhabitants, and took their effects in his little boat, which he sent back to Placentia, and he himself continued his course to *Bonneviste*, where he found the inhabitants entrenched on the island. He attacked them and, without much resistance, they surrendered to about 50 men. The commander of the English, who was a merchant, asked to ransom himself for 4,000 pounds sterling, which he paid by a draught on Mr. Nelson, of Boston. De Montigny, on receipt of the money, retired to Placentia, promising the people that they should not be further molested by the French, and that they might pursue their fishery in peace.

After that another Canadian went to Bonavista and seized more prisoners, who also had to offer round sums to secure their ransom.

In the month of June, M. Levire, commander of a vessel, captured a prize which was going from Boston to St. John's, and brought her to Placentia. The two citizens in charge of her, Geffry and Quion, asked to be allowed free on parole, which was granted; but a few days afterwards Quinn managed to get a shaloupe and escape to St. John's. Geffry was afterwards exchanged for a Basque named Melle Roup, whom the St. John's people had taken.

(i.) GENERAL NOTE.

These narratives do not by any means exhaust the matter preserved about this troubled year, but have been chosen as illustrating the period best. Lieut. Moody kept a diary recording the events of each day; it is very interesting but too long to print, and not easy to condense. The evidence of Campbell and Sampson must be received with discrimination. Sampson, who was Campbell's servant, made a further affidavit that he had been made drunk by Major Lloyd and compelled to sign his first and afterwards signed a third, reciting that the second had been obtained by Campbell placing a pistol at his head.

II. Lord Dartmouth's Report, 1706.
(Abstract.)
[Written by MATTHEW PRIOR, January 16, 1706.]

The English have at all times used this Fishery on the Eastern coast and in Harbours and Fishing places on that side, wherein they are protected against the French in the Summer Season by yearly convoys and men of war sent thither. A Fort was erected some years past in Bay St. John's for the defence of the inhabitants and retreat of others that may come for protection from other harbours during the winter.

The French who usually fish from Placentia on the south to westward, and Northward of the Island; have their fortifications in Placentia Bay for defence of their Trade and Protection of their fishery

Since the beginning of the last war, the Convoys and men of war sent to Newfoundland have at times very much molested the French in their trade and fishery, taken considerable number of ships and destroyed their fishing Materials on the South Coast, so the French have taken all advantage to annoy her Majesty's subjects by their shipping; but chiefly by land, with assistance of Canadians as well French as Indians.

Mons. Subercase, Governor of Placentia. came in January last with about 430 men, surprised the fishing places to the Southward of St. John's and possessed himself of that Harbour, Forts excepted, where garrisons maintained themselves against the enemy abt. thirty days when they retired.

They marched from St. John's to Ferryland and then Northward to Bonavista and committed barbarities and destroyed boats and flakes in the harbours.

Mons. de Subercasse took away with him a hundred and fifty of our ablest men, forcing them to work in the French Fishery; at the end of the season sent several of the young men to Canada and to France, the rest are still at Placentia, they are said to have entered French service particularly the Irish.

Placentia is the only place fortified by the French in Newfoundland, Two Forts there. In lower Fort thirty-six Guns and in the Castle on the Hill eleven Guns and two Mortars. Three company's of soldiers, in whole one hundred and twenty men. Inhabitants—two hundred fighting men and can draw further supply's from Settlements in Canada, besides Indians.

Our chief Fishery is on the East of Newfoundland from Cape Race to Cape Bonavista and French employ craft around rest of Island. Fish coming from the Southward reach the French in the beginning of April, whereas they do not come to our most southern Harbours before the end of the month and not to St. John's till the middle of May; the French having beach on the coast side, to dry and cure fish can be ready to Fish in four or five days after their arrival and on the E. and N. side of the Island, having not met with molestation from us in these desolate harbours, find their stages and flakes in condition they left them, whereas we have suffered much in destruction of houses flakes and stages by incursions of French of Placentia assisted by their neighbours of Canada.

We have upon the petition of Merchants reported our opinion that two or more men of war might be appointed early in the year to convoy the Fishing Ships and two others to convoy sack ships, which have been accordingly ordered.

Salt for fishery chiefly supplied from Portugal; ordered convoy's for salt ships from Lisbon to Newfoundland.

Has been our care, to prevent Irregularities committed by inhabitants and Fishermen, to give Instruction to Commodore, with regard to the late Act of Parliament.

We further offer; That the English that continue yearly in Newfoundland are dispersed into about thirty greater harbours besides coves and other Fishing places above Eighty leagues distant from N. to S. according to following scheme :—[Omitted.]

That the English live there the whole year without civill or Military Government except St. John's where are fortifications with a Captain who commands only his own officers and soldiers; By reason of the distances of the habitations from each other and the inhabitants being under no discipline they will be exposed to incursions of the enemy, who are under strict rules of Government.

For better security of the harbours of St. John's a boom and chain has been placed at the entrance of the harbour on representation to Her Majesty. And for benefit of Merchants and Planters, we represented to Her Majesty that the officers of the Garrison of St. John's be strictly prohibited from trading for thereby they have opportunity of engrossing trade and forestalling the Market.

And that the Prize officer settled there be for the same reasons forbidden to trade except for disposal of ships and goods brought as prizes into Newfoundland. Orders in this behalf have in like manner been given.

Our Fishery has not of late years been so considerable as formerly, imputed chiefly to the interruptions occasioned by war as well in winter as Fishing Seasons and in the passage of our ships to and from Europe as also by want of a vent for our Fish in the dominions of Spain and other parts of the Mediterranean.

This trade was first supported by an Act of Parliament in the second year of King Edward the Sixth; a commission was sent in 1615 for enquiring into abuses; several regulations having been thereupon agreed in the Star Chamber the same were framed into a charter in 1633 known as the western charter—this continued in force till 1699 when an Act of Parliament was past to Encourage Trade to Newfoundland by which the same is at present regulated—and we, having carefully observed the management of the Fishery in pursuance of the said Act, do find by Information, of divers matters prejudicial to this Trade.

That in general the inhabitants have not due regard to the Regulations of the Act of Parliament it being found that N. of St John's as far as Carbonier and S. as far as Ferryland, the trees have been rinded and woods destroyed as much as before the Act.

Fishing Admirals and masters of ships do not exactly observe the Rules of the Act. There are few Admirals capable of keeping Journals and Accounts as the Act directs. Fishing Admirals before the 20th of August will hear complaints, but none received after; they being generally the greatest offenders themselves.

Vessels from New England supply Newfoundland with provisions viz Bread, Beef, Pork, Flour, Pease, Butter, Boards, and great Quantitys of Tobacco. European commodities carried to Newfoundland by masters of ships as follows ; from France in time of peace, Brandy, Wine, Salt linnen canvas, paper, Hats and Silks; from Spain, Wine, Brandy, Iron; from Portugal Wine, Brandy, Salt, Oyle and Linnen; all which goods sold or truckt with traders from New England for Tobacco Sugar &c. which they carry to Foreign Parts so at the end of the year masters are wholy taken up in Management of that illegal trade.

New England Traders seldom depart till men of war are sailed and then carry away handy-crafts-Men, Seamen and fishermen whom they entice in expectation of great wages.

Masters of ships negligent in bringing their men home, whereby they save the charge of their passage, men so left are inticed and carried away to New England.

The Reason why the New England men fish upon the coast of Newfoundland besides carrying on illegal trade is that they may get those men; they having otherwise a most advantageous fishery on their own coast.

The preventing of which Irregularities we humbly offer to this Honble. House our opinion, that a power be given by a clause in an Act that shall be passed to commanders of Her Majesty's Ships of war, and to admirals of each Harbour in Newfoundland, to lay fines and penalties upon offenders against the said Act, such fine not exceeding the sum of £5. stg and power likewise given them of confining such offenders in case of non-payment, such confinement not exceeding the space of ten days.

That the commanders of Her Majestys Ships may have the power of a custom house officer to search New England Ships upon their coming, and to take account of the number of their crew and Passengers and to take bond from each of the masters that they shall not carry away a greater number of men than they brought, which we hope would in a great measure prevent irregularities committed by New England Traders.

As early as the year 1615 the fish killed by English amounted to 300,000 Quintals, and we have been well informed, that in several years after ye year 1650, we have taken (season favourable) above 400,000 Quintals, but that about ye year 1651, (until which year and some time afterwards, we furnished France itself with fish) the French entered upon that Trade, and have possession of a large part of the Island, and have by degrees advanced their Fishing so as to be superior to ours, by which means our trade has decreased, they having since furnished the Dominion of France and even other nations before solely supplied by us.

Upon all which foregoing considerations, we cannot but conclude that whilst Placentia does remain in the hands of the French, our Fishery will be under continual discouragement all which is most humbly submitted.

III. Capture of St. John's in 1708.

(a.) CHARLEVOIX'S ACCOUNT.

I have already observed that the centre and stores of all the English settlements on that island were on St. John's Bay. De St. Ovide proposed to M. de Costebelle to reduce St. John's at his own expense. . . . . He arrived on the last day of the year [with one hundred and sixty-four men including Indians] about five leagues from St. John's without being observed. Two hours before day, they pushed on in a clear moonlight to the head of St John's harbour, whence he reconnoitred the whole place leisurely. He then marched on, led by bad guides, whom he should have distrusted.

As soon as he detected their treachery, he moved from the centre where he was, to the van, where the volunteers were and put himself at their head. He was discovered three hundred paces from the fort he designed attacking, so that some musketry fire opened on him as he approached the first pallisade. Some of his volunteers abandoned him, but this did not prevent his pushing on to the covered way, the entrance to which they had fortunately neglected to close. He entered shouting *Vive le Roy*, a cry that raised the courage of his men and made the English lose all heart. Leaving fifteen or sixteen men to guard the covered way, he crossed the ditch under the fire of two other forts, which wounded ten of his men, planted two ladders against the rampart, which was twenty foot high, and scaled in with six men, three of whom were dangerously wounded.

At that moment Despenseus arrived with his detachment and planted his ladders. He was the first to ascend, entering the fort with two or three others. Renou, Johannis, du Plessis, la Chesnaye, d'Argenteuil and d'Aillebout his brother followed close on this brave man; some seized the barracks, others the Governor's quarters, some others ran to the drawbridge connecting this fort called Fort William with that of the colonists and the Governor, who was hastening to throw in three hundred settlers, was struck down with three wounds. Despenseus immediately lowered the drawbridge and opened the gate. Then all the rest of the army entered and the English cried quarter.

Thus in less than half an hour the French took two forts, either of which might have resisted a whole army; one had eighteen guns mounted, four mortars for bombshells, twenty for grenades and a garrison of over a hundred men, commanded by a very brave officer. The other had six hundred colonists well entrenched, ready to come to the succour of the first fort, but a subterranean door by which they expected to pass when occasion required, was found so well closed that it could not be forced open in time. A small fort still remained at the entrance of the port. De St. Ovide sent to summon it, and the commander asked twenty-four hours to reply, and although he had eighty men in a strong work, provisions for several months, quite a good supply of artillery, large cannon and a bomb mortar, as well as a bomb-proof vault, he surrendered.

Ovide dispatched a messenger to inform Costabelle of his success. Learning that some English had escaped to Belle Isle and had embarked from there to England, he sent word at once by a small ship to France, that the Court there might learn what had been achieved as early as that of London. This step offended M. de Costabelle, who considering it useless to expect troops from

THE CAPTURE OF ST. JOHN'S IN 1708.

France and not having men enough to defend both places, ordered De St. Ovide to demolish the forts and return to Placentia by the end of March at least. They brought away large stores, as three hundred English were on the point of marching to surprise Placentia.

(b.) First English Account.

Letter from H. E. Harbargrace Island 4 Jany 1709. On the 21st December, the French from Placentia to the number of one hundred and sixty came to the fort of St. John's and there with scaling ladders got over the work without any assistance, only two small guns the sentry fired; Major Lloyd then asleep in his bed and after the French got into the fort, the inhabitants in the New Fort rose in arms and would have taken the fort again from the French but the soldiers could not get the keys out of the Major's house; but when the French came he could find them; so from some of those men that made their escape to those respective islands Harbargrace and Carboniere Islands; the fort was actually sold to the French or else that number could never have taken it. They surrendered the Castle next day being never an officer in it to command it.

(c.) The Post Boy, Feby. 8.

On Tuesday last an express arrived from Lisbon that the French have made themselves masters of Fort St. Johns by treachery; the wooden palisadoes that defended the same having been cut down upon notice of the enemy's advancing that way under pretence of putting iron spikes in their stead.

(d.) John Collins' Account.

About four in the morning the sentinel of the S.W. corner of the New Fort discovered the enemy but his gun would not go off so he called to the sentinel of the N.W. corner who fired his piece which allarmed the place; this deponent being one of the Captains of Militia for the New Fort went to his appointed quarters which was the guard house of the fort where two other companies besides his were appointed their quarters. He then heard firing at the N.W. corner between the enemy and our men. The deponent saith to the best of his remembrance at the time of the firing he heard quarter called in the old fort and presently after the French there cried *Vive le Roy* three times upon which this deponent and others in the old fort gave three *Huzaas* and the enemy immediately fired at them and they at them and eight of our men were killed and seven wounded. They of the new fort called to those in the old fort to have the sally port opened and the bridge let down but could have no answer; some of the soldiers of the old fort got into the new fort and said there were five hundred French and that they gave no quarter (upon which we accepted the offer of quarter on the 26th [?]).

This deponent heard Sarjeant Steel say at Mr. Winchen's house, that when the French entered the old fort but one man was beside himself on the works and that Major Lloyd came as far as the ramparts and said "Fight boys," and went away and he never saw him afterwards, until the garrison was taken which was within half an hour of the alarm and that he believed it was lost by neglect [and not by treachery].

(e.) Mr. Wm. Keen's Journal.

Decr. 21 1708. About 4 this morning we were allarmed by the firing of small musketts and were within half an hour's time surprized to hear the fort was taken without meting resistance; some small time after the Fort surrendered, the Castle took the alarm and fired two guns, all the inhabitants of that side being about sixty men were retired into the Castle; about 7 this morning two French officers came to assure the inhabitants of good quarters and took with them the Most Master Inhabitants and Merchants into the Fort where I saw Major Lloyd very heavy eyd'd and little notice taken of him; in entering the fort the French lost three killed by the inhabitants; about five in the evening the inhabitants and servants were imprisoned in storehouses, excepting some few that were kept in their own houses.

A fire happened and burnt two streets of houses; Mr. Russell was committed to the guard house, Mr. Wm. Keen was confined in his own house; Captain Dennis was sent to have the castle surrender, which was at first refused but next day the 22nd the people gave it up; the French hoisted a white flag and fired three guns; the people were to have their clothes and provisions and be reinstated in their houses which was not complied with; on the 24 the Comiss'r St. Ovide de Brouillon sent four hundred and seventy-seven men prisoners to the church and the house of Mr. Collins allowing them one pound of bread four ozs. of pork and four ozs. of pease per diem—the prisoners were set in ranks and counted by the Indians who threatened if any escaped they would kill an equal number in their room; on the 25th an account was taken of the goods in the town; on the 26 an express was sent to Placentia which returned in nineteen days—the French did not resort with the English during this time. With the express arrived two hundred more soldiers from Placentia. The French sent Major Lloyd, Lieut. Philips, Engineer Vane and his wife by ship to Placentia on Jany. 8.

M. St. Ovide gave the inhabitants 24 hours to consider his proposals of ransom which if rejected he would send them all prisoners to Canada; he said it was His Master's intention to keep the country. The inhabitants under threat of burning the town were forced to agree to terms of ransom. A party of men were sent to Ferryland under M. Larond but failed to take it, the inhabitants refusing to admit a flag of truce. The French retreat was hindered for a month by ice. After the destruction of the fort M. St. Ovide retired to the castle where he was nearly blown up by powder, one officer was killed.

March 27 M. St. Ovide sailed for Placentia taking R. Cole, Allyn Southmayd, Wm. Keen, Thomas Russell, Wm. Nicholls, John Collins, and Squarry and arrived at Placentia the 5th of April.

On the 13th May Mr. Lloyd and Mr. Phillips sailed for Canada. On the 26th of May arrived the Fiddell man-of-war from France with two hundred soldiers for reinforcing St. John's and St. Ovide received news of his being created Knight of St. Lewis and Governor of St. John's. On the 26th of June, the principal merchants arrived back in St. John's having been kept several months longer than they had been told they would be upon St. Ovide's word of honour.

(f.) TERMS OF SURRENDER.

The inhabitants of St. John's, Petty Harbour, Bay Bulls, Quidi Vidi, Tar Bay, Portugal Cove and Parlican have this day (2nd Feby. 1709) desired M. St. Ovide to grant us liberty to ransom or buy our goods as specified in the 9 following articles:—

First. We promise to pay M. St. Ovide or his order, a hundred quintals for each shallop and fifty for each half-shallop sent fishing of the fish first cured or if the English take this port, to St. Ovide's order in London seventy and thirty-five pounds sterling respectively in August or October.

Second. That our houses and clothes be preserved.

Third. That no damage be done to our stages, boats, &c.

Fourth. That the said St. Ovide is to furnish us twenty hogsheads of salt per shallop ransomed.

Fifth. That the French do not waste our victuals.

Sixth. That our boats be allowed to go fishing.

Seventh. That any French plundering us shall make restitution and be punished by M. St. Ovide.

Eighth. We promise to be neuter until our ransom be paid.

Ninth. If the French retain Newfoundland, to have liberty to go to New or Old England or remain in the country and retain our houses.

	St. John's.	Petty Harbour.	Bay Bulls.	Quidi Vidi.	Tar Bay and Portugal Cove.
Signed	19	14	15	12	4

The whole ransom was computed at £7,280.

(g.) GOVERNOR COLLINS' PETITION.

By Captain JOSEPH TAYLOUR Commander of her Maj. ship Litchfield and Commander-in-chief of her Majesties forces in Newfoundland to JOHN COLLINS Esqre. hereby appointed Governour and Commander in Chief of the Fort and Harbour of St. John's and all the sea coasts between Ferryland and Carbonear Island.

By virtue of the power given me by Her Maj. I do hereby Constitute and appoint you, until further order Governour and Commander in chief of the Fort and Harbour of St. John's and all the sea coasts between Ferryland and Carbonear Island, Willing and requiring you forthwith to take upon you the said charge and command; Requiring all officers inhabitants and others to be obedient to you as their Governour: and you are to take care to secure and defend the said fort against the enemy and to keep good order and disciple amongst those under your command and to order all the inhabitants into the said fort and to compel them to bring their provision there and for your better security and guard of the said Fort and Harbour of St. John's, you are hereby empowrd to make as many Captains, Lieuts. Ensigns, and inferior officers as you find necessary and to do what is further for Her Majesties service.

Given under my hand and seal H.M.S. Litchfield in St. Johns Harbour 6 Oct. 1709.

JOSEPH TAYLOUR.

TO THE QUEEN'S MOST EXCELLENT
MAJESTY.

The humble pet[n]. of JOHN COLLINS Esq[r]. your Maj. present gov. of St. John's Fort.

Sheweth:

That about Decm. 1708 the said fort was surprized by the French and the then governour Capt. Loyd taken therein, at which time y[r] pet[r] being Commander of the Militia raised the best force he could and attempted the Relief of the said garrison with great hazard of his life, the two nearest persons to him being, the one killed and the other wounded: But the town being altogether defenceless and under the garrison, y[r] pet[r] was forced (after all possible resistance) to submit with the rest of the inhabitants and to pay a considerable ransom after which he was treacherously carry[d] away to Placentia and detained there to his great prejudice several months before he was permitted to return.

That in Oct. 1709 Capt. Taylour y[r] Maj. Commodore being there, and impowered and authorized to grant a commission to whomsoever he should find most deserving upon the place. (The former Governour Captain Loyd being carried into France and since killed there) your petioner was appointed gov[r]. and

Com^r in chief of the Fort of St. John's which he accepted at the request of the s^d Commodore the several Merchants and Traders and all other the inhabitants of the Place and y^r pet^r has ever since held the same at his own great charge and to the satisfaction of all concerned in the Trade there. Wherefore y^r pet^r having supplanted no other pretension (coming in upon an entire vacancy) pet^s for Governour's pay and continuance in Govt. and not to be removed without just Reason and your pet^r &c. &c.

TO THE QUEEN'S MOST EXCELLENT MAJESTY.

The humble address of the inhabitants in Newfoundland.

Dread Sovereign :

We your most dutiful subjects inhabiting yr province of Newfoundland do humbly beg leave to tender our unfeigned gratitude . . . . for favours . . . . which with God's assistance have in a great measure contributed to our being protected against the violent outrages of our barbarous neighbours the French, whose bold attempt upon our coast have rendered the adjacent unfortified harbours most dangerous as they would our residing at St John's had not yr Maj. Royal Wisdom thought proper to order our being regulated into a Militia and to be put under command of John Collins whose extraordinary vigilance and prudent conduct in guarding and repairing yr Maj. Fort in St. John's and regulating and ordering us for its defence have been manifested to our entire satisfaction.

We therefore beg leave to recommend him for the care he has taken and the great and necessary expence he has been at to the prejudice of his private affairs.

Subscribed by all the best inhabitants that are masters of families.

Concurring pet^n from a number of principal Merchants and Masters of ships in London (and more are ready to do it if needful).

IV. Captain Crowe's Laws.

By Captain Jos. CROWE, Commander-in-Chief of HM ships, forts, and garrison in Newfoundland.

A record of several laws and orders debated at several courts. Present, commanders of merchant ships, chief inhabitants; and witnesses being examined, it was brought to following conclusion, between 23rd August and 23rd October 1711 :—

1st. That a sum of money should be collected by voluntary gift from commanders of ships, merchants, masters of families, and others, for repairing church which was demolished, and subsistence of minister.

2nd. That orders be put up at publichouses and other places for suppressing drunkenness, cursing, and swearing. Fines and punishment according to annexed copy [omitted].

3rd. A body of seamen or others should keep guard in the night to prevent mischiefs by spyes of the enemy and others to be raised as follows, viz., from the complements of the ship in the harbour, one man for every fifteen, and one man for every three boats of inhabitants and by boat keepers ; a commander of a ship and a merchant to command them each night.

4th. The tenements, store-houses, and stages which are now in possession of persons under-mentioned (to wit). Richard Colesworthy, upper stage-house and room at ffort at Bursthart Hill; Captain Stafford, in behalf of Henry Perden, one store-house on vice-admiral's room ; Thomas and John Squary, one store-house on admiral's room ; Mrs. Turf's, in behalf of Mrs. Anne Earll, the upper stage adjoining to his own two boats room; Governor Collins, in behalf of Mrs. Holeman, one store-house on the vice-admiral's room ; Hugh Tucker, in behalf of John Harris, Esq., of Exon, one store house on the admiral's room ; Captain Holsworth in behalf of Michael Martin, one store house on the admiral's room. Being proved formerly belonging to ffishing ships and ingrossed since the year 1685 contrary to Act of Parliament to prejudice of said ships, &c. I do therefore hereby dispossess them of same in right of ffishing ships.

5th. Inhabitants, ffishermen, and servants to repair to winter quarters allotted them by 1st of October, and be under command of several governors for better security against the enemy in small bodies to particular places (to wit) :—

St. John's.
Quitty Vitty.   } Into Fort William, under
Torbay.   }   Governor Collins.
Petty Harbour.   }

Conception Bay upon { Carbinear Island, Little Bell Isle, and Harbergrass Island. } Under their respective governors

Trinity Bay, on Foxe's Island and Dildo Island.

Bay of Bull, Wittless Bay, and Toad's Cove. } On Gull Island, under Governor Colesworthy.

From Isle of Speer, Southerly, into fort at Ferryland.

6th. Houses in ffort William not to be sold or let, but in case the person who built it does not inhabit it themselves, said houses to be at the disposal of Governor Collins, to put in persons destitute of habitation in said fort.

7th. Owners of such houses not having proportion of people to said house, at discretion of Governor Collins to put in others.

8th. If not sufficient ground in fort to build habitations, Governor Collins to give leave for building proper habitations under the guns within outwork of fort.

9th. To prevent servants hiring themselves to one, two, or three masters at once, governor to oblige them to pay for such offence £2 10s., or otherwise cause them to be whipt three times forward and backward along some public place.

10th. Five men for each ship in harbour shall go into the woods and cut twenty stockades and pallasadoes to repair works of fort of St. John's, and boat keepers for every boat to fetch as many.

11th. Plantation of John Drue, of St. John's, proved to be ship's room, yet, in regard to his age, and thereby past labour, may enjoy same during life, but after his decease to return to right of ships.

12th. Mr. Turf's confirmed at second application to loose upper stage adjoining his own two boats room that he now holds in behalf of Mrs. Anne Earl, mentioned in 4th Article.

13th. Whosoever shall demolish, deface, or break down any stage, cooke room, house, or flakes by removing raffters, rinds, floorings, shoars, stakes, or layers, except to employ them on same room next year, shall forfeit £10 for repairing same to possessor of said stage and room.

14th. House in possession of Captain Arthur Holdsworth that formerly belonged to Mr. Lint, confirmed to said Captain Holdsworth, right being assigned to him by Mr. Richard Colesworthy.

15th. Minister to have subscription for ensuing year from shollups, three, the two men boats, two, and the ship one quintol of dry merchandable fish to be levied as followeth :—One from owner of stage, one from boat keeper, and one from servants.

16th. A plantation of three boats rooms in possession of Abraham Barrot and Richard Sutton in Torbay. Being ships rooms, they are dispossessed in right of ships that have occasion for them next year.

Jos. Crowe.

V. Sir N. Trevanion's Orders and Fishery Scheme.

(a.) By Sir Nicholas Trevanion, Knight, Commander of H.M. Ships and Garrisons, and Governor-in-Chief at Newfoundland.

(Decr. 10, 1712.)

A Record of several Courts held at St. John's for better discipline and good order of people, &c. Debated at Courts held. Present: Admiral and Vice-Admiral, Merchants, and Chief Inhabitants ; and witnesses being examined, it was brought to the following conclusions :—

1st. That orders be put up at public houses and other places for suppressing drunkenness, &c.

2nd. Confirmed last year by Captain J. Crow, that Mr. Jacob Rice, minister of St. John's, should have as follows :—

From shallops - three ⎫ quintals of dry
From two-men boat two ⎬ merchandable
From the skiffs - one ⎭ fish.

And planters very backward in paying, he got only one hundred quintals of fish this season.

Confirms what Commander Crow and Court agreed to for minister's subsistence, and to encourage him to remain.

3rd. Confirms John Collyns, Esq., Governor of Fort William, and it is appointed, during cessation, that twenty men lie in fort every night.

4th. Warrant granted to call Mr. Benger before him [the Governor] relating to Sir William Hopkins' place at Ferryland, now in possession of Widow Clapp, and tenement formerly in possession of Sir David Kirk; but Mr. Benger did not appear.

5th. Mrs. Benger, wife of James Benger, appeared relating to a tenement formerly in possession of William Bennet, deceased. Mrs. Benger willing to allow to heirs of William Bennet, deceased, to one Tomson Reeve £10 per annum till further decided.

6th. Other matters between masters of ships and planters and boat-keepers relate to debts not mentioned, parties being satisfied.

(b.) Fishery Scheme for 1712.

1st. Referred to annexed scheme for number of English planters [always given on a separate sheet].

2nd. Planters receive little sustenance from the countries, and kill few beavers and other wild beasts.

3rd. Inhabitants have most salt provisions from Ireland; fresh provisions, as bread, pease, &c., from New England and Pensilvania ; salt from Lisbon and Isle of May, and in war time from prizes brought in.

4th. Strict orders that no trees be cut down or rinded, nor woods set on fire, except for building, nor trees cut down on account of making oyle.

5th. Has taken all care to settle matters between fishing ships and planters, to give each their rights.

FISHERY SCHEME FOR 1712.

6th. No complaints of fishing ships.

7th. Care taken that bye boat keepers and fishing ships do carry such number of fresh men and green men as Act directs.

8th. No complaints of marks of any boats or train vats being altered.

9th. No complaints of any person leaving the country; do not destroy or injure stages, &c.

10th. No complaints that any admiral, vice-admiral, and rear-admiral do ingross more beach or flakes than they pitch upon at their arrival.

11th. Orders sent to admirals and chief planters of every little cove, to give account of boats and fish and of inhabitants, which is hereunto annexed.

12th. General court held twice a week with admiral and vice-admiral to assist, and endeavoured to settle differences relating to planters and boat keepers, servants, &c.

13th. Orders to captains of men-of-war and admirals of harbours, that no ballast be thrown out of ships in harbours.

14th. Care taken that offals have not been offensive, stages so near water, when thrown in it is washed away.

15th. Care that Lord's Day duly observed. Corrections to all so offending.

16th. None but Her Majesty's subjects fish or take bait in ports inhabited by English.

17th. Care taken that fish be preserved with good salt and sent to market in good condition.

18th. No wine nor brandy brought from New England, only rum and molasses, which is the liquor drunk by servants. Bad year of fishing. Planters in debt to masters of ships and merchants to pay ensuing year it able.

19th. 17th of September when governour arrived, so could not get master's names; most of them gone before his arrival, but by scheme it is found there were twenty sail belonging to America, brought bread, pease, rice, rum, tobacco, mollasses, and cattle, &c., &c.

20th. Provisions from England, Ireland, and New England. New England men return home in their ballast.

21st. Account in former article of provisions brought hither, there is sugar and tobacco, but cannot find any cotton wooll, indico, ginger, fustick, or any dying wood, nor any put on board ships to Spain, Portugal, or any foreign part.

22nd. Refers for information to scheme for number of boats and men employed by inhabitants.

23rd. As to 27th Article, refers to scheme for number of fishing ships and boats, with burthens, &c. Men's food is beef, fish, pease, &c. Beer brewed with molasses and spruce. Go out of harbours in shallops, seven men and five men in a boat; catch fish with hook and line, first part of year their bait is muscles and lances; about middle of June bait is capeling, squid, and fresh herring, and end of year they fish with herring only—nets purposely for taking the sort of bait.

24th. Price of fish this year from thirty to thirty-six ryalls per quintal good merchandable fish. Broken fish which they call refuse fish sold for twenty ryalls per quintal, and carried to Spain and Portugal and oyl made of livers carried to England; value of oyl 16*l.* per tun.

25th. Refers to scheme for number of sack ships. They load with dry fish bound to several ports as Spain and Portugal. But eight ships this year could not get loading and forced to go in ballast to Virginia to seek freight.

26th. Strict charge to carry back men brought from England.

27th. Best enquiries made to know what inhabitants at Placentia; five hundred men, two hundred women, and children. Great quantities of fish catched there this year and sold for twenty-two ryalls a quintal.

28th. Fort and platform of sixty guns, ammunition, and victoals from France and Canada. Quantities of ammunition not informed of and provisions no want of.

29th. Thirty sail from Placentia this year—most came to make fishing voyage, and some to buy fish to carry to market—ships that fish upon banks taking cod and salting and carrying them in bulk to France, and in bay they fish upon coast of Canada, and salt fish after same manner.

30th. No other nation besides England and France, except Spaniards, come by stealth into harbours where they are not discovered.

31st. Care taken to see all New England men out of port, so that they do not carry away any of Her Majesty's subjects.

CHAPTER XI.

REIGN OF GEORGE I.
1714-1727.

1714.—Difficulties about fishing rooms in Placentia sold by French to planters and officers.

1715.—Spaniards not allowed to fish, by order of Governor of Placentia.

1718.—Difficulties with the French about English settlers' fishing establishments near Cape Bonavista.

1719.—Claim again made by Biscayans to fish in Newfoundland disallowed.

1723.—Grant of salmon fishery to Skiffington between Cape Bonavista and Cape John.

Under the sovereignty of the first Hanoverian King there were few stirring events in the Colony; the history of our Island in this reign is a chronicle of the piping times of peace. English trade flourished, settlements increased, the poor Newfoundland planter no longer listened for the dreaded war-whoop of the Abenaquis, or the tramp of the invading French soldiers.[1]

The immediate result of the peace is best shown by the enormous increase of the English fishery. Whilst in 1713 there were only forty-six fishing ships, with one hundred and sixty two boats, one hundred and ninety-five bye-boats, and two hundred and eighty-eight inhabitants' boats, in the following years the figures were :—

	Fishing Ships.	Boats.	Bye-boats.	Inhabitants' Boats.	Fish caught by Ship Fishermen. Quintals.	Fish caught by Inhabitants and Bye-boats. Quintals.
1714	106	441	133	362	115,000	45,000
1715	108	376	197	468	89,622	35,531
1716	86	319	184	408	88,469	33,830

---

[1] In 1717 the "Second Somersetshire Regiment," now the First Battalion Prince of Wales' Volunteers, the "Fighting Fortieth"—a corps familiarly known by the sobriquet of "Excellers" (XL-ers)—was formed of eight independent companies raised in Nova Scotia and Newfoundland. The field officers carried half-pikes; the company-officers, spontoons; the serjeants, halberds, and the rank-and-file, flint-lock muskets and short swords. Having served in the Colonies for nearly fifty years, the regiment was transferred to Ireland in 1764, where it remained throughout a decade, having six years previously to its recall from Canada won the first "honour" inscribed on its colours at the memorable siege of Louisburg.

The Regimental Records have been edited by Captain Raymond Smythies.

In 1711 and 1712 the common danger had united the ship fishermen and the planters in arrangements for orderly government. Their town meetings lasted, however, only for the two years. When once the stern pressure of war was removed by the peace of 1713 all the old quarrels revived, the fishing admirals and the merchant adventurers returned to their normal habits of disorder tyranny, and persecution.

The Commodore and his officers were gradually curtailing the fishing admirals' powers. If we are to judge by Mr. Larkin's report, in some instances this was going from bad to worse. The lieutenants in Captain Poulton and Captain Fairbourne's time all took bribes of fish. "The present Commander, Captain Graydon," he says, "had taken much pains to do the country justice and to settle religion amongst them." Larkin gives a doleful picture of the disorders prevalent in the Colony.

GEORGE I.
From an engraving after Kneller.

This unfortunate condition of affairs was due to the extraordinary imbecility of the British Government. They endeavoured to rule the Colony without a Governor, to defend it from invasion without adequate military or naval force, to distribute justice without duly constituted courts or laws made by the authority of the Imperial Parliament; in fine, they went on administering the affairs of the Island in the most blundering manner, and then stupidly wondered because the inevitable result was chronic disorder and chaotic confusion.

After the Treaty of Utrecht, by a very singular and ill-conceived arrangement, Placentia was placed under the government of Nova Scotia, whilst the rest of the island was ruled by the admiral or commodore. A very troublesome question arose out of the Queen's sympathy with the sufferings of the French Protestants undergoing the hardships and cruelties of the galleys by order of Louis XIV. In order to get these poor slaves released, she made the following liberal arrangement.

The Treaty of Utrecht was signed on the 31st of March 1713; on the 23rd of June of the same year Queen Anne wrote to Nicholson, Governor of Nova Scotia:—

"Whereas our good brother the most Christian King hath at our desire released from imprisonment aboard his galleys such of his subjects as were detained there on account of their professing the Protestant religion, we being willing to shew by some mark of our favour towards his subjects how kind we take his compliance therein, have therefore thought fit hereby to signify our will and pleasure to you; that you permit such of them as have any lands or tenements in places under your Government in Acadia and Newfound Land, that have been, or are to be yielded to Us by virtue of the late Treaty of Peace, and are willing to continue our subjects, to retain and enjoy their said lands and tenements, without molestation, as fully and freely as others of our subjects do or may possess their lands or estates, or to sell the same, if they shall choose to remove elsewhere. And for so doing this shall be your warrant."

PLACENTIA.
B.M. MSS. 22,873.

Legal questions arose out of this transaction. Most of the Frenchmen, before leaving Placentia, sold their places; Governor Moody and the English officers bought several pieces of land; some of these at the gut were required for fortifications, and, after some delay, Moody was paid for his land by order of the Board of Trade. The ship fishermen complained bitterly of this transaction, which deprived them of free ships' rooms, and as Placentia was renowned for fishing, they could not benefit by the new acquisition without paying high rents to officers and the Governor.

It appears, notwithstanding Costabelle's urgent appeal, many French remained behind in Placentia, and secretly encouraged Biscayans and French Basques to fish there. The poor Biscayans were misled by the Spanish authorities; they believed that, under Article XV. of the Treaty of Utrecht, they had fishing rights in Newfoundland.

This Article declares:—

"And because it is contended on behalf of Spain, that the Biscayans and other subjects of His Catholic Majesty have a certain right of fishing in Newfoundland His Britannic Majesty agrees that to the Biscayans and other Inhabitants of Spain be reserved *all the privileges to which they can with right pretend.*"

The English declared the Biscayans had no fishery rights in Newfoundland, and under no circumstances would they tolerate the Spanish pretensions. In the year 1715, according to the Spanish records, some Biscayan vessels arrived at Placentia and, as they had expected, the English Governor of Placentia ordered them off. He said:—

"He had no orders from the king to consent that the Spaniards should enjoy any fishing privileges under the Treaty of Utrecht."

The unfortunate ship masters had to return empty to Spain, losing their voyage and the large expense of outfit; however, notwithstanding this order, many Biscayan ships fished out of Placentia, and when the English Government became very strict, they transferred their vessels nominally to English owners, and sailed under the English flag. A case is mentioned as late as 1765, in which two ships were found to be owned by Spaniards.

It has been contended by the French that the English never settled or fished north of Cape Bonavista prior to 1765. This statement is contradicted by many facts recorded in contemporary history. There can be no doubt that in the sixteenth and in the early part of the seventeenth century the French fished about Notre Dame Bay, and it was in this locality that they came in collision with the Red Indians, but afterwards we find all their fishing establishments were further north, only an occasional ship locating east of Fleur-de-Lys, in Notre Dame Bay.[1] In proof of this we have the expedition of Captains Underdown and Lloyd in 1706; all the French places mentioned are on the line of coast extending from White Bay to Quirpon, none were found elsewhere.

The reason why our opponents selected this portion of the coast is very obvious; it contained a number of excellent harbours, it was removed from their dreaded enemies the Red Indians and the English, and for fishing vessels it afforded the very best field for operations. We know from the records that the French moved about a good deal, shifting their quarters oftener than the English; here, at Petit Nord, they had the best part of the north-east coast and the Straits of Belle Isle, then, as now, the very best fishing ground in the Colony.

Subsequent to the French attack of 1696-7, from about 1700, the English settlements were gradually extended north from Bonavista;

---

[1] "Thomas Mitchell captured and taken to White Island 7th June 1697. This island lies half a mile from the shoare and is fourteen leagues N. of Cape Frills. No more ships there, *but there were thirty or forty further along the coast.*" (*B. of T., Nfld.*)

STARVE HARBOUR, ON THE OLD FRENCH SHORE.
From a drawing by the Hon. and Rev. W. Gray.

some of the first "liviers," in Old Newfoundland parlance, had by this time built their huts and fishing stages as far north as Twillingate, Exploits, and Fogo.

T. COUR LOTTER'S MAP OF 1720.
B.M., 70620 (5).

There can be no surer guide to the nationality of the occupiers of the Newfoundland coast than the names of the various harbours. Placentia Bay, St. Mary's Bay, Fortune Bay, and the western shore towards Cape Ray, all testify by their nomenclature to French occupation; similarly such vulgar English names as Bett's Cove, Tilt Cove, Seldom-Come-By, Nippers Harbour, Joe Batts Arm, Leading Tickles, undoubtedly prove the presence of English fishermen as the occupiers and first settlers in these localities. Turning Partridge Point we find from the bottom of White Bay to Quirpon mainly French names, showing that these harbours were used by our opponents. The following historical evidence bears out the same conclusion:—

"LETTER from Wm Coca of Bonavista to Col. NORRIS 7 Sep. 1698.

"I think it my duty to acquaint your Honour that to the North side of this bay are many extraordinary harbours and better fishing; one William Wyng has fished there some years (it being 14 leagues N We N° from this place) who has still increased the inhabitants of this place very considerably, and this year one Nowill has been that way who has more fish for his two boats than they have for shallops, so that next summer severall of the inhabitants of this harbour design to remove thither and their masters of ships that have fished there this year intend to be likewise, for it is certain the fewer boats are kept in a place the better the fishing.

"I write this that those sent to settle affairs may have power as far as Cape Frills. I think a draught [chart] ought to be drawn of that place. There is room for five hundred sail."[1]

The English settlements north of Bonavista grew so rapidly that in 1732 the commodore was instructed to include in his "scheme" an account of Fogo, Twillingate, and any other places he thought fit, but none appears to have been furnished until that of Captain Vanbrugh in 1738.

The most important particulars then were:—

	Fishing Ships.	Sack Ships.	Passengers.	Boats of Fishing Ships.	Boats of Inhabitants.	Byeboatmen.	Fish. Qntls.	Seal Oil. Value. £	Furs. Value. £	Families.	Farmers.	Inhabitants.	Remained last Winter.
Fogo	7	4	70	14	24	135	19,000	770	300	21	None	215	143
Twillingate	2	3	50	8	16	130	12,000	440	100	16	None	184	152

In 1739, 386 persons remained during the winter. In 1742 Fogo and Twillingate were credited with making £2,550 from seal oil.[1]

These official returns prove conclusively the English occupation prior to 1763, and there can be no doubt that there were a number of smaller settlements which never made any returns.

Palliser, in his report of 1768, says Twillingate was never formerly used by the French; and the master of the *Bon Ami* admitted that he received an extra bounty from the French Government to fish there, in order to annoy and drive away the English settlers.

There are entries in the books of Messrs. Gundry, Bridport, showing purchases of nets, lines, and cordage by the Nobles as far back as 1760, and thirty years later (1790) Rowsell's accounts with this most ancient firm showed very large dealings and very extensive fishery operations,

---

[1] *Records, Board of Trade, Newfoundland.*

amounting in some cases to £1,000 for the year. John Slade of Poole, who carried on business in Twillingate early in the eighteenth century, died in 1792, leaving a fortune computed at £70,000 sterling, all made out of the Newfoundland trade.

All these facts form a complete answer to the French contention that the English never occupied any place north of Cape Bonavista prior to 1763. It is well known that during the celebrated Seven Years' War which commenced in 1756 the French virtually abandoned Newfoundland; they were chased from the North American seas by British cruisers during the ten years prior to 1763, and English fishermen occupied all the deserted French establishments as far north as Quirpon. There is abundant evidence on this point from the records. Many years, however, prior to 1763 there were British settlements sparsely scattered all around Green Bay and along the Newfoundland coast from Cape Bonavista to Cape John.

By the treaty of Utrecht the boundaries of the Newfoundland coast on which the French were permitted to fish extended from the well-known point Cape Bonavista to Point Riche. The French claimed that Point Riche was Cape Ray, citing in proof of their contention a map of Hermann Moll. The merchants and planters of Newfoundland, in a petition presented to Parliament in 1716, declared the Point should be fixed at fifty and one-half degrees of North latitude. A letter was found from Prior, settling the limits, and was admitted by the French as conclusive, in 1764.

MOLL'S MAP.

Later on our opponents alleged that they had found a map drawn by Jean Denys, to which reference had been made in the negotiation of 1713, which placed Point Riche at 49°, upon the borders and to the north of the Bay of Three Islands (Bay of Islands), now called North

---

[1] Moll was led astray by La Hontan, who was then in London. Moll's knowledge of the interior of Canada was also mainly derived from La Hontan.

Head. "This," said the Abbé Reynal, "was a reasonable and just "demand, and yet the French, who ventured to frequent the contested "space, experienced the loss and disgrace of having their boats "confiscated." This dispute continued between the two nations until 1778. As a matter of fact, both nations showed a marvellous ignorance of geography; Point Riche is really situated a little to the north of Ingornachois Bay.

There were other difficulties with the French besides the question of Point Riche. Many English settlers had fishing establishments and dwelling-houses north of Cape Bonavista; the French claimed that they interfered with their fishery rights under the treaty, and that they should be removed. The English Government, as usual, did nothing.

This question arose again in a still more troublesome and complicated form in 1763, at the Treaty of Paris, when there was a still larger English settlement, extending from Bonavista to Cape John, some stray English fishermen having fixed establishments as far north even as Quirpon. An Irishman—a Mr. Dunien—was so obstreperous in his altercations with the French at St. Julian's, that Admiral Palliser ordered him to be banished from the Colony.

Whilst the French had occupied Placentia, all the best places on the beach, and the most convenient positions for fishing stations, had been appropriated by the Governor and his officers; a regular part of the business of the soldiers, marines, and sailors was to catch fish for their masters; a small share was allowed them, but, of course, the lion's portion went to the officers. The Frenchmen complained bitterly that they had not so much beach room and conveniences for the fishery at Louisbourg as they had enjoyed for many years at Placentia.

When the English took possession, Governor Moody and his successor, Governor Gledhill, followed the same practice as their predecessors; Moody, and some of his subordinates, bought out the French officers, and, as we have seen before, their rights were confirmed. This military dominion and military trading was too much for the West Countrymen, and a peremptory order was sent to the lieutenant-governor of Placentia, Colonel Gledhill, putting an end to their trading and fishing. In defence of the officers, it should be remembered that they were always very badly paid, often not paid at all, and frequently in arrear. They had no alternative but to eke out a living in some way.

Other peculiarities were copied from the French; in Placentia disputes were decided according to French rules, and it was some considerable time before Plaisance became a thoroughly English settlement and settled down to English ways. It remained under the government of Nova Scotia until 1729.

In the records we find an account of a large salmon fishery carried on by Mr. Skeffington, from Bonavista, between Cape Bonavista and Cape John, which it is expressly stated was never used by fishing ships. After considerable delay and a reference to the law officers of the Crown, Skeffington obtained a grant in 1723 for twenty-one years in a sole fishery for salmon in Freshwater Bay, Ragged Harbour, Gander Bay, and Dog Creek. About this time the salmon fishery was also extended to Exploits and various other rivers in Notre Dame Bay, and with this new enterprise there was a corresponding increase of the resident English population in this portion of the Colony.

GREAT AUK.
From the English Pilot, 1755.

The whole of this period, 1714 to 1727, was like the heavy prosaic Hanoverian monarch—dull, uneventful, peaceful, and prosperous. Population and the fishery increased considerably; the trade with England for provisions almost entirely ceased; salt beef, pork, butter, bacon, all came from Ireland; fresh meat, live stock, corn, flour, lumber, lime, and bricks were all imported from the North American colonies; woollen cloths were largely shipped from Ireland; linen, &c., from France and Spain, and from the latter country iron, for which the Basque provinces have always been famous.

The tyranny of the fishing admirals still prevailed, but it was very much tempered by the interference of the naval officers, who assumed their functions, and in a rough-and-ready sort of way administered justice. The want of a ruler and a settled government was felt acutely at this period; representation after representation was made to the home Government on the subject, and, at last, after many delays, in 1729, a Governor and Commander-in-Chief was appointed.

CHAPTER XII.

REIGN OF GEORGE II.

1727-1760.

1729.—Lord Vere Beauclerc recommended for first Governor, but Captain Osborne, R.N., eventually appointed Governor and Commander-in-Chief; Placentia placed under him; Island divided into six districts; J.P.'s appointed; contests between fishing admirals and justices: Osborne's letter to the Duke of Newcastle; J. P. Taylor, of St. John's, allowed to open a shop in Boston.

1730.—Court House and Prison at St. John's completed in September. St. John's magistrates threaten to resign on account of indignities and obstructions expected during the winter.

1731.—Captain Clinton, R.N., appointed Governor.

1732.—Captain Falkinham, R.N., of H.M.S. *Durseley Galley*, Governor; Governors requested to furnish account of inhabitants, &c. at Fogo and Twillingate.

1733.—Lord Muskerry, Governor.

1735.—Great complaints of French competition in European fish markets.

1737.—Court of Oyer and Terminer appointed, owing to inconvenience of trying two cases of murder in 1736. Captain Vanbrugh, R.N., Governor.

1738.—Captain Vanbrugh's account of inhabitants at Fogo and Twillingate.

1740.—Lord George Graham, Captain, R.N., Governor.

1741.—Hon. Jno. Byng, R.N., Governor. Mr. William Keen appointed Naval Officer to collect returns about the fishery, also to be Health Officer and Judge of the Vice-Admiralty Court.

1742.—War between France and England; Captain Welch prosecuted at Boston for bringing passengers from Newfoundland without reporting them.

1743.—Captain Byng appointed Naval Officer to prevent smuggling.

1745.—Louisbourg, Cape Breton, captured by Pepperell and Admiral Warren; great rejoicings in England over the victory; won principally by New England troops; Admiral Watson, Governor.

1747.—British-American officers recruiting in Newfoundland.

1748.—Peace of Aix-la-Chapelle between England and France; Louisbourg restored to France; great indignation in New England; Col. Bradstreet, Lieut.-Governor.

1749.—Captain George Brydges Rodney, R.N., Governor (celebrated as Lord Rodney).

1750.—Captain Francis W. Drake, Governor. Commission of Oyer and Terminer to try felons in Newfoundland. R. Carter, Esq., J.P. for Ferryland. Murder of William Keen, the magistrate.

1753.—Confederation of British North American Colonies for mutual defence against the French. Governor Bonfoy. Grant of Isle aux Bois to R. Carter.

1754.—Lord Baltimore renewed his claim upon part of Avalon; ruled that his title had lapsed.

1755.—Richard Dorril, Governor. Roman Catholics prosecuted for celebrating Mass Bradley reports from Fogo, presence of forty French armed ships surveying and fishing; also capture of French spies; complaint by Harbour Grace fishing admiral of destruction of property by loose characters living in huts at the end of the harbour.

1756.—Commencement of the Seven Years' War.

1757.—Local Militia appointed; Michael Gill, J.P., honorary colonel. Governor Edwards. Small-pox epidemic. Number of French prizes captured; a captured Waterford vessel recaptured by her own crew.

1759.—Quebec captured by Wolfe; great power of France in America destroyed. New English church built at St. John's; Rev. Edward Langman, minister. The Molasses Act.

1760.—Governor Webb; Gundry's of Bridport supplying lines and seines to Noble at Fogo.

The period covered by the reign of the second Hanoverian king is distinguished by two of the most stirring events in the history of North America, the capture of Louisbourg and the fall of Quebec. For Newfoundland there was the dawn of a brighter day: England at last determined to confer the blessings of government on the unfortunate Colony.

During the preceding years of peace the trade and fisheries of the Island had wonderfully increased. The average catch for the years 1749, 1750, and 1751 was about four hundred and thirty thousand quintals of fish and two thousand five hundred tons of cod oil; the population had become about six thousand permanent inhabitants.

Whilst no rude alarms of war disturbed the Newfoundland colonists, the mother country all through this reign experienced the perils and dangers of '45—the Jacobite rebellion. The air was full of war and warlike preparations.

GEORGE II.
From an engraving by Faber.

To the alarm caused by Prince Charles Edward we owe the efficient fortification of St. John's, Trinity, Carbonear, Ferryland, and the maintenance of garrisons and artillery; it was all allowed to fall into decay just before the French again made another successful attack on St. John's.

Acting on the most urgent representations of the naval commanders the Ministry determined to appoint a Governor. The Committee of Council had recommended that Lord Vere Beauclerc, who had been Commodore on the Newfoundland station, should be appointed—

"Governor and Commander-in-chief in and over the Island of Newfoundland, our fort and garrison at Placentia, and all forts and garrisons erected and to be erected in the Island, with authority to appoint Justices of the Peace and to erect Court Houses and Prisons; that a person skilled in the laws should be sent annually to the Island with His Majesty's Commission of Oyer and Terminer; and that Placentia should be separated from the Government of Nova Scotia and placed under the control of Newfoundland."

As usual with the Home Government, this wise and practical measure was frustrated and marred in its execution; instead of the learned counsel skilled in the law being sent out, it was thought quite sufficient to forward copies of the Acts of Parliament and eleven sets of "Shaw's Practical Justice of the Peace," impressed on the covers in gold letters—Placentia, St. John's, Carboneer, Bay of Bulls, St. Mary's, Trepassey, Ferryland, Bay de Verd, Trinity Bay, Bonavista, and Old Parlekin, in Newfoundland. This ancient treatise—as dull and pedantic as were all law books before Blackstone wrote in the language of a scholar, and with the style of a gentleman—were to guide the Governor in all matters of justice; in place of a lawyer to advise him, he was to have unintelligible law books.

Instead of the able and energetic Lord Vere,[1] who had experience of the Colony, and was both a politician and a naval officer, a subordinate, Captain Henry Osborne, Commander H.M.S. *Squirrel*, was appointed the first Governor of Newfoundland.

Osborne proved himself a painstaking, honest, and conscientious ruler, but he had neither the weight nor the strength of will to contend successfully with the great difficulties that surrounded him; he was both badly advised and badly supported by the Home Government.

The Governor, in all his ways and works, was vigorously attacked by the West Country adventurers. They argued, with a show of reason, that their fishing admirals had authority under an Act of Parliament, whilst Osborne's justices derived their authority only from one estate of the realm, the king; of course, the great mistake made was in not passing an Act of Parliament for the government of Newfoundland and the establishment of courts of justice.

Subservient Crown lawyers in the Georgian era might hold that the king had absolute power over the plantations, and could, by his mere motion, create governments and constitutions and courts of law for the Colony. Intelligent public opinion took a different view; independent lawyers advised that an Act of Parliament was necessary for the constitution, law, and government of the Island, but from this date until

---

[1] Lord Vere would have had to vacate his seat in Parliament on accepting an office of emolument under the Crown; the Ministry wanted his vote, so this arrangement fell through.

1791 the necessary measure was not passed; in consequence there was nothing but contention, confusion, and uncertainty. The following letter explains the new Governor's proceedings:—

"GOVERNOR OSBORNE to the DUKE OF NEWCASTLE.

"St. John's Newfoundland, 14th October 1729.

"Transmits to His Grace particulars of his proceedings since his arrival in Newfoundland; as the principal powers he had to execute were establishing Justices of the Peace and other Ministers of Justice, has divided the Island into convenient Districts and has appointed over each—of those the little time I have been here would admit me to visit—out of the Inhabitants and Planters of the best characters—such a number of justices of the Peace and Constables according to the bigness of the fishery they preside over, as he judged necessary, in case they did their duty, to preserve peace and quietness in the Island. Further particulars of which he has enclosed for His Grace's approbation, as likewise a copy of the Commission given to justices drawn up in the best manner he was capable of doing not being well acquainted with forms of such Commissions nor with powers granted him not having time enough to prepare himself with them before he received His Majesty's commands to be gone. In consideration of which he begs His Grace to look favourably upon it. Could set apart no house proper for a prison and in regard many delinquents escape with impunity for want of places to secure them, has ordered a rate presented to him by justices of the Peace of little burthen to the people, to be raised in Districts of St. John's and Ferryland for building a prison in each of these places—rate half a quintal of Merchantable fish per boat, and half a quintal for every boat's room, including the ships rooms of those fishing on the Banks that have no boats, with like proportionable rate upon persons in trade and not concerned in the fishery and only for one fishing season.

"For punishing of petty crimes has erected several pairs of stocks. Makes no doubt but all these measures will be sufficient to suppress great disorders in the Island. But what is yet to be feared is that as the best of these magistrates are but meen people and not used to be subject to any Government, that no longer than they have a superior amongst them will they be obedient to any orders that are given. Besides these measures my Lord Vere and he have done many acts of justice to inhabitants and planters and particularly at Placentia where they had restored several Planters which Col. Gledhill had unjustly dispossessed for several years and apprehend would have taken from him many more which he holds by very unjust 'Tenners,' had the proper proprietors been on the spot to have sued."

By September 1730 the Governor had the satisfaction of completing his new court house and prison in St. John's; he hoped his stocks and his jails would be a sufficient terror to evil doers and to all his opponents. The opposition, however, to the Governor's authority increased rather than diminished. The admirals declared the justices were only *Winter Justices*, and accordingly they had licensed public-houses, seized, fined, and whipped at their pleasure, and entirely set aside his new-fledged magistrates. Their worships were not the men to resist these bullying old ship-fishermen. In September 1730, just before the

Governor sailed, the St. John's magistrates, Wm. Keen, William Weston, and A. Southmayd, wrote:—

"They have reason to think that they are like to meet with some obstructions in the execution of their office from Admirals whose authority is limited to disputes relating to the fishery, but who oppose all authority but their own. Rather than suffer any indignities as justices shall resign their authority."

The Attorney-General very properly advised that Osborne's taxes were illegal; he suggested there should be a grand jury to fix the rates, and that they should be assessed, not on property, but on persons,—a nice distinction which the Newfoundlanders do not seem to have appreciated. No doubt the Crown could appoint justices, it is part of the prerogative. When, however, it came to the creation of a superior court of record and taxation, it was clear that the authority of an Act of Parliament was required. After a time this fact dawned upon the authorities at home. The contest between the Western Adventurers and the fishing admirals on one side, and the Governors and the justices on the other, continued for more than half a century.

The merchants declared that some of the justices were New England men—probably referring to M. Gill, who was a provincial, and that they supplied the fishermen with intoxicating liquors at higher rates than the merchants. Their great offence, however, was that they summoned masters and merchants to pay wages—an unknown thing in the Colony—the merchants having been specially exempted from the jurisdiction of the fishing admirals.

Owing to an affray in Torbay, in which one of the ancient family of Gosse was killed by a man called Blackmore, and another case of murder by one Steele, with the expense and delay of sending home the accused and the witnesses for trial, generally at Exeter. In 1737 in Governor Vanbrugh's Commission a clause was inserted giving him authority to hold one Court of Oyer and Terminer whilst he was resident in the Colony, but not to suffer any sentence to be executed "till report thereof be made to His Majesty."

When the Commission went before the Privy Council, the clause was struck out; it was ultimately granted in Governor Drake's Commission in 1750. All these difficulties about creating an efficient court of justice were really prompted by West Country influence, and by narrow commercial jealously; they lasted until about the year 1828. The story of the fight against the Courts and Government was as bitter a controversy as the design to extirpate the settlers.

In following the course of our history through this period we find amongst our naval Governors such distinguished names as Lord George

THE FALL OF LOUISBOURG.

Graham in 1740, and the Hon. John Byng in 1741. In this year Mr. William Keen, a merchant of St. John's, one of the first justices, was appointed Naval Officer, Health Officer for the port, and Judge of the Vice-Admiralty Court—another attempt to create a court of justice, which subsequently led to a curious conflict between this tribunal and the rival civil court.

In 1742 war was declared between France and England, and in 1745 that most brilliant victory—the capture of Louisbourg—was achieved by the American colonists under the gallant Pepperell and Admiral Warren. The siege was being carried on under great difficulties, until the timely arrival of the English squadron from Newfoundland gave the besiegers the necessary additional force and supplies to capture the great French fortress.

When the French retired from Placentia in 1713, Cape Breton became the head-quarters of their fishery.[1] Always bent on aggression, they spent millions of dollars in raising a great fortress at Louisbourg. The fishery carried on by the French in Cape Breton, St. John's Island (Prince Edward's Island), Gaspé, and Newfoundland employed at this time sixteen thousand men. France was at the height of her power in North America. Her constant raids and insidious attacks on the neighbouring colonies raised such a spirit of resentment in New England that, immediately the war broke out in 1742, preparations were commenced for an attack on the great Island fortress.

HON. JOHN BYNG.
From an engraving after Houston.

Both in England and British America the fall of Louisbourg was

---

[1] Besides the fishery the French carried on a large smuggling business in Cape Breton; French brandy, silks, &c., and West India produce were clandestinely exchanged with New England traders for fish, fur, lumber, flour, &c. Whole cargoes of English Newfoundland fish were exchanged with the French traders. All North America joined in this extensive smuggling trade, and in cheating the French and English governments. The very fortifications of Louisbourg, in defiance of laws which prohibited trading with the enemy, were built with Yankee bricks, boards, lime, and stone.

hailed with a far wilder excitement and enthusiasm than the fall of Sebastopol in our own days. In 1747, when a French attack to recover the fortress was expected, Shirley and Pepperell's officers were busy recruiting all over the provinces; many soldiers for the service were obtained from Newfoundland. At the Peace of Aix-la-Chapelle in 1748, Cape Breton was restored to France. New England was naturally indignant over this base surrender of a conquest achieved at the cost of so many valuable lives, which they looked on with just pride, not only as a proof of their own prowess, but also as a material guarantee for the security of their fisheries and commerce. They were furious that this great fortress should be given up in exchange for "a petty factory (Madras) in the East Indies." The Colonies, after a time, received £235,200 sterling to recompense them for their expenditure incurred in the capture of Louisbourg. Colonel John Bradstreet of Massachusetts, who had distinguished himself in the siege, was made Lieutenant Governor of St. John's, our second colonial ruler.[1]

In 1749 arrived the most distinguished of our early naval governors —Captain George Brydges Rodney[2]— the heroic admiral who broke

---

[1] Bradstreet, whose name appears in our records as Lieutenant-Governor of St. John's in 1749, was a very distinguished American officer. Besides his brilliant services at Louisbourg, he was conspicuous for his gallantry in several other encounters with the French. In the absence of the Commodore he was the real Governor of the Colony for nine months of the year.

John Bradstreet, soldier, born in Horbling, England, in 1711; died in New York city, 25th September 1774. When a young officer he was sent to join the British forces in America, where he remained for the rest of his life. In 1745 he served with the expedition against Louisbourg, as lieutenant-colonel of Pepperell's (York, Me.) regiment, and contributed largely to its success by his zeal, activity, and judgment, and by his particular knowledge of the circumstances of the place. On the 5th of September 1745, he was made a captain, and on 16th September 1746, was appointed to the lieutenant-governorship of St. John's, Newfoundland, a sinecure. In 1755 he was ordered by General Braddock to Oswego, and became the adjutant-general to Governor Shirley. During the following summer he conveyed from Albany a great quantity of stores, with six months' provisions, to Oswego, and on his return from the fort was attacked by a strong party of French whom he defeated.

In March 1757 he was appointed to a company in the 60th Regiment, Royal American, and in December was made lieutenant-colonel and deputy quartermaster-general with the rank of colonel. On 27th August 1758, he captured Fort Frontenac, which he razed to the ground, and destroyed such stores as could not be removed. He served under Amherst in his expedition against Ticonderaga and Crown Point in 1759, received his colonelcy in February 1762, and was advanced to the rank of major-general on 25th May 1772. During Pontiac's war he commanded an expedition against the western Indians, with whom he negotiated a treaty of peace in Detroit 7th September 1764.

[2] Rodney, next to Nelson the most renowned British naval hero, when appointed Commodore, Governor, and Commander-in-Chief in Newfoundland, in 1749, was only thirty-one; he was a post captain at twenty-four, and two years before coming to the Colony had distinguished himself in Hawke's great victory off Ushant. As Governor of the Island Rodney showed shrewd common sense, firmness, a great regard for justice and fair play, and, what is most remarkable in that age, a kindly benevolent feeling for our hardy toilers of the sea; he carefully protected them from their grasping employers. As Wellington has been immortalized in a boot, so Rodney is for ever remembered in the name of a small boat. One remarkable event in Rodney's life shows the character of the age. Disappointed at not obtaining the

the line, and achieved the great victory over the French in the West Indies. In Rodney's time the Newfoundland appointment was one of the coveted prizes of the service. Though a very young man Rodney showed marked ability. In giving instructions to his surrogate, Lieutenant Frankland, R.N., lieutenant of H.M.S. *Rainbow*, he says:—

"In case any other complaints shall appear before you of crimes and misdemeanours committed upon the land you have full power and authority to adjudge and determine the same according to the custom of the country *and the best of your judgment.*"

Governor Rodney figures largely in our colonial records. Two letters of his are characteristic; one is in reply to George Garland, and the magistrates in Harbour Grace, who asked leave to reduce the servants wages on account of a bad fishery:—

"In regard to what you have laid before me concerning the merchants request that the servants may bear an equal proportion with them in their losses— I can by no means approve of it, as both law and equity declare the labourer to be worthy of his hire.

"Mr. Drake and myself would be glad to ease the merchants in all that lay in our power, but we are by no means capable of committing so flagrant a piece of injustice as desired to serve any people whatever. I have only one question to ask namely; had the season been good, in proportion as it has proved bad, would the merchants or boat keepers have *raised* the men's wages?

"I am Sir
"Your most obedient humble servant
"G. B. R.

"To
"George Garland Esq."

LORD RODNEY.
From an engraving after Reynolds.

Governorship at Jamaica, Rodney was living in Paris; by election expenses and high play he was in terrible money difficulties. On the breaking out of the war he was in great straits; from this he was relieved by his noble French friend Maréchal Biron, and enabled to take command and destroy the prestige of the French Navy. When the French Prince Philippe Egalité asked Rodney what would happen if he, the Duke, met the English at sea off Brest: "That your Highness will have an opportunity of learning English," was the Admiral's ready answer. Within two years he had taken two Spanish, one French, and one Dutch admiral, and on the 9th of April 1782 came his crowning victory over De Grasse at Dominica, when he broke the line. Rodney was remarkable for decision, boldness in attack, and confident self-reliance; these qualities were conspicuous in his character both as a young commodore and as an experienced and victorious admiral.

The other letter is to the same Harbour Grace magistrates, about their neglect to summon John Pike, who was charged with cruelly whipping David Careen and Michael Moreen. Pike, after a sharp reprimand from Rodney to the magistrates, appeared before the court on the 25th of September. He was fined £25 sterling and costs in Careen and Moreen's cases, and ordered to pay £100 to Amos Vincent, whose fish he had seized illegally. The Governor was not a man to be trifled with.

Rodney was succeeded, in 1750, by Commodore Francis William Drake, R.N. He appears to have been Rodney's senior officer, for whilst in the Colony, Rodney acted as his surrogate. Drake remained in command until 1752, when Captain Hugh Bonfoy, R.N., succeeded him.

Several horrible murders were committed about this time, the most notable being the killing of the magistrate, William Keen. Nine persons were involved in it.

FREDERICK LORD BALTIMORE.
From the London Magazine, 1768.

Four were hung, two the day after the conviction, and two the next day; the other five were respited on condition of their leaving the Colony. Keen was murdered partly out of revenge for the punishment of a man charged with larceny, and partly for the sake of money he had hid under his bed. The details, which are given at length in the records, are most revolting. A woman, dressed in man's clothes, was one of the prime instigators of this horrible crime; three of the murderers were soldiers. The principal culprits were hung on a gallows erected at the end of Keen's Wharf, west of Hunter's Cove.

Another case about the same time illustrates the curious way in which justice was dispensed. A man named Martin Doyle was charged with causing the death of his servant at Bay Bulls in a drunken fray. The jury acquitted him " by reason no man saw him lift hand against " the deceased, so we all give in our opinion for the man to be not

" guilty." Whereupon Doyle was set at liberty *on payment of the charges of the court.*

In 1753 the North American Colonies confederated for mutual defence against the French. In the next year a descendant of Lord Baltimore's attempted to renew his claim to the exclusive possession of part of Avalon. The Council decided unanimously that the title had lapsed.

We find from the records that the defences of the Colony were considerable compared with former times There was one company of infantry and a train of artillery in St. John's, sixty-six foot and nineteen artillerymen at Placentia. Fort William mounted in 1753 seven twenty-four-pounders, six eighteen-pounders, and ten six-pounders; Fort George—the lower gun battery—thirteen twenty-four-pounders, and ten guns on the platform; and the south side battery—Fort Frederick—four eighteen-pounders.

In this year a grant was made to Robert Carter, of Ferryland, of Isle aux Bois, described in the application as Little Bog Island. In 1755 Christopher Bradley, residing at Fogo, reports the arrival of forty French ships on the north-east coast, engaged in the fishery, well armed, and surveying the harbours. He also mentions the capture of French spies at Fogo. In the next year, 1756, the Seven Years' War commenced, and the French virtually abandoned the Newfoundland fishery, English fishermen during this period taking possession of the French fishing establishments at Petit Nord.

Governor Dorrill's administration of the Government in 1755 and 1756 is distinguished by intolerant bigotry and the persecution of Roman Catholics for exercising their religion. The Governor and other officials naively lament that these poor Irish—hunted down like wild beasts—were disloyal. What else could anyone expect them to be?

In 1755 Governor Dorrell wrote to the magistrates of Harbour Grace :—

"Whereas I am informed that a Roman Catholic priest is at this time at Harbour Grace, and that he publicly read mass, which is contrary to law, and against the peace of our sovereign lord the king. You are hereby required and directed on the receipt of this, to cause the said priest to be taken into custody and sent round to this place. In this you are not to fail."

The magistrate replied :—

"As concerning the Roman priest of whom you were informed that he read public mass at Harbour Grace, it was misrepresented, it was at a place called Caplin Cove, somewhat below the Harbour; for if he read it in the Harbour I should have known it and would have secured him. After he was informed that I had intelligence of him, immediately [he] left the place, and yesterday [I] was informed he was gone to Harbour Main."

The matter was, however, not allowed to drop, as the following record shows :—

"By THOMAS BURNETT, Esq., deputy or surrogate,
  to RICHARD DORRELL, Esq., governor, &c.

"At a court held before me at Harbour Main the 20th of September, at which you, Charles Garland, was present, at which time Michael Katem did appear before us, and by his own confession did admit a Roman priest to celebrate public mass according to the Church of Rome, in one of his fish-rooms or store-houses, and he, being present himself, which is contrary to law, and against our sovereign lord the king, we think proper to fine him the sum of fifty pounds, and to *demolish the said fish-room or store-room where mass was said*, and I do likewise order the said Michael Katem to sell all the possessions he has or holds in this harbour, on or before the 25th day of November ensuing. At the same day appeared before us Michael Landrican, who was guilty of the same crimes, for which we think proper to fine him the sum of twenty pounds, *to burn his house and stage down to the ground*, and he to quit the said harbour by the 25th of November ensuing. At the same time appeared before us, Darby Costley, Robert Finn, Michael Mooring, and Ronold McDonald, all which by their own confession are Roman Catholics and inhabitants of this place, which is contrary to law that they should hold any property in this island. We therefore think proper to fine the said Darby Costley ten pounds, Robert Finn ten pounds, Michael Mooring the sum of eight pounds, and Ronold McDonald the sum of two pounds ten shillings, all the said fines in sterling money of Great Britain, and all the said persons to quit the said island by 25th of November ensuing.

"T. BURNETT.

" To Charles Garland, Esq., one of His Majesty's
" Justices of the Peace at Harbour Main."

These were not the only sufferers; sixteen others in Harbour Main and many at Harbour Grace and Carbonier were convicted, and in every case the building where the service had been held was destroyed.

In 1757, owing to the breaking out of the great Seven Years' War in the previous year, a local militia was formed in St. John's. Mr. Michael Gill, judge of the Vice-Admiralty Court, was appointed colonel, Wm. Thommasley captain of the first company, John Stripling of the second, Wm. Baird of the third, Robert Hutchings of the fourth, Messrs. Green, Robert Hutchings, junr., Cocking, Morley, Stokes, Fly, Chafe, Tucker, and George Hutchings, lieutenants. Every officer had to take the oath of allegiance, supremacy, and abjuration.

In 1755 there is a complaint from the fishing admiral of Harbour Grace, signed by Webber, Parsons, Snow, Martin, Sheppard, &c., "com-
" plaining of the destruction of their sheep and cattle by people living
" in huts at the upper end of the harbour [River Head], loose and bad
" characters, harbouring numbers of idle persons."

In 1757, under the active and spirited Governor Edwards, a number of French prizes are brought into St. John's. Judge Gill and his officials reaped a rich harvest of fees and commissions; in one case a vessel from Waterford was captured by a French privateer, and afterwards gallantly recaptured by her own crew. An unfortunate epidemic of small-pox broke out this year. The magistrate was ordered to take steps to prevent its spreading.

In 1759 it appears that four hundred pounds had been collected towards the building of a new English church, near the site of the present Anglican cathedral. The building committee and trustees were Michael Gill, treasurer, the Rev. Edward Langman, B.A., of Balliol College, Oxford, incumbent, John Monier, William Bevill, and William Thomas:—

"Decided at a meeting of the Treasurer, Trustees. Subscribers &c. 29 Oct. 1759— That the pulpit, Communion Table, clerk's desk &c. be as in the old church. The West Gallery for the boat keepers as in the old Church; the North Gallery to be divided into three pews, the middle one for the Governor, one for the officers of the garrison and the other for the officers of the Navy. Bells to be put up in the belfry at the west end.

"That William Keen should have the first pew on the right coming in at the west door and Michael Gill the first on the south door.

"That the Parson should have a pew built for himself and family under the pulpit next the clerk's desk.

"First choice of pews to subscribers from £25 to £15 to be settled by lot.

"That those of £10 should have one square pew setled in the same manner.

"£5 to £10 subscribers to have single pews setled in the same manner.

"That the Gallows should be removed and put on Gallows Hill.

"That the bodys which is buried in the old church should be left at the election of their friends whether they would remove them or no."

Governor Edwards' method of completing the new church was eminently practical; he did not beat the drum ecclesiastic, or hold a bazaar, or appeal to anyone's religious feelings, but following the naval practice in vogue, he simply made prisoners of all the leading persons of the town who had not paid their subscriptions like "the well disposed inhabitants." He satisfied his own conscience by putting down his name for £25; there is no reference to its payment. The thirty-four substantial residents mentioned in the margin, who were apparently, judging from their names, chiefly Roman Catholics, Presbyterians, and Nonconformists, all had to work on the church or pay a carpenter, or else go to jail. The whole proceeding was illegal. The Governor's proclamation reads thus:—

"By RICHARD EDWARDS. Esquire, Governor, &c.

"Whereas the Church of this place, St. John's, has been carried on by the subscription of well disposed persons and it being highly necessary that the same should be covered as soon as possible. you are therefore hereby required and directed, to cause the men mentioned in the margin to repair to work on the said church from the date hereof to the 4th day of November next, as it appears that they are livers in this place and have not subscribed towards the building of the same; or to cause each of them that shall neglect complying herewith to pay the usual price given to carpenters daily in this place [till that time].

"For which this shall be your order.

"R. EDWARDS.

"To His Majesty's Justices of the Peace   By command of the Governor,
"for the District of St. John's.   B. PAYNE."

The end of George II.'s reign was signalized by Wolfe's victory at Quebec, and the complete destruction of the great French empire in America.

Lieutenant Griffith Williams, R.A., who was stationed at Carbonear Island in 1745 (afterwards promoted to St. John's, where he lived for some twelve or fourteen years), was a very active, enterprising young officer. He cleared the present Grove Farm, Quidi Vidi, and obtained a grant of two hundred acres. Subsequently he served in the American war and attained the rank of general. He was connected with the old family of Williams in this Colony; the late Sir Robert Pinsent, D.C.L., and the distinguished Sir Monier-Williams are his collateral descendants. In 1765 he published an account of the Colony. Commenting on the very irregular and unsatisfactory manner in which the fishery returns were made up at the time, he says:—

"I remember one of the above kind of Returns being sent to the Governor with an account of the number of boats kept, the quantity of fish, the oil caught &c. Having a boat and men of my own I had the curiosity to know how near they came to the truth,

GENERAL WOLFE.
From an engraving after Schaak.

and therefore began at Bay de Verds in Conception Bay and went into every creek and cove quite round to Portugal Cove and found they had not got within a third part in any one account.

"I found in Conception Bay 496 boats kept, and computed on an average each boat caught 500 qtls. of fish (though many caught 750 and several at Trinity Harbour 900). These made 248,000 qtls.; I allow for the shipping about 10,000, which I make 258,000 and allow for men, women and children employed in catching and curing the fish of each boat (as they all equally work) ten, which will make 4,960 and for the shipping 300 making in all 5,260 people.

"It is not so easy to come at the exact quantity of oil as some years the livers of the fish yield so much more than in others; and some years the Cape Cod men meet with great success in the whale fishery and at other times little or none, either in that or the seal fishery. Some years from the shore fish you have three hhds. of oil to 100 qtls. of fish and from the bank fish you have but a small quantity, however I shall allow one hhd. to the 100 qtls. which will be 645 tuns of train oil.

BOIS ISLAND FERRYLAND   LATTONEAU ISLAND

ST. JOHNS

I have known that oil sell at Newfoundland from £8 to £16 per tun and in England from £14 to £36 per tun.

"As the fishery of Conception Bay was reckoned equal to one quarter part of the whole fishery of Newfoundland from the year 1745 to 1752 i.e. Trinity, Bonavista, Catalina with the creeks thereunto belonging one quarter; Bay de Verd, Carboneire Harbour Grace and the several creeks and coves thereunto belonging one quarter; Torbay, Kidivide, St. John's and Petty Harbour a quarter; Bay of Bulls, Firiland, Firmoves, Trepassey and Placentia Bay another quarter part; so that the whole produce of fish and oil for one of the aforesaid years will be (exclusive of the whale and seal oil) of fish 1,032,000 qtls. and oil 5,160 tuns.

"Fish upon an average sell at foreign markets from eighteen to thirty shillings per quintal but suppose it at 20,- it will then amount to £1,032,000. Oil is often sent to Spain which upon an average sells at £18 per tun, it will then amount to £92,880 sterling.

"I shall make no calculation on the fur trade, which was very considerable before the French had such vast possessions to the northward. The salmon fishery is of no great consequence, though before the French were so powerful many a hundred tierces were sent to the Italian markets."

Referring to the forts, he says :—

"St. John's from 1745 to 1750 was very well garrisoned by four companies of Foot, a captain of artillery with about 50 men. It was also well supplied with all manner of stores and about 40 pieces of cannon. Feriland, Carboniere and Trinity Harbours had each an officer of artillery with about 18 or 20 men and an officer of Foot and 30 men. There were 200 small arms at each place for the use of the Inhabitants. If those defences had been kept up the French would not have succeeded in capturing these places in 1762."

The gallant major is very bitter against Irishmen, says they are not half so good as Newfoundlanders and English to catch fish. He gives us a life-like description of the fishery at this period, its wonderful productiveness. Nine hundred and ninety quintals a boat seems to us an enormous catch, but on the Labrador, even within my recollection, some of Hunt & Henley's men have equalled this. We must remember there were five men in a boat, or rather a large skiff.

Williams complains of the large expense of olive oil, owing to its having to be brought to England. The fishermen could not do without it to cook their salt fish; butter was scarce and dear. Olive oil is universally used for cooking in Spain, and, when good, it is the best to fry fish with. The native Spaniard does not care for the mild Lucca liquid, he likes his oil with a flavour—"que huele."

We still hear a good deal in these records about the bye-boat men[1]— the planters who brought out West Country servants. The late Hon. Stephen Rendell has often told me that even when he came to the Colony in 1834, hundreds of sturdy Devonshire lads came out every spring to Rowell's, Boden's, Bulley's, Mudge's, Job's, and many others on

---

[1] Bye-boat keepers were what we should now call planters or middlemen. They were not possessed of fishing ships, but they generally either had fishing establishments or hired them; they fitted out a number of men and boats; all who were independent sold their fish for the best price to sack-ships, traders, &c.

the South Side and in Hoyle's Town (Magotty Cove), and to Torbay, Bay Bulls, Petty Harbour, &c. All these "youngsters" were shipped for two summers and a winter.

Mr. Rendell said nearly every labouring man about Coffinswell had been a servant in Newfoundland. The regular place for shipping was at Newton Abbott, in the still existing hostelry, "The Dartmouth Inn and Newfoundland Tavern." Here the engagement was "wetted" with cyder, strong beer, and the still more potent Jamaica. There were the same scenes enacted every spring. The coming and going of the Newfoundland men was an event in Devonshire. The rurals reckoned the time by the old Church of England lectionary: "Jan! the Parson be in Pruverbs, the Newfanlan men will soon be a coming whome."

Dartmouth, Teignmouth, Exmouth, and "the seven strong firms" of Poole, every year sent out their contingent of West Countrymen to fish and work in Newfoundland. Jersey men and Newman's crew, even in our day, all had their passenger vessels sailing spring and autumn.

What helped to keep more Devonshire men in the country later on in the eighteenth century was the development of the ship seal fishery. Most writers on Newfoundland have described the seal fishery as only commencing about 1790, but this is a mistake. Ever since Newfoundland had permanent settlers there was more or less of a seal fishery, carried on at first simply as a shore fishery, with nets, afterwards in punts, and gradually in larger boats, until schooners came into play. The statistics show how it fluctuated, rising from £1,016 worth of seal oil in 1749 to £12,664 in 1768; at the price of oil ruling then, this latter figure shows quite a respectable "haul," even in those early days. Every "Room" and every merchant's establishment at that time had its vats, both for seal and cod oil, the latter always called "Train." But besides the seal fishery there was more or less of a whale fishery. New Englanders from Cape Cod were expert whale men, and with their splendid Hampton boats killed the cetaceans around our southern coast, particularly about Fortune Bay.[1]

---

[1] Of the whale fishery in Fortune Bay the Rev. P. Toque says:—

"It appears from evidence given by Henry Butler, before a committee of the House of Assembly, in 1840, that the whale fishery was carried on by the Americans to a great extent in Hermitage Bay, Bay of Despair, and Fortune Bay, during the years 1796, 1797, 1798, and 1799; that during the three first years, twelve vessels were employed by them, manned by fifteen men each; that all of the vessels returned nearly loaded; that they carried on the whale fishery in this part of the country until about the year 1807, when it was discontinued, owing to some dispute arising between Great Britain and the United States; that three years after this a schooner was fitted out by the Americans, which arrived at Burin, but on account of a man-of-war being stationed there, the schooner proceeded to St. Mary's Bay, where she remained until the month of August, and had nearly completed her load when she was taken by a British sloop-of-war, and ordered to St. John's; but the crew being too strong for the prize-master, the schooner shaped her course for America, and arrived in safety at Cape Cod. With this ended the American whale fishery on the western shores of Newfoundland. Mr. Butler stated that a whale fishery commenced in Hermitage Bay, under the firm of Peter

Considering the large intercourse between Newfoundland and New England at this period, American records contain very little information on the subject. In 1729, in the Boston Records, there is an entry about the admission of James Pulman Taylor, of St. John's, and "liberty " granted to him to open a shop on giving Bond in £100 to indemnifie " the Town." In 1742 Captain Nathaniel Welch was to be prosecuted for bringing passengers from Newfoundland without reporting them at the impost office. In 1735 there are great complaints about French competition in the European fish markets.

England, in 1759, imposed a duty of sixpence per gallon on molasses, rum, and sugar imported from the West India Islands other than British. It caused great excitement in Massachusetts and New England; the colonists declared they were ruined to appease the clamours of the British West India planters; all the same, the Americans

A VIEW OF LOUISBOURG, IN THE POSSESSION OF THE PEPPERELL FAMILY.
From Winsor's N. & C. H. of America.

never paid any duty. In 1764 the Act was renewed, and larger powers given to the Admiralty courts to try smuggling cases without a jury,

Le Messurier & Co., which continued for four years only, when the partnership dissolved; that the natives of Hermitage Bay, having some idea of the fishery, began a whale fishery on a very small scale; that a person of the name of McDonald had made a large property by it; that the house of Newman & Co. being aware of these proceedings, purchased the premises that had been Peter Le Messurier & Co.'s, and began the whale fishery on a large scale."

On Messrs. Newman's establishment at Gaulton, Hermitage Bay, there are still the buildings and machinery for carrying on an extensive whaling business. The premises are situated on an Island in that beautiful land-locked harbour; they have not, however, been used for some years past.

besides arming the Custom House officers with formidable power under writs of assistance. The Yankees evaded this law by lading their vessels in the French islands and purchasing clearances signed with the name, if not in the handwriting, of the Governor of Anguilla, who acted as collector. Anguilla—a British island—was so small as not to afford a cargo for a single vessel, yet the collectors in New England allowed all vessels with these clearances to pass without inquiry. Suddenly this was all changed; a vessel putting into Bermuda was seized and sold, the Governor getting one-third, the Colony one-third, and the informer one-third of the forfeiture.

Most American writers admit that this molasses difficulty was one of the primary causes of the Revolution. England was absolutely within

CANNON FOUND AT LOUISBOURG.
From Bourinot's History of Cape Breton.

her right in protecting her sugar islands, but Americans, in their ignorant impatience of taxation, thought they had good cause to be angry. Both Burke and Josiah Quincy declared these Acts were amongst the causes which led to separation. The result of the Molasses Act was to increase the direct trade between Newfoundland and the British West Indies, from whence rum, sugar, and molasses could be imported free, and to decrease the imports from New England.

APPENDIX TO CHAPTER XII.

Persons appointed to administer Justice in the several Districts of Newfoundland in 1732.

Each particular District.	Limits of the same.	Places within ye same.	No. of Justices.	Names of Justices.	No. of Constables.	Names of Constables.
Bonavista	From Cape Bonavista to the No'ward.	Bonavista, Bayleys Cove	Three.	Mr. John Clerk, the Rev. Mr. Henry Jones, Mr. John Hemming.	Three.	Mich. Reed, Will. Tully, Will. Trasler.
Trinity	From Cape Bonavista all within Trinity Bay to ye Bay de Verds.	English Harbour, New Parlikin, Trinity—Old Parlikin, Bay de Verds.	Three.	Mr. Jacob Taverner, Mr. Thos. Floyd, Mr. Richard Waterman.	Five.	Richard Archer, Wm. Martin, Duval Langer, Tho. Wiliaucs, Tho. Stone.
Carbonier	From the Bay de Verds as far So'ward as Cape St. Francis.	Muskete, Carbonier, Harbour Grace, Bay Roberts,	Two.	Mr. Will. Pynn, George Garland.	Seven.	Mr. Fred Ash. Hugh Perry, Robt. B. G. Grenves, Jno. Sheppard, Tho. Thistle, Wm. Badcock, Richd. Porter.
St. John's	From Cape St. Francis to So'ward as far as the Bay of Bulls.	Torbay, Quidi Vidi, St. John's, Petty Harbour, Bay of Bulls.	Four.	Mr. Will Keen, Mr. Will. Weston, Mr. Abr. Southmayde, Mr. Nathl. Brooks.	Four.	Jno. Huddle, Jno. Curtis, Adam Lendon, Jno. Clenck.
Ferryland	From the Bay of Bulls to the So'ward as far as Cape Race and to the We'ward as far as Cape Pine.	Tods Cove, Ferryland, Fermouse, Renowse, Trepassey.	Five.	Mr. Jno. Ludwic, Mr. John Kates, Mr. Saml. Hutchins, Mr. Jno. Jenkins, Mr. Will. Jackson.	Nine.	Mr. Henry Rex, Mr. Wm. Pidgrom, Mr. Dolton and Packer, Mr. Rouse and Stevens, Mr. John Rose, Mr. Thos. Cury, Andrew Armstrong.
Placentia	From Cape Pine to Placentia and the western side of that Bay.	St. Marys, Placentia, Petty Placentia.	Three.	Mr. Peter Sigmut—dead, Mr. Tho. Salmon, Mr. Tho. Buchanmon.	Three.	Lawrence Harden, Mr. Henry Huxford, Mr. Jno. Brand.

This list was enclosed in Capt. Falkingham's Report, Oct. 1, 1732. Another list of Districts of the same description is enclosed in Governor Osborne's letter, Sep. 25, 1730, without the names of the Justices, the only change being in St. John's.

CHAPTER XIII.

REIGN OF GEORGE III.

1760–1820.

1760.—Captain Webb Governor.

1761.—Captain (afterwards Lord) Graves Governor.

1762.—St. John's, Carbonear, and Trinity captured by the French; re-captured same year, in September, by Colonel Amherst; battle of Quidi Vidi.

1763.—War with Spain; importation of fish from Newfoundland prohibited. Treaty of Paris; St. Pierre and Miquelon confirmed to France; all the rest of North America given up to England. Survey of the Island by Cook. Labrador re-annexed to Newfoundland.

1764.—Sir Hugh Palliser Governor. Collector of customs appointed in St. John's. Court of Vice-Admiralty, St. John's.

1765.—Rev. Laurence Coughlan introduced Wesleyanism.

1766.—Riots in St. John's and Harbour Grace. Lieut. Cartwright made an unsuccessful attempt to effect friendly intercourse with Beothics. Repeal of the American Stamp Act.

1772.—Lord Shuldham, Governor, issued Proclamation 24th June, regulating river salmon fishery; French not mentioned.

1774.—Continental Congress in America; all exportation to Newfoundland from North American States prohibited. Quebec Act, 14 Geo. III. c. 83; Labrador annexed to Canada.

1775.—Rev. John Jones first Congregational minister in St. John's. Heaviest storm ever known in Newfoundland; 300 persons drowned. Palliser's Act, 15 Geo. III.; Commodore Duff issues Proclamation about salmon fisheries at Exploits, Gander Bay, &c.

1776.—Declaration of Independence, United States.

1777.—Admiral Montague fitted out armed vessels to cruise against American privateers.

1782.—Independence of United States acknowledged by England.

1783.—Treaty of Versailles; French allowed to fish from Cape John to Cape Ray; Declaration of King George III. that English were not to interrupt French fishery by their competition.

1784.—Religious freedom established in the Colony; Dr. O'Donel, first Roman Catholic Prefect Apostolic, arrived.

1786.—Act 26 Geo. III. c. 26; continuing bounty to Bank fishery for ten years. Jurisdiction of Courts of Vice-Admiralty to try fishery cases transferred to Sessions Courts. Prince William Henry arrived in Newfoundland.

1787.—Bishop Inglis appointed as Anglican Bishop of Canada, New Brunswick, Nova Scotia, and Newfoundland.

CHRONOLOGY.

1788.—Bermudian vessels fishing in Newfoundland.

1789.—French Revolution. Court of Common Pleas established for the Colony.

1791.—Reeves appointed Judge of "the Court of Civil Jurisdiction of Our Lord the King at St. John's, in the Island of Newfoundland."

1792.—"Supreme Court of Judicature of the Island of Newfoundland" created.

1793.—Chief Justice D'Ewes Coke.

1794.—Murder of Lieut. Lawrie, R.N. France declares war against England.

1795.—Royal Newfoundland regiment embodied; Commander, Colonel Skinner.

1796.—French destroyed Bay Bulls. England and Spain at war. Dr. O'Donel consecrated Bishop of Thyatira *in partibus*, and Vicar Apostolic of Newfoundland; first Roman Catholic Bishop.

1797.—Battle of Cape St. Vincent. Mutiny of the Nore.

1799.—First grammar school opened.

1800.—Mutiny in the garrison at St. John's.

1802.—Treaty of Amiens, signed by England, France, Spain, and Holland.

1803.—"The Newfoundland Light Infantry" formed.

1805.—The first Post Office established in the Colony.

1806.—Benevolent Irish Society formed. Dr. Lambert, Roman Catholic Bishop of Chitra *in partibus*, arrived. Volunteer Corps, Newfoundland Rangers, embodied.

1807.—The "Royal Gazette and Newfoundland Advertiser" first published.

1808.—Formation of Volunteer Corps for defence of the Capital and Island. Lieut. Spratt, R.N., sent with paintings to the Beothics.

1809.—Labrador and Anticosti re-annexed to the Government of Newfoundland by Act 49 Geo. III., which also established permanent Courts of Judicature in Newfoundland.

1810.—Proclamation to protect Red Indians. Sir John Thos. Duckworth, Governor.

1811.—Lieut. Buchan's expedition to Beothics. Waterside in St. John's cleared of ships' rooms; leased by auction to the public. Permission first granted to erect permanent houses.

1812.—Second American war. Harbour of St. John's full of prizes. Volunteer force reorganised.

1813.—Capture of the *Chesapeake* by H.M.S. *Shannon*. Sir Richard Godwin Keats, Governor. First grants of land. Publication of Dr. William Carson's pamphlet; agitation for Colonial Parliament.

1814.—First Treaty of Paris.

1815.—Second Treaty of Paris; last Treaty made between England and France about the Newfoundland fishery; confirms Treaty of Versailles, 1783. Numerous failures caused by the peace and the depreciation of fish in foreign markets.

1816.—St. John's nearly destroyed by fire; cargo of provisions sent in winter by benevolent people of Boston, U.S. Francis Forbes, Esq., afterwards Sir Francis, Chief Justice, arrived. First visit of an Anglican Bishop to Newfoundland. Dr. Scallan, Roman Catholic Bishop of Drago *in partibus*, and Vicar Apostolic of Newfoundland.

1817.—St. John's again visited by fires, November 7th and 21st; 200 houses destroyed. "The winter of the Rals."

1818.—Convention with the United States respecting the fisheries. Admiral Pickmore, first resident Governor, died in St. John's. Captain Bowker, Administrator. Sir C. Hamilton, Governor.

1819.—Case of Butler and Lundrigan. Great fire in St. John's.

The reign of our sovereign lord King George, "the good King George," of our forefathers, is the longest and most eventful in English history. It begins in an age which appears to us remote; it ends in a period in which many of us have lived, and with which we are all familiar.

It witnessed great disasters and great victories—the loss of the American colonies, the overthrow of France in three great wars. It commenced when the British navy was neither well organised nor in uniform; it ends with making England the greatest sea power the world has ever seen, and the British fleet a real invincible armada, which had beaten every nation in fair fight, a fleet from which Spanish and gallant French officers were carefully instructed by their respective Governments to flee away on the wings of the wind.

GEORGE III.
From an engraving after Ramsay.

It begins with the bungling appliances of the eighteenth century; it ends with steam, macadamised roads, the electric telegraph, the railway, and the steamboat.

Our own history also advances with this age of progress. We pass away from the fishing admirals into the modern epoch, with roads, education, responsible government, and courts of justice. This later Georgian era is the transition period in our history between the bad old days of tyranny, corruption, and violence, and the dawning of the brighter days of civilisation and progress.

In the first year of this reign the Governor and Commander-in-Chief was Webb.[1] All the captains appointed on this station were given the honorary rank of commodore whilst in this commission. The new Governor was active and vigilant. He captured a large number of French vessels; one of these, the *Tacignor*, realised at the Admiralty sale, by order of Michael Gill, Judge of the Vice-Admiralty Court, the handsome sum of £2,570 sterling for three thousand five hundred quintals of fish, the price being fairly good, with a brisk demand in the Mediterranean markets. The French merchant navy was almost

---

[1] Captain James Webb became a commander in 1745. In 1746-7-8, he distinguished himself very greatly by the capture of a large number of French privateers. He took command of the *Sunderland* (60), on the recommencement of the war with France in 1756. He died on the 14th May 1761 on board the *Antelope*, which was then prepared to sail to Newfoundland.

annihilated by English privateers and men-of-war. The merchant fleet convoyed from Newfoundland in 1761 consisted of seventy sail of vessels, armed with two hundred guns, and manned by six hundred and eighty hardy West Country sailors. They all arrived safely, and sold their fish well.

Governor Webb seems to have given most of his time to capturing stray French vessels. The civil business of the Government was of a very petty character—writing threatening letters to some of the merchants' debtors, and settling the titles to land.

Newman's land at the foot of McBride's Hill, Keen's property at the foot of Prescott Street, extending to Hunter's Cove (then called Hudson's Cove), the property of Peter Weston, Esquire, J.P., at Ferryland (ancestor of Sir F. B. T. Carter, K.C.M.G.), and, amongst others, the titles of the Gosses and Codners in Torbay, were thus disposed of by his Excellency. There is a curious report about a murder at St. Pierre, then in possession of the Grandys of Belloram and other English families, which will be found in the chapter on the French colony of St. Pierre and Miquelon.

Though war was raging with France, the Colony seems to have been very peaceful and orderly, and fairly prosperous up to the end of 1761. After their numerous defeats the French were anxious for peace. To secure favourable terms, and especially a share of the fishery, it was most desirable that they should capture some English possession. Their well-served Intelligence Department informed them of the defenceless state of St. John's, its neglected military condition and weakened garrison. On our capital, therefore, they made their successful attempt.

Whilst England had been spending millions of dollars on the colonisation and defence of Nova Scotia, St. John's was left with less than a single company of soldiers—sixty-three men—and all the forts in a state of decay.

The French Government, in the spring of 1762, sent out four ships of war, thirty-two officers, and nearly seven hundred troops, under the command of Count D'Haussonville. They managed to elude the British cruisers by sailing from Brest in a thick fog. Sir Edward Hawke was sent in pursuit of them, but they escaped, and the squadron under Admiral De Ternay, with the troops and transports, took Bay Bulls on the 24th June, and marched towards the capital.

On the 27th they arrived before St. John's. Against such an overwhelming force no resistance could be made by a handful of men and one English sloop-of-war—the *Grammont*, of twenty-two guns. After this easy capture, the French general set to work to repair the ruined fortifications and erect fresh defences on Signal Hill, where the remains of the old French barracks are now crumbling into decay.

When the intelligence of the capture of St. John's, Carbonear, and Trinity, and the devastation of the trade and fishery reached England, the English Ministry were loudly and universally blamed for their neglect of the great Chatham's advice about the defence of the Colony.

FORT AMHERST, ST. JOHN'S.
From a photograph by S. H. Parsons.

Preparations were at once made on an extensive scale to retrieve their negligence. Fortunately for our Island the governorship of Newfoundland had been entrusted to one of the bravest and most skilful naval officers of the period—the distinguished Captain Graves, afterwards Lord Graves.

Captain Douglas, R.N., of H.M.S. *Syren*, happened at the time of the French invasion to be on a cruise off Cape Race. As soon as he heard of their arrival in Bay Bulls he pressed into the service two English merchant vessels in St. Mary's Harbour—the brig *William* and the sloop *Bonetta*. The master of the *Syren*, Peter Burne, was given charge of the sloop, and a petty officer was placed in charge of the brig, with orders to cruise on the banks and endeavour to intercept Captain Graves[1] in H.M.S. *Antelope*, with the English convoy.

---

[1] Thomas Lord Graves entered the navy at an early age, and was present at the unsuccessful attack on Carthagena in 1741. He was a lieutenant in the *Romney* at the notorious action off Toulon on 11th February 1744; was on the *Monmouth* in Anson's action off Finisterre, and Hawke's action in the Bay of Biscay in 1747. He was tried by court-martial in 1757 for not endeavouring to discover whether a French ship he met was

Lieutenant General
William Amherst

The *William* missed the fleet, and proceeded with her intelligence to Halifax, U.S. Burne, however, met Graves at the outer edge of the Grand Bank with his large convoy. The Governor ordered him to land a party of marines at Ferryland, and then to proceed at once with despatches to Halifax. Graves in the meantime put the defences of Placentia in order, and Captain Douglas looked after Ferryland.

QUIDI VIDI, LOOKING TOWARDS THE SCENE OF THE ACTION.

Colonel William Amherst,[1] who commanded the troops, was in New York at the time. He at once proceeded to embark with part of the Royal Americans—a fine regiment, mostly composed of Swiss and

[1] General Amherst was an ensign 3rd Foot Guards, 1753; lieutenant and captain, 1757; colonel, 1766; colonel 32nd Regiment, a man-of-war or an East Indiaman, and was reprimanded. In 1759 he was at the bombardment of Havre de Grace; he was appointed to the *Antelope* immediately on the death of Webb, in May 1761. In 1778 he went with Byron to North America and the West Indies, and in 1781 became commander-in-chief on the North American station. He was unsuccessful in an action with De Grasse at the mouth of the Chesapeake, for which he was much blamed. In 1787 he was vice-admiral, and next year commander-in-chief at Plymouth. He became admiral in 1794 and had an important share in Lord Howe's victory; for his gallant conduct he was created an Irish peer, and received a pension. He was wounded in this engagement, so he resigned his command; he died in February 1802. (STEPHEN's *Dict. of Nat. Biography*.)

1775; major-general, 1777; and lieutenant-general, 1779. During his distinguished career he held the appointment of Lieutenant-Governor of Portsmouth, adjutant-general at head-quarters, and aide-de-camp to the King. He died 13th May 1781. He married a Miss Patterson, a celebrated beauty at George III.'s Court. The portrait of him is from a painting by Sir J. Reynolds at Montreal, Sevenoaks, in the possession of the Right Hon. Earl Amherst; it is reproduced from a photograph by Mr. E. Essenhigh Corke, Sevenoaks. Amherst's pen was as sharp as his sword; he tells D'Haussonville, in answer to his gasconading, "If any injury is done to the fort, he will put every man to the sword." In pith and point the gallant Colonel's despatches remind one of the Duke of Wellington's. General Amherst's son, William Pitt, who succeeded his uncle as second Baron, served as Ambassador to China, and as Governor-General of India; he was created Earl Amherst.

Germans; troops were also despatched from Louisbourg.[1] On the 11th of September the fleet, under the command of Lord Colville,[2] and the transports with the troops, were off the narrows of St. John's.

The French, besides the strong, almost impregnable position which they occupied in St. John's with seven hundred soldiers, had a squadron consisting of the *Robuste* (74), *L'Eveille* (64), *La Garonne* (44), *La Sicorne* (30), and a bomb ketch. The whole English force was less than seven hundred.

Amherst had distinguished himself at Louisbourg and Quebec, and right gallantly he led his troops. The French attempted to stop his landing at Torbay but the light infantry, under Captain McDonnell, soon drove them back. The English then advanced rapidly on Quidi Vidi, where there was a sharp fight. The French retreated up Signal Hill with such precipitation that they left several prisoners in our hands.

Before daylight the next morning an assault was made on Signal Hill; the heroic McDonnell actually passed the sentries, and was not discovered by the enemy until they saw him

FRENCH SOLDIER, 1755.
From Winsor's N. & C. H. of America.

---

[1] The British troops were composed of companies of the—
  Royals, now the Royal Scots (Lothian Regiment).
  77th, or Montgomery's Highlanders; disbanded in 1763 [1775?].
  78th, or Fraser's Highlanders; disbanded in 1763.
  Royal Americans, afterwards 60th Rifles.

Montgomery's was raised in 1757 by A. Montgomery, afterwards Earl of Eglinton; Frazer's by Sir Simon Fraser, son of the celebrated Lord Lovat; the Royal Scots is the most ancient and one of the most distinguished of the British regiments. The French were very much afraid of these kilted warriors; no better troops could have been chosen for the work; they were thoroughly at home in the difficult country around Quidi Vidi.

[2] Alexander Lord Colville, the fourth Baron, served in the Mediterranean in 1744 as captain of the *Dursley galley*. He distinguished himself by capturing a French vessel, and destroying eight others off Genoa. In 1755 he was sent to North America; and in 1757 was present at the unsuccessful attack on Louisbourg, by Admiral Holburne, and at the taking of the same place next year. He was left on the station with temporary commodore's rank during the winter. He served under Sir C. Saunders in the expedition against Quebec in 1759. He wintered at Halifax, and was engaged in 1760 trying to intercept supplies to the French army then besieging Quebec. He continued to serve in North America during 1761 and 1762. On returning to England after the recapture of St. John's in 1762, he was made Rear-Admiral of the White. He subsequently served as commander-in-chief on the North American station. He returned to England in 1768, and died in 1770. (CHARNOCK's *Biographia Navalis.*)

at the top of the hill. Against such determined bravery the French could not stand. The gallant McDonnell was badly wounded in the moment of victory,[1] and Lieutenant Schuyler of the Royal Americans and about thirty men were killed. Under cover of a thick fog, the French admiral slipped his cables, and left the troops to their fate. On the 20th the whole French garrison surrendered.

The retaking of St. John's in 1762 is represented as one of the best conducted, most splendid, and most important of all the successes of the glorious war which resulted in the capture of Havanna and Manilla.

QUIDI VIDI FROM SIGNAL HILL.
From a drawing by Col. Skinner about 1793, B.M. MSS., etc.

The fleet and the army co-operated with singular harmony and success; both the whole plan and the subordinate parts of the expedition were conducted with consummate wisdom and heroic bravery.[2]

In order to understand the surroundings of the Treaty of Paris,[3] which concluded the war in the next year, it is necessary to explain shortly the preceding events.

---

[1] Captain McDonnell, the hero of this gallant attack, though severely wounded, was not killed; he finally recovered and returned to England. During his illness he was most carefully nursed by Mrs. Horwood, of Quidi Vidi, great grandmother of Mr. John Horwood, best known amongst us as "Protestant John, of Quidi Vidi."

[2] A very full account of these gallant actions will be found in the Appendix to this chapter taken from the "Gentleman's Magazine" of October 1762, kindly lent to me by Dr. Pilot.

[3] TREATY OF PARIS.
Article V.—It is agreed that the subjects of France shall have the liberty of fishing and drying fish on a part of the coast of the Island of Newfoundland such as is specified in Article XIII. of the Treaty of Utrecht, which article is renewed and confirmed by the

When George III. came to the throne the Seven Years' War was still in progress; Frederick the Great was gallantly fighting France and Austria—the alliance "des trois cotillons"—three petticoats—Maria Theresa Empress of Austria, Madame de Pompadour, and the Empress of Russia. The English had beaten the French at sea, in the East and West Indies, and in America; there had been one fatal miscarriage at Minorca, for which Admiral Byng was shot, according to Voltaire, "killing one admiral to encourage the others." Pitt, in order to balance the loss of Minorca, captured Belle Isle in the Bay of Biscay.

Whilst negotiations for peace were being carried on throughout 1761, Pitt suddenly found the French growing bolder in their demands; they insisted that the Spaniards, as well as themselves, should have the right of fishing in Newfoundland. He declared he would not consent to this, even if the Spaniards captured the Tower of London. Pitt found out through his agents that there was a secret treaty between France and Spain — the family compact — and that Spain was only awaiting the arrival of her treasure ships to declare war.

LORD CHATHAM.
From an engraving by Brompton.

The genius of Chatham saw through their designs, and to counteract them he resolved to immediately begin the fight with Spain. George III. opposed him, his colleagues were timid, and as he could not carry out what he believed to be the true policy for England, he resigned on the 5th October 1761.

---

present Treaty (except what relates to the Island of Cape Breton as well as to the other islands and coasts in the mouth and in the Gulf St. Lawrence),and His Britannic Majesty consents to leave to the subjects of the most Christian King the liberty of fishing in the Gulf of St. Lawrence on condition that the subjects of France do not exercise the same fishery, but at the distance of three leagues from all the coasts belonging to Great Britain as well those of the continent as those of the islands situated in the Gulf of St. Lawrence. And as to what relates to the fishery on the coast of the Island of Cape Breton, out of the said Gulf the subjects of the most Christian King shall not be permitted to exercise the said fishery but at a distance of fifteen leagues from the coast of the Island of Cape Breton, and the fishery on the coasts of Nova Scotia or Acadie, and everywhere else out of the said Gulf shall remain on the foot of former treaties.

Article VI—The King of Great Britain cedes the Islands of St. Pierre and Miquelon,

On the 2nd of January 1762, his feeble and corrupt successor, Bute, had to declare the very war against Spain which he had foreseen was inevitable. In one short year the unfortunate Spaniards saw their armies beaten in Portugal, Cuba and Manilla torn from their grasp, their commerce destroyed, and their fleets annihilated.

Both our antagonists were now clamorous for peace. Pitt had declared to Choiseul, the French minister, that he would make no second Treaty of Utrecht. On the 10th of February 1763, the Treaty of Paris was signed. It excited even more indignation in England than the former one of 1713.

The great Chatham, so ill that he had to be allowed to sit in the House, denounced, in one of his most magnificent speeches, the terms of this infamous treaty. Almost in the language of prophecy he predicted what the cession of St. Pierre and Miquelon would be to this Colony; he vehemently attacked the surrender of the right of fishery in Newfoundland to the French, and the restoration of Cuba—the pearl of the West Indies—to the Spaniards.

LORD BUTE.
From an engraving in the B.M.

Bute was openly charged in the House of Commons with bribery; the very sum, £300,000, was named, that had been paid to him by the French.[1] There can be no other explanation of this shameless surrender of territory actually in our possession.

The folly of the English Ministry in ceding the fishery and St. Pierre and Miquelon to France had nearly been eclipsed by a still more

---

in full right, to His most Christian Majesty, to serve as a shelter to the French fishermen; and his said most Christian Majesty engages not to fortify the said Islands, to erect no buildings upon them, but merely for the convenience of the fishery, and to keep upon them a guard of fifty men only, for the police.

[1] Junius, in his celebrated letter to the Duke of Bedford, does not scruple to charge his Grace, who was one of Bute's colleagues, with bribery:—"Belle Isle, Goree, Guadaloupe, St. Lucia, Martinique, The Fishery, and the Havana, are glorious monuments of your Grace's talents for negotiation. My Lord, we are too well acquainted with your pecuniary character to think it possible that so many public sacrifices should have been made without some private compensation. Your conduct carries with it an internal evidence, beyond all the legal proofs of a Court of Justice.'

outrageous proposition. A strong party in the Ministry were in favour of restoring Canada to France; it was mainly due to the strong protests of the American Colonies, through their most able diplomatist, Benjamin Franklin, that this was prevented.

The secret history of the treaty, which is now laid bare, shows the ministry in their very worst light. They voluntarily offered to restore the fishing privileges given under the Utrecht Treaty. In the commencement of the negotiations, France agreed to surrender Canada, provided she was allowed to keep Cape Breton, and to enjoy the fishery in the St. Lawrence and on the banks and Island of Newfoundland. The fortifications of Louisbourg were to be destroyed, and the harbour laid out for common use.

The English Ministry flatly refused all concession of Cape Breton, Nova Scotia, or Canada. They would give the right of fishing in Newfoundland, if the stipulations about the dismantling of the French fortifications at Dunkirk were agreed to. They might have St. Pierre on four conditions:—

" 1. That the Island should not be fortified or troops be stationed there.

" 2. That no other vessels should be admitted there even for shelter; that the harbour should be used for her own fishermen alone. [This was meant to keep out Basques and to prevent smuggling; an utterly unworkable condition.]

" 3. That the possession of St. Pierre should not be deemed to extend in any way the stipulations of the Treaty of Utrecht: that is to say—

" A loco Cap Bonavista non cupato, usque ad extremitatem ejusdem insulæ septentrionalem, indique at latus occidentale recurrendo usque ad locum Pointe Riche appellatum."

" From the place called Cape Bonavista to the northern extremity of the said Island and thence running westerly to the place denominated Point Riche."

" 4. That an English Commissary should be allowed to reside at St. Pierre, and the Commander of the British Man of War on the Newfoundland station should have liberty to visit the Island and see that these four conditions were complied with."

The French were dissatisfied. They did not want St. Pierre. They said it was too small, that it was so near Placentia, that it would not serve as a shelter, and that it would create disputes between the two nations. They would prefer Prince Edward Island or Cape Breton; finally they agreed to accept Canseau.

The British Ministry would not consent to give up Canseau. Of course New England and Nova Scotia had strong influence, and they did all in their power to prevent the French getting any settlement on the continent. Finally, when the English Ministry threw in Miquelon, they then accepted the terms offered.

The French agreed to keep up no military establishment, only a guard of fifty men to support police regulations, *and that as much as possible with so weak a force they would prevent all foreign vessels from sheltering as required.*

How childlike and bland were these French diplomatists. By the light of the present day, when St. Pierre is the common resort of all the smugglers in North America, and when on no consideration will France allow England to have a consul in their Colony, this paragraph reads very humorously.

The French agreed that their fishery in Newfoundland should be regulated by the terms of the Treaty of Utrecht; they made no objections whatever to the residence of the commissary.

As usual, the whole commercial world of England was opposed to any concession of the Newfoundland fishery to France. The commerce of England had suffered very much from the French navy and the privateers of Dunkirk. They knew that the fishery was a great source of wealth to their enemy, and the chief nursery for her seamen; on strong national, as well as commercial grounds, they sternly opposed the concession. The Common Council of London, as representing the whole mercantile interest of Great Britain, transmitted to the House of Commons peremptory instructions to the city members. The Newfoundland fishery, it was said, was worth more than all Canada. They declared " that the sole and exclusive right of fishing in the American seas should be reserved to the subjects of the British Crown." All the ablest and most patriotic Englishmen of the day were opposed to the fishery clauses of the treaty; the pamphlets and periodicals of the time are full of denunciations of Bute. The literature on the subject is fuller and far more fierce than the famous opposition to the Treaty of Utrecht; the scurrilous Wilkes, and the unscrupulous Churchill, abused and caricatured the authors of the treaty in every mood and tense of objurgation.

Notwithstanding all these attacks and all the intelligent opposition, the treaty was carried by the immense majority of three hundred and nineteen against sixty-five in the corrupt House of Commons. All Pitt's splendid eloquence was wasted on members that were bribed and bought by the ministry. Chatham said, in his great philippic against Lord Bute, that England's exclusive right to the fishery and to the possession of St. Pierre and Miquelon was an object worthy to be contested by the extremity of war.

Under the governorship of Lord Rodney, 1749, begin a series of records preserved in the Colonial Secretary's Office. Through the courtesy of the Hon. Robert Bond, I have been allowed to peruse them; they make reference to other record books, which are either mislaid or were removed to England, or destroyed in the French invasion. They are not quite complete, but for the period over which they extend are an excellent guide to our local history.

Amongst the names in these books, distinguished amongst many celebrities, is that of Thomas Graves, R.N., Captain of H.M.S. *Antelope*. One cannot peruse these musty old papers without forming pictures in the mind's eye of the various worthies whose acts are recorded in these gubernatorial diaries. I must confess to a strange liking for this worthy hero; as I read his crabbed old writing I fancy him presiding with dignity in the Placentia court house, then held in a dingy room in Thomas Kennedy's house.

The cool, methodical way in which he sets to work to defend the Colony, his admirable arrangements, his lucid judgments, his entire freedom from the bigotry of the age, mark the high qualities of one who, in an age of naval heroes, was distinguished for his undaunted courage and skill. His fight with the French admiral largely contributed to Lord Howe's victory on the memorable first of June 1794. This terrible duel is one of the most stirring passages in English naval history. For his gallantry he was created Lord Graves.

LORD GRAVES.
From an engraving after Northcote.

Both before and after the peace he had difficult and arduous work, settling claims arising out of the war—restoring property plundered from the inhabitants. Many had taken advantage of the war to rob their merchants; Graves disposed of all these various questions promptly and fairly. I gather from these records that whilst the French held St. John's from the 27th of June until the 20th of September following, the English remained in possession of the other fortified places. Carbonear Island, however, for the only time in our history, was captured and the fortifications destroyed. Placentia, Ferryland, Carbonear, and Bay Bulls were peaceably occupied by part of Colonel Amherst's forces. Mr. Nathaniel Brooks of Bay Bulls, Mr. Robert Carter of Ferryland, and Mr. Charles Garland, the Harbour Grace magistrate, furnished supplies to Carbonear, Ferryland, and Bay Bulls. These fine old merchants not only supplied the garrisons, but were most energetic in getting men, providing boats, and fitting out small vessels to aid in the defence of the Colony.

Besides the St. John's records, books were kept at Placentia, Ferryland, Harbour Grace, &c., containing the judgments of the surrogate courts. The most amusing are the papers from Placentia, under Robert Edgecumbe and Haddock, justices of the peace. Their worships were not contented with administering the law after an erratic fashion of their own, taxation even did not satisfy their lust for power—they determined the prices at which goods should be sold to the fishermen. In these records is a copy of an agreement made by their orders between Simon Honeyburn, on behalf of William Turner, Little Placentia, and his planters :—

"Bread and flour at 20/- per cwt. except when bought in Little Placentia then to be 22/-, Pork £3. 10/- per brl., Spanish Salt 16/- per hhd., Soap and Candles 8d. per lb., Rum 4/6 per gall., boots 25/- per pair, Leather 3/- per lb., Powder 2/- per lb., Tobacco 9d. per lb., Molasses 4/- per gall. 15 % to be allowed on all slops supplied to their men; one-third of balance to be paid in Bills of Exchange. Little Placentia 8th Oct. 1761."

After settling the prices the court further ordered that no fisherman was to deliver his fish to the supplying merchant until he received his winter's supplies.

Honeyburn was evidently litigious and obstinate; he figures largely in the courts. He had a dispute with a spirited Irishman named Lawrence Reilly, who had struck him. Reilly charged Honeyburn with keeping his wages back and charging him twenty-four shillings for neglect of duty. The magistrates ordered Reilly to ask Honeyburn's pardon before the public court; he refused in a very emphatic manner, whereupon he was sentenced "to be confined for twenty-four hours in the black hole of the guard-house." William Collins was charged by John Green, his servant, with having beaten and turned him away; Collins was ordered to pay his servant's passage home "in order that the place may not be troubled with vagabonds." Collins evidently had the ear of the court. The reign of these burlesque justices came to an untimely end in 1764. They were summarily dismissed by Sir Hugh Palliser with a stinging reprimand, and Jervis Grossard, Richard Braithwaite, and William Bennett reigned in their stead.

In 1762 the first custom house came into existence, and the first collector, Mr. Hamilton, was appointed; he was under the control of the department in Boston, Mass., then the capital of the British North American Colonies. The West Country merchants were so reluctant to pay him any fees that, after trying to live there for one season, he threw up the post in disgust. He was succeeded the next year by a Scotchman, Alexander Dunn, who appears to have been made of sterner stuff; either his ominous name, steady perseverance, or better defined legal rights, enabled him to get in the fees.

In 1763 the survey of the Island was commenced by the immortal navigator, Cook. He had been employed as master in the navy at the siege of Louisbourg; with great gallantry, in face of the enemy's shot and shell, he had sounded and surveyed the St. Lawrence, and piloted the fleet in Wolfe's last fight. Cook was master of the *Northumberland* in Lord Colville's squadron in 1762, and had also been in Newfoundland under Governor Graves. He returned in 1764 with Sir Hugh Palliser, who highly appreciated his scientific ability and sterling qualities. Cook was engaged in the arduous work of surveying for four years, until 1767.

CAPTAIN COOK.
From an engraving by Hogg.

His account of an eclipse of the sun, seen at Burgeo, was published in the "Philosophical Transactions," and added greatly to his reputation as a skilled scientist; at Burgeo Islands, and several other places on the Newfoundland coast, his survey marks are still pointed out.

The great navigator, unlike his superior officer, Palliser, took a most hopeful view, both of the resources and the future of Newfoundland. He told his friends of the great mineral wealth of the Island, especially of the supply of coal; on what grounds he based this latter statement we are not informed; however, he declared that he had personally seen the coal, probably on the west coast, where it has been long known to exist.

To this day Cook's chart of our island is noted for its minute accuracy; it shows the indomitable perseverance and genius of the man who, from the very lowest origin, a poor cabin boy, solely by his own exertions, rose to the rank of captain in the Navy, and the highest

COOK'S MAP.[1]

position in his age as a navigator, nautical astronomer, and scientific observer.

[1] For convenience of reproduction the small copy of Cook's map given by Major Holland has been used. This map shows what was known of the interior prior to 1800.

In 1764 Admiral Graves was succeeded by Sir Hugh Palliser,[1] who was afterwards brought into notoriety by his charge against Admiral Keppel, and the subsequent court-martials held upon both accuser and accused. Public feeling was undoubtedly in favour of the gallant Keppel, and deservedly so.

One of the first duties of the new Governor was in connexion with the treaty of the previous year. He was instructed by the home government to issue the following proclamation. It begins with reciting the Treaty of Utrecht, enjoining:—

"1. That there should be no distinction or interruption given to the subjects of France in injoyment of the Fishery allowed them by the stipulations of the Treaties.

"2. The Harbor Admirals and all officers were to take care that the said subjects of France be permitted and allowed in common with the king's subjects to choose their stations during the Fishery season according as they shall respectively arrive in the Harbors, and occupy such a space of Beach as shall be proportioned to their number of boats, as long as the said subjects of France shall be actually employed in fishing and drying of fish. In case of dispute the Captains of H.M.'s ships and Harbor Admirals were to proceed with the strictest justice and report their proceedings; the subject matter to be taken in writing and transmitted by the admirals duly authenticated to the Commander in Chief or to the Governor, to be confirmed or annulled as justice may require.

"3. The officers were not upon any pretence whatever to interfere in disputes which might arise between French subjects.

"4. The French were not to be disturbed in their persons, properties and effects, carrying or fishing within the limits aforesaid according to the treaties.

---

[1] Palliser was born in Yorkshire in 1722; he was sent at an early age to sea, under the care of a relation; became a lieutenant in 1742, and was at the action off Toulon in 1744. He commanded the *Weazle* sloop in 1746, and was promoted for capturing four French privateers off Beachy Head. He was wounded by an accidental discharge of fire-arms at Dominica, and became ever after lame in the left leg, having a perpetual and sometimes very excruciating pain; this wound eventually caused his death. While serving in Scotland he made many enemies, and being enticed on shore, was arrested and imprisoned in the Tolbooth for some days, until he was released by the Lords of Session. He went with Keppel to Virginia in 1755. By taking a more southerly course his men arrived in good health, while Keppel's were all invalided. He was at the capture of Quebec in 1759; he arrived too late to take part in the recapture of St. John's in 1762. On account of his spirited policy while Governor of Newfoundland, the French ambassador presented many memorials against him, but he was fully supported by the English ministry. In 1770 he was Controller of the Navy, and 1773 was created a baronet. In 1774 he represented Scarborough in Parliament; and in 1775 received his flag. In 1775 he was lieutenant-general of marines; and Vice-Admiral of the Blue in 1778. The dispute between Keppel and Palliser (who had been great personal friends), owing to the indecisive action of the 27th July 1778, was connected partly with differences of opinion on the political aspect of the American war. During the events succeeding the court-martial which he demanded on Keppel and himself, he resigned his appointments, but was subsequently made Governor of Greenwich Hospital. He again entered Parliament, and sat for Huntingdon. He died Admiral of the White in 1796. There is a monument to him in Chalfont St. Giles Church, Bucks, where he was interred. His life was written by R. M. Hunt in 1844. (CHARNOCK's *Biographia Navalis*.)

"5. His Majesty having been informed that boats left in the harbors the winter before by the French were burnt or destroyed; H.M.'s subjects are enjoined to desist from such practices.

"6. These Rules to be put up in some conspicuous place in every harbor."

Palliser has been highly praised in our histories; in some respects he is entitled to our gratitude; the bounty for the fishery in the Act 15 Geo. III. cap. xxxi.—Palliser's Act—is undoubtedly due to his exertions. He defined the French rights under the Treaty of Paris honestly and clearly. According to his lights, he was an excellent Governor—in labours incessant, the very spirit of unrest, remarkably clear-headed, but very dictatorial.

The Governor had only one great fault; beyond his own circumscribed vision he could see no horizon; he had no faith, no hope, no future for the Colony; the one narrow insular idea of the age pervaded his official mind, that it should be a fishing colony, used for one great purpose only in his eyes, supplying men for the Navy. With this aim every other consideration, every attempt to promote settlement, cultivation, and civilisation, must be ruthlessly swept aside. On all who opposed his views he poured out the vials of his wrath. He could see clearly enough that settlement could not be prevented, so he abused the Colony and the colonist. No ruler since the days of Charles II. hated the country he was set over more bitterly than Sir Hugh Palliser.

SIR H. PALLISER.
From an engraving by Orme.

The statement that he gave the servant by this Act a first claim on the fish for his wages, is altogether erroneous. It was an ancient custom of the fishery, proved over and over again; it is really founded on the principle of lien, which dates back to the very foundation of English law.

Much of Palliser's usefulness as a Governor was undoubtedly due to his able secretary, Jno. Horsenaill, whose beautiful writing and well-expressed letters are contained in our records during four years. Horsenaill must have been either an original genius, or else have been well trained; all the documents in his writing are distinguished for precision, clearness, and conciseness.

The Treaty of Paris, which Palliser was to put in force, extinguished the last hopes of the Basques to participate in the Newfoundland fishery; by Article XVIII. Spain "for ever relinquished all claims and pretensions to a right of fishing on the Island." In the brief war of 1763 the Spaniards had procured from His Holiness full liberty to eat meat instead of Newfoundland fish; the order, however, seems to have had small effect, the export of our staple commodity for that year being as large as in former years. Dried cod is one of the most convenient, portable, and, when nicely cooked, one of the most succulent articles of food for a warm country; it always has been, and always will be, a favourite dish in Spain, Italy, Portugal, Brazil, and the West Indies. In 1765 an ingenious attempt was made to get over the English law by sending out Basque vessels with English names, such as the *Bilbao Merchant*, with an English master and an Anglo-Spanish crew. The Governor allowed them to proceed to the banks.

Palliser's interpretation of the treaties is very clear and distinct. Whilst it was a concurrent fishery between the two nations, the control and regulation remained entirely in the hands of the English authorities. Great Britain, owning the territory and being the sovereign power, alone had authority to exercise coercive jurisdiction; under no circumstances were the French allowed to take the law into their own hands.

Palliser had no scruple or hesitation in vigorously enforcing the English view of the treaty.[1] Some Frenchmen captured a whale at

---

[1] "BY HIS EXCELLENCY HUGH PALLISER, &c., &c.

"Whereas by the proceedings had before the Judge of the Vice-Admiralty Court here relating to a French snow, named *Le Montaran*, of Sables D'Olonne, arrested for being employed on a trading voyage upon that part of the coast of Newfoundland where by treaties the French are allowed to fish but not to trade, it appears by evidence on oath, as follows:

"That so soon as the said snow arrived on the coast, which was not till the 13th July, the person named Andrew Colenet, who has charge of the cargo and the management of the voyage, went on shore at Engelie, and offered to sell to the inhabitants sundry merchandize (prohibited in this country) for fish, and this is in this part owned by . . . . . . the said Colenet, on his examination, pleading in excuse that he did not know it was contrary to the laws of the country.

"It also appears by the ship's papers and the examinations that she had aboard (exclusive of the provisions, necessaries, and fishing utensils for the voyage) merchandize prohibited in this country, and which was offered as above for sale by the said Colenet, though the said merchandize is pretended to be consigned to South America.

"It also appears by a written agreement between the said Colenet and the owners of the said snow (which writing the said Colenet acknowledged to be his hand), that he was authorised by them to trade on the coast of Newfoundland on their account, for fish and other merchandize.

"After duly considering all the proofs and circumstances attending this case, and finding that this vessel was actually employed trading as well as on a fishing voyage, I have examined the several laws relating to the trade of His Majesty's plantations, and considered the treaties subsisting between the two Crowns, and find that by the several laws no foreign ship or vessel can, on any pretence whatever, resort to or carry on any commerce to, from, or in any of His Majesty's plantations,

Great Orange Harbour, but it was taken from them and sold. Others who remained behind after the 20th of September to cut wood and build boats, were seized and sent to France. His ships captured English and American smugglers in St. Peter's Roads, confiscated their vessels and cargoes, and banished them. He made one Frenchman, who had put a deck on his fishing boat, take it out; and another, who had built a small vessel, was compelled to pull her to pieces. Frenchmen and their vessels caught on the Newfoundland shore were promptly seized, the ship confiscated, and the owners landed at St. Pierre. On the other hand, English subjects who improperly interfered with Frenchmen were dealt with severely.

John Duneen, evidently an Irishman, had opposed Forterie, a Frenchman, in the possession of a room at Great St. Julien's. The Frenchman's vessel having been the first to arrive, he was therefore entitled to first choice of fishing places. Duneen and all concerned were to be arrested and brought before the Governor, then to be put on board a man-of-war and sent home, and if they ever returned to Newfoundland they were to be arrested again, whipped, and banished. I think the bold Duneen was never caught, and this cruel sentence was only so much *brutum fulmen*.

In the time of the vigorous Sir Hugh there was no truckling to France; an English naval officer had no fear then of offending a Gallic admiral. We have a description, in 1762, of the treaty and its interpretation from a popular French point of view in a pamphlet freely circulated from Paris, and copied into the "Scots Magazine" of December of that year, when the terms of peace were known:—

"When we consider the vile concessions made of our territories, rights and possessions, which shall we most wonder at—the ambition and arrogance of the British ministry, or the pusillanimity, or perhaps open treachery, of our own. Let us begin with what relates to the very valuable fishery in the North American seas. In the first place, then, we have given up Isle Royale, or Cape Breton, to regain which, at the last peace, we relinquished all Flanders and every conquest in Europe.

"In the next place, we have abandoned all the most valuable coasts from whence the dry cod was usually got.

"By the second article of the Preliminaries, France cedes to Great Britain, besides Cape Breton, all the other Islands in the Gulf and River of St. Lawrence without restriction; and by the third article we are excluded from fishing within three leagues of any of their coasts. The consequences of these cessions are obvious. We have nothing left us but a *precarious right*, subject to cavil and insult, to the '*morue verte*,' [literally green fish], a commodity not marketable in

but by the treaties the subjects of France are allowed to resort to a certain part of the coast of Newfoundland to fish, and to land and dry their fish during the fishing season; therefore, whilst they employ themselves in the business of fishing only, they are *under His Majesty's protection* from any molestation or hindrence therein."

1 p. 2729.

Portugal, Spain or Italy, but only fit for our own home consumption. Ever since the happy Treaty of Utrecht France has enjoyed great advantages in the dry cod fishery. At the breaking out of *this* war we had in the Bay of Fundy, in Acadia, in Cape Breton, in St. John's (P. E. Island), Great Gaspe, and other places in the Gulf, above 16,000 fishermen, who carried on most successfully in shoal water the *pêche sédentaire*—'shore fishery.' Now all this is in the hands of the British; all our settlements are unpeopled. From the single island of St. John's (P. E. I.) Admiral Boscawen removed 5,000 inhabitants. What, then, is left to France? Nothing but the North coast from Cape Riche to Cape Bonavista, with liberty to land and erect stages for a short season, so that we must carry and recarry both our fish and fishermen, whilst the British, settled on the spot, and carrying on the *pêche sédentaire*, will forestall us and undersell us in every market in the Mediterranean. Miquelon and St. Peters, two barren rocks indeed, are to be ours; yet even for them we have pledged the Royal Word, engaging not to erect in them any fortifications, so that even they, with their guard of fifty men for the police, will always be at the mercy of the British."

BEOTHICS OF THE INTERIOR.
From an engraving after a drawing by Cartwright.

Palliser's interpretation admits of no doubt. It was held to be a concurrent fishery in which all disputes were to be decided by English authorities alone. It only included a cod fishery, and gave no right whatever to the French to catch salmon, to trade or traffic; they were only to fish for codfish, and dry them on land; they were not even permitted to cut spars or to build boats.

This same treaty is still in operation; it controls to-day the French fishery on the treaty shore of Newfoundland. Beyond the alteration of coast-line from Cape St. John to Cape Ray, in place of Bonavista and Point Riche, and the declaration of King George in 1783 that the English should not interrupt the French by their competition, this old international difficulty stands precisely on the same ground as it did in 1763.

The Governor was directed by the authorities at home to give his special attention to the prevention of smuggling. In 1764, the Act had been passed which caused such disturbance in New England; it armed the Custom House authorities with new powers of seizure, arrest, &c., and directly gave a bounty to the Governor and informer in all such cases, His Excellency getting one-third of the plunder; this accounts for Palliser's abnormal activity in searching out illicit traders.[1]

The Newfoundland Government, in addition, had special instructions to look after the New Englanders, well known for their smuggling proclivities. No doubt Sir Hugh gave them a great deal of trouble, but they beat him, as they had beaten all the Custom House officers in America; they had an invincible prejudice and objection to the payment of duties of any kind to King George, and they lied like

JOHN CARTWRIGHT.
From an engraving after Hoppner.

---

[1] BY HIS EXCELLENCY HUGH PALLISER, &c., GOVERNOR.

"Mr. Thos. Stout, master of the *Good Intent* brigg, being convicted before me of having carryd in the said brigg sixty fishermen and seamen from this countrey to the continent of America, contrary to the king's express commands published the last year:

"For this disobedience and contempt of His Maj's. commands, I hereby order and direct the said Thomas Stout to pay into the hands of His Majesty's Justices of the Peace at St. John's the sum of sixty pounds, which sum of sixty pounds to be laid out in payment for the passages of such poor needy people to Britain or Ireland as shall be ordered by me or the said justices, and till the said sum of sixty pounds is paid the said brigantine is not to be permitted to go out of the harbour. And whereas William Cocking hath complained that two of the men carried away by the said Stout were in his debt, one of them in the sum of £6 6s. 0d., the other £6 7s. 9d. I hereby order and direct the said Stout to pay to William Cocking the said sums of £6 6s. 0d. and £6 7s. 9d. when Cocking swears to the said debts, over and above the aforementioned fine of sixty pounds. Given at St. John's, 16th Sept. 1765.

By command of HUGH PALLISER.
 His Excellency,
  Jno Horsnaill."

troopers. The following letter is the only one that I can find about this time relating to American smugglers:—

"SIR, Great St. Lawrence Harbr. 8 July 1765.

I have sent to St. John's three New England schooners seized by Lieut. A. Dickson, Commander of Her Majestys snow *Egmont* in St. Pierres Road. I desire you will proceed against them in Court according to law, and immediately on receipt of this to cause the proper notice to be put up of the time allowed for claims to be put in, in order to their being sold as soon as possible and most for the benefit of the seizures.

"Such vessels are wanted for the fishery . . . . The vessels are the *Industrious Pretence* [good name for a smuggler] belonging to Cape Ann, the *Robin Hood* belonging to the same place, and the *Industry* of Marblehead."

There must have been some flaw in the proceedings, as they never came to anything. The New Englanders found some way to get their vessels out of the rapacious clutches of the Admiralty Court and the Governor. There is not even a suggestion in this letter that the traders were either selling or purchasing anything; they declared they had gone in to water, which was a transparent fiction.

Governor Palliser took a great interest in Labrador and Anticosti, which had been annexed to his Government in 1763; he encouraged the salmon fishery, and laid down rules for the regulation of the cod fishery in Labrador as a ship fishery. His Excellency was the first to establish friendly relations with the Eskimos and Mountaineer Indians; one of his proclamations threatens the most severe punishments against the French, whom he declares did last year—

"Invite over to Quirpont the savages named Caralits and Esquemeaux's and had a considerable trade with them, and used many infamous, wicked, savage arts to prejudice those ignorant barbarous people against the English nation."

Sir Hugh made a treaty with the Labrador Indians. In his dealings with the savages[1][2] and in looking after the interests of the fishermen he

---

[1] Amongst the various attempts to open up friendly intercourse with the Red Indians, perhaps the most remarkable is the story told by Anspach of the adventures of a shipmaster, Scott. In 1762 he landed with another master and a strong crew at Exploits, and built a kind of fort. Some days after, a party of Indians appeared; they made a full stop, and would not come nearer; Scott then proposed to go and meet them; they proceeded with part of the crew unarmed. Scott went up to them, mixed with them, and shook hands; suddenly an old Indian, in pretended friendship, put his arm around Scott's neck, at the same instant another Indian stabbed him in the back; a shower of arrows fired at the party killed the other master and four of the crew; the remainder fled to their vessel, and brought one dead man to St. John's, with the arrows sticking in his body. Exactly the same conduct was shown to Buchan's expedition later. Whatever may be said about the Beothics, there can be no doubt they were a most bloodthirsty, treacherous race.

[2] Lieutenant John Cartwright, R.N., is mentioned several times as Sir Hugh Palliser's surrogate for Trinity and Conception Bays. He was sent in 1768 to the Exploits with a proclamation to protect the Red Indians, whom, however, he did not succeed in meeting, though they had only recently deserted some of the camps which he passed. On his return he wrote an interesting account of the Indian remains which he had inspected;

INCREASE OF THE FISHERY.

was kind, humane, and considerate; for French aggressors, for smuggling New Englanders, and for the riotous Irishmen, he seems to have been full of all the narrow prejudice of the age. He was specially distinguished for his barbarous treatment of Roman Catholic Irishmen; he would not allow any two of them to live in one dwelling, and none were permitted to keep public-houses.

During Palliser's reign of four years, Newfoundland increased rapidly in trade and population. In his report of 1765 he gives the resident population as follows:—

" Men	9,976
Women	1,645
Children	3,863
	15,484
Fishermen employed exclusive of Inhabitants	9,152
Total	24,636 "

FRENCH TRADING WITH ESQUIMAUX.
From Potherie's Histoire, 1722.

this has been printed by his niece, as an appendix to the biography. Cartwright was very strenuous in his efforts to protect the poor Irish in Conception Bay, and was generous in relieving their distress. He has often been confused with his cousin Major George Cartwright (who accompanied him on his expedition to the Exploits), the founder of Cartwright, Labrador, and the author of a long and most peculiar diary of his sixteen years' experience on the coast.

John Cartwright afterwards rose to great distinction; he took a prominent part in the discussion of all the great questions of the day, American independence, the supply of timber for the navy, the threatened French invasion, &c., and, as a Member of Parliament, supported the Reform Bill. A statue was erected to his memory in Burton Crescent, London. Cartwright was the first European who visited Red Indian Lake.

The catches of the English fishermen during the four years of his government were:—

	1764.	1765.	1766.	1767.
Quintals	561,310	532,512	559,985	553,310

In 1765 he estimates the French resident population of St. Pierre and Miquelon at nearly sixteen hundred, the whole number of men employed in the French Newfoundland fishery at nearly fifteen thousand, and their catch at half a million quintals.

In reading our local records it is remarkable that whilst there was not a single lawyer in the Colony, the legal jargon was as copious, complicated, and absurd as anything to be found in the pages of "Chitty on Pleadings." Out of many examples I select one, the case against William Kitchen, a drunken soldier, for stealing a lamb of Mr. John Stripling's "grazing on the *Barons* of St. John's."

"The Jurors of our Sovereign Lord the King upon oath present William Kitchen for that he did feloniously kill and bear off a certain lamb being the property of Mr. John Stripling and that the said William Kitchen of St. John's, a soldier, not having God before his eyes but moved and seduced by the instigation of the devil on . . . . did feloniously of his forethought and mallice seize and kill a lamb the property of Mr. John Stripling grazing on the Barons of St. John's, and the said William Kitchen did with a knife skin and bear away the said lamb . . . . The sentence of the Court is as follows:

"That you William Kitchen be returned to the gaol from whence you came and there remain till tomorrow at ten o'clock in the forenoon, when, before the Court House of St. John's, you receive punishment of being burnt in your right hand with a hott iron marked with the letter R, your goods and chattels forfeited, and *after paying the charge of the Court* be set at liberty. Then the Court was adjourned during the Governor's stay in the Island.

"MICHAEL GILL.
"EDWARD LANGMAN, &c."

This mild sentence is probably due to the influence of Parson Langman, as sheep stealing was punishable by hanging in those days.

It is only fair to the character of Sir Hugh to give the reverse of the shield, an example of his humanity and care in the protection of a poor fisherman from extortion and bad treatment. I therefore append his short judgment in the case of Fling v. Cochran, an action for assault in which Fling injured Cochran in the hand; the amusing part of these proceedings is the high-handed way in which His Excellency takes the case out of the hands of Gill and Langman, and deals with it himself:—

"On a case of quarrel between James Cochran and James Fling it apearing James Fling was the first agresser, I therefore hereby order and direct that he shall be alowed nothing for his loss of wages and time. The two doctors for their

exorbitant charge on account of a poor man shall have nothing, and Joseph Cochran to pay £6. 10. 0. for Fling's maintenance during the cure of his head, also £3. 19. 0. for his passage home.

"Given at St. John's 27th September 1765.

"By command of His Excellency,   "HUGH PALLISER.

"JNO HORSENAILL."

Commodore Palliser's administration lasted for the unusual period of four years; his records are the longest and by far the most complete; he was an admirable man of business—orderly, methodical, and industrious. He had set his heart on making his newly-acquired territory of Labrador, Anticosti, and the Magdalen Islands, into a great fishery, governed by the Rules of William's Act. His first object was to build a fort at Port Pitt, Chateau Bay; this he carried out with his accustomed energy. Visiting all the places within his territory both in Newfoundland and Labrador, he encountered obstacles and difficulties from the resident population, from the French, the French Canadians, but most of all from the American whalers. In a letter to Governor Bernard of Massachusetts, 7th August 1766, he states:—

FORT YORK, LABRADOR.

"The great trouble and difficulty I meet with in keeping good order amongst the fishers in a part of this government (Labrador) is occasioned chiefly by a number of disorderly people from your Province. You will I hope excuse me for giving you this trouble, to beg you will permit the enclosed advertisement to be put up in the Towns within your Government where the vessels employed in the whale fishery mostly belong; which I apprehend will greatly facilitate my proceedings in the execution of the King's orders for the benefit of H.M. subjects carrying on the fishery within this Government.

"The last year whilst a tribe of four to five hundred of the Esquemeaux's savages were with me at Pitt's Harbour (and by means of interpreters) I made a peace with them and sent them away extremely well satisfied, without the least offensive thing happening.

"I am well informed some New England vessels contrary to the orders I have published went to the Northward, and robbed, plundered, and murdered some of their old men, women and children, who they left at home, so I expect some mischief will happen this year; revenge being their declared principle.

"I am Your Excellencies
"Most obt. & humble servant
"HUGH PALLISER.

"P.S.—If you think proper to take any other method properer than what is above proposed for the reformation of those concerned I shall be extreamly obliged to you, for the complaints I have of the mischiefs committed by them are many great and barbarous."

The result of Sir Hugh's abnormal activity, and the rules he promulgated for his successors, was to stir up a determined hostility on the part of many Canadians and Englishmen who had fixed posts and settled property at Labrador, which were all to be destroyed under the Fishing Admiral rules; with the aid of the New Englanders they persistently resisted the Newfoundland Government, until at last the Home authorities restored Labrador to Canada, and reversed all Palliser's regulations in 1774 by the Quebec Act, 14 Geo. III. Cap. lxxxiii.

Coming nearer home Palliser found trouble in the garrisons of St. John's and Placentia; Captain McDonald and his officers were at open war, half the soldiers at Placentia had deserted; they were short of beds, bedding, and clothing; both garrisons seem to have been badly paid, and worse provided. Palliser put an end to many abuses, and he pulled down a number of houses that had been built around Fort William which were looked upon by officers and soldiers as their private property. On the 3rd of September 1766 he makes this order:—

"The house owned by Mr. William Newman standing under the Fort having been built by a soldier of the former garrison by sufferance of his commanding officer and pretended to be sold by the soldier in payment of debts contracted for liquor and other unjustifiable dealings—Notice is given to Mr. Wm. Newman to take down the said house or he may dispose of the materials thereof. . . Michael Gill's house built also by sufferance may remain only during Gill's lifetime; no liquor to be sold there. . . . . . . Wood's house also built by sufferance may remain; no liquor to be sold there; to remain only during Wood's lifetime, at his death to be pulled down."

These records show there was much grumbling against Alexander Dunn, the collector, about his fees, which were certainly heavy. There were several New England vessels seized for having rum on board without certificates or cockets; they mostly gave bonds from their agents in St. John's, and always appear to have got off without penalty; they evidently knew how to manage the collectors of the Georgian era, as in nearly every case of theirs the Custom House officials reported favourable and mitigating circumstances.

The whole New England trade with the Colony was one vast smuggle. Palliser estimates it in 1765 at "£102,304 stg., carried in one hundred and forty-two vessels, nine-tenths of which is paid for in Bills of Exchange on England." The real amount was at least two hundred thousand pounds; the year before the Revolution it was three hundred thousand pounds, or probably nearer four hundred thousand. During Palliser's and Byron's administrations a commercial war had begun between England and America; the Molasses Act commenced the fray in New England; the narrow commercial policy of England kept fanning the flame, until it culminated in the Stamp Act. Some regulations of the English Government indicate the absurd lengths to which they carried their trade laws; they stopped coal-mining in Nova Scotia, fearing that it would interfere with English coal and encourage provincial manufactures; they were always jealous of colonial home-spun woollen and coarse linen cloths. Palliser's letters show the strong prejudice that existed against New England long before the revolutionary war.

Nothing appeals more to the higher sentiments, the poetic feeling that is implanted in us, than the self-sacrificing devotion of a religious community to its worship and its ministers, typified amongst us by the warm attachment of the Irish to the poor hunted and silenced priests who ministered to their spiritual needs in Newfoundland. The following official correspondence shows how the English colonial rulers appreciated the religious sentiments of the poor French exiles and the Indians of Acadia. Sober history, it must be admitted, takes some of the beautiful bloom off Grand Pré and Evangeline.[1]

THE LORD'S PRAYER, WRITTEN BY NEWFOUNDLAND MIC MACS.
B.M., Add. MSS., 11,638.

"LIEUT.-GOVERNOR OF NOVA SCOTIA TO GOVERNOR PALLISER.

"SIR, Halifax, Nova Scotia, 11 Sep. 1766.

"I have the honour to forward to Your Excellency a packet from the Secretary of State's office which came to me enclosed the 9th inst.

"I think it necessary to acquaint Your Excellency that last summer the greatest part of the Indians of this Province assembled on the Isle of Breton, and by the flying reports which were spread by them, together with an unusual deportment to some of the neighbouring settlements, the people were much alarmed; however by

---

[1] See "The true story of Evangeline," by Rev. T. B. Stephenson, D.D., in the *Sunday Magazine*, November 1893.

sending some gentlemen amongst the savages they were prevailed on to disperse—this summer they have also assembled again, although they behaved very peaceable; but as I find that Holy Water, Relicts, Books and other articles that relate to the superstition of the Romish religion are furnished to them, it is an evident proof they find means to hold communication with the Islands of St. Peter's and Miquelon, if they do not even receive from thence priests to officiate amongst them, which may in time prove of very ill consequence to this young province, as our settlements are very straggling and defenceless. I must therefore entreat your Excellency to give directions to the several cruisers under your command which may be stationed near these Islands to prevent as much as possible all communication between the savages and Acadians [or neutral French] of this Province with the French at St. Peter's or even with the Island of Newfoundland and that if any extraordinary occurrence should happen I may be informed of it.

"MICHAEL FRANCKLIN."

To the fly thus cast by the Nova Scotian Governor, the Ultra-Protestant Palliser rose at once. In one respect, no doubt, they were right; the French have ever been inflated with the idea of recovering their lost empire in America, and St. Pierre has always been a thorn in our side, but to accomplish their great design France would need better and stronger allies than the Mic Macs and the poor simple Acadians. Neither Palliser nor Francklin seemed to realise their attachment to the clergy, which was signally manifested later on, when the whole body of Acadians left Miquelon, with their good curé, for the Magdalen Islands, sooner than subscribe to the hated doctrines of the Revolution. Palliser's reply is a smart reprimand to his fellow governor :—

"GOVERNOR PALLISER to the HON. MICHAEL FRANCKLIN Lieut.-Governor of Nova Scotia.

"SIR, St. Johns 16 Oct. 1766.

"Two days ago I had the honour to receive your letter of the 11th Sepr. and with it a packet from the Secretary of State's office which you was pleased to forward to me.

"The information you give me of the motives and behaviour of the Nova Scotia Indians is somewhat alarming and seem to require attention, but I confess it is nothing more than I have expected from the banefull effects of a communication with the French.

"As soon as I came to this Government I perceived the extensive views of France in contending for these two insignificant Islands (as they were called) St. Pierre and Miquelon and that the uses for which they demanded them was the least part of their view, that of communicating with and preserving their influence over the bigoted savages and the rebellious and more dangerous Acadians was a more important part of their object.

"I did not fail to inform H.M. Ministers of my apprehensions of this, and that this part of H.M. Dominions would thereby be endangered and the fishery and trade of his subjects here be greatly prejudiced as well as the New Colonies on the Continent be disturbed. The occurrences since that time have proved those apprehensions to be well founded. . . . The intercourse you complain of between these people and the French is carried on by *your* clandestine traders with these Islands from the Island Breton and especially Miganich, likewise by passports granted to the Indians. Last year the Chief, John Peqidawa-Oalaut, with two hundred men returned with passes from the Secretary's office in Halifax.

"Miquelon is full of Acadians, who have come there with passes from different officers in your Government. . . I shall leave two ships all the winter to drive away the Indians and keep the French off."

Two important events in the religious history of the Colony occurred during Sir Hugh's government—the commencement of the Moravian Mission at Labrador, and the first introduction of Wesleyanism into the island by the Rev. Lawrence Coughlan, a Church of England clergyman sent out by the S.P.G. in 1765. Coughlan was a devoted follower of John Wesley, whose method he followed, and in whose footsteps he endeavoured to tread. The great founder of Methodism lived and died a member of the Church of England, and there is nothing at all incongruous in the first Wesleyan in the Colony being an Episcopalian; the new body was practically driven out of the Church and compelled to form themselves into a separate society.

The Rev. Lawrence Coughlan, an Irishman, a most earnest man, like most enthusiasts in a good cause, was persecuted, but worse still, was not paid his legal salary; it is recorded that, in November 1765, a bond was signed by "the principal inhabitants of Harbour Grace, "Musquito, and Carbonier, in Conception Bay, for the rest of the "inhabitants of the Bay, by which they agreed to cheerfully contribute "annually the full sum of £100." Governor Byron, on the 18th July 1770, thus adjudicated upon this bond :—

"Whereas I am informed that the Revd. Mr. Coughlan is the Minister so procured and residing amongst you, and that, so far from your paying him cheerfully the stipend aforesaid, great numbers of you have refused to contribute towards it, insomuch that he is annually much in arrear to the disgrace of religion and dishonor of yourselves: I do therefore desire and command you and every one of you as aforesaid to pay him what sums are in arrear, and that you also comply with your said agreement in paying him annually his sallary of £100, every one of you according to your abilities."

Commodore Byron appointed Coughlan a justice of the peace for Harbour Grace, and was his firm friend and supporter until the last year of his government. The Harbour Grace merchants, finding that they were obliged to pay the salary, petitioned the Governor against him as a justice. Evidently Coughlan had made himself obnoxious by upholding the rights of the servants. To please the merchants, the stout old commodore bowed the knee to Baal, and dismissed Coughlan from the Bench, who thereupon left the Colony. Coughlan's memory, as a just and good man, was long held in pious reverence in Conception Bay.

A recent writer on the ecclesiastical history of the Colony has thought fit to take exception to the founders of the Newfoundland

Methodists and the Moravian missionaries. The results of the Brethren's one hundred and thirty years of work and labour of love in the Arctic Labrador are visible to all men; out of the most hopeless savages they have brought up a Christian, educated, church-going, moral, and respectable population. It is a mistake to state that the mission is self-supporting; Captain Linklater informs me it is not so, the expenses are paid out of voluntary contributions, the two vessels employed alone costing £2,500 a year each. The character of the missions of the humble Moravian Brethren in Africa and America needs no defence. From the records it appears that Jans Haven, one of their first missionaries, had been sent by Palliser, in 1764, to conciliate the Eskimos and Mountaineer Indians. Next year the Brethren received the following passport:—

"By His Excellency Sir HUGH PALLISER Governor &c.

"Whereas the Society of the Unitas Fratrum under the protection of His Majesty have from a pious zeal of promoting the knowledge of the true God and of the religion of our blessed Lord and Saviour Jesus Christ amongst the heathen, formed a resolution of establishing a mission of their brethren upon the Coast of Labrador,

ESQUIMAUX.
From Potherie's Histoire, 1722.

and for that purpose have appointed John Hill, Christian Drachart, Jans Haven, and Christian Andrew Schlozer to effect this pious purpose. And whereas the Lords Commissioners of the Admiralty and the Lords Commissioners of Trade and Plantations have signified to me their entire approbation of an undertaking so commendable in itself and that promises so great benefit to the publick and are desirous of giving all reasonable encouragement and assistance thereto. These are therefore to certify all persons whom it may concern that the said Brothers are under His Majesty's protection and all officers Civil and Military and all others His Majesty's subjects within my Government are hereby strictly charged and required not to give any interruption or hinderance to them but to afford them every aid and friendly assistance for the success of their pious undertaking for the benefit of mankind in general and His Majesty's subjects in particular 13 April 1765.

"By command of His Excellency. "JNO. HORSENAILL."

On the eve of his final departure from the Colony in 1768 the Governor cancelled the commission for the trial of murder, and the High Sheriff's appointment. Sir Hugh had lavished every kind of office on the Gills and the Keens, and now, at the last, he seems to have been dissatisfied with the close ring of officials that surrounded him. The Gills seem to have held most of the Government offices; Michael was Judge of the Vice-Admiralty Court, Keeper of the Rolls, J.P., public auctioneer, sole sworn broker, and sole notary public, and, later on, lieutenant-colonel of militia; his brother Nicholas seems to have had all the other posts. What caused Palliser to alter his mind about his subordinates is not known; he states, "My reasons will be laid before the King." Perhaps he did not get enough share of the prize money. He finds great fault with the resident naval officers; probably he found the clique around him too greedy.

Everything went on peaceably during his administration; there was, indeed, a war scare in 1764 owing to alarming news brought home by a man-of-war to England, that the French had a fleet at St. Pierre, and were fortifying it; Palliser sent a frigate, and soon found out that the whole story was a mere canard. During the last years of his administration there was a growing spirit of disaffection all through the North American Colonies, owing to the new taxes and the increased severity of the Custom House officials; a very mild outbreak in Newfoundland; in New England the precursor of the civil war.

A French vessel, *Chere Marie*, Jacques Quenal, master, having taken a parcel of furs on board at Port-au-Choix, was seized by Lieutenant Stanford, and brought into the Vice-Admiralty Court for adjudication and condemnation as contrary to the treaty. The following plain-spoken letter shows the Governor's view of the French rights :—

"To M. GEO. LE NOUVEE Master of the French ship *La Rada*,
M. FRANCOIS JAHAN Master of the French ship *L'Etoile*.

"GENTLEMEN, 14 Aug. 1767.

"The Governor directs me to acquaint you that your audacious attempts to encroach on the fisheries on this Coast are in violation of the Treaties and in disobedience to the strict orders you have received from Your King. . . . . He directs me to acquaint you that you need not give yourselves the trouble to make any further application or enquiry about either your boats or people; that in future, not only the boats that come on the Coasts, but the ships to which they belong will be seized and confiscated for encroaching and violating the Treaties.

"JNO. HORSENAILL."

On the 8th of July 1769 the Honourable John Byron,[1] Sir Hugh Palliser's successor, was sworn in with the usual oaths and honours as Governor of Newfoundland, Labrador, Magdalen Islands, and Anticosti. He made no alterations whatever in the rules and regulations established by his predecessor; he commanded the officers not to fire on ships leaving the harbour, and then claim the cost of the powder and shot from them, as had been the former practice; he was a martinet, and there is quite a long correspondence about the disposal of the old pickets when a new fence was put up at Fort William. Michael Gill, Parson Langman, and the other magistrates still presided in the courts of justice at St. John's, Mr. Weston and Mr. Carter at Ferryland, and Mr. Garland with Parson Coughlan at Harbour Grace.

AMERICAN BANKER AND FISHING BOAT IN 1741.

In 1771 Byron sent special orders to Captain Gower, of H.M.S. *Pearl*, to put a stop to the disorderly proceedings of New England men in the Magdalen Islands, and not to permit them to carry on the sea-cow fishery without a licence from him. Frenchmen were also vigorously prosecuted for venturing to fish outside the treaty limits; several were arrested, brought to St. John's, and sent home to France.

The Honourable John Byron is best remembered as the grandfather of the great poet, who refers to him in "Don Juan" as "my grand dad." The marvellous description of the shipwreck in that poem is partly taken from the Commodore's adventures in H.M.S. *Wager*, as well as from his celebrated voyage to the South Pacific. Governor Byron

---

[1] Byron was born in 1723; was the second son of the fourth Lord Byron; was wrecked in the *Wager* on the Chili coast in 1741; after great hardships, he reached Valparaiso. In 1757, in the *America*, he was at the futile attack on Rochefort. In 1760 he was sent, with a small squadron, to superintend the destruction of the fortifications of Louisbourg. In 1764 Byron was Commander-in-Chief in the East Indies, flying his pennant on the *Dolphin* (the first vessel in the English Navy to be copper-sheathed). At Rio he met Lord Clive, who wanted to go in the *Dolphin* to India; but Byron refused, for his real instructions were to explore the Southern Seas. It was on this voyage that the Patagonian giants were said to have been seen. As a voyage of discovery it was a failure; Byron had no genius for such work. He was appointed Governor of Newfoundland in January 1769; Rear-Admiral in 1775; Vice-Admiral in 1778. His expedition in this year to intercept the Count d'Estaing was a failure. Byron, though brave, had not enough originality or ability to distinguish himself. He died, Vice-Admiral of the White, in 1786. There is a portrait by Reynolds, painted in 1759.—(STEPHEN's *Nat. Dict. of Biography*.)

was made a commodore for his gallantry at the second siege of Louisbourg. He was a very plain, straightforward old sailor; like all the family, rather eccentric. He was known throughout the navy as "Foul-weather Jack." In the American War he did not distinguish himself.

Byron's administration was marked by the same humane treatment of the Eskimos that had characterised Palliser's dealings with them. An endeavour was again made to open up friendly intercourse with the Beothics, but without effect.

The Governorship from this time forward appears to have been a regular three years' commission. Commodore Molineux Shuldham, R.N., afterwards Lord Shuldham,[1] was appointed in 1772; during his command, which extended to 1774, the commercial war between England and America culminated in the Continental Congress of September 1774. One of the first acts of this assembly was to prohibit all exportations to England or the British Colonies. War, however, did not actually begin until the 18th of April the following year in the skirmish at Lexington, dignified by American historians into a battle.

---

[1] Molineux Shuldham was the second son of the Rev. S. Shuldham, of the diocese of Ossory, Ireland. He went to sea at ten years old; was Captain of the *Sheerness* in 1746. He saw very little fighting till, in 1756, he had the misfortune to be captured by three French men-of-war, which he had mistaken for merchantmen. He was honourably acquitted before a court-martial. He distinguished himself at the capture of Guadaloupe, but was unfortunate in losing his ship when again in the West Indies with Rodney; when attacking some coast batteries in Martinique, his ship struck and was wrecked. In 1772, on his return from Newfoundland, he brought an Esquimaux chief, who was presented to George III. Was Rear-Admiral of the White in 1775, and became Member for Fowey; Vice-Admiral of the Blue in 1776, when he was appointed to command on the American station. He convoyed Howe's army to Halifax from Boston in 1776, and thence to Staten Island; in June of this year he was created an Irish peer. Nothing remarkable occurred during the remainder of his stay on the American station. In 1778 he successfully convoyed the outward-bound West Indian and American fleets, and on his return became Port-Admiral at Plymouth, which post he held till 1783. Made Admiral of the White, 1779; Admiral of the Blue, 1787; and Admiral of the White, 1793.—Charnock's *Biographia Navalis.*)

REIGN OF GEORGE III.

The year before the outbreak of the American War was remarkable for a terrific storm at sea, which destroyed a vast amount of fishing property. The water rose suddenly twenty feet above its usual level; this great tidal wave caused immense destruction, both by land and sea, and three hundred persons along our coast lost their lives. It is known in Newfoundland annals as the "Year of the Great Storm."

With the exception of this event, and the passing of Palliser's Act (15 Geo. III.), nothing remarkable occurred during Shuldham's tenure of office; the same questions, the same routine, prevail all through this period. The New Englanders still gave trouble on the Labrador. The officer in command at Fort Pitt is complained of for having engaged in the seal fishery. A small "Behring Sea difficulty" arose at the Magdalen Islands, owing to the reckless and barbarous way in which the New Englanders were killing the sea-cows, driving them away from their quiet haunts, and preventing them from breeding; there is a long correspondence on this subject.

During this period the great Michael Gill died, and Edward White, Ordnance Storekeeper, became Judge of the Vice-Admiralty Court and Master of the Rolls; Edward Langman,[1] Charles Garland, Robert Gray, Nicholas Gill, and James Brooks, were the remaining justices of the quorum for St. John's; Robert Carter, J.P., was Keeper of the Rolls for Ferryland, William Keen for Bonavista, and D'Ewes Coke (afterwards Chief Justice) for Trinity; Nicholas Gill was Notary Public and Vendue Master, and John Philips, High Sheriff.[2] A proclamation was issued

---

[1] Langman, however, succeeded White as Keeper of the Rolls in 1773. The Gills seem to have soon recovered their old prestige. Nicholas Gill in 1774 became Master of the Rolls and Judge of the Vice-Admiralty Court, which posts he held until his death in 1787.

[2] The following local events in 1773 are noticeable:—

We notice in these records how property was acquired; for instance, the collector Alexander Dunn received a grant of Friendly Hall, Engineer Pringle the property now owned by Sir James Winter (Pringle's Dale); the hill now called Robinson's Hill was originally Dover's Hill.

William Spurrier, of the great firm of Spurrier's of Poole, was made Naval Officer for St. Mary's, Oderin, Burin, and Mortier, where his firm carried on their extensive business. Mr. John Slade, of the great firm of Slade's of Poole, was made Naval Officer for Twillingate. In Spurrier's bill for expenses of a proceeding out of the Vice-Admiralty Court against a servant, 2s. is charged for the *Whipper*. In 1773 Fort Townshend was commenced and the road to it from the Queen's Wharf, also the King's Road, the Military Road between Fort William and Fort Townshend, and the Signal Hill Road. The way in which titles to property were acquired in St. John's is curiously illustrative of the corruption and favouritism which prevailed in the days of our naval Governors; all around Fort William officers and soldiers had been allowed to take in land as far as the margin of Quidi Vidi Lake; on removal, soldiers and officers sold these to civilians in the town; valuable properties, both on the south and north side of Water Street, were purchased sometimes for a winter's provisions; a good building lot on the north side of Water Street, east of McBride's Hill, was given to one large firm for their cook's passage to England.

Ann Ellis acquired Ellis's estate in a curious way: her brother had left it all to a woman not his wife; the sister produced to Governor Shuldham an opinion in her favour from the celebrated English lawyer, Dunning, embodying an admirable set of regulations for the government of the salmon fishery on the coasts of Newfoundland and Labrador; the French are not mentioned, and it was evidently the practice at this time to completely exclude them from all occupations outside the cod fishery.

Commodore Duff's[1] appointment lasted during 1775. The following proclamation, issued in July by him, is of so much importance, and in such striking contrast to the manner of dealing with obstreperous French naval officers at the present day, that it is given in full. The stout old commodore took the strictly correct legal view of the treaties and the rules of international law; would that the same spirit were infused into the British Governments of to-day, which calmly permit French officers to put up proclamations on British territory, ordering British subjects to sell their herrings only to Frenchmen, and allow them to enforce such arbitrary decrees. The proclamation reads:—

"Whereas I have received authentick accounts that in the month of July 1763 a French ship of war named the 'Unicorn' visited several Ports within my Government, particularly 'Cremellaire,' where the Captain of the said ship interfered in matters relating to the laws and government of the Country. In case you should meet with any French ships of war within the limits of your station you are in the most civil and friendly manner to enquire of the Captain the occasion of his coming, and should he be driven there by necessity or distress you are to offer him assistance, and every other friendly office in your power, but should he pretend to come there for the protection and defence of French fishers or any other pretence whatsoever, other than distress, you are to signify to him that the subjects of France resorting to any port of H. Britannick Majesty's dominions to follow any business or trade by virtue of the Treaties subsisting between the two nations are, whilst in H.M. Dominions, *under the protection of H. Britannick Majesty only*; and that in conformity to H. Majestys sentiments and firm resolution

and on this *ex parte* opinion she obtained her grant.

Stripling, a stout Protestant and a publican, through the interest of the officers and soldiers, obtained a piece of land at Quidi Vidi, and afterwards, when he became a justice and sheriff, though utterly ignorant and illiterate, a grant of the land on the east side of King's Bridge Road, and all Stripling's plantation, were given to him.

The title of the Thomas's dates back to the reign of Charles II., and was continued through the Bevils, and William Thomas, a justice in Palliser's time, down to the William and Henry Thomas of our own time.

The Keens, Gills, Williams, and others of the clique that surrounded Governor Palliser, all gained their properties through Court influence. Hutchings' estate was acquired by George Hutchings for his valuable services in keeping a watch on Admiral de Ternaye's fleet in 1762.

[1] Duff, a cousin of the first Earl of Fife, became a commander in 1744. In 1758 he was with Commodore Howe in the squadron convoying the expeditions against St. Malo, Cherbourg, and St. Cas, and in 1759 was senior officer of a small squadron covering the Brittany coast while Hawke blockaded Brest. He was not present at Lord Hawke's victory over the French, but it was in chasing Duff's ships that the French came in sight of the main English fleet. He was with Rodney, in 1762, at the reduction of Martinique. He endeavoured to relieve Gibraltar in 1779, but the Government were not able to strengthen his command, so he was recalled. He became Vice-Admiral in 1778, and died in 1787. There is a portrait of him at the Royal United Service Institute.—(STEPHEN's *Nat. Dict. of Biography*.)

I p. 2729.

of maintaining with the utmost exactness probity and good faith the Treaties relating to the fishery I shall with an unbiassed and impartial justice to the subjects of both Crowns in my station inviolably observe H. Majesty's commands upon that head; but that I cannot permit any officer with a commission from His Most Christian Majesty and *with an armed force to resort to or exercise any authority within any part of* H. Majesty's dominions under my Government, their doing so being directly contrary to the spirit and words of the 13th section of the Treaty of Utrecht, by which the sovereignty, property, and full possession of this country is ceded to the Crown of Great Britain and the French expressly excluded from having forts or forces in any part of it, and the tenor of the whole article is to provide against the French encroaching on H.M. Territories and on H.M. rights and privileges. That therefore I will not allow any Foreign officer with an armed force to resort to this country without first applying for and obtaining the King's leave for that purpose. In case you should meet with any French officer within the limits of your station you are to appoint a reasonable time for him to depart; beyond which time you are not to allow him to stay and for your justification herein you are to deliver to him a copy of this my order to you.

"ROBERT DUFF."

Several writers on Newfoundland history, in their anxiety to make out a case against the American colonists in their struggle with England, have magnified a street row—an ordinary Irish faction fight—in Harbour Grace, in 1766, into a serious battle, and the merchants' opposition to the new custom house as treason; they have exaggerated and perverted these small affairs into a sinister plan and preconcerted scheme of rebellion. There is not the slightest foundation for such a statement; at the time of the Declaration of Independence there was, no doubt, a good deal of lawlessness in the Colony, and some disaffection, but there was some little common sense amongst our islanders; the republicans were few and scattered, the loyalists were in an overwhelming majority; there were four or five men-of-war always on the coast, a strong garrison, and at least ten thousand sturdy West Countrymen. A rebellion in Newfoundland would not have stood for an hour against such overwhelming odds.

Underhand attempts, no doubt, were made to seduce all the colonies from their allegiance. They met with no favour in Newfoundland; against none were the new republicans more vindictive than against us; they knew that we were largely dependent on them for food, yet one of the first acts of the Congress of 1774 was to decree non-intercourse; this was not fully carried out, with all its dire effects on our population, until the following year; but in 1775—a terrible year of storm and suffering—our late colonial brethren, who had been on such friendly terms, did their utmost to starve us and to destroy our trade with their privateersmen, who knew every creek and cove along the Newfoundland coast. The extreme animosity of the Americans against us seems to be

THE AMERICAN REVOLUTION.

a very clear indication that in the great struggle our population were loyal to the core.

It is not necessary to repeat again the oft-told story of the American revolution: how the obstinacy and stupidity of George III. and his ministers drove the colonists into rebellion; how the greatest statesmen in England—Chatham, Fox, and Burke—Franklin, Washington, and others, in America, tried to prevent war; how the gallant colonists at last achieved their liberty through the powerful assistance of France and a combination of nearly all Europe against England; this great history has been written in every form, from the "Spread-Eagle" one-sided view of some American historians, to the newest and fairest description of the events by Goldwin Smith. The

GRAND BANK, FORTUNE BAY.
From a photograph by J. Vey.

greatest blot on the character of the first American republicans is their treatment of the loyalists; in the words of Goldwin Smith:—

"The first civil war was followed not by amnesty, but by an outpouring of the vengeance of the victors upon the fallen. Some royalists were put to death, many others were despoiled of all they had and driven from their country. . . . Massachusetts banished by name three hundred and eight of her people, making death the penalty for a second return."

These loyalist exiles peopled Nova Scotia, New Brunswick and Upper Canada; some few of them came to this Colony; to one of these

---

The following local events in 1775–6 are noticeable:

Rev. Edward Langman, who appears to have been a very spirited and decided character, accused his brother justices of being partial and perjured; whereupon Edward White, Michael Gill, T. Dodd, John Stripling, and John Swingston complained of him to Governor Duff, and he was struck off the Commission of the Peace; he was restored by Governor Montagu. There was a grant to A. Dunn, collector, of a site for the Custom House in its present situation, to the east of King's Road (a path leading to the New Fortifications), on a hillock at the top of the Admiral's Beach, bounded on the north by a garden belonging to the late W. Delgrave. In 1776 General Howe removed the 65th Regiment, which was replaced by a company of the Royal Highland Emigrants.

banished Tories—Dr. Gardner of Boston, U.S.—we are indebted for a very interesting account of our Island.[1]

Rear-Admiral Montague,[2] who succeeded Duff, was sworn in, May 1776; one of his first acts was to graciously permit the French to cut wood in the Bay Despair and other places, and to build houses, &c. On war breaking out between France and England in 1778 he nevertheless promptly took possession of St. Pierre and Miquelon, destroyed all the buildings, and sent away all the inhabitants, thirteen hundred and ninety two persons, prisoners to France.

In 1776 Montague, who had been specially selected for Newfoundland on account of his activity and daring, picked out a number of

CAPTURE OF A CONTINENTAL BRIG BY AN ENGLISH CUTTER.
From a drawing in the B.M.

the best fast sailing vessels in the trade and fitted them as armed cruisers, putting young lieutenants, masters, mates, midshipmen, and petty officers in charge of them. With the men-of-war under his command and these improvised sloops and cutters, he most effectually protected our coasts from the American privateers, who had done considerable damage the year before. The petition given below throws a flood of light on our social history in 1775; it shows clearly that the

[1] The fierce attacks of the Republicans on their Tory brother colonists, who had done them no wrong, and their treatment of the loyalists are some of the most serious blots and scandals of American history.

[2] John Montague was Commander of the *Hinchinbroke* in 1745; in 1747 he represented Huntingdon in Parliament. He held various commands, but saw very little service during the wars except off Toulon, where he helped to destroy the French fleet which endeavoured to effect a junction with De la Clue at Carthagena. Became Rear-Admiral of the Blue in 1776, and Commander-in-Chief at Halifax. After his return from Newfoundland in 1778 he never accepted any active command; he was Port-Admiral at Portsmouth, and a member of the Keppel court-martial. He died in 1795 at Fareham, Hants.—(CHARNOCK's *Biographia Navalis*.)

old West Country ideas were still prevalent, also that St. John's had become quite a town, and that there was (in spite of the stern edicts of the naval Governors) considerable cultivation of land going on near the city; foremost in this innovation were the officers of the garrison. There are many names around St. John's to remind us of these old soldiers who took to farming. The well-known Major's Path is named after Major Brady, R.N., 1787; Pringle's Bridge, Pringle's Dale (Sir James Winter's residence), after Chief Engineer Col. Pringle, R.E., who built Fort Townshend; Bally Haly after Col. Haly. I recommend to my readers the perusal of this remarkable letter; it is copied from an admirable lecture on the fisheries by the late M. H. Warren in 1853, which is quite out of print, and was kindly lent to me by Mr. J. H. Noonan, of H.M. Customs, St. John's.[1]

[1] "TO THE HONOURABLE THE COMMONS OF GREAT BRITAIN IN PARLIAMENT ASSEMBLED:—

"The Petition of the Merchants, Boat-keepers, and Principal Inhabitants of St. John's Petty Harbour, and Tor Bay, in the Island of Newfoundland, 1775.

"Most Humbly Sheweth:

"That your petitioners having Maturely Considered a Bill for amending and rendering more Effectually an Act made in the Fifteenth year of His present Majesty (George 3rd, 1776,) entitled 'An Act for the encouragement of the Fisheries carried on from Great Britain, Ireland, and the British Dominions in Europe, and for securing the return of the fishermen, sailors, and others Employed in the said fisheries to the ports thereof at the end of the fishing season,' and for repealing certain provisions in the said Act relative to the said fisheries, are of opinion that its General tendency is well calculated for the Benefit of this Island, at the same time beg leave to lay before you some amendments and additions, which we apprehend will also be of public utility.

"Relative to Bounties granted ships or vessels employed in the British fishery, on the Banks of Newfoundland, having been found inadequate to its intention (as to obtain it the adventurers were obliged to be at a considerable expense in outfitting their Vessels, carrying extra men, to entitle them to receive the same) that the said Bounties may be appropriated and allowed to such ships or vessels employed in the said fishery, navigated with ten men each, at the rate of six shillings per Ton, agreeable to their registers, subject to all the rules and restrictions as reserved in former Acts.

"That all the Plantations, Houses, Gardens, and so forth, in this Island, on being established property, to be nevertheless liable to the payment of debts, otherwise those merchants and *others* who supply the Boat-keepers and Inhabitants will be deprived of that resource, for the discharge of their just debts.

"That all Oil, Blubber, and Seal Skins, exported from this Island, caught by British subjects, may be imported into Great Britain free of Duty; oath being made by the Master or person having the charge of the said ship, that it was caught and cured as aforesaid.

"If a Master or the person acting under him, should at any time see it necessary to correct any servant under them with moderation, (free from harshness or cruelty) for not doing his duty in a proper manner, that the said servant may not be allowed, for every frivolous disagreement or complaint to have his Master summon'd before a Justice of the Peace, which in the height of the fishery has been found very detrimental and often known to be the case without a just cause of complaint.

"Fishing Admirals being authorized to hear and determine matters relative to the fishery, the Trading People are often deprived of an immediate resource to them, they being employed fishing on the Banks.

"That such fishing Admirals may be allowed to appoint deputy or deputies to act under them to hear or determine, on such matters as may come before them relative to the fishery aforesaid, with liberty to preside at any Court of Justice held in their different districts as a Justice, and also for their deputations to remain in force until the Twentieth of November, before which time the transactions, relative to the said fisheries are not adjusted, as frequently, the fishing Admirals are obliged to sail from this Island, early in October.

"As Lumber is at present a scarce commodity, and the intercourse of supply from Quebec, and Port Roseway, not yet warranted, from whence no doubt large quantities will be sent to this Island, in the intermediate space, Regard should be paid to

As a further illustration of the state of society, and of the manner in which the administration of justice was carried out at

the Timber Trees growing in this Island, which if not wantonly cut down would in a few years, become large spars, for Masts of Ships and other uses, as well as to saw into boards.

"To prevent the said Trees from being unnecessary cut down the principal person of each crew (of which there are a great many who prosecute the Business of making Shingles for covering houses, stores, &c.; also hoops in the winter season) should be competent to judge such Timber as would suit his purpose, and not wantonly cut down any Trees but for their immediate use under certain restrictions.

"Rinding Trees is also of a pernicious tendency, altho' that article is very necessary in the fishery, yet should be subject to Regulations, not for more *Trees* to be rinded than is necessary for curing and preserving the fish and for the covering temporary houses and huts, where boards are not to be obtained.

"Codd Seans we deem a great nuizance as by them we destroy a great quantity of small fish, which after being inclosed in the sean (and not worth the attention of the person who hauls them) are left to rot, by which means a multitude of fish that would grow to maturity, perish.

"Contiguous to the Northern Part of this Island are a great many Islands where Birds breed in vast abundance which were of great service to the inhabitants residing near them, for food in the winter, and also for bait in catching of fish during the summer, of which valuable resource they are now almost entirely deprived, as great part of the birds are destroyed within a few years by the crews of men who make it their business to kill them in their breeding season, for their feathers (of which they make a Traffic) and burning the carcasses, we have applied to get this with many other grievances redressed but have yet only retained a partial relief, therefore pray that an entire stop may be put to destroying the birds otherwise than for food or bait as before excepted.

"Olive Oil and Cork, both articles very necessary for the fishery if allowed to be imported here duty free, we apprehend would not be detrimental to the revenue, and at the same time of public utility, as at present we are not allowed to import either, except its being first sent to England, which is attended with additional expense.

"When Bread and Flour is to be purchased in Great Britain Ireland and Quebec at Twelve Shillings per cwt. it can be supplied the inhabitant of this Island at such moderate prices as not to be a burthen or tax on the fishery, but when it exceeds the price before quoted, a bounty to be granted on what is exported from Great Britain and Ireland, to reduce it to the said price of twelve shillings per cwt. (in British vessels).

"Every Ship or Vessel that brings Passengers to Newfoundland not provided with Masters (which is often the case) the Master of such Vessel on his arrival should be obliged to enter into Bond, that such men as do not get employed during the summer (by which means they become very burthensome here, and frequently through Idleness and want commit Outrages, Breaking open Stores and Shops for plunder) and are not provided with a Master in the fall, either to carry them back from where they came or give proper security for their passages so that they may not be burthensome here, which would prevent a number of Idle Men remaining here the winter, all of that description being a great nuizance.

"It has been a Custom lately with several Masters of Vessels on their arrival, to land many Passengers (great part thereof unprovided for) and then go off with most of their Cargoes (chiefly provisions) supposed for some part of the United States, leaving the said Passengers and others without even the resource of their Cargoes, for supplying them as also the Inhabitants, and by this means doubly distressing the Trade. This we pray may be prevented in future by a clause, that every Vessel bringing provisions to this Island, should not be suffered to carry away more than sufficient Stock for said Vessel's intended Voyage, by suffering the Exportation the Price here is consequently enhanced and the Inhabitants much distressed thereby.

"As our Season for prosecuting the Fish is of a short continuance the utmost industry during that period is very requisite, and therefore the fewer innovations or incentives to draw the Servants off from their duty the strictest their attention will be in the discharge of it.

"Some few years back when the Fishery was prosecuted in the Harbour of St. John's, with great vigour, three to four Houses Public by Licence for vending Spirituous and Malt Liquors were found sufficient, then the servant was obliged to apply to his Employer for Liquor when, if he made bad use of it getting intoxicated and thereby neglecting his duty, it was in the said Master's Power to prevent the like happening in future, but within a few years the number of Licenced Houses in the said Harbour are amounted to more than Eighty in number, many of which are houses of Ill-fame, where the fishermen and seamen resort, and get drunk, neglecting their duty to the great detriment of their Employers, it often happening through one this period, I give in the notes an account of a few of the cases tried in 1777.[1]

servant's neglect of a few hours a considerable loss ensues, as fish is a perishing commodity too much care and attention can't be paid it. To prevent the like in future we pray that the number may be reduced (of Houses Licenced for Selling Liquors) to twelve, which we deem full sufficient for the Entertainment both of the Inhabitants, as well as Strangers resorting to the Harbour, and that each person so authorized to Vend Liquors should be obliged to keep a Fishing Shallop and cure all the Fish said Shallop may catch.

"The number of Shopkeepers and Retailers of Goods have increased lately in St. John's to the great detriment of the Fish Catchers, as formerly every Employer had the supplying his own Servants, which we apprehend in Equity they are entitled to, from the very great wages given to them for the short season of prosecuting the Fishery, the profits arising from such supply was a small emolument to reduce the enormous wages given, but at present the Masters are deprived of this, by their Servants being supplied at those Retail Shops before alluded to, who in the fall of the year collect their Bills, in consequence of which the servants are often reduced to great distress during the winter, to prevent which we pray that each Shopkeeper of Goods may in future be obliged to keep a Shallop on the Fishery otherwise to have six months liberty to sell off his Goods and leave this Island, as we deem every person not immediately concerned in the Fishery (except his Majesty's Servants) is a burthen to the Island, and that every Tavern-keeper, or other person, known to supply a Servant belonging to or Employed by Merchants or Boat-keepers in the Fishery, on Proof to be fined Fifty Pounds.

"His Majesty's Officers having lately inclosed large Spots of Ground contiguous to this Harbour for erecting Houses, Planting Gardens, Farms, &c., by which means many of the public pathways leading to the woods are stopped, to the prejudice of the residents here, we therefore request that no more ground may be inclosed for farms, or otherwise, except as Gardens for the use of the said Officers families, which, when they may be recalled should go to the next that arrives according to their rank.

"We therefore request you will deign to take the preceding matters into your serious consideration and grant us such redress as your Honourable House shall seem meet and as in duty bound your Petitioners shall ever pray, &c." — (WARREN'S *Lecture*, Apps. pp. x-xv.)

[1] CRIMINAL CASES TRIED IN 1777.

The jurors for our Lord the King, upon their oath, present that Richard Power, a native of the kingdom of Ireland, labourer, not having God before his eyes, but being moved and seduced by the instigation of the Devil on the first day of October in the 15th year of our sovereign Lord, George the Third, of Great Britain, France, and Ireland, &c., &c. . . . At the hour of about 9 o'clock in the evening of the same day, with force and arms at St. John's, &c., in and upon one John Cahill, of St. John's, aforesaid, merchant, in the peace of God and our sovereign Lord the King, then and there being, the aforesaid John Cahill not having any weapon then drawn, nor the aforesaid John Cahill having first stricken, the said Richard Power feloniously did make an assault, and that he the aforesaid Richard Power, with a stone of no value which he the said Richard Power in his right hand then and there had and held, hit the said John Cahill in and upon the side of the head of him the said John Cahill, the aforesaid John Cahill as is aforesaid then and there not having any weapon drawn nor the aforesaid John Cahill then and there having first stricken, the said Richard Power then and there feloniously did strike, giving unto him the said John Cahill then and there with the stone aforesaid, in form aforesaid, in and upon the left side of the head of him the said John Cahill one mortal stroke or blow, of which he the said John Cahill languished until the evening of the 24th November and then died, &c., &c. . . . .

This is an abbreviated form of the indictment against Power; there was no evidence to sustain it. It appears that Cahill, a shopkeeper or merchant, was having a drunken spree in his house; some boys looked in through the window, so he and other guests rushed out and struck the spectators with sticks; the accused, an Irish "youngster," was passing, and was struck violent blows on the head by Cahill and Lawrence Power, who were too drunk to distinguish anyone; after being struck, Richard Power immediately went home, and next day had his wounds dressed by Dr. Delaney. The jury found the prisoner not guilty, and he was discharged *on payment of the fees of the court.*

Lawrence Hallahan, found guilty of forging a bill of £8, was sentenced as follows: "That you be carried back to the place from whence you came and thence be led to the place of execution and there to be hanged by the neck until you are Dead, Dead, Dead, and the Lord have mercy on your soul."

Next Lawrence Dalton, for forging two orders for 20s. and 17s., received the same sentence. Patrick Knowlan, for stealing a counterpane, value 10d., from Peter Prim, sentence: "That you P. Knowlan be whipped by the common whipper with a halter about

In the year 1776 came into operation the statute known in the Colony as "Palliser's Act," 15 Geo. III. c. xxxi. This important measure was very ably drawn, and, although somewhat encumbered with the involved and redundant verbosity of the period, it was remarkably clear and definite; Sir Hugh's hand can be traced in every line. The distinct purpose of the measure was to make the Newfoundland business a British fishery, carried on by fishermen from England and the King's dominions in Europe; American colonists were rigidly excluded from any participation in the bounties and other benefits granted by it. The preamble clearly explains this object :—

"Whereas the fisheries carried on by H. M. subjects of G. Britain and of the British dominions in Europe have been found to be the best nurseries for able and experienced seamen, always ready to man the Royal Navy when occasions require; and it is therefore of the highest national importance to give all due encouragement to the said fisheries, and to endeavour to secure the *annual return* of the fishermen, sailors, and others employed therein to the Ports of Great Britain &c. at the end of every fishing season.

"Now in order to promote these great and important purposes and with a view in the first place to induce H. M. subjects to proceed early from the ports of G. Britain to the Banks of Newfoundland, and thereby to prosecute the fishery on the said banks to the greatest advantage it is enacted &c. . . . .

"That from and after 1st Jany. 1776 the bounties hereinafter mentioned shall be paid and allowed annually for 11 years . . . . such vessels must be British built and owned by British subjects residing in England &c., not less than 50 tons burthen, not less than 15 men (three fourths of whom must be H. M. subjects), to be fitted and cleared out from an English Port on the 1st January each year; they must catch on the Banks not less than 10,000 fish to be landed on the E. coast of Newfoundland before the 15th July each year.

"Bounty of £40 per ship to the first 25 vessels making two trips to the Banks— next 100 vessels £20 each. Bounty for whale fishery £500 to the first vessel arriving with the largest quantity of oil.

"No person allowed to fish in Newfoundland except those arriving from H. M. Dominions in Europe [intended to exclude the Americans]. Provisions to be brought from England, Ireland, &c. free. Fishing vessels to be free from restraint and only pay a Custom House fee of 2s. 6d. Seal skins and oil to be free of duty.

"No fishing vessels to carry passengers to Newfoundland without permission. Agreement in writing with fishermen obligatory. No advance to fishermen to be more than half their wages—other half on return home. Master must produce Shipping paper. Fish and oil liable preferentially for payment of servants wages.

your neck, that is to say you are to receive on your bare back twenty lashes at the common whipping post, then to be led by the halter to the Publick Path just opposite Mr. Peter Prims door and there receive twenty lashes as before, and then led as before to the Vice-Admiral's Beach and there to receive twenty lashes as before; to forfeit all your goods and chattels; to pay the charges of the Court, and to depart this Island by the first vessel bound for Ireland never to return on pain of having the same punishment repeated every Monday morning; to be kept in prison till you go aboard."

Thus ended the assizes.

MCHL. GILL.
JOHN STRIPLING.
EDWD. WHITE.
THOS. DODD.
EDWARD LANGMAN.
ROBT. BULLEY.

Hallahan was hung 10th May 1777.

Penalties for misconduct of fishermen. All disputes to be determined by Sessions Courts in Newfoundland or by Vice Admiralty Court [this was repealed as regards Admiralty Courts by 26 Geo. III. cap. xxvi. sec. 25].

" Fishermen to be free from press gang. Duty of 1/- per gallon on rum from America, &c. . . . ."

Palliser's Act was one of the results of the troubles with America. The bounty was given to encourage the loyal Colony of Newfoundland; by a provision in the Act, Americans, as well as all Colonists outside Newfoundland, were excluded from all participation in the colonial fishery. The bank fishery was specially reserved for the subjects of His Majesty's dominions in Europe. Hanoverians, Jersey men, &c. might fish; but Canadians, Nova Scotians, and Bermudians were rigidly excluded by this extraordinary narrow policy. As Ireland was at the time in strong sympathy with the American insurgents, it was thought desirable to win over the Celts by granting them the much-desired boon of free trade with the Colonies, and a bounty for their fishery. The Irish were so much concerned with Newfoundland at this time that historians speak of the bounty on our bank fishery as given to the *Irish Newfoundland fishery*. The trade between the two countries at this period was large; Arthur Young speaks of the farmers around Waterford fattening pigs for our markets; legal or illegal, the trade was carried on.

BERMUDIAN SLOOP OF THE EIGHTEENTH CENTURY.

The West Countrymen always made a provision that the convoy out to Newfoundland should remain forty-eight hours in Cork. The effect of Palliser's Act was to increase the bank fishery, it had no other result. The provisions about servants' wages were bitterly disliked by the West Country merchants, and in every way they tried to evade the new law.

In the years 1787 and 1788 a new trade question arose. The Devonshire men found a formidable competitor in a most unlooked-for quarter, Bermuda. The whole story of this sudden irruption into our island of the Somers Islanders and their lusty negroes is so graphically described by Jeremiah Coghlan, that I give his report in full; it is dated 25th October 1788, St. John's:—

" This new and alarming undertaking consisted this year of thirty four sloops of 30 to 60 tons burthen, from 8 to 12 men each, three parts of whom consist of robust able black men, natives of Bermuda, and slaves to owners of said vessels, other part were old country men, hired for splitting, salting, and conducting things aboard said vessels on the Banks, and the large vessels had each one of our expert fishermen to instruct the crew in managing their lines and disengaging the hooks with quickness when swallowed by the cod.

" These vessels came early in the spring from Bermuda, laden with salt which was brought from Turks Island. Part of them paid Masters of our fishing rooms 2/- per quintal for curing the fish they should take. The other part, particularly large size sloops, took possession of vacant ship's or admiral's rooms at different parts to the southward of St. John's and hired one experienced Master of voyages to manage and inspect the curing of fish, occupying the said fishing rooms in the same manner as British ships are entitled to do.

" The first trips these our rivals made to the Grand Bank, they appeared as if they could not undergo the hardships of such a business, and as natives of a more southern climate could not endure fatigues; but they soon convinced the English fishers that they were equal to any young beginners who came before them; and to aid their endeavours they were greatly favoured by a most uncommon mild moderate season which was a great encouragement to their exertions, and which men, to the surprise of our fishermen, exceeded them in despatch, which appears by the following account.

" The smallest of these vessels, in July and August seldom exceed eight days in making fishing trips to the Grand Bank and in returning loaded from thence. For being not only remarkably fast sailors, but also, when it became calm, frequently the case in those months, these blacks (shewing example of attention for good of their Masters' interest worthy notice of our people) rowed their sloops from 2½ to 3 miles per hour and in working in and out of narrow harbours excelled the best of our fishing lugger shallops. No wind prevented them from getting on the Banks. Have been told that the Master of one of our banking ships being stopped in the Narrows of St. John's by a strong wind blowing from the sea when bound on the Grand Bank, two of these Bermudian sloops passed him and worked out under low sail; the next evening the former got his vessel out of Harbour also and meeting a contrary time was five days after before he got on the fishing ground, at which time he fell in with one of the sloops before mentioned returning with her full take of fish which her crew were but four days in catching.

" Also learned from Masters of our Bankers who have been in company with Bermudians on Banks fishing in August, that the black men aboard of them became as expert in catching fish as old country men and as eager and attentive to catch as any of ours who are paid £4 10s. per 1000 fish for catching only—some of which men have earned this year £45 stg. for their separate share of a Banker's voyage.

" This information discovers to you the very great take of fish there has been on the Grand Bank this past season, which to a great degree exceeds any single year's take of that article within the memory of the oldest trader to this Country; a circumstance that (with many encouraging advantages these new Adventurers have in view superior to fishers from England) must terminate to the latter's prejudice if not speedily taken under the consideration of the Lords of Committee of Trade and Plantations and must cause great decline to this valuable nursery of British seamen.

" These Bermudian fishing vessels are to sanction the subtle views of Americans, who to evade the late restrictions laid on their exports, the wise check given their navigation, a wound their boasted liberty cannot readily heal, are now become concerned with their second selves, the Bermudians, in imposing this new and unexpected undertaking on Great Britain.

" The said fishing vessels, the alarming rivals of British European fishers, being manned with proprietors' own slaves and fitted out in much cheaper manner than English Bankers will have great superiority over the latter in case of a bad fishery happening, the former having no claim on owners for wages, which will enable them to undersell the English taken fish and also introduce a new mode of smuggling New England fish at all our West India Islands, where they can afford to supply them with fish of first quality as cheap as we can; what the Spanish market will not consume being such as we call refuse at this market.

"Under colour of the said Banking vessels taking their fish from hence when cured to be reshipped on board larger size vessels at Bermudas and transported from thence to the Mediterranean markets, protected by our passes, said vessels will proceed to America and there receive New England fish to the amount of two thirds their cargoe, and proceed with such to the former markets which will be rivalling us at the same. The Americans not daring to face the Mediterranean or get within reach of being made slaves by the Algerines, which also burdens their voyages made to the Straights with an additional premium for insurance that no markets can support and which markets we command at present.

"The fishing crews, being slaves, the property of people of Bermuda and many American blacks, not being within reach of our men of war in case of rupture with European powers are only for the service of America [for manning ships of war]. The major part of these vessels will be supplied with cordage, canvas, iron work, &c. from America and, being a great field for smuggling produce of that country into bays and creeks of Newfoundland, these vessels, under sanction of taking fish, will set aside the restrictions on importation of provisions &c. from the Continent, which the greatest attention of the King's ships on this station cannot prevent, and they will be enabled thereby to undersell us at this market, and maintain their crews much cheaper than we English fishers.

"The chief agent who came with our rival codfishers from Bermuda, whose name is Harvey, is a shrewd American. He openly declares there will be 100 sail of Bermudian sloops fishing on the Grand Bank next season, and is now going to London, having all the bluster of the American party to support him in case of need, to make good their establishment at this Island. The other agents are rank Americans; also Nathaniel Philips of St. John's who discovered himself so implacable a stickler for the Bostonians during the late troubles, is the person who undertakes to defray all matters and costs these mock Bermudians are subject to; and, though notwithstanding the Act of Parliament, these Bermudians, as they call themselves, have been permitted by the Government to all rights of British Europeans' ships to the surprize of every Englishman, who lay this evil at the door of the former's secretary [Aaron Graham] a much greater man than his master and governs this Island as he thinks fit, of which all the surrogates complain loudly. To set aside any right of claim those mock Mudians can have to disinherit English fishers, I am solicited by a body of English fishers to lay those threatening *national grievances* before you, praying representation to Lord Hawkesbury (as owing to your judicious measures when our Governor, the rise and consequence of this Island is become *the envy of all nations*) that a better check to New England fishers [be arranged]."

The Bermudians were allowed to dry their fish this year, but they were afterwards rigidly tabooed.[1]

This letter, addressed to Sir Hugh Palliser—the most virulent opponent of our native resident fishermen—gives a very clear statement of the case from the West Country standpoint. There can be very

---

[1] The Bermudians had fished in Newfoundland before this date, and after they were prohibited from landing and curing their fish, they carried it home green to Bermuda. The damp climate of their Island was found, however, unsuitable for fish curing, and the enterprise had to be abandoned. I have received valuable information on this subject from T. Reid, Esq., Bermuda. Further information will be found in the Appendix.

little doubt that the shrewd Yankees had a hand in this new dodge. The Nathaniel Philips referred to was a well-known merchant in St. John's; he had been the general agent for the New England trade in Newfoundland; a close-fisted, penurious old fellow, who had become very rich "by saving of candle ends and sich"; he died in 1790, and was buried in the cathedral burying ground, at the corner near St. Andrew's Kirk.[1] Three of his clerks were Henry Shea (father of Sir Ambrose, and the Hon. Edward D'Alton Shea), Geo. Lilly (afterwards Judge Lilly, father of the late R. R. W. Lilly, Q.C.), and William Lilly, of Harbour Grace. Philips was navy agent all through the first American war; Hunt Stabb & Preston during the war of 1812. Philips' name figures largely in the judicial records; he had very large dealings, and appears frequently as a harsh creditor, screwing and selling up some unfortunate out-harbour planter.

Under the administration of the admiral-governors, there was a curious blending of judicial and executive functions; their excellencies wanted to have a hand in everything. We find, for instance, Governor Montague issuing an order to the sheriff, John Philips, to hang Hallahan, and fixing the time for his execution. On many occasions he not only manufactured a law to suit the special exigencies of the case, but also invented a punishment. He fined publicans for a first or second offence, deciding that for a third they are to be banished to Ireland. For fishermen disobeying the commands of their skippers he ordered first a forfeiture of all their wages, and secondly that they should be imprisoned and then sent on board a man-of-war, never to return to the Colony.

At this period of our history there had grown up a considerable trade with Greenock, Glasgow, and Belfast, besides the long standing commercial intercourse with Waterford. Representations were made by the chief magistrates of these towns about the state of the civil government in the Colony, or rather the want of any efficient and orderly administration of law or government.[2] Being anxious to increase

---

[1] In Philips' time clerks had a very hard life, they were treated almost like menial servants. One day Michael, Philips' faithful old Irish servant, told his master the appalling news that the young gentlemen wanted a change in their dinner—all three had declared they would eat pork no longer. "Not eat pork," said the old man in a furious rage, "I'll make 'em eat pork until the bristles grow on 'em."

[2] WRECK OF THE "TROIS FRERES."

"As every part of the conduct of the people at and about St. Marie's concerned in this transaction appears to me the most inhuman and barbarous proceeding I ever heard of in a Christian country I rely on your doing that justice to the injured parties their unhappy case requires, and doubt not there may be some well disposed people there who will be happy to render you every assistance towards this discovery, and am gentlemen,

"Your very humble servant,
"J. MONTAGUE.

"To John Follett &
Jas. Jackson, J.P.'s,
Trepassey."

[This letter relates to the wreck and plundering of the French schooner *Trois Freres*, of Guadaloupe, Pierre Barthelemy Bloum, master, in April 1777.]

their profitable business with the Island, they represented the deplorable state of affairs to the Ministry, but all to no purpose. Grievous complaints were made, especially about the administration of justice—Governor after Governor represented the matter to the Crown, but without effect.

Rear-Admiral Montague remained until 1778. In July of that year France recognised the independence of the United States, and declared war against England. This step had been in contemplation for some time; in the autumn of 1777 all the French fleet in Newfoundland, both men-of-war and merchantmen, had been suddenly ordered to return to France. On the Governor's departure from the Colony at the usual time, in both the autumn of 1776 and 1777, he had left two frigates and two armed vessels at St. John's and Placentia, and at the earnest request of the merchants in 1777 a frigate remained on the coast up to the 25th of November to convoy the fish vessels to the Mediterranean.

There is very little interesting matter in the records during Governor Edwards' tenure of office.[1] He was a very careful and attentive administrator. All available means were used to strengthen the defences of the Colony; nine men-of-war, between three and four hundred volunteers, and about four hundred and fifty regular troops were under his command; batteries were established at Quidi Vidi, Cuckold's Cove, Amherst Tower, Frederick's Battery, Chain Rock Battery, Fort William, Fort Townshend, and at Petty Harbour, and in the Torbay and Bay Bulls Roads; a ship was moored at River Head to defend the path leading into the town from Bay Bulls; the volunteers when under arms were allowed rations, pay, and each half a pint of rum per diem. About £5,000 in specie to pay troops and volunteers, and eight hundred stand of arms, were sent out from England. Edwards acknowledges in

GOVERNOR RICHARD EDWARDS.
From an engraving after Dance.

---

[1] Richard Edwards must not be confused with the Governor of the same name in George II.'s reign. He was appointed a Commander in 1747, and in 1777 was Captain of H.M.S. *Sandwich* (90) at Ushant, under Admiral Keppel, where his ship suffered very severely. He was a witness at the subsequent court-martial. On 19th March 1779, he became Rear-Admiral of the Blue, and soon after was sent to the Newfoundland station; he resigned this post in April 1782 on the change of administration. Edwards saw very little active service; he died, at an advanced age, in 1794. — (CHARNOCK's *Biographia Navalis*.)

grateful terms the loyalty of the Newfoundland population; their active exertions to defend the Colony, their cheerful submission to military rule and discipline, and their valuable aid in perfecting the defences, both of the capital and the outports. Beyond tampering with the guns at Renews, there is not a single complaint of disloyalty or disaffection.

All through 1780 St. John's was kept in a state of vigilant watchfulness about the great French fleet, with a hundred transports, that had sailed from Brest on May 2nd; its destiny, however, was the United States, not Newfoundland. During all the first American contest no foreign men-of-war—either French, Spanish, or American—made any serious attack on the Island. Newfoundland suffered much from

TWILLINGATE.
From a photograph.

the scarcity and dearness of provisions which had all to be imported from England, as well as coal. On the other hand she enjoyed all the fishery—bank and shore—without a rival; prices were good and the harvest of the sea abundant. On the whole, the war time was a prosperous period in Newfoundland history.

There were, however, many American privateers hovering about the coast. They did most damage to the planters at Fogo and Twillingate. In August 1780 Edwards writes that " already he has captured five American privateers, but they are in force on the coast." With the strong naval armament then cruising about Newfoundland they did not venture on our shores, except in the early spring, when they might do mischief to the northward, or late in the autumn, when the fleet had sailed for England. Beyond destroying a few fishing boats and stages they did not do much serious injury on the south coast. Some of the small outlying settlements were plundered by skippers who had been traders to the Island. They boldly sailed their vessels right into the wharves, and then requisitioned the inhabitants and carried off all the sailors they required. Several attempts were made to attack Carbonear and Harbour Grace, but they were successfully defended by the well-manned batteries on the islands. They seldom ventured near St. John's; one privateer—a brig of twelve guns—is mentioned in a letter from Renews, but she did not dare to enter the harbour, which was fortified with six guns.

Many of their ships were captured. A silent witness to the smartness of the Royal Navy in these days lay for a long time sunk at River Head—the American privateer *George*. In 1781, in the early spring, H.M.S. *Pluto* was lying in St. John's Harbour dismantled; news was brought in by a fisherman at daybreak that two American privateers were cruising off Bay Bulls, and had captured several fishing vessels; before eight o'clock that morning the *Pluto* was made ready for sea, and before sundown she returned to St. John's with the two captured Americans. One of these, the *George*, was found in 1882, when the dock was being built. In the second American war of 1812 there were far more Yankee vessels captured than in the revolutionary conflict.

In 1780, one of the English squadron, H.M.S. *Antelope*, Captain Keppel, R.N., cruising on the banks, fell in with and captured the American armed packet *Mercury*, with Mr. Lawrence on board. As the vessels approached each other a packet was thrown by Henry Laurence, the American envoy to Europe, from the American vessel; a sailor from the English frigate dived overboard, and brought up the package, which contained the secret negotiations then being carried on by the Americans with France and Holland; by the smartness of this plucky tar, England was put in possession of all the designs of her enemies.

In 1781 the memorable capture of York Town and the surrender of Lord Cornwallis demonstrated, even to the obstinate old king, that the Americans were not to be brought back to their allegiance; next year (1782) preliminaries of peace were signed between England and America, although the United States had solemnly bound themselves with France to make no separate treaty.

During the American war England had been gallantly fighting the three greatest naval powers of Europe and their colonies, as well as her own rebellious provinces. The British lion was a little torn and ragged after these desperate encounters with French, Spanish, Dutch, and Americans, but everywhere he had held his own. Incapable generals, timid admirals, and divided counsellors had blundered and quarrelled over their stupid mistakes, yet England, in 1783, was more than a match for her four antagonists. France, Spain, and Holland were utterly beggared and routed, America was at her wits' end, the old country was full of pluck and vigour, the national spirit was aroused, ships and regiments were being offered to the Government. Our old Governor Rodney's crowning victory at Domenica showed the world what English sailors could do when properly led.

In 1783 came the Treaty of Versailles, in which the Imperial Government had once more an opportunity of settling her North American fisheries on a permanent and satisfactory basis. The United States—always the spoiled child of diplomacy—though she had separated from England, claimed a right to the coast fishery in the English provinces. One of her first modest demands from England was Canada—she had previously divided Newfoundland provisionally with France. However, as Mr. Oswald, the first English diplomatist, an English merchant well acquainted with American affairs, would not listen to any of these proposals, they dropped Canada after their first interview, but they actually gained the right, in a modified form, to the coast fishery about Newfoundland and the maritime provinces. In brazen effrontery and diplomatic roguery the simple Quaker printer, Benjamin Franklin, taught European diplomatists a lesson which they have never forgotten.[1]

With respect to Newfoundland, we were again sacrificed by Mr. Alleyne Fitzherbert, afterwards Lord St. Helen's. Every detail of this important treaty had been agreed on after protracted discussion, only the fisheries remained. The French claimed the exclusive right to the Newfoundland fishery from Cape John to Cape Ray. Fitzherbert told them the English Ministry dared not give away British territory on the Island, and he could put no such terms in the treaty. There was a dead-lock: the French would not give way, both nations were anxious for peace. The diplomatists wanted to show their ability by finding some way out of the difficulty. At last, says Fitzherbert, "I ventured to propose as " a mezzo-termine (taking care, however, to add that the proposition " came from myself) that the exclusive right should not be mentioned " in the treaty, but that we should promise *ministerielment* to secure " it to the French fishermen by means of proper instructions to that " effect to the government of Newfoundland." To this the Count de Vergennes assented. The whole transaction was dishonest; there was

---

[1] Read Wedderburn's attack on Franklin about the stolen Whateley correspondence.

THE TREATY OF VERSAILLES.

to be a sham treaty, signed and set before the English House of Commons; the real treaty was to depend on the word of the minister, and afterwards on the declaration of the king. The *treaty* says:—

"Article IV.—That His Majesty the King of Great Britain is maintained in his right to the Island of Newfoundland and to the adjacent Islands, as the whole were assured to him by the 13th article of the Treaty of Utrecht, except the Islands of St. Pierre and Miquelon, which are ceded in full right by the present Treaty to His Most Christian Majesty.

"Article V.—That the King of France, in order to prevent the quarrels which have hitherto arisen between the two nations of England and France, consents to renounce the right of fishing which belongs to him in virtue of the aforesaid article of the Treaty of Utrecht from Cape Bonavista to Cape John. And His Majesty the King of Great Britain consents on his part that in the fishery assigned to the subjects of His Most Christian Majesty, beginning at the said Cape John, passing to the north and descending by the West Coast of Newfoundland to Cape Ray, the French fishermen shall enjoy the fishery as they had the right to enjoy that which was assigned to them by the Treaty of Utrecht."

The *declaration* 3rd Sept. 1783 states:—

"The King having entirely agreed with the French King upon the articles of the definite treaty, will seek every means which shall not only insure the execution thereof, with his accustomed good faith and punctuality; but will besides give, on his part, all possible efficacy to the principles which shall prevent even the least foundation of dispute for the future.

LORD ST. HELENS.
From an engraving in the B.M.

"To this end, and in order that the fishermen of the two nations may not give cause for daily quarrels, His Britannic Majesty will take the most positive measures for preventing his subjects from interfering in any manner *by their competition*, with the fishery of the French during the *temporary exercise* of it, which is granted to them upon the Coasts of Newfoundland; and he will for this purpose cause *the fixed settlements which shall be formed there to be removed*. His Britannic Majesty will give orders that the French fishermen be not incommoded in cutting the wood necessary for the repairs of their scaffolds, huts and fishing vessels."

It is perfectly clear that the English envoy virtually promised to give France exclusive rights from Cape John to Cape Ray, but the Ministry dare not put it in the Treaty—the clauses about Newfoundland were most unpopular. Fox and Burke tore away every vestige of credit from the Peace of Versailles, and the Ministry were turned out. This is the secret of the dubious character of the declaration; nowhere does it mention exclusive rights, neither in the proclamation issued by the Governors, nor in the Act 28 George III. c. xxv.; Lord Palmerston might well say:—

"In no similar instrument which has ever come under the notice of the British Government, is so important a concession as an exclusive privilege of this description, announced in terms so loose and indefinite.

"Exclusive rights are privileges which from the very nature of things, are likely to be injurious to parties who are thereby debarred from some exercise of industry in which they would otherwise engage. Such rights are therefore certain to be at some time or other disputed, if there is any maintainable ground for contesting them; and for these reasons when negotiations have intended to grant exclusive rights, it has been their invariable practice to convey such rights in direct, unqualified, and comprehensive terms, so as to prevent the possibility of future dispute or doubt.

"In the present case, however, such forms of expression are entirely wanting, and the claim put forward on the part of France, is founded simply upon inference and upon an assumed interpretation of words."

This is a very ably written despatch. It appears to me, however, after having carefully read the immense correspondence on the subject, that, notwithstanding all the hair-splitting letters, the French argument that they have a prior claim to the fishing on the Treaty Shore had great force, and if they had been able to occupy every inch of the ground with their fishing operations, from Cape John to Cape Ray, they could maintain their position: but, unfortunately for them, they never could do so, and the inexorable logic of events—the failing shore fishery and the permanent settlement of so many British subjects on the shore (which was originally *encouraged* by the French), and the settlers' persistence in fishing—has, at present, reduced the French treaty rights to mere barren privileges. They can have no permanent buildings of any kind, they cannot remain behind to look after their property, and the codfish—their chief end and aim—has forsaken the coast, except in the early spring, when the western shore men snatch a voyage before the French arrive, and in the autumn take another good trip or two after they have left. The assertion of French right has, in our days, become a mere dog-in-the-manger policy. Add to this the fact that they have virtually abandoned the treaty shore, and that about a dozen old brigs and two hundred French fishermen now represent the whole commercial status of France on this much-disputed territory.[1]

		Vessels.	Tons.	Men.
[1] The exact figures for 1888 and 1889 are the following. Since then they have much decreased	St. Juliens	1	204	11
	Port au Choix	1	204	11
	Ile St. Jean	3	407	51
	Cap Rouge	2	235	33
	Le Croc	2	598	36
	Ile Rouge	1	112	7
	West Coast	4	614	85
		14	2,374	234

Whilst the French have diminished, the English population has increased, and now numbers over *thirteen thousand permanent settlers.*

The whole French case at the present day rests on the declaration of George III., a secret, fraudulent proceeding: foreign diplomatists would at once have found a way out of such a promise—England did not do so The strongest assurance the Emperor Nicholas could give was " on the honour of an English gentleman." Whatever one may think, therefore, either of the legality or of the morality of the Royal declaration, it was clearly binding on the English Government until abrogated by war; the original Treaty of Utrecht had a clear meaning it gave the French a *concurrent* fishery, regulated and controlled *exclusively* by English authorities; our history shows that this was the uniform system on which it was carried on up to 1783. It is an elementary rule of international law that the sovereign power alone exercises authority within its own territory. Whatever rights France may have on the Newfoundland treaty shore, they must be carried out under English supervision and control; neither France nor any other foreign power can exercise coercive jurisdiction on English territory. It will appear strange to many English readers, but it is nevertheless true, that England has never maintained this principle until the last few years. Lord Salisbury was the first English minister to put his foot down firmly and declare that no French officer would be permitted to seize English boats, cut English nets, or to drive English fishermen out of their own harbours.[1]

We have seen in the foregoing pages some of the outrageous proceedings of the courts of justice in their criminal proceedings, mainly directed against poor Irish Roman Catholics: subsequently these absurd tribunals went further and filled up the measure of their iniquity. A more incongruous caricature of law and justice can hardly be imagined than the so-called Court of Oyer and Terminer. The chief justice at one time was the Church of England minister, the Rev. Edward Langman; at another time the ordnance storekeeper, White (later on the naval officer, sworn broker, sole notary public and sole auctioneer). The most cruel proceedings were under his tenure of the chief justiceship. In 1785 he had grown so arrogant that he refused to serve as a justice unless he was made keeper of the Rolls: on the 6th of October of that year Governor Campbell therefore struck his name off the Commission of the Peace. The two cases I am about to

---

[1] The House of Commons, in October 1893, was much amused at a notice given by the Commander of H.M.S. *Pelican* to the English inhabitants of St. George's Bay, prohibiting them from selling herring except to French vessels, and, it follows as a consequence, at the prices the French chose to give for them.

refer to are set forth fully in the parliamentary report on the courts of justice in Newfoundland, and also in the manuscript history of Dr. Gardner of Boston, U.S.[1] In the summer of 1784 a French brig was lost at Greenspond.

Dr. Gardner says:—

"Finding that the vessel must be lost altogether, some of the Planters at Greenspond made free with some of the property on board which occasioned the French Captain to go to St. John's and complain to the judge of the Vice-Admiralty Court, who immediately issued out a summons against sixteen of the principal planters, who he pretends had plundered his ship, and in the height of the fishing season they were sent prisoners to St. John's to be tried for their lives and for that purpose detained there in custody until October; at the same time, previous to the trial, their effects were attached; the consequence was that upwards of £1500 is said to have been lost by this unlawful act.

"The men were all acquitted except one who, being found guilty of having endeavoured to secrete some goods from on board the wreck, was condemned to die, but so shocking was this decree for a fault or crime which in this country [America] would be deemed petit larceny that the French Captain and the prosecutors petitioned the Governor to pardon him, who humanely complied with the request. The poor man, by name George Clarke, was so shocked at the treatment he sustained together with the loss of his property which was all sold by order of the Judge of the Vice-Admiralty Court (and the amount is now in his hands), that he came to England and soon died of grief.

"It is melancholy to relate that some of these poor men were tried for their lives merely for having a dozen spike nails found upon them, which they delivered up to the first person who appeared to receive them. The cruelty of these proceedings needs no comment. Had a Court been instituted directly, and a person acquainted with the laws appointed to try them on the spot, the injured would have been redressed, and the guilty, if any, punished, and these industrious men by being employed in the fishery during the season enabled to make good their payments to their employers, or bail might have been taken for their appearance after the fishing season was over. But that would not have suited the purpose of the Admiralty Court at St. John's, the fees of which are most enormous. . . ."[2]

The following statement is taken from the sworn evidence of Richard Routh, Collector of the Customs—afterwards appointed Chief Justice by the British Government:—

"For the sole purpose of fees the Magistrates licensed 108 Public Houses in St. John's alone at 4½ guineas each; one-half of this went to the three Justices, the other half to the Public funds.

---

[1] Dr. Gardner was a leading physician in Boston, the first to introduce vaccination into New England; besides his practice he carried on a large wholesale drug business, supplying all the Eastern States with his medicines; by this means, which was a great innovation on established practices, he made a large fortune, with which he founded the town of "Gardner," in Maine; he was an ardent Royalist, and when the British troops left Boston he followed them, and came down to Newfoundland; after the Revolution he returned to Boston, where he died at a very advanced age. He was a man distinguished for high character, for active benevolence, and stern unbending loyalty. His history is in manuscript (B.M. MS. 15493), I regret I have only space to make a few extracts from it.

[2] This story is not a bit exaggerated. The case is reported shortly in the Records, 23 Oct. 1784.—The French brig was called *L'Actiffe*, the master's name Y. le l'omelle, Louis Gouillon was second master, and Frans. Gouillon, surgeon.

"There were other means of increasing their incomes by fines the most oppressive. . . . A poor inoffensive taylor [Foreham] had for several days [in the summer of 1783] been intoxicated and was by that means rendered insane; in this situation he affronted his neighbour, a widow woman, with improper language, accusing everyone of robbing him. She being unacquainted with the state of his mind applied to the magistrates. The taylor was summoned but regardless of every event [in his insane condition] he did not appear. He was fined for contempt of Court *one hundred and fifty pounds* and his property attached for the amount. . . ."[1]

The three magistrates divided the fines; this would not be a bad day's work. Routh says there was not a single instance of a poor man recovering against a merchant before these justices except one. A judgment was given against a man named O'Driscoll, of Bay Bulls, in the matter of Brook's estate; as he was passing along the street, down-hearted about his case, which spelled ruin for him, a friend pointed out Prince William Henry (afterwards William IV.); "get him to plead your case agen," said the Irish friend, "and bedad you will win before ould judge"; so O'Driscoll accosted the Prince, told him his miserable story, and the Prince, a jolly good-natured sailor, went off with him hot foot to the justice, and pleaded his cause so ably that judgment was given in his favour; the first case, it is alleged, old Mr. Gill ever gave against a merchant.

The following account of the Newfoundland courts of law was written in 1784 by Dr. Gardner:—

"The present Government of Newfoundland such as it is, is in the Admiralty; they send out an Admiral annually for the Governor, who resides at St. John's the capital of the Island during the fishing season, which generally lasts near or quite four months. His Commission authorizes him to appoint Courts of Oyer and Terminer and Justices of the Peace in any Harbour in the Island; there are likewise Justice Courts appointed by him to be held at St. John's once every week [they were held twice a week—on Tuesdays and Fridays]. These, with the Court of Vice-Admiralty, are the only Courts instituted in the Island.

"The present Judge of the Admiralty, who the Governor seems to make the head of the Law Department, was obliged to leave this country about thirty years ago, and went to the Bay of Bulls at Newfoundland, where he lived as a Clerk to a gentleman concerned in the fishery. After some time he went to St. John's and kept a small school which he did not find answer his expectations, he therefore became a retailer of spirituous liquors. However he may be found qualified for the business of a gin shop, those who are best acquainted with him declare with one voice that he is unworthy of holding the posts he now sustains.

"The Judges who compose the Court of Oyer and Terminer are usually, the Judge of the Admiralty who presides, two or three justices, one or two Merchant men not the least acquainted with law or the form of it. Their Commission is during the session and renewed every year. They have no salaries and therefore

---

[1] Gardner says the magistrates were well aware of Foreham's condition of mind. He was a man of means, and therefore a good subject to be mulcted.

we may suppose make the most of their places. The expense of the most trifling cause is commonly £20 and the poor wretches by paying it feel much misery and distress. The six persons usually on the Bench on these occasions with the sheriff have each two guineas for every trial. The clerks, gaolers, and constables' fees make up the rest; so that rather than be at so heavy an expense to prosecute, the culprit often goes without punishment."

The final result of all this cruelty and injustice was to create a terrible feeling of indignation against the courts. I have mentioned before that their constitution was illegal. Governor Edwards, after his return from Newfoundland, was sued at Exeter. The presiding judge, unwilling to have his Excellency's judgment exposed and his illegal proceedings published to the world, suggested a compromise. This case made the governors more cautious; they never took part again in open court. The final change came about in rather a curious way.

Admiral Mark Milbanke,[1] who entered on the government of Newfoundland in 1789, was advised by his admirable secretary, Aaron Graham, to create a court of common pleas, with regular judges, instead of justices of the peace. It was a fortunate mistake, as it led to a more careful investigation and inspection of our judicial system by the House of Commons. Grievous complaints were made by the merchants against Sir Mark's new tribunal. Finally, in 1791, the House of Commons passed an Act—31 Geo. III. c. xxix.—creating a court designated "The Court of Civil Jurisdiction of our Lord the King at St. John's, in the Island of Newfoundland." This was presided

JOHN REEVES.
From an engraving after Dannsman.

[1] Mark Milbanke, the third son of Sir Ralph Milbanke, of Halnaby, Yorkshire, entered the Navy in 1737 as a scholar at Portsmouth. After serving in various ships without seeing much service, he was sent in 1758 in the Guernsey, on a mission to the Emperor of Morocco. He sat on the Keppel court-martial, was made rear-admiral of the White in 1779. During the following years he occasionally acted in place of Admiral Shuldham as commander-in-chief at Plymouth. In 1782 he held a command in the grand fleet under Lord Howe, with whom he took part in the demonstration in the North Sea, the relief of Gibraltar, and the action off Cape Spartel. From 1783 to 1786 he was port admiral at Plymouth, and 1790-1-2 Governor of Newfoundland. He was commander-in-chief at Portsmouth, 1799 to 1803, but had no active command during the war. He died in 1805.—(STEPHEN'S Nat. Dict. of Biography.)

over by Chief Justice Reeves,[1] and was only to continue for one year; next year it was properly set forth by 32 Geo. III. c. xlvi., as "The Supreme Court of Judicature of the Island of Newfoundland." It was also only for one year, but was continued annually until 1809. John Reeves, again made Chief Justice, had been law adviser to the Board of Trade; he was an admirable official—industrious, painstaking, firm, and resolutely impartial; the whole reformation in our judicial system is due to him, Aaron Graham,[2] and Admiral Mark Milbanke.[3]

It was a terribly up-hill struggle; the West Country merchants fought as resolutely against the courts as they had formerly done against the

---

[1] Chief Justice Reeves, to whose high qualities I have endeavoured to do justice, shows in one of his judgments that, even under his able administration, the quality of mercy was not strained. He tried some fishermen for taking eggs at the Funk Islands, which was forbidden by Proclamation; it was proved that one of the culprits, Clarke, lived at Greenspond; he was in want of food for his family, and the eggs were taken solely to obtain some for his wife and children. Whilst sentencing the other prisoners to be *publicly* whipped, he solemnly ordered that, out of regard to these mitigating circumstances in Clarke's case, he was only to be *privately* flogged. We do not think this unfortunate victim of a cruel law appreciated the distinction.

[2] Aaron Graham had been secretary to the two former governors; to his advocacy we are largely indebted for our courts of justice, and every improvement in their administration. He was a most able and enlightened official, and, as Coghlan truly says, was the virtual governor of the Colony. He afterwards filled the important position of police magistrate in London.

[3] THE FORMATION OF THE SUPREME COURT.

Whitehall, 22nd March, 1794.
MY LORDS,
I am to inform your Lordships that in the sessions of Parliament of 1791, 1792 and 1793, there were passed the annual Acts for instituting Courts of Judicature in Newfoundland (Stat. 31 Geo. III. cap. xxix., 32 Geo. III. c. xlvi. and 33 Geo. III. c. lxxvi.).

Under the first of these Acts, His Majesty was pleased by the authority thereby vested in him, to appoint Mr. Reeves Chief Judge of the said island; and the Governor of the said island, in conjunction with Mr. Reeves, under the authority vested in them by the said Act, appointed Mr. Aaron Graham, the Governor's secretary, and Mr. D'Ewes Coke, a magistrate resident in the said island, to be assessors in the said Court.

Mr. Reeves accordingly proceeded to Newfoundland, and there, with the assistance of those two gentlemen, discharged the duties of his office and returned back to England.

In the year 1792 His Majesty was pleased by virtue of the power vested in him by the second of the said Acts to appoint Mr. Reeves Chief Justice, and that gentleman did accordingly a second time proceed to Newfoundland, and return back to this kingdom. In this second Act there was no direction as to appointing any assessors.

In the last session of Parliament, His Majesty was in like manner again authorized to appoint a Chief Justice and he was pleased to appoint the before mentioned D'Ewes Coke to be Chief Justice in the court established by the third of the said Acts. For the trouble these gentlemen have had in discharging the duties of their respective offices, I am of opinion they should be paid the following sums, viz.:—

For the first year, Mr. Reeves, £500, Mr. Graham, £200, Mr. Coke, £200.
For the second year, Mr. Reeves, £500.
For the third year, Mr. Coke, £300.

By the first of the before-mentioned Acts of Parliament, the Governor and the Chief Justice are authorized to settle the allowance to be made to the assessors, and they have recommended the above sums as reasonable compensation. The Governor and Chief Justice have also authority under all the acts to settle what should be paid to the clerks for their trouble, and it has been agreed by them as follows:—

For the first year, to the first clerk, £40, to the second clerk, £25.
For the second year to the clerk, £40.
For the third year, £40.

It has been found since the first year that one clerk is sufficient to conduct the business . . . . These salaries were to be allowed in lieu of all fees or emoluments whatsoever.

I am, &c.
HENRY DUNDAS.

Lords Commissioners
of the Treasury.

settlers. The two most determined antagonists were Mr. Peter Ougier, a Devonshire merchant in Bay Bulls, and Mr. William Newman of Dartmouth. As a sample of their reasonable proposals, I will quote one case only. Judgment was given against a merchant on a bill of exchange for £12 for a servant's wages; the defendant would not pay, on the ground that the bill was endorsed by a marksman. The court, holding the endorsement good, gave judgment accordingly, and, as the merchant's agent would not pay, execution had to issue. The defendant considered himself most cruelly ill-treated because the Privy Council, on his urgent appeal, refused to send home, as prisoners to England, the judges, the sheriff, and all officers of the court concerned in the transaction. Reeves, by his firmness, courtesy, and resolute impartiality, finally triumphed over all opposition; it was, however, a very long time before things quieted down.

The records of the first courts, in the beautiful handwriting of the Chief Justice, are still preserved. Besides his well-known "History of Newfoundland" we have his voluminous evidence given before the House of Commons Committee, and a treatise on the new court. Reeves was succeeded in 1792 by D'Ewes Coke. He had settled in Trinity as a surgeon; to eke out his small income as a doctor he had acted as a scrivener, justice of the peace, and keeper of rolls. From Trinity he migrated to St. John's, became chief judge, and, later on, assessor with Aaron Graham in the first court of 1791. D'Ewes Coke continued to preside in the Supreme Court as Lord Chief Justice until 1797, when he was succeeded by Richard Routh, Collector of the Customs—a man of considerable ability, and firm, determined character.

The Governors required the Chief Justices to reside in the Colony. Routh prayed the Governor very earnestly that this rule might be relaxed on his behalf for one season (1800), which was granted; the vessel on her passage home was lost with all hands. His widow was allowed a pension for several years afterwards. D'Ewes Coke had only £300 a year, but I think his successors had £500. During 1801 no Chief Justice was appointed, but in 1802 Jonathan Ogden was made Acting Chief Justice. He had been Supreme Surrogate and Deputy Naval Officer under Richard Hatt Noble, Naval Officer, who was allowed to remain in England and execute the office by deputy, a common practice in the Georgian era. Jonathan Ogden had been sent out as a surgeon's mate to the St. John's Hospital; he seems only to have occupied the position for a short time, and appears to have been a man of sound judgment, on whom the Governor placed great reliance. After two doctors and a collector, the next Chief Justice was a merchant, Thomas Tremlett, or

VIEW OF QUIDI VIDI

THE NARROWS, ST. JOHN'S

Trimlett His firm had been very large Newfoundland merchants; they came to grief through some outside speculation, and, in accordance with the custom of the country, he received a Government office. There never was a more independent, upright judge than Tremlett; his decisions gave great offence to his quondam friends in the trade. They made constant complaints against him; finally they embodied their grievances in a long, elaborate petition containing three specific charges of injustice. The Governor, Admiral Duckworth, furnished the old chief with the complaints against him. His reply was unique.[1] I give it in full:—

"To the first charge Your Excellency I answer that it is a lie, to the second charge I say that it is a d——d lie, and to the third charge that it is a d——d infernal lie, and Your Excellency I have no more to say. Your Excellency's obt. Servant

"THOMAS TREMLETT."

Tremlett was sustained in his position both by the Governor and the authorities in England.[2] It was, however, considered desirable that a man of more legal knowledge, of more popular manners, and unconnected with local interests, should be appointed. His Lordship was therefore transferred to Prince Edward's Island. The choice next fell upon an eccentric Irish gentleman of good family, Cæsar Colclough, who was Chief Justice of that Island. Tremlett was the last of the unlearned;

---

[1] Of course, besides this letter, there was a formal official one from Tremlett.

[2] DESPATCH OF GOVERNOR SIR J. T. DUCKWORTH ON THE CHARGES AGAINST CHIEF JUSTICE TREMLETT.

"The chief justice of Newfoundland, as far as my intercourse with him has enabled me to judge, is a person who will not be influenced in the discharge of his duty by the approbation or disapprobation of any man. Of his legal knowledge I can form no opinion, but of his abilities I am far from thinking poorly, and a salary of seven hundred pounds a year is not likely to induce a more competent person to accept the office. He is certainly a man of great diligence and application, but he has by an irritability of temper, and a certain rudeness of manner which are natural to him, and by separating himself entirely from the society of the people of the town, rendered himself in the last degree unpopular; and however circumspect his future conduct may be in the discharge of his public duties, he will never be approved by them. How far, in the cases now under discussion, he may have been to blame, it is extremely difficult for me to know. They occurred chiefly before I came to the Government and there is scarcely any person capable of giving information relative to them who is not influenced in some measure by a feeling of party. The complainants are urgent for a *public examination* of evidence upon the spot, alleging that they are not equal to a discussion with the chief justice on *paper*; that his representations are filled with falsehood, and that there is no other method of proceeding effectually than that of a public enquiry at which they may be able to bring forward their witnesses upon oath. Your lordship will perceive from my correspondence with the complainants that they reserve to themselves to transmit additional statements. I have shown to them the defence of the chief justice which is enclosed herewith, and they aver that it is filled with misrepresentation. If your lordship or the Lords of the Committee of Council should be pleased to require from me more minute information in this matter, I beg to be honoured with your commands, but it is my duty to state distinctly in this report that in whatever instances his judgement may have erred, I have not found in any part of the chief justice's conduct the most remote appearance of corruption, nor when I have called upon the complainants, have they ventured to charge him with it in any instance. As your lordship will perceive that the accompanying statements are not of subsequently the head of the Supreme Court was a barrister of not less than seven years' standing.

Vice-Admiral John Campbell was Governor from 1782 to 1785; he appears to have been an able and enlightened ruler.[1] John Jones, a dissenting preacher, who founded Congregationalism in the Colony in 1782, gives a pleasing picture of his Excellency, "as beyond all expression gentle, mild, and good-natured." In 1784 he issued the

a nature to admit of my sending duplicates to the Lords of the Committee of Privy Council for Trade, I take the liberty of requesting that they may be forwarded when your lordship has done with them.

"I have the honour to be very respectfully
"My Lord,
"Your Lordship's
"Most obedient humble servant,
"J. T. DUCKWORTH.
"To the Earl of Liverpool."

REPORT BY THE LORDS OF THE COMMITTEE OF COUNCIL FOR TRADE AND FOREIGN PLANTATIONS.

Downing Street, 13 June, 1812.

"Referring to papers sent on 28 October 1811 of complaints preferred by the Merchants of St. John's against the Chief Justice of Newfoundland . . . . .

"Their Lordships have averted in the first instance to the charge made against John Reeves Esq., late Chief Justice ' that he had for several years together participated in the salary of the Chief Justice after he had ceased to fill that situation . . . . .'

"Their Lordships say that they have no reason to doubt the truth of Mr. Reeves' declaration that he has never received any money or money's worth in consideration of the office of Chief Justice of Newfoundland or any office place or thing relating to Newfoundland. . . . . .

"After a full enquiry and deliberation it does not appear that any act of wilful injustice has been sanctioned by Chief Justice Tremlett nor is there any well attested proof of partiality or oppression or of any unaccountable delay or unwarrantable decision.

"Under these circumstances their Lordships have not recommended His Royal Highness to dismiss the Chief Justice from the high and important situation which he fills and H.R.H. is therefore pleased to continue to confide to him the charge of administering justice in the Island of Newfoundland. . . . . .
"BATHURST.

[In a separate paper.]

"Their Lordships attribute the unpopularity of the Chief Justice not to any actual misconduct in his judicial capacity but in some degree to the invidious nature of the duties which he is called upon to execute as well as to the ungracious manner in which they may be occasionally performed. Although there may have existed no ground for serious complaint and still less for any charge of partiality or corruption there can however be little doubt that whilst the Chief Justice is continued in his present situation there will not be that general satisfaction and confidence which ought in all cases to accompany the administration of justice; and although H.R.H. will on no account consent to the dismissal of the Chief Justice or to any act which might imply the least suspicion of his integrity or even any disapprobation of his past conduct H.R.H. would nevertheless be desirous that some arrangement should be made by which Mr. Tremlett might be employed with less embarrassment and inconvenience to himself and with greater prospect of advantage to the public service. . . . . .

"Should an opportunity offer of placing Mr. Tremlett in a judicial situation of equal emolument in some other settlement he will not object to transfer his services from that which he now fills."

Witnesses to be sworn against the Chief Justice—

JOHN BLAND, High Sheriff.	JOHN BURKE, cooper.
GEO. LILLY, auctioneer.	CHRISTOPHER BROOM.
PATK. BRAZELL, cooper.	

[1] John Campbell, the son of a minister of Kirkbean, in Kirkcudbrightshire, was born in that parish about, but probably before, the year 1720. At an early age he was bound apprentice to the master of a coasting vessel, and is said to have entered the Navy by offering himself in exchange for the mate of this vessel, who had been pressed. After serving three years in the *Blenheim*, *Torbay*, and *Russell*, he was, in 1740, appointed to the *Centurion*, and sailed in her round the world with Commodore Anson, as midshipman, master's mate, and master. On his return home he passed the examination for lieutenant, and his certificate, dated 8th January 1744-5, says that he appears to be more than 24 years of age. Through Anson's interest he was very shortly afterwards made a lieutenant, then commander, and was advanced to post rank on the 23rd of November 1747, and appointed to the *Bellona* frigate, which he commanded with

following order, which stands in pleasing contrast to the proclamations of his predecessors:—

"Pursuant to the King's instructions to me you are to allow all persons inhabiting this Island to have full liberty of conscience and the free exercise of all such modes of religious worship as are not prohibited by law, provided they be contented with a quiet and peaceable enjoyment of the same, not giving offence or scandal to Government.

"JNO. CAMPBELL."

Under the benign sway of this excellent Governor the first Roman Catholic chapel was built in this year, on the site known in St. John's as the "old chapel," then called "Parson Langman's garden." Bishop O'Donel came to the Colony first as Prefect-Apostolic, with power to administer confirmation; on the 5th of January 1796 he was appointed Vicar Apostolic of Newfoundland, and Bishop of Thyatira *in partibus*. Bishop O'Donel's name is one of the most honoured in this Colony; his deeply religious character, his polished manners, and his inherent gentleness and goodness won all hearts. He had to overcome terrible obstacles—the prejudice and opposition of the strait-laced old admiral, Milbanke, and the rampant Protestantism of his surrogate.

Bishop O'Donel's career deserves every attention at the hands of the local historian. His arrival and his sojourn in the Colony are of far more importance to us than the advent of half-a-dozen admiral-governors. He brought peace, quiet, and good order; instead of silenced priests there was an authorised ecclesiastical organisation, an open administration of the rites of the church. The fugitive priests, by their example and teaching, were not conducive to harmony. In fulfilment of the divine injunction to render to Cæsar the things that are Cæsar's, Dr. O'Donel taught his people to be good Christians and good citizens. I quote from Bishop Howley an extract from the body of

---

some success till the peace. He afterwards commanded the *Mermaid*, in 1755, the *Prince*, of 90 guns, and in 1757 the *Essex*, of 64 guns, and was flag captain to Sir Edward Hawke in 1759 in the *Royal George*, and served in that capacity in the decisive battle of Quiberon Bay, 20th November 1759. Campbell was sent home with the despatches, and was taken by Anson to be presented to the king. According to the received story, Anson told him, on the way, that the king would knight him if he wished. "Troth, my lord,' answered Campbell, "I ken nae use that will be to me." "But," said Anson, "your lady may like it." "Aweel," replied Campbell, "His Majesty may knight her if he pleases." He was, in fact, not knighted. He afterwards commanded the *Dorsetshire*, of 70 guns, till the peace, and in 1770 he was in the *Royal Charlotte*, in which he remained till promoted to his flag in 1778. In the following spring he was chosen by Admiral Keppel as first captain of the *Victory*, and had thus an important share in the conduct of the fleet in the indecisive action with the French fleet under D'Orvilliers, on the 27th of July, as well as on the previous days. His loyalty to Keppel, and the rancour which the subsequent courts-martial excited, prevented his having any further employment as long as Lord Sandwich was in office, though he attained, in course of seniority, the rank of vice-admiral in 1779. In April 1782, when his friend Keppel was installed as First Lord of the Admiralty, Campbell was appointed Governor of Newfoundland and commander-in-chief on that station. He held this office for four years, and ended his service in 1786. He died in London on the 16th of December 1790.

the Diocesan Statutes of 1801 for the guidance of priests in the Colony, prepared by Bishop O'Donel. He directed:—

"That public prayers be offered up every Sunday and holiday (though but few of the latter can be observed in this Mission, and the Superior will hereafter, by a private notice, designate such as can be observed) for our Most Sovereign King George III. and his Royal family; that the priests should use every means to turn aside their flocks from the vortex of modern anarchy; that they should inculcate a willing obedience to the salutary laws of England, and to the commands of the Governor and magistrates of this Island. . . . We most earnestly entreat, and by all the spiritual authority we hold, ordain that all missioners oppose with all the means in their power all plotters, conspirators, and favorers of the infidel French, and use every endeavour to withdraw their people from the plausible cajolery of French deceit; for the aim of this conspiracy is to dissolve all bonds, all laws, by which society is held together, and more especially the laws of England, which are to be preferred to those of any other country in Europe."

The patriotic services of Bishop O'Donel at the particular crisis of the French Revolution, when rebellion and anarchy were rampant, his especial service in putting an end to the conspiracy amongst the soldiers and United Irishmen to murder the whole population of St. John's,[1] the dangers he voluntarily encountered, the secret influence his deep religious fervour exercised over these poor ignorant dupes, are only known to the Omnipotent. Under such obligations, can we wonder that Protestant vied with Catholic to do him honour, and to show their love for one who, with Colonel Skerret, under Providence had been the saviour of their lives?[2]

In recognition of his loyal conduct he had a pension from the Crown of £50 a year; it was only obtained after much petitioning and persistent application by the Governors, especially Waldegrave; everyone must agree with Bishop Mullock, that he was very poorly rewarded. A friendship existed not only amongst the Catholic and the Protestant laity, but also between Father Yore and the Church of England minister, Parson Dingle. The following letter shows, however, that all the priests were not of the same amicable disposition as their gentle chief pastor:—

"Sir,   St. Johns 19 Oct. 1785.

"Mr. WILLIAM SAUNDERS having represented to me that there is a Romish Priest named Landergan at Placentia of a very violent and turbulent spirit, who

---

[1] See the letter on this subject from Chief Justice Ogden to Governor Waldegrave, in the Appendix, p. 418.

[2] In a petition to the King from Bishop O'Donel, praying for a continuation of his pension after his retirement from the Island, he declares "that his own loyalty and services have been acknowledged and fully approved of by every Governor and particularly by General Skerret who found himself under great embarrassment in 1799 as having no force either by sea or land to oppose a most dangerous conspiracy formed against all the people of property in the Island. Petitioner was fortunate enough to bring the maddened scum of the people to cool reflection and dispersed the dangerous cloud that was ready to burst on the heads of the principal Inhabitants of this Town and even of the whole Island for which he often received the thanks of the very deluded people who were led into this dark design of robbery and assassination."

PRINCE WILLIAM.

has given great interruption to Mr. Burk, a regular and sober man of the Catholick persuasion, and that unless the former is sent out of the Country the peace of the place is in imminent danger of being disturbed—I desire that you will cause the said Latedergan to be put aboard the first vessel that may sail from Placentia for England or Ireland.

"JNO. CAMPBELL.

"H.M. Justices of the Peace at Placentia."

The toleration shown to the Roman Catholic Church had great influence on the permanent settlement of the Colony. The country boys who came out from Ireland were full of the earth hunger which distinguishes their race; they cherished the little spots of land they cleared and cultivated; the best farms around the capital are the work of either West Countrymen or Irishmen; to these two classes of settlers we owe the good cultivation and picturesque homesteads around St. John's and Conception Bay.

It is impossible, in a history of this character, to give details about the various administrations of the twenty-three governors who ruled the Island during the long reign of George III.[1] Two events, however, require more than a passing notice—the arrival of Prince William Henry (afterwards William IV.) as captain of H.M.S. *Pegasus*, in 1786, and the last attack of the French, in 1796.

His Royal Highness, in accordance with the naval rule of the day, was appointed surrogate by his commanding officer, Governor Elliott. In his letters to the Governor, the Prince appears as an attentive, careful subordinate, most respectful towards his superior officer. Later on we have a very animated and lengthy correspondence between his younger brother, the Duke of Kent (father of Her Majesty) and Governor Waldegrave, who sternly refused to recognise the Duke's authority, as lieutenant-general of the forces in Nova Scotia, over the military in Newfoundland. "Your Royal Highness has no more control over me

PRINCE WILLIAM.
From an engraving after Holmes.

---

[1] The appointment of each governor, and the principal events during his tenure of office, will be found in orderly sequence in the chronology in Chapter XXIII.

366   REIGN OF GEORGE III.

them you have over the Emperor of China," said the Governor of Newfoundland. The Duke was right, but still, all through the discussion, His Royal Highness is most respectful in his language to our haughty ruler.

Our naval Royal Highness—the Duke of Clarence—was not a model prince, but he was very good natured, and a good friend to the Colony; he ordered the building of the English church in Placentia (1787), contributed handsomely to its erection, and furnished the massive communion service, long in the custody of Dr. Bradshaw's family at Placentia. He gave a commission to one of the Collins family, who afterwards became a lieutenant.[1]

FLAKES OVER THE ROAD AT QUIDI VIDI.
From a photograph by S. H. Parsons.

On the 20th of July 1786 a great event happened in Placentia; on that memorable day His Royal Highness presided as surrogate in the noble court house of the ancient capital; the justices showed their respect for the Protestant succession by issuing an order, " That no more Catholics should be buried in the graveyard."

One of his judicial decisions is given in the Records:—

"A riot happening on shore at 4 o'clock, the Magistrate attending to suppress it, was insulted. The Prince came on shore with a guard of marines, arrested the ringleader, called a Court, and sentenced him to receive 100 lashes—he was only able to receive 80. *Not then inquired into the facts of the case*; (and report has it that they had whipped the *wrong man*)."

[1] The story goes that, in order to test the courage of the boys to be selected for commissions, the Prince made a feint to give them a tremendous blow with a stick. Young Collins, a stolid, strong fellow, never budged, and was accordingly chosen for His Majesty's service.

Many tales are told of his stay in Newfoundland. Mr. Warren, afterwards a partner in Stuart and Rennie, was going home under the flakes which covered the streets in those days; he carried a lantern; suddenly he had it seized from him by the Prince, who walked before him until they arrived opposite to where his ship lay at anchor. His Royal Highness wished him good night and returned the lantern. A lieutenant's wife got her husband's company for him by presenting a Newfoundland wild goose. But the best is about an old gentleman, who had known the Prince well in Newfoundland, calling at Kensington Palace. His Majesty was delighted to see him, gave him a glass of calabogus, and talked pleasantly over a pipe. The Newfoundlander considered it the right thing to ask after the Queen's health. His Majesty said Queen Adelaide was quite well, and would have had much pleasure in seeing him, but unfortunately it was *washing day*.

Many other anecdotes are current in the Colony about our Royal visitor. One told by Bishop Howley, about his being fired at is, apparently, a perversion of the well-known story of Sir John Harvey's son being shot by Mitchell, the butcher, for robbing his garden on Circular Road, and I cannot believe his account of the insults to Bishop O'Donel.

The great and ominous events of the year 1789—the outbreak of the French Revolution, followed by the murder of Louis XVI. and Marie Antoinette in 1793—again brought on war between England and France. On the 14th of May, our Governor, Vice-Admiral King, took possession of St. Pierre.[1] A far more memorable event even than the arrival of His Royal Highness, is the last attack of the French on the Colony, under Admiral Richery in 1796; the story is told in the Colonial Records, but is more graphically described by

ADMIRAL SIR R. KING, BART.
From an engraving of an oil portrait.

---

[1] An account of this capture will be found in the chapter devoted to the history of the French Newfoundland Colonies of St. Pierre and Miquelon.

Sir R. King, born in 1730, entered the service in 1738 on the *Berwick*, on which his father was master, but was soon moved to the *Dragon*, in command of his uncle, Curtis Barnett, whom he accompanied to the Mediterranean and the East Indies; he became a lieutenant in 1746, and commanded the boats at the capture of Calcutta in 1757.

an eye-witness, quoted by the Rev. P. Tocque. Mr. George Hutchings, grandfather of the present Mr. George A. Hutchings, rendered valuable service to the Colony by reconnoitring the movements of the invading fleet; he was specially distinguished by the Governor for his patriotic conduct.

In the mute testimony of the Records we can see the gallant old Admiral, Sir Richard Wallace, superintending, ruling, and managing everybody, the young merchants and gentlemen of the town vying with each other who should get guns and stores first up the long steep hill to the Block House, the careful watch and reports of the various parties sent along the coast from Cape Spear to Cape Race. No country has produced more gallant soldiers and sailors than fair France; Citizen Richery was not one of them; with his big fleet he never dared to come in contact with Wallace[1] and his hastily improvised levies. I quote the Rev. P. Tocque's account of the attack:—

"1794. Estimates had been prepared and approved of for repairing and improving the existing defences, and plans had also been submitted to the Board of Ordnance for fortifying Signal Hill, which having met the approbation of the Honourable Board, preparations were entered into for that object proportionate to the magnitude of the undertaking. Early this summer, Colonel Skinner, Commanding Royal Engineer, received a letter of service directing him to raise a Regiment of Fencible Infantry, to be called the Royal Newfoundland Fencibles, of which he was appointed Colonel; and having the appointment of his officers, selections were made here and at the out-ports, of such gentlemen as were likely, from their loyalty, responsibility and influence, soon to raise the quotas of men required for their respective commissions. The recruiting service commenced with great spirit about the latter end of September, at the close of the fishery, and in two months more than half the number were enlisted. An Adjutant, late a non-commissioned officer of the Royal Artillery, a Quartermaster, and Sergeant-major, arrived from England.

"1795. It has been stated that the Nova Scotia Regiment was chiefly formed of old refugee soldiers from the American Army, many of whom were well disciplined non-commissioned officers, and were of great service in drilling and forming the young recruits of the Royal Newfoundland Regiment; and it was

He saw some service on the home station in 1760, and in 1762 went with General Draper to the East Indies again, took part in the Manila expedition, and assisted Captain Parker in the capture of a rich Spanish galleon, his personal share of prize money amounting to £30,000. After various services he was again in the East Indies in 1779 in the *Exeter*, and was made an established commodore and second-in-command to Sir E. Hughes. In the action off Sadras in February 1782, the *Exeter* received the whole brunt of the French attack, King's flag captain being killed by his side, and his ship dismasted; asked what was to be done, he replied, "Nothing but to fight her till she sinks." King took part in the four actions between Hughes and Suffren, and the *Exeter* became so unseaworthy that she was condemned at the Cape. King was knighted on his return to England, and became rear-admiral in 1787; he was made a baronet in 1792, and after his return from Newfoundland was elected M.P. for Rochester. He became a full admiral in 1795, and died in 1806.—(STEPHEN's *Nat. Dict. of Biog.*)

[1] The existing memorial of Sir James Wallace is the pointed rock often called Crow's Nest, but properly named Wallace's Battery; it is being gradually destroyed being used by spoilers as a stone quarry

THE LAST FRENCH INVASION.

astonishing how soon the latter became fit for duty; when this service was performed the Nova Scotia Regiment were ordered to return to Halifax.

"In the meantime some buildings were erected at Signal Hill, and the first block-house commenced . . . . There being no carriage road to Signal Hill, all the guns required for the Hill were taken by men of the garrison, and parbuckled up the face of the rock at Crow's Nest, and thence to the respective batteries—a most laborious and dangerous service.

"Preparations for the more effectual defence of the Narrows were also going on, in the formation of three furnaces for heating shot, viz.: At Fort Frederick, Chain Rock, and Fort William. A large naval force from different stations met here that summer, consisting of the *Monarch* (74), the Governor's ship, the *Romilies* (74), the *Meteor*, and another six; four frigates, and three sloops of war, all in the harbour at the same time.

"1796. The levy of the Royal Newfoundland Regiment had been completed the preceding fall; and it was found that the barracks at Forts Townsend and William were insufficient to contain so many men; it was therefore ordered that

the garrison should go under canvas for a few months while the old barracks were being repaired and cleansed, and some of the new barracks at Signal Hill finished, and also for the greater facility of practising the officers and men of that young regiment in the indispensable tactics and operations of the field. A camp was accordingly formed on the general parade ground with a small park of artillery, of which the troops took possession about the middle of June. The improved defences of the Narrows being finished, some experiments were tried with heated shot before His Excellency Admiral Sir James Wallace, the Governor, which gave general satisfaction. A large platform of wood was built on South Point called the Duke of York's Battery, on which were mounted eight 24-pounder guns, three or four 18-pounder carronades, and two 10-inch mortars. The Blockhouse was so forward as to admit six guns to be mounted on the second floor. The regiment by this time—the latter part of August—was approaching fast to systematic regularity and discipline, and of approved internal economy.

1 p. 2729.

"Such being the state of the garrison and fortifications, together with the efficiency of the volunteer companies—a fine set of men particularly the company of volunteer artillery selected from among the flower of the Inhabitants of St. John's—as well as the undoubted loyalty of the Inhabitants, a wish seemed to be inspired that something might happen to test the fidelity of the whole. If such was the case it was not long before that wish was realised, for early in the morning of the first day of September the signal was made for an enemy's fleet to the Southward, which proved to be the French Admiral with seven sail of the line, two frigates and some other small vessels of war. The signal of alarm in the town was instantly made at Signal Hill and all the forts. There was only the Governor's ship and one frigate in Port. [The Governor's own report says there was one fifty-gun ship, two frigates, and a sloop of war.] His Excellency Admiral Sir James Wallace,[1] a Governor of warlike celebrity, immediately proclaimed martial law and ordered all the men in the town fit for service—merchants with their domestic and wharf establishments, Captains of vessels with their crews, planters with their fishermen and sharemen—to muster in front of the camp where they were enrolled and told off to the forts and batteries and they were not to be dismissed until the Governor's pleasure was known.

"The enemy stood off and on near Cape Spear all that day and during the night the road was open from Magotty Cove Bridge through the enclosures leading to Signal Hill, by direction of the Governor, in order to expedite the transport of ammunition, stores, and provisions to Signal Hill, as well as the camp equipage, which had been struck in the evening; and by daylight in the morning of the 2nd the tents were all pitched on the summit of the Hill—from the Duke of York's battery to Cuckold Head and also on the south side Hills over Fort Amherst. This warlike demonstration with the display of three or four thousand men on the Hill must have had a very intimidating effect on Monsieur when viewed from the sea.

"This day passed off under something like a passive hesitation on the part of the enemy a great deal of telegraphing and boat communication took place with the flagship and towards the evening the fleet stood a little further off to sea; reconnoitring parties were out along the shore day and night in anticipation of a landing being effected. A great many seamen were employed that day in raising the chain across the Narrows, the great capstan at the south side being assisted by three schooners placed at equal distances from Chain Rock and by grappling the chain with their anchors and heaving all together they raised it to the surface of the water. These vessels were also charged with combustibles and were intended

---

[1] The first notice of Wallace is his command of the *Trial* sloop in 1763, on the Newfoundland station; in 1774 he was again on this station, in the *Rose* (20). He was sent by Admiral Shuldham from St. John's to Boston, with a detachment of the 65th Regiment. An armed mob having seized cannon and ammunition in Fort George, Newport, and carried them to Providence, he demanded to know why the Governor had allowed the fort to be dismantled. The reply was: "To prevent them falling into the hands of the King's servant, and to make use of them against any Power that shall molest us." Wallace was in many of the engagements in 1775-6-7-8 at Rhode Island and New York. He very gallantly repulsed the French squadron sent to take the Channel Islands in 1779, and went with Admiral Darby to the relief of Gibraltar in 1781. His attack upon a French 74 in this same year is one of the most brilliant examples of British valour and perseverance. He was soon appointed to the *Warrior* (74); in 1793 became colonel of marines; in 1794 Rear-Admiral of the White, and to command at Newfoundland; and in 1795 Vice-Admiral of the White. For his exertions to repel Admiral Richery, he was voted the sincere and heartfelt thanks of the merchants of St. John's. He undertook no further service after retiring from the Newfoundland command, and died in 1803. He was knighted in 1777. His services during the American War were very brilliant; but, in spite of his abilities and worth, he did not receive the degree of attention and reward he was entitled to.—(From ROLFE's *Naval Biography*, vol. i., p. 413.)

to be used as fire ships on the enemy coming in contact with the chain. The flag ship and the frigate were also placed in enfilading distances in the Harbour to give them a warm reception on entering the Narrows. On the first appearance of the enemy the shot furnaces were kindled, it was found difficult however to preserve the proper degree of heat and to prevent fusion which happened to some of the shot.

"On the 3d the enemy formed a line and stood in for the Narrows, when it was expected their intention was to attempt a landing; they stood on until the van ships came within the extreme range of the guns of Fort Amherst, when she and all of them put about and stood out to sea. They remained in sight for several days and at last bore away to the southward and arrived at Bay Bulls where they landed and to consummate their dastardly conduct, they drove the poor defenceless inhabitants to the woods."

In the words of the local poet of the southern shore—

"Burnt their stores and houses,
Took their fish and oil,
The hard-earned produce
Of their yearly toil."

Thus terminated the great excitement occasioned by the appearance of this formidable armament. The detachments at the respective posts were all continued until the French fleet had entirely left the coast. Only one man and a boy were allowed on each merchant's establishment, all the rest were stationed at the forts and batteries. The enemy remained in Bay Bulls from the 4th to the 8th. On the 5th they set the town on fire; on the 6th a gale of wind came and prevented their further progress; on the 8th they unmoored and left. Their further exploits were to destroy what remained of St. Pierre— then in possession of the English; they also burnt some fishing rooms in the straits of Belle Isle. In Bay Bulls the French captured a couple of merchant vessels, and Mr. Dingle,

MILITARY COSTUME.

the magistrate. One captain was brought on board of Admiral Richery's flag ship, the *Jupiter*. When asked about the strength of St. John's, he lied "like an ambassador for the good of his country"; he said there were five thousand troops; that they could not enter St. John's on account of the boom and chain, and that two hundred guns would fly on them if they came in. The French seemed to doubt the number of troops, but on his boldly repeating his statement the Admiral gave up the idea of attacking the town.

The French Republican newspapers gave a flaming account of Richery's great warlike exploit; that he had landed fifteen hundred men at Bay Bulls, two thousand at Portugal Cove, and had captured a large number of ships and fishing vessels and a thousand sailors which had been sent to St. Domingo.

The Honourable William Waldegrave[1]—the last naval Governor in the eighteenth century, 1797-8-9—was a son of the Earl of Waldegrave. No administrator of the Colony, with the exception of Palliser, did more for the island. He had greatly distinguished himself as a dashing captain of a frigate and as admiral. The period of his government was a very troubled one, the mutiny of the Nore extending even to Newfoundland. A rebellion broke out on board H.M.S. *Latona*, and was only quelled by the officers drawing their swords and the marines presenting their bayonets; they actually had to prick the mutineers before they would give in. In his address to the ship's crew on the following Sunday the Admiral told them:—

LORD RADSTOCK.
From an engraving after Hopner.

"You are all eager for news and newspapers. I thank God I have the satisfaction to inform you that your great delegate Parker is hanged, with many other of his atrocious companions. You looked up to him as an example whilst he was

---

[1] William Waldegrave, first Lord Radstock, G.C.B., born 9th July 1753, was second son of John, third Earl of Waldegrave (by Elizabeth Gower, sister of Granville, first Marquess of Stafford, K.G.); entered the Navy about 1766. As early as 1775 he obtained command of the *Zephyr* sloop, and was shortly afterwards—May 30th, 1766—posted into the *Ripon*, 60, bearing the broad pennant of Sir Edward Vernon, in the East Indies. He afterwards commanded the *Pomona*, 28, in which ship he captured the *Cumberland*, a notorious American privateer of 20 guns and 170 men; and in the *Prudente*, 38—aided to some extent by the *Licorne*, 32—he succeeded in capturing 4th July 1780—the French frigate *La Capricieuse* of 32 guns and 308 men, more than 100 of whom, in the course of an obstinate engagement of four hours, were either killed or wounded, with a loss to the *Prudente* of 17 killed and 28 wounded; he afterwards, in the same ship, took *L'Americaine* privateer of 32 guns and 245 men. He accompanied Admiral Darby to the relief of Gibraltar, and assisted under Admiral

in his glory, I recommend you to look to his end as an example also. . . . .
. . . . I have now to tell you that I have given orders to all your officers, that in case of any further signs of mutiny they are not to think of confining the ringleaders, but to put them to death instantly, and what is still more, I have given orders to the batteries to burn the *Latona* with red-hot shot in case you drive me by your mutinous conduct to that extremity. I know in this case the officers must perish with you, but there is not one of them but is ready to sacrifice himself for the good of his country in any mode whatever . . . . And now go to church and pray God to inspire you with such sentiments as may acquire you the respect and love of your Countrymen in this World and eternal happiness in the next."

The fire-eating old sailor who made this address was most sincerely religious, and, in private life, the kindest and most benevolent of men; he looked carefully after the food and comfort of the soldiers and sailors, organised a society for the relief of the poor in St. John's, and was all his life a permanent subscriber of £20 annually to this fund. It was mainly through his exertions that the old Anglican church in St. John's was thoroughly repaired and improved; it had fallen into such a dilapidated condition that it could not be used, and divine service had to be held every Sunday in the court house. Through Waldegrave's active exertions over £1,500 was obtained from the king, the Society for the Propagation of the Gospel, and private friends—His Excellency being the most liberal subscriber of all. He exerted himself also to increase the miserable salaries of the clergymen in the Colony. Bishop O'Donel, and all who came in contact with the Admiral, pay a warm tribute to his fine character. It was very fortunate for our island that in such troublous times as the Irish rebellion, the conspiracy in St. John's, and the mutiny of the *Latona*, the Government was in the hands of a ruler at once so benevolent, so just, and above all so courageous.

Kempenfeldt in capturing part of a French convoy under M. De Guichen, and obtained possession of another privateer, the *Boulogne*, of 16 guns. During the subsequent peace, Captain Waldegrave, with the exception of a short period in command of the *Majestic*, 74, was on half-pay. In 1793, on the commencement of the French revolutionary war, he was appointed to the command of the *Courageux*, 74, when he served under Lord Hood in the Mediterranean. He was nominated a colonel of marines on 11th of April 1794, and was advanced the 4th of July following to the rank of rear-admiral, and on the 1st June 1795 was made a vice-admiral. In the spring of 1796 he was sent with five ships of the line to conduct a negotiation of great delicacy with the Bey of Tunis. Subsequently he fought as third in command in Sir John Jervis' victory over the Spanish fleet off Cape St. Vincent, February 14th, 1797. For his cool, steady, and meritorious conduct on that memorable occasion, he was offered a baronetcy, which he declined, as being inferior to the rank of an earl's son. He was shortly afterwards appointed Governor of Newfoundland, where he remained for three years; and on the 29th of December 1800 was raised to the peerage of Ireland as Baron Radstock of Castle Town, Queen's County. In April 1802 he became a full admiral. About the same period he was nominated commander-in-chief in the East Indies, but in consequence of the cessation of hostilities he did not accept the appointment. He was created a G.C.B. in 1815, and died on the 20th August 1825.

The opening years of the present century were peaceful and uneventful in our island Colony; the fisheries were successful, the country prosperous. After the dangerous conspiracy of the United Irishmen had been put down with a strong hand, and the mutiny on board the *Latona* quelled by the firmness and severity of Waldegrave, the magistrates report to the new Governor for 1800—Vice-Admiral Charles Morice Pole—that peace and good order prevail both in the city and the Colony. Next year there was neither Governor nor Chief Justice. Admiral Pole never returned to the Colony, and poor Routh was drowned on the passage home in November; Newfoundland, however, does not appear to have felt their loss. Later on, at the end of the summer, Doctor J. Ogden was made Acting Chief Justice, and Captain Robert Barton, of H.M.S. *La Concorde*, Lieut-Governor. Barton gave himself more airs and assumed more authority than a duly commissioned administrator. His presumption caused a little friction with Brigadier-General Skerrett, an old campaigner, with six hundred troops under his command, who could not brook being ordered about by a young captain in the Navy. The magistrates for St. John's—Ogden, Rev. J. Harris, and George Williams,

---

Sir C. M. Pole, born in 1757, entered the Royal Naval Academy, Portsmouth, in 1770; was a lieutenant in the commodore's ship in the action with the French off Trincully, and commanded a body of seamen and marines at the siege of Pondicherry; on the surrender of that place he was made master of the *Cormorant* sloop; he became post-captain in 1779. He gallantly captured a large Spanish frigate, the *Santa Catalina*, in 1782, for which he was praised by Nelson, who wrote: "In seamanship he showed himself as superior to the Dons as in gallantry"; ..."he was a young man who bore his own merits with so much modesty." In 1788 he he was made a groom of the bedchamber to the Duke of Clarence. He served with Lord Hood at Toulon, and in 1795 became Rear-Admiral of the Blue. He was in command at the unsuccessful attack on the Spanish fleet at the Isle of Aix in 1799, and next year was appointed to the Newfoundland station; he only held the post for one year, as he was appointed to succeed Nelson, who was indisposed, in the Baltic. He was made a baronet in 1801 and vice-admiral in 1802; he sat for Newark. In 1803 he was president of the Board of Naval Commissioners to investigate abuses, and 1806 became one of the Lords of the Admiralty. In 1805 he was made Admiral of the Blue, and in 1818 G.C.B. (From Ralfe's *Naval Biography*, vol. ii., p. 129.)

Chief Justice Ogden received his formal commission and was actually sworn in May 1802.

chief magistrate—appealed strenuously to Barton to allow the licences to remain at thirty-six instead of being reduced to twenty-four; they urged that the publicans were paying high rents, that they had laid in a choice stock of liquor, and that they would be ruined; His Honour's reply was very curt and peremptory—his order must be obeyed.[1] There were strict instructions from England about the change in the flag—the Union Jack—consequent upon the union of England and Ireland, consummated on July 2nd, 1800.

All this time war was raging, but its effects never reached Newfoundland; Englishmen had the whole island and banks to themselves, including St. Pierre and Miquelon; our only competitors were a few American fishermen. We had large well-armed convoys with resolute naval officers to protect our fishing fleets, and men-of-war permanently stationed on the coast.[2] American vessels going to the Mediterranean were always in danger from the Algerine pirates, and they therefore smuggled a good deal of their cod abroad in English bottoms. This year, and each succeeding year, licences were issued to import provisions strictly in British vessels manned by British crews but it appears very evident from the Governor's proclamation that these rules were evaded; American traders came disguised as fishing vessels, sold and bartered their goods in the outports, and stole away the men just as usual. Admiral Gambier strongly recommended support being given to the seal fishery, as a powerful incentive to keep the men in the Colony during the winter, and thus prevent the constant emigration to America.

James Gambier,[3] Vice-Admiral of the White, who was Governor from 1802 to the end of 1803, was not only a very gallant naval officer, but

---

[1] List of Persons who have obtained Licenses to keep Public Houses from Michelmas, 1797, to Michelmas, 1798.

Michael Little.	John Widdicomb.
John Cox.	Edmond Doyle.
John Bolan.	Michael Hanlon.
Sarah Martin.	Patrick Redmond.
John Cahill.	John Power.
Wm. Power.	Thomas Murphy.
Patk. Flannery.	Wm. Prendergast.
Augustus McNamara.	Dominic King.
Wm. McCarthy.	George Shepherd.
Wm. Welsh.	David Power.
Patrick McDonald.	Michael Welsh.
Andrew S. St. John.	John Nevean.
Peter Lyons.	Phil Harrahan.
Michael Mara.	Daniel Delaney.
James Maher.	Mark Codey.
John Flood	Michael Welsh.
John Brophy.	

[2] Captain Edgell, H.M.S. *Pluto*, had a house and farm near St. John's, and resided here many years. The *Pluto*, a sloop, appears to have remained in Newfoundland for about twenty years, off and on.

[3] James Gambier, born in 1756 at New Providence, was placed on the books of the *Yarmouth*, guard-ship at Chatham, when eleven years old, under the care of his uncle. Became lieutenant in 1777 while serving on the North American station; was captured in 1778 by the French, but was soon exchanged; he took part in the relief of Jersey in 1779, and the capture of Charlestown in 1780. He had no further appointment afloat till 1793, when he commissioned the *Defence* (74), for the Channel fleet. Gambier's notions of religion and morality were much stricter than those in vogue at that time; his ship was known as "a praying ship," but she proved

was far in advance of his age, both in regard to his views on the future prospects and government of the Colony, and in the furthering of all humane and benevolent ideas for educating the settlers' children, and civilizing the poor Beothics. The naval ruler has been much abused in our histories, it will therefore probably astonish many of my readers to find a naval governor strongly urging on the British Ministry the necessity of granting responsible government to Newfoundland in 1802. This communication of Gambier's shows that he was a Liberal far in advance of his time; he had seen the benefits of local government in America and Nova Scotia, and knew that it was necessary for the progressive advancement of the Colony. He wrote to Lord Hobart on December 12th 1802, as follows:—

"I am led to apprehend that the present system of policy observed towards this Island is defective, being insufficient to effecting the happiness and good order of the community which is the chief end of all government. This I attribute to the want of *a power in the Island for framing laws for its internal regulation*, and for raising the sums necessary to promote any measures of public utility by which expense must be incurred. . . . . No money can be raised here except by voluntary contribution, and that mode must be always inadequate for the many useful purposes for which it is required. . . . . . I therefore feel it incumbent on me to propose to your Lordship's consideration *the establishment of*

LORD GAMBIER.
From an engraving after Beechey.

she was also "a fighting ship" by being the first to break the line on 1st June 1794. His ship suffered severely; the story is told that Captain Pakenham passing within hail said to Gambier, "I see you've been knocked about a good deal; never mind, Jimmy, whom the Lord loveth He chasteneth." Gambier's conduct was noticed by Howe, and he received a gold medal. In 1795 he was an Admiralty Lord, and though made rear-admiral and vice-admiral in 1799, he remained at the Admiralty till 1801, when he became third in command in the Channel. In 1802 he was Governor of Newfoundland, and in 1804 again went to the Admiralty. He was mainly responsible for the omission of the order from the "King's Regulations" requiring foreign ships within the Narrow Seas to salute the flag, an order maintained since King John's time, if not from the days of William the Conqueror. In 1807 he was made a peer for his conduct at Copenhagen and again went to the Admiralty. Gambier was strongly opposed to Lord Cochrane's attempt to use fire-ships against the French in Basque Roads in 1809. Hearing that Cochrane would oppose a vote of thanks, Gambier applied for a court-martial, and was acquitted by one expressly selected as friendly to him. In 1814 he was a commissioner for negotiating a treaty with the United States. Was made a G.C.B. in 1815, and Admiral of the Fleet in 1830; he died in 1833. He was only at sea five and a half years between his promotions to lieutenant and rear-admiral; his naval experience was thus extremely limited.—(STEPHEN's *Nat. Dict. of Biography*.)

a Legislative power in Newfoundland, similar to that which *has been found necessary to the prosperity and good government* of other parts of H.M. foreign dominions."

The British Government would not listen to his proposal; they had given Nova Scotia Home Rule years before, but poor Newfoundland had still to struggle thirty years more for this great boon. Even when the privilege of a proper court of justice was granted after a long fight—though an able lawyer like Reeves was sent out for the first two years—the salary of the chief justice on the second appointment was reduced to £300 a year, resulting in cheap and inefficient judges—an out-port doctor, a worn-out poor old navy surgeon, a broken-down merchant, and an impecunious Irish squireen.

One important event occurred during Gambier's administration, the peace of Amiens in 1802. All the conquered territory was to be given back; so St. Pierre and Miquelon were again returned to the French,[1] and the right of fishery restored to them " in the manner they were " entitled to enjoy the same under the Treaty of Utrecht "; so runs the Governor's proclamation.

The utmost harmony seems to have prevailed between the Governor, Bishop O'Donel, and the Protestant clergyman. Two schools, known as the St. John's Charity Schools, were established, mainly through Gambier's influence, one for Roman Catholics and the other for Protestants. The Grammar School, established in 1799, with the Rev. Louis Amadeus Anspach as master, lasted only a few years, as in 1802 we find the author of the "History of Newfoundland"[2] a justice of the peace in Harbour Grace, and Church of England missionary there. Besides his efforts to promote education and to increase the clergy in the island, Gambier took a deep interest in the unfortunate Beothics. An Indian woman was brought to St. John's by the notorious William Cull, for which he received a reward of £50. Cull evidently did not take kindly to His Excellency's ideas about the savages; in his opinion the only decent Indian was a dead Indian; he writes to the Governor: "The people do not hold with civilizing the Indians, as they " think that they will kill more than they did before." All thoughtful care and attention was shown to the poor Beothic woman, and she was to be sent back to her kindred loaded with presents. With the views held by Cull and his companions, it is very doubtful if she ever reached the wigwams of her tribe.

---

[1] An account of the surrender will be found in the chapter on St. Pierre.

[2] Anspach's *History of Newfoundland* is a valuable addition to our knowledge of the Colony; it is rather too full of his own affairs, his own importance, and his narrow religious views. It is also, unfortunately, very inaccurate and unreliable.

378   REIGN OF GEORGE III.

Sir Erasmus Gower[1] succeeded Gambier in 1804; he is principally remembered for the street thirty feet wide, bearing his name, which he laid out. The population at this time was increasing rapidly; six hundred and seventy Irish emigrants landed in St. John's in one year. In 1804 the population is returned as more than twenty thousand, the quantity of fish caught as over six hundred thousand quintals; for the same year the returns of the seal fishery show a net result of thirty-four thousand seals, and boat or schooner fishery of seventy-three thousand.[2] The records show great activity in ship-building, thirty vessels of two thousand three hundred tons having been built this year on the island. One important fishery seems to have been entirely neglected; the whole pack of herrings is given as about a hundred barrels. The imports are very large: 234,162 gallons of rum, bread and flour 83,389 cwt.; pork and beef, 10,522 cwt., not allowing for all the smuggled provisions brought in by Americans. One of these Yankee vessels was nearly caught at Tilton Harbour, but all that the naval captain could actually find out that she had on board were *garden seeds*.

We find in the annals of this time, and all through the history of the Colony, bitter complaints of the tyranny of the merchants towards

---

[1] Sir E. Gower, eldest son of Abel Gower, of Glandovey, Pembrokeshire, entered the Navy in 1755 under the care of his uncle, Captain Donkley. He served through the war on the American and home stations, passed for lieutenant 1762, and was sent to Portugal for service against the Bourbons; served under Commodore Byron, and in 1768 under Sir George Rodney in Jamaica. In 1779 was first lieutenant in the *Sandwich*, Rodney's flag-ship, at the capture of the Spanish convoy off Cape Finisterre, and took command of the *Conception* prize. He gallantly captured the *Leopard*, a Dutch ship of 50 guns, under the batteries at Cuddalore, and soon after the *Crescent* sloop with important despatches to Suffren. From 1786 to 1789, Gower was Commodore Elliot's flag captain on the Newfoundland station, and in 1792 took Lord Macartney and his embassy to China in the *Lion*, for which service he was knighted. In 1794 he commanded the *Triumph*, one of the ships with Cornwallis in his celebrated retreat. During the mutiny at the Nore he hoisted a broad pennant on the *Neptune* for the defence of the Thames, which ship he continued to command till he became rear-admiral in 1799; he was made vice-admiral in 1704, and admiral in 1809. He died at Hambledon, in Hampshire, in 1814. —(STEPHEN's *Nat. Dict. of Biography*.)

[2] In the Appendix will be found a long and very interesting account of the early seal fishery, written by Mr. John Bland to Governor Gambier. 1817 was another year like 1862; a continuation of N.E. gales drove twenty-five vessels ashore, but no lives were lost.

their dealers. They never gave out the prices of the articles sold on credit to the fishermen, and they "broke the price of fish in August," just at the amount they liked.[1] In good years some relief was obtained from the competition of the sack ships, who bought fish from the independent planters and gave good cash prices. The labouring men complained to Governor Gower that the merchants "price their own "goods and ours also as they think most convenient to them."[2] To remedy this intolerable state of affairs His Excellency adopted the following drastic remedy:—

"Whereas I am informed that a practice has prevailed in some of the outports of this island among the merchants of not informing their dealers of the prices of the supplies advanced for the season, or the prices they will allow for the produce, until they are in possession of the planter's voyage, whereby

---

[1] There were numerous complaints from outports about merchants' prices and their dealings with the fishermen. The one from Fogo says: "For a number of years back we have been struggling with the world, as we suppose, through the impositions of the merchants and their agents by their exorbitant prices on shop goods and provisions, by which means we are from year to year held in debt so as not daring to find fault, fearing we may starve at the approach of every winter. We being at the distance of seventy leagues from the Capital, where we suppose they arrogate to themselves a power not warranted by any law, in selling to us every article of theirs at any price they think fit, and taking from us the produce of a whole year at whatever price they think fit to give. They take it on themselves to price their own goods and ours also as they think most convenient to them." The petition is signed by many Irishmen—Patrick Murray, Peter Fowler, Toby McGrath, Michael Burke, James Meehan, John Geary, Wm. Broders, and Wm. Keefe.

[2] Prices of Provisions and other Commodities in Newfoundland during the Summer of 1805, in Barter for Fish.

	At St. John's.		In Conception Bay.	At Trinity, Bonavista, Fogo.	In Placentia Bay.
	For Fish.	For Bill.			
Bread, per cwt.	40s. to 45s.	32s. to 42s.	45s.	40s.	44s. to 47s.
Flour, per barrel	60s. to 70s.	50s. to 68s.	67s. to 72s.	77s.	75s.
Pork, per barrel	105s. to 120s.	95s. to 100s.	120s.	130s.	130s.
Butter, per lb.	11d. to 1s. 2d.	10d.	1s. 3d.	1s. 3d. to 1s. 6d.	1s. 4d. to 1s. 6d.
Rum, per gallon	5s. to 5s. 6d.	3s. 3d. to 3s. 9d.	6s. 6d.	7s.	6s. to 7s.
Molasses, do.	6s. to 6s. 6d.	4s. to 4s. 6d.	7s. 6d.	6s. 6d. to 7s.	7s.
Salt, English, per bushel	1s. 6d. to 1s.	11s. 6d. to 15s.	18s.	20s.	20s. to 22s.
Do., Foreign, per bushel	18s. to 25s.	18s. to 20s.	21s.	25s.	22s. to 20s.
Cordage, new, per cwt.	100s.	100s.	—	112s.	112s.
Do., twice laid, per cwt.	50s. to 56s.	50s.	—	75s.	70s. to 80s.
Grapnels and anchors, per lb.	8d.	7d.	—	9d.	—
Pitch, per barrel	60s. to 63s.	55s. to 60s.	—	6d. per lb.	70s.
Tar, per barrel	42s. to 50s.	35s. to 42s.	—	{ 2s. 6d. to 2s. 9d. per gallon }	6s.
Tea (common), per lb.	3s. 6d. to 4s. 6d.	2s. 11d. to 3s.	—	5s. to 7s. 6d.	8s.
Tobacco, per lb.	1s. to 1s. 3d.	8d. to 9d.	—	1s. 6d.	1s. 6d.
Peas, per bushel	—	—	—	11s. to 13s.	12s.
Oatmeal, per cwt.	—	—	—	25s. to 32s.	20s.
Canvas, per piece	84s.	—	—	97s.	9s. to 10s.

Of course it must be remembered that it was war time, and wheat was from 9s. to 12s. per bushel, and pork and beef relatively high. The prices of molasses and salt are exorbitant.

An old fisherman informs me that, in the "spring of the Wadhams," he was wrecked at Greenspond, and lived part of the winter there; some of the people, he says, had never seen money from their birth to their grave, they were in debt to the merchant all their lives long.

the latter are exposed to great impositions, the merchants are hereby required to make known to their dealers before the 15th day of August in every year, or at the time of delivery, the prices of provisions and other commodities sold by them, and the prices they will give for fish and oil, and to fix a schedule thereof in some conspicuous part of their respective stores; and in case any merchant shall neglect to comply with this useful injunction, and a dispute shall arise between him and any dealer respecting the prices charged on such merchant's account, and such dispute shall be brought into a court of justice, the same shall be determined according to the *lowest* price charged for such goods, and the *highest* price given for fish and oil by any other merchant in that district. And the judge of the Supreme Court, the surrogates and the magistrates, are hereby strictly enjoined in all such cases to govern themselves by this regulation.

"Given under my hand, September 12, 1805.

"E. GOWER."

The evils of the truck system have been exposed by many able writers on political economy; a parliamentary commission showed its workings amongst the Shetland fisher folk, how men lived and died without ever once getting their necks free from the yoke of the shop. In Newfoundland this terrible evil is almost coeval with the fishery. To this very day there are places in the Colony where neither the wages of the labourers on the merchants' wharves nor Government roads, nor even the widow's poor relief, are paid in cash. Truck had to be killed by a stringent Act of Parliament in the United Kingdom, but no Government in Newfoundland has yet had the courage to declare that the labourer is really worthy of his hire—that payments in truck are illegal, and all such paymasters liable to a penalty. Truck is not a crying evil in St. John's; it is "the dark places of the earth that are full of wickedness," and it is in the distant out-ports, and amongst petty traders and old-fashioned houses, that it still flourishes in full vigour.

It is not necessary, for a clear view of our history, to dwell much on minute details. From this period onwards the Colony began steadily to improve; a primitive post office was instituted in 1805, under Simon Solomon (father of our first postmaster-general, William Solomon);[1] a newspaper, the *Royal Gazette*, which still flourishes, was instituted by Mr. John Ryan, an American loyalist, in 1806; it was published as a possible evil thing, under the most severe restrictions; security in £200 sterling had to be given, and the magistrates were to have the perusal

---

[1] The postage rates in 1815 were as follows:—

From Canada:
On a ½-oz. letter the postage from—

	s.	d.
Quebec	1	8
Montreal	2	1
Three Rivers	1	10½
Berthier	2	1
York (Toronto)	2	9
Niagara	2	9½

From Nova Scotia:
On a ½-oz. letter the postage from—

	s.	d.
Winsor	0	4½
Digby	0	9
Horton	0	7
Yarmouth	1	1½
Pictou	0	7
Parrsboro	0	7

of the contents of the paper before publication! I am thankful that duty is not incumbent on us now, especially during the elections, when each party organ is full of audacity, mendacity, and scurrilous personal

VIEW ON THE NEWFOUNDLAND COAST.
From a drawing in the B.M.

abuse. Nothing better indicates the pleasant social relations of St. John's at this time than the founding of the Benevolent Irish Society; this

[1] PERSONS LICENSED 21ST SEPTEMBER 1807 TO KEEP TAVERNS IN THE TOWN OF ST. JOHN'S FOR THE ENSUING YEAR.

From the "Royal Gazette," December 24, 1807.

Persons licensed.	Sign of Tavern.
Robert Parsons	West India Coffee House, High Constable.

UPPER DIVISION.—From River Head to Mr. Boucher's, Bulley's Farm.

William Best	Bunch of Grapes.
John Widdicombe	Rose and Crown.
James Hayse	Ship.
Edward Angell	Britannia.
John Williams	Nelson.
John Cahill	Tavern for all Weathers.
Patrick Murine	Flower Pot.
William McCarthy	Hope.
Richard Heaney	Struggler.
Michael Murphy	Dove.
Mary Hennessey	Royal Standard.

MIDDLE DIVISION.—From Boucher's to Hudson Cove, Mr. Hunter's (now Job's Cove).

Patrick Redmond	Ship Assistance.
William Power	Angel.

Angus Mochannat	Agincourt.
William Welsh	Swan.
Robert Dooling	Red Cow.
John Fitzgerald	Jolly Fisherman.
Edmond Doyle	Blue Ball.
Michael Hanlen	Shoulder of Mutton.
Dominick King	White Hart.
Graham Lattle	
Richard Pritchard	Royal Oak.
Margaret Walsh	Sailor.

LOWER DIVISION.—From Hudson's Cove to the easternmost part of St. John's.

Cornelius Quirk	London Tavern.
Dennis Murphy	Wheatsheaf.
Daniel Driscoll	Broken Hand.
Patrick Walsh	Union Flag.
Robert Brine	Butchery and at Pringle's Farm.
William Welsh	
Michael Maza	Sun.
John Murphy	Duke of York.
Thomas Murphy	Three Crowns.
Charles Power	Plough at Brine's Bridge.

All persons licensed to keep publichouses are constables for the district of St. John's.

institution, which still flourishes in full vigour, was instituted under the happiest circumstances. James McBraire was the most active amongst the founders, and president from 1809 to 1821, when he left the Colony. I quote from Bishop Howley:—

"The preliminary meeting 'of a number of Irish gentlemen, desirous of re-
' lieving the wants and distresses of their countrymen and fellow-creatures at
' large, was held at the London Tavern, in St. John's, on Wednesday, the
' 5th February, 1806. It was unanimously agreed "That a society, formed upon
' true principles of benevolence and philanthropy, would be the most effectual mode
' of establishing a permanent relief to the wretched and distressed." Under this
' conviction, it was proposed to elect a committee from the gentlemen present to
' form a code of rules and regulations for the government of the society, the
' extension and regulations of the charity, and to consult with the Rt. Rev. Doctor
' O'Donel and others, whose local knowledge of this country could best inform
' them as to the most effectual and beneficial mode of establishing a CHARITABLE
' IRISH SOCIETY upon firm principles of loyalty, true benevolence, and philanthropy,
' when the following gentlemen were nominated and unanimously chosen:
' Lieut.-Col. John Murray, James McBraire, Esq., John McKellop, Esq.,
' Mr. Joseph Church, Captain Winckworth Tonge.'

" From this it will be seen that the society was purely unsectarian in its origin, and all denominations of Christians were admissible to its ranks, the only qualifications required being that one should be either an Irishman or a descendant of an Irishman."

James McBraire, who figures prominently in the social and political life of the Colony at this period, was a very remarkable character. Originally a sergeant in the Army, he came out to Newfoundland a poor man; he soon acquired the reputation of being one of the shrewdest and most prosperous business men of the place. On the constitution of a volunteer corps he was appointed captain; he drilled his companies admirably, if severely; some of the gentlemen, like Magill, complained of his being a martinet, and terribly overbearing; finally he rose to be major-commandant of the St. John's Volunteer Rangers.[1] McBraire was of a very fine, commanding presence, and never looked better than when at the head of his table, dispensing hospitality. In all riots the major was a terror to the mob. In the year 1816 a transport, with troops for England, put into St. John's for water, with Dr. Leslie on board. He

---

[1] In 1806 the Royal Newfoundland Rangers were embodied under Major McBraire, Commandant; Captains Parker, I. Williams, Bouchier, T. Williams, and Batten; Lieutenants Henry Shea, Solomon, Lilly, Stevenson, Haire; Ensigns Parker, Gill, Thomas, Melledge, Parsons; Surgeon Coughlan; Quarter-Master Beenlen.

In 1812 the corps had fallen into a disorganised state, and was reconstructed, on the breaking out of the American war, with the following officers:— Major McBraire, Commandant; Captains Bouchier, T. Williams, Lilly, McAllister, G. R. Robinson, Crawford, Haynes, Ryan, Trimingham, Thomas; Lieutenants Melledge, Broom, Stewart, McLea, Simpson, Livingston, Grieve, Arnott, Clift, Shannon; Ensigns Morris, McCalman, Rendell, Scott, Willis, N. Gill, Niven Lang; Adjutant Hughes; Quarter-Master Barnes; Surgeon Dr. Duggan.

Major-General Campbell commanded the troops, which at this time numbered seven hundred and fifty.

mentions dining in state at Major McBraire's with the principal merchants and officers of the garrison. After an excellent dinner, as the gentlemen were smoking, there was a great noise heard outside; McBraire immediately put on his hat and rushed out with a long staff. The Doctor describes with delight the prompt way in which the redoubtable Major quelled the disturbance; everyone went down before his terrible wand, and in five minutes the mob dispersed. McBraire left this Colony about 1822,[1] and settled with his only son at Berwick-on-Tweed; he carried off a fortune of about £80,000 sterling. He was reputed to have made a great deal of money in the American war; one of the prizes had a load of grind-stones, some twelve hundred, of course these went for a song. Someone asked McBraire, who had purchased them, what he was going to do with such a lot? "You will see," said he, and they did see. In the winter the town was short of biscuit, McBraire had his stores full, every man who bought a bag of bread had also to buy a grind-stone for two dollars.

Sir Erasmus Gower not only distinguished himself by his benevolence, his promotion of religion and education, he was equally remarkable for his zeal in reforming the courts of justice; he raised the salary of the Chief Justice from £300 to £500 per annum, and the stipendiary magistrates were under his administration first given permanent pay; he significantly hints to all these officials that, for the future, they must not be concerned in any private or professional business in the town. In his recommendations to the Home Government he endeavoured to impress upon them that St. John's was no longer a mere fishing station, but a large commercial seaport; that the promotion of agriculture and a secure tenure of lands was absolutely necessary for its future welfare and progress. He said:

"It is eighteen years since I was first on this station, and the great improvements and changes that have taken place in that time, render it now absolutely

ADMIRAL HOLLOWAY.[2]
From an engraving by C. S.

---

[1] The story is told that as McBraire was going out of the Harbour he waved his hand and said: "Goodbye, Newfoundlanders; good-bye, you poor fools."

[2] Admiral Holloway was Governor from 1807 to 1810. His name does not appear in any of the usual biographical works, nor in Stephens's *Nat. Dict. of Biography*.

From the Census of 1794 it appears that at that date Chief Justice D'Ewes Coke owned and operated a fishing room at Quidi Vidi.

REIGN OF GEORGE III.

necessary that the capital of this Colony should no longer be cramped, cabined, and confined by laws and restrictions, which at present are entirely unsuited to its condition and progress."

He had to use at all times great pressure upon the Imperial Government to obtain their consent to the free importation of American provisions. There was evidently a bitter dislike and jealousy of the United States, and it was only the absolute requirement of food for the Island that made the British Government reluctantly give way on this point. In accordance with a strong petition from the merchants, he tried to obtain for Newfoundland the exclusive privilege of supplying the West Indies with salt codfish, and the British Army and Navy with regular rations twice a week of our great staple, but failed. In 1809, Labrador and Anticosti were again re-united to the Newfoundland Government, and the courts made permanent under an Act of Parliament.

In 1810 the celebrated Admiral, Sir John Thomas Duckworth,[1] became Governor. He made another and more serious attempt to conciliate the Red Indians. Lieutenant Buchan, R.N. of H.M.S. *Pike*, was sent to Exploits with a party of seamen and marines. It was in the winter, and after undergoing unparalleled hardships they at last came up with the Boëothics. The gallant Buchan did all in his power to promote friendship with the savages; he left two of his marines with

MARY MARCH.
From a drawing by Lady Hamilton.

---

[1] Sir J. T. Duckworth, born in 1748, was the son of Rev. A. Duckworth, afterwards Vicar of Stoke Pogis and Canon of Windsor; entered the Navy at eleven, and was present at the destruction of M. de la Clue's squadron in Lagos Bay and the Battle of Quiberon Bay. Duckworth served in Byron's ship in the action off Grenada in 1779, and was immediately promoted to be commander of the *Rover*. He was praised specially by Lord Howe for his behaviour in the *Orion* (74), in the action off Ushant, and received a gold medal. He was present at the capitulation of Minorca in 1798, and expected to receive a baronetcy. In 1799 he became Rear-Admiral of the White; was with Lord St. Vincent in his unsuccessful pursuit of Admiral Bruix. In 1800, when blockading Cadiz, he captured a rich Spanish convoy; his share of the prize-money has been said to have amounted to £75,000. Was made a K.B. for his services in the West Indies in 1801; he directed, in 1803, the operations which resulted in the surrender of General Rochambeau at San Domingo. The operations conducted by him during 1805–6–7 were not at all successful. He was Governor of Newfoundland from 1810 to 1813; on his return he was made a baronet; he became a full admiral in 1810. Of all the men who have attained distinction in the English Navy, there is none whose character has been more discussed.—(STEPHEN's *Nat. Dict. of Biography*.)

[2] One of the last survivors of the Boëothics.

them, and some Indians accompanied him. The blood-thirsty character of these aborigines and their treachery is most forcibly exhibited by the terrible tragedy with which this promising effort to conciliate their savage nature ended. The two marines left by Buchan with the Indians were found lying about two hundred yards apart; that of the corporal, being first, was pierced by one arrow in the back, three had entered that of Bouthland; they were laid out straight, with their feet towards the river, and back upwards; their heads were off, and had been carried away. No blame can attach to Buchan for this melancholy disaster; the whole object of the expedition was to gain the friendship of the Indians by exhibiting confidence in them, and trusting white men unarmed amongst them.

Whatever our sentimental feelings may be for these primitive inhabitants, all their history shows that the one ineradicable feature in their character was an insatiable hatred of the pale faces. They must have known, if we give them credit for any intelligence, that this was a mission of peace, and that there was no intention of injuring them. Every other motive in them seems to have been overpowered by their instinct to kill the white man. There can be no doubt that the settlers hunted them like wolves, and shot them in cold blood whenever they encountered them. The captured Indian woman, Shanditith, declared that the hatred of the white man was so strong amongst her people that she would not be again tolerated by her tribe after speaking with Englishmen. With such feelings against Europeans all attempts at reconciliation were fruitless. There are many conjectures about the ultimate fate of the Red Indians. Bonnycastle thinks they may have emigrated in a body to the Canadian Labrador, and he mentions, in confirmation of this view, the arrival at the Bay of Seven Islands of a body of Indians who were neither Mountaineers nor Mic Macs, whom he therefore conjectures were the remnant of our Beothics. This may be so, but the general opinion of those who have studied the subject most

SIR J. T. DUCKWORTH.
From an engraving of Peter Buchan.

1 p. 2729.

closely is that the Red Indians were exterminated partly by the settlers, and the Mic Macs, partly by famine and disease.[1]

To the energy of Sir John Duckworth St. John's is indebted for many improvements; it was through his exertions that the Act 51 Geo. III. was passed in 1811. In September of that year His Excellency issued the following notice:—

"Whereas by an Act passed in the fifty-first year of His Majesty's reign, entitled 'An Act for taking away the public use of certain ships' rooms in the town of St. John's in the Island of Newfoundland, &c.,' it is enacted that the several ships' rooms therein mentioned, shall and may be granted, let and possessed as private property. Notice is, therefore, hereby given, that His Excellency the Governor will, by virtue of the authority in him vested by the said recited Act, proceed to let or lease the said several fishing rooms in lots, for the accommodation of those who may be inclined to build thereon, conformably to a plan which may be seen by application at this office, on or before the 7th day of October next."

In a very short space of time the whole of this area was let on leases for thirty years, renewable at a rental amounting to £1,000 sterling per annum. A considerable space, both in the east and west end of the town, was reserved for ships' rooms and flakes; it is within the memory of most of us when all the frontage below Brooking's and near Newman's was covered with flakes.

Anspach says of this leasing of the ships' rooms:—

"They were divided into a certain number of lots, and put up to public auction, in leases for thirty years, renewable at the expiration of that time upon payment in way of a fine of a sum equal to three years' rent of the lot so purchased if built with timber, and of a sum equal to one year's rent if built of stone or brick. The purchaser of a lot might at his option take the next lot adjoining backward at the same price that he paid for the first. Party walls between adjoining lots were to be built of brick or stone of twenty inches thick, to stand equally on each lot. The buildings were to be of the height of two stories, or not less than eighteen feet from sill to wall-plate, and no encroachments were to be made on the space allotted for the streets by bow-windows, porches, or other erections."

MR. EWEN STABB.

The merchants petitioned the Crown that this money might be retained in the Colony, for the purposes of providing police, lighting, and sewering of the town, and to afford protection from fire. This reasonable request was not complied with; however, through Sir Thomas' representations, a few permanent police were established, but in order to protect themselves from fire, the Merchants' Society had to organise an association which was both a fire brigade and a

---

[1] Mr. James Howley tells me that the whole trouble was caused by the chief of the tribe. He understood Buchan had the presents on the river at the outlet from the lake. He went thither with the English, and when he found they were a long way further down, he turned back, and created a suspicion amongst the Indians that Buchan's force was to capture them. On his return he took them all off into the woods.

vigilance committee; it was managed and controlled by the astute and ubiquitous McBraire.

In 1812 began the second American War. The ostensible cause was the right of search claimed by England, and the impressment of seamen. The real reason, as is now admitted by all candid American historians, was Madison's re-election as President. He did not want war, but felt that his chance of being elected again depended upon his taking that course. All the blood that was shed, and the English and American property destroyed in this terrible conflict, was simply to gratify the inordinate political ambition of this unscrupulous man. For once, the British Government were ready and prepared for the struggle; in St. John's alone there were three sail of the line and twenty-one frigates, with thirty-seven sloops, brigs, and schooners of war. Mr. Ewen Stabb told of thirty American prizes being brought into the harbour. I have heard a gentleman describe his walking across from Bennett's (now Duder's) to Alsop's, on the south side, on American prizes chained together.[1]

During the whole of the conflict Newfoundland was in a great state of prosperity; wages were high, provisions were very dear having all to be brought from England and the British provinces, but fish and oil and all our produce was also abnormally high. On board the captured vessels were all sorts of valuable freights—Lyons silks and whole cargoes of champagne. The clerks at Hunt, Stabb, Preston & Co., prize agents,[2] spent their Sunday afternoons firing at champagne bottles on

ADMIRAL KEATS.
From an engraving after Jackson.

---

[1] Licences were granted in September 1815 to seventeen vessels from St. John's to proceed to the United States for provisions and live stock; out of these eleven were American prizes. They included the *Mercury*, brig, 156 tons, owned by Laing, Baine, & Co. (Baine, Johnston, & Co.); *Ad*, schooner, 60 tons; *John Dunscombe*, Dunscombe & Harvey, now Harvey & Co.; *Morell*, 61, schooner, Brown, Hoyles, & Co.; and the *Express*, 131, W. & H. Thomas & Co.

[2] Thomas Stabb, the resident partner in this firm, was the father of the late Ewen, Nicholas, and Dr. Henry Stabb—of the Lunatic Asylum. The clerks in the firm who shot for champagne were Ewen Stabb, Thomas Brooking, and Samuel Prowse (afterwards collector at Twillingate). During this period, William Carter, Esquire, held the lucrative position of judge of the Admiralty Court; a most impartial and efficient judge. P. W. Carter was naval officer (afterwards the well-known senior magistrate of St. John's); he was the son of Judge Carter, and father of our esteemed Chief Justice, Sir F. B. T. Carter, K.C.M.G.

a gumphead at the end of the wharf; the man who knocked the head off the bottle won a case, the one who missed had to pay for one.

In the autumn of 1812, after the breaking out of the second American War, Newfoundland lost the valuable services of Sir John Thomas Duckworth; he was invited by the electors of New Romney to stand for Parliament, and had to resign his commission; he was succeeded by a still more distinguished admiral, Sir Richard Godwin Keats, K.B.[1] The naval career of this gallant officer ranks with the most brilliant in the heroic annals of that age. Nothing could exceed his activity and zeal for the protection of the island from the attacks of the French and Americans.

Our American cousins pride themselves on their naval exploits in their two great wars with England; the Newfoundland records contain ample evidence of their losses and defeats by English cruisers, and very few instances of their success. Occasionally they made a raid on some

---

[1] Sir R. G. Keats was born on the 16th of January 1757. He served at the commencement of the American War, at the burning of Norfolk, in an attack upon Hampton, Virginia, and at the capture of New York, Fort Washington, and Rhode Island. As a lieutenant he was on board the *Ramilies* in the action between Keppel and D'Orvilliers, the 27th July 1778; also at the defeat of Don Juan de Lomgena by Rodney on 16th January 1780, and at the ensuing relief of Gibraltar; was promoted Commander into the *Rhinoceros* sloop of war, in September 1783, as a reward for the skilful manner in which he had conducted the naval part of an expedition against the enemy's small craft at New Brunswick. Captain Keats also bore a distinguished part at the capture of the French 40-gun frigate *L'Aigle*. In 1789 he attained post rank. In the ensuing war, in command of the *Galatea*, he attended the expedition to Quiberon, and participated in the capture and destruction of several of the enemy's frigates and other vessels. He was a long time employed in the *Boadicea* in watching the port of Brest, and, on the 2nd July 1799, commanded part of the force under Rear-Admiral Charles Morice Pole in an attack on a Spanish squadron in Aix Roads; and, in the *Superb*, distinguished himself in the defeat of the Franco-Spanish squadron by Sir James Saumarez in the Gut of Gibraltar, 12th July 1801. Keats ran his ship alongside two Spanish three-deckers, and engaged them both at the same time; then making sail, he passed out from between them unnoticed, and overtaking another of their fleet, whose force was more proportionate to that of the *Superb*, he soon compelled her to a surrender. The two three-deckers, not perceiving his escape, continued, in the darkness of the night, to engage each other, until they both caught fire and were consumed together; thus giving to Captain Keats the honour of having, by a masterly manœuvre, occasioned the destruction of two first-rate line-of-battle ships belonging to the enemy, and capturing another of equal force, with a comparatively trifling loss on his own part. He accompanied Lord Nelson to the West Indies in 1805 in pursuit of the combined fleets, and fought as flag-captain to Sir John Duckworth in the action off San Domingo 6th February 1806, and was in consequence presented with a sword valued at 100 guineas. In October 1807 he became a rear-admiral, and shortly afterwards, on the outbreak of war with Russia, was appointed third in command to the fleet destined for the Baltic, under the command of Sir James Saumarez; and, in August 1808, being detached by the Commander-in-Chief, he was the instrument, with his flag on board his old ship, the *Superb*, of emancipating from French thraldom the Spanish troops stationed in the Danish provinces under the Marquis de Romana. For the able management displayed by him on this occasion he was created a K.B. He afterwards served, in 1809, under Sir Richard Strachan during the operations against Walcheren, and assumed charge in 1810 of the squadron employed at the defence of Cadiz; and in 1811 was second in command in the Mediterranean. From 1813 to 1816 he was Governor and Commander-in-Chief at Newfoundland. In 1818 he was nominated a major-general of Marines, and made a full admiral in 1825; and from 1821 till his death, in 1834, he held the Governorship of Greenwich Hospital. He died an Admiral of the White.

remote outport of the Colony;[1] Major George Cartwright, in his long diary, gives a graphic account of the way his fine business at Labrador was spoiled and plundered by an enterprising New England privateer in the American war; there is also an account of the capture of three of our sealing schooners in 1817, given in the statistics of the Seal Fishery.[2] The destruction of American commerce and the capture of American vessels by British cruisers in our waters exceeded by ten to one the gains on the Republican side; the English fleet on our shores far outnumbered their enemies. Under two such distinguished naval officers as Duckworth and Keats, the Governors of Newfoundland from 1812 to 1814, captains vied with each other in their activity, vigilance, and smartness. The Admiral Governor had no hours, he was always on duty.

I am indebted to my friend, Mr. Robert Pike of St. Lawrence, for the two stories given below[3] about privateering on our coast.

---

[1] Mr. Robert L. Newman furnishes me with the following information about the capture of their vessels by American and French privateers in the war of 1812, taken from the letter-books of their firm:—

"1812. The *Duck* sailed from Little Bay, Fortune Bay, 5 Decr. for Oporto. On the 22 Decr. was taken by two French frigates, Lon. 16·04 Lat. 42·35, who let her proceed after heaving overboard about 900 qtls. of fish in order to put aboard 100 prisoners, recaptured by an English frigate and taken to Halifax.

"On Jany. 23 1812. The *Gosport* was taken by a French privateer *La Gavotte*, of 16 guns, who let her proceed after plundering her of 150 qtls. fish.

"In 1813. The *St. Lawrence* boarded by an American privateer, who plundered, destroyed, and disabled the vessel in every way possible, flinging overboard the cargo. She bore up for Dartmouth arriving 10 April.

"Dec. 1813. The *Syren* captured and scuttled on her voyage from Oporto to Newfoundland by an American privateer.

"12 March 1814. The *Duck* was captured and given up, to bring upward of 100 Prisoners to England, after throwing all the fish that was between decks overboard to make room for the men.

"14 April 1814. The *Selby* captured on her voyage from Little Bay to Portugal on the Newfoundland coast, but given up.

"13 Aug. 1814. The *St. Lawrence* on her passage to Bilbao with a cargo of fish was captured by an American privateer, recaptured by a British frigate, and again captured by another American privateer, the *Way*, and sent to America, recaptured again by the English and sent to Portsmouth."

[2] *See* statistical chapter.

[3] In 1813 an Irish youngster ran away from his master, Mr. Bonnell, in St. Lawrence, and went to Lauu, found an American privateer there, went on board of her and joined the crew. He came down to Great St. Lawrence with the Americans, and captured a Jersey brig belonging to a firm of three brothers, then carrying on a trade there. The privateer was commanded by a little Irishman named Conolly. She was afterwards captured in the passage between Columbier and St. Pierre—known as Hell's Mouth—by H.M. cutter *Lictor*, under command of Lieut. McKillop, R.N. The privateer got in the Doldrums (becalmed there), and surrendered without a fight.

In the last French war, before the battle of Waterloo, Mr. Henry Beck, an old Englishman, ancestor of the Becks of St. Lawrence, had his fishing skiff armed. In the spring of 1814 he captured a large French banker, by boarding her and driving the crew off the deck. He was taking his prize into Harbour Breton. It was a fine day. The French cook was in the galley getting dinner for all hands. An altercation took place between one of Beck's fishermen and the cook; as the vessel was passing Little Cape the cook threw the contents of the frying pan into the Englishman's face, blinding him. This was a preconcerted signal agreed on among the French crew; they seized Beck's men, and threw Beck into the hold, breaking his bones; he died soon after. The Frenchmen took the banker to Boston, U.S., where the St. Lawrence men were kept prisoners until the autumn, when they returned home.

The following ships were captured in 1808:—

The *Alfred*, Park, Master, from Newfoundland to Poole, and *Duke of Kent* from

One of the most striking events of this war was the capture of the American frigate *Chesapeake*, by Broke, in the *Shannon*; the boarders were led by their heroic captain, and the ship struck in eleven minutes. Mr. Emerson, grandfather of the Honourable the Speaker, had a brother a midshipman in the *Shannon*, and he has often described the excitement in Halifax when young Lieut. Provo Wallis brought the prize into the harbour. In connexion with this immortal combat there was one very curious circumstance. A number of Irish labourers were on board the brig *Duck*, belonging to Newman & Co., going out to Newfoundland; their vessel was captured by the American privateer *Governor Plumer*; she was in turn captured by the English privateer brig *Sir John Sherbrooke,* and as the *Shannon* was short of men the Irishmen were put on board of her; one of these labourers, Darby Murphy, used often to relate to his friends how he captured the Yankee frigate.

Cæsar Colclough,[1] Tremlett's successor on the Supreme Court bench, arrived in St. John's in September 1813, from Prince Edward's Island, in place of Tremlett, who was sent there in a king's ship.[2] He writes to his friend Reynolds, who was Postmaster-General at Lisbon, in the closing year of the great Peninsular War :—

                                                       " St. John's Newfoundland,
" My dear Reynolds.   Sep. 29, 1813.

" Fate has removed me for my sins to this cursed spot as Chief Justice and I have by chance just heard that you are Postmaster-General at Lisbon. I write this in the counting house of a fish merchant, whose ship is bound to Lisbon. I have been here but a few days . . . . . ."

Colclough remained in St. John's for three years; he was not much of a lawyer, and a very sorry administrator; he had, however, shrewd mother wit, and the true Hibernian faculty of "gammoging the Saxon," and paid particular court to old Sir Richard Keats, impressing on His Excellency the great and patriotic services of Cæsar Colclough.

Newfoundland captured; recaptured by H.M.S. *Melpomene*. Sent for Oporto; captured again 1st November.

Union of Poole from Newfoundland captured; recaptured by H.M.S. *Plover*.

Nancy captured by French privateer; retaken by H.M.S. *Dragon*.

Live Oak, Wimboro, Master, from Newfoundland to Oporto, captured by three Spanish rowboats; carried into Vigo after an engagement in which one man was killed and three wounded.

Acorn from Newfoundland to Portugal captured and taken into Corunna.

Margery and Mary from Newfoundland to Demerara captured; recaptured and taken to Dominica.

[1] Chief Justice Colclough lived in the house near Mr. Eden's shop, Rawlin's Cross. He had a Royal coat-of-arms over his door, and compelled every one to take off his hat when passing the house. When one of the Daltons was a trifle vociferous in court his Honour appealed to him, "If you can't be civil, Mr. Dalton, be as civil as you can."

[2] On the 28th October 1811 charges of partiality and corruption were made by the Society of Merchants in St. John's against

The result was eminently satisfactory; he had practically the dormant commission in the Governor's absence, and had his salary raised from £500 to £1,000 a year. I regret the inexorable requirements of space prevent me from quoting more from this humorous and fantastic Irishman's letters, but it is quite clear that in a difficulty he was little better than an old woman; he got out of all troubles by simply relying on the strong common sense, personal influence, and energy of McBraire, who was now magistrate, major-commandant, and president of the Commercial Society. The quondam serjeant, with his long staff, and humorously forcible way of knocking down all opposition, had a thousand times more power and influence over the people than this absurd Don Pomposo.

Colclough reminds us forcibly of Thackeray's Malloney of Bally. Malloney, who invites him to "come over to O'Dowd's town, my boy; we "are all English there, with a brogue as broad as from here to the Cove "of Cork." The Chief Justice was always running down his countrymen; he exaggerated a "combine" to raise wages in the fishery into a terrible political conspiracy; he hints at murder—the only evidence he could produce was one soldier, whose evidence was worthless. When all this blew over, then he begins again about the Irish faction fights on the Barrens, when General Finn stripped to fight General Muldowney for the honour of Waterford against the "yallow bellies" of Wexford. These

the Chief Justice, Thomas Tremlett. The Society at the same time charged the former Chief Justice, John Reeves, Esq., Law Clerk to the Council for Trade, with peculation and having received a portion of the salary of each of his successors. The accusations against both Tremlett and Reeves were proved to be wholly malicious and unfounded. In his report on the case (p. 361) Sir J. T. Duckworth declared that Tremlett was a most independent Judge, that he had good ability and great industry, that in all his conduct there was not the most remote appearance of corruption, and that when the complainants were called upon they did not venture to charge him with corruption in any instance. There is no doubt Tremlett was an irritable old bachelor; his manner was rude, and he swore terribly. He exchanged in 1813 with Cæsar Colclough, Chief Justice of Prince Edward's Island. Both these legal luminaries were at the time under a cloud, and it was considered a good arrangement to give each a new sphere, so a man-of-war carried Chief Justice Tremlett to the Island, and on her return voyage in October brought back the illustrious Cæsar. I am indebted to Lieut.-Governor Howland and Judge Alley for the following notes on the careers of both these Judges in Prince Edward's Island:— Colclough, an Irish barrister belonging to an old family in Wexford, was appointed Chief Justice of the Island on the 1st May 1807. For the first few years he gave great satisfaction; afterwards he got into trouble with Governor Des Barres, and was suspended in September 1812. Colclough claimed the right to appoint the sheriffs; he showed himself a partisan on the side of the proprietors against the settlers' society, known as the "loyal electors." Des Barres was recalled through the influence of the proprietors, and Colclough was reinstated; but as he was greatly disliked in Prince Edward's Island, and Tremlett was unpopular in Newfoundland, they exchanged offices. Tremlett as a Chief Justice in Prince Edward's Island was a complete failure. Complaints were made against him, but the Tory Governor shielded him. At last, in 1824, both Governor and Chief Justice were removed on an appeal to the king, supported by resolutions from an influential county meeting. Tremlett died at Truro, Nova Scotia. His ignorance of law and practice was a great bar to his success in his last situation. He was surly and unpopular everywhere.

fights were simply for "divarsion"; the town was dull after the fishery was finished; there were no politics or House of Assembly, no police office, no theatres, not even a bazaar; what could an Irish boy do in those times without a bit of lively fun? McBraire, who knew the Irish well, laughed at the whole thing.

The Chief Justice's description of the great riot is very good in its way. The constables came in to say that if he did not go out the town would be in ruins. This message, he writes, "was delivered without "any alleviation by a beast of an Irish maid servant, whilst I was "sitting in Mrs Colclough's sick room with all her children down in "the measles, with the addition, 'Madam, don't let him out, he will "'probably be killed, and what will become of us?'" We picture the scene of Mrs. Colclough weeping on his neck. He said he was not to be stigmatized as a coward, so out he must go. Guns were fired from the Hill, Fort Townshend, and Fort William—a signal that the troops were coming. When the gallant Chief Justice arrived on the Barrens: "lo! behold! there was nobody there," he says: "McBraire had driven them off." Whatever may have happened, it is clear the riot did not disturb old Coote, Mr. Blaikie, P. W. Carter, and the other magistrates, who were having a good dinner at the hospitable board of David Tasker. The fun of the whole thing was that the crowd followed Colclough, and hurrahed him, trying to make him believe that they were his assistants. In his letter, he seems to have had a lurking suspicion that the mob were mocking him. McBraire would have invited them all in to drink at the store. Neither priests, bishops, Colcloughs, nor justices, could have put down the faction fights; they died out in time, and were succeeded by the more legitimate "divarsion" of politics.

I judge Cæsar Colclough was no lawyer from a correspondence with the very able Attorney-General of Nova Scotia, Uniacke. The Act provided for a sole judge; the Chief Justice wanted the Governor to appoint an associate judge, as he was afraid he could not get through the term; Uniacke pointed out that an acting Chief Justice could be appointed in case Colclough was sick or absent, but when the law provided for *one* judge, the court would be illegally constituted with *two* on the bench. Colclough was a mere tool of the Governor's, a striking contrast to Tremlett, who possessed the highest qualities of a judge— independence and impartiality. Tremlett's manners were, unfortunately, against him; a crusty, ill-tempered, old bachelor, he did not make friends.

There was a merchants' society in St. John's in these days which had been constituted about 1800; its object was to afford a medium of

PORTUGAL COVE, CONCEPTION BAY.

official communication and consultation between the Governor and the mercantile body about convoys, &c.[1]

The two leading men on whom Colclough, during the absence of the Governor in England, relied to guide him in his difficulties were McBraire and young Mr. James Stewart,[2] a very able, intelligent, gentlemanly man.

It is very doubtful if the conspiracy referred to by Colclough really ever existed, except in his own imagination; there was, however, a good deal of excitement amongst the people,[3] especially the Irish, who formed the great bulk of the "shipped" servants in St. John's, concerning the change in wages; the rumour had gone abroad that "wages were to be cut." Some of the merchants were very shrewd business men; they knew that the war was drawing to a close; France and America were exhausted, Napoleon's star was on the wane, Trafalgar and Wellington's Peninsular campaign had delivered Europe from his thraldom; they fully realized that if men were shipped on the old terms, should peace be suddenly proclaimed, the war prices for fish they were then getting would come down with a crash, with the high prices they had to pay for provisions and outfit, and with large sums for wages falling due in the autumn, they would all go under. McBraire forcibly impressed this on his brother merchants, but they had all been making money, the war had lasted with the French almost continuously since 1789, most of them believed it would still continue; they did not, therefore, take the wise precaution of preparing for a sudden fall in the markets.

Not only Newfoundland, but all British North America had prospered by the war. Compared with the United States, the British Provinces were very small and very thinly populated; during hostilities, however, all the trade with Newfoundland, hitherto monopolized by the Americans, had fallen into their hands. They supplied all the lumber, cattle, butter, oats, corn, hay, and other produce that had always been

---

[1] The Chamber of Commerce of St. John's was founded on the 26th December 1823. First President, N. W. Hoyles (father of Sir Hugh Hoyles); secretary, John Boyd (father of Mrs. James Baird).

[2] I have heard several persons speak in rather disparaging terms of this gentleman (who founded the firm of J. & W. Stewart), so I consulted the late Mr. Brown, who knew him well. He says Stewart was a fine man of very superior parts, a perfect gentleman. In contradistinction to the old firm of Rennie Stuart & Co., in which he had been resident partner, his establishment was afterwards generally know as "Foxy Stewart's."

[3] In 1813 a very large Commission of the Peace was issued, under which the following gentlemen were appointed Justices:— Coote, Broom, Rev. Mr. Roland, and Blaikie magistrates for St. John's; Rev. F. Carrington and Lilly for Harbour Grace; Rev. J. Church and Burrell, Trinity; Egar, Greenspond; Ford, Bonavista; McKie and Angell, Bay Bulls; W. Carter, Ferryland; Bradshaw and Blackburn, Placentia; Gosse, Carbonear; Anthoine, Fortune Bay; Bryant, Ferryland; Phippard, St. Mary's; Pinson and S. Prowse for Labrador. For the Island generally, the following naval officers:—Captain Elliott, Cooksley, Skekel, Campbell, Holbrook, Buchan; also the Rev. F. Carrington, and P. C. Le Geyt, the Governor's Secretary.

procured from America; of course, they could not furnish all the flour that was required, but it shows what progress they were making that out of eighty-five thousand cwt. of bread and flour, British America supplied Newfoundland in 1813 with nearly twelve thousand cwt., also with fourteen hundred oxen, fourteen hundred sheep, and two and a quarter million feet of board. As an illustration that it was war time and high wages, we have the enormous quantity of four hundred and twenty-six thousand gallons of rum and spirits imported, besides all the French brandy captured in the French and American prizes. There were nearly seventeen thousand men employed in the fishery and trade; this would give about twenty-six gallons per man; but the amount imported was only a small portion of the liquor brought into the Colony, there were prizes with whole ship loads of champagne and large cargoes of French brandy and wines; all were sold by the prize agents in St. John's. It has always been told as a tradition that the head of the firm of prize agents never asked anyone to his table under a first lieutenant; as there were from thirty-five to forty vessels of war on the coast, it was about as much as he could be expected to do.

Whatever were the intentions of the merchants about wages, no reduction was attempted. In 1814, £60 and even £70 was paid to a common hand at the fishery, whilst a splitter obtained from £90 to £140 for the season. No doubt the merchants were either encouraged to give these high wages by the results of 1813, or else they were compelled to do so against their will: I think most probably they acted on compulsion; certainly no prudent men would run such fearful risks if they could help it.[1]

FARMER AND GIRL SPLITTING FISH.
From a drawing in the B.M.

---

[1] In Lieut. Chappell's book, "The Cruize of the *Rosamond*," we have an account of the social life of the Colony written in a very superficial manner. He describes the trial of an Irish fisherman for getting drunk at the latter end of the fishing season. The jury in the Surrogate Court having found the prisoner guilty, Captain Campbell, R.N., the surrogate, passed the following sentence on the culprit: "Prisoner, you have been found guilty, after the most mature deliberation, of unruly and disorderly conduct; the law in such a case warrants the court to cancel all your claim for

TITLES TO LAND.

The greatest event occurring under the governorship of Sir Richard Keats was the order from the Home Government to grant titles to lands in the Colony. This change was brought about by various causes, by the suggestions and recommendations of Gower and Duckworth, but at the last chiefly by an organized determination on the part of the Merchants' Society to build houses without His Excellency's consent. A fund was provided to test the legality of the prohibitory orders against the erection of buildings;[1] this movement, which was peaceable and constitutional, is stigmatized by Pedley as refractory; no doubt it was thought so by the Governor. The author and instigator of this opposition

---

wages, but in consideration of your former industrious character, of your large family, and of your master having himself supplied the means of intoxication, you are hereby sentenced to be mulcted of *only one half of your wages* as a penalty for your drunkenness and misconduct." "The effect," says Chappell, "produced by this righteous judgment was instantaneous; the countenances of the fishermen brightened, whilst those of the masters fell. . . Our good Captain maintained the same impartiality and lenity throughout the whole line of his judicial career. . . ."

The prices of fish mentioned by Chappell are very high; 20s. per quintal in outports, 32s. in St. John's, and 42s. sterling in Portugal. No wonder the merchants made fortunes. Glorious times when $30,000 in gold was obtained for an ordinary 3,000 quintal cargo. The fish was smuggled into Spain from Portugal, and the Newfoundland merchants had the whole Peninsular markets and Italy without a rival. Their immense success in these days led to reckless trading, and the final crash at the peace in 1818.

Under Sir Richard G. Keats in 1813 three men of war wintered in the Island, H.M.S. *Crescent* in St. John's, H.M.S. *Pheasant* at Ferryland, H.M.S. *Prometheus* at Placentia. Chappell mentions the public reading room in St. John's supplied with all the English daily papers, the "St. John's Gazette," and most of the British monthly publications. He says: "The President of the committee of merchants was an Irishman of low origin who had been a serjeant in the rebel army at the battle of Vinegar Hill." Evidently McBraire had not invited the lieutenant to dinner. There were over a dozen men-of-war in port. The convoy did not sail from St. John's until 14th December 1813, and the fishing fleet joined the convoy again at Queenstown in the February following. Chappel mentions the LONDON TAVERN; this was kept by Cornelius Quirk; it was in Gower Street and Duckworth Street. On 25th August 1806, Quirk was allowed to extend his large public room, to widen his kitchen, and to enlarge his store. This is the tavern mentioned by Dr. Chappell as being the best in St. John's; it had a good billiard room. Quirk was ancestor to Quirk who used to live at Bally Haly.

Ross's Valley was called after Captain Ross, R.E., commanding the Royal Engineers in 1806.

[1] LETTER from the Governor, M. K. MILBANKE, to GEORGE HUTCHINS, Esq., dated Government House, St. John's, Newfoundland, 15th October 1790.

"SIR,—I have considered your request respecting the alteration which you wish to make in your Storehouse, near the waterside, and as it appears that the alteration will not be any ways injurious to the Fishery, you have hereby permission to make it. As to Alexander Long's house which has been built contrary to His Majesty's express commands, made known to the inhabitants of this place by my Proclamation of the 13th of last October, it must and shall come down. The pretence now set up of its being intended as a craft-house serves rather to aggravate than extenuate the offence, for by the confession of your tenant to the Magistrate who forbade him to go on with the work after it was begun, as well as to me when I viewed the house on Saturday last, no such use was to be made of it: as he said it was intended only as a covering to his potato cellar, though there is a complete chimney, if not two in it, and lodging for at least six or eight dieters. I shall embrace this opportunity of warning you against making an improper use of any other part of (what you are pleased to call) your ground, for you may rest assured that every house or other building erected upon it hereafter, without the permission (in writing) of the Governor for the time being (except such building and erection as shall be actually on purpose for the curing, salting, drying, and husbanding of Fish, which the fishermen from any part of His Majesty's European dominions, qualified agreeable to the Act of the 10th and 11th of William the to English tyranny was Dr. William Carson,[1] the real founder of agriculture and constitutional government in the Colony. Governor Duckworth wrote to the Home Government asking leave to confiscate a number of pamphlets "coming from Scotland, which are of a very libellous character concerning the authorities and the system of government in the Colony"; he also understood "that another is being prepared by the same pen, of a still more infamous character, and he thought these monstrous proceedings should be stopped." The pamphleteer was Dr. Carson. After reading the whole correspondence, there can be very little doubt that the doctor was largely influenced by personal rancour in making these attacks; both Governors—Duckworth and Keats—treated him with unpardonable rudeness. They declined to let him peruse the records, and what stung more than anything else, refused to pay his legal salary as surgeon to the volunteer of the house above mentioned, which you will no doubt assist him in executing.

"I am, &c.,
"To George Hutchings, Esq."
—WARREN'S *Lecture*, App., pp. xv.-xvi.

DR. CARSON.
From a silhouette in the possession of his daughter, Mrs. Job.

Third, and the 15th of George the Third, have a right to erect without asking permission) must unavoidably be taken down and removed to obedience to his Majesty's said commands. And it may not be amiss at the same time to inform you, I am also directed not to allow any *possession as private property to be taken of, or any right of property whatever to be acknowledged in any land whatever* which is not actually employed in the Fishery, in terms of the aforementioned Act, whether possessed by pretended grants from former Governors or from any other (no matter what) unwarrantable pretences—therefore it behoves you, with all possible dispatch, to employ the whole of the ground which you now lay claim to in the Fishery, lest others should profit by your neglect, and make that use of it which the Legislature of Great Britain intended should be made of all the land in this Country, and without which no one has a right to claim it as his own. The Sheriff will have directions about the removal

[1] Dr. William Carson came to St. John's in 1808. He had practised for fourteen years in Birmingham, England; he obtained the highest medical honours from the University of Edinburgh; his character and standing is certified by the eight principal physicians of Birmingham. He was appointed surgeon to the Loyal Volunteers of St. John's in 1809, but when the corps was augmented to ten companies, denominated " The Loyal Volunteer Rangers." Carson was dismissed from the position of surgeon. In an indignant letter to Governor Duckworth occurs the following high-flown passage:—" The dark and secret machinations of the malignant may tease but cannot irritate me, the arm of power may humble my mind but cannot subdue it."

brigade.[1] Carson, a determined, pertinacious character, was not to be put down by any number of old admirals or hangers-on, like Colclough and the Government House clique; he stuck to his point, and ultimately got his pay.

Carson was an old Whig, of the same school as Sydney Smith and the Edinburgh Reviewers; there were many abuses in his time, and he exposed them. Douglas Jerrold says of the Conservatives of his day, "they would not allow a rat hole to be a rat hole, but a healthy ventilator." In the same spirit, Dr. Carson was attacked and persecuted by the Governors and their minions; the profound learning of Cæsar Colclough was invoked by His Excellency as to what should be done to this daring pamphleteer; but Colclough, though he breathed anathemas on the head of the doctor, gave forth but a very uncertain sound on the subject of prosecuting him. The authorities at home gave the Governor also but little satisfaction; there were plenty of libels at the time on the Prince Regent, and very little satisfaction had been got out of prosecuting the libellers. The fat Adonis of forty had not raised his reputation by libel information, so the English Ministry recommended their Excellencies, Duckworth and Keats, to possess their souls in peace, and to let Dr. Carson alone. The following extracts show the character of these slanders. They appear very logical, moderate, and well expressed. The statement of facts is unanswerable, and the conclusions on the subject of the government of the Colony are the only ones that a reasonable man could arrive at. The first, published in 1811, contains "the libellous and scurrilous attack" complained of by Governor Duckworth:—

"A naval commander accustomed to receive obedience, whether his orders are dictated by justice or injustice, by reason or false prejudice, cannot be expected to brook with temper any opposition to his will. The man whose duty calls upon him to defend his rights, and the just interest of his family, in opposition to the opinion and passions of such a Governor, will have but a small chance of success. An act of independence would be arraigned as an act of mutiny. All the influence of his office, all the arts of his satellites would be marshalled to effect his overthrow. Accustomed to use force to knock down opposition—force being the power he knows best how to direct—the toils of investigation, deliberation, and judgement, are seldom had recourse to by a Naval Governor."

The following is from the Doctor's second tract, "the poisonous publication and vicious pamphlet," referred to by Sir Richard Keats. If these ancient admirals could only have lived to see our local press at

---

[1] He mentions in his second pamphlet, 1813, that he had been dismissed from his offices of surgeon to the volunteers and the gaol, an office now held by his grandson, Dr. Henry Shea.

electioneering time, how would they feel when Dr. Carson's papers so hurt their pride?—

" I am far, very far indeed, from wishing to impugn the motives of the Governors. I am even disposed to allow, that they have been, for the most part, actuated by the best intentions. It is the habits of Naval Commanders, generating a fondness for arbitrary rule, and thereby requiring a passive submission to their will, utterly unfitting them to preside at the head of a Government not possessing the usual necessary restraints. It is the undertaking a high situation, with the duties of which they cannot be acquainted, that I wish to expose and deride, as inconsistent with just moral conduct, derogatory to the character, and hostile to the privileges of Britons.

" The inhabitants of Newfoundland are truly loyal, and attached even to enthusiasm, to the glory and interest of the British nation. They are uniformly desirous of obtaining the good opinion, and the good will of their Governors. This fact has been strongly manifested, on the arrival of each succeeding Governor; but, no sooner did they become entangled in the Gothic system of pulling down fences, stages, and houses; no sooner did they commence the blasting system of favouritism and proscription, than all hopes of improvement were dissipated, and the mind recoiled into gloomy despondency.

" The only remedy against the evils flowing from the present system, will be found in giving to the people, what they most ardently wish, and what is unquestionably their right, a civil Government, consisting of a resident Governor, a Senate House and House of Assembly.

" I shall as briefly as possible, endeavour to point out the advantages that would flow to this island, and the mother country, from the establishment of a civil Government, and from the appropriation and cultivation of the lands. In doing this I shall have to combat some prejudice, and some error. The island of Newfoundland has been represented as destitute of soil; the atmosphere as unfriendly to vegetation; agriculture as injurious to a fishery; and the country colonized as contrary to the interest of the British merchants, and incompatible with the policy of the mother country."

As the result of the action of the merchants and the animadversions of the doctor, Sir Richard Keats' instructions from England

"Directed his attention to the propriety of authorising the cultivation of those lands of the colony which might be applicable to that purpose. He was therefore to consider himself authorised to grant leases of small portions of land to industrious individuals for the purpose of cultivation, taking care, however, to reserve an annual quit-rent, either nominal or real, according to the circumstances of each individual case. In furtherance of the design contemplated by this instruction, the following notice was published, bearing date June 26, 1813:—

" ' All resident and industrious inhabitants desirous of obtaining small grants of land for the purposes of cultivation in the neighbourhood of St. John's, subject to very moderate quit-rents, are desired to give in their applications to the office of the Secretary to the Governor, before the last day of July.'

" Before issuing this order, His Excellency had called for a return of all lands that were already claimed outside the town of St. John's, with the titles on which the several claims were based, when it appeared that the inhabitants were proceeding rather rapidly to do for themselves what they had tardily received from

GRANTS OF FARM LANDS.

the Government permission to do, and this without the condition annexed in the latter case. The return showed that between October 25, 1812, and July 10, 1813, twenty-six persons had enclosed plots of land of various dimensions, but amounting in the aggregate to seventy-five acres.

"The following extracts are taken from the letter of the Governor to Lord Bathurst, reporting the success of this measure. They also afford a glimpse of the squatting system which had begun to prevail, and of new ideas which were dawning in people's minds as to the agricultural capacities of the country:—

"'The measure which I was authorised to adopt, of making small grants of land to industrious individuals for the purpose of cultivation, has been generally

FARM SCENE NEAR ST. JOHN'S ABOUT 1790.
From a water colour painting in the B.M. MS.

received with becoming gratitude, notwithstanding pains have been taken to induce the lower classes to ascribe the bounty of Government to a wrong motive. In proceeding to execute this part of my instructions, it became necessary to make some enquiry into the lands at present enclosed, or in cultivation, and into the titles by which those in occupancy in the vicinity of St. John's are held. And it is evident that the possessors of a considerable portion of them have no other claims than that which occupancy may be permitted to establish. St. John's, with a population of nearly 10,000, seems to have grown out of its original situation, and to be changing its character from a fishery to a large commercial town, and for a considerable time past has offered such advantages to the farmer and gardener, as to overcome all the restraints which nature and the policy of Government have laid on the cultivation of a soil certainly less sterile than it has generally been considered. More than a thousand acres are in cultivation, and as many more perhaps enclosed, the produce of which is confined to hay, potatoes, and vegetables of various kinds, crops of which may be seen as plentiful as in England, whilst the environs of the town, the natural beauties of which are very striking, present to the view several neat, well-cultivated, and productive little farms.

"'It is a circumstance particularly favourable to agriculture that husbandry does not interfere with the fisheries, and that the fisheries supply the farmer with manure. The lands may be prepared, and the crops put in and taken out, before the commencement of, and after the fishery is over. With these advantages, and that of a certain and profitable market, the desire to possess land for several years has been eager and general. Proclamations repeated by my predecessors, forbidding persons to take possession of lands, have been disregarded. In cases where grants or leases have been obtained from Government, the limits have commonly been exceeded. Pretexts of every sort which ingenuity could devise have been resorted to to found titles, and by paying attention to claims or pretexts of private property, of which they are peculiarly jealous (and they have not been invaded by me) I have found but little land in the neighbourhood of St. John's to dispose of.

"'The total number of grants made this season by the Governor under the authority afforded by his instructions was one hundred and ten small plots of land not exceeding four acres. These were subject to annual quit-rents of from 2s. 6d. to 5s. per acre, renewable at the expiration of thirty years at moderate fines. The above grants were not equal to the number of applications. Many of the latter had yet to be decided on; His Excellency governing himself chiefly by the recommendation of the magistrates, paying attention to character, and considering the circumstances and family of the applicant.

"'The scarcity of provisions which had prevailed in the early part of the year 1813, had been well calculated to stimulate the people to make trial of what the land could produce towards their support. During the first months of 1812, before the declaration of war by America, supplies were in sufficient abundance, and to be had at a moderate price. But after the breaking out of hostilities, the prices gradually advanced to an unprecedented height. Fortunately, a seasonable importation was received from Canada, of 12,000 cwt. of bread, and 4,000 barrels of flour, which barely dissipated the prospect of starvation during the winter. Even with this welcome addition, so dire was the scarcity, that at one period common biscuit "was retailed out in small parcels of a few pounds as a peculiar favour to the poor, at the rate of £6 sterling per cwt. Potatoes were sold at 35s. per barrel (two bushels and a half), and the inhabitants were reduced to the most alarming state of need, when a vessel arrived from Greenock with relief." Before the arrival of this vessel, a committee of gentlemen had paid General Moore £7 sterling per barrel as a deposit for flour out of the public stores, to bake up for the poor. Even in the summer of 1813, the following high prices prevailed—Biscuit, 70s. to 84s. per cwt. Flour, 120s. to 126s. per barrel. Beef, 140s. to 147s. per barrel. Pork, 180s. to 200s. Potatoes, 22s. 6d. to 25s. per barrel. On July 16, the society of merchants reported to His Excellency that the quantity of provisions on hand was not more than sufficient to supply the demand for two months, and there was little prospect of any considerable importations.'

"On this subject the Governor made urgent representations to the Secretary of State, and, probably as the result of those representations, though apparently coming in the ordinary way of trade, large imports were received, mostly from Great Britain, which replenished the stores, brought down prices, and removed all apprehensions of famine for the ensuing winter." [1]

---

[1] From PEDLEY's *History of Newfoundland* and *Newfoundland Records*.

In June 1814 there is a letter in the Records from Hunter & Co. praying permission to export a quantity of flour, "that the market is " now so glutted that it is impossible to sell it, and that if not allowed " to send it away it will be spoiled."

In 1815 both Colclough and Sir Richard Keats left the Colony. The Chief Justice was evidently terrified by the following letter. He put forth a proclamation immediately, offering a reward of £100 for the discovery of the writer or of the person who affixed it to the Court House gate, of course without result.

" To the Honorable CESAR COLCLOUGH, Esq., Chief Judge in the Supreme Court of St. John's, and in and over the Island of Newfoundland, &c., &c., &c.

" The humble petition of the distress^d of St. John's in general most humbly sheweth :—

" That the poor of St. John's are very much oppressed by different orders from the Court House, which they amigine is unknown to your Lordship, Concerning the killing and shooting their doggs, without the least sine of the being sick or mad. Wee do hope that your Lordship will check the Justices that was the means of this evil Proclamation against the Interest of the poor Families, that their dependance for their Winter's Fewel is on their Doggs, and likewise several single men that is bringing out Wood for the use of the Fishery, if in case this business is not put back it will be the means of an indeferent business as ever the killing the Doggs in Ireland was before the rebellion the first Instance will be given by killing Cows and Horses, and all other disorderly Vice that can be comprehened by the Art of Man.

" Wee are sorry for giveing your Lordship any uneasines for directing any like business to your Honour, but Timely notice is better than use any voilance. What may be the cause of what we not wish to men^t at present, by puting a stop to this great evil. Wee hope that our Prayrs will be mains of obtaining Life Everlasting for your Lordship in the world to come.

" Mercy wee will take, and Mercy wee will give."

The Chief Justice should have known, as one experienced about his countrymen, that the threatening letter is a common Hibernian device; that, whilst it is sometimes malignant, often enough it is the mere wanton trick of some idle vagabond who can write, and wants to worry his neighbour. Magistrates of any standing, either in Ireland or amongst Irish people, could " paper a trunk " with such epistles. This one is in very mild tone; it has not got even the traditionary coffin and cross bones at the head of it; it is more of a respectful remonstrance than a threat of murder, as the affrighted Colclough translated it. During the troublous times that were coming on the Colony, it was a good thing he left. Colclough was succeeded in the Chief Justiceship by Francis Forbes, Esq., a distinguished barrister of Lincoln's Inn. He was appointed on the 4th August 1816, and commenced the discharge of his duties on the 15th July 1817, and remained resident in the Colony up to the 6th of May 1822. Chief

Justice Forbes won golden opinions from all classes; the pages of "The Select Cases in the Supreme Court of Newfoundland" are an abiding monument to his profound learning and serene intelligence.

The faction fights went on for many years after Colclough left. "Yallow-belly Corner," on the east side of Beck's Cove, commemorates the spot where the wounded in the melee used to be washed in the little brook flowing into Beck's Cove. The Tipperary "clear airs," the Waterford "whey bellies," and the Cork "dadyeens" were arrayed against the "yallow belly" faction—the "Doones" or Kilkenny boys, and the Wexford "yallow bellies." There were besides the "young colts" and a number of other names for the factions. They fought with one another "out of pure devilment and diversion," as an old Irishman explained it to me. Besides these scrimmages there were plenty of fights when the "fools" or mummers came out from Christmas to Twelfth Day. These men were dressed up with high paper caps of a triangular form, ornamented with ribbons. They wore white shirts, sewn all over with ribbons and streamers. A good "rig-out" cost both time and money. The "swabs" were made of a bladder, covered with canvas or a switch, made sometimes of a cow's tail fastened to a stick. Some were dressed as women, with long garments, known as "eunchucks." They were all masked, and ran at passengers with an Indian yell, and spoke in a falsetto voice. Men were often beaten badly for old grievances by the fools. I remember, as a boy, how proud I used to be to shake hands with a fool, and to know what "rigs" Noah Thomas or Mick Toole were going out in. Each company had one or more hobby-horses, with gaping jaws to snap at people. The fools had to be put down by Act of Parliament. Mummers and fools were English customs, dating back to the Saxon time, brought to this Colony by the old Devonshire settlers.

The returns for the year 1814 show unexampled prosperity—an enormous fishery, a large catch of seals (a hundred and twenty thousand) and splendid prices; 1815 was also a good season,[1] the fish exported amounted to one and a quarter million quintals. Fish was quoted in St. John's at nineteen and twenty-one shillings per quintal, cod oil at thirty-three pounds, and seal oil at thirty-six pounds per ton. 1814 is, wrongly, generally stated to have been a regular *annus mirabilis*, nine hundred and fifty thousand quintals of fish having been reported to have been taken and sold, at

---

[1] In 1815, 1816, and 1817, Newmans built several fine vessels at Great Jervois, which were highly commended by Trinity House for their excellent models and staunch construction, all constructed out of timber obtained in Bay Despair.

two pounds sterling per quintal, the whole exports being valued at the enormous sum of over two million pounds sterling.[1] With the close of the year 1815 came the crash.[2] In December 1815 Mr. Coote, the Supreme Surrogate, and Captain Buchan, R.N., on whom the whole judicial business of the capital devolved, wrote to Sir R. G. Keats:—

"In November 1815 there have been upwards of seven hundred writs issued since the closing of accounts in October [in all over nine hundred summons], and forty declarations of insolvency; notwithstanding which we are happy to inform your Excellency that the public peace has not in any material degree been interrupted, nor do we perceive the smallest ground for apprehension of any change of sentiment likely to disturb the present tranquillity."

What a contrast between these calm words of two brave coolheaded men in the midst of dire calamity and the fears and forebodings of Colclough. Peace had come after the crushing defeat of Waterloo,

WEXFORD HERRING COT.[3]

18th June 1815; the United States had made peace with England by the Treaty of Ghent; American and Norwegian fish flowed into the Mediterranean markets; produce was selling abroad for less sometimes

---

[1] The official returns of exports for this year, from October 1813 to October 1814, do not show either such high prices or quantities. Fish is put down at 20s. to 26s. per quintal; value of seal oil, &c. and furs at £38,570; salmon, 3,425 tierces, at £4 per tierce. There is a significant item of 2,049 quintals of fish *exported to the Brazils.* James Stewart is credited with being the first merchant in Newfoundland to inaugurate this important business. In one of his letters he writes, "30,000 quintals of fish, well handled, should make any man's fortune."

[2] PRICES, 1812–1816.

"Price of cod oil, Liverpool, 1812, £38 sterling per ton.

"Price of cod oil, Liverpool, 1813, £49 sterling per ton.

"Price of cod oil, London, 1813, £42 10s. sterling per ton.

"Tar in England, 1813, 43s. per barrel, and expected to rise higher.

"April 1816, the price of cod oil continues low at £28 per ton. The introduction of gas light for the streets and shops lessens the consumption very considerably, and will be worse."—*From* NEWMAN & Co.'s *Books.*

[3] It was from this handy little craft that our fishermen got the idea of the boat now in such general use all over the Colony; it displaced the lug-sails towards the end of last century.

The fishing boats in the cod and seal

than one-third of its cost to the merchant. A panic ensued, and nearly all the houses in the trade went down. The catch of 1816 was considerable[1]—over a million quintals were exported. Prices, however, had become abnormally low—fourteen, twelve, and even ten shillings per quintal.

The winters of 1815, 1816, and 1817–18 are memorable in the annals of the Colony. In the winter of 1815 the capital and all the outports were in a state of actual starvation. The losses and insolvencies referred to by Coote had ruined the credit of our merchants. Importations of provisions were quite inadequate, and, to add to the general misery, emigrants were flocking in from Ireland.[2] By Christmas 1816, when communication with the outside was virtually shut off, the dread spectre of famine threatened our unfortunate Colony. Fortunately, at this terrible crisis, the virtual control of the Colony was in the hands of Captain David Buchan, R.N. The most fulsome panegyric is really but faint praise for the cool courage, able management, and humane exertions of the heroic commander. During this trying winter he put his own men on H.M.S. *Pike* on short allowance, when the following address was presented to him by the Grand Jury:—

"You, sir, were seen conspicuous in public exertions to afford the only refuge to which those suffering the calamities of impending famine could address themselves for succor."

fishery were formerly called shallops and shalloways, these words often occurring in our history. The shallop was a large boat, decked at both ends and open in the centre, with moveable deck-boards and pounds; there were cuddies both fore and aft where the fishermen could sleep. There were never less than three men in a shallop; their dimensions were—30 to 40 feet keel, 10 to 40 feet beam; many of the larger shallops had five men, and would carry 200 qtls. dry fish. The shalloways were open boats, what are now called punts. The sails in common use until after 1780 were lug sails. The spritsail boats were probably copied from Irish models, like the picture of the Wexford herring cot. There was no fire below deck; the cooking apparatus, or galley, was built of stone, and was generally on the forecastle. The fishermen's clothing was made commonly of whitney and barked swanskin (oiled clothing had not been invented, and the barvel was universally used by the fishermen all over North America); for the seal fishery the men had bluchers and buskins; pewter pots were mostly used for cooking and drinking vessels. The first decked vessels for the seal fishery were about the size of ordinary Western boats, 40 to 50 feet keel, and 14 to 15 feet beam. The schooners all had deep, heavy keels; both the bottom planking and keel were made of birch and witch hazel. It took about seven men to haul out the birch stick for a keel. For the boat's frame juniper was generally used; the timbers were about a foot apart, and the planking was about an inch and a half thick, generally of pine, with black spruce for spars. The schooner rig came into vogue about the time of the commencement of the ship seal fishery. In the early accounts of this industry a distinction is made between the fishery as prosecuted in shallops and in schooners. The only novelty introduced about 1798 was the use of larger vessels in this business. There was always more or less of a seal fishery carried on by the residents with nets, pursuing them on the ice, and following them up with shallops and punts.

[1] Pedley, in his history, states the catch was small. The records show that the amount was about 1,083,452 quintals.

[2] Eleven thousand Irish came to St. John's between 1814 and 1815. There is an instructive correspondence between Kent and Morris of Waterford about the cubic space required for an emigrant. Their sufferings in crossing must have been terrible, only exceeded by the horrors of the middle passage on board an African slaver.

If Buchan deserved all these encomiums for his services in 1815-16, what praise shall we give him for his still more difficult task in the terrible season of 1817-18, known in Newfoundland as the "Hard Winter," and still more generally as the "*Winter of the Rals?*" In the former season, starvation alone had to be contended with; now famine, frost, and fire combined, like three avenging furies, to scourge the unfortunate Island. A frost that sealed up the whole coast commenced early in November, and continued almost without intermission through the entire season, and on the nights of the 7th and 21st of November 1817, three hundred houses were burnt, rendering two thousand individuals, in depth of that cruel winter, homeless.[1] Nothing can add to the simple pathos of the grand jury's presentment:—

"Calamities so extensive would have been in our most prosperous times productive of severe distress, but on retrospecting to our situation for the last three years, during which period we have alternately suffered by fire, by famine, by lawless outrage, and numerous mercantile failures, which have greatly injured the commercial reputation of the town, the recent conflagrations seemed only wanting to consummate our misfortunes. Several hundred men in the prime of life, without money, or the means of being employed, without adequate clothing or food, are at the hour of midnight wandering amidst the smoking ruins to seek warmth from the ashes, and food from the refuse of the half-consumed fish. In dwelling-houses the misery is little less. Many families, once in affluence, are now in absolute want. Within these two days, two men have been found perished of cold, and many hundreds must inevitably experience a similar fate if humanity does not promptly and effectually step forward to their relief."

To add to this misery, gangs of half-famished, lawless men everywhere threatened the destruction of life and property; vigilance committees were formed in every settlement. Mr. George Kemp, then residing in Brigus, tells of the confidence and safety the planters felt when Captain Buchan came amongst them. In St. John's and every outport his presence brought tranquillity; all caught the contagion of his splendid courage. The suffering endured during that winter no pen can fully describe.

A vessel with provisions put into Bay Bulls in distress; the people flocked down *en masse* to board her, and they would not let the ship leave the harbour until half her cargo had been unloaded by the authorities and distributed. In Renews, two West Country crews were frozen up; a mob, headed by the village blacksmith, attacked the room, threatening to murder the Devonshire men unless they surrendered their provisions; one of the skippers, an old captain of a privateer, had been expecting an attack, and had his store loopholed for musketry; he fired a volley over the heads of the crowd, and all fled; afterwards the same captain and his merchant shared all their provisions with the Renews

[1] There had also been a very destructive fire in February 1816.

people. Many more incidents could be related about the winter of the "Rals" or "Rowdies." Near Renews, a lot of Irish emigrants left their ship at the edge of the ice, and crawled on shore on their hands and knees, to add more sharers in the already inadequate rations. During these three unhappy years everything was against us; even the seal fishery failed in 1817.[1]

In the spring of 1818 this period of calamity came to an end. The seal fishery was unusually productive, in less than a fortnight

WOODLANDS COTTAGE, ST. JOHN'S.
From a drawing by Lady Hamilton, in the possession of Sir F. A. Hamilton, Bart.

scores of little vessels returned, loaded to the scuppers with fat; hope revived, the fisheries were good, the markets improved, and the poor old Colony again began to lift up her head. The Governor, Sir Francis Pickmore,[2] had been ordered to remain through the winter in Newfoundland. Dr. Carson's pamphlet had shown up the absurdity of Governors coming out for two or three months in the year. Henceforth all their Excellencies were perennials, not fleeting annuals. Admiral Pickmore was a firm, courageous old man, but the toil, exposure, and

---

[1] 1817 is the worst seal fishery on record, only thirty-seven thousand seals being killed over the whole Island.

[2] There appears to be no information about Sir F. Pickmore beyond what can be gathered from the Navy Lists. The family appears to have died out, as none of this name can be found in the Navy, Army, Church, &c.

anxiety of the last terrible winter told on his enfeebled constitution, and on the 24th of February he died. One can form some idea of the severity of the season from the fact that it took all the crew of H.M.S. *Fly*, with the assistance of civilians, a whole fortnight to cut a channel through the ice, which was between four and five feet thick. The faithful admiral's obsequies were carried out with great state, the grandest ceremony ever known in the Colony.

> "So past the strong heroic soul away.
> And when they buried him the little port
> Had seldom seen a costlier funeral."

The sufferings of the Newfoundland colonists called forth humane response from all quarters. The British Government sent £10,000, Halifax contributed liberally, but the most touching and generous gift was from the large-hearted people of Boston. A few years before they were fitting out privateers to destroy our fishing vessels, now they sent us a welcome ship-load of provisions. In the most inclement month of the year, January, the brig *Messenger* came into St. John's, bearing the following address:—

"To His Excellency FRANCIS PICKMORE, Esq., Vice-Admiral and Governor, &c., President of the Society for the Improvement of the Poor of St. John's.

"SIR,—The recent conflagration of a great part of the town of St. John's, at a period of the year when it may be impracticable to obtain relief from the parent country, and the calamity which must necessarily ensue to a large number of our fellow-beings, have been felt in this town with all the sympathy which they are calculated to inspire. A subscription, for the purpose of affording some immediate aid to the sufferers, has been consequently opened in this place, and the means of purchasing a quantity of such articles as are considered to be best adapted to the exigencies of the moment, have been readily contributed by a number of its inhabitants.

"The American brig *Messenger*, Captain Peterson, having been chartered for the exclusive object of carrying this offering to St. John's, we have now the honour to enclose you a bill of lading, and manifest of her cargo, consisting of the following articles:—

| 174 barrels of flour | 125 barrels of meal |
| 11 tierces of rice | 27 barrels and 963 bags of bread, |

which, on behalf of the contributors, we request that you will have the goodness to receive, and cause the same to be distributed among the sufferers by the late conflagration, in such manner and in such proportions as their respective circumstances may require. We beg leave to recommend the bearer, Captain Peterson, to your kind protection. . . The cause of humanity alone has induced him to undertake, at this inclement season, such a voyage which, under other circumstances, he would have felt himself obliged to decline.

"We have the honour to be, with all due consideration, very respectfully, your Excellency's obedient humble servants.   (Signed)

"JAMES PERKINS
"JONATHAN AMORY, Junr.
"TRISTRAM BARNARD
"Boston, December 27, 1817."

ARNOLD WILLIS
BENJAMIN RICH
JOHN HOUSTON.

Bishop Lambert, of the Franciscan order, had succeeded the eminent Dr. O'Donel as Roman Catholic Bishop of Newfoundland; he was consecrated at Wexford, April 1806, Bishop of Chitra *in partibus*. Dr. Lambert was rather an old man when appointed, and of very delicate constitution. All his contemporaries speak of him as a perfect gentleman, sometimes a little hasty, but genial, kind, and of pre-eminent social qualities; he dined out a good deal with the Governor and the officers and merchants, entertaining them in return at his own hospitable board. Dr. Lambert received an allowance from the British Government.[1] In 1811 Dr. Scallan came out to assist, and was afterwards his successor. The first three Roman Catholic bishops in this Colony, by their suavity of manner, and their liberal, enlightened policy, contributed perhaps more than any others to promote harmony and peace in the community.

There were two treaties of peace with France—in 1814 and in 1815. St. Pierre and Miquelon had been formally given back to our enemies in 1814, when suddenly, in 1815, Captain Buchan was sent again to retake the islands and plant the Union Jack on the Governor's staff; the taking and retaking of these little islands was a regular "Jack-in-the-box" affair. Before the peace the merchants of St. John's had sent a very strong memorial to the Prince Regent praying that in any future settlement foreigners might be excluded from our fisheries; the Governors vigorously supported the prayer of the memorial. His Royal Highness promised favourable consideration, but, as usual, our interests were deliberately sacrificed. France had been completely conquered. Why, then, did she recover her position on the Newfoundland coast? Castlereagh's answer is characteristic: "The European sovereigns wanted to make the Bourbons popular with the French people." For the sake of the incapable, unteachable Louis XVIII., a galling yoke was thrown round the necks of British colonists. It is the flimsiest and most paltry excuse for a great diplomatic blunder.

On the death of Admiral Pickmore, Captain Bowker, of the admiral's ship, was Acting-Governor until the arrival of Sir Charles Hamilton[2] in July 1818. In the beginning of September of that year another fire broke out in St. John's, which consumed twelve houses and part of the

---

[1] A stipend of £75 per annum was granted to Dr. Lambert. "1814, April. In consideration of the respectability attached to your situation as Head of the Catholic Church in Newfoundland, and of the highly creditable and meritorious manner in which you discharge the duties of your important office, His Royal Highness has been graciously pleased to direct that an annual allowance of £75 shall be paid to you whilst you continue to hold that important situation."

[2] Sir C. Hamilton, born 1767, was entered on the books of his father's ship, the *Hector*, in 1776; in 1784 he succeeded to the baronetcy; was captain in 1789. In 1794 he was present at the sieges of Bastia, Calvi, &c. He was in command of the *Melpomene* for seven years, serving on the coasts of Holland, Africa, the East and West Indies. In 1801

SIR CHARLES HAMILTON.

Ordnance property, and in 1819 yet another destructive conflagration, which destroyed one hundred and twenty houses at the western end of the town; the loss was estimated at £120,000 sterling. There can be very little doubt that these fires were the work of incendiaries. Although, for the time, these recurring calamities caused great privations and misery, the result was a great improvement in the laying out of the city; Water Street and Duckworth Street, formerly narrow lanes, were now built up with good substantial houses, and were widened to fifty feet.[1] The new Governor was chiefly remarkable for his stern, unbending Conservatism. The most important event during his tenure of office was the convention of 1818 with America.

SIR C. HAMILTON, BART.
From a portrait in the possession of Sir E. A. Hamilton, Bart.

It was agreed:—

"That the inhabitants of the United States should have for ever, in common with the subjects of His Britannic Majesty, the liberty to take fish of every kind on that part of the southern coast of Newfoundland extending from Cape Ray to

he was returned for Dungannon, and in 1807 for Honiton, which he represented till 1812, though away on active service. Was made rear-admiral in 1810, and vice-admiral in 1814. From 1818 to 1824 he was Governor of Newfoundland; became admiral in 1830, a K.C.B. in 1833, and died at Iping, Sussex, in 1849. Lady Hamilton was the first Governor's wife to reside in the Colony; she lived in Fort Townshend, St. John's, for four years, and drew the portrait of Mary March.

[1] THE ST. JOHN'S FIRES OF 1817–20.

1 Geo. IV. Cap. li.

AN ACT TO REGULATE THE RE-BUILDING OF THE TOWN OF ST. JOHN'S, IN NEWFOUNDLAND, AND FOR INDEMNIFYING PERSONS GIVING UP GROUND FOR THAT PURPOSE.
[15th July, 1820.]

WHEREAS the Town of *Saint John*, in the Island of *Newfoundland*, hath recently been visited by very great and destructive Fires, the ravages whereof have been chiefly occasioned by the narrowness of the Streets, and the difficulty of arresting the progress of the flames: And whereas it will greatly contribute to the convenience of the said Town, as well as to its future security, if certain regulations be made for the rebuilding of such parts thereof as have been destroyed, and also for the erection of any Houses or Buildings in the said Town hereafter; Be it therefore enacted by the King's Most Excellent Majesty, by and with the advice and consent of the Lords Spiritual and Temporal, and Commons, in this present Parliament assembled, and by the authority of the same, that the Lower Street in the said Town, commonly called *Water Street*, shall not be less than Fifty Feet in width in every part thereof, extending from the house and stores occupied by *Brown, Hoyles & Co.*, at the East end, to the public Ships Room, commonly called the *Western Ships Room*, at the West end thereof; and that the Upper Street, commonly called *Duckworth Street*, shall not be less than Forty Feet in width; and that all and every Houses, Stores, Erections and Buildings whatsoever, built and erected since the first day of *June* One Thousand Eight Hundred and Eighteen, or which shall at any time or times hereafter be erected and built in the said street or either of them, whether the same be upon any vacant spot of Ground or upon the site of any former Building, shall be made to conform to the width of the said the Rameau Islands; on the western and northern coast, from Cape Ray to the Quirpon Islands; on the shores of the Magdalen Islands, and also on the coasts, bays, harbours, and creeks, from Mount Joli on the southern coast of Labrador to and through the straits of Belleisle; and thence northwardly, indefinitely along the coast, without prejudice, however, to any of the exclusive rights of the Hudson's Bay Company."

The convention further provided:—

"That the American fishermen should also have liberty for ever to dry and cure fish in any of the unsettled bays, harbours, and creeks of the southern part of the coast of Newfoundland above described, and of the coast of Labrador; but so soon as the same, or any portion thereof, should be settled, it was not to be lawful for the said fishermen to dry or cure fish at such portion so settled without previous agreement for such purpose with the inhabitants, proprietors, or possessors of the said ground."

LADY HAMILTON.
From a portrait in the possession of Sir E. A. Hamilton, Bart.

Streets, as the same is respectively hereby established and directed; Provided always, that nothing herein contained shall be construed to extend to any House, Store, Erection or Building, which since the said first day of June One Thousand Eight Hundred and Eighteen, may have been or at any time hereafter may be erected in *Water Street* aforesaid, the same being built and made entirely of Stone or Bricks, and covered with Slates or Tiles, and always having a clear width in the said Street of not less than Forty Feet.

II.—*And be it further enacted,* That there shall be Four Cross Streets or open spaces to serve as Fire-breaks, and intersect the said Streets called *Water Street* and *Duckworth Street* as nearly as might be at right angles; and that all and every of the said Cross Streets shall not be less than Sixty feet in width, and shall run in the following directions, that is to say, the first or western Cross street from the Water Side, in a line with the corner of *Dinah Elliot's* Shop and *Maddock's Lane* to *Duckworth Street*; the second from the Water Side, running in a line with the corner of *James Clift's* and *Perkins and Winter's* tenements leading up the *Church Hill*, the third to run from the Water Side between *Clapp's* and *Keen's* Properties, lately held by *George Niven* and *A. Chambers,* the middle of the Cove to be the centre of the Street, through the Ground lately occupied by *William Barnes* and others; and the last or Eastern Street from the Ordnance Wharf up to the *King's Road*; and that no House, Store, Erection or Building whatsoever, shall be erected or built so as to front above *Water Street*, upon any or either of the said Cross Streets, but that the same shall be and remain open and free from any Buildings whatsoever, other than the inclosures thereof; and also, that in case any other Cross Streets may be hereafter required as a security against Fire, upon the same being marked out and presented by the Grand Jury, and approved by the Governor for the time being, there shall be such other Cross Streets or Fire-breaks, of the like dimensions of those hereinbefore mentioned, and according to the Boundaries so presented and approved; and the Ground and Property necessary to be taken shall be estimated and paid for in like manner as is herein-after mentioned; Provided always, that nothing herein contained shall authorise the taking of any Fishing Room, Flakes, or any part thereof, which may be actually occupied and employed for the purpose of curing Fish.

The agitation for representative government in the year 1819 received great impetus from the well-known case of Butler and Lundrigan. At a surrogate court held in Harbour Grace, before Captain David Buchan, H.M.S. *Grasshopper*, and the Rev. John Leigh, Episcopal Missionary, Lundrigan, not appearing upon a summons, was held to be guilty of contempt of court, and sentenced to receive thirty-six lashes on his bare back. Lundrigan was tied up and flogged by the boatswain of the ship until he fainted under the severity of the punishment.[1] At a meeting held in St. John's on the 14th of November 1820, Patrick Morris chairman, the following resolutions were passed:—

"Resolved that we yield to no body or class of men in loyalty to our King, in obedience respect and support of the laws of our country, or in love and veneration to our glorious constitution.

"Resolved that we have beheld with abhorrence and detestation the cruel and ignominious punishment inflicted on the bodies of Philip Butler and James Lundrigan for the trifling causes elicited in evidence on the late trial in our Supreme Court.

"Resolved that we shall pursue such legal and constitutional means as may be within our power to have the law repealed which, it appears, sanctions such arbitrary proceedings in the Surrogates, and that a committee be appointed to carry our intentions into effect.

"Further resolved that we defray Butler's and Lundrigan's expenses and maintenance and that thanks be passed to the Lawyers Dawe and Geo. Lilly for their disinterested conduct in conducting the cases in the Supreme Court.

"WILLIAM CARSON, M.D.,	PATRICK DOYLE,
"PATRICK MORRIS,	JOHN RYAN,
"JOHN ROCHFORT, M.D.,	GEO. GADEN,
"GEORGE NIVEN,	THOMAS BECK,
"HENRY SHEA,	THOMAS BURKE,
"TIMOTHY HOGAN,	ROBT. R. WAKEHAM,

"LEWIS W. RYAN."

The case of Butler and Lundrigan was taken up solely for the purpose of being used as a lever to obtain a legislature for the Colony. Petitions were presented to both Houses of Parliament, and Dawe was sent to England to work up the case. There is no doubt that this agitation very much forwarded the demand for local government. The immediate result of the appeal, which was warmly supported by Lords Holland and Darnley in the Lords, and by the celebrated Sir James Macintosh and Dr. Lushington in the Commons, was the Judicature Act and the suppression of surrogate courts.

[1] Sir Charles Hamilton was so disgusted with the way that Government suits were conducted in the courts, that he requested the Government to send him out a lawyer who could act as attorney-general; a gentleman called Westcott was accordingly sent out to His Excellency. Sir Charles found his new law adviser very glib at recommending measures in the Council, but utterly incapable of defending their legality in the courts; the imported adviser made the last state of things worse than the first, and he was soon sent back again to England; both Westcott and his wife enjoyed a pension for the valuable services he rendered the Colony.

APPENDIX TO CHAPTER XIII.

I. The Recapture of St. John's in September 1762.

FROM THE "LONDON GAZETTE."

Whitehall, October 12. This morning arrived Captain Campbell, of the 22nd regiment, from St. John's, Newfoundland, being dispatched by Lieutenant-Colonel Amherst with the following letters to the Earl of Egremont.

(*a.*) COL. AMHERST to the EARL OF EGREMONT.

St. John's Newfoundland,
MY LORD,   Sept. 20 1762.

According to the orders I received from Sir Jeffery Amherst at New York, of which your Lordship will have been informed, I proceeded from New York to Halifax with the transports, to take up there the troops destined for the expedition. I got into the harbour the 26th of August; and finding Lord Colvill sailed, determined to embark the troops there, and at Louisbourg, as expeditiously as possible, and proceed after his Lordship. The men-of-war being sailed, who were to have taken part of the troops on board, I was obliged to take up shipping to the amount of 400 tons. I had everything embarked, ready to sail on the 29th, but contrary winds kept us in the harbour till the 1st of September, when we got out and arrived at Louisbourg on the 5th. The next day the troops were embarked, and we sailed out of the harbour the 7th in the morning.

I had the good fortune to join Lord Colvill's fleet on the 11th, a few leagues to the southward of St. John's; and by the intelligence his Lordship had received, I was obliged to change my resolution of landing the troops at Kitty Vitty (a narrow entrance close to the harbour of St. John's), the enemy having entirely stopped up the passage in, by sinking shallops in the channel. From the best information I could get, it appeared that Torbay, about three leagues to the northward of St. John's, was the only place to land the troops at, within that distance. Lord Colvill sent the *Syren* man-of-war into Torbay with the transports; and it was late at night on the 12th, before they all came to an anchor. Capt. Douglas, of His Majesty's ship *Syren*, went with me to view the bay, and we found a very good beach to land on. It blew hard in the night, and one of the transports, with the provincial light infantry corps on board, was driven out to sea.

I landed the troops early the next morning, at the bottom of the bay, from whence a path led to St. John's: a party of the enemy fired some shots at the boats, as they rowed in. The light infantry of the regulars landed first, gave the enemy one fire, and drove them towards St. John's. The battalions landed, and we marched on, the path for four miles very narrow, through a thick wood, and over very bad ground. Capt. M'Donell's light infantry corps in front came up with some of the party we drove from the landing place: they had concealed themselves in the wood, fired upon us, and wounded three men. A part of Capt. M'Donell's corps rushed in upon them, took three prisoners, and drove the rest off.

The country opened afterwards, and we marched to the left of Kitty Vitty. It was necessary to take possession of this pass to open a communication for the landing of artillery and stores, it being impracticable to get them up the way we came. As soon as our right was close to Kitty Vitty river, the enemy fired upon us from a hill on the opposite side. I sent a party up a rock, which commanded the passage over, and under cover of their fire, the light infantry companies of the Royal and Montgomery's, supported by the grenadiers of the Royal, passed, drove the enemy up the hill, and pursued them on that side towards St. John's, when I perceived a body of the enemy coming to their support, and immediately ordered up Major Sutherland, with the remainder of the first battalion, upon which they thought proper to retreat, and we had just time before dark to take post. Capt. Mackenzie, who commanded Montgomery's light infantry, was badly wounded. We took ten prisoners. The troops lay this night on their arms.

The next morning, the 14th, we opened the channel, where the enemy had sunk the shallops; they had a breast work which commanded the entrance, and a battery not quite finished. Lieutenant-Colonel Tullikin, who had met with an accident by a fall, and was left on board, joined me this day, and Captain Ferguson, commanding the artillery, brought round some light artillery and stores from Torbay, in the shallops. The enemy had possession of two very high and steep hills, one in the front of our advanced posts, and the other near to St. John's, which two hills appeared to command the whole ground from Kitty Vitty to St. John's. It was necessary that we should proceed on this side, to secure at the same time effectually the landing at the Kitty Vitty; from the first hill the enemy fired upon our posts.

On the 15th, just before daybreak, I ordered Captain M'Donell's corps of light infantry, and the provincial light infantry, supported by our advanced posts, to march to surprise the enemy on this hill. Captain M'Donell passed their sentries and advanced guards, and was first discovered by their main body on the hill as he came climbing up the rocks near the summit, which he gained, receiving the enemy's fire. He threw in his fire, and the enemy gave way. Captain M'Donell was wounded, Lieutenant Schuyler of his company killed, and three or four men, and 18 wounded. The enemy had three companies of grenadiers, and two picquets at this post, commanded by Lieutenant-Colonel Belcombe, second in command, who was wounded; a captain of grenadiers wounded and taken prisoner, his lieutenant killed, several men killed and wounded, and 13 taken prisoners. The enemy had one mortar here, with which they threw some shells at us in the night; a six-pounder not mounted, and two wall pieces. This hill, with one adjoining, commands the harbour.

The 16th we advanced to the hill nearer St. John's, which the enemy had quitted. Twenty-nine shallops came in to-day with artillery and stores, provision and camp equipage, from Torbay, which we unloaded. I moved the remainder of the troops forward, leaving a post to guard the pass of Kitty Vitty on the other side. Last night the enemy's fleet got out of the harbour. This night we lay on our arms.

The 17th a mortar battery was completed and a battery begun for 4 twenty-four-pounders and 2 twelve-pounders; about 400 yards from the fort made the road from the landing for the artillery, and at night opened the mortar battery with one 8 inch mortar, seven cohorns and six royals. The enemy fired pretty briskly from the fort and threw some shells.

The 18th in the morning I received a letter from Count D'Haussonville, of which I do myself the honour to enclose your Lordship a copy, with copies of other letters that passed and of the capitulation. As Lord Colvill at this time was some distance off the coast and the wind not permitting his lordship to stand in, to honour me with his concurrence in the terms to be given to the garrison, I thought no time should be lost in so advanced a season and therefore took upon me to determine it, hoping to meet with his Lordship's approbation; and he has given me the greatest pleasure by entirely approving of everything that I have done.

I must beg leave to say, my Lord, that every assistance we could possible desire from the fleet has been given us, Lord Colvill upon the short notice he had of our joining him having laboured to get together all the shallops he could and with which we were amply supplied; it was a measure of essential service and without which our operations must have been considerably retarded. The indefatigable labour and persevering ardour of the troops I have the honour to command, so necessary towards completing the conquest before the bad season set in, did indeed exceed what I could have expected. Lieut.-Col. Tullikin seconded me in everything that I could wish. Captain McDonell of Col. Fraser's regiment having Sir Jeffrey Amherst's leave to go to England, was to have delivered this to your Lordship, but his leg was broken by the wound he received, which keeps him here. May I humbly presume, my Lord, to recommend this gentleman to your Lordship's protection as a real brave and good officer.

Lord Colvill intends sending H.M.S. *Syren* immediately to England. I send Capt. Campbell of the 22nd Regiment with these despatches who will inform your Lordship of any particulars you may desire to know. I do myself the honour to transmit to your Lordship such returns as I can possibly get in time, to show the true state of the French troops and garrison here.

I am, &c.
WILLIAM AMHERST.

Capt. Campbell has brought with him the French colours which were hoisted on the fort at St. John's.

(*b.*) COL. AMHERST to the FRENCH COMMANDER.

Camp before St. John's,
SIR, Sept. 16, 1762.

Humanity directs me to acquaint you of my firm intentions. I know the miserable state your garrison is left in and am fully informed of your design of blowing up the fort on quitting it; but have a care, as I have taken measures effectually to cut off your retreat, and so sure as a match is put to the train, every man of the garrison shall be put to the sword. I must have immediate possession of the fort in the state it now is, or expect the consequences.

I give you half an hour to think of it.

I have the honour to be Sir,
Your most obedient humble servant,
WM. AMHERST.

To the officer commanding in St. John's.

(*c.*) COUNT D'HAUSSONVILLE to COL. AMHERST.

16 Sep. 1762.

With regard to the conduct that I shall hold, you may, sir, be misinformed. I wait for your troops and your cannon; and nothing shall determine me to surrender the fort unless you shall have totally destroyed it and that I shall have no more powder to fire.

I have the honour to be Sir,
Your most humble and most obedient servant,
The COUNT D'HAUSSONVILLE.

(d.) COUNT D'HAUSSONVILLE to LIEUT.-COL. AMHERST.

SIR,
Under the uncertainty of the succors which I may receive either from France or its allies, and the Fort being entire and in a condition for a long defence, I am resolved to defend myself to the last extremity. The capitulation which you may think proper to grant me, will determine me to surrender the place to you, in order to prevent the effusion of blood of the men who defend it. Whatever resolution you come to, there is one left to me, which would hurt the interests of the Sovereign you serve.

I have the honour to be Sir
Your most obedient humble servant,
LE COMPTE D'HAUSSONVILLE.
Fort St. John,
Sept. 17, 1762.
[N.B.—This date should be the 18th.]

(e.)
Camp before St. John's,
Sept. 18th 1762.
SIR,
I have just had the honour of your letter. His Britannick Majesty's fleet and army co-operating here will not give any other terms to the garrison of St. John's than their surrendering Prisoners of war. I don't thirst after the blood of the garrison but you must determine quickly or expect the consequences for this is my final determination.
I am Sir &c.
WM. AMHERST.
To Count D'Haussonville.

(f.) COUNT D'HAUSSONVILLE to COL. AMHERST.
Sept. 18, 1762.
I have received sir your letter which you did me the honour to write to me. I am as averse as you to the effusion of blood. I consent to surrender the fort in a good condition as I have already acquainted you, if the demands which I enclose herewith are granted to my troops.
I have the honour &c.
LE COMPTE D'HAUSSONVILLE.

(g.) ARTICLES OF CAPITULATION.

Demands of the garrison of St. John's, and, in general, the troops that are in it:—

The French troops shall surrender prisoners of war.—*Agreed to.*

The officers and subaltern officers shall keep their arms to preserve good order among their troops.—*Agreed to.*

Good ships shall be granted to carry the officers, grenadiers, and private men, either wounded or not, to France in the space of one month, on the coast of Britanny.—*Agreed to.*
(*Lord Colvill will, of course, embark them as soon as he can.*)

The goods and effects of both the officers and soldiers shall be preserved.—*His Britannick Majesty's troops never pillage.*

The gate will be taken possession of this afternoon, and the garrison will lay down their arms.

This is to be signed by Lord Colvill, but it will remain at present, as afterwards, in full force.
Camp before St. John's, 18 Sept. 1762.
WM. AMHERST.
LE COMPTE D'HAUSSONVILLE.

(h.) TOTAL OF THE FRENCH TROOPS MADE PRISONERS IN ST. JOHN'S FORT.

1 colonel, 1 lieut.-colonel, 13 captains, 13 lieutenants, 4 ensigns, 27 serjeants, 45 corporals, 40 sub-corporals, 12 drummers, 553 fusiliers.

Staff Officers.

M. Le Compte D'Haussonville	- Colonel.
M. De Bellecombe	- Lieut.-Colonel.
M. De Mongore	- Major and Adjutant
M. Seire	- Engineer.
Henry	- Surgeon Major.
Michel	- Chaplain.

(i.) ENGLISH KILLED AND WOUNDED.

RETURN of the killed, wounded, and missing of the troops under the command of Lieut.-Col. Amherst, from the 15th Sept. inclusive.

Captain Maxwell's light infantry.—3 rank and file killed ; 10 rank and file wounded.

Captain McDonell's light infantry.—3 rank and file killed ; 1 lieutenant, 1 serjeant, 5 rank and file killed ; 1 captain, 15 rank and file wounded.

Captain Barrow's provincial light infantry.—1 rank and file killed ; 3 rank and file wounded.

First battalion—
2 captains, 1 serjeant, 1 drummer, 3 rank and file wounded.

Second battalion—
1 rank and file killed ; 1 rank and file wounded.

Provincial battalion—
1 rank and file killed.

Total, 1 lieutenant and 11 rank and file killed ; 3 captains, 2 serjeants, 1 drummer, 32 rank and file wounded.

Names of the Officers.

Lieut. Schuyler, of the Royal Americans, killed.

Captain McDonell, of Frazer's
Captain Baillie, of the Royals } wounded.
Captain McKenzie, of Montgomery's

WM. AMHERST.
St. John's,
Sept. 20, 1762.

THE RECAPTURE OF ST. JOHN'S.

(*k.*) LORD COLVILL to Mr. CLEVLAND.

COPY of a letter from Lord Colvill, Commander-in-Chief of His Majesty's ships in North America, to Mr. Clevland. Dated on board the *Northumberland*, in St. John's Harbour, Newfoundland, Sept. 20, 1762.

SIR,

I had the honour of sending you an account of my proceedings until the 18th of August by a vessel which sailed from Placentia for England at that time, and on the 22nd I sailed with his Majesty's ships the *Northumberland*, *Antelope*, *Gosport*, and *Syren*, and the *King George*, belonging to the province of Massachusetts Bay.

On the 25th we chased a schooner off St. John's, and took her close to the harbour's mouth. She had been an English privateer, taken by the enemy, had eight carriage guns mounted, and was manned with thirty Frenchmen, commanded by an ensign de Vaisseau.

The enemy had sent away great part of St. John's men, women and children, by giving them vessels and provisions to carry them where they pleased; two of these, a sloop and a schooner, we met with on the coast, and took twenty-three Irishmen that were single men out of them, to replace in part the marines of the squadron that were left in the garrison at Placentia and the Isle of Boys. These Irishmen said, that if I would go into the Bay of Bulls, numbers of their countrymen would resort to me and enter on board the squadron; but during two days which I stayed in that bay, not a man joined me. The few inhabitants that remained there, quietly followed their business of fishing, and it is possible the enemy prevented any others at St. John's from coming.

Mr. Garland and Mr. Davis, two of the principal inhabitants of Harbour Grace and Carbonera, in Conception Bay, having acquainted me that a number of men in their neighbourhood were willing to serve in the squadron during the present exigency, I sent the armed schooner for them, and she returned with fifty men, which I have distributed among the ships. And the same gentlemen, representing that the enemy sometimes sends small parties by land to Portugal Cove, which have threatened to molest them in shallops from that place, desired, in behalf of themselves and all their neighbours, that the schooner might be stationed in Conception Bay, for their protection and defence, which request I complied with.

The island of Carbonera, in Conception Bay, has had no other garrison for many years but a few old men of the artillery, to take care of the guns and ordnance stores. Had some of the inhabitants of the adjacent coast taken post here, they might easily have defended it against any force, as the island is inaccessible on all sides, except one narrow landing place, and no safe road in the neighbourhood for great ships; but the enemy landed in boats, and destroyed the whole without resistance. And the island of BOYS, near Ferryland, would probably have shared the same fate, had it not been possessed in due time by the *Syren's* marines.

In frequently passing the harbour's mouth of St. John's, we could plainly see that the fort, which fronts the entrance, was fortified all round with new works; and that a redoubt, or something like one, was raised at the little Harbour of Kitty Vitty. The old battery at the south side of the harbour's mouth was repaired with additional works, and a new one erected on the same side nearer the entrance. All these were to be seen from the sea; and I could not learn that the enemy intended any thing more than the finishing these works.

On the 8th of September I received, by a sloop express from Halifax, letters from Sir Jeffery Amherst at New York, acquainting me that he had come to a resolution to send a body of troops, in order to dislodge the enemy as soon as possible from St. John's; and that Lieutenant-Colonel Amherst was to command these troops. The same conveyance brought me letters from Colonel Amherst, acquainting me with his arrival at Halifax on the 26th of August, his departure from thence on the 1st of September, and with his intention to call at Louisbourg for the troops there, and then proceed round Cape Race, to join me on this coast. Upon receipt of these letters, I sent the sloop which brought them to look out for Colonel Amherst and the transports off Cape Race, and in order to join them the sooner, to concert measures for the ensuing operations, before the enemy could have notice of their arrival. I dropped down with the squadron to Cape Broyle; but Mr. Gill of St. John's, who had been sent out of the town in a cartel schooner, sending off advice from Ferryland, that he was sure the enemy intended to sail in a very little time, I returned with the squadron to our station off St. John's.

On the 11th we were joined by Colonel Amherst, with the troops in ten transport vessels; and I proposed Torbay as the proper place to land at; it is to the northward of St. John's, about seven miles by land, and the roads pretty good, but the bay is not reckoned safe anchorage, being open to the easterly winds, which usually begin to prevail at this season.

By one of the transports from New York I received a duplicate, the original not yet come to hand, of their Lordships' order of the 7th of June, directing me to repair myself or send a sufficient force, to enable Captain Graves of the *Antelope* to defeat the designs of the squadron commanded by M. de Ternay.

On the 12th we proceeded to Torbay. I sent Capt. Douglas in the *Syren* to anchor with the transports, accompanied by the boats of the squadron, and a number of shallops, or fishing boats, which I collected from different parts for the king's service. With the rest of the ships I returned to my station close to St. John's harbour.

Next morning Col. Amherst landed with the troops in the head of the Bay, having only four men wounded from the distant bush firing of the enemy; he marched directly to Kitty Vitty and made himself master of that important post in the evening without having a man killed, and only two or three wounded. Everything belonging to the army was carried from Torbay to Kitty Vitty in shallops escorted by boats from the squadron. And this service was conducted with diligence and care by Mr. Dugdale, my first lieutenant, Captain Douglas having joined the squadron again.

The enemy's fleet was to have sailed the morning I passed the Harbour with the transports; and three hundred men only were to be left in St. John's for the winter—but upon seeing us they landed the grenadiers again.

The 15th it being strong from E. to E.S.E. with thick rainy weather. In the evening the wind shifted to the westward, light breezes and thick fog. At six next morning, it being calm with a great swell, we saw from the mast head, but could bring them down no lower than half-way to topmast shrouds, four sail bearing S.S.E. distant seven leagues; the mouth of St. John's Harbour at the same time bore W. four leagues. We lost sight about seven, though very clear, and some time after a small breeze springing up from the S.W. quarter I stood towards Torbay in order to cover the shallops that might be going from thence to Kitty Vitty.

In the afternoon I received a note from Col. Amherst acquainting me that the French fleet got out last night. Thus after being blocked up in St. John's Harbour for three weeks by a squadron of equal number, but smaller ships with fewer guns and men, M. de Ternay made his escape in the night by a shameful flight. I beg leave to observe that not a man in the squadron imagined the four sail when we saw them were the enemy; and the pilots were of opinion that they must have had the wind much stronger than with us to overcome the easterly swell in the Harbour's mouth. I sent the *King George* as far as Trepassy to bring me intelligence if the enemy should steer towards Placentia; and I directed Captain Douglas of the *Syren* to get the transports moved from Torbay, a very unsafe road, to the Bay of Bulls.

A bomb battery was opened against the fort, in the night of the 17th, and next day it capitulated before any other batteries had begun to play; and I herewith enclose a copy of the capitulation.

The squadron got into the harbour yesterday morning; and in the evening I received their Lordships' order of the 2nd of August, sent me by Captain Palliser of the *Shrewsbury*, who with the *Superb*, *Bedford*, and *Minerva*, had just arrived on the coast. I have directed Captain Palliser, with the other ships, to come into the harbour as soon as convenient opportunity offers for so doing.

We have about 800 prisoners, grenadiers piequets, and some marines, being a very fine body of men and nearly equal in number to the regulars of our army. I am now preparing transports to carry them to Brest. The enemy did not intend to leave so great a part of their force here; their grenadiers were ready for embarking, but M. de Ternay seemed determined at all events to grasp an opportunity, which if once lost might never be regained; therefore in the utmost confusion he left behind his grenadiers, anchors, and turned his boats adrift, when they had towed him out. The fog was so thick that Lieut. Col. Tullikin who was posted on an eminence in the narrowest part of the harbour's mouth could hear their noise but could not discern any of the ships; the fog even altered the direction of the sound, which seemed to come from another part of the Harbour whilst they must have been directly under him.

There is a considerable quantity of provisions and other goods at this place collected and tumbled promiscuously into different storehouses by the enemy. Many of the Irish servants have also been robbing and plundering their masters. To ascertain properly in order to make restitution as far as can be, and to restore regularity to a country so long distracted by being in the enemy's possession, will be the particular care of Governor Graves who in my opinion is well qualified for such an office, and as he will stay here he will be able in a great measure to restore the affairs of this country. Captain Douglas of the *Syren* has behaved with spirit and activity and exerted every talent of a good officer during the expedition; (and without adding any more officers to the corps) I am happy in the opportunity of sending him to wait on their Lordships.

II. Bermudians in the Bank Fishery.

(*a*.) Messrs. HULL & HARVEY to JOHN BRICKWOOD, Public Agent for the ISLAND OF BERMUDA.

Newfoundland Aug. 11th 1788.

Since arrival of Governor Admiral Elliot are confirmed by him, in indulgence of making and drying fish on any part of the coast of Newfoundland for present year; but he is of opinion that the clause in the Act of 14th Parliament 15th year of Reign of present Majesty is against us, insomuch that they may not in future land to cure and make their fish on any part of coast, unless a different explanation of that clause take place. Notwithstanding by Act of William III. 10 & 11. c. xxv. His Majesty's subjects residing within the realm of England or dominions belonging, trading to Newfoundland have equal right to making and husbanding &c. of fish on the shores, as well as taking it on the Banks—appears to be no repeal of that Act, unless the explanatory clause of Act alluded to be construed to repeal so much of Act of William III.

By the Boston Port Bill, Bermudians are particularly named encouraged and licensed to engage in this business. The force of that law was done away by change of Government in United States so far as respected them only, and as no repeal has taken place, conceive no doubt, but that it still has effect with all subjects therein described who continued subjects to the Crown of Great Britain. Act [Boston Port Bill] speaks not of landing or curing fish, but of general licence of taking it on the Banks; Query! will not landing and curing be considered as a natural consequence of taking? Otherwise indulgence of law will not avail them, for if forbidden to Bermudians to land fish for drying and husbanding in Newfoundland ports, it would be little short of total prohibition of indulgence granted—distance from Banks to Bermuda being too great to carry green fish, with security, and if carried safe, the severity of the weather in all the fishing season will not admit husbanding and curing fish in their island fit for market—the attempt would be preposterous.

There are many reasons for indulging Bermudians in present pursuit. They have no staple commodity for exporting, they are altogether supported by our Navigation. All supplies of Cordage Sail canvas, nails &c. for ship building are mostly received from England. Before the War they were carriers of a large proportion of the produce of America from thence to the Sugar Colonies, but now that trade is loaded with difficulties and expenses, they cannot continue it with any advantages. We apprehend great exertions will be made by Merchants from the West of England to prohibit them in their present pursuit, and we request that their [Bermudian] agent loses no time nor exertion to get Acts alluded to explained, or anything contained that tends to obstruct them in making and husbanding fish on shore in harbours and bays about Newfoundland, or in bringing into port for curing and manufacturing oil on shore, either whales or blubber, killed and taken in and about Coast, to get such obstruction removed by most certain means possible. We shall take the earliest opportunity of laying before the Legislature of Bermuda a representation of their difficulties. They have now employed in their Bermuda Vessels upwards of 200 men, four-fifths of whom are natives, and a large proportion raw inexperienced men, and but few blacks. May not Bermuda be said to become a nursery for seamen for America, with good affect that fewer will be encouraged to leave His Majesty's dominions in Europe. We further hint that the difficulties that are started are founded on the expression in the 4th Clause of the first Act alluded to.

(*b.*) GOVERNOR ELLIOT TO THE GOVERNOR OF BERMUDA.

SIR,
St. John's, Newfoundland,
20th August 1788.

On my arrival here a few days since, I was surprised to find a number of vessels belonging to Bermuda engaged in the fishery of this island contrary to an Act of Parliament past in the 15th year of His present Majesty, entitled "An Act for the encouragement of the fisheries carried on from Great Britain, Ireland, and the British Dominions in Europe, and for securing the Return of the Fishermen, Sailors, and others employed." [As] I am inclined to believe [they came] without any intention on their part of infringing the law, I shall allow them to continue till the end of the present season, but must request of your Excellency to warn them against coming here next year, as the most positive orders will be given to the Custom House not to admit them upon any consideration whatever, to land and dry their fish contrary to the before mentioned Act of Parliament.

I have the honor to be, Sir,
Your Excellency's Most Obedient
and Most Humble Servant,
ELLIOT.

His Excellency
The Governor of Bermuda.

(*c.*) G. ELLIOT, GOVERNOR, TO LORD SYDNEY.

St. John's, 26th Oct. 1788.

Soon after my arrival from England this year I was informed that Bermudian ships were engaged in the Newfoundland fishery, and in course of ten days nineteen sail of them came into the port of St. John's with their second cargoes of fish from the banks. Had I arrived in time I should have thought it my duty to refuse them the privilege of landing and drying, but in consideration of the vessels being owned and navigated by British subjects, and understanding they had been misled by Act 15 of His present Majesty, which although it deprived them of most of the privileges enjoyed by vessels arriving from our British Dominions in Europe did not preclude them from catching fish on the Banks and bringing them into harbours of Newfoundland for sale, I permitted them to compleat their voyages, and I hope my conduct therein, together with my letters to the Governor of the Bermudas upon the subject, will meet with H.M. approbation.

(*d.*) (*From the Bermudian Records.*)

Friday, June 27th, 1788.

Colonel Tucker, Mr. James Tucker, and Mr. George Bascome [were appointed] a committee in conjunction with a committee of council to correspond during recess of assembly with John Blackwood, Esq., public agent at Lamlin.

(e.) Tuesday, November 11th, 1788.

EXTENSION ADDRESS OF THE GOVERNOR (HENRY HAMILTON) ON THE OPENING OF THE SESSION.

The promotion of the Newfoundland fishery appears to me an object calling for your immediate attention if any obstacles have occurred which have rendered the first adventure less profitable than might have been expected, your prudence will surmount them or weaken their effect by legal restrictions or adequate encouragement. Should it appear to you advisable to resort to the favour and protection of the British Legislature, the earliest intimation must be given to the principal agent whose endeavours, I am persuaded, will not be wanting to advance a branch of commerce in the said fisheries to the said Ports thereof at the end of the Fishing Season which by the following Clause ("and in order to obviate any doubts that have arisen or may arise to whom the Privilege or Right of drying Fish on the Shores of Newfoundland does or shall belong under the before mentioned Act made in the 10th and 11th years of the Reign of King William III. which Right or Privilege has hitherto only been enjoyed by His Majesty's Subjects and the other British Dominions in Europe be it enacted and declared by the authority aforesaid that the said Right and Privilege shall not be held and enjoyed by any of His Majesty's Subjects arriving at Newfoundland from any other Country except Great Britain or one of the British Dominions in Europe") of course incapacitates the Bermudians and all other His Majesty's Subjects arriving there in vessels not fitted in letters of the said Act from landing and drying their Fish. But in consideration of their having been at considerable expense and the very great loss they would sustain if at this period they were to be prohibited from prosecuting their voyages, which were undertaken so advantageously to "these Islands."

(f.) EXTRACT FROM REPLY OF THE HOUSE OF ASSEMBLY TO THE GOVERNOR'S ADDRESS AT THE OPENING OF THE SESSION.

To people destitute of a staple, nothing can be more desirable than the establishment of some productive substitute. In this point of view, the cod fishery demands our immediate and serious attention. We shall therefore endeavour to promote such measures as shall [tend] to remove the difficulties which have arisen to the prosecution of the first adventure, and to afford in future a greater probability of success.

III.—The Conspiracy in St. John's in 1799-1800.

St. John's, Newfoundland,
SIR,   July 2, 1800.

I am sorry to inform you, that a spirit of disaffection to our Government has manifested itself here last winter and in the spring. The first symptoms made their appearance about the latter end of February, by some anonymous papers posted up in the night, threatening the persons and property of the magistrates, if they persisted in enforcing a proclamation they had published, respecting hogs going at large, contrary to a presentment of the grand jury. We advertised a hundred guineas reward for the discovery of the author or authors, and the inhabitants viewing it in a very proper light, as the commencement of anarchy and confusion, and destruction of all order, handsomely came forward in support of the magistrates, and offered two hundred guineas more, but I am sorry to say without effect. The next step, still more alarming, was a combination of between forty and fifty of the Royal Newfoundland Regiment, to desert with their arms, with a declared intention, as appeared by a letter left behind them, of putting every person to death who should attempt to oppose them. This they put in execution on the night of the 24th April. Their place of rendezvous was the powder shed, back of Fort Townshend, at 11 at night, but were not joined in time from Fort Townshend or Fort William. We know not the reason why the party from Fort Townshend did not join them, but at Fort William Colonel Skinner happened to have a party at his house very late that night, preventing the possibility of their going out unperceived at the appointed hour, and the alarm being made at Signal Hill for those who quitted that post, the plot was blown, when only nineteen were met, who immediately set off for the woods, but from the vigilance and activity used in their pursuit, in about ten days or a fortnight, sixteen of them were taken, two or three of whom informed against the others, and implicated upwards of twenty more, who had not only agreed to desert, but had also taken the oaths of United Irishmen, administered by an arch-villain Murphy, who belonged to the regiment, and one of the deserters, who with a sergeant Kelly, and a private, have not as yet been taken. We do not know, nor was it possible to ascertain, how far this defection and the united oaths extended through the regiment. General Skerret ordered a general court-martial upon twelve of those taken, five of whom were sentenced to be hanged, and seven to be shot; the former were executed on a gallows erected upon the spot where they met at the powder shed, the other seven were sent to Halifax, to be further dealt with as His Royal Highness should think proper, those also implicated by the king's evidence were sent in irons to Halifax; and the Duke of Kent has at length removed all the regiment, except two companies of picked men, to head quarters, and has relieved them by the whole of the 66th regiment, who are now here. Various have been the reports on this business; the town to the amount of 2, 3, or 400 men mentioned as privy or concerned in this business, and of acting in concert with them, at least so far as to destroy, plunder, and set off for the States, but no names have been particularly mentioned, so as to bring the proof home. In fact, we were at one time in such a situation, as to render the policy of acting very doubtful, until more force should arrive, as we knew not who we could depend upon for support in case of resistance, having every reason to believe the defection was very extensive, not only through the regiment, but through the inhabitants of this and all the out harbours, particularly to the southward, almost to a man have taken the United Oaths, which is "to be true to the old cause, and to follow their heads of whatsoever denomination." Although those heads are not to be known to them till the moment a plan is to be put in action, all this one of the evidences has declared originated from letters received from Ireland. Although a United Irishman, he was yet but a novice, and was not so far let into the secret as to know who the letters were addressed to, or who from. Although we are at present without any immediate apprehension of danger, we have no reason to suppose their dispositions have changed, or that their plans of plunder, burnings, &c., are given up, but only waiting a proper opportunity to break forth. The most probable time for such an event would be towards the close of the winter, when the ships of war are absent, the peaceable and well-disposed part of the community off their guard, and no possibility of succour for two or three months, or of even conveying intelligence of our situation. If such has been their plan, of which there is little room left for doubt, though I believe more for motives of plunder than of conquest, either of which would be equally destructive, it would be absurd to suppose it might not take place again—I should therefore imagine it behoves Government not to risk another winter without obviating its possible effect; and I am firmly of opinion, after taking the whole of what has passed into view, that the security of the trade and fishery, nay, the security and salvation of the island itself, will entirely depend upon a proper military force at this place with sufficient strength to afford small detachments to some of the out harbours to the southward to watch their motions, and assist the magistrates when necessary. This force to render security effectual cannot be less than 800 or 1,000 men, particularly while Ireland is in such a state of ferment as it has been and is likely to continue till the business of the union is settled, for the events of Ireland have heretofore and will in a great measure govern the sentiments and actions of the far greater majority of the people in this country.

I omitted observing that the regiment now here (the 66th) have but little more than half their complement of men, and are mostly composed of drafts from the Irish brigade sent three or four years ago to Halifax, of course not so well adapted for the protection required, as a full and complete regiment from England, staunch and well-affected.

I have thus ventured to offer my opinion upon the public situation of affairs in this island, and have only to regret in common with the real well-wishers to its prosperity, that by the triennial mode of appointing governors we are to be deprived of the aid of your influence and counsel, at a time when from your real knowledge of the island and its internal affairs, they might be of such essential service.

I have the honour to be, &c.
J. OGDEN.
To the Hon. Vice-Admiral Waldegrave,
&c. &c. &c.

IV.—The Early Seal Fishery.

Described by J. BLAND, of Bonavista, in a Letter to Governor GAMBIER.

SIR, Bonavista, 26th September 1802.

Your Excellency has been pleased to request of me some information respecting our seal fishery, and as far as my own experience and general observation can lead, I shall endeavour to comply with that request.

This adventurous and perilous pursuit is prosecuted in two different ways—during the winter months by nets, and from March to June in ice-skiffs and decked boats, or schooners. The fishery by nets extends from Conception Bay to the Labrador, and in the northern posts there is most certainty of success. About fifty pounds weight of strong twine will be required to make a net, the half worn small hawsers, which the boats have used in the summer fishery, serve for foot ropes; new ratline is necessary for head ropes, and each net is required to be about forty fathoms in length, and nearly three in depth. I am thus minute that your Excellency may form some idea of the expense attending this adventure, as well as of the mode in which it is conducted.

Four or five men constitute a crew to attend about twenty nets, but in brisk sealing this number of nets will require a double crew in separate boats. The seals bolt into the nets while ranging at the bottom in quest of food, which makes it necessary to keep the nets to the ground, where they are made to stand on their legs, as the phrase is, by means of cork fastened at equal distances along the head ropes. The net is extended at the bottom by a mooring and killock fixed to each end, and it is frequently placed in forty fathoms water, for we observe that the largest seals are caught in the deepest water. To each end of the head-rope is fixed a line with a pole standing erect in the water to guide the sealers to the net, and when these poles are torn away by ice, or other accident, they are directed by landmarks and find their nets with creepers. The seals, in their efforts to get free, cable the nets at the bottom, and none but experienced sealers can disengage them without cutting the net. This description, sir, may not be interesting, but it will convey to your Excellency a correct idea of this laborious business, and show that none but men active and inured to hardship, can be qualified to engage in it. On the Labrador coast the seal fishery begins in November and ends about Christmas, when the nets are taken up. With us, it begins about Christmas and continues through the winter, the ice in this quarter being seldom stationary for any considerable length of time.

Should strong East and N.E. winds prevail through the months of December and January, the seals towards the end of the latter month never fail to appear in large companies, always going before the wind and ice till they find themselves inbayed. The seals upon this coast are of many species, they are classed and distinguished by names only to be found in the Newfoundland nomenclature, and only understood by the Newfoundland naturalists. *Tars, Doaters, Gunswails*, and many others, breed upon the rocks in the summer season, and may be called natives, but these make but little part of our fishery, our dependance rests wholly upon *Harps* and *Bedlemers*, which are driven by winds and ice from the north-east seas. The harp in its prime will yield from ten to sixteen gallons of oil, and the bedlemer, a seal of the same species, only younger, from three to seven. About the middle of March the female harp whelps upon ice, and, in the course of a few days, becomes reduced to less than half of her largest bulk. The male, also, from this period reduces, but not in the same proportion. There is, therefore, an evident advantage in catching the seals in the winter.

I will now, sir, proceed to bring into view the produce of this fishery in Bonavista Bay for some years back, in doing which I shall be as precise as the nature of the case will now admit of. In the winter of 1791-2, a succession of hard gales from the north-east brought the seals in great numbers, before the middle of January, unaccompanied by any ice, a circumstance that rarely occurs. In Bonavista about two hundred men might have been employed in attending the nets, and the number of seals caught amounted to about seven thousand. The entire catch at Bonavista Bay may be taken at ten thousand, and two-thirds of the whole reckoned *Harps*. The harps yielded thirteen shillings each, and the bedlermers seven shillings and sixpence, which at that time afforded the merchant a large profit in the English market.

The winter of 92-3 the nets were unproductive, but the ice-skiffs in the spring were generally successful, killing from five to six thousand seals, principally young, which yielded five shillings each.

For the winter and spring 93-4, we may reckon about five thousand.

In 95 the nets were successful in the prime part of the season, and the numbers taken about six thousand, two thirds of which were harps.

The five succeeding years may be averaged at six thousand each, and three-fourths of these may be reckoned young seals. In the spring of 1801 we may count about twenty thousand, the greatest part of which were dragged on the ice by men, women, and children, with incredible labour. These seals were principally of the *hooded* kind, and about nine-tenths of them young. The old yielded about fourteen shillings and the young seven. The last season may have produced six thousand, yielding on an average about seven shillings each. I do not know, sir, if what I have written will be thought satisfactory. I have confined myself to the district in which I live, not having materials from which to give anything like a correct statement of the other sealing ports of the island and of Labrador. It may, nevertheless, be proper to say, that your Excellency ought not to form an estimate of these, from the foregoing sketch. The ports on the coast of Labrador, on the northern shore, now possessed by the French, and southward to Fogo, have been out of all comparison more successful in this fishery by nets.

The sealing-adventure by large boats, which sail about the middle of March, has not been general longer than nine years. It has been pursued with various success, and unquestionably has a tendency to promote the first intention of government beyond any other. From two to three thousand men have been employed in this perilous adventure, and it may excite surprise that so few fatal accidents have happened. It is, however, in my opinion, for various reasons, upon the decline, and it may properly become a question whether Government ought to suffer it to fall, if it can be supported to its full extent through the medium of a premium or bounty. Out of the harbour of Saint John's this adventure has been followed with uncommon spirit, and your Excellency, it is likely, may obtain useful information on this subject from the merchants of that quarter.

I have the honour to be with great respect, Sir,
 Your Excellency's obedient humble servant,
  JOHN BLAND.

His Excellency
James Gambier, Esquire.

CHAPTER XIV.

REIGN OF GEORGE IV.
1820-1830.

1822.—Richard Alexander Tucker, Esq., Chief Justice.

1823.—The last of the Red Indians of Newfoundland seen; Indian women brought to St. John's. Newfoundland School Society established. Mr. Cormack crossed the Island. Dr. Scallan, Bishop of Drago, and Vicar Apostolic of Newfoundland and Labrador. Chamber of Commerce, St. John's, instituted 26th December.

1824.—Imperial Act, 5 Geo. IV. cap. 67, for the better Administration of Justice in Newfoundland; appointing Supreme Court, with Chief Justice and two assistant judges. First fire company, Eastern Ward, St. John's.

1825.—Sir Thomas Cochrane Governor. First roads constructed.

1826.—Supreme Court of Newfoundland constituted by Royal Charter. First assistant judges, with Chief Justice Tucker, were John William Molloy and A. W. Des Barres; Molloy soon removed; E. B. Brenton appointed.

1827.—Bishop Inglis, Anglican Bishop of Nova Scotia and Newfoundland, first visited Newfoundland and consecrated St. John's Church. Beothic Institution: W. E. Cormack, President.

1828.—Publication of P. Morris's pamphlet. Great agitation for representative institutions.

1829.—Bishop Fleming consecrated Bishop of Carpasia *in partibus*.

REIGN OF WILLIAM IV.
1830-1837.

1831.—First coach road opened to Portugal Cove.

1832.—Representative Assembly granted to Newfoundland.

1833.—1st January, first Session of the Newfoundland House of Assembly opened by Sir Thomas Cochrane, Governor.

1834.—Captain Prescott, R.N., Governor. George Lilly, Esq., appointed Acting Judge, Supreme Court; first native judge. Savings Bank constituted.

1836.—First Light erected on Cape Spear. Bank of British North America established in St. John's.

In 1820 the long reign of George III. came to a close. The agitation about Butler and Lundrigan caused the British Government to consider the whole question of the administration of justice, and the formation of constitutional government in the Colony. Sir Charles Hamilton was recalled, for the purpose of consulting with the Ministry, Chief Justice Tucker[1] acting as Governor during his absence. As the

[1] Chief Justice Forbes resigned in 1822.

REIGN OF GEORGE IV.

result of these deliberations, the Royal Charter, the Imperial Act 5 George IV. cap. lxvii.—An Act for the better administration of justice in Newfoundland—was passed.

The preamble states:—

"Whereas it is expedient to make further provision for the administration of justice in the Colony of Newfoundland, it is therefore enacted by the King's Most Excellent Majesty, by and with the consent and advice, &c., in this present Parliament assembled, and by the authority of the same, that it shall and may be lawful for His Majesty by his charter, or letters patent, under the Great Seal, to institute a Superior Court of Judicature in Newfoundland, which shall be entitled 'The Supreme Court of Newfoundland,' and the said court shall be a Court of Record, and shall have all civil and criminal jurisdiction whatever in Newfoundland and in all lands, islands, and territories dependent upon the government thereof, as fully and amply to all intents and purposes as His Majesty's courts of King's Bench, Common Pleas, Exchequer, and High Court of Chancery, in that part of Great Britain called England have, or any of them hath, and the said Supreme Court shall also be a Court of Oyer and Terminer, and general gaol delivery in and for Newfoundland, and all places within the Government thereof, and shall also have jurisdiction in all cases of crimes and misdemeanours committed on the banks of Newfoundland, or any of the seas or islands to which ships or vessels repair from Newfoundland for carrying on the fishery."

The principal provisions of the Act were to the effect that the Supreme Court shall be—

"Holden by a chief judge and two assistant judges, being respectively barristers in England or Ireland of at least three years' standing, or in some of His Majesty's colonies or plantations; that it shall be lawful for the Governor to divide the colony into three districts, as may appear best adapted for enabling the inhabitants to resort with ease and convenience to the circuit courts to be therein established,—that it shall be lawful for His Majesty to institute circuit courts in each of the three districts, such courts to be holden at least once every year by the chief judge, or one of the assistant judges of the supreme court; that the circuit courts shall have the same jurisdiction within the district in which they were severally held, as is vested in the supreme court for the whole colony, with the exception of trying certain crimes specified, or of hearing or determining any suit arising out of a violation of any Act of Parliament, relating to the trade and revenue of the British colonies in America. Such crimes and such suits to be tried, heard, and determined only in the supreme court. To persons who feel themselves aggrieved by any judgment given in the circuit court, there is granted power of appeal to the supreme court, for a reversal of such judgment. A power is given to the Governor to institute a court of civil jurisdiction on the coast of Labrador."

Although the Act was passed in 1824, the Supreme Court was not duly constituted until the 2nd January 1826, when it was opened with

THE SUPREME COURT.

the following imposing ceremonies by His Excellency Captain Sir Thomas Cochrane :—

"The honourable judges, the honourable Lieut. Colonel Burke, C.B., commanding His Majesty's forces, the magistrates and heads of all the public departments, civil and military, the clergy, the chamber of commerce, the grand jury, and most of the principal inhabitants assembled at the Government House, when the oaths of office were administered to the chief judge and assistant judges, after which His Excellency delivered to the chief judge His Majesty's Royal Charter, which was handed by the judge to the chief clerk of the Supreme Court, to be borne by him to the Court House, and to be there read.

"After these preliminaries were over, the assembled parties formed themselves into a procession, the order of which had been fixed by a programme previously issued. The constables (two and two)—fort-major—gentlemen of the learned professions (two and two)—clerks of the central, southern, and northern circuit courts—magistrates (two and two),—the chief magistrate, &c. &c. On arriving at the Court House, the Charter was solemnly read; at the conclusion of which proceeding, all the prisoners confined in the gaol (with the exception of five) were called to the bar, and, after a suitable admonition from the chief judge, were informed that His Excellency the Governor had been graciously pleased to exert on their behalf the prerogative of pardon entrusted to him by the Crown."

The judges appointed under the Act were Chief Justice Tucker and Assistant Judges John William Molloy and Augustus Wallet Des Barres.[1] Molloy was soon removed, and Judge Brenton appointed in his stead. The full dress of the chief justice, as superior civil officer, was appointed by the king—a blue coat, but no epaulettes nor lappets, button-holes upon the cuff and collar only, but the same pattern as worn by Lords-Lieutenants. The chief magistrate was ordered to wear a blue coat,

JUDGE DES BARRES.
From a photograph taken in 1861.

---

[1] The two puisne judges first appointed to the Supreme Court in 1826 presented a marked contrast. John William Molloy was a reckless, gay, squandering squireen, who soon ran into debt, and was got rid of. The Hon. Augustus Wallet Des Barres was, on the contrary, a most prudent and correct man. His father, Governor Des Barres, was a distinguished French engineer officer in the English service; his surveys of the Maritime Provinces were celebrated; he is alleged to have been present at the battle on the heights of Abraham when Wolfe was killed; and was Governor of Cape Breton and Lieut.-Governor of Prince Edward's Island. He was a man of consummate ability and immense influence; he is reported to have danced on a table when he was a hundred. He died at Halifax, N.S., in 1824, aged 102. His son, A. W. Des Barres, was so young when he received his first appointment—I believe as Attorney-General of Cape Breton—that, by the advice of his friends, he wore a pair of false whiskers when he went to receive his commission. He was celebrated for his ready wit and repartee. Once when the late Judge Hayward was quoting Chitty to the Bench, his Lordship retorted: "Chitty, Mr. Hayward! Goodness me, what does Mr. Chitty know about this country? He was never in Newfoundland."

with red cuffs and collar, buttons with crown, and G. R. cockade on the side of the hat. Constables were to wear blue coats and buttons, with the crown and G. R., a red waistcoat with the same buttons, and a cockade on the hat, and were required always to carry the insignia of office. His Excellency had a great taste for official forms and ceremonials. Lieut.-Col. W. Haly, Thomas H. Brooking, John W. Dunscombe, and Newman W. Hoyles, were in 1825 appointed His Excellency's colonial aides-de-camp, with the rank of lieut.-colonels of militia.

Sir Thomas Cochrane is now universally admitted to have been the best Governor ever sent to Newfoundland; everywhere are monuments erected to his memory. He inaugurated our system of roads, promoted agriculture, and laid out the beautiful grounds of Virginia as his country seat. Cochrane Street and the Military Road remind us of the great administrator. I cannot say much in praise of His Excellency's taste in the erection of Government House. The site is an admirable one, the grounds are well laid out, but the building

N. W. HOYLES.
From a portrait in the possession of Mrs. A. O. Hayward.

COLONIAL BUILDINGS AND GOVERNMENT HOUSE IN 1856.
From Mullock's Trip to Newfoundland.

itself looks more like a prison than a vice-regal residence; the ditch all round is a trap to catch snow, and in winter the north entrance is as cold as Siberia. I can give him credit for every other improvement, but am compelled to say that Government House is a huge pile of unredeemed ugliness.

The two great leaders in the struggle for a local legislature in Newfoundland were Doctor William Carson and Patrick Morris. Both were distinguished, able men, but in marked contrast to each other. The Doctor, the originator of the movement, was a stiff-mannered, pedantic old gentleman; dogmatic, self-opinionated, and independent, a very clever man both in his profession and the conduct of public affairs. Morris, on the other hand, had all the qualities of a popular tribune; you can see both in his writings and his speeches that he was an impetuous Irishman; everything was done with a rush; in place of the doctor's calm reasoning and carefully polished periods, his pamphlets are full of go, flashes of Irish wit and sarcasm; when he comes down to personalities he is as truculent and scurrilous as a Western editor. Morris once tried to cross swords with the great tribune O'Connell; the arch-agitator annihilated his colonial antagonist simply with a wink. At a great repeal meeting near Waterford, Morris, who was opposed to O'Connell's views, attempted to address the meeting; O'Connell called out in his broadest Kerry brogue, "Well, Pat, when did you come across, was there much fog on the Banks?" and then with his finger to his nose said: "Boys, do you smell the fish." Amidst the roar of laughter that followed, Morris quietly disappeared.

HON. P. MORRIS.
From an old portrait.

Sir Thomas Cochrane's government lasted from 1825 to 1834. During the first part of his administration his popularity was unbounded; he was the first civil Governor, the first real administrator and ruler of the Colony. An eminently practical man, he not only organised improvements, he personally superintended their execution. His activity was unbounded; in the early mornings he was out on horseback inspecting the roads, directing his workmen, laying out the grounds at Virginia, having interviews with the farmers, giving them practical hints about agriculture; everywhere he impressed his strong personality on Colonial affairs. He was very sociable, and his hospitality was unstinted; no Governor ever entertained in the style of Sir Thomas Cochrane. Mr. Morris in his pamphlet thus speaks of him:—

"Our present Governor is allowed, I understand, about £3,000 per year,[1] out of which he has to support the 'splendour of vice-regal authority,' a large retinue of servants, entertain the principal inhabitants of Newfoundland at his table, and all strangers who visit the seat of his government, to subscribe to all public charities and institutions. A great part of his income is expended in the country, so that if the author of the pamphlet only just takes an enlarged view of the subject, he will find that he was egregiously in error in supposing that his favourite *Admiral-Governor* was a *cheap governor*, for it appears that the matter of pounds, shillings, and pence, is his only criterion of judgment. If a comparison be made between the relative systems, the difference will appear more striking; our present Governor has been, since his arrival, improving the condition of the country and the people; and . . . . I maintain that he has done more real good to the colony, since his appointment, than all his predecessors put together.

He has, as far as his limited authority permitted him, given every encouragement to the cultivation of the soil, and has himself shown the example; he has encouraged every measure calculated to promote the internal resources of the country; he has made roads, some of them at his own expense; he has been the patron of education for the poor and the rich; and he had scarcely landed on our shores when he recommended the establishment of a university for the education of our respectable youth, to prevent the necessity of sending them to the United States and other parts; in short, he has felt a sympathy for the country and the people beyond what was ever felt by his predecessors, and the country feels grateful to him for it."

SIR THOMAS COCHRANE.
From a photograph by Maull and Polyblank.

Both Bishop Fleming[2] and Doctor Carson were equally loud in their praises of His Excellency.

[1] The salary was only £3,000 per annum.
[2] *A View of the Rise, Progress, &c. of the Newfoundland Fishery.* Poole, 1828.

Dr. Scallan, the third Roman Catholic bishop of Newfoundland, was appointed in April 1815 bishop of Drago *in partibus*, and in 1816 coadjutor to Dr. Lambert; he was consecrated the same year at Wexford; he had been labouring as a priest in St. John's since 1812. No man was more beloved in his diocese than Bishop Scallan; he was in every sense a gentleman. Both Bishop Mullock and Bishop Howley censure him for his extreme liberality. The Right Rev. Michael Anthony Fleming was appointed his coadjutor, and consecrated in the old chapel Bishop of Carpasia *in partibus* in 1829. Carpasian, the Bishop's farm, now owned by John Duder, Esq., was named after his titular episcopate.

All the great improvements around St. John's may be said to date from Sir Thomas Cochrane's time. The roads to Topsail, Bay Bulls, Torbay, and Portugal Cove had been commenced before his arrival; it was, however, his energy that pushed them forward. At this time officials and merchants vied with each other in creating country residences and farms—Mount Pearl, cleared by Sir James Pearl, Holbrook's Farm, cultivated by Surveyor-General Holbrook, and the finest of all, Brookfield, the property of William and Henry P. Thomas. Everywhere around the capital land was being cultivated; a perfect *furore* seemed to have seized everyone to become landed proprietors. The great pioneer in this movement was Dr. Carson, though it must be remembered to their honour that Major Griffith Williams, Col. Skinner, and Lieut.-Col. Haly had been farming before he cleared "Rostellan," formerly known as "Billies." Amongst the public-spirited merchants of that day the chief place must be given to the Thomases, and especially to the senior partner William Thomas.[1]

During the whole of the first part of Sir Thomas's administration, there was a continued agitation for a local legislature; whilst the Irish were probably the most busy workers for a form, many of the leading Protestant merchants took an active part. Besides the committee, the most conspicuous supporters of the movement were William Thomas, Thomas H. Brooking, his partner, G. R. Robinson (afterwards member of the English House of Commons), Benjamin Bowring, founder

---

[1] The family of the Thomases are probably the most ancient in this Colony; their connection can be traced back to the Shapleighs (one of whom was grandfather to John Treworgie, the Cromwellian Governor of the Colony), thence through the Bevils to William Bevil Thomas.

The Thomases carried on business at Dartmouth and St. John's in partnership with a Mr. Stokes, as Thomas & Stokes. William Bevil Thomas was born in St. John's in 1757; he married Elizabeth Way, in 1785, at Dartmouth, and had two sons, William Thomas and Henry Phillips Thomas.

William Thomas was foremost in every benevolent work. As a very young man he was secretary to the society for improving the condition of the poor; he was equally distinguished as a merchant and a politician. He filled all positions well, whether presiding at a religious meeting or as president of the Chamber of Commerce. Though a professedly religious man, sometimes the old leaven broke out in him. He was very active, and fond of directing everybody. Often, as he paced his long wharf, if one of his ships was beating in the Narrows, say his fine brig the *Cynthia*, Captain Goldsworth, he could be heard muttering, "Luff, cot round you, Goldsworth, luff, you lubber!" Brookfield, the fine house at Devon Row, their Water Street premises, and the beautiful cottage at Topsail, are monuments of the large progressive ideas of the Thomases, and especially of the constructive ability of Henry Phillips Thomas.

of the firm of Bowring Brothers, a very active, intelligent Liberal (cousin of Sir John Bowring), Charles T. Bowring, who afterwards filled a high position in the Corporation of Liverpool (father of William Benjamin Bowring, recently Lord Mayor of Liverpool), R. R. Wakeham, the genial secretary of the committee (brother-in-law of Sir W. V. Whiteway, K.C.M.G.) and Henry Winton, the able and independent editor of the *Public Ledger*. The opposition consisted of all the officials and those dependent on the Governor's good will; James Simms — afterwards Judge Simms — seems to have been their mouthpiece at all public meetings.

THE LATE C. T. BOWRING, ESQ.
From a photograph by
Hart, Exeter.

The bitterest antagonists of the measure were, however, the old West Country merchants; the idea of Newfoundland having a legislature was to their minds simply outrageous. One of them — Peter Ougier — stated in his evidence, "they are making roads in Newfoundland, next thing they will be having carriages and driving about." In his pamphlet Mr. Patrick Morris scarifies the author of a work entitled, "A view of the rise and progress of the Newfoundland Fishery." The whole object of this writer was to recommend a return to the rule of the fishing admirals; the pamphlet was published in Poole, and the writer declared his object was to give an *enlarged* view of the fisheries and trade of Newfoundland.

There can be no doubt that it was the influence of these West Country merchants that retarded the grant of a local legislature; a good deal could be said against the movement. Bishop Fleming, in a letter to Lord Glenelg, declared that he never approved of it; but the reply to every objection was the unanswerable argument that all the British Colonies, even to little

ALDERMAN W. B. BOWRING.
From the Illustrated London News.
Photo by Brown, Barnes, & Bell.

Bermuda, had a local government; Nova Scotia had obtained it in 1758, the older American Colonies had always governed themselves, and Newfoundland could no longer be denied. English statesmen clearly saw that, with all its defects and possible evil consequences, it was the only way in which free men could be governed under the British constitution, and it came at last as a matter of course.[1] In July 25th, 1831, Mr. Robinson objected to the Vote for Newfoundland in the House of Commons, adding, "that if a local "legislature were granted, the colonists would never ask the House "for another farthing." Lord Howick, in reply, stated "that the time had come for such a boon to be granted." In January 1832, Mr. Brooking, Chairman of the Newfoundland Committee in London, writing to William Thomas, Deputy Chairman in St. John's, stated that Viscount Goderich informed him that it was the intention of His Majesty to give Newfoundland a representative government similar to that of Nova Scotia and New Brunswick. The agitators had hit upon a fortunate time in English politics—the era of the great Reform Bill. In 1832 the Bill was passed in the House of Commons granting a representative assembly to Newfoundland; on August 26th of that year Sir Thomas returned to St. John's armed with full powers to carry out the great constitutional change. The general election took place in the autumn of 1832.

The first House of Assembly seems to have been a very respectable body. The only contest in which there appears to have been any excitement was in St. John's; the candidates were Dr. Carson, Mr. Patrick Keough, Mr. William Thomas, Mr. John Kent (a relative of Bishop Fleming's, from whom he received strong support), and Mr. W. B. Row, who does not appear to have gone to the poll. The great Doctor was defeated; the author of the new constitution was the first to test the proverbial fickleness of the public:—

"Fantastic as a woman's mood,
And fierce as frenzy's fevered blood."

He had been the pioneer of the new movement, had suffered in the people's cause, and yet the public, "that many-headed monster thing —the mob"—were the first to cast aside their leader in the fight for Home Rule, and to give their votes and support to a new and

---

[1] Note the items of expenditure under this government of officials; the whole revenue swallowed up in enormous salaries, and only £300 allowed for roads, show that it was high time to make a change. (See in the statistics the expenditure in 1830, 1831, and 1832, prior to grant of Legislature.)

untried man. Carson was a veteran in the Liberal cause; compared with him, Kent was a mere neophite. The Doctor's defeat was due, so the story goes, to an old electioneering trick. An Irishman called Bennett came into the booth where a number of Wexford men were casting their votes. "Well," he said, "I hear the Doctor say he did not "care how it went, so long as he could bate Keough and them blooming "yallow bellies." Mr. Keough was a Wexford man, and after that he got every Wexford vote. The story was a barefaced lie, but it served its purpose.

Our old friend Mr. John Kent, who then fleshed his maiden sword, was a very young man. His address shows how thoroughly he had grasped the political situation, that there was no finality about the existing Legislature; it was merely a lever to force greater concessions from the British Government.

In his address to the electors of St. John's, 4th September 1832, he states:—

"Our constitution has, as yet, only half developed itself; but in that partial development, a sufficient evidence is given of the desire of power to hedge round its prerogative with a force ductile to its will, but irresponsible to the people. In a council nominated by the Governor, composed of those holding offices under Government, or expectants for place, and in which the leading interests of the country are misrepresented, oligarchical principles must prevail. The task of prostrating those principles, or of so modifying them as to make them useful, now devolves on the people. . . . Your extensive franchise, amounting almost to universal suffrage, will enable you to do this."

Mr. James Simms, who had been a merchant, carrying on business in St. John's, was appointed Attorney General of Newfoundland on the 2nd of January 1826. The first law officer of the Crown was one of the most prominent opponents of the new Legislature, and, as senior member of the Council, his conduct towards the Lower House was most overbearing. Many of us can remember him as a handsome, gentlemanly old man, very stiff in his opinions, and of fearless courage, in his own house hospitable and generous. He had a very high-pitched voice, and very slow, measured speech, which gave more point to his sarcasms. Once, in the Amalgamated House, Mr. Kent declared: "I will "attack Her Majesty's Attorney-General." Simms rose, slowly, to reply: "I know not," said he, "with what weapon the Honourable Member will "attack me, except it be with the jawbone of an ass."

THE OPENING CEREMONY.

On the 1st of January 1833, with all due pomp and ceremony, the first House of Assembly was opened. The newspaper report says:—

"His Excellency the Governor left Government House a little before two o'clock, attended by some of the principal military officers and by his staff, and proceeded to the Court House, at the doors of which he was received by a guard of honour, and was saluted with nineteen guns from the fort. Having been conducted to the door of the High Sheriff's house, His Excellency was received by the High Sheriff and the Sergeant-at-Arms to the Council, who led the way to the throne, &c. . . ."

The speech of the Governor dwelt at considerable length on the new era which had arisen in the political condition of the island, and the new responsibilities imposed thereby, concluding with the following declaration of His Excellency's own sentiments:—

"The experience of the past will afford the best criterion by which to judge of my wishes and feelings towards those you are here to represent. Uninfluenced by any local prejudices, and without a single personal desire to gratify, I can have but one object before me—their happiness and prosperity; and I assure you, gentlemen, from the bottom of my heart, that it will be my most anxious and increasing endeavour to co-operate with you in every measure that can best attain those objects, for which the privileges now about to be enjoyed have been solicited by the people, and graciously conceded to them by their sovereign."

The following members were elected for the nine districts to the first House of Assembly of Newfoundland in 1832:—

St. John's	- Patrick Keough.	Bonavista	- William Brown.
,,	- John Kent.	Trinity	- John Bingley Garland.
,,	- Wm. Thomas.	Ferryland	- Robert Carter.
Conception Bay	- Peter Brown.	Burin	- Wm. Hooper.
,,	- James Power.	Fortune Bay	- Newman W. Hoyles.
,,	- Charles Cozens.	Placentia	- Roger F. Sweetman.
,,	- Robert Pack.	,,	- John Hill Martin.
Twillingate and Fogo	Thomas Bennett.		

The House of Assembly of 1833 was the youngest constituent body in America, but it was not one whit behind any of them in stately parliamentary pageant and grandiloquent language. H. B. (Doyle) in London caricatured it as the "Bow-wow Parliament," with a big Newfoundland dog in wig and bands as Speaker putting the motion: "As many "as are of that opinion say—bow; of the contrary—wow; the "bows have it." The Clerk of the first House of Assembly, appointed by the Crown, was Mr. E. M. Archibald[1]; he had been admirably trained in his father's office, and he kept the Speaker and the new House

---

[1] E. M. Archibald, afterwards Sir Edward Archibald, Consul-General in New York, a very able man, was one of the younger sons of the celebrated Hon. S. G. W. Archibald, the most distinguished Nova Scotian of his day, a man with influence enough to secure for himself the position of Attorney-General of Nova Scotia, Speaker of the House of Assembly, and subsequently Chief Justice of Cape Breton; his son, Charles Dixon Archibald, was Clerk of our Supreme Court, and was succeeded in this office by his brother Edward, who afterwards became Attorney-General.

REIGN OF WILLIAM IV.

straight on all questions of parliamentary form; his journals are admirably written.

The first journal contains election petitions from Dr. Carson and Hugh Alexander Emerson. The former shows some queer ways of

THE BOW-WOW PARLIAMENT.

working a contest. It appears there were at first only four candidates, John Kent, William Thomas, William B. Row, and Patrick Keough; afterwards the Doctor came forward. Each candidate agreed to bring his voters to the poll in tallies of ten; Carson alleged that Kent and

Keough broke this agreement by both of them bringing forward two fictitious candidates, who crowded out his voters. The Doctor also contended that as Mr. Keough had been employed "filling up several places and appointments in the court house for the opening convenience

" of the local Legislature, the said Patrick Keough is therefore utterly
" disqualified for being a member of this Honourable House. Elections
" are fountains from whence flow the purity of parliaments; if the
" sources are permitted to be impure the accumulated mass will soon be
" corrupt." The complaint of Hugh Alexander Emerson, candidate for
Bonavista, is all directed against Peter Le Messurier, the returning
officer. The House of Assembly dismissed both petitions.

John Bingley Garland was elected Speaker. In 1834 on the removal
of Mr. William Thomas to the Legislative Council, and Garland's retirement, William Carson was elected for St.
John's, and William Bickford Row for
Trinity. There was a sharp contest between Dr. Carson and Mr. Thomas Bennett
for the speakership; Bennett won.

The most absurd thing about the constitution was the creation of a Colonial
House of Lords—the Legislative Council.
It looked as if it had been formed on purpose to render the whole machinery unworkable; it consisted wholly of officials.
The Governor's instructions, besides directing him to summon a House of Assembly,
commanded him also to call together the
following persons appointed to be members of His Majesty's Council in the Island, viz:—

J. B. GARLAND.
From a portrait in the possession of Mrs. Morison Carlisle.

"The chief justice for the time being, the officer in command of the land
forces for the time being, the attorney-general for the time being, the colonial
secretary for the time being, the collector or other chief officer of the Customs for
the time being, and William Haly, Esq. 'With all due and usual solemnity' the
Governor was to cause his commission to 'be read and published before the
'Council, and to administer to each of the members thereof the oaths therein
'required.' He was also to communicate to the said Council such of the instructions wherein their advice and consent were mentioned to be requisite, and to
permit the members to have and enjoy freedom of debate, and vote in all affairs of
public concern submitted to their consideration in council."

The two bodies, as might be expected, immediately disagreed; Chief
Justice Tucker, a Bermudian, contended that the Assembly had no *right
to pass a Revenue Bill*. The matter was referred to England, and, as a
matter of course, the Ministry supported the Lower House; Richard
Alexander Tucker resigned his office, and left the Colony in disgust.

Chief Justice Henry John Boulton succeeded Mr. Tucker; he had
been Attorney-General of Upper Canada.[1] The difficulties between the

---

[1] Subsequent to his dismissal from the Chief Justiceship in 1838, Boulton returned to Toronto, and afterwards represented Niagara, and also Norfolk in Parliament. He was taken prisoner during the year 1814 by a French privateer called the *Grand Duke de Berg*, when crossing the Atlantic in the *Mercator*, and kept a prisoner until 1814 at Verdun.

House and the Council were rendered much more bitter by his appointment. He was most overbearing to the Lower House, always calling himself most improperly—*The Speaker*! With him were associated in the Council Colonel Sall, Commandant; James Crowdy, Colonial Secretary; James Simms, Attorney-General; the Collector of the Customs; and Lieutenant-Colonel William Haly. Next year (1834) J. B. Bland and William Thomas were added.

Carson and Kent in the House of Assembly, kept up a continual quarrel with Boulton and Simms. They fought over the most trivial details. When the lower branch styled themselves the *Commons* House of Assembly in *Parliament* assembled, they were ordered to strike out the word "*Parliament*." Their controversies were of the most puerile character; each side displayed vile temper and utter incapacity. The essence of politics is compromise, a principle that neither side seems to have understood. On the whole, the Council were the most cantankerous. Boulton had undoubted ability, but he was the worst possible selection for both the Council and the Bench. His views both of law and legislation, were most illiberal; as a technical lawyer he was mostly right and sublimely independent, but his harsh sentences, his indecent party spirit, and his personal meanness caused him to be hated as no one else was ever hated in this Colony. Forbes and Tucker were both able men, especially Forbes; they were not only learned, but, better still they were shrewd men of the world, thoroughly polished, courteous gentlemen. *Apropos* of Boulton's character for inhospitality, a good story is told by Bishop Strachan, the genial old Anglican Bishop of Toronto. Boulton in a hot argument with a young lawyer, committed the unpardonable crime of stopping the bottles at the Bishop's table. Strachan stood it for a few minutes; at last he called out, in his broad Scotch: "Henry John, pass the bottles; ye're nae in yer own hoose noo, mon."

The fiercest controversy between the two bodies was over the Contingency Bill of the Lower House. These contingencies were swelling up each session, the Council tried to cut them down; strictly speaking they had no authority to touch them at all. They could throw out the

---

This shows Boulton to have been a very small-minded man, and either ignorant or presuming. The presiding officer in all Colonial Legislative Councils is styled the President. When rebuked by the Secretary of State for using the term Speaker, he signed himself Henry John Boulton in full, with a very small r.c.

Bill, which would include their own charges, but they could not amend it. The Council not only refused to pass the Contingency Bill, but year after year, also, threw out the Supply and Revenue Bills. In the meantime, the Governor drew warrants on the Colonial Treasury for the civil expenses of the Government, an extremely high-handed proceeding. The quarrel between the House and the Council was inflamed by the press and the mercantile body. I give two examples of the amenities of the press:—

"And we believe a greater pack of knaves does not exist than that which composes the House of Assembly for the Colony. Take them for all in all, from the Speaker downwards, we do not suppose that a greater set of low-life and lawless scoundrels as Public men can be found under the canopy of Heaven.

"As for the arrogant scoundrelly House of Assembly with which the country is cursed, His Excellency will in this instance do well to, as far as possible, wash his hands clear from it, and take upon himself a judicious responsibility, in which all honest men will bear him out, And let the House of Assembly take any course which it may deem fit."

The men to be pitied in all these childish squabbles were the English Ministry; they were worried to death with long memorials from each side, volumes of despatches; the Colonial Legislature they had called into existence was a veritable political Frankenstein, that unceasingly haunted and disturbed them.

Viewing the events between 1833 and 1838—an unfortunate time for the Colony—we see clearly that free institutions never had a fair trial. The upper and mercantile classes were on the whole bitterly opposed to them; the Legislative Council, with Chief Justice Boulton at its head, was an uncompromising opponent; Boulton brought his powerful but narrow mind in antagonism to the Lower House on all questions; he was almost invariably wrong in his constitutional doctrines, as he was astray in his decision about servants' wages not having a prior claim on the fish and oil. As I have shown, the custom of giving the fishery servants the first claim on the voyage had existed in the Colony since the fishery began.

We had also another element that worked against our infant assembly—the violence of the mob; this gave support to all the arguments of the Tory and mercantile party, and it helped to kill out some of the very best blood in the Colony—the very cream of the most important element in the community—the Irish middle-class Liberals (afterwards designated with the odious name of "mad dogs"). How these men and their families were insulted, attacked, and many driven from the Colony, is one of the most deplorable chapters in our political history. The worst effect, however, of free government was the sectarian discord it produced. Previous to the introduction of the Legislature, the community was harmonious and united; for years afterwards there was nothing but strife and discord. The House gave a handle to their opponents by providing little jobs and pickings for their supporters; as their Contingency Bills show, they were not very large. The new Government was, after all, preferable to the ring of officials.

In the politics of this period the Roman Catholic bishop always played a prominent part. It is told, as an example of Bishop Fleming's skill and sagacity, that when a delegation, consisting of Messrs. Nugent and O'Brien, were sent to the Colonial Office, he suggested that the Hon. Lawrence should always go first, as a very handsome Colonial specimen, but, when it came to speaking, Nugent, who was a scholar, should do the work. At the close of his life, Bishop Fleming deeply deplored the unhappy divisions politics had produced in the Colony; he held out the right hand of fellowship to all who had been at enmity with him; his friendship with Dr. Carson was warm and sincere. On all matters, both public and private, his confidant, friend, and legal adviser was Mr. Wakeham. In the latter part of his episcopate, which extended over the long period of twenty-one years, he was ably assisted by Dr. Mullock.

In 1834 Sir Thomas Cochrane was rather suddenly called home. The Ministry seemed to have entertained the idea that he was in some way responsible for the unsatisfactory state of affairs in the Colony. It is painful to relate that many of those who had been loud in his praises as the best Governor ever sent to the Colony, had now turned against him, and loaded him with abuse. The conduct of the mob was most disgraceful. When His Excellency sailed for England they hooted, and actually threw dirt at Sir Thomas and Miss Cochrane as they passed down Cochrane Street to embark at the Queen's wharf. Every respectable man in the community, except a few political agitators, regretted his departure, and addresses were presented to him from the leading inhabitants all over the Colony.[1] 1835 witnessed the barbarous outrage on Mr. Henry Winton, editor of the *Public Ledger*.[2]

Captain Prescott, R.N., was sent out to succeed Sir Thomas Cochrane in 1834. No doubt the idea of the Ministry was that Sir Thomas might

---

[1] In 1834 an Act was passed for the creation of a savings bank. Newman W. Hoyles was appointed first treasurer and cashier; at his death, Patrick Morris succeeded to both positions. J. R. M. Cooke, a son-in-law of Mr. Hoyles, was clerk to the bank.

[2] Henry Winton, on whom this most disgraceful outrage was perpetrated, was a man of remarkable intrepidity, an able and most independent editor. He was one of a very convivial circle, which included Mr. John Boyd, whose Baillie Nicol Jarvie was considered by good judges the best amateur acting ever seen either here or elsewhere. Boyd was being sharply cross-examined about Winton's habits in a libel suit. Winton was of rather a saturnine habit, except when under the influence of good liquor, which brought out all his talents. "Now, sir," said Mr. Emerson, pointing at Boyd, "did you never see Mr. Winton the worse for liquor?" "Nae, nae," said Boyd, "never. I often saw him the better of it."

have been too rigid in his views, and that, with a new man at the helm, matters might work smoother in the distracted colony. After all Governor Cochrane's great services, he was superseded in a discourteous and shabby manner; his first intimation of the change of government was the arrival of Captain Prescott, with a fresh commission. During the new Governor's stay, from 1834 to the summer of 1840, the political condition of the Colony did not improve, the quarrels between the Council and the Assembly were rather intensified. In 1838 an

PORTUGAL COVE ROAD, OPENED IN 1851.
From a photograph by Sir T. N. O'Brien, K.C.M.G.

attempt was made to infuse a more popular element into the Council; it then consisted of the following (the Hon. Patrick Morris was added in 1840):—

"Lieut. Col. William Sall, Commanding the troops.
James Simms, Attorney-General.
James Crowdy, Colonial Secretary.
James Morton Spearman, Collector of Customs.
John Dunscombe.
William Thomas.
John Bayley Bland.
John Sinclair.
Patrick Morris, Colonial Treasurer."

438 REIGN OF WILLIAM IV.

The first House of Assembly by statute, ended in 1836. The elections of this year were very hotly contested; there were riots at Harbour Grace and all around Conception Bay, and great disturbances in St. John's. The Attorney-General indicted a number of persons for riot and assault; six of these were members of the House of Assembly.[1] There was not a tittle of evidence to sustain the charges against the members, and they were acquitted. In the other cases, the sentences passed by Chief Justice Boulton were considered so unnecessarily severe that they were remitted by the Home Government. The most preposterous proceeding of all was the disannulling of the 1836 elections, on the ground that one returned writ was *unsealed*.[2] Both Boulton and Attorney-General Simms declared the elections invalid. New writs were ordered; at the second contest the Conservatives or Protestants made no fight, and a very inferior set of members were returned, one of them being the celebrated Tom Fitz-Gibbon Moore, of Diddo. The new House contended for its right to appoint its own officers. Mr. E. M. Archibald, the clerk, and other officials had been appointed by the Crown. The new House, however, appointed its own clerk, Mr. R. R. Wakeham. Between the Legislative Council and the Assembly there was war to the knife. The Council threw out Supply, Revenue, and Contingency Bills; as fast as the Lower House enacted measures the Upper House annulled them. There was only one way out of the deadlock: the Ministers at home had to be appealed to.

P. H. GOSSE.
From an old photograph.

[1] One of the parties indicted was the Hon. Patrick Morris. The only evidence of violence at the great political meeting held at Roe Island was that young Mr. John Kent rode a spirited blood horse, and a man called Power sang out "Bah." The rioting and disturbance in Conception Bay was disgraceful. Nearly all the election fights were between rival Roman Catholic candidates. The Hon. T. Talbot, in his pamphlet on Newfoundland, gives a graphic description of one of these scenes. Some of the Conservatives who could not be frightened were bullied and threatened; another member, however, who was not to be intimidated in any way, they punished by setting fire to his house. Lord John Russell sharply rebuked Governor Prescott for his laxity in not sending troops to Carbonear in 1840. His Lordship said this place, Carbonear, should be disfranchised. An old man named Farrell, who was one of the leaders of the mob, complained that "after all the murdering and blackguarding he had done in these elections, he had no berth, whilst the men he put in had a fat office, and was aiting and drinking the best in the land."

[2] In the elections of 1836 and 1837 to the House of Assembly there was a complete change; nearly all the leading men seem to have retired. Peter Winsor replaced Mr. Carter in Ferryland; Peter Brown, John McCarthy, Anthony W. Godfrey, and James Power were elected for Conception Bay; John V. Nugent and Patrick Doyle were returned for Placentia; Trinity was represented by Tom Fitz-Gibbon Moore, Fogo by Edward James Dwyer, Bonavista by the Solicitor-General, Hugh A. Emerson, Fortune Bay by W. B. Row, whilst the St. John's members were Dr. Carson, John Kent, and Patrick Morris.

[3] Tom Fitz-Gibbon Moore used to walk from his home to the Assembly every session, carrying his "nunny" bag on his back; a wild, eccentric individual, he was as excited as an Indian bravo over the arrest of Judge Lilly. Only one of his many speeches has come down to us. His father was a soldier, and Tom had been a drummer in the Navy; in one of his famous orations he described himself "As born in the Glorious British Army, reared in the Navy, and Musician under our Most gracious Sailor King." A rival of Moore's—Dwyer—was the Hon. Member for Lion's Den, Fogo.

[4] A very interesting sketch of the social and political history of the Colony from 1827 to 1835 is given in the life of Philip Henry Gosse (1810-1888), the eminent naturalist, by his son, the well-known author and critic, Edmund Gosse. It appears from this biography that William Gosse, an elder brother (who survived until 1893), went out to Carbonear in 1822 to the old firm of Pack, Gosse and Fryer; the youngest brother, Philip, later on became a clerk in the house of Slade, Elson & Co. A graphic account is given of the outfitting, tallying, seals, and settling the shareman's accounts, the wrangle over what was "took up;" all the phases of outharbour life in the thirties are admirably told. The firm had a branch establishment at St. Mary's, ruled by a pompous little West countryman, John Hill Martin, one of the first members for Placentia. Gosse was packed off to this out-of-the-way place, so we get a description of St. Mary's, of Phipard and his pretty daughters, and a very graphic account of the journey overland from St. Mary's to Carbonear with Byrne, prototype of Tom Kelly, at the Head, and other noted country guides. Gosse was living at Carbonear when the dastardly attack was made on his friend Henry Winton. He mentions the name of the surgeon who cut off Winton's ears. Philip Henry Gosse's character, with all its faults and foibles, is admirably portrayed—his generosity, his high sense of honour, his absorbing passion for natural history, and his rigid religious convictions. In these days Carbonear was the most turbulent district in the colony. It is not, therefore, to be wondered at that Gosse's views of his religious and political opponents are unfavourable. A few persons still living in Carbonear and Harbour Grace remember him, his mania for collecting, his friendship with the talented St. John family, the Elsons, and many other Carbonear worthies, whose memory is fast fading away from the present generation. In 1833 P. H. Gosse wrote and copiously illustrated a volume which he entitled *Entomologia Terræ Novæ*. This was the earliest attempt made to describe the insects of Newfoundland, but the young naturalist did not find a publisher, and his work has never been printed.

APPENDIX TO CHAPTER XIV.

The Tariff and Contingency Bill, 1835.

THE TARIFF.

A Table of Duties upon Goods, Wares, and Merchandize (except Wines and Spirits) imported into Newfoundland and its Dependencies.

	£	s.	d.
Beef and pork (salted) the cwt.	0	0	9
Flour, the barrel, not exceeding in weight 196 pounds	0	0	9
Oatmeal, the barrel, not exceeding in weight 200 pounds	0	0	6
Bread or biscuit, the cwt.	0	0	3
Butter, the cwt.	0	1	6
Molasses			Free.
Salt			Free.
Implements and materials fit and necessary for the fisheries,—videlicet, lines, twines, hooks, nets and seines			Free.
Coin and bullion			Free.
Apples, the barrel	0	0	6
Coals, the ton	0	0	6
Horses, mares, and geldings, each	0	10	0
Neat cattle, each	0	5	0
Calves			Free.
Sheep, each	0	0	6
Hogs, each	0	0	6
Lumber, one inch thick, the thousand feet	0	1	0
Ton timber, and balk, of all kinds, including scantling, the ton	0	0	6
Shingles, the thousand	0	0	4
Goods, wares, and merchandise (except wines and spirits), not otherwise enumerated, described or charged with duty in this Act, and not herein declared to be duty free, for every £100 of the true value thereof	2	10	0

CONTINGENCIES.

The sum of £3,137 17s. 2d. to be applied towards remunerating the officers of the Legislature for their services, and towards defraying the contingent expenses of Her Majesty's Council, and of the House of Assembly, as follows:—

The clerk of Her Majesty's Council for his services, £100.

The master in Chancery attending Her Majesty's Council, £100.

The usher of the Black Rod, for his services, £70.

The door-keeper of Her Majesty's Council, £55.

The assistant door-keeper and messenger of Her Majesty's Council, £10.

The clerk of Her Majesty's Council, for preparing and superintending the printing of the Journals for the present session, £25.

The clerk of Her Majesty's Council, to defray the expenses contingent on his office, £9 13s. 3d.

Probable amount of printing and binding the Journals of Her Majesty's Council for the present session, £100.

The usher of the Black Rod, to defray the expenses contingent on his office, £11 13s. 10d.

Richard Perchard, house-keeper, for cleaning the Council Room the present and last sessions, £10.

The librarian of the Legislature for salary of one year and a quarter, omitted in Contingency Bill of last session, £18 15s.

The librarian of the Legislature for salary of the current year, £15.

To the Hon. the Speaker of the House of Assembly, £200.

To the chairman of the Committee of Supply, towards defraying the charges of attendance during the present session, at the rate of £1 per diem, for forty-two days, travelling charges, postages, and extra expenses of the members of the House of Assembly (exclusive of the Speaker) resident at St. John's, and in the out-ports, £753.

The clerk of the House of Assembly, £100.

Hugh W. Hoyles, Esq., for preparing and superintending the printing of the Journals, £50.

The Serjeant-at-Arms, for his attendance during the present session, £70.

John Delaney, door-keeper, for his attendance this session, £35, and a further sum of £10 for extra services.

David Walsh, messenger, for his attendance, £35, and a further sum of £5 for extra services.

Philip Brown, under door-keeper, for his attendance, £25, and a further sum of £5 for extra services.

John B. Cox, assistant door-keeper, for his attendance, £25, and a further sum of £5 for extra services.

Mortagh Dunn, assistant messenger, for his attendance, £25, and a further sum of £5 for extra services.

The solicitor of the House of Assembly, for his services, £100.

CONTINGENCIES.

The solicitor of the House of Assembly, for extra services, £50.

Richard Holden, assistant clerk, for his services, £80.

The chairman of Supply and Finance, for his services, £50

Alexander M'Iver, for stationery, £32 1s. 9d.

William Firth, for coals, 15s. 4d.

William Freeman, for fitting up the Assembly for the present session, £24 17s. 2d.

David Walsh, for his services as special messenger to Conception Bay, £5.

Ryan and Withers, for account of the Legislature, £18 1s.

Stephen J. Daniel, for stationery and engrossing, £3.

Robert R. Holden, for engrossing petitions in 1837, £10 18s. 4d.

The chairman of the Committee of Audit, for his services, £50.

The proprietor of the *Newfoundlander*, for balance due for printing the journals, £53 9s. 9d.

The proprietor of the *Newfoundlander*, for printing the Journals of the present session, £150.

The proprietor of the *Patriot* newspaper, for the general printing of the House of Assembly during the present session, £279 18s.

The representatives of the late Timothy Kelly, for painting the Court room, £4 3s. 4d.

The assistant clerk, towards paying for the newspapers of the Colony, £7 18s. 2d.

The reporter of the House of Assembly, £50.

The door-keeper, for expenses contingent on his office, 7s.

Henry Winton, for stationery, £1 3s. 1d.

Richard Holden, junior, for copying since the last, and during the present, session, £30.

Robert R. Wakeham, for office rent and coals, £13 10s.

Richard Holden, assistant clerk, for extra services, £50.

Ambrose Shea, for binding the Journals of the two last sessions, £19 10s. 2d.

The under door-keeper and the assistant door-keeper, to defray the expenses of cleaning the House of Assembly, £10.

And a further sum of £50 to Thomas Beck, Esq., for his services during the present session.

And a further sum of £130 to the acting clerk of the House of Assembly towards the defraying of law charges incurred by order of the House of Assembly.

And a further sum of £10 to Walter Dillon, Esq., for his services the present session.

CHAPTER XV.

REIGN OF VICTORIA.

1837-1857.

1838.—First geological survey by J. Beete Jukes. Boulton, C.J., removed, and Bourne appointed. Great case of Kielly v. Carson.

1839.—Newfoundland constituted a separate see; Bishop Spencer, first Anglican Bishop.

1840.—Regular fortnightly sailing packets established between St. John's and Halifax. H.M.S. *Spitfire* first steamer to visit St. John's.

1841.—Foundation stone of the Roman Catholic cathedral laid.

1842.—Amalgamated Assembly constituted by Act of Parliament. First Presbyterian kirk established. Agricultural Society formed. Captain Fabvre and Mr. W. Thomas, President Chamber of Commerce, appointed Commissioners on French Fishery Question.

1843.—Amalgamated House opened by Sir John Harvey. Act for the Encouragement of Education passed by Richard Barnes.

1844.—Edward Feild, D.D., appointed Bishop of Newfoundland. The first steam packet, the S.S. *North American*, arrived in St. John's from Halifax, N.S.: sixty hours' passage. Chief Justice Norton, first Roman Catholic Chief Justice.

1846.—Public meeting on 26th May in the Court House, St. John's, in favour of Responsible Government; petition sent to Queen and Parliament. Terrible and destructive fire consumed the town on the 9th June. Tremendous gale on 19th September. Colonel Law, Administrator.

1847.—Sir Gaspard Le Marchant, Governor. Chief Justice Brady appointed. Foundation stone of English Cathedral of St. John the Baptist laid; also Colonial Building and Custom House, St. John's.

1848.—First Session of Legislature, after return to Constitution of 1833, opened on December 14th by Sir Gaspard Le Marchant. Bishop Mullock arrived on 6th May. Free Kirk established.

1849.—Customs' Department placed under control of the local Government.

1850.—Death of Bishop Fleming.

1851.—Public meeting to promote direct steam communication from St. John's to England.

1852.—Ker Baillie Hamilton, Governor. First steamer in Conception Bay. Hon. J. Crowdy, Administrator. Electric telegraph introduced into St. John's by F. N. Gisborne. Terribly disastrous seal fishery; "Spring of the Wadhams."

1854.—Reciprocity treaty between British America and the United States. New York, Newfoundland, and London Telegraph Company incorporated.

1855—Governor Darling. Responsible Government introduced; Hon. P. F. Little first Premier. Roman Catholic Cathedral consecrated.

1856.—Direct steam by the Galway Line. The American steamer *James Adger* arrived in St. John's; endeavoured to lay the cable across the Gulf.

1857.—Hon. L. O'Brien, Administrator. Sir Alexander Bannerman appointed Governor. The Anglo-French Convention about the Newfoundland fishery; indignation meetings; delegates sent to Canada, Nova Scotia, &c. Gulf cable laid by S.S. *Propontis*.

On the 20th of June 1837 begins the reign of Victoria, Her present Majesty, the noble Queen whose virtues have won the hearts of all English-speaking people, whose fine character and statesmanlike ability have done so much to quicken the loyalty of her subjects, to—

"Keep her throne unshaken still,
Broad based upon the people's will."

Her accession ushered in the dawn of a happier era of peace and marvellous progress. To treat of all the important events that have occurred during the Victorian age, even in this small portion of Her Majesty's dominions, is quite beyond the space at my disposal.[1]

The very first subject brought under the notice of the English Ministry in the year of the Queen's accession concerning our Island was the old trouble and dispute between the Council and Assembly. In 1837 the House of Assembly sent home delegates on the complaints against Chief Justice Boulton, and respecting the disputes between the House and the Council. The Assembly was represented by Dr. Carson,

---

[1] The first Anglican Bishop of Newfoundland, Aubrey George Spencer, was appointed in 1839—a most amiable and godly prelate. He founded the Theological College, and laid the first stone of the Cathedral. His feeble health soon gave way under the strain of his arduous episcopal labours. The successor of Bishop Spencer was the Right Rev. Edward Feild, our great Anglican prelate, whose life has been admirably written by the Rev. H. W. Tucker, M.A. A striking personality, his powerful influence changed the whole character of the Church and the clergy in the Colony. The ministers had all belonged to the Evangelical or Low Church type; one of this school is now a *rara avis* in the diocese. The Bishop's predominant trait was the true missionary spirit; to the service of his Divine Master he was consecrated, body and soul. He scorned popularity and all the pomps and vanities of the world. To his opponents he seemed narrow and intolerant; but to his admirers, and they now embrace the whole Anglican Church, he was the embodiment of all that is saintly and holy. In social life the Bishop was a delightful companion, full of pleasantness and humour, a dear lover of children. The marvellous work he performed in his great diocese is well known; one of the results of his powerful influence was the sub-division of the Protestant educational scheme. With all my admiration for the great prelate, I cannot say that it was a good movement; I believe its influence in dividing the grant, and in giving many localities two poor schools in place of one good one, has been very detrimental to the progress of education in the Colony.

P. Morris, and J. V. Nugent. As the result of this appeal in 1838, the Queen recommended the adoption of the Appropriation Bill by the Council. The Assembly in the main succeeded; both Houses, however, were severely blamed for their discourteous and improper conduct towards each other, and were informed that they ought to show each other proper consideration. The success of the British Constitution, as the best Government in the world, is largely dependent on the fact that it is worked out by gentlemen and men of honour, who, notwithstanding all the acerbities of party, are governed by the rules of courtesy and propriety. As a result of the appeal, the Chief Justice was dismissed. With all Boulton's faults, he was shabbily treated by the Home Government. In the first place his appointment was an injudicious one; he was an extreme partizan, a rigid Tory and too fresh from the heated political strife of Upper Canada to suit the calm atmosphere of the Bench; in order to make amends for the loss of the Attorney-Generalship of that province, the Ministry had appointed him Chief Justice of Newfoundland; his pecuniary loss by the change was a very great one. The popular attacks on Boulton were most disgraceful and unfair. The serious charges, that his judgments were biassed by his political views, and that his decisions were corrupt, were all proved to be untrue. The Privy Council should have considered his anomalous position as President of the Council and Chief Justice; they were wholly incompatible offices. There was, however, sufficient evidence of his party speeches, his attendance at political meetings, and of his intemperate and injudicious behaviour, to warrant the Privy Council in advising his removal. As he was made the scapegoat for an unworkable political system, he should certainly have been pensioned, and not cast adrift penniless after filling such high office.

The advice of the English Ministers does not seem to have been acted on, for in 1838 we find the House and the Council more seriously at variance than ever; this was largely due to the celebrated case of Kielly v. Carson. On Tuesday, 7th August 1838, Doctor Kielly met Mr. John Kent on the street; both were very high-spirited gentlemen. Mr. Kent declared that Dr. Kielly had put his fist up to his face and had then and there threatened to pull his nose. This amounted, as anyone can see, to an ordinary case of assault, and the remedy lay in proceedings before the magistrates or the Supreme Court; that, however, would not have suited the insulted and impetuous Kent; he appealed to the House. The Assembly sat with closed doors, and finally decided to summon Dr. Kielly to the bar. Mr. Speaker Carson informed him that he had been brought there on a charge of having violated the privileges of the House by making an attack on one of their members. The clerk was ordered to read the report of the committee appointed to consider the matter with the evidence. The report declared "the "conduct of Dr. Kielly is a gross breach of the privileges of the House, "and, if allowed to pass unnoticed, would be a sufficient cause for "deterring members acting in the independent manner so necessary for

WATER STREET, ST. JOHN'S, LOOKING WEST, IN 1837.
From a drawing by William Gosse, Esq.

"a free Assembly." The doctor requested to be allowed to produce witnesses on his own behalf; this was refused. The Speaker informed him that his only course was to plead ignorance of the privileges of the House, to express regret, and to throw himself on the clemency of the Assembly. Far from apologizing, the doctor pointed his finger at Mr. Kent who was sitting in the House, and said he was a liar and a coward. For this ebullition of temper Kielly next day sent a written apology. When brought to the bar the second time he was ordered to

---

[1] John Kent, examined, said: "He was a member for the District of St. John's, he and Dr. Kielly had some difference, provoked by him [Dr. Kielly], about 12 o'clock that day. Dr. Kielly had put his hand clenched up to his [Mr. Kent's] face several times and said, 'he had it in him for him, the lying puppy, and his privileges should not protect him,' alluding to certain statements made by him [Mr. Kent] in his place in the House upon the subject of the St. John's Hospital."

apologise in the following terms: "I exceedingly regret that I have been guilty of any act or expression which has been considered by your Honourable House to be a gross breach of its privileges." The prisoner refused to make this apology. With the Conservative party, the doctor now became the hero of the hour.[1] In charge of the celebrated Tommy Beck, Serjeant-at-Arms, with the mace, Dr. Kielly was marched down to the prison, situated on the east side of Church Hill, now Market House Hill. Mr. Bryan Robinson,[2] then a rising young barrister, applied to Judge Lilly for a habeas corpus, on the grounds that the House of Assembly had no such rights and privileges as were assumed in their late extraordinary proceedings, and that the warrant for Kielly's arrest was informal. Judge Lilly[3] decided that the commitment was deficient in those essentials necessary to constitute it legal. Three days afterwards his lordship delivered a long and very able judgment.

The House of Assembly seem to have completely lost their heads; instead of submitting to the law, and thus setting a good example, they were guilty of the most outrageous absurdities. It was the Wild Westerner—Tom Fitz-Gibbon Moore—and Mr. Kent who proposed that Mr. Robinson, for taking up Dr. Kielly's case, should not be permitted to communicate with the House as Master in Chancery of the Legislative Council.[4] Another motion proposed was that the *Newfoundlander's*

DR. KIELLY.

---

[1] "Oh! Did you see Dr. Kielly, oh!
With his boots and spurs and style oh."

[2] Mr. B. Robinson was charged by John O'Mara and Edward Morris that, in his argument before the court on the habeas corpus for Kielly, he had compared the privileges of the House to those of the Mechanic's Society. He had said that the House had simply the power of turning people out that disturbed it.

[3] In their address to the Queen, the House of Assembly made a most unjustifiable attack on Judge Lilly. They spoke of him as a judge who had rendered himself conspicuous by publicly subscribing to most outrageous calumnies on the persons and political character of the members; Mr. E. M. Archibald, the Clerk of the Court and Clerk of the Assembly, who assisted the judge in the preparation of his judgment, was also denounced as a violent partizan.

[4] The House, considering "that B. Robinson, Esq., Master in Chancery, attendant on H.M. Council, by contemptuous language and observations respecting the House of Assembly and the Members thereof, and by the issuing out of certain writs at the suit of one Edward Kielly for alleged damages against the Speaker, &c., has been guilty of a gross breach of the privileges of this House, and the said B. Robinson being an officer of H.M. Council, this House cannot proceed against him for such contempt.

"Resolved, That the said Bryan Robinson be not admitted as the bearer of any message to this House until a message be despatched to H.M. Council acquainting the Council with their resolution."

Two days later the House of Assembly came to their senses and rescinded the resolution against the obnoxious Master in Chancery. Of all the absurd proceedings proprietors and printer should be brought to the Bar *for publishing Judge Lilly's judgment*. These, however, were mild outbreaks of legislative insanity compared with their last act. The Speaker issued his warrant to arrest Dr. Kielly, who had been discharged from custody, also to arrest the High Sheriff, who had liberated him under a judge's order, and, lastly, to arrest Judge Lilly. The spectacle was seen in the town of Tommy Beck, with the mace, dragging a highly respected judge of the Supreme Court through the streets, with a great mob hurrahing and following the cortège. After being taken to the Speaker's room, the judge was confined in the house of the Serjeant-at Arms. Governor Prescott immediately prorogued the Legislature, and thus promptly and properly put an end to these undignified proceedings. In the autumn the case of Kielly v. Carson came up before Chief Justice Bourne, in the Central Circuit Court, for adjudication. The decision of the court was reserved for the opinion of the three judges in the Supreme Court. The judges differed; Assistant-Judge Lilly decided that the plea of justification, on the ground of privilege, had not been made out, and that the plaintiff should have judgment on the demurrer; Des Barres, A.J., and Bourne, C.J., gave judgment in favour of the defendants. This judgment was appealed against to the Privy Council, and the final decision was pronounced as follows, on the 11th of January 1841, by Chief Baron Parke :—" The House of Assembly of Newfoundland " is a Local Legislature with every power reasonably necessary for the " proper exercise of their functions and duties ; but they have not, what " they erroneously supposed themselves to possess, the same exclusive " privileges which the ancient law of England has annexed to the " House of Parliament." The fantastic tricks of our legislators furnished the leading case on the question of the powers of colonial parliaments ; Kielly v. Carson established the law on the subject for all time.

One word more and we have finished with the legislatures of 1833 and 1836 and the short-lived parliament of 1841. The terrible election riot at Carbonear, in the autumn of 1840, so disgusted the British Ministry with Newfoundland affairs, that Governor Prescott was ordered to dissolve the Legislature, which he did on the 26th April 1841,[1] and the

---

[1] GOVERNOR PRESCOTT'S Speech in Closing the HOUSE OF ASSEMBLY, 26th April 1841.

" Mr. President and Hon. Gentlemen of the Council, Mr. Speaker, and Gentlemen of the House of Assembly,

" As a Committee of the House of Commons has been appointed to enquire into the state of Newfoundland, before which Committee I shall have to appear, I will on the present occasion confine myself to the expression of my regret that such a proceeding should have become indispensably necessary to the tranquillity and welfare of the Colony."

all the ways to Outer Cove, Middle Cove, and all the other coves Constitution was suspended from that date until the 17th January 1843. In 1842, under the Conservative ministry of Sir Robert Peel, a new constitution was given to the Colony—the Amalgamated Legislature. The members of the Legislative Council sat with the fifteen elected members; the Acts were worded, "Be it therefore enacted by the Governor, Council, and Assembly in General Assembly convened." It was one of the queerest forms of a statutable parliament ever invented; there was an executive council, but it did not contain a single one of the popularly elected members. As usual, the whole patronage of the Government was in the hands of the Executive.

In the summer of 1841 Captain Henry Prescott, C.B., ceased to govern us. He is universally acknowledged to have been a polished gentleman, his speeches are able and above all concise, but the last of the naval administrators, with all his good qualities, was neither a strong Governor nor a good diplomatist; the whole period of his rule was troubled with political squabbles and sectarian animosities. He disliked Boulton, but appears to have been either unable or unwilling to control him. The dawn of a brighter day, however, was already breaking; our old friend Byrne, most able and practical of road surveyors, was laying out the great roads to Placentia, the road around Conception Bay and the Bay Bulls line. Mr. James Douglas and Mr. O'Brien—named the "Colossus of roads"—were busy getting all the ways to Outer Cove, Middle Cove, and all the other coves

---

[1] Admiral Sir H. Prescott, G.C.B. (1783–1874), was the only surviving son of Admiral Isaac Prescott (who was on the Newfoundland station in 1785) and was born at Kew Green, Surrey. He entered the navy at the usual age; was engaged in action with four ships that escaped from Trafalgar; was employed off Sardinia from 1808 to 1810, and took part in the defence of Sicily. He was promoted to the rank of Captain, after distinguishing himself in the destruction of several vessels at Amatia; was Governor of Newfoundland from 1834 to 1844; was a Lord of the Admiralty during the later half of 1847 and was Admiral Superintendent of Portsmouth Dockyard from December 1847 to the end of 1852. In 1862 he became Admiral of the Blue and was a magistrate for Surrey. He was created a G.C.B. in 1869. (*Men of the Reign*, 1885.) Further full details of Sir H. Prescott's early life will be found in O'Byrne's Naval Biography.

about the capital improved. Sir Bryan, then Mr. Robinson, was also what my friend Justice Harvey would call an enthusiastic "projector of viaducts."

The arrival of Sir John Harvey, on the 16th of September 1841, marks an important point in our history ; for the first time the control and management of the Colony were placed in the hands of two able politicians, two statesmen of consummate tact and ability, Sir John and his colleague, the Hon. Jas. Crowdy, for fourteen years the Colonial Secretary. Crowdy had been for many years endeavouring to smooth over difficulties and to make peace, but Boulton was too overbearing, and the House too extreme. From this time forward the political wheel ran smoother.

Sir John had one rather awkward habit, he always wrote his speeches, and, though excellent, they were uncommonly long. He had been known in the Army as "the handsome Colonel Harvey"; his manners were the perfection of courtesy, nothing disturbed him. In those days Cassidy the tailor was a great sporting man, and prided himself on his knowledge of farming in general. At the great agricultural meeting at Mount Pearl,

SIR JOHN HARVEY.
From Bonnycastle's Newfoundland.

when His Excellency made the speech memorable in every history of the Colony, the irate tailor came in to complain of Murray, another sporting tailor, who insisted on judging a ploughing match. Cassidy, very excited and inebriated, strode up to the head of the table where His Excellency was being entertained by the magnates of the land: "Your Excellency," says he, "is a shoemaker to be a judge of a tailor's "work, your Excellency, or a tailor to be a judge of a shoemaker's work, "your Excellency?" With a bland bow, "Mr. Secretary Templeman,"

450   REIGN OF VICTORIA, 1837-1857.

said Sir John, turning to that fat official, "be good enough, sir, to take "a note of these most valuable suggestions of Mr. Cassidy."

The Amalgamated House was a makeshift assembly, but under the presidency of its admirable speaker, Mr. Crowdy, it worked better than the former arrangement; there was fierce debate, scurrility, and vituperation, but at any rate the Acts were passed, and the public service was not embarrassed. In the first session Mr. Richard Barnes introduced and passed a valuable Education Act, and large grants were made each year for roads. All the country was prosperous—the seal fishery had immensely increased; exports of all kinds were very large; in 1840 over nine hundred thousand quintals of fish and over six hundred thousand seals rewarded the labours of our hardy fishermen; taxation was very light, the revenue for 1840 being only £43,863, and the whole civil expenditure £39,347—dear, delightful days of Arcadian simplicity! when we had no debt and port wine was a shilling a bottle!

The Governments of Captain Prescott and Sir John Harvey mark the parting of the ways, the interregnum between the last days of the cook-room¹ and the fishing ships and the new departure.

HON. J. CROWDY.
By Southwell.

The wonderful growth of the spring seal fishery just about this period completely changed the social habits of the people; the work required for fitting out the vessels, building punts, repairing and strength-

---

¹ On every large mercantile establishment the cook-room was a necessary institution. All the planters and servants were boarded and lodged on the premises during their stay in the capital; the men slept in bunks ranged round the cook-room like the berths in a ship; generally an ancient retainer of the house, with an assistant, often a man and his wife, cooked for all.

I have heard an old Newfoundland merchant describe his experiences. When he came out, as a young man, to the Colony in 1808, he became great friends with Mrs. Pollard, the presiding genius of the cook-room on John Hill & Co.'s premises; as the smallest clerk in the shop he had the privilege of getting the ends of listing off the West of England cloth, which were used to make moccasins; he generally bartered his listing with Mrs. Pollard for sweets—bull's-eyes.

A great institution on the merchant's premises, always called in the vernacular "The Room," was the periodical serving out of grog; morning, eleven o'clock, noon, and in the afternoon, all employed in the room had a glass of rum; on the Jersey and on Newman's place this continued up to my own time. Various attempts were made by reformers to alter this practice. A most worthy Scotchman—Mr. Johnson, familiarly known as Willie Johnson (managing partner of the old firm of Baine Johnson)—tried to improve it by watering the grog; he went on diluting it until he raised a rebellion. Mr. Robert Job was the first man to make a firm stand against the practice; he was execrated at the time, but he stood steadfast, and lived to see his example followed by all his brother merchants. Mr. Job and his brother, Mr. Thomas Job, were zealous promoters of all civic improvements. Mr. Robert Job was largely instrumental in getting the Long Bridge, known as Job's Bridge, built; he introduced gas, and helped greatly to form the first Water Company.

ening the sealing schooners, kept masters and crews at work all through the winter; what had formerly been a carnival of drinking and dancing now became a season of hard, laborious toil.[1] The seal fishery, besides

MR. T. JOB.
By Saxony, Scarborough.

MR. J. MUNN.
By Negretti & Zambra.

MR. RIDLEY.
By Selva, Bayswater.

altering social customs, largely increased the importance of the out-ports; the statistics of the early part of the century show us that there was a considerable foreign trade in the Island outside of St. John's. Many resident merchants carried on a large business in such places as Trinity, Greenspond, Twillingate, Fogo, Bonavista, King's Cove, Harbour Grace, Carbonear, Brigus,[2] Port de Grave, &c. Some of these men were Catholic Liberals; injured by politics, many of them later on left the Colony, others were ruined. The effect of the seal fishery was to add materially to the wealth of the various settlements where it was carried on. First of all there was the building of the ships; as prior to about the Forties, when the Conception Bay merchants began buying the slop-built vessels from the Provinces, nearly every vessel in the seal fishery was native built; the crews belonged to the place; in many cases the seals also were manufactured into oil in the same harbour— Twillingate, Fogo, Greenspond, Trinity, besides the Conception Bay ports, had vats. All this, as my readers can readily understand, brought

---

[1] From Mr. Daniel Ryan, of King's Cove, and from other sources of information, it appears that sharemen were always clear of service by 20th September; after that there was dancing, drinking, and card-playing every night, from house to house in the out-ports, often ending in a fight; when the Hibernian element was present, generally a faction fight. On the first of May all hands set to work again. A large number of English and Irish went home every autumn, and returned in the spring; Jersey men always left. From about 1820 the spring seal fishery changed all this. There was always, however, a carnival of dancing, mumming, and, of course, drinking, from Christmas to Twelfth day.

[2] Brigus in the Forties, as we can see from the returns, was the head-quarters of a great seal fishery. In 1844 Mr. and Mrs. Gilbert Harrison (brother of Mrs. T. Ridley) were making a tour of the bay, accompanied by Mr. Addison, chaplain to Bishop Spencer. They were people of great refinement and culture. Mr. Brown tells the story how he took them over to see old Billy Ribbets; of course the "broke" sugar and the hot water and spirits were immediately produced, and a toast had to be proposed. "Bloody decks to en," said Billy, as he raised his glass. Addison was horrified. "Really, my dear sir, as a minister of religion, I could not drink to such a sanguinary wish as that." Mr. Brown had to explain it was a customary toast of success to the seal fishery, and homicide was not intended.

F F 2

strength and wealth to the out-harbours, and nourished the growth of a great middle class—the traders and sealing skippers; the two occupations were often combined. Enormous amounts of money were made in those days. Steam completely changed the whole aspect of affairs. The men now get much smaller shares; the big bills of the Forties and the Fifties are no longer earned; a man's share to-day hardly ever goes over £8 or £10, and the great army of sealing skippers and great planters, where are they? Their descendants, the Ashes, Dawes, Delaneys, Blandfords, Kanes, Knees, Jackmans, Bartletts, and others, are still the

KILLING SEALS.

most skilful ice masters, and their crews of Newfoundlanders the best sealers in the world. Dundee has splendid sealing steamers, but her men can never have the same aptitude as ours for this perilous pursuit. The following anecdote of the late Mr. Smith Mackay's, apropos of copying (jumping from pan to pan of ice), shows how much at home the Newfoundlander feels on the ice floe:—

"There was a Canadian on board one of our sealers who was very smart at going on the ice; there were also some boys on half their hand; a great rivalry existed between them. One day the master called out that there were seals on the starboard bow; over the side went the Canadian, followed by the boys; there was a channel just caught over, which the Canadian did not see, and down he went; as he rose the boys, seven in number, came to the edge, and successfully coped over the Canadian's head and shoulders. Well might a Dundee captain exclaim 'barbarous!' when he heard the story."

PANNING SEALS.
From a photograph by Walter Monroe.

When Mr. Walter Grieve sent the first sealing steamer to the ice it was a poor day for Newfoundland. The only consolation we can lay to our hearts is that steam was inevitable; it was sure to come, sooner or later, the pity of it is that it did not come later. Politics and steam have done more than any other cause to ruin the middle class, the well-to-do dealers that once abounded in the out-ports. Contrast the statistics of 1848 with 1878. It was as bad for the merchants as for the men.

Another aspect of our trade, which is almost forgotten by the present generation, was the great influx of Spanish vessels between 1840 and 1860; the direct cause was the Spanish duty known in the Peninsula as "el derecho de la bandera"—the deferential duty in favour of the Spanish flag, amounting to over a dollar a quintal. For several years there were often sixty and seventy Spanish vessels loading fish in this port, and a large number in Harbour Grace. C. F. Bennett & Co. had thirty-two in one year. The most numerous at first were our old acquaintances the Biscayans; their ships, however, compared with the Spaniards' from the Mediterranean, were small and poorly equipped, a great many of them simply luggers of sixty and seventy tons. Barcelona, Malaga, and Valencia vessels were splendid craft; many of them were slavers; you could see the ring-bolts in the hold to which the poor Africans were chained. Mr. Henry Le Messurier informs me that one beautiful vessel of this class upset, and in getting her up a number of secret places were found in her hold. The captains of these ships nearly always brought gold Spanish onzas and Mexican dollars to pay for their cargoes, and Mr. Le Messurier speaks with gusto of the cartloads of Spanish bullion sent up to the bank. Whilst it lasted it must have been a large source of profit to the trade. For many years these Spanish vessels carried away between one hundred and sixty and one hundred and seventy thousand quintals of fish.[1] The alteration of the tariff—doing away with the preference given to Spaniards—ended this trade.[2]

Under both Captain Prescott and Sir John Harvey there was great activity both in agriculture and road making.[3] In 1838 the first geological survey was commenced under the distinguished J. Beete Jukes, who arrived in St. John's in Mr. John Stuart's clipper brig

---

[1] In 1850 there were seventy Spanish and Portuguese vessels in St. John's alone, aggregating 8,673 tons; navigated by 678 men, they loaded 154,415 qtls. of cod-fish and 378 tons of oil. In the same year American vessels loaded 16,582 qtls. of fish; a German and Danish vessel took 200 tons of oil and 6,430 seal skins.

The trade with Hamburg in oil continued for many years; Munns sent as much as 500 tons of pale seal oil in a year to Hamburg, the greatest factory of adulterated goods in the world, there to be converted by German science and dexterity into the finest quality of "*Pure Cod-liver Oil.*"

[2] PORTUGUESE FISHING COMPANY.

"In 1835, a Portuguese company was formed in Lisbon, under the title of the Companià Piscarias, for the prosecution of the Bank fishery; they sent to England and purchased seven English schooners, of about 100 tons each, and shipped in Devonshire, at high wages, men who had been accustomed to the Bank fishery. After being fitted out at a large expense with all the luxuries they thought Englishmen were fond of, such as cheese, brandy, porter, &c. (and fine feasting these old Bankers had), the vessels proceeded to Lisbon, and on arrival there, an equal number of Portuguese were put on board, to be instructed in the method of fishing; then taking in sardines for bait, they proceeded to the Banks, and when they had completed their first trip, they returned to Fayal, in the Western Islands, where they landed their fish and then went on a second voyage, on the return from which those who had been successful landed the second cargo, and proceeded on their third voyage, the catch of which they took green to Lisbon, where it was sold in the same condition. In Fayal the fish was taken in waggons to the tops of the mountains, where flakes had been previously made, covered with boards, as a screen to protect the fish from the scorching rays of the sun, and it was there cured by the winds and heats, which in those climates are very drying, and when cured the fish was thence exported to Portugal, where it is admitted at a nominal duty. At the end of the season the Englishmen so employed were discharged and sent home, the Portuguese having thus obtained from them all the information they required (they now fish with bultows); the Company, however, is not in a flourishing state, having laboured under many disadvantages. So ignorant were many of the Directors, at the time the Company was formed, that at one of their meetings, the Vice-President proposed drying the fish on the Banks! Their Government, I believe, have made overtures to Great Britain to take off a portion of the heavy duties they now impose upon our fish, on condition of having granted a portion of the Newfoundland coast, for them to form a settlement for the cure of fish; if such is the case, the Portuguese Government not having the means of granting bounties, it would be wise policy in Great Britain to accede to the proposal, as the consumption is much curtailed by the high prices the consumers have to pay, the duties being in many instances more than the price we obtain for the fish itself, and the quantity consumed would increase in a greater ratio than the difference of quantity the Portuguese would catch."—(WARREN's *Lecture*, pp. 17, 18.)

[3] In two years, 1837 and 1838, the Legislature voted $175,000 for roads.

Diana, in company with the celebrated Plantagenet Harrison. Two very important elements in the commercial life of the Colony—a bank[1] and regular postal communication with Halifax—were established during this period. The first steamer to visit our waters was H.M.S. *Spitfire*, a paddle steamer, in 1840; she put into St. John's with a detachment for the Royal Newfoundland Company. J. B. Jukes returned to England in her. In 1842 the steamship *John McAdam* arrived, and several pleasure trips were made to Trinity and Conception Bay, and duly astonished the natives. By 1844 we had a regular packet steamer plying between St. John's and Halifax, Nova Scotia; most of us can remember the excitement caused in the town when the *North American*, with her huge walking beam and a figure-head of an Indian painted white, first came into Mr. Matthew Stewart's wharf; she had made a wonderful passage of *sixty hours* from Halifax, and her captain,

J. B. JUKES.
From an engraving.

MR. J. W. SMITH.
By S. H. Parsons.

MR. R. BROWN.
By S. H. Parsons.

Richard Meagher, was duly congratulated on his remarkable voyage. From this time forward the sailing packets which had been run by

---

[1] The Bank of British North America commenced business about 1836. Mr. Andrew Milroy, father of Lady Thorburn, was the first manager. For many years they carried on business in Tobin's Building, Water Street, below Mr. Stott's; for some reason the Legislature refused for several years to grant the bank a charter. In April 1844 the Newfoundland Bank was incorporated, the capital was £50,000, half paid up. The following were the principal shareholders: Charles Fox Bennett, William Bickford Row, Lawrence O'Brien, Robert Prowse, George H. Dunscombe, Richard Barnes, John Dillon, John Kent, Richard O'Dwyer, John P. Mullowney, Robert Roberts Wakeham, Lawrence Macausey, James B. Wood, John Stuart, Edward Kielley, Thomas Ridley,

Bland & Tobin were discarded, and we have had continuous steam communication ever since. The service for many years was carried out by Cunard & Co., in conjunction with their Liverpool line, and, though several vessels were lost, it was maintained very efficiently by the well-known Captain Corbin, and afterwards by the dashing Guildford, two as fine seamen as ever trod a deck.

The Amalgamated House[1] lasted all through Sir John Harvey's administration; it worked far more harmoniously than the first House; a glance at its composition will show us that it contained nearly all

NARROWS, OR ENTRANCE OF THE HARBOUR OF ST JOHN'S, NEWFOUNDLAND

the best and ablest men in the Colony. In the memorable year of the fire (1846), an agitation was set on foot to obtain responsible government; it was not entirely successful, but in 1848, when the

William Walsh, and Charles Loughlan. The money was returned to the shareholders. The very existence of the new concern probably influenced the existing bank, and made it discount with more liberality and less favouritism, and the *raison d'être* for the Newfoundland Bank ceased. . . . Nearly the same proprietors founded in 1854, the Union Bank of Newfoundland; the success of this institution was due, in the first place, to the able management of Mr J. W. Smith, manager, carried out afterwards by his successor, Mr. Goldie. The Commercial Bank was established in 1857; the first manager was Mr. R. Brown, under whose careful administration the bank was a marked success. He was succeeded by Mr. Henry Cooke.

[1] The last session of the House of Assembly, under the first constitution, was closed by Governor Prescott on the 26th April 1841. His Excellency making the shortest speech on our parliamentary records, the constitution being suspended until 1842, when an election was held on the 20th December of that year. Sir John Harvey opened the new Legislature, the Amalgamated House, on the 14th January 1843 with the longest speech on record.

The House consisted of the 10 following members appointed by the Crown:—Hon J.

world was agitated with revolution, and crowns were falling in a very promiscuous manner all over Europe, our original constitution of Queen, Lords and Commons, was restored to us. I should have mentioned that Chief Justice Boulton was succeeded in 1838 by John Gervase Hutchinson Bourne; he was a scholar, a Fellow of Magdalen, Oxford, and an able lawyer. He was, however, unfortunately cursed with a violent temper; at the bar he was uniformly favourable to Mr. George Henry Emerson and antagonistic to Mr. Robinson (afterwards Sir Bryan).[1] Many stories are told of Bourne's temper; the best one I know is in connexion with the crier of the court, Lambert. The old man was helping the chief with his gown, the sleeve was inside out, and Bourne could not get his arm through; in his wrath he swore, "The devil's in the gown"; old Lambert, who was getting the sleeve right, said, quite innocently, "Not yet, my Lord, not yet." Sir John Harvey dismissed the Chief Justice in 1844; he was succeeded by Thomas Norton, a most accomplished Irish gentleman, who had been sent out as assistant judge to Demerara.[2] Norton was the first Roman Catholic Chief Justice; he was a universal favourite, an able, impartial judge, a most humorous and fascinating companion off the Bench; he only remained in Newfoundland a few years; he loved gay society, and had most influential friends to promote his advancement.

During the Governorship of Sir John Harvey, St. John's was devastated by the "Great Fire"; what the Hejira is to the Mussulman, the 9th of June 1846 was to Newfoundlanders, a date constantly referred to. The previous year, 1845, had been remarkable for the disastrous fire at Quebec, and a month later the terrible conflagration at St. John, New Brunswick. St. John's, to its honour, had contributed

Simms, Attorney-General; Hon. Jas. Crowdy, Colonial Secretary; Honbles. Jno. Dunscombe, Wm. Thomas, P. Morris, Colonial Treasurer, W. B. Row, Jas. Tobin, Jo. Noad, Surveyor-General, C. F. Bennett, Jno. Kent.
The 15 members elected were:—
For St. John's: Dr. Carson, L. O'Brien, J. V. Nugent.
Conception Bay: Thos. Ridley, John Munn, J. L. Prendergast, E. Hanrahan.
Trinity: Richard Barnes.
Bonavista: Robt. Carter.
Ferryland: T. Glen.
Placentia: Jno. Dillon, Simon Morris.
Fortune Bay: B. Robinson.
Fogo: J. Slade.
In 1846 there were three sessions, and members and officers got three sessions' pay; H. W. Hoyles, Solicitor to the House. In June 1846, owing to the absence of Mr. Speaker Crowdy, Mr. Kent was appointed Speaker. The House sat in the Eastern Chamber of the Orphan Asylum School House.

[1] Chief Justice Bourne was terribly antagonistic to Mr. Robinson, who petitioned the Imperial Government against him. The Chief Justice then made charges against the Colonial Secretary, Mr. Crowdy, and Sir John Harvey; his complaints were shown to be unfounded, and he was quietly removed. He was a man of ability and learning, but his ungovernable temper utterly unfitted him for a position requiring calmness and cool judgment.

[2] Chief Justice Norton was an intimate convivial friend of Sir Alexander Cockburn. One day on circuit Cockburn sent him a note, "Master in Lunacy dead; will this suit your book, Tom?" Norton answered at once, "Your servant Tom will accept this crumb that falls from your Lordship's table."

liberally to the sufferers by both calamities. Our fire was the most disastrous of all; it began in Hamlin the cabinet maker's shop, about 8 a.m., and by nightfall it had destroyed the city; the suburbs, then very unimportant, were left; by sundown nothing but a forest of chimneys remained to mark the site of our flourishing town. The citizens and the fire brigade worked manfully; Sir John, Major Robe, Colonel Law, and the military were untiring in their exertions; His Excellency was everywhere. An attempt was made at Messrs. E. & N. Stabb's, now Blair's premises, to blow up the corner building, and thus make a break. One artilleryman and two citizens were killed; many had narrow escapes. By mid-day the heat of the fire became so intense that no one could do anything. The conflagration reached everywhere; the beautiful new convent at the head of Long's Hill, far away from the flames, was destroyed by sparks carried by the high wind; when the huge wooden building, St. John's Church, caught, the heat to leeward became overpowering. With the burning of the many substantial wooden buildings and seal vats on Water Street, and with several ships on fire in the harbour, it seems now almost miraculous that the south side escaped. Out of sixty large mercantile warehouses, Newman's old premises at River alone remained.[1]

[1] A plan of the town, showing the extent of this fire, will be found at p. 522.

(*Newfoundlander, June* 18, 1846.)

"The fire broke out at 8.30 a.m. on Tuesday, 9th June 1846, in the shop of Hamlin the cabinet maker, in George Street, off Queen Street, and was caused by the overboiling of a glue-pot. The fire immediately communicated to Queen Street, and in a short time the whole collection of stone and wooden houses in the locality were on fire. It was hoped that a stand might be made at the corner of Queen Street and Water Street, but the fire spread on, consuming Messrs. Rogerson's, Stewart's, and C. F. Bennett's premises; it was stopped by an heroic effort at Newman's premises, River Head. The wind began to blow from the westward. The terrified cry now arose that Bennett's and Stewart's oil vats were on fire; at that sound despair seized on every mind and paralysed every nerve; it was then seen that the total annihilation of the town was inevitable, and the scene of consternation that arose defies description. Sir John Harvey ordered Mr. Stabb's house (O'Dwyer's corner) to be blown up. The break, however, was not of sufficient extent, and the wind, which was strong at first, seemed to act here with redoubled violence, hurrying on the flames with fearful rapidity to the back of Stone Buildings, commencing with Mr. Pierce Grace's house, and ending with Messrs. McBride and Kerr's, and the entire range of wooden dwellings at the opposite side. The next suites of buildings at both sides were soon enveloped, and the fire, now rendered all powerful by the immense quantities of oil and combustible materials of every description which it had consumed, and with which it had been fed, hastened on the work of destruction with inconceivable rapidity, laying waste completely every erection at both sides, stone and wood without distinction, as far as the break at Messrs. Douglas & Co's. The Custom House next took fire, and lured the flames forward to Messrs. Gill's premises; hence they extended rapidly along, consuming everything intermediate to the premises of Messrs. Robinson, Brooking & Co. These fine buildings were soon involved, and the ravages continued with unabated violence even to the premises of Messrs. Parker and Gleeson, at the extreme end of Magotty Cove, after the consumption of which, it might with truth be said, the fire died out from the utterness of exhaustion, having left nothing to sustain it, and having laid the entire way for more than a mile in extent a barren waste, its two principal streets. The loss of life, if the extent of the havoc be remembered, is inconsiderable; we believe there were but three—one artilleryman and two civilians—who met death on this occasion. The public buildings consumed were, besides the Custom House above mentioned, the beautiful convent of the Presentation Nuns, and schoolroom opposite, St. John's Church,

Not one of us who witnessed the terrors of that awful fire will ever forget the 9th of June 1846. The weather was fortunately warm, otherwise the misery of the poor families who were huddled together on the Barrens for the first night or two would have been still greater;

PLAN OF THE APPROACH TO ST. JOHN'S HARBOUR.

with military promptness, tents were provided for their shelter, and in the course of a very short time long lines of wooden sheds were erected, called "the camps." The leading men in St. John's showed great spirit

the Court House and jail, the theatre, the Commercial buildings, the Bank of British North America, the Colonial Treasurer's Office, and Savings Bank. The public moneys fortunately were all saved and deposited in Government House. The Roman Catholic Chapel, the Orphan Asylum School, the Native Hall, and the Factory were immediately thrown open for the shelter of the many houseless and destitute of our fellow creatures, who had been in the short space of a few hours deprived of their homes and means of subsistence.

"We cannot speak in too high terms of praise of the conduct of His Excellency Sir John Harvey in these melancholy circumstances. He was to be seen during the day in the midst of the scene of horror, aiding the people by the suggestions of a superior judgment and experience, counselling against the commission of irretrievable errors, and evincing all that sympathy for the afflicted which is so strikingly characteristic of his humane and tender heart. To Lieut.-Col. Law and M. A. Robe and every officer of the garrison we feel an expression of public thankfulness is a just debt. Their actions were judiciously directed, and most energetically continued, and the troops under their command have ably sustained the high character they had achieved on many and similar occasions of public distress.

"The fire destroyed the premises of Messrs. Hounsell, Schenk & Hounsell, Stabb Row, and alacrity in taking measures to relieve the distressed, and to reconstruct the town. The very next morning some of the citizens were at work excavating amongst the ruins of their dwellings, and preparing to erect temporary sheds; thousands were ruined, but everywhere there was a hopeful, determined spirit that St. John's should rise again. Sir John and his advisers acted with great promptitude and good judgment; an admirable relief committee was appointed; property was carefully guarded by the military. On the very next day His Excellency adopted measures to meet the pressing emergency of the situation.

Pedley says:—

"He issued a proclamation convening the local legislature to meet in six days. He laid an embargo for a limited period on the exportation of provisions. He addressed a circular letter to the Governor-general and the lieutenant-governors of all the British American colonies, and the British consuls at Boston and New York, making known the deplorable disaster and the immediate wants arising from it. He authorised the chartering of two vessels, one to Halifax and one to New York, for provisions. Lastly, he called a meeting, held on the 10th, at which he presided, of all the heads of the mercantile establishments, as well as of the principal inhabitants, the clergy, judges, and officers of the Government. One of the resolutions passed at the public meeting deserves to be recorded, as evincing the strong brave heart of the citizens amidst the still smouldering embers of the fell ruin which had suddenly come upon them:—

"'Resolved: That this meeting is aware that the well-established credit and stability of the trade of St. John's, coupled with the natural and inexhaustible resources of its fisheries, will speedily enable it to recover its usual current, but that in the meantime it is necessary that publicity should be given to the demand for provisions and building materials which at present exists in this market.'

"Great sympathy was displayed, accompanied by a bounteous liberality, towards the inhabitants of St. John's suffering under such a fearful calamity, in the neighbouring colonies and in the United Kingdom. Halifax was the first to exhibit its practical charity. At a meeting of the citizens held the day after the news arrived, a subscription was commenced which in a very short time reached £1,500. This munificent contribution was expended in provisions, which were forwarded by the steamer, and was in addition to £1,000 transmitted in specie by the Government of Nova Scotia. Prince Edward's Island also forwarded a large sum, as did also the towns of St. John and Fredricton. The Government of Canada sent £2,000, and the citizens of Quebec subscribed even a larger sum for the same object. The news arrived in England at the time when Mr. Gladstone was holding the office of Colonial Secretary only until the appointment of his

and Holmwood, William Grieve & Co., Wilson & Meynell, Robert Alsop & Co., Rennie Stuart, & Co., Wm. Warren, Boyd & McDougall, P. Rogerson & Son, J. & W. Stewart, C. F. Bennett & Co., John Warren, Langley & Tessier, F. & W. Carter, E. Taylor, Shea & Murphy, Thomas Glen, John McWilliam, E. & N. Stabb, Pierce Grace, I. & I. Kent, R. O'Dwyer & Co., Neil McDougall, Begg Keir, & Co., Bowring Bros., R. & A. Rutherford, M. Stewart & Co., Robt. Finlay, McBride & Kerr, Michel Nowlan, John Renouf, Richard Howley, Saml. Mudge, Warren Bros., Baine Johnston & Co., Edward Smith, Wilson & Co., James Clift, Richd. Perchard, S G Archibald, J. Fox & Co., R. Prowse, R. N. Goff & Co., W. & H. Thomas & Co., J. M. Rendell & Co., Gilbert Clapp, J. B. Barnes & Co., Job Bros. & Co., Hunters & Co., Jas. Tobin & Co., L. O'Brien & Co., James Douglas & Co., Parker & Gleeson, Edward Morris, Nicholas Gill, G. F. Bown, Walter Dillon, J. Cusack & Sons, Dunscombe & Harvey, Robinson Brooking & Co., John Brocklebank, John P. Mullowney, Richard Hillman."

successor: but he at once sent present relief to the extent of £5,000; and immediately afterwards the new secretary, Earl Grey, with the sanction of Parliament, added to that sum £25,000. Besides this large public grant, the Queen issued a letter to the Archbishops of Canterbury and York, authorising them to bring before the clergy and congregations under their charge the case of the sufferers in Newfoundland, in the manner that might seem best calculated to draw forth the liberality of the benevolent."[1]

The year of the fire was a most unfortunate one for the Colony. On the 19th of September a terrific gale destroyed an immense amount of property, both by land and sea; the unfinished Native Hall was blown down, St. Thomas's Church was moved bodily, a large number of houses in St. John's, partly built, were injured; there was also an extraordinary high tide, the water came up to the floors of several houses on the south side of Water Street.[2]

There were addresses and most sincere and universal regret from all classes when Sir John Harvey left this Colony to assume the Government of Nova Scotia, in August 1846; he went there, as he went everywhere, to calm the troubled sea of politics. His success in promoting peace and harmony among the able but excitable politicians of that province was the final achievement of his long and active life. Lady Harvey, to whom he was tenderly attached, expired rather suddenly in 1851. Sir John never rallied from this blow; in March 1852 he also died, at Halifax.[3] His merits as an able diplomatist and politician were rightly appreciated in Nova Scotia, but he has received scant justice from our local politicians and historians. We have only to

---

[1] Pedley's *History of Newfoundland*.

[2] In the June session of the House of Assembly (1846) Mr. Glen proposed to spend £100 to increase the gas lamps in Water Street; clergymen, doctors, and out-harbour planters complained of the dangers and darkness of the streets. R. J. Parsons, E. Hanrahan, R. Carter, and Hon. W. B. Row voted against it; Parsons vehemently denounced the expenditure.

[3] Major-General Sir John Harvey, K.C.B., entered the army in 1800; he served with great distinction in India and in Egypt. As Deputy Quartermaster General he went through the American war of 1812. On one occasion, when opposed to General Wingfield Scott, U.S.A., his opponent admired his gallantry so much that he gave orders to his soldiers not to fire at the handsome, dashing colonel. After the war, Sir John was appointed Inspector-General of the Police in Ireland; even in this difficult position he became a universal favourite. In 1835 he was made Lieut.-Governor of Prince Edward's Island, and two years later was promoted to the larger governorship of New Brunswick. His Excellency had to inaugurate responsible government in the province, and it need not be said that he carried out the liberal policy of the English ministry in an eminently satisfactory manner. During his tenure of office, there was great excitement over the Maine Boundary question; Sir John and his old opponent General Scott, by their wise and pacific measures, kept peace between England and the United States. For his action in opposition to the Commander-in-Chief in Canada, Sir John was dismissed; after explanations, his valuable services were rewarded by a K.C.B. and promotion to the Governorship of Newfoundland.

In 1845 the Cunard steamer *Hibernia* struck near Cape Race; she got off all right, and the passengers came on to St. John's. One of them wrote to the *Frederickton Loyalist*, "St John's Harbour is quite a business place, the harbour full of shipping, everybody actively employed, and apparently profitably so. . . . Political feuds have vanished, religious differences are unknown, Protestants and Catholics are living in Christian charity and perfect harmony with each other, the society is excellent, and the people hospitable in the extreme, and this state of things, I am happy to say, is mainly attributed to the propitious administration of contrast the violence and party animosity that existed under his predecessors, both excellent Governors, to rightly value the tact and the ability with which Sir John Harvey managed all parties. Both sides have always declared that, with his infinite grace and smooth speech, he humbugged them all, perhaps he did, at any rate he was a skilful peacemaker, one of the first duties of a Governor.[1]

Sir John Harvey was succeeded in 1847 by Sir Gaspard Le Marchant, a distinguished soldier.[2] His Excellency will long be gratefully remembered in this Colony for the deep interest he took in promoting agriculture. He was a thoroughly practical man and not a diplomatist, like his august predecessor; Sir John talked admirably about farming, Sir Gaspard acted. He introduced Ayrshire and Jersey cows, and in a few years completely transformed the breed of cattle throughout the Colony. He liked to see after everything personally; when he heard that the mob were burning him in effigy, he went down to see if his

SIR G. LE MARCHANT.
By Bassano.

Sir John Harvey, their present Governor, and the former Governor of New Brunswick; he is certainly the most kind-hearted, hospitable, excellent man; he is doing a great deal of good here, and is respected and beloved by by all classes, I believe...."

[1] Mr. Timothy Mitchell, afterwards the well-known Inspector of Police, had been in the police force, under Sir John Harvey, in Ireland and New Brunswick, and at His Excellency's suggestion he came on to St. John's. In the old days the Inspector did splendid work, both in the detection of crime and in the capture of criminals. I remember on one occasion when he was attempting to arrest a rioter in Carabus, the man caught up an old pocket with a long rusty nail in it; as he was going to make a blow at Mitchell the Inspector drew from his pocket the case of a long French pipe he had borrowed from me; the man thought it was a revolver, and dropped his weapon at once. In the witness-box Mitchell showed as much ability as in the performance of his other duties. Judge Robinson had rather a sharp way of cross-examining police and magistrates; he was asking the Inspector, rather peremptorily, about the confession made to him in an arson case. "You searched the prisoner, sir, what did you find on him?" "His insurance policy in one pocket, my Lord, and the Key of Heaven in the other," was the imperturbable reply.

[2] Sir John Gaspard Le Marchant, Knt. Bachel. (creat. 1858); G.C.M.G., 1860; K.C.B., 1865. Entered the army in 1821; became a colonel in 1851, and held local rank as a major-general till fully promoted to that rank in March 1858; retired from the command of the 85th foot in 1846 on proceeding to Newfoundland; was Governor and Commander-in-Chief of Newfoundland from February 1847 to June 1852; Lieut.-Governor of Nova Scotia from June 1852 to December 1857, when he was appointed Governor of Malta, and received local rank of lieut.-general there, 1859; was a brigadier-general in the service of Her Catholic Majesty; a knight of the 1st class and a knight commander of the orders of San Fernando and of Charles III. of Spain; received the honour of knighthood from the Queen, with permission to wear his foreign orders, which were conferred for services in Spain. He died in 1874.

image was properly got up, and if his bold aquiline nose had been successfully copied.[1]

In December 1848 the first session of the new Legislature was opened under the old Constitution of 1832, with separate Council and Assembly. 1848 was a year of revolution in Europe; with the exception of Her Gracious Majesty the Queen's, every throne in Europe was tottering and tumbling. The wave of political excitement which Thackeray describes—

> "When pursuing of their shindies,
> They broke the lovely windies,
> Upon the Shannon shore"—

reached our Island home. Responsible government was the war cry of our modest rebellion, and the only outbreak of violence, burning the Governor's image. The revolutionary fever has so far always attacked us in a mild form. Both the Whig Earl Grey and the Conservative Sir John Pakington refused point blank to grant the Colony local self-government. Earl Grey wrote:—

"Until the wealth and population of the Colony shall have increased considerably beyond their present amount, the introduction of what is called Responsible Government will by no means prove to its advantage. . . . . . The institutions of Newfoundland have been of late in various ways modified and altered, and some time must unavoidably elapse before they can acquire that amount of fixity and adaptation to the colonial wants of society which seems an indispensable preliminary to the future extension of popular Government."

Sir John Pakington, in 1852, also took the same view; in a despatch of April 3, he says:—

"Her Majesty's Government see no reason for differing from the conclusions at which their predecessors had arrived in the question of the establishment of Responsible Government, and which were conveyed to you by Lord Grey. . . . I consider on the contrary that the wisdom and justice of these conclusions are confirmed by the accounts since received from Newfoundland."

---

[1] POSTAL COMMUNICATION, 1847.

"James Hodge begs to acquaint the Public at large that he intends to run a four-sail boat between Kelligrews and Brigus and Port de Grave during the winter months; a steady and confidential man will leave St. John's every Wednesday morning, with the packages and letters for transmission, which will be forwarded to their destination as regularly as the weather will permit: single letters 1s., double letters 2s., packages in proportion to their bulk and weight.

"Mr. Doyle begs to announce to the communities of St. John's, Harbour Grace, and Carbonear, that he has engaged a confidential packet man to travel around the Bay during the winter months and while the boat is necessarily laid up . . . . . .

In 1841 Messrs. W. Thomas and Jos. Noad recommended that there should be no postal communication outside of St. John's and Conception Bay.

			$
The Postal Revenue in 1841	was	1,084
,,	,,	1851	,, 4,329
,,	,,	1861	,, 5,170
,,	,,	1871	,, 10,000
,,	,,	1878	,, 15,609
,,	,,	1892	,, 44,000

The agitation still went on, notwithstanding Earl Grey and the sturdy Sir John Pakington. Responsible government had been conceded to every one of the North American Colonies; the Home Government ought to have had wisdom enough to see that it was inevitable, and conceded it gracefully, instead of having it wrung from them. Each successive House of Assembly had pronounced in favour of executive responsibility; even the Amalgamated House, in which two-fifths of the members were nominees of the Crown, had voted in favour of the same principle.

This political agitation, begun at the May meeting in 1846, continued up to the introduction of our present form of government in 1855. The actors in the final scenes of our great constitutional drama, however, were new men. Mr. John Kent, in 1849, became Collector of the Customs in place of Mr. Spearman (who retired with a pension). Dr. Fleming, worn out with incessant toil and labour in his diocese, in 1848 obtained as coadjutor Dr. Mullock, who arrived in St. John's on the 6th of May 1848. From this time forth the leaders of the Liberal and Catholic party were Mr. P. F. Little and the new Bishop. Both were men of great ability, liberal and enlightened in their views.[1] Dr. Mullock was a scholar, full of wit and eloquence; he did much to forward the interests of the Colony, and was one of the first to promote telegraphic communication, local steam, and practical agriculture.

P. F. LITTLE.
By Lafayette, Dublin.

Mr. P. F. Little, afterwards Assistant Judge of the Supreme Court, and brother of the present excellent judge, J. I. Little, came from Prince Edward's Island, where he was born in 1824; he began practice as a lawyer about 1845. He had a very up-hill fight, but his ability, his attention to business, with his shrewdness and knowledge of affairs, soon

---

[1] Bishop Mullock's good sayings, however, are quite eclipsed by the wit of his brother, familiarly known as Tom, organist of the Cathedral, the "Parish Piper" as he styled himself. On one occasion there was a discussion at the Bishop's table about the interior of the Colony; Dr. Mullock, in his impetuous way, said it was a wilderness, only fit for the bears. "That's what I was saying," said Tom, "it was *barely* known." On another occasion, Tom, for want of a better conveyance, sent down to Don Hipolito De Uriarte, the Spanish Consul, a piano he had purchased for him, on a hearse. The Don was very indignant; a crowd had collected before his door to witness this novel method of moving a piano. "What for, Mr. Mullock," said Uriarte, "you send down my piano on the funeral cart?" "Sure," said Tom, "I wanted to convince you that you had a *dead bargain*." Tom's peculiar drawl and brogue, and his rubicund countenance, gave a fine flavour to his jokes, which is lost in the telling.

brought him clients; from the first to the last he enjoyed the complete confidence of Dr. Mullock. He was elected to the Legislature in 1850, and almost at once became the real leader of the Catholic and Liberal Party in the House.[1] In the agitation for responsible government Mr. P. F. Little was the leader, the organiser, and by far the most powerful man in the movement; he was not so polished a speaker as Mr. Robinson, or as eloquent and ornate as Mr. Kent, but in astuteness, in assiduity, in political sagacity, in the management of his party, and in constitutional knowledge, he was a match for all his opponents.

Sir Gaspard was appointed Governor of Nova Scotia, and left the Colony on July 28, 1852. His last speech at the close of the House of Assembly was neither courteous nor dignified, and was accordingly assailed by a portion of the local press in very scurrilous terms; his enemies specially sneered at his devotion to agriculture; the introduction of cocks and hens, cows, horses, and sheep were the subjects of infinite ridicule. Administrations come and go, politics pass away, but an improved breed of cattle is a permanent benefit to the country that possesses it; the fight between the Governor and his political enemies has long been forgotten, but many an old farmer in the country even to-day will point out with pride a beautiful cow as " of ould Sir Gaspar's breed." The rough old soldier was a very poor politician, but he was loyal, honest, and sincere; he did far more practical work in encouraging the cultivation of land, and especially the breeding of cattle, than any former Governor.

His Excellency Ker Baillie Hamilton,[2] who assumed the reins of the government in December 1852, was in marked contrast to his predecessor. Sir Gaspard went about everywhere, and knew every farmer around St. John's; Mr. Hamilton was an exceedingly shy,

---

[1] LEGISLATIVE COUNCIL.
Hon. Col. Law, President.
  „ E. M. Archibald, Attorney-General.
  „ Jas. Crowdy, Colonial Secretary.
  „ W. B. Row.
  „ Jo. Noad, Surveyor-General.
  „ C. F. Bennett.
  „ J. J. Grieve.
  „ L. O'Brien.

HOUSE OF ASSEMBLY.
Speaker, Hon. J. Kent.
St. John's: John Kent, Little, Parsons.
Placentia: G. Hogsett, A. Shea.
Burin: C. Benning.
Fogo: G. H. Emerson.
Ferryland: P. Winsor.
Conception Bay: Hayward, Nugent, Talbot, and Hanrahan.

Fortune Bay: H. W. Hoyles.
Bonavista: J. H. Warren.
Trinity: S. March.

[2] Ker Baillie Hamilton, C.B., was educated for the Army at the Royal Military Academy at Woolwich; entered the Indian military service in 1822; appointed a writer in the civil service of the Mauritius in 1826, and assistant private secretary to Governor Sir Lowry Cole there; appointed clerk of the council, at the Cape of Good Hope, in 1829; afterwards acted there as colonial secretary; appointed Lieut.-Governor of Grenada in 1846; administrator of the Government of Barbados and, the Windward Islands in 1851; Governor of Newfoundland in 1852; Governor-in-Chief of Antigua and the Leeward Islands in 1855 to January 1863.

[1] p. 2729.

taciturn man; he wrote well, and was very pious and good, but he never tried to please the public; he could not speak, and in the crisis and agitation for responsible government he was about as unfit a man as the British Government could possibly have selected to fill a difficult position. Lord Dufferin humorously compared himself to the humble individual in a paper cap who goes about with a long-spouted tin can oiling the machinery, and his Lordship's marvellous success as an administrator is largely due to his tact and good judgment, and his faculty as a political lubricator. Poor Ker Baillie Hamilton, excellent, good, honest man, had not this gift; he never tried to conciliate parties or to make the government work smoothly; as a Governor he was a complete failure; at the same time nothing can palliate the indecent manner in which the majority of the House of Assembly assailed him.

It is not necessary to go over all the long discussion about responsible government. When the British Cabinet, represented by the Duke of Newcastle, finally agreed to grant the Colony Home Rule, they attached two main conditions—the old office holders should receive fair treatment, and there should be a proper Representation Bill. The Secretary of State for the Colonies wrote to Governor Hamilton that—

"Her Majesty's Government had come to the conclusion that they ought not to withhold from Newfoundland those institutions, and that civil administration, which, under the popular name of Responsible Government, had been adopted in all Her Majesty's neighbouring possessions in North America, and they were prepared to concede the immediate application of the system as soon as certain preliminary conditions had been acceded to on the part of the Legislature."

On the question of the pension to the retiring officers, there was a most contemptible wrangle; a Committee of the House, consisting of A. Shea, Little, Benning, Hogsett, and Hanrahan, decided to give E. M. Archibald, Attorney-General, after twenty years' good service as a public officer, and now compulsorily retired, £140 per annum. Governor Hamilton very properly refused to accede to such an unfair allowance, and the Home Government approved of his conduct. Finally, the pensions were fixed as follows:—J. Crowdy, Colonial Secretary, £400; Archibald, Attorney-General, £350; Noad, Surveyor-General, £285; H. A. Emerson, Solicitor-General, £90. Over the Representation question both sides fought bitterly. Mr. Little's party wanted to "gerrymander" the districts to secure his party majority, whilst the

Conservatives with equal pertinacity opposed him. In such a difficulty a wise and diplomatic Governor would have stood between the opponents and have endeavoured to work out a fair compromise; during the three years' struggle he certainly should have had a census taken. Responsible government was brought in in 1855, and the only return of population that both sides had to work on was the imperfect census of 1845; it was owing to the Council, ruled by the Governor's friends, that a census Bill passed by the Assembly had been thrown out. We know now that if a census had been taken in 1853 or 1854 it would have shown a very different basis from the one on which representation was ultimately carried. The most disagreeable feature in this interminable discussion was the desire for sectarian ascendency evinced by both sides. Subsequent history shows that the Conservative party were in the main right in their contention that Bonavista and Twillingate with one member each were under-represented, whilst less important and less populous districts, like Placentia and Ferryland, had each two members. It is clear, however, that the Protestant Party were unwise in stolidly resisting any change. They should have known that responsible government was sure to come sooner or later, and have stood out firmly for a census before the Representation Bill was agreed to, and endeavoured to make the best of the coming event. Too much importance was given to the personal interests of the office holders, and too little regard to the future good government of the Colony. There should have been a fairer distribution of offices. No one can doubt now that the Roman Catholics had been unfairly treated; under the new Government that came into office in 1855[1] there was a complete change. After a lapse of forty years we can now view the whole matter dispassionately, and it must

HON. T. R. ROW
By Cox and Lorrequet.

[1] LEGISLATIVE COUNCIL.

Hon. L. O'Brien, President.
 „ Jas. Tobin.
 „ John Rochfort, M.D.
 „ Geo. H. Emerson, Solicitor-General.
 „ John Munn.
 „ S. Carson, M.D.
 „ T. R. Row.
 „ J. J. Rogerson.
 „ T. H. Ridley.
 „ Jas. Furlong.
 „ P. Duggan.
 „ J. Cormack.

HOUSE OF ASSEMBLY ELECTED 7TH MAY 1855.

The first House of Assembly under responsible government consisted of the following members :—

St. John's West: Hon. P. F. Little, Attorney-General and Premier; Hon. A. Shea, Speaker; John Fox.

St. John's East: Hon. J. Kent, Colonial Secretary; R. J. Parsons; Peter Winsor.

Harbour Grace: J. Hayward; J. L. Prendergast.

be admitted that Mr. Little played his hand in the political game artfully, and the Conservatives' stolid opposition to any change in the constitution was a political blunder. We may give them credit for honesty of purpose, but all the same they committed a grave mistake.

It is due to Governor Hamilton's memory to record that when important questions of telegraphic and steam communication arose during his administration he showed both liberal and enlightened views; he also wrote very able despatches on the French fishery question. On the subject of the telegraph, I have carefully consulted the records of the time, and, as far as possible, endeavoured to state the history of its introduction into the Colony correctly in Chapter XXI.

In 1855 the new administration under responsible government was appointed, with the Hons. P. F. Little, Premier and Attorney-General; J. Kent, Colonial Secretary; T. Glen, Receiver-General; E. Hanrahan, Surveyor-General; G. H. Emerson, Solicitor-General; and L. O'Brien, President of the Legislative Council. It was purely and entirely a Liberal administration, all the members of the Government representing Roman Catholic constituencies; Mr. Emerson did not count, as he had been defeated in Twillingate, and now sat in the Council. The three principal officers, Little, Kent, and Glen, were able men; in the words of Mr. Hanrahan, as an administration "*it was as near perfection as possible.*" They had the rare good luck of prosperous years, "the sunshine of prosperity," in the words of Mr. Kent, beamed on the Government. 1855, 1856, and 1857 were years of plenty; the new Cabinet, under the firm hand of the Premier, was able, liberal, and progressive.

In 1854, the cholera was brought into St. John's by infection from a sailor's clothes; it spread destruction with frightful rapidity; all the efforts

---

Carbonear: Hon. E. Hanrahan, Surveyor-General, and Chairman of the Board of Works.
Holyrood: Talbot and Byrne.
Port de Grave: R. Brown.
Ferryland: Hon. T. Glen, Receiver-General; E. D. Shea.
Burin: Benning and Morris.
Bonavista: R. Carter, Warren, and Walbank.
Fogo and Twillingate: Ellis and Knight.
Fortune Bay: H. W. Hoyles.
Burgeo and La Poile: R. Prowse.
Placentia: Hogsett, Delaney, and Kelly.
Trinity: F. Carter, March, and Winter.
Bay de Verds: Bemister.

The first administration under responsible government was composed of able and enlightened politicians; the Governor guided their footsteps, and was their firm ally and supporter. The Attorney-General, P. F. Little, very wisely associated himself with members from the opposite side; Messrs. Walter Grieve, Munn, Ridley, Rogerson, G. H. Emerson, and Hayward (afterwards Judge Hayward), were amongst his Protestant supporters. Mr. Little was an able leader, and always kept his party well in hand; from first to last he enjoyed the unbounded confidence of Bishop Mullock. Mr. Kent made an excellent Colonial Secretary, and T. Glen was a heaven-born Receiver-General, one of the best party men that ever sat in a cabinet. At a political meeting an out-harbour member, who was under obligations to the Government, said to Glen, in a patronizing tone: "I believe you are right, Mr. Receiver-General; I will support you." "Confound you," said Glen, "I don't want your support when I am right; it is when I am wrong you must back me up."

of medical skill, the humane exertion of the clergy and of self-devoted women, were powerless to stay the plague; however, it was practically confined to the lowest and dirtiest parts of the city. Whilst the cholera lasted, the number of deaths was appalling. Bishops Mullock and Feild and Archdeacon Bridge were conspicuous during the epidemic by their heroic, self-sacrificing labours for all—Catholics and Protestants alike were personally attended by these devoted servants of God. Bishop Feild lived to a good age, but Archdeacon Bridge, the idol of his congregation, almost equally adored by rich and poor of all creeds, fell a victim to duty soon after. No one who has ever seen his beautiful countenance, or heard his magnificent tones in the sublime service for the dead, will ever forget Thomas Finch Hobday Bridge, the most beloved Anglican minister that ever set foot on our soil; his place has never been filled; generous, warm-hearted, and deeply religious, Nature had endowed him with every gift and grace, even the divine gift of humour; religion had purged away all the earthly dross of selfishness and ambition from a truly noble character, and made him one of the most lovable of men. After escaping the deadly peril of the cholera, he died from fever contracted whilst attending one of the very poorest of his congregation. Readers of to-day may think this language exaggerated, but the generation that heard that earnest voice will bear witness to the deep affectionate feelings of all St. John's for the Archdeacon.

ARCHDEACON BRIDGE.
From a miniature in the possession of his son, Admiral Bridge.

Direct steam to England by the Galway line, the completion of the telegraph, and finally, in 1858, the laying of the first Atlantic cable, are the striking events of this period. In 1858 Judges Des Barres and Simms were pensioned, and Hons. P. F. Little and B. Robinson became the assistant judges of the Supreme Court.

Sir Charles Darling, who inaugurated responsible government in 1855, remained only until 1857.[1] He was a remarkably able man, of

---

[1] Sir Charles Henry Darling, K.C.B. (created 1862), entered the Army as ensign on the 7th December 1826, by recommendation from the Royal Military College, Sandhurst, after public examination; became, in 1827, assistant private secretary to the late General Sir Ralph Darling, then Governor of New South Wales and Major-General com-

470 REIGN OF VICTORIA, 1837-1857.

vast experience; he taught his new ministry how to work the new constitution, and ruled them like a pack of schoolboys. The Conservative party came into collision with him, first as regards his authority to inaugurate the new constitution, and again when they insisted on naming members of their own party for the new legislative council: on both these questions Sir Charles was clearly and constitutionally right.

VIEW OF VIRGINIA WATER, ST. JOHN'S.

It will be remembered that Louis Napoleon was just about this time, after the Crimean War, our "good ally," and the English Government were most anxious to please the French, and for that purpose the

manding the Forces in that colony and Van Dieman's Land; and was also appointed military secretary to that officer in 1830. In 1833, while a student in the senior department of the Royal Military College, was appointed secretary to the late Lieutenant-General Sir Lionel Smith, upon that officer's nomination to be Governor and Commander-in-Chief of Barbados and the Windward Islands, and was employed in that capacity until 1836; Sir Lionel Smith having been in that year nominated to the government of Jamaica, Mr. Darling was appointed Governor's secretary for that colony, and retained the appointment until the termination of Sir Lionel Smith's Government in 1839; in that year obtained an unattached company, and retired from the army in 1841; in 1843 appointed by the Earl of Elgin, then Governor of Jamaica, Agent-General of Immigration for the colony, and held also the office of Adjutant-General of Militia, was a member of the assembly and of several executive boards; was again appointed Governor's secretary during the ad-interim administration of the government of Jamaica by Major-General Sackville H. Berkeley, and continued to hold that office during the earlier period of the government of the Right Hon. Sir Charles Grey in 1846-47; in 1847 was appointed Lieutenant-Governor of the island of St Lucia; in 1851 appointed Lieutenant-Governor of the Cape of Good Hope, an office specially created for the conduct at Cape Town of the civil government while Sir George Cathcart, the Governor and Commander-in-Chief, might be engaged in his military and civil duties on the frontier. After the departure of Sir George Cathcart, administered the government of the Cape from May 1854 to December 1854, during which period the parliamentary constitution of the settlement was interests of this Colony were as usual to be sacrificed. There can be no doubt that Governor Darling, eager to please the Home Government, lent himself to this policy; his famous No. 66 Despatch was a strong argument, ably put no doubt, but entirely in the interests of the French, and opposed to the rights and claims of the Colony. There was much indignation in St. John's when it was published with the other papers concerning the great Convention with the French of 1857.

In order to comprehend the wild outburst of popular indignation which arose in 1857, it is necessary to go back for some time, and also to understand the character of the previous negotiations which had been going on between the representatives of the two Governments for several years; all these various discussions and draft settlements have one unvarying characteristic: the French gain all the advantages, and the Colony gets nothing in return. The principal English negotiator, Sir Anthony Perrier, appears to have been either a French tool or thoroughly incapable official. All the fine diplomacy of France was directed to three principal points: first, to secure an unlimited supply of bait; second, to get the right to arrest and remove Colonial fishermen and their vessels; third, to get a secure territory and to extend their rights on the treaty shore. It is a fortunate thing for us that the French were so over-reaching and so covetous of territory that even Perrier could not concede all their demands, and that the final Draft Convention of 1857 was an outrageous abandonment of our fishery rights. Labouchere and Perrier were aghast when they heard of the excitement these unfair propositions created in the Colony; the Newfoundlanders held indignation meetings as hot and fiery as the Tea riots of Boston; not only was Newfoundland aroused, all British North America rose with her.

The Earl of Derby, the Secretary of State for the Colonies, in a despatch in 1884 to Sir John Glover, summarized the negotiations resulting in the Convention of 1857 as follows:—

"In the year 1844 the French Government proposed negotiations to be held in London, and previous to opening them it was determined to appoint a British and French Commissioner in Newfoundland to report upon the question.

inaugurated and established; was nominated to the government-in-chief of Antigua and the Leeward Islands, previously to his sole administration of the government of the Cape; but never assumed the duties of that Government, having shortly after his arrival in England been required to proceed to Newfoundland as Administrator of the government of that colony, of which he was subsequently appointed Governor and Commander-in-Chief; in February 1857 was appointed Captain-General and Governor-in-Chief of Jamaica, an office which embraces the general superintendence of the affairs of British Honduras and the Turks' Islands, and at that time included also the government-in chief of the Bay Islands; received the Order of the Bath (K.C.B.) 1862, for his "long and effective public services." Appointed Governor of Victoria, 1863; recalled, March 1866; died in 1870.

"Captain Fabvre, commander on the French naval station, and Mr. Thomas, President of the Chamber of Commerce at Newfoundland, were, in consequence, appointed by their respective Governments.

"On the 30th July 1844, Mr. Thomas made his report to the Governor. In this report he suggested with regard to the French claim of 'exclusive rights,' that the respective fishermen of both nations should be kept separate and distinct in their fishing places. He also suggested the extension of the French fishery limits to Belle Isle North, and made suggestions with regard to the sale of bait to French fishermen.

"This report resulted in negotiations being held in Paris in the month of March 1846.

"The British Commissioner, Sir A. Perrier, was authorised to offer, in exchange for the French cession of all rights between Cape Ray and Bonne Bay, the following concessions :—

"Admission of *exclusive* right of fishery from Bonne Bay to Cape St. John, going round by the north ;

"Exclusive right of French fishery, drying, and curing at Belle Isle North ;

"Permission for English fishermen to sell bait at St. Pierre.

"At preliminary conferences held in Newfoundland, these measures had nearly been agreed to by Mr. Thomas and Captain Fabvre ; but Captain Fabvre was desirous of retaining for France, in addition to the exclusive rights above mentioned, her rights of fishing, curing fish, &c., at Cod Roy, Red Island, Port-a-Port, and Lark Harbour, and to acquire for the French a 'concurrent' right of fishery on the coast of Labrador.

"The instructions, however, to the French Commissioner did not admit of his negotiating on the above-mentioned principles, and as no new propositions were brought forward by the French Government up to the month of May 1847, the negotiations fell through.

"On the application of the French Government in 1854 negotiations were renewed, Sir A. Perrier being again directed to proceed to Paris to act as British Commissioner, M. de Bon being appointed on the part of France.

"The British Commissioner was instructed to invite proposals from the French Commissioner such as might form a starting point in the negotiations.

"M. de Bon accordingly proposed, on the part of France, to admit the right of British subjects to inhabit the Bay St. George, or, in other terms to give up the exclusive right of fishery in that bay, to which they considered themselves entitled by the Treaty of 1783. In return for this concession he demanded—

"1. The right to fish for bait (herring and caplin) on the south coast of Newfoundland, without restriction.

"2. The right to fish during two months of the year (without curing or drying on shore) on that part of the coast of Labrador situated between the Isles of Vertes and the Isles St. Modeste, both included ; and

"3. The right of fishery at Belle Isle North, in the Straits, which the French Commissioner asserted was enjoyed by the French up to 1841, without any demur on the part of Great Britain.

"The concessions demanded by the French negotiator were not considered admissible, and the British Commissioner, in order to overcome the difficulties arising out of the claim of Great Britain to a concurrent right of fishery, suggested that the question would be best settled if the rights of the fishermen of the two nations were kept separate and distinct. In order to carry out this suggestion, he proposed that the French rights should be made exclusive as against British subjects from Cape St. John to some point on the western coast, such as Cape Verde (Green Point, to the north of Bonne Bay) ; the French, on the other hand, to renounce their right altogether on the remainder of the coast, which would be that part where the British had been in the habit of carrying on the herring fishery and other fisheries incidental to the requirements of a fixed population.

" The French negotiator offered no objection to the plan of recognising the French 'exclusive right' on a diminished extent of coast; but he contended for the retention of a 'concurrent right' on that portion on the coast on which the exclusive claim might be renounced, and for other advantages as well, such as admission, concurrently with British fishermen, to the fisheries of Labrador and North Belle Isle, and to the 'bait fishery' on the southern coast, all of which, he maintained, were necessary, as an equivalent for admitting British subjects to a free 'concurrent right' on the lower portion of the western coast.

" The British Commissioner was disposed to accept the demands of the French so far as to extend the French fishery to North Belle Isle, and also to remove all restrictions on the purchase of 'bait,' on condition that the French should entirely renounce their rights between Cape Verte and Cape Ray; and in June 1855, he forwarded to the Foreign Office the above suggestions in the form of a counter proposal to those which had been made by France.

" Mr. Labouchere, Her Majesty's Secretary of State for the Colonies, concurred in the adoption of the British negotiator's project of a 'compromise' as the basis of negotiation to be offered to the French Government. It corresponded, he believed, with the views of the Colonial authorities; deprived neither nation of any advantage of real value; and there would only be a reciprocal abandonment of barren rights and useless or nominal restrictions; and he prepared a draft treaty which might be substituted for the whole of the existing engagements on the Newfoundland Fisheries question.

" The negotiations were continued in the year 1856 by Captain Pigeard, who arrived in London in the month of July of that year, and by Mr. Merivale, the Under Secretary of State for the Colonies. The basis of these negotiations was founded upon the counter proposals made by Sir A. Perrier, and also upon the draft of the treaty proposed by Mr. Labouchere. The negotiations finally terminated by the signature of a Convention in London on the 17th January 1857.

" According to the stipulations of this Convention, an exclusive right of fishery and the use of the strand for fishery purposes was conceded to the French from Cape St. John, on the east coast of Newfoundland, to the Quirpon Islands, and from the Quirpon Islands, on the north coast, to Cape Norman, on the west coast, in and upon the following five fishery harbours, namely, Port-au-Choix, Small Harbour, Port-a-Port, Red Island, and Cod Roy Island, to extend, as regarded these five harbours, to a radius of three marine miles in all directions from the centre of each such harbour. On other parts of the west coast (the five harbours excepted) British subjects were to enjoy a 'concurrent' right of fishing with French subjects, but French subjects were to have the exclusive use of the strand for fishery purposes from Cape Norman to Rock Point, in the Bay of Islands, north of the River Humber, in addition to the strand of the reserved harbours.

" A 'concurrent' right of fishing was also granted to French subjects on the coast of Labrabor, from Blanc Sablon to Cape Charles, and of North Belle Isle."

The excitement in the Colony over the Convention of 1857 was most intense and wide spread; the British flag was hoisted half-mast; other excited citizens flew American flags; everywhere there was burning indignation over this proposal to sell our birthright for a mess of pottage. The proceedings of our Legislature in 1857 are a guide to us as to what our conduct should always be in dealing with the fisheries, "there none were for a party but all were for the State." Government and Opposition united to maintain our rights. Our Chief Justice, Sir F. B. T. Carter, K.C.M.G., Sir A. Shea, Hons. E. D. Shea, P. F. Little, Mr. Prendergast, Mr. J. J. Rogerson, and Mr. Kelly, alone survive of those who took a leading part in that famous struggle. Sir Frederick (then Mr. Carter, M.H.A.) went with Hon. John Kent as a delegate to Canada, and won golden opinions for himself by his ability in this matter. Immediately the House closed, Hon. P. F. Little and H. W. Hoyles were sent as delegates to England; all worked unitedly and with a will to destroy the convention. H. W. Hoyles (leader of the Opposition), P. F. Little (the Attorney-General), J. Kent (Colonial Secretary), R. Prowse, W. H. Ellis (Opposition members), and

HON. E. D. SHEA.
By S. H. Parsons.

J. J. ROGERSON.
By S. H. Parsons.

R. J. PARSONS.
From an old photograph.

R. J. Parsons, were the committee appointed to draft resolutions and addresses on the subject. The resolutions adopted by the Newfoundland Legislature were worthy of the occasion. I will quote only the concluding paragraph :—

"We deem it our duty, most respectfully, to protest in the most solemn manner against any attempt to alienate any portion of our fisheries or our soil to any foreign power, without the consent of the local legislature. *As our fishery and territorial rights constitute the basis of our commerce and of our social and political existence, as they are our birthright and the legal inheritance of our children*, we cannot, under any circumstances, assent to the terms of the convention; we therefore earnestly entreat that the Imperial Government will take no steps to bring this Treaty into operation, but will permit the trifling privileges that remain to us to continue unimpaired."

The result was a great triumph for the Colony. Before Governor Darling left in May 1857, he had received and laid before the

Legislature the celebrated despatch known as "The Labouchere letter":—

> "The proposals contained in the Convention having been now unequivocally refused by the Colony, they will of course fall to the ground; and you are authorised to give such assurance as you may think proper. That the consent of the community of Newfoundland is regarded by Her Majesty's Government as the essential preliminary to any modification of their territorial or maritime rights."—(H. Labouchere.)

Mr. Darling had informed the House during the winter of his promotion to Jamaica. The publication of His Excellency's own despatch (No. 66, July 23rd, 1856) created a very strong feeling against him; on a careful perusal of this document, I think the irritation it produced was rather extreme. He states emphatically, in regard to the French proposals:—

> "Their proposition may be, indeed, justly described, when regarded in its national bearing, as one of which *the advantage is wholly on the French side.*"

The objectionable paragraph in the paper is on the question of French exclusive rights.

Governor Darling's letter is in marked contrast to his predecessor's communication of September 1853 (No. 57).[1] Governor Hamilton's views are both more logical and more correct; they are founded on a more complete knowledge of the history of the fishery. The despised and insulted Ker Baillie Hamilton was really a far more sincere and loyal friend of the Colony, and a far abler defender of our fishery rights than Sir Charles Darling, the popular introducer of responsible government and the patron of the Liberal party. We must give both of them credit for honesty of purpose; but it is clear that Hamilton had the advantage of superior information on the subject. This, I think, was largely due to his advisers, Messrs. Archibald and Crowdy, as well as his mercantile friends.

On the question of "fixed settlements," the correct definition of the term is undoubtedly given by Governor Hamilton. It is clear, that under the administration of our naval Governors, the fishery carried on by both French and English on the coast was a *ship* fishery without permanent stages, &c.; under these arrangements each ship as she arrived selected a fishing place for her crew and made the necessary erections for carrying on their operations. Owing to the French being driven off the coast during the wars between 1756 and 1818, English fishermen had monopolised all the north-east coast; but long before this,

---

[1] These despatches, unfortunately, are both too long to reproduce; they will be found in the Journals of the House of Assembly, 1857.

as far back as 1698, Newfoundland "planters" had extended themselves from Bonavista gradually as far north as Quirpon. It was the permanent establishments of the English fishing ships which interfered with the free exercise of French rights, when the French fishermen came back in such overwhelming numbers after the last treaty of peace in 1815; the English ship fishermen had to be forced away, but the real permanent settlers were never interfered with; the French encouraged their presence as guardians and keepers of their fishing establishments; originally they never claimed a right to interfere with these small farmers and permanent settlers on the coast, whose occupations in the winter were furring and sealing, and it is to this direct encouragement that the present English settlements on the north-east and west coasts are largely due. The English fishery at this time was changing its character from a ship fishery into a shore fishery, and the men who had been using the west and north-east coasts now betook themselves to the more lucrative fishery at Labrador. The fight made against the French by one of these old ship fishermen is told in the narrative of the stubborn old West Countryman Tory.[1] Fixed settlements only referred to the permanent establishments of their rivals, the English ship fishermen. Governor Hamilton's advisers were well aware of this historical fact; Governor Darling seems to have entirely ignored it.

The treaties on this subject must be construed according to their real legal meaning, and the principles of International law, and also by the *expositio contemporanea* showing how they were interpreted and understood. Whatever was not given to France remains with the proprietor and Sovereign Power, England; we have therefore the right to clear and cultivate land, to work mines, to carry on a salmon fishery, and any other business that does not actually interfere with the French cod fishery. Our opponents may claim that either or any of these interferes with their limited fishery rights, but the injury must be proved, their claim for damages must be a reasonable claim, and the question must be decided in a reasonable and rational manner by the

---

[1] The case of the firm of Richard & Mellam Tory, of Poole, carrying on a large business at Sop's Arm, White Bay, for twenty-four years (set forth very fully in a long memorial to Governor Elliott in 1786), represents very high-handed proceedings on the part of the French naval officers. First, two bateaux with fifty men attempted to take possession of Tory's premises, but they would not allow them to land; next day two French men-of-war came to Sop's Arm, and officers and men armed came ashore, drove the Torys from their premises, took away two-thirds of their dwelling-house, dragged another English planter, Craze, on board the French sloop-of-war, and kept him prisoner for two hours; they also took possession of a salmon fishery up a brook which had been occupied and used by an Englishman, named Craze, for thirty years, made him leave the brook and take up his nets, &c. The French let the Newfoundland planter Craze remain in possession of his dwelling-house and premises. The great antagonism of the French at the time was against their rivals the English ship fishermen; the fixed settlements referred to were their rooms, not the humble establishments of the resident fishermen, which the French rarely disturbed.

British Government, the only authority who can execute a treaty on English territory. For instance, on the west coast of Newfoundland there are several small settlements on rivers. These streams are barred at their mouths by sand banks, and are therefore entirely unsuited for a ship cod fishery; for a century and more Englishmen have cleared and cultivated land at these places, and latterly some lobster factories have been carried on in these localities; will any reasonable man contend that we cannot occupy these places? We have done so, and will continue to do so.

It may be asked, is there no fair solution and settlement possible of this venerable international difficulty? The French, as business men, are the most reasonable, clear-headed people in the world. If this question could be once approached in a fair and reasonable spirit, it might be amicably settled. At the present time the French fishery is a ship fishery, carried on principally on the banks; their sedentary or shore fishery is relatively insignificant;[1] as a French friend of mine

[1] "LIST OF FRENCH LOBSTER FACTORIES AND COD FISHING ROOMS ON THE TREATY COAST OF NEWFOUNDLAND DURING THE SEASON OF 1893.

LOBSTER FACTORIES.

Where situated.	Number of Men approximately.	Manager.	Where from.	Remarks.
Brig Bay	—	Belin	—	Not worked since 1892.
Bartlett's Harbour	32	Baudgren	France.	
St John's Island	30*	Marie	France.	
Port au Choix	12*	Vilala	France.	
Port au Choix	17*	Belin	France.	
Black Duck Brook	15	Tajan	St. Pierre.	
Les Vaches	24	Farvacque	St. Pierre.	
Red Island	(All lobsters canned at Les Vaches.)			

COD FISHING ROOMS.

Red Island	60	Poirier	St. Pierre.	
Tweed Island	28	Hacala	St. Pierre.	
Port au Choix	80*	Belin	France.	
Savage Islands	35	Belin	France.	
Port au Choix	80*	Vilala	France.	
Port au Choix	34	Budeau	France.	
Berbice Cove	34	Budeau	France.	
St. John Island	70*	Marie	France.	
Fishot Islands	46	Foliard	France.	
St. Juliens	68	Eyon	France.	
Rouge	35	Dollo	France.	
Rouge	35	Pedron	France.	

* The numbers marked * vary according to the fishing, as their services are most required for either cod or lobsters."

[This return contains the French lobster factories; these erections, with boilers and chimneys, are a clear infraction of the treaty, which only allows temporary stages and scaffolds (flakes) for curing and drying of fish (i.e., codfish).]

explained, it is "an affair of a dozen old fishing brigs." The first requisite for a successful bank fishery is a certain supply, at reasonable prices, of the three varieties of fresh bait—herring, caplin, and squid. Our Gallic neighbours know well that Fortune Bay, in close proximity to St. Pierre, furnishes the best possible supply of bait in the world; it is abundant, easily accessible, and reasonable in price. Without a certainty of this supply at a moderate rate the bank fishery is unremunerative; every French fisherman thoroughly understands and appreciates this great fact.[1] This supply is entirely in our hands; we can at any moment paralyse the movements of the whole French fishing fleet by stopping their supplies of bait. We did so in 1888. Their full complement for their first baiting on herring amounts to fifty-four thousand barrels; by the 4th May in that year the French had only obtained four thousand and forty barrels; their spring fishery was in consequence a complete and disastrous failure. The effect of the Bait Act, which began in 1888, is clearly shown by the tables given below.[2] That year was a favourable one in the bank fishery, as both the English and American fishermen made good voyages in 1888.

There can be no possible doubt about the effect of the Bait Act on the French fishery; besides the convincing proof of the returns, we have the following extract from a letter published at Paris, in the *Petit Journal*, dated St. Pierre and Miquelon, July 15th, 1889:—

"Our Colony is very severely tried this year; the cod-fishing, which consti-tutes its principal—we might say its only—industry, has, up to this date, given

---

[1] The value of our bait is shown by the following:—

"According to the report of Captain Loch, of H.M.S. *Alarm*, in 1848 there were 360 French Banking vessels, of from 150 to 300 tons each, carrying from 16,000 to 17,000 Frenchmen, which vessels caught annually 1,200,000 quintals of fish on the Banks. He also states that Monsieur Delucluse, the French Governor of St. Pierre's, had the honesty to tell him, it was the supply of bait obtained from the Newfoundland fishermen that alone enabled them to carry on the Bank fishery. Captain Loch also remarks:—'It is obvious that, by withholding from the French the supply of bait from our shores, their catch on the Banks would sensibly diminish, and their trade could not increase beyond the limits controlled by the comparatively very scanty supply of bait afforded by their own coasts and islands.' All naval officers who have been on the Western station, as well as all disinterested persons who are acquainted with that coast, unite in stating that it is only by means of the bait supplied to them by British subjects, that the French are enabled to carry on the Bank fishery. Is it not, then, a source of wonder, that our Legislators are so blind to the interests of the country as to permit this evil to continue? Is it not surprising they should be so supine as to neglect their great and important duty of passing such laws, and adopting such measures, as will effectually check and prevent our foreign rivals from obtaining their supplies of bait from our shores?"—(WARREN's *Lecture*, p. 14.)

[2] EXPORTS OF FRENCH FISH, FROM OFFICIAL RETURNS.

	Total catch calculated in dry qtls.	Bounty paid. Francs.
1878	201,982	
1879	233,923	
1880	254,939	
1881	236,250	
1882	255,671	2,056,619
1883	304,580	2,528,442
1884	404,604	3,342,114
1885	497,284	3,849,221
1886	579,390	5,109,680
1887	453,058	4,673,240
1888	338,126	
1889	300,000	

(See also p. 586.)

deplorable results. During the first trip, seven-eighths of the fishermen have barely paid for their wine; all have returned from this trip with an average of from four to eight thousand fish, sixty-five to one hundred and thirty quintals for each craft, which represents nearly nothing. The whole of this fish has been sent to Bordeaux, and we have nothing left, and the future prospects look almost like a complete failure, consequently consumers will have to pay very dearly for the fish which they have hitherto been able to buy at a low price. *The schooners from St. Pierre are obliged to go to the east coast on the French shore of Newfoundland in search of bait, which means a month's fishing lost."*

And from the French journal, *Le Progrès*, of June 2nd, we get the following incontrovertible testimony:—

"This bait is made of small fish, which is only to be found in any quantities in the warmer waters of the south coast of the island, and is the necessary bait for cod-fishing, and which, until 1887, the French could buy, according to their want, at St. Pierre, Miquelon. *The law forbidding its sale was thus a great blow for them*, as they were reduced to bring from France a salted bait less liked by cod, or else to find for themselves, on the French Shore, a fresh bait which would always be costly, and the supply of which would be irregular. *Thus the Bait Bill entailed both loss of time and money to the French, and they found their fishing much less productive than before."*

The French are a very shrewd people; in each and all the various commissions to frame a settlement, one of their principal demands was a free supply of bait from our waters. It is clear then that we have something exceedingly valuable to give the French; what should we ask in return for this immense boon of free bait? I think, if the French would be reasonable, we could settle the whole question something after this manner, or at least have a *modus vivendi*:—

1. Let the French have exclusive possession for the fishing season within the three-mile limit around each harbour which they actually occupied with their fishing ships and crews last season, one or two guardians to be allowed in each harbour to protect their property;

2. Concurrent rights of fishing over the whole north-east coast, and on the west coast as far south as Cow Head;

3. An absolute right to purchase, paying port charges and light dues, a full supply of bait at anchor in any port of entry in Newfoundland during the fishing season, subject only to the same regulations as our local fishermen.

In return for these valuable privileges, what should we ask? I think we might demand:—

1. That the French give up their impracticable and absurd claims, and give us a free and uninterrupted right of fishing on all

the north-east and west coasts of the treaty shore, except where the French are allowed exclusive rights; and should also give us—

2. An English consul at St. Pierre;
3. And an undertaking to prevent the export of intoxicating liquors in their fishing vessels except for ship's use.

This simple arrangement would solve a great many of the present difficulties. It would not wound French pride, they would have the inestimable advantage of obtaining at all times a sure and certain supply of bait fresh from the nets, it would prevent the present wanton destruction of the bait fishes, and put an end to smuggling. The plan could be easily carried out. Some Newfoundlanders might object to it, and no doubt the St. Pierre shopkeepers would strongly oppose any arrangement which would put an end to their lucrative trade of smuggling. This suggestion is entirely my own; it is a good working arrangement, and should be acceptable to all but the extremists on both sides. Under no circumstances should bait be allowed to be exported to St. Pierre. Recent experience has taught the bait dealers that the indiscriminate sale of bait to the French is suicidal folly even for them. Every sensible man in Fortune Bay will approve of my proposal.

CHAPTER XVI.

REIGN OF VICTORIA.

1857-1895.

1858.—First Atlantic cable landed in Trinity Bay, but soon ceased to act.

1860.—Prince of Wales visited the Island. Formation of the Volunteer Corps.

1861.—H. W. Hoyles became Premier; political riots in St. John's, Harbour Grace, and Harbour Main.

1862.—Great distress owing to bad fisheries. Steamers used in the seal fishery.

1863.—Hon. L. O'Brien, Administrator. Revenue collected at Labrador.

1864.—Sir A. Musgrave, Governor. Confederation of the Dominion of Canada. Copper mining commenced at Tilt Cove. The Currency Act confirmed.

1865.—Present Geological Survey commenced. F. B. T. Carter became Premier, and Sir H. W. Hoyles, Chief Justice.

1866.—Second Atlantic Cable successfully landed at Heart's Content.

1867.—Fishery very successful. The British North America Act for the Confederation of the Provinces is passed. Dominion of Canada proclaimed.

1868.—Proclamation issued by the Carter Administration suppressing able-bodied poor relief.

1869.—Sir Stephen Hill appointed Governor. General Elections; Confederation candidates defeated. Census taken. Dr. Mullock died.

1870.—Hon. C. F. Bennett became Premier.

1871.—Garrison withdrawn from Newfoundland. Treaty of Washington.

1873.—Direct Steam to England by Allan Line commenced. General Election; Bennett Government defeated.

1874.—The largest cod-fishery ever known in Newfoundland. Sir F. B. T. Carter became Premier. The Royal Commission; Sir B. Robinson, J. Goodfellow and J. Fox, Esquires.

1875.—The first Government Railway Survey under direction of Sandford Fleming, Civil Engineer.

1876.—Sir J. H. Glover, G.C.M.G., Governor. Halifax Fishery Commission met; $5,500,000 awarded as compensation to be paid by the United States to the British Provinces; Newfoundland's share, one million; Sir W. V. Whiteway, Commissioner for Newfoundland. Bishop Feild died, in Bermuda.

1877.—Sir F. B. T. Carter appointed Acting Assistant Judge. Commander W. Howorth, R.N., appointed first Stipendiary Magistrate, West Coast, by Imperial and Colonial Governments; duties first collected there.

1878.—Sir W. V. Whiteway became Premier.

1880.—Sir F. B. T. Carter appointed Chief Justice; Colonial Government allowed to make grants of land on the West Coast or "French Shore" so-called. Sir F. B. T. Carter, K.C.M.G., Administrator. First Railway Bill passed.

1881.—Serious disturbance on the railway line (Battle of Fox Trap). Sir Henry Fitz-Hardinge Maxse, Governor. First Railway under construction in Newfoundland; St. John's to Harbour Grace.

1882.—An Act passed for the construction of the Great American and European Short Line Railway. Charter granted for the construction of a Graving Dock. Sir W. V. Whiteway became Premier.

1883.—St. Stephen's Day Harbour Grace riots. Sir F. B. T. Carter, Administrator. Sir H. Maxse died in St. John's. Sir John H. Glover, G.C.M.G., appointed Governor. Dry Dock at Riverhead, St. John's, opened. H.M.S. *Tenelos* docked. Fishery Exhibition held in London; Sir A. Shea, K.C.M.G., Commissioner for the Colony. Railway to Harbour Grace opened for passengers. Hon. E. Morris, Administrator in absence of Sir F. B. T. Carter, K.C.M.G.

1885.—Ford-Pennell Convention on French fishery claims. Sir F. B. T. Carter Administrator. Sir Robert Thorburn, Premier. General Election.

1886.—Report of Joint Committee on Fishery question. Placentia Railway commenced. Sir F. B. T. Carter, Administrator. Sir G. W. Des Vœux appointed Governor.

1887.—The Bait Act became Law. Sir H. A. Blake, Governor. Ballot Act passed. Queen's Jubilee: Service in English Cathedral attended by all denominations of Protestants. Sir A. Shea, K.C.M.G., appointed Governor of the Bahamas. Colonial Conference held in London; Colony represented by Sir R. Thorburn, Premier, and Sir A. Shea.

1888.—Second Washington Treaty negotiated; Hon. J. S. Winter represented the Colony. *Modus vivendi* established for two years. Bait Act put in operation in March. Placentia Railway opened for traffic. Act to provide Municipal Council for St. John's passed. Sir T. N. O'Brien appointed Governor. Sir F. B. T. Carter Administrator to January 1889.

1889.—General Election; Thorburn Government defeated by an immense majority. Sir W. V. Whiteway, Premier.

1890.—Act authorising new Railway Line North. Agitation concerning the *modus vivendi* with the French about Lobster Factories West Coast. Reciprocity Treaty with United States by Hon. R. Bond, Colonial Secretary; prevented being carried into effect by Canada. Delegation to England on difficulties with the French.

1891.—Municipal Council Act amended. Delegation to England on difficulties with French. International arbitration on Lobster question to be held at Brussels. Hall's Bay Railway completed to Trinity and Bonavista Bays. Celebrated case of Baird v. Walker, arising out of *modus vivendi*, determined by Supreme Court in favour of plaintiff; confirmed by the Privy Council. Newfoundland Bill in the House of Commons.

1892.—Death of the Duke of Clarence, January 14th. Terrible calamity and loss of life in Trinity Bay, February 28th. Great fire in St. John's on 8th and 9th of July.

1893.—General election; Sir W. Whiteway's Government returned by a large majority.

1894.—Election petitions, sixteen members unseated. Goodridge Government formed. Failure of the Commercial and Union Banks and many mercantile houses. Greene Government formed.

1895.—Disability Bill sanctioned by the Imperial Government. Sir W. V. Whiteway, Premier.

I am conscious of many sins of omission and commission in the preparation of this most difficult part of my subject; whilst endeavouring to write a true history of the period, I have had also to walk, like Agag before Saul, delicately, in order to avoid offence. Many minor events which I have not included in the text will be found in the notes and the chronology. The history of St. Pierre and Miquelon, one of the most amusing episodes in our Island story, and an account of the Labrador, will be found in a separate chapter.

Many persons have imagined that the frequent election rows in Newfoundland, about this period, were the outcome of religious bigotry, but a better understanding of the facts will show us that this is an incorrect view. There is no real bigotry or sectarian intolerance in Newfoundland; all these riots were made to order. Dr. Johnson has defined

ANGLICAN CATHEDRAL AND THE NARROWS, ST. JOHN'S, IN 1857.
From a drawing by the Hon. and Rev. W. Grey.

patriotism as "the last refuge of a scoundrel." The sham patriots who instigated their dupes to get up these disturbances often made religion a stalking horse for their designs on the Treasury; the blatant demagogues who cried out that the Catholic Church was in danger, or that the sacred rights of Protestantism were being trampled on, always bloomed out after the *mêlée* as fat officials. Instigated by these designing rogues, a few rowdies and bludgeon men led the way, and the simple crowd that followed were led to believe that their rights or their religion were in danger; in American political slang this is known as "bulldozing."

For a few years after the inception of the Legislature these tactics were pre-eminently successful, especially in Conception Bay. We hear most about riots by Catholic mobs, but the attacks on Catholics by Protestants, in Bay Roberts and other places, were equally disgraceful. The riots of 1861 marked the end of this discreditable violence; it was all caused by unscrupulous politicians, there was no strong popular sentiment to sustain it; disorder and political rowdyism completely died away shortly after these events of 1861; it would never have arisen had the principles of amalgamation[1] and fair play to all parties been carried out on the introduction of responsible government; but the Protestants and the Merchants' party blindly resisted the new movement, and the Liberals and Catholics, being wiser in their generation, and more skilful politicians, though representing really a minority of the population, gained the ascendency, and kept it from 1855 to 1861. Having kept power so long, they were loth to give it up; they made a terrible outcry when they were turned out in 1861. When the elections were fairly contested, the Protestant party, representing a majority of the people, easily won. In their turn they kept all the departmental offices for themselves; it is due to Sir Hugh Hoyles's memory, however, to state that he offered his opponents a fair share in the Government—the Presidentship of the Council, held by Hon. L. O'Brien, and two departmental offices—but the Catholics either could not, or would not, coalesce with him. The principle of amalgamation, giving all classes and creeds a fair share of the offices and patronage, was not carried into effect until 1865, under the Liberal Administration of Sir Frederick Carter. Since then, the relative position of the great religious bodies has completely changed; formerly their numbers were nearly balanced, now the Protestants outnumber the Catholics by nearly two to one.

Sir Alexander Bannerman's administration of the Government lasted from 1857 to 1863; the period was marked by prosperity. In the year following his arrival, Hon. P. F. Little, the able leader of the Liberal

SIR B. ROBINSON.
Bro Hoyles, K

---

[1] Mr. Little offered Mr. Hoyles the Attorney Generalship if he would assist in the movement for responsible government; Hoyles refused. No offers were made on the formation of the first Ministry in 1855.

party, retired from politics, and was appointed an assistant judge of the Supreme Court; the Hon. A. W. Des Barres and J. Simms, assistant judges of the Supreme Court, having been pensioned, Mr. B. Robinson and Mr. Little were appointed in their places; two more able and efficient judges never graced the Bench.

One of the most notable events in 1859 was the hotly contested election of that year. Burin was what the Americans call the pivotal district; there has never been in this Colony anything like the struggle which took place there; every office holder of the old Assembly, and every Liberal supporter, was requisitioned for the campaign fund. Mr. Glen, who managed this part of the business, was inexorable; members and officials fought against the demands of the stern old Receiver-General, but all had to pay down their money. Hoyles and Evans were the Conservative candidates, the Liberals were represented by A. Shea and J. J. Rogerson; they were well matched opponents. Mr. Shea, now Sir Ambrose, was the greatest politician of his party, one of the most able men the Colony has produced, and amongst his co-religionists far away the greatest of them all; he had an opponent worthy of his steel in the Conservative leader, Sir Hugh Hoyles. What the contest cost has never been made public, purity of election was then undreamt of. The Liberals were credited with spending about £2,000; Mr. Hoyles paid all his own expenses. The contest was exceedingly close, but the tactics of Mr. Shea, and the intimidation of electors by the celebrated Cody ("who had a claim") at Flat Islands and elsewhere, helped materially to gain the day.

JOHN STUART [1]
By S. H. Parsons.

The Liberals again carried the Government—the Hon. J. Kent was Premier and Colonial Secretary; Hon. G. J. Hogsett, Attorney-General, Mr. Shea, Speaker. The new administration was inferior in strength to Mr. Little's cabinet. Mr. Kent, as Premier, was a most honest and capable official, but his temper was uncertain, he never enjoyed the complete confidence of the Catholic party and of Dr. Mullock

---

[1] John Stuart, of the old firm of Rennie Stuart & Co., was the most popular man in Newfoundland; for over 30 years he performed the duties of the two responsible offices of clerk to the House of Assembly and the Board of Works. A most able official, kindliest and most genial of men, his death left a void in the House and our hearts which can never be filled.

like his predecessor; the real leader was Mr. A. Shea. Though the sunshine of prosperity had risen upon them, it did not last; from 1859 to 1861 there were serious divisions in the party, the strong and skilful hand of Mr. Little was no longer felt, and the great Liberal party began to fall to pieces. Shea and Kent did not work harmoniously together. In 1860 the fisheries partially failed, there was consequent distress, and a lavish expenditure of relief to able-bodied poor; Mr. Kent, I believe, was opposed to this indiscriminate expenditure. In the autumn of 1860 there was a special session of the Legislature held before Christmas; it was soon manifest to outsiders that there was war in the Liberal camp.

A serious conflict had arisen earlier in the year, between Bishop Mulock and the administration, which called out the celebrated letter given below.[1] His lordship and Mr. Justice Little, on a visit to New York, had virtually made a contract with the owners of the steamer *Victoria* to run this vessel

HON. JOHN KENT.
By Chisholm.

---

[1] "To the Catholic people of the Diocese of St. John's.

"My dear people,   June, 1860.

"I address you this letter on a matter of vital importance to your interests, and I consider that my advocacy of everything connected with the improvement of the country gives me a right to offer you a few words of advice. The great and paramount want of Newfoundland is a facility of communication between the capital and the outports; as long as the outports are left isolated, so long will education, religion, and civilization, be left in the background. Newfoundland must remain in that state of darkness to which ages of bad government have reduced it. I solemnly declare that without steam communication the people must remain poor, degraded, and ignorant. Forced by the indignant voice of the people, those whom you call your representatives passed a Bill granting £3,000 a year for five years for outport steam. It appears that by a dishonest quibble, intended to defeat the project, two steamers were smuggled into the Bill so as to render the offer illusory, in plain English a humbug.

"A beautiful steamer, in every way adapted for the purpose, engaged to do the service north and south twice a month, was offered in New York; I visited the ship myself, and if she was not all that was specified, the contract could be terminated at three months' notice. She had every accommodation for passengers and would have done more to develop the interests of the out-harbours than all the Houses of Assembly that ever met on the Island.

"The Government, when they saw the matter brought to a point, refused to engage her. What was intended only to delude the people was about to become a reality, and the contract was repudiated. How does it happen that an enormous revenue, wasted in providing useless places for *State paupers*, cannot afford the sum of £3,000 a year for outport accommodation? Year by year every improvement is put off for want of means, though every infant even in Newfoundland pays in taxes £1 a head. Will strangers believe that in a British Colony the shire town of Fortune Bay is in reality further from us than Constantinople? but then we have the satisfaction of seeing thousands upon thousands of pounds distributed amongst our *locust-like officials*. We pay heavy taxes, but get comparatively no return; almost all goes in salaries and pretended compensations, and I have no hesitation in saying that the collection of a revenue under the present system is nothing but *legalized robbery*. I am aware

THE PRINCE OF WALES AT ST. JOHN'S.

twice a month north and south. An Act had been passed granting £3,000 a year for local steam, and the bishop, a most vigorous supporter of improved communications both by steam and telegraph, was terribly wroth when his own particular Government refused to recognise his authority to commit them to a contract; when his lordship found that the Government firmly refused to charter the *Victoria*, he then unceed Mr. Kent's administration in this scathing epistle.

The year that marked the publication of Bishop Mullock's letter is also distinguished in our annals by the arrival of His Royal Highness the Prince of Wales on his way to Canada and the United States. The visit, which lasted from the 22nd to the 25th July 1860, was a complete success; the town was given up to festivity and rejoicing, the young heir apparent won all hearts by his grace and courtesy. We did honour to our future sovereign by a grand ball, a regatta, a review, and the gift of a dog[3] from the breed of the celebrated Earl Sullivan. Much of the success of the Prince's visit was due to Sir Alexander and Lady Bannerman, the Duke of Newcastle's tact, and the geniality and refined courtesy of old Earl St. Germains, the excellent management of General

THE PRINCE OF WALES.

---

that my name has been made use of to prop up the supporters of this system, but I consider it due to myself, and to those whose interests I advocate, to repudiate any connexion with a party who take care of themselves, but do nothing for the people. This is not a political or a religious question, it is one of civilization, in which Catholics and Protestants, priests and ministers, are equally interested."

[1] Newfoundland owes a deep debt of gratitude to Dr. Mullock; he was not only the active, earnest promoter of steam communication, both local and transatlantic, for the Colony, he was the first to advocate a railway to Harbour Grace and telegraphic communication. The steamer *Victoria*, Captain Culworth, eventually inaugurated local steam communication north and south; she was utterly unfitted to the service; in September 1861 she completely broke down, and had to return to New York. In 1863, the S.S. *Ariel* was put on the route north and south, by her owner, Hon. Captain Cleary; under her most careful commander, Hagan, she did excellent work, until she was finally replaced by the steamers *Tiger* and *Leopard*. In 1877 the *Curlew* and *Plover* began a very efficient service. In 1888 the fine steamers *Volunteer* and *Conscript* of the Coastal Steamships Company performed the work. These splendid boats were a vast improvement on the former coastal steamers.

[2] This dog, "Cabot," was afterwards the subject of an amusing law suit. Cabot was a very fine animal, and Sullivan charged a royal price for him, which the committee thought exorbitant.

Bruce, the Prince's Governor, and the popular gay young Captains Grey and Teesdale, the hero of Kars. All went merry as a marriage bell during the three lovely summer days of the Prince's stay amongst us; one and all did their best to make the auspicious occasion a truly joyous time; our volunteer turn-out and review was a great success.

The spring session of 1861 was marked with more dissensions in the Government ranks about poor relief.[1] An injudicious utterance of the Premier brought matters to a climax; the strife in the party was so keen that there would have been a split even if this untoward event had not happened. Mr. Kent, in his place in the House of Assembly, openly accused Sir Alexander Bannerman of conspiracy with the judges,[2] the lawyers, and the minority in the House of Assembly, to defeat the Government Bill fixing the value to be given to sterling money in the payment of official salaries. This accusation appeared in the newspapers. The Governor wrote to the Colonial Secretary asking for an explanation; Mr. Kent replied that he did not consider himself called upon to give an account of his utterances as a member of the Legislature to His Excellency.[3] Immediately on receiving this communication, Sir Alexander dismissed his ministry and called upon the leader of the Opposition, Mr. Hoyles, to form a new administration. Mr. Hoyles selected his Government, and announced its formation to the Assembly.

SIR H. HOYLES.
By the Stereoscopic Company.

The House was immediately dissolved, and a general election took place in April 1861.[4] There was no contest in Burin, and no conflict or

---

[1] Bishop Mullock wrote an indignant letter about the distribution of poor relief. Mr. Kent tried honestly to curtail and regulate the expenditure. He found a conspiracy against him, headed by Mr. Shea. Mr. P. Nowlan brought in a resolution "that any regulations made on the subject of poor relief should not ignore the just influences of the representatives of the people." Mr. Kent declared he "was attacked by a miserable faction who sought his political destruction; a set of frozen serpents, which having been warmed into life had stung the breast which gave it vitality. There was no doubt a Judas at the bottom of all these proceedings . . . It was well known who was the person behind the scenes, some designing, cozening, cunning rogue who for ambition or vindictive purposes had devised this treason against the Government."

[2] Judge Robinson had always contended that *sterling* could only mean British sterling, i.e., dollars at 4s. 2d. It had been the practice to use two sterlings, one a colonial sterling dollar at 4s. 4d. and another, designated as British sterling, at 4s. 2d. Judge Robinson petitioned the House against the passage of this Bill, urging his claim to be paid his official salary in British sterling.

[3] In a debate on this question, Mr. Hoyles stated that Mr. Kent had not consulted his colleagues before replying to the Governor. Mr. Hogsett contradicted him; "He consulted me," said the ex-Attorney-General. "Then if he consulted you," replied Mr. Hoyles, "he would be sure to put his foot in it."

[4] For the result of the election, see p. 664.

riot, except in the districts of St. John's, Harbour Grace, and Harbour Main. The result completely changed the position of political parties. There was a serious disturbance in Harbour Main between the rival Catholic candidates, Hogsett and Furey, on one side, Nowlan and Byrne on the other. The attempt to invade Cats Cove (now Conception Harbour) with a strong Harbour Main contingent caused terrible bitterness, the death of one man, and the looting and destruction of property. After a protracted contest before the election committee, Nowlan and Byrne were subsequently declared duly elected.

On the 13th of May 1861, the Governor opened the new House of Assembly, His Excellency was hooted, and a violent mob surrounded the Colonial Building and attempted to break through the doors.[1] Messrs. Hogsett and Furey, who claimed to be elected for Harbour Main on a certificate from the returning officer, which it was afterwards stated was obtained by intimidation, took their seats in the House. They were ordered to withdraw from the Assembly; they refused; Mr. Hogsett was then removed by the police, and Mr. Furey followed.

Later on the same day, there was a serious riot in St. John's; a mob broke into the premises of Messrs. Nowlan and Kitchen (relatives of Mr. P. Nowlan, the member for Harbour Main), on Water Street. The soldiers were ordered out, Col. Grant and Judge Little and Father Jeremiah O'Donnell did all in their power to calm the violence of the mob and to persuade them to retire; the magistrate read the Riot Act, but all to no purpose; stones were thrown at the military, an attempt was made to drag Colonel Grant from his horse. Finally, it is alleged, a shot was fired at the soldiers, and reluctantly the commander was then compelled to give the order to fire.[2] Three people were

---

[1] I remember looking at the mob from the windows of the House of Assembly. A crowd tried to break in at the lower western door; a tall Irishman, whose name was never known, put his back against the door and defended it against the whole excited rabble.

[2] It is but fair on this question to place side by side with my own views the arguments put forward on the Liberal side. They contend that the Governor should not have dismissed his Ministry for the act of one member; that it was unlawful to exclude Hogsett and Furey from the House of Assembly; that the police force and special constables should have been used to stop the riot—to all who were present at the *mêlée* of 13th May this idea of the police maintaining order is simply absurd; in presence of such a mob the small police force of that day were utterly powerless. A review of the whole evidence given on the inquest clearly exonerated the authorities from all blame; there is not a shadow of a case against either Mr. Carter or Mr. Bennett, the magistrates. The behaviour of Col. Grant was most forbearing; for nearly two hours he endeavoured to make the mob retire peaceably. The *Newfoundlander* that attacked Mr. Hoyles and the Governor so bitterly on this subject, made the same attack on the Government about the Harbour Grace election. What was the result there when order was restored and the election fairly conducted? Both Messrs. Hayward and Moore were returned by double the number of votes received by Prendergast.

No one can doubt now that Sir Alexander was fully justified in dismissing the Premier and his Ministry when he made such a charge against the Queen's Representative, and refused to withdraw or apologise. Hon. T. Talbot, sheriff (the Protector of the District Judges), an eminent and devout Catholic, says, in his short History of the Colony: " No Governor fit for his position would have taken any other course than the one adopted killed and twenty wounded; amongst the injured was the estimable Father O'Donnell, for whom great sympathy was expressed among all classes.

The whole trouble was due to the turbulence of the defeated candidate Hogsett and the violence of a few rowdies. The unfortunate riot in St. John's was the direct outcome of the Harbour Main election. For a time it appeared like an organised attempt to make parliamentary government impossible; thanks, however, to the exertions of Bishop Mullock and his clergy, and the general good sense of the community, order was completely restored. The next day the town was as quiet as usual; Colonel Grant walked up through the city alone with his cane and a little dog to attend at the inquest. It was fortunate for us at this stage of our history that the reins of government were in the hands of one who, in this terrible crisis, showed a firmness, and cool, undaunted courage that won the admiration of his fiercest opponents. Sir Hugh Hoyles, the leader of the new Government, and, we may say, the whole Administration rolled into one, soon after 1861, when the angry passion of this evil time subsided, became not only the most respected, but the most popular, man in the Colony, beloved by all classes.[1]

HON. J. TALBOT.

by Sir Alexander Bannerman." After all, the best answer to all objections made against both the Governor and Mr. Hoyles is the result of the appeal to the constituencies; when the elections were fairly conducted a good working majority of their own party, over and above their Catholic allies, was obtained to sustain their action.

[1] THE RIOTS OF 1861.
Newfoundlander, May 14th, 1861.

"The military should never be called out, and never are called out, where prudence and good order prevail, until the civil powers of repression have been proved insufficient, and this was notoriously not the case here, for the means of increasing them to efficiency in the way we suggest had been neglected. Well, what might have been anticipated followed; the presence of the troops excited anew the fury of some of the townspeople. Those who had been before then dispersing began to collect again; stones were thrown at the soldiers; Colonel Grant was insulted and struck; provocation followed provocation, and the order was given to fire. Then came that terrific discharge which yet thrills with horror every soul who heard it, that sound which told of slaughter to the innocent and guilty, perhaps to the innocent alone, as the blow might chance to fall; and then was the air rent with such shrieks as the sudden and awful sense of the death summons can alone produce. Seven shots told, three of them mortally; one man, named Clifford, an aged widow's only son and support, died on the instant. The two others, Hunt and Fitzpatrick, lingered but a short time; the latter was an elderly invalid, who had only the day before come out of the hospital, and though, unhappily for the poor fellow, making one of the crowd, quite incapable of mischief, both from age and infirmity. Amongst the wounded, we grieve to say, was the Rev. Jeremiah O'Donnell, one of the most esteemed and loved priest in the island. Exhausted from his previous labours of the day, he called a respectable man, named Patrick Mirick, whom he saw in the crowd, and took him to lean on and help him through, while he entreated and implored them, for the love of God, to keep the peace and retire to their homes. While thus engaged in the divine work of peace, this most amiable and worthy priest received a shot which passed through his ankle. He was taken into a neighbouring house for a while, and then, in a most painful and prostrate condition, carried home on a bed; poor

Out of evil sometimes comes good; the direct result of all this rioting and violence, all this storm of violent partisanship and sectarian strife, was to put an end for ever to religious ascendency on both sides. After a short respite, it became the settled rule in the formation of our Government that all religious parties should be fairly represented in the arrangement of an administration and in the distribution of offices. As a direct result, sectarianism in politics, bigotry, and intolerance, have year by year diminished.

The year 1861 witnessed the commencement of the great civil war between the North and South; many of the blockade runners made St. John's a port of call on their way to and from the Southern States.

The following year, 1862, will always be remembered as "the spring of the *Polynia* and *Camperdown*," two Dundee whalers that were sent out to prosecute the seal fishery. Within the memory of man there has never been such an ice blockade; for weeks and weeks it blew a "solid" north-easter; the sealing steamers did not take a seal. The ill wind, however, blew wealth untold into Green Bay; all along our

---

Mirick, who was with him, was shot in the thigh, and, of course, very seriously injured. When the alarm rang through the crowd that the priest had been shot down, their strongest feelings were aroused to a degree, seemingly, beyond all control, and infuriated demands for vengeance were heard in every direction. At this critical juncture came again the most praiseworthy services of the Catholic clergy and Judge Little. They positively left no means unemployed to restrain the people, and had they done less than they did, we are assured by undoubted eye-witnesses that direful retaliation would have followed. The judge, at imminent peril to his life from stones on the one hand and musket balls on the other, rushed into the middle of the mêlée. He called upon the magistrate, Mr. Bennett, to retire the troops for the safety of the town. Mr. Bennett declined. The judge then asserted his own superior authority, and assured Colonel Grant of peace if he would withdraw his soldiers. This assurance was strongly endorsed by Crockwell, J.P., who came up at the moment, and with wise and cool discernment saw and declared the judge's proposed course to be the right one in all respects. The Colonel at once consented, with an expression of deep regret for what had taken place, and requested the judge to accompany him and his men to barracks, which was accordingly done. Meanwhile, between eight and nine o'clock, the powerful summons of the cathedral bells bade the terrified and enraged multitude repair from amidst scenes of crime and blood to the House of God, there to hear the voice of their chief pastor. The thoroughfares began at once to empty themselves in that direction, and in a few minutes a vast multitude had assembled within the cathedral. The Right Rev. Dr. Mullock appeared on the altar in pontificals, and, with heartfelt and melting supplications, conjured the people to be calm, to keep the peace, and to go to their homes. He then presented to them the Chalice containing the Most Holy Sacrament, and exacted a promise from all present that, for the honour of the Divine Presence, they would obey his instructions, and endeavour to induce all within their influence to do the same. Soon after this all externally was restored to tranquillity, and no disturbance or breach of the peace took place in the night. His Lordship, on the following evening, repeated his exhortation to peace, and with such excellent effect that, thank God, all is well up to the time we write. The present is not the moment for recrimination or for any other words than those which may tend, with Heaven's help, to soften down passion stimulated to madness.

"At a more fitting period responsibility for the present state of the community will doubtless be fixed upon its causes and accessories. But now the immediate and paramount duty of all is to strain every nerve for the conservation of peace and order, and to avoid, as far as possible, every subject or proceeding calculated to freshen or keep alive the bitter aching memories of those events we have endeavoured to describe. We are happy to be enabled to add that Father O'Donnell, for whom such universal sympathy exists, is satisfactorily recovering from the effects of his accident."

northern coast the catch of seals by shore men was the largest on record; £25,000 was made by one firm, Muir and Duder, out of this remarkable windfall. The cod fishery of this year was a partial, and the ship seal fishery almost a complete failure [1]—the worst season since 1845—the whole export of seal skins amounting only to two hundred and sixty thousand.

In the following year Sir Alexander Bannerman [2] resigned his Governorship; he was a man well stricken in years, and died in the year following his retirement from Newfoundland. He will long be honoured in our memories as an honest, straightforward administrator; a genial, kindly, liberal old Scotchman, with a dry, pawky humour, essentially Aberdonian. I do not remember that he had any prejudice in the world except against the Galway line.

The early spring of this year was marked with the terrible shipwreck of the S.S. *Anglo-Saxon* at Clam Cove on 27th, accompanied with great

SIR A. BANNERMAN.
From an old portrait.

---

[1] The season of 1862 was unprecedented; for fifty-two days the wind was inshore, N.E. to E.N.E., and for more than two months not a drop of rain fell. The papers of the day speak of the certain decline of the seal fishery. They attribute the losses made in this industry to the large size and expense of the more modern vessels. The *Newfoundlander*, of 7th April, 1862, says:—

"New capital will certainly not be invested to any amount in the costly ships that have been in vogue of late years, and it looks as though the choice will be between the vessels of the olden time and screw steamers. We think, whether we will or no, the trade will come to be carried on by means of steamers. Their failure in the present year [*Polyna* and *Camperdown*], when all have failed from causes without precedent, and beyond all human control, will, perhaps, not deter the same parties from another attempt; and should the adventure succeed, we must go to work with all the same means, or be content to abandon the enterprise altogether."

LETTER FROM CAPTAIN E. WHITE TO JOB BROS, 6th April 1862.
Eranthes at Sea.

After referring to the wind, N.N.E. and E.N.E., and sea, he says:—

"As to losses, I am afraid the number will be fearful. I have seen some six or eight go down the last few days, among which are the *Emily Tobin*, *Melrose*, and the *Margaret*, besides several others I cannot name. While I am writing there is so much sea, and the ice is so heavy, that I cannot tell the minute the sides of my vessel will be driven in. I have driven from the Funks since the 28th ult. tightly jammed. We are now off Cape St. Francis and expect to drive to Cape Race before getting clear. . . . . The young harps are all in Green Bay and White Bay, the vessels cannot enter more than half a mile in the jam of ice, and then they subject themselves to damage and loss from the fearful sea." The spring of 1894 very much resembled this extraordinary season.

[2] Sir Alexander Bannerman, Knt., born 1783, died 1864, a cousin of the baronet of that name, was for many years an extensive shipowner, merchant and banker of Aberdeen, and M.P. for Aberdeen in the Liberal interest from 1832 to 1847. He was elected Dean of the Faculty in Marischal College, Aberdeen, and appointed, by Lord Melbourne, Commissioner of Greenwich Hospital; knighted in 1851 on his appointment as Governor of Prince Edward's Island, thence to Bahamas in 1854, Newfoundland in 1857 to 1863. Lady Bannerman, née Margaret Gordon, survived her husband several years; she was an intimate friend of the great General Gordon, and the celebrated Margaret beloved by Thomas Carlyle.

SEALING VESSELS LEAVING ST. JOHN'S NFLD.

SEALING STEAMER "VANGUARD"

STEAMERS AT THE SEAL FISHERY.

loss of life. The steamer *Bloodhound*, belonging to Baine, Johnston & Co., commanded by the late Captain Alexander Graham, and the *Wolf*, belonging to Walter Grieve & Co., William Kean master, inaugurated the employment of steam in the seal fishery. The first attempt was a comparative failure; the *Bloodhound* arrived, 22nd April, with three thousand, and the *Wolf*, with thirteen hundred seals, on the 28th.[1]

A limited supply of water was provided for St. John's by the water company instituted in 1848. The flow was derived from George's Pond, Signal Hill, and was found very beneficial; later on there was a demand for a larger and fuller supply. In 1863 the town was at length furnished with an almost unlimited quantity of water from Winsor Lake, by the General Water Company. A great blunder was made in the engineering by an official whom the company had distinctly refused to employ. Sir A. Shea and the other directors weakly gave way, and the works cost the Colony about $120,000 more than they should have done. However, we cannot grumble, the supply of pure water is simply invaluable, and, if properly managed, it offers a complete protection against fire. No town in the world has such a water supply as St. John's, in proportion to its population. The natural pressure is sufficient to reach the highest points in the city. The supply is beautifully soft, clear, cool, and absolutely pure drinking water; much of the success of the water company is due to the good management of our veteran sportsman, John Martin.

WALTER GRIEVE.
By Moffatt, Edinburgh.

HON. L. O'BRIEN.
From an old photograph.

During the interval between the departure of Sir Alexander in 1863, and the arrival of Governor Musgrave in 1864, Hon. Lawrence O'Brien,

---

[1] The next trip of the SS. *Bloodhound* is commemorated in a local poem:—
"The *Mary Joyce*,
 Is stuck in the ice,
   And so is the *Bloodhound* too,
 Young Bill Ryan left Terry behind
   To paddle his own canoe."

President of the Council, administered the government with dignity and efficiency. During the four years of Mr. Musgrave's tenure of the Governorship there were great changes, progress, and poverty. Sir Anthony was an amiable and painstaking administrator; he was thought a great deal of at the Colonial Office as an able writer of despatches, and no doubt he made the Home Government believe that he was able to carry confederation in the Colony; he never, however, had any real power or influence in Newfoundland.[1] By the end of 1864 Sir Hugh Hoyles' health had so completely failed that he was no longer able to bear the heavy burthen of his office; he had literally worked himself to death's door. In 1865 he became Chief Justice of the Supreme Court, a position of comparative ease—as a lawyer Sir Hugh was unrivalled. He made a model judge, the most painstaking, able and impartial administrator of justice that ever graced the bench of any British colony—an indefatigable worker, he gave no complaints for the law's delays. His decision of character, his amiable manners and his extreme courtesy endeared him to all. We were all proud of Sir Hugh as the most distinguished Newfoundlander of our day. The leadership of the party naturally fell on the shoulders of the present Chief Justice. In the election of 1865 Sir Frederick's Government was sustained by a large majority.

SIR A. MUSGRAVE, K.C.M.G.
By Dorner Abbott.

SIR F. B. T. CARTER, K.C.M.G.
By S. H. Parsons.

The great political movement of the time was the confederation of British North America. To complete the union our Island was necessarily included in the scheme; Sir Frederick and Sir Ambrose Shea were sent as our delegates to the great confederation conference, and returned

---

[1] Sir Anthony Musgrave, K.C.M.G. (1875) C.M.G. 1871, was Private Secretary to Mr. Mackintosh when Governor-in-Chief of the Leeward Islands, 1850-54; entered as student at the Inner Temple, 1851; appointed treasury accountant at Antigua, 1852; resumed legal studies at the Temple in 1853; appointed Colonial Secretary of Antigua, February 1854; administrator of the Colony of Nevis, October 1860; Administrator of Government of St. Vincent, April 1861; appointed Lieutenant-Governor of St. Vin-

with a draft of the terms on which we might become united with the Dominion. The proposals to unite our destinies with Canada were not received with enthusiasm. The main question was one of terms; what would Canada give us in return for surrendering our independence? The offer from the Dominion on the all-important subject of a railway and a steam ferry has hitherto been vague and uncertain; but even if any such tangible offer had been made before 1869, looking back now at the excited condition of our population on the subject, I very much doubt if any terms would have been accepted. The anti-confederate party were strong in numbers, powerful in organisation, and their leader, Mr. Charles Fox Bennett, showed himself a most able and indefatigable political campaigner. The awful tales that were told about taxation, about ramming the new-born babes down Canadian cannon, "bleaching their bones on the desert sands of Canada," had a tremendous effect on the simple out-harbour people. There still lingers amongst them a traditionary remembrance of the sufferings their forefathers endured from the French Canadian and Indian raids made in the seventeenth and eighteenth century, and this partly accounts for their dread of Canada: Irish national feeling, their hatred of the Union, brought about by fraud and bribery, was also appealed to. The result was an overwhelming defeat for the Confederate party; they were simply annihilated, and from that day to this Confederation has never been put forward before the country as a practical political question.[1]

Both from an Imperial and Colonial point, the union of the British North American Colonies is a consummation devoutly to be wished: it is all a question of terms. There are, however, some objections to union. Since the death of the great Sir John A. McDonald there is no statesman in Canada strong enough to guarantee us such terms as we would accept. There are also great drawbacks in Canada's protectionist tariff; the Dominion is a fish producer and not a fish consumer; our business relations and our future market lie with the United States; the customers and consumers of our inexhaustible fisheries are the sixty-three million Americans. Canada's latest move on the Blaine

---

cent, May 1862; Governor of Newfoundland, April 1864; Governor of British Columbia, June 1869; Lieutenant-Governor of Natal, May 1872; Governor of South Australia, 1873; Governor of Jamaica, 1877; Governor of Victoria, where he died. He married the only daughter of David Dudley Field, of New York. Sir Anthony came to this Colony with the full assurance of carrying confederation. He was a good writer, and an amiable man, who made few enemies.

[1] Our modern Newfoundland legislators have earned fame in various ways. Sir W. V. Whiteway will be handed down to posterity as the introducer and successful promoter of the railway; Sir Robert Thorburn is immortalized by a great road—the Thorburn turnpike; Mr. Goodridge as the Rupert of debate; Sir James Winter for his connexion with the Chamberlain-Blaine Treaty; Mr. Murray for his amusing campaign literature; but all these celebrities sink into insignificance compared with the first introducer of the public grindstone, where every man could grind his own axe at the public expense. Skipper John Bartlett, the anti-

Bond Convention has alienated the feelings of many Newfoundlanders who were formerly Confederates.

Great impetus was given to mining by the operation of C. F. Bennett and Smith McKay in the great Tilt Cove Mine in 1864, to-day one of the finest copper deposits in the Colony. The geological survey was commenced under the late Mr. Alexr. Murray, C.M.G. in 1865, continued by his able successor, Mr. Jas. Howley, F.R.G.S. In 1866 the telegraph cable was successfully landed in Hearts Content; in August the end of the 1865 cable was picked up, and the gulf cable repaired by McKay in the *Bloodhound*. 1867 is noted as the year of the "great fishery" and the great Labrador gale; the destruction of boats, shipping, and stages was enormous. The large firms had most of their losses covered by insurance; to the poor settlers and small planters it was a terrible calamity. In 1868 a vigorous effort was made by the Carter Government to suppress able-bodied poor relief; it was a bold move, all the best men in the party supported the measure, and it was pre-eminently successful.

HON. JOHN BEMISTER.
By S. H. Parsons.

Sir Frederick's administration and all his party were overthrown in 1869, and Mr. Bennett formed an administration, which in its turn was again defeated in 1873, through the defection of three of its supporters. Mr. Bennett's tenure of office corresponded with the Governorship of Sir Stephen Hill, K.C.M.G. In July 1869, direct steam to England by the Allan Line was permanently established. Vessels of the same line had been making calls each year since the S.S. *North American* first came to St. John's in January 1862.

HON. C. F. BENNETT.
By L. Abell.

The Bennett Government was a most able and progressive administration. The Premier had always been an indefatigable promoter of

---

confederate member for Brigus, was the prime mover in this great public improvement—a most popular move. Besides the public grindstone at Brigus, there are subsidiary public grindstones at Bareneed, Port de Grave, Clarke's Beach, and Pick Eye. The late T. D. Scanlan is my authority; he says: "I have used the public grinder myself, and ground my own hatchet at the public expense."

roads; the present efficient police is due to Mr. Bennett's statesmanlike sagacity; during his tenure of office there were successful fisheries, good harvests, and general prosperity; the revenue rose in 1871 to $831,160. In the mining industry, the increase was very marked under the fostering care of the great pioneer of this industry (Mr. Bennett); the large expenditure of wages in Green Bay to the copper workers added largely to the resources of our working population, and helped to diffuse general prosperity throughout the Colony.

The most exciting subject in 1872-73, next to the all-absorbing question of confederation, was the right of our Government under the Charter to pre-empt the New York, Newfoundland and London Telegraph Company's rights and plant.

SIR STEPHEN HILL.

With the exception of a few cool headed individuals, everyone went mad about monopoly and pre-emption. Mr. H. Labouchere, M.P., a leading shareholder in the Direct Cable Company, has always had the credit of engineering this great financial dodge. Our telegraph company's stock, known amongst financiers as "Dogs," stood at a high figure (above par), as it was a highly speculative stock, it probably was rated above its real value. A shrewd operator discovered this point about *pre-emption*. He saw that if sufficient pressure or influence could be gained over the Newfoundland Government to get them to decide that they would pre-empt, or that they would not waive their right of pre-emption, the stock could be beared to a large extent. To accomplish this end the great writer Lawrence Oliphant was sent to influence Governor Hill. The Duke of Buckingham wrote to the Premier on the subject; the Hon. J. Tobin and a Mr. Cole were also sent out to the Colony. Lawyers' opinions were published that the Newfoundland Company's plant might be taken over by our Government as so much old wood and iron; we were to receive a handsome yearly revenue for the right to land on our shores; even ministers of the Gospel were dragged from their sacred functions to go sounding in Placentia Bay; money was spent like water, and at last the desired result was obtained. At the moment that it suited the stock-jobbers, a telegram was sent by our Government that "they would not waive their right of pre-emption." "Dogs" declined 9*l*. a share, and a ring of speculators who had prepared this elaborate plan pocketed £400,000 sterling. Pretty nearly all the influential men in the Colony were drawn into this clever, unscrupulous game, and the most respectable individuals amongst us were paid agents in working out this great financial dodge.

Pre-emption was the wildest, maddest, most absurd proposal ever entertained by a Government; to commit us, with our small revenue, to the purchase of a speculative concern like a cable and a telegraph; to risk our revenue for about ten years on a thing that might be gold to-day and utterly worthless to-morrow.—George Law's Mississippi scheme was not more fantastic.

THE EAST END OF WATER STREET BEFORE THE FIRE OF 1892.
From a photograph by S. H. Parsons.

The most humorous thing about the whole affair was the way in which it was managed; that the agents, the paid pamphleteers, the subsidized press and the whole army of claqueurs should gird at the monopoly and attack the Anglo-American Company, was only meet and right. They were paid for it, and I am bound to say they did it well, they earned their money; but that the whole outside public, unpaid and disinterested, should clamour for the same object, that virtually the whole Colony should aid and abet a great stock-jobbing trick, seems really too absurd; however, there are men amongst us, even to this day, who will not believe that the offers made to our Government were a sham and the whole affair a delusion and a snare.

The high moral tone assumed by Labouchere and all these financing agents is quite delightful. Our Government was quite prepared to pre-empt if they could obtain a good guarantee for reimbursement in case of loss; they applied for this purpose to the British Government but none could be obtained, and so Sir F. Carter's Government very properly, therefore, refused to entertain the subject.

The following extract of a letter from Mr. Labouchere to Governor Hill shows the kind of vague promises on which our Government were requested to run so enormous a risk :—

"Should you, Sir, terminate the existing monopoly in 1874, and take over the land lines of the island, for the value of their plant and material, I am informed by responsible capitalists that they will be ready, if it be wished, to take over your lines at a rental, agreeing to lower the tariff, and to allow all cables to land on your shores, and to advance money on the guarantee of the rental to enable your colony to pay off Mr. Field. In fact, they are ready to enter into any arrangement with you which may facilitate the operation, so anxious are all commercial houses and our daily press to reduce the heavy cost of transatlantic telegrams.

"I have the honour to be, Sir,
"Your Excellency's most obedient humble servant,
"To Sir S. Hill, K.C.M.G.   HENRY LABOUCHERE."

One of the most humorous things was the final result. The big telegraph monopolist, John Pender, of the Anglo-American, gained a controlling influence over the Direct Cable Company, and the balances due to the lawyers and claqueurs against the Anglo-American and their monopoly were all ultimately paid through the company's agent, A. M. Mac Kay; so ended the farce.

The election returns of 1873 gave a small majority to the Bennett Government, but it was of a doubtful character; by a series of intrigues well understood at the time, Mr. T. R. Bennett member for Fortune Bay, and the Surveyor-General, Hon. Henry Renouf, took office as District Judges, and Mr. C. Duder joined Mr. Carter; this left the Government in a minority of one.[1] Mr. Carter was called on to form an Administration, and he worked along through the session of 1874 with only the Speaker's casting vote; in the autumn he dissolved the House, and a general election gave him a good working majority. To this period belongs the incident of the Royal Commission, consisting of Sir B. Robinson, James Goodfellow, and J. Fox, Esquires. The evidence was not taken on oath, only the Report was published. The Opposition demanded the evidence, which was never produced. From the known high character of the Commissioners, we may rest assured that the inquiry was honestly conducted; the non-production of the evidence, however, seriously impaired its value; it is known in our annals as

---

[1] If Bennett's party had remained steadfast he had a majority of three. When T. R. Bennett and Renouf took office, and C. Duder left his party, Mr. Carter had fifteen to fourteen, with the Speaker. The return of 1875 shows the immense advantage of going before the country with the control of the Executive machinery.

the "Jim Dobbin" Commission.[1] Sir Frederick's Administration in 1874 was happily favoured with prosperity and the largest fishery ever known in the Colony.

In 1875, Sir Stephen Hill, in his speech at the opening of the session of the Legislature, said:—

"The period appears to have arrived when a question which has for some time engaged public discussion, viz., the construction of a railway across the Island to St. George's Bay, should receive a practical solution. . . . . . As a preliminary to this object, a proposition will be submitted to you for a thorough survey to ascertain the most eligible line, and with a view to the further inquiry whether the Colony does not possess within itself the means of inducing capitalists to undertake this great enterprise of progress."

SIR A. SHEA.
Ba Bassetere.

A sum of money was voted for the preliminary survey; it was completed during the summer of 1875 by a number of Canadian surveyors under the superintendence of Sandford Fleming, the eminent Canadian engineer. The result of the survey, which was carried out in a very rapid manner, and over quite a different course from the one followed in the actual construction of the railway, clearly demonstrated that a line was feasible, that there were no great engineering difficulties to be overcome, and that a light railway might be constructed at a very reasonable rate per mile. Mr. Bellairs' previous survey established the same result.

Sir Stephen Hill's term of office having come to a close in 1876, he was succeeded by Sir John H. Glover, G.C.M.G.[2] The new administrator proved himself a most energetic ruler.

---

[1] This nickname was given to it by the sheriff, Hon. T. Talbot, a member of Mr. Bennett's Government; he stated that the Commission was got up entirely for party purposes. He compared it to a dispute between two neighbours who had fallen out—Jim Dobbin and Pat Ellard—and Jim Dobbin got all the friends on his side to blacken the character of Pat Ellard. Badinage apart, there are very grave objections to the appointment of a judge on a political inquiry of this character.

[2] Sir J. H. Glover, R.N., G.C.M.G. (1874) entered the navy in 1841 on board the *Queen*, bearing the flag of Vice-Admiral S Edwaird Owen, in which ship he sailed to the Mediterranean; transferred, in May 1842, to the Mediterranean Survey until 1850; for two years commanded the cutter *Auxiliar*; in 1841 served on the West African station until promoted to lieutenant in October of that year; in 1852 served in the *Winchester* frigate on the East Indian station; transferred to the steam sloop *Sphinx*, shared in the attack and capture of Pegu, and in the action at Donibew, was especially mentioned in despatches on both occasions; senior lieutenant in the steam sloop *Rosamond* in the Baltic in 1854; commanded the *Otter*, steam, 3 guns, from 1st March 1855 to March 1857, and was employed in her on "particular service" in the rivers Elbe and Weser, in 1855; from March 1857 to March 1861 was employed on the service of the Niger Expedition, surveyed the lagoons at Lagos, and that portion of the River Niger comprised between Boressa and the sea; during 1861-2 he commanded the *Handy* gunboat on the lagoons

In the following year, 1877, after protracted negotiations, and repeated applications to the Imperial Government, Commander W. Howorth, R.N., was appointed the first stipendiary magistrate on the west coast, and, in accordance with the undoubted rights of the Colonial Government, Custom House officers were appointed and duties collected there.

In 1877 Sir Bryan Robinson was compelled by age and increasing infirmities to retire from the Bench; Sir Frederick Carter took his place, and Sir W. V. Whiteway became acting Attorney-General. One of the important subjects that required the attention of the new Cabinet was the Washington Treaty, ratified between England and the United States on the 8th of May, 1871.

SIR J. GLOVER.
By Bosch, Frankfort a M.

Under the compensation clause of this treaty a Commission was arranged to sit in Halifax, Nova Scotia, which commenced on the 15th June and closed on the 23rd November 1877, after the examination of some hundreds of witnesses, and the production of a vast quantity of documentary evidence.

There had been much controversy, negotiations, and correspondence before the arrangements for the assembling of the Commission were finally concluded.

Both in the Newfoundland Cabinet and amongst outsiders very influential people ridiculed the idea of our ever getting anything out of the Americans. Notwithstanding, however, these opposite views,

---

at Lagos, until promoted to the rank of commander; first commission as Administrator of the Government of Lagos, 21st April 1863; Colonial Secretary, Lagos, 5th May 1864; Administrator of the Government from 21st February 1866 until the 9th of July 1872; received the thanks of the Secretary of State for Foreign Affairs and of the Secretary of State for War for services rendered on different occasions; also received the thanks of the Administrator and Council of the Government of the Gold Coast for his survey of the River Volta, from the rapids to the sea, and for the assistance he rendered in destroying the pirates of the island of Daffoe on that river in 1870; Special Commissioner to friendly native chiefs in the eastern district of the protected territories on Gold Coast, 18th August 1873; engaged and defeated the Ahoonah tribes, December 1873, and having left Mr. Goldsworthy in command in that quarter, marched with about 700 Houssas into Ashanti, and made his way to Coomassie, through the ruins of which he passed on the 12th of February 1874. Received the Grand Cross of Saint Michael and Saint George for these services. Sir John succeeded Sir Stephen Hill as Governor from 1876 to 1881. On the death of Governor Sir H. Maxse, he was reappointed in 1883. Sir John died in London in 1885. A monument to his memory was erected in the Anglican cathedral of St. John's. No more honourable, generous, kind-hearted, or active ruler ever presided over our Government.

Sir William Whiteway, then Solicitor-General, held strongly to his opinion that we were now entitled to, and would receive, compensation. He accepted the position of British counsel for Newfoundland at the Commission. Messrs. Doutre, S. Thompson Weatherbee and L. H. Davies, all eminent lawyers, were appointed British counsel to conduct the Canadian branch of the inquiry.

In conjunction with the Hon. W. J. S. Donnelly, Mr. J. O. Fraser, Judge Bennett, and Mr. W. Kelligrew, Sir William prepared our case. In this important work his assistants were not only experienced and able men, but probably the best that could be selected in the Colony. Judge Bennett's practical knowledge of the fishery on the southern and south-western parts of the island, and the operations of American and French fishermen on our shores, was unequalled; both Mr. Donnelly, Mr. J. O. Fraser, and Mr. Kelligrew were thoroughly versed in the general trade in the Colony. Their duty in assisting to prepare the evidence and select witnesses was very well performed. Whilst we give them every credit for their valuable labours, their work does not in the least detract from the eminent services before the Commission of our counsel. Sir A. Shea, who was always pre-eminently clear and lucid in his statements, whilst praising their work, put Sir W. V. Whiteway's services in the right light when he declared that they were rendered *in a case of greater importance and involving larger responsibilities than have ever fallen to the lot of any public man in connection with the affairs of this Colony*. Addresses to Sir W. V. Whiteway from both Houses were passed in the following complimentary terms :—

"Resolved, That the Legislative Council has pleasure in recording its thankful appreciation of the services of the Hon. William Vallance Whiteway, as counsel for Newfoundland, before the Halifax Fishery Commission, in the year 1877.

"The Council feel assured that the successful issue of the inquiry there held into the claim of Newfoundland was in large measure due to Mr. Whiteway's able and zealous exertions in behalf of the interests of this Colony.

"EDWARD MORRIS,
"Legislative Council, "*President.*
" April 18th, 1879.

"Resolved, That the thanks of the House be accorded to the Hon. William V. Whiteway, Premier of the Colony, for the ability and energy displayed by him in successfully conducting the case of this island before the Fisheries Commission which sat at Halifax in 1877, appointed as a Tribunal of Arbitration under the terms of the Washington Treaty.

"A. I. W. MCNEILY,
"April 18th, 1879. "*Speaker.*"

The result of the Halifax Commission is well known; its great success was largely due to the tact and ability of the secretary, Sir Henry G. Bergne. Five-and-a-half million dollars were accorded by the Commissioners, and out of this amount the handsome sum of one million to Newfoundland under the following award :—

"The undersigned Commissioners, appointed under Articles XXII. and XXIII. of the Treaty of Washington, of the 8th of May 1871, to determine, having regard to the privileges accorded by the United States to the subjects of Her Britannic Majesty, as stated in Articles XIX. and XXI. of the said Treaty, the amount of any compensation which, in their opinion, ought to be paid by the Government of the United States to the Government of Her Britannic Majesty in return for the privileges accorded to the citizens of the United States under Article XVIII. of the said Treaty, having carefully and impartially examined the matters referred to them according to justice and equity, in conformity with the solemn declaration made and subscribed by them on the 15th day of June 1877, award the sum of five millions five hundred thousand dollars in gold to be paid by the Government of the United States to the Government of Her Britannic Majesty, in accordance with the provisions of the said Treaty.

"Signed at Halifax this 23rd day of November 1877.

"MAURICE DELFOSSE.
"A. T. GALT."

A number of gentlemen in the Council and Assembly took part in the discussion when the award was considered. I have given portions of the speeches of Hon. A. W. Harvey, Sir Ambrose Shea, and Sir William Whiteway, as they throw light on the subject; they bring out in a very distinct and emphatic way the immense value of our fisheries—the greatest cod-fishery in the world—and the magnitude of the interests at stake before the Commission.

The Hon. A. W. Harvey spoke as follows on this occasion:—

"The amount of the award made by the Commission is declared by the Americans to be out of all proportion to the privileges of fishery they have obtained, and to no part of the award did they object so vehemently as to the portion allotted to Newfoundland; in fact, they insisted that Newfoundland should be ruled out of court altogether. By reference to the terms of the Washington Treaty it will be seen that they do not specify what the remuneration, if any were awarded, was to be paid for. They do not say, for instance, that if the fishery privileges granted are ten times more valuable than those given to us on the coasts of the United States, the award should be proportioned to that. Nor do they say that the extent to which the United States fishermen used those fisheries over and above the extent to which British fishermen used the United States fisheries, should be the gauge of compensation. It is the value of the privilege of fishing the claim was based on, which was a very difficult and intricate matter to get hold of and decide upon. If the value of the fisheries were to be a basis, then five million dollars would not be a tithe of what the United States should have to pay for their use of the fisheries of Newfoundland, New Brunswick, and Nova Scotia; and he should have said that one million dollars would be utterly inadequate to represent the value of our fisheries, if that were to be the standard, as we contended they were worth more than all the fisheries the United States fishermen were admitted to participate in on the coasts of the other provinces. There would be hardly a disputation that the fisheries between Cape Ray and Cape John were of more worth than the combined fisheries of the neighbouring colonies; and if upon that principle the award had been decided, we should have received more than two million five hundred thousand dollars of the whole sum. But as that would have been manifestly unfair, I consider the ends of justice were more conserved by paying this Colony one million dollars than the larger amount. No doubt the Nova Scotia fisheries are far more interfered with by the United States fishermen than are ours, and the extent to which they use, and will use them, is four times greater than the use they will make of ours; therefore I consider we had made an uncommonly good bargain in securing the proportion of the award that has been paid to us."

HON. A. W. HARVEY.
By S. H. Parsons.

The Hon. A. Shea said:—

"He regarded this issue as involving much more than the money consideration, for it established the value ascribed by an impartial authority to a right to participate in our fisheries for 12 years, and the House would see the importance of this decision in the event of any future negotiation in which it became necessary to appraise the worth of the fisheries of this country. And it had this further great value, that looking at the temper of the American people on the subject of the award, they would not be likely to ask for a renewal of the case, and in thus becoming rid of the presence of active competition in our fisheries, we should be gainers in a degree far beyond any supposable amount to be desired as alleged compensation for the privilege of participation."

VALUE OF THE NEWFOUNDLAND SHORE FISHERY.

Sir W. V. Whiteway, the Attorney-General, after acknowledging the vote of thanks, concluded by saying:—

"For some years after the signing of the Washington Treaty it appeared to be very doubtful whether or not the Halifax Commission would ever sit. The question was international between Great Britain and the United States. Numerous despatches were interchanged between the two Governments in reference to the subject. At length, in the year 1876, official information reached us to the effect that the Commission would probably sit in 1877, and we were required by the Imperial Government to prepare our case. Two members of the Executive, the Hon. Mr. Donnelly and myself, were nominated to perform this duty. We did so, and had our case ready to submit to the British Agent, Mr. Ford, who with Mr. Bergne visited St. John's on his way to England from Canada, where they had been engaged for about two months with the fishery officials of the Dominion and several eminent counsel in the preparation of the Canadian part of the case. The stay of Messrs. Ford and Bergne here was short, some two weeks only, as our prepared case needed little or no alteration, a re-arrangement being all that was required to make it accord with the case of Canada. And here it affords me infinite pleasure to refer to the eminent services rendered by the hon. Surveyor-General, Mr. Donnelly. The services rendered by Judge Bennett, Mr. Fraser, and Mr. Kelligrew may be gathered from the records of the Commission. By their evidence and by about twenty affidavits our case was sustained, and there was not a point which was not secured. I may say it was not only nailed home, but each nail was clinched, and our position rendered invulnerable. On the part of the United States there were about seventy witnesses examined and a similar number on behalf of Canada, in addition to which they each produced between two and three hundred affidavits. A treaty had been entered into between Great Britain and the United States, by which the United States had conceded to Great Britain the right of fishing upon a certain part of the American coast and a free market in the United States for Canadian and Newfoundland caught fish and produce, and in return Great Britain had conceded to the United States the right of fishing in Canadian and Newfoundland waters in common with British subjects. We alleged that the value of our concession was greater than that made by the United States. This Commission, appointed by virtue of the treaty, was to try that question, and to award the difference in value, if any, to Great Britain. Now, the United States counsel candidly admitted, first, that the concession to us to fish in American waters was of no value to us, as we could never use it; and secondly, it was our argument at the trial and clearly proved that for us to have the right of importing into the United States our fish and fish produce duty free was an advantage to the United States as a nation; it gave them a cheaper article, upon the principle that the consumer always paid the duty, and in this case it was shown by conclusive evidence that, duty or no duty, the Canadian exporter of mackerel had averaged about the same returns in his account sales. A duty simply operated as a protection to the United States fishing interests as a distinct business. To take it off was an injury to that interest, but a benefit to the United States as a nation. It was with the nation that Great Britain was dealing: therefore the concession of a right of fishing on the American coast was admitted to be valueless, and the right of free market was shown to be a benefit to the United States and no additional value to us. On the other hand, Newfoundland conceded to the United States a free right of fishing on the coast from Ramea Islands by Cape Race to Cape John. What was the value of this concession? Had the Commission found nothing in our favour, what would have been the effect hereafter in British negotiations with the United States and with France? Let us for a moment suppose the case of Great Britain proposing to us to give the French a free right of fishing all along our coast, with a view to the solution of our so-called French Shore difficulty. We know that this course would prove our ruin, but the argument of Great Britain to us would have been unanswerable:—' You have had the opportunity of a solemn inquiry before a disinterested tribunal sitting in the very centre of your fisheries, where every facility was at hand for fully investigating their value, and the conclusion arrived at, after six months inquiry by that tribunal, was, that a right to fish along your coast was not worth anything.' I venture to say that probably the true position and importance of this inquiry was not generally appreciated here at the time of this Commission, or we should not have had loose, ill-considered opinions expressed. The decision had established that which would for all time endure to the benefit of the country. It has been decided after a most rigid investigation that the right to fish along a portion of our coast for 12 years, under the facts given in evidence, is worth one million dollars. We have now an established basis, and I look upon this as of the greatest importance, and that upon which we cannot set too high a value."

SIR W. V. WHITEWAY, K.C.M.G.
By S. H. Parsons.

Sir Frederic Carter having taken his seat upon the Bench, first as Assistant Judge, and in 1880 as Chief Justice, in succession to Sir Hugh W. Hoyles, who had been compelled to retire by failing health, the conduct of affairs devolved on Sir William Whiteway, K.C.M.G.; he showed himself most progressive in his ideas. In 1880 he passed the first Railway Bill for a light railway from St. John's to Hall's Bay.

THE HALL'S BAY RAILWAY.

The Bill was founded on the following report, prepared by a Joint Committee of the Legislative Council and the House of Assembly, and is an admirable résumé of the reasons for building the railway:—

"April 2nd, 1880.

"The Joint Committee of the Council and House of Assembly appointed to consider the question of constructing a railway in this island, have to report that they have given the most careful consideration to this matter, and beg to state the result of their deliberations.

"The question of the future of our growing population has for some time engaged the earnest attention of all thoughtful men in this country, and has been the subject of serious solicitude. The fisheries being our main resource, and to a large extent the only dependence of the people, those periodical partial failures which are incident to such pursuits continue to be a source of recurring visitations of pauperism, and there seems no remedy to be found for this condition of things but that which may lie in varied and extensive pursuits.

"This reflection would apply with force to the present population, but when we contemplate it in relation to our increasing numbers, the necessity of dealing with the subject urgently presses itself on our consideration.

"Our fisheries have no doubt increased, but not in a measure corresponding to our increase of population. And even though they were capable of being further expanded, that object would be largely neutralised by the decline in price which follows from a large catch, as no increase of markets can be found to give remunerative returns for an augmented supply.

"It is evident, therefore, that no material increase of means is to be looked for from our fisheries, and that we must direct our attention to other sources to meet the growing requirements of the country. Our mining industry may now be regarded as an established fact. Large areas of geological formation similar to that in which the mines are being successfully worked are known to

In the autumn of 1880 the survey was completed from St. John's to Harbour Grace. Tenders were received from various capitalists

exist, and there is every reason to believe from recent explorations that a great amount of wealth in copper and other ores is waiting the application of enterprise and capital to bring them into profitable use. Our agricultural industry, though prosecuted to a valuable extent, is yet susceptible of very enlarged development. Vast stretches of agricultural land, extending from Trinity Bay north, along the heads of Bonavista Bay, Gander Bay, and Exploits River, as well as on the west coast, need only the employment of well-directed labour to convert them into means of independent support for thousands of the population.

"We have in this town a large market for agricultural produce and live stock, which at present is mainly supplied from abroad, and as an illustration of what may be done by the cultivation of the land when a market is within reach, we have the fact that amongst the most prosperous of our labouring people are those who live by the land in the vicinity of St. John's, though the average conditions of fertility are far below those which exist in the interior of the Island. There are indications, moreover, leading to the conclusion that we shall hereafter be more dependent than before on home supply of live stock, for in those places from which we have hitherto received our meat supplies, attention is being given to the English market, which is supposed to offer better prospects, and an advanced value may therefore be reasonably anticipated.

"With an improved market on the spot the inquiry is further suggested whether this Colony should not become an exporter of live stock to England, and we have little difficulty in affirming this position. For grazing purposes we have large tracts that, we believe, cannot be surpassed in British North America; and when we regard our proximity to England, and the all-important consideration of a short voyage for live stock, the advantages we possess in this connection are too manifest to be subject of question or argument.

"But to what end do these elements of wealth exist if they continue to remain neglected? For they will as before be outside the reach of the people if some energetic effort be not made to render them accessible to our centres of population. We have means of remunerative employment in those dormant resources, coincident with the spectacle so often about us of unemployed labour; and we cannot but feel that the Government fails in its duty if it have the power and does not employ it in connecting those resources with that industry, which ought to receive its satisfactory reward.

"Your Committee believe that no agency would be so effective for the promotion of the objects in view as that of a railway; and when they consider that there is no Colony of equal importance under the Crown without a railroad, and the advantages thereby conferred elsewhere in the enhancement of the value of property and labour, it is felt that in our circumstances no effort within the means of the Colony should be wanting to supply this great *desideratum*.

"They are not unmindful of the financial considerations involved, but having regard to the influence of such a work in elevating the people and enlarging the area of profitable industry, the Committee are convinced that ample compensation will be found in the improved condition of the country for any outlay the undertaking may require.

"We do not regard it *per se* as an enterprise that will pay, or as one that offers attraction to speculators, but as the work of the country, and in its bearing on the promotion of the well-being of the people, in which the returns are alone sought and will be found, it eminently commends itself to our judgment. In this sense we believe that, in time, it will amply pay its cost, and that the consequent advance in the comfort and independence of the people will fully attest the wisdom of its establishment.

"The Committee are of opinion that the present financial condition of the Colony makes the time favourable for entering on the project, and that it may be undertaken on conditions which will not unduly press upon our resources.

"The Committee believe that a narrow gauge road might be constructed at a comparatively moderate cost, and that it would be found well adapted to the circumstances of this Colony, as well in regard to our means as to the physical condition of the country. The road should be made from St. John's through the peninsula of Avalon, and the favoured agricultural and timber regions north, to the mineral district, connecting the principal towns and settlements in Conception Bay and along the proposed line. Your Committee have had reference to the survey made in 1875, and it would seem to be ample for preliminary purposes, so far as it affects the district of Avalon and along the route already examined to the northern point indicated; but a further survey would be required to establish the immediate location of that, as well as of such branch lines as shall seem to be necessary and practicable for the carrying out of the proposed project.

"Your Committee therefore recommend the introduction and passage of an Act to construct the line. The Premier moved a resolution to refer the consideration of the various proposals to a joint committee of both Houses. On the recommendation of this committee, a provisional contract was made and a charter afterwards granted to the Newfoundland Railway Company. The principal points in the contract provided that the company were to build a substantial, reliable, and efficient railroad of three feet six inches gauge, subject to the approval of the Government engineer, and were to continuously operate and maintain the same, and to complete the whole line to Hall's Bay within five years; the Government to pay an annual subsidy of $180,000 per annum for thirty-five years, the subsidy to attach as each five miles of road was completed and passed by the Government engineer; a large land grant of five thousand acres per mile was to be given for each completed mile. It is due to Sir William Whiteway to say that he was always in favour of the Government constructing the line themselves.

On the 9th of August 1881 the railway was actually commenced, and at the close of the working season twenty miles were graded, and ten miles metalled; very large sums of money were expended in labour on the line. During the ensuing winter hundreds of men were employed north and south cutting sleepers. The money thus spent in construction and in purchase of the right of way was found most beneficial; it came on the whole community like the gentle rain from Heaven; its refreshing dews descended alike on the friends and opponents of the new enterprise; its rills trickled into everyone's pocket—merchant, trader, small shopkeeper, all alike experienced the good results of this large outflow of money to the railway labourers. In his opening speech to the Legislature in 1882, Sir

authorising the raising by loan of the required amount in sums not exceeding five hundred thousand dollars in any one year, and providing an organisation for carrying out the object in accordance with the views contained in this Report. The Committee further recommend that the Executive Government apply to Her Majesty's Government, requesting that they will guarantee the interest on the bonds of the Colony for such amount as may be required for the purpose of constructing the railroad, within the sum of one million pounds sterling, and we cannot doubt that this will meet with a favourable response when Her Majesty's Government are made aware of the exceptionally sound and healthy condition of our finances.

"All of which is respectfully submitted.
" (Signed) W. V. WHITEWAY,
" *Chairman.*
" P. G. TESSIER.
" C. R. AYRE.
" ROBT. THORBURN.
" A. SHEA.
" JOHN RORKE.
" JOSEPH I. LITTLE.
" ROBT J. KENT.
" A. M. MACKAY."

Ordered, That the said Report be received.

Frederic Carter, Administrator of the Government, announced to the Legislature:—

"That the leading industries of the country had, during the previous year, been prosecuted successfully on the whole, and that mining showed a considerably enlarged export of copper ore, and prospects of a further development in the immediate future. He referred to the railway as progressing satisfactorily in construction, conferring important benefits on the people, and causing a large monetary expenditure in the country. This great work, he said, is an enterprise which, in the increase of commercial and social communication, and the development of our agricultural and mineral resources, contains the elements of solid and lasting prosperity for Newfoundland.

"The revenue was found to be in a very flourishing condition, amounting to $1,063,803, being the largest ever received."

THE DRY DOCK, ST. JOHN'S.
From a photograph.

"The Administrator further informed the Legislature that the imperial authorities had at length authorised the local Government to make land grants, and issue mining licences on that part of the coast on which the French have fishery privileges. This was the boon for which the Colony had been pleading in vain for many years. Its importance to the people of Newfoundland can hardly be overrated. It is a virtual settlement of the vexed French Shore question, and a removal of a serious and long-standing grievance. It opens the half of the island, which had hitherto been closed to the people, to settlement and industrial enterprise. It enfranchises the population of this part of the island, who are in future to have two representatives in the local Legislature, and removes all restrictions on the exercise of territorial rights. The Administrator very justly connected this concession with the name of Sir William Whiteway, to whose able and persevering representations the country is largely indebted for a settlement of this vexed question.

"The coincidence, said the Administrator, of the improved conditions to which I have adverted with the inauguration of the Newfoundland railway, marks an era of progress which is a meet subject of congratulation to the country."

1882 was a period of enterprise, a shaking up of the dry bones; besides the railway, two other great works were initiated, the construction of the dry dock at River Head and the Rope Walk. The dock is over 600 feet long, one hundred and thirty-two at its widest part, with twenty-five feet over the gate sill at high water; it is large enough to admit the largest ocean steamer afloat. It was built by the patentees, J. E. Simpson & Co., of New York. The work began in May 1883, and in December 1884 H.M.S. *Tenedos* was docked, and the great work formally occupied. The patentees agreed to lease the dock for ten years at $15,000 per annum. Owing to a dispute between the lessees and the Government about the cost of dredging and the nonpayment of rent, the dock has been taken out of Messrs. Simpson's hands, and is now under lease to Messrs. Harvey & Angel for $11,000 per annum. The dock has been a magnificent success; it is of very great benefit and convenience to the trade, gives almost constant employment to tradesmen, and keeps in the colony thousands of dollars which would be otherwise expended abroad.

The most important social industry in St. John's is the Rope Walk. As a great fishing country Newfoundland uses an enormous amount of lines and twines, netting, cordage, and cables; until quite recently all these articles were imported, principally from the West of England, latterly from New England. The Colonial Cordage Company was founded by the energy and enterprise of the Hon. M. Monroe, a brother of the distinguished Judge Monroe of the Higher Court in Ireland. Aided by local and foreign capital, he inaugurated a work which gives employment to a large number of workpeople, and circulates money in the

HON. M. MONROE.

Colony. The goods turned out by this company are all of the very finest quality. Instead of importing all our cordage from abroad, the bulk of the lines, twines, nets, and cables used in our fishery are now made in the country. Whilst the initiation of the enterprise was the work of the Hon. M. Monroe, its successful working is mainly attributed to the practical skill, tact, and good judgment of his brother, the sole managing partner, James H. Monroe.[1]

THE COLONIAL CORDAGE COMPANY'S MILL.

The events of the next succeeding years, from 1883 forwards, are fresh in the memories of all, and it is not needful to dwell with minute particularity over circumstances with which all Newfoundland readers are familiar. One unpleasant subject I should like to pass over, the virulence, mendacity, and misrepresentation with which the promoters of the railway and the graving dock were assailed. The most monstrous fictions were invented to set the people against these new enterprises. This resulted in a very serious disturbance.

In 1881 the inhabitants of the south shore of Conception Bay, believing that all unutterable evils would happen to them if the line

---

[1] The Rope Walk is owned and operated by a local joint stock company, the Colonial Cordage Company, Limited, of St. John's, Newfoundland. It gives constant and steady employment to upwards of 500 people—men, boys, and girls—in the manufacture of cables and cordage of all kinds, fishing lines of every description, and all sorts of netting, sieves, and cod traps. It is situate at Monday Pond, convenient to the railroad. This concern was originally built in 1882, and burned down in December 1885. The present buildings are of a more substantial nature in brick and stone. They were pushed forward with great energy, operations being commenced the following July, only six months after the destruction of the old buildings. The machinery is of the most improved description, and the goods manufactured are quite equal to anything produced in England or the United States.

went through their lands, stoned the engineers, took away their instruments, and drove them from their work. The inspector of police, Mr. Carty, and the police magistrate, with only eleven men, were left to contend with a mad, excited crowd of about five hundred men and women armed with guns and every variety of weapon. The arrest of the ringleader at the point of the bayonet, and the firm action of the police authorities, eventually restored order. All this unseemly,

THE ROPE WALK.

dangerous disturbance was directly caused by the unscrupulous fabrication of falsehoods to stir up these poor, ignorant people to oppose the railway.[1]

For five days the whole population from Topsail to Indian Pond were in an insane state of excitement. Though it was the busiest time of the year, they never did a stroke of work; all day long they watched

[1] This riot has been generally known as the "Battle of Fox Trap." The people of the south shore were told by a leading merchant in the west end of St. John's that if the railway were carried out a "tall gate" (toll gate) would be erected near the Long Bridge, and every man going into town with a horse and cart would have to pay fifty cents; that their little farms and horses would be taxed, and they would be ruined. They further believed that if the tape was once carried over their ground, it would be taken from them.

the engineers and the small posse of police, and followed them from place to place. From Topsail to Indian Pond the whole population believed the advent of this terrible monster, the railway, meant their ruin. Thanks to the wise counsels of the Rev. Jeremiah O'Donnell, the people of Holyrood and Harbour Main never made the slightest opposition to the line.

It is not necessary in the present day to say anything in favour of one of the greatest factors in the promotion of modern civilization and progress—the railway; however useful and beneficial it may be in an old settled country, it is a positive and absolute necessity for the development and settlement of new territory. Looking at the position of our most important northern out-ports,

SIR HENRY MAXSE.

with their great timber and mineral wealth, developed and undeveloped, communication with them by railway, especially in winter, is the only possible means of intercourse. It was one of the insuperable objections to the line that it could never run in severe winter weather; however, experience shows us that by good management the railway will never be retarded, even by the worst weather, beyond a few hours. When the coast is blocked by ice, when all travelling by road is impossible, the trains to Whitbourne and Placentia have run their course almost as punctually as in the finest summer weather. So far the railroad is the most complete, the most safe and convenient road and mode of communication the wit of man has been able to devise; no other enterprise of modern times so benefits the working man or distributes labour in so generally beneficial a manner.

HON. J. I. LITTLE.
By S. H. Parsons.

The year 1883 is distinguished for the painful episode of the Harbour Grace riot; it was not only a most regrettable incident, owing to the deplorable loss of life, but also for the dire feelings of revenge and hatred it called forth. Three men were killed belonging to the Orange procession and one on the Catholic side. The police authorities at Harbour Grace had full warning, yet no precautions were taken to keep the rival factions apart; this fatal error produced most disastrous effects, both social and political. It upset the parties in the Assembly and the trials, with their exhibition of perjuries and prejudice, were by no means edifying. The whole trouble was begotten of fanaticism, and it ended in a complete fiasco.

In 1885 there was a new deal of the political cards, and considerable shuffling. Sir W. V. Whiteway, who had been Premier during two parliaments, resigned, and a new party was formed, known as the "Thorburn Administration." It was intended at first to be a genuine Protestant Government, worked on sound commercial principles; it was to inaugurate a new reign of moderate progress, economy, and no amalgamation; it ended by building the expensive railway to Placentia, and the Thorburn turnpike road to Broad Cove, the best constructed and the most costly road in the Colony. Its stern principles of "no amalgamation with Catholics" soon died away.

The Thorburn Administration will ever be memorable for their bold policy in the inauguration of the Bait Act, the construction of the Placentia Railway,[1] and the inception of the new line to Hall's Bay. They added one fine touch of humour to the annals of our constitutional history, the construction of the Placentia Railway under the disguise of a road. One member of the Executive, when attacked in the Legislative Council on this subject, solemnly declared that he was not aware that the Government were building a railway, and when he found out that the so-called road was the veritable Placentia Railway he resigned.

SIR R. THORBURN.
By Bassano.

---

[1] This railway was built, so it is said, to obtain the adhesion of the two Members for the district, Hon. W. J. S. Donnelly and the Speaker, G. H. Emerson. Each of these eminent legislators cost the Colony $250,000. Another account of the reasons for building the Placentia Railway and the admission of Catholics to the ministry is given by a friend of Sir G. Wm. Des Voeux. He and the Governor were standing on Colinet Bridge; they were on their way to Placentia; they could plainly hear the sound of the railway whistle at Whitbourne. The Governor then and there determined to use his influence to build the Placentia branch railway. My informant also states that it was the Governor's objection to the gentleman named as Colonial Secretary that caused the Ministry to seek for Catholic allies.

To some of the stern unbending Tories of Water Street, the railway was the unclean thing, hence this thin disguise; it was altogether too transparent to deceive the public.

The convention between England and France, made in 1884 relative to French fishery rights in Newfoundland, was submitted to the Newfoundland Government in 1884, by Sir Clare Ford and Mr. E. B. Pennell, C.M.G.; with certain modifications it received a qualified approval, but the Whiteway Cabinet absolutely refused to hold a special session of the Legislature to recommend its adoption. In 1885, on the change of Government, Mr. E. B. Pennell, C.M.G., of the Colonial Office, was again sent out to Newfoundland with an amended convention to confer with the local authorities on the subject, and to endeavour to make an arrangement. The negotiations resulted, however, in the Joint Committee of the House of Assembly and the Council absolutely refusing to ratify the Ford-Pennell Convention, unless the French would agree to withdraw or modify their bounties; concurrently the committee drafted, and both Houses passed, the first Bait Act of 1886. In substance it empowered the Executive to prohibit the capture in our waters for exportation or sale of bait fishes, except under special licence to be issued by the Receiver General under the authority of the Governor in Council.

SIR G. W. DES VŒUX, K.C.M.G.

If carried out efficiently it would stop all the supply of bait to the French from our south coast. The French made every effort to induce the Imperial Government to refuse their sanction to the Act, and in the Governor's speech of 1887 Sir G. W. Des Vœux informed the Legislature that Her Majesty would not sanction the Bill. The Governor's despatch in favour of the proposed measure, and the address from the House of Assembly sent home with the second Bait Bill in 1887, are both very able and well-written documents.

Sir G. W. Des Vœux wrote on January 14, 1887, to Sir H. Holland; after referring to the matter generally, he concluded :—

"25. Though this measure, if allowed, would to a large extent place the fish production in this neighbourhood within the control of the people of this Colony, they have no desire to monopolize it, and I feel satisfied that they would willingly

K K 2

modify the provisions of the measure in favour of such Governments as would grant a proportional reciprocity.

"26. Without of course being able to speak with certainty as to the amount of concession that would be granted by the Legislature in any particular case, I have very good reason for believing that, as regards the United States, the right of obtaining bait would be restored on the opening of the American markets to Newfoundland fish, or (if common cause be made with Canada) to all British fish; while in view of the greater expense involved in maintaining the fishery from head-quarters on the other side of the Atlantic, I believe that in the case of the French the abolition or a substantial reduction of the export bounties would alone be held sufficient, even though the other bounties and the prohibition of the import of British fish were still retained. In a word, the principle that the colonists desire to maintain is, 'Live and let live,' and they merely object to that of 'Let others live by killing us.'

"26. But whether the views of the colonists on this subject are just or not (and after much and anxious consideration of the subject I am bound to say that, in my opinion, they are based on very substantial grounds), the proposed measure of prohibition, as in no way affecting the Treaty rights of foreign Powers, can scarcely be contended to be otherwise than such as is within the competence of the local Legislature under the existing constitution of the Colony; and, indeed, if the same object had been aimed at by more indirect means, and a Bill had been passed imposing a prohibitive duty on bait exported in foreign vessels, it appears open to doubt whether, under my existing instructions, I should have been justified in refusing assent to it.

"27. But however this may be, any question as to the competence in the matter of the Colonial Legislature has been practically set at rest by the recent allowance of the Canadian Bill, which, I am informed, adopts almost precisely similar means for procuring an analogous object. And as the importance of the fisheries to the Dominion is moreover incomparably less, for the reasons above given, than to this Colony, it may be presumed that the disallowance of the Newfoundland Bill, which would appear probable from the long delay of decision, is due to some Imperial consideration which applies either not at all, or in a considerably less degree, to the case of Canada. If this be so, as indeed there are other reasons for believing, I would respectfully urge that in fairness the heavy resulting loss should not, or at all events not exclusively, fall upon this Colony, and that if in the national interest a right is to be withheld from Newfoundland which naturally belongs to it, and the possession of which makes to it all the difference between wealth and penury, there is involved on the part of the nation a corresponding obligation to grant compensation of a value equal, or nearly equal, to that of the right withheld.

"31. I would respectfully urge that, in the absence of a fixed decision against this measure, the delay which has already taken place in respect of its allowance should not be further prolonged.

"32. Now that I fully comprehend the present position of the Colony, it is to me no longer a matter of wonder that the Legislature has hitherto failed to ratify the proposed Arrangement with France; indeed, I can scarcely conceive it possible that this Arrangement will ever be accepted so long as the Bait Clause remains in it, and no security is taken that the export bounties will not be maintained on their present footing.

"33. For though all the other articles have the appearance of concession on the part of the French, and some are, no doubt, substantial concessions, they are all immeasurably outweighed by the single concession required on the part of this Colony. For if there were granted to the French an inalienable right to procure bait here, the future, not only of the coast where they already have fishing rights, but of the whole Colony, would practically be placed within the control of their Government. Even if the present bounties should prove insufficient, it would require but a slight addition to them, involving an exceedingly small cost by comparison with the enormous expenditure of France, to destroy the trade of this Colony altogether, and at once; and in view of the great importance attached to these fisheries by the French, as the means of maintaining the strength of their navy, it would appear by no means improbable that such an attempt would be made if there were thus withdrawn the only means of preventing its success. And this probability appears the greater, when it is considered that the cessation of British productions with the cause in operation that would render its recovery impossible would, in all probability, produce a rise in the market value of fish, which would eventually render unnecessary the continuance of any bounty, so that the additional expenditure on the part of France would be only a temporary sacrifice that would secure a permanent economical gain.

"34. As the matter at present appears to me, it seems deserving of the consideration of Her Majesty's Government whether it would, under any circumstances, be politic to place in the hands of the French a weapon capable of being used with such terrible effect against British interests, and whether, without the security for the discontinuance of the bounties on their present footing as above referred to, it would be wise to make further effort for the passing of the Arrangement while the Bait Clause is included in it.

"35. In conclusion, I would respectfully express, on behalf of this suffering Colony, the earnest hope that the vital interests of 200,000 British subjects will not be disregarded out of deference to the susceptibilities of any foreign Power, and this especially when the privilege which that Power desires to retain cannot be pretended to be matter of right, but is a benefit which may be lawfully withdrawn, as in the nature of a tenancy at will, and may now be justly withdrawn as being used for the infliction of fatal injury on those who have hitherto permitted its enjoyment. Sincerely hoping that the fulfilment of the desire of Newfoundland may be no longer delayed, and that I may be able to meet the Legislature next month with the announcement that this important Bill has already received Her Majesty's gracious allowance and confirmation, I have, &c.

"G. WILLIAM DES VŒUX."

The House declared:—

"It was with feelings of profound disappointment and regret that we learned from His Excellency's speech, at the opening of the present Session of the Legislature, and from your despatch to him of the 3rd instant, that Her Majesty will not be advised to give her sanction to this Bill.

"This announcement awakened a public sentiment that has had its expression in the immediate passage of another similar Bill, which took precedence of all other business in the Legislature, and will be transmitted immediately for the approval of Her Majesty's Government. We most earnestly trust that the result of this renewed effort in support of our rights may not be another disappointment with its ruinous consequences.

"When we learn from your despatch that the main reason for the refusal of our Bill is that its present adoption would 'inflict grave loss on the French fishermen,' we cannot forbear from the expression of our surprise at this apparent disregard of the sufferings of our fishermen, and of the British interests which are thus made subservient to the purposes of foreigners. The people of this Colony have the right in our fisheries, and foreigners have not; and we cannot see those rights surrendered in defiance of our appeals without expressing our deep sense of the injustice to which our people are thus called on to submit.

"Your despatch sets forth that further information is required to enable Her Majesty's Government to appreciate the true character and bearings of our Bait Bill. The Address of the Legislature, already referred to, in possession of Her Majesty's Government, is pregnant with facts in justification of that measure, and appears to us to exhaust the whole subject. But while we fail to see any want of completeness in the evidence already supplied, every desire is felt to satisfy any further reasonable requirements in this respect.

"It would further appear from your despatch that, in support of the objections to the measure, much importance is given to the fact that the bait traffic has been long recognised, and has only of late been resisted. We thought the reasons for this change of view had been fully explained in the representations recently made to Her Majesty's Government. The traffic was permitted so long as the bounty-assisted fisheries of France found a market in that country for their produce. But within the last three years the great increase in their fisheries has gone far beyond the requirements of their home markets; and we find them meeting us in Spain, Italy, and other European countries, and, with the bounty equal to 60 per cent. of the value of the fish, they are fast supplanting us; the reduced value of our staple industry from this cause already representing a fairly estimated sum of £250,000 per annum, under conditions that menace us with a still more serious decline. In these facts, our change of view of the bait traffic is but too well warranted, and we have abundant reason for the application of the remedy provided in the Bait Act. In furnishing our rivals with bait, we promote the evils we have to contend with, and our only course is to terminate this suicidal traffic.

"We are but too conscious that, from the causes referred to, the condition of our trade awakens a sense of great anxiety at the present moment; while we have full trust in the future, if only permitted by Her Majesty's Government to legislate as we see fit for the protection of what belongs to us. We regret we cannot safely accept your view of waiting to test, by further experience, the question how much longer and to what further extent our trade will bear up against the adverse influences that now prevail. Our ability to sustain ourselves against undue competition would be no argument for obliging us to contribute to its continuance, while the perils of such an experiment are too obvious to warrant its acceptance.

"Her Majesty's Government, in proposing that they should be the judges of the effect of our measures on our local interests, are not, we humbly submit, in a position to discharge that duty with safety or advantage. When it is suggested that, as regards our Bait Act, a consultation with the French may lead to a remedy being found in some other direction for the admitted evils, this proposal would appear to have originated with a want of knowledge of the situation. A free supply of bait to the French from our coasts means the effacement of our British trade and the exodus of our population, and forbids all thought of possible equivalents. We, moreover, must decline respectfully to accept the view that the French, or any other foreign Power, has a status or consultative claim in the control or disposition of our property, and we humbly demur to any recognition of their pretensions in this respect. We acknowledge no authority but that of the Imperial Government, and their rights of dominion are wisely limited by our constitutional powers, which secure for us the free exercise of our instructed intelligence in the management of our local affairs.

"The decision of Her Majesty's Government leaves us to deal with disheartening prospects for another year, the effects being already seen in the restriction and abandonment of proposed enterprise; but we cannot believe that any alleged difficulties will be allowed further to supersede the rights and mar the fortunes of the loyal people of this Colony struggling to maintain their position as an independent and honourable appendage of the British Crown."

In 1887, when our delegates were sent to England to press on the sanction of the Bait Act, their arrival, most fortunately for our interests, coincided with the holding of the Colonial Conference in London. Our Premier, then Mr. Thorburn, soon made Sir Robert, represented the most ancient colony; he was the premier of colonial premiers. In claiming our rights to control and legislate for our own fisheries we had all the colonies on our side but Canada; she demanded from the Colonial Office that the Act should be disallowed, and even if allowed, the penal clauses should be altered. Our representatives gave an assurance that Canadian fishermen were "to be placed upon the same footing as our own." Whilst we must all do justice to the able and earnest efforts of our delegates, Sir A. Shea and Sir R. Thorburn, the fortunate coincidence of their visit and the conference of all the Colonial Premiers gave great weight to our demand for the Imperial sanction to the Bait Act; in the Jubilee Year of Her Majesty's accession, the Colonial Office dare not be so ungracious as to refuse us the exercise of a right in which we would be sustained by every Colonial statesman then in London.

The British Government, having most reluctantly assented to the Bait Act, made it a condition that the Act should not be put in force until the following spring (1888).

HER MAJESTY THE QUEEN.
By Bassano.

The year 1887 will be ever memorable as the Jubilee of our Gracious Sovereign Queen Victoria. The occasion called out a grand exhibition of loyalty over the vast Empire whose drum-beat now encircles the world. In St. John's an impressive Jubilee service was held in the Anglican cathedral of St. John the Baptist, and was attended by all denominations.

The subsequent history of this important question of the Bait Act is well known to Newfoundland readers. I was requested by the Thorburn Government to put the Act in operation. In March 1888 I found myself one morning suddenly transformed from a peaceful District Judge into the commander of a fleet; the French called me "Bombarde Admiral," and our tugs "the Ironclads." We had very great difficulty in getting free from the ice; the old *Hercules*, however, butted her way round Cape Spear, and the S.S. *Lady Glover* followed in her wake; we managed to "clear our skirts," whilst the *Curlew* and *Portia* were detained for a long time at Trepassy. The initial difficulties attending a very arduous undertaking were thus overcome.

The year 1892 will ever be memorable in the Colony as a period of calamity, beginning with the great disaster in Trinity Bay, and followed by the fire of July. In January all the English-speaking world mourned for the death of the Duke of Clarence; sincere and widespread sympathy was felt for the bereaved prince and for the mother, the beloved Danish princess, endeared to all English hearts. In February occurred one of those terrible calamities and loss of human life which vividly impress us with the terrible dangers to which our hardy fishermen, who earn their bread upon the waters, are daily and hourly exposed.

Saturday, the 28th of February 1892 is a dark day in the annals of Trinity, a day to be ever remembered and mourned. The morning sun ushered in a lovely dawn, the sky was clear, a soft, bright, balmy air blew from the land over the treacherous sea, the light breeze scarcely ruffled its bosom. From Trinity and every harbour adjacent, boats were out by early dawn in pursuit of seals, which had been seen the previous evening. From Trinity, Ship Cove, Trouty, English Harbour, Salmon Cove, and other

SIR HENRY BLAKE, K.C.M.G.
By W. & C. Downey.

small places, the daring ice-hunters set off with high hopes and buoyant spirits to chase the wary seal; in this most exciting and dangerous pursuit the Newfoundlander recks not of danger; difficulties and perils that would affright one unaccustomed to the ice-fields are mere sport to the hardy native. On this eventful day seals were few and scattered; in the fierce excitement of the chase many went far out into the bay, heedless of the coming tempest; a few of the older fishermen, especially those from Trinity, more wary, and probably less vigorous, noticed the first signs of the storm, and before the icy blast came down with full force they were under the lee of the land and could row in. Two hundred and fifteen men were out on that day; the majority got safe to land after a tremendous struggle for their lives; the rest of the unfortunate fishermen, in spite of their heroic exertions, were finally overpowered; with strong arms they rowed for their lives, but the freezing icy tornado swept down upon them and paralysed their efforts; they had done all that men could do against the blizzard; they fought with the gale whilst instant death appeared on every wave. One bold crew from English Harbour, seeing all their attempts to stem the tempest were in vain, made for the ice; so chilling was the blast that before the boat had reached the floe, flying before the wind, one young fellow became paralysed with the cold; however, Newfoundlanders in a difficulty are never without resource. They climbed on to a pan higher than the rest, where they made a rude shelter; their boat was broken up to make a fire; with this and some seals they managed to live through that awful night. Thirteen fishermen were found frozen to death in their little punts; eleven others were driven up the bay and perished in that dark cold night of death. The hardships that were endured, the sufferings of the poor fellows that were saved, the agony of suspense for the dear ones on shore, the heroism of these poor humble souls in their hour of agony is known only to the Almighty Power " that rules the raging of the sea." All that could be done was done to alleviate the distressed; a gallant crew from Heart's Delight saved the sixteen men on the ice; the generous Captain Fowlow put out in the schooner and succoured some and brought them home to their agonised families. Charity flowed in to the widows and orphans; kindness, open-handed liberality, tender human sympathy was called forth for the mourners, for those, alas, whose sorrow for the dead will never die, who all life long will grieve over the death and destruction of that dark day of storm.

In the course of this History I have often had to chronicle the ravages of fire; thrice our capital has been destroyed by the devouring flame; the conflagration of the 8th and 9th of July 1892 far exceeded all former calamities in suddenness and in the immense value of the property destroyed. The great fire of 1846 began with the upsetting of a glue-pot in the shop of Hamelin the cabinet-maker, the still greater fire of July 1892 commenced in a stable, and was, in all probability, caused by the spark from a careless labourer's pipe. Commencing on a fine summer's evening, fanned by a high wind, the fire burnt all through the night, and in the bright dawn of that ever-memorable 9th of July, ten thousand people found themselves homeless, a forest of chimneys and heaps of ashes marking where the evening before had stood one of the busiest and most flourishing towns in the maritime provinces. Lest I should be accused of prejudice, I prefer giving an account of the disaster

from another pen. Nearly all the following description is taken from the *St. John's Evening Herald* of 10th September 1892 :—

THE FIRE OF 1892.

Ever memorable in the annals of St. John's will be the 8th day of July 1892. For generations to come the great fire of this year will form a subject for conversation, a period to date from, in the same manner as for the past forty-six years the great fire of the 9th of June 1846 has been. Exactly forty-six years and one month had passed away since the great fire of 1846, and the inhabitants of St. John's had come to look upon the fire demon as one that would never again destroy any great portion of our city. We felt secure in the great water power we had, and the almost unlimited quantity which was stored in the natural reservoir at Windsor Lake. In fact, such was our faith in the power of the fire department, and in the supply of water, that when a fire occurred, even at night, but few people ever troubled to arise from their beds to ascertain its whereabouts.

Such was the feeling of security, that when the bells rang the double alarm on Friday, the 8th July, but few people paid any attention to it. The weather had been extremely hot for some weeks before; so much so, that the grass had withered on the high lands, and vegetables were being dried up. Forest fires prevailed in the surrounding country, and for days the air had been laden with the smoke and heat of burning bush and moss. Friday was one of the hottest days of the summer, the thermometer registering 87° in the shade at 2 p.m. Although the thermometer ranged so high, an unusually strong breeze of wind prevailed all day, decking the harbour with "white caps," and the dust flew about in blinding showers. About five o'clock the Central fire bell rang out an alarm, which was quickly responded to by the firemen, who proceeded to the scene of the conflagration at the junction of Freshwater and Pennywell Roads. By the careless handling of a match the stable of Mr. T. Brien had caught fire, and there is not the least doubt that it might have been easily extinguished in its incipient stage, but that not a bucketful of water could be had, for the water-pipes had been undergoing repairs that day, and although the water is said to have been turned on at 3 p.m., the water at 5 had not reached the higher levels of the town, and the reservoir, close to the scene of the outbreak, was found to be empty, having been pumped out by the fire brigade at a practice about one month previously. With no water to check the devouring element, and a stable full of hay to feed, and a gale of wind to fan the flames, the fire spread with incredible rapidity, leaping from house to house. It was speedily seen that the fire was going to assume large proportions, and a call was made for extra aid, which brought many townsfolk to the spot, but although there were many willing hands, there was no water. This fact seemed to paralyse the firemen, and the leaping flames flying with such rapidity from house to house, passing over an occasional one, demonstrated the fact that no human effort could stay their onward rush. Whilst one stream of fire rapidly descended Carter's Hill, another swiftly destroyed the buildings on the south side of Harvey Street, and those on Long's Hill, taking in its course the magnificent Methodist College Hall, School, and Home; the Masonic Temple, a comparatively new building, and one that was justly looked upon with great pride by the Masonic fraternity. The destruction of Presbyterian Manse and building near by followed.

People began to realise that the fire was going to be one of huge proportions; household goods were hastily packed and taken to places which were thought to be safe, such as the Church of England Cathedral, the Gower Street Methodist Church, and the St. Patrick's Hall. Soon flying pieces of shingle and light wood were scattered over the city, and in less than two hours fires had started in several places. Scotland Row, on Church Hill, was on fire before the Masonic Temple had caught, and a building inside of Chain Rock was burnt down before the fire reached Water Street. The Court House and W. Campbell's supply store caught simultaneously, and before Gower Street Church was on fire. Standing near the Synod Hall one could see a mass of flames rushing down Long's Hill and across the road from the Fire Hall, licking up the brick buildings in front of Victoria Hall as though they were chips. A few firemen, with a short hose, through which feebly filtered a small stream of water, endeavoured to put out a spark of fire which fell on the building north of Mr. Mariott's house; presently it was seen that the Clergy House adjoining Bishop Jones's residence was on fire, and then the roof of the Synod Hall caught. A ladder and some water would have saved these buildings, but there was none at hand, and the chief of the Municipal Council stood and gazed in a helpless manner at the empty hose and the burning buildings.

The fire had now reached that noble edifice the Church of England Cathedral, a work of art, of Gothic design, by Sir Gilbert Scott. Although not quite complete, it was the pride of the city. It had been erected at a cost of about $500,000, the transepts and chancel having been lately added to the nave, which latter had been built forty years previously. Alas, it now lies a magnificent ruin. With the onward sweep of the fire, the heat and the wind increased. Sweeping down over Gower and Duckworth Street, the brick and stone buildings, warehouses, stores, halls, public buildings, and houses on Water Street fell before the flames as speedily as did the wooden buildings higher up. The Union Bank had a narrow

VIEW OF THE ANGLICAN CATHEDRAL AND THE UNION BANK AFTER THE FIRE.
From a photograph.

escape, due no doubt to the fact that it was protected in the front by the large poplar trees standing in the Cathedral grounds.

By 8 o'clock the fire had reached Water Street, and Messrs. Harvey and Co.'s premises, Campbell's, Job Bros. and Co.'s, were on fire in the east, and the Court House to the west of Market House Hill. People on the upper levels were fast hurrying away with their household goods, those who could employing teams and paying exorbitant prices for their hire. Many deposited their belongings in the streets, only to be consumed by the relentless flames, or stolen from them. As the night advanced, the fire swept on from Long's Hill west down over Playhouse

THE FIRE OF 1892.

Hill to Beck's Cove, where a vigorous stand was made, which was effectual in stopping its progress west. On Playhouse Hill, near Bates Street, a vigorous effort was made by some noble workers, who formed a fire break by tearing down Dougherty's Forge, thus saving the upper part of the town. The fire, which had taken possession of the buildings on Garrison Hill, was communicated to the St. Patrick's Hall, and notwithstanding the great efforts made by the Christian Brothers and others to save this fine building, it was soon one mass of flames. It was then feared that the fire would spread to the Convent and buildings on Military Road, and a stand was made to save the houses on the north side of Queen's Road. All on the south side were in flames, but the stone chapel belonging to the Congregationalists stood intact. It was here that great want of tact was displayed by those in charge of the fire department. A hose which was engaged in playing on some wooden buildings further to the eastward, and which could not possibly do any service at the time, should have been employed in wetting the side of the Congregational Church. Had such been done, this building, the one opposite, and in all probability the houses of Mr. Greene and of Maxse Terrace, would have

THE ANGLICAN CATHEDRAL AFTER THE FIRE.
From a photograph.

been saved. The fire which had swept down Gower, Duckworth, and Water Streets, crept slowly up Prescott Street, and at the top of King's Road a great effort was made to save the Eastern Fire Hall, which was successful. Had this taken fire all the buildings on Military Road would have been destroyed. Another danger menaced Military Road in the presence of a stable to the south-east of the

Drill Shed, which could not be reached by the hose. On this building for over half-an-hour three of the members of the force worked right valiantly, being supplied with water by a body of citizens, who vied with each other in carrying buckets. It was here that Constable Manning fell, injuring himself somewhat. Owing to the exertions of these policemen and citizens, the Military Road Buildings, the Methodist School on Carew Street, and the Church of England Academy Buildings were saved.

The fire had now reached Cochrane Street, and it was hoped that the upper portion of this fine street might be saved. A few lengths of hose were obtained, but not sufficient to reach the burning houses, and the water supply was not what it ought to have been. Several attempts were made to pull down buildings, but as they were supplied with very staunch chimneys, the efforts proved futile until the fire had reached next door to the Hon. G. T. Rendell's residence. The house to southward was partially torn down whilst on fire, saving Mr. Rendell's, the only house now standing on the east side of Cochrane Street.

About two o'clock, the fire had reached the buildings west of Devon Row. The waterside premises, stores, warehouses, wharves, &c., from Bowring's to Murray's were a mass of ruins. Pitts' Tobacco and Soap Factory was in flames, and it was feared that Devon Row would go, but a vigorous effort on the part of its residents saved it, and the destroying element swept past, consuming the stores of Hon. A. M. McKay, The Tannery, Messrs John Woods & Son's premises, Harvey's Tobacco Factory and Bakery, the Coastal Company's Wharf and Stores, a portion of Hoyles Town, including the Convent School, and the buildings on Signal Hill, including the Bavarian Brewery, Lindberg's, W. Canning's, and the American Consul's residences. The preservation of that part of Hoyles Town adjoining the Railway Depôt is due to the hard work done by Manager Noble, of the Railway Company, and his men, who successfully fought the sparks and flames. The St. George's Barracks, which was used as a fever and diphtheria hospital, and several buildings on the crest of the hill had taken fire, and were destroyed early in the evening. Several vessels lying at the wharves had narrow escapes. The *Nelly*, *Ethel*, and *Prince Le Boo* moved into the stream, and their rigging and sails caught fire several times. The steamer *Sharpshooter*, brig *Dovre*, the coal hulk *Huntress*, and a number of small boats were burned.

About 5.30 a.m. of the ninth the fire had completed its work of destruction; fully three-fourths of the city lay in ruins. $20,000,000 worth of property had been destroyed, only covered by an insurance of $4,800,000.[1] Nearly eleven thousand people were homeless, some two thousand houses and stores had been destroyed, and the following public buildings: Church of England Cathedral, Rectory,

---

[1] AMOUNT OF INSURANCE EFFECTED ON PROPERTY IN ST. JOHN'S DESTROYED BY THE FIRE.

	$
Liverpool, London, and Globe	375,000
Phœnix, London	750,000
Atlas	100,000
Queen	550,000
Northern	300,000
Royal	500,000
Norwich Union	45,000
Guardian	200,000
North British	235,000
London and Lancashire	500,000
Carried forward	3,555,000

	$
Brought forward	3,555,000
Manchester	100,000
Commercial Union	200,000
Imperial	240,000
Lion	50,000
City of London	37,000
Lancashire	30,800
General	120,000
Phœnix of Hartford (U.S.)	38,000
Citizens	20,000
London Assurance	50,000
Sun (London)	150,000
Total	4,590,800

ST. JOHN'S AFTER THE FIRE OF 1892

GIVING OUT RELIEF AT THE PARADE GROUND

WHARVES AT ST. JOHN'S AFTER THE FIRE OF 1892

Clergy House, Synod Hall, Orphanage and Sunday School House; Gower Street Methodist Church, Parsonage, College Hall, School and Home; Presbyterian Church (St. Andrew's), Manse and School House; the Congregational Chapel, Queens Road; Colonial and Continental Church Society's School and Dwelling; the Old Factory; the following public halls: St. Patrick's, Athenæum (including the offices of the Savings Bank, Surveyor-General, Government Engineer, and Fisheries Commission), Star of the Sea, Masonic, Victoria, Total Abstinence, Temperance, Mechanics and British, Commercial Bank, City and Academia Club Houses, Temple Billiard Room, Court House and Custom House; St. John's Laundry; Hotels: Atlantic, Waverly, Central, and Gordon; City Skating Rink; Factories: Harvey's Bakery and Tobacco, Pitts' Tobacco and Soap, Terra Nova Boiler Works, Lindberg's Brewery, Boot and Shoe Company's Tannery; Printing Offices: *Herald*, *Times*, *Gazette*, *Advocate*, *Telegram*, *Colonist*, and Bowden and Sons; every lawyer's office; all the offices and residences of the principal physicians; the druggist shops of McMurdo & Co., J. T. O'Mara, Kavanagh, and Hatton; the S.P.G. Depôt, and principal stationers' shops; the business premises and wharves from Bowring's hardware shop to Chain Rock, including Bowring Bros.' dry goods shop and eastern store, J. & W. Pitts, Goodfellow & Co., Ayre and Sons, G. Knowling, Prowse and Sons, J. Baird, Baine Johnston & Co., Clift Wood & Co., S. Woods, W. Frew, Thorburn and Tessier, West and Rendell, Marshall and Rodger, T. J. Edens, W. Campbell & Co., J. H. Martin & Co., Job Bros. & Co., Rothwell and Bowring, Hearn & Co., J. Stott, Harvey, & Co., Gleeson, S. March and Sons, W. P. Walsh, W. and G. Rendell, Shea & Co., H. J. Stabb, J. Murray, J. Woods and Son, and A. J. Harvey, were among the principal ones burnt.

The boundaries of the burnt district may be thus particularly described: from Beck's Cove, up Beck's Hill, along Bates Street to New Gower, west along New Gower, up Carter's Hill to corner of Wickford Street, thence west to back of houses on east side of Good View Street, thence north to Cabot Street, thence up Carter's Hill to Le-Marchant Road, and on to Freshwater Road, thence east along Freshwater Road and down Harvey Street to Roman Catholic Cathedral. Down Garrison Hill and along Military Road, thence along Queen's Road, south to Fire Hall, thence south of Church of England Academy, and east along Bond Street. Up Cochrane Street and along Military Road to King's Bridge Road, thence south down Ordnance Square to Temperance Hill, up Signal Hill Road (the fire destroying many detached houses in the neighbourhood), thence west along Water Street, including all the waterside premises.

The loss of life was comparatively small. It is known that Ellen Molloy, Mrs. Stevens, daughter and servant were burnt. All the shipping at the wharves had to make for the stream, and there anchor out of reach of the flames, and all the wharves, in many instances with valuable contents, were destroyed. All through the long night the crowds continued passing and repassing, those who had friends gladly availing themselves of the welcome shelter of their houses, while those who had no better places, settled themselves with their belongings in Bannerman Park, the Roman Catholic Cathedral grounds, and even by the road sides waiting for day to break. Few there were who closed their eyes in sleep that night—the homeless too heartsick and weary to seek relief in slumber, while those more fortunate found themselves burdened with relatives and friends, or gave way to the natural excitement engendered by such an occasion, and wandered aimlessly from place to place fascinated by a scene at once magnificent and awe inspiring. The misery of that awful night will long be borne in the memories of the witnesses, and the scenes of utter desolation and hopeless ruin which became evident at every step were sufficient to unman the strongest nerves. When morning broke the thick clouds of smoke still ascended from the burning ruins, and it was hours before it had cleared sufficiently to admit of a view of the track or the desolating scourge.

A walk through the deserted streets demonstrated that the ruin was even more complete than seemed possible at first. Of the whole easterly section scarcely a building remained. In the extreme north-east a small section of Hoylestown was standing protected by massive Devon Row, but the remainder of St. John's east had vanished. Of the immense shops and stores which displayed such varied merchandise and valuable stocks gathered from all parts of the known world; of the happy homes of artisans and middle classes, where contentment and prosperity went hand in hand; of the comfortable houses where the labouring man sought rest and refreshment; and of the costly and imposing structures and public buildings which were the pride and glory of our people, scarcely a vestige remained; and St. John's lay in the morning sun as a city despoiled of her beauty and choicest ornaments, presenting a picture of utter desolation and woe. But hungry mouths were to be fed; houseless people provided with shelter, and with the advent of the morning the work commenced. Temporary shelters were erected in Bannerman Park, and substantial provisions provided.

The temporary telegraph offices enabled us to communicate the details to the outside world, and on Saturday the first offers of relief came pouring in. To

ENCAMPMENT NEAR QUIDI VIDI FOR FIRE SUFFERERS.
From a photograph.

Halifax belongs the glory of first assisting us, and that evening H.M.S. *Blake* started from there with a large stock of provisions and tents. The *Ulunda* left about the same time, and the *Portia* followed her on Monday. Subsequently the s.s. *Havana*, with a full cargo of relief stores, arrived from Halifax, followed by the Dominion steamer *Newfield* with a contribution of $10,000 worth from the Dominion Government, and the s.s. *Newfoundland* from Montreal, with a cargo of relief stores. Besides the large amount collected for the relief of the city throughout the length and breadth of the Dominion, the Ontario Government voted $10,000 towards our needs, and the Dominion Government $20,000. We cannot too highly extol the magnificent spirit of charity which pervaded our fellow subjects in the Dominion . . . . . All honour to the noble-hearted and generous people of the Dominion, and may they never meet such a dire calamity as we have passed through. From Great Britain generous donations poured in, and by the influence of our Governor,

THE FIRE OF 1892.

Sir T. N. O'Brien, K.C.M.G., and Lady O'Brien were in England, enjoying a brief holiday; the moment they heard of the great calamity they at once cancelled all their engagements, and during the remainder of their stay at home devoted themselves to the relief of the sufferers. By their personal influence and untiring zeal in the cause of the distressed, very large and generous donations were sent from England, both in money, clothes, and materials; all these Lady O'Brien, with a committee of ladies in St. John's, afterwards dispensed to the fire sufferers; only those who have been concerned in such work of relief can realise the time, the trouble, the worry and anxiety involved in such labours. In his exertions on behalf of the Colony Sir Terence was ably assisted by the Newfoundland colonies in London and Liverpool, also by Sir J. S. Winter, the Honourable A. W. Harvey, and afterwards by Bishop Jones. A Mansion House fund was started, which reached £20,000 sterling. From the United States many contributions were received, notably the gift from Boston, raised principally among our fellow-countrymen there by the zeal and energy of two warm-hearted Newfoundlanders, Messrs. Taylor and Whittle.

SIR T. N. O'BRIEN, K.C.M.G.
By Bieber, Hamburg.

On the 12th July a Relief Committee was appointed by His Excellency the Administrator of the Government, the Hon. Sir F. B. T. Carter, K.C.M.G., consisting of the following gentlemen:— Hon. Judge Little, President; Honbles. Sir W. V. Whiteway, H. J. B. Woods, E. P. Morris, J. S. Pitts, E. D. Shea, G. T. Rendell; J. J. Rogerson, Sir R. Thorburn, J. Outerbridge, H. C. Burchell, Thomas Mitchell, J. R. McCowan, W. P. Walsh, A. Marshall, C. Tessier, Col. Fawcett; J. B. Sclater, Secretary, and Alfred Pike, Clerk.

The most important event in the year 1893 was the general election in November. Both sides entered into the contest with the greatest enthusiasm; the utmost vigour and energy was displayed in the contest; it was the most stubbornly-contested party fight in our annals. Both the Whiteway party and the Opposition everywhere had good candidates, the Conservatives being largely composed of the mercantile party, with a powerful wing of the Catholic or old Liberal Party. The contest was so keen, the chances appeared so evenly balanced, especially in St. John's, that no one under the Ballot Act could foretell the result. Mr. Monroe, one of the ablest politicians in the island, conducted his own election in the west end of St. John's with immense spirit, leaving no stone unturned to gain his seat; Mr. Walter Baine Grieve made an equally determined fight against Sir William and the Hon. R. Bond in Trinity. The merchants used their influence to the full, and the Whiteway party employed the machinery of Government to the very utmost extent; both sides were sure of victory. The old leaven of prejudice against the mercantile monopolists of a former time has still immense influence in the Colony; antagonism between capital and labour shows in a very pronounced degree under the Ballot Act. This feeling, and the unlimited use of the machinery of Government, gained the day for the Whiteway party.

LADY O'BRIEN
By S. H. Parsons.

The prejudice against the merchants, however reasonable and natural in olden times, should not exist now; employers and employed are mutually dependent on each other. We have seen the effect of the withdrawal of large mercantile houses from the outports. No one has filled their places; their beneficial influence in giving labour and employment to the people has been entirely lost.

It should always be remembered that a fishery business like ours is a most precarious enterprise; it is exposed to a thousand accidents, from the dangers and perils of the sea, from the chances and changes of a variable climate, quite apart from the risks of markets abroad. Whatever great fortunes were made in the old days, they are not gained now; occasional large profits are a necessity in such an exceedingly risky business. The men who stir up strife between capital and labour in the Colony are no true friends of Newfoundland; what we require is more money introduced into the Colony, more patriotism and less politics.

SIR R. PINSENT.

The election campaign of 1893 was marked by a remarkable outburst of personal abuse; both the political parties vied with each other in keeping up this indecent carnival of scurrility. There was not even a stray gleam of coarse humour to palliate the nauseous dose; the one and only comic element in the campaign literature of 1893 was the political manifesto of Mr. Murray, who posed as "the fisherman's friend."

The year 1893 was saddened by the untimely deaths of Sir R. J. Pinsent, D.C.L., on April 28th, and the Most Rev. Dr. T. J. Power, Roman Catholic Bishop of St. John's, on December 4th. Sir Robert was a native that any Colony might be proud of; he was not only an able lawyer and a distinguished judge, he took a deep interest in all that concerned the welfare of the Colony, and was active in every good work to promote the best interests of his native land; his mild, amiable character and his polished courtesy made many friends; few men in the Colony were more beloved, few who are more missed. His clear intellect, his untiring industry, and his intense love of his profession, combined to make a lawyer who would have been an ornament to the Bench and the Bar of any portion of Her Majesty's dominions. Sir Robert's courtesy and kindness to the Bar were proverbial. He had all the qualities of an able judge, strong in his law, clear in the marshalling of his facts; always prompt in his decisions, no charge could ever be laid against him of that terrible delay which is a practical denial of justice.

SIR R. J. PINSENT, D.C.L.
By S. H. Parsons.

The period between 1884 and 1894 was marked by a number of negotiations with other countries. Besides the Ford-Pennell Conventions of 1884 and 1885, and other questions concerning the Treaty shore and the lobsters, we had the Washington Treaty of 1888, in which England and Canada were represented by Mr. Chamberlain, M.P., and Sir Charles Tupper, Newfoundland by Sir James Winter, K.C.M.G. An admirable Reciprocity Treaty was arranged between the United States, Canada, and our Colony; it was not, however, ratified. The United States treated us in rather a dishonourable manner; they obtained the benefit of a *modus vivendi* for two years, and then repudiated the solemn international engagement.

SIR J. S. WINTER, K.C.M.G.

In 1890 we had the *modus vivendi* about the lobster controversy with France. Two delegations were sent to England: the one from the Patriotic Association consisted of Sir James Winter, P. Scott, and A. B. Morine, Esqrs. (also one to Canada, composed of D. Morrison, P. R. Bowers, and D. J. Greene, Esqrs.); the other was the official delegation of Sir W. V. Whiteway and the Hon. A. W. Harvey (who went first to England), and the Hons. R. Bond and G. H. Emerson, Speaker, who followed later on. In the same year the Hon. R. Bond was sent to Washington to negotiate the Blaine-Bond Reciprocity Treaty. In 1891, again, a delegation, consisting of Sir W. V. Whiteway, the Speaker, G. H. Emerson, and A. B. Morine, with Honbles. A. W. Harvey and M. Monroe, was sent by the Legislature to oppose the French Fishery Treaty Bill, known in popular parlance as the "Coercion Bill," then before the House of Lords. These were all very important questions for the Colony; they brought us a good deal into public notice, and it is necessary for the due elucidation of our history to state the leading points in each question. I will take first the abortive Convention with the United States, known as the Blaine-Bond Treaty, leaving the French Fishery dispute to be dealt with in a separate chapter.

According to the Parliamentary papers laid before the House of Assembly, the Colonial Secretary went to Washington with the concurrence and at the request of Lord Knutsford. The terms of the Convention to be made between Newfoundland and the United States were approved of by the Colonial Office, and it was only after the whole matter was definitely arranged that the Imperial Government intervened at the instance of Canada and refused to ratify the Treaty. Sir John A. McDonald's opposition to the arrangement, and his imperious order to the Home Government to put an end to it, was given on the eve of an election; it was done to secure his Government's return. For the English Government to act as election agents for Canada seems a very extraordinary proceeding; our rights as an independent Colony have been made entirely subservient to the political exigencies of the Dominion. Because Canada could not get a suitable Reciprocity Treaty with the United States, she should not have stopped our Convention with America.

D. MORRISON, ESQ.

Nothing did more to stir up a hostile feeling against the great Dominion than this interference in our affairs. A conference met at Halifax, Nova Scotia, in 1893 to endeavour to arrange in an amicable manner matters between the two Colonies. One of our demands was that Canada's opposition to the Blaine-Bond Treaty should be withdrawn. Matters still remain *in statu quo*. Canada has a considerable trade with Newfoundland, but our Colony sends very little produce to the Dominion. She is not one of our consumers, but our rival in the fish trade; our great market of the future lies in the United States. The American deep-sea fishery is a decaying industry; the consumption of salt-water fish is very small compared with Europe. We can supply the great Republic with all the fish she can consume from our most abundant and extensive cod and herring fisheries. We have immense advantages to offer the Americans in the pursuit of their own bank fishery; we are not like Canada, rivals with the States in manufacturing and agriculture. America, from its position and its immense population, is our best customer. Every West India island is allowed to make an arrangement with the States; why should we alone be forbidden to carry on our trade in a way which is most beneficial to ourselves? The position of the British Government on this subject was rather undignified. The points of our case against both Canada and the British Government were very clearly set forth in the Resolutions proposed in the House of Assembly on March 6th, 1891, by the Hon. R. Bond, Colonial Secretary, and adopted by that body.

HON. R. BOND.

Any fair-minded person reading the correspondence on the intended Treaty will be convinced, first, that the Secretary of State for the Colonies authorised Mr. Bond to negotiate for the Blaine-Bond Convention; that England made no objection; that the only opposition to the proposed Treaty emanated from Canada. If after the Colonial Minister submitted the Convention to the Dominion Government it was then to entirely fall to the ground, the Secretary of State should have stated that such was his decision clearly to the Newfoundland Cabinet; that his sending Mr. Bond again to Washington, after hearing Canada's objections, could have only one meaning and intention, viz., that the Imperial Government, notwithstanding Canada's objections, proposed to allow Newfoundland to carry out the proposed Convention, and this is further proved by the despatch from the Colonial Office to Canada that the Convention could not be indefinitely postponed. Colonists are wont to rely upon the honour and word of an

English Minister. If he was not all the time playing with Newfoundland, if he really meant serious business, then the only obvious meaning and true intent of his words, the only construction that any honourable man can put upon his language and action, is that he intended and determined that this Colony should be allowed to make a Convention with the United States. In the negotiations now going forward between the Governments respecting the union of Newfoundland with the Dominion, it is to be hoped that the Canadian statesmen will show themselves liberal, and even generous, towards the Colony, otherwise they will make the path of the Island delegates very thorny and difficult. No terms whatever will satisfy the opponents of the Newfoundland Government, but if the conditions are eminently reasonable, all sensible men in the Colony who are now disposed towards confederation as the best available way out of our difficulties will be satisfied.

The other alternative, making the Island into a Crown Colony, which is put forward very earnestly by many persons and the Opposition, is really not a practical solution; we must remember that an English Cabinet would never take away a constitution from its British subjects unless there was tremendous pressure brought to bear in its favour; the least opposition to it on the part of the Colony or the Assembly would decide against it. The Home Government would also object to administer the government and make themselves responsible for its finances and general control. The Crown Colony idea is obsolete and impracticable.

The whole of this chapter was printed in 1894, and the book was intended to end with that year; owing, however, to my absence from England, final publication was delayed until 1895, and in order to bring this History up to date it becomes my very unpleasant duty to comment on the disasters and disgrace of 1894. These events are too near, some of the details are still *sub judice*, and the whole circumstances are too recent, to be calmly discussed and impartially considered; all the facts want to be brought forward, and a certain distance of time and space allowed, before we can fairly adjust the blame for all these disasters and humiliations. One thing, however, comes out very clearly, that merchants and politicians on both sides have helped to bring the unfortunate Colony into disrepute by the fierce rancour and bitter personal hate which characterised their party struggles; in their mad desire for revenge on each other true patriotism disappeared, and the vital interests of our unfortunate Colony were entirely ignored.

The merchants' party having suffered ignominious defeat in the General Election of 1893, were determined to be revenged on the Whiteway side, their avowed object being to ruin its leader; for this purpose petitions were filed in the Supreme Court under the Corrupt Practices Act against seventeen members of the majority. The English opinion that measures all political questions in the Colonies by its own imperial bushel has been extremely severe on the Whiteway party, and laudatory of their opponents. Persons well acquainted with Newfoundland politics see clearly that there was no real principle involved, that there was not a pin to choose between the Goodridge and the Whiteway politicians, that this clever political trick to kill Sir William, all the turmoil, disorder, and bad feeling caused by these election petitions and the contests they created, the disgrace and degradation of the Colony, were simply the outcome of rage and vindictiveness.

HON. A. F. GOODRIDGE.
By Bradlaw, Torquay.

The Corrupt Practices Act is a very severe and drastic measure, but standing alone it is quite an inadequate remedy for the rotten method of electioneering pursued everywhere in North America. The spoils system lies at the root of all political corruption at contests. It is only, therefore, by the reform of the Civil Service on the English model that elections can be carried out in a fairly decent and honourable way. In the distribution of patronage and the allocation of public work to their supporters the Whiteway party continued the bad practices of their predecessors, and the Goodridge party did much the same. It was acknowledged at the election trials by the judges that the public road-money had been fairly well spent, and that no charge of personal dishonesty could be brought against the unseated members.

How any set of politicians, aware of the condition of the Colonial finances, and, as directors of the banks, cognisant of the state of the trade, could have ventured on this wild career and rushed the Island down headlong to ruin, seems utterly unintelligible, except on the supposition *quem Deus vult perdere, prius dementat*. The real interests of the Colony were never considered.

No one can deny that the findings on the election petitions were technically right, but the manner and mode of delivering the first judgment was, to put it in the mildest way, not judicious. The first decision, which was to govern all the cases, should certainly have been the act of the full Court; the judgment should have been delivered by the Chief Justice as the united act of the Bench, not as the isolated opinion of the one judge, who had only recently been an extreme opponent of the Whiteway party.

Our successive disasters, the fire of 1892, and the jarring of the political factions, seemed enough to fill up the cup of our woe; but worse was in store for us. Up to fatal Black Monday, 10th December 1894, Newfoundland credit stood high. Our principal monetary institution, the Union Bank, had for forty years maintained the highest reputation at home and abroad; suddenly credit, financial reputation, confidence in both mercantile houses and banks, fell like a house of cards. For several days we were the most distracted country in the world—a community without a currency; the notes of the banks had been the universal money of the Colony—circulating as freely as gold on Saturday, on Monday degraded to worthless paper.

It would be too painful a task to enumerate all the causes that led to this terrible financial crisis. The death of a commission merchant in London disturbed nearly the whole monetary affairs of the Colony. If his executor had gone on accepting, probably the crisis might have been postponed for some months. The only excuse that can possibly be alleged for the directors of the banks, their large borrowings and crass mismanagement, was that, like Micawber, they were waiting for "something to turn up"—some rise in the fish markets, or some other lucky chance that would lift them out of the mire of insolvency.

The misery caused by these failures of banks and mercantile houses was as disastrous, as widespread, and as universal within our border as the bursting of the South Sea bubble was in the United Kingdom. All our prospects still seem black and gloomy, and in most countries such disastrous events could have but one result—irretrievable ruin; the prospects of Newfoundland, however, cannot be judged by outside standards. Once before, in 1817, she suffered far more severely and rose again; may we not, therefore, reasonably hope that Newfoundland and her bold and adventurous sons will once again emerge from her present unhappy condition? Populations that live by the sea and earn their bread upon its treacherous waters are always liable to dire disaster; but the same spirit that leads them to face the dangers of the troubled waves, nerves them also with a spirit to rise again from calamities that would for ever daunt the courage of a landsman. One change was inevitable; the dishonest credit system on which the business of the Colony was transacted had to die out; demoralising to the people and disastrous to the merchant, there could be no genuine prosperity whilst this old truck system existed; recent events have effectually banished it, we may hope, for ever. Terrible misery will be caused before the change can be effectually carried out, but in the end it will be beneficial. If commercial gambling finally ceases, trade and finance will rest on a firmer and safer foundation. Not only must there be a new mercantile method of carrying on the fish business, the old antiquated system of curing and handling our staple product must also be superseded by modern ideas, and newer and more scientific methods adopted both in preparing, packing, and transporting.

We must remember that whilst much of the working capital of the Colony has been lost in recent failures, the wealth-producing power of the Island has not been seriously impaired. Fish must always remain one of the staple foods of the world, but the products of the sea, which have hitherto been our chief, we may almost say our only resource, should in time be augmented by the labours of the lumberman and the miner. Newfoundland is still almost an unexplored country; her geological formation points to much hidden wealth, which we may fairly hope the development and completion of the railway will help to bring forth; the natural result of speedy and convenient communication is to attract capital and start new enterprises.

On the morning of the 24th June 1897, four hundred years will have rolled away since John Cabot first sighted the green Cape of Bonavista; four centuries will have elapsed since the stem of the *Matthew's* boat grated on the gravelly shore of Keels, and since King's Cove witnessed the setting up of the Royal Ensign, the feudal ceremony that proclaimed to the world the possession of a new continent for England, the grandest field for the expansion of our race. May we not confidently hope that when the morning sun shines out again on the anniversary of that great Baptist's day in 1897 evil times will have passed, and our Island, closely united with her prosperous younger sisters, will once again become a happy and contented New-found-land?

APPENDIX TO CHAPTER XVI.

I.—Convention between Great Britain and the United States of America.

ARTICLE I.

United States fishing vessels entering the waters of Newfoundland shall have the privilege of purchasing herring, caplin, squid, and other bait fishes, at all times, on the same terms and conditions, and subject to the same penalties, in all respects, as Newfoundland vessels. They shall also have the privilege of touching and trading, selling fish and oil, and procuring supplies, in Newfoundland, conforming to the Harbour Regulations, but without other charge than the payment of such light, harbour, and customs dues as are or may be levied on Newfoundland fishing vessels.

ARTICLE II.

Dry codfish, cod oil, seal oil, seal skins, herrings, salmon, trout, and salmon trout, lobsters, cod roes, tongues and sounds, the product of the fisheries of Newfoundland, shall be admitted into the United States free of duty. Also all hogsheads, barrels, kegs, boxes, or tin cans, in which the articles above-named shall be carried, shall be admitted free of duty. It is understood, however, that "green codfish" are not included in the provisions of this Article.

ARTICLE III.

The officer of the customs at the port where a vessel laden with the articles named in Article II. clears, shall give to the master of said vessel a sworn certificate that the fish shipped were taken in the waters of Newfoundland, which certificate shall be countersigned by the consul or consular agent of the United States, and delivered to the proper officer of customs at the port of destination in the United States.

ARTICLE IV.

When this Convention shall come into operation, and during the continuance thereof, the duties to be levied and collected upon the following enumerated merchandise imported into the Colony of Newfoundland from the United States shall not exceed the following amounts, viz.:—

Flour, 25c. per brl.
Pork, $1.50 per brl.
Bacon, hams, tongues, smoked beef, and sausages, 2 1.4c. per lb., or $2.50 per cwt.
Beef, pig's heads, hocks and feet, salted and cured, $1.00 per brl.
Indian Meal, 25c. per brl.
Peas, 30c. per brl.
Oatmeal, 30c. per brl.
Bran, Indian corn, and rice 12 1.2c. ad valorem.
Salt, in bulk, 20c. per ton.
Kerosene oil, 6c. per gal.

And the following articles imported into the Colony of Newfoundland from the United States shall be admitted free of duty:—

Agricultural implements and machinery imported by agricultural societies for the promotion of agriculture.
Crushing mills, for mining purposes.
Raw cotton.
Corn for the manufacture of brooms.
Gas engines, when protected by patent.
Ploughs and harrows.
Reaping, raking, ploughing, potato digging, and seed-sowing machines to be used in this Colony.
Printing presses and printing types.

ARTICLE V.

It is understood that if any reduction is made by the Colony of Newfoundland, at any time during the term of this Convention, in the rates of duty on the articles named in Article IV. of this Convention, the said reduction shall apply to the United States.

ARTICLE VI.

The present Convention shall take effect as soon as the laws required to carry it into operation shall have been passed by the Congress of the United States on the one hand, and the Imperial Parliament of Great Britain and the Provincial Legislature of Newfoundland on the other. Such assent having been given, the Convention shall remain in force for five years from the date at which it may come into operation, and further until the expiration of twelve months after either of the high contracting parties shall give notice to the other of its wish to terminate the same; each of the high contracting parties being at liberty to give such notice to the other at the end of the said term of five years, or at any time afterwards.

ARTICLE VII.

This Convention shall be duly ratified by the President of the United States of America, by and with the advice and consent of the Senate thereof, and by Her Britannic Majesty: and the ratification shall be exchanged at Washington on the 1st day of February 1891, or as soon thereafter as practicable.

CHAPTER XVII.

THE PRESENT POSITION OF THE FRENCH FISHERY QUESTION.

The French Government were very indignant over the failure of the Ford-Pennell Conventions of 1884 and 1885. M. De Freycinet immediately afterwards gave instructions "to seize and confiscate " all instruments of fishing belonging to foreigners, resident or other- " wise, who shall fish on that part of the coast which is reserved for " our use." As Lord Rosebery pointed out to M. Waddington, these instructions were a direct infringement of the Treaty; they ignored the sovereign rights of Great Britain which the French Government solemnly undertook by the Treaties never to question or dispute. Incensed, however, as the French were by the failure of the one-sided Convention, they were still more enraged by the passing of the Bait Act; they realised far more fully than we did, that the Colony had by this measure obtained an immense advantage in maintaining the struggle against French aggression. Whether we actively use this formidable weapon, or hold it in reserve, it will always have great influence in this vexed question.

In 1888, after the Bait Act had been successfully put in operation for the first season, the French retaliated upon us by stopping Messrs. Murphy & Andrew's lobster factory, and by erecting a French canning business in the same locality. Two years before, in 1886, Commander Browne, of H.M.S. *Mallard*, reported the existence of a French lobster factory at Port-aux-Choix, worked by a Captain Dameron, a substantially-built structure, roofed with corrugated iron. The French admitted that this erection was contrary to the Treaty, and when the French commodore arrived in the *Drac*, he ordered it to be removed. This was all a trick, for the captain of the French man-of-war schooner *Perle*, which came into port just after, allowed the factory to go on again, and later on a whole cargo of lumber was permitted to be imported in the French brigantine

Tombolo to complete the buildings. The French cod fishery was failing, and ingenious traders from St. Pierre thought it would be a clever stroke to carry on this business, of course in defiance of law. The French knew what all this would lead to; they calculated that the British Government would not firmly oppose their lobster factories, and if all came to the worst they would compromise the matter and allow English lobster factories to be erected in return for the permission to legalise the erection of French factories. The final result was the *Modus Vivendi*.

FOREST AND SHEARER'S LOBSTER FACTORY, BRIG BAY, N.W. COAST.
From Black and White.

It must be remembered that in this lobster question the French, by their own admission, are entirely in the wrong. They solemnly promised to remove the French factories as illegal; no reasonable man could for a moment argue that temporary stages made of boards and scaffolds, or flakes for drying fish, would include a substantial building roofed with corrugated iron, containing a solidly-built boiler with a brick foundation. The whole proceeding on the part of our clever opponents was part of a well-arranged scheme. English lobster factories have been long established on the coast, and we have the emphatic testimony of the English naval authorities that they in no way interfered with the French fishery. The whole history of this fishery is given in an excellent and most impartial report[1] by Captain Campbell,

[1] See Captain Campbell's Report, map, &c., in the Appendix to this chapter.

of H.M.S. *Lily*. The complaint of France against our fishermen and lobster catchers on the West Coast is purely factious. The French captain, Landgren, and the other two French traders, admitted to Captain Campbell that they had really no complaint whatever to make against English fishermen, but were requested by their naval officers to make one, and it was ante-dated twenty days. It would be possible to multiply instances of the bad faith and dishonesty of French officials on this question by the score, if necessary; it is, and always has been, their policy to keep up this fishery question as a sore to irritate and annoy England. Unfortunately all English Governments have been too conciliatory with France; they put up with flagrant violation of international laws and courtesies, which Germany would not tolerate for a moment.

In the course of the discussion between Lord Salisbury and M. Waddington about the lobster question, there were two very interesting letters in which the ancient history of the dispute between England and France was very fully discussed. In the French letter occurs this remarkable passage:—

"France preserved the exclusive right of fishing she always had. The right of France to the coast of Newfoundland reserved to her fishermen is only a part of her ancient sovereignty over the island which she retained in ceding the soil to England, and which she has never weakened or alienated."

This bold statement of French claims was evidently made by some smart official of the Quai D'Orsay, who had been reading his Mirabeau to advantage, and remembered the motto, "*l'audace, l'audace, toujours l'audace*"; a more audacious perversion of history was never before put on paper even by a French official. Lord Salisbury proceeds elaborately to controvert this extraordinary travesty of facts. Our case was very fairly got up by the Foreign and Colonial Offices with the slender historical details at their command; but it is not absolutely correct, and it does not make out nearly so strong an argument on our side as can be obtained from authentic records.

The ancient possession and sovereignty of England over this Island dates back to its discovery. It is proved by continuous evidence of dominion, the making of laws, granting of charters, and the enforcement of taxation on foreigners. Lord Salisbury only refers to the dues obtained by Sir David Kirke from the French, against which the French Ambassador complained; but the exaction of taxes from Frenchmen and all other foreigners by the Cromwellian Governors is much more to the point. Kirke, it might be said, and truly, was only the manager of a trading company. Treworgie, Governor under the Commonwealth, had a formal commission from the Home Government in which he was specially required to exact the taxes from foreigners. The only break in the English sovereignty occurred when Charles II. allowed the French to occupy Placentia and to oust the English settlers who were then in possession there. Under that most fraudulent concession our opponents never permanently occupied any part of the Island outside Placentia and, possibly, St. Pierre and Trepassey. There is clear evidence that whilst they carried on very extensive fishing operations on the South and South-West Coast, and at Petit Nord, nowhere did they reside on the coast all the year round, except at Placentia, &c. Even at Placentia the French attempt at colonisation was a complete failure. The English population, natives of the soil, spread themselves all over the East and North-East Coast. Even as early as 1698 they had sent out offshoots from the considerable settlement of Bonavista, and by 1738 we have official records of an English resident population at Twillingate and Fogo.

However, it is happily not necessary to further discuss this question of English occupation and sovereignty; it is purely academic; all the rights of France in this Colony were definitely and finally surrendered and completely extinguished by the Treaty of Utrecht in 1713. The English negotiators were very careless about our fishery rights, but they were exceedingly careful and tenacious on the question of sovereign rights; they left no loophole whatever for doubt and ambiguity. They not only declared in emphatic terms " that the Island of Newfoundland " shall belong of right wholly to Great Britain," but, further, they made the vanquished surrender, in the most absolute and perfect manner, all possible or pretended claims; " the French king, his successors and " subjects, shall not lay claim to any right to the said island or islands, " or to any part of it or them." This impudent attempt of France at the present time to base her claim on a " sovereignty which she has " never relinquished or alienated," in face of these words of the Treaty of Utrecht, which still govern and control the fishery rights of the French on the Newfoundland coast, are examples of the method in which France carries on this controversy.

The next and most serious point in the discussion of this important question is as to the French rights of fishery—are they exclusive or concurrent rights? On this topic Lord Salisbury omits to particularly mention the manner in which the Treaty was carried out between the two nations, from 1713 to 1783. We have the proclamations and acts of our naval governors to show that not only was the fishery carried on as a concurrent fishery, but, further, that the sole control over the fishery was always exercised by the English Governor. Palliser settled all disputes about rooms and the priority of claims between the French and English fishermen; he confined the French rigidly to the limits of the Treaty shore; he confiscated boats that attempted to trade and barter, and threatened that if he caught them again he would confiscate their ships; he would not allow them to retain possession of a whale, nor would he permit a Frenchman to build a boat with a deck. Commodore Duff went further, and actually prohibited French men-of-war from visiting our coast. "I cannot permit any officer with a commission from " His most Christian Majesty, and with an armed force, to resort to or " exercise any authority within any part of His Majesty's dominions " under my government." The cod fishery on the Treaty shore was a concurrent fishery, entirely controlled by the English during this long period. This *expositio contemporanea* has a most important bearing. The French submitted to the rule in all cases. It will be seen from Lord Salisbury's references to the correspondence about the Treaty of Versailles, that in 1783 the French tried in every way to get the word exclusive inserted, but the English Minister dare not permit such language. At the Treaty of Amiens, in 1802, Joseph Bonaparte tried hard to obtain exclusive fishery rights and the grant of a portion of Newfoundland. The British Government were fully aware of the clamour such a concession would arouse, and they most emphatically refused to give the French exclusive rights. All facts, all history, all practical experience, show distinctly that the contention of the British Government is correct; that English fishermen may at all times pursue their calling upon that portion of our coasts where the French have fishery rights, provided they do not actually interfere with and molest the French in their fishing operations.

It is sound law and common sense, that when an owner grants a limited easement like the present very restricted grant to the French of fishery privileges, whatever is not included in such licence to fish and to dry fish, is retained by the owner; this is the position of England, the Sovereign Power and grantor. The privileges of the French are strictly limited to three things: first, they have the right to catch fish; secondly, to dry them on land in temporary huts and stages made of boards; thirdly, they are allowed to cut wood on land for the strictly limited purposes of repairing these stages and huts and their fishing vessels. Outside these limits they have no authority or rights whatever; they may remain on the Island *only* during the fishing season; they cannot trade or barter goods, and they are specially prohibited from erecting any permanent buildings, fortifications, &c. England, as the Sovereign Power, retains the right to use this part of her dominions for every other purpose that does not limit or unduly prejudice this licence to the French. As the Sovereign Power on her own territory she has the undoubted right to decide how her treaty obligations in this matter shall be carried out; it amounts to a complete abrogation of her sovereign rights when a foreign nation comes upon her territory with an armed force, and arrogantly exercises or attempts to exercise a coercive jurisdiction over English subjects in an English Colony. It follows as a clear matter of right that, where Frenchmen do not temporarily occupy the coast and do not fish, English subjects may occupy and may fish and utilize their own territory; to taboo this whole extensive coast, to make the whole land into a barren wilderness, simply because a dozen old French brigs fish in three or four harbours, is too absurd to be discussed.

FRENCH HUTS, RED ISLAND.

The French know well how weak their case is on the treaties, so in all their official correspondence they fall back on the declaration of George III. in 1783 attached to the Treaty of Versailles. I have shown under what fraudulent circumstances that declaration was made. It was part of a treaty. Now, it is a well-recognised principle that a treaty, and all its concomitants, is abrogated by war. To make that declaration legal and binding upon the English Government it should have been repeated in succeeding treaties, but it was never renewed. If the French fishery was an exclusive one, why did Joseph Bonaparte at the Treaty of Amiens endeavour to get the word *exclusive* introduced, and Lord Cornwallis firmly refuse? The indiscrect letter of Governor Darling, which is quoted by M. Waddington, or the stupid despatches of other officials, Imperial and Colonial, are nothing to the point, and cannot alter a principle which English statesmen have maintained, and none more firmly than Lord Salisbury, that the fishery is a concurrent fishery, although in exercising this right, English subjects are not to interrupt the subjects of France when fishing on the Treaty shore.

The French are constantly demanding that England shall honourably discharge her treaty obligations, and they have to admit that the Imperial Government in all good faith does endeavour to fulfil these most unpleasant duties with her accustomed fidelity. Why, on the other hand, should not France in the same honourable way respect the obligations which the French Government voluntarily took upon themselves with respect to St. Pierre, that the French king would give his constant attention that it should not become an object of jealousy between the two nations? St. Pierre was ceded to be a real shelter to French fishermen; in no way was the island so generously given up to our rivals to be hurtful or antagonistic to our interests. This is the plain meaning and intention of these general words of obligation. How has this gallant chivalrous French nation carried out the undertaking? Ever since its transfer to our opponents St. Pierre has been a perpetual nuisance to all British North America. Every nation in Europe or America that chooses to have a representative is allowed a resident consul; Great Britain alone is rudely refused. This petty little island, which was not to be an object of jealousy between the two nations, carries on a huge smuggling trade, to the detriment of all our British colonies, under the direct encouragement of the French Government. Every other stipulation of the treaty also is openly or secretly evaded. For this offensive conduct on the part of the French we have not retaliated except in name. The able and accomplished gentleman, M. C. Riballier Des Isles, who represents France so efficiently in our Colony, is not nominally recognised, but actually he is allowed to exercise all the duties of his office. Every courtesy is shown to him; he has every facility for obtaining information; whilst if anyone attempts to look after the large interests of our island at St. Pierre, he is rudely driven out of the little colony. So much for the courtesy and honour of France.

The next important subject is as to the manner in which the treaty is to be carried out and enforced. England, as the Sovereign Power, is the only authority that can enforce law or exercise coercive jurisdiction on her own territory. The French are well aware of this rule, this unquestioned axiom, of international law, yet, in defiance of all principle and all the rights of Great Britain, French officers are continually taking up our fishermen's nets in our own territorial waters, using force to expel English fishermen from English territory, and in one case issuing a proclamation at St. George's Bay, forbidding English fishermen to sell herrings except to French vessels. Until the accession of Lord Salisbury all this aggression and usurpation of authority was acquiesced in by the English Government and naval officers. The late Lord Derby characteristically declared that whilst these forcible acts of French naval officers on English soil were illegal and not defensible, still they might be allowed, as they only legalise an authority which had long been exercised *de facto*.

The mischief of the whole matter arises from the fact that the French have a very big navy and a very small colony to deal with in North America; hence, all the fuss and fume, annoyance and correspondence with the Foreign and Colonial Offices, about the most petty and contemptible affairs, in which the French are invariably in the wrong. Their officers are instructed to get up as many complaints as possible (witness the case of Captain Landgren), and when they are guilty of a more than usually outrageous act of illegal violence and assumption of authority, and complaints are made to the French Foreign Office, the course pursued is to clear themselves out of the scrape by the most unblushing lies. There is a most amusing instance of this peculiar French style of doing things. The captain of a small French cruiser had been more than usually violent on the West Coast; he told the stipendiary magistrate, Mr. G. Lilly, that he would not recognise any English rule, that if Custom House officers attempted to board any vessels he would capture them and carry them off, and the magistrate also if he dared to enforce any authority. Mr. Lilly duly reported the whole proceeding. The English Senior Naval Officer, most hospitable and generous of men, entertained this vapouring little commander; over the walnuts and wine he expatiated on the way he had sat on the Newfoundland authorities, giving full vent to the language he had used towards Mr. Lilly. The English captain's clerk heard the whole scene; like careful officials, he and the captain made a note of the Frenchman's remarks. When the charge was made through the Foreign Office, the French Naval Commander calmly denied that he had ever used the language ascribed to him. It is happily the case that all French officers are not of this class; more moderate, more sensible, and more competent officers no Navy possesses than France; Admiral Humann, Captain Reculoux, and others, being specially distinguished for their high qualities, both official and social.

The trouble is that the character of the naval officers, both French and English, is a most uncertain quantity; weak, incompetent men may at any time make trouble between the two nations; when we realize from the official statement how small the real French interest is in this shore fishery, the immense fuss made about it by French officials is ludicrous. The French nation is excited, sometimes to madness, about these trumpery affairs, the facts of which are carefully concealed from them; outside those immediately concerned in the business, the true state of things is practically unknown in France. Most Frenchmen believing that they own a large portion of Newfoundland, it is a pity the nation cannot be made to understand how heavily they are taxed to support their beggarly colony and small fishery, and how useless is this waste of money for national purposes.[1]

The argument that the main object of all this expenditure is to man the navy is another fiction. Most of their men are brought out in steamers nowadays. Every intelligent French naval officer recognizes that the English system of training boys for the service is the only method of providing man-of-war sailors. The Newfoundland French fishery, as a method of manning the navy, is to-day played out. A close ring of capitalists guard these enormous fishery bounties, and the whole French protective system. The voice of intelligent public opinion in France on these heavy burthens is completely stifled by this selfish gang of monopolists, who virtually rule France far more firmly even than the "combines" and trusts in the American Republic. The more democratic the Government, the more corrupt the rule, is strikingly exemplified in these great Republics. The useless expenditure of public money by France on her colonies is well known to be enormous: compared with the vast sums wasted on Tonquin, the cost of St. Pierre and Miquelon will appear very small. In Newfoundland there are probably not more than 2,500 genuine Frenchmen sent out to the cod fishery. They cost annually to the French exchequer at least three million francs,[2] made up of the bounty (nearly equal to the prime cost of the dried fish), the cost of administration over and above the local revenue, and the expense of the warships employed. At a rough

---

[1] A resident of St. Pierre, well versed in the liquor trade, says, that the wooden cases of gin, painted green and marked "De Kuyper's Prime Geneva," containing 12 large square bottles, over a quart each, are invoiced at 4 francs 80 centimes per case. St. Pierre is really one of the largest supporters of the German manufacturers of this delectable compound.

[2] Formerly it cost double this amount, the bounty alone in 1886 being 5,000,000 francs. The fishery has now become very small; see p. 479.

calculation, every one of these French "métropolitain" fishermen costs the nation fifty pounds sterling a year. If this expenditure, now wholly thrown away, were directly used for the great national purpose of manning the navy, it would provide annual maintenance for three thousand French naval recruits.

The excitement which commenced in 1886 about the lobster factories, culminated in the *Modus Vivendi* of 1890. M. Jusserand, of the French embassy, strolls into the Foreign Office one fine morning, and suggests a simple little understanding for the current season: it is very simple: like a good diplomatist, this distinguished scholar has made a little note of its terms.[1]

Behold how great a matter a little fire kindleth; this little agreement produced a debate in the House of Commons, a hot discussion in the French Chamber; it created that eminent body the Newfoundland Patriotic Association; it drew forth a very sensible and moderate article from the great French critic, John Le Moinne, and an eloquent oration from Mr. P. R. Bowers. Looking now calmly at this storm in a teapot, the delegations, the great meeting in Bannerman Park, and all the excitement of 1890, it appears after all that, though the *Modus Vivendi* was a clever French trick, it was not on the whole an unsatisfactory arrangement; there were only half-a-dozen small French lobster factories doing a very small business, whilst we had over forty making quite a large pack. It put all establishments on the same footing, and secured peace for a time. Serious charges were made against the British Government of having given way to the French, of having relinquished our rights, of having violated the Magna Charter of the Colony (the Labouchere Despatch); but on calmer reflection these accusations are now seen to be unfounded. The whole history of this Colony is one long indictment

---

[1] AMENDED DRAFT "MODUS VIVENDI."

"The questions of principle and of respective rights being entirely reserved on both sides, the maintenance of the *status quo* can be agreed upon on the following bases:—

"Without France or Great Britain demanding at once a new examination of the legality of the installation of British or French lobster factories on the coasts of Newfoundland where the French enjoy rights of fishing conferred by the Treaties, it shall be understood that there shall be no modification in the positions ('emplacements') occupied by existing establishments of the subjects of either country on the 1st July 1889, except that a subject of either nation may remove any such establishment to any spot on which the Commanders of the two Naval Stations shall have previously agreed.

"No lobster fisheries which were not in operation on the 1st July 1889 shall be permitted, unless by the joint consent of the British and French Senior Naval Officers on the station. In consideration of each new lobster fishery so permitted, it shall be open to the fishermen of the other country to establish a new lobster fishery on some spot to be similarly settled by joint agreement between the Naval Commanders.

"Whenever any case of competition in respect of lobster fishery arises between the fishermen of either country, the Commanders of the two Naval Stations shall proceed on the spot to a provisional delimitation of the lobster fishery grounds, having regard to the situations acquired by the two parties.

"N.B.—It is well understood that this arrangement is quite provisional, and shall only hold good for the fishing season which is about to open."

FRENCH ROOMS AT FISHOT ISLAND

FRENCH ROOMS AT ST. JULIAN HARBOUR

FRENCH ROOMS AT CAPE ROUGE HARBOUR

CLOSING OF BAIRD'S FACTORY.

against the Imperial Government; I have not failed to set it forth but on this subject I do not think that we can lay to their charge any very heavy faults. No doubt many Newfoundlanders believe that the Home Government might have made our case stronger; that they might have pushed our claims with more vigour; that they should have resented the encroachments of the French with more firmness, and sternly forbidden French naval officers from exercising any coercive jurisdiction over our fishermen on the Treaty shore; whatever other Administrations have done in the past, it is clear that Lord Salisbury, at any rate, has strongly supported our rights.

Out of this lobster question arose another difficulty, and a far more serious one. Amongst the factories on the West Coast, was one belonging to Mr. James Baird of St. John's, managed by E. Leroux. It was claimed by the French Commander that the factory was not protected by the *Modus Vivendi* inasmuch as it had been erected after the 1st of July 1889. It was situated in a locality where the French had never carried on any establishment, and where a cod fishery could not be prosecuted; the French Commander, however, insisted that Mr. Baird's factory should be shut up.¹ The owner stood upon his rights, and at the closing of the factory a sight was witnessed which happily does not occur in any other territory under the English Crown, a party of English man-of-war sailors landing on English soil to close up an English industry at the bidding of a French naval officer. No other reason can be given for this act than the orders of a French commander. I believe Sir Baldwin Walker had direct orders from the English Admiral to carry out

---

¹ "Sandy Point, Bay St. George,
"July 7, 1892.

"Edward Leroux, of Sandy Point, Bay St George, Newfoundland, do certify that during the season of 1889 Captain Reculoux of the French war vessel *Drac* called upon me; in the course of the conversation we had together, he threw all the blame of the obnoxious Bait Act upon the merchants of St. John's, observing the St. John's merchants are the sole cause of all this unpleasant business. He then asked me whether there were any parties here doing business with any of the St. John's merchants; without suspecting any ulterior purpose I answered, 'Well, yes, Mr Haliburton and others are doing business with Mr. Baird.' He answered, 'Why, these are the people we want to get at.' Shortly after this conversation, Sir Baldwin Walker, Captain of H.M.S. *Emerald*, forcibly closed our Fishels Brook Lobster Factory at the instigation of the French Commander.

"I strongly objected to this act, and later I objected to the inconsistent permission given to Mr. Garnier to erect and operate a lobster factory at Fishels whence I had been excluded. I made this objection to Sir Baldwin Walker in the presence of Mr. Dwyer, our stipendiary magistrate, and observed there would be malice at the bottom of my exclusion. Sir Baldwin Walker protested, but when I related the foregoing conversation with Captain Reculoux to him, Sir Baldwin energetically observed, 'Why, this conversation throws a great deal of light upon this matter, and explains very much.'"

this eviction. If all these facts be true, and I believe they are substantially correct, it was a most un-English proceeding. Mr. Baird immediately took proceedings against Sir Baldwin Walker in the Supreme Court, which decided in his favour, and on an appeal to the Privy Council the decision was upheld.[1] When the Home Government discovered that through the repeal of the old Acts for the Enforcement of the Treaties and of George III.'s declaration of 1783, they were powerless, they proposed to re-enact *verbatim et literatim* these obsolete Georgian statutes.

In order to avert this unfortunate state of affairs, delegates from both sides of the House went to England in 1891—Sir W. V. Whiteway, K.C.M.G., Hon. A. W. Harvey, Hon. M. Monroe, Hon. G. H. Emerson, Speaker, and Mr. Morine, M.H.A. When they arrived in London, a Bill was before the House of Lords for second reading on the 23rd of April; this measure was a virtual re-enactment of 51 Geo. IV., giving almost absolute powers to naval officers, a most barbarous old-fashioned Act. The first object of the delegates was to stop the passage of this Bill, and in the promise to pass a temporary measure through the Newfoundland Legislature in order to carry out the Treaty obligations, the delegates concurred; this is admitted by all, was so stated by the Colonial Secretary, and is also corroborated by a private message sent by Messrs. Monroe and Morine to Mr. Pitts. The delegates found themselves in a sorry predicament; the Ministry absolutely refused to withdraw the obnoxious Bill; in order, therefore, to avert what they considered a most serious calamity, they promised to get a temporary measure passed, and to discuss and arrange a permanent measure to enable Great Britain to carry out her Treaty obligations with France. Speaking only for myself, I think their acts bound the Assembly, and it was in honour bound to carry out their promise to the British Government.

MR. A. B. MORINE.

[1] BAIRD v. WALKER.

The judgment of the Privy Council was delivered by Lord Herschell on the 4th of August 1892; it sustained the decision of the Supreme Court of Newfoundland; that naval officers had no authority to invade the rights of private individuals whenever it was necessary to enforce the provisions of a treaty or convention; that in order to confer such authority upon officers to invade the rights of individuals and private property, legislation was necessary. The court completely demolished the argument of defendant's counsel that the act complained of being an affair of State done under the authority of the Crown, the Newfoundland Court was not therefore competent to inquire into it; they declared that such a doctrine was wholly untenable.

The main difference of opinion arose first on the appointment of the Judicial Commissioners; the delegates claimed that they should be appointed by the Governor in Council, with the approval of the Home Government. Lord Knutsford, Sir William and Mr. Harvey declare that from the first the British Government claimed the right of appointment of two judges, allowing the Colony to nominate the third. From this determination the Secretary of State will not deviate.

The whole matter now stands *in statu quo*; the House of Assembly refuses to pass a permanent measure, the French decline to proceed with the arbitration on the lobster question, and each year we have had a renewal of the *Modus Vivendi*, and the Temporary Treaties Act is now extended to December 1895. Most Newfoundlanders are afraid of arbitration. England is always on the losing side; she is like a rich corporation—a railway or insurance company—against whom juries always give verdicts; they are always in the wrong. As regards the Fishery Treaties Bill it really is not of such serious consequence as its opponents make out. Great Britain virtually concedes to us the third judge; if our local nominee is a strong man he will make his presence felt; his local knowledge and experience will outweigh the other two, and he will be there to prevent hardships and injustice; besides, according to the latest despatches, the Home Government seems now willing to allow an intermediate appeal to the Newfoundland Supreme Court, and from thence to the Privy Council. All these appear unnecessary precautions; judges nowadays have to work in presence of a watching public, and a still more observant Press; this serious responsibility will be sure to keep them straight. To all appearances the cases that will come before them will be very trivial and very easily disposed of; the importance of these high commissioners has been most ludicrously exaggerated.

The great object of the Bill was to take away the jurisdiction of the English naval officers. A careful consideration of their reports shows that

MR. GEO. H. EMERSON.

they do their delicate and difficult work on the whole admirably, nor, with one or two exceptions, can any serious complaint be made against them. Theoretically they may be wholly unfitted for their magisterial and judicial work; practically they perform it in a most satisfactory manner.

There was one observation to which no one seems to have taken any objection, either when made by Lord Herschell, or on its repetition by Lord Knutsford :—" There can be no difference of opinion as to the "nature of the obligation that rests on the Government of this country "to see that its treaties which are in existence are enforced and "fulfilled. The rights under the treaties which we are considering, "whatever those rights may be, are ancient, and came into existence "at *a time when there was no inhabitant population on the coasts in* "*question. These treaty obligations were not imposed on an existing* "*community,* but the community that has since grown up has come "into being subject to the existence of these treaty rights." Lord Herschell is entirely astray on the historical question. There was a British population on the coast when these ancient treaties were passed, even the earliest of them all. The records show that there was a small resident population; they and the larger floating population were deliberately sacrificed in spite of the protests and urgent resistance of Newfoundlanders and all interested in the Island. There was a settlement at Bonavista when the French were allowed fishing rights there in 1713, even a small settled population at Fogo and Twillingate, and it appears from evidence given before Governor Palliser that premiums were given to French masters to fish there, and thus annoy the English residents. It was the annoyance and the hostilities between the English resident population and the ship fishermen from France that caused the change to be made from Cape Bonavista to Cape John, and that produced the declaration of George III., 1783. Lord Herschell, as a great constitutional lawyer, must be aware of all the protests and violent outbursts of public indignation against the fishery clauses of the Treaties of Utrecht, Paris, and Versailles. Newfoundland in those days had powerful friends and supporters, who made a very loud outcry at the way her interests were sacrificed to France. Lord Salisbury may well refer to us as "the sport of historic misfortune," but it is the cruel, treacherous, and imbecile policy of Great Britain that has laid this heavy load upon our unfortunate islanders. It is the bounden duty of every honest and patriotic public man in England to lighten the burthen; instead of this, the object, apparently, of every English Ministry has been to please France, to shunt us, to get rid of us as the importunate beggar at the gate. If the English Foreign Office would only once stand firm and resolutely resist French aggression, give instructions to our naval officers that all violent and wanton attacks on our fishermen are to be firmly resisted, that men-of-war are sent on our coasts to protect and not punish our poor settlers, matters might soon be settled. The French are our neighbours in all four quarters of the world; aggressive and

FRENCH TRADING ON THE WEST COAST.

irritating, everywhere they are difficult to get on with; the worst possible policy is to be afraid of them. It is this fear of France that has caused all the trouble in Newfoundland.

What makes all of us distrust and fear English negotiation on our behalf is the manner in which our rights have been thrown away in the various Conventions. Our negotiators have been almost invariably ignorant of the subject, whilst their opponents have been thoroughly acquainted with the real points at issue. It is on this account that most Newfoundlanders prefer the policy of drift.

Under the anomalous *Modus Vivendi* things are going on very fairly on the Treaty shore; the arrangement, though temporary, works well; the English lobster packers are protected in their fishing, and each side keeps, on the whole, to its own part of the coast. Sir Baldwin Walker had some trouble with Commander Marechal, but a deter-

PORT-AUX-BOIS, ON THE FRENCH TREATY SHORE.

mination on the part of the English Commodore not to permit our opponents to meddle with English traps put an end to the dispute. The French, however, are not satisfied with the present peaceful state of affairs, they want to create trouble, and for this purpose the Municipal Council of St. Pierre now gives an extra bounty to parties who will carry on a shore fishery and pack lobsters.[1] Such a proceeding

[1] The Municipal Council of St. Pierre has lately given a premium of 50 francs to every French cod and lobster fisherman on the Treaty shore; this is in addition to the national bounty. Desertion from French vessels is also connived at to increase the resident French fishermen. Probably a hundred additional Frenchmen fished on the Treaty shore last season.

as a shore fishery, not carried on from ships, is against both the letter and the spirit of the Treaty, and our Government would be fully justified in demanding duties on all goods thus brought into the Colony. The only goods exempted from duty are the actual supplies and stores brought by the fishing ships for the maintenance of the crews during the season; goods brought into the Colony in any other way than in fishing ships, and for the maintenance of the fishing crew, are clearly liable to duty.[1] This was the point which the French Admiral came to St. John's about last summer; when he found the Imperial authorities maintained the position taken up by our local Government, he refused all invitations, and went away in a rage. It is to be hoped the Government of the Republic in future will send Admirals with a little more common sense and courtesy. If the French disturb the present peaceful state of affairs our course is clear, we will put the Bait Act in operation and enforce it rigorously.

LITTLE RIVER, WEST COAST.

I have endeavoured to deal with this most important international question of the Treaty shore as fairly and impartially as possible; I am free, however, to confess that I view it mainly from a colonial standpoint; every Newfoundlander holds strong opinions upon the subject, and I am possibly not exempt from local bias. It is a mighty unpleasant, irritating question, and the French are mighty unpleasant

---

[1] The French are inveterate smugglers. Under pretence of stores for their ships, they always carry a large supply of liquor, tea, sugar, and tobacco, to sell and barter with the Newfoundland fishermen. One French master actually required the magistrate to summon a number of parties who owed him money for goods supplied during the fishing. All trading of this kind is clearly illegal, and our Custom House authorities should keep a sharp lookout on all French vessels, and chiefly on parties from St. Pierre. Their stocks of goods should be carefully inspected.

neighbours in all four quarters of the world; it says little for English diplomacy that it has not been disposed of long ago. The real interest of France is ridiculously small on the coasts in question; they have not a dozen vessels, and less than two hundred fishermen, whilst we have at least twelve thousand people, permanent and transient, in the same localities. England, apparently, has really never made any tangible offer of exchange of territory as a basis of settlement; it is the only way in which the question can be approached. France will not take money, but she might accept territory and money combined. The recent occurrence in the hinterland of British Sierra Leone, in which English and French troops came into collision, and so many gallant men lost their lives, points to a region where we might satisfy French ambition and lust of territory, and really not seriously interfere with the extent of "England in Africa." The cession of the English island of Dominica, which is practically French, lying between Martinique and Guadaloupe, is another territory that would also be acceptable to our Gallic neighbours.

It would be wrong to declare that the French have no rights; they have well-defined rights within the strict limits set out in the Treaty. Of course, it is quite clear that if the French were able to occupy the whole of this extensive coast with their fishing operations, English subjects would have no right to interfere with them, or actually to interrupt them. There was a time when the French fishery on the Treaty shore was very large, and the English very small, but that day is long past; year by year the business of our opponents has been growing smaller. The fish on the shore have been continually failing, and the French have consequently practically abandoned this mode of fishing. Our western fishermen make a voyage or two before the Frenchmen arrive about June, and often obtain another after they leave in October. The bank fishery also, from St. Pierre, has never recovered from the effects of the Bait Bill; so that now the whole French business in Newfoundland is artificially propped up; the moment the bounty is withdrawn the French trans-Atlantic fishery will cease to be prosecuted; time, the inexorable logic of events, and the failure of the fishery, are all working on our side.

APPENDIX TO CHAPTER XVII.

The Lobster Factories on the West Coast.

REPORT by CAPTAIN CAMPBELL, R.N.

Enclosure 8 in No. 126.

Captain Campbell to Captain Hamond.

(Extract.)

Lily, at Channel, Newfoundland,
October 10, 1888.

IN compliance with my sailing orders of the 29th August last, with reference to the lobster industry on the west coast of Newfoundland, where the French have certain Treaty privileges, I have the honour to report as follows :—

1. *Historical Retrospect.* — It appears that the first lobster was canned on this coast about thirty years ago; a party from Nova Scotia had been canning salmon from the Humber, and at the close of the salmon fishing they went to the north shore of Bay of Islands, and started the first canning of lobsters.

(*a.*) The first attempt to build a factory was, so far as I have been able to ascertain, made in St. Barbe's Bay, fifteen years ago, by a Mr. Rumkey, of Nova Scotia, who subsequently parted with it as a going concern to Messrs. Forest and Shearer, factory owners in Nova Scotia, who next, in 1881, purchased the factory at Brig Bay, built in 1880, from Mr. Forsey, capable of canning 10,000 lobsters daily, and erected one at Port Saunders in 1884.

(*b.*) The industry then seems to have attracted more Nova Scotians.

(*c.*) Messrs. Payzant and Frazer, who built a large factory on Woody Point, Bonne Bay, and later on Mr. Carter and Mr. Neville and Messrs. Stabb and Roach, who all built in Bay of Islands. Mr. J. Cairns, of Prince Edward Island, Mr. Baird, of St. John's, Newfoundland, started in and about Port-à-Port; and the local inhabitants of Bay St. George have started numerous factories, and are fishing that district.

(*d.*) The numbers rose to sixteen in 1887, and at the close of this season there are twenty-six factories at work, employing a total of about 160 from Nova Scotia and Prince Edward Island, and about 1,000 natives.

2. *Process.*—The factories are worked on the same principle throughout; their canning capacity varying with their size and the number of hands employed.

(*a.*) They usually consist of a boiling and bath room, and a packing-room, cookhouse, and sleeping apartment for girls.

(*b.*) Lobsters are taken in three ways; the first and most common is by buoyed lines of cages.—Figure I.

FIGURE I.

Secondly.—By hand trap, a circular hoop of iron with a net stretched across it, upon which are fastened three or more herrings.—Figure II.

FIGURE II.

(*c.*) This trap is important, as it could perfectly well be used when the cages justifiably interfere with the Treaty rights of the French; and, thirdly, handed by "claw-nipping" in shallow water.

(*d.*) In this way as many as 1,000 have been taken in one day by one boat.

(*e.*) Local fishermen, assisted on the rougher portions of the coast by men from Nova Scotia, work the traps, &c. along the parts which feed their particular factory, and deliver them at the pier, or to the collecting schooners, at 70 to 80 cents per 100, which may be said to be the cost of the raw material.

(*f.*) The lobsters are then handed in and boiled for half-an-hour, after which they go to a smasher, who breaks the claws and takes out the meat, which is then washed and packed in the tins by one set of girls, another set then dry the edges of the tins for soldering, which are then closed up and bathed for an hour-and-a-half, then punctured to let out the vapour, and again bathed for a second period of the same duration.

(*g.*) The tins are then packed in four-dozen cases, and are mostly shipped to Halifax and St. John's without being labelled, with the exception of Messrs. Payzant and Frazer's factory at Bonne Bay, which varnishes and labels on the spot.

(*h.*) The cost of building varies, but it may be roughly estimated at from 2,000 to 3,000 dollars, and the daily cost of maintenance may be roughly stated to average 6 to 8 dollars.

(*i.*) The value of a case at present is 6 dol. 25 c., and the profit from a dollar to 2 dollars a case in average years.

(*j.*) Generally the "take" is sold or mortgaged to the outfitter, before the season commences.

3. The lobster industry has become, and will become more and more, year by year, the mainstay of the inhabitants of the west coast of Newfoundland; it employs men, women, and children, winter and summer.

(*a.*) Trapping lobsters pays better than fishing for cod, is far more regular, and gives the fishermen a "night in bed." This to some extent accounts for the falling-off in the local takes of cod.

(*b.*) Nothing but a personal inspection can give any idea of the good the factories are doing along the whole of the west coast, and of the number of men, women, and children that are dependent upon them; it would send the whole coast back to ruin and starvation if this industry were suppressed, or even curtailed.

(*c.*) The profits are not so great to the owners as is supposed, but the people benefit all the same, and the Government has thus a most magnificent system of out-door relief for its poor, with all risks taken and the capital found.

4. *French Interference.*—There is only one factory on the whole coast which can possibly in any way interfere with the temporary fishing rights of the French. It is situated on "Two-Hill Point," inside Port Saunders, and it has been in the habit of purchasing lobsters from the local fishermen who set their traps in the bays and along the shore, practically from Gargamelle Cove to about a mile to the northward of Mal Bay.

(*a.*) Part of the coast thus fished is undoubtedly used by the men from the French rooms at Port-au-Choix, Barbese, and Savage Island to seine and bar herring for bait, but only at certain times and in certain places, notably Keppel Harbour, in June and July.

(*b.*) It was the bad arrangement of the manager and the local fishermen in setting their traps after the arrival of the Frenchmen which gave Captains Belin and Villala (agents for Auguste Lemoine and Guibert et Fils) an apparent ground for complaining "that the cages along the shore from Mal Bay to Point Riche prevent them from provisioning themselves with bait on the appearance of the various schools of herring, capelin, squid, &c., during the fishery season, and that when they attempt to seine for bait gave them an excuse for complaint that their nets are destroyed."

(*c.*) The justice of their demand was so far allowed this season by you, that the fishermen who supply the Port Saunders factory were limited to a very small lobster area, and the harbours and bays complained of were prohibited.

(*d.*) Notwithstanding this prohibition, I have been able to ascertain that since your order the bays in question have not been fished by the French for bait.

(*e.*) The real reasons why Captains Belin and Villala wish to prevent the fishermen who trap for this factory from setting their traps are:—

(1.) Personal animosity to Mr. Shearer, the manager, the reason for which is difficult to arrive at, but it was in connection with the purchase of bait.

(2.) If they could get this factory closed, they would be enabled to feed their own small boiling-houses at a cheap rate, through the fishermen who work on the prohibited coast, and possibly set up themselves at Port Saunders.

(*f.*) The lobster factory at Port Saunders is unfortunately situated, in so far that it is about 10 miles from the French rooms at Port-au-Choix; but there is no just reason for closing it, and under proper restrictions, which could be regulated annually by the west coast ship or senior officer, there can be no possible ground for complaint on the part of the French.

(*g.*) In September this year Mr. Shearer pulled down half of his canning buildings, and transplanted them to the north of Castors River, a place not fished at present, leaving sufficient sheds at Port Saunders to carry on the industry on a reduced scale suitable to the curtailed lobster fishing-ground.

5. In compliance with your Memorandum dated the 10th June 1888, I have carefully investigated the Black Duck Brook (No. 8 on Chart) trawl cutting case (*vide* special letter No. 2 of the 22nd June) on the 18th and 19th June. There is not, and cannot be, any just complaint against this factory; but on my last visit Mr. Halliburton told me, in conversation, that he intended to move north of Bonne Bay early next season.

(*a.*) No other factory on the west coast is near to any French fishing-station, or can in any way interfere with their Treaty rights, and none other has ever been complained of.

6. After the most careful and repeated inspection of the west coast from Cape Ray to Cape Norman, the conviction has been forced upon me that the wholesale closing of the British lobster factories, and the suppression of this great industry, because "the only

two French firms, Auguste and Anatole Lemoine, and Guibert Fils, of St. Malo, employing 510 fishermen," who fish this coast, complain that they are hindered in obtaining bait at one spot (they themselves having four lobster factories working), would be as cruel as it would be unjustifiable on the part of these two firms to demand it.

7. Your thorough knowledge of this coast will, I venture to hope, enable you to bear me out in my statement, that there exist at this moment fixed settlements and fixed fishery establishments all along the line of coast from Cape Ray to Cape St. John, on which the French rights extend, and not only do they exist without protest, but with even greater harmony than is usual between rival settlements of the same nationality.

(*a*.) According to the present policy and manner of working the fishery on the west coast, these settlements are permitted and recognized where they do not interrupt by their competition the fishery of the French, and should there be any complaint as to any particular settlement or locality, it is, by your instructions, reported to you, and dealt with on its individual merits.

(*b*.) This manner of treating the fishery settlements has been this season, by your orders, extended to the lobster factories, and I would advocate, with all the fervour at my command, that Her Majesty's Government sanction this means of dealing with the difficulty caused by the unreasonable demand of the French to crush a thriving industry on a starving coast, where it in no possible way interferes by competition with their fishermen.

8. I have prepared the accompanying Chart in order to show clearly the position of the factories with reference to the French rooms on the west coast.

9. *Close Season.*—I am informed that the Legislature of Newfoundland contemplate a close season from the end of July, and I would beg to point out that between the third week in July and the third week in August the lobsters go through a process of changing shells, during which time they lay by, and do not crawl into the traps, and if caught are thrown back, but after the 20th to 25th August they come on strong during September and October, which, except for the weather, are the two best months of the year.

10. If the factories are closed either at the end of July or August, it will not be worth while to open them at all. They open, as a rule, on the 8th to 12th June, and close during October, the ice period establishing a close season of its own.

Enclosure 9 in No. 126.

Memorandum.—(*Vide accompanying Chart.*)

No. 1. Cod Roy, owned by Mr. McDougal, is the most southern factory on that part of the coast where the French have certain

The regular French fishing stations are shown thus ‡‡‡‡‡ ; occasional fishing grounds thus ≡≡.

Treaty rights of fishing. It was closed on account of bad weather and scarcity of lobsters.

No. 2. Next in order, going north, is a factory owned by Mr. E. Leroux, trader, of Sandy Point, Bay of St. George, a Frenchman who left his country to evade conscription, and became a native of Newfoundland; he employs about thirty hands at the highlands near Cape Anguille, and is doing fairly well.

No. 3. A few miles to the northward again Mr. C. R. Bishop, trader and postmaster of Sandy Point, has a factory at Crabbs Brook on about the same scale.

No. 4. At Sandy Point, belongs to Mr. E. Leroux, employs about twenty hands. This factory does not open until after the herring and the French schooners have left Flat Bay.

No. 5. On the south side of Flat Bay, belongs to Mr. N. Butt, trader, a native of Sandy Point; he employs about twenty hands, and does not open until after the French leave.

No. 6. The Gravels, Bay of St. George, owned by Messrs. Abbott and Hill, natives of Newfoundland. They were obliged to close at the end of July owing to scarcity of lobsters, having little more than paid their expenses.

No. 7. Cape George. This factory also belongs to Messrs. Abbott and Hill; the fishing-ground is very open, and exposed to the south-west gales, but has made a fair profit.

No. 8. Black Duck Brook, or Shoal Cove Factory, owned by Mr. James Baird, of St. John's, Newfoundland. The fishermen who supply it fish the outer coast of Long Point, Port-à-Port, and are also at the mercy of the weather. The French from Red Island, 18 miles away, complain that the traps off Shoal Cove interfered with their seining for herring, and they landed at Black Duck Brook, and cut some of the trawls. Their complaint was proved to be ridiculous, and I am informed they were punished for the outrage committed. The manager, Mr. John Halliburton, informed me he would move further north next season.

No. 9. The Gravels, Port-à-Port, is also owned by Mr. James Baird. Cans salmon and lobsters. It is situated on the inside of the Gravels, and fishes the harbour of Port-à-Port. They had a fairly good season.

No. 10. Middle Point, Port-à-Port. This factory is in ruins, and need no longer be taken into account.

No. 11. Long Point. This factory is owned by Mr. J. Cairns, of Prince Edward Island. He employs about sixty men, but does not open until after the departure of two schooners from Red Island, who leave towards the end of June.

No. 12. Broad Cove Bluff Head, also owned by Mr. J. Cairns, has done well, but not quite as well as in 1887.

No. 13. Bay of Islands. This factory is situated on the eastern extremity of Wood Island, and is owned by Mr. Carter, an enterprising resident of ———. They have only canned half the number of cases that they reached in 1887.

No. 14. Bay of Islands, also on Wood Island, in Thibaut Cove. A Mr. Neville is managing for a Halifax firm; this is their first year, and they have done little more than pay expenses.

No. 15. Bay of Islands, Liverpool Cove. This factory also belongs to Mr. Carter. It was opened for a short time in 1887, but did not pay, and was again tried in July this year, with no better result. I doubt its being opened again.

No. 16. Bay of Islands. Lark Harbour, owned by Mr. Forsey, from Grand Bank. It was burned down last year, but rebuilt before the commencement of this season, during which it has done fairly well.

No. 17. Bay of Islands. North side Crabbs Brook, owned by Messrs. Stabb and Roach, the former from St. John's. They are outfitted and send all their cans to Halifax. It is feared that the firm who fit them out may fail.

No. 18. Outside Bay of Islands, near North Head, known as Shoal Point, also owned by Messrs. Stabb and Roach. As is the case with almost all the lobster fishing, they have the advantage of the sea fishing and quantity of lobsters, with the disadvantage of being open to all weather. They find that they are obliged to get Nova Scotian fishermen for the rougher portions. I was obliged to find fault with No. 18 on account of the accumulation of offal on the beach, and the overcrowding of the girls' shed, but I am glad to report that on my second visit I observed that both these faults had been remedied.

No. 19. Woody Point, Bonne Bay, owned by Messrs. Payzant and Frazer, of Halifax. This is one of the most complete and well-built factories on the coast. It is situated in the middle of the large fixed fishing settlement of Woody Point, and with the aid of three small hired schooners fishes the coast from Bonne Bay northwards, and what they can take inside, which gets yearly less. They are not doing so well this year, owing to traps being three years old. They take 200 tons of wood annually from natives at about 2 dollars a cord, thus giving winter employment. They are the only firm who varnish and label their cans on the spot. A large schooner belonging to the firm runs between Halifax and the factories.

No. 20. Sally Point lies between Bonne Bay and St. Paul's Bay. It has only been erected this year, but should do well in 1889. Owners, Messrs. Payzant and Frazer.

No. 21. St. Paul's Bay. This also belongs to Messrs. Payzant and Frazer, and has taken more lobsters than any other factory on the coast this season. When there are too many here the surplus is sent to Bonne Bay.

No. 22. Cow Head, belongs to Messrs. Taylor and Cooper, of St. John's and Halifax. They are also doing well.

No. 23. Cow Cove. I was unable to land either time I called owing to heavy sea, but factory reported to be doing well.

No. 24. Port Saunders, belongs to Messrs. Shearer and Forest, of Halifax. This is the only factory of which the French can have any reason to complain (*vide* General Remarks). They have lost money on it this year, but next season it will be worked on a reduced scale suitable to the fishery area available.

No. 25. St. Margaret's Bay. This bay has, up till now, been fished by Messrs. Shearer and Forest for their Brig Bay factory, but this year Mr. Chetwynd, of Halifax, has built a factory, and is fishing concurrently with them. There are at present plenty of lobsters.

No. 26. Brig Bay. Belongs to Messrs. Shearer and Forest, and is the best conducted and most paying factory on the coast, averaging 8,000 lobsters a day during the best part of the season, one day's catch being canned before leaving off work on the next.

No. 27. Current Island, owned by Mr. Chetwynd; has been erected this season on the mainland just inside Current Island. Fishes in Geneviève Bay; will probably do well next year. Can be visited by walking four miles from St Barbe's.

No. 28. Salmon River, St. Geneviève Bay. A small factory owned by Messrs. Evans and Matthews, of Halifax. They will probably increase their scale of operations next year.

No. 29. St. Barbe's Bay, belongs to Messrs. Shearer and Forest; is the oldest factory on the coast, having been worked for 15 years; was closed last year, but has paid fairly well this season.

Besides the above, there are factories about to start, which will probably be in working order by the beginning of next season.

(1.) By Mr. E. Leroux, along the Highlands, between Cape Anguille and Sandy Point.

(2.) Mr. Chetwynd, along the Highlands, between Cape Anguille and Sandy Point.

(3.) Mr. Le Grandais, along the Highlands, between Cape Anguille and Sandy Point.

The portions of the coast marked +++++ in the Chart are occupied by the French permanently during the fishing season. The portions marked ≡≡≡ are where the French fish during a small period of the season; all the remainder is open to British enterprise.

(Signed)   CHARLES CAMPBELL,
Captain.

(*See* p. 558.)

LOBSTER FACTORIES.

Enclosure 10 in No. 126.

[ENGLISH] LOBSTER FACTORIES on the West Coast.

No.	Name of Place.	Date.	Owners.	Where from.	Girls. Foreign.	Girls. Native.	Men. Foreign.	Men. Native.	Fishermen. Foreign.	Fishermen. Native.	Cases, 1887.	Cases, 1888.	Remarks.
1	Cod Roy	Passed	McDougall	St. John's	Nil	Nil	Closed	Nil	Nil	Nil	Nil	Nil	Not sufficient lobsters to pay.
2	Highland, Bay of St. George	"	L. Levoux	Sandy Point	12	7	6	10	11	850	Not started	850	
3	Crabbs R., "	"	C. R. Bishop	"	7	4	11	11	800	700	800		
4	Sandy Point, "	"	E. Leroux	"	7	4	8	11	500	500	300		
5	" " Bay of St. George (south)	May 9	N. Butt	Sandy " Point (south side)	8	8	8	300					
6	The Gravels, "	Aug. 5	Abbott and Hill	Gravels	10	10	10	10	700	400	Closed from scarcity end of July.		
7	Cape George, "	June 20	James Baird	St. John's	15	8	8	20	First year	1,000	Propose to move northward.		
8	Black Duck Brock "	Aug. 5	"	"	24	12	23	2,400	1,900	Has done well with salmon.			
9	Gravels, Port-á-Port	June 20	"	"	Closed and going to run	2,000	Will not re-open.						
10	Middle Point, Port-á-Port	"											
11	Long Point, "	" 20	J. Cairns	Prince Edward Island.	Nil	Nil	10	Nil	35	900	850	Start after French schooners leave.	
12	Broad Cove, Bluff Head	" 20	Carter	St. John's	22	10	11	36	2,000	1,700	Lobsters falling off in the bays.		
13	West Island, Bay of Islands	—	Neville	"		4	31	1,400	700	Only started this year.			
14	Thibaut Cove, "	—	Carter	Grand Bank		8	24	Not started	500	Packed again, 1888.			
15	Liverpool Cove, "	—	Forsey	St. John's		5	12	700	600	Burnt down, 1887; rebuilt by June, 1888.			
16	Lark Harbour, "	—	Stabb and Rauch	Halifax	13	3	8	1,025	1,000	Weather very rough.			
17	Crabbs Point, "	—			15	3	6	Nil	10	Not started	1,000		
18	Sisal Point, "	—	Payzant and Frazer	"	16	4	6	2,800	2,000	A very complete and well-managed factory.			
19	Woody Point, Bonne Bay	—			Not started this year	Will open in June, 1889.							
20	Sally Point, "	—	Taylor and Cooper	Halifax and St. John's	Nil	15	4	11	Nil	21	2,000	3,000	A very good catch this season.
21	St. Paul's Bay	—			12	3	11	17	1,600	1,600			
22	Cow Head	—			18	3	8	15	1,600	1,400	Weather very rough here.		
23	Cow Cove	—	Shearer and Forest	Halifax	7	8	23	2,340	900	Catch greatly diminished on account of prohibition.			
24	Port Saunders	—											
25	St. Margaret's Bay	—	Chetwynd	"	4	5	13	Not started	600	The most paying and best managed.			
26	Brig Bay	—	Shearer and Forest	"	20	21	17	2,500	2,800	Will probably be enlarged.			
27	Current Island	—	Chetwynd	"	Nil	8	3	12	Not built	1,000	Ditto		
28	Salmon River (Genevieve Bay)	—	Levonard Matthews	"		2	6	400	400	Was closed last year, but has paid this, and will open in June.			
29	St. Barbe's Bay	—	Shearer and Forest	"	3	11	7	2	16	1,210			
				Total	3	302	12	188	20	444	21,325	27,880	

Total number employed: Foreign, 91; native, 934.

(Signed) CHARLES CAMPBELL, Captain.

Enclosure 12 in No. 126.

Captain Campbell to Captain Hamond.

(Extract.)

Lily, at Channel, Newfoundland,
October 10, 1888.

In compliance with my sailing orders of the 29th August, with reference to the lobster factories established by the French on the west coast of Newfoundland, I have the honour to report as follows:—

Five years ago a small boiling-shed was set up on the right hand side going out of Port-au-Choix, by Guibert et Fils, of St. Pierre and St. Malo; tins were imported from France, and an attempt was made to copy the lobster canning at that time in full swing at St. Barbe's and Brig Bay. [By English factories.—Richd. H. Hamond.]

One, two, or three boats, as they could be spared from the cod fishery, were employed to catch lobsters, and the cases were taken to France on the return of the brigs and schooners.

Not to be outdone, Auguste Lemoine started a similar establishment on their side of Port-au-Choix Harbour, on about the same scale, capable of canning 300 cases a year at their best.

They fish along the coast from Point Riche to old Port-au-Choix.

The following year Anatole Lemoine, who fishes St. John's Islands, erected a small boiling-house on the left bank going into Sesostris Bay, and started canning there, and Captain Dameron, of the barque *Puget,* as his agent, built a roofed shed at the head of Old Port-au-Choix.

This roof being contrary to Treaty, was removed by order of the French "Chef de Division Navale," and only the skeleton now remains, but Captain Dameron removed with his roof to Barred Bay, St. John's Island, where his barque, the *Puget,* was, and is still moored, and the only building which can be termed a lobster factory was erected.

The following year bricks and mortar were brought from France, and a permanent store added to the factory.

The *Puget* and crew from this date devoted their time to the lobster industry, assisted by some of the local fishermen, and a few foreign girls, who pack the cans.

The Barred Bay factory is the only French factory on this coast doing real lobster business, and this year it has reached 1,600 cases.

Taking into consideration the increased expenses of maintaining the *Puget* and crew, bringing out stores, &c., the profit for 1888 may have reached £400, but certainly not much more.

It is built contrary to Treaty rights, as reported in my special letter of the 24th July.

On the 4th September, when bidding me good-bye at Port Saunders, Commander Reculoux, of the aviso transport *Drac,* informed me that he was the bearer of orders to Captain Dameron to remove the corrugated iron roof and permanent building, but a fortnight after the French ships of war had sailed from St. Pierre for France, and a few days before Captain Dameron's departure, I made a special visit to Barred Bay, and found that there had been no alteration made, neither did there appear to be any intention of carrying out the orders I had been assured were given.

I venture to hope I may be permitted to point out, as is clearly proved by the accompanying statistical tables, showing British take as 27,880 cases, as against French 2,500, that whereas the suppression of the French lobster factories would scarcely affect the Brothers Lemoine or Guibert Fils, let alone France, the suppression of the British factories would renew the fearful misery so often and so strongly represented by the British naval officers who have had charge of the fishery on this coast, which misery is now so happily averted by the apparently ever-increasing swarms of lobsters which infest the shore.

It would, therefore, be a heavy sacrifice on our part to remove the lobster factories along the west coast, in order to prevent these two firms from canning 2,500 cases of lobsters per annum, and I doubt if they will do that for long.

If I might venture to suggest a line of policy with reference to the French lobster factories, it would be to recognise them under certain conditions and laws for their guidance, and obtain an equivalent concession in return. I can scarcely think they would do more harm to our interests than a French firm setting up business in London would to its ordinary rivals in trade.

Then let the captains of Her Majesty's cruisers deal with individual cases with reference to British factories as they occur, forwarding reports as heretofore, and await the reduction or abolition of the bounty, which is inevitable as soon as the French nation become aware of that which is already known to their naval officers, viz., that the fishermen bred on the banks and shores of Newfoundland are next to useless in a modern ironclad.

I have not heard of any intention on the part of the French to erect new buildings or start more factories on this coast, and I feel confident that the poor success of those existing will not encourage a fresh outlay of capital.

LOBSTER FACTORIES.

Enclosure 13 in No. 126.

TABLE of French Lobster Factories working in 1888 on the West Coast of Newfoundland.

No.	Name of Place.	Date of Visit	Owners.	From	Managers.	No. employed.	Catch, 1887.	Catch 1888.
							Cases.	Cases.
1	Port-au-Choix	Frequently	Auguste Lemoine.	St. Malo	Capt. Belin	5 to 8	320	300
2	Port-au-Choix	"	Guibert et Fils	"	Capt. Villala	4 to 7	290	250
3	St. John Harbour	"	Anatole Lemoine.	"	Capt. Landgren	4 to 7	300	300
4	Barred Bay, St. John Island.	"	Anatole Lemoine.	"	Capt. Dameron	60	1,500	1,600
						73	2,410	2,450

Remarks.—Very difficult to get the exact truth about the catch, but these figures may be taken as fairly accurate.

(Signed) CHARLES CAMPBELL, Captain.

PLAN OF ST. JOHN'S BAY.

CHAPTER XVIII.

ST. PIERRE AND MIQUELON, THE FRENCH COLONY.

The French Empire in North America, once a magnificent dominion that extended from the St. Lawrence to the Gulf of Mexico, to-day consists of a small cluster of islands off the south coast of Newfoundland.

OX-CART, ST. PIERRE.
From a photograph.

Miquelon, the largest of the group, has a few fishermen and farmers, but no harbour; all the interest in the little archipelago centres in the port and town of St. Pierre, a bustling little seaport, a lively little Franco-American town, containing a mixed population of about six thousand resident inhabitants. It is like a bit of Old France transported to the New World, the creaking ox-cart, the click of the sabot on the ill-constructed trottoir, the Breton, Basque, and apple-cheeked Norman women, the patois, the French windows, the gay colours, and last of all the fanfare of the bugle as the town crier proclaims at each corner of the streets and squares, after a preliminary blast of the trumpet, that

A STREET CORNER, ST. PIERRE.
From the Century.

M. Solomon will sell some "bonnes vaches à lait" at the Quai de la Roncière punctually to-morrow at ten o'clock—all these varied sights and scenes remind us of La Belle France.

The history of St. Pierre and Miquelon is a small fragment of the history of France, a Liliputian reproduction of that ancient and tragic story. The little island has had, like the mother country, its Revolution, its Reign of Terror, its Tree of Liberty, its Jacobin Club, and under the Empire a miniature *coup d'état*; all, however, was on a very small scale, a veritable tempest in a teapot. The diminutive French colony in Newfoundland has suffered most extraordinary vicissitudes of fortune, and it speaks volumes for French enterprise and energy that, after all its disasters by fire and foe, it is to-day as gay, brilliant, and as bustling a little seaport as exists in the world, of its size.

The early history of St. Pierre is embraced in the history of Newfoundland; it was frequented by Bretons and Normans early in the sixteenth century, and later on, from about 1545, by the Biscayans. In the list of Newfoundland harbours contained in the records of San Sebastian, the name of the island is given in the French form *Pierre*, and not in the Spanish *Pedro*, which appears to afford unmistakable evidence that it was first so named by French fishermen; it is mentioned by Cartier, and in several of the early English voyages; Captain Rice Jones fished there in 1594. Its commodious inner harbour and convenient situation early attracted the attention of the ship fishermen—English, French, and Biscayans; it was not formally taken possession of by the French until after their arrival in Placentia in 1662,[1] and it appears very doubtful whether it was ever permanently inhabited until about the end of the seventeenth century. There was a small fort at St. Pierre, mounting six guns, which was destroyed in 1702 by Captain Leake, R.N., but it is probable that St. Pierre was only occupied by the French in the same way that St. Mary's, Colinet, and a number of other places were, that is, simply as summer fishing stations. When all the French inhabitants in Newfoundland were compelled to leave in 1713, under the Treaty of Utrecht, the official return shows only one hundred and eighty persons.

From 1713 to 1763 St. Pierre and Miquelon remained in the possession of the English. The earliest reference we have to the islands, after they passed into the English possession, occurs in 1714, when William Cleeves, the first English fishing-admiral of St. Peter's, complained that Captain Taverner charged the French like Beloran, who had taken the oath of allegiance, fees for surveying their rooms, and also took bribes of salt, fish, wine, and brandy. Taverner was originally a Newfoundland fisherman. Wine was so cheap in those days that the Newfoundland

---

[1] Charlevoix says, "Gargot, the first Governor of Placentia, was appointed in 1660, but did not obtain possession until 1662."

fishermen complained bitterly that, in the purchase of salt, for every ten hogsheads they were obliged also to take a butt of wine.

The islands remained in English possession for fifty years. By the Treaty of Paris in 1763, they were given to France to serve as a port of refuge for her fishermen; the history of the negotiations concerning this retrocession will be found in the portion of this history relating to that Treaty.[1]

It must be borne in mind that these colonies had then been for half a century the permanent home of a considerable English population. The Imperial Government were well acquainted with the immense value of St. Pierre as a fishing station, and especially as head quarters for the Bank fishery. They were also well aware that its dangerous proximity to Newfoundland rendered it—as Lord Chatham declared—a constant menace to our Colony. Notwithstanding these facts, under this disgraceful treaty of 1763, the rights of the Colonists and the property of the permanent English settlers at St. Pierre were ruthlessly sacrificed.

The extraordinary story of the alleged murder of McKeown and his crew at Miquelon, given in the following despatch of Governor Lawrence, of Nova Scotia, to Governor Webb, of Newfoundland, in 1759, sheds some light on the social condition of the quondam French islands during this period of English occupation, from 1713 to 1763. It was very much like an ordinary Newfoundland outport settlement of the period, the substantial planters all kept public houses. The story of the murder is of the most vague indefinite character; there was no legal evidence against Shaughroo and his companions, nor was the matter ever fully investigated; we can see that the accusation arose out of a drunken quarrel, and reading between the lines we easily perceive the inveterate hostility existing between the Protestant Jerseyman, Edward Grandy, and the West-country planter, Mr. Thomas Meader, and his Irish servants, Shaughroo, Curtis, and Molloy:—

"Hallifax. 25 Sep. 1759.

" The Deposition of Mr. Jeremiah Soward of Old York taken before Comander Crawley One of His Majestys Justices of the peace for ye County of Hallifax.

" This Deponent being duly sworn sayeth that about a month ago he was at St. Peters in Newfoundland, when he heard Mr. Edwd Grandy of St. Peters Declair that he was afraid Mr. McKowing and his vessels crew, which was cast away upon the Island of Mechlin was murdered by James Shockney & Co. Upon their coming ashore in a boat from the vessel after she was cast away and likewise that it was ye common talk of the Inhabitants of St. Peters, that some of Shockneys people when in liquor had at several times told of the said talk and that this Deponent further sayeth, that ye said Shockneys said to him that he had a suit of clothes which he Took out of a Trunk not much damaged that belonged to

[1] See pp. 312, 313.

some of the Gentlemen that was cast away in that vessel this deponant further sayeth that he learnt that one Curtis was of the party concerned in ye s^d murder.

"JER. SOWERD."

"Sworn before Com^d Crawley Halifax.

"The Deposition of Jno. Johnston, Fisherman, taken before Commander Crawley 25th Septr 1759.

"This Depenant being Duly Sworn, sayeth that between two & three Months ago he was Drinking at the House of Mr. Thos Meader in St. Peters Newf^dl^d in company with One Curtis Alias Courting, Jos^h Blake and Ja^s Shockney, when a quarrell insued Concerning Catching fish, when Jos^h Blake Charg'd Curtis with Killing a Man in the Stern of the Boat coming ashore from ye Rock upon ye Island of Mechling and that this Deponant further sayeth it was ye general talk upon ye Island that Jos^h Blake should say that the Body was Buried in ye Sand in a Cove on ye Back Side of Meckling Island.

"Jno
"The mk × of
"Johnston."

"Sworn before Com^d Crawley Halifax.

"The Deposition of Mr. R^d Viguers, taken before Com^d Crawley ye 25th Septr 1759.

"This Deponant being Duly Sworn, sayeth that about a month ago he was at St. Peters in Nf^dl^d when he heard that Jos^h Blake should have reported that Jam^s Shockney fir'd on killed Mr. Alex^r McKowin in a boat coming ashore from ye Rock on ye Island of Mechling and that James Curting had shot the remainder of the people in ye boat and this Deponent further sayeth that he was informed that one Edmond Mulloy or some such name Servant to Mr. Thomas Meader had charged one Edward Grandy of murdering one of his men and offering to show some of ye company then present where the man was buried.

"RD. VIGUERS."

On the 14th July 1763, Baron de L'Esperance, captain of infantry, was given possession of the islands; a considerable portion of the new settlers were Acadians, who had refused to become English subjects. The local catch of fish, from 1765 to 1777, averaged about six thousand quintals a year; there being besides, according to French records, the fish caught by the two hundred and twenty fishing ships from France of twenty-four thousand tons, manned by eight thousand sailors and fishermen. St. Pierre, during this period, carried on a considerable contraband trade, both with Newfoundland and the British provinces; numerous visits were paid to the islands to catch these smugglers, chiefly New Englanders, but though the clandestine trade in French brandies, wines, silks, velvets, &c. was known to be extensive, hardly any of the smugglers, Americans or Newfoundlanders, were ever captured by the English men-of-war.

The celebrated astronomer Cassini's account of his voyage in 1768 to St. Pierre and Salee, in Africa, to make experiments on M. Le Roy's chronometers, is the best contemporary account of the island; at the time of his arrival the Governor of St. Pierre was M. Dangeac. Cassini says:—

"They have fixed their dwellings in a little plain along the sea coast; they have small gardens, where, with much ado, they grow a few lettuces that never come to perfection, but which they eat greedily when they are still quite green. Owing to the prevention of all intercourse with the English, fresh meat is very scarce; if by any means an English ship [American smuggler] finds means to convey a few head of oxen or other cattle, it is by eluding the vigilance of a number of vessels stationed there to prevent this contraband trade; our arrival at St. Pierre was celebrated by the death of a bullock; it was the noblest reception they could bestow upon us."

From Cassini's narrative we gather that the Acadians soon became dissatisfied with St. Pierre and Miquelon:—

"Many [he says] went at first, but the difficulty of subsisting in such a barren country soon determined them to quit it; the greatest part desired leave to remove to France; it was granted, but they were no sooner there than they regretted the Island of St. Pierre, and wanted to go back. A cargo of nearly three hundred arrived there just before us. Their unexpected return put the Colony in some confusion; those who were left behind had seized upon the habitations which the others had forsaken; they had pulled down some of the wooden houses, and made use of the materials. The new comers were sent to Miquelon, which with this addition may contain 500 or 600 inhabitants, St. Pierre about half as many."

The Acadians are very romantic figures in poetry and romance, but both France and England found them most difficult and disagreeable people to manage; essentially farmers, accustomed to the rich dyke lands of Nova Scotia, to a country ever famous for its orchards, they found themselves transported to a hopeless desert like St. Pierre, a barren rocky little islet, where nothing would grow, and where the fishery was the only possible occupation of the settlers. They had not the pluck and daring of the Normans, Bretons, and French Basques, so they longed for France; but they found, alas, that even the barren soil of Miquelon and St. Pierre, with liberty, was preferable to the conditions of a peasant under the grinding tyranny and oppression that prevailed under Louis in 1768.

Cassini gives us an interesting account of the French fishery as carried on at that time. He says:—

"The vessels destined for the [bank] fishery sail from France from the end of February to the end of April; happy those, however, who can get there by the middle of April. From that time until the 15th June the fishery is most plentiful, [then] the capelin draw away the cod, who forsake the Grand Bank until the middle of September; the fishery again in September and October yields almost as much as it did in May and June. Many ships, consequently, go twice a year to the Great Bank, and employ the interval in returning to France to dispose of their cargo and recruit their provisions and salt; few ships, except those from Olonne, go twice a year to Newfoundland; the rest are stationed there for six or seven months together, and never come home till they begin to be in want of provisions, unless they have made a speedy and plentiful capture, which is seldom the case. The principal ports in France where vessels are fitted out for the codfishery are Saint Maloes, Granville, Honfleur, St. Jean de Luz, Olonne, and Bayonne. The fishermen all complain that the fishery grows worse and worse. Before and after the war of 1744, prodigious shoals of cod flocked to the Banks of Newfoundland, and made the fortunes of fishermen and privateers; but since the last peace, the produce of the fishery is reduced to one-third of what it was before; doubtless, the bait of a small fortune has increased the number of vessels, and proportionably divided the profit . . . . The salt fish is landed at

THE "PARKS," OR MOVABLE ENCLOSURES ON BOARD A MODERN FRENCH BANKER.—
THE "DÉCOLLEURS" AT WORK.
From the Graphic.

Bordeaux, Rochelle, or Nantz; sells dearer or cheaper, according to the scarcity or plenty of the capture . . . Those who are so lucky as to bring in the first cod make 360 livres of the great hundred, which contains 124 large fish. The second may be worth 260 livres, but the last seldom fetches more than 50 crowns. At Olonne, St. Jean de Luz, and Bayonne, the crew commonly come in for one-third of the landing; in other places, as at Granville, they have but one-fifth, but every sailor on his return, is entitled to a gratuity of 100 to 240 livres, according to the dexterity shown in fishing. Elsewhere, as at St. Maloes, the crew are hired for the whole season, as high as 400 livres per man."

During the years between 1763 and the breaking out of the American War in 1778, the inhabitants and trade had slowly increased. In the first summer after the declaration of war Rear-Admiral Montague,

Governor of Newfoundland, captured the islands without even a show of resistance. According to his instructions, he destroyed all the buildings, and deported to France nineteen hundred and thirty-two inhabitants—fishermen and farmers.[1]

From the records we gather that during the various periods of English dominion between 1778 and 1815, St. Pierre contained a mixed population of English and French; there were frequent disorders. At the close of the American War, most of the inhabitants of St. Pierre and Miquelon returned. One hundred and fifty

FISHING FOR COD ON THE BANKS FROM A DORIS.
From the Graphic.

residents came back in 1783, and immediately set to work to restore their buildings, and to prosecute the fishery; even before the formal restitution the energetic French had commenced the fishery. In 1784 seven hundred and thirteen residents once more inhabited their old homes. The business was prosecuted with increased energy, as shown by the returns; three hundred and eighteen French vessels, of nearly thirty-five thousand tons, manned by nine thousand five hundred hardy French mariners and fishermen, carried on the Bank and shore fishery.

[1] The French account says only thirteen hundred.

The tragic events of 1789 found a re-echo in the little isle. The great wave of the French Revolution was felt even at distant St. Pierre. In July of that year there was a General Assembly and a Committee of Notables. Some of the commandants, strange to say, were Republicans, and acted in common with the Assembly; the first official to proceed in this remarkable manner was M. du Mesnilambert, acting Governor, then M. Danseville, incumbent since 1785. The controller and the judge also took part in this extraordinary Parliament; and even the prefect apostolic seems to have caught the Republican fever. Meetings of the Assembly

DOUARNEZ, NEAR CAPE DU RAS, BRITTANY.

were announced from the pulpit, and were commonly held in the sacred edifice. M. Allain, the curé of Miquelon, was made of sterner stuff than the pliant prefect. He took no part in these wild Jacobin orgies and travesties of a deliberative assembly; in 1789, when required to take the oath of allegiance to the Republic, he refused to swear, and sooner than serve under the French Government, he and nearly all his flock in Miquelon transported themselves to the Magdalen Islands. They preferred living under the English dominion, where they could exercise their faith and freedom, to the infidel rule of France. The renowned Chateaubriand passed through St. Pierre about this period, and he has given us, in his

"Memoires d'outre Tombe," a graphic description of the little French colony.[1]

In 1792 the affairs of the island were regulated by "The Assembly-General of the Commune of St. Pierre and Miquelon." They met sometimes in the church at St. Pierre, sometimes in the hall of Government House. A decree of this Assembly, dated 13th January 1792, decided that its meetings should be held under the presidency of M. Danseville, the Commandant; M. Bordot, Interpreter and Registrar of the Admiralty Court, and ex-Secretary of the Committee of Notables, was appointed Secretary-General of the Commune.

In February of this year a Jacobin club was formed, under the fantastic title of "Le Club des Amis de la Constitution"; for a short time there was a veritable reign of terror, and in a riot caused by members of the club, a woman named Geneviève Larache was killed. Order was at length restored through the firm and energetic action of the Commandant; the revolutionary club was dissolved, and the most violent of its members, in true French fashion, were expelled from the Colony in April.

Following, in a ludicrous way, the example of the Mother Country, a Committee of Public Safety was formed. When M. Pelegrin, Commander of the frigate *Richemond*, arrived in July, he at once put an end to some of these absurd proceedings. He pointed out to the Commandant that it was against the laws that he should be, at one and the same time, Governor of the Colony and President of the Communal Assembly; Danseville accordingly resigned. M. Bordot was appointed in his place, whilst Gachot was made Secretary-General. There was soon war between the new officers. Old Danseville had kept his stern Republican hand on the turbulent Assembly; but when once it was withdrawn, these brave "citoyens" could do nothing but quarrel. There was an immense conflict between St. Pierre and Miquelon; never, in the most stormy days of the French Chamber, even in conflicts between Derculede and Paul de Cassagnac, have there been more violent scenes, more vituperation, or more rage and fury than between Citizen Bordot and his opponents. There were resignations and re-appointments, and dissolutions; everything but duels. The shop element was too strong for that last alternative of the bellicose Gaul. A day memorable in the annals of Republican St. Pierre was the 8th of April 1793; a big spruce tree was transported from the opposite shores of Newfoundland, and solemnly planted in the square, towards the seashore, as a "Tree of Liberty," with all the pomp and ceremony the Colony could muster for the grand occasion.

[1] *See* Appendix to this chapter.

All this fantastic Republican farce and playing at Parliament suddenly came to an end. On the 5th of May 1793 the Newfoundland boats brought word to the fire-eating citizens that war had been declared between France and England. On the 7th and 9th of May there were sittings of the Assembly of the Commune, the last of the puny Republic; a Committee of Defence was appointed, cannon were to be planted, and provisions procured, as their stock of food was nearly exhausted, and the Colony was on the brink of starvation. On the 14th, Vice-Admiral King, with two ships of the line, three frigates, and four other vessels, with troops under the command of Brigadier-General Ogilvie, came into the Roads. St. Peter's and all its gallant citizens surrendered without striking a blow; all the inhabitants, fifteen hundred and two persons, were taken to Halifax, N.S., and from thence sent to France. Some of the unfortunate Acadians, by the irony of fate, were deported for the fourth time from their homes. This time St. Pierre was not destroyed by the English; it was the French Republican Admiral, Richery, after complete failure on the Newfoundland coast, who turned his guns against the French buildings at St. Pierre. Immediately after the departure of the French many Newfoundland families from Placentia and Fortune Bay settled in the little French town. The O'Gormans of Burin, Cluetts and Grandys of Fortune Bay, lived there for many years. Subsequent to the capture of the island by Admiral King, Major Thorne, of the 4th Regiment, was left in command of the island. From Aaron Thomas, purser of H.M.S. *Boston*, who visited the island in 1794, we get a humorous account of a dinner party given by the gallant Governor.[1]

---

[1] *Boston* Frigate, St. Pierres 2nd July 1794. We left Cabling Bay, on Monday 30th June and Anchor'd in the Road, before the Town, in the Island of St. Pierres, or at St. Peters, this afternoon.

The Governor of St. Pierres, Major Thorne of the 4th Regiment, gave a Dinner to the Officers of the *Boston*, in the late French Governors House, in the Town of St. Pierres, and as there was some singularitys attending it, I noted a few of them down.

It being understood that it was intended, by the British Government to Evacuate & afterwards burn St. Pierres so of course, every Officer, here, kept up, but as small a stock of necessarys, as the nature of their situation would admit, amongst other articles which muster'd short was Wine Glasses, Every House in which Inhabitants were left; (for many of the French, had been sent to Halifax,) were viseted, to procure, these useful Vessels, for this Grand occasion. The day came, Dinner was served to about 30 persons, the Wine went round to a late hour, Jollity, Gaiety, Merriment, & good humour.—Were prominant in the countinance of all.—God Save Great George our King, was repeated a number of times, expressions of attachment & Loyalty, were carried to the extreme (altho', by the by, Two of the Party, not quit a Thousand Years ago, had nearly been thrown out of a window, for, favouring somewhat Republicism.)—But to do the business, in a more exalted manner, all hands must needs mount the Table, to drink, Success to the *Boston*;—The Table was so cover'd with Decanters, Glasses, Bottles, Fruit Plates, Knives, Punch Bowls, etc. etc.;—That it was with dificulty, a foot could be shoved on. But as there is but few enterprizes, but what the British Army & Navy, will overcome, so in this particular, all impediments, were soon overcome, & the Table was soon covered with the Officers of the Navy & Army.— Success to the *Boston*, was given,—And just as each mans Glass, came to his mouth, —— Down, Comes the Table.—With as terrible a crash,—as if all the Masts, of the *Boston*, had

In 1802, by the peace of Amiens, St. Pierre was restored to France, but war breaking out next year it was again taken possession of, and not finally restored until after the final peace of 1815. On the 22nd June 1816, the Colonists returned to their old home, conveyed in the frigates *La Caravane* and *La Salamandre*. One hundred and fifty old families, numbering six hundred and forty-five souls, re-populated St. Pierre. In the same year St. Malo sent four thousand six hundred fishermen to try their fortune on the perilous Grand Bank.[1]

During the remainder of the period of its history there have been no wars. The little French town has had fires to contend with, not foes. It has been seriously damaged by the devouring element in 1865, 1837, and lastly in 1879. It has risen Phœnix-like from its ashes, and now contains a very considerable population; its fishery operations are

gone overboard at Once!—Here was curious, Sprawling. — Amongst. — broken Glasses, Platters, and Bottles. By the same heavy stroke, All the Lights in the room, were extinguished, so that the Caterstrophe, was the more darker, & lamentable. *Each man, not being perfectly himself*—And having the stump of a broken Glass, in his hand, he ran it, against his neighbours face, maiming & wounding one another some of them thought, that they had been suddenly assailed, by the Enemy, and that a Shot, from a Cannon;—had upset the Table, For they cryed aloud to Arms,—To Arms.—To Arms.—Beat To Arms.—I Gad thinks I, you are to Arms, At Legs,—And Faces, too —For Old Nick himself would not wish, to be in the midst of ye.

When Candles came, I looked at them, & saw this heap of superior beings, struggling in friendly, Agitation, to regain their Legs. But to see a Red Coat & a Blue Coat, alternately moving & tumbling about in a Cluster, I could not but compare them, to a pile of Lobsters, some alive and some boiled.

Propper assistance having arrived, & the Party regained their Legs I need not comment, on the friendly, *Look*, given, to one another!—Two Companys of Light Infantry, came in and moved the broken remnants, the wreck was soon cleared.

But to the great discomfiture of all, not a whole glass remained!—I mean, not only in the Governors House,—But not, in all the Island,—Bowls, Bottles & all, shared the same fate.

It getting a late hour it was proposed, by way of, Finile.—That the whole Company should March (as well as they could) in Procession, Drums & Fifes, at their head, round the Room & Hall, in the Hall, the Band of the Regiment, had been playing all the Evening. They had been supplyed, plentifully with Liquirs and as the Bottles were emptyed, they, put them under, their Table.

The Procession came unawares on the Band, they suddenly moved the Table for them to pass, but in the hurry the candles fell down, it became dark, the Table was withdrawn, but the empty Bottles, remained, *Point Blank* in the way of the Procession.—Captain Johnson was the first!—Right in he goes amongst the Bottles, he trod upon Ten or Twelve, but like a true Hero, he did not notice them, but advanced. The rest of the Gentlemen followed in *Tolerable* order cracking the Flint, Cutting their Shoes, Cursing the Bottles as they burst, and asking if they were full or empty. One or Two of the Rear, fell amongst them, but no serious mischeife happened.

St. Pierres was the head Quarters of the 4th Regiment. All their Band was, here, which is a Capital one. It played all the Evening, at intervals, Drums & Fifes. Our Officers, on the morrow said.—That.—They were Drumed Drunk.

On our return to the Ship which was late at Night, the Band played for us to the waters edge.—Some were so inebriated, as to get up to their Arms, in water, in mistaking the Boat. We got on Board all safe, with the satisfaction, of having left not a single Wine Glass, within the Governors Juridiction, Nor one solitary Bottle of Wine, in Major Thorn's Celler.

[1] FRENCH FISHERY OF 1802.

It speaks volumes for the indomitable industry of the French fishermen that in their one year of activity after the short peace of Amiens, 1802, they were able so quickly to re-organise their trade, to erect their buildings, and to carry on a fishery which, according to the returns given below, obtained from the English naval officers, and Mr. John Thomey of Harbour Grace (who had a fishery on the north-east coast), produced in one year 100,000 qtls., or at the rate of 50 qtls. per man. This is about the same proportion as large, entirely the result of the enormous bounties; practically the prime cost of the catch of codfish is paid by the French Government. Its

OFF ST. PIERRE.
From the Century.

contraband trade is also extensive; in former years, whilst the imports of Newfoundland were about $36 per head, the imports of St. Pierre the whole catch of the English in 1885, 14,557 fishermen having caught about 700,000 qtls., of which 587,000 were exported that year, the balance of the 700,000 being made up of fish left over, and the quantity retained by the inhabitants for food.

REPORT ON THE FRENCH FISHERY IN NEWFOUNDLAND, 1892.

Places	Vessels	Tonnage	Men	Fish caught.	Oil.	Remarks.
				Quintals.		
Pacquet Harbour	2*	84 / 36	42	2,400	40	Bounty: 5 livres per quintal, 10 if exported again; 50 livres for each fisherman employed this season in the Island. *Note.*—The amount of fish caught at St. Pierre and Miquelon is not given, but at the same proportion per man it would make the total catch 84,180 quintals. If the seven other vessels are added, it would give about 2,000 men and 10,000 quintals. (a) Employed on the banks, on shore, and fishing in two-handed skiffs.
La Scie	2*	102 / 104	86	3,000	14	
Fleur de Lys	1‡	200	74	3,350	60	
	2*	230 / 207				
Carouge		124 / 113 / 115 / 150	258	11,200	218	
	1*					
Conche	2*	129 / 150	44	2,400 dry / 500 green	40	
St. Julliens		1† / 3*	—	11,000	200¶	
Fischot		1† / 1*	—	6,000	90¶	
Zealot		1† / 3*	—	11,050	200¶	
Goose Cove		3*	—	7,000	100	
St. Anthony		2*	—	3,000	—	
St. Pierre		2	—	—	—	
Miquelon		5	(a1200)	—	—	
Total		35	—	904	61,340	—

* Brig. † Ship. ‡ Schooner.
§ Barrels. ∥ Tons. ¶ Hogsheads.

There were five vessels at Quirpon, one at Grignet, and two at Canada Bay. No account received of any French vessels on the west coast of Newfoundland.

amounted to over $480 per head, at least $450 of which was smuggled into Newfoundland and Canada. The operation of the Bait Act in 1888 and succeeding years was a serious blow to the commercial success of St. Pierre, a blow from which the little French Colony has never recovered. All the great trade which it boasted of is an inflated, artificial prosperity, it rests entirely on the support of the Home Government; withdraw the bounties, and St. Pierre would come down like a house of cards.

La Grande Nation has always set the fashion for Europe, and latterly for America. The French have always been distinguished for their excellent taste, their art, the politeness of their manners; the French colonies in America, for this reason, had a remarkable attraction for their English neighbours. Both in Cape Breton and at St. Pierre New Englanders and Newfoundlanders carried on a large clandestine trade with their Gallic friends; in peace and war the old smuggling trade progressed with scarcely any interruption; this trade with Newfoundland rose to its height after the " Forties." The Pierrois in this business plundered the revenues not only of Canada, Newfoundland, and the Maritime Provinces, for years they made even greater depredations on the revenues of France; thousands of quintals of English-caught fish were surreptitiously taken in St. Pierre by sale and barter, received the enormous bounty, and went to swell fictitiously the French catch of fish; later on the vigilance and superior honesty of the officials put an end to this business on a large scale, but it is impossible to extinguish it altogether. The author of the "Annuaire" of 1883 speaks of the immense benefit of the bait trade to St. Pierre, but he very judiciously avoids all mention of the smuggling.

The following extract is taken from the "Annuaire" of St. Pierre for 1883:—

"Les grosses transactions qui ont pour objet la vente et l'achat des morues s'entament et se dénouent le plus souvent en France. Aussi le petit commerce qui gravite autour du grand commerce a-t-il une action plus directe et plus immédiate sur les affaires qui se traitent dans la colonie. Pour ne citer qu'un exemple, on estime à près de 800,000 francs le prix payé cette année (1883) par les pêcheurs Français aux Anglais qui ont fourni le hareng. En échange du prix de la boitte, les Anglais font des achats relativement considérables à St. Pierre, et c'est ainsi que les îles St. Pierre et Miquelon sont sur la côte méridionale de Terre-Neuve un débouché très important, le centre d'affaires le plus actif par lequel s'écoulent les marchandises soit de provenance française soit de provenance américaine. Ce système d'échanges n'a pas lieu seulement que pour la boitte, mais encore pour le bois à feu apporté à l'automne par les mêmes galopeurs."

"The large transactions which have for their object the sale and purchase of cod fish begin and end most frequently in France, whilst the small trade which gravitates around the great trade has an action more direct and immediate on the affairs of the Colony. For instance, it is calculated that this year (1883) 800,000 francs is the price paid by the French to English fishermen for herring. In exchange for the price of the bait the English make quite considerable purchases at St. Pierre. Thus these islands of St. Pierre and Miquelon are on the west

SPREADING FISH, ST. PIERRE.
From the Century.

coast of Newfoundland, a large outlet, the centre of an active business; here are collected together the merchandise furnished both from France and America.

Not only bait, but firewood, brought in the autumn, is used in this system of exchange."

When that most excellent official, Mr. James Hayward, of Her Majesty's Customs, visited St. Pierre in 1864, he appeared such a nice simple man that the French gave him every facility to acquire information; in his report he stated that the Newfoundland revenue was robbed every year by St. Pierre of about $50,000; latterly it has been quite double that sum. The amount so taken from the revenue of Canada cannot be ascertained, but it has been stated that half the spirits and tobacco formerly consumed in Lower Canada was smuggled from the French colony. Increased vigilance on the part of the Canadian cruisers has largely curtailed this clandestine business, and the imports of St. Pierre (largely through the influence of the Bait Act) show the result: from 20,199,062 francs in 1885 they have come down in 1892 to 8,560,908 francs, and the exports of fish have fallen from 46,240,817 kilos. in 1886 to 22,098,075 kilos. in 1892.

The following account of the clandestine trade between St. Pierre and Lower Canada, taken from a Montreal paper, shows the *modus operandi*. The writer is not correct about the price of the German gin.[1] Some Newfoundlanders are in the trade; they sail from St. Pierre to some unfrequented part of Canadian Labrador, where (choosing foggy weather for the run), amongst the inner islands, they meet smaller craft; these smaller boats again tranship their cargo into punts and dories farther up the St. Lawrence; and, lastly, it is distributed about Quebec by farmers in carts. It is an immense business, and has enormous evil effects on the French Canadians. The activity of the Canadian cruisers and the operation of the Bait Act has now largely curtailed this illicit traffic. The statistics of St. Pierre show that from these causes their imports have fallen from twenty million francs to eight millions.

"Quebec, May 25.—With the disappearance of icebergs and the opening of the season of navigation in the St. Lawrence between Quebec and the gulf, the bold smugglers of the north have again forced themselves upon public attention by the persistence with which they have resumed their traffic of former seasons, and the readiness with which they show fight when attacked or pursued by vessels of the Canadian customs fleet. The head-quarters of the smugglers of the St. Lawrence and New England ports is at the French Island of St. Pierre, Miquelon, off the south coast of Newfoundland. Hitherto their chief traffic has been spirituous liquors. This year they are extending their operations and doing a large business in tobacco. The French Government has recently reduced the duties on all classes of tobacco landed at St. Pierre to 4 francs 70 centimes a hundred kilos. The duty previously was 50 to 150 francs, according to quality. The new duty, amounting to 41 cents a hundred pounds, means that St. Pierre is

[1] *See* p. 547.

practically a free port for the entry of tobacco, so that smuggling it thence to Boston, Quebec, or more convenient ports on the Atlantic coast or shores of the St. Lawrence is now quite a profitable one for coasters.

"Spirituous liquors are admitted into St. Pierre, Miq., free of duty. A fleet of three large three-masted schooners are constantly employed by the smugglers, conveying cargoes of alcohol, 60 over proof, from Boston to St. Pierre. There is no concealment about this part of the traffic—the difficulty consisting in landing the alcohol at Canadian ports so as to avoid the duty of $2 a gallon. There are two and sometimes three transhipments of the liquor from the time it leaves the entrepot at St. Pierre until it is safely put ashore upon the banks of the St. Lawrence. The immense profit of the traffic may be judged of by the fact that the whiskey or alcohol, which is the chief staple of the trade, sells for only $1.40 a gallon in Boston, and is worth here, with the duty added, no less than $3.75 a gallon. Jamaica rum and French liquors and brandies, etc., which are also admitted duty free into St. Pierre, form a portion of most cargoes of the smuggling schooners from St. Pierre to Quebec and other points, and, as the Canadian duty upon these is very high, there is even more profit upon the smuggling of them than upon that of the whiskey.

"The large gulf schooners that leave St. Pierre with the liquor aboard never risk a total loss of vessel and cargo by venturing as far as Canadian inland waters. Before leaving the gulf for the mouth of the St. Lawrence river they are each met by three or four smaller craft, generally schooners of very small value, which divide among them the cargo of the larger craft. One of these may be seized and confiscated, and yet the profit upon the operations of the others will make the entire trip a lucrative one, and often they all escape capture. Small boats land the liquor from the schooners, often under cover of the night, at some of the parishes of the island of Orleans or elsewhere in the vicinity of the city.

"Some of the parishes of the lower St. Lawrence has become completely demoralized by the proportions to which this traffic has grown. Farmers entirely neglect their land and fishermen their nets to engage in ventures that promise so large returns, and the excitement and sailor life attendant upon it offer great attractions to the French Canadian character. The parish priests complain bitterly of the demoralizing effects upon their people and of the fearful drunkenness that prevails wherever the whiskey blanc—as the fiery alcohol is called by the Canadians—is landed or sold, and many of the country curés turn informers to the Government upon the smugglers.

"There is no doubt that encouragement has been given the smugglers by the unfortunate failure of justice some time ago in the case of the noted smuggler Captain Bouchard, who fought and compelled the retreat of a Government revenue cutter last season, and was only subdued and captured after he had been besieged in and dislodged from the smuggler's stronghold on the Isle aux Coudres in the lower St. Lawrence. Yet when his case was brought to trial here a few days ago, he was only convicted before the court of simple assault, and got off with a fine of $25.

"Only last week the Government cruiser *Constance* was set at defiance by the crew of a little smuggling schooner opposite the mouth of the Moisie rivers. The name of the vessel, which turns out to be the *Steadfast*—of St. John's, Nfld.— had been painted over on her stern, and she refused to come to when summoned in the Queen's name, and when about to be boarded by the Government officers her crew fought with their axes and wounded a couple of them. Finally the prize, with her cargo of $15,000 worth of liquors, was secured, and her crew put in irons. They are now in jail awaiting trial, and the vessel and cargo are in port, and have been confiscated, but her two consorts have escaped arrest, and have probably safely landed their cargoes."

In July 1890 the schooner *Mary*, owned by Mr. Deidy, of Fox Harbour, John Kelly master, put into St. Pierre; she had on board freight shipped by Mr. Chafe to A. Goodridge and Son, St. John's—six hundred and thirty quintals of dried codfish. Kelly and his crew were caught landing some cod-roes and other articles for liquor. The law of St. Pierre is that " the introduction of foreign fishery products into " the Islands of St. Pierre and Miquelon involves necessarily the " confiscation of those products, without distinction between those which " have been or are about to be landed and those which may be found in " the hold of any ship which has put into a roadstead of the Colony." Under this law Goodridge's fish was confiscated and sold, and the schooner belonging to another innocent owner confiscated and cut up, all because a rascally skipper chose to sell some cod-roes to get liquor at St. Pierre. It is a monstrous injustice to punish innocent parties for another's technical wrong-doing. It is well known that Frenchmen, both on the north-east and west coast, and about the south coast, barter liquor, sugar, tea, tobacco, and other goods for fish and oil—the usual currency in the Newfoundland outports. One French master on the west coast wanted the magistrate at St. George's Bay to issue process against his English debtors on the coast. Besides the usual items of liquor, tea, sugar, and tobacco, one account included bonnets and millinery.

Under the old regime the government of St. Pierre was always entrusted to a distinguished admiral. Amongst the more modern administrators under the Second Empire we have the names of the genial Admiral Cloué and the stately old Baron Ronciere Le Noury. These fine old sailors are now replaced by a lawyer from Paris, or a press writer.

In 1857 the Baron and La Baronne paid a visit to St. John's. The Baroness was a splendid singer and musician. I remember one evening how she astonished the amateurs who had been singing their little songs at Government House. She sat down to the piano, and as she pulled off her long gloves, as a preliminary, she asked for a *petit verre* of brandy, and then came forth her glorious notes. The audience were carried away by her splendid performance; the unfortunate amateurs who had sung before her hid their diminished heads. We found out afterwards that she had been one of the stars of the Grand Opera at Paris.

In all French colonies *l'administration* is always more or less of a despotism. In St. Pierre the surrounding Anglo-American atmosphere has had a marked influence, and there has always been a sturdy resistance to absolute government. About nine years ago it took the form of a struggle against the strict rebuilding laws enacted after the fire of 1879. A French bourgeois does not make much fuss over the curtailment of his individual liberty, but he is terribly touchy about his pocket. Clapboards were not to be allowed; all houses in certain streets were to be faced with brick or covered with iron. When the edict went forth to pull down the clapboards there was for a time a fierce resistance. Men, and especially the hardy Norman and Breton women, struggled with the officers; all the available force had to be called out to quell the rebellion, known in the annals of St. Pierre as "the Clapboard Revolution."

I have spoken of the *coup d'état*. It was on a small scale, a travesty of the tragic events of the 2nd of December 1851; it followed, however, the Napoleonic method of silencing political opponents by imprisonment and deportation. Amongst the sturdy sea captains who largely compose the society of the little French colony there were many earnest Republicans in the days of the Empire. The fear of the Administration kept them, however, mute and inglorious. One dashing "capitaine aux long cours" was not to be repressed; he was an able man, and, though only a sea captain, he acted as the principal lawyer of the little port. As oracle of the café he held forth nightly on the corruption and imbecility of the miserable Government; the Governor, a relative of Paul de Cassagnac, vowed vengeance on his rebellious head. At last the opportunity came; our Republican hero became mixed up in an insurance case at Miquelon. In some technical way he infringed an article of the Code. Complaisant judges at once condemned him to the maximum punishment — twelve months' imprisonment, and to be deported from the Island. On the advent of the Republic, this corrupt decree of the Colonial tribunal was promptly quashed by the Court of Cassation at Paris. In the meantime, however, the sturdy opponent of absolute government was ruined. For neatness and despatch there is nothing like the French method of silencing a political opponent. About the same time as this occurred, a rich merchant of St. Pierre shot one of the disciplinaires[1] dead in his hall; the poor hungry prisoner was coming forward to ask for bread. The murderer was sentenced to one

HACKELA, CAPITAINE DES SAPEURS POMPIERS.

---

[1] Disciplinaires are military prisoners who have committed offences against the discipline of the army; there are always a number of them at St. Pierre; they are employed on public works, and are always accompanied by guards with loaded rifles.

ST. PIERRE LOOKING SEAWARD

TOWN OF ST. PIERRE

month's imprisonment, which he spent interned in his own luxurious house.

In the June number of the "Revue Maritime et Coloniale," 1894, Doctor Du Bois Saint Sevein, after giving a graphic account of the state of the French fishing fleet in Newfoundland, Iceland, and the North Sea as regards medical aid and appliances, strongly recommends the adoption of a service on the model of the "Deep Sea Mission." Reading between the lines in this excellent article, one can see clearly that "Les Armateurs," the fitters out of the French fishing fleet, are all powerful with the French Government. To satisfy the greed of these merchants, the carrying of medicine chests and doctors in the fishing fleet has been practically swept away until quite recently. The wretched state of the French bank fishermen is quite as deserving of charity as the poor Labrador men; anything so dirty, poor, and miserable as their condition on board the banking vessels can hardly be imagined.

POINT AUX CANONS, ST. PIERRE.

In the preparation of this chapter I have freely used the excellent "Annuaire" of St. Pierre. Other information has been obtained from the Colonial Records and miscellaneous sources. The account of Major Thorne's dinner party is from a MS. volume belonging to Mr. James Murray, written by Aaron Thomas, purser of H.M.S. *Boston*—a very curious production. I have not mentioned the affair of the Commercial Bank notes, unique in the annals of crime. Personal association prevents me from describing this remarkable transaction; besides I do not wish to say anything that might in the least offend the feelings of my numerous kind friends of St. Pierre.

In taking leave of this brave little island, monument of the indomitable industry, energy, and recuperative powers of the French people, I will conclude with the words of the St. Pierre historian: "After many misfortunes this small group of St. Pierre and Miquelon,

FRENCH FISHING BOAT.

" the last parcel afloat out of the great wreck of the French dominion " in North America, can with legitimate pride sum up its position thus: " Six thousand inhabitants, trade amounting to thirty millions of francs " a year, and a public revenue of half a million francs."

APPENDIX TO CHAPTER XVIII.

I.—Chateaubriand's account of St. Pierre in 1790.

"We steered towards St. Pierre and Miquelon looking for a fresh anchorage. When we approached the first between 10 a.m. and mid-day, we were almost on shore before we were aware, the land suddenly appearing in the form of a black lump through the mist. We anchored opposite the principal town of the island. We did not see it but we heard the noise from the shore. The passengers hastened to land; the superior of St. Sulphice was so ill that he had to be carried on shore. I took a lodging apart, waiting until a squall dissipating the fog, should show me the place which I inhabited, and, so to speak, the countenances of my hosts in this country of shadows.

"The harbour and roadstead of St. Pierre are on the eastern side of the island, facing another smaller island of a long shape, called the Isle of Dogs. The harbour surnamed the Barachais eats deep into the land, and terminates in a blackish pool. Several sterile hills are closely grouped together in the centre of the island; some, detached, overhang the shore, whilst others are surrounded by a tract of level and boggy soil. From the town can be seen the Hill of the Watch-Tower.

"The Governor's house is directly opposite the landing place. The church, the parsonage, and the storehouse for provisions are in the same locality. Then comes the dwelling-house of the Commissioner of the Army and that of the Captain of the Port. After these commences the only street of the town, which extends along the pebbly shore. I dined twice or three times at the house of the Governor, an officer full of politeness and friendly zeal. He cultivated a few European vegetables in one of the glacis. After dinner he showed me what he called his garden. The delicate odour of heliotrope exhaled from a square plot of beans in flower was not wafted to us on the breeze of our native country, but by the savage wind of Newfoundland, without any relation to the exiled plant, without any sympathetic feeling of recollection or delight.

"From the garden we proceeded to climb the hills, and stopped at the foot of the flag-staff of the watch tower. The new French flag floated over our head. Like the women of Virgil we gazed at the sea *flentes*. It separated us from our native land. The Governor was uneasy. He belonged to the Breton side, and, moreover, was weary in this retreat, suitable enough for a dreamer of my species, but a rude dwelling for a man occupied with business, or not carrying within himself the lesson which fills all space and banishes from men the rest of the world. My host made inquiries respecting the revolution. I asked him in return for some information about the north-west passage. He belonged to the advance guard of the desert, but he knew nothing of the Esquimaux, and only received from Canada a few partridges.

"One morning I proceeded alone to the Eagle Cape to see the sunrise in the direction of France. There a winter torrent had formed a cascade which fell in its last bound into the sea. I seated myself on a rock overhanging the sea. While thus employed, I perceived a young fisherwoman advancing along the hill above me. She had bare legs and feet, though it was cold and the dew was on the ground. Her black hair was gathered in knots beneath an Indian handkerchief, which was wrapped around her head. Over this she wore a bonnet, made of reeds of the country, fashioned like a boat or cradle. A bouquet of blue heath was fastened in her bosom, the contour of which was displayed beneath the white lace frill of her chemise. For a time she gathered the leaves of an aromatic plant called in the island *Indian tea*. She saw me, and, without appearing terrified, seated herself at my side, and allowing her limbs to hang over the edge of the cliff, like mine, she gazed at the noisy sea. We remained a few minutes without speaking. At last I said, 'What are you?' She raised her large black eyes, at once timid and haughty, and replied, 'My father is at the fishing with Guillammy. . . . We weave nets, and fish on the lakes by making holes in the ice in winter. On Sunday we go to Mass and Vesper, and then we have games on the snow, and look at the young men shooting the white bears . . . . the Captain is gone with Guillammy to Genoa, who will return next season and bring me a corset of striped silk, a muslin petticoat, and a black collar.' . . . . 'Would you like a corset from me?' 'Oh, no!' Guillaume, the image of the young sailor, hanging on the yard in the midst of the tempest, changed into a land of delight for her the frightful rock of St. Pierre. 'L'isole di Fortuna ora Vedete.' She rose, and rushed away, singing one of the missionary hymns:—

"'Tout brûlant d'une ardeur immortelle,
C'est vers Dieu que tendent mes desirs.'

"We stayed a fortnight on the island. From its shore can be seen the more desolate shores of Newfoundland. The hills stretch away into the interior in divergent lines; the loftiest extends as far as Rodrigo Bay. In the valleys the granite rocks are clothed with a dense carpet of sphaigues, lichens, and dicranum."

[The rest of the narrative relates to the flora, &c. He says the puny woods of St. Pierre form a striking contrast to the forests of Newfoundland seen near at hand. He calls St. Pierre the island of J. Cartier.]

II.—Statistics.

TABLE of the Exports of Dry and Green Fish from St. Pierre and Miquelon for the following Years; also Value of Imports.

Years.	Dry Fish.	Green Fish.	Imports Value.	Years.	Dry Fish.	Green Fish.	Imports Value.
	Kilogs.	Kilogs.	Francs.		Kilogs.	Kilogs.	Francs.
1841	3,121,950	1,566,505	1,965,094	1867	8,197,550	7,873,792	7,897,614
1842	7,757,900	1,520,275	2,307,761	1868	7,355,604	7,747,777	8,174,712
1843	9,007,194	794,036	1,991,211	1869	6,399,461	8,152,603	8,535,086
1844	7,783,608	1,572,079	3,050,834	1870	7,024,704	8,632,125	7,842,902
1845	9,948,307	1,047,629	2,641,511	1871	6,634,543	8,851,905	6,835,702
1846	10,225,333	1,488,516	3,111,827	1872	7,316,444	12,560,927	7,984,151
1847	9,401,489	1,248,062	3,019,102	1873	5,878,108	12,404,378	8,130,338
1848	7,267,927	2,026,234	2,257,662	1874	5,757,614	12,428,898	8,639,951
1849	7,104,872	1,724,059	2,263,276	1875	4,331,161	10,305,184	8,858,694
1850	8,305,765	2,085,303	2,445,339	1876	3,810,175	11,269,566	8,941,519
1851	10,454,093	1,885,720	2,918,745	1877	2,276,611	13,021,814	8,971,473
1852	9,681,494	1,781,532	2,988,340	1878	2,055,437	16,087,418	6,184,262
1853	10,541,484	1,545,557	3,213,002	1879	3,114,039	17,164,379	9,469,099
1854	10,138,966	1,144,719	3,261,042	1880	4,635,292	16,223,495	9,158,711
1855	8,461,261	1,115,060	3,158,434	1881	4,584,175	14,456,725	8,953,556
1856	9,341,180	1,368,445	3,519,073	1882	4,593,916	16,379,946	10,035,408
1857	9,345,042	94,663	3,776,183	1883	3,457,063	23,543,926	17,036,623
1858	10,074,519	495,741	4,715,203	1884	8,285,666	23,889,162	16,639,229
1859	11,097,908	1,209,070	3,821,001	1885	7,945,091	33,838,240	20,199,062
1860	10,102,677	1,280,872	4,084,861	1886	11,198,342	35,042,475	11,404,776
1861	7,783,685	1,614,205	4,239,567	1887	6,881,173	31,543,567	18,230,272
1862	10,327,285	1,004,380	3,528,763	1888	5,836,782	22,139,297	17,709,077
1863	7,629,166	3,213,253	3,971,581	1889	6,130,130	20,877,261	18,120,336
1864	9,844,881	4,694,063	3,632,784	1890	5,969,122	19,723,555	17,335,445
1865	11,974,309	6,033,842	4,441,817	1891	3,210,219	17,720,557	10,084,435
1866	10,437,464	8,258,051	6,467,089	1892	4,855,070	17,243,005	8,560,908

CHAPTER XIX.

HISTORY OF LABRADOR.

UNDER THE JURISDICTION OF NEWFOUNDLAND.

The Great American Peninsula known as Labrador is washed on one side by Hudson's Bay and Straits, on the other by the Atlantic and the Gulf and River St. Lawrence. This vast territory is little known, and only very partially explored; whilst on the Atlantic coast it is one of the most bleak and barren regions of the earth, recent Canadian explorers have discovered in the interior great mineral wealth and large belts of timber.

The portion of Labrador under the dominion of this Colony is alone referred to in this chapter.[1]

The discovery of this peninsula by Europeans has given rise to more wild conjectures and more points for discussion even than the vexed question of the landfall of Cabot in North America and Newfoundland. Passing over the voyages of the Northmen, which the Danish chronicles state were in A.D. 770 and the Icelandic chronicles in A.D. 982, we come to the whaling voyages of the hardy Biscayans in the North Atlantic in the fourteenth and fifteenth centuries. It is alleged that on one of these expeditions in 1470 they discovered and fished at Labrador. One such story is given by Navarrete.[2] It is quite probable that these daring whalers from Northern Spain in pursuit of their dangerous avocation sailed as far west as Greenland, but considering the vague and uncertain geographical knowledge of the middle ages, it is more than probable that Greenland, a shadowy country then, only dimly known, was mistaken for Labrador. The old sailors of that age

---

[1] The part of Labrador belonging to Newfoundland is defined as extending from Hudson's Straits to a line to be drawn due north and south from Anse Sablon to the 52° of north latitude. This division is very unsatisfactory and uncertain. The correct mode of dividing Labrador would be to carry the dividing line due north from Anse Sablon to the height of land, and then to continue along the natural boundary to Ungava Bay.

[2] *See* The Basque Fishery, p. 47.

trusted entirely to a good look-out; their latitude was generally several degrees wrong, their longitude equally vague; they relied on their keen observation—the compass, the run of the ship, and the sign of birds. On Cartier's celebrated voyages it was the vast numbers of great auk and penguins off our coasts that led him into the land. Against the very

FALLS OF THE EAGLE RIVER.
From a drawing by the Hon. and Rev. W. Gray.

dubious claims of the Basques we have some hard, unanswerable facts. Juan de la Cosa,[1] a Basque, whose map was made in 1500, shows Newfoundland as just discovered by the English. Would such an experienced Biscayan navigator ignore the claims of his countrymen if they really had found Labrador and North America? Again, there are no

[1] See p. 13, and note Juan de la Cosa.

Biscayan papers to support such a discovery; on the contrary, the records of San Sebastian[1] prove that the voyages of the Biscayans to Newfoundland and Labrador began from 1525 to 1541. Reliance has been placed on the use of the word "Baccalao" in the account of Cabot's voyage, but this was an ordinary trade word in general use at that period; the cod fishery was pursued by Biscayans and English, centuries before the discovery of America.

As a further confirmation that the English and not the Biscayans discovered Labrador, in the Spanish official maps of 1529, made by Diego Ribero, the great cosmographer of the "Casa de Contratacion" of Seville, we read, "Tierra de Labrador: esta tierra descubrieron los "Ingleses, no hay en ella cosa de provecho"—"Labrador, this land "was discovered by the English, nothing in it of any value"; and in another by "los Ingleses de la villa de Bristol"—"the English from "the town of Bristol."

The claims of the Bretons to be the first discoverers of Labrador rest also on vague tradition, unsupported at the present time by historical documents; 1504 is the earliest date at which their presence can be proved in the Newfoundland and Labrador fishery. In the absence of any authentic evidence to the contrary we must therefore ascribe the discovery of southern Labrador to John Cabot in 1498. There may have been earlier discoveries, but so far his claim is the only one that now rests on recorded unimpeachable testimony. It has been argued that John Cabot's landfall of 1497 must have been Labrador, because he speaks of the white bears. At the time of the discovery of North America, the range of the white bear and the walrus extended far up the Gulf of St. Lawrence; the walrus bred at the Magdalen Islands as late as 1770.[2] Parmenius, in his letter to Hakluyt in 1583, mentions the white bears in Newfoundland.

Whilst the French and Portuguese in the sixteenth century fished about the Straits of Belle Isle, the English carried on their fishing further north. The clearest proof of the presence of the different nationalities on the Labrador shores is shown by the nomenclature of the coast; whilst the occupation of the Straits is proved by the French names, on the northern portions of this most extensive territory all the names are exclusively English.

The origin of the name "Labrador" is obscure; it is stated to have been given by the Portuguese on Cortereal's expeditions, as designating the hardy Indian slaves brought home to Portugal, whom the king

---

[1] *See* pages 43 and 44.   [2] *See* p. 336.

stated were the best labourers—"Labradores"—he had ever seen. Some writers have stated that these slaves were Eskimos, but the description given of them "as tall and well formed" shows plainly that they must have been either Montagnais or Mic Macs, the Eskimos being a remarkably low-sized, thick-set race. The designation Labrador is supposed by other writers to have been derived from a Basque or Navarrese vessel, "La Bradore." Now, as the hardy Basques did not frequent the North American coast until forty years after the known expeditions of English, French, and Portuguese, and as Navarre at the end of the fifteenth century was an inland province, we may dismiss the Navarrese and Basque legends as purely romantic. We have the first attempt at an explanation of the word in the Wolfenbüttel Map B. of 1530, of Sevillian origin; the inscription on Labrador, after referring to its discovery by Bristol men, adds, "And as the one who first sighted "the land was a farmer of the Azores, they gave it the name of "Labrador."

The early navigators, though shrewd observers, were not ethnologists; all the savage tribes were simply barbarous people in their eyes; they discovered, however, that one race—the Eskimos—were persecuted by all the rest. In the sixteenth century the Eskimos are said to have numbered seventy thousand; probably at present from the Atlantic to the Pacific there are not five thousand of their nation remaining.

The Eskimos are the most remarkable people in North America; the most interesting to the ethnologist, distinct from all other savage tribes on the American continent in appearance, manners, customs, stature, and habitat. This extraordinary race of Mongolians, remnant of one of the great primitive stocks that peopled the world, has spread over five thousand miles of coast-line from Asia to Labrador; one in language, customs, weapons, and occupation. the Tuski on the Asiatic side of Behring's Straits being as veritable Eskimos as the settlers at Hopedale, Labrador.

Linke divides the Eskimos into seven groups:—1, the East Greenlanders, very few in number; 2, the West Greenlanders, mostly civilised; 3, the Northern Greenlanders, the Arctic Highlanders of Ross, who all live north of the Melville Bay glaciers in the arctic regions, a pure, primitive race; 4, the Labrador Eskimos, mostly civilised; 5, the Eskimos extending from Cape Chidley to Hudson's Bay and beyond Mackenzie's River, heathen; 6, the Western Eskimos, extending from Barter Island to the Pacific; 7, the Asiatic Eskimo, or Tuski. The name Esquimaux is a French corruption of the Abenaki word "Eskimatsic," an eater of raw flesh. The native name is "Innuit," meaning "the people." Eskimo is the Danish form of the name, and has now quite supplanted the old French name, Esquimaux. The old English voyagers called them "Huskimaws," or, shorter, "Huskies."

The theory now generally accepted by ethnologists about the Eskimos is that they are Mongolians who, in the remote ages, crossed from Asia to America. In the early period, before Cabot's discovery, they had spread as far as the St. Lawrence and Newfoundland, possibly as far south as Nova Scotia, and perhaps to Maine. There, says Crantz, in his History of Greenland, they were first met with in the eleventh century by the Icelandic discoverers of Wineland. When they were compelled to evacuate these possessions by the hostility of the North-American Indians, they receded to the Arctic regions, and crossed over from Labrador to Greenland. Eskimo tradition all points to this fact, that Greenland was peopled by their race from Labrador, not Labrador from Greenland; there is also very distinct tradition amongst their tribes of the arrival of the Northmen in Greenland.

From the fifteenth century up to the time of Sir Hugh Palliser in 1764, there is clear proof that the Eskimos frequently visited Newfoundland. Their object in crossing the Straits every season was to procure a special kind of wood for the making of arrows, and to kill deer and other game, then marvellously abundant in Newfoundland. They seem also to have had friendly intercourse with the Red Indians, as amongst the Beothic remains is the well-known Eskimo lamp. Palliser, in his prejudice against the French, accuses his Gallic neighbours of having invited these savages over to Newfoundland and prejudiced them against the English.[1] This was quite true as regards all the other Indians—Montagnais, Nascopees, Mic Macs, Algonquins—whom the French excited against our countrymen all over North America. The Eskimos, however, were always opposed to the French. There was a certain amount of trade carried on between the French and the savages about the Straits of Belle Isle, including to some extent the Eskimos, but the records show that from the very first the French joined with their enemies, and thereby earned the deadly hatred of these relentless savages.

There are many traces of the Eskimos and their wars with the American Indians along the Gulf of St. Lawrence as far as Anticosti. The Eskimos held their ground against all comers until the French joined their enemies, and put firearms into the hands of the Montagnais. At Esquimaux Island, near St. Paul's, a great battle was fought about

[1] See p. 324.

1640; the French and the Mountaineers and Nascopees drove the Eskimos from their entrenched camp, the remains of which are still visible, composed of stones and turf. About a thousand are said to have been killed in this battle; human bones in innumerable quantities lie scattered over the island. In revenge for their defeat the Eskimos made

ESKIMO ABOUT 1864.
From Dr. Packard's Labrador.

frequent raids on the French rooms on both sides of the Straits of Belle Isle. It is quite probable, knowing as we do now the dire hostility between the French and the Eskimos, that the murder of the French fishermen related by Kirke[1] was really committed by Eskimos, and not by our Newfoundland Red Indians. The teaching of the Moravians, and the good influences of Lucas and Cartwright, soon

[1] See p. 63.

pacified these cruel barbarians; they are now as quiet and as peaceable a race as exists in the world.

The yearly life of the civilised Eskimos of Labrador is thus described by Dr. K. R. Koch, who spent thirteen months on the coast:—

"During the summer, and especially in the hunting season, that is from May to December, the Eskimos with their families are scattered along the shore at their different fishing places. After the men return in May from the reindeer hunting, they take their whole families with them to the islands lying near the seashore to hunt seals. On their return to the Northern Seas the seals follow the outside edge of the drift ice, and the hunters are often obliged to drive far out in their dog-sledges to reach the seals' course. Hence they wait with their wives and children upon the outer islands until the coast ice has left the bays and straits between the islands; this takes place about the last of June. Then they hasten back in their kayaks to the stations where they have passed the winter months in order to prepare their large sail-boats, which are generally purchased from the Newfoundland fishermen. With these they fetch their families, which have in the meantime remained at the spring fishing grounds, and go trout-fishing in the inlets on the river courses. Then follows, from three to four weeks, the season of the cod-fishery.[1] .... In autumn the season of the reindeer hunting again returns. From November until Christmas the Eskimo is employed at the seal fishery, catching them in nets, or killing them in their kayaks through the thin ice. This work is exceeding tiresome and dangerous. .... About Christmas time all the Eskimos, with their families, assemble in their winter houses at the various Mission stations. Now comes the time for the children's schooling and the season of rest and religious duties for the older persons. ...."

ESKIMO BOY.

The Eskimos have extraordinary memories; they know well by heart the usual Church tunes. Through close personal contact with the Moravian missionaries they try to gain information regarding European customs. Every Sunday afternoon they are allowed to come to the Mission houses, where illustrated papers which have been sent as presents are shown to them. They are specially attracted by music. The harmonium used in the Church service is played by them, and the organ is accompanied by a small orchestra, likewise composed of natives.

[1] The cod-fishery is pursued in large boats which the Eskimos purchase from the Newfoundland fishermen. It is stated that prior to 1864 the natives had no sail-boats except one large schooner built by themselves at Hopedale. They are now, however, learning to build boats, all constructed on the old Newfoundland model.

The Moravian Brethren, or "Unitas Fratrum," comprise a small religious body whose origin dates back to 1457. At the present time it is divided into three provinces, German, English, and American, each under its own synod, but all governed by a general body, which meets at Herrnhut, Germany, every ten years. This most estimable body of Christians, numbering at the present day about fifty thousand, is specially remarkable for the great success of its missionary efforts in Asia, Africa, and America.

The history of the efforts made by the Moravian Brethren to evangelize the Eskimos forms one of the most remarkable episodes in the annals of Christian missions. These devoted servants of God braved all the perils and privations of savage life in the Arctic regions of Labrador; heroic soldiers of the Cross, they faced death in order to win the souls of these poor benighted heathen. The Eskimos had been so hunted and persecuted by the other Indian tribes and Europeans, that in their mad fury of revenge, their hand was turned against every white man.

The first attempt of the Moravians to found a mission to the Labrador Eskimos was made in 1752. Christian Erhart, a Dutch member of the brotherhood, with a boat's crew of five men, landed in July of that year in Nisbet's Haven;[1] all the company were cruelly murdered by the savage Eskimos. The next effort was made by Jans Haven, in 1764,[2] who arrived in St. John's in May of that year: he had to meet with many vexatious delays before he was finally landed on the Labrador Coast; the fear of the savage Eskimos was so great that no one would send a ship or venture amongst them; finally he was conveyed in one of the English men-of-war, and landed at Chateau Bay. Here he found no signs of an Eskimo population; later in the season, however, he was taken to Quirpon, where he first met the natives. "On the 4th September 1764, was the happy day," he writes, "when I "saw an Esquimo arrive in the harbour. I ran to meet him." He addressed him in Greenlandic; Haven had been stationed for some years amongst the Eskimos in Greenland, and had learned Eskimo. The Eskimo was astonished to hear a European speak his language, and answered back in broken French. The next day Haven met thirteen Eskimos. On July 17, 1765, Haven and three companions landed at Chateau Bay. Haven and Schlotzer went north, Drachart and John Hill remained, and had intercourse with several hundred Eskimos for about a month. The early labours of the missionaries were very much interrupted by the quarrels and fights between the traders, especially

---

[1] Nisbet's Harbour is marked in Reichel's map of Northern Labrador as "Ford's Bight, or Nisbet's Harbour, 1752," and lies a few miles south of Cape Ailik.

[2] See ante, p. 332.

the New Englanders, and the natives. The first mission at Nain was founded in 1771; Okak, one hundred and fifty miles north of Nain, was established in 1775, Hopedale in 1782, Hebron in 1830, Zoar in 1865, and Ramah, the most northern station, in 1871.

Besides attending to the spiritual wants of the Eskimo, the Moravians have done much to improve their condition in other ways. Instead of miserable huts and kayaks, they now have wooden houses and boats on the European model; they are not wealthy, nor even well fed, according to our standard, but they never now suffer from actual privation; the missionaries, in a patriarchal way, not only managing and controlling their religion and education, but also all their trade and business. Notwithstanding the very able management of the brethren, the missions are not self-supporting. About twenty thousand dollars a year are received from the parent society to carry on their work at Labrador. The principal station and head-quarters of the Moravian Brethren is at Nain, where they have substantially-built premises, well laid out gardens, &c.; from six to eight missionaries superintend their work here. Their other stations are Hopedale, with six missionaries; Zoar, two; Hebron, four; Okak, four; and Ramah, two. The missionaries are all well-educated, earnest men; considering the dreary field of their labour, the isolation, privations, and hardships they necessarily undergo in carrying out their laborious work, even the prejudiced observer must acknowledge that only the highest Christian motive of self-devotion, and earnest zeal for the conversion of the heathen, could induce these men to labour so abundantly, both in torrid Africa and arctic Labrador. The most rabid opponents of Christian missions are unanimous in their praises of the Moravians.

MARTIN HEAD,
Moravian Missionary.

It has been argued, and with some show of reason, that civilizing the Eskimos, means destroying their virtues and self-reliance as a savage race; it is, alas, only too true that they are a decaying race, but the same may be said of the heathen Eskimos of the further north, they are also fast decreasing; the absence of game and the terrible vicissitudes of the Arctic climate is decimating the Arctic Highlanders more surely than civilization is killing out their Greenland and Labrador brethren.

The great opponents and life-long enemies of the Eskimos, the Montagnais and Nascopees, have always been hunters. With their families they wander all over the vast peninsula of Labrador, shooting and trapping. The cariboo, their principal supply of food, is yearly diminishing; starvation, whiskey, and the contagious diseases of the whites have so decimated these hardy tribes, that now only a few hundred poor degraded savages represent this once flourishing branch of the fierce Algonquin race.

In the Dictionary of Commerce, by Lewis Roberts, printed in London, 1638, there is an account of the French Settlement of Brest, afterwards Bradore, in the Straits of Belle Isle. "It was," he says, "the chief town of New France, the residence of the Governor, Almoner, and other public officers; the French draw from thence large quantities of baccalao, whale fins, and train [oil], together with castor [beaver] and other valuable furs." It is computed that it contained two hundred houses and a thousand inhabitants in winter.[1] About 1600, Brest began to decay. In 1630 a grant "en seigneurie" of four leagues of the coast embracing the town was granted to a Seigneur Courtemande. After the conquest of Canada by the English, Bradore and the surrounding coast west was monopolised by a company in Quebec known as "the Labrador Company."

From about 1545 to about 1700 Basque whalers and cod-fishers in considerable numbers frequented the Straits and the Gulf of St. Lawrence. The western end of Belle Isle Straits, where it widens out into the Gulf of St. Lawrence, is marked on the old maps as the "Grand Bay"; here the Biscayans at first had Brest as their headquarters; their rendezvous, however, for general convoy to Spain was always at St. John's for the first half of the sixteenth century. After the Armada year they

A MODERN MOUNTAINEER INDIAN.
After a photograph by H. G. Bryant.

---

[1] The remains of works at Bradore are still traceable, though all the buildings have long since disappeared. The settlement was deserted by the French early in the seventeenth century, on account of the hostility of the Eskimo and the decay of the fur trade.

AMERICAN WHALERS.

consorted more with the French; fishing at first about St. Pierre and Fortune Bay, they gradually advanced round by the west coast up to the Straits. From a very early period, probably to keep away from the turbulent English, the French fished on the north-east coast of Newfoundland from White Bay to Quirpon, called by them "Le Petit Nord," and in the straits of Belle Isle. From Bonne Esperance to Cape Charles was about the extent of their fishing operations, and within this limit only are French names.

The first authentic account of a settled English Labrador fishery occurs after the peace of 1763, when Labrador and Anticosti were annexed to Newfoundland. Prior to that date a few English green fish catchers, traders and furriers from Lower Canada, and New Englanders had been doing a desultory sort of business on the coast; there were few, if any, settlers between the Straits and Hamilton Inlet; probably a score or two of white men and "courriers du bois" had intermarried with the Indians, and carried on a salmon and winter seal fishery. Governor Palliser[1] made regulations for the Labrador fishery to be carried on as a ship fishery, and to protect English interests he built Fort Pitt in Chateau Bay, and garrisoned it with an officer and soldiers. Through the opposition of the Canadians and New Englanders, who then frequented the coast, Labrador was taken away from the jurisdiction of Newfoundland and placed again under Canadian rule in 1774 by the Quebec Act (14 Geo. III. cap. lxxxiii.).

In 1820, according to the estimate of Captain Hercules Robinson, R.N., five hundred and thirty sail of American vessels, with a few sloops and brigs, employing five thousand eight hundred and thirty men, caught five hundred and thirty thousand quintals of fish, whilst the whole catch of English fishermen at Labrador was at the same time only one hundred and thirty-four thousand five hundred and eighty quintals. The trade, indeed, had attained very considerable dimensions prior to the war of 1812, and Sabine's statement, that American fishermen and traders did not frequent the Labrador shores before 1794, appears very doubtful. We gather from our Records that American whalers and traders visited the coast, and were of a very lawless, troublesome disposition, even prior to 1760. It was a common thing at that period to combine whaling fishing and trading for furs in one adventure; the ubiquitous New Englander had his market in our northern outports as early as 1698, not long after the formation of the settlements of Fogo and Twillingate; the Slades and other merchants of Fogo and Twillingate sent trading and

---

[1] See p. 324.

fishing vessels to Labrador; in 1770 we have an authentic account of these voyages; it appears very improbable, therefore, that the enterprising New Englanders, hearing all about the Labrador from Newfoundlanders, did not also push their operations into this new and fruitful field of adventure.

Many years before the formation of English establishments at Labrador (such as Noble and Pinson's at Temple Bay about 1768, Nicholas Darby's at Cape Charles in 1767, and Cartwright's at the same place in 1770), the Newfoundland merchants sent fishing ships to Labrador. Newmans, Hunter, and the Slades from Twillingate and Fogo were amongst the earliest adventurers in this new business. Their operations were confined to the coast between the Straits and Cape Charles. North of this there was perpetual danger from the Mountaineers and Eskimos. The French excited the Indians against the English, and latterly gave the Mountaineers firearms, with which they waged a relentless war against the Eskimo.[1] This trade did not commence until after the Treaty of Paris, 1763.[2]

The most full and accurate information about Labrador from 1770 is afforded us by the ponderous diary of Cartwright. The gallant major used very humane measures towards the Indians, both Eskimos and Mountaineers, completely won their confidence, and did a large trade with them. Until Cartwright's and Lucas's friendly intercourse with them, they were accounted the most savage tribe on the whole American continent. Cartwright appears to have succeeded in winning the attachment of both Mountaineers and Eskimos to the English. Before a Committee of the House of Commons he expounded his plans for overcoming the hostility of the Red Indians of Newfoundland. In his testimony he mentions his successful efforts to promote amicable relations with the savages on the Labrador coast. It is largely due to his humane efforts and the ministry of the Moravian missionaries that both Mountaineers and Eskimos became friendly to Europeans.

---

[1] *See* p. 327, Palliser's letter to Governor Bernard of Massachusetts. At Forteau old settlers point out the battlefield of the great fight between the Eskimos and Montagnais; the country around is strewed with flint chippings. It is a tradition that the Mountaineers descended on the coast at this point, and here occurred the great struggle between the Highlanders and Lowlanders of Labrador. The Lowlanders were beaten and driven north.

[2] Noble *v.* Kennoway.—The case of Noble et al. *v.* Kennoway, an action on a policy of insurance, tried before Lord Mansfield in 1780, arose out of the capture of Noble and Pinson's vessels, *Hope* and *Anne*, on a fishing voyage from Dartmouth and Waterford to Temple Bay, Labrador; on the 13th of August the American privateer *Minerva* captured both vessels. Noble and Pinson's master, Astwick, said there were no settlements at Labrador but those belonging to the plaintiffs. This was not correct, as Cartwright and Darby had a fishing establishment at Cape Charles, beginning 1767. French, Newman, and Hunter were called to prove the practice of the Labrador trade. In his judgment, Lord Mansfield said, "Since the Treaty of Paris (1763) a new trade has been opened to Labrador."

One of the most remarkable books ever written is "A Journal of "Transactions and Events during a Residence of nearly Sixteen Years "on the Coast of Labrador," by George Cartwright. He was born 1739. After serving in the army he came out to Newfoundland with his brother, John Cartwright, R.N., first lieutenant of H.M.S. *Guernsey*, under Sir Hugh Palliser, in 1766. John Cartwright was sent to try and make peace with the Red Indians, and had command of a small schooner; George accompanied him on these trips. He came out again to Newfoundland with his brother in 1768. In March 1770 he entered into partnership with a Lieutenant Lucas, and Perkins and Coghlan of Bristol, to carry on business at Labrador under the firm of Perkins, Coghlan, Cartwright, and Lucas. Their objects were two-fold: to trade and promote friendly intercourse with the savage Eskimos. In 1767, Nicholas Darby, of Bristol, father of the celebrated Mrs. Robinson, had an establishment at Cape Charles; three of his men were murdered by the Indians, and he had in consequence abandoned the post. This was the first place Cartwright took possession of in 1770. Lucas, who had previously lived at Cape Charles with Darby, had taken an Eskimo woman to England about 1768, and had learned the language from her, and had brought her back again. On his cruise up the Labrador coast in 1770 Lucas made friends with an Eskimo family, and brought them to Cape Charles, where they lived the first winter with Cartwright; by this means friendly intercourse was opened with the whole tribe, who were afterwards on the best terms with the English, and especially friendly with the major, who invariably treated them kindly and honestly. In 1772 he brought two Eskimo families to England, who were presented to the King, and created great excitement in London; all died in England of small-pox, except one woman.

The gallant Major's journal is in three large volumes; all the incidents in his career are told with the utmost frankness. His only rivals in the Labrador business, the only other firm having establishments of any importance on the whole dreary coast of Labrador, were Noble and Pinson's, of Temple Bay. The two houses were always at war; no language is too strong for Cartwright to use towards his hated rivals; in vituperation Cartwright could give points even to a local editor. Every day's work and every animal killed is noted in this immense diary; even the most inveterate sportsman would tire a little after perusing sixteen years of this daily work of slaughter. Cartwright was an honest, upright man, but a total failure in business; his interest in sport and his love of natural history were far keener than his attention to codfish and seals. He met with great losses; the worst of all was the plundering of all his possessions, ships, servants, stores, fish oils, and skins by that "lying rascal John Grimes," commander of the privateer *Minerva*, of Boston, mounting twenty nine-pounders and manned by one hundred and sixty men. One of his own servants, "that villain Dominick Kinnien," as he calls him, piloted them and joined the privateer's crew with his six men. Poor Cartwright lost £14,000; he would have made a clear profit of £1,500 upon the year's transaction. There can be no doubt that Cartwright did immense service in reconciling the Eskimos

GEORGE CARTWRIGHT.
From an engraving in his Journal.

to English rule; his treatment of these savage tribes was uniformly kind and considerate; his honourable and straightforward transactions won their complete confidence. He was a curious anomaly; whilst frankly immoral, he was at the same time most regular in his religious devotions; his ruling passion was the love of sport. Latterly he removed from Cape Charles and founded the establishment at

Cartwright, Sandwich Bay, now occupied by the Hudson's Bay Company.[1] Cartwright, in his diary, mentions the presence of the Moravian missionaries on the Labrador, but he attached very little importance to their devoted labours.

The more rigid proceedings of English and French naval officers after 1783 against the ship fishermen on the north-east and west coast so harassed our traders that they began to extend their operations on the Labrador coast, and about the same time, from 1783 to 1800, Jersey houses commenced business at Blanc Sablon, Forteau, and other places in the Straits. In the petition to the Governor of Newfoundland

ST. FRANCIS HARBOUR IN 1857.
From a drawing by the Hon. and Rev. W. Gray.

De Quettville[2] sets out the price he had paid for his room at Blanc Sablon (now owned by Job Brothers, and under the able management of the Hon. S. Blandford). About this period also other West-country houses, besides Noble & Pinson, commenced business at Lance-a-Loup, Grady, and Henley Harbour. In 1813 Sir Richard G. Keats appointed

---

[1] Cartwright sold to Hunt & Henly, from whom the Hudson Bay Company purchased their present establishment.

[2] In our Records of 1813 there is a letter from De Quettville to Governor Keats about his fishing establishments at Forteau and Blanc Sablon. In 1784 two vessels were sent there by Pointestre & Robinson. Forteau Great Room and Admiral's Point were bought by Thomas Falle and De Quettville in 1795; in 1802 De Quettville bought both rooms, Forteau and Blanc Sablon, for £755 sterling. The Jersey house of Robin began their fishing operations at Cape Breton in 1750.

Pinson, of Temple Bay, and Samuel Prowse, of Cape Charles, justices of the peace for the Labrador; it was the first attempt to create courts of justice on this desolate coast.

Planters from Conception Bay were amongst the first pioneers in this great fishery; to-day the contingent from Harbour Grace, Carbonear, Brigus, Bay Roberts, Port de Grave, Harbour Main, Holyrood, Bonavista, Twillingate, and Fogo form the bulk of the Newfoundland fishermen on the Labrador coast. Year by year enterprising Newfoundlanders have extended their operations farther and farther up the coast towards Cape Chidley.

The expansion of the English fishery at Labrador began about the middle of the eighteenth century; for the first period it was confined to the Straits and Cape Charles; Cartwright was the first Englishman to extend his operations to the settlement now bearing his name. The next extension was from Cape Charles to Seal Islands by green fish catchers. The third move forward was to Spotted Island and Sandwich Bay. The fourth was from Spotted Island to Grosewater Bay. Settlers in all cases followed in the wake of the green fish catchers. Mr. Charles Cozens, of Brigus, about 1850, was the first trader who adventured as far as Indian Harbour. Thomas Brown, Downer, and Wade, of Conception Harbour, were the most adventurous of these later green fish catchers, and were the first to go north of the Moravian settlements. Spracklin's, at Cape Harrigan, a dealer of Messrs. Job's, is to-day the most northern fishing establishment occupied by Newfoundlanders. Downer had fished at Nachvak for twelve years, and Wade had been to Iron Strand below Eclipse Harbour for several seasons.

T. R. JOB, ESQ
By S. H. Parsons

Thirty years ago Mr. Nathan Norman's establishment at Indian Harbour, now owned by Job Brothers, was the most northern of the Newfoundland establishments, though a few schooners from Holyrood and Harbour Main soon after ventured to fish farther up the coast. To-day Newfoundland fishing extends far beyond, and last summer the Hon. S. Blandford in the steamer *Nimrod* explored and fished as far north as Cape Chidley.[1]

In the olden times, planters, with their families and household belongings, including their dogs and goats, used annually to transport themselves to the Labrador for the fishing season. Until within the last few years all this immense traffic was carried on by sailing vessels, mostly small

---

[1] Cape Chidley, called after "The worshipful Mr. John Chidley, of Chidley, in the county of Devon, Esquire, chief promoter and general of an expedition to Chili in 1589."

schooners; there was overcrowding, and a great want of proper accommodation for the women; to-day, thanks to Mr. Rogerson and his Bill regulating the Labrador passenger traffic, and also to the more general use of steamers, the emigration of our hardy fisher folks to Labrador is conducted in a safer, more orderly, and more decent way; a voyage in a planter's vessel to and from Labrador even now, however, is not exactly luxurious travelling.

I have a lively remembrance of one episode in this Labrador emigration. All the first three weeks of November 1868 there was terrible anxiety in Brigus about William John Rabbit's brig, *Hunter*; she was known to be an old vessel, and was much over due. Everyone had faith in William John, but his coming was long delayed. All day long the distracted relatives strained their eyes for a vision of the *Hunter* coming up the Bay. The vessel was short-handed and full of women and children. By many she was given up for lost; women went about wringing their hands, weeping and wailing and lamenting for the dead. One morning I was awakened by an unusual noise and disturbance in the settlement; it was just daylight. As I peered through the window I saw a bare-headed fellow, with his garments loose about him, mad as an Indian Fakir, rushing through the streets, shouting at the top of his voice, "The *Hunter* is coming! The *Hunter* is coming!"

The shout electrified Brigus; women and men half dressed, wild with intense excitement, rushed out to see her; and in a short time the battered old brig was seen slowly coming round the point; her sails hung about her loose and ragged, her old gear was weather-beaten and dilapidated, her stumpy spars bore only her topsails; but what joy! what intoxication of delight! that clumsy old vessel brought to Brigus on that fine sunny November morning.

With many others I went on board the *Hunter*, and as long as I live I shall never forget the scene—the women and children, goats, pigs, and dogs, crowded in her hold. After seeing and smelling, I believe I can now form an idea of the horrors of the middle passage, and the odours and sufferings of the chained negroes in the slaver's hold.

For many years past the Newfoundland Government has sent down a doctor each season to visit the Labrador residents; valuable medical assistance has also been given by the surgeons of the English men-of-war, who periodically visit a portion of the coast. It has long been felt that more should be done for the health and comfort of this large population, scattered over such an extensive coast; the colonial doctor and the man-of-war surgeon's calls were like angels' visits, very few and far between. All this miserable state of affairs has now been remedied to a large extent by the operation of the Deep Sea Mission.

For the following account of the inception and work of the mission, I am indebted to the superintendent, Wilfred T. Grenfell, M.R.C.S.:—

In 1891 Mr. F. S. Hopwood, of the Board of Trade, England, and a member of the council of the above mission, passed through St. John's, Newfoundland, on his way from Canada. Here he was convinced that the exigencies and privations of the Labrador fisher folk constituted a clear call on the society to extend their medical and mission work to the poor British toilers of the sea on dreary Labrador. On his return to England the council of the Society adopted his suggestion, and in 1892 appointed their superintendent, Wilfred T. Grenfell, to fit out one of their vessels for a trans-Atlantic voyage and proceed to Labrador, in order that they might be better informed about this claim on their resources. Accordingly, in June 1892, their hospital vessel *Albert* sailed from Great Yarmouth (England), with a crew of nine men and the doctor on board. A considerable sum was spent in alterations and outfit, the largest item being the sheathing of the vessel's bows with hard wood to protect her from the ice. In twenty-one days she arrived at St. John's, where a pilot was provided for her by the Newfoundland Government, and a week later she made a landfall at Domino on the east coast of Labrador.

The *Albert* is a ketch of ninety-seven tons register, one hundred and fifty-five tons gross measurement, and was built as a sister ship to the mission's first hospital vessel *Queen Victoria*. She was named by permission of Her Majesty, who is patron of the mission, and has from the first taken a deep interest in its charitable work, and been a constant subscriber to its funds.

The *Albert* remained three months on the coast visiting the settlements as far north as Hopedale (Moravian mission station), and as far south as Red Bay in the Straits of Belle Isle. On the return to St. John's a careful report was

MR. W. B. GRIEVE.
By S. H. Parsons.

drawn up by the superintendent and read to a meeting of merchants and planters called by his Excellency Sir Terence O'Brien, K.C.M.G., Governor of Newfoundland, at Government House.

It was explained that the mission was neither sectarian nor political, but simply a philanthropic work, aiming at alleviating the condition of the poor Labrador fishermen and their families, and preaching the Gospel. At the close of the meeting it was decided to raise funds to build two hospitals on the coast; a house ready built was presented by Mr. Walter Baine Grieve, at Battle Harbour, to serve as the first. The

Society in June 1893 sent out the *Albert* a second time, with a nurse and doctor for each hospital; also a small steam launch called the *Princess May* was provided by the mission to enable the superintendent to visit as many intermediate stations as possible. Indian Harbour, at the entrance of Hamilton Inlet, was chosen for the site of the second hospital. The Report for 1893, given in the Appendix, shows the progress of this good work. During the year there were only two deaths in the hospitals, one more patient died at Battle Harbour, and another soon after reaching St. John's.

At the close of the season of 1893, two of the doctors, Grenfell and Bobardt, visited Canada in order to endeavour to raise an interest and gain funds for the mission in the Dominion. They were eminently successful. A branch of the society was formed in Halifax, N.S., where numbers of Canadian vessels fishing in the gulf and off the Labrador coast come for supplies. A second branch of the society was formed in Montreal. Here Sir Donald A. Smith, K.C.M.G., who in early life had spent several years in the Hudson Bay Company's service, at North West River, Hamilton Inlet, presented the mission with a suitable steam yacht, seventy-eight feet long, fourteen feet beam, which was adapted and fitted out for the special work she has now to perform. Sir Donald took a deep interest in the success of the mission; he has not only given the yacht to the society, but also a handsome yearly contribution towards the expenses of running the steamer.

Besides this noble charity, Lady O'Brien, the most benevolent and kind-hearted wife of our esteemed Governor, each season sends down boxes of clothing to the more distressed inhabitants of the Labrador: these gifts are generally distributed by the captains of the English men-of-war. For several years some benevolent ladies in Portland Maine, headed by Mr. James Phinney Baxter, have sent to the Moravian missions a large stock of warm clothing for the Eskimos.

Terra Novian Labrador bears a very marked resemblance to Norway in the deep indentation of its coast line; the celebrated Norwegian fiords with their beetling cliffs and grand picturesque coast scenery, beloved of artists and tourists, have almost their exact counterpart in the deep inlets of Northern Labrador. The island zone of the Norwegian coast commences just below the arctic circle; so in a corresponding manner the very remarkable insular portion of Labrador begins well to the North. From St. Lewis Sound to Spotted Islands the coast line is nearly due north and south; with few exceptions there are no islands off the coast in this distance; as soon, however, as the coast line trends to the north-west, islands become numerous and continually increase in numbers and extend until Cape Mugford is reached; from Cape Mugford to Cape Chidley the coast line and the island-studded ocean forms a labyrinth of archipelagos and deep fiords. From the mouth of these deep indentations of the coast to the far-off rocks and islets, there is an estimated depth all along this portion of Labrador of not less than twenty miles. Outside of this island zone for thirty miles are valuable fishing banks, and off from these again at a distance variously estimated at from one hundred to one hundred and fifty miles are other banks, the feeding ground of innumerable cod, corresponding to the great banks off Newfoundland.

Professor Hind states that there are extensive banks lying off the shore all along this northern part of Labrador. Captain Blandford believes, from the number of stranded icebergs seen on his voyage of discovery, that these banks are at least thirty miles off from the archipelago of islands that fringe the coast north from the Bull Dog Islands to Cape Chidley. This portion of the coast has never been properly surveyed, and when fully laid down in a chart, Captain Blandford believes the islands and fiords will be found very differently situated from the present vague idea of coast line. It is calculated that the codfishing grounds on this vast Northern Labrador are equal in extent to the whole area of our Island's coast fishery; to a large extent it is a *terra incognita*, but from the information already obtained it would appear to afford in the future an almost indefinite extension of our fishery.

HON. S. BLANDFORD
By J. ——

I am indebted to Captain the Hon. Samuel Blandford for a very interesting account of his exploring trip to Cape Chidley in 1893. He started from Blanc Sablon on the 1st of August, in the s.s. *Nimrod*, with a crew of forty-five men, ten trap boats, five traps, and four cod seines; on the 6th August he arrived at Nachvak Bay. This bay he describes as a long inlet, about a mile wide, and fifteen miles deep, the land on both sides being precipitous, rising to the height of about three thousand feet; it is indented with coves, some of which have a strand; at its head it divides into two arms; into the north-west branch a large brook pours its waters; the land is lower here than in any other part of Nachvak; there is a large trout fishery at the mouth of the brook. Captain Blandford describes the bay as resembling one of the romantic fiords of Norway, with deep water and towering cliffs. An enterprising Newfoundlander, Captain Downer, master of the schooner *Laddie*, belonging to Mr. Scott, of Fogo, has frequented this remote spot for the past ten years. There is a Hudson's Bay post at Nachvak. Fish struck in, and in three days Captain Blandford secured three hundred quintals; five other Newfoundland schooners came in whilst the *Nimrod* was at Nachvak. On the 17th of August, in the evening, he arrived off the Kickkertaksoak Islands, south of the bill of Cape Chidley. Here the current runs at the rate of six knots; the steamer was headed to the south-west, and about seven miles from Cape Chidley the Captain found a beautiful land-locked port which he named "Blandford Harbour"; moving on again, he found another commodious port about half a mile inside of Kickkertaksoak Islands, which he named after Sir T. N. O'Brien. There were plenty of codfish here, but the terrible race of the tide and the danger to his traps from floating ice induced him to move further towards the Cape; south of Cape Chidley he found a harbour which, in compliment to his owners, he named "Lady Job Harbour." Captain Blandford describes this northern haven as a beautiful land-locked port; there was just room for the s.s. *Nimrod* to swing. "For the month I was there," he says, "we could "only see the sun at three o'clock, when it then crossed a notch in the "hills which are about three thousand feet high, with absolutely per- "pendicular cliffs rising sheer out of the water; so high was the "surrounding land, and so completely was the little port sheltered from "the breezes, that we could never tell in the harbour how the wind was "blowing." Inside the Openigevik Islands lies a narrow channel leading into Hudson's Straits; nowhere is it more than a mile and a half wide, and the tide rushes through this narrow passage at a fearful rate; the master of the Hudson Bay Company's steamer *Eric* has been offered a large sum to navigate this channel, as it would considerably shorten the passage to Hudson's Straits, but as the vessel would not steer, he did not dare to run the risk. I have a very strong idea that the intrepid Blandford with his bold Newfoundland crew will somehow get through this strait and solve the problem of its difficult navigation. The captain believes that there is good cod fishing around both the Button Islands and Resolution Island in Hudson's Straits; he intends to fully investigate all the extensive fishing grounds in this high northern latitude.

Labrador is a truly extraordinary country, but probably the most remarkable peculiarity of the great Arctic Peninsula, so sparsely occupied by humanity, is the Labrador Post; twice during the winter, which extends from 1st December to 1st June, a mail is carried each way from Quebec to Ungava in Hudson's Straits. Possibly in Siberia there may be long and difficult postal communication, but I doubt if there is in all the world a longer or more dangerous mail route for men and dogs than the course of the Labrador mail of nearly two thousand miles of land travel.

This unique postal route commences at Bersimis, about one hundred and fifty miles below Quebec, and connected with the lower Canadian capital by highways. Next the mail man on snow shoes and comatik takes the letters to Mingan, and from Mingan to Esquimaux Point. At Esquimaux Point the Bonne Esperance mail man delivers the up mail for Quebec, and receives the down mail for Northern Labrador. From Esquimaux Point the route goes by Natashquan, a distance of a hundred miles, and from Natashquan to Bonne Esperance, over Augustine and Shecatica Bays, the most difficult parts of the coast. In extremely dry cold weather the traveller may be lucky enough to get along the frozen coast line, but generally there are breaks in the weather, and the

BATTLE HARBOUR IN 1857.
From a drawing by the Hon. and Rev. W. Gray.

unfortunate courier has to climb over the mountains and morasses of the back country. The whole distance from Bersimis to Bonne Esperance is seven hundred and fifty miles. From Bonne Esperance to Blanc Sablon, the western limit of Canadian Labrador, a special carrier conveys the mail to Long Point. The mail route from Bersimis to Bonne Esperance is difficult, and from Natashquan to the western end of the line is specially tiresome and troublesome to the mail man, but this course is easy, civilised, and commonplace compared with the carriage of the mails to the frozen north. From Blanc Sablon, the first carrier takes the mail to Battle Harbour, from Battle Harbour

another postman carries it a stage further to Seal Islands, and another from Seal Islands to Rigoulette in Hamilton Inlet.

The Canadian mail route ends at Long Point, near Blanc Sablon; from this place to Rigoulette, Hamilton Inlet, is a Newfoundland postal route. From Rigoulette on to the furthest northern post office at Fort Chimmo, a Hudson Bay Company's station, the mails are conveyed in charge of the Company's men. From Rigoulette the next stages forward are Stag Bay and Davis Island. At Davis Island Mr. John Ford takes charge of the mail to Ungava and the northern Hudson Bay posts; here the most difficult part of this extraordinary postal journey begins. Mr. Ford, formerly manager of the Hudson Bay post at Nachvak, now in charge of the Hudson Bay Company's post at George's River, Ungava Bay, takes the mail from Davis Inlet across Labrador to Fort Chimmo, Ungava Bay. From George's River twice during the Labrador winter with his team of dogs and two hardy Eskimos, he runs this perilous post over an immense barren wilderness. The stages are so long, inhabitants so few, that the three daring postmen have to trust to snow houses and the wonderful sleeping bags of the Hudson Bay travellers. They must brave all the cold of an Arctic winter, all the horrors of a blizzard from the icy north, blinding and cutting like a razor, the short Arctic day, the long, cold, dreary Arctic night. The ordinary post is such an important ingredient in our daily existence that life would hardly seem worth living without the intercourse with our loved ones; but, after all, the post in civilised countries is a commonplace, every-day occurrence. Every trip of the Labrador postmen is an adventure, every journey is a daring exploit. The letters are carried over two thousand miles of wilderness, in peril of the lives of men. The postman is always a welcome visitor to our homes, but to the Frozen North the arrival of the mailman's comitik is the event of the season, the mailcarrier the hero of adventure, his advent the one pleasant break in the dreary monotony of the poor, isolated settlers' lives.

MR. JOHN FORD.
By Hicks, Plymouth.

I am indebted to J. O. Fraser, Postmaster-General of Newfoundland, for the following information about the Labrador post in summer. This mail service to the Labrador is performed by steamers of a superior class. Leaving St. John's generally in the first week in July, the boats call at—

Harbour Grace, thence to Flower's Cove or Nameless Cove, L'anse-au-Loup, Blanc Sablon, Bonne Esperance and Salmon River, thence going North, calling at Bonne Esperance, Blanc Sablon, Forteau, L'anse-au-Loup, and Red Bay.

N.B.—Red Bay will, after the first trip, be the Southern terminus of the Labrador steamer's route, and the coastal steamer, leaving St. John's Tuesday, July 17th, will connect with the Labrador Boat at that place on or about the 23rd July, and fortnightly thereafter.

Going North, after leaving Red Bay, the following ports will be called at, viz.:—Chateau and Henley Harbour, *alternately*, Chimney Tickle, Cape Charles, Assizes Harbour, Battle Harbour, Spear Harbour, Mecklenburg, Francis Harbour, Fishing Ships Harbour, Square Island, Dead Island, Snug Harbour, Venison Island, Bolster's Rock, Punch Bowl, Batteau, Domino, Indian Tickle, Grady, Long Island, Pack's Harbour, Indian Harbour, Smoky Tickle, White Bears, Emily Harbour, Holton, Cape Harrison, Ragged Islands, Adnavick, Long Tickle, Mannock's Island, Turnavick Islands, Winsor's Harbour, Paradise, Hopedale, Fanny's Harbour, *Nain, Queen's Lakes, Freestone Islands, and Ramah*. To the last four ports only two trips will be made, on which occasion Battle Harbour will be the Southern terminus.

Returning South, steamer will call at Spracklin's Island, Cape Harrigan, Davis's Inlet, (*last trip only*), Fanny's Harbour, Hopedale, Malta, Paradise, Winsor's Harbour, Turnavick Islands, Ilack, Macovick, Iron Bound Island, Long Tickle, Adnavick, Ragged Islands, Cape Harrison, Sloop Cove, Tinker's Harbour (*first two trips*), Holton, Emily Harbour, White Bears, Smoky Tickle, Indian Harbour, Rigoulette, Indian Islands, Pack's Harbour and Independent (*alternately*), Cartwright, Long Island, Grady, Indian Tickle, Domino, Black Tickle, Batteau, Punch Bowl, Seal Islands, Bolster's Rock, Venison Island, Snug Harbour, Dead Island, Square Island, Fishing Ship's Harbour, Francis Harbour, Merchantman's Harbour (*last two trips only*), Mecklenburg, Battle Harbour, Assizes Harbour, Cape Charles, Chimney Tickle, Chateau, and Henley Harbour, *alternately*. and Red Bay.

Fortnightly trips are made to and from the Labrador during fishery operations on the coast, commencing on the first week in July and ending about the first week in November.

Of late years Labrador has excited considerable interest amongst American tourists, and various admirable works have been written by these adventurous Republican travellers, notably Mr. Stearns, and the admirable work of Professor Packard, by far the best late work extant on Labrador; besides the valuable information it contains respecting the geology and natural history of the Peninsula, the author has compiled a most complete bibliography of Labrador, for which all future students will bless his memory.

About this great peninsula there is the "glamour of the arctic." Tourists, without running any of the imminent perils of the frozen North, can enjoy in a summer cruise the bracing atmosphere and all the healthy influences of high northern latitudes; to the sportsman, the lover of grand coast scenery, and to the adventurous explorer, Labrador offers unparalleled attractions. This great unknown land has very recently been visited by several parties of tourists both from England and America. The great attraction was the tremendous falls on the Grand River, Hamilton Inlet. This great natural curiosity had been described, briefly, but very correctly, by John McLean,[1] an officer of the Hudson Bay Company, who visited it in 1839. In 1887 Mr. Randle F. Holme made a bold attempt to reach the Grand Falls with a boat and two men; he very pluckily surmounted the difficulties of river navigation, and ascended one hundred and forty miles; unfortunately he had miscalculated the distance, and the failure of his provisions obliged him to return without accomplishing his main object. An account of his journey was read by Mr. Holme before the Royal Geographical Society, and contained much valuable information.[2]

Two successful attempts were made in 1891 by Messrs. Bryant and Kenaston, and by two students of Bowdoin College, Austin Cary and D. M. Cole. The latter reached the falls on the 13th August; Mr. Cary published an account of his journey in the "Bulletin American Geographical Society," Vol. xxiv., p. 1. There has seldom been recorded a more adventurous and dangerous trip than the journey of these two bold American boys: without any assistance from guides, and with the most slender resources, they surmounted every obstacle, and finally, after losing their boat by an accidental fire, they descended the river on a raft of their own construction, and arrived half famished at Rigoulette. Nothing in fiction can exceed the marvellous risks and hair-breadth escapes these young students went through in order to accomplish their object. By far the fullest and most complete account of the Grand Falls and of the surrounding country has been given to the world by Mr. Henry G. Bryant, in his pamphlet "A Journey to the Grand Falls of Labrador"; space only permits of his description of one of the grandest waterfalls of the world.

HENRY G. BRYANT.
By Gilbert and Bacon, Philadelphia.

"September the 2nd was a day memorable as marking the date of our arrival at the Grand Falls. . . . . A single glance showed that we had before us one of the greatest waterfalls in the world. Standing at the rocky brink of the chasm, a wild and tumultuous scene lay before us, a scene possessing elements of sublimity, and with details not to be apprehended in the first moments of wondering contemplation. Far up stream one beheld the surging, fleecy waters and tempestuous billows, dashing high their crests of foam, all forced onward with resistless power towards the steep rock, whence they took their wild leap into the deep pool below.

"Turning to the very brink and looking over, we gazed into a world of mists and mighty reverberations. Here the exquisite colours of the rainbow fascinated the eye, and below and beyond the seething caldron the river appeared, pursuing

---

[1] *Notes of a twenty-five years' service in the Hudson Bay Territory.* London, 1849.

[2] *Proceedings of the Royal Geographical Society,* 1888.

its turbulent career, past frowning cliffs, and over miles of rapids. . . . A mile above the main leap the river is a noble stream four hundred yards wide, already flowing at an accelerated speed. Four rapids, marking successive depressions in the river bed, intervene between this point and the Falls. At the first rapid the

Copyright 1892, by THE CENTURY CO.

THE GRAND FALLS.

width of the stream is not more than seventy-five yards, and from thence rapidly contracts until reaching a point above the escarpment proper, where the entire column of fleecy water is compressed within rocky banks, not more than fifty yards apart.

"Here the effect of resistless power is extremely fine; the maddened waters, sweeping downwards with terrific force, rise in great surging billows high above the encompassing banks, ere they finally hurl themselves into the gulf below.

"A great pillar of mist rises from the spot, and numerous rainbows span the watery abyss, constantly forming and disappearing amid the clouds of spray.

"An immense volume of water precipitates itself over the rocky ledge, and, under favourable conditions, the roar of the cataract can be heard for twenty miles.

"Below the Falls, the river turning to the south-east pursues its maddened career for twenty-five miles, shut in by vertical cliffs of gneissic rock, which rise in places to a height of four hundred feet. The rocky banks above and below the Falls are thickly wooded with firs and spruces, among which the graceful form of

PORTAGING AROUND THE NISIPI FALLS.

the white birch appears in places. . . . . . . The height of the fall may be considered something more than three hundred feet. The vertical height of the chute, thirty-two feet; and from the head of the chute to the surface of the water in the chasm, about three hundred and forty-eight feet. . . . . . . The Grand Falls of Labrador, with their grim environments of time-worn, archaic rocks, are one of the scenic wonders of the western world, and if nearer civilization would be visited by thousands of travellers every year. They are nearly twice as high as Niagara, and are only inferior to that marvellous cataract in breadth and volume of water. . . . . . . The Indian name for the Grand Falls—Pat-ses-che-wan—means 'The narrow place where the waters fall.' Like the native word 'Niagara,' 'Thunder of waters,' this Indian designation contains a poetic and descriptive quality which it would be hard to improve."

APPENDIX TO CHAPTER XIX.

I. Report of the Deep Sea Mission to Labrador, 1893.

At a meeting of sympathisers in the work of the "Mission to Deep Sea Fishermen," which was held at Government House on October 27th, 1892, His Excellency Sir Terence O'Brien in the chair, a resolution was proposed and carried that a Committee be formed for the purpose of co-operating with the directors of the Deep Sea Mission, to extend the service by private and Government aid, and to institute at least two hospitals, or lazarettes, on the coast of Labrador, for the benefit of the fishermen engaged on the coast.

On November 3rd, a second meeting was held at Government House, when the following resolution was carried:—"That this representative Committee will undertake to provide two suitable buildings which may be used as hospitals by the 'Mission to Deep Sea Fishermen,' should the Council of the mission signify their intention to continue their operations on the coast of Labrador, and this Committee will heartily co-operate in any way that the Council of the society may suggest."

A copy of the foregoing resolution was sent to Dr. Grenfell in London. On February 14th, 1893, at a meeting held at Government House, a letter was read from Mr. Francis A. Wood, secretary of the Council of the "Mission to Deep Sea Fishermen," thanking the local Committee for offer of assistance, and it was then resolved that a subscription list be at once opened, with a view to obtain the necessary funds towards the erection of the hospitals referred to and to furnish the sum of £250 stg., as a contribution towards the objects of the Mission.

The following gentlemen were appointed by His Excellency Sir Terence O'Brien as an Executive Committee:—Sir W. V. Whiteway, Sir R. Thorburn, Hons. A. W. Harvey and M. Monroe, and Messrs. W. B. Grieve and W. C. Job, who have now the honour to submit their report.

After careful consideration it was decided by the Committee to establish one of the proposed hospitals at Battle Harbour and one at Indian Harbour.

At Battle Harbour a very suitable building was placed at the disposal of the Committee by W. B. Grieve, Esq., which has greatly assisted the work of the Mission, and the Committee would desire to express their deep sense of their obligation to Mr. Grieve for his generous benefaction.

For the Indian Harbour hospital, a new and complete building was erected after plans sent out by Dr. Grenfell. This building was prepared in St. John's and forwarded to Indian Harbour by the S.S. *Windsor Lake*. Some difficulty was experienced and consequently delay in getting this building erected, and it was not until late in the season that it was in readiness to receive patients.

A subscription list was opened and contributions solicited, and the amount of $1,385.09 has been received as donations to the fund.

BATTLE HARBOUR HOSPITAL.

In addition to the substantial building already erected, the Committee, under the kind direction of Mr. Hall, Messrs. Baine, Johnstone, & Co.'s agent at Battle Harbour, have expended in completing the hospital the sum of $366.00, and for provisions, bedding, and utensils for this hospital, a further sum of $280.67, an expenditure in all of $647.67 on the Battle Harbour hospital.

INDIAN HARBOUR HOSPITAL.

The cost of the building, freight, and erection was $1,712.20, and the sum of $341.64 has been expended in provisions and fittings, making a total expenditure of $2,053.84 on Indian Harbour hospital.

The council of the "Deep Sea Mission," in order to make the service more complete, sent out the fine steam launch *Princess May*, in which Dr. Grenfell has been able to get over the coast much more expeditiously than he could have done in the *Albert*.

Certain necessary expenditure had to be incurred in coaling and provisioning the *Princess May*, and on this an outlay has taken place of $153.91, which, however, the Committee would state, is outside the undertaking and objects originally agreed upon.

In addition to the foregoing, a list of outstanding debts has been handed to the Committee by Dr. Grenfell, which, with the wages of the engineer and man engaged on the *Princess May*, amounts to $902.01.

The following is a condensed statement of the expenditure and receipts:—

BATTLE HARBOUR HOSPITAL.

	$ c.	$ c.
Expended on building	366 00	
Food, fittings, &c.	280 67	
		646 67

INDIAN HARBOUR HOSPITAL.

	$ c.	$ c.
Expended on building	1,712 20	
Food, fittings, &c.	341 64	
		2,053 84
Total on two hospitals		2,700 51

"PRINCESS MAY."

	$ c.	$ c.
Sundries, coal, food, &c.	153 91	
Wages, engineer and steward, four and a half months	247 50	
		401 41

GENERAL.

Sundry accounts for Dr. Grenfell		655 51
		3,757 43
Less amounts collected on account		1,385 00
Balance to be yet raised		2,372 43

The Committee desire to express their sense of the great interest taken in the entire work of the Mission by His Excellency Sir Terence O'Brien, who threw his influence into the work of the Committee, and placed Government House at their service for meetings. He, by his presence, as Chairman of the general meetings of the Committee, rendered the greatest possible benefit to the whole work.

St. John's, Newfoundland, 20th November, A.D. 1893.

W. V. WHITEWAY, WILLIAM BARTLETT,
ROBERT THORBURN, AD. NIELSEN,
A. W. HARVEY, ROBERT S. MUNN,
M. MONROE, SAMUEL BLANDFORD,
W. B. GRIEVE, N. FITZGERALD,
WILLIAM C. JOB, P. G. TESSIER,
JAMES H. WATSON, CHARLES H. EMERSON,
Secretary.

RESULTS OF THE LABRADOR MISSION OPERATIONS IN 1893.

The following are a few figures from Dr. Grenfell's report, rendered to the St. John's Auxiliary Branch of the Mission to Deep Sea Fishermen at the close of the fishing season in November 1893:—

In Labrador, the Straits of Belle Isle, and on the French shore of Newfoundland there were treated by—

	In-patients.	Out-patients.
Dr. Bobardt, at Battle Harbour	33	647
Dr. Curwen, on the hospital ship *Albert*	3	1,052
on the steam-launch *Princess May*	1	794
Total	37	2,493

These cases, for your better information and that of the public, I have analysed as follows:—

MEDICAL CASES.
Diseases of—

Digestive system	633
Respiratory and circulatory system	194
Nervous system	60
Excretory	40
Women	64

Diseases of Special Organs.

Eye (including 34 cases of night blindness)	211
Ear	40
Nose and throat	93
Skin	105
Minor cases—headaches, colds, strains	167
Cases of rheumatism	64

SURGICAL CASES.

Affections of the upper limbs	306
Affections of the lower limbs	94
General surgical cases—glands, bones, special agues, rickets, tumour, fistula, &c.	188
Sundry minor cases	210
Total	2,493

Operations performed under chloroform	17
Major operations without chloroform	11
Minor surgical operations, including teeth	269

The Battle Harbour Hospital was opened July 29th, and kept open till October 31st—in all, 94 days. Dr. Bobardt and Nurse Cawardine had charge of this hospital. The building was a gift from W. B. Grieve, Esq., and was fitted up by the Committee. The warmest thanks of the Committee are due to Mr. Hall, Mr. Grieve's agent at Battle Harbour, for his untiring kindness and help, in spite of a very busy season. Without his assistance the work could not have been done.

Owing to a variety of untoward and unforeseen circumstances, it was found impossible to get Indian Harbour Hospital ready in time for occupation. Dr. Curwen and Nurse Williams, to whom the charge of this hospital had been allotted, worked on the Mission ship *Albert* till the middle of August, when, owing to the press of work at Battle Harbour Hospital, Nurse Williams was directed to go there to assist Nurse Cawardine.

The great need of hospital work on Labrador is seen when it is considered how many cases occur of blindness, deformities, or loss of certain faculties, affecting the bread-winners of families, most of which might have been prevented if treated in time, and thus much personal suffering spared, and also a great loss to the community. During the season the medical men were able to render such aid that several who had been compelled to give up work found themselves capable of resuming their duties. When sick persons are thus saved from losing their season's work, or saved the time and expense involved in returning to Newfoundland for advice, in cases of minor importance; or when, as happened in several instances during the season, the lives or limbs were saved, or in some hopeless cases, life was prolonged so as to allow them to reach home and end their days in the bosom of their families, the value of this hospital work becomes more apparent.

To the sick of Labrador these hospitals will be an inestimable boon. Only those who have known what it is to toss on a bed of pain, perhaps unable even at night to find rest, their tongue parched with thirst, and fever raging in their system, can properly appreciate the meaning of the skilful help of the physician, the delicate attention of the trained nurse, the hushed house, the subdued voices, and the gentle light of the half-darkened room. When this is contrasted with the sad sight so often witnessed on Labrador, of delicate women, and even children, undergoing sufferings, which are hard to bear even amid the comforts and gentle attentions of home, on the dreary coast of Labrador, far from every helping hand, or in the dark hold of some small fishing vessel, where the atmosphere is poisonous, and the noises to the sick distressing and almost maddening, it is then we realise the value of the noble humane work in the hospitals erected on storm-beaten Labrador for the relief of suffering humanity. Who would not aid in such a good work?

DISTRIBUTION OF CLOTHING.

The *Albert* brought from England a very large stock of clothing, both new and cast-off, the gift of kind charitable friends. This was distributed with the greatest care and discrimination, every precaution being used to guard against imposition. The cases of utter or partial destitution of clothing, among families who reside permanently on the Labrador coast, were numerous, and much timely aid was given, especially to women and children. Food was also given in cases of extreme destitution. Many families were thus helped to provide for the long, cold winter of this region. There is no doubt that every spring some families are driven to subsist on mussels and seaweed they can gather along the land-wash. With ice on the coast no help can reach them.

DISTRIBUTION OF BOOKS, PERIODICALS, AND TRACTS.

A very large supply of wholesome literature was carried on board the Mission ship, and, wherever she went, was freely distributed among the fishermen. Wherever it was found in any family that anyone could read, a gift was made either of illustrated or plain literature, or both.

RELIGIOUS SERVICES.

Wherever the *Albert* or *Princess May* called, when opportunity offered, especially on Sundays, religious services were held, which all were invited to attend. Hymns were sung, prayers offered, and simple addresses given on Scriptural subjects. These services were much appreciated among these lonely sea-toilers; and thus something was done to make known that Gospel which has brought such blessings to mankind, but without any reference to creed or sect being made.

The steam launch *Princess May* proved to be of great service in the Mission work. Dr. Grenfell was enabled to go up uncharted bays in her, so as to visit a large number of the small settlements which would otherwise not have been within reach. He was thus able to make a thorough examination into the condition of the residents, and to collect accurate statistical information regarding them to an extent never before attempted. In all, he visited 87 different settlements on the Labrador coast, as far north as Okkak. Dr. Curwen in the *Albert* visited 35 more settlements; and Dr. Bobardt visited all the places in the vicinity of Battle Harbour.

II. The Labrador Trade.

The following list gives the names of the localities, supplying merchants, and agents in Labrador:—

Names of Places.	Supplying Merchants.	Agents.
Bonne Esperance	Job Bros. & Co.	W. H. Whitely.
Salmon River	Do.	Jas. Brown.
Middle Bay	Do.	Wm. Smith.
Bradore	Penny Bros.	— Powell.
Grundy Island	Job Bros. & Co.	S. Blandford.
Blanc Sablon	Do.	S. Blandford.
Do.	Frewing & Co.	Thos. Moral.
Isle-au-Bois	Penny Bros.	Edgar Penny.
Forteau	Job Bros. & Co.	S. Short.
Lance-au-Loup	Do.	J. H. Watson.
Lance-aux-Morts		Davis.
Red Bay	Penny Bros.	Jos. Penny.
Do.		Jos. Udell.

TRADE AND POPULATION.

Names of Places.	Supplying Merchants.	Agents.
Chateau	Joyce Bros.	— Joyce.
Henley Harbour		Wm. Butt.
Cape Charles	Baine, Johnston, & Co.	Soper.
Battle Harbour	Do.	Geo. Hall.
Cape Charles	Kinealy	Kinealy.
Fishing Ships Harbour	Jno. Munn & Co.	Ed. Parsons.
Dead Island	W. Ross & Co.	Chas. Payne.
Seal Island	B. Greene	Greene.
Punch Bowl	J. Munn & Co.	M. Poreen.
Cape Harrison	Do.	Levi Frost.
Do.	J. Rorke	
Indian Tickle	Crummy	Crummy.
Spracklin's Island	Job Bros. & Co.	Thos. Spracklin.
Cape Harrigan	Do.	
Merchantman's Harbour	Duff	Winsor.
Francis Harbour	J. Rorke	Penny.
Venison Tickle	Do.	Hawker.
Griffin's Harbour	Goodfellow & Co.	Power.
Batteau	J. Ryan	
Do.	Ben. Boyles	Boyles.
Domino	Isaac Bartlett	Bartlett.
Indian Tickle	J. Munn & Co.	Winsor.
Grady	Do.	R. McRae.
Pack's Harbour	Do.	Lawrence.
Cartwright	Hudson's Bay Company	Jas. Fraser.
Indian Harbour	Job Bros. & Co.	J. Simms.
Smoky	Geo. Jerritt	Jerritt.
Emily Harbour	J. Munn & Co.	Geo. Apsey.
Holton	J. Ryan	
Do.	Do.	
Turnavick, W.	Job Bros. & Co.	W. Bartlett.
Turnavick, E.	Do.	Wm. Hennessy.
Winsor Harbour	John Hennessy	Jno. Hennessy.
Hopedale	Moravian Mission	Kissiover.
Rigoulette	Hudson's Bay Company	Wilson.

III. Census of Labrador, 1891.

LOCALITIES AND POPULATION.

Isle au Bois	6	Deep Water Creek	10
Blanc Sablon	47	Petty Harbour	3
L'anse au Clair	79	Little Harbour	8
Forteau	103	Seal Bight	23
L'anse au Mour	12	William's Harbour	13
L'anse au Loup	78	Francis Harbour Bight	8
L'anse au Diable	27	Sloop Cove	6
Capstan Island	23	Square Island	35
West St. Modeste	92	Nowlan's Harbour	14
Pinware	63	George's Cove	25
East St. Modeste	56	Soug Harbour	17
Carrol's Cove	29	Tub Harbour	7
Red Bay	152	Venison Tickle	69
Frey's Cove	9	Hawke Harbour	10
Barge Bay	19	Bolster Rock	33
Chateau	15	Seal Island	67
Henley Harbour	20	Black Bear Bay	15
Chimney Tickle	8	Pennock's Cove	12
Camp Islands	34	Spotted Island	67
Cape Charles	52	Black Tickle	10
Assizes Harbour	4	Domino	2
Indian Harbour	45	Salmon Point	27
Battle Harbour	281	Sandhill	20
Trap Cove	58	Mullin's Cove	9
Mathew's Cove	31	Table Bay Point	7
Fox Harbour	47	Grady	10
		Sandwich Bay	318
		Hamilton Inlet	486

LOCALITIES AND POPULATION—cont.

Hopedale	341
Nain	272
Zoar	92
Hebron	256
Okak	362
Ramah	64
Total	4,106
As taken in 1884	4,211

RELIGIOUS CENSUS.

	1884.	1891.
Church of England	1,974	1,749
Church of Rome	566	354
Methodist Church	305	604
Presbyterian Church	17	2
Moravian Church	1,349	1,397
Total	4,211	4,106

POPULATION OF MORAVIAN SETTLEMENTS IN 1891.

	Missionaries.	Eskimos.	Children attending School.
Hamilton Inlet	—	10	—
Hopedale	6	341	28
Nain	8	272	45
Zoar	2	92	63
Hebron	4	256	47
Okak	4	312	63
Ramah	2	64	11
Total		1,327	257

IV. A. P. Low's Survey.

The most complete survey of Labrador has been recently carried out by A. P. Low, of the Geological Survey of Canada, assisted by T. D. V. Eaton. Leaving Ottawa in June 1893, Mr. Low crossed the Labrador area from south to north and from east to west, and his detailed report, when published, will contain the first trustworthy account of the vast region. Surveys were made over 2,000 miles of rivers and lakes, including the greater part of the courses of the East Main, Koksoak, or Ungava River, and Hamilton River. All these regions will now, for the first time, be accurately mapped out. Large iron fields and great timber regions were discovered. Considering the immense area to be traversed and the difficulties to be encountered, the exploration was a splendid success, and reflects the greatest credit on this energetic and daring traveller.

CHAPTER XX.

RAILWAY CONSTRUCTION IN THE COLONY.

The progress of Newfoundland has been terribly retarded by the want of internal communications; until after the first quarter of the present century we had no public highways—primitive paths through the woods were the only means of communication between the settlements by land. The population earned their living on the sea, cultivation of the soil was prohibited, and until the arrival of Sir Thomas Cochrane, the advancement of the Colony, its civilization and material prosperity, was crippled for want of roads. Our first legislators very wisely gave their almost undivided attention to the construction of highways, and, in consequence, now we have probably the best common roads in North America. To-day, however, the common road, as a medium of communication, is practically useless; it is too slow; we want the swifter, safer, and more convenient road, the Railway.

There were three purposes for which railways were urgently required. First, to connect the population around Conception Bay; it was the earliest settled part of the Colony, and is still the most thickly populated. Dr. Mullock was the first to see that a line of railway through this district was not only practicable but would pay.

The next most important purpose for which a railway was urgently needed, was to bring the great mining region of the north, and the prosperous settlements of Bonavista, Trinity, Twillingate, and Fogo, into unbroken connection with the capital, during the season's ice, which comes periodically on our coast in the spring. These important localities are cut off from the capital by sea for the six months of winter. Their only communication during this long dreary period was a precarious post by dog teams and Indians; this was felt to be a scandal and reproach, and one of the first objects of the Newfoundland Railway was to reach the Exploits. Under Mr. R. G. Reid's management, this important work has now been accomplished; trains run as regularly, and mails are delivered to these distant outports as punctually, as the daily mails to Harbour Grace.

The opponents of railways always argued that they would carry nothing, and develop nothing, in the country; the results of the very short time in which the Northern Railway has been in operation shows how ignorant and short-sighted was their antagonism.

Besides giving access to a great undeveloped country, and the consequent facilities to the merchant, the miner, the sportsman, the tourist, and the furrier (the latter being turned to such good account that one party of trappers at Soulis Brook has already secured $500 worth of furs), the railway opens up several fine tracts of agricultural land, and in the near future will inaugurate a great mining industry.

Although only in operation for one season, the Northern Railway has developed splendid granite quarries and a lumber business which bids fair to be one of the greatest industries of the Colony, already consisting

OLD SAW MILL, SHOAL HARBOUR.

of several great mills, besides smaller operators and hand loggers, whose united turn-out this year will not be less than twenty million feet of lumber. Botwoodville, owned by the Exploits Wood Company of London, will cut six million feet of lumber; the Benton Mill, at Soulis Brook, owned by Mr. Reid, another six million; the Campbell Mill, at Terra Nova River, three million; Sterritt's Mill, at Gander Crossing, Glenwood, about one million. At Gambo there are the fine mills of Messrs. John Murphy and Osmond; at Gander Arm, Philip's Mill, with unrivalled facilities for collecting and shipping; Arthur's Mill; and some smaller establishments. The whole cut of timber for the season of 1893 may be safely estimated at twenty million feet, which, at the low average price of $15 per thousand feet, amounts to $300,000. The lumber business in time will develop many minor industries connected with it, the making of wood pulp, matches, spools, and gunpowder charcoal, for which our abundant aspen is admirably suited.

All the new mills on the line owe their creation and their successful working entirely to the railway. Formerly every article required for all our northern out-ports had to be laid in by November; no communication was possible during the winter. The railway has changed all this; every

SAW MILL, BOTWOODVILLE.

day, every week, the lumberman in his camp gets his provisions and all necessaries for his work, his daily paper, and his daily food, as conveniently as if no distance intervened between the forest and the capital. Anyone who understands the lumber business can see at once the immense advantage of the railway to the minor mills, smaller operators, and hand loggers; less capital will be required, less advances given out, and much greater facilities will be given for doing business when the lumberman can get his supplies from time to time as he requires them; virtually he can get paid as he works along; all these advantages naturally increase the output of timber. But not only the lumberman and the merchant, but the miner and the fisherman equally profit by the railway. In time it will kill out all the old abuses of the out-harbours;

the isolation, the outrageous prices—all will die away before the magic influence of the iron road.

The third great object for which a railway was required in Newfoundland, and by far the most important of all, was to unite us with the Continent of America, to bring us into closer contact with the civilization and superior advancement of the Continent, to make us an integral portion of the go-ahead America of to-day. At present we lie outside the strong currents of progress; our Island lies remote, unbefriended, and practically unknown; our insular position is a tremendous drawback to our material prosperity. The new railway to Port-aux-Basques, which is being rapidly pushed forward by Mr. R. G. Reid, will

MR. REID AND HIS LABOURERS.

put an end to this isolation, and in a few years will change the moral, social and commercial conditions of our Colony. Our Island is like a great estate around whose borders and outer limits there has been digging and delving, whilst the great interior, the boundless expanse of the great property, is ignored, under-valued, and undeveloped.

A railway policy is always a progressive policy; like the proverbial snowball, it gathers strength as it rolls; when once a line is built, however short the distance, it must go forward; its benefits are so obvious, its accommodation to the public is so apparent, its advantages to the great labouring population are so striking, that its extension goes forward as a matter of course. In the inception of our first railway, Sir William Whiteway strongly advocated its construction by the local Government; the committee, however, were almost unanimously of opinion that it should be built by outsiders and by a company. The

THE HARBOUR GRACE LINE.

first promoters of our little line to Harbour Grace turned out to be men of straw; all the money put in the railway was borrowed money; there was a good deal of jobbery and robbery in connexion with it. We accepted the lowest tender from an American Company, who bound themselves to build the line to Hall's Bay for an annual subsidy of $180,000 for thirty years, and a land grant of five thousand acres per mile. With the exception of the line to Harbour Grace, all the remainder was over a country which had never been surveyed; Sir Hugh Allan's Company undertook to build the Harbour Grace Railway, but they declined to commit themselves to any definite offer over the unsurveyed country. The committee considered that the American Company, by depositing $100,000, and by agreeing to build the line subject to the approval of the Government engineer, were practically safe people to bargain with, and they made a contract, which, after much discussion in committee, was finally accepted. The chronic impecuniosity of the contracting company produced endless difficulties and delays in the completion of the line; even before the metals were laid half-way to Whitbourne, the company was in the hands of a receiver, and the mortgagees had to complete the line to Harbour Grace; but for the exertions and advances of A. M. Mackay, Sir W. V. Whiteway, and others, it would never have gone forward at all.

Experience has shown us that we might have built the line for about half the money it cost, and that it would have been one of the best paying short lines in North America.[1] The engineering was very unsatisfactory and incomplete; instead of running into Topsail, the most important pleasure resort and best paying station on the railway, the line has to be reached by a steep uphill road a mile long; a much better

[1] NEWFOUNDLAND RAILWAY.

	Total Earnings.	Total Expenditure.	No. of Passengers carried.	Passenger Receipts.	Tons of Freight carried.	Freight Receipts.
	$	$		$		$
1885	47,624	98,959	—	—	—	—
1886	46,772	—	27,649	29,010	4,996	10,156
1893	81,091	72,210	58,791	48,815	10,181	22,294

The receipts for mail service are $7,200 per annum, Government subsidy $75,000 per annum, total earnings $153,200 per annum. At the present time the railway gives a fair return to the bondholders. Under the careful management of the Receiver, Sir Francis Evans, and his manager, Captain Noble, the road bed has been put in good order, wooden bridges and trestle work have been replaced by solid mason work and steel structures, and the whole line has in many places been practically rebuilt.

route could have been selected if there had been a more complete preliminary survey.

For a colony railways should be run to secure traffic or to encourage settlement; the Topsail Line should have commenced at the west end of St. John's; Nature has made River Head into a wet dock; by removing the gasworks and reclaiming a large part of this area for a goods station, a dock and a broad quay, carried down to Steers, could have been made; here should have been the passenger station, with a tramway turning up Queen's Street, and running to the old garrison by Duckworth Street; no town of the size of St. John's exists on this side of the Atlantic without the immense convenience of a street railway.

The Newfoundland Railway Company having failed to complete the line to Hall's Bay, proceedings were taken against them by the Government to recover damages for their breach of contract. This suit has been dragging its slow length along for several years, and through two administrations. It was a long time in the hands of the lawyers; it has now been for several years before the Supreme Court; some time, probably towards the end of the century now drawing to a close, it may be confidently hoped the final decision in this Railway Jarndyce and Jarndyce will be arrived at.

The Thorburn Government, following out the policy of their predecessors, built the Placentia Railway, and commenced the extension of the line north to Hall's Bay. About sixteen miles had been graded when their administration was defeated at the polls in 1889.

In 1890 the Whiteway Administration invited tenders for the construction and operation of a line of railway from a point on the Placentia line to Hall's Bay north. After the receipt of a large number of tenders, and a very full consideration of all these various offers, the committee finally recommended the acceptance of the tender of R. G. Reid and G. H. Middleton, to build the line for $15,600 per mile. This was the lowest efficient tender, and the most satisfactory one; the principal contractor was known to be wealthy, and his financial standing was unexceptionable. Besides the deposit of one quarter million dollars as security for the fulfilment of the contract, it was well known that the contractor would take our three-and-a-half per cent. bonds at par. The Government had had enough to do with impecunious promoters, and when it was found that the contract had been given to Mr. R. G. Reid, it was universally approved of. Subse-

MR. R. G. REID.
By Marshall, Guelph.

quent experience has shown that the committee made a wise selection. Mr. Reid has fulfilled all his obligations with the utmost honour and punctuality; his able and energetic sons, W. D. Reid and Harry Reid, are universal favourites with the labourers on the line; the men are well treated, good honest work has been done on the new line, obstacles overcome which appeared at the outset almost insurmountable. Only those who have organised an operation like railway building through a wild country can appreciate all the difficulties that have to be faced, the organisation required, the careful forethought, the toil and labour of providing food and shelter for a small army of workmen; the precautions that have to be taken against the thousand and one accidents, perils, and casualties that are almost inevitable in connexion with a big railway contract in a new country.

On the 16th June 1890 the Government made the contract with Messrs. Reid and Middleton to construct and equip a line of railway, beginning at Placentia Junction on the Placentia Railway, and extending

RAILWAY BRIDGE OVER THE TERRA NOVA RIVER.
From a photograph by H. Parsons.

north to Hall's Bay, a distance of two hundred and sixty-two miles. The contractors were also to operate the Placentia Railway free of charge, and they were to take over at a valuation the work already carried out by the Thorburn Government on the new northern line; five years was the limit of time within which the line to Hall's Bay was to be completed; the railway was to be furnished with rolling stock, machine shops, &c. The work is now completed on the northern route to Exploits. The construction is of a very solid character. 50 lbs. per yard steel rails for a narrow gauge railway of 3 feet 6 inches; the sleepers are of the best obtainable material, the road is well ballasted with gravel, the culverts are of stone, granite from local quarries, and iron is used in all the bridges, and the line generally is properly equipped. The work is all done in a most substantial and workmanlike manner, to the complete satisfaction of the Government Inspecting Engineer, Mr. H. C. Burchell. In 1890 the work did not commence until the autumn; fifteen hundred men were employed, and ten miles of railway completed and metalled; in the following year, 1891, eighteen hundred men had work on the line, and fifty miles were finished. In May 1892 Messrs. Reid and Middleton dissolved partnership, and the work henceforward was entirely carried out by R. G. Reid. This year the work was pushed ahead with vigour, two thousand two hundred had employment on the line, and eighty miles of railway were finished.

On the 16th May 1893 Mr. Reid entered into a further arrangement with the Newfoundland Government, on precisely the same terms as the first contract, to construct and equip a line of railway from the terminus at Exploits to Port-aux-Basques When the Government decided to carry the railway west to Port-aux-Basques, Mr. Reid had a survey made by his own engineers and an excellent line was found. The new contract was—

"To construct and equip a line of railway commencing at the terminus of the road, to be constructed under the Northern Railway contract, being a point two hundred miles distant from Placentia Junction, and running by the best, most desirable, and most direct route to the north-east end of Grand Lake; thence to the north-east end of Deer Lake, and westerly along the north side of Deer Lake and down the Humber River; thence by way of the north side of Harry's River; and thence to Port aux-Basques." This contract was signed on the 16th May 1893. On the same day another contract was signed, in which Mr. Reid undertook to operate the Placentia Branch Railway and also the "Newfoundland Northern and Western Railway," as the new line from Placentia Junction to Port-aux-Basques was to be called, for a period of ten years, commencing 1st September 1893. The whole length of the new line, from Placentia Junction to Port-aux-Basques, is estimated to be about five hundred miles.

For constructing and equipping the railway "payments shall be made to the Contractor upon the completion of each continuous and consecutive section of five miles, or a fraction of a section at the end of the work, at the rate of $15,600 per mile of main line, the said payments being in full for all the works and materials provided for under this contract and necessary for the thorough and complete construction and equipment of the line of railway herein provided for. All such payments shall be made by the Government and accepted by the Contractor in debentures of the Government of Newfoundland in sterling money of the United Kingdom of Great Britain and Ireland, maturing on the 1st day of January 1947, with interest thereon at the rate of $3\frac{1}{2}$ per cent. per annum, payable half-yearly; principal and interest payable in London, England," "Payments will be made to the Contractor on the written certificate of the Engineer and the approval of the Government that works have been duly executed." The whole line is to be completed in three years from 1st September 1893, and to be a narrow gauge of three feet six inches. The specifications are such as will secure a thoroughly safe and well-equipped line.

The contract for maintenance and operation of the Placentia Branch and of the Newfoundland Northern and Western Railway, for a period of ten years from

1st September 1893, provides that the Contractor shall maintain these in a safe, efficient, and satisfactory manner, and continuously and efficiently operate the same (the number of trains to be run being specified); also, shall erect telegraph lines along the whole line of railway for the purposes of its operation and work them at his own expense, and also shall, if required, work them as part of the Government Telegraph System on certain conditions. On the faithful performance of these engagements, the Government agreed "to grant in fee-simple to the Contractor, five thousand acres of land for each one mile of main line or branch railway throughout the entire length of the lines to be operated. Should the line, therefore, be five hundred miles in length, the land grant would be two million five hundred thousand acres. "The said fee-simple grants shall be made by the Government to the said contractor as follows: 250,000 acres upon the completion of the northern line to Exploits; 250,000 acres upon the completion of the western line to Deer Lake; 250,000 acres upon the completion of the western line to St. George's Bay; 250,000 acres upon the completion of the line to Port-aux-Basques; and the balance at the end of five years from the date of this

RAILWAY BRIDGE AT CLODE SOUND.
From a photograph by H. Burchell.

contract, or as soon thereafter as practicable." "The land shall be located on each side of the railway in alternate sections of one or two miles in length with the railway, at the option of the contractor, on meridian or base lines, as the case may be, and eight miles in depth, the Government retaining the alternate sections, and until the contractor has made his selection under this section, the Government shall not dispose of any Crown Lands, timber, or mineral rights within eight miles on either side of the line of railway." "Where such sections from any cause are not obtainable along the line, the said contractor may select Crown Lands elsewhere to make up deficiencies, the last mentioned selections to be made in sections or blocks of not less than one mile square, and not more than ten miles square."

The contract contains stringent provisions for the due execution of the various agreements, so as to secure the construction of a first-class line of railway. One section stipulates that the wages of daily labourers shall not be less than one dollar per day, payable monthly.

In order to make the railway really valuable to the settlements along the line, it is necessary to connect the small villages and towns with the railway; much good work has been done, but much more remains to be done. The population in Fortune Bay and the whole western shore could avail themselves of the line for mails and passengers by a road from the bottom of the bay to Black River, or by a short road between Bay de l'Argent, Buck Cove, and Boat Harbour, with a ferry to the Placentia shore opposite. Good work has already been done in this direction; Mr. Reid, acting under the instructions of the Government, has made a good waggon road, forty miles in length, from Trinity to Shoal Harbour, via Goose Bay; this opens up a large quantity of good land for settlement, and secures access to the railway to a considerable population. Another road, ten miles in length, has been built to connect Indian Arm Bay with the railway; while a third, five miles in

RAILWAY BRIDGE OVER DARK HOLE BROOK, RANDOM.
From a photograph by H. Parsons.

length, runs from Alexander Bay to the railway near Gambo. A long line of road from Hall's Bay to Badger Bay has been surveyed and partly built, and another from Arnolds Cove and Come-by-Chance is finished. The Hall's Bay line may be completed this year and will connect with the railway. A line of road four miles long has been surveyed from Northern Bight to the line, and another is projected from Exploits to Botwoodville and Gander Bay. Wherever there is good land along these waggon roads it will be occupied by settlers, and farms will multiply.

Starting from Placentia Junction, seven miles from Whitbourne, the new line runs from thence northerly, crossing the isthmus which connects the peninsula of Avalon with the main body of the island, which at its narrowest part is less than three miles wide. On either side of the isthmus are the heads of the great bays of Placentia, Trinity,

HUMBER RIVER, BAY OF ISLANDS

LITTLE RIVER

and Fortune, the waters of which are only a few miles distant from Placentia Bay. Still following a northerly course the railway traverses the Terra Nova, Gambo, and Gander Valleys, and enters the great valley of the Exploits at Norris's Arm. At this point it turns westerly and follows the Exploits River to Badger Brook, where it leaves the river and takes a more north-westerly course, and at Bishop's Falls, ten miles up, it crosses the Exploits River on a fine steel bridge, having many piers of solid masonry.

Following this north-westerly route the portion to be immediately constructed will cross the White Hill Plains and thence down the valley of Kitty's Brook to the north-eastern end of Grand Lake. The course will then be along the southern side of Deer Lake to Bay of Islands, thence through the valley of Harry's Brook to Bay St. George. From this point the line will pass to the east of the Anguille range of hills, down the valley of the Codroy Rivers, and thence along by the coast to Grand Bay and Port-aux-Basques, the terminus of the line.

With the exception of the first portion of the route, which lies amongst the barren lands of the Avalon peninsula, the course of the railway runs through most picturesque wild scenery; there are no more beautiful vistas in North America than Exploits Arm and its river valley, the noble expanse of Grand Lake, the fertile vale of Deer Lake, the Humber River, and the majestic coast scenery of Bay of Islands. An American writer—S. G. W. Benjamin—in the *Century Magazine*, thus describes this noble view:—"The sun also came out, the clouds rolled "away, and the magnificent scenery of the Bay of Islands lay around "us. We felt more than repaid for the effort required of us to reach it. "The coast scenery of the world offers few prospects more grand, more "varied, more enchantingly beautiful than this; certainly on the "Atlantic coast of North America it is not to be found." After an eloquent description of the varied beauties of this lovely bay, in almost prophetic tones, the writer says, "The time is not very distant when the "world will wake to a consciousness of the mineral wealth and abundant "timber resources of Newfoundland."

The railway is already awakening the world to a dim consciousness of our vast latent wealth—the wealth of the sea, the vast harvest of the ocean, seems to have obscured all our other resources; even this undoubtedly rich mine of wealth is only half developed. In Europe, the fisheries of the North Sea produce more than eighty millions of dollars, the value of British fish alone representing about forty millions, whilst the whole deep sea fisheries of the United States, exclusive of the oyster fishery, is to-day probably less than twelve millions of dollars. With half the population, England consumes three times as much fish as America. The reason for this vast difference lies in the cheapness of fish food in Europe as compared with America, owing to improved methods of fishing, more fishermen, and greater facilities for transportation. The deep sea fishery of America is a decaying industry; were it not for Canadians and foreigners, and excessive Protection, it would die altogether. The whole state of things is artificial and unsound.

The North Sea of America lies around Newfoundland, a fishery far vaster in extent and more abundant than the famed fishing grounds of Europe; in order to bring it to the European standard we must adopt European methods, the old-fashioned plan of salting and drying the cod fish must be abandoned; it is most absurd and wasteful to actually destroy two-thirds of a most valuable article of food in order to render

RAILWAY BRIDGE OVER BISHOP'S FALLS, EXPLOITS RIVER.
From a photograph by H. Burchell.

the remainder uneatable. What we require is a new method of selling our fish in its most palatable form fresh; frozen mutton is carried fourteen thousand miles through the Tropics, and fish is brought fresh and sound three thousand miles across the American continent; as certainly the vast fish wealth of our Island, the lordly salmon, the magnificent and abundant cod of the winter fishery at Channel, the tempting lobsters, the magnificent herring of Bonne Bay and Bay of Islands will find their way into the American market when the new railway and the steam ferry across Cabot Straits give us constant access to the Continent. Given the facilities for trade, and trade will follow, when our silvery salmon, fat and fresh from the cold waters of the Atlantic are worth five cents a pound in Newfoundland, and fifty in New York; when one hundred lobsters fetch sixty cents in our Island,

the price of a single good crustacean in New York. Frozen cod and most delicious cod's tongues, fresh every morning, will be transported from our shores; every train from Cape Breton, and every steamer across the ferry will carry frozen fish as regularly as the fish trains run in Europe. The supply from Newfoundland is simply inexhaustible, all that is required are facilities—the train and the twenty knot steamer, and the enterprise to transport it regularly to the ever-ready market of the States and Canada. When the time comes we shall wonder why we were asleep so long; why this obvious trade was so long delayed. Twenty-five years ago there was no frozen herring trade between Newfoundland and America; to-day it is an immense and profitable business. So it will be with the fresh and kippered fish, bloaters, Findon-haddocks, boneless cod, and frozen fish. My prediction of years ago, "Fresh fish and Fulton Market," will soon cease to be the dream of an enthusiast; the railway and steam ferry will soon convert it into a reality. The business is there: let us hope the right persons will take it up.

The new Northern and Western Railway will probably be metalled to Bay of Islands by the end of 1896, the end of the track is now only eighty miles distant from the mouth of the Humber; by the close of

MAP
showing
SHORTEST SEA VOYAGE
and
QUICKEST ROUTE
between
EUROPE & AMERICA

1896 it will reach the terminus at Port-aux-Basques, where docks and warehouses are to be erected by the contractor. This admirable harbour is the centre of a large winter cod fishery, whilst Bay of Islands is celebrated for its splendid herrings, also caught in winter; the railway and the steam ferry will open a way for their transportation, all the winter through, to the Continent. Besides the fisheries there are large deposits of iron, copper, coal, asbestos, gypsum, marble, granite, and other building stone of the finest quality to provide freight for the new iron road.

To the sportsman, the tourist, the angler, and the canoeist, the new railway will offer unrivalled attractions. For the hunter of big game there is the noble cariboo, a species of reindeer peculiar to the Island;

NEWFOUNDLAND CARIBOO.

they range over the woods and barrens in countless thousands, the whole interior is one vast deer park; so numerous are these magnificent animals that at least one thousand are killed every winter on the south coast, and eight hundred were slaughtered swimming across Gander Lake in the autumn of 1893, a barbarous practice, which is now to be put down by law. The new railway will bring the sportsman right on to the deer park at Grand Lake (fifty miles long), down which he can proceed by boat and place his camp; by careful stalking and straight shooting he will be sure to obtain some splendid heads. To the less ambitious sportsman our Island offers some of the finest grouse shooting in America (the best localities are on the southern parts of the Island), and wild geese, ducks, snipe, and curlew are abundant. To the fisherman Newfoundland offers unrivalled attractions; lakes and rivers full of noble trout and silvery salmon, an angler's Paradise that would have delighted old Izaak Walton's heart. There is not only plenty of sport for the coarse and common bait fisher, the refined artist of the rod and the fly will be still more gratified with sea trout, brown trout, and salmon, the former abundant in every lake and river. By virgin streams and lovely placid lakes, past woods and mountains, the canoeist, the angler, and the mere camper-out may wander at his own sweet will.[1]

An immense advantage of the new line to Newfoundlanders will be the complete and entire change of our present communications with the outside world; instead of fortnightly mails we shall have tri-weekly posts to Europe and America, and in a short time daily communication with Canada, the West Indies, and the United States. Besides being more frequent, postal and passenger communication will be much more regular, and many degrees swifter than is possible under existing arrangements.

WILLOW GROUSE IN SUMMER PLUMAGE.   PTARMIGAN IN WINTER PLUMAGE.

At first it is proposed to have a tri-weekly service between Port-aux-Basques and Sydney, Cape Breton, but when the railway in Cape Breton is completed to Neil's Harbour, thirty miles nearer to Cape Ray, there will be a daily service across the Straits.

[1] The game laws will be found at the end of Chapter XXV.

CHAPTER XXI.

TELEGRAPHIC COMMUNICATION IN NEWFOUNDLAND.

1850-1894.

The history of Telegraphic Communication has been a good deal written about, but always with a certain amount of bias. The first written communication in Newfoundland about a telegraphic line across the Island to connect us with Cape Breton came from Dr. Mullock, and was published by him in the *Courier* at St. John's, Nov. 8, 1850, in the following letter :—

"To the Editor of the Courier,   St. John's, November 8, 1850.

"I regret to find that in every plan for Transatlantic Communication Halifax is always mentioned and the natural capabilities of Newfoundland entirely overlooked. This has been deeply impressed on my mind by the communication I read in your paper of Saturday last, regarding telegraphic communication between England and Ireland, in which it is said that the nearest telegraphic station on the American side is Halifax, twenty-one hundred and fifty-five miles from the west of Ireland. Now would it not be well to call the attention of England and America to the extraordinary capabilities of St. John's, as the nearest telegraphic point? It is an Atlantic port, lying, I may say, in the track of the ocean steamers, and by establishing it as the American telegraphic station, news could be communicated to the whole American continent forty-eight hours, at least, sooner than by any other route. But how will this be accomplished? Just look at the map of Newfoundland and Cape Breton. From St. John's to Cape Ray there is no difficulty in establishing a line passing near Holy-Rood along the neck of land connecting Trinity and Placentia Bays, and thence in a direction due west to the Cape. You have then about forty-one to forty-five miles of sea to St. Paul's Island, with deep soundings of one hundred fathoms, so that the electric cable will be perfectly safe from icebergs. Thence to Cape North, in Cape Breton, is little more than 12 miles. Thus it is not only practicable to bring America two days nearer to Europe by this route, but should the telegraphic communication between England and Ireland, 62 miles, be realised, it presents not the least difficulty. Of course we in Newfoundland will have nothing to do with the erection, working, and maintenance of the telegraph; but I suppose our Government will give every facility to the company, either English or American, who will undertake it, as it will be an incalculable advantage to this country. I hope the day is not far distant when St. John's will be the first link in the electric chain which will unite the Old World and the New.—J. T. M."

The pioneer of telegraphic communication in the Colony was the celebrated Frederic Newton Gisborne. In the winter of 1849 he was employed as an engineer in extending the telegraph from Lower Canada through New Brunswick to Sackville, N.S., to connect with the Nova Scotia lines which had been begun in 1848-49; he then conceived the idea of also connecting Newfoundland with the continent. In 1851 Mr. Gisborne came to St. John's, appeared before the Legislature, explained his plans, which were to lay a telegraph line from St. John's to Cape Ray, and to connect with Cape Breton by carrier pigeons, steamer, or, eventually it was hoped by a sub-marine cable. The House of Assembly granted £500 for a survey and passed an Act authorising the construction of the line.[1]

F. N. GISBORNE.
From an old photograph.

In the same year Mr. Gisborne commenced building the St. John's and Carbonear Electric Telegraph Company's line.[2] The survey of the route for the line to Cape Ray proved a most arduous undertaking. Mr. Gisborne began his journey in September and on the 4th December 1851 he writes: "I accomplished the survey through three hundred

---

[1] FIRST PROPOSED ACT.
(*Newfoundlander.*)

Frederic N. Gisborne may form the Newfoundland Electric Telegraph Company with capital of £100,000 in 1,000 shares of £100 each. That such company may construct and complete the line of magnetic electric telegraph from St. John's towards Cape Ray and branch lines to Trepassey and other places, but not to interfere with the St. John's and Carbonear Electric Telegraph Company. That the company shall have granted to them blocks of land not exceeding five square miles each, and in all not exceeding 35 square miles, subject to such reservation and condition respecting all mines of gold, silver and coal, and other matter, as may be just and reasonable. That as soon as a good traversable path on the line of survey to Cape Ray shall be made, not less than four feet in width and opened to the public, the Government shall pay the proposed sum of £1,000 for every 100 miles of such road. Lastly the Government reserves to itself the right at any time, after giving 12 months' notice, to assume the proprietorship of the said main line and all branch lines and everything connected therewith on payment of the actual outlay and expenses of the company, with an addition of 50 per cent. thereto. The New York and Galway steam packet proposition of making this the intermediate port of call, both homeward and outward, for their fine line of steamships, will form the subject of another Bill.

[2] (*Newfoundlander*, March 11, 1852.)

"The electric telegraph between St. John's and Conception Bay was put in operation for the first time on last Saturday (6 March 1852) and has transmitted several messages from Brigus and Harbour Grace each day of this week. Yesterday, particularly, the telegraph office was the scene of a general attraction throughout the day."

The first telegraph office was in the Commercial Building, Duckworth Street. For the first time in 1852 the papers have news headed per Electric Telegraph. The Carbonear line was a very poor affair; it was, however, a never-ceasing wonder. There were constant complaints of malicious injuries to the line; the out-harbour boys could not resist the temptation to throw stones, in the vernacular, "fire rocks," at the insulators.

and fifty miles of woods and wilderness."[1] On the 6th March 1852, Mr. Gisborne delivered a lecture, before the Mechanics' Institute in the Old Factory, on the electric telegraph; a battery in the room was connected with the St. John's and Carbonear telegraph wires, and messages were sent forth and back from Harbour Grace, Carbonear, and Brigus; the experiments duly astonished the natives; Judge Robinson and the Attorney-General Archibald gave Mr. Gisborne great praise, and he thoroughly deserved it. To the energy, spirit, and disinterested exertions of Gisborne, Newfoundland owes the great advantage of telegraphic communication; he was the pioneer, but he reaped no benefit from all his labours and privations on our behalf.

In the spring of 1852 an Act was passed incorporating "The Newfoundland Electric Telegraph Company," giving the company the exclusive right to erect telegraphs in the Island for thirty years, and a large grant of land on the completion of the line. The *Ellen Gisborne* came to St. John's in December 1852, but it was not until the spring of 1853 that Mr. Gisborne organised a company in New York, with Horace B. Tibbetts, Darius B. Holbrook, and others; he then proceeded vigorously with the work of building the line to Cape Ray. His agents in St. John's were Gisborne and Henderson; everything was progressing favourably in the summer of 1853, when the New York agents dishonoured his bills and the whole concern collapsed; Gisborne himself was stripped of everything he possessed. This unfortunate result produced intense distress amongst the unfortunate labourers; on 31st January 1854, the Governor, Ker Baillie Hamilton, refers to the widespread poverty amongst the people, "aggravated, moreover, by the failure of the electric telegraph company."

---

[1] From the *Manchester Examiner and Times*.

"Testimonial to Mr. F. N. Gisborne. A very beautiful, valuable, and appropriate piece of plate has been prepared as a testimonial to Mr. Frederic Newton Gisborne, eldest son of Hartley P. Gisborne, Esq., of this city, contributed and to be presented by the inhabitants of St. John's, Newfoundland, as marking their sense of the energy and perseverance he has displayed in traversing the previously unexplored parts of the island, in anticipation of the introduction of the electric telegraph. The design is bold, and highly characteristic of the subject portrayed. At the summit of a rocky eminence, in frosted silver, stands a figure of science, with a wreath of *immortelles* in her upraised and extended left hand, ready to crown the deserving enterprise—a figure of Roman character, with a hatchet in one hand, evincing vigour and determination, and in the other a pair of compasses, indicative of skill and calculation, has struggled to nearly the highest point, and is handing the compasses to science. The rocky heights are studded here and there with North American fir-trees. Upon the front of the base an oval is formed by a cable, and within the coil is the inscription; on the opposite side is represented a vessel at sea, laying down the cable for the electric telegraph. A group of seals and a group of beavers occupy parts of the space between these. There are also engraved representations of American scenery, with Indian wigwams. The specific character of the testimonial is further indicated by the whole being encircled by telegraph posts and wires. Manchester may justly take some credit to itself, on account of its relation to the gentleman whose enterprise this testimonial commemorates."

In none of Mr. Gisborne's written communications about this time is there one word about an Atlantic cable or telegraphic communication with Europe; there can be no doubt, however, that an able man like Gisborne had thought of the project, as had others, long before. The written and printed papers, the prospectus and plans of his company make no reference whatever to the larger and grander conception. In January 1854, Gisborne came in contact with Cyrus W. Field, then a young merchant who had made a handsome fortune and retired from active business. Field at once took hold of the larger idea of cable communication with Europe; for Gisborne's project of the limited Newfoundland line he cared nothing and would have nothing to

PETER COOPER.
By Falk, N.Y.

C. W. FIELD.
By Falk, N.Y.

do with it, but when he found from Professor Morse, Lieut. Maury, and Brett, that an Atlantic telegraph was a practicable undertaking, he threw himself into the project with all his marvelous zeal and pertinacity. No one claims for Mr. Field any originality of thought about this great enterprise, but nothing can rob him of the credit of being the first organizer, the moving spirit, the vital force and power that from first to last completed the Atlantic cable. His enthusiasm brought over Peter Cooper, Moses Taylor, Marshall O. Roberts, and Chandler White, the financiers of the new company, founded in March 1854, and granted a charter by the Newfoundland Government as "The New York, Newfoundland, and London Telegraph Company."[1]

There is a marked contrast between the prospectus of Mr. Gisborne's Company and Mr. Field's. The indefatigable Cyrus came down in the

[1] Field, Cooper, Taylor, Roberts, and Wilson G. Hunt are known as the "Five Immortals"; the men who first risked £500,000 in 1854, and paid up the balance of the million sterling to keep up the connection with Newfoundland until the Atlantic cable was completed in 1866.

Merlin in March 1854, and returned in her, leaving his able brother, David Dudley Field, and Chandler White to secure and perfect the charter. There was a good deal of discussion in the Executive Council and in the House on the grant to the new company, especially the Government guarantee of £50,000 worth of bonds, not a penny of which was ever required; it was, however, practically passed unanimously, and immediately the poor labourers on the line and all outstanding liabilities

MOSES TAYLOR.
By Sarony, N.Y.

M. O. ROBERTS.
By Moss, N.Y.

of the defunct company were paid off. Chandler White remained for a year as manager; he gave rise to more law-suits in that short period than the Anglo-American has had ever since.

Whilst his associates were busy settling the affairs of the company in St. John's, C. W. Field was in England getting the first cable made for the Gulf. It was very unfortunate for the company that Mr. Field could not be, like "Boyle Roche's bird," in two places at once; the company's affairs in the Colony were managed with reckless extravagance and woful incapacity. One Sunday I remember seeing the *Victoria's* crew landing glass insulators at Burgeo; three out of every five were smashed on a lot of ballast at the head of the wharf. "There goes ten cents for Peter Cooper's," said the profane Shuyter.

It has been argued by many persons in our day that the charter to Field's Company was extravagant and unjustifiable, that harder terms should have been exacted, and particularly that the Colony should have secured a revenue out of the company. Now let us look at the facts as they appeared to the highly intelligent and able men who arranged this question in 1854. I admit, at the outset, that the Act was ably drawn, drafted in the interest of the company by the first lawyer in America, David Dudley Field, but were its provisions unreasonable? In the first place Mr. Cyrus Field would accept nothing less than the Act; if there had been any important modification he would simply have let the matter drop and have retired to New York to enjoy his well-earned leisure. We must remember that whilst one part of the project, the land line and the connection across the Gulf, was practicable and feasible, the main project of an Atlantic cable was looked upon by ninety-nine men out of every hundred as the wild project of a Yankee lunatic; even on the very eve of its completion, the London *Times* declared it was a visionary and utterly impracticable undertaking. Our Legislature had

THE "VICTORIA" TOWING THE "S. L. BRYANT."
From Mullaly's Trip to Newfoundland.

before them an offer from wealthy Americans to pay off the debts of the bankrupt company, to expend a million dollars in the Colony, to give the Island telegraphic communication with England and America, and a local line to Cape Ray and Cape Race absolutely for nothing! Would the Legislature have been justified in rejecting such an obviously advantageous offer, and was it unreasonable for daring capitalists, who were willing to risk their millions in such a risky enterprise, to require

[1] Until the local lines were begun by Mr. Mackay in 1877, this Colony had not spent a farthing on telegraphs beyond the Carbonear line, which was taken over at par by Mr. Field. All the other North American Colonies expended large sums on local lines. In 1877, Trinity, Catalina, and Bonavista were connected by telegraph; in 1878 Government lines were extended to St. George's Bay, Bay of Islands, Betts Cove, Tilt Cove, and Little Bay Mines; in 1885 the telegraph was extended to Greenspond and Twillingate, Burin, St. Lawrence, Lamaline, Grand Bank, and Fortune; in 1887 it was extended to Fogo, Seldom Come By, Change Islands, &c.

exclusive rights subject to a right of pre-emption? Our Legislature would have been wrong to refuse such an obviously favourable offer, the rights of the Colony being carefully guarded by rather onerous restrictions.[1]

The land line to Cape Ray was completed in October 1856. In anticipation of its operation Mr. Field and a party of friends came to St. John's in the steamer *James Adger*, and went to Port-aux-Basques to lay the cable across the Gulf; in towing the barque *Sarah L. Bryant* with the cable, a gale arose, and the cable had to be cut to save the barque; a little later in the same year, however, the cable was successfully laid to Cape Breton by Sir Samuel Canning, Mr. T. D. Scanlan[2] representing the Newfoundland Company.[3] When Mr. Field arrived in New York in December 1856, he found the Gulf cable broken, and all the Newfoundland telegraph line in a state of disorder, the superintendent Simpson, having abandoned the country in despair. He put

T. D. SCANLAN.
By S. H. Parsons.

PORT-AUX-BASQUES IN 1857.
From Mullock's Trip to Newfoundland.

himself in communication with James Eddy and the well-known D. H. Craig, founder of the New York Associated Press, and asked

---

[1] There is a very able article in the *Newfoundlander* in April 1854 on this subject, evidently written by Hon. E. D. Shea.

[2] The line Mr. T. D. Scanlan was associated with the New York, Newfoundland, and London Telegraph Company, from its birth in 1854 to its amalgamation with the Anglo-American Company in 1873.

[3] The first message sent was a cable from J. & W. Pitts to A. & M. Cameron, Baddeck.

them to select for him the best man in America to take charge of the Newfoundland lines; without communication with each other, they advised him to appoint Mr. A. M. Mackay, then twenty-two years old, the Superintendent of the Nova Scotia Telegraph.[1] When Mackay came here in January 1857 he found everything in confusion, not a single section of the line was in working order; he ascertained where the break was in the cable, repaired it in June 1857 with the small steamer *Victoria*, walked over the line from Cape Ray, organised the staff of operators and repairers, and put the whole concern in working order. From this period until the successful laying of the cable in 1866, the New York, Newfoundland, and London Telegraph Company in this Colony was kept in existence as a going concern by two men, Field and Mackay[2]; a dozen times the other directors would have dropped it altogether but for Field's enthusiasm and perseverance, and Mackay's activity and careful, economical management in the Island. The laying of the cable of course put life into the local lines, made the worthless valuable, and from that day to this everything has gone well under the same able management.[3]

HON. A. M. MACKAY.
By S. H. Parsons.

All in Newfoundland who remember the 27th July 1866, when the Atlantic cable was landed, can bear witness to the excitement and enthusiasm that pervaded all classes. I was present with a party in Heart's Content at the time, and I believe Cyrus W. Field hardly slept for three nights whilst in port. The cable is no longer a wonder and a marvel, but as one sits through the long watches of the night, with both continents at rest, and notes the beginning of the business day in

---

[1] The best proof of Mr. Mackay's energy and economy in management is the actual work accomplished. In 1867 he rebuilt the whole telegraph line from St. John's to Cape Ray, which had originally cost $1,000,000, for $90,000, in recognition of which service the Company presented him with a magnificent service of plate; and in 1885 he built for the Newfoundland Government branch lines from Burin and Twillingate, to connect with the New York, Newfoundland, and London telegraph system, 340 miles through the wilderness for $15,000.

[2] The receipts from the Newfoundland lines throughout this period of hope deferred were very small and very precarious. In 1859 a news boat was placed at Cape Race by the Associated Press to intercept ocean steamers; the first ship met was the S.S. *Lowe*, of the Inman Line. The public constantly saw the heading in English and American papers, "*Via Cape Race*," but few had any idea of those daring trips of bold John Murphy to catch the outward and homeward-bound steamers; considering the imminent peril of landing and launching boats from such a wild spot, it is marvellous how much news was sent in this extraordinary way.

[3] The Anglo-American Telegraph Company has spent in this Colony more than $4,000,000 in salaries, renewals, and repairs over and above the entire receipts from Newfoundland sources.

Europe, and later on the rush from America, watching by the cable instrument, we appear almost to hear the eager steps of the busy multitudes in two worlds; to the tired operator it is mere ordinary business, but to the onlooker, this joining of the hemispheres, and the complete annihilation of time and space, will always appear as the most wonderful achievement in an age of scientific marvels. To Mr. F. Perry, the able Superintendent of the Anglo-American Cable Company, I am indebted for the chapter on the landing and working of the cable. Mr. Perry was at Heart's Content in 1866, and has for many years been the very efficient general manager there, one of the busiest and best-equipped telegraph stations in the world.

THE ATLANTIC CABLE AND HEART'S CONTENT.

By F. PERRY.

Superintendent of the Anglo-American Cable Office at Liverpool.

The 27th of July 1866 will long be remembered by the inhabitants of Newfoundland as a red-letter day in its history, for on that morning the S.S. *Great Eastern*, with the living end of the Atlantic cable on board, accompanied by the steamships *Medway* and *Albany*, might be discerned from the settlement of Heart's Content, two or three miles in the offing; the hopes and fears which had been entertained in reference to this undertaking were then within an ace of being successfully determined. It is true that some years previously (1858) an attempt had been made to unite Ireland and Newfoundland by a submarine cable, which had been landed in Bay Bull's Arm, at the head of Trinity Bay, but its life had been short and at best precarious; the instruments used in its manipulation were cumbrous, while the signals recorded were sluggish, and the working painfully slow. About mid-day on the date above-mentioned the shore-end of the cable was successfully landed, and from that moment until the present, if we except a few months between November 1870 and May 1871, the communication between Valentia and Heart's Content has never for an instant been interrupted.

To connect Heart's Content with the United States, Canada, and the continent of America, lines had been erected between Newfoundland and Cape Breton, where the wires belonging to the Western Union Company

MR. F. PERRY.
From an old photograph.

of America had their terminus—the New York, Newfoundland, and London Telegraph Company had been incorporated. This latter company owed its creation to the almost superhuman efforts of Mr. Cyrus Field, a prominent citizen of the United States, to whose energy and perseverance also the formation of the companies in the United Kingdom, primarily the Atlantic Telegraph Company, and subsequently the Anglo-American Telegraph Company, was at the same time mainly attributable.

The lines of the New York, Newfoundland, and London Telegraph Company consisted of an air-line suspended on poles along the southern shore of the island terminating at Port-aux-Basques, at its south-western corner; from this point to Aspée Bay, in the island of Cape Breton, a distance of some seventy miles, a submarine cable had previously been submerged, although at the time of the completion of the ocean cable to Heart's Content this short cable was unfortunately interrupted, fast steamers being employed for the time in conveying batches of messages at frequent intervals. Towards the autumn, however, this short section was repaired by A. M. Mackay, the General Superintendent in Newfoundland of the New York Company, thus completing telegraph communication between the two great continents, Europe and America.

HUMOROUS PLAYBILL ABOUT THE CABLE.
By Dudley.

In the ensuing summer (1867), it having been found that the land line across the breadth of Newfoundland, from the severity of winter storms and the tardy means at hand for restoration, was generally unreliable and unsatisfactory, it was determined to lay a submarine cable from Great Placentia in Newfoundland to North Sydney in Cape Breton, taking the French island of St. Pierre by the way, and so bringing that colony within the fold of telegraph communication, and at the same time rendering the company independent of the somewhat precarious communication by the air line across the island of Newfoundland. From that time until the present the cables between Placentia and North Sydney have been multiplied and strengthened, while the line *via* Port-aux-Basques has not of late been in use for through traffic:

it is merely serviceable for local messages and for completing the network of telegraphs throughout the island.

It was part of the *Great Eastern's* mission, if the cable of 1866 should be successfully accomplished, to endeavour to recover the lost end of the 1865 cable which had been attempted to be laid by the Atlantic Telegraph Company with the same steamer in the summer of the previous year. This feat, which has been compared to fishing with a bent pin at the end of a string from the dome of St. Paul's, was also an accomplished fact towards the middle of September in the same year, when the ship having recovered the cable from a depth of nearly two thousand fathoms spoken through the line to Valentia and spliced it on to the cable on board brought that end also safely to shore at Heart's Content.

The instruments at first used in manipulating the cable were an ordinary double-current key and a mirror-reflecting galvanometer, the

PAYING OUT THE LAND END OF THE CABLE FROM THE STERN OF THE "NIAGARA."
From the Illustrated London News.

former for transmitting the signals, and the latter for receiving them; some sixteen to twenty cells of the form known as "Menotti" were used for generating the current, while boxes of "condensers," which are composed of alternate sheets of tinfoil and mica, or other insulating material, were employed to keep the movements of the "spot," or column of reflected light, obedient to the movements of the mirror, suspended by a fibre of silk within the convolutions of fine wire contained in the galvanometer, within control. These instruments, although simple in construction and somewhat crude in comparison with those in use in the present day, were proved to be satisfactory, and continued to hold their place for seven years. The speed of working at the beginning was six to eight words a minute, but this was improved upon as time went on and the operators gained experience in what to them was an entirely new system.

In 1873 the siphon recorder, an invention of Lord Kelvin, then Sir William Thomson, the eminent electrician and Professor of Philosophy at Glasgow University, was introduced. The advantage of this instrument was that the signals transmitted through the cable were no longer interpreted by the movements of a flash of light, but were permanently recorded on a paper tape or ribbon by ink flowing through a glass tube or siphon, not much thicker than a hair, one end of which was bent into a small tank or metal box containing ink, and the other moving near the surface of the paper, which was kept continually moving onward by the revolutions of a "mouse-mill" worked by a "quantity battery" of large surface, the mouse-mill also fulfilling the duty of electrifying the ink and forcing it through the bore of the narrow siphon. This system was greatly in advance of the mirror-galvanometer, inasmuch as the record could be preserved for reference in case of errors, and the eyes were relieved from the tedium and constant strain involved in the old method.

In the year 1878 "duplex" was successfully placed on the cables after a long period of painstaking research and perseverance by Mr. J. B. Stearns, a citizen of the United States, thus permitting a message to be sent and received on the same cable at the same time, and so nearly doubling its working power. In this system a mock cable or artificial line was employed, an instrument, or rather succession of instruments, made up so as to represent the cable as nearly as possible, both as regards *resistance* and *capacity*; these latter had to be adjusted, or, to use a common term, "balanced," with such nicety that when outgoing signals were sent into the cable, the in-coming signals would not be affected or disturbed; when this result was attained the rest was easy, and duplex from that time to the present remains an undoubted possibility.

The Anglo-American Telegraph Company, by its cables between Valentia and Heart's Content, makes a great point in transmitting the quick-time messages, or "stocks" as they are termed; the wires are brought into the Stock Exchange at New York, while the Company's office in Throgmorton Street, London, is within a few steps of the Stock Exchange in that city. The land lines are placed alongside the cable instruments at Valentia, Heart's Content, and North Sydney, so that while the messages are being transcribed by one operator they are forwarded a stage on their journey by another, with the minimum delay at each station. By this method it is a thing of frequent occurrence for a broker in New York to telegraph an order to his client in London and receive a reply that the business has been completed, all within the space of five minutes, thus compassing the journey of two thousand five hundred miles in each direction, or five thousand miles in all, within that short space of time.

When the first cable was landed at Heart's Content in 1866, some nine or ten individuals were landed from the *Great Eastern* to work it; in the present day there are forty-five persons composing the staff at that station; some are there yet who were the original operators. The first public message that passed over the cable was at the rate of one pound

W. DICKENSON.
By Turner, Edmonton.

SAMUEL TROTT.[1]
By Harrison, Edmonton.

sterling a word; now the same service is performed for one shilling. In the early days it was considered a good day's work to pass two hundred telegrams per diem; now it is by no means uncommon by this one route alone to exchange three thousand.

Thus has an enterprise, which at first may have provoked the jeers or the ridicule of the incredulous as a scheme altogether too wild in design or too impossible of accomplishment, been proved by the persevering to be an undertaking well worthy of imitation, and may render those who initiated it, and those who have assisted in bringing it to its present state of perfection, as men deserving well of their country and posterity, and leaving, as the poet tells us, "footprints on the sands of time."

[1] The Anglo-American Co. possesses most devoted and valuable servants; none of them are more remarkable than the captain of their cable steamer *Minia*, Samuel Trott. John W. Mackay correctly designated him "the greatest cable-catcher in the world"; no difficulty, no depth of ocean, can keep the cable from his grasp. His latest feat, in the summer of 1894, in grappling and splicing successfully the two ends of the seventy-four cable, over 200 miles apart, in 2,700 fathoms of water, with a current running six knots, is the crowning achievement of his remarkable career.

CHAPTER XXII.

THE NEWFOUNDLAND FISHERIES COMMISSION.

By Rev. M. Harvey, LL.D.,

Secretary to the Commission.

In 1887 a Commission was appointed by His Excellency the Governor in Council, to investigate the operations of Fisheries Departments in other countries, with the view to the establishment of a similar department in Newfoundland should it be found desirable and practicable. This appointment was made in accordance with a resolution passed by the House of Assembly.

The Commission, of which the Hon. A. W. Harvey was chairman, presented their first report in March 1888. In it the various steps taken in carrying out the objects in view were stated in detail. By means of a circular addressed to the Departments of Fisheries in the Dominion of Canada, the United States of America, England, and Norway, much valuable information regarding the organisation and working of their respective departments was obtained, as well as the results of their operations in the artificial propagation of food fishes, and their methods of constructing hatcheries. The report, after giving a summary of the information thus collected, went on to contrast the intelligent guardianship over their fisheries exercised in the United States, Canada, Norway, and England with the almost complete neglect of the fisheries in Newfoundland, where there was no department charged with the duty of investigating, reporting on them, or furnishing any useful help or guidance to the fishermen; while there were no proper regulations to protect these industries, on which the mass of the people were dependent for their subsistence, from the effects of ignorance and reckless greed. As a consequence, the Newfoundland cod fisheries were declining to an alarming extent, especially those around the shores, and the rivers were largely depleted of salmon. The methods of curing and drying the fish had deteriorated, and no attempt had been made to replenish exhausted waters by artificial propagation as practised in other fishing countries. The report recommended the organisation of a permanent Fisheries Commission as a branch of the public service.

Accordingly, in June 1889, the Legislature passed an "Act to " provide for the formation of a Fisheries Commission, and other " purposes," in which the powers, duties, and functions of the said Commission were defined. Provisions were also made for the appointment of a chairman, a secretary, and a superintendent of fisheries, and the erection of fish hatcheries. The Hon. A. W. Harvey, a member of the Legislative Council, who had made a speciality of the fisheries, and with commendable zeal and ability had for many years urged on the Legislature the vital importance of a scientific examination of the fisheries and a proper supervision of their working, was appointed chairman, and the Rev. M. Harvey, who had given much attention to the same subject, and written extensively on fish and fisheries, was nominated as secretary.

The Commission was fortunate in securing the services of Mr. Adolph Nielsen, a Norwegian Inspector of Fisheries, as Superintendent of Fisheries in Newfoundland. His accurate and extensive knowledge of fisheries, scientific and practical, and his lengthened experience fitted him admirably for the position, and, as subsequent events proved, his zeal, energy, and devotion to his duties were all that could be desired. The names of forty-two gentlemen were placed on the roll of the Commission, but the business was conducted by an Executive Committee of seven members.

The first step was the erection of a hatchery in April 1889, for the propagation of cod and other fish, on Dildo Island in Trinity Bay. This was fitted up with proper apparatus embodying all the latest improvements, and had sufficient capacity for hatching between two and three hundred million of cod ova in the season. At a later date a salt-water pond was added in which the fish were allowed to spawn in the natural way, an arrangement which enabled the Superintendent to hatch from sixty to seventy per cent. of the ova and plant the young fry in good condition in the waters of the bay. Both cod-fish and lobsters were hatched here.

The Commission then commenced a careful study and investigation of the fisheries of the Colony, in all their branches, with a view to devising rules and regulations for their protection, of ascertaining the habits of the commercial fishes, the causes which injuriously affect the fisheries, the best means of restoring them, and the effects of the various appliances used in the capture of fish. The results of these investigations conducted by the Superintendent were embodied in annual reports, which were presented to the Legislature, printed, and circulated. Rules and regulations for the guardianship of the fisheries were submitted for approval to the Legislature, and proper arrangements made for the enforcement of these when they became law.

The artificial propagation of lobsters on an extensive scale was carried on by means of floating incubators, invented by Mr. Nielsen. These were worked in nearly all the large bays each season.

The Superintendent drew up an exhaustive account of the "Cure of Cod-fish and Herrings," in which were given full directions for the proper cure of these fishes according to different methods, and the errors committed in the treatment and packing of herrings were pointed out. This valuable paper has been reprinted by the Irish Department of Fisheries, for the use of the fishermen, and has also been translated into French. A large edition was distributed in Newfoundland by the Commission.

A Bait Intelligence Service has also been established for the purpose of informing the captains of vessels engaged in the Bank Fishery, on touching at any port, where bait was to be obtained, thus saving much time which would otherwise have been spent in searching for bait.

Seven years have now elapsed since the formation of a Fisheries Commission. A great change for the better has been accomplished. The fisheries have been brought under control by judicious rules and regulations based on a knowledge of fish life, and these are enforced by fishery wardens. Injurious practices and destructive modes of fishing, by which vast quantities of immature fish were destroyed, thus causing deterioration of the fisheries, are being gradually suppressed. The salmon rivers are, to a great extent, cleared of those obstructions which prevented the ascent of the salmon for spawning purposes. The ruinous practice of "barring" rivers, which was almost universal, has been almost entirely ended. The pollution of salmon rivers by sawdust from lumber mills is greatly checked. Improvements in the cure and packing of our sea products are making way. The manufacture of boneless cod-fish, of glue from the skins of cod, of improved cod-liver oil on the Norwegian plan, have been introduced, and will enhance the value of our cod-fishery. The proper cure and packing of herrings, so as to fit them for different markets on both sides of the Atlantic, has been practically exemplified by the Superintendent, and those treated under his supervision have secured enhanced prices Model smoke-houses have been erected in Placentia Bay, in which some of the finest smoked herrings have been packed for market, and have readily sold at remunerative prices. Model refrigerating rooms have also been built for the preservation of fresh bait by the freezing process, which if brought into general use will be the means of greatly increasing the annual catch of cod by having constantly on hand a supply of fresh bait.

The artificial propagation of cod-fish and lobsters has given satisfactory results, and promises great things in the future. The following figures exhibit the total number of young cod hatched at Dildo Hatchery in four years:—

1890	-	Cod-fish hatched	-	-	17,000,000
1891	-	,,	,,	-	39,550,000
1892	-	,,	,,	-	165,254,000
1893	-	,,	,,	-	201,435,000

Fishermen report having seen large shoals of fry and small cod-fish during last summer in various localities in Trinity Bay, where they were never seen before, and in such numbers and under such conditions as to satisfy them that they were the products of the hatchery. In the near future a great increase of cod-fish in this bay may reasonably be anticipated.

In the artificial propagation of lobsters by means of the Nielsen floating incubators, Newfoundland is now far ahead of all other nations.

The following table shows what has been done in four years:—

1890	-	Lobsters hatched and planted	-	390,934,000
1891	-	,,	,,	-	541,195,000
1892	-	,,	,,	-	427,285,000
1893	-	,,	,,	-	517,353,000
				1,876,767,000

To the foregoing must be added 32,889,000 lobsters planted from Dildo Hatchery in five years. Grand total, 1,909,656,000 lobsters hatched and planted.

The Fisheries Commission has had to encounter many difficulties and much opposition, but that its labours have been appreciated, and that public confidence in it is now established, may be inferred from the fact that the legislative grant for this service was doubled, and is now $20,000 per annum. Besides, in 1893, it was advanced to the dignity of a Government Department, with the Hon. A. W. Harvey at its head as Commissioner of Fisheries, and Mr. Nielsen, as before, Superintendent of Fisheries. A prosperous and useful career may be confidently anticipated for this Department.

M. HARVEY.

[In publishing this valuable paper it is only due to myself to state that my opinions do not coincide with all the views expressed by the author. No one appreciates more highly than I do the value of the Fisheries Commission, and the deep debt of gratitude we all owe to the Chairman, the Hon. A. W. Harvey, for the dogged perseverance with which for years past he has fought for its appointment, and to the learned Secretary for his valuable papers in the promotion of its objects. In the practical part of its business, improvement in the cure of cod, herrings, and the packing of lobsters, its work is already bearing good fruit. The cod hatching is a valuable experiment, carried out in the most complete and scientific manner by Mr. Nielsen, but I look upon it, however, simply as an experiment, though one well worth trying. My investigations do not confirm Dr. Harvey's view that the artificial hatching of cod has been a complete commercial success, either in Newfoundland, Norway, or the United States. The theory on which it is founded, that all the pelagic fishes return to the home of their birth for the purposes of reproduction, is not proved; this idea has been pushed too far. It is only partially true as regards salmon and sea trout. With respect to cod, it seems now to be ascertained by the careful investigation of the Scotch Fishery Board that they spawn in the ocean from seven to one hundred and seventy miles from land; that such a rapacious fish, whose migration has been proved to extend over five hundred miles, returns to the home of its birth, or has any settled home at all, is a theory with no scientific proofs to sustain it.

D. W. PROWSE.]

CHAPTER XXIII.

CHRONOLOGY, JUSTICIARY, HOUSE OF ASSEMBLY.

I. Chronology.

GEORGE III., 1760 to 1820.

1760.—**Captain WEBB** captured French vessel *Tavignor*, with 3,500 quintals fish, which was sold in St. John's for £2,570 sterling.

1761.—**Captain (afterwards Lord) GRAVES** sailed in December, 1761, with convoy to Spain and Portugal; seventy sail of vessels, 7,000 tons; 680 men and 200 guns.

1762.—St. John's, Carbonear, and Trinity captured by French squadron under Admiral de Ternay; re-captured same year, in September, by Colonel Amherst, brother of Sir Geoffrey Amherst, Capt. McDonel, with Highlanders and Provincials (Loyal Americans) Light Infantry; battle of Quidi Vidi.

1763.—War with Spain; importation of fish from Newfoundland prohibited. R. Carter, Esq., garrisoned Isle Bois, Ferryland; C. Garland, Carbonear. Treaty of Paris; St. Pierre and Miquelon confirmed to France; all the rest of North America given up to England. Survey of the Island by the immortal navigator Cook. Labrador re-annexed to Newfoundland. Population 13,112; 386,274 qtls. fish; 106 fishing ships; 123 going foreign voyages; 142 vessels from New England and other parts of British North America, Cork, Waterford, Belfast, and Glasgow, engaged in Newfoundland trade.

1764.—**Sir Hugh PALLISER** Governor. Collector of Customs appointed in St. John's, under the Commissioner of the Custom House in Boston, Mass.; soon after Comptroller appointed. Court of Vice-Admiralty, St. John's; Major Griffith Williams, R.A., resident in St. John's and commanding Royal Artillery, published an account of the Newfoundland fishery.

1765.—Large increase in fishery; total catch for this year 493,654 qtls. 1763—348,294 qtls. 1764—470,118 qtls. Rev. Laurence Coughlan, Church of England minister, introduced Wesleyanism into the Colony. Sir H. Palliser's report very severe on Newfoundland.

1766.—Riots in St. John's and Harbour Grace. Lieut. Cartwright made an unsuccessful attempt to effect friendly intercourse with Beothics; first European to visit Red Indian Lake; wrote a history of the Red Indians, or Beothics of Newfoundland. Repeal of the obnoxious American Stamp Act.

1769.—**Commodore BYRON,** grandfather of Lord Byron, the poet, Governor.

1770.—John Stretton, Wesleyan minister, has hot dispute with Rev. David Balfour, Episcopal Minister, Harbour Grace, about the right to preach in Carbonear chapel.

1772.—**Commodore MOLYNEAUX** (afterwards Lord Shuldham) Governor. Rev. John Hoskins Wesleyan minister. Governer issues Proclamation 24th June, regulating river salmon fishery for the Colony; French not mentioned.

1773.—Engineer Pringle began to build Fort Townshend, and to construct King's Road and Military Road.

1774.—Placentia Court House built. Continental Congress in America. All exportation to Newfoundland from North America States prohibited 17th September, 1774; caused great distress in Newfoundland. Imports from colonies £345,000 stg. prior to Revolution. Quebec Act, 14 Geo. III. cap. 83; Labrador annexed to Canada.

1775.—Rev. John Jones first Congregational Minister in St. John's. Heaviest storm ever known in Newfoundland; 300 persons drowned. Palliser's Act, 15 George III. Bounty for bankers to continue eleven years; first Act requiring written agreement between masters and servants in the fishery; wages first charge on fish, &c.: all cases to be tried summarily by Court of Sessions or Court of Vice-Admiralty. Duty of one shilling per gallon on rum from America; caused excitement in New England. **Commodore DUFF**, Governor, issues Proclamation about salmon fisheries at Exploits, Gander Bay, &c.

1776.—4th July, Declaration of Independence, United States. 7th May, **Rear-Admiral MONTAGUE**, Governor, arrived.

1777.—July. Admiral Montague fitted out several armed vessels in Newfoundland seas to cruise there against the American privateers, by which measure he kept the coast clear, so that vessels might sail without danger.

1778.—Independence of the United States recognised by France. France declared war against England. Admiral Montague captured St. Pierre.

1779.—Spain declared war against England. **Rear-Admiral EDWARDS**, Governor, completed Fort Townshend. New Anglican Church on site of present cathedral being built.

1781.—The lower road (Water Street) and the upper road (Duckworth Street) ordered to be kept twelve feet wide. First regiment formed in St. John's, under Colonel Pringle; Wm. Lilly, Ensign. Smart fitting out of H.M.S. *Pluto*, in St. John's, and capture of two American privateers at Petty Harbour, one called *The George*; part of her timber now in the Museum, St. John's.

1782.—**Vice-Admiral John CAMPBELL** Governor. Independence of United States acknowledged by England.

1783.—N. Gill, D'Ewes Coke, George Williams, Archibald Buchanan, Magistrates, St. John's. Treaty of Versailles; French allowed from Cape John to Cape Ray; declaration of King George III. that English not to interrupt French fishery by their competition.

1784.—Royalist province of New Brunswick created; divided from Nova Scotia 1784. Religious freedom established in the Colony; Dr. O'Donel, first Roman Catholic Prefect Apostolic, arrived. Lease for 99 years to Rev. J. (Bishop) O'Donel, and certain trustees, of the premises known as "Parson Langman's Garden" (Old Chapel); Rev. Walter Price appointed Episcopal minister, St. John's.

1785.—Judges of Oyer and Terminer, D'Ewes Coke, Geo. Williams, Wm. Gaden, Richard Hutchings, Richard Routh, Nicholas Lechmere and Thos. Dodd. John McGeary, Wesleyan missionary, arrived in Newfoundland. Permission given to import bread, flour, and livestock from United States in British bottom.

1786.—Act 26 George III. cap. 26, continuing bounty to Bank fishery for ten years. Jurisdiction of Courts of Vice-Admiralty to try fishery cases transferred to Sessions Courts. Rev. Jno. McGeary Wesleyan minister. **Rear-Admiral ELLIOT** Governor. Prince William Henry, afterwards William IV., arrived in Newfoundland as Captain H.M.S. *Pegasus*; presided in Court at Placentia; instrumental in building present English Church, Placentia, towards which he contributed fifty-five guineas and the present handsome communion plate.

1787.—Wm. Carter, grandfather of Sir F. B. T. Carter, appointed Judge Vice-Admiralty Court, vice N. Gill, deceased. Bishop Inglis appointed as Anglican Bishop of Canada (formerly Rector Trinity Church, New York), New Brunswick, Nova Scotia, and Newfoundland. John Jones allowed to erect Meeting House (Old Congregational Church). Dr. John Brown appointed J.P. Placentia (grandfather of Sir H. W. Hoyles). Year of peace and plenty; no prisoners in the jail.

1788.—Many Bermudian vessels fishing in Newfoundland; complaints against them by West of England adventurers. Serious riot at Ferryland. McAuslan appointed Deputy Postmaster, October, 1778.

1789.—**Admiral Mark MILBANKE** Governor. French Revolution. Court of Common Pleas established for the Colony. Seal fishery prosecuted in small decked vessels and open boats.

CHRONOLOGY.

1791.—**Chief Justice REEVES** presided in Court, designated as "the Court of Civil Jurisdiction of Our Lord the King at St. John's, in the Island of Newfoundland," appointed by Act 31 George III. Canada divided into two Provinces. Rev. W. Black, Wesleyan minister, arrived in the Colony.

1792.—"Supreme Court of Judicature of the Island of Newfoundland," presided over by C. J. Reeves, opened 7th Sept., 1792; first case tried—Andrew Thomson *v.* George Williams. This Act was renewed annually until 1809. Surrogate Courts established. The Floating Surrogates. Cottage Farm, Quidi Vidi, cleared by Captain Skinner, R.E. **Admiral KING** Governor.

1793.—Louis XVI., King of France, beheaded. Chief Justice, **D'EWES COKE.**

1794.—Murder of Lieut. Lawrie, R.N. Farrell and Power convicted of the murder. H.M.S. *Boston* pressing men for Navy in St. John's. France declares war against England.

1795.—Royal Newfoundland Regiment embodied; Commander, Colonel Skinner.

1796.—**Admiral Sir James WALLACE** Governor. All St. John's under arms. French under Admiral Richery destroyed Bay Bulls. England and Spain at war. Newfoundland fishery very prosperous. £1,500,000 invested in fisheries. Dr. O'Donel consecrated, at Quebec, Bishop of Thyatira *in partibus*, and Vicar Apostolic of Newfoundland; first Roman Catholic Bishop. George Williams appointed Chief Magistrate.

1797.—Battle of Cape St. Vincent. Mutiny of the Nore. The ringleader, Parker, hung. Bishop O'Donel received a grant of land 500 yards frontage at River Head. Governor, **Hon. Wm. WALDEGRAVE, Vice-Admiral,** afterwards Lord Radstock. **R. ROUTH** Chief Justice.

1798.—Irish Rebellion. Nelson's great victory over French fleet. Battle of the Nile.

1799.—First Grammar School opened, Rev. L. Anspach Head Master. Census of St. John's this year (1799), 3,132 inhabitants, besides military; General Skerett in command of the troops.

1800.—Mutiny in the Garrison at St. John's. Ringleaders captured and punished. **Admiral POLE** Governor of Newfoundland. Richard Routh, Chief Justice, drowned on his passage to England.

1801.—Union of England and Ireland. **J. OGDEN** Chief Justice.

1802.—**Admiral Lord GAMBIER** Governor. Treaty of Amiens, signed by England, France, Spain, and Holland.

1803.—Regiment of Volunteers, under the name of "The Newfoundland Light Infantry," formed 1,000 strong; Colonel Skinner in command. Former regiment Newfoundland Fencibles disbanded, 1802. Saint John's Charity School Society instituted, August 1803. **Thomas TREMLETT** Chief Justice. Thomas Coote Chief Magistrate, vice Williams, deceased.

1804.—Phœnix Insurance Company, of London, presented a fire-engine to the town; British and Imperial Insurance Companies gave 35 fire-buckets. Sunday schools re-established. **Sir Erasmus GOWER,** Governor, opened Gower Street.

1805.—Post Office established in the Colony. Simon Solomon Postmaster-General. Battle of Trafalgar. Death of Nelson. Population of St. John's, 5,564.

1806.—Benevolent Irish Society formed at the London Tavern by Jas. McBraire, Esq., Major Commandant of the St. John's Volunteer Rangers; President Captain Winckworth Tonge. Dr. Lambert, Roman Catholic Bishop, arrived; consecrated in Wexford Bishop of Chitra *in partibus*. Volunteer Corps Newfoundland Rangers embodied; officers—Captains Parker, J. Williams, Bouchier, T. Williams, Batten; Lieuts. Shea, Solomon, Lilly, Stevenson, Haire; Ensigns Parker, Gill, Thomas, Mellege, Parsons; Surgeon Coughlan; Quarter-master Beenlan.

1807.—Four actors ask permission to open a theatre. **Admiral HOLLOWAY,** Governor, arrived July 26th, 1807. The "Royal Gazette and Newfoundland Advertizer," first published, 27th August 1807, under most careful restrictions. John Ryan, editor and publisher. Abolition of the slave trade by England.

1808.—Formation of Volunteer Corps for defence of the capital and island. Lieut. Spratt, R.N., sent with paintings to the Beothics.

1809.—Labrador and Anticosti re-annexed to the Government of Newfoundland by Act 49 Geo. III., which also established permanent Courts of Judicature in Newfoundland.

1810.—Proclamation to protect Red Indians. **Sir John Thomas DUCKWORTH** Governor. Magistrates for St. John's—T. Coote, J. Broom, R. Sconce, James Blaikie, Esqrs., and Rev. D. Rowland. Population, St. John's, 6,000. Major-General Moore in command of the troops.

1811.—Lieut. Buchan's expedition to Beothics. Two marines killed. Waterside in St. John's cleared of ships' rooms; leased by auction to the public. Permission first granted to erect permanent houses.

1812.—Second American War. St. John's in a flourishing condition North American fleet consisted of 3 sail of the line, 21 frigates, 37 sloops, brigs, and schooners of war. Harbour of St. John's full of prizes. Napoleon's retreat from Moscow. Volunteer Force re-organised ; Major McBraire, commanding ; Captains—Bouchier, T. Williams, Lilly, McAllister, G. R. Robinson. Crawford, Haynes, Ryan, Trimingham, Thomas; Lieutenants—Melledge, Broom, Steward, McLea, Simpson, Livingston, Grieve, Arnott, Clift, Shannon ; Ensigns—Morris, McCalman, Rendell, Scott, Willis, N. Gill, Niven Lang; Adjutant—Hughes ; Quarter-master—Barnes ; Surgeon—Duggan.

1813.—June 1st, Capture of the *Chesapeake*, American frigate, off Boston, by H.M.S. *Shannon*. Twenty-two Irishmen, bound to Newfoundland, were in *Shannon*. Coming out in Newman & Co.'s brig, *Duck*, they had been captured by American privateer, *Governor Plummer*, recaptured by English privateer brig, *Sir John Sherbrooke*, and then put aboard *Shannon*. **Cæsar COLCLOUGH** Chief Justice, from Prince Edward Island, in place of Tremlett, who was sent there in a King's ship. **Sir Richard Godwin KEATS**, Governor, laid foundation stone of St. John's Hospital, Riverhead. First grants of land ; 110 grants issued the year. Decisive victory of Wellington at Vittoria, Spain. French driven across the Pyrenees. Publication of Dr. William Carson's pamphlet ; agitation for Colonial Parliament. The following magistrates were appointed this year :—Coote, Broom, Roland, Blaikie, for St. John's ; Carrington and Lilly, Harbour Grace ; Rev. J. Church and Burrell, Trinity ; Edgar, Greenspond ; Ford, Bonavista ; McKie and Angell, Bay Bulls ; W. Carter, Ferryland ; Bradshaw and Blackburn, Placentia ; Gosse, Carbonear ; Jackson, Trepassey ; Butler and Bishop, Burin ; Spooner and Anthoine, Fortune Bay ; Bryant, Ferryland ; Phippard, St. Mary's ; Pinson and S. Prowse, Labrador ; and for the Island, Captains R. N. Elliott, Cooksley, Skekel, Campbell, Holbrook, Buchan, and Rev. F. Carrington and P. C. Le Geyt, the Governor's Secretary. Major-General Campbell commanding troops numbering 750.

1814.—Battle of Lundy's Lane, between Loyal Canadians and Americans. Treaty of Ghent ; end of second American War. First Treaty of Paris ; allies enter Paris. 1,200,000 qtls. fish exported ; whole value of exports, $11,144,000. Newfoundland Mercantile Journal established. P. W. Carter, Esq., Registrar Vice-Admiralty Court.

1815.—Battle of Waterloo. Abdication of Napoleon ; banished to St. Helena. Second Treaty of Paris. Last Treaty made between England and France about the Newfoundland Fishery. Confirms Treaty of Versailles, 1783. Numerous failures, caused by peace and depreciation of fish in foreign markets. Wesleyan Mission Stations organised into districts. 26th August, Captain David Buchan, R.N., took possession of St. Pierre and Miquelon.

1816.—12th February, St. John's nearly destroyed by fire ; great distress ; loss, £100,000 sterling ; cargo of provisions sent in winter by benevolent people of Boston, U.S. **Francis FORBES**, Esq., afterwards Sir Francis, Chief Justice, arrived ; a most able and competent Judge ; continued on the Bench for six years. First visit of an Anglican Bishop to Newfoundland by Dr. Stanser, Bishop of Nova Scotia. Dr. Scallan, third Roman Catholic Bishop, consecrated Bishop of Drago *in partibus*, and Vicar Apostolic of Newfoundland. Church at Harbour Grace burnt. H.M.S. *Comus* and transport *Harpooner* lost at St. Shott's, November 10th. **Admiral PICKMORE** Governor.

1817.—St. John's again visited by fires, November 7th and 21st ; 200 houses destroyed. Great distress ; severe winter ; riots ; known in Newfoundland history as "The Winter of the Rals," and the Hard Winter.

1818.—Convention with the United States respecting the Fisheries. **Admiral PICKMORE**, first resident Governor, died in St. John's. **Captain BOWKER** Administrator. Coldest winter ever experienced in Newfoundland. Arrival of brig *Messenger* in January with cargo of provisions, sent by the benevolent people of Boston. **Sir C. HAMILTON** Governor.

1819.—Queen Victoria born, 24th May. Red Indian woman, Mary March, brought to St. John's. Celebrated case of Butler and Lundrigan. Great fire in St. John's.

1820.—Death of George III., aged 81, his reign of 60 years being the longest of any English sovereign.

GEORGE IV., 1820 to 1830.

1822.—Richard Alexander **TUCKER**, Esq., Chief Justice, appointed 1st October.

1823.—The last of the Red Indians of Newfoundland seen; Indian women brought to St. John's. Newfoundland School Society established by Samuel Codner, Esq., of Dartmouth, Devon. Mr. Cormack crossed the Island. St. John's Library Society instituted February 14th; President, Hon. R. A Tucker; Librarian, James Clift. Surrogate Courts abolished. J. Broom Chief Stipendiary Magistrate. *vice* Coote resigned. James Blakie and P. W. Carter, Esqrs., Stipendiary Magistrates, St. John's. Dr. Scallan Bishop of Drago and Vicar Apostolic of Newfoundland and Labrador. Chamber of Commerce, St. John's, instituted 26th December; Newman Hoyles first President; Secretary, John Boyd. Naval establishment removed from St. John's.

1824.—Imperial Act, 5 Geo. IV. cap. 67. Act for the better Administration of Justice in Newfoundland; appointing Supreme Court with Chief Justice and two Assistant Judges. First fire company, Eastern Ward, St. John's; N. W. Hoyles, Captain. St. John's Dorcas Society instituted October 29th; Mrs. Ward, wife of Rev. D. S. Ward, Congregational minister, first president; Mrs. R. Job, second President. Peace of Ghent between England and the United States, December 24th.

1825.—Sir Thomas **COCHRANE** Governor. First roads constructed.

1826.—Supreme Court of Newfoundland constituted by Royal Charter, and opened with great ceremony by the Governor January 2nd, 1826. First Assistant Judges, with **Chief Justice TUCKER**, were Jno. William Molloy and A. W. Des Barres. Molloy soon removed. E. B. Brenton appointed. Orphan Asylum erected; Orphan Asylum school instituted February 17th, 1826; Chairman, T. Hogan; Master, Henry Simms. Fire Company, Middle Ward, St. John's, October 16th, 1826; P. Kough, Captain. Lieut.-Governor of St. John's, Col. Sir George Elder, Knt.; Lieut.-Governor, Placentia, Col. George Reeves.

1827.—Bishop Inglis, Anglican Bishop of Nova Scotia and Newfoundland, first visited Newfoundland and consecrated St. John's Church. Mechanics' Society formed 3rd March, 1827. J. Crowdy Colonial Secretary. Beothic Institution; W. E. Cormack, President.

1828.—Publication of P. Morris's pamphlet. Great agitation for representative institutions; movement led by Dr. W. Carson and others.

1829.—Roman Catholics emancipated. Bishop Fleming consecrated Bishop of Carpasia *in partibus*. Duel fought on Robinson's Hill between Captain Rudkin and Lieut. Phillpotts; the latter killed; Rudkin tried and convicted of manslaughter. Shawnandithit, a captive Boethic, died in St. John's.

WILLIAM IV., 1830 to 1837.

1830.—Liverpool and Manchester Railway opened September 15th. Bishop Scallan died. Government House completed.

1831.—First coach road opened to Portugal Cove.

1832.—Representative Assembly granted to Newfoundland. Opening first Parliament under Reform Bill in England. Great fire in Harbour Grace. Factory opened by benevolent ladies of St. John's.

1833.—1st January, first Session of the Newfoundland House of Assembly opened by Sir Thomas Cochrane, Governor. John Bingley Garland first Speaker; Chief Justice Tucker President of the Legislative Council; he resigned this year, and was succeeded by **Hy. John BOULTON**, Chief Justice. First Convent of Presentation Nuns in St. John's founded by Bishop Fleming.

1834.—**Captain PRESCOTT**, R.N., Governor. George Lilly, Esq., appointed Acting Judge Supreme Court; first native Judge. August 1st, Abolition of Slavery in the British Colonies. Heavy Criminal Calendar; four persons convicted of murder. Savings Bank constituted; N. W. Hoyles, Colonial Treasurer, Cashier.

1836.—First light erected on Cape Spear. Bank of British North America established in St. John's. Second General Election.

VICTORIA, 1837.

1837.—Accession of Her Majesty to the Throne, June 20th. First Session of Second General Assembly commenced, 3rd July. Father Matthew's Temperance Missions. Daguerrotype process discovered.

1838.—First Geological Survey made by J. Beete Jukes, who arrived in St. John's, in company with the celebrated Plantagenet Harrison, by the brig *Diana*, belonging to Stuart and Rennie. Chief Justice Boulton removed, and **John Gervase Hutchinson BOURNE** appointed. Legislature voted $175,000 in two years for roads. Great case of Kielly *v.* Carson.

1839.—Newfoundland constituted a separate see; Bishop Spencer, first Anglican Bishop.

1840.—First regular sailing packet established between St. John's and Halifax, N.S.; trips once a fortnight. H.M.S. *Spitfire*, paddle steamer, arrived with troops; Jukes left in her; first steamer in St. John's. Native Society formed. St. Thomas's Church consecrated. Penny Postage established in England.

1841.—Legislative Union of Upper and Lower Canada. Foundation Stone of Roman Catholic Cathedral laid by Dr. Fleming. **Major-General Sir John HARVEY**, K.C.B., appointed Governor.

1842.—Sisters of Mercy arrived in St. John's, 10th June. Amalgamated Assembly of Newfoundland constituted by Act of the Imperial Parliament—5 & 6 Vict. cap. cxx., passed August 12th; Hon. J. Crowdy, Colonial Secretary, first Speaker. First Agricultural Society formed. S.S. *John McAdam* arrived. Steamship Company incorporated in St. John's to run steamer between St. John's and Halifax, N.S. First Presbyterian kirk established; Rev. Donald A. Fraser minister. Captain Favbre and Mr. W. Thomas, President Chamber of Commerce, appointed Commissioners on French Fishery Question. General Election of Members to the Amalgamated House held on 20th December. The Assembly consisted of 15 elected members and 10 nominees of the Crown. Hon. J. Crowdy Speaker.

1843.—Act for the Encouragement of Education introduced by Richard Barnes. Death of Dr. Wm. Carson. Nugent introduced Bill to abolish oath of supremacy and abjuration, and to substitute oath of allegiance. Amalgamated House opened by Sir John Harvey on 17th January; longest opening speech on record. St. Andrew's Kirk opened December 3rd.

1844.—Edward Feild, D.D., appointed Bishop of Newfoundland. The first steam packet arrived in St. John's from Halifax, N.S., S.S. *North American*, commanded by Captain Richard Meagher, sixty hours' passage. Non-denominational Academy at Castle Rennie, St. John's, Charles D. Newman, M.A., Oxford, Principal; J. Nugent and T. Talbot, Masters. **Chief Justice NORTON** first Roman Catholic Chief Justice; most excellent Judge.

1845.—Prince Henry, son of the King of the Netherlands, in war steamer *Rhine*, visited St. John's; great demonstration. Gas introduced into St. John's. Geo. Lilly appointed Judge, Supreme Court.

1846.—26th May, public meeting in Court House, St. John's, in favour of Responsible Government; petition sent to Queen and Parliament. 9th June, terrible and destructive fire consumed the town. 19th September, tremendous gale. Sir John Harvey appointed Governor of Nova Scotia. **Col. LAW** Administrator.

1847.—**Sir Gaspard LE MARCHANT**, Governor, arrived 23rd April. **Chief Justice BRADY** appointed. Foundation Stone of English Cathedral of St. John the Baptist laid; also Colonial Building and Custom House, St. John's.

1848.—Great Revolution in Europe. December 14th, first Session of Legislature, after return to Constitution of 1833, opened by Sir Gaspard Le Marchant. Bishop Mullock arrived, May 6th, in S.S. *Unicorn*, Captain R. Maher. First Water Company; supply from Signal Hill. Free Kirk established.

1849.—Discovery of gold in California. Customs Department placed under control of local Government; J. Kent first collector; Mr. Spearmen retired on a pension. Steamer *Kestrel*, Captain Maher, lost.

1850.—Death of Bishop Fleming. Market House opened. Free Kirk opened.

1851.—Public meeting to promote direct steam from St. John's to England. The great Exhibition of the Industries of all Nations held in London, May 1st. Great demonstration of Sons of Temperance, St. John's. General Election.

1852.—Ker Bailie **HAMILTON** Governor. Death of the Duke of Wellington. Louis Napoleon Emperor of the French. First Steamer in Conception Bay. Hon. J. Crowdy Administrator. Electric telegraph introduced into St. John's by F. N. Gisborne; St. John's and Carbonear Electric Telegraph Company; R. Prowse Managing Director. Terribly disastrous seal fishery; "Spring of the Wadhams."

1853.—English and French fleet enter the Dardanelles. Turkey declares war against Russia. The Electric Telegraph Company, Gisborne's Company, incorporated, 1853.

1854.—Union Bank established. Outbreak of cholera in St. John's. Crimean War. Victories of the English and French. Battles of Alma, Balaclava, Inkerman. Reciprocity Treaty between British America and the United States. F. B. T. Carter appointed Acting Judge, Supreme Court. New York, Newfoundland, and London Telegraph Company incorporated.

1855.—Governor **DARLING**. Increased Representation Act, giving 30 members, including Burgeo and La Poile. Responsible Government introduced. Taking of Sebastopol; great rejoicings over the British Empire. First General Election under Responsible Government. Hon. **P. F. LITTLE** first Premier. Roman Catholic Cathedral consecrated. The American steamer *James Adger* arrived in St. John's with Mr. and Mrs. Cyrus Field, Peter Cooper, Bayard Taylor, and a distinguished company; endeavoured to lay the cable across the Gulf; failed owing to bad weather; cable parted; forty miles paid out.

1856.—Newfoundland divided into two Roman Catholic dioceses, St. John's and Harbour Grace; Dr. Dalton first Bishop of Harbour Grace. Telegraphic communication established with the American continent. First message sent across Gulf from J. and W. Pitts to A. and M. Cameron, Baddeck. Foundation Stone Gower Street Methodist Church laid. Fire in St. John's (Tarehin's Town). Direct steam by the Galway Line. Gulf cable laid by S.S. *Propontis*; Sir Samuel Canning; T. D. Scanlan represented New York, Newfoundland, and London Telegraph Company.

1857.—Hon. **L. O'BRIEN** Administrator, on the promotion of Sir C. Darling to the Governorship of Jamaica. Sir Alexander **BANNERMAN** appointed Governor. The Indian Mutiny. The Anglo-French Convention about the Newfoundland fishery; indignation meetings. Delegates sent to Canada, Nova Scotia, &c. Gower Street Wesleyan Church completed. Commercial Bank established.

1858.—First Atlantic Cable landed at Bay Bulls Arm, Trinity Bay; great rejoicings in St. John's in honour of Cyrus Field, to whose indefatigable energy final success was due. First cable soon collapsed. Hon. P. F. Little and B. Robinson appointed Judges Supreme Court, and the Hons. J. Simms and A. W. Des Barres retired on pensions.

1859.—News boat placed at Cape Race by the New York Associated Press to intercept ocean steamers. First ship intercepted, *Vigo*, of Inman Line. General Election; great contest at Burin. Act for Local Steam passed. **Hon. John KENT** Premier.

1860.—His Royal Highness the Prince of Wales visited the Island. Formation of Volunteer Corps.

1861.—**H. W. HOYLES** Premier. Time of great political excitement. Political riots in St. John's, Harbour Grace, and Harbour Main. Commencement of the American Civil War between North and South.

1862.—January, first Allan Steamer, *North American*, left St. John's. S.S. *Polynia*, S.S. *Camperdown*, total failure at seal fishery. Great haul of seals at Green Bay. Colonial and Continental Church Society incorporated. Great distress owing to bad fisheries. S.S. *Victoria* inaugurated local steam north and south.

1863.—27th April, loss of *Anglo-Saxon*, Clam Cove; great loss of life. St. John's provided with water from Windsor Lake. S.S. *Bloodhound*, Captain Graham, arrived 22nd April, 3,000 seals; S.S. *Wolf*, W. Kane, arrived 28th, 1,340 seals. Fire Brigade established. Revenue collected at Labrador. Hon. L. O'Brien Administrator. S.S. *Ariel* put on route, north and south.

1864.—Sir Anthony **MUSGRAVE** Governor. Confederation of the Dominion of Canada. Meeting of Delegates in Maritime Provinces and Quebec to inaugurate Confederation; Sir F. B. T. Carter and Sir A. Shea represented the Colony.

1864—1880.

Copper mine opened, Tilt Cove, by C. F. Bennett, the pioneer of mining in the Colony, and Smith McKay, the discoverer. Three steamers, *Bloodhound, Wolf,* and *Osprey,* at the seal fishery. The Currency Act confirmed. Hon. J. Hayward appointed Acting Assistant Judge.

1865.—Present Geological Survey commenced. American Civil War ended with the complete conquest of the Southern States, and abolition of slavery. **F. B. T. CARTER** Premier. **Sir H. W. HOYLES** Chief Justice. General Election.

1866.—Second Atlantic Cable successfully landed at Heart's Content, Newfoundland, by the *Great Eastern,* August 1866; the end of 1865 cable also picked up, and successfully landed at Heart's Content same year. A. M. Mackay successfully repaired Gulf Cable in S.S. *Bloodhound.* First business message sent across the Atlantic by W. J. S. Donnelly, fee £20 sterling.

1867.—Fishery very successful. Great gale at Labrador, much shipping destroyed. The British North America Act for the Confederation of the Provinces is passed. Dominion of Canada proclaimed. Bishop Kelly consecrated coadjutor to Bishop Feild.

1868.—Proclamation issued by the Carter Administration suppressing able-bodied poor relief. 7th August, Hon. J. Hayward appointed Assistant Judge Supreme Court, on the retirement of P. F. Little. Cunard contract ceased and Inman Company carried mails and passengers from St. John's to Halifax, N.S., during winter months.

1869.—Large increase in the Public Debt caused by the bad fisheries. **Sir Stephen HILL** appointed Governor in July. Central District Court constituted. General Election; Confederation Candidates defeated. Census taken. Dr. Mullock died.

1870.—The Most Rev. T. J. Power, consecrated at Rome Bishop of St. John's, arrived in St. John's 9th September. Diocesan Synod of Church of England established. **Hon. C. F. BENNETT** Premier.

1871.—Garrison withdrawn from Newfoundland. Increasing prosperity consequent on good fisheries, &c. Treaty of Washington. S.S. *Ariel* discontinued coastal service, carried out by S.S. *Tiger* and *Leopard.*

1872.—First Exhibition held in Newfoundland, opened by the Governor; Rev. E. Botwood, R.D., projector. Agitation about pre-emption of the New York, Newfoundland, and London telegraph lines; continued through 1873.

1873.—Direct steam to England by Allan Line commenced. George Street Methodist Church opened. General Election; Bennett Government defeated by the withdrawal of three members.

1874.—The largest catch of cod fish ever taken in Newfoundland. **Sir F. B. T. CARTER** Premier. Newfoundland Conference of Methodist Church of Canada organised; Rev. G. S. Milligan President. The Royal Commission; Sir B. Robinson, J. Goodfellow, and J. Fox, Esquires.

1875.—The first Government Railway Survey under direction of Sandford Fleming, Civil Engineer.

1876.—Christian Brothers arrived in St. John's. **Sir J. H. GLOVER**, G.C.M.G., Governor. Dr. J. B. Kelly, D.D., appointed Bishop of Newfoundland. Halifax Fishery Commission met; $5,500,000 awarded as compensation to be paid by the United States to the British Provinces; Newfoundland's share one million; Sir W. V. Whiteway Commissioner for Newfoundland. Bishop Feild died, in Bermuda. Both Presbyterian kirks burnt.

1877.—Sir F. B. T. Carter appointed Acting Assistant Judge, on the retirement of Sir B. Robinson. Commander W. Howorth, R.N., appointed first Stipendary Magistrate, West Coast, by Imperial and Colonial Governments; duties first collected there. St. Andrew's Kirk built by United Presbyterians. Trinity, Catalina, and Bonavista connected by telegraph. S.S. *Curlew* and *Plover* on coastal service.

1878.—Dr. Ll. Jones, D.D., appointed Bishop of Newfoundland. **Sir W. V. WHITEWAY** Premier. Telegraph extended to St. George's Bay, Bay of Islands, Bonne Bay, Betts Cove, Tilt Cove, and Little Bay Mines.

1879.—First issue "Evening Telegram."

1880.—**Sir F. B. T. CARTER** appointed Chief Justice, and R. J. Pinsent Judge Supreme Court. Colonial Government allowed to make grants of land on the west coast, or "French Shore" so-called. **Sir F. B. T. CARTER**, K.C.M.G., Administrator. First Railway Bill passed.

T T 2

1881.—Serious disturbance on the Railway line (Battle of Fox Trap). **Sir Henry Fitz-Hardinge MAXSE** Governor. First railway under construction in Newfoundland, St. John's to Harbour Grace.

1882.—First issue "Evening Mercury." An Act passed for the construction of the Great American and European Short Line Railway. Charter granted for the construction of a graving dock. **Sir W. V. WHITEWAY** Premier. Inauguration of St. Patrick's Hall, B. I. Society.

1883.—St. Stephen's Day, Harbour Grace Riots. **Sir F. B. T. CARTER** Administrator. Hon. J. I. Little appointed Assistant Judge, Supreme Court, in place of Hon. Judge Hayward, retired. Sir H. Maxse died in St. John's. Fishery Exhibition held in London; Sir A. Shea, K.C.M.G., Commissioner for the Colony. **Hon. E. MORRIS** Administrator, in absence of Sir F. B. T. Carter, K.C.M.G.

1884.—Union of Methodist Bodies in Canada. Newfoundland Conference of Methodist Church organised in Gower Street Church; Rev. Dr. Milligan, President. July, **Sir J. H. GLOVER** arrived in St. John's as Governor. Dry Dock at Riverhead, St. John's, opened. H.M.S. *Tenedos* docked in December. Railway to Harbour Grace opened for Passengers in December.

1885.—Ford-Pennell Convention on French Fishery claims. **Sir F. B. T. CARTER** Administrator. **Sir Robert THORBURN** Premier. General Election. Choir and transepts of English cathedral consecrated by Bishop Jones. First issue "Daily Colonist." Great Storm in Newfoundland and Labrador. Atlantic Hotel opened, May. Telegraph extended to Greenspond and Twillingate, also Burin, St. Lawrence, Lamaline, Grand Bank, and Fortune. Sir W. V. Whiteway resigned Premiership in October. General Election November. **Sir R. THORBURN** Premier. Death of Sir J. H. Glover in London.

1886.—**Sir F. B. T. CARTER** Administrator. **Sir G. W. DES VŒUX** Governor. Building of New Post Office. Corner Stone of Methodist College laid by Sir G. W. Des Vœux. Report of Joint Committee on Fishery question; approved of Bait Act and refused to sanction the Ford-Pennell Convention. Placentia Railway commenced.

1887.—The Bait Act became Law. **Sir H. A. BLAKE** Governor. Ballot Act passed. Queen's Jubilee; Service in English Cathedral attended by all denominations of Protestants. Sir A. Shea, K.C.M.G., appointed Governor of the Bahamas. Methodist College and Alexander Street Methodist Church opened. Colonial Conference held in London; Colony represented by Sir R. Thorburn, Premier, and Sir A. Shea.

1888.—Second Washington Treaty negotiated; Hon. J. S. Winter represented the Colony. *Modus vivendi* established for two years. Methodist College Home opened. Bait Act put in operation, March. Placentia Railway opened for traffic. Act to provide Municipal Council for St. John's passed. S.S. *Volunteer* and *Conscript* on coastal service. Governor Blake appointed to Jamaica. **Sir F. B. T. CARTER** Administrator to January 1889.

1889.—**Sir T. N. O'BRIEN** appointed Governor; arrived in January 1889. General Election. Thorburn Government defeated by an immense majority. Roman Catholic Cathedral, Harbour Grace, burnt. Act granting manhood suffrage passed.

1890.—**Sir W. V. WHITEWAY** Premier. Act authorising new Railway Line North. Agitation concerning the *modus vivendi* with the French about Lobster Factories West Coast. The *modus* was accepted by French Ambassador, 11 March. Protest from both Houses 14 March. Meeting of Patriotic Association, Bannerman Park, 26 March. Tax on all Canadian vessels purchasing bait. Reciprocity Treaty with United States by Hon. R. Bond. Colonial Secretary; prevented being carried into effect by Canada. Delegations to England on difficulties with the French, consisting of Sir W. V. Whiteway, Hon. A. W. Harvey, Hon. R. Bond and the Honble. The Speaker, G. H. Emerson (official); from the Patriotic Association Sir J. S. Winter, P. J. Scott, and A. B. Morine to England, and D. J. Greene, D. Morison, and P. R. Bowers to Canada.

1891.—Municipal Council Act amended. Delegation to England on difficulties with French, consisting of Sir W. V. Whiteway, Hon. A. W. Harvey, G. H. Emerson, Hon. M. Monroe and A. B. Morine. International Arbitration on Lobster Question to be held at Brussels. Hall's Bay Railway completed to Trinity and

1891—1895.   661

Bonavista Bays. Celebrated case of Baird v. Walker, arising out of *modus vivendi*, determined by Supreme Court in favour of plaintiff; on appeal to Privy Council, judgment confirmed. Newfoundland Bill in the House of Commons; Temporary Act (Treaty Bill) passed for two years.

1892.—Death of the Duke of Clarence, Jan. 14th. Terrible calamity and loss of life in Trinity Bay, Feb. 28th; death of 24 men caught in a northerly gale, driven to sea, and frozen to death. Visit of Deep Sea Mission to Labrador. Conference at Halifax, N.S., between Canadian Ministers and Members of the Newfoundland Government. Great fire in St. John's on July 9th.

1893.—Bait Act suspended in April by Proclamation. Temporary French Treaty Bill extended to end of 1895. April 28th, death of Sir R. J. Pinsent, D.C.L. November, General Election. The Whiteway Government sustained by a large majority. December 4th, the most Rev. T. Jos. Power, D.D., Roman Catholic Bishop of St. John's, died. Dispute with the French about payment of duty on goods landed on West Coast not carried in fishing vessels.

1894.—January 6th, nine petitions against 17 members Whiteway party filed under Election Act. February 16th, Houses of Assembly opened. March 27th, two members for Bay de Verde unseated and disqualified. April 2nd, judgment communicated to the House of Assembly. April 3rd, deputation of 20 members of Whiteway party waited on Governor asking for a dissolution. April 4th, counter deputation of Goodridge party protested against dissolution. April 10th, dissolution refused. April 11th, Whiteway Government resign. **A. F. GOODRIDGE** Premier; Whiteway party withdraw Supply and Revenue Bills. April 14th, House of Assembly prorogued to 23rd; April 21st, prorogation extended till 23rd May. May 5th, two members of St. John's East unseated and disqualified. May 22nd, Bay de Verde bye election resulted in return of one Government and one opposition candidate. May 23rd, prorogation extended to 7th June. May 31st, three members St. John's West unseated and disqualified. June 7th, prorogation extended to 7th July. June 11th, Revenue Act expired. June 14th, one member for Burgeo and La Poile unseated and disqualified. June 23rd, H.R.H. the Duchess of York safely delivered of an infant Prince. July 7th, prorogation extended to 7th August. July 25th, two members for Trinity unseated and disqualified and a third member unseated only. July 31st, two members for Placentia unseated and disqualified. August 2nd, House of Assembly opened. August 9th, House of Assembly closed. September 10th, Burgeo and La Poile election resulted in return of a Government candidate. October 2nd, Bonavista bye-election; Colonial Secretary and Attorney-General returned. Fogo election; Duder, Government candidate, returned. Twillingate election, 16th October. Foote, Opposition candidate, returned. Three Opposition members elected for Trinity. 10th November, Placentia, St John's, and Burin all returned Whiteway candidates. Carty, Government candidate, returned for St. George's, 12th November; 20th, severe storm. December 10th, Black Monday; failure of Commercial and Union Banks and several mercantile houses; December 12th, resignation of Goodridge Government; 13th, appointment of Cabinet with **D. J. GREENE** Premier.

1895.—New Administration formed; **Sir W. V. WHITEWAY** Premier. April, Conference at Ottawa on the Confederation of Newfoundland with Canada.

II.—Judiciary.

CHRONOLOGICAL TABLE OF THE CHIEF JUSTICES AND ASSISTANT JUDGES OF THE SUPREME COURT.

1. **JOHN REEVES**, C.J., 1791-1792. Appointed in 1791, under Act 31 Geo. III. c. xxix., sole Judge of the Court of Civil Jurisdiction of Our Sovereign Lord the King, at St. John's, Newfoundland; next year, by 32 Geo. III. c. lvi., the Supreme Court of Judicature of the Island of Newfoundland was created, Reeves, C. J., sole Judge, D'Ewes Coke and AARON GRAHAM assessors.

2. **D'EWES COKE**, C.J., 1792-1797. Coke, originally a surgeon in the navy, settled in Trinity; was afterwards supreme surrogate at St. John's.

3. **RICHARD ROUTH**, C.J., 1797-1800. Was formerly collector of the customs; on his appointment as Chief Justice he was required to reside permanently in the Colony; in 1800 he requested permission to visit England, and was drowned on the passage; his widow enjoyed a pension for many years.

4. **JONATHAN OGDEN**, C.J., 1801-1803. Surgeon, R.N.; sent as assistant surgeon to hospital by H.R.H. Duke of Kent, commanding in Nova Scotia; became naval officer and supreme surrogate; appointed acting C.J. in 1801; received his commission in May 1802; resigned in 1803, and was pensioned.

5. **THOMAS TREMLETT**, C.J., 1803-1813. Was an insolvent merchant of Poole; became naval officer and supreme surrogate in succession to Ogden, and, on the latter's retirement from ill health, Chief Justice; he was translated to Prince Edward's Island as Chief Judge, in exchange for Judge Colclough, 1713.

6. **CÆSAR COLCLOUGH**, C.J., 1813-1815. An Irish gentleman of good family; an amusing writer, but a very inefficient judge, and no lawyer; salary increased to £1,000; retired on a pension.

7. **FRANCIS FORBES**, C.J., 1816-1822. Appointed by commission bearing date 4th August 1816; took his seat on the bench 1st July 1817; resigned 30th September 1822; resided on the Island during the whole of the period; a most able and popular judge.

8. **RICHARD ALEXANDER TUCKER**, C.J., 1822-1833. Commission dated 1st October 1822; took his seat on the Supreme Court Bench 5th May 1823; sole Judge until 2nd January 1826, when the Royal Charter granted by His Majesty to the Supreme Court of Newfoundland, under the provisions of the Act 5 Geo. IV. cap. lxvii. s. 17, was promulgated, and the bench then filled by—

HON. R. A. TUCKER, Chief Judge
HON. JOHN WILLIAM MOLLOY   } Assistant Judges.
HON. AUGUSTUS WALLET DES BARRES }

On 26th September 1826 HON. EDWARD BRABAZON BRENTON was appointed A.J. in the room of Mr. Molloy, who had been removed from his office.

JAMES SIMMS was sworn in, 2nd January 1826, as H.M. Attorney-General. In September 1826, during the absence of the Governor, Sir T. Cochrane, Tucker, C.J., was Administrator of the Government, Brenton Acting C.J., and JAMES COCHRANE Acting Assistant Judge, until Sir Thomas's return on 12th August 1828.

JUDICIARY.

9. **HENRY JOHN BOULTON**, C.J., 1833-1838. Was formerly Attorney-General of Upper Canada; removed from office and appointed C.J. of Newfoundland; removed by order of the Privy Council in 1838. Charges having been made against Judge Des Barres, he retired temporarily, and E. M. ARCHIBALD, Clerk of the Court, was Acting Assistant Judge in December 1833, and in part of 1834.

10. **JOHN GERVASE HUTCHINSON BOURNE**, C.J., 1838-1844.
    DES BARRES and BRENTON, A.J's.
    Bourne was dismissed by Sir John Harvey in 1844.
    J. Simms, Attorney-General, made Acting Chief Justice on 10th June 1844, and continued to act until the arrival of C.J. Norton.

11. **THOMAS NORTON**, C.J., 1844-1847. Commission dated 5th November 1844.
    Des Barres and Brenton, A.J's.; Brenton died in 1845; and
    GEO. LILLY was appointed A.J.; Lilly died in 1846; and
    J. Simms was appointed Assistant Judge on 27th November 1846.
    Des Barres was Acting Chief Justice from 3rd September 1847 to 29th November 1847.

12. **SIR FRANCIS BRADY**, C.J., 1847-1865. Sworn in 29th November 1847.
    F. B. T. CARTER became acting A.J. on 6th April 1854, in place of Des Barres, A.J., who resumed in the fall term of the same year.
    G. H. EMERSON, Acting Judge in 1856.
    Des Barres and J. Simms, A.J's. until November 1858.
    P. F. LITTLE appointed A.J. on 1st November 1858.
    BRYAN ROBINSON appointed A.J. on 2nd November 1858.
    P. F. Little was Acting Chief Justice on 30th November 1858.
    CHARLES SIMMS was acting A.J. on 30th November 1858, and again on 7th February 1859.

13. **SIR HUGH WILLIAM HOYLES**, C.J., 1865-1880. Sworn in on 20th May 1865. P. F. Little retired, 20th November 1866, when Geo. Hy. Emerson was appointed acting A.J. on 19th August 1867.
    JOHN HAYWARD was appointed A.J. on 7th August 1868.
    F. B. T. Carter, Attorney-General, was acting A.J. on 20th May 1865, on 20th May 1868, and again on 20th May 1878.

14. **SIR FREDERIC BOWKER TERRINGTON CARTER**, C.J., K.C.M.G., 1880, present Chief Justice. Sworn into office 20th May 1880.
    SIR R. J. PINSENT, D.C.L. Made Judge of the Supreme Court on 20th May 1880; died April 1893.
    J. I. LITTLE. Made Acting Judge on 27th November 1883, and Judge on 7th May 1884.
    SIR J. S. WINTER. Made Judge on 27th May 1893.

III.—House of Assembly.

District.	1832.	1837.	1842.	1848.	1852.	District.	1855. 7th May.	1859.	1861.
Bonavista	Wm. Brown	H. A. Emerson	Robert Carter	Robert Carter	J. H. Warren	Bay de Verde	J. Bemister	J. Bemister	J. Bemister.
Burin	Wm. Hooper	Henry Butler	C. Benning	J. G. Falle	C. Benning	Bonavista	R. Carter	S. March	S. March.
Ferryland	Robert Carter	Peter Winser	T. Glen	P. Winser	P. Winser	"	J. H. Warren	J. H. Warren	J. H. Warren.
Fogo	T. Bennett	E. J. Dwyer	J. Slade	G. H. Emerson	G. H. Emerson	Burgeo & La Poile	M. W. Walbank	M. W. Walbank	M. W. Walbank.
Fortune Bay	N. W. Hoyles	W. B. Row	R. Robinson	H. W. Hoyles	H. W. Hoyles	Burin	C. Benning	James Seaton	H. W. Prowse.
Conception Bay	Peter Brown	Peter Brown	Thomas Ridley	J. L. Prendergast	J. Hayward	"	P. Morris	A. Shea	H. W. Hoyles.
"	James Power	James Power	John Munn	Nicholas Molloy	J. V. Nugent	Carbonear	E. Hanrahan	J. J. Rogerson	Ed. Evans.
"	C. Cozens	John McCarthy	J. L. Prendergast	Richard Rankin	T. Talbot	Ferryland	T. Glen	E. Hanrahan	E. Hanrahan.
Placentia and St. Mary's	Robert Pack	A. W. Godfrey	E. Hanrahan	E. Hanrahan	E. Hanrahan	"	E. D. Shea	T. Glen	T. Glen.
"	R. F. Sweedman	J. V. Nugent	John Dillon	A. Shea	G. J. Hogsett	Fortune Bay	H. W. Hoyles	E. D. Shea	E. D. Shea.
St. John's	J. H. Martin	Patrick Doyle	Simon Morris	J. Delaney	A. Shea	Harbour Grace	J. Hayward	Capt. Carter, R.N.	Capt. Carter, R.N.
"	P. Kough	W. Carson	W. Carson	J. Kent	John Kent	"	J. L. Prendergast	J. Hayward	J. Hayward.
"	John Kent	John Kent	L. O'Brien	L. O'Brien	P. F. Little	Harbour Main	T. Talbot	J. L. Prendergast	H. Moore.
Trinity	Wm. Thomas	Patrick Morris	J. V. Nugent	R. J. Parsons	R. J. Parsons	Placentia & St. Mary's	T. Byrne	P. Nowlan	P. Nowlan.
"	J. B. Garland	T. F. Moore	Richard Barnes	T. B. Job	S. March	"	G. J. Hogsett	C. Fury	T. Byrne.
						Port de Grave	J. Delaney	G. J. Hogsett	R. Shea.
						St. John's East	J. Kelly	J. Delaney	R. McGrath.
						"	R. Brown	J. English	W. G. Flood.
						St. John's West	J. Kent	J. Leamon	J. Kent.
						"	R. J. Parsons	J. Kent	J. Leamon.
						"	Peter Winsor	J. Kavanagh	J. Kavanagh.
						Trinity	P. F. Little	R. J. Parsons	R. J. Parsons.
						"	A. Shea	J. Casey	J. Casey.
						"	John Fox	T. S. Dwyer	T. Talbot.
						"	P. B. T. Carter	P. M. Barron	Henry Renouf.
						Twillingate and Fogo	S. March	P. B. T. Carter	F. B. T. Carter.
							J. Winter	S. Rendell	S. Rendell.
							W. H. Ellis	J. Winter	John Winter.
							T. Knight	W. V. Whiteway	W. V. Whiteway.
								T. Knight	T. Knight.

HOUSE OF ASSEMBLY.

House of Assembly—*continued*.

District.	1865.	1869.	1873. November.	1874. November.	1878. November.	1882. November.	1885. October 31st.	1889. November 6th.
Bay de Verde	J. Bemister	J. Bemister	J. J. Rogerson	J. J. Rogerson	A. Penny	E. Garland	S. R. March	E. White.
Bonavista	J. T. Oakley	J. L. Noonan	C. Bowring	J. H. Warren	F. Winton	W. B. Grieve	A. J. W. McNeily	H. J. B. Woods.
"	J. H. Warren	F. Winton	A. J. W. McNeily	A. J. W. McNeily	G. Skelton	G. Skelton	J. L. Noonan	D. Morison.
"	J. T. Burton	W. M. Barnes	J. T. Burton	C. Bowring	J. Saint	F. Winton	A. Kean	S. Blandford.
Burgeo & La Poile	D. W. Prowse	P. Emerson	P. Emerson	P. Emerson	A. M. McKay	A. M. McKay	E. White	A. B. Morine.
Burin	Ed. Evans	F. B. T. Carter	J. S. Winter	C. R. Ayre	J. J. Rogerson	J. S. Winter	A. M. McKay	J. Murray.
"	F. B. T. Carter	Ed. Evans	C. R. Ayre	J. S. Winter	J. S. Winter	J. E. P. Peters	J. E. P. Peters	E. Rothwell.
Carbonear	J. Rorke	J. Rorke	J. Rorke	J. Rorke	J. Rorke	A. Penny	H. Le Messurier	Dr. Tait.
Ferryland	T. Glen	T. Glen	T. Glen	R. Raftus	D. J. Greene	D. J. Greene	A. Penny	W. Duff.
Fogo	M. Kearney	T. Battcock	T. Raftus	J. G. Conroy	J. G. Conroy	A. F. Goodridge	D. J. Greene	G. Shea.
Fortune Bay	T. R. Bennett	T. R. Bennett	W. O. Wood	R. Alexander	J. O. Fraser	A. F. Goodridge	G. Shea	D. J. Greene.
Harbour Grace	J. Hayward	J. Munn	W. O. Wood	A. Shea	C. Dawe	A. Shea	J. Rolls	J. Rolls.
"	W. S. Green	W. S. Green	A. Shea	J. Godden	A. Shea	C. Dawe	J. S. Winter	J. Studdy.
Harbour Main	G. J. Hogsett	J. I. Little	J. I. Little	J. I. Little	J. I. Little	J. I. Little	C. Dawe	W. H. Whitely.
Placentia and St. Mary's	Charles Furey	J. Kennedy	P. Nowlan	P. Nowlan	P. Nowlan	R. McDonnell	J. Godden	E. Dawe.
"	A. Shea	C. F. Bennett	J. Collins	C. F. Bennett	W. J. S. Donnelly	W. J. S. Donnelly	J. Veitch	R. S. Munn.
"	P. M. Barron	H. Renouf	H. Renouf	J. Collins	J. Collins	A. Bradshaw	R. McDonnell	W. J. Woodford.
Port de Grave	T. O'Reilly	R. J. Parsons, Jr.	C. F. Bennett	M. E. Dwyer	M. E. Dwyer	M. Tobin	J. F. McGrath	G. H. Emerson.
St. Barbe	J. Leamon	J. B. Wood	J. Bartlett	N. Rabbits	N. Norman	J. Bartlett	W. J. S. Donnelly	R. O'Dwyer.
St. George						J. H. Boone	G. Emerson	J. F. McGrath.
St. John's East	J. Kent	W. P. Walsh	J. J. Dearin	R. J. Kent	M. J. O'Mara	M. H. Carty	G. A. Hutchings	J. A. Clift.
"	J. Kavanagh	J. A. Jordan	R. J. Parsons	R. J. Parsons	R. J. Kent	R. J. Dearin	A. Bradshaw	G. C. Pearn.
"	R. J. Parsons	R. J. Parsons	R. J. Kent	R. J. Dearin	R. J. Parsons, Jr.	R. J. Parsons, Jr.	M. H. Carty	M. H. Carty.
St. John's West	J. Casey	T. Talbot	L. Tessier	L. Tessier	L. Tessier	P. J. Scott	A. Shea	T. J. Murphy.
"	T. Talbot	H. Renouf	P. J. Scott	M. Fenelon	M. Fenelon	P. D. White	M. J. O'Mara	Dr. Dearin.
Trinity	H. Renouf	P. Brennan	M. Fenelon	P. J. Scott	P. J. Scott	J. J. Callanan	E. P. Morris	J. Halaren.
"	S. March	S. Rendell	J. Steer	W. V. Whiteway	W. V. Whiteway	W. V. Whiteway	P. J. Scott	E. P. Morris.
"	S. Rendell	T. H. Ridley	J. H. Warren	J. H. Watson	J. H. Watson	R. Bond	J. J. Callanan	J. Day.
Twillingate	E. J. Wyatt	R. Alsop	W. V. Whiteway	J. Steer	J. Rendell	J. Boyd	R. Thorburn	L. Gearin.
"	W. V. Whiteway	S. McKay	F. B. T. Carter	F. B. T. Carter	A. J. W. McNeily	N. McKay	W. B. Grieve	W. V. Whiteway.
"	T. Knight	C. Duder	C. Duder	C. Duder	S. R. Carter	R. P. Rice	A. F. Goodridge	R. Bond.
"			S. McKay	W. Killigrew	E. P. Rice	J. P. Thompson	S. McKay	D. C. Webber.
"							M. T. Knight	E. R. Burgess.
"								J. P. Thompson.
"								T. Peyton.

* By Redistribution Act three members were given to Twillingate and one to Fogo.

CHAPTER XXIV.

BIBLIOGRAPHY, MANUSCRIPTS, RECORDS, &c.

I.—Chronological Bibliography.

Works marked thus * have not been traced in the British Museum.

The earliest references to Newfoundland are contained in FABIAN's *Chronicle*, STOWE's *Annals*, EDEN's *Gatherings*, in the reign of the first Tudor Sovereigns. There are also brief references to the Island in GOMARA, OVIEDO, PETER MARTYR, and the great works of RAMUSIO and HERRERA, also, later, in CHARLEVOIX, ABBÉ RAYNAL, and the great Spanish classic, NAVARRETE.

1515—**MARTYR, Peter.**—Decades. [First printed account of Cabot's voyages.]

1582—**HAKLUYT, R.**—Divers voyages touching the discovery of America, 1582.

1583—**PECKHAM, Sir George.**—A True Reporte of the late discoveries and possession of the Newfoundlandes, by Sir Humphrey Gilbert. At London: Printed by I. C. for John Haide, dwelling in Paule's Churchyard at the Signe of the "Golden Hinde."

1589—**HAKLUYT, R.**—The principal navigations, &c. G. Bishop and R. Newberie, Deputies to C. Barker. *London*, 1589.

1598-1600—**HAKLUYT, R.**—The principal navigations, &c. 3 vols. G. Bishop, R. Newberie, and R. Barker. *London*, 1598-1600.

1608—**BACON, Lord.**—Essay on Plantations.

1609—**LESCARBOT, M.**—Histoire de la Nouvelle France. *Paris*, 1609.

1610—*****HARLEY, John.**—Discovery of a New World. Tuterbelly, Newland, Forliana. No date, prob. 1610. *London*. [*Vide* Watt.]

1620—**MASON, Captain John, R.N.**—A brief discourse of Newfoundland. *Edinburgh:* Printed by Andro Hart.

1620—**WHITBOURNE, Sir Richard.**—A Discourse and Discovery of Newfoundland. Imprinted at London, by Felix Kingston, for William Barrett, 1620.
[Several editions with slight alterations in 1621, 1622, and 1623. Wynne's, Captain Daniel Powell's and N. H's Letters add., slight alterations of title page.]

1623— **ANON.**—A short discourse of the Newfoundland, containyng divers reasons and inducements for the planting of that Colony. Published for the satisfaction of all such as shall be willing to be adventurers on the said Plantation. *Dublin*, 1623. [Lord Falkland's Advertisement.]

1624—***EBURNE, Richard.**—A Plaine Pathway to Plantations [principally relating to Newfoundland]. *London:* Printed by G. P., for John Marriott, 1624. [In Carter-Brown Library.]

1625—**PURCHAS, Rev. S. M. A.**, His Pilgrims. *London*, 1625.

1625—**VAUGHAN, Sir William, D.C.L.**—Cambrensium Caroleia, Reportata a Colchide, Cambriola ex Australissima Novæ Terrae Plaga. *London:* William Stanbieus.

1626—**VAUGHAN, Sir William, D.C.L.**—The Golden Fleece, &c. Transported from Cambriol Colchos out of the Southernmost part of the Island, commonly called Newfoundland. *London:* Printed for Francis Williams, and to be sold at his shop, at the Signe of the Globe, over against the Royal Exchange, 1628.

1628—**HAYMAN, Robert.**—Quodlibets lately come from New Britaniola, old Newfoundland; all of them composed and done at Harbour Grace in Britaniola, anciently called Newfoundland, by R. H., sometime Governor of the Plantation there. *London:* Printed by Elizabeth All-De for Roger Michell, dwelling in Paule's Churchyarde, at the Signe of the Bull's head, 1628.

1630—**VAUGHAN, Sir William, D.C.L.**—The Newlander's Cure . . . . Published for the Weale of Great Britaine, by Sir Wm. Vaughan, Knt. Imprinted at *London*, by N. O., for F. Constable, and are to be sold at his shop, in St. Paule's Churchyard, at the Signe of the Craine, 1630.

1633 ——————— A Commission for the well-governing of our people inhabiting in Newfoundland. Imprinted in *London*, by Robert Barker and by the Assignes of John Bill.

1638—**ROBERTS, Lewes.**—The Merchant's Mappe. [Many editions.] *London:* 1638.

1640—**LAET, J. de.**—L'histoire du Nouveau Monde. *Leyde:* 1640.

1648 ——————— *Remonstrance on behalf of the Merchants trading to Spain, East Indies, and Newfoundland.

1670—***YOUNG, James, F.R.S.**—Remarks on Debate on Newfoundland Fishery. [*Vide* "Western Antiquary," 1886, Mar.] 1670.

1681 ——————— *Ordinance of Louis XIV. concerning Marine. [See Anspach's History.] *Fontainebleau*, 1681.

1680—**PHILANGLUS** Brittania Languens. *London*, 1680.

1687 ——————— *The present state of His Majesty's Isle, and Territories in America, July 20, 1686. *London*, Printed for Dorman Newman, 1687.

1689—**CLARKE, S., Minister of St. Benet Fink.**—A new description of the World. *London*, 1689.

1691—**LECLERCQ, Chrétien.**—Nouvelle Relation de la Gaspesia [Account of Indians on West Coast of Newfoundland]. *Paris*, 1691.

1693—**GORDON, Patrick.**—Geography anatomized, &c. *London:* 1693. [Twenty editions. 20th inlarged by E. Bowen. *London:* 1754.]

1694—**CHILD, Sir Josiah.**—Discourse on Trade. 2nd edit. *London:* 1694.

1698 ——————— *House of Commons Report.—Account of the Trade and Fishery of Newfoundland, and of the Planters. Answer of the Commissioners for an order of the House of Commons. 1695 to 1706.

1699—*DESBOROW, Chas.—The Humble Address of the Lords Spiritual and Temporal, with regard to the Petition of Chas. Desborow; also an Act to encourage the Trade of Newfoundland, 1699.

1700—MORDEN, Robert.—Geography rectified, 4th Edit. [illus.]. *London*, 1700. [1st Edition in 1688.]

1700—WHITE.—Relation de Terre Neuve [in Bernard, J. F., Recueil de voiages au Nord, V. 3, 1716]. *Amsterdam*, 1715-27.

1700—BRAY, T., D.D.—A memorial representing the present state of Religion. *London*, 1700.

1705—HARRIS.—Collection of Voyages. Discovery of plantation of Newfoundland from 1497 to 1610. *London*, 1705.

1708—*MOLL, Herman, Geographer.—The British Empire in America—Newfoundland. Printed for John Nicholson, *London*, 1708.

1708 ——————— A Proclamation by the Queen to encourage the trade more to Newfoundland, and to observe the Rules relating to the Fishery better. *Kensington*, June 26, 1708. London Gazette.

1708—*GREAVE, Allen H.—Ebenezer—A monument of thankfulness; true account of the miraculous preservation of nine men in a boat, on a voyage from Plymouth to Newfoundland. By Allen H. Greave, chief mate of the ship, and principal sharer in misery and mercy. *London*: Printed by Sam. Smith.

1710—COLLINS, John.—Petition for Governour's pay for services rendered, &c. [In B. M. cat'd as from Capt. J. Taylour, of *H.M.S. Litchfield*.] 1710?

1711—THOMPSON, Thomas.—An Account of the Colony and Fishery of Newfoundland. (With additions, by Sir Peter Thompson.) [Printed sheet and MSS.] B.M. MS., 13,972.

1712—A WEST INDIA MERCHANT—Letter to a gentleman at Tunbridge, concerning Treaty about Newfoundland. *London*, 1712.

1713 ——————— *Copies of Letters and other documents relating to the Peace of Utrecht and the Newfoundland Fishery.

1713 ——————— *Extracts from Lord Oxford's Impeachment, &c., relating to the Newfoundland Fishery.

1718—LORDS COMMISSIONERS FOR TRADE, &c.—Representation to His Majesty relating to the Newfoundland Trade and Fishery. [*See* Leclerc's Biblio. Amer.] 1718.

1722—POTHERIE, Bacqueville de la.—Histoire de L'Amerique Septentrionale depuis 1534 jusqu'à 1704. 4 vols. *Paris*, 1722. [Contains very full account of the Abenaquis.]

1728—COLLIBER, S.—Columna Rostrata, or a critical history of the English Sea-Affairs, &c. *London*, 1728.

1732—CHURCHILL, A. and J.—Voyages—Vol. iii., Sir Wm. Monson's Naval Tracts . . . concerning Fish and Fishing. *London*, 1732.

1735—LA HONTAN, Baron.—New Voyages to North-America [English Edition]. Letters XXIII. to XXV. and Memorial. Map of Newfoundland by Moll. 2 vols. Illus. *London*, 1735. [French 1st Editn., published at La Haye in 1703, has plan of Placentia, but no map.]

1741—OLDMIXON, John.—British Empire in America. [*London?*], 1741.

1745—HARLEIAN Collection of Voyages, &c.—Considerations on the trade of Newfoundland. Ebenezer, A Monument, &c. *London*, 1745.

1749—DOUGLASS, Wm., M.D.—A summary, historical and political, of the first planting, progressive improvements, and present state of British Settlements in North America. Boston, 1749-50; London, 1755-60.

1749 ——————— Considerations on the State of the British Fisheries in America. [See Watt.] London, 1749.

1753—CHABERT, Joseph Bernard de.—Voyage fait en 1750 dans L'Amerique Septentrionale pour certifier les cartes des Côtes de l'Ile de Terre Neuve. Paris, 1753.

1755 ——————— *Histoire et Commerce de Colonies Angloises dans l'Amerique Septentrionale. [Royal Institution Library.] Paris, 1755.

1755 ——————— *French Policy defeated, being an account of all the hostile proceedings of the French against the English in North America for the last seven years, with an account of the Naval engagement of Newfoundland, &c. [See Winsor's N. & C. H. of America.] London, 1755.

1756 ——————— *A new and complete history of the British Empire. London, 1756.

1759—*ADDRESS to Rt. Hon. Wm. PITT.—Considerations on the Importance of Canada, &c., and the North American fisheries dependent on Isle of C. B. and St. John's, Newfoundland, and the seas adjacent. [See Watt.] London, 1759.

1761—WINDTHROP, John, Hollisian Prof. of Astronomy, Camb., Mass.—Observations of transit of Venus, St. John's, Newfoundland, June 6, 1761. Phil. Trans.

1761—WINDTHROP, J.—Relation of a voyage from Boston to Newfoundland for obs. transit of Venus. [Boston Athenæum Library.] Boston, 1761.

1761—CHOISEUL-STANVILLE, Duke de.—Memoire historique. Leipzig, 1761.

1762—MASSIE, J.—Historical account of Naval power of France; state of English Fisheries in Newfoundland. London, 1762.

1762 ——————— Papers relative to the rupture with Spain. London, 1762.

1762—HEATHCOTE, George.—A letter to the Rt. Hon. the Lord Mayor, &c. of London, concerning the Peace now in Agitation between Great Brittain and Ireland. From an old servant. [A very vigorous letter against allowing the French rights in Newfoundland.] London, 1762.

1762—FROM AN HONEST MAN.—A reply to Mr. Heathcote's letter. London, 1762.

1762—BOLLAN, W.—Colonae Anglicae, Illustratæ, or the Acquest of Dominion and the Plantation of Colonies. [Royal Institution Library.] London, 1762.

1762 ——————— [French view of the Treaty of Paris.] Scots Magazine, December, 1762.

1763 ——————— Reflections of the Terms of Peace. London, 1763.

1764—BOLLAN, Wm.—The Ancient Right of the English Nation to the American Fishery, with a map. London, 1764.

1765—WILLIAMS, Captain Griffith.—Account of Island of Newfoundland, by Capt. G. Williams, of the Royal Regiment of Artillery, who resided there 14 years when a lieutenant, and now has the command there. An account of the Island, with the nature of the trade, method of carrying on the fishery, with reasons for the decrease of that most valuable branch of trade. To which is annexed a Plan to exclude the French from that trade, by Capt. Cole. [London], 1765.

1766—COOK, Capt. James.—Directions for navigating on part of the South Coast of Newfoundland, including St. Pierre and Miquelon. London, 1766.

1766—*LORDS COMMISSIONERS FOR TRADE, &c.—Representation relating to the Trade and Fishery of Newfoundland. 2 tables. [See Leclerc's Biblio. Amer.] 1766.

1767—ROGERS, Major Robert.—A concise account of North America [including Newfoundland]. London, 1767.

1767—COOK, Captain.—Account of eclipse of sun at Newfoundland. Phil. Trans.

1767 ——————— *The true interest of Great Britain in regard to the Trade and Government of Canada, Newfoundland, and Labrador, showing the absurdity of appointing Military and Naval officers to rule over a Commercial people. [See Watt.] London. Williams, 1767.

1768—COOK, Capt. James.—Directions for navigating the West Coast. London, 1768.

1768—CARTWRIGHT, Lieut. J., R.N.—Remarks on the situation of the Aborigines of Newfoundland. [Printed in Miss Cartwright's Life of Major Cartwright, Vol. ii., p. 307. London, 1826.]

1770—WYNNE, J. H.—A general history of the British Empire in America, &c. 2 vols. London, 1770.

1772—*CARTWRIGHT, Major John.—On the Rights and Interests of Fishery Company. [Vide his Life, p. 299.]

1774—*ANON.—A brief account established among the Esquimaux on the coast of Labrador. [See Dr. Packard's Labrador.] London, 1774.

1775—LANE, Michael.—The North American Pilot, being a collection of charts and plans drawn from surveys by James Cook and M. L. 1775.

1775—COOK, Capt. James; LANE, M.; GILBERT, J., and others.—The North American Pilot for Newfoundland, Labrador, and the Gulf of St. Lawrence, chiefly engraved by Jefferys, T. London, 1775.

1776—*JEFFRIES, Thos.—The American Atlas; description of America, chiefly the British Colonies. London, 1775-6.

1776—*COUGHLAN, Rev. L.—[Account of the early history of Wesleyanism in Newfoundland.] 1776.

1778 ——————— *Verses to the memory of Col. Ackland, with a letter on advantages arising from Newfoundland fishery trade. [See Watt.]

1778—D'AUTEROCHE, Abbe J. Chappe.—A voyage to California. Also contains J. D. de Cassini's voyage to Newfoundland. London, 1778.

1779—MILES, Wm. Aug.—Remarks on the Act for the encouragement to the Newfoundland fisheries from England. London, 1779.

1783—CARTWRIGHT, Geo.—Labrador, a poetic epistle. [See Dr. Packard's Labrador.] Reprinted by W. H. Whiteley. [St. John's?], 1882.

1784 ——————— The manner of determining disputes among the fishermen, and the quantity of cod fish annually shipped from Newfoundland. Voyage to Newfoundland. Monthly Review, Vol. xiii., 276.

1785-89 ——————— Value of our fisheries in Newfoundland. Monthly Review, Vol. lxxiii., 405.

1785—SHEFFIELD, John, Lord.—Observations on the commerce of America. 1785.

1786—*LORDS COMMISSIONERS FOR TRADE, &c.—Representation of, relating to the Trade and Fishery of Newfoundland. [See Leclerc's Bibl. Amer.] 1786.

1786—FORSTER, J. R.—Voyages and discoveries made in the North. [Anspach refers to a work of Dr. Forster which I cannot trace.] *London*, 1786.

1787—HOLLINGSWORTH, S.—The present state of Nova Scotia and the British Islands on the coast of North America. *Edinboro'*, 1787.

1787—POWNALL, Thos.—Hydraulic and Nautical observations on the currents in the Atlantic Ocean; with Notes by Dr. Franklin. *London*, 1787.

1790—*LORDS COMMISSIONERS FOR TRADE, &c.—Representation relating to the Trade and Fishery of Newfoundland. [See Leclerc's Bib. Amer.] 1790.

1792—CARTWRIGHT, Geo.—A journal of transactions and events during 16 years in Labrador. *Newark*, 1792.

1793—EARNSHAW, J.—Abstract of Acts of Parliament relating to Greenland and Newfoundland fisheries. *London*, 1793.

1793—REEVES, John, F.R.S., Chief Justice.—History of the Government of Newfoundland. *London*, 1793.

1793—PARLIAMENTARY BLUE BOOK.—Report of Michael Angelo Taylor's Committee on Newfoundland.

1793—REEVES, Judge.—Evidence before a Committee of the H. of C. [Reprint of his evidence before the Committee.] [*London?*], 1793.

1797—*RADSTOCK, Lord.—Propositions of.

1799—LAURIE, R., and WHITTLE, J.—Newfoundland Pilot. New and enlarged edition. 1799.

1801—TRADE AND SHIPPING OF NEWFOUNDLAND, Account of the, 1799.—Custom Returns, 1799. Mass. His. Soc. Col., Vol. 7., 1801.

1809—ANSPACH, Rev. Louis.—Summary of the Laws of Commerce and Navigation, adapted to the present state, Government, and trade of the Island of Newfoundland. *London*, 1809.

1810—LANE, M. [Revised by Dessiou, J. F.].—Directions for navigating the Bay of Placentia, the Coast of Labrador, Newfoundland from Point Lance to Cape Spear [three separate books]. *London*, 1810.

1810—MORSE, Jedidiah.—American Gazetteer. *Boston*, 1810.

1810—STEELE, Sir Robert.—Tour through part of the Atlantic . . . Recollections of Newfoundland. *London*, 1810.

1812—*CARSON, Wm., M.D.—Letter of a member of Parliament on the address of the Inhabitants of St. John's to the Prince Regent. [*St. John's*], 1812.

1813—*CARSON, Wm., M.D.—Reasons for colonising Newfoundland. [*St John's*], 1812.

1813—SCHULTES, Henry.—A dissertation on the Public Fisheries of Great Britain, &c. *London*, 1813.

1815—*ADAMS, J. Q.—Letters on the Fisheries. [New York State Library.] [*N.Y.*], 1815.

1790-1816 ——— Regulations respecting the Government of Newfoundland. Monthly Review, XI., 458. Particulars relating to Newfoundland. LXXII., 99.

1817 ——— *Monument of a beneficent mission from Boston. [Brig *Messenger* with supplies after great fire, 1817. Appended to Friend of Peace. Boston Athenæum Lib.]

1817—**CHAPPELL, Ed., Lieut. R.N.**—Narrative of a Voyage to Hudson's Bay and the N.E. coast of N. America. *London, 1817.*

1818—**CHAPPELL, Ed., Lieut. R.N.**—Voyage of H.M.S. *Rosamond* to Newfoundland. *London, 1818.*

1818—*****SABINE, Rev. J.**—View of the moral state of Newfoundland. [Boston Athenæum Library.] *Boston, 1818.*

1818—*****SABINE, Rev. J.**—Sermon in commemoration of benevolence of Boston citizens, St. John's, February 22. [Boston Athenæum Library.] *St. John's, 1818.*

1819—**ANSPACH, Rev. Louis.**—History of Newfoundland. *London, 1819.*

1819—**CHAPPELL, Lieut. Ed.**—Reise nach Neufundland und der südlichen Küste von Labrador. A. d. Engl. *Jena, 1819.*

1823—**ST. DONAT, Coupé de.**—Histoire de l'establissement des Français dans l'Amerique du Nord. 1823.

1824—**COLONUS.**—Observations on the Government, Trade, Fisheries, and Agriculture of Newfoundland. *London, 1824.*

1824————— Report of the Trial of an action brought by Mr. Wm. Dawe against Sir C. Hamilton, Bart. [Copy in the Library of Sir E. A. Hamilton, Bart.] *London, 1824.*

1824————— Specimen of the Language of Newfoundland.—In R. Kerr's General History and Collection of voyages. Vol. VI., pp. 32, 33. *London, 1824.*

1826—**CARTWRIGHT, F. D.**—The Life and Correspondence of Major Cartwright. Vol. I. *London, 1826.*

1827—*****HOLMES, Rev. John.**—Missions of the United Brethren for propagating the Gospel [in Labrador]. [York Gate Library.] *London, 1827.*

1828—**MORRIS, Patrick.**—Arguments to prove the policy and necessity of granting to Newfoundland a Constitutional Government. A letter to the Rt. Hon. W. Huskisson, &c. *London, 1828.*

1828—**McGREGOR, John.**—History and descriptive sketches of the Maritime Colonies of British America. *London, 1828.*

1828————— *Newfoundland.—A view of the rise, progress, &c. of Newfoundland. *Poole, 1828.*

1829—**FORBES, Francis, Chief Justice of Newfoundland.**—Select cases from Records of Supreme Court. *St. John's, 1829.*

1829—**BADDERLEY, Lt.**—Description of Devil's Dining Table, Labrador.—Lt. and Phis. Soc. *Quebec, 1829.*

1830?—**RELIGIOUS TRACT SOCIETY.**—Dangers on the ice off the coast of Labrador, with some particulars concerning the natives. *London, 1830?*

1832—**McGREGOR, John.**—British America. 2 vols. *London, 1832.*

1832—**BOUCHETTE, Joseph.**—The British Dominions in North America; a description of Newfoundland, &c. *London, 1831–1832.*

1832—**ESTANCELIN, L.**—Recherches sur les voyages et decouvertes des Navigateurs Normands . . . . en Amerique. *Paris, 1832.*

1832—BIDDLE, R.—Memoirs of Sebastian Cabot. *London*, 1832.

1832—WIX, Rev. Ed.—The guilt of a denial of God's providence [a sermon on Zeph. i. 12]. *St. John's*, 1832.

1832—WIX, Rev. Ed.—Divine Visitations [a sermon on Luke xiii. 4, 5]. *St. John's*, 1832.

1832—WIX, Rev. Ed.—A retrospect of the operations of the S.P.G. in N. America [a sermon on Gen. xxxii. 10]. *St. John's*, 1833.

1833—GOULD, N.—Sketch of the trade of British N. America. [Royal Institution Lib.] 1833.

1834—ROBINSON, Capt. H., R.N.—Private journal on H.M.S. *Favorite* on Newfoundland Coast. Journal R. Geog. Soc., Vol. IV. 1834.

1834—LEIGH, Rev. J.—Vocabulary of the language of the natives of Newfoundland; procured from Mary March in 1818. Journal R. Geog. Soc. 1834.

1834 ——————— Newfoundland Dog. Penny Magazine, Vol. 3, p. 15. 1834.

1835 ——————— The Moravians in Labrador. *Edinburgh*, 1835.

1835—*ST. JOHN, W. C.—Catechism of the History of Newfoundland. *St. John's*, 1835.

1836—WIX, Ed., Archdeacon.—Six months of a Newfoundland Missionary's journal. *London*, 1836.

1836—*CORMACK, W. E.—Journey across Newfoundland. *Edinboro'*, 1836.

1837—*MONTGOMERY, R. Martin.—History of Nova Scotia and Newfoundland. *London*, 1837.

1838—*LAVAND, C.—Instructions pour Naviguer sur la côte Oriental de l'Ile de Terre Neuve. *Paris*, 1838.

1839—JUKES, J. B.—Report on the geology of Newfoundland. *St. John's*, 1839. [*See also* Edin. New Phil. Jrnl., Vol. xxix., p. 103.]

1839—MURRAY, H.—An account of British America comprehending Newfoundland. Edinburgh Cabinet Library, Vol. ii., pp. 275-328. *Edinburgh*, 1839.

1841—A LATE RESIDENT.—A sketch of the state of affairs in Newfoundland. *London*, 1841.

1841—MARTIN, R. Montgomery.—Geography, colonisation, fisheries—Article in Simmond's Colonial Magazine, IV., 372. 1841.

1842—BONNYCASTLE, Sir R. H.—Newfoundland in 1842. *London*, 1842.

1842—JUKES, J. B.—Excursions in and about Newfoundland. *London*, 1842.

1842?—LOWELL, Rev. O.—The new priest in Conception Bay. [*Boston*, 1842?]

1842 ——————— Newfoundland in 1842. Monthly Review, Vol. 159, p. 142.

1842 ——————— Newfoundland. Eclectic Review, Vol. 77, p. 316. 1842.

1843 ——————— Newfoundland. Penny Mag., Vol. 11, p. 289. 1842.

1843—ROBERTSON, Saml.—Notes on the coast of Labrador. Trans. Lit. & Hist. Soc. Quebec, February, 1843.

1843 ——————— Colonial Tariff of 1843, Vol. 10, p. 380. Hunt's Merchants' Magazine, *New York*, 1843.

1843—ANON.—Canada, Newfoundland; with the prospects of those colonies in regard to emigration. [*London?*], 1843.

1843—*JUKES, J. B.—General Report on the Geological Survey of Newfoundland during 1839-40. [R. C. Int. Lib.] *London*, 1843.

1844—FEILD, Bishop.—Order and uniformity in the public services of the Church; substance of a charge to the Clergy in 1844. *St. John's*, 1844.

1844—HUNT, R. M.—Life of Sir H. Palliser. 1844.

1844—VITET, L.—Histoire de Dieppe. *Paris*, 1844.

1845—HOUSE OF ASSEMBLY.—Report of Committee appointed to inquire into the state of the Fisheries. *St. John's*, 1845.

1845 ——————— Newfoundland Fisheries. Simmond's Colonial Magazine, Vol. VI., 1845.

1845—FEILD, Bishop.—Journal of voyages and visits on coasts of Newfoundland and Labrador. [Church in the Colonies Series, S. P. G. publication.] *London*, 1845-53.

1845—FEILD, Bishop.—List of contributions for the diocese, with a letter from the bishop to the contributors. 1845.

1845 ——————— Day's Excursion in Newfoundland. Frazer, Vol. 32, p. 740, 1845.

1846—*TOCQUE, Rev. Philip.—Wandering Thoughts. *London*, 1846.

1847—PURDY, John—completed by FINDLAY, A. G.—British American Navigator. Sailing Directory for Newfoundland. *London*, 1847.

1847—MORRIS, Hon. Patrick.—A short review of the history, government, constitution, fishery, and agriculture of Newfoundland. The series of letters addressed. . . . . . Earl Grey, &c. *St. John's*, 1847.

1847—FEILD, Bishop.—Charge to Clergy of Newfoundland. [*Bermuda?*] 1847.

1847—JUKES, J. Beete.—Notices of the Aborigines of Newfoundland. Brit. Assoc. for 1846; Trans. of Sections, p. 114.

1849—CHATEAUBRIAND, V. de.—Memoires d'outre-tombe. Vol. II., 156. [*See also* Colburn's Standard Lib., Pt. II., 1848, and the Parlour Lib., Vol. I., 1849.] *Paris*, 1849.

1849—LEGISLATIVE COUNCIL.—Rules and regulations to be observed in Legislative Council. *St. John's*, 1849.

1849—McLEAN, J.—Notes of a twenty-five years' service in the Hudson's Bay Territory. *London*, 1849.

1849—SCORESBY, Wm.—The Northern Whale Fishery. *London*, 1849.

1850 to 1895.

*FILLEAU, Aug.—Memoire sur la colonie de S. Pierre et sur les vrais moyens de consolider cet établissement. [N.L., Paris.] *Paris*, 1850.

*CARPON, C. T. A.—Voyage à Terre Neuve, observations et notions curieuses . . . . de plus importants travaux de marins français et étrangers. [N.L., Paris.] *Caen*, 1852.

1850—1860.

DISNEY, Rev. H. P., and **GIFFORD, Rev. A.**—The Labrador Mission. [Church in the Colonies. No. 26.] 1850.

BAYFIELD, Capt. H. W., and others.—Sailing directions for Newfoundland, Labrador, &c. *London*, 1851.

SABINE, Lorenzo.—Report of the principal fisheries of the American seas. *Washington*, 1853.

ANDREWS, Js. D.—Report on Trade and Commerce of British N. American Colonies. *Washington*, 1853.

WARREN, Matthew, H.—Lecture on Newfoundland and its Fisheries [with statistics]; before the Mechanics' Institute at St. John's, 14th March 1853. *St. John's* [1853?].

———— American Tract Society.—Newfoundland Fishermen. Illus. 18°. 1853.

MULLALY, John.—A trip to Newfoundland; its scenery and its fisheries, with an account of the laying of the cable. Thirty illustrations by Hitchcock. *New York*, 1855.

*****ST. JOHN, W. C.**—Catechism of the history of Newfoundland. *Boston*, 1855.

ANON.—A sketch of history of Newfoundland from 1846 to 1854, &c. The crisis, emigration, &c. [1855?].

MULLALY, John.—Trip to Newfoundland. Harper, XII. 1856.

———— Newfoundland Fishermen, Art in. Harper, IX. 1854.

LATHAM, R. G.—Table showing affinities between Bethuck and various Algonku dialects. Philological Soc. Trans., 1856.

*****CORMACK, W. E.**—Narrative of a journey across the island of Newfoundland. *St. John's*, 1856.

MOUNTAIN, Rev. J. G.—Church in the Colonies Series. Some account of sowing time on the rugged shores of Newfoundland. 1856.

BOWEN, Noel H.—The social condition of the coast of Labrador. Trans. Lit. and Hist. Soc. of Quebec. 1856.

FIELD, C. W.—Statement of advantages attendant upon making St. John's, Newfoundland, a port of call. *London*, 1856.

BAYFIELD, Admiral H. W.—Maritime positions in Newfoundland. *London*, 1857.

*****MAURY, M. F.**—Letter on Nautical Directions for sailing from Valentia to Newfoundland. *Washington*, 1857.

MULLALY, John—The Laying of the Cable in 1855. *New York*, 1858.

GRAY, Hon. and Rev. W.—Sketches and Views of Newfoundland. [B.M., 204 (24).] *Ipswich*, 1858.

DAYMAN, Joseph—Deep sea soundings between Iceland and Newfoundland. *London*, 1858.

———— Pêche de la morues. Repartition des places de pêche assignées aux armateur français. *St. John's*, 1859.

*****PAGE, F. R.**—History and description of Newfoundland, with chart. *London*, 1860.

DAWSON, J. W.—Notice of tertiary fossils from Labrador, &c., &c. [Reprinted from Vol. V. of Canadian Naturalist.] *Montreal*, 1860.

TAYLOR, B.—At home [Notice of Newfoundland in 1855]. *New York*, 1861-62.

WELLS, W. V.—Newfoundland Fisheries. Harper, XXII., 456, 1860-1.

MULLOCK, Rt. Rev. Bishop.—Two Lectures on Newfoundland. *St. John's*, 1860.

NOBLE, L. L.—After icebergs with a painter; a summer voyage around Newfoundland. *New York*, 1861.

GOBINEAU, Count A. de.—Voyage à Terre Neuve. [N.L., Paris.] *Paris*, 1861.

——— [Normand Voyages.]—Transactions of the Quebec Literary and Historical Soc., 1862 [p. 116].

ANON. [H. WINTON?].—A chapter in the history of Newfoundland for the year 1861. *St. John's*, 1851.

ASHE, Lieut. E. D.—Journal of voyage from New York to Labrador. Nautical Magazine, 1861.

[ASHE, Lieut. E. D.?]—Journal of voyage from New York to Labrador. Trans. Lit. and Hist. Soc. of Quebec, 1861.

HALLOCK, Chas.—Three months in Labrador. Harper, April, May, 1861.

LATHAM, R. G.—Elements of Comparative Philology. [Beothic Language.] *London*, 1862.

WALLICH, G. C.—The North Atlantic Sea-bed. *London*, 1862.

WINTER, J.—A lecture on the decline of the Fisheries. *St. John's*, 1863.

HIND, H. Y.—Explorations in the interior of the Labrador Peninsula. Illus., 2 vols. *London*, 1863.

PEDLEY, Rev. Charles.—History of Newfoundland from the earliest times to 1860. *London*, 1863.

*****MORETON, J.**—Life and work in Newfoundland. [*London?*], 1863.

——— Lives of Missionaries.—C. K. Soc. [of Rev. J. G. Mountain]. *London*, 1863-5.

——— British North America. Religious Tract Society. *London*, 1864.

*****CAMPBELL, J. F.**—Frost and Fire [Labrador]. *Edinboro'*, 1864.

MORETON, J.—Physical Geography of Newfoundland. J. R. Geog. Soc., 1864.

HIND, H. Y.—Explorations up the Moisie River of Labrador. J. R. Geog. Soc., 1864.

*****CAMPBELL, J. F.**—Short American tramp in 1864 [in Newfoundland]. [R. C. Inst. Lib.] *Edinboro'*, 1865.

HAMILTON, Captain R. V.—Coast of Labrador. J. R. Geog. Soc., 1865.

——— Sailing directions for Island and Banks of Newfoundland. *London*, 1865

*****WILSON, Rev. Wm.**—Newfoundland and its Missionaries; History of Wesleyan Church. *Cambridge, Mass.*, 1866.

SHEA, J. G.—History and description of New France, with notes. [Translation of CHARLEVOIX. P. F. X. de. Paris, 1744.] *New York*, 1866-72.

FEILD, Bishop.—Charge to Clergy of Newfoundland, June 25, 1866. *London*, 1867.

CHIMMO, Wm.—Visits of the *Gannet* to Labrador. J. R. Geog. Soc., 1867.

McCREA, Col. R., R.A.—Lost amid the Fogs. *London*, 1869.

AVEZAC, M. d'.—Les Navigations Terre-Neuviennes de J. and S. Cabot. *Paris*, 1869.

BROWN, Richard, F.G.S., F.R.G.S.—History of Cape Breton, including notices of Newfoundland. *London*, 1869.

*HOWLEY, Richard.—Letters on the present state of Newfoundland and on Confederation. *St. John's*, 1869.

LITTLE, John.—The Constitution of Newfoundland. [*St. John's*, 1869?]

KOHL, J. G.—Discovery of Maine. *Portland*, 1869.

WHITBURN, T.—Westward ho to Avalon! [A partial reprint of Whitbourne, with notes.] *London*, 1870.

———————— Newfoundland. New Dominion Monthly, Vol. 7, pp. 77-279, 335. 1871.

HARVEY, A.—Record of extinct Race of Newfoundland. New Dominion Monthly, Vol. 8, p. 11. 1871.

BENJAMIN, S. G. W.—Summer trip to Newfoundland. Scribner, Vol. 2, p. 618. 1871.

HARVEY, A.—Early History of Newfoundland. New Dominion Monthly, Vol. 8, p. 79. 1871.

KIRKE, H.—The first English Conquest of Canada; with some account of the earliest settlements in Newfoundland. *London*, 1871.

*DASHWOOD, R. L.—Chipoloquargan, or life by the camp fire in Newfoundland. [R. C. Inst. Lib.] *Dublin*, 1871.

BROWNE, C. A.—Letters and extracts from the addresses and occasional writings of J. B. Jukes. [Letters from Newfoundland to Mr. J.'s family.] *London*, 1871.

MURRAY, A.—Report upon the Geological Survey for 1870 [1872]. *St. John's*, 1870-3.

*CORMACK, W. E.—Narrative of a journey across the island of Newfoundland. [R. C. Inst. Lib. Pamp., Vol. V.] *St. John's*, 1873.

———————— Newfoundland. Blackwood, 114-53. 1873.

GOSSELIN, E.—Documents authentiques et inédits . . . . . . de la Marine Normande et du commerce Rouennais pendant les xvie et xviie siècles. [*See also* Nouvelles glanes historiques Normandes.] *Rouen*, 1873.

HOWARTH, Comr., R.N.—Report on the Newfoundland and Labrador Fisheries. [R. C. Inst. Lib.] *St. John's*, 1874.

*GILPIN, E.—Sketch of the Carboniferous District of St. George's Bay. [R. C. Inst. Lib. Pamp., Vol. V.] *Halifax, N.S.*, 1874.

*MURRAY, A.—Resources of the interior of Newfoundland. [R. C. Inst. Lib., Pamp. A.] *St. John's*, 1874.

*ANON.—Les Pêcheries de Terre-Neuve et les traités. [R. C. Inst. Lib., Pamp., Vol. LXX.] *Paris*, 1874.

LLOYD, J. G. B.—Beothuks. Jnl. of the Anthropological Inst. *London*, 1874.

WHITMAN, J.—French Fishery Claims on the Coast of Newfoundland. Frazer, Vol. 93, p. 22. 1875.

CORDEIRO, M. Luciano.—La part pris par les Portugais dans la découvert de L'Amérique. Compte-rendus du Congrès des Americanistes. 1875.

──────── R. Col. Inst. Proceedings.—Report on the Newfoundland Fishery Question. 1875.

*****MORRIS, Father.**—Proposed railway across Newfoundland. [R. C. Inst. Lib., Pamp., Vol. V.] St. John's, 1875.

──────── Beschreibung einiger Häfen, Buchten und Auker-plätze an den Küsten von Neufundland und Labrador. Annalen de Hydrographie, *Berlin*, 1876.

MURRAY, A.—Summary of the Newfoundland Railway Survey, 1875. *St. John's*, 1876.

*****PATTERSON, W. J.**—Resources, industries, &c. of Newfoundland. [York Gate Library.] *Montreal*, 1876.

HOWLEY, J. P., F.R.G.S.—Geography of Newfoundland. *London*, 1876.

IMRAY, T. F.—Sailing directions for the Island of Newfoundland. *London*, 1876.

LLOYD, T. G. B.—A further account of the Beothucs and the stone implements of Newfoundland. Anthropological Journal, Vol. 5, p. 222. 1876.

──────── Geological Survey of Newfoundland. Nature, Vol. 14, p. 254. 1876.

TOCQUE, P.—Climate of Newfoundland. Canadian Monthly, Vol. 10, p. 156. 1876.

TOBIN, Jas.—Newfoundland; Tangled Lands and Tangled Laws. [R. Col. Inst. Pamp., Vol. V.] *London*, 1877.

MURRAY, A.—Geography and Resources of Newfoundland. J. R. Geog. Soc., xiv., 267. 1877.

*****MURRAY, A.**—Roads—Newfoundland : A lecture. [R. C. Inst. Lib.] *St. John's*, 1877.

ROBINSON. G.—Journey across the Island. J. R. Geog. Soc., 1877.

TUCKER, H. W.—Memoir of life and episcopate of Ed. Feild, D.D., Bp. of Newfoundland, 1844-76, with portrait and map. *London*, 1877.

HIND, H. Y.—Fishery Commission, Halifax, 1877. The effect of the fishery clauses in Treaty of Washington on Fisheries, &c. of British North America. *Halifax, N.S.*, 1877.

*****HIND, H. Y.**—Notes on the influence of anchor ice in relation to fish offal and the Newfoundland fisheries. *St. John's*, 1877.

HARVEY, Rev. M.—This Newfoundland of ours : A lecture. *St. John's*, 1878.

TOBIN, Jas.—A letter to the Colonial Secretary, Oct. 5, 1878, protesting against the abolition of his appointment as Magistrate on the West Coast of Newfoundland. *London*, 1878.

BERGNE, Sir H. G., K.C.M.G.—The Halifax Commission. Blackwood, March 1878.

MORRIS, M. P.—Crisis in Newfoundland. Irish Monthly, Vol. 6, p. 101. 1878.

MACDONALD, D. C.—Notes of a trip to Newfoundland. Lippincott, Vol. 23, p. 116. 1878.

WHITEAVES, J. F.—Primordial Fossils from Newfoundland. Amer. Jrnl. Science, Vol. 116, p. 224. 1878.

BENJAMIN, S. G.—Atlantic Islands as resorts of health. . . . . Newfoundland. *London*, 1878.

FISHERY COMMISSION.—Award and Documents of Halifax Commission. 3 vols. *Washington*, 1878.

*****PROWSE, D. W.**—Episodes in the early history of Newfoundland. *St. John's*, 1878.

CHAVANNE, Josef.—Die Literateur über die Polar-Regionen der Erde. [*Vienna*], 1878.

OWEN, R.—Memoirs on extinct Wingless Birds of New Zealand, with appendix on those of Newfoundland, &c. 1879.

*****TOCQUE, Rev. P.**—Newfoundland as it was, and as it is in 1877. [York Gate Library.] *Toronto*, 1879.

*****HARVEY, Rev. M.**—Across the Island with Sir John Glover. [York Gate Library.] *St. John's*, 1879.

*****WOODBURY, C. Levi.**—Relation of the Fisheries to the discovery of North America. *Boston*, 1880.

BROWN, Richard, F.G.S., F.R.G.S.—Notes on the Northern Atlantic. *London*, 1880.

DUNRAVEN, Earl of.—Glimpse at Newfoundland, XIX. Cent., Vol. 9, p. 86. Living Age, Vol. 148, p. 410. 1880.

MURRAY, A.—Mineral Resources of Newfoundland. Nature, Vol. 23, p. 46. 1880.

HANNAY, J.—The History of Acadia. *London*, 1880.

MURRAY, A., and HOWLEY, J. P.—Geological survey of Newfoundland, 1866-1880. *London*, 1881.

DURO, C. F.—Arca de Noé. La Pesca de los Vascongados zel descubrimiento de Terra Nova. *Madrid*, 1881.

RAE, W. F.—Newfoundland to Manitoba. *London*, 1881.

——— Early French voyages to Newfoundland. Mag. American History, Vol. 8, p. 286. 1881.

BAIRD, S. F.—The History and Condition of the Fishery Industry [U.S. Census Report.] 1881.

——— John Mason. Including his tract on Newfoundland. Reprint by Prince Society. *Albany, U.S.A.*, 1881.

LANMAN, C.—Curious characters. [Notice of Newfoundland.] *Edinburgh*, 1881.

*****SOUBEIRAN, J. Leon.**—Terre Neuve, étude sur son passé, son présent et son future. *Montpellier.* [Extract from the *Bulletin de la Société languedocienne de géographie*, Septembre 1882.] [N.L., Paris.]

BROWN, R.—Review of Harvey's Newfoundland. Academy, Vol. 23, p. 199. 1882.

CLOUÉ, G. C., and others.—Pilote de Terre-Neuve, par le contre-amiral, &c. [First edition in 1869.] 2 tom. *Paris*, 1882.

——— Mag. of Amer. Hist., 1882, April. [About Basque voyages.]

HARTWIG, Georg.—The Polar World. Newfoundland, its Aspects, Forests, Animals, Climate, Fisheries, Fogs, and Storms. [*See also* reprints in 1882, &c.] *London*, 1869.

*****TALBOT, Hon. T.**—Newfoundland in relation to its circumstances and condition. *London*, 1882.

DOYLE, J. A., M.A.—The English in America. *London*, 1882.

HALL, E. Hepple.—The Home Colony; a guide book to Newfoundland. *London, 1882.*

HEYDEN and SEWYN.—Physical Geography, Agricultural Capabilities, Fisheries, &c. of Newfoundland in Stanford's North America. *London, 1882.*

GOODE, Geo. Brown.—A review of Fishery Industries of the U.S. Fishery Exhibition Paper. *London, 1883.*

HATTON, J., and HARVEY, Rev. M.—Newfoundland; the oldest British Colony. *London, 1883.*

——————— Magazine of American History, Oct. 1883—Oct. 1885. [Article on Lord Baltimore's departure from Newfoundland.]

SHEA, Sir A., K.C.M.G.—Newfoundland; its Fisheries. Fishery Exhibition Paper. *London, 1883.*

WINSOR, J.—Narrative and Critical History of America. 8 vols. *Boston, 1883, &c.*

——————— Newfoundland, the oldest English Colony. Spectator, Vol. 57, p. 227. 1884.

HOWLEY, M. F.—Presentation Nuns in Newfoundland. Irish Monthly, Vol. 12, p. 487. 1884.

STEARNS, W. Alden.—Labrador; a Sketch of its People, &c. *Boston, 1884.*

HARVEY, Rev. M.—Labrador and Newfoundland. Articles in Encl. Brit., 1884.

MARQUER.—Société bretonne de géographie de Lorient. Conférence sur l'Ile de Terre Neuve fait dans la séance du 4 janvier, 1884. *Lorient, 1884.*

GILLPATRICK, W. W., and GIBSON, J.—The coasts and banks of Newfoundland and the coast of Labrador. [N.L., Paris.] *Washington, 1884.*

——————— Sport in Newfoundland. Spectator, Vol. 58, p. 1342. 1885.

WADSWORTH, M. E.—Rocks of Newfoundland. Amer. Jrnl. Science, Vol. 128, p. 94. 1885.

PARKMAN, F.—Collected works on Canadian History. *London, 1885-1886.*

GRIEVE, Symington.—The Great Auk or Garefowl. *London, 1885.*
[For further information on this subject, *see* the Bibliography of the Great Auk, in Prof. A. NEWTON's *Dictionary of Birds*.]

PINSENT, Sir R.—Our oldest Colony. R. Col Inst. Proceedings, 1885.

KENNEDY, Admiral W. R.—Sport and Travel in Newfoundland and West Indies. *Edinboro', 1885.*

GATSCHET, A. S.—Beothucks. Amer. Phil. Soc. Trans. *Philadelphia, 1885-6.*

HARVEY, Rev. M.—Text Book of Newfoundland History. *Boston, 1885.*

FARNHAM, C. H.—Labrador. Harper, Sept., Oct., 1885.

——————— Her Majesty's Colonies: Papers issued under authority of Commissioners of Colonial and Indian Exhibition. *London, 1886.*

LA CHAUME, Henri de.—Terre Neuve et les Terre-Neuviennes. *Paris, 1886.*

BONWICK, Jas.—The British Colonies and their resources. . . . . Newfoundland, St. Pierre, and Miquelon. *London, 1886.*

SULLIVAN, J.—Newfoundland; its Origin, its Rise and Fall. *Jersey, 1886.*

LLOYD, F.E.L.—Two years in the region of icebergs. *London*, 1886.

DAVENPORT, R. G., and others.—Newfoundland and Labrador Pilot. Supplement, No. 1. *Washington*, 1886.

———— Newfoundland and Labrador. Chambers' Journal, Vol. 64-65. 1887.

MAXWELL, Staff-Comn. W. F., R.N.—Admiralty. Newfoundland and Labrador Pilot. *London*, 1887-1891. 2nd edition. [An edition, 1878 to 1884.] [Supplement No. 2 corrects to 17th June 1892.]

ISHAM, C.—The Fishery Question. *New York*, 1887.

JAY, J.—Fisheries dispute. *New York*, 1887.

HOWLEY, R.—Fisheries and fishermen of Newfoundland. Month. Magazine. 1887.

———— [Account of Labrador Fishery.] Lund und vater. *Berlin*, 1887.

———— *Newfoundland: Treaty Rights of French Fishermen in British Waters. [R. Col. Inst. Lib.] *London*, 1887.

GOODE, Geo. Brown, and others.—U. S. Commission of Fish and Fisheries, 1887.

AGASSIZ, A.—A contribution to American Thalossography. *London*, 1888.

LE BEAU.—Terre Neuve, la pêche de la morue, la pêche du homard. [N.L., Paris.] *Nantes*, 1888.

HESSE-WARTEGG, Ernst von.—Kuada und Newfundland nach vongen Reisen und Beobachtungen. *Freiburg*, 1888.

DORAN, J. I.—Our Fishery Rights in the North Atlantic. *Philadelphia*, 1888.

DE RICCI, J. H.—Fisheries dispute. *London*, 1888.

HOWLEY, Most Rev. Bishop.—Ecclesiastical History of Newfoundland. *Boston, U.S.*, 1888.

*PILOT, Rev. Dr.—Geography of Newfoundland. *Glasgow*, 1888.

BLAKE, Lady.—Beothucks. Nineteenth Century, December, 1888

HOLME, R. F.—Journey in the interior of Labrador. Proc. R. G. S. [N.S.] X., 189, 1888.

KINGSFORD, Wm.—History of Canada. *London*, 1888, &c.

BOAZ, Franz.—Notes on Geography of Labrador. Science, *New York*, Feb. 17, 1888.

PACKARD, A. S.—Who first saw the Labrador coast? and the geographical evolution of Labrador. Bull. Amer. Geog. Soc. June, 1888.

*PACKARD, A. S.—Sealing on the Newfoundland Coast. The Orphanage Record. Providence, R.I. April, 1888.

GOODE, Geo. Brown—American Fishes. A popular treatise. *London*, 1888.

BLAKE, Lady.—On Seals and Savages. Nineteenth Century, April, 1889.

ROBINSON, Capt. Geo., R.N.—A Report on the movements of the ice, currents, and tidal streams of Newfoundland to Gulf of St. Lawrence. *London*, 1889.

MACKAY, A. H.—Fresh-water sponges of Canada and Newfoundland. Trans. Roy. Soc., Canada. 1889.

RECLUS, J. J. E.—Nouvelle géographie, Vol. 15. Labrador et Terre Neuve. *Paris, 1890.*

BOWRING, W. B.—Home Rule for Newfoundland. Subjects of the Day. November, 1890.

——————— Dispute about the Lobster Fisheries. [*Map.*] Review of Reviews, Feb., June, July, Aug., Dec., 1890.

ROBERTSON, A.—Dispute about the Lobster Fisheries. Law Magazine, August, 1890.

MORRIS, E. H.—The Newfoundland Dog. Outing Mag., N.Y., 1890.

MORISON, D.—Discontent in Newfoundland. Forum Mag., 1890.

PATTERSON, Rev. Geo., D.D.—The Portuguese on the North East Coast of America. Royal Society of Canada Proceedings, Vol. VIII., 1890.

HARVEY, Rev. M.—A short History of Newfoundland. *London, 1890.*

WHITEWAY, Sir Wm. V.—The Newfoundland Fishery Dispute, by Sir Wm. V. Whiteway, Honbles. A. W. Harvey, R. Bond, and G. H. Emerson. Fortnightly Review, Sept. 1890.

WINTER, Sir James S.—French Treaty Rights in Newfoundland. The case for the Colony stated by Sir J. S. Winter, P. J. Scott, and A. B. Morine. *London, 1890.*

*****WINGFIELD-BONYN, W.**— Agricultural and Mineral Lands of Newfoundland. [R. Col. Inst. Lib., Pamp. 91.] *St. John's, 1890.*

*****NIELSEN, A.**—Cure of Codfish and Herrings, Newfoundland. [R. Col. Inst. Lib., Pamp. 91.] *St. John's, 1890.*

PINSENT, Sir R. J.—Fishery Claims in Newfoundland. R. Col. Inst., 19th April 1890.

GEFFCKEN, Dr. F. H.—North American Fishery Disputes. Fortnightly Mag., May 1890.

GOLDSMITH, H. C.—Newfoundland Fishery Question. Naturalist, May 1890.

GOSSE, Edmund.—The life of P. H. Gosse [who lived in Newfoundland from 1828-1835]. *London, 1890.*

HAYNES, T. H.—International Fishery Disputes. [*London, 1890.*]

BAYLEY.—Newfoundland loyal to England. *London, 1890.*

GRESWELL, W. H. P.—Geography of Canada and Newfoundland. *Oxford, 1891.*

THOULET, J.—Un Voyage à Terre Neuve. *Paris, 1891.*

PACKARD, Dr. A. S.—Labrador Coast—A journal of two summer voyages, with notes on its early discovery, on the Eskimo geology, natural history, &c. *New York, 1891.*

——————— The Grand Falls of Labrador. Goldthwaite's Geographical Magazine, Feby. 1891.

APPLETON, Lewis, F.R.H.S.—The Newfoundland Fishery Question. [Pub. for the British and Foreign Arbitration Association by J. Heywood.] *Manchester* [1891].

BLAKE, Lady.—Chat about Newfoundland. North American Review, June, 1891.

WHEATLEY, R.—Newfoundland. Methodist Review, 1891.

——————— Newfoundland and the French fishery question. Spectator, 1891.

——————— Newfoundland Fisheries dispute. Saturday Review, Vol. 71, pp. 345-493. 1891.

MINISTÈRE DES AFFAIRES ÉTRANGÈRES.—Documents diplomatiques Affaires de Terre-Neuve. *Paris, 1891.* [N.L., Paris.]

MAYO, Isabella F.—The tribulations of Newfoundland [*ill.*]. Victorian Magazine, August, 1892.

——————— Newfoundland Fisheries. Board of Trade Jrnl., July, 1892.

HOLBERTON, W.—A trip to the White Hills [*ill.*]. Outing Mag., January, 1892.

COLLET, C.D.—Newfoundland and the Lobster Fisheries. Asiatic Quarterly, April, May, 1892.

LAROCHE, C.—Newfoundland and the Lobster Fisheries. Review of Reviews, May, 1892.

SPEARMAN, E. R.—Sacrificing the first-born. Westminster Review, April, 1892.

LANGTRY, John.—History of the Church in Eastern Canada and Newfoundland—Map, &c. [*See* Colonial Church Histories.] 1892.

*****WINGFIELD-BONYN, W.**—Newfoundland Colonization Handbook. [Pamp., R. C. Inst. Lib.] *London. 1892.*

HARRISSE, H.—Discovery of N. America. *London, 1892.*

PATTERSON, Rev. Geo., D.D.—The Beothics, or Red Indians, of Newfoundland. Royal Society of Canada Proceedings, Vol. IX. 1892.

WINSOR, J.—The results in Europe of Cartier's explorations, 1542-1603. *Boston, 1892.*

BRYANT, Henry G., M.A., LL.B.—A Journey to the Grand Falls of Labrador. 1892.

WORTH, R. N.—Municipal Records of Plymouth. *Plymouth, 1893.*

PASCOE, C. F.—Digest of the S.P.G. Records. *London, 1893.*

HATTON, J.—Under the Great Seal: A Novel. *London, 1893.*

HARVEY, Rev. M., LL.D.—Newfoundland as it is in 1894. *St. John's, 1894.*

——————— Newfoundland Illustrated. The Sportsman's Paradise. [Introduction by Rev. M. Harvey, LL.D.] *Concord, N.H, 1894.*

DAWSON, S. E.—The Voyages of the Cabots. Royal Society of Canada Proceedings, Vol. XII., 1894.

*****LOW, A. P.**—The Recent Exploration of the Labrador Peninsula. Canadian Record of Science, 1894.

WHITEWAY, A. R.—The Commercial Collapse of Newfoundland. National Review, February, 1895.—Politics in Newfoundland. New Review, March, 1895.

GRESWELL, Rev. W.—The Crisis in Newfoundland. Fortnightly Review, March, 1895.

MARKHAM, C. R.—Life of Captain S. Martin. *London, 1895.*

PROWSE, D. W.—History of Newfoundland. *London, 1895.*

PROWSE, G. R. F.—The Discovery of Newfoundland and Labrador. The Courses taken by Cabot, Cortereal, and the French and Spanish Explorers traced by the Liturgical Evidence of the Early Maps. [Preparing.]

*****ANSPACH, C. A.**—Geschichte und Beschreibung von Neufundland und der Küste Labrador. Ausdem Engl. 3o Bd. der Bibliothek der neuesten Reisebeschreibungen von Bertuch. [*See* Dr. Packard's Labrador.] *Weimar.*

*****SIDDALL, E. J.**—The Origin of Nonconformity in St. John's, Newfoundland. *St. John's.*

II.—Index of Authors' Names.

Ackland, Col., verses to, 1778.
Adams, J. Q., 1815.
Agassiz, A., 1888.
Andrews, J. D., 1853.
Anspach, C. A. [1895].
Anspach, L., 1809, 1819 [1895].
Appleton, L., 1891.
Ashe, E. D., 1861.
Avezac, M. d', 1869.

Bacon, Lord, 1608.
Badderley, Lt., 1829.
Bavid, S. F., 1881.
Bayfield, H. W., 1850, 1857.
Bayley, —, 1890.
Benjamin, S. G. W., 1871, 1878.
Bergue, Sir H. G., 1878.
Biddle, R., 1832.
Blake, Lady, 1888, 1889, 1891.
Boaz, F., 1888.
Bollan, W., 1762, 1764.
Bond, R., 1890.
Bonnycastle, Sir R. H., 1842.
Bonwick. J., 1886.
Bouchette, J., 1832.
Bowen, N. H., 1856.
Bowring, W. B., 1890.
Bray, T., 1700.
Brown, R., 1869, 1880, 1882.
Browne, C. A., 1871.
Bryant, H. G., 1892.

Campbell, J. F., 1864, 1865.
Carpon, C. T. A., 1850.
Carson, W., 1812, 1813.
Cartwright, F. D., 1826.
Cartwright, G., 1783, 1792.
Cartwright J., 1768, 1772.
Cassini, J. D. de, 1778.
Chabert, J. B. de, 1753.
Chappell, E., 1817, 1818, 1819.
Chateaubriand, V. de, 1849.
Chavanne, J., 1878.
Child, Sir J., 1694.
Chimmo, W., 1867.
Choiseul-Stanville, Duke de, 1761.
Churchill, A. & J., 1732.
Clarke, S., 1689.
Cloué, G. C., 1882.
Collet, C. D., 1892.
Colliber, S., 1728.
Collins, J., 1710.
Colonus, 1824.

Cook, J., 1766, 1767, 1768, 1775.
Cordiero, M. L., 1875.
Cormack, W. E., 1834, 1856, 1873.
Coughlan, L., 1776.

Dashwood, R. L., 1871.
D'Auteroche, Abbe, 1778.
Davenport, R. G., 1886.
Dawson, J. W., 1860.
Dawson, S. E., 1894.
Dayman, J., 858.
De Ricci, J. H., 1888.
Desborow, C., 1699.
Disney, H. P., 1850.
Doran, J. I., 1858.
Douglas, W., 1749.
Doyle, J. A., 1882.
Dunraven, Earl of, 1880.
Duro, C. F., 1881.

Earnshaw, J., 1793.
Eburne, R., 1624.
Emerson, G. H., 1890.
Estancelin, L., 1832.

Farnham, C. H., 1885.
Feild, Bp., 1844–1847, 1867.
Field, C. W., 1856.
Filleau, A., 1850.
Findley, A. G., 1847.
Forbes, F., 1828.
Forster, J. R., 1786.

Gatschet, A. S., 1885.
Geffcken, F. H., 1890.
Gibson, J., 1884.
Gifford, A., 1850.
Gilbert, J., 1775.
Gillpatrick, W. W., 1884.
Gilpin, E., 1874.
Gobineau, Count A. de, 1861.
Goldsmith, H. C., 1890.
Goode, G. B., 1882, 1887, 1888.
Gordon, P., 1693.
Gosse, E., 1890.
Gosselin, E., 1873.
Gould, N., 1833.
Gray, Hon. W., 1858.
Greave, A. H., 1708.
Grieve, S., 1885.
Greswell, W., 1895.
Greswell, W. H. P., 1891.

Hakluyt, R., 1582, 1589, 1600.
Hall, E. H., 1882.
Hallock, C., 1861.

Hamilton, R. V., 1865.
Hannay, J., 1880.
Harleian Voyages, 1745.
Harley, J., 1610.
Harris, —, 1705.
Harrisse, H., 1892.
Hartwig, G., 1882.
Harvey, A., 1871.
Harvey, A. W., 1890.
Harvey, M., 1878, 1879, 1883, 1884, 1885, 1890, 1894.
Hatton, J., 1883, 1893.
Hayman, R., 1628.
Haynes, T. H., 1890.
Heathcote, G., 1762.
Hesse-Wartegg, E. von, 1888.
Heyden, —, 1882.
Hind, H. Y., 1863, 1864, 1877.
Holberton, W., 1892.
Hollingsworth, S., 1787.
Holme, R. F., 1888.
Holmes, J., 1827.
Howarth, Comr., 1874.
Howley, Bp., 1888.
Howley, J. P., 1876, 1881.
Howley, M. F., 1884.
Howley, R., 1869, 1887.
Hunt, R. M., 1844.

Imray, T. F., 1876.
Isham, C., 1887.

Jay, J., 1887.
Jeffries, T., 1776.
Jukes, J. B., 1839, 1842, 1843, 1847, 1871.

Kennedy, W. R., 1885.
Kerr, R., 1824.
Kingsford, W., 1888.
Kirke, H., 1871.
Kohl, J. G., 1869.

La Chaume, H. de, 1886.
Laet, J. de, 1640.
La Hontan, Baron, 1735.
Lane, M., 1775, 1810.
Langtry, J., 1892.
Lanman, C., 1881.
Laroche, C., 1892.
Latham, R. G., 1856, 1862.
Laurie, R., 1799.
Lavand, C., 1538.
Le Beau, —, 1888.
Leclercq, C., 1691.
Leigh, J., 1834.
Lescarbot, M., 1609.
Little, J., 1869.
Lloyd, F. E. L., 1886.

INDEX OF AUTHORS.

Lloyd, J. G. B., 1874, 1876.
Lord Commissnrs. for Trade, 1718, 1766, 1786, 1790.
Low, A. P., 1894.
Lowell, Rev. O., 1842.

McCrea, R., 1869.
MacDonald, D. C., 1878.
McGregor, J., 1828, 1832.
Mac Kay, A. H., 1889.
McLean, J., 1849.
Markham, C. R., 1895.
Martyr, P., 1515.
Marquer, —, 1884.
Mason, J., 1620, 1881.
Massie, J., 1762.
Maury, M. F., 1857.
Maxwell, W. F., 1887.
Mayo, I. F., 1892.
Miles, W. A., 1779.
Moll, H., 1708.
Montgomery, R. M., 1837, 1841.
Morden, R., 1700.
Moreton, J., 1863, 1864.
Morine, A. B., 1890.
Morison, D., 1890.
Morris, E. H., 1890.
Morris, M. P., 1875, 1878.
Morris, Hon. P., 1828, 1847.
Morse, J., 1810.
Mountain, J. G., 1856.
Mullaly, J., 1855, 1856, 1858.
Mullock, Bp., 1860.
Murray, A., 1870, 1874, 1876, 1877, 1880, 1881.
Murray, H., 1839.

Newton, Prof. A., 1885.
Nielsen, A., 1890.
Noble, L. L., 1861.

Oldmixon, J., 1741.
Owen, R., 1879.

Packard, A. S., 1888, 1891.

Page, F. R., 1860.
Parkman, F., 1885.
Pascoe, C. F. 1893.
Patterson, G., 1890, 1892.
Patterson, W. J., 1876.
Peckham, Sir G., 1583.
Pedley, C., 1863.
Philanglus, 1680.
Pilot, Dr., 1888.
Pinsent, Sir R., 1885, 1890.
Potberie, B. de la, 1722.
Pownall, T., 1787.
Prowse, D. W., 1878, 1895.
Prowse, G. R. F. [1895].
Purchas, S., 1625.
Purdy, J., 1847.

Radstock, Lord, 1797.
Rae, W. F., 1881.
Reclus, J. J. E., 1890.
Reeves, J., 1793.
Roberts, Lewes, 1638.
Robertson, A., 1890.
Robertson, S., 1843.
Robinson, G., 1877, 1889.
Robinson, H., 1834.
Rogers, R., 1767.

Sabine, J., 1818.
Sabine, L., 1853.
St. Donat, C. de, 1823.
St. John, W. C., 1835, 1855.
Schultes, H., 1813.
Scoresby, W., 1849.
Scott, P. J., 1890.
Sewyn, —, 1882.
Shea, Sir A., 1883.
Shea, J. G., 1866.
Sheffield, Lord, 1785.
Siddall, Mrs. [1895].
Soubeiran, J. L.
Spearman, E. R., 1892.
Stearns, W. A., 1884.
Steele, Sir R., 1810.
Sullivan, J., 1886.

Talbot, Hon. T., 1882.
Taylor, B., 1861.
Taylor's, M. A., Report, 1793.
Thompson, Sir P., 1711.
Thompson, T, 1711.
Thoulet, J., 1891.
Tobin, J., 1877, 1878.
Tocque, P., 1846, 1876, 1879.
Tucker, H. W., 1877.

Vaughan, Sir W., 1625, 1626, 1630.
Vitet, L., 1844.

Wadsworth, M. E., 1855.
Wallich, G. C., 1862.
Warren, M. H., 1853.
Wells, W. V, 1860.
West India Merchant, 1712.
Wheatley, R., 1891.
Whitbourne, Sir R., 1622.
Whitburn, T., 1870.
White, —, 1700.
Whiteaves, J. F., 1878.
Whiteley, W. H., see 1783.
Whiteway, A. R., 1895.
Whiteway, Sir W. V., 1890.
Whitman, J., 1875.
Whittle, J., 1799.
Williams, G., 1765.
Wilson, W., 1866.
Windthrop, J., 1761.
Wingfield-Bonyn, W., 1890, 1892.
Winsor, J., 1883, 1892.
Winter, J., 1863.
Winter, Sir J. S., 1890.
Winton, H., 1861.
Wix, E., 1832-1836.
Woodbury, L., 1880.
Worth, R. N., 1893.
Wynne, J. H., 1770.

Young, J., 1670.

III.—Manuscripts.

1521—*DRAPERS' RECORDS.—Proceedings of Drapers' and other guilds respecting the fitting out of ships for the Newfoundland [See HARRISSE's *Discovery of N. America*, 1892. 747]

1527—THORNE, Robert.—Letter to Henry VIII. concerning the discovery of new lands, wherein is also mentioned the project of dividing the whole world between the Kings of Spain and Portugal, by Robert Thorne, 1527. B.M., Cott. MSS. Vitellius C.—VII., 324. [See HAKLUYT's *Divers Voyages*, Hak. Soc. Pub.]

1527—*THORNE, Robert.—Letter to Dr. Leigh. "This inclination and desire of this dis- "covery I inherited from my father, who, with Hugh Elliott, were the discoverers of the "Newland." [Record Office.]

1527—RUT, John, and DE PRADO, Albert.—Letters from St. John's. [Printed in PURCHAS and in BREWER's *State Papers*.]

1530?—*DENYS, Jean.—Legal notice about boats, &c. left in Newfoundland for the winter. Paris Nat. Lib. MSS Français, 24209.

1597—LEIGH, Chas.—A Brief platforme for a voyage with three ships unto the iland of Ramea to leave inhabitaunts which shall keepe the iland to Her Majesties use, as also forbid the Frenchmen from the trade of fishing in that place. Oct. 1597. B.M. MSS.

1609—*GUY, John.—[A discourse] to animate the English to plant in Newfoundland. [Purchas had a copy of this MS.]

1610—JAMES I.'s Charter to London and Bristol Co. B.M., Harl., 589.

1610—LONDON AND BRISTOL CO.'S instructions to John Guy about management of the Colony. B.M. MSS. Otto E., VIII. [5].

1612—*GUY, John.—A journall of the voiadge of discouverie made in a boate built in Newfoundland, called ye *Indeavour*. Lambeth MSS. 250, f. 405.

1619—*WHITBOURNE, Sir R.—Letter to Lord Carew, Governor of Jersey. An abstract of some material points in my discourse of Newland, which was presented to His Majesty at Huntingdon, the 17th day of October 1619. Lambeth MSS., 494, f. 273.

1620?—WHITBOURNE, Sir R.—A brief discourse [MS. of his book, with author's alterations]. B.M. MSS., 22564.

1623 ——————— Charter of Avilonia [in Latin and English]. B.M., Sloane MSS.

1629 ——————— *Relations about Lord Baltimore's priests returning to England in September, 1629. Southampton Municipal Archives.—Book of Examinations, Informations, and Depositions, No. 42, A.D. 1622–1643.

1630—HAYMAN, Robert.—A Proposition of Profit and Honour proposed to my dread Sovereign, Lord King Charles I., relating to building a city in Newfoundland, by Robert Hayman, 1630. B.M. MSS., Eg. 2541.

1660 ——————— (Baltimore *v.* Kirke.)—Narrative and other Papers concerning Newfoundland. MSS., B.M., Eg. 2395. Letter from Chas. Hill to John Kirke, *re* Lord Baltimore's Claim. B.M. MSS., 2395.

1661 ——————— Papers concerning Lord Baltimore's interest in Newfoundland, 12 Sept. 1661. B.M. Eg. 2395.

1666—L'ALMEY, H.—Articles for Newfoundland fishing. B.M. MSS., 5489.

MANUSCRIPTS.

1666 ———— Petition of Inhabitants of Avilonia to George Kirke, 18 March 1666[7]. B.M. MSS. Eg. 2395.

1670—**MATTHEWS, John.**—Attestation concerning the French in Newfoundland—Taking possession of Placentia, 27 Jany. 1670. B.M. MSS., Eg. 2595.

1670—**NEWFOUNDLAND SETTLERS.** — Reply to declarations of Dartmouth, Plimouth, &c. B.M. MSS., Eg. 2395.

1676—**DOWNING, John.**—A Breif Narratiue concerning Newfoundland, 24 Oct. 1676. B.M. MSS., Eg. 2395.

1677 ———— MSS. History of the Colonisation of the Province of Avalon in Newfoundland in 1670. B.M., Sloane MSS., 3662.

1680 ———— MSS. account of the Plantations in America—Newfoundland.—An Account of the People settled on East Coast of Newfoundland "who live by catching fish." B.M. MSS.

1680 ———— List of Inhabitants in English ports of Newfoundland. B.M. MSS., Add. 15898.

1696-7—***BAUDOIN, Sieur de, Missionaire.**—Journal de Voyage que jay faie avec M. de Iberville en L'Isle de Terre Neuve, 1696-1697. MSS. Quebec.

1697 ———— Correspondence respecting certain duties on fish and oil imported by Englishmen in English built ships from the English settlements in Newfoundland and elsewhere. B.M. MSS., 5540.

1697 ———— Papers relating to Newfoundland and the expedition for the protection of the fisheries from the French; consisting of Official Reports and Letters from the Transport Office, Admiralty, &c., 1696-7. B.M. MSS., 15492.

1697 ———— Warrants for Ordnance and Lists of Officers, 1697-1705.—B.M., Add. 5795.

1705-8 ———— Trade to Newfoundland, Account of.—B.M. Eg. MSS., 921.

1705—**ANON.**—MS. account by a French officer supposed to be Chaussegros de Lery or Gedeon de Catalogue, of the Campaign of 1705. Quebec MSS.

1711—**THOMPSON, Thomas.**—An account of the Colony and Fishery of Newfoundland, with additions by Sir Peter Thompson. [Printed sheet and MSS.] B.M. MSS, 13972.

1719—**PROVINCE OF GUIPOSCOA.**—Memorial on their rights of fishery at Newfoundland. B.M., Add. 33028.

1729 ———— Report of a Committee of the Privy Council on the state of the Newfoundland Fishery. 19th April 1729. B.M. MSS., 33028.

1734—**WALDEGRAVE, Lord**—Memoire par le Compte de Waldegrave, Ambassadour Extraordinaire, sur l'Isle de Terre Neuve, 9 January 1734. B.M. MSS., 32785.

1737 ———— Contract for victualling the Garrison of Placentia.—B.M. MSS., 33028.

1744 ———— Appointments of Lieut.-Governors to Forts, 1744.—B.M. MSS., 33029.

1744—**AUCHMUTY, Robt.**—Paper on the Importance of Cape Britton, situate between Newfoundland and N. Scotia, to the British Nation, 10 April 1744. B.M. MSS., 32702.

1749 ———— Fort William and Plans of Batteries erected 1749. Crown, cxix. 105.

1749—**BASTILE, T. H.**—New and exact plan of Fort of Placentia.—T. H. Bastile's Reports to Board of Ordnance, March 5, 1749-50. Crown, cxix. 101b, 109.

1751—**SMELT, Leonard.**—Report of Fort of Placentia to Board of Ordnance, 22 Nov. 51. Crown, cxix. 101c.

[1751]—**DAWSON'S** report [undated] of Fort of Placentia. Crown, cxix. 1.

1754 —————— *Report of Attorney and Solicitor General on Lord Baltimore's Claim, April 5, Shelburne MS. Historical MSS. Commissioners' Report, Vol. V.

1758 —————— MSS. Papers relating to Newfoundland. B.M., Add. 32882.

1761 —————— Terms of Peace between England and France.—Consideration of the Newfoundland Fishery, 13 April 1761. MSS., B.M., Add. 33030.

1762 —————— Letters from Grenville to Mitchell, and despatch from Col. Amherst about the taking of St. John's by H.M. Arms, Oct. 12, 1762. MSS., B.M., 6820. *Also* B.M. Add. MSS., 32943.

1766 —————— Remarks on Labrador.—B.M., Add. 33,030, f. 220.

1766—***BANKS, Sir Joseph, F.R.S.**—Jnl. of a voyage to Newfoundland and Labrador, April 7 to Nov. 17. MSS. of plants, insects, &c., description of cod fishery and curing of fish, both by English and French. Also of the state of St. John's; the Government, &c. [York Gate Library.]

1782*—**PLAIRE, Sieur A. de la.**—Précis alphabetique des traites de Pais, presentis au Roi en MSS. par le sieur Ama. de la Plaire, grand maitre des eaux et fonds [notes in French Gazette, March 27, 1782], f.f. 435, large 8vo. XVIII. century MS. in Versailles Library.

1786—**GARDNER, Dr.**—Some facts collected and observations made on the fishery and government of Newfoundland, by Dr. Gardner, late of Boston, in New England. B.M. MSS., 15493.

1795—***THOMAS, Aaron.**—Paymaster of H.M.S. *Boston*. MSS. diary of events in Newfoundland in 1794–5. [In the possession of Mr. James Murray.]

1796 —————— Natives of Newfoundland, Specimen of writing of.—B.M., Add. 11038.

1820 —————— *Vocabulary of the Language of the Aborigines of Newfoundland. [MS.] 1820. [Royal Institution Library.]

[1834?]—**ROBINSON, Capt. H.**—Vocabulary of the Beothick language. B.M., MSS. Add. 19350.

1835—***GOSSE, Philip Henry.**—MSS. on Entomology of Newfoundland, 1835. [*Vide* P. H. Gosse's Life.]

IV.—Plans.

1689—**THORNTON, J.**—Plans of St. John's (p. 204), Carbonear, Bay Bulls, Harbour Grace, and Ferryland. B.M., 1804, b. 21.

1693—**FITZHUGH.**—Plans of St. John's (p. 198), Harbour Grace (p. 198), Bay Bulls, and Ferryland. B.M. MS., 5414 (30).

1698 —————— Draught of St. John's harbour, with soundings, 100 toises to inch. B.M. K. 119, 103.

PLANS.

1703—**LA HONTAN, Baron.**—Plan of Placentia (p. 184). La Haye, 1703.

1704—**THORNTON, J.**—Plans of St. John's, &c. B.M., S. 100 (18).

1708—**MONSEGUR, Michael de.**—Plan of Port of Placentia, presented to the Prince of Denmark (p. 248). B.M., K. 119, 99.

1709 ——————— *Fort William, Plan of, as rebuilt by Captain Taylour in 1709. Records, B. of Trade, Newfoundland, No. 6, K. 21.

1714—***TAVERNER, Captain.**—Survey of St. Peter s [*vide* Board of Trade Records].

1725 ——————— Plan of the Fort and Castle of Placentia, and of the new Fort. B.M., K. 119, 100.

1741—**BONACHE, P.**—Port de Plaisance. B.M., K. 118-57, a and b.

1745-74 ——————— Plans, of various dates, prepared for military purposes. B.M. MSS. 33231, II.
  1. Proposed fort [Townsend], showing chain rock and chain.
  2. Contour map of St. John's.
  3. Battery to be erected at South Head. A.—Amherst Tower. B.—Barbet Battery. C.—Lower Battery. D.—Bridge over gully on the road to St. John's.
  4. Contoured plan from Quidi Vidi and Signal Hill to Fort William and King's Bridge, showing proposed batteries to defend Signal Hill from Quidi Vidi and St. John's, and Crossfire, with Fort Amherst in the narrows, barracks and magazines.
  5. Plan of entrance of St. John's Harbour, showing the additional works erecting. A.—Block House, on Signal Hill, with additional works. B.—Batteries on the south point of Signal Hill. C.—Battery for defence of narrows. D.—Wallace's Battery. E.—Chain Rock Battery; Amherst's Tower; Frederick's Battery. [NOTE.—Two chains seem to have gone straight across from Chain Rock, and another from there to Frederick's Battery.]
  6. Entrance of harbour from Chain Rock Point to Fort Charles or South Battery, showing plan for a gun battery at Chain Rock Point, and the points the guns would cover in their fire.
  7. Section of hills around St. John's; views of Fort Townsend, Block House, and Fort Wallace.
  8. Plan of a proposed Palliser's Tower at the S. head for ten 24-pounders, and four 8-inch howitzers, and garrison (round fort).
  9. Elevation of proposed Palliser Tower.
  10. Project for fortifying Admiral's Point going into Trinity Harbour. October 1745.
  11. Plan proposed for fortification of Carbonniere Island, by Jno. Chamberlain, 1763.
  12. Plan of part of Placentia Harbour.
  13. Plan of Placentia, March 1, 1774, showing defences proposed by Lieut. Robt. Pringle, engineer.
  14. Plan of Ferryland Head and Capeling Bay.
  15. Plan of Buoy Island batteries and barracks, by Francis Assiotte, 1762.
  16. Plan of Fort Frederick, as it is now, with the new additions.

1746 ——————— Plan of Carbonere Island in Mr. Brewse's letter, dated St. John's, 18 Oct. 1746. B.M., K. cxix., 109.

1749 ? ——————— Trinity Harbour. B.M., K. cxix., 108.

1749 ? ——————— Plan of Boys Island, Ferryland. B.M., K. cxix. 110.

1749-50 ——————— New and exact plan of Fort of Placentia in J. H. Bastide's report to Board of Ordinance. March 5, 1749-50. B.M., K. cxix., 101-a, b.

1749 ?—**DAWSON'S** coloured plan of Town and Harbour of Placentia. (Undated.) B.M., K. cxix., 102.

1749—**FOURNIER, A. G.**—A coloured plan of Fort William, and of the batteries erected at the entrance of the harbour on the south side, 1749, by A. G. Fournier, done by order of Captain Bastide; also plan of harbour. B.M., K. cxix., 105.

1749 ——————— A coloured plan of Trinity's Harbour, 1748, received with Col. Cook's letter, dated 11th November 1748, accompanied by MS. report of J. H. Bastide, to Board of Ordinance, relating to Ferryland, Carboniere, and Trinity. B.M., K. cxix., 107.

1751—**SMELT, Leonard.**—Report made to Sir John Legorier by Leonard Smelt, engineer in ordinary, of present state of fortifications at Placentia, what has been done, and what is still necessary, should it be thought requisite to proceed in the repairs, accompanied by plans, 22 November 1751.
    i. An elevation of pallisading of stone-work of new fort. ii. Plan of Fort Frederick. iii. Plan of the New Fort. K. cxix., 101, c, d, e, f.

1751—**BRAMHAM, J., and HYLTON, E. S., Engineers.**—Plan of St. John's in 1751 (p. 292). B.M., K. cxix., 104.

1752?—Small book of very neatly executed plans. B.M. MS., 22875.
    100—Fort Porchartrain, Labrador.
    101—Plan of part of St. John's (p. 296).
    102—Plan of Carboniere Island (p. 296).
    103—Ferryland Head and Buoy Island (p. 296).
    104—Enlarged plan of Buoy Island, with forts, &c.
    105—Plan of Admiral's Point, Trinity Harbour (p. 296).
    106—Plan of Placentia (p. 276).
    107—Plan of Placentia under Nova Scotia, showing salaries of Lt.-Governour, &c.

1760—**RODGERS, Capt. Lieut. David, R.A.**—Plan of York Harbour, Labrador, taken in August 1760 on board H.M.S. *Antelope*. B.M, Add. 14036 a

1764 ——————— MS. plan of Bay of Three Islands, taken on board H.M.S. *Guernsey*, June 1764, 2 ft. 7 in. × 2 ft. 0 in. B.M., Add. 17693 a.

1764? ——————— MS. plan of York Harbour and Lark Bay, within the Bay of Three Islands B.M., Add. 17963 b, c.

1766 ——————— Plan of York Fort, Labrador, 1766. B.M. MSS., 33231, k.k.

1766? ——————— A view of Bona Vista (p. 238), the northernmost port for the fishery (excepting Fuego, lately settled). B.M. MSS. 31357 M.

1798—**BRENTON, J. P.**—View of St. John's (p. 374). K. cxix., 106.

1799?—**SKINNER, Col.**—Views (p. 326, 360, 381, 399). Add. 32233.

1858—**GRAY, Hon. and Rev. W.**—Sketches and views of Newfoundland and Labrador. S. H. Cowell, Ipswich. S. 204 (24).

V.—English Public Records.

The following papers in the Record Office have not yet been calendared. As they will be differently arranged when printed, no attempt has been made throughout the History to refer to them specifically. Records up to 1674 are included in Mr. George Sainsbury's Colonial Papers or in the Calendar of State Papers, &c.

Colonial Papers, No. 56.—1676 to 1684.
Colonial Entry Books, No. 65.—1623 to 1671.
Colonial Entry Books, No. 66.—1677.
America and West Indies, No. 32.—1706, Oct. 12. to 1745, Dec. 6.—Governors Crowe, Gledhill, Osbourne. Clinton, &c.
America and West Indies, No. 33.—1748, June 9, to 1752, Jan. 11.—Lieut.-Governor Hamilton, Governors Bradstreet, Drake, Rodney, &c.
America and West Indies, No. 570.—1702 to 1710.
America and West Indies, No. 571.—1711 to 1760.
Board of Trade :—
No. 3.—1696 to 1699—A. B.
No. 4.—1699 to 1703—C. D. E.
No. 5.—1703 to 1706—F. G. H.
No. 6.—1706 to 1710—I. K.
No. 7.—1710 to 1715—L.
No. 8.—1715 to 1720—M.
No. 9.—1720 to 1725—N. Governor Gledhill.
No. 10.—1725 to 1730—O.
No. 11.—1730 to 1735—O. Governor George Clinton.
No. 12.—1735 to 1740—P. Governor Edward Falkingham.
No. 13.—1739 to 1742—P. Governors Fitzroy Henry Lee, Philip Vanbrugh, Thomas Smith, John Byng.
No. 14.—1743 to 1751—Q. Governors Charles Watson, G. Brydges Rodney.
No. 15.—1751 to 1757—Q. Governors Francis W. Drake, Hugh Bonfoy, Richard Edwards.
No. 16.—1757 to 1760—R. Governor Richard Edwards.
No. 23.—1730 to 1760—Misc. papers.
No. 25.—1696 to 1701—Entry Book A.
No. 26.—1701 to 1705　 　 　" B.
No. 27.—1705 to 1708　 　 　" C.
No. 28.—1708 to 1715　 　 　" D.
No. 29.—1715 to 1719　 　 　" E.
No. 30.—1719 to 1741　 　 　" F.
No. 31.—1742 to 1760　 　 　" G.

VI.—Newfoundland Records and Newspapers.

The most interesting of the Newfoundland manuscripts are the records kept by the Admiral Governors. They contain very full details on the naval, military, legal, and diplomatic subjects of the various years. The present series begins with Governor Rodney's administration, 1749. There are traces of anterior records from Osborne's time, but all have disappeared. From 1749 the series is complete, with the exception of one or two years at the close of the 18th century. There are most complete statistics of the exports and imports of the Colony, floating and resident population, &c.

There are also incomplete records of the Surrogate Courts, particularly of Harbour Grace, Placentia, and Ferryland. Records of the Supreme Court, begun in 1791, are not complete; fire, damp, and gross neglect has made sad havoc with these invaluable papers. —Mr. J. W. Withers possesses a complete file of the Newfoundland Royal Gazette, from 1809, with the original list of subscribers. Files of all the local papers are kept in the Colonial Secretary's Office, and in the Legislative Library. They are fairly complete.

CHAPTER XXV.

STATISTICS, CLIMATE, SOIL, TIMBER, MINES, MINERALS, SPORT, AND GAME LAWS.

I.— Table of Trade, Revenue, and Expenditure from 1805 to 1860.

Year	Revenue. £	Expenditure. £	Public Debt. £	Imports. £	Exports. £	Qtls. Fish Exported. No.	Tuns of Cod and Seal Oil Exported. No.	Seal Skins Exported. No.	Ships Entered. No.	Ships Cleared. No.
1805*	—	—	—	531,700	530,450	568,922	4,590½	81,988	550	467
1810*	—	—	—	417,040	763,330	773,557	4,678½	118,080	619	660
1815*	—	—	—	659,290	1,183,809	1,245,503	7,632	125,315	852	874
1820*	—	—	—	580,040	907,000	901,159	9,280½	213,679	740	732
1822	9,174	—	—	407,752	225,198	881,476	1,529	306,982	749	748
1825	14,236	11,969	—	823,329	651,486	804,544	6,440	230,440	753	711
1826	25,614	11,753	—	802,443	732,305	863,942	9,343	232,097	851	825
1835	12,297	30,280	—	671,374	765,977	—	—	—	—	833
1836	16,187	31,082	—	622,576	850,334	800,354	9,319½	394,321	810	785
1837	30,471	36,019	—	702,205	904,705	—	—	—	851	800
1838	34,527	34,480	—	689,258	829,005	—	—	—	925	832
1839	32,640	17,472	—	710,557	901,383	724,515	8,623½	273,361	817	834
1840	41,863	42,822	—	784,045	983,361	865,377	8,906	137,501	861	834
1841	44,143	39,347	—	804,423	952,535	915,795	12,724½	631,385	1,005	952
1842	—	40,787	—	—	—	1,009,725	10,609½	417,115	904	920
1843	50,884	59,820	—	741,963	960,411	1,097,980	12,300	344,983	—	—
1844	60,253	66,379	—	770,016	882,305	833,292	12,363	651,370	1,171	1,071
1845	60,303	62,703	—	801,330	831,496	852,102	10,280	685,590	1,130	1,045
1846	76,760	78,050	—	802,247	751,103	1,000,533	8,804½	352,702	1,180	1,123
1847	49,019	74,873	—	813,499	906,565	879,085	6,703	295,469	1,219	1,222
1848	59,300	62,071	—	789,628	837,581	837,973	9,535	436,881	1,155	1,181
1849	64,405	66,362	—	770,119	926,567	920,306	10,321½	521,404	1,101	1,040
1850	82,552	71,807	106,701	867,314	975,770	1,175,167	10,307½	528,840	1,149	1,077
1851	80,395	75,770	103,718	963,191	959,771	1,089,182	10,302½	611,650	1,220	1,102
1852	85,925	90,409	111,712	795,753	965,772	1,017,132	10,882½	534,378	1,216	1,080
1853	58,857	93,066	114,820	912,605	1,170,603	972,921	11,683	521,783	1,221	1,015
1854	81,097	72,493	113,558	964,527	1,013,572	922,718	12,220½	398,870	1,074	1,050
1855	126,448	120,925	151,404	1,152,304	1,182,212	771,117	9,272	283,083	1,077	925
1856	118,831	105,845	167,257	1,271,404	1,318,797	1,107,388	8,405	361,317	1,327	963
1857	145,324	116,748	176,704	1,413,432	1,454,171	1,288,334	9,650½	496,113	1,534	1,140
1858	111,128	123,965	175,680	1,172,862	1,318,836	1,302,322	12,187½	507,024	1,440	1,314
1859	124,799	114,509	177,013	1,323,298	1,357,113	1,068,089	12,107½	329,185	1,423	1,266
1860	133,698	120,728	182,139	1,254,128	1,271,712	1,105,729½	10,579½	144,202	1,421	1,278

*For these years the returns do not furnish the value of the goods imported or exported, only the quantities of each article; so that the sterling amount for either the imports or exports is only an approximation, being based upon the prices paid and given for the various articles at the present time.

STATISTICS.

II.—Table of Trade, Revenue, and Expenditure from 1861 to 1893.

III.—A Statement of the Newfoundland Fishery in the following Years, taken from the Returns of the Admirals who commanded on that Station.

STATISTICS. 695

IV.—A Statement of the Newfoundland Fishery in the following Years.

(Table too faded and low-resolution for reliable transcription.)

V.—Recapitulation of the aforegoing Account.

Average of Years.	Number of Ships.	Burthen of Ships.	Number of Men belonging to the Ships.	Number of Passengers.	Number of Boats.	Quintals of Fish made.	Quintals of Fish carried to Market.	Tierces of Salmon carried to Market.	Tuns of Train Oil made.	Number of Inhabitants remaining in the Country during the Winter.
1699, 1700, 1701	152	7,891	1,026	—	1,314	216,320	154,370	—	1,049	3,506
1714, 1715, 1716	161	9,198	2,119	—	982	97,730	102,365	—	891	3,501
1749, 1750, 1751	288	33,512	4,108	—	1,370	432,318	422,116	—	2,532	5,855
1764, 1765, 1766, 1767, 1768, 1769, 1770, 1771, 1772, 1773, 1774	516	40,630	5,435	3,149	2,163	626,236	524,236	1,368	2,882	12,340
1784, 1785, 1786, 1787, 1788, 1789, 1790, 1791, 1792	480	48,950	4,422	4,617	2,258	637,953	622,108	2,974	2,364	13,253

Office of the Committee of Privy Council for Trade,
Whitehall, 19th March 1793.

A true copy, taken from the Admiral's returns in this office.
(Signed) GEORGE CHALMERS,
Chief Clerk Commissioners Commercial Trade.

VI.—State of the French Fishery at Newfoundland in the following Years, taken from the Returns of the British Admirals who commanded upon that Station.

Years.	Number of Ships.	Their Tonnage.	Number of Boats.	Number of Men employed in the Fishery.	Quintals of Fish taken and cured.	Oil made.
1769	131	44,727	1,155	12,367	215,030 And 470,000 of fish by tale.	3,153 hhds.
1770	437	45,541	1,170	12,855	455,340	3,511 "
1771	419	42,369	1,327	12,610	138,864	4,259 "
1772	330	37,257	1,468	15,248	388,800 And 470,000 of fish by tale.	4,687 "
1773	284	33,332	1,452	14,476	336,250	3,358 "
1774	273	31,880	1,614	15,157	386,215	3,377 "
1786	86	22,640	1,532	7,859	426,400	1,059 tuns.
1787	73	15,600	1,319	6,402	128,530	823 "
1788	89	20,130	1,560	7,433	241,262	103 "
1789	58	15,900	1,035	7,314	239,000	—
1791	43	10,417	628	5,895	40,580	120 tuns,
1792	46	9,180	689	3,397	94,000	174½ "

The average tonnage of each ship employed in this fishery for the years 1769 to 1774 was 108, and the average tonnage from 1786 to 1792 was 239 tons. The number of men in the former period—35 to every 100 tons shipping, and in the latter period, 40 to every 100 tons shipping.

Whitehall, 10th March 1793.

A true copy taken from returns of Admirals,
GEORGE CHALMERS,
Chief Clerk Commissioners Trade.

STATISTICS. 697

VII.—Returns of the Quantities of Fish caught at, and Exported from, Newfoundland.

Years ending 10th October

		1804.	1805.	1806.	1807.	1808.	1809.	1810.	1811.	1812.	1813.	1814.	1815.	1816.	1817.	1819.	1820.
Fish made		Qntls. (No return.) 706,314	Qntls. 706,314	Qntls. (No return.)	Qntls. 520,522	Qntls. 478,435	Qntls. 677,761	Qntls. 731,066	Qntls. 618,491	Qntls. 708,103	Qntls. 816,000	Qntls. 865,132	Qntls. 866,550	Qntls. 819,290	Qutls.	Qntls.	Qntls.
Cod fish exported, and where.	Spain, Portugal, and Italy	354,466	377,223	438,919	262,368	154,030	325,781	No particulars returned.	611,920	515,451	706,939	768,010	952,115	812,145	713,238	648,979	618,481
	British Europe	189,320	65,959	84,241	130,160	208,254	292,068		139,561	67,020	50,678	55,791	46,180	49,109	70,774	44,593	90,295
	West Indies	55,498	81,188	100,936	103,418	115,677	133,359		122,154	97,867	119,314	97,249	158,250	175,003	149,927	127,995	140,672
	British America	18,167	22,776	32,555	23,541	40,874	41,884		18,621	4,121	11,389	24,712	28,750	43,548	20,206	3,680	21,711
	United States	43,131	77,993	116,159	154,085	56,658	16,117		1,214					3,017	2,848		
	Brazils									2,600							
Total of cod fish exported		661,277	625,519	772,869	674,810	576,152	810,219	884,474	923,540	711,059	891,320	917,762	1,086,296	1,046,626	956,094	825,197	901,159
Salmon exported.	British markets	Tierces. —	Tierces. 680	Tierces. —	Tierces. 2,303	Tierces. —	Tierces. 3,337	Tierces. —	Tierces. 2,323	Tierces. 3,444	Tierces. 2,910	Tierces. 2,247	Tierces. —	Tierces. —	Tierces. —	Tierces. —	Tierces. —
	Foreign markets	—	1,307	—	1,166	—	727	—	371	337	827	1,178	—	—	—	—	—
	Total of salmon exported	3,739	1,916	2,040	3,469	3,272	4,064	5,717	2,694	3,831	3,737	3,425	—	2,659	2,858	2,125	1,773

At Labrador, 27,000.

VIII.—Duties imposed on British Fish imported into Spain during the under-mentioned Years.

	Real.	Per Hard Dollar.
1792	21 per quintal, at 4s. exchange is equal to 4s. 2d. ⅓ per Castilian quintal or 4s. 7d. ½ per English cwt.
1802	43	8s. 6d. ⅓	9s. 6d. ½
1808	16½	3s. 3d.	3s. 8d.
1814	46	9s. 3d.	10s. 2d.
1816	47, 31 mrs.	9s. 7d.	10s. 6d. ½

IX.—Population, &c.

The figures given in these early annals about population, fishery statistics, &c. are vague and very incorrect.

In 1654 the resident population is set down at 350 families distributed over 15 small settlements between Cape Race and Cape Bonavista. In the Parliamentary Paper of 1713, the figures are:—

	1675	1676	1677
Planters	140	138	152
Servants	1,250	943	1,355
Boats	277	263	287

The usual number allowed to a boat in these statistics is five men.

This will give in 1675 — 1,385 men
                  1676 — 1,630 ,,
                  1677 — 1,385 ,,

In computing it is necessary to take account of the families, which average quite five, and nearly every family had at least one woman servant. This would make the households for each year as follows:—

	1675	1676	1677
Households	840	828	912
Servants	1,385	1,630	1,385
Total	2,225	2,458	2,797

In 1680 the resident population is put down at 2,280, and in 1698 at 2,640.

1684 — 270 vessels; 21,300 tons; 16,800 seamen; boats, 2,160 with five men; average catch 250 to 300 qtls. each.

	1675	1676	1677
Fishing ships	105	126	100
Seamen	3,275	1,556	1,475
Boats	677	804	822
Planters	140	138	152
Men servants	1,250	943	1,355
Boats	277	263	287

	1682	1684
Fishing ships	52	65
Seamen	1,642	1,489
Boats	183	224
Inhabitants' boats	250	504

X.—Population in 1697.

The fishermen purposely underrated the population. Many families of English were residing amongst the French in Placentia, St. Lawrence, Trepassey, Fortune Bay, &c.; many had migrated north of Cape Bonavista. No early returns of population are therefore satisfactory. In 1696-1697 we have an estimate of the population made from actual survey, and in the winter, by a foreigner, Abbé Baudoin.

Census of Population, &c. of Newfoundland from Père Baudoin's Journal, 1697.

Names of Places.	Men	Fishing Establishments	Number of Boats	Quintals of Fish Caught
Renews	120	7	8	4,000
Fermeuse	40	7	8	4,000
Ferryland	108	12	16	8,000
Capelin Bay	12	2	2	1,000
Cape Broyle	5	1	1	500
Brigus by South	15	3	3	1,700
Caplinbay probably, Tom's Cove	30	3	5	2,500
Witless Bay	15	2	3	1,700
Bay Bulls	120	13	20	10,000
Aquaforte	25	4	5	2,500
St. John's	300	50	125	6,270
Petty Harbour	60	14	16	8,000
Quidi Vidi	40	5	5	4,500
Torbay	18	3	4	2,500
Portugal Cove	25	3	3	2,100
Foxtrap	13	6	7	4,500
Harbour Main	12	1	2	1,000
Brigus	70	11	12	6,000
Cupids	11	2	2	1,000
Port de Grave	136	14	20	10,000
Fayline Cove	18	3	3	1,700
Bay Roberts	10	3	3	1,700
Brim's Cove	30	4	6	3,000
Harbour Grace	100	14	15	7,500
Musquito	35	4	5	2,500
Carbonear	220	22	36	12,000
Crocker's Cove	10	4	5	2,500
Kelm Cove	22	3	3	2,000
Freshwater	20	2	4	2,000
Old Pelican	130	18	27	15,000
Bay de Verds	85	14	16	10,000
Hants Harbour	20	4	5	3,000
Scilly Cove	40	4	7	4,500
New Perlican	60	9	11	6,000
Hearts Ease	12	1	2	1,000
Hearts Content	20	4	4	2,500
Trinity	24	2	4	2,000
Bonavista	300	10	20	5,000
Total	1,581	195	246	160,000

To this must be added settlements not named—Fogo, Twillingate, and other scattered population in the northern part of the Island. About 150 — 30 — 15 — 4,000

STATISTICS.

XI.—A List of Inhabitants and their Concerns from Trepassey to ye Cape Bonavista in 1677.

	House-Keepers	Wives	Sons	Daughters	Men Servants	Women Servants	Dwelling Houses	Store Houses	Lodging for Men	Boates	Stages	Train Fats	Rooms	Horses	Cattle	Sheep	Hoggs	Gardens	Knits. fish per Boat
Trepassey	4	2	4	9	34		4	7		11	3	2	11		4	3	12		780
Renoze	6	3	4	2	39		6	10	5	13	6	4	13		14	7	35		1,160
Fermoze	2	5	2	1	14		7	6	9	11	7	4	10		22		33		1,100
Ferryland	7	3	5	5	108	3	8	15	24	27	9	5	27	4	15		63	6	1,240
Caplin Bay	1	1	3	4	20		1	4	2	5	3	1	5				20	28	200
Bereekus	3	3	4	2	33		3	4	1	7	3	2	7				13		480
Balene	2	2	3	1	19		3	4		5	3	3	5						350
Toad Cove	1	1	2	3	12		3	4		4	1	1	4				7	12	160
Whitleys Bay	3	3	2	2	19		3	4		6	5	3	6		16	5	32	4	510
Bay of Bulls	6	6	8	16	57		6	20		15	5	5	13			9	50	9	660
Petty Harbour	2	2	1	2	44		7	7		10	5	4	10		112	11	59	1	1,020
St. John's Harbour	27	15	18	27	139	3	27	30		13	29	18-5	46	8	112	29	184	28	
Tarr Bay		2	4	6	2		3	6		2	3		2		6		21		350
Carboneer	11	9	15	20	107		14	12		25	11	10	25		79	22	48	12	2,136
Musketta	2	2	4	2	22		2	4		5	3	4	5		38	2	20	4	410
Harbour Grace	10	2	7	6	35		7	8		11	9	3	11		38		27	9	1,800
Bay of Roberts	2	2	2	2	19		2	2		6	2	2	6		34	22	13	1	400
Brian's Cove	1	1	2	1	12		1	2		4	1	1	4						330
Port Grave	4	2	2	2	49		5	10		10	4	4	10		34	18	33	4	880
Bergues	3	1	3	3	14		2	6		4	3	1	4		12		11	2	580
Harbr. Main	1	1	3	3	26		3	3		5	1	1	5			1	14	3	200
Bay of Vardis	8	4	9	8	100		8	13		20	9	8	20				36	11	1,700
Old Parlican	13	9	15	2	167		16	18		35	14	12	35		22	3	29	12	2,820
Silly Cove	3	2	5	8	33		4	4		5	3	4	8		11			4	780
New Parlican	2	2	2	3	11		2	10		3	2	2	3				13	2	380
Bonaventura	3	1	1	2	27		3	8		7	3	2	7		9		16	3	610
Salmon Cove		1	1	2	9		1	1		2	1	1	2						140
Bonavista	16	13	21	13	96		18	19		28	18	11	28	8	8	28	51	13	3,040
Total	162	94	137	130	1,327	13	167	363	42	334	163½	121¼·7*	334	12	480	131	843	114	24,360

Total of Inhabitants, 1833. *Casks.

STATISTICS.

XII.—A List of Inhabitants in the District of St. John's, Newfoundland, residing the Winter of 1794.

Families. No.	Where situate.	Boundaries.	Men.	Women.	Children. Males.	Children. Females.	Servants. Males.	Servants. Females.	Dieters. In Family.	Dieters. On own Account.	Protestants.	Catholics.	Total.
43	1st Division St. John's	From River Head to Roper Cove.	41	21	37	22	43	4	13	39	43	177	220
81	2nd "	From River Head to Nobles Cove.	69	54	70	63	33	15	8	10	177	205	382
139	3rd "	From Nobles Cove to Engine House.	130	90	122	111	147	34	58	24	154	552	706
198	4th "	From Engine House to King's Beach.	178	142	174	140	229	53	123	—	356	682	1,038
92	5th "	From King's Beach to Old Garrison.	82	71	91	97	60	13	51	13	141	327	468
39	6th "	From Old Garrison to Chain Rock.	29	19	22	26	21	7	6	16	55	121	176
41	Quiddy Viddy		38	19	33	16	24	6	—	29	59	106	165
20	South side of St. John's		6	5	9	13	56	—	—	—	44	45	89
			563	427	548	488	702	132	259	179	1,029	2,215	3,244
53	Petty Harbour		50	28	46	49	23	4	32	23	133	122	255
49	Torbay		48	28	45	34	14	3	15	20	108	99	207
34	Portugal Cove		33	27	75	52	11	2	—	—	165	35	200
13	Bell Isle		11	11	28	21	8	5	1	5	54	33	87
901			705	515	742	644	758	143	307	179	1,489	2,504	3,993

XIII.—Population of St. John's and District, 1815.

A RETURN of the NUMBER of WINTER INHABITANTS residing within the Town and District of St. John's, Newfoundland, in February and March 1815, taken by order of the Magistrates, by Lionel Chancey, Clerk of the Peace.

	Heads of Families.		Children.		Servants.		Boarders.		Religion.		Total.
	Male.	Female.	Male.	Female.	Men.	Women.	Men.	Women.	Protestant.	Roman Catholic.	
District of St. John's:—											
No. 1. River Head to Pye Corner	135	118	13	137	137	18	352	8	198	66	1,064
" 2. From Pye Corner to Burst Heart Hill Cove.	195	190	207	242	208	57	417	31	424	1,153	1,577
" 3. Burst Heart Hill Cove to Church Hill.	195	190	243	207	371	61	478	38	154	1,592	1,746
" 4. Church Hill to Hudson Cove (Hunter's Cove, now Job's Cove).	142	139	191	173	216	54	211	30	406	750	1,156
" 5. Hudson Cove (John's Cove) to the King's Wharf.	216	213	254	219	187	62	438	40	353	1,276	1,629
" 6. King's Wharf to Fort William.	148	138	167	177	117	32	255	29	257	806	1,063
" 7. Fort William to the eastern part of St. John's.	96	90	113	115	65	13	80	16	253	344	97
" 8. Quidi Vidi and north of the Pond.	145	125	164	174	178	14	190	9	323	663	989
" 9. South side of St. John's	24	11	23	12	74	—	45	3	118	79	197
	1,296	1,214	1,476	1,456	1,603	311	2,465	197	2,486	7,532	10,018
Torbay	98	70	124	90	79	13	72	7	181	375	556
Portugal Cove	98	81	114	112	58	20	12	6	360	140	500
Belle Isle	58	37	59	41	50	5	30	—	74	209	280
Petty Harbour	66	50	101	100	79	2	37	5	195	248	440
Pouch Cove	14	11	17	10	16	5	3	1	47	30	77
	1,622	1,463	1,891	1,809	1,888	356	2,629	216	3,313	8,531	11,874

STATISTICS.

XIV.—Population.

Year	Population	Year			Population
1804	20,380	1857 (Labrador included)			124,288
1825	55,719	1869 (do. do.)			146,536
1827	59,571	1874 (do. do.)			161,374
1832	60,000	1884 (do. do.)			197,589
1836	75,094	1891 (do. do.)			202,040
1845	98,703				

XV.—Denominational.

	Church of England.	Church of Rome.	Methodists.	Presbyterians.	Congregational.	Baptists, &c.	Salvation Army.	Moravians.	Reformed Church of England.
1845	34,294	46,983	14,239	478	539	44	—	—	—
1857	44,285	57,214	20,229	838	317	10	—	—	—
1869	55,184	61,040	28,990	974	338	165	—	—	—
1874	59,561	64,317	35,702	1,168	461	165	—	—	—
1884	69,646	75,330	48,943	1,478	768	65	—	—	—
1891	69,824	72,696	53,276	1,449	782	37	2,092	1,397	487

XVI.—Census of 1891.

District.	Total.	Church of England.	Church of Rome.	Methodists.	Presbyterians.	Other Denominations.	Chief Town.	Population.
St. Barbe	6,690	3,362	1,784	1,027	14	3	Bonne Bay	1,112
Twillingate	16,780	3,916	2,449	9,661	58	696	Twillingate	3,585
Fogo	6,700	2,829	1,174	2,692	4	1	Fogo	1,020
Bonavista	17,849	8,550	3,069	6,045	14	171	Bonavista	3,551
Trinity	18,872	9,947	1,613	6,888	11	413	Trinity	1,401
Bay de Verde	9,708	503	2,135	7,062	—	5	Western Bay	1,043
Carbonear	5,765	1,011	1,896	2,734	10	114	Carbonear	4,127
Harbour Grace	13,881	8,033	5,494	1,964	157	233	Harbour Grace	6,095
Port-de-Grave	7,986	2,969	1,990	2,722	1	273	Brigus	1,541
Harbour Main	9,189	2,157	6,813	248	—	—	Harbour Main	841
St. John's, East	20,776	5,376	11,644	2,767	652	337	St. John's	29,007
" West	15,251	3,174	9,112	2,368	378	219		
Ferryland	5,853	160	5,673	5	5	1	Ferryland	549
Placentia	12,801	1,643	10,614	527	13	5	Great Placentia	1,303
Burin	9,059	1,797	2,930	3,845	2	485	Burin	2,729
Fortune	7,671	5,292	1,817	120	4	438	Harbour Briton	748
Burges and La Poile.	6,471	5,162	138	1,166	4	1	Channel	1,024
St. George	6,632	2,252	3,965	261	121	3	St. George	1,112
Labrador	4,106	1,749	354	604	2	1,397	Battle Harbour	281
		69,824	72,696	53,276	1,449	4,795		

XVII.—Sexes, 1891.

Males		100,084
Females		97,259

	Males.	Females.
65–70 years of age	1,536	1,486
70–75 "	1,062	983
75–80 "	608	587
80 and upwards	376	468

XVIII.—Occupations.

Merchants and traders	767
Clerks and shop assistants	1,948
Mechanics	2,681
Factory operatives	1,058
Lumberers and miners	1,923
Fishermen	53,502
Farmers	1,545
Clergymen	180
Teachers	601
Lawyers	43
Doctors	62
Government officials	608

XIX.—Nationality, &c., 1891.

Natives	193,550
British	3,049
Colonies	1,163
Other countries	369
Deaf	159
Deaf and dumb	136
Blind	187
Crippled and disabled paupers	2,485
Lunatics	280
Orphans	690

XX.—Agriculture in 1891.

Acres, improved land		64,494
" in pasture		20,524
Wheat and barley	bushels	491
Oats		12,900
Hay	tons	36,632
Potatoes	barrels	481,024
Turnips	"	60,235
Horses		6,138
Milch cows		10,863
Other horned cattle		12,959
Sheep		60,840
Swine		32,011
Fowl		127,420

XXI.—Factories, Mills, &c., in 1891.

Number of saw mills	53
" tanneries	3
" breweries and distilleries	2
" iron foundries	2
" bakeries	4
" furniture factories	4
" other factories	24
Value of above factories	$893,860
" goods produced	$1,450,456
Number of employees	1,299
Number of lobster factories	349
" employees	4,807
Value of lobster factories	$179,288
Number of cases exported, 1890	77,580

XXII.—Statistics of the Seal Fishery.

(a.) 1804.

WINTER.

District.	Men employed.	Seals taken.	Value.	Tuns of Oil made.
Fogo	Uncertain.	21,120	—	264
Bonavista and Greenspond	370	11,500	—	169
Trinity	46	1,345	—	19
Total	416	33,965	—	452

SPRING.

District.	Vessels.	Tons.	Men employed.	Seals taken.	Price.	Tuns of Oil made.
St. John's	35	1,589	430	17,000	5s. 6d. to 12s.	220
Fogo	11	400	108	1,330	6s. to 11s.	16
Greenspond	6	180	70	2,000	—	25
Bonavista	12	407	130	3,583	5s. 6d. to 11s.	77
Trinity	14	628	152	6,093	5s. 6d. to 12s.	85
Conception Bay	*43 / †25	2,479	729	40,704	8s. ‡	540
Ferryland	3	100	30	1,114	7s. 9d. to 11s.	16
Total	149	5,783	1,639	72,774	—	949

* Schooners. † Shallops. ‡ Average.

(b.) 1834.

Ports.	Vessels.	Tons.	Men.
St. John's	125	11,020	2,910
Conception Bay	218	17,785	4,894
Other Ports of the Colony	31	2,511	682
Total	374	31,316	8,486

(c.) 1844.

Ports.	Vessels.	Tons.	Men.
St. John's	121	14,088	3,775
Conception Bay	173	16,031	5,065
Other Ports of the Colony	64	1,755	1,687
Total	358	31,874	10,527

(d.) 1847.

	Vessels.	Tons.	Men.
St. John's and Southward	95	9,355	3,245
Harbour Grace	49	4,957	1,407
Mosquito Bay	1	72	28
Spaniards and Bay Roberts	4	354	141
Carbonear	37	3,054	996
Brigus, Cupids, Port de Grave, &c.	96	5,956	1,963
Trinity and Catalina	12	3,901	1,361
New Perlican and Hants Harbour	27	2,159	740
Greenspond, &c.	13	854	334
Harbour Briton	2	204	73
La Poile	1	47	19
Total	337	30,899	10,365

(e.) 1853.

	Vessels.	Tons.	Men.
St. John's	101	11,264	3,967
Conception Bay	184	19,235	6,964
Other Ports of the Colony	107	10,464	4,000
Total	392	40,963	14,931

(f.) 1867.

Ports.	Vessels Steam.	Vessels Sail.	Tons.	Men.
St. John's	6	—	1,493	685
Do.	—	19	2,058	868
Conception Bay	2	—	437	229
Do.	—	105	13,347	5,653
Other Ports of the Colony	2	—	532	—
Do.	—	42	3,558	2,042
Total	10	166	21,415	9,468

STATISTICS.

STATISTICS.

(k.) FERRYLAND—continued.

Years.	Vessels.	Tons.	Men.	Seals taken.	Tuns of Oil made.
1808	4	159	56	3,500	33*
1813	2	52	29	1,500	—
1814	4	206	57	1,654	—
1815	—	—	—	1,700	—
1818	—	—	—	90	—
1819	1	48	12	950	9
1820	—	—	—	1,230	—
1821	—	—	—	1,250	16
1822	3	82	36	1,887	19
1823	3	143	47	620	—

* Fell in with ice and seals off St. Francis.

(l.) BONAVISTA AND GREENSPOND.
[W.=Winter; S.=Spring.]

Years.	Vessels.	Tons.	Men.	Seals taken.	Tuns of Oil made.
1804 W.	18	587	370	11,500	169
S.			190	5,583	102
1805 W.	—	—	252	4,222	126
S.	13	465	139†	5,378	68
1808 W.	—	—	210	2,000†	38
S.	17	371	107	16,790	107
1813 W.				7,711	121
S.	3	118	35	615	7
1814 W.	—	—	150	4,547	67
1815 W.	—	—	—	20,108	—
1817 W.	—	—	106	1,399	29
1818 W.	—	—	—	17,714	155
S.	4	58	—	3,488	41
1819 W.	—	—	—	14,878	153
S.	4	212	69	4,013	45
1820 S.	—	—	—	7,503	—
1821 W.	—	—	—	2,448	42
S.	6	—	97	7,738	83
1822 W.	—	—	—	17,776	388
S.	5	301	72	9,427	160

* 60 more in skiffs. † Taken in nets.

(m.) FOGO AND LABRADOR.
[W.=Winter; S.=Spring.]

Years.	Vessels.	Tons.	Men.	Seals taken.	Tuns of Oil made.
1804 W.	—	—	—	8,424	128
S.	5	210	19	1,576	17
1808 W.	—	—	6	490	16
S.	3	126	32	950	9
1815 W.	—	—	—	1,400	—
1819 W.	—	—	—	1,200	30
1820 S.	—	—	—	27,989*	—

* Fogo very few.

(n.) ST. JOHN'S.—1852.

Vessels marked * sailed from outports.

SUPPLIED BY BROOKING & SON.

Vessels.	Masters.	Tons.	Men.
*Packet	Rockwood	84	34
Helen Stares	Sheehan	129	43

STABB, ROW, & HOLMWOOD.

Vessels.	Masters.	Tons.	Men.
*Charles	Benson	101	40
Lady Young	Geran	121	44
Swift	Geran	65	30
Mary	King	72	33
Pursuit	Knight	135	50

McBRIDE & KERR.

Vessels.	Masters.	Tons.	Men.
*John & Maria	Benson	76	35
*Elizabeth	Benson	81	35
Scottish Lass	Neil	143	45
Anna	Hally	163	50
Gannet	Cahill	51	21
Avalon	Byrne	45	21

W. & H. THOMAS & CO.

Vessels.	Masters.	Tons.	Men.
*Two Brothers	Hopkins	111	40
Caledonia	Houlahan, Jr.	114	42
Coquette	Houlahan, Sr.	154	56
Gem	Ebsary	78	27

BAINE, JOHNSTON, & CO.

Vessels.	Masters.	Tons.	Men.
Sea Nymph	Pike	187	66
Swift	Woodford	107	45
Triton	Keefe	94	40
Rover	Aylward	88	40
M. A. Fleming	Kearney	154	50
Johanna	Goss	47	25
Spartan	Cullen	57	30
Eagle	Pike	55	26
Hero	Pike	106	40

BROCKLEBANK & ANTHONY.

Vessels.	Masters.	Tons.	Men.
*Prosperity	Brien	84	36
Hecla	Martin	121	44
Creole	Staunton	140	48

W. BODEN & CO.

Vessels.	Masters.	Tons.	Men.
Telegraph	Sheehan	135	45
Piscator	Lacey	129	45

R. ALSOP & CO.

Vessels.	Masters.	Tons.	Men.
Empress	Kennedy	136	44
Ajax	Carew	126	45
Friends	Duff	90	34
Dolphin	Goss	79	32
Margaret	Mealey	103	35
Brothers	Ryan	70	32
E. M. Dodd	Nurse	67	30
*Harmony	Brien	85	33
*Active	Brien	76	30

L. O'BRIEN & CO.

Vessels.	Masters.	Tons.	Men.
Kingaloch	Burke	143	45
Normal	Lynch	114	40
St. Margaret	Fitzgerald	98	40
Shamrock	French	143	45
Western Trader	Power	114	43

J. & W. STEWART.

Vessels.	Masters.	Tons.	Men.
Kirtland	Lynch	160	42
Chedabucto	Cole	83	35
Resolution	Phoran	122	46

JOB BROTHERS & CO.

Vessels.	Masters.	Tons.	Men.
Sarah	White	125	50
Delmont	Ashman	122	50
Margaret	Cummins	164	60

T. HALERN.

Vessels.	Masters.	Tons.	Men.
Emily Tobin	Halern	85	32

HUNTERS & CO.

Vessels.	Masters.	Tons.	Men.
Ellen	Hally	94	35
Escape	Cummins	116	44
Howard Primrose	Walsh	90	35

MUDGE & CO.

Vessels.	Masters.	Tons.	Men.
William	Withycombe	116	40
Cora	Jackman	126	43

M. O'DWYER.

Vessels.	Masters.	Tons.	Men.
Clipper	Gearin	132	45
Lovely Mary	Silvey	135	43
Elizabeth	Silvey	117	40

WILSON & MEYNELL.

Vessels.	Masters.	Tons.	Men.
Panda	Mountain	75	32

E. & N. STABB.

Vessels.	Masters.	Tons.	Men.
Maria Grace	Morry	139	50
Favorite Lass	Rhodes	117	46
Sisters	Chafe	79	39
Georgina	Butler	107	38

STATISTICS.

J. B. Barnes & Co.

Vessels.	Masters.	Tons.	Men.
Iris	Knight	143	48
Hunter	Davis	113	36

D. Steele.

Champion	Mullowney	115	48
Ann Catherine	Kough	64	19
Munroe.			
Dartford	Jackman	70	34
Queen Victoria	Mullowney	35	19

P. Rogerson & Son.

Glenara	Graham	126	45
Bridgewater	Knight	106	38

P. Brennan.

Mary	O'Connor	70	35

Wm. M. Blake.

Christiana	Houlahan	98	38

Hounsell, Schenk, & Hounsell.

Vesta	Bursell	114	44
Orestes	Ryan	154	45
Sea Flower	French	121	45
Juno	Prior	100	40
George	Linnegar	82	35
Ann	McLoughlan	95	30
Billow	Comerford	60	31

C. F. Bennett.

Superior	Furneaux	122	41
Active	Pike	54	25

M'Kay & M'Kenzie.

Clara	Power	174	69
Tweed	Shea	94	36

Bowring Brothers.

Lena	Feehan	147	48
Regina	Foster	137	45
Helen	Noseworthy	70	30

J. H. Warren.

Warrior	Chafe	130	45

J. Barron.

Dash	Callahan	160	52
Nisibis	Cody	151	42
Acorn	Walsh	80	35
Isabella	Costello	76	30
James	Barrington	43	16

Clift, Wood, & Co.

Morning Star	Wood	40	18

J. Cusack & Sons.

Star	Reddy	118	40

97 Vessels.   10,236   3,862

(o.) ST. JOHN'S.—1855.

Supplied by Brooking, Son & Co.

Vessels.	Masters.	Tons.	Men.
*Packet	Rockwood	82	35

W. & H. Thomas.

*Apollo	Hopkins	133	
*Native	Hopkins	87	3
Caledonia	Houlahan	104	

Bulley, Mitchell.

*Avalon	Andrews	48	20

Hounsell & Co.

*Seaflower	Perry	123	45
Wyoming	Kelly	127	37
Juno	Prior	10	38
George	Stark	80	30

Brocklebank & Anthony.

*Prosperity	Brien	54	35
Active	Brien	76	34
Harmony	Brien	85	35

Baine, Johnston, & Co.

Vessels.	Masters.	Tons.	Men.
Guitar	Joy	129	48
Maggie	Goose	93	45
Heather	Goss	150	50
Swift	Woodford	109	45
Triton	Silvey	94	38
Rover	Hennbury	88	36

Job Brothers & Co.

Margaret	Cummins	164	51
Evanthes	White	147	55
Sarah	Brien	124	50

Hogsett.

Howard Primrose	French	91	35

L. O'Brien & Co.

Kingsloch	Butler	143	50
Helen	Colbert	100	40
Shamrock	French	143	50
Iris	Keefe	117	45
Nancy	Moore	78	30

P. Rogerson & Son.

Jessie	Graham	151	55
Francis Patrick	Howley	114	46

Barron, Fraser, & Co.

Swift	Coady	105	42
Nimrod	Barrington	100	40
James	Mulloy	40	22

Bowring Brothers.

Ann	Lynch	116	40
Fanny Bloomer	Silvey	142	45
Roxana	Jackman	134	48
Mary	Lacy	76	35
Lena	Feehan	147	50
Swallow	Glindon	124	48

McBride & Kerr.

Scottish Lass	Sheehan	142	45
Hope	Scott	63	25
Gannett	Cahill	51	19

Goodridge & Kelligrew.

Lioness	Jackman	93	30

Hunter & Co.

St. Fillan	Mullowney	160	50
Escape	Cummins	116	50
Jasper	Haily	60	30

R. Alsop & Co.

Dolphin	Hinds	79	33
Margaret	Mealey	165	35
Brothers	Ryan	70	32
Friends	Neale	90	30
Dove	Ryan	98	41
John and Maria	Carew	76	34

Stabb, Row, & Co.

Emily Tobin	Scanlan	85	32
Charles	Gearan	102	37
Mary	King	72	31
Panda	King	76	29
Pursuit	Knight	136	45

P. & L. Tessier.

Cadmus	Shea	101	35
Free Trade	Cottar	61	23
E. M. Dodd	Nurse	77	26
Helen Stares	Chafe	129	46
United Brothers	Scott	75	35
Spartan	Beddy	64	23

Mudge & Co.

Gazelle	Kennedy	102	40
Cora	Jackman	102	41

Ewen Stabb.

Three Sisters	Rhodes	165	45
Sisters	Chafe	79	37
Margaret	Hickey	60	27
Favourite Lass	Bursell	132	45

L. Macassey.

Juno	Bolan	112	40

J. & W. Stewart.

Kirtland	Lynch	160	46
Chedabucto	Cole	83	35

STATISTICS.

W. W. LE MESSURIER.

Vessels.	Masters.	Tons.	Men.
Gold	Hally	104	40
Britannia	Morey	66	30

73 Vessels.   7,484   2,813

(p.) ST. JOHN'S.—1861.

SUPPLIED BY BAINE, JOHNSTON, & CO.

Vessels.	Masters.	Tons.	Men.
Zambesi	Gosse	199	85
Quango	Keefe, Jr.	194	85
Maggie McNeil	Connors	173	75
Noel	Martin	135	65
Balaclava	Keefe	118	75
Guitar	Duff	113	70
Maggie	Gosse	93	55

BOWRING BROTHERS.

Contest	Breen	228	65
G. M. Johnson	Lynch	177	55
Wm. Stairs	Walsh	143	55
Roxana	Jackman	134	54
Rainbow	Woodford	127	56
Fanny Bloomer	Silvey	136	55
Emma	Roberts	89	30

STABB, ROW, & HOLMWOOD.

Livingstone	Halern	174	66
Arthur Leary	Galshue	174	66
Leader	Gearan	153	55
Prima Donna	Delaney	125	50
Sarah Grace	Silvey	125	54
Scottish Chief	Wade	96	36

McBRIDE & KERR.

Triumph	Feehan	208	70
Sonora	Glindon	208	70
Rover's Bride	Rhodes	154	60
Afton	Foster	131	50
Jenny Lind	Power	48	24

THOMAS & DICKINSON.

Henry Thomas	Houlahan	198	69
St. Fillan	Aule	147	59
Dash	Snook	100	40
Sweet Home	Taylor	81	40

BROOKING, SON, & CO.

Peerless	Andrews	144	50
George William	Sheehan	120	42
*Hope	Rockwood	114	54
Rosalie	Sheehan	80	30

J. & W. STEWART.

Dumbarton	Cole	178	60
Flora	Callahan	141	53
Hunter	Pike	136	55
*James Henry	Bryant	106	50

R. ALSOP & CO.

Isabella	Ryan	140	55
Seamew	Moore	135	57
Jane	Gosse	104	45
Friends	Walsh	90	30

J. KAVANAGH.

Christian	Malone	197	60
Tiger	Lynch	171	60
Dolphin	Malone	74	40

P. ROGERSON & SON.

Dove	Percey	145	55
Jessie	Percey	142	57
Orion	Knight	110	45

CLIFT, WOOD, & CO.

Naiad	Colbert	153	60
Comet	Flinn	148	65
Dash	Ainsworth	111	40

GOODRIDGE & KELLIGREW.

Reindeer	McCarthy	147	50
Maggie	Jackman	145	50
Lioness	Bradshaw	93	30

J. M'LAUGHLIN.

Eleanor J. Davis	M'Laughlin	175	55
Wyoming	M'Laughlin	118	48

JOB BROTHERS & CO.

Vessels.	Masters.	Tons.	Men.
Margaret	Cummins	149	53
Sophia	Brien	131	57

L. O'BRIEN.

Arrow	French	169	60
Hollyhock	Houlahan	152	55

P. & L. TESSIER.

Margaret	Mackay	130	45
Mary Bell	Day	124	55

E. WHITE.

Evanthes	White	134	55
Sarah	Hudson	104	45

H. W. BARRON.

Swift	Callahan	105	45
Celt	Joy	79	39

M. WOODFORD.

*Stirling Clipper	Woodford	112	48

A. GRAHAM.

Glance	Graham	142	50

K. McLEA & SONS.

Nightingale	Mullowney	136	56

STEPHEN MARCH.

Corsair	March	130	60

MUDGE & CO.

Gazelle	Kennedy	93	40

A. GOODRIDGE & SONS.

Mary	Goodridge	118	50

P. BRENNAN.

Maid of Erin	Duff	159	50

W. HOUNSELL & CO.

Juno	Prior	100	

73 Vessels.   9,729   3,836

(q.) ST. JOHN'S.—1881.

SUPPLIED BY W. STEPHEN & CO.

Vessels.	Masters.	Tons.	Men.
Arctic s.s.	Walsh	522	310
Thetis s.s.	Dawe	492	325
Aurora s.s.	Fairweather	386	295

D. S. & W. FISHING CO.

Esquimaux s.s.	Blandford	456	295
Resolute s.s.	Jackman	424	275
Narwhal s.s.	Dawe	362	270

JOB BROTHERS & CO.

Neptune s.s.	White	468	329
Hector s.s.	White	299	220

J. & W. STEWART.

Proteus s.s.	Pike	467	226
Ranger s.s.	Delaney	353	222

W. GRIEVE & CO.

Wolf s.s.	Smith	353	237

BAINE, JOHNSTON, & CO.

Panther s.s.	Bartlett	246	165

M. TOBIN.

Oban	Ashburn	129	69

P. & L. TESSIER.

New Havelock	St. John	112	65

ALAN GOODRIDGE & SONS.

New Mary	Sullivan	50	25

15 Vessels.   5,107   3,294

Full details about the sealing steamers will be found in Mr. Chafe's book on the subject.

STATISTICS.

(r.) HARBOUR GRACE.—1861.
SUPPLIED BY PUNTON & MUNN.

Vessels.	Masters.	Tons.	Men.
Caroline	Avery	159	64
Islay	Brine	143	56
Iona	Hanrahan	151	66
Dash	Smart	156	60
Curlew	O'Neill	163	60
Gem	Green	168	60
Jura	Snelgrove	127	58
Alfrida	Pike	128	45
Eclipse	Stoyles	146	55
Union	Parsons	105	50
Thrasher	Strapp	141	55
United Brothers	Fitzgerald	126	45
Maria	Keefe	131	42
Elizabeth Margaret	Power	108	50
Emily	Hennessey	112	42
Mary	Newell	107	50
Penguin	Parsons	106	42
Shannon	Bray	102	35
Jane & Mary	Parsons	101	40
*Estelle	Henneberry	176	60
*True Friend	Antle	169	55
*Glencoe	G. Taylor	133	50
*Superb	Sol. Taylor	109	48
*Bride	Rob. Taylor	134	50
*Emily Tobin	Brown	90	30

RIDLEY & SONS.

Jane	Scully	131	49
Isabella Ridley	Thomey	154	65
Linda	Benson	121	46
Elizabeth & William	Stephenson	134	44
Union	Pike	135	50
Wave	Pike	110	50
William	Costello	93	50
Rosina	Alcock	125	56
Glide	Pumphrey	128	50
Argo	Fitzgerald	114	46
Avalon	Cleary	134	55
Elizabeth Jane	Ryan	131	50
Lord Clyde	Pumphrey	134	55
Alabama	Heater	104	45
Prince Edward	Hamilton	140	56
Terra Nova	Pike	120	50
Harriet Ridley	Joyce	134	52
*Medora	Murphy	139	50
*Adamant	Murphy	128	50
*True Blue	Hopkins	152	50
*Mary	—	77	50
*Melrose	Pike	152	50
*Rob Arthur	Roberts	129	40

W. DONNELLY & CO.

Chanticleer	Stapleton	137	50
Ticino	Farrel	130	48
Hecla	Davis	117	46
Roe	Thompson	106	41

RUTHERFORD BROS.

Commissary	Noel	143	60
Sir J. G. Le Marchant	Vise	118	50
Brothers	Noel	101	45

M. PARSONS.

Christiana	Davis	142	45

D. GREEN.

Laurel	Green	154	63

(s.) HARBOUR GRACE.—1881.
SUPPLIED BY J. MUNN & CO.

Vessels.	Masters.	Tons.	Men.
Confederate	Greene	171	95
Isabella Ridley	Thomey	154	90
Rescue	Fitzgerald	147	75
Sisters	Sheppard	113	70
Consort	Parsons	96	60
Sneezer	Hennessey	128	65
Matilda	Hanrahan	111	50
Creole	Pike	140	66
Commodore	H. Thomey	290	220
Mastiff	Gosse	245	180
Iceland	Wilcox	259	200
		1884	1175

BRIGUS.—1847.

Vessels.	Masters.	Tons.	Men.
Mary	Wilcox	74	28
Lady Ann	French	82	30
Isle of Skye	Heddison	59	20
Isaac and Elizabeth	Richards	100	30
Jane Dalrymple	Delaney	106	40
Billow	Fitzgerald	114	40
Express	Whelan	103	37
Glenfalloch	Dawe	87	34
Hebe	Pomrey	85	32
Elizabeth	Smart	126	35
John and Maria	Burke	75	34
Pearl	Andrews	85	33
Isabella	Andrews	106	36
Norval	Sheppard	111	36
Newfoundlander	Mercer	89	35
Eclipse	Delaney	117	40
Emily	Walsh	102	40
Rolla	Burke	82	34
Nimrod	Rabbits	72	31
Theresa	Walker	69	30
Sarah	Bartlett	91	34
Hound	Whelan	96	40
Jane Isabella	Taylor	130	40
Willow	Le Drew	89	30
Sisters	Clarke	98	37
Brothers	Bartlett	107	34
Mary	Bartlett	100	35
Jane	Munden	113	36
Witch	Bartlett	100	33
Gleaner	Wilcox	104	37
Gem	Munden	123	35
Providence	Antle	93	34
Five Brothers	Antle	75	31
Ellen	Gushue	94	37
Bickley	Penny	82	31
Hare	Dawe	96	35
Unicorn	Le Drew	86	33
Lady Norman	Norman	102	35
Nymph	Norman	88	32
Ann	Strange	71	27
Rake	Batten	116	35
Margaret Ellen	Norman	83	26
Montezuma	Brown	74	27
Antigonish	Russel	83	35
James Clift	Delaney	90	34
Charlotte	Russel	78	28
Charles	Richards	84	29
Isabella	Mercer	76	28
Falcon	Whelan	61	22
Jane	Curtis	93	30
John Alexander	Roberts	96	22
Sarah Jane	Munden	88	33
Orestes	Nurse	92	37
Rose	Norman	103	35
Terra Nova	Percy	106	35
Speedwell	Spracklin	80	27
Stranger	Rabbits	77	30
Herald	Roberts	100	38
Henrietta	Wells	86	30
Isabella	Spracklin	81	28
Racer	Smith	83	29
Four Brothers	Munden	98	33
Mary	Wells	76	33
Swift	Burke	60	20
Argo	Woodford	82	32
New Packet	Woodford	73	31

(t.) BRIGUS.—1881.
SUPPLIED BY GOODFELLOW & CO.

Vessels.	Masters.	Tons.	Men.
William	Whelan	141	75

J. MUNN & CO.

Atlanta	Whelan	143	95

P. BUTLER.

Mary	Fowler	37	25
3 Vessels.		321	165

708

STATISTICS.

(u.) TRINITY.—1847.
SUPPLIED BY EXECUTORS OF R. SLADE.

Vessels.	Masters.	Tons.	Men.
Caroline	J. Dwyer	80	34
Dorothy	G. S. Field	125	40

BAINE, JOHNSTON, & Co.
| Syren | R. Coleman | 96 | 33 |
| Margaret Jane | J. Coleman | 103 | 36 |

ROBINSON, BROOKING, & Co.
| Gazelle | S. Crocker | 128 | 36 |
| Dart | J. Morris | 147 | 38 |

E. VERGE.
| Thomas & Elizabeth | C. Ainsworth | 59 | 30 |

HUNTERS & Co.
| St. John's Lass | E. Eagan | 87 | 38 |

RENNIE, STUART, & Co.
| Alexander | A. Graham | 84 | 30 |

J. DOUGLAS & Co.
| Wave | J. Ainsworth | 70 | 24 |

J. TOBIN & Co.
| Argo | G. Christian | 92 | 36 |

J. & J. KENT.
| Victory | G. Rix | 84 | 29 |

WM. STONEMAN.
| Times | L. Christian | 72 | 31 |

(v.) CATALINA.—1847.
SUPPLIED BY EXECUTORS OF R. SLADE.

Vessels.	Masters.	Tons.	Men.
Thomas	Robert House	117	36
Anna	Thos. Wells	67	27
Joseph	Joseph Clark	49	19

JAS. TOBIN & Co.
Elizabeth	Martin Smart	126	41
Elizabeth	Joseph Manuel	81	30
Cumberland	Michl. Smart	51	20

PUNTON & MUNN.
| Jane | Jas. Dalton | 81 | 27 |

EDGAR STIRLING.
| Hebe | Geo. Pomery | 81 | 28 |

McBRIDE & KERR.
| Reform | Jos. Mifflen | 99 | 25 |

BAINE, JOHNSTON, & Co.
| Packer | Jno. Martin | 82 | 32 |

JNO. DIAMOND.
| Hope | John Diamond | 63 | 24 |

JOS. SHEARS.
| Troubadour | Saml. Mifflen | 95 | 25 |

WM. WARREN, JR.
| Catalina | Jno. Beasley | 60 | 29 |

FREDERICK HISCOCK.
| Sisters | Frederick Hiscock | 50 | 21 |

WM. NORMAN, SR.
| Victory | Wm. Norman, jr. | 49 | 23 |

WM. WALSH.
| Amity | Wm. Walsh | 82 | 31 |

RENNIE, STUART, & Co.
| Post Boy | Jas. Brine | 46 | 23 |
| Dartford | T. Jackman | 70 | 82 |

JOS. SHEARS.
| Hibernia | Wm. Clouter | 86 | 23 |

(w.) NEW PERLICAN.—1847.
SUPPLIED BY W. & H. THOMAS & CO.

Vessels.	Masters.	Tons.	Men.
Henry	Warren	80	31
Native	Hopkins	81	35
Mayflower	Benson	116	43
Charles	Hopkins	108	39
Caledonia	Houlahan	113	42

W. W. BEMISTER & CO.
| Britannia | Rockwood | 87 | 35 |
| Victoria | Burton | 84 | 33 |

J. & W. STEWART.
| Leah | Shea | 77 | 32 |

CHARLES McCARTHY.
| Dart | Green | 81 | 35 |

JOB BROTHERS & CO.
| Crusader | Pittman | 111 | 38 |
| Kingfisher | March | 81 | 34 |

RICHARD HOWLEY.
| Native Lass | Walsh | 117 | 37 |
| Mary | Furneaux | 115 | 36 |

HUNTERS & CO.
| Sandy | Row | 73 | 28 |

(x.) HANTS HARBOUR.—1847.
SUPPLIED BY EXECUTORS OF R. SLADE.

Vessels.	Masters.	Tons.	Men.
Robert and James	Hindy	80	27
Thomas and Sarah	Green	81	37

JOB BROS. & CO.
Afghan	March	95	40
Frederick	March	84	28
Mary	Willcocks	74	29

NATHANIEL NORMAN.
| Indian Chief | Norman | 120 | 36 |

STEPHEN RENDELL & CO.
| Charles | Cox | 65 | 36 |

HUNTERS & CO.
| Daniel O'Connell | Blundon | 94 | 33 |

ROBERT ALSOP & CO.
| Tryon | Neill | 84 | 30 |

SHEA & MURPHY.
| John and Rachel | Benson | 93 | 46 |

(y.) The following is a LIST of SEALERS reported to date, 1862.

Vessels.	Masters.	Suppliers.
Eliza	Winser	Baine, Johnston & Co.
Rosebud	Dawe	"
Roxana	Jackman	Bowring Brothers.
G. M. Johnston	Lynch	"
Wm. Stairs	Welsh	"
Jessie Brown	Norman	"
Emily Tobin	White	Punton & Munn.
Christina	Parsons	"
Jura	Snelgrove	"
E. Margaret	Power	"
Carolina	Avery	"
Melrose	Pike	Ridley & Sons.
Elizabeth Jane	Rivan	"
Hunter	Pike	J. & W. Stewart.
Mary Ann	Winser	"
Margaret	Cummins	Job Brothers & Co.
Alinn	Winser	McBride & Kerr.
Victoria	Egelton	P. Rogerson & Son.
Hope	Andrews	Brooking & Co.

STATISTICS.

XXIII.—Salmon Fishery, 1804.

In what Harbour.	Merchants and Planters by whom it is carried on.	Tierces caught.	Price per Tierce.
Dog Bay	Benjamin Lester & Co.	35	55s.
Indian Arm	Do. do.	22	—
River Exploits	Harry Miller	90	—
Loo Bay	John Creasy	6	—
Halls Bay	George Rowsell, senr.	45	—
New Bay	George Rowsell, junr., and Rd. Ridout	19	—
Nippers Harbour	Jno. Noble and Jno. Ridout	76	—
Round Harbour	Cox and Round	10	—
Indian Burying Place	Adams and Palmer	60	—
Shoe Cove	A. Tilsey and Wm. Shepherd	12	—
Fogo	J. Slade, B. Lester & Co., Ad. Kennedy	85	—
Toulinquet	Sundry planters	117	—
Gander Bay	Thomas Street	250	50s.
Indian Bay	Ben. Lester & Co.	70	—
Freshwater Bay	Do. do.	80	—
Trouty	Sir J. Lester and George Garland	1	60s.
New Harbour	Do. do.	33	—
English Harbour	Sundry inhabitants	25	—
Trepassey	Michael Kearney	32	40s.
St. Mary's	Wm. Phippard & Co. and Spurrier	129	—
		1,197	—

A quantity of salmon has been caught in Fortune Bay, of which no particular account has been received.

XXIV.—Salmon Fishery, 1814.

Trinity Bay.	Tierces caught.	Prices.
		s.
English Harbour	57	80
Bonaventure	19	80
Hearts Delight	18	80
New Harbour	12	—
Bonavista (no return)	—	—
Fogo	106	80
Straits of Belle Isle and Labrador.	—	—
English Point	212	—
River Esquimaux and St. Modeste.	200	—
Francis Harbour	150	—
Sandwich Bay	1,000	—
Black Bay	70	—
Battle Harbour	46	—
Matthew Cove	30	—
Cape Charles	70	—
Wall Island	15	—
Camp Island	116	—
Hawkes Bay	220	—

Caught by inhabitants with nets.

XXV.—Exports of Salmon, &c. for the under-mentioned Years.

Year.	Salmon.	Herring.	Mackerel.	Fur Skins.
	Tierces.	Barrels.	Casks.	No.
1817	2,858	1,726	941	4,820
1818	1,663	1,601	1,158	3,975
1819	2,125	1,668	780	2,217
1820	1,783	3,233	Herring & Mackerel.	2,482
1821	1,777	526	700	3,211
1822	2,651	305	923	3,934
1823	2,249	333	436	3,300
1824	1,927	349	357	2,684
1825	2,958	263	560	3,565
1826	3,172	267	752	—
1829	4,340 bls.	970	621 bls.	4,685
1830	4,322	1,524	560	—
1831	2,763	3,365	916	£1,185
1832	2,729	3,285	635	£3,341

Exports of Salmon, &c. for the under-mentioned Years—cont.

Year.	Salmon.	Herring.	Mackerel.	Fur Skins.
	Tierces.	Barrels.	Casks.	No.
1835	2,564	2,271	149	3,216
1836	1,847	1,534	79	2,959
1837	2,262	5,815	None caught.	—
1838	4,408	15,276	do.	2,200
1839	2,922	20,806	None caught.	3,815
1840	3,396	14,686	do.	3,083
1841	3,642	9,685	do.	2,325
1842	4,715	13,839	do.	—
1843	4,058	9,649	do.	—
1844	3,753	13,410	do.	2,281
1845	3,845	20,903	do.	2,037
1846	5,201 bls.	12,119	do.	2,375
1847	4,917	9,908	do.	3,053
1848	3,822	13,872	do.	3,903
1849	5,911	11,471	do.	2,106
1850	3,108	19,556	do.	—
1851	4,375	36,259	do.	2,526
1852	4,048	42,715	do.	—
	Value in $.	Value in $.		
1860	91,336	—	—	—
1865	61,272	—	—	—
1869	—	242,804	—	—
1870	82,915	—	—	—
1871	—	449,838	—	—
1874	—	578,168	—	—
1875	85,010	—	—	—
1877	—	558,736	—	—
1878	—	200,296	—	—
1880	—	229,100	—	—
1881	—	269,556	—	—
1882	—	174,145	—	—
1883	—	183,241	—	—
1884	—	174,145	—	—
1885	64,044	112,294	—	—
1886	63,080	68,628	—	—
1887	79,526	149,120	—	—
1888	82,050	255,658	—	—
1889	71,736	245,247	—	—
1890	96,359	241,268	—	—
1891	80,311	77,941	—	—
1892	37,425	212,678	—	—
1893	45,608	227,478	—	—

STATISTICS.

XXVI.—Vessels built in Newfoundland, 1804.

Vessel's Name.	How rigged.	Tonnage.	Where built.
Capelin Bay	Sloop	31	Capelin Bay.
Mary	Schooner	30	St. John's.
Brothers	Do.	45	Cupids.
Race Horse	Do.	61	St John's.
Mary	Do.	45	Bare Need.
Sisters	Do.	46	Conception Bay.
Musquitto	Do.	31	Brigus.
Brothers	Lugger	40	Belle Isle.
Industry	Schooner	70½	Carbonear.
Adventure	Do.	44	Do.
Fly	Do.	74	Western Bay.
Betsy	Do.	58	Belle Isle.
William	Do	60½	Brigus.
Industry	Do.	49	Bay Roberts.
John	Do.	48	Tilton Harbour.
Belle	Do.	69	Clodes Sound.
Mary	Do.	31	Holyrood.
Falcon	Do.	67½	Hearts Content.
Flora	Do.	47	Do.
Cabot	Brig	80	New Harbour.
Benjamin	Do.	173	Trinity.
Fanny	Schooner	9½	Bay Despair.
Victor	Do.	53½	Audierne.
Hope	Brig	132½	Trinity.
Stork	Do.	167½	Do.
Trepassey	Schooner	52	Trepassey.
John	Brig	154	Trinity.
Chance	Schooner	32	Bonavista.
Alicia	Ship	232	Great Placentia.
Marianne	Do.	196	Bay of Islands.

XXVII.—Population, Fishery, Shipping, &c. 1804.

Bankers, English	21
" Newfoundland	61
Sack ships	249
Ships from the N. A. Colonies	168
West Indies	38
U. States	21
Passengers from England	163
Ireland	443
Jersey	40
No. of boats kept by inhabitants in the fishery	2,070

Quintals of Fish caught.

	Qtls.
By English bankers'	23,650
Newfoundland bankers	54,950
Inhabitants	531,084
Total	609,684
Stages	1,870
Private dwelling-houses	3,403
Public houses	72
Population in summer	24,922
Protestants	12,345
R. Catholics	8,035
Population, St. John's	7,390
Private houses	760

XXVIII.—Exports, &c., 1813.

	Qtls.
Codfish—To Spain, Portugal, and Italy	727,738
" " British Europe	50,701
" " West Indies	119,554
" " British America	14,389
	912,183

	Tierces.
Salmon exported	3,761

	Tuns.
Train oil to British Europe	4,054½

	Skins.
Seal skins	133,847
	Tuns.
Seal oil made	1,583½
Value of seal oil made	50,161*l*.
Furs taken by inhabitants	585*l*.
In truck with Mic Macs	331*l*.

Prices.

Fish, merchantable, per qtl.	32*s*.
Salmon, per tierce	95*s*.
Train oil, per tun	30*l*.
Seal oil, per tun - 44/	32*l*.

Population.

Protestants	17,179
R. Catholics	15,570
	32,749

XXIX.—IMPORTS.—11th October 1803 to 10th October 1804.

	Shipping.	Bread and Flour.	Beef and Pork.	Butter and Cheese.	Sugar.	Molasses.	Rum.	Coals.	Oxen.	Sheep and Pigs.
		Cwts.		Cwts.	Lbs.		Gallons.	Chaldrons.		
British Europe	216	24,877	13,986	7,158	18,534* 14,329†	13,973	47,142	1,438	—	—
Foreign Europe	46	—	—	—	—	—	—	—	—	—
West Indies	36	—	—	—	206,662	161,702	182,110	—	—	—
British America	149	18,053	1,910	947	—	—	727	1,836	511	533
United States	28	25,078	1,778	1,108	—	—	—	—	97	533
Total	476	68,008	17,674	9,303	18,624* 221,091†	120,710	229,979	3,274	608	1,066

* Refined.   † Muscovado.

XXX.—EXPORTS.—11th October 1803 to 10th October 1804.

To what Countries.	St. John's, distinguished from Outharbours.	Shipping. No.	Tons.	Men.	Dry Codfish.	Core Fish.	Seal Skins.	Oil. Cod. Tons.	Oil. Seal. Tons.	Salmon. Tierces.	Herring. Barrels.	Furs.
British Europe	St. John's	79	7,633	631	53,770	14,866	No. 41,369	17	72	361	88	Value Uncertain. £3,000
	Outharbours	83	9,598	633	118,198	2,486	68,524	2,003	63½	1,398	5	
	Total	162	17,531	1,264	171,968	17,352	109,893	4,409		1,759	93	£3,000
Foreign Europe	St. John's	58	8,094	585	16,884	—	—	—	—	145	—	—
	Outharbours	82	11,182	567	208,777	—	—	—	—	551	—	—
	Total	140	19,276	1,152	354,661	—	—	—	—	696	—	—
West Indies	St. John's	28	3,846	310	50,385	—	—	1½	—	312	11	—
	Outharbours	5	577	46	5,613	—	—	—	—	204	—	—
	Total	33	4,463	356	55,994	—	—	1½	—	516	11	—
British America	St. John's	113	11,968	730	6,513	—	—	—	—	—	—	—
	Outharbours	40	3,749	222	11,574	80	—	—	—	32	—	—
	Total	153	15,717	952	18,087	80	—	—	—	32	—	—
United States	St. John's	31	3,545	241	37,669	—	—	—	—	694	14	—
	Outharbours	4	704	44	5,523	—	—	—	—	42	—	—
	Total	35	4,249	285	43,131	—	—	—	—	736	14	—
Grand Total		523	61,236	4,009	643,845	17,432	109,893	4,410½		3,739	118	£3,000

XXXI.—Imports, 1813-1819.

	1813.	1814.	1816.	1817.	1819.	
Shipping	656	741	792	675	710	
Ships	89,638	145,228	165,427	131,465	90,411	Tonnage
Men	5,645	31,331	24,532	26,160	6,014	
Bread and Flour	156,713	14,074	16,671	13,262	21,746	Cwts
Beef and Pork	20,018	376,004	293,352	226,619	14,353	Barrels
Butter and Cheese	13,807	389,771	548,315	164,325	378,410	Cwts
Molasses	257,881	4,658	8,537	4,248	297,728	Gallons
Rum	441,133	3,535	1,342	1,038	517	
Coals	4,658	1,379	1,913	891	722	Chaldrons
Oxen	1,451	1,471	160,150	72,851	140	
Sheep and Pigs	1,949	258,399	245,465	107,251	137,834	Lbs.
Tea	103,080	439	679	154,008	295	Tuns
Wine	2,134	179,114			149,257	Hhds.
Salt	91,247	163,178	5,858,176	1,386,050	2,078,290	Lbs.
Tobacco	88,896	1,069,659				
Potatoes and Turnips	25,158	8,431	8,051		1,738	Feet
Lumber	250,225	4,089		1,252	935	Lbs.
Coffee						Hhds.
Beer	3,361		49,307			Ells
Russian Linen						

XXXII.—Revenue and Expenditure prior to the introduction of Representative Government.

REVENUE OF NEWFOUNDLAND FROM CUSTOMS, AND PAYMENTS TO OFFICERS.

Years.	Duties.	Payments.
	£	£
1781	1,047	422
1782	474	363
1783	727	331
1784	223	349
1785	396	410
1786	529	410
1787	605	469
1788	338	380
1789	1,346	413
1790	1,004	459
1791	428	381
Total	7,131	4,394

N.B.—The salaries of the officers were largely increased by seizures, quite equal to their salaries. The value of the seizures for the period amounted to £4,949 11s. 1d., out of which the King received one third, the remainder being distributed amongst the Custom House officers. They also received large fees. At this period there were no duties levied on English goods or on molasses or rum, &c. imported from the British possessions in the West Indies. The tax on foreign rum and molasses was only 6d. per gallon. This duty is the celebrated "Molasses Duty" that raised such an outcry amongst New Englanders, and indirectly led to the American Revolution. This charge gave a virtual monopoly of the rum and molasses business to Jamaica, &c. There was, however, a great deal of smuggling; large quantities of foreign rum were imported as "Real Jamaica," like the "Pure Havannah" made by the Hamburgh Jew pedlar, and pawned off on an unsuspecting public as a genuine article; so all British North America was supplied with more liquor under the name of "Fine Old Jamaica" than the Island could ever have produced.

DUTIES COLLECTED AT THE CUSTOM HOUSE, NEWFOUNDLAND, FROM 1813-22.

[Rum, British West Indies, 6d. per gall.; foreign, 1s. 6d. per gall. Wines, French and Spanish, 7l. per tun; Portuguese, 10s. per tun.]

Years.	British W.I. Rum.	Foreign Rum.	Fr. & Sp. Wines.	Portuguese Wines.	Molasses.	B. Coffee.	Sugar (Foreign).	Total.
	£	£	£	£	£	£	£	£
1813	12,724	896	183	103	1,067	23	—	14,939
1814	10,460	6,462	57	230	942	22	—	18,174
1815	10,220	5,579	569	231	864	289	207	16,954
1816	10,349	1,539	63	64	1,471	160	—	13,651
1817	2,373	807	122	37	780	—	—	4,122
1818	8,668	1,216	97	18	1,023	72	—	11,097
1819	6,594	1,559	153	64	1,508	49	—	9,280
1820	9,443	2,297	547	73	1,598	29	—	13,908
1821	9,308	854	442	87	1,286	61	—	12,039
1822	4,522	647	148	2	1,206	38	—	6,587
Total	85,368	19,982	2,380	†33	11,687	*858	207	122,008

* £111 added, duty on sundry articles.
† £574 added, duty on sundry articles.

The Collector's salary was £401 9s. 1d.; fees, £1,599 8s. 2d. Comptroller's salary, £373 6s. 9d.; fees, £1,547 6s. Surveyor's salary, £25; fees, £789 8s. 5d. Landing Waiter's salary, £35; fees, £157 11s. 6d.

Note on the duties collected in Newfoundland from 1813-22:—

Rum was 6d. per gallon from B. W. Indies, 1s. 6d. from other parts not English. Molasses, 1d. per gallon. Sugar from English W. Indies was 5s. per cwt., foreign, 22s. British Plantation coffee, 7s. per cwt., foreign coffee, £2 18s. 9d. per cwt. Portuguese wines from our allies, 10s. per tun; French and Spanish wines, £7 per tun; this was protection with a vengeance. Note the tremendous falling off in the unfortunate year 1817. Nearly all the revenue was made out of rum.

XXXIII.—Civil List, 1815.

SALARIES AND ALLOWANCES.

	£
Governor	800
Governor's Secretary	182
Chief Justice	1,000
Clerk Supreme Court	70
Marshal	50
Gaoler	36
Supreme surrogate	100
Seven surrogates at 60l. per annum	420
Judge of the Admiralty	500
Naval officer	100
Surveyor of lands	25
Schoolmaster	25
Allowance to the sheriff	252
To John Ogden, Esq., late Chief Justice, in consideration of his long services, and of his infirm state of health	200
Allowance to the clerk to the secretary	60
Agent	100
To the Society for the Propagation of the Gospel in aid of the expenses of the Society in Newfoundland	1,000
On account of fees for receipt and audit	159
	£5,080

The expenditure of the Government under the Admiral Governors before Sir Thomas Cochrane's time was moderate.

	£
Governor	1,000
Secretary	182
Clerk in secretary's office	60
Chief Justice	1,000
Judge of the Vice-Admiralty Court	500
Sheriff	252
Clerk Supreme Court	70
Surrogates, seven, at 60l. each	420
Chief Magistrate St. John's	200
Ordinary relief of the poor, police expenditure, repairs, &c. roads	1,535
	£5,220

The whole expenditure, exclusive of relief after the fires of 1817, &c., averaged £5,220 per annum.

These figures are taken from the accounts of Sir Charles Hamilton, 1819. Prior to this date, the expenditure was much smaller, as all the official salaries were much lower.

The salary of the Governor was first raised to 3,000l. on the appointment of Sir Thomas Cochrane. Former Admiral Governors had their pay as Admirals and Commanders-in-Chief as well as their salaries as Governors.

XXXIV.—Expenditure.

1831.

Prior to grant of Local Legislature.

	£	£
Governor	3,000	
Colonial secretary and clerk to Council	700	
Two clerks in secretary's office	400	
Office keeper 60l., messenger 37l.	95	
Surveyor-General	300	
Chainman to Surveyor-General	15	
Colonial agent	300	
School of Industry, St. John's	104	
Newfoundland School Society	100	
School in Conception Bay	25	
Making fishery returns	56	
Customs Establishment	4,498	
		9,594
Judicial Department—		
Chief Justice	1,200	
Two Assistant Judges	1,400	
Attorney General	450	
Clerk of the Supreme Court	400	
Three clerks, Circuit Courts	650	
Crier of Supreme and Central Courts	20	
High Sheriff	513	
Labrador Court Judge	700	
Clerk, 200l., sheriff, 150l.	350	
Two constables, 26l. each	52	
Judge of Vice-Admiralty Court	500	
		6,235
		15,829
Police Establishment—		
Chief Magistrate	360	
Two Police Magistrates	320	
Nine constables	320	
		1,000
Ecclesiastical Department—		
Archdeacon	300	
Five lay readers	65	
Catholic Bishop's allowance	75	
		440
Pension.—Wm. Armstrong, late Marshal Supreme Court	50	
Mrs Wescott, wife of late Attorney-General	35	
		80

	£	£
Contingencies—		
Civil Department	238	
Judicial Department—		
Expenses of civil and criminal prosecutions	634	
Circuit Judges on Circuit	300	
Labrador Court	270	
Fuel and light	91	
Stationery and printing	132	
Gaol expenses, dietary, medicines, medical attendance	747	
Washing	26	
Coroners' accounts	131	
Attorney-General's fees	250	
		2,654

Miscellaneous Expenditure.

	£	£
Expenses of supporting paupers, orphans, and bastards	780	
Supporting and lodging of sick paupers	257	
Medical attendance on do.	200	
Expenses of providing passages for paupers, &c.	60	
		1,299
Expenses of making and repairing public roads	350	
Repairs and preservation of public buildings	693	
Repairs of bridges and Government fences	54	
Other incidental charges	565	
		1,663
Total expenditure, 1831		£23,204

Note. During this period the whole revenue of the Colony seems to have been expended in the payment of enormous salaries to such officials as the Judge of the Labrador Court, £700 sterling a year, whilst £350 was expended on all the roads in the Colony. The care bestowed by the new Legislature on roads was in marked contrast to the policy of their predecessors.

Road Expenditure in Colony by First Legislature, 1833 to 1837.

1834.

£
500 on roads, north and south, appropriated.
43 towards paying Henry Thomas for opening the road to Brookfield.
1,200 seed potatoes.
400 roads in St. John's.
56 do. St. Mary's.

£2,200

Treasury Notes, £5,600 sterling, to bear interest at 6 per cent.:

£
20 at 100
50 at 50
44 at 25 for public improvements.

1835.

£
450 for competent persons to lay out roads.
1,640

£2,090

1836.
£7,539 7s. for roads.

1837.
The large sum of £16,801 for new roads and improvements.

XXXV.—Climate and Soil.

There has been a fierce controversy waged over the climate and soil of our island. I am not writing a Government guide-book, and I therefore state definitely that Newfoundland does not rejoice in the balmy airs of California, and her soil is not equal to the black loam of Manitoba. On the other hand, old Terra Nova is not a barren waste and howling wilderness, and her temperature is by no means arctic. On the east coast, where there has been the earliest settlement and most cultivation, the earth is frequently thin, with underlying gravel. This naturally poor soil is wonderfully productive, grasses and all vegetables grow with astonishing quickness. Connoisseurs declare that the Newfoundland peas, beans, turnips, potatoes, cabbage, and cauliflower, are the sweetest and the richest they have ever tasted. Wheat has been ripened over and over again; barley, oats, and all leguminous plants come to perfection. The greatest drawback to our climate is the tardy and uncertain spring, caused by the presence of ice on the coast. The summer is always delightful, and, except in the extreme north of the island, there is generally no severe weather before Christmas. During the winter, when the cold is much less severe than either in Canada or Maine, there are a few very extreme days, and a few snowstorms, but very seldom a continued hard frost. We are quite free from the violent thunderstorms and tornadoes that devastate other countries. We have no venomous reptiles. The hardy, robust appearance of our stalwart fishermen, the blooming complexions of our girls, all bear testimony to the healthiness of our sea-girt isle. On the west coast, after Cape Ray is turned, there is some excellent land about the Codroy Valleys and St. George's Bay; with the rudest and most primitive farming fine crops are raised. That a large portion of Newfoundland is rocky and barren is unfortunately too true; both Nova Scotia, New Brunswick, Maine, and Canada, also contain some of the most barren and sterile soil in the world. Our country has been condemned because the rocky and sterile parts, the haunts of the deer-stalker, are known, whilst large portions of the good soil lies up river valleys and amidst forests, mostly unexplored and unknown except to the surveyor and the lumberer. Newfoundland contains many fine stretches of grazing land. Even about the comparatively shallow soil of Avalon cattle and sheep become wonderfully fat and flourishing. The truth about the country lies between the picturesque enthusiasm of our own writers and the fierce depreciation of some English and American travellers, who, from hasty observation of the most unfavourable portions, have cursed the whole country.

XXXVI.—Timber.

Whatever questions may arise about our soil, there can be no question about our forest wealth; the best answer to all our detractors is the price of our pine lumber in London, Newfoundland yellow pine fetching the very highest price in that market. The principal varieties of our forest timber are:—

White Pine, Yellow or Red Pine, Scrub Pine, Black Spruce, White Spruce, Red Spruce, Fir, called here Var; Larch, called Hackmatack in New Brunswick, Tamarack in Canada, and very erroneously Juniper in Newfoundland.

White Birch, Yellow Birch, called Witch-hazel; Black Birch, Low and Alpine Birches, two inferior varieties.

White Ash, Black Ash, Mountain Ash or Rowan Tree, called here Dogwood.

Balsam Poplar or Balm of Gilead, Aspen Poplar.

Willow in several varieties, Alders, Choke, and Wild Cherry.

XXXVII.—Mines and Minerals.

The mineral wealth of Newfoundland has only been developed very partially. Large deposits of copper have been found principally in Nôtre Dame Bay. Whilst so much of the country is unsurveyed, it is only reasonable to suppose that there is much latent wealth over a wide and unknown area, displaying much the same geological formation as Tilt Cove and Bett's Cove Mines. Every facility is given to explorers; licence fees to secure a large mining area are only $20. Valuable information can be obtained on the subject of our mineralogy from the yearly geological reports furnished to the Government. The following account is taken principally from Mr. Howley's Geography.

The metals and economic minerals known to exist in Newfoundland are as follows:—Gold, found only in traces in quartz veins, and associated with iron ore; native silver is found in Fortune Bay. Silver, associated with galena; nickel ores, viz., copper nickel, cloanthite, and millerite. Copper in various forms, viz., native copper, variegated copper ore, grey and yellow sulphurets, copper pyrites, &c.; galena, or sulphuret of lead; graphite, or plumbago; molybdenum. Iron ores in great variety, viz., magnetic, chromic, specular, iron pyrites, or sulphuret of iron, iron sand, hæmatite, vivianite, or phosphate of iron; manganese and zincblende, coal, and several other less important minerals. Various other important substances, such as marbles, white, black, and variegated, limestone in abundance, barytes, gypsum, shell marl, kaolin clay, brick clays, roofing slates, granites, syenites, serpentines, sandstones, whetstones, steatite, asbestos, petroleum, &c., and many others. The following are the localities where the more important of these substances have been found. Copper ores, at Shoal Bay, south of St. John's, in the neighbourhood of St. John's Town; at Holyrood, Turk's Gut, and Crow's Gulch, in Conception

Bay; at Tickle Harbour, and head of Random Sound, in Trinity Bay; at Pit Sound Island and Bloody Bay, Bonavista Bay; at Twillingate Island, Trump Island, New Bay Head, Pilley's Island, Sunday Cove Island, Three Arms, Green Bay, Burton's Pond, Bett's Cove and Tilt Cove, in the Great Bay of Nôtre Dame. In Mings Bight, Bay Vert, or Little Bay; on Groais Island, in St. Julien Harbour, in Goose Cove and Howe Harbour, Hare Bay; in St. Mary's Bay. At Placentia Harbour, and La Manche, in Placentia Bay; at Bennoits Brook, Lewis Brook, and Serpentine River, Port-à-Port Bay, and several other localities.

Lead is known to exist near St. John's Harbour, in Conception Bay, Trinity Bay, St. Mary's Bay, Placentia Bay, principally at La Manche; in Fortune Bay, Bay Despair, on the west coast, at Red Rocks, near Cape Ray; in East and West Bays, Port-à-Port, and other parts of Port-à-Port Peninsula, besides various other localities. Iron ores are found on every side of the island, and in all the bays. A valuable supply of the finest ore is now being worked by a Nova Scotia Company at Belle Isle, Conception Bay. Nickel is almost invariably found in the serpentines; but has only been developed in workable quantity at the Union Mine, Tilt Cove. Coal, as already mentioned, in St. George's Bay. It is stated to exist in workable seams, but its commercial value has not yet been fully ascertained; some of the seams are on the new line of railway, and will be opened up by the Construction Company. Petroleum, in Port-à-Port Bays, at Cow Head, and Cape Rouge Peninsula; gypsum, in immense volume in St. George's Bay, and at Great Codroy River. Excellent roofing slates in Smith's Sound, and on Random Island, Trinity Bay; white and variegated marbles at the mouth of the Humber River, at Canada Bay, and other places. An immense deposit of asbestos is now being worked very successfully by a company on the west coast. Building stones of every description and good quality, limestones, &c., are found in vast profusion at many parts of the island, the latter especially on the north-eastern and western shores. There are only a few places where the more valuable ores were worked to any extent so far, viz., at the Union Mine, Tilt Cove, and at Bett's Cove and Little Bay, Nôtre Dame Bay. At the former nickel and copper are mined to a large extent; at the latter, only copper as yet. Lead has been worked at La Manche Mine, Placentia Bay, and at Lead Cove, Port-à-Port Bay.

XXXVIII.—Sport.

As a sporting country Newfoundland has no rival in North America. The whole interior of the island, unvisited by man, is the home of immense herds of Cariboo (*Cervus Tarandus*), a species of reindeer peculiar to this Colony. Soon after the birth of their young, in the spring, the Cariboo herds migrate north and return again to the milder southern coast in the autumn; many deer also remain in the woodlands about the Gander River and other northern streams all the winter. Throughout the interior the deer-paths abound, even the stones in places are worn smooth by the countless herds who have been making their pilgrimage through endless years. At some places lakes and streams lie across their track. At one of these crossing places, Gander Lake, fifteen hundred deer, so Garrett Kelly informed some tourists lately, had been killed; his original statement to me was seven hundred. The very best deer grounds in the island can now be reached quite easily by the new railway or by coastal boats, north and south. With camp and canoe, the deer-stalker can be transported in a few hours to grounds that formerly could only be reached by three and four days, often a week, of most laborious toil and travel. Deer-stalking, the sport of princes in Europe, the common occupation of Newfoundland fishermen, requires endurance, nerve, and straight shooting; with these qualifications and sufficient leisure, nowhere in North America can better sport be obtained. Grouse-shooting comes next to deer-stalking in the Terra-Novian sporting bill of fare, and is a most fascinating, health-giving amusement. Whilst the best deer-stalking is at the north and west, by far the most extensive moors and the largest number of broods are found in the south-east part of the island, Avalon Peninsula, St. Mary's, and Placentia Bay. The local game laws are well observed, and by the 15th September grouse are generally to be found in fair numbers; even around St. John's, ten or a dozen miles from the capital, bags of eight and ten brace are made on the first day by good shots and hard walkers. For successful grouse-shooting, next to straight powder, the most important factor is a well-trained setter; with these concomitants and fine weather, a good Newfoundland barrens affords glorious sport. I have heard Admiral Kennedy, R.N., a very prince amongst shooters, declare that he preferred the wild shooting in Newfoundland to any other sport in the world. To ensure success a knowledge of the habits of your game is also essential. The grouse, a semi-arctic bird, takes no heed of cold, but is extremely sensitive to wet and north-east winds; in fogs they are found on the highest and barest rocks, always, as the fishermen say, "standing," on the alert, hard to get at. There are two distinct species of grouse, the Willow Grouse (*Tetrao salicensis*), and the true Ptarmigan, known amongst the fishermen as the rock partridge; this latter bird is found on the highest and barest hills, west of Fortune Bay. It is entirely unknown on the east coast, where the Willow Grouse, the great sporting bird of Newfoundland, is most abundant. Besides grouse, there are geese, ducks, and snipe, &c. Salmon fishing has been specially good during the season of 1894; one commander killed thirty fair-sized salmon and grilse for his own rod in one day. Sea trout are even more abundant than salmon in some streams; they run small, from a ½ pound to 2 pounds, but in all the good rivers, both north and south, the average is from 1 lb. to 3½ lbs. I have never seen a sea trout over 5 lbs., though I understand they run much larger at Labrador, up to 7 lbs. Brown and fresh-water trout are of all sizes, and marvellously abundant. Recently rainbow trout and Loch Levens have been introduced; many of these fish were caught this season near St. John's weighing 4 lbs. to 5 lbs., and one 6¾ lbs. (a beautiful fish). The American or blue hare, as it is known in Scotland, is extraordinarily abundant. The large arctic hare is common, but never in large numbers. Our local natural history is very incomplete. A good catalogue of indigenous plants has been made by the Rev. Mr. Waghorne. The one and only list of birds was made by Mr. Henry Reeks, F.L.S., and published in the *Ornithologist*; it applies more especially to the west coast of the island. Valuable notes on Newfoundland natural history were also made by Philip H. Gosse, but have not been published.

Game Laws of Newfoundland.

For WILLOW GROUSE, locally named partridge, and other varieties of grouse and eggs of same, close time begins 12th January, ends 15th September; birds, however, may be sold up to 22nd January, provided they are shot in season.

CURLEW, PLOVER, SNIPE, or other wild or migratory birds, or eggs of same, close time 12th January to 20th August.

WILD GEESE may be shot at any time or their eggs taken.

CARIBOU, close time 15th February to 15th September.

MOOSE or ELK (imported), close time 10 years from 1st January 1886.

OTTER and BEAVER, close time 1st April to 1st October.

RABBITS and HARES, close time 1st March to 15th September.

SALMON, close time from 11th September to 30th April.

TROUT, land-locked salmon and other fresh water fish not to be taken in any lake, river, or stream, between 15th September and 31st December.

CARIBOU. *Note.*—Licence is required by non-residents to shoot deer, fee $100; only five stags and three does can be killed by each sportsman. The licences are granted by Justices of the Peace and Custom House officers in the form prescribed by the Act.

INDEX.

Abhott and Hill, 559, 561.
ACT:
  8 Henry VI. c. ii., 27.
  22 Edward IV., c. ii., 28.
  11 Henry VII. c. xxiii., 28.
  1 Henry VIII. c. 1., 27.
  33 Henry VIII. c. xi., 33.
  2 & 3 Edward VI. c. vi., 53.
  5 Elizabeth c. v, 27, 28, 55.
  23 Elizabeth c. vii., 28, 56.
  Charles I. thrown out by Lords, 121, 138.
  12 Charles II., 173.
  15 Charles II. c. xvi., 173.
  10 William III. c. xxv., 225, 233, 267, 416.
  George II. (1759), 299.
  George III. (1764), 299, 323.
  14 George III. c. lxxxiii., 328.
  15 George III. c. xxxi., 319, 336, 344.
  26 George III. c. xxvi., 345.
  31 George III c. xxix., 358.
  32 George III., c. xlvi., 359.
  33 George III. c. lxxvi., 359.
  49 George III. c. lxxvi., 384.
  51 George III. c. lxxvi., 386.
  1 George IV. c. li., 409.
  5 George IV. c. lxvii., 422.
  William IV. c. lxvii., 429.
Adams, —, 252.
Addison, Rev. Mr., 451.
Adnavick, 610.
Africa, Sierra Leone, 555.
Ailik, Cape, 594.
Aillebout, d', M., 268.
Akarman, S., 174.
Alexander Bay, road to, 628.
  R., 665.
Allan, M., 572.
Allan's, Sir H., tender for railway, 623.
Alley, Judge, 391.
Alsop, firm of, 387.
  R., 665.
  R., & Co., 460.
Amherst, Sir G., 412-416.
  Col. Wm., 307.
  despatches, 412-416.
  portrait of, 306.
Andrews (Murphy & Co.), 539.
  Capt., 224.
  Elias, 175.
Angell, 393, 655.
  E., 381.
Anguille, Cape, 559, 560, 561.
  Hills, 629.
Anspach, Rev. L. A., 377.
Anse, Sablon, 587.
Anthoine, —, 393, 655.
Apsey, G., 617.
Aquafort, view of, 227.
Archer, R., 301.
Archibald, C. D., 431.
  portrait of, 432.
  Sir E. M., 431, 439, 446, 465, 466, 475, 636, 663.
  portrait of, 432.
  S. G., 460.
Armstrong, A., 301.
ARMY:
  fortifications at Cupids, 126.
  power to build, 143.
  at Ferryland, 157.
  Kirke's, 205.
  in N. in 1745, 297.
  in 1780 at St. John's, 349.
  troops sent to St. John's in 1697, 222.
  winter in St. John's, 223.

ARMY—cont.
  picture of English soldier in 1710, 224.
  troops permanently stationed at St. John's, 224.
  failure of the, in America, 236.
  Moody's defence of St. John's, 242.
  Lloyd's defence of the outlying settlements in 1705-6, 246.
  colonial militia, 249.
  Collins' command, 249.
  troops in St. John's, 267.
  officers engrossing trade, 267.
  local militia, 268, 269.
  local militia formed, 270.
  regiment raised in N., 274.
  recruiting for, in N., 290.
  troops at St. John's and Placentia, 293.
  local militia reformed, 294.
  church accommodation in St. John's for, 295.
  sketch of cannon found at Louisbourg, 300.
  recapture of St. John's, 306, 412.
  60th Rifles, 308.
  Montgomery's Highlanders, 308.
  Frazer's Highlanders, 308.
  Royal Scotch, 308.
  trouble with garrison at St. John's and Placentia, 328.
  soldiers acquire land, 336.
  change of regiments, 339.
  soldiers farming, 341, 342.
  garrison of St. John's and neighbourhood, 349.
  sedition in St. John's, 364, 418.
  Nova Scotia, jurisdiction of, over, N., 365.
  troops in St. John's in 1794-8, 368.
  Royal N. Regiment, 368, 654.
  Nova Scotia Regiment, 368.
  volunteer corps formed, 382.
  Royal Newfoundland Company, 455.
  St. Pierre, troops at, in 1794, 575.
  duel in St. John's, 656.
  garrison withdrawn from St. John's, 659.
ARMY OFFICERS:
  Amherst, Sir G., 412-416.
  Col. W., 307, 412-416.
  portrait of, 306.
  Baillie, Capt., 414.
  Barrow, Capt., 414.
  Bennet, Col., 167.
  Brady, Major, 341.
  Bruce, Genl., 488.
  Campbell, Capt. See.
    M. Genl., 382, 655.
  Cartwright, Major G. See.
  Darling, Sir C. See.
  Desborrow, Genl., 167.
  Elder, Sir G., 656.
  Elford, Major, 202.
  Fawcett, Col., 529.
  Ferguson, Capt., 412.
  Gibson, Col., 222.
  Gledhill, Col., 282, 287.
  Grey, Capt., 488.
  Haly, Lt. Col. See.
  Handyside, Lt. Col., 223.
  Harvey, Sir J. See.
  Howe, Genl., 339.

ARMY OFFICERS—cont.
  Latham, Lt. See.
  Law, Col. See.
  Le Marchant, Sir J. G. See.
  Lilburne, Lt., 224.
  Lloyd, Major. See.
  Maxse, Sir H., 513, 660.
  McDonell, Capt. See.
  Moody, Lt. See.
  Moore, M., Genl., 655.
  Murray, Col., 382.
  Norris, Col., 280.
  O'Brien, Sir T. N. See.
  Ogilvie, B., Genl., 574.
  Pearce, Capt. See.
  Philips, Lt., 269.
  Phillpotts, Lt., 656.
  Pringle, Col., 341, 652, 653.
  Pynn, Sir H., 176.
  Raynor, Capt. J., 156, 178, 179.
  Reeves, Col. G., 656.
  Richards, Major, 223, 252.
  Rivers, Col., 237.
  Robe, Major, 458.
  Rudkin, Capt., 656.
  Sale, Lt. Col., 434, 437.
  Schuyler, Lt., 309, 413, 414.
  Skerret, Col. See
  Skinner, Col. See
  Stapley, Col., 167.
  Sutherland, Major, 412.
  Teesdale, Capt., 488.
  Thorne, Major, 574.
  Tomlinson, Col., 167.
  Tonge, Capt. W., 382, 654.
  Tucker, Col., 417.
  Tullikin, Lt. Col., 412.
  Vane, Engineer, 269.
Arnold's Cove, road to, 628.
Arthur's Mill, 621.
Arnott, —, 382, 655.
Ash, F., 301.
  family, 452.
Ashenhurst, T., 4, 13.
Assises Harbour, 610.
Augustine, Labrador Post from, 608.
Auk, Great, view of, 283.
Auten, Capt., 239.
Aylon, L. V. de, 43.
Aylrod's, John, description of Placentia, 185, 206.
Ayre & Sons, 527.
  C. R., 508, 665.
Azores farmer discovers Labrador, 590.

Back Cove, road to, 628.
Badcock, W., 301.
Badger Bay, road to, 628.
  Brook, 629.
Baillie, Capt., 414.
Baine, Johnston & Co., 460, 493, 527, 614, 617.
  (Lang & Co.), 387.
Baird J., 527, 548, 556, 559, 561.
  portrait of, 549.
  Mrs. J., 393.
  W., 294.
Baleine, 259.
Balfour, Rev. D., 652.
Baltimore, Lord, 132, 137.
  portrait of, 113.
  arms, 110.
  character, 113.
  charter, 131.

INDEX.

Baltimore, Lord—*cont.*
  colony, true boundaries of, 109, 110.
  colony, Wynne's letter, 128.
  mansion, 132, 151, 155, 156.
  Leonard Calvert, 133.
  Cecil, Lord, 133, 155, 159.
  claim to Avalon in 1660. 156.
  Frederick, Lord, claim in 1754, 133, 293.
  portrait of, 292.
Bank, Savings, 436, 459, 656.
  Union, 658.
  Commercial, 658.
  failure of, 536, 661.
Banking, 455.
Bannerman, Sir A., 484, 487, 488, 492.
  portrait of, 492.
Barbese, 557.
Bareneed, 496.
Barge Bay, 617.
Barjery, J., 262.
Barnes, J. B., & Co. 460.
  Quarter-master, 382.
  R., 450, 455, 457, 664.
  W., 410.
  W. M., 665.
Barron, P. M., 720.
Bartlett's family, 452.
  harbour, 477.
  J., 496, 617, 665.
  W., 615, 617.
  crew, view of, 604.
Barton, Capt., acting Governor, 374.
Barred Bay, 562.
Barrot, A., 272.
Barrow, Capt., 414.
Bas, Cape de, 40.
Bascombe, G., 417.
Basques, Port-aux-, 626, 629, 631.
  railway to, 622.
  cable to, 640.
  in 1857, view of, 640.
Battcock, T., 665.
Batteau, —, 610, 617.
Batten, Capt., 382.
  —, 664.
Battle Harbour, 604, 610, 614, 617.
  hospital, 615.
  post to, 608.
  view of, 608.
Batts, Joe, Arm, 279.
Baudoin, 216, 220, 230.
Baxter, J. Phinney, 105, 605.
Bayley's Cove, 301.
Beauclerc, Lord Vere, 284, 285.
Beaucourt, M., 264, 265.
  (Boocore, M.), 261.
Beck family of St. Lawrence, 389.
  H. of St. Lawrence, 389.
  T., 411, 441, 446.
Beenlan, Quarter-master, 654.
  —, 382.
Begg, Keir & Co., 460.
Belcombe, Lt. Col., 413, 414.
Beletre, M. de, 261.
Belin, Capt., 557, 563.
Bellair's survey, 501.
Bellater, M., 253.
Belle Isle, 222, 268, 471, 472.
  Little, 271.
  straits of, 39, 45, 278, 410, 596.
  French burn rooms at, 371.
Belloram, 305.
Beloran of St. Pierre, 566.
Benger, T., 252, 253, 272.
Bennet, Col., 167.
  Wm., 272, 315.
Bennett, —, 430.
  C. F., 455, 457, 458, 658, 465, 495, 496.
  portrait of, 496.
  C. F. & Co., 453, 460.
  portrait of, 502.
  T., 431, 433, 664.
  Judge, T. R., 489, 499, 502, 506, 665.

Benning, C., 465, 466, 468, 664.
Benton Mill, 621.
BEOTHICS, 96, 151, 183, 278, 324.
  Whitbourne's description of the, 63–65
  in north of N., none in south, 107.
  Guy's meeting with, 128, 133.
  settlement, view of, 322.
  Gambier attempts to civilize the, 376, 377.
  Buchan's expedition, 384.
  Mary March, portrait of, 384.
  Shandithit, 385.
  disappearance of the, 385, 386.
  wars with the Eskimo, 591.
  G. Cartwright's plan to reconcile, 598.
  G. Cartwright accompanies his brother to, 599.
  Spratt sent with painting to, 654.
  murder of Lawrie, 654.
  proclamation to protect, 655.
  Institution, 656.
  Society formed, 657.
Berbice Cove, 477.
Bergne, Sir H., 503, 505.
Bermuda, 89, 151, 300, 418, 429, 433.
  view of, 89.
  fishery at N., 345, 416.
Berry, Sir John, 194, 196.
Bersimis, post from, 608.
Best, W., 381.
Bett's Cove, 279.
  telegraph, 639.
Beverley, T., 174.
Bevill's family, 427.
  title, 337.
  Wm., 295.
Bickford, Elias, 222.
"Billies," 427.
Biscayan Cove. 20.
Bishop, C. R., 559, 566.
  —, 655.
Bishop's Falls, 629.
Black Bear Bay, 617.
  Duck Brook, 477, 557.
  River, road to, 628.
  Tickle. 610, 617.
  Rev. W., 654.
Blackburn of Placentia, 393, 655.
Blackmore, —, 288.
Blackwood, J., 418.
Blaikie, —, 392, 393, 655.
Blake, Sir H., 660.
  portrait of, 519.
  J., 568.
Bland & Tobin, 456.
  J., 362, 419.
  J. B., 434, 437.
Blandford Harbour, 607.
  Hon. S., 661, 662, 615, 616, 665.
  portrait of, 606.
  voyage to Cape Chidley, 606.
  family, 452.
Blanc, Sablon, 473, 601, 606, 608, 609, 616.
  Boat, Harbour, road to, 628.
Bobardt, Dr., 605.
Bodens, firm of, 297.
Boisbriand, M., 232.
Bolan, J., 375.
Bolster Rock, 610, 617.
BONAVISTA, Cabot's landfall at, 10, 537.
  origin of name, 11.
  French fishing, 186.
  French attack on, 245, 238, 240, 261, 262, 263, 264, 266.
  planters, go to, 232.
  18th century plan of, 238.
  Montigny's attack on, 241.
  defence of, 249.
  difficulties with French, 274.
  law books for, 286.
  fishery at, 297.

BONAVISTA—*cont.*
  magistrates, &c., of, 301.
  treaty limit, 312.
  justices for, 336, 393.
  seal fishery at, 419, 451.
  settlements north of, 280, 542, 552.
  under-represented, 468.
  election petition, 433.
  members for, 438, 455, 465, 468, 664.
  farming land in, 597.
  trade to Labrador, 602.
  advantages of railway to, 619.
  telegraph to, 639.
  Cape, 258, 537.
  Green Island, 246.
Bond, Hon. R., 530–538, 665.
  portrait of, 533.
Bonfoy, Capt., 284, 292.
Bonne Bay, 472, 556, 557, 560, 561.
  herring fishery, 630.
Bonne Esperance, 597, 608, 609, 616.
  view of, 608.
Bonnell, —, 389.
Book first printed about N., 76.
Books on N., p. 666.
Boone, J. H., 665.
Booth, Sir G., 175.
Bordot, M., 573.
Botwood, Rev. G., 659.
Botwoodville Saw Mill, view of, 621.
  view of, 624.
Bouchier, —, 382, 654, 655.
Boulton, Chief Justice, 433, 434, 438, 444, 448, 449, 663.
  portrait of, 434.
Bourne, Chief Justice, 447, 457.
Bouthland, —, 385.
Bowers, P. R., 532, 548.
Bowgan, N., 84.
Bowker, Capt., 408, 655.
Bown, G. F., 460.
Bowring, B., 427.
  Bros., 460, 527.
  C., 721.
  C. T., 428.
  portrait of, 428.
  (Rothwell and), 527.
  W. B., 428.
  portrait of, 428.
Boyd and McDougall, 460.
  J., 393, 436, 656, 665.
Boyles, B., 617.
Bradore, 616.
  remains of French town at, 596.
Bradley, —, 284.
  Chris., 293.
  T., 4, 12.
Bradshaw, —, 393, 655.
  A., 665.
Bradstreet, Col. John, 284, 290.
Brady, Chief Justice Sir F., 226, 663.
  Major, 341.
Braithwaite, R., 315.
Brand, J., 301.
Brazell, P., 362.
Brazil, trade to, 14, 53, 403.
Brennan, P., 721.
Brenton, E. B., 662.
Breton Harbour, 380.
  Cape, *see* Canada.
Brett, —, 637.
Brest, Labrador, 46, 596.
Brickwood, J., 416.
Brien, T., 523.
Brig Bay, 477, 560, 561, 562.
Bridge, Archdeacon, 469.
  portrait of, 469.
  Commodore, 241.
Brigus, 232, 262, 496, 602.
  view of, 104.
  return of the "Hunter," 643.
  seal fishery, 451.
  trade to Labrador, 602.

INDEX.

Brigus—*cont.*
  telegraph to, 635, 636.
  the Goulds, view of, 136.
Brine, R., 381.
Bristol's Hope, 110.
Brittaniola, 137.
Brocklebank, J., 460.
Broders, W., 379.
Brookfield, 427.
Brooking's family, 227.
  (Robinson & Co.), 458, 460.
  T. H., 387, 424, 427, 429.
Brooks, J., 336.
  N., 301, 315.
Broom, C. 362.
  J., 382, 393, 655.
Brophy, J., 375.
Brown, J., 616.
  Hoyles, & Co., 387, 409.
  John, J.P., at Placentia, 709.
  P., 431, 438, 440, 664.
  R., 393, 451, 455, 456, 463, 664.
  portrait of, 455.
  T., 602.
  W., 431, 664.
Browne, Capt., 539.
Browning, A., 174.
Broyle, Cape, 132, 415.
Bruce, Gen., 488.
Bryant of Ferryland, 393.
Bryant, —, 655.
Buchan, Capt., 384, 393, 403, 404, 411, 655.
Buchanan, A., 709.
Buchannan, T., 301.
Bull Dog Islands, 606.
Bulley, R., 344.
Bulley, firm of, 297.
BULLS, BAY, 152, 157, 174, 205, 242, 261, 262, 264, 266, 271, 286, 292, 297, 301, 315, 349, 357, 360, 393, 405, 415.
  D'Iberville at, 215.
  losses in 1705, 246.
  French land at, 306, 371.
  road, 427, 448.
  Arm, Trinity Bay, 133, 233, 245, 264.
  cable to, 642.
Buraleet, M., 217.
Burchell, H. C., 529, 625.
Burgeo, eclipse observed at, 316, 468.
  members for, 664.
Burgess, E. R., 665.
Burin, 48, 165, 298, 336, 465, 468, 574.
  members for, 720.
  telegraph to, 639, 641.
Burke, J., 362.
  M., 379.
  T., 411.
Buoy's Island, 249, 415.
  plan of, 298.
  (Isle-aux-Bois), 293.
  (Isle-au-Bois), Labrador, 616.
Burrell of Trinity, 393, 655.
Burne, Peter, 306.
Burnett, T., 294.
Burt, —, 253.
Burton, J. T., 665.
Bushell, Wm., 108.
Butler, —, 655.
  Hy., 298.
  P., 411.
  W., 720.
Butt, N., 559, 566.
  W., 617.
Button Islands, fishing at, 607.
Byng, Hon. John, 284, 289.
  portrait of, 289.
Byrne, T., 448, 468, 489, 664.
  — 438.
Byron, Lord, 334.
  decision about Coughlan's salary, 331.
Cabot, J., 6, 7.
  at Labrador, 587.
  Ayala's letter, 29.

Cabot—*cont.*
  charters, 8.
  voyages, 9-13.
  landfall, 9-10, 30, 589.
  Sebastian, 8, 12, 16, 30.
  portrait of, 17.
Cahill, J., 343, 375, 381.
Cairns, J., 556, 559, 561.
Callanan, J. J., 665.
Calvert, Leonard, 133.
Cambriol Colchos, 111.
Camp Islands, 617.
CAMPBELL, Admiral, 355, 362.
  Capt., 393, 412, 541, 655.
  report on lobster fishery, 556.
  Colin, 239, 242, 244, 253, 262, 263, 265, 266.
  Maj.-Gen., 382, 655.
  Mill, 621.
  W. & Co., 523, 527.
Canada Bay, 576.
CANADA, DOMINION OF.
CANADA, 245.
  French agree to surrender, 312.
  produce, 394.
  Government send aid for fire of 1846, 460.
  deputation to, 474.
  to have full right of taking bait, 519.
  Government relief from, in 1892, 528.
  smuggling from St. Pierre, 578-581.
  Quebec Act joins Labrador to Canada, 597.
  supports Labrador Deep Sea Mission, 605.
  confederation, 494, 532.
  confederation conference, 658.
CANADIANS.
  Allan, Sir H., 572.
  Alley, Judge, 391.
  Davies, L. H., 502.
  Dawson, Dr. S. E., 30.
  Doutre, —, 502.
  Eaton, T. D. V., 618.
  Francklin, M., 330.
  Hind, H. Y., 606.
  Howlan, Lieut.-Governor, 391.
  Lawrance, Governor, 567.
  Low, A. P., 618.
  McDonald, Sir J. A., 532.
  Nicholas, Governor, 276.
  Paterson, Rev. G., 10.
  Reid, R. G. *See.*
  Smith, Sir D. A., 605.
  Strachan, Bishop, 434.
  Thompson, —, 502.
  Tupper, Sir C., 531.
  Uniacke, Judge, 392.
  Weatherbee, —, 502.
ANTICOSTI, 324, 327, 334.
  joined to N., 384.
CAPE BRETON, 21, 78, 257, 258, 259, 260, 290, 312, 329, 423, 431, 601.
  discovery of, 4.
  Hore's voyage to, 41.
  cable to, 640.
  Baddeck, first cable sent to, 640.
  Louisbourg, 259, 282, 284, 289, 312.
  view of, 299.
  cannon found at, 300.
  troops from, 308.
  Scatari, 259.
  Sydney, proposed steamers to, 633.
  Sydney, North, cable to, 643.
  Cameron, M., received first cable from N., 640.
HUDSON BAY, 605.
  D'Iberville's attack on, 215.
  Company, 410, 617.

CAPE BRETON—*cont.*
HUDSON BAY—*cont.*
  stations and steamer, 601, 606, 607.
  postal service, 607.
  straits channel leading to, 607.
NEW BRUNSWICK, 21, 429.
  created, 709.
  Chedabuctou garrison to Placentia, 209, 210.
  Fredericton, N.B., 460.
  St. John, fire at, 457.
  aid from, 460.
NOVA SCOTIA, 20, 21, 147, 257, 290, 392, 429, 431, 460.
  government of Placentia, 275.
  Placentia separated from, 286.
  coal mining, 329.
  obtains local government, 377.
  Sir J. Harvey made governor, 461.
  fisheries, 504.
  lobster packers in N., 556.
  Acadians at St. Pierre, 568, 569.
  Eskimo in, 591.
  Annapolis, 20.
  Canseau, 312.
  Halifax, N.S., 307, 329, 389, 419, 567.
  assistance from, in 1817, 407.
  communication with, 455.
  aid from, in 1846, 460.
  meeting of Commission, 502.
  conference, 532.
  inhabitants of St. Pierre with, 455.
  branch of Deep Sea Mission formed at, 605.
  Port Royal, 20.
ONTARIO, Government relief from, in 1892, 529.
PRINCE EDWARD ISLAND, 312, 391, 423, 464.
  (St. John's Island), 289.
QUEBEC.
  Gaspe, 289.
  Magdalen Islands, 20, 327, 334.
  (Ramea Islands), 52.
  French curé and flock go to, 330, 592.
  sea cow fishery, 334, 589.
  Quebec, 45, 249, 264.
  captured by Kirke, 147.
  Labrador Co., 569.
Canaries, Grand, 248.
Canynge, W., 7, 27.
Caplin Bay, 574.
Cove, 293.
Capstan Island, 617.
CARBONEAR, 105, 196, 232, 249, 261, 262, 285, 286, 297, 301, 315, 331, 351, 393, 415, 468.
  D'Iberville's attack on, 220.
  views of, 244.
  defence of, 245.
  losses in 1705, 246.
  persecution of Roman Catholics at, 294.
  troops at, 297.
  magistrates, &c. of, 301.
  captured in 1762, 306.
  riots at, 438.
  riot, 447.
  seal fishery, 451.
  post to, 463.
  trade to Labrador, 602.
  telegraph line, 639.

INDEX

CARBONEAR—*cont.*
    dispute about right to preach in, 652.
    riots in, in 1766, 652.
    members for, 664.
    Island, 266, 270, 271.
    view of, 244.
    successfully defended in 1705, 264.
    plan of, 296.
    captured, 314.
Careen, D., 292.
Carleton, Capt., 247.
Carmel, Bay of, 266.
Carolinopole, 137.
Carouge, 247, 576.
Carrington, Rev. F., 393, 655.
Carrol's Cove, 617.
Carson, Dr. W., 396-398, 411, 427, 429, 432, 433, 436, 438, 444, 445, 457, 467, 664.
    death of, 657.
    portrait of, 396.
Carter, Sir F. B. T., 305, 468, 474, 494, 499, 501, 506, 509, 529, 658, 663, 664.
    portrait of, 494.
    J., 4, 12.
    Mr., 559, 561.
    P. and W., 460.
    P. W., 387, 392, 489, 711.
    R., 284, 293, 315, 334, 336, 652, 664.
    Capt. R., R.N., 431, 457, 461, 468, 664.
    S. B., 665.
    Val, 213.
    W., 387, 393, 653, 655.
Cartier's, J., voyage, 10, 45, 587, 588.
    at St. Pierre, 565.
Cartwright, 601, 610, 617.
    view of, 608.
    G., 325, 592, 598, 602.
    account of Labrador, 598.
    character, 600.
    diary, 599.
    dislike of Noble and Pinson, 599.
    treatment of Eskimo, 599.
    portrait of, 600.
    John, 323, 324.
    portrait of, 323.
Carty, Mr., 512.
    M. H., 665.
Cary, T., 301.
Casey, J., 720.
Cassidy, the tailor, 449.
Cassini's description of St. Pierre, 569.
Castors River, 557.
Cat Bay, 16.
Catalina, 297, 639.
Cawardine, Nurse, 615.
Chafe, Lieut., 294.
    Mr., 581.
Chambers, A., 410.
Change Islands, telegraph to, 639.
Channel winter fishery, 630.
    view of, 630.
CHANNEL ISLANDS. Guernsey, 103.
    Jersey, 52.
    Raleigh encourages trade to N., 76.
    settlers, 183.
    ship, 239, 389.
    men, 298.
    rooms, 450, 451.
    men at St. Pierre, 567.
    Robins of, 601.
Chapeau Rouge, 180.
Chappell, Lieut., 394.
Charles, Cape, 473, 597, 599, 602, 610, 617.
Charters, Cabot's, 8.
    Ashenhurst's, &c., 13.
    Gilbert's, 62, 66.

Charters—*cont.*
    Guy's, 93, 122.
    Western, 142, 154.
    Sir D. Kirke's, 148.
    Sir J. Kirke's, 155.
Chasco Portu, 48.
Chateau, 594, 610, 617.
Chetwynd, Mr., 560, 561.
Chidley Cape, 602, 605.
Child, Sir Josiah, 188, 189.
    portrait of, 190.
Chimmo, Fort, Post, 609.
Chimney Tickle, 610.
Choix, Port au, 333, 354, 473, 477, 539, 557, 562.
    view of, 553.
Christian, R., 213.
Church, J., 382, 655.
Church, Rev. J., 393.
Claim Cove, loss of *Anglo-Saxon* at, 658.
Clapp, G., 460.
    widow, 272.
    property, 410.
Clark, R., capture by Sancé, 77, 78.
    narrative of Gilbert's expedition, 70.
    George, 356.
    of Greenspond, 359.
    S., 78.
    beach, 97, 406.
    views of, 101, 104.
Cleary, Capt., 487.
Cleer, John, 213.
Clenick, J., 301.
Cleeves, W., 566.
Clerk, John, 301.
Clift, —, 352, 655.
    J., 410, 460, 656.
    J. A., 665.
    Wood & Co., 527.
Climate. *See* N. Miscellaneous.
Clinton, Capt., 284.
Clode Sound, view of, 624.
Clotworthy, —, 161.
Cluetts at St. Pierre, 574.
Coch, Wm., 280.
Cocking, Lt., 294.
    Wm., 323.
Cochran, J., 326.
Cochrane, Sir J., 662.
    Sir T., 423, 424, 619.
    recalled, 436.
    portrait, o', 426.
Codey, M., 375.
Codner's title, 395.
Codroy, 472, 473, 558, 629.
Cody's claim at Flat Islands, 485.
Coffin, John, 169.
Coghlan (of P. C. C. and Lucas), 599.
Coghlan's, J., account of Bermudians fishing in N., 343.
Coke, D'Ewes, 336, 359, 360, 653, 662.
Colclough, Chief Justice C., 361, 390, 662.
    threatening letter sent to, 401.
Cole, R., 270.
    Mr., 497.
Colesworthy, Governor R., 271.
Colinet, 185, 210, 246, 514, 566.
    view of Bridge, 216.
    Admiral's Beach, 185.
    Island, 173.
Collins, —, 366.
    Governor John, 249, 255, 270-2.
    account of, 1708, 269.
    appointed governor, 270.
    petitions for governor's pay, 271.
    J., 665.
    W., 315.
Colston, W., 94.
    letter, 128.
Columbier, 389.

Columbus, 5.
Colvill, Lord, 308, 412-6.
Come-by-Chance, road to, 623.
Conception Bay, 245, 266, 296, 438, 457, 465.
    names in, 19.
    chosen for Guy's Colony, 95.
    raided by Montigny, 263.
    views in, 326.
    road, 448.
    riots, 483.
    trade to Labrador, 602.
    members for, 664.
Conche Harbour, 247, 576.
Conolly, —, 389.
Conroy, J. G., 665.
Content Harbour, 232.
Cook, Capt., 316.
    portrait of, 316.
    map, 317.
Cooke, J. R. M., 436.
Cooksley, Capt., 393, 655.
Cooper (Taylor and), 560, 561.
Coote, T., 392, 393, 463, 652, 653.
Corbin, Capt., 456.
Cormack, J., 467.
    crossed N., 654.
Cortereal's voyage, 4, 10, 14, 15, 590.
Costabelle, —, 249, 259, 264, 268, 276.
Costley, Darby, 234.
Cotton, Master, 62.
Couch, Wm., 174.
Coughlan, Rev. L., 331, 334.
    Surgeon, 382, 654.
Courtemande, Seigneur, 596.
Courting, 568.
Cow Head, 497, 560, 561.
Cox, J., 375.
    J. B., 440.
Cozens, C., 431, 602, 664.
Crabb's Brook, 559, 561.
Craig, D. H., 640.
Crantz's History of Greenland, 591.
Craudley, R., 149.
Crawford, —, 382, 653.
Crawley, Capt., 567, 568.
    family, 137.
Craze, —, 476.
Cremellaire, 337.
Crowe, Capt., 254, 272.
    laws, 254, 271.
Crowdy, Hon. J., 434, 437, 449, 456, 457, 465, 466, 475.
    portrait of, 450.
Crummy, —, 617.
Cruse, T., of Ashprinton, 157.
Cuckold Head, 370.
    Cove, 349.
Cudworth, Capt., 487.
Cull, W., 377.
Cunard Line, 453.
    steamer ashore at Cape Race, 461.
Cupids, 97.
    view of, 97.
Curwen, Dr., 615, 616.
Curtis, J., 301.
Curtis, —, 567, 568.
Cusack, T., and Sons, 460.

Dalton, —, 301.
    L., 343.
Dameron, Capt., 539, 562, 563.
Danby, Lord, 208.
Dangeau, M., 569.
Daniel, S. T., 441.
Danseville, M., 572, 573.
Darby, N., of Bristol, at Cape Charles, 598, 599.
D'Argenteuil, M., 268.
Darling, Sir C., 469, 474, 545.
Davies, L. H., 502.
Davigrand, M., 245.

INDEX.

Davis, —, 215.
—, 616.
Capt., 194, 196.
Mr., 415.
Inlet, 610.
Davis Island, Post to, 609.
Davy, Capt., 252.
Dawe, Lawyer, 411.
C., 665.
E., 665.
family, 452.
Day, J., 665.
Dead Islands, 610, 617.
Deady of Fox Harbour, 581.
Dearin, J. J., 665.
De Bellievre, P., 148.
De Bon, —, 472.
De Brouillon, M., 209, 210.
St. Ovide, 249, 268, 269, 270.
De Catalogne, G., 264.
Deep Sea Mission to Labrador, 604, 614.
Deep Water Creek, 617.
Deer Lake, 626, 629.
view of, 622.
De Frontenac, M., 211.
Delaney, D., 375.
Dr., 343.
J., 440, 468, 665.
family, 452.
De la Cosa, J., 13, 30, 47, 589.
De La Peiriere, M., 232.
De La Poype, 182.
Delean, M., 265.
Delepiney, M., 264.
De Lery, C., 264.
Delfosse, M., 504.
De Grave, W., 339.
De Linctot, M., 261.
De Lo, Chevalier, 261.
Delucluse, M., 478.
De Mins, M., 217, 231.
De Mongore, M., 414.
De Montorgueil, M., 211.
Denmark, fishery negotiations with, 25-28.
chronicles, 587.
vessels, 454.
Dennis, Capt., 269.
Denys Jean, in N., 4.
at Renew's, 17.
map, 281.
De Prado, A., 39.
De Quetville at Forteau, 601.
Dermer, Thomas, 104.
letter, 129.
De Sancé, —, 77.
De Sapiain, M., 48.
Des Barres, Judge, A. W., 423, 447, 469, 662.
portrait of, 423.
family, 391, 423.
Desborow, Commander Charles, 213.
Desborrow, Genl., 167.
Deschaufours, M., 232.
Des Isles, C. R., 545.
portrait of, 545.
Despair Bay, 298, 340, 402.
Despenseus, M., 269.
Destrick, Stephen, 185.
De Ternay, Admiral, 306.
Dettrick's, Isaac, account of the occupation of Placentia, 178.
De Vandreuil, Marquess, 264.
De Villedonné, M., 261.
De Vœux, Sir G. W., 514.
portrait of, 515.
Devonshire. See England.
De Witt on the English Navy, 17.
D'Haussonville, Count, 305, 413-415.
D'Iberville, Bienville, 215.
P. Le Moyne, 215-219.
portrait of, 215.
Dickenson, W., portrait of, 646.
Dickson, Lt., 324.

Dildo, 271, 439.
Island, fish hatchery at, 648, 650.
Dillon, J., 455, 457, 664.
W., 446, 460.
Dingle, Rev. —, of Bay Bulls, 364, 371.
Dodd, T., 334, 339, 653.
Dog Creek, 283.
Dollard, —, 450.
Domino Run, 604, 610, 617.
Donelly, Hon. W. J. S., 502-506, 514, 659, 665.
portrait of, 502.
Dooling, R., 381.
Dorrill, Governor R., 284, 293.
Dougherty's forge, 524.
Douglas, Capt., 306, 412.
J., 448.
J., and Co., 458, 460.
Doutre, Mr., 502.
Downer, Capt., 606.
at Nachvak, 602.
Downing, John, 176, 194.
narrative, 205.
petition, 207, 208.
John, senr., 205.
instructions, 150.
William, 176.
Doyle, E., 375, 381.
(H. B.), 431.
J. A., English in America, 17.
Martin, 292.
Mr., 463.
P., 411, 438, 664.
Drachart, C., 332, 594.
Drake, Sir B., 79.
Sir F., 54.
portrait of, 54.
Commodore F. W., 291, 292.
Drew, John, 272.
Wm., scalping of, 216, 230.
Driscoll, D., 381.
Ducarrow, J., 174, 185.
Duckworth, Sir J. T., 361, 384.
Carson's attack on, 397.
portrait of, 385.
Duder, C., 492, 499, 665.
Dudley's map, 160.
Duff, —, 617.
W., 665.
Governor, 337.
Dugdale, Lt., 416.
Duggan, P., 382, 467.
Surgeon, 382, 655.
Du Mesnilambert, M., 572.
Duneen, John, 321.
Dunien, Mr., 382.
Dunn, A., 316, 328, 339.
M., 440.
Dunscombe and Harvey, 387, 460.
G. H., 455.
Hon. J. W., 424, 437, 457.
Du Plessis, M., 268.
Durant, M., 266.
DUTCH ships in N., 83, 109, 103, 127.
supplies of fish to Spain, 138.
attack on Ferryland, 156.
traders, 162.
defeat English, 174.
war, 177.
at St. John's, 193, 197.
Admiral Ruyter, 197.
missionary to Labrador, 594.
Prince Henry in St. John's, 657.
Dwyer, E. J., 438, 439, 664.
S., 664.
T., 549.

Eagle, Lt., 248.
River, Labrador, view of, 588.
Earle, family of, 222.
Earll, Mrs. Ann, 271, 272.

Easton's, Peter, piracies, 101, 128.
Echarde, Portu, 48.
Echevete, —, 37.
Eclipse Harbour, 602.
of the sun observed at Burgeo, 316.
Eddy, James, 640.
Edens, T. J., 527.
Edgar, —, 393, 655.
Edgcombe, R., 315.
Edgell, Capt., 375.
Education, Castle Rennie school, 657.
Gambier encourages, 376, 377.
subdivision of Protestant schools, 444.
Richard Barnes' Act, 450.
first grammar school, 654.
Edwards, Governor R. (1757), 284, 294.
Governor R. (1780), 349.
sued at Exeter, 358.
Eguillete, 247.
Elder, Sir G., 656.
Elford, Major, 202.
Eliot, Hugh, 4, 14.
Sir John, 108.
Elliott, Capt., 393, 655.
Governor, 365, 476.
letters of, about Bermuda, 416.
Ellis, Capt., English pirate, 103.
W. H., 468, 474, 664.
Elson (Slade & Co.), 438.
Emerson, G. H., 390, 436, 457, 465, 467, 615, 663, 664.
G. H., jun., 514, 532, 550.
portrait of, 551.
H. A., 432, 438, 466, 664.
P., 665.
Emily Harbour, 610, 617.
Engelie, 320.
English Cape, 10, 13.
English Harbour, 20, 301, 520, 521.
English, J., 664.
English fishery and trade in N., 12-18, 33-35, 39, 40, 57, 53, 69, 70, 81, 83.
Armada, 82.
Pine's picture of, 82.
frequent 40 harbours, 103.
Star Chamber rules, 140, 154, 267.
girls pressed, 147.
"Rump of ye Parliament," 169.
Government in Anne's reign, 256.
Jacobite rebellion, 285.
Union Jack, 375.
Government aid in 1817, 407, 1846, 461.
Crimean War, 470.
Colonial Conference, 519.
Mansion House Fund, 529.
ENGLISH MEN AND WOMEN:
Addison, J., 257.
Anglesey, Lord, 208.
Archibald, Sir E. M. See.
Bacon, Lord, 91-97.
portrait of, 92.
Baltimore, Lord. See.
Bannerman, Sir A. See.
Beauclerc, Lord V., 284, 285.
Bergne, Sir H., 503, 505.
Blake, Sir H. See.
Booth, Sir G., 175.
Bowring, Sir John, 428.
Bridgewater, Lord, 208.
Buckingham, Duke of, 109.
—, 497.
Burke, Edmund, 300, 353.
Bute, Lord, 311.
portrait of, 311.
Canning, Sir S., 640.
Carbery, Lord, 110.
Carlisle, —, 77.
Lord, 208.

INDEX.

ENGLISH MEN AND WOMEN—cont.
　Charles I., 121, 135, 141, 146, 148, 152, 155.
　　portrait of, 135.
　Charles II., 153, 172, 175, 176, 180.
　　portrait of, 172.
　Chatham, Lord, 306, 310, 313, 567.
　　portrait of, 310.
　Child, Sir J. See.
　Churchill's attack on Treaty of Paris, 313.
　Clarence, Duke of, death of, 520.
　Claypole, —, 151, 161.
　Cockburn, Sir A., 457.
　Cochrane, Sir J., 662.
　Coke's argument for freer fishing, 121.
　Conway, Lord, 109.
　Cornwallis, Lord, 544.
　Cottington, Sir F., 133.
　Craven, Lord, 208.
　Cromwell's, Oliver, policy, 159.
　　recapture of Nova Scotia, 147.
　　rule, 205.
　　proposed Protestant missions, 228.
　　portrait of, 159.
　Danby, Lord, 208.
　Darling, Sir C. See.
　Darnley, Lord, 411.
　Dartmouth's, Lord, report, 236, 266.
　Derby, Earl of, 471, 546.
　Desborrow, General, 167.
　De Vœux, Sir G. W. See.
　Doyle (A. B.), 431.
　　J. A., 17.
　Drake, Sir —, 54.
　　portrait of, 54.
　Egremont, Earl of, 412.
　Elizabeth, Queen, 54, 55, 80, 81.
　　portrait of, 53.
　Eliot, Sir T., 108.
　Exeter, Bishop of, 150.
　Falkland, Lord. See.
　Fauconberg, Lord, 208.
　Ford, Sir C., 505, 515.
　Fox's attack on the Treaty of Versailles, 353.
　Frobisher, Sir M., 55.
　George I., 274.
　　portrait of, 275.
　George II., 285.
　　portrait of, 285.
　George III., 304, 599.
　　portrait of, 304.
　George IV., portrait of, 422.
　Gilbert Sir H. See.
　　Sir J., 79.
　Glenelg, Lord, 429.
　Gladstone, W. E., 461.
　Goderich, Viscount, 429.
　Gorges, Sir F., 104.
　Grey, Earl, 460, 463.
　Hawkesbury, Lord, 347.
　Hamilton, Duke of, 143, 151.
　　portrait of, 142.
　　K. Baillie. See.
　Hampshire, Sir T., 61.
　Harley, Earl of Oxford, 255.
　　portrait of, 255.
　Harrison, General, 167.
　　Plantagenet, 455.
　Harvey, Sir J. See.
　Hinton, W., 175.
　Howick, Lord, 429.
　Henry VII., 5, 23.
　　portrait of, 5.
　　seal of, 8.

ENGLISH MEN AND WOMEN—cont.
　Henry VIII., 32.
　　portrait of, 32.
　Herschell, Lord, 549, 551, 552.
　Holland, Lord, 151.
　　—, 411.
　Hopkings, Lady, 155, 180.
　Hopkins, Sir R., 272.
　Howard, Lord E., 39.
　James I., 91.
　　portrait of, 87.
　　seal of, 94.
　James II., 196, 204, 210.
　Jones, Colonel, 164, 167.
　Jukes, J. B., 454, 455.
　Junius letter, 311.
　Kelvin, Lord, 645.
　Kent, Duke of, 365, 419.
　Kirke, Sir D. See.
　Knox's, W., report. See Introduction.
　Knutsford, Lord, 515, 550.
　Labouchere, H., 471-475.
　　H., 467.
　Larkin, Mr., 227, 275.
　Laud, Archbishop, 146, 155, 238.
　Leslie, Dr., 382.
　Lushington, Dr., 411.
　Macintosh, Sir J., 411.
　Manering, Sir H., 101.
　Mansfield, Lord, 598.
　Mason, Capt. J., 104-109.
　Mavericke, —, 151.
　Maxse, Sir H., 513, 660.
　Meadus, Dr., 109.
　Merivale, Mr., 473.
　Mitchell, T., 278.
　Monier-Williams, Sir E., 296.
　Monk, General, 172.
　Montgomery, Lord, 151.
　Musgrave, Sir A., 494.
　Newcastle, Duke of, 287.
　　Duke of, 487.
　Noakes, —, 139.
　Oliphant, L., 497.
　Ormonde, Lord, 208.
　Packington, Sir J., 463.
　Palmerston, Lord, 354.
　Parke, Baron, 447.
　Pearl, Sir J., 427.
　Peaseley, W., 132.
　Peckham, —. See.
　Peel, Sir R., 447.
　Pembroke, Earl of, 150.
　Pender, Sir J., 499.
　Pennell, E. S., 515.
　Perrier, Sir A., 471, 473.
　Pickering, Sir G., 167.
　Povey, Mr., 169.
　Powell, York, 26.
　Prior, M., 236, 257, 281.
　　portrait of, 237.
　Raleigh, Sir W. See.
　Redwood, —, 161.
　Reynolds, —, 390.
　Rigby, Mr., 151.
　Robinson, G. R., 427.
　　Mrs., 599.
　Rosebery, Lord, 539.
　Rupert, Prince, 161.
　Russell, Lord J., 438.
　Salisbury, Lord, 541.
　Scott, Sir G., 524.
　　Sir J., 105.
　Shea, Sir A. See.
　Shirley, Sir A., 57.
　Sikes, W., 161.
　Slaney, J., 109.
　Smith, Capt. J. See.
　Stafford, Lord, 132.
　Steele, Sir R., 255.
　St. Germains, Earl, 487.
　St. Helens, Lord, 352.
　　portrait of, 353.
　Swift, Dean, 257.
　Sydney, Sir P., 77.

ENGLISH MEN AND WOMEN—cont.
　Talbot, Sir R., 12.
　Taylor, Jeremy, 110.
　Temple, Sir R., 148.
　Thoroughgood, T., 161.
　Vaughan, Sir W. See.
　Victoria, Queen, 443, 461, 519, 520.
　　portrait of, 519.
　Wakeham, R. R. See.
　Wales, Prince of, 487.
　　portrait of, 487.
　Whitbourne, Sir R. See.
　Wilkes, attack on Treaty of Paris, 313.
　William III., 224.
　　portrait of, 211.
　William IV., 357, 365-367.
　　portrait of, 365.
　Willoughbee, Sir P., 137.
　Wolfe, General, 296.
　　portrait of, 296.
　Wolsey, Cardinal, 39.
ENGLISH TOWNS:
　Barnstaple, 154, 161, 196.
　Berwick-on-Tweed, 383.
　Bideford, 196.
　　losses of, in 1696, 221.
　　ships at the Armada, 81.
　　view of, 221.
　Birmingham, 396.
　Bridport, 280.
　　cordage, 19, 145.
　　—, 145.
　Bristol, 7, 49, 68, 152, 176.
　　Custom House, view of, 13.
　　men discover Labrador, 590.
　　ship in N. in 1620, 103.
　　trade from, 12.
　　to Iceland, 27.
　　to Labrador, 599.
　　to N., 16.
　Chester, 84.
　Cockington, 174.
　Coffinswell, 298.
　Dartmouth, 37, 154, 159, 161, 163, 196, 222, 298, 360, 427, 598.
　Devonshire, fishermen in N., 297.
　　influence at Court, 188.
　　in N., 144.
　　share in the Armada, 82.
　Exeter, 271, 288, 358.
　　view of 115, port of, 115.
　Exmouth, 298.
　Fowey, 154.
　Gloucester ship, 153.
　Golden Grove, 110.
　London, 176, 239.
　　merchants, 149.
　　ships, 108, 153.
　　trade from, 12.
　Lowe, East, 154.
　Melcombe Regis, 154.
　New Romney, 388.
　Newton Abbot, 298.
　Plymouth, 39, 52, 146, 154, 161.
　　view of, 78.
　Poole, 58, 78, 196, 239, 281, 298, 389, 390, 428, 476.
　　mayor of, 146.
　　ships built in N., 165.
　Portsmouth, 199.
　　governor's house, 108.
　Scilly Islands, 40.
　Southampton, 62, 154.
　Teignmouth, 298.
　Weymouth, 146, 154, 176, 196.
　Widdicombe, 118, 381.
　　See also Army, Channel Islands, Navy, Ship Fishermen.
Erhart, C., 594.

INDEX.

Eskimo, Palliser's attempts to trade with, 324.
   treaty with, 327.
   Moravian mission to, 332.
   Byron's treatment of, 335.
   description of, 590, 595.
   divisions of race, 590.
   in N., 591.
   traces of, in Labrador, 591.
   derivation of the name, 591.
   Island, battle at, 592.
   modern mode of living, 592.
   effect of civilization, 595.
   treatment of, by Cartwright and Lucas, 598.
   battle at Forteau, 598.
   in England in 1772, 599.
   reconciled by Cartwright, 600.
   portraits of, 332, 592, 593.
Esquimaux, Post from, 608.
Evans, E., 485, 664.
   Sir F., 623.
      portrait of, 623.
   and Mathews, 560, 561.
Everson, Capt., 174.
Exploits River, 279, 283, 629.
   Cartwright's expedition to, 324.
   farming land on, 507.
   Wood Co., 621.
   land grant to railway, 627.

Fabvre, Capt., 471.
Fabyan, P., 78.
Fairhourne, Capt., 275.
Falkingham, Capt., 284, 301.
Falkland, Lord, 137.
   portrait of, 119.
   Colony and proposals, 118-20.
   Colony, boundaries of, 110.
Falle, T., 601.
   J. G., 664.
Fanny's Harbour, 610.
Farrell, —, 438, 654.
Fawcett, Col., 529.
Fearn, G. C., 721.
Fearne, Capt., 133.
Feild, Bishop, 444, 469.
Fenelon, M., 665.
Fermeuse, 120, 176, 301.
   (Firmoves), 297.
Ferguson, Capt., 412.
Fernandez, J., 4, 13.
FERRYLAND, 142, 150, 155, 179, 183, 196, 197, 225, 209.
   view of, 111.
   defence of by Holman, 212.
   d'Iberville at, 215.
   planters losses at, in 1696, 221.
   Holdsworth's house at, 227.
   French attack on, in 1705, 244.
   losses in 1705, 246.
   Larond's attack on, 249.
   French attack on, 261, 262, 263, 266, 269, 276.
   fort at, 271.
   Baltimore house, 272.
   fortifications at, 285.
   law books for, 286.
   R. Carter of, 293.
   troops at, 297.
   Firiland, 297.
   magistrates, &c. of, 301.
   captured in 1762, 306.
   Weston's property, 305.
   troops landed at, 307.
   English retained possession of, 314.
   parties at, 334, 336, 393.
   H.M.S. "Pheasant," at, 395.
   member for, 438, 457, 465, 468.
   over-representation of, 467.
   riot at, in 1788, 653.
   members for, 664.

Field, Cyrus W., 637-41, 643.
   portrait of, 637.
Finlay, R., 460.
Finn, R., 294.
Firth, W., 448.
Fishing ship's harbour, 610, 617.
Fishot Island, 477, 576.
   view of, 548.
Fitzgerald, J., 381.
   N., 615.
Fitzherbert, A., 352.
Flannery, P., 375.
Flat Bay, 559, 561.
   view in, 630.
   Islands, 485.
Fleming, Bishop, 429, 436, 464.
   Sandford, 500.
Fleur de Lys, 247, 278, 576.
Pling, J., 326.
Flood, J., 375.
   W. G., 664.
Flower's Cove, 609.
Floyd, Thos., 301.
Fly, Lt., 294.
Fogo, 279, 280, 284, 293, 350, 379, 438, 451, 457, 465, 468.
   settlement at, 542, 552.
   trade to Labrador, 597, 602.
   Scott, of, 606.
   advantages of railway to, 619.
   telegraph to, 639.
   members for, 664.
Follett, J., 348.
Forbes, Chief Justice, 402, 421, 434, 662.
Ford, —, 393, 655.
   John, 609.
Ford's bight, 594.
Foreham, fined for contempt of court, 357.
Forest and Shearer, 558, 560, 561.
   factory, view of, 540.
Forsey, —, 556, 559, 561.
Forteau, 598, 601, 616.
Forterie, —, 321.
Fortune, 48.
   telegraph to, 639.
Fortune Bay, 185, 279, 298, 389, 393, 438, 457, 465, 478, 479, 499.
   settlers go to St. Pierre, 574.
   road to, 628.
   members for, 664.
   Grand Bank, view of, 437.
Fowler, T., of St. Mary's Church, 157.
   P., 379.
Fowlow, Capt., 321.
Fox Harbour, 581, 617.
   J., 467, 500, 664.
   J. & Co., 460.
   Trap, battle of, 512.
Foxes Island, 271.
Francis Harbour, 610, 617.
Frankland, Lt., 291.
Frazer (Paysant, and), 557.
   J., 617.
   J. O., 502, 506, 609, 665.
   portrait of, 502.
Freels, Cape, 278, 289.
Freeman, W., 441.
Freestone Islands, 610.
French Protestants, 276.
   defeat at Quebec, 296.
   Bishop O'Donel attacks the French infidels, 364.
   Revolution, 367.
FRENCH AT ST. PIERRE.
   not to fortify, 312.
   traders to, 329.
   reported to be fortifying, 333.
   captured by English, 367.
   recovered, 377.
   early history of, 565.
   revolution at, 572.
   tree of liberty at, 573.
   committee of public safety at, 573.
   Jacobin club at, 573.

FRENCH AT ST. PIERRE—*cont.*
   Coup d'état at, 582.
   clapboard revolution at, 582.
   disciplinaires at, 582.
   fortification at, view of, 583.
FRENCH, EFFECT OF BAIT ACT ON.
   the Bait Act, 478.
   view of the Bait Act, 478.
   opinion of Governor and the Legislature on the Bait Bill, 516, 518.
   Bait Bill sanctioned by English Government, 519.
   effect of the Bait Act, 539.
FRENCH FISHERY.
   fishery, commencement of, 17.
   fishery methods, 22.
   fishery in N., 49.
   grievance against English pirates, 68.
   French vessel at St. Mary's captured by Clark, 78.
   fishing at Harbour de Grace, 103.
   ships captured by pirates, 103.
   fishing at Carbonear, 103.
   prizes taken in 1628, 133.
   fishery, 137.
   bank fishery, 138.
   fishing regulations of Louis XIV., 139.
   prud'homme, 140.
   complaint of Kirke, 148.
   in Nova Scotia, 148.
   resent Kirke's duties, 148.
   captures a sham man-of-war, 149.
   boats, 165.
   to pay licence duties, 167.
   summer fishermen, 173.
   Busseaux's, S. de, complaint of English, 178.
   fishing fleet captured by Dutch, 183.
   fishing north of Bonavista, 183.
   fishing associates, 184.
   bounty to fishermen, 185.
   bounties, 187.
   fishery, increase of, 187.
   fishing at Placentia, 188.
   no alien to take bait, 192.
   destruction of boats, 205.
   duties claimed from, 224.
   pretensions in N., 224.
   bounties to recruit the navy, 256.
   meaning of "fish," 259.
   trade to N., 267.
   aliens forbidden to fish in English harbours, 273.
   difficulties with, at Bonavista, 274.
   giving bounties to fishermen to annoy English settlers, 280.
   abandon N., 281.
   ships and spies at Fogo, 293.
   abandon the fishery, 293.
   prizes to St. John's, 294.
   ship "Tavignor" captured by Capt. Webb, 304.
   fishery estimate, 322, 326.
   extent of their fishery on the treaty shore, 354.
   privateers in 1812, 389.
   supply of bait, 478.
   dues enacted for fishing from, 541.
   no French fishing on the west coast in 1802, 576.
   recruiting, 576.
   fishing at straits of Belle Isle, 589.
   Basque consort with, 597.
FRENCH NAVY, 256, 303, 546, 547.

FRENCH SETTLEMENT AT PLACENTIA, &c.
  occupation of Placentia, 176, 180.
  Gargot's commission, date of, 566.
  Placentia strongly fortified, 175.
  Placentia re-fortified, 211.
  fortifications at Placentia, 267.
  danger of occupation of Placentia, 268.
  Garneau's description of Placentia, 182.
  Downing's account of Placentia, 206.
  Costabelle's report of condition of Placentia, 237.
  insecure tenure of Placentia by, 210.
  winter in Placentia, 180.
  customs at Placentia, 282.
  stay at Placentia after the evacuation, 276.
  attempt to induce English to settle at Placentia, 182.
  English remove to Placentia, 202.
  encourage English to settle at Placentia, 206.
  take fishermen to Placentia, 261.
  take fishermen to France, 263.
  settlement at Brest, 596.
  number of settlements, 185.
  settlements, 279.
  danger of settlements, 202.
  settlers at Trepassey, 183.
  no settlement up to 1662, 178.
  settlements in N., 259, 260.
  leave St. Pierre, 330.
  permitted to build houses and cut wood in Bay Despair, 340.
FRENCH SMUGGLING, 289, 312, 313, 320, 553.
  agree to an English Commissary at St. Pierre, 312.
  at St. Pierre, 577.
FRENCH TOWNS.
  Bayonne, 68, 570.
  Bordeaux, 84, 186, 570.
  Brittany, Douarnez, view of, 572.
  Breton pilots, 43.
    in St. Pierre, 565.
    fishery, 60.
    discoveries in Labrador, 589.
    fishing in 1527, 41.
  Burgundian with Cabot, 9.
  Dieppe, 4.
    Kirke born in, 148.
    view of, 46.
  Douarnez, view of, 572.
  Dunkirk, 176, 312.
  Granville, 570.
  Harfleur, 17.
  Jumieges, 49.
  La Bonille, 49.
  Marseilles, 84.
  Nantes, 570.
  fishermen, 35.
    fishing in 1527, 41.
    in St. Pierre, 565.
  Rochelle, 89, 570.
  St. Bridgeon, 49.
  St. Malo, 45, 46, 49, 138, 186, 215, 247, 562, 570, 575.
    view of, 46.
  Toulon, 84.
  Vaterville, 49.
FRENCH TRADE with Eskimo, 324.
  trading, view of, with Eskimo, 325.
  dealings with Indians, 591.
  help Indians against Eskimo, 592.

FRENCH TRADE—cont.
  Eskimo raid French rooms in Straits of Belle Isle, 592.
  murder of fishermen by natives, 63, 592.
  excite Eskimo against the English, 598.
FRENCH TREATY RIGHTS.
  Treaty of Utrecht, 252.
  view of Treaty of Utrecht, 260.
  Treaty of Paris, 309.
  Palliser's interpretation of Treaty of Paris, 317, 320.
  view of Treaty of Paris, 321.
  forbidden to catch salmon, 322.
  aggression resisted by Palliser, 325.
  Palliser's opinion of French intentions at St. Pierre, 330.
  furs seized at Port au Choix, 333.
  captured for violating treaty, 334.
  excluded from salmon fishery, 337.
  Duff's proclamation about the observance of Treaty of Paris, 337.
  Declaration of 1783, 352.
  Treaty of Versailles, 352.
  Lord Palmerston's opinion of Treaty of Versailles, 354.
  rights on the Treaty shore, 354, 355.
  Treaty of Amiens, 377.
  Treaty of Paris, 408.
  indignation in St. John's, 471.
  negotiations in 1844-57, 471.
  resolution of the Legislature, 474.
  the Labouchere letter, 475.
  Darling's despatch, 475.
  Hamilton's letter, 475.
  the *expositio contemporanea* of the Treaty rights, 476.
  proposals for a settlement, 479.
  aspect in connection with the Halifax award, 506.
  Convention of 1884, 515.
  Legislature refuse to accept, 515.
  failure of Ford-Pennell Convention, 539.
  confiscation of English ship's cargo at St. Pierre, 581.
FRENCH TREATY SHORE.
  rights upheld at St. Julian's by Palliser, 321.
  fixed settlements on the French shore to be removed, 353.
  "Fixed settlements," 475.
  treatment of R. and M. Tory, 476.
  first stipendiary appointed to the West Coast, 501.
  land grants allowed by the English Government on the treaty shore, 509.
  bounty at St. Pierre, 553.
  attempt to serve process by French master in St. George's Bay, 581.
  lobster factories in 1893, 477.
  lobster dispute, 539.
  Report on lobster factories, 556.
  arbitration on lobsters, to be held at Brussels, 660.
FRENCH WARS.
  F. at Trepassey, attacked by Baltimore, 133.
  English attacks on F., 237.

FRENCH WARS—cont.
  F. settlements destroyed by Leake, 246.
  Petit Nord, English attack the, 246.
  attacks cease, 204.
  account of campaign of 1705, 261.
  attack in 1705, Prior's account, 266.
  movements in 1708, 249.
  claims for ransom in 1708, 249.
  terms of surrender to planters, 270.
  soldier of 1755, 308.
  attack on St. John's in 1696, 214, 215.
  attack on St. John's, &c., 1696, 230.
  treatment of Drew, 216.
  attack on St. John's in 1705, 242, 245.
  attack on St. John's in 1708, 248.
  attack on St. John's in 1708, 268.
  propose to occupy St. John's permanently, 270.
  capture of St. John's, 305.
  English recapture of St. John's, 412.
  expected attack by, on St. John's, 350.
  last attack on St. John's, 367.
  attack on Cape Broyle Harbour, 132.
  attack on Little Belle Isle, 222.
  attacks on Trinity and Conception Bays, 234.
FRENCHMEN.
  Aubert of Dieppe, 4.
  Bonaparte, J., 543.
  Cassini's account of the French fishery, 569.
  Chateaubriand's account of St. Pierre, 585.
  Cloué, Admiral, 581.
  Colbert, Minister, 139.
  Freycinet, M. de, 539.
  Harrisse, H., 17.
  Humann, Admiral, 547.
  Jusserand, M., 547.
  Le Noury, Baron R., 581.
  L'Esperance, Baron de, 563.
  Louis XIV, 177.
  Louis XVIII., 408.
  Reculoux, Capt., 549, 562.
  Waddington, M., 539, 541.
Frenchman's Cove. 20.
Freshwater Bay, 283.
Frew, W., 527.
Frewing & Co., 617.
Frey's Cove, 617.
Friend's map, 250.
Frost, L., 617.
Fryer (Pack, Gosse and), 438.
Funk Islands, 359, 402.
Furey, C., 483, 664.
Furlong, J., 467.

Gaden, G., 411.
  W., 709.
Galway line, 469, 635.
Galt, A. L., 504.
Gambier, Lord, 375.
  portrait of, 376.
Gambo, 621.
  road to, 628.
  River, 629.
Game Laws, 717.
Gander Arm, 621.
  Bay, 283.
  Bay, farming land in, 807.
  crossing, 621.
  River, 629.

INDEX.

Gardner, Dr., 340, 356.
Gargamelle Cove, 557.
Gargot, Governor, 182, 566.
Garland, family of, 224.
    Charles, 294, 315, 336, 352.
    —, 334.
    E., 665 (should be Levi).
    Geo., 291, 301.
    J. B., 431, 433, 664.
    portrait of, 433.
    Mr., 415.
Garnier, M., 549.
Gastaldi's map, 42.
Gaultois, Hermitage Bay, 299.
Gearin, J., 721.
Geary, J., 379.
Geffry —, 266.
Gelman, R., 230.
Geneviève Bay, 560, 561.
George's Cove, Labrador, 617.
    River, Labrador Post to, 609.
German vessels, 454.
    Hamburg, 454.
    gin at St. Pierre, 479, 547.
Gibson, Col., sent to St. John's in 1696, 222.
Gilbert's, Sir H., voyage; reason for calling at St. John's, 57.
    expedition, 61, 65, 74.
    portrait of, 72.
    map, 66.
    Sir John, 79.
Gill, Michael, 239, 284, 288, 294, 295, 305, 326, 344, 357, 382, 415, 654.
    house in Fort William, 328, 333, 334.
    death of, 336.
    Nicholas, 333, 336, 339, 460, 653, 655.
    death of, 386.
    family, 241.
    premises, 458.
    title, 357.
Gisborne, F. N., 633.
    presentation to, 636.
    portrait of, 635.
    G., and Henderson, 636.
Gladstane, Capt., 241.
Gledhill, Governor, 282, 287.
Gleeson, —, 527.
    (Parker and), 459, 460.
Glen, T., 457, 460, 461, 468, 485, 664.
Glover, Sir J., 471, 501.
    portrait of, 501.
Godden, J., 665.
Godfrey, A. W., 433, 664.
Goff, R. N., & Co., 460.
Goldie, J., 456.
Goldsworthy, —, 427.
Gomez's voyage, 43.
Gonzalo, J., 4, 13.
Goodridge, Hon. A. F., 495, 535, 661, 665.
    portrait of, 535.
    A., and Son, 581.
Goodfellow, J., 500.
    & Co., 527, 617.
Goodyeare, S., 153.
Goose Bay, road to, 628.
    cove, fishing at, 576.
Gorges, Sir F., 104.
Gosse, murder of, 288.
    —, 393, 655.
    Edmund, Prefatory Note by, ix.
    P. H., 438, 717.
    portrait of, 438.
Gosse's title, 305.
Gouillon, L. and F., 356.
Gould, Wm., 196, 199.
Gouling, Jesuit priest in St. John's, 228, 263.
Gower, Sir E., 378.
    portrait of, 378.
Gowge, R., 19.

Grace, Harbour, 103, 137, 176, 232, 246, 262, 271, 291, 293, 301, 331, 334, 351, 377, 415, 453, 468, 609.
    early settlement of, 99.
    view of, 104.
    "Bristol's Hope," 137.
    view of, 139.
    Montigny at, 245.
    lawlessness at, 294.
    faction fight in 1766, 338.
    magistrates, 393.
    riots, 437.
    seal fishery, 451.
    post to, 463.
    riots, 489.
    railway to, 507.
    riot, 513.
    Thomey of, 1575.
    trade to Labrador, 602.
    railway to, 623.
    telegraph to, 635, 636.
    church burnt, 655.
    R. C. cathedral burnt, 660.
    member for, 664.
    Island, 269.
Grace, P., 458, 460.
Grady, 601, 610, 617.
Graham, Aaron, 347, 358, 359, 662.
    Capt., 284, 658.
    Lord George, 289.
Grand Bank, view of, 437.
    telegraph to, 639.
Grand Bay, 63, 95, 596, 629.
    Falls, exploration of, 610, 613.
    Lake, 626, 629.
Grandy, E., 567, 568.
Grandy's family, 305, 574.
Grant, Col., 489.
Grates, 114, 133.
Graves, Lord, 300, 314, 415, 652.
    Thomas, 152.
Gray, R., 336.
Graydon, Admiral's attack on Placentia, 237.
Graydon, Capt., 275.
Grave, l'ort de, 97, 232, 262.
    view of, 326.
    seal fishery, 451, 468, 496.
    trade to Labrador, 602.
    members for, 664.
Greaves, D. G., 301.
Green Bay, 127, 281.
    seals in, 491, 497.
    J., 315.
    Lt., 294.
    W. S., 665.
Greene, D., 617.
    D. J., 661, 665.
    M., 625.
Greenland discovered, 1.
    Basques in, 588.
    Eskimo, 590.
    populated from Labrador, 591.
    Crantz's History, 591.
    J. Haven, a missionary in, 594.
Greenspond, 356, 359, 379, 393.
    view of, in 1846, 450.
    seal fishery, 451.
    telegraph to, 639.
Grenfell, W. T., 604, 605, 614-616.
Grey, Capt., 438.
Grieve, —, 382.
    J. J., 465.
    W., 453, 468.
    portrait of, 493.
    W., & Co., 460, 493.
    W. B., 530, 604, 614, 615, 665.
    portrait of, 604.
Griffin's Harbour, 617.
Griggs, —, 161.
Griguet, fishing at, 576.
Grimes, J., 600.
Grosewater, 602.
Grossard, J., 315.
Grube's ships, 39, 40.

Grundy Island, 616.
Guilbert et fils, 557, 558, 562.
Guilford, Capt., 456.
Gull Island, 271.
Gundry's lines, 19.
    of Bridport, 290.
Guy, John, 65, 652.
    letters, 125.
    secession from the company, 137.
    Colony, 93, 94.
    negotiations for sale of part of, 109.
    company, arms of, 93.
    charter, 122.
    boundaries, 122.
    birth of a boy, 128.

Hackela of St. Pierre, 582.
Haddock, W., 161.
    —, 315.
Haire, Capt., 382, 654.
Haliburton, J., 549, 557, 559, 561.
Hall, G., 617.
    Mr., 614.
Hallahan, L., 343.
Hallaren, J., 721.
Hall's Bay, line planned to, 620.
    road to, 628.
Haly, Lieut.-Col. W., 341, 424, 427, 433, 434.
Hamilton, Mr., 315.
    Sir C., 408, 421, 409.
    portrait of, 409.
    Governor H., of Bermuda, 418.
    K. B., 465, 466, 475, 636.
    portrait of, 466.
    Lady, 409.
    portrait of, 410.
    Inlet, 617, 618.
Hamlin, —, 468.
Hamond, Capt., 556.
Hampshire's, Sir T., regulations, 61.
Handyside, Lieut.-Col., 223.
Hanlon, M., 375, 381.
Hanrahan, E., 457, 461, 465, 466, 468, 664.
Hants Harbour, 232.
Harden, L., 301.
Harney, Justice, 449.
Harques, M. de, 68.
Harrahan, P., 375.
Harrigan, Cape, 602, 610, 617.
Harris, John, of Exon, 271.
    Rev. J., 374.
Harrison, Cape, 610, 617.
    Gilbert, 451.
Harrisse, M., 17.
Harry's River, 626.
    Brook, 629.
Harvey, —, 347, 416.
    (Dunscombe and), 387, 460.
    A. J., 527.
    A. W., 504, 529, 532, 550, 614, 615, 647.
    portrait of, 504.
    and Angel, 509.
    & Co., 524, 527.
    Sir J., 449, 456, 457, 459, 488.
    portrait of, 449.
    departure of, 461.
    son shot at, 367.
    Rev. M., the Newfoundland Fisheries Commission, 647.
    T., 199.
Hatch, Capt., 252.
Hatton, —, 527.
Haven, Jans, 332, 594.
Hawke, Sir E., 305.
    Harbour, 617.
Hawker, —, 617.
Hayes, —, 67.
    narrative, 35, 70.

INDEX.

Hayman's, Robert, poetry, 109.
 proposition, 137.
 map, 137.
Haynes, —, 382, 655.
Hayse, J., 381.
Hayward, Judge, 423, 465, 468, 579, 659, 663, 664.
Head, M., portrait of, 595.
Heaney, R., 381.
Heard, John, 163.
Hearn & Co., 527.
Heart's Content, 133.
 landing cable, 642.
 Delight, 521.
Hebron, 595, 618.
Hemming, John, 301.
Henderson (Gisborne and), 636.
Hendy, — 161.
Henley Harbour, 601, 610, 617.
 Island, view of, 64.
Hennessey, M., 381.
Hennessy, —, 617.
 W., 617.
Henry, M., 414.
Hermitage Bay, 298.
Hill (Abbott &), 559, 561.
Hill's, Charles, letter, 156.
 John, 332.
 J. & Co., 450.
 Sir S., 497.
  portrait of, 497.
 Captain W., 155.
Hillman, R., 460.
Hind's, Professor, account of Labrador, 606.
Hinton, Wm., 175.
Hodge, J.,
Hody, Peter de, 68.
Hogan, T., 411, 656.
Hogsett, G. J., 465, 466, 468, 485, 488, 489, 664.
Holbrook, —, 393, 655.
 D. H., 636.
Holden, R. R., 441.
 R. jun., 441.
Holdsworth, family of, 227.
 Capt., 228, 255, 271, 272.
 Mr., 159.
Holeman, Mrs., 271.
Holloway, Admiral, 383.
 portrait of, 383.
Holman's, W., defence of, Ferryland, 209.
 defence of St. John's, 212.
Holmwood (Stabb, Row, &), 460.
Holme's, R. F., attempt to reach the Grand Falls, 611.
Holton, 610, 617.
Holyrood, 245, 262, 468, 513.
 trade to Labrador, 602.
Honeyburn, Simon, 315.
Hooper, W., 431, 664.
Hopedale, 595, 610, 617, 618.
 Deep Sea Mission at, 604.
Hopkings, Lady, 155, 180.
Hopkins, Sir R., 272.
Hopwood, F. S., 604.
Hore's voyage, 41.
Horsenaill, John, 318.
Horwood, John, 309.
 Mrs., 309.
[Hoskins], N., letter, 131.
Hounsell, Schenk, & H., 459.
Howlan, Lt.-Governor, 391.
Howorth, Capt. W., 501.
Howley, J., 386, 496.
 J. P., on Cabot's landfall, 9.
 R., 460.
Hoyeda's charter, 4.
Hoyles, Sir Hugh, 387, 393, 409, 440, 457, 465, 468, 474, 484, 488, 494, 656, 663, 664.
 portrait of, 488.
 N. W., 393, 424, 431, 436, 656, 664.
 portrait of, 424.
Huddle, J., 301.
Hughes, Capt., 247.

Hughes—*cont.*
 —, 382, 655.
Hull & Harvey, 416.
Humber River, 473, 626.
Hunt, Thomas, 104.
Hunt, Stabb, & Preston, 348, 387.
 W. G., 637.
Hunters & Co., 401, 460.
 trade to Labrador, 598.
Huntingdon, Sound, view of, 604.
Hutching's title, 337.
 Geo., 294, 368.
 letter to, about erection of houses, 396.
 G. A., 368, 665.
 R., 294, 653.
 R., junr., Lt., 294.
 S., 301.
Huxford, H., 301.

ICELANDIC discoveries, 1.
 trade, 7.
 fishery, 16, 25.
 chronicles, 587.
 meet Eskimo, 591.
Ilack, 610.
Independent Harbour, 610.
Indian Arm Bay, road to, 628.
 Harbour, Labrador, 602, 610, 617.
 Hospital, 615.
 Pond, 512.
 Tickle, 610, 617.
Inglis, Bishop, 655.
Ingram, Davy, 67.
India Co., East, 188.
 Madras, 290.
INDIANS, 242, 243, 245, 263, 269.
 methods of warfare, 231.
 attempt to murder Moody, 244.
 in Newfoundland from Cape Breton, 329.
 Abenaquis, 240, 264.
 Algonquins, 591.
 Canadian, 179, 214, 230, 239.
 Canada, natives of, 65.
 Caralits, 324.
 Mic Macs, 591.
  writing, 329.
 Montagnais, Cortereal describes the, 15.
  mention of, 590.
  French dealings with, 591.
  decimation of, 595.
  battle at Forteau, 598.
 Mountaineer, 324, 332.
  portrait of a modern, 596.
 Nascopees, 591.
  decimation of, 595.
 Nescambiouit, 261.
 Squantum, 104.
INDIES, WEST, early English trade to, 41.
 trade, 241, 346, 384.
 planters, 299.
 Anguilla, 300.
 Bahamas, 163.
 Barbadoes, 158, 205.
 Demerara, 390, 457.
 Dominica, 390, 555.
 Guadaloupe, 555.
 Jamaica, 19.
 Martinique, 555.
 St. Bartholomew, 257.
 St. Domingo, 372.
 St. Kitts, 190.
 St. Martin, 257.
IRISH at Placentia, 259.
 prisoners enter French service, 263.
 on the *Shannon*, 390.
 at St. Julian's, 282.
 at Little Placentia, 315.

IRISH—*cont.*
 at St. Pierre, 567.
 "youngsters," 201.
 banished to Ireland, 344.
 conspiracy of, to murder the inhabitants, 364.
 Benevolent Society, 381.
 faction fights, 391, 392.
 United, 418.
 middle-class planters, 435.
 Newfoundland fishery, 345.
 fisherman, trial of, 394.
 Wexford herring cot, 403.
 fishermen, 451.
 provisions for, 58.
 trade with Ireland, 200.
 provisions from Ireland, 272.
 trade from Ireland, 283.
 trade, 348.
 ships from Ireland, 652.
 Palliser's treatment of, 325.
 treatment of, 232.
 Catholics persecuted, 293.
 Williams' attack on, 297.
 Cartwright's treatment of, 325.
 population, 201.
 immigration in 1804, 378.
  in 1814-5, 404.
 immigrants land on the ice, 406.
 O'Connell, D., 425.
 Cork, 201.
  ships stay 48 hours at, 345.
 Crookhaven, 108.
 Valentia, 44.
  cable communication with, 642.
 Waterford, 201, 206, 295, 345, 404, 598.
 Wexford, 430.
Iron Bound Island, 610.
Island Cove, 262.
Islands, Bay of, 556, 559, 561.
 railway to, 631.
 description of, 629.
 herring fishery, 630.
 view of, 630.
 telegraph to, 639.
Italy, Gallipoli, 685.
 Genoa, 585.
 Leghorn, 103.
 Venice, view of, 7.
 Florence, Duke of, 128.

Jackman's family, 452.
Jackson, Rev. John, 228.
 persecution of, 231.
 Jas., of Trepassey, 348.
 W. of Ferryland, 301.
 —, 655.
Jacob, Capt., Dutch pirate, 103.
Jahan, F., 333.
Jenkins, J., 301.
Jerritt, G., 617.
Jervois, Great, 402.
Job Bros. & Co., 460, 492, 524, 527, 601, 602, 616, 617.
 Lady, Harbour, 607.
 R., 450.
 Mrs. R., 656.
 T. B., 450, 664.
  portrait of, 451.
 T. R., portrait of, 602.
 W. C., 614, 615.
Jobs, firm of, 297.
Johannis, M., 268.
Johnston, J., 568.
Johnstone (Baine) & Co., 450, 493, 527, 614.
Joli, Mount, 410.
Jones, Bishop, 529.
 Rev. H., 301.
 Rev. John, 362, 653.
 Rice fishing at St. Pierre, 77, 565.
 Thomas, 161.

INDEX.

Jordan, J. A., 665.
Joyce, —, 616.
  Bros., 617.
Juggler's Cove, 272.
Jukes, J. B., 454.
  portrait of, 455.

Kane W., 668.
  family, 452.
Katem, Michael, 294.
Kates, J., 301.
Kavanagh, J., 527, 684.
Kean, A., 721.
Kearney, M., 721.
Keats, Sir R. G., 388, 403, 601.
  Carson's attack on, 397.
  leaves Newfoundland, 401.
  portrait of, 387.
Keefe, W., 379.
Keels, 30, 537.
Keen, William, 248, 270, 284, 288, 289, 301, 336.
  diary 1708, 269.
  murder, 292.
  wharf, 292, 410.
  property, 305.
  title, 337.
Kelligrew, W., 502-506, 665.
Kelly J., 468, 474, 581, 664.
  Sargeant, 418.
  Timothy, 441.
  T., at the Head, 439.
Kemp, George, 405.
Kennedy's, T., house as Court house, 314.
  T., 665.
Kennaway v. Noble, 598.
Kenaston, Mr., 611.
Kent, John, 404, 429, 430, 431, 432, 433, 445, 455, 457, 464, 465, 467 474, 657, 664.
  portrait of, 486.
  I. and I., 460.
  R. J., 665.
Keough, P., 429, 431, 432, 664.
Keppel Harbour, 557.
Kerr (McBride &), 458, 460.
Kickkertaksoak Islands, 607.
Kielly, Dr. E., 444, 447, 455.
  portrait of, 446.
Kinealy, —, 617.
King, Admiral, 367.
  takes St. Pierre, 574.
  portrait of, 367.
  D., 375, 381.
  map, 10.
  Richard, 262.
King's Cove, 30, 537.
  seal fishery, 451.
Kinnien, D., 600.
Kirke, Sir D., 147, 155, 161, 164, 179, 205, 541.
  charter, 142, 143.
  fortifications, 207.
  house, 272.
  account of murder of French fishermen, 592.
  George, 155, 157, 176, 194.
  Sir James, 161.
Kissioner, —, 617.
Kitchen, W., 326.
  —, 439.
Kitty's Brook, 629.
? Knee's family, 452.
Knight, T., 468, 664, 665.
Knowlan, P., 343.
Knapman, F., 174.
Knowling, G., 527.
Koch's, K. R., description of modern Eskimo, 593.

LABRADOR fishery, 25.
  origin of name, 47.
  Basque fleet frozen up, 47.
  Palliser's interest in, 324.

LABRADOR—cont.
  Pitt's harbour, 327.
  fort at, 327.
  plan of Fort York, 327.
  English trading ports in, 328.
  New England, 328.
  annexed to Canada, 328.
  under Newfoundland, 334.
  New Englanders at, 336.
  joined to Newfoundland, 384.
  supposed emigration of Beothics to Canadian, 385.
  justice for, 393.
  American rights, 410.
  seal fishery at, 419.
  civil jurisdiction in, 422.
  French to have a concurrent right in fishery, 472.
  gale of 1866, 496.
  origin of the name, 590.
  Eskimo emigrate to Greenland, 591.
  Moravian mission, 594.
  number of Moravian missionaries, 595.
  Company, 596.
  English fishery, 597.
  American traders, 597.
  liviers tilt, views of, 598.
  Cartwright's diary, 599.
  English fishing at, 601.
  the voyage of the "Hunter," 603.
  medical aid for Labrador, 603.
  Rogerson's Bill to regulate the passenger traffic to, 603.
  liviers, views of, 604.
  Deep Sea Mission, 604.
  description of the coast of, 605.
  winter post, 607.
  green fishers, view of, 608.
  visited by Americans, 610.
  Grand Falls, 610, 613.
  Deep Sea Mission Report, 612-616.
  Trade, 616.
  census, 1891, 617.
  A. P. Low's survey, 618.
  revenue collected at, 658.
La Chesnaye, M., 268.
La Grange's attack on Bonavista, 239.
Laine, B., 85.
Lambert, Bishop, 408.
  General, 167.
  court crier, 457.
Lamaline, 418.
  telegraph to, 639.
Landgren, Capt., 541, 546, 563.
Landrecan, 294.
Langer, D., 301.
L'anse-au-Clair, 617.
L'anse-au-Diable, 617.
L'anse-a-loup, 601, 609, 616.
L'anse-au-Mour, 617.
Lance-aux-morts, 616.
Lang, Niven, 382, 387, 655.
Langley and Tessier, 460.
Langman, Rev. Ed., 295, 326, 336, 339, 344, 355.
La Poile, 468.
  members for, 664.
Lark harbour, 472.
Larkin's, Mr., Report, in 1701, 227, 275.
L'Argent Bay, road to, 628.
Larond, Capt., 249, 269.
La Scie, fishing at, 576.
Latham, Lt., 241, 244, 261, 263.
Laun, 389.
Law, Colonel, 459, 465.
  administration, 657.
Lawrance, Governor, 567.
Lawrence, —, 617.
Lawrie, Lt., murder of, 654.

Leading tickles, 279.
Leake, Sir John, 185, 246, 565.
  portrait of, 246.
Leamon, J., 664, 665.
Lechmere, N., 653.
Le Croc, 354.
Le Geyt, P.C., 393, 655.
Le Grandais, Mr., 560, 561.
Leigh's, Charles, voyage, 78.
  Rev. J., 411.
Le Marchant, Sir J. G., 462.
  departure of, 465.
  portrait of, 462.
Le Messurier, H., 454.
  H., junr., 665.
  P., 299, 433.
Lemoine, A., 557, 558, 562.
Le Moinne, J., 548.
Lendon, A., 301.
Le Noury, Baron R., 581.
Le Nouvee, G., 333.
Le Pomelle, Y., 356.
Leroux, E., 548, 559, 566.
Le Roy's chronometer, 569.
Lescarbot's, M., description of the fishery, 20.
Levire, M., 266.
L'Hermite, M., 265.
Lilburne, Lt., 224.
Lilly, Capt. G., 382, 393, 654, 655.
Lilly, George Judge, 348, 362, 411, 439, 446, 656, 663.
  George, junr., 546.
  W., 348, 653.
Linke's division of the Eskimo, 590.
Linklater, Capt., 332.
Lint, Mr., 272.
Lion's Den, 439.
Little, G., 381.
  Judge, J. I., 464, 529, 660, 663, 665.
  portrait of, 513.
  M., 375.
  P. F., 464, 465, 466, 467, 469, 474, 484, 489, 663.
  portrait of, 464.
  Bay, 389.
  view of, 216.
  telegraph to, 639.
  River, view of, 554.
Littlebury, John, 161.
Livingston, —, 382, 655.
Lloyd, Major, 247, 248, 249, 266, 269, 270.
  suspended, 241.
  re-appointment, 246.
  persecution of Jackson, 252.
  indictment, 253.
  death of, 270.
Loch, Capt.'s report on bait, 478.
Logy Bay, view of, 10.
Long, A., 395.
  Pond, view of, 326.
  Island, Labrador, 610.
  Tickle, 610.
Lotter's map, 279.
Loughlan, Charles, 455.
Lovelace, Dudley, 157.
Low, Ann, 155.
Luce, N. of Dartmouth, 157.
Lucas, —, 592, 598, 599.
Ludwig, J., 301.
Lundrigan, J., 411.
Lushington, Dr., 411.
Lyons, P., 357.

Mabb, Edward, 149.
Maccassey, L., 455.
MacKay, A. M., 496, 499, 526, 623, 639, 641, 643, 665.
  portrait of, 641.
  S., 452, 496, 659, 665.
MacKenzie, —, 412, 414.
MacLea, —, 655.
MacNamara, A., 381.

INDEX.

Macovich, 610.
Magill, —, 382.
Maher, J., 375.
Main, Harbour, 232, 262, 293, 573.
    riots, 489.
    trade to Labrador, 602.
    members for, 664.
Maiollo map, 15.
Mal bay, 557.
Malta, Labrador, 610.
Manering, Sir H., 101.
Manning Constable, 525.
Mannock's Island, 610.
Mansfield, Ann, 164.
MAPS OF—
    Stephanius, 3.
    Ruysch, 14.
    Rotz, 34.
    Thorne, 38.
    "Harleyan," 40.
    P. Descellier, 40.
    Gastaldi, 42.
    Martinez, 57.
    D. Homem, 58.
    J. Dee, 58.
    Gilbert, 66.
    Pistolet, 69.
    Cupids, 98.
    Mason, 106.
    Six colonies, 110.
    Jacobsoz, 120.
    Ile Laet, 138.
    Champlain, 138.
    Dudley, 160.
    Sellers, 177.
    Thornton, 193.
    Fitzhugh, 198.
    Thornton, 203.
    1698 campaign, 218.
    Friend, 250.
    Lotter, 297.
    Moll, 281.
    Cook, 317.
    West Coast, 558, 563.
    Atlantic, Short Route, 631.
Mara, M., 375, 381.
March, Mary, portrait of, 384.
    S., 465, 468, 664.
March, S. R., 665.
March and Sons, 527.
Marechal, Commander, 553.
Marshall and Rodger, 527.
    A., 529.
Martin, —, 294.
    C., 174, 197.
    J., 493.
    J. H., 431, 433, 664.
    J. H. & Co., 527.
    M., 271.
    S., 375.
    W., 301.
Martinez' map, 57.
Martyr, Peter, 48.
Mason, Anne, 107, 108.
    John, 104-109.
    inscription about Cabot, 10.
    map, 106.
Massie, W., 84.
Masters, John, 239.
Mathew's cove, 617.
Matthews (Evans and), 560, 561.
Matthews's, John, account of French occupation of Placentia, 179.
Maury, Lieut., 637.
Maxse, Sir H., portrait of, 513.
    died in St. John's, 660.
Maxwell, Capt., 414.
May, Isle of, 102, 272.
    Samuel, 230.
McAllister, 382, 655.
McAuslan, appointed deputy postmaster, 653.
McBraire, J., 381-383, 391.
    Chappell's description of, 395.
McBride and Kerr, 458, 460.

McCalman, —, 382, 655.
McCarthy, J., 438, 664.
    W., 375, 341.
McCowan, J. R., 529.
McDonald at Hermitage Bay, 299.
    P., 375.
    Ronold, 294.
McDonell, Capt., 308, 412, 414.
    R., 665.
McDougal, Mr., 558, 561.
McDougall, Neil, 460.
    (Boyd and), 460.
McGeary, J., 653.
McGrath, J. F., 665.
    R., 664.
    Toby, 379.
McIver, A., 441.
McKellop, J., 382.
McKeown, alleged murder of, 567, 568.
McKie, —, 393, 655.
McKillop, Lt., R.N., 389.
McLea, —, 382.
McLean's, J., visit to Grand Falls, 611.
McMurdo & Co., 527.
McNamara, A., 375.
McNeily, A. J. W., 503, 665.
McRae, R., 617.
McWilliam, J., 460.
Meader, T., 567, 568.
Meadus, Dr., 109.
Meagher, R., 456.
Mechlin, 567.
Mecklenburg, 610.
Meehan, J., 379.
Melledge, —, 382, 654, 655.
Mercator's map, 15.
Merchantman's Harbour, 610.
Merchants attack Tremlett, 360-362.
    effect of Palliser's Act, 344.
    oppose the New Court, 359.
    the Custom House, 338.
    local government, 428.
    the House of Assembly, 435, 464.
    petition of 1775, 340.
    Society, 392.
    tyranny of the, 379.
    Harbour, 610.
Merivale, Mr., 473.
Merrett, Samuel, 239.
Meynell (Wilson and), 460.
Michael, M., 414.
Middle Bay, Labrador, 616.
    Cove road, 449.
Middleton, G. H., tenders for railway, 624.
Milbanke, Admiral, 358.
Millegan, Rev. G. S., 659.
Milroy, A., 455.
Minerals. See N., Miscellaneous.
Miner's, Mr., defence of St. John's in 1696, 217, 231.
Mingan, post from, 608.
Minshew, Mr., 253.
Miquelon, 48.
    (Mechlin), 567. See also St. Pierre.
Mitchell, T., 278.
    T., 462.
    T., 529.
    shoots at Harvey, 367.
Mollins, —, 185.
Molloy, —, 567, 568.
    E., 527.
    J. W., 423, 662.
    N., 664.
Moll's map, 281.
Monier, John, 295.
Monier-Williams, 296.
Monroe, J. H., 511.
    Hon. M., 510, 530, 532, 550, 614, 615.
Monsengs, M., 265.

Montague, Governor, 340.
    takes St. Pierre, 570.
Montigny, M., 217, 230, 245, 261, 263, 264, 266.
Moody, Lt., 241, 246, 261, 262, 265, 282.
    Governor at Placentia, 276.
    diary of 1705 campaign, 266.
Moore, H., 664.
    Major-Gen., 655.
    T. F., 438, 439, 446, 664.
Mooring, M., 294.
Moral, T., 618.
Moreen, M., 292.
Morey, Mr., 227.
Morgan, Miles, 67.
Morine, A. B., 532, 550, 665.
    portrait of, 550.
Morison, D. —, 665.
    portrait of, —.
Morley, Lt., 294.
Morris, of Waterford, 404.
    —, 382, 655.
    Hon. E. P., 411, 425, 436, 437, 438, 444, 446, 457, 460, 468, 503, 529, 664, 665.
    portrait of, 425.
    F. J., 665.
    S., 457, 664.
Morrison, D., 532.
    portrait of, 532.
Mortier, 336.
Moyer, Mr., 167.
Mudge, S., 460.
    firm of, 297.
Mugford Cape, 605.
Muir and Duder, 492.
Mullins Cove, 617.
Mullock, Bp., 436, 464, 486, 487, 488, 490.
    on telegraphic communication, 634.
    proposes a railway, 619.
    T., 464.
Mullowney, J. P., 455, 460.
Munn, J., 457, 467, 664, 665.
    portrait of, 451.
    J., & Co., 617.
    R. S., 615, 665.
    firm of, 454.
Murine, P., 381.
Murphy, —, a deserter in 1800, 418.
    (Shea and), 460.
    and Andrews, 539.
    and Osmond, 621.
    D., 381.
    Darby, 381, 390.
    J., 381.
    J., 641.
    M., 381.
    T., 375, 381.
    T. J., 665.
Murray, the tailor, 449.
    A., 496.
    J., 495, 527.
    Col. J., 382.
    James, 531, 583, 665.
    Nicholas, 146.
    P., 379.
Musgrave, Sir A., 494.
    portrait of, 494.
Musquito, 301, 331.

Nachvak Bay, 602, 606.
Nain, 595, 610, 618.
Nameless Cove, 609.
Natasquan, post from, 608.
NAVAL OFFICERS:
    Barton, Capt., 374.
    Berry, Sir J., 194, 196.
    Bobardt, Dr., 605.
    Bonfoy, Capt., 284, 292.

INDEX.

NAVAL OFFICERS—cont.
Bowker, Capt., 408, 655.
Bridge, Commodore, 241.
Browne, Capt., 539.
Buchan, Capt. See.
Byng, Hon. John. See.
Byron, Lord. See.
Campbell, Admiral, 355, 362.
 Capt. See.
Carleton, Capt., 247.
Cartwright, Lt. J. See.
Chappell, Lt., 394.
Clinton, Capt., 284.
Cochrane, Sir T. See.
Colvill, Lord, 308, 412–416.
Cook, Capt., 316, 317.
Cookesley, Capt., 393, 655.
Crawley, Capt., 567, 568.
Crowe, Capt. See.
Davy, Capt., 252.
Desbrow, Capt., 213.
Dickson, Lt. A., 324.
Dorrill, R., 284, 293.
Douglas, Capt., 306, 412.
Drake, F. W., 291, 292.
Duckworth, J. T. See.
Duff, Admiral, 337.
Dugdale, Lt., 416.
Edzell, Capt., 375.
Edwards, Capt. R. See.
Elliott, Capt. See.
Fairbourne, Capt., 275.
Falkingham, Capt., 284, 301.
Frankland, Lt., 291.
Gambier, Lord, 375, 376.
Glover, Sir J., 471, 501.
Gower, Sir E., 378.
Graves, Lord. See.
Graydon, Capt., 275.
Hamilton, Sir C. See.
Hamond, Capt., 556.
Hatch, Capt., 252.
Hawke, Sir E., 305.
Holloway, Admiral, 383.
Howarth, Capt. W., 501.
Hughes, Capt., 247.
Keats, Sir G. See.
King, Admiral, 367.
La——e, Lt., 654.
Leakes, Sir J., 185.
Loch, Capt., 478.
Mason, Capt., 104–109.
Maxwell, Capt., 414.
McKillop, Lt., 389.
Milbanke, Admiral, 358.
Montague, Admiral, 340, 570.
Norris, Admiral, 222, 223.
Osborne, Capt. See.
Palliser, Sir H. See.
Pickering, Capt., 252.
Pickmore, Sir F., 406.
Pole, Sir C. M., 374.
Poulton, Capt., 375.
Prescott, Sir H. See.
Radstock, Lord. See.
Rodney, Lord, 284, 290, 291.
Russell, Capt., 205.
Rut, John, 38–41.
Shuldham, Lord, 335.
Spratt, Lt., 654.
Stanford, Lt., 333.
Taylour, Commodore, 249, 270.
Trevanion, Sir N., 254, 272.
Underdown, Capt., 247, 253.
Vanbrugh, Capt., 280, 284.
Walker, Admiral, 182, 237.
 Sir B., 549.
Wallace Sir R., 368, 370.
Wallis, Admiral Provo, 390.
Warren, Admiral, 289.
Watson, Admiral, 284.
Webb, Capt., 285, 305, 567.
Wheler, Capt., 183.
Whetstone, Admiral, 237.
Williams, Commodore, 182, 211.

NAVY, effect on, of discovery of Newfoundland, 17.
Henry VIII., efforts to found a navy, 32.
English seamen, 35.
ships used for trade, 37.
Mason, treasurer of the, 109.
naval convoy in 1623, 112.
dock and storehouse, 142.
"men of war," 149.
picture of man of war, 149.
sham man of war, 149.
captain of convoys to obey the Governor's orders, 167.
"ducking," 174.
Drake's destruction of St. Pierre, 185.
Sir John Berry, 194.
French power augmented in America, 178.
Admiral Walker's attack on Placentia, 182.
Williams' attack on Placentia, 182.
attack on Placentia, 211.
incompetence of the, in America, 236.
Leakes' attack on Trepassey, &c., 246.
naval rule, 253.
French power in America, 256, 257.
Keen appointed naval officer, 289.
Church accommodation for, 295.
making of England, 304.
prize money, 305.
English officers enforce their interpretation of the treaty, 321.
Palliser complains of resident naval officers, 333.
French men-of-war forbidden to come on the coast, 337.
fishermen freed from press-gang, 345.
frigates remained on the coast during the winter, 349.
men-of-war at St. John's and Placentia, 349.
gallant fight against France, Spain, Holland and America, 351.
Rodney's victory at Dominica, 352.
smart capture of an American privateer, 351.
mutiny of the Nore extends to Newfoundland, 372.
Pluto stationed for 20 years in Newfoundland, 375.
fleet at St. John's in 1812, 387.
prizes, 387.
American vessels captured, 387, 389.
capture of the Chesapeake, 390.
naval officers in 1813, 393.
ships winter in Newfoundland, 395.
Carson's attack on naval administration, 395–398.
Morris' attack on naval governors, 426.
first steamer to enter St. John's, 435.
officers on the west coast, 546.
efficient work done by naval officers, 551.
pressing men in St. John's, 654.
St. John's full of ships, 655.
naval establishment removed from St. John's, 656.

NAVY—cont.
H.M.S.:—
Adamant, 369.
Alarm, 478.
Ann and Joyce, 161.
Antelope, 306, 314, 351, 415.
Bedford, 416.
Boston, 574.
Centurion, 199.
Crescent, 161, 395.
Dreadnought, 231.
Durseley galley, 284.
Egmont, 324.
Falkland, 247.
Fly, 407.
Gosport, 415.
Grammont, 305.
Grasshopper, 411.
Guernsey, 599.
La Concorde, 374.
Latona, 372.
Lictor, 389.
Lichfield, 270.
Lily, 541.
Mallard, 539.
Medway, 247.
Minerva, 416.
Monarch, 369.
Nonsuch, 247.
Northumberland, 316, 415.
Oxford, 231.
Pearl, 334.
Pegasus, 365.
Pheasant, 395.
Pike, 384, 404.
Pluto, 351, 375, 653.
Prometheus, 395.
Rainbow, 291.
Ramilies, 369.
Reserve, 205.
Sapphire, 211.
Shrewsbury, 416.
Spitfire, 455.
Squirrel, 286.
Superb, 416.
Syren, 306, 415.
Tenedos, first ship docked, 509.
Virgin Prize, 212.
Wager, 334.
Negro servant, 176.
Negroes from Bermudian fishing, 346.
Nesmond, Chevalier, 209, 223.
attack on St. John's, 213, 223.
Nevean, J., 375.
Neville, Mr., 559, 561.
Newfoundland coast scene, 391.
NEWFOUNLAND. See also EDUCATION, MERCHANTS, SEALING, SETTLEMENT, SHIP FISHERMEN; also under N., Miscellaneous, see Climate, Soil, Timber, Mines and Minerals, Sport and Game Laws, &c.
NEWFOUNDLAND CHURCHES:—
CONGREGATIONAL Church refounded, 362.
CHURCH OF ENGLAND, 155, 202, 204, 255.
no, at Bay Bulls, 157.
English Church in Conception Bay, 101.
C.C.C. Society formed, 653.
Coughlan's salary, 331.
church at St. John's, 228.
Harbour Grace Church burnt, 655.
church in St. John's, 263, 265.
description of the feeling between the churches, 461.

INDEX.

NEWFOUNDLAND—cont.
NEWFOUNDLAND CHURCHES—cont.
  Diocesan synod formed, 659.
  dispute about Carbonear chapel, 652.
  Dingle, Rev. —, 364.
  established in Newfoundland, 71.
  foundation stone of cathedral laid, 657.
  Jackson's persecutions, 251.
  minister's salary, 272.
  Labrador population, 618.
  Lent, stricter observance of, 172.
  non-observance of, 188.
  new church, 295.
  note on, 443.
  petition for minister, 194.
  prayer book, 154.
  repair of church in 1701, 271.
  school established, 377.
  Sunday schools re-established, 654.
  St. John's church, 458.
  St. Thomas' consecrated, 657.
  St. Thomas' church moved, 461.
  S.P.G., founding of the, 228.
  Waldegrave helps to restore the church, 373.
MORAVIAN Mission; Labrador population, 618.
  Mission, 331, 332, 592, 594, 617.
  mentioned by Cartwright, 601.
METHODIST CHURCH compelled to subscribe to the new church, 295.
  Wesleyanism introduced, 331.
  dispute about Carbonear Chapel, 652.
  Wesleyan Mission stations organised, 655.
  George Street Methodist Church, 659.
  Labrador population, 618.
PRESBYTERIAN Labrador population, 618.
  first church established, 657.
  Free kirk established, 657.
QUAKERS, 241, 265.
  at Bonavista, 264.
ROMAN CATHOLIC Biscayan priest in Newfoundland, 47.
  Bishop Fleming, 426.
  Bishops Lambert and Scallan, 408.
  Bishop Mullock, 487.
  Bishop O'Donel. See.
  Capuchin friar, 263.
  chapel built, &c., 363-365.
  church at St. Pierre, 573.
  compelled to subscribe to the new church, 295.
  description of the feeling between the churches, 461.
  English at Placentia compelled to become, 186.
  forbidden to use churchyard at Placentia, 366.
  establishment of, in Newfoundland, 110.
  Gouling the Jesuit, 263.
  in Cape Breton, 330.
  influence in politics, 436.
  Labrador population 618.

NEWFOUNDLAND—cont.
NEWFOUNDLAND CHURCHES—cont.
  Lent, permission to eat fish in Spain during war, 320.
  loyal to the Government, 364.
  Norton first Roman Catholic judge, 457.
  persecution of, 293.
  Presentation Nun's convent, 656.
    burnt, 458.
  priest in St. John's, 228.
  propaganda, 228.
  school established, 377.
  service at Ferryland, 101.
  Jesuits, 155.
  M. Allain at St. Pierre, 572.
CUSTOMS HOUSE formed, 315.
  seizures, 328.
  opposition to, 338.
  site of, 339.
  Collector Routh, 356.
CUSTOMS:
  fishing in Newfoundland, 19-24.
  share of a wreck, 19.
  stages and barrelling fish, 29.
  fishery customs at Cromer, 33.
  "half seas over," 34.
  Devonshire customs in Newfoundland, 61.
  fishing admirals, 70.
  "Cruizing," 114.
  derived from Devonshire, 114.
  ancient, of fishing admirals, 139.
  "scaffold of the Grapple," 139.
  French rooms at Placentia, 182, 183.
  French Fishing Company, 184.
  green men, 192.
  casks for oil, 204.
  ship fishermen's legal, 226.
  "triangulation," 226.
  character of the fishery, 258.
  officers taking bribes, 275.
  fishing at Placentia, 276.
  "liviers," 279.
  in Placentia, 282.
  "Tenners," 297.
  Bye-boat-men, 297.
  "youngsters," 298.
  winter supplies, 315.
  servants' wages, 318.
  new regulations, 323.
  "whipper," 336.
  whipper, 343.
  mentioned in petition of 1775, 347.
  whipping, 359.
  faction fights, &c., 401.
  cook room, 450.
  public grindstone, 496.
  Ox cart, St. Pierre, view of, 564.
  at St. Pierre, 564.
  English settlers at St. Pierre, 567.
  wine obliged to be taken with a cargo of salt, 567.
  French method of paying seamen, 570.
  the Labrador passenger traffic, 603.
FARMING, sheep, 96.
  Guy's attempt at, 100.
  Mason's account, 106.
  at Cupids, 126.

NEWFOUNDLAND—cont.
FARMING—cont.
  at Ferryland, 129, 130.
  Baltimore cattle, 156.
  encouraged, 164.
  Downing's farm, 195.
  in 1675, 207.
  grazing, 326.
  near St. John's, 341, 342, 365.
  Capt. Edgell's farm, 375.
  Governor Holloway advocates, 383.
  allowed, 398, 399.
  view of, near St. John's, 399.
  around St. John's, 427.
  agricultural meeting, 449.
  great development about 1840, 454.
  Sir G. Le Marchant's interest in, 462.
  "ould Sir Gasper's breed," 465.
  land in Newfoundland, 507.
  Cottage farm cleared, 654.
  first grants of land, 655.
  first agricultural society, 657.
FISHERY, view of a stage, 22.
  barrelled fish, 29.
  Bacalao, meaning of, 81.
  charter party in 1580, 84.
  leave to export fish in 1599, 84.
  policy of insurance on Newfoundland fish, 84.
  season, men summoned in, 100.
  customs, 100.
  seine, "halinge of a seyne," 103.
  caplin, 106.
  admirals, 139.
  cost of outfit, 204.
  green men, 233.
  bye-boat-men, 228, 297.
  "Room," 298.
  "Train," 298.
  "cod seines," 342.
  green fish men in Labrador, 602.
FISHERY, description of Mason's, 106.
  description of, 206.
  account of, in 1705, 267.
  description, 273.
  Williams' account of, 296.
FISHERY, REGULATION of the, 29.
  number of voyages made, 37.
  Act, to compel fish to be eaten on Wednesdays and Saturdays, 55.
  forbidding importation of foreign caught fish, 56.
  Raleigh's opinion upon the, 69.
  supplies for the army, 75.
  under Treworgie, 164.
  losses in 1705, 246.
  convoy for, 1761, 305.
FISHERY, ENGLISH.
  Newfoundland first mentioned in Act of Parliament, 33.
  English ships in Newfoundland, 60.
  in English hands, 350.
FISHERY, ESTIMATE of ships in, 1527, 40.
  estimate, 136.
  in 1661, 156.
  spoilt by the wars, 159.

INDEX. 733

NEWFOUNDLAND—*cont.*
FISHERY—*cont.*
quantity of catch, 186.
estimate of, 190, 203, 210.
reduction of the, 250.
estimate of, 268, 273, 274, 285, 296, 326, 346.
successful, 374.
effect of the war, 393.
enormous catch, 402.
partial failure, 486, 492.
"great fishery," 496.
largest known, 500.
estimate, 652, 654.
FISHERY, FRENCH, confined to English, 375.
French, from June to October, 183, 187, 322, 568.
French, 575.
St. Pierre statistics, 586.
FISHERY, IMPORTANCE OF, 256.
value of, according to delegates to Halifax, 504, 506.
capable of enormous development, 629, 630.
price of fish in 1512, 19.
price of fish, 28, 140, 387, 395, 402, 403.
profitableness of the, 106.
FISHERY, BAIT, birds for, 100.
supply in Fortune Bay, 478.
Act passed, 514.
effect of, 577.
French paid for, 578.
intelligence service, 649.
FISHERIES COMMISSION, 647.
fish hatcheries, 647.
cure of codfish and herrings, 649.
Model freezing rooms, 649.
Codfish hatched, 650.
D. W. Prowse's opinion on cod-hatchery, 650.
FISHERY, LOBSTER report, 556.
lobster hatchery, 650.
Fish Exhibition, 660.
FISHERY, SALMON, 274, 283, 297.
French not right, 322.
regulations, 337.
failing, 647.
FISHING, BANK, account of, 569.
banks, French fishermen, view of, on the, 570, 571.
bank fishing, number at the, 575.
LEGAL AND JUDICIAL:
Laws proclaimed by Guy, 99.
Whitbourne's court in 1615, 114.
"some way of judicature," 155.
trial of four men for plundering French rooms, 173.
process served in 1650, 179.
offenders to be brought to England, 192.
abuses in St. John's, 204.
want of, effect in Act of William III., 225.
abuses of the fishing admirals, 226.
powers of Act of William III., 233.
Capt. Crowe's laws, 254.
courts appointed, 273.
want of courts, 275.
districts appointed, 284.
court house, St. John's, 284.
courts appointed, 285.

NEWFOUNDLAND—*cont.*
LEGAL AND JUDICIAL—*cont.*
Shaw's "Practical Justice," 286.
aspect of new courts, 286.
winter justices, 287.
Vanbrugh's commission, 288.
Drake's Commission, 288.
Keen's murder, 292.
Rodney's treatment of, 292.
districts in 1732, 301.
surrogate courts, 315.
abuses, 326.
Coughlan appointed a justice, 331.
offices held by the Gills, 333.
change of judges, 336.
Dunning's opinion on, 336.
lawlessness in Newfoundland, 338.
Fishing admirals to have power to appoint deputies, 341.
criminal cases in 1777, 343.
Philip's cases, 348.
Admiral's proceedings, 348.
want of civil government, 348.
abuses, 355.
description of the courts in 1784, 357.
Act of 31 George III., 358.
salaries of the judges and clerks, 359.
high constable, 381.
officials forbidden to trade, 383.
chief justice's salary, 383.
police established, 386.
chief justice's salary advanced, 391.
Colclough's attempt to appoint an associate judge 392.
trial of a fisherman, 394.
writs issued in 1815, 403.
Butler v. Lundrigan, 411, 421.
supreme court constituted, 422.
dress of the judges, &c., 423.
supreme court opened, 423.
Attorney-General Simms, 430.
Boulton's decisions reversed, 438.
Boulton's anomalous position, 444.
Kielly v. Carson, 445.
Court of Common Pleas established, 653.
session courts, 653.
no prisoners, 653.
first case in supreme court, 654.
surrogate courts abolished, 654.
judiciary, 662.
NEWFOUNDLAND MISCELLANEOUS:
auk, great, view of, 283.
bears, white, 59.
beer, price of, 19.
boots, 200.
bottomry, 189.
calabogus, 226, 367.
cariboo, 631.
view of, 632.
casks, 96.
chronometers, Le Roy's, 569.
cod oil, 95.
commerce, 198.
commercial, 403.
compass, 36.
crisis in 1815.
cranberries, 153.
Cunard Line, 456.
Cunard SS. ashore, 461.
Deep Sea Mission, 604, 614.

NEWFOUNDLAND—*cont.*
NEWFOUNDLAND MISCELLANEOUS—*cont.*
duties, power to levy, 144.
levied on French by William III., 224.
eclipse at Burgeo, 316.
expenditure, 429.
exports in 1814, 655.
famine threatened in 1812, 400. 1817, 405.
fires, forest, 103, 131.
freight, rates of, 107, 136.
ships, 153, 273.
to Newfoundland, 39, 40.
wine obliged to be taken with a cargo of salt, 567.
furs, 109, 179, 184, 297.
at Soulis Brook, 620.
game, 136, 179.
glass-making, 96.
granite quarries, 620.
view of, 624.
Great Eastern, 642, 644.
hawks in Newfoundland, 16.
health officer, 289.
imports, 394, 653.
insurance on fish, 86.
land grant to railway company, 627.
lumbering development, 620, 621.
lynx in Newfoundland, 16.
log line, 37.
marine insurance, 37, 84.
meat, price of, 19.
mineral found by Gilbert, 73.
at Tilt Cove, 496, 497.
mines and minerals, 715.
molasses, 198.
Newfoundland Records, 314.
dog, 487.
olive oil, expense of, 297.
Papers :—
Royal Gazette, 380.
St. John's Gazette, 395.
Public Ledger, 430.
Newfoundlander, 441.
Patriot, 441.
Royal Gazette started. 654.
Newfoundland Mercantile Journal established, 655.
Evening Telegram, 659.
Daily Colonist, 660.
Evening Mercury, 660.
partridge, picture of, 633.
population, 142, 195.
understated, 176.
Irish, 201.
in 1765, &c. 325, 652.
in 1804, 378.
of St. Pierre, 571.
census in 1869, 659.
postal rates in 1815, 380.
communication, 455, 463.
revenue, 1841-1892, 463.
Victoria S.S., 486, 487.
Allan line, 497.
Labrador winter post, 607.
summer post, 609.
McAusand deputy, 653.
post office established, 654.
potashes, 96, 127.
Press abuse the House of Assembly, 435.
prices, 387.
of commodities, 315, 379.
effect of crisis, 403.
prize agents, 242, 246, 267, 348.
ptarmigan, picture of, 633.
rackets, snow, 264.
revenue, 450, 497, 509.
rum, 198.
salt, cargoes of, 95.
cost of, 136.
proposals, 137.

734 INDEX.

NEWFOUNDLAND—*cont.*
NEWFOUNDLAND MISCELLANEOUS—*cont.*
saltmaker, 128, 130.
sarsaparilla, 96, 109.
saw mill, 96, 100, 103.
views of, 620, 621, 624.
servants, excitement among the "shipped," 393.
wages, 394.
shipbuilding, 35-37, 165, 378, 402, 403, 404.
boat-building at Cupids, 126.
Eskimo boats, 593.
Columbus caravels, 5.
size of ships, 23.
ships of Charles II.'s time, 165.
picture of small craft, 173.
French fishing boat, 570, 571, 576.
small-pox, 295.
soil, 715.
sport in, 62.
Cartwright's Journal, 600.
opportunities for, 631, 632.
sport, 716.
game laws, 717.
spruce beer, 136, 273.
steamers, first, 465.
steam communication, Galway line, 469, 635.
Sunday observance, 234, 253, 273.
survey, Mason's, 104.
Cook's, 316.
geological, 454, 496.
Fleming's, 500.
Bellair's, 501.
tariff of 1835, 440.
tavern licences, 356.
taverns, 157, 168, 204, 234, 271, 342, 373.
at St. Pierre in 1750, 567, 568.
names of, in John's, 381.
telescope, 131.
tilts, 264.
timber exports, 95, 620, 621.
timber, 715.
truck system, evils of, 380, 537.
tobacco, 108.
Yorke, 200.
trade to, 12, 107.
through, 145.
in, in Commonwealth, 162.
under Treworgie, 164.
walrus, killing, 60, 589.
weather in 1611-16, 125, 128.
great storm, 336.
in 1817, 405.
"winter of the Rals," 405.
in 1846, 461.
climate, 715.
wine to be exported from, to England, 95.
woollen trade with Ireland, 201.
POLITICS, Governor Treworgie, 160.
Governor's pay, Collins petitions for, 271.
Governor appointed, 283.
first appointed, 285.
want of civil government, 348.
poor relief, society for, in 1799, 373.
Gambier advocates local government, 376.
Carson's attack upon the system of government, 396.
first governor Pickmore, 406.
Butler v. Lundrigan, 411.
agitation for local government, 411.
Morris' pamphlet, 425, 426.

NEWFOUNDLAND—*cont.*
POLITICS—*cont.*
renewed agitation for local government, 427.
merchants' opposition, 428.
first house of assembly, 429.
local government granted, 429.
Kent's address, 430.
bow-wow parliament, 431.
opening of first house of assembly, 431.
legislative council formed, 433.
dispute between the two houses, 433, 435.
merchants' opposition, 435.
violence of the mob, 435.
contingency Bills, 436.
end of the first house of assembly, 438.
riots by Roman Catholic candidates, 438.
supply thrown out, 439.
house of assembly claims to appoint its own officers, 439.
elections declared invalid, 439.
contingency Bill, 440.
disputes between the houses, 443.
Privy Council advise moderation, 444.
Boulton dismissed, 444.
Kielly v. Carson, 445.
privilege of colonial members decided by Privy Council, 447.
the amalgamated legislature, 447.
House of Assembly dissolved, 447.
the amalgamated house, 450, 456.
original constitution restored, 457.
opening of the new legislature, 463.
English Government refuse responsible government, 463.
grant of responsible government, 464.
compensation to office holders and Representation Bill, 466.
the Representation Bill, 467.
first administration purely Roman Catholic, 468.
election note in 1861, 483.
attempt to form an amalgamated ministry, 484.
the election of 1861, 484.
the Burin election, 485.
Mr. Kent's administration, 485.
dispute about the coastal steamer, 486.
Bishop Mullock's letter, 486.
poor relief, 486.
Act for coastal steamers, 487.
dissension about poor relief, 488.
dispute about "sterling," 488.
Kent's accusation of Sir A. Bannerman, 488.
Sir H. Hoyle's administration, 488.
Riot in St. John's, 1861, 489.
Sir F. Carter's administration, 494.
poor relief, attempt to suppress, 496.
Bennett's administration, 497.
collapse of the Bennett administration, 499.

NEWFOUNDLAND—*cont.*
POLITICS—*cont.*
the "Tim Dobbin" commission, 500.
Sir W. V. Whiteway's administration, 506.
riot at Fox Trap, 512.
Harbour Grace riot, 513.
Sir R. Thorburn's administration, 514.
election of 1893, 529.
election petitions, 532, 661.
Ballot Act passed, 660.
manhood suffrage, 660.
Newman, C. D., 657.
Newman, R. L., 389.
Newman, W., 360.
house in Fort William, 328.
men, 298, 402.
and Co., 299, 390.
land, 305.
premises secured in 1846, 458.
rooms, 450.
trade to Labrador, 598.
Nicholls, Wm., 270.
Nicholson, Governor, 276.
Nielsen, A., 615, 648.
Nippers Harbour, 279.
Nisbet's Haven, 594.
Neven, G., 410, 411.
Noad, J., 457, 463, 465, 466.
Noble, —, 280.
Captain, 623.
Mr., 526.
and Pinson, 598, 599, 601.
J. Hatt, 360.
v. Kennoway, 598.
Noll, John, 239.
Noonan, J. H., 341.
Noonan, J. L., 665.
Norman Cape, 473, 557.
N., 665.
Norris, Adm., 222, 223.
portrait of, 222.
Col., 280.
Arm, 629.
Northmen, discoveries of the, 1, 587.
Eric, statue of, 2.
Norton, Chief Justice, T., 457, 663.
Norway, trade with, 25, 28.
Notre Dame, 278, 283.
Nowill, —, 280.
Nowlan, M., 460.
P., 488, 489, 664, 665.
Harbour, 617.
Nugent, —, 465.
J. V., 436, 438, 444, 657, 664.
portrait of, 444.

Oakley, J. T., 665.
O'Brien, Mr. (Colossus of Roads), 448.
L., 436, 455, 457, 465, 467, 484, 493.
portrait of, 493.
L. and Co., 460.
Lady, 529, 605.
portrait of, 530.
Sir T. N., 529, 604, 614, 615.
portrait of, 529.
harbour, 607.
Oderin, 165, 336.
O'Driscoll, —, 357.
O'Donel, Bishop, 363, 364, 382.
insult to, 367.
speaks well of Governor Waldegrave, 373.
O'Donnell, Father J., 489, 513.
O'Dwyer, R., 455.
R. & Co., 460.
Ogden, C. Justice J., 360, 374, 419, 662.
Ogilvie, B. Genl., 574.
O'Gormans of Burin, 574.

INDEX.

Okak, 595, 618.
Olonne, 570.
O'Mara, J., 446.
  J. T., 527.
  M. J., 665.
Openigevik Islands, 607.
Opot Portu, 48.
Orange, Great, Harbours, 321.
O'Reilly, Constable, 16.
Osborne, Capt., 284, 286, 301
Osmond (Murphy and), 621.
Oswald, Mr., 352.
Ougier, P., 390, 428.
Outer Cove road, 443.
Outerbridge, J., 529.
Oxford, Thomas, 176, 197.
  description of, destruction done in, Newfoundland, 194.

Pack, Gosse, and Fryer, 438.
Pack, R., 431, 664.
Packard's, Dr., book on Labrador, 610.
Packer, —, 301.
Pack's Harbour, 610, 617.
Pacquet Harbour, 576.
Paine, Mr., 109.
Palais, Cavalier de, 211.
Palliser, Sir H., 282, 317, 416, 599.
  portrait of, 318.
  Coghlan's letter to, 347.
  dismisses Placentia justices, 315.
  interest in Labrador, 324.
  letter to Bernard, 598.
  letter to Francklin about French Mic Macs, 330.
  protection of fishermen, 326.
  regulations for Labrador fishery, 537.
  support of the Moravians, 332.
  charges the French with bringing savages to Newfoundland, 591.
Paradise, 48, 610.
Parker, Ensign, 382.
  and Gleeson, 458, 460.
  Capt., 382, 654.
  Richard, 157.
Parkhurst's narrative, 34, 60.
Parmenius, 589.
Parsons, —, 294, 382, 654.
  E., 617.
  R., High Constable, 381.
  R. J., 431, 465, 468, 474, 664.
    portrait of, 474.
  R. J., junr., 665.
  family, 137.
Pasquiligo's letter, 11.
Paterson, Rev. G., on Portuguese discoveries, 10.
Payne, B., 296.
  C., 617.
Payzant and Frazer, 557, 559, 561.
Pearce, Capt., 156, 179.
  Mr., 226.
Pearl, Sir J., 427.
Peaseley, W., 132.
Peckham, —, 67.
  narrative, 76, 70.
Pelegrin, M., 573.
Pemberton, —, 244, 263.
Penhallow's description of the losses in 1696, 221.
Pennell, E. B., 515.
Pennock's Cove, 617.
Penny, —, 617.
  A., 665.
  Bros., 616.
  E., 616.
  Jos., 616.
Pepperell, —, 289.
Pepperill, W., 109.
Perchard, R., 381, 440, 460.
Percy, T., 19.
Perden, Henry, 271.

Perkins and Winter, 410.
  —, 599.
Perlican, New, 232, 301.
  Old, 232, 246, 270, 286, 301.
Perry, F., account of Atlantic cable, 642.
  portrait of, 642.
  H., 301.
Peters, J. E. P., 665.
Peterson, Capt. (Boston), 407.
Petit Maitre, 139, 248.
Petit Nord, 185, 246.
PETTY HARBOUR, 103, 230, 242, 281, 262, 263, 264, 266, 270, 271, 297, 301, 341, 349, 617, 653.
  D'Iberville's fight at, 215.
  view of, 242.
Peyton, T., 665.
Philips, Lieut., 269.
  mill, 621.
  J., 336.
  Mr., 270.
  N., 347.
Phillpotts, Lieut., 656.
Phippard, —, 393, 438, 655.
Pick Eye, 496.
Pickering, Capt., 252.
  Sir Gilbert, 167.
Pickmore, Sir F., 406.
Pidgeon, W., 301.
Pigeard, Capt., 473.
Pike, Alfred, 529.
  family, 137.
  John, 21, 292.
  R., 389.
Pinsent, family of, 222.
  Sir R., 71, 98, 296, 531, 663.
    portrait of, 521.
Pinson, 393.
  a justice for Labrador, 393, 602, 655.
  (Noble and), 598, 599, 601.
Pinware, 617.
Pirates attack St. John's, 174.
  damage by, 136.
  defence against, 183.
  Mason's Commission to suppress, 109.
Pistolet's map, 69.
Pitcher, T., 157.
Pitt's factories, 526.
  J. S., 529, 550.
  J. and W., 527.
  J. and W., send first cable, 640.
PLACENTIA, 48.
  description of, under the French, 180.
  Crevecour, 181.
  Castle Hill, 181.
  fortifications, 181.
  attacked by English, 182.
  views of, 182.
  plan of, 184.
  Aylrod's, John, description of Placentia, 185.
  view of farm and fishing stage, 186.
  Aylrod's account of, 206.
  garrisoned from Chedabucto, 209, 210.
  escape of English from, 213.
  D'Iberville at, 215, 216.
  Costabelle, Governor of, 217.
  Castle Hill, 237.
  Graydon's and Walker's attacks on, 237.
  defences of, 237, 239.
  Subercase, Governor of, 242.
  plan of, 248.
  compensation to Costabelle, 249.
  French surrender of, 258.
  terms of surrender, 259.
  attack from, 262.
  French chaplain at, 263, 266, 269, 270.
  fortifications at, 273.

PLACENTIA—cont.
  under government of Nova Scotia, 275.
  plan of, 276.
  Bay, 279.
  Governors Moody and Gledhill, 282.
  under Nova Scotia, 283.
  separated from Nova Scotia, 286.
  fishing at, 297.
  magistrates, &c. of, 301.
  Petty, 301.
  Graves defends, 307.
  English troops at, 314.
  Court House, 314.
  justices dismissed, 315.
  surrogate records, 315.
  Little, 315.
  trouble with the garrison, 328.
  William IV. at, 366.
    393, 395, 415, 438, 448, 457, 465, 467, 468, 498.
  advantages of railway to, 513.
  French occupation of, 542.
  date of Gargot's Commission, 566.
  settlers go to St. Pierre, 574.
  Junction, 625, 626.
  cable from, 643.
  model smoke-houses, 649.
  court house built, 653.
  J. Brown, appointed J.P., 653.
  members for, 664.
Pointestre and Robinson, 601.
Pole, Sir C. M., 374.
  portrait of, 374.
Pollard, 174.
  Christopher, 220.
Poutrincourt, 20.
Port-a-Port, 472, 473, 559, 561.
Porcen, M., 561.
Porter, R., 301.
Portucho, 48.
Portugal Cove, 20, 222, 232, 270, 296.
  French pretended to have landed troops at, 372.
  view of, 392.
  road, 427, 656.
  view of, 438.
PORTUGUESE, discoveries and names in Newfoundland, 10.
  claim to Newfoundland, 14, 15.
  fishery, 15.
  (Anglo-), trade to Newfoundland, 16.
  fishery, commencement of, 17.
  fleet, 20.
  fishery methods, 22.
  fishermen's dread of collector, 35.
  fishing in 1527, 41.
  fishery, 60.
  treatment of Gilbert, 70.
  ships captured by pirates, 102, 103.
  at Petty Harbour, 103.
  trade to Newfoundland, 267.
  Lisbon, 269, 272, 390.
  Oporto, 389.
  Fishing Company, 454.
  fishing at Straits of Belle Isle, 589.
Poulton, Capt., 275.
Povey's report, 169.
Powell's, Daniel, letter, 122.
Power, 438, 617.
  Bishop, 531.
  C., 381.
  D., 375.
  J., 375, 431, 438, 664.
  Lawrence, 343.
  R., 343.
  W., 375, 381.
Prendergast, J. L., 457, 468, 474, 664.

INDEX.

Prescott, Sir H., 436, 438, 447, 448, 456.
  portrait of Sir H., 448.
Preston (Hunt, Stabb, and) 348, 387.
Prim, P., 343.
Pring, M., voyage to New England, 86.
Pringle, Colonel, 341, 652, 653.
Prior's, M., report, 266.
Prowse & Sons, 527.
  at Calais roads, in the fireships, 82.
  D. W., 650, 664.
  R., 179, 196, 455, 460, 468, 474, 658, 664.
  S., 387, 393, 602, 655.
Punch Bowl, 610, 617.
Pyle, —, 161.
Pynn, J., 176, 194.
  family, 137.
  —, 249.
  W., 301.
Pynne, —, 245.

Queen's Lakes, 610.
Quenal, J., 333.
QUIDI VIDI, 176, 194, 196, 232, 261, 265, 266, 270, 271, 297, 301, 308, 349, 383, 412.
  view of, 10.
  losses in 1705, 246.
  Grove Farm, 296.
  view of, looking towards the scene of the fight in 1762, 307.
  view of, from Signal Hill, 308.
  Horwoods of, 309.
  land at, 337.
  views of, 360.
Quinn, —, 266.
Quirk, C., 381.
  N., 395.
Quirpon, 278, 281, 324, 410, 473, 476, 576, 594, 597.

Rabbit, W. J., 603.
Rabbits, Billy, 451.
  N., 665.
Race, Cape, 10, 461.
  via, 641.
Rade, de la, 132.
Radstock, Lord, 365, 372.
  letter to, 419.
  portrait of, 373.
Rae Island, 438.
Raftus, R., 721.
Ragged Harbour, 283.
  Islands, 610.
RAILWAY, proposed, 500.
  prosperity resulting from, in 1882, 509.
  Hall's Bay line, 506.
  advantages of a, 513.
  inception of the Hall's Bay line, 514.
  Placentia railway constructed, 514, 524.
  construction, 622.
  contractors fail, 623.
  line completed by the receiver, 623.
  Sir H. Allan's tender, 623.
  Sir W. Whiteway advocated construction by the Government, 623.
  receipts, 623.
  new tenders for Hall's Bay line in 1890, 624.
  proceedings against the contractors, 624.
  views on the, 624.
  proper terminus in St. John's, 624.
  bridges, views of, 622, 625, 627, 628, 630.

RAILWAY—cont.
  further contract of 1893, for Port-au-Basque line, 626.
  land grant, 627.
  connecting roads, 628.
Raleigh, Sir W., 66, 67, 68.
  portrait of, 75.
  fleet revictual in Newfoundland, 57.
  captain in Newfoundland, 103, 111.
Ramah, 595, 610, 618.
Rameau Island, 506.
Random Sound, 64.
Rankin, R., 664.
Ray, Cape, 353, 410, 506, 557, 558, 635, 636.
Raynor, Capt. John, 156, 178, 179.
Rebou [Bay Bulls?] 261.
Reculoux, Capt., 547.
Red Bay, Labrador, 604, 610, 616.
  Indian Lake, 325.
  Island, 472, 473, 477.
  views of French huts at, 256, 544.
Redhood, N., 179.
Redmond, P., 375, 381.
Redwood, 161.
Reed, M., 301.
Reeks, H., 717.
Reeve, Thompson, 272.
Reeves, Chief Justice, J., 358, 662.
  accused of peculation, 391.
  portrait of, 358.
  Col. G., 656.
Reichel's map of Labrador, 594.
Reid, R. G., 620, 621.
  and his labourers view of, 622.
  portrait of, 624.
  and Middleton's contract, 625, 626.
  T., 347.
Reilly, L., 315.
Rendell, —, 382, 655.
  G. T., 526, 529, 676.
  J., 665.
  J. M. & Co., 460.
  S., 297, 665.
  W. & G., 527.
Renewse, 120, 242, 301, 351, 405, 406.
  Denys at. 17.
  French propose to settle at, 230.
Rennie, Stuart, & Co., 367, 393, 450, 657.
Renou, M., 268.
Renouf, J., 460.
  Hon. H., 499, 664.
Resolution Head, fishing at, 607.
Rex, H., 301.
Reynell, Mr., 196.
Reynolds, Colclough writes to, at Lisbon, 390.
Ribero's map, 15, 599.
Rice, Rev. Jacob, 255, 272.
  R. P., 655.
Richards, Major, 223, 252.
Riche Point, 258, 289, 312, 557, 562.
Richery, Admiral, 367.
  destroys St. Pierre, 574.
Ridley, Mr., portrait of, 451.
  T., 455, 457, 664.
  T. H., 467, 685.
Rigoulette, 610, 617.
  post to, 609.
Rivers, Col., 237.
Roach (Stabb and) 556, 558, 561.
ROADS, primitive paths through the woods, 114.
  Baudoin's description of the, 233.
Road making, 336, 427, 448, 454, 619, 656.
  expenditure, 429.
  connecting with railway, 628.
Robe, Major, 458.

Robinson, Sir B., 446, 449, 457, 465, 469, 488, 500, 501, 636, 663, 664.
  portrait of, 484.
  Capt. Sir R., 174, 175, 202.
  G. R., 382, 427, 429, 655.
  Brooking & Co., 458, 460.
  Mrs., celebrated, 599.
  (Pointestre, and), 601.
Roberrow, John, 93.
Roberts Bay, 301, 484.
  trade to, Labrador, 602.
  Lewis, 596.
  M. O., 637.
  portrait of, 638.
  Philip, 217, 230, 231.
Roberval's voyages, 45.
Robins of Jersey, 601.
Rotz map, 34.
Rochfort, J., 411, 467.
Rock Point, Bay of Islands, 473.
Rodger (Marshall and), 527.
Rodney, Lord, 284, 290.
  portrait of, 291.
Rogerson, J. J., 474, 485, 467, 529, 664.
  portrait of, 474.
  P., & Co., 458, 460.
Rogerson's Bill to regulate the Labrador passenger traffic, 603.
Roland, Rev. Mr., 393, 655.
Rolls, J., 665.
Rolson, —, 174.
Roope, John, 241, 244, 246, 262, 263.
Rorke, J., 509, 617, 665.
Rose, J., 301.
Ross, W., & Co., 617.
Rothwell, E., 665.
  and Bowring, 527.
Rouge, Cape, view of French stages at, 258, 548.
  Ile, 354.
Roupe, Melle, 266.
Rouse, —, 301.
Routh, Chief Justice R., 356, 360, 653, 662.
  drowned, 374.
Row (Stabb, and Holmwood), 459.
  T., 467.
  portrait of, 467.
  W. B., 432, 433, 438, 455, 457, 461, 465, 664.
Rowland, Rev. D., 655.
Rowsell's, 280, 297.
Rudkin, Capt., 656.
Rumkey, Mr., 556.
Russell, Capt., 205.
  Mr., 179.
  Thomas, 269, 270.
Rutherford, R. & A., 460.
Rut's voyage, 38–41.
Ruyter, Admiral, 197.
Ruysch's map, 14.
Ryan, —, 382, 655.
  —, 441.
  Bill, 493.
  D., 451.
  J., 380, 411, 617.
  L. W., 411.
  T., 654.
Ryoes, Matt, 78.

Sabine's statement about Labrador, 597.
Saint, J., 665.
Sale, Lt.-Col., 434, 437.
Sallee Rovers, 108, 145.
Salmon Cove, 131.
  view of, 136.
  Trinity, 520.
  Labrador, 617.
  River, 609, 616.
  T., 301.
Salmonier, views of, 187, 216.
Salvage, 186.

INDEX.

Sampson's, R., account of campaign of 1705, 262, 266.
Sandhill, 617.
Sandwich Bay, 617.
Saunders Port, 557, 560, 561, 562.
Savage Harbour, Trinity Bay, 123.
  Islands, 477, 557.
Savalet, Captain, 20, 37.
Sawley, John, 199.
Scaffold of the grapple, 139.
Scallan, Bp., 408, 426.
Scanlan, T. D., 196, 640.
  portrait of, 640.
Schenk (Hounsell, and Hounsell), 459.
Schlozer, —, 594.
Schlozer, C. A., 332.
Schuyler, Lt., 309, 413, 414.
Scuffington, George, 241, 245, 264, 274, 283.
Scilly Cove, 232, 239.
Solater, J. B., 529.
Sconce, R., 655.
Scotchman, 316.
  Cull, Laird of, 704.
  Dundee whalers at the seal fishery, 491.
  trade, 348.
Scotland, Orkney fishery, 16.
Scott, Ensign, 382, 655.
  Mr., of Fogo, 606.
  P. T., 532, 665.
  Sir J., Mason's letter to, 105.
Scott's expedition to exploits, 324.
SEAL FISHERY, 20, 43, 62, 186, 230, 296, 298, 378, 402, 406, 450.
  sea cow fishery, 334.
  Gambier advocates, 375.
  of 1814-5, 402.
  account of, in 1802, 419.
  Spring, 450.
  Dundee sealers, 452, 491.
  steamers at the, 493.
  pictures of, 452, 453.
Seal Islands, 602, 609, 610, 617.
Seeley, W., 699.
Seire, M., 414.
Seldom-Come-By, 279.
  telegraph to, 639.
Seller's map, 177.
Selman, C., 157.
Señoria, 48.
Sesostris Bay, 562.
SETTLEMENT, winter crews, 59.
  at St. John's, 72.
  ship fishermen's rule, 83.
  in early times, 93.
  attempt to grant land to Guy's Company possessed by Englishmen, 94, 195.
  saw mill damaged, 96, 98, 103.
  carts loaded with caplin, 106.
  fishing in December, 106.
  by poor Devonshire fishermen, 113.
  of Torbay, Pouch Cove, Grates, and Bonavista, 114.
  early, at Harbour Grace, 137.
  early, 140.
  planters not to build within six miles of the coast, 143.
  rents — "a flat hog," 157.
  planters encouraged by Treworgie, 163.
  Hinton's application for governorship, 175.
  necessity for governor, 175.
  method of collecting taxes, 176.
  at Placentia, 178.
  opposed at Placentia, 184.
  Child's argument against settlement and a governor, 188.
  Board of Trade recommend deportation of settlers, 191.
  wealth of settlers, 195.

SETTLEMENT—cont.
  stay of order for depopulation, 196.
  petition for fortification, 201.
  23 March 1697, permitting settlement near the shore, 204.
  permitted, 205.
  planters' aid to fishermen, 206.
  Downing's account of, 207.
  order for stay of depopulation order, 208.
  attacks on by French in 1695, 209.
  Beaudoin's account of the, 218.
  wealth of the, 219, 232.
  character of the, 221.
  losses in 1676, 221.
  allowed by Act of William III., 225.
  Act of William III., 233.
  losses in 1705, 246.
  statistics, 251.
  Capt. Crowe's laws, 254, 271.
  planters do observe the Act of William, 267.
  planters' terms of surrender, 270.
  Sir N. Trevanion's laws, 272.
  at Bonavista, 278, 285.
  at Twillingate, 279.
  occupation of French rooms, 281, 282, 283.
  Court House erected, 287.
  servants' wages, 291.
  planters' loyalty, 338, 350.
  fixed settlements to be removed on the French shore, 353.
  houses built contrary to the law, 395.
  titles to land granted, 395.
  north of Bonavista, 476.
  at Twillingate and Fogo, 552.
  wine obliged to be taken with a cargo of salt, 567.
  settlers right at St. Pierre sacrificed, 567.
  permission to erect permanent houses, 655.
Settlers occupy French rooms, 281.
Shannon, Lieut., 382, 655.
Shapleigh family, 163, 427.
Shaughroo, —, 567.
Shea and Murphy, 460.
Shea and Co., 527.
Shea, Sir A., 348, 440, 465, 466, 467, 474, 485, 493, 494, 504, 505, 508, 658, 660, 664.
  portrait of, 500.
  Hon. E. D., 348, 468, 474, 529, 640, 664.
  portrait of, 473.
  G., 665.
  Dr. H., 348, 382, 397, 411.
  Lt., 654.
Shearer (Forest and), 540.
  factory, view of, 540.
Shearer, Mr., 557.
Shecatica Bay, post from, 608.
Shephard, G., 375.
Sheppard, J., 294, 301.
Ship Cove, 520.
SHIP FISHERMEN, English rule over foreign fishermen, 29.
  for stalling fish, 33.
  Sir T. Hampshire's regulations, 61.
  Reception of Gilbert, 68.
  completely rule Newfoundland, 83.
  hostility to Guy's settlement, 99.
  duties levied on, by Guy's company, 100.

SHIP FISHERMEN—cont.
  petition against planters, 100.
  "West and by law," 130.
  monopoly, 138.
  exempted from Kirke's government, 145.
  royalties, 152.
  duty on salt remitted, 173.
  remission of all duties on fish, 173.
  Child's defence of, 188.
  Board of Trade recommend deportation of settlers, 191.
  destroy stages, 194.
  Losses in 1696, 221.
  Rights under, 225.
  description of fishing admirals, 225, 226.
  "Governors," 226.
  "King," 226.
  bye-boat keepers, 228, 297.
  attitude of, in 1705, 242.
  selling prices, 252.
  Western Charter, 267.
  reception of Captain Crowe's laws, 255.
  Sir N. Trevanion's regulations, 272.
  unite with planters, 275.
  tyranny of, 283.
  attack Governor Osborne, 286.
  Rodney's reply to, 291.
  opposed to Treaty of Paris, 313.
  neglect to pay customs, 316.
  Palliser favoured, 318.
  Labrador under William III.'s rules, 327.
  opposition to Custom House, 338.
  Cleeves, William, first admiral of St. Pierre, 591.
  wine obliged to be taken with a cargo of salt, 567.
  early English fishery at Labrador, 589.
  ships' rooms abolished, 655.
Shirley, Sir A., 57.
Shoal Harbour, road to, 628.
  view of, 622.
Shockney, J., 567.
Short, S., 616.
Shuldham, Lord, 335.
  portrait of, 335.
Signat, P., 301.
Simms, C., 459, 663.
  H., 656.
  Hon. James, 430, 434, 437.
  portrait of, 430.
Simms, J., 617.
Simpson, Lieut., 382, 655.
Simpson, J. E., and Company, 509.
Sinclair, J., 437.
Skekel, Capt., 393, 655.
Skelton, G., 721.
Skerret, Col., 364, 374, 418.
Skinner, Col., 368, 418, 427, 654.
Slade, John, 281, 336, 457, 664.
  Elson, and Company, 438.
Slade's trade to Labrador, 597, 598.
Slaney, John, 109.
Sloop Cove, Labrador, 610, 617.
Sluyter, —, 638.
Small Harbour, 473.
Smith, Captain John, 88.
  Edward, 460.
  J. W., 455.
  portrait of, 455.
  Sir D. A., present of a yacht to the Deep Sea Mission, 605.
  W., 616.
Smoky, 617.
  Tickle, 610.
Snell, George, 199.
Snow, —, 294.
Snug Harbour, 610, 617.

INDEX.

Solomon, S., 380, 382, 654.
W., 380.
Soncino's letter, 11.
Soper, —, 617.
Sop's Arm, 476.
Soulis Brook, 621.
   Furring at, 610.
Southmayd, A., 270, 288, 301.
Soward, J., 567.
SPANISH claim to Newfoundland, 15.
   Ayala's letter, 29.
   Agramonte's charter in 1511, 43.
   San Sebastian law suit, 44.
   method of annoying, 66.
   treatment of English prisoners, 68.
   Sir B. Drake's expedition to Newfoundland, 79.
   Elizabeth's policy in fighting, 80, 81.
   Armada, 81.
   fleet, destruction of the, 81.
   claim to Virginia, 89.
   voyage to, 153.
   ships' pay and licences, 168.
   fishing fleet, 186.
   with French in 1705, 265.
   claim to fish in Newfoundland, 310.
   war declared with, 311.
   traders, 453.
   slavers in St. John's, 454.
   San Sebastian records, 589.
   Navarrese traditions about Labrador, 590.
   importation of fish forbidden, 652.
   Biscayans, 35, 78, 133, 183, 186, 206, 273, 453, 589.
   fishery, 43–45, 47–49, 60, 63, 137.
   at Labrador, 587.
   tradition about Labrador, 590.
   in Newfoundland in December, 95.
   at Placentia, 276, 277.
   rights in Newfoundland, 274.
   rights finally relinquished, 320.
   in St. John's, 266.
   at St. Pierre, 565.
   sealers, 20.
   whalers, 596.
   Bilboa, 152.
   Corunna, 390.
   Malaga, 104, 152.
   Seville, 38.
   San Sebastian, 565.
   St. Jean de Luz, 20, 48, 68, 186, 570.
   St. Mary's Port, Murcia, 47.
   Cuñega, Don Pedro, 89.
   Navarrete, 43, 587.
Spaniard's Bay, 20.
Spear, Cape, 49, 270.
   Lighthouse at, 656.
   Harbour, 610.
   Isle of, 271.
Spearman, J. M., 437, 464, 757.
Spencer, Bp., 443, 451.
Spenser, —, 163.
Sport. See N., Miscellaneous.
Spotted Island, 602, 605, 617.
Spracklin's, 602, 617.
   Island, 610.
Spracklin, T., 617.
Spratt, Lt., R.N., 654.
Spooner, —, 655.
Spurrier, W., 336.
   firm of, 165.
Square Island, 610.
Squary, T. and J., 270, 271.
Stabb, Ewen, 387.
   portrait of, 387.

Stabb—cont.
   E. & N., 458, 460.
   Dr. H., 387.
   H. J., 527.
   Hunt, and Preston, 348, 387.
   N., 387.
   Row, and Holmwood, 459.
   and Roach, 556, 559, 561.
   T., 387.
Stafford, Capt., 271.
Stag Bay, post to, 609.
Stanford, Lt., 333.
St. Antony, fishing at, 576.
Stapley, Col., 167.
Starve Harbour, 278.
St. Barbe, 556, 560, 561, 562.
   Members for, 655.
Stearns, J. B., system of duplexing, 645.
   Account of Labrador, 610.
Steel, Sargeant, 269, 298.
Steer, J., 665.
Stephanius, map of, 8.
Stephenson, Capt., 382, 654.
Sterritt's Mill, 621.
Stevens, —, 301.
   Mrs., 527.
Stewart, Broom, 382, 655.
   J., 393, 403.
   J. and W., 458, 460.
   M., 455.
St. Francis, Cape, 492.
St. George's Bay, 472, 546, 549, 581, 629.
   settlers forbidden to sell bait, except to the French, 355.
   view of, 639.
   telegraph to, 639.
   Members for, 655.
   Cape, 39.
St. Jean, J., 354.
St. John, A. S., 375.
   family, 438.
   Cape, 274, 353, 472, 505, 552, 558.
ST. JOHN'S:
   Admiral's Beach, 339, 344.
   Amherst Tower, 349.
   Alsop's, 387.
   Bally Haly, 341, 395.
   barons of, 326
   Barter's Hill (?), 271.
   Beck's Cove, 401.
   Bennett's wharf, 387.
   Boucher's farm, 381.
   Brooking's flakes, near, 386.
   Bursthart Hill (Barter's Hill), 271.
   Bulley's farm, 381.
   Carpasian, 426.
   Chain rock, 267, 369.
   Battery, 349.
   boom for, 224.
   Chamber of Commerce, 393, 427.
   Church Hill, 410, 446.
   Clapp's, 410.
   Cochrane Street, 424.
   Colonial Buildings begun, 657.
   Commercial Society, 391.
   Commercial Buildings burnt, 459.
   Cordage Company's mills, 511, 512.
   Cottage farm, 654.
   Court House, burnt, 459.
   finished, 287.
   Crow's Nest, 368.
   Custom House begun, 657.
   burned, 458.
   Devon Row, 427.
   Dock at River Head, 509.
   view of, 510.
   Dover's [Robinson's] Hill, 336.

ST. JOHN'S—cont.
   Duckworth Street, width of, 709.
   Duder's farm, 426.
   wharf, 387.
   Duke of York's battery, 369.
   Eden's shop, 390.
   Elliott's, D., shop, 410.
   Ellis estate, 336.
   Fort William, 203, 223, 230, 231, 340, 369, 418.
   description of, 231, 263, 258.
   houses in, 271.
   Wood's house in, 328.
   destroyed, 270.
   houses around, pulled down, 328.
   houses in, 271.
   rebuilt, 249.
   taken, 248.
   repair of, in 1709, 271.
   Fort Amherst, 370.
   Fort Frederick, 369.
   Fort George, 223.
   Fort Townshend, 336, 341, 349, 418, 652, 708.
   completed, 653.
   Frederick's battery, 349.
   Friendly Hall, 336.
   Gallows Hill, 295.
   George Street, fire of 1847 commenced in, 458.
   Gill's, 458.
   Gower Street opened in 1804, 654.
   Holbrook's farm, 427.
   Hospital, 360, 655.
   Hudson's Cove, 305, 381.
   Hunter's Cove, 292, 305.
   Keen's, 292, 410.
   King's Road, 336, 339, 410, 652.
   Langman's garden, 363.
   London Tavern, 382, 395.
   Maddock's Lane, 410.
   Maggott's Cove, 241, 298, 370.
   Magotty Cove, fire of 1846, 458.
   Major's Path, 341.
   McBride's Hill, 305.
   site on, 336.
   Market House opened, 657.
   Military Road, 336, 424, 652.
   Mount Pearl, 427, 449.
   Newman's flakes, 386.
   Old Chapel, 363.
   Ordnance Wharf, 410.
   Orphan Asylum School, 656.
   Post Office built, 660.
   Prescott St., 305.
   Pringle's Bridge and Dale, 336, 341.
   Queen's Wharf, 142, 244, 262.
   Rawlin's Cross, 390.
   River Head, ship stationed at, 349.
   grant of land to Bishop O'Donel at, 654.
   Robinson's Hill, 336.
   duel on, 656.
   Rope walk, 510.
   Ross' Valley, 395.
   Rostellan, 427.
   St. Andrew's Kirk opened, 657.
   St. Patrick's Hall, 660.
   St. Thomas's Church moved, 461.

INDEX

St. John's—cont.
  Signal Hill, French barracks, 306.
    road, 336.
    fortified, 368, 418.
    water from, 657.
  South side, 230, 294.
    castle, 241, 249, 263, 265.
  Stabb's house, 458.
  Stripling's plantation, 337.
  Taverns, names of, 381.
  Tobin's buildings, 455.
  Virginia Water, 424.
  Water Street properties, 336.
  Water Street, width of, 709.
  Yallow Belly Corner, 401.

St. John's, EVENTS CONNECTED WITH.
  first mention of, 41.
  Roberval at, 45.
  Gilbert at, 67.
  importance of the trade at, in 1583, 69, 70.
  grant of land by Gilbert, 72.
  Peckham's proposal to fortify, 77.
  Sir B. Drake in, 79.
  value of the fish caught in 1620, 106.
  colony, boundaries of, 110.
  the metropolis of the fishery, 113.
  colony, 131.
  attacked by Dutch, 174, 175, 176, 183.
  disorder in, 192, 194, 196.
  fort at, begun, 203.
  Kirke's fortifications at, 205.
  DeBrouillon's attack, 215.
  losses in 1696 at, 221.
  fortification of, 223.
  boom for, 224.
  Privy Council decide to fortify, 224.
  church at, 228.
  scalping of William Drew, 230.
  description of, 232.
  attack on, 242.
  losses in 1705, 246, 264.
  attack on in 1708, 248, 266, 268.
  centre of the English trade, 238.
  St. Ovide appointed governor, 270.
  fortifications at, 285.
  stocks, 287.
  French prizes, 294.
  new church, 295.
  magistrate, &c. of, 301.
  French capture, 306.
  Signal Hill, McDonell's captur of, 308, 412.
  doctors in, 324, 343.
  trouble with garrisons, 328.
  justice at, 336.
  "a town," 341.
  expected attack on, in 1780, 350.
  not attacked by U.S.A. privateers, 351.
  courts, 357.
  chain across the harbour, 370.
  magistrates, 374.
  Beothic woman in, 377.
  constables, 381.
  a commercial port, 383.
  appearance of, in 1811, 386.
  fire brigade, 386.

St. John's, EVENTS CONNECTED WITH—cont.
  lease of rooms, 386.
  full of ships of war, 387.
  faction fights, 391, 401.
  population of, 397.
  fires in 1816, 1817, 405, 408.
  Act to regulate the rebuilding of, 409.
  rebuilt, 409.
  conspiracy in 1800, 418.
  disturbances in, in 1836, 438.
  fire of 1846, 457.
  church burnt, 458.
  jail and bank burnt, 459.
  municipal improvements advocated, 461.
  cholera, 468.
  riot of 1861, 489.
  water supply, 493.
  fire of 1892, 521.
  insurance, 526.
  encampment after the fire of 1892, 528.
  Baron le Noury at, 581.
  Moravians at, 594.
  Basques rendezvous at, 596.
  riots in, in 1766, 652.
  Charity School Society formed, 654.
  presentation by Phœnix Insurance Co., &c., 654.
  grant of land to Bishop O'Donel at Riverhead, 654.
  population, 654, 655.
  theatre, permission asked to open, 654.
  duel on Robinson's Hill, 656.
  Library Society formed, 656.
  Mechanic's Society formed, 656.
  gas introduced, 657.
  water from Signall Hill, 657.
  exhibition in, 657.
  garrison withdrawn, 657.
  municipal council for, 658.
  members for, 664.

St. John's, VIEWS OF.
  view of the Narrows, 67.
  Thornton's, plan of, 193.
  plans of, 204, 292, 296.
  views of, 348, 360.
  Crow's Nest, view of, 369.
  view of, 374.
  view of Woodland Cottage, 406.
  view of Colonial Buildings and Government House, 424.
  view of Water Street in 1837, 445.
  views of, 450, 458.
  Narrows, view of, 456.
  plan of the harbour, 459.
  the Narrows, view of, 483.
  landing of Prince of Wales, 486.
  view of sealing ships, 492.
  before the fire, view of, 498.
  Cordage Co.'s Mills, view of, 511, 512.
  plan of, 522.
  view of, 522.
  views of Anglican Cathedral after the fire, 524, 525.
  view of, 526.
  view of encampment for fire sufferers, 528.

St. John's Island, 477.
  Isles, 562.

St. Julian, 248, 282, 321, 354, 477.
  views of French stages at, 256, 548.
  fishing at, 576.
St. Lawrence, 48, 165, 185, 246, 324, 389.
  telegraph to, 639.
St. Lewis Sound, 665.
St. Lucia, Cape, 30.
St. Margaret's Bay, 540, 561.
St. Mary's, 48, 78, 179, 185, 186, 210, 246, 262, 279, 286, 298, 301, 306, 336, 344, 393, 566.
  Members for, 664.
St. Modeste, Isles, 472, 617.
St. Nicholas, 39.
Stokes, Lt., 294.
  Mr., 427.
Stone, T., 301.
Stott, J., 527.
Stourton, Rev. Erasmus, 101, 138.
St. Ovide. See De Brouillon.
St. Paul's Bay, 559, 561, 592.
ST. PIERRE, 48, 185, 186, 259, 389 472, 477, 478, 479, 562.
  Rice fishing at, 52.
  fortifications at, 206.
  murder at, 305.
  cession of, 311, 312.
  English Commissary to reside at, 312.
  not to be fortified, 312.
  smugglers captured at, 321.
  French opinion of, 322.
  not to be fortified, 322.
  smuggler captured at, 324.
  population at, 326.
  French curé and flock leave, 330.
  French traders to, 330.
  Palliser's opinion of, 330.
  French reported to be fortifying, 333.
  taken by the English, 346, 367.
  French destroy, 371.
  surrendered to the French, 377.
  taken in 1814, 408.
  fishery failing, 540.
  French occupation of, 542.
  all attempts to appoint a Consul refused, 545.
  ceded for a shelter only, 545.
  German gin at, 547.
  bounty given and men encouraged to desert on the Treaty Shore, 553.
  description of, 564-586.
  Chateaubriand at, 572.
  revolution in 1785, 572.
  Tree of Liberty at, 573.
  taken by Admiral King, 574.
  fishing at, 576.
  spreading fish, view of, 577.
  revenue derived from smuggling, 579.
  smuggling into Canada and Newfoundland, 579, 580.
  confiscation of codfish, 581.
  views of, 582.
  Clapboard revolution, 582.
  coup d'etat, 582.
  disciplinaires at, 582.
  Chateaubriand's account of, 585.
  imports, &c. of, 586.
  cable to, 643.
  taken by Buchan in 1815, 655.
Strange, R., 52.
  fishing at Magdalen Islands, 77.
Street, T., 164.
Stretton, Rev. J., 652.
Strickland, Mr., 167.
Stripling, John, 294, 326, 339, 344.
St. Shotts, 210.
  wreck at, 655.

INDEX.

Stuart, Rennie, & Co., 367, 460, 657.
— J., 454, 455, 485.
— portrait of, 485.
Studdy family, 227.
Studdy, J., 665.
Subercase, Governor, 242, 244, 261, 264, 266.
Sullivan Bat, 487.
Sutherland, Major, 412.
Sutton, R., 272.
Sweetman, R. F., 431, 664.
Swingston, J., 339.

Table Bay Point, 617.
Tait, Dr., 665.
Talbot, Hon. T., 438, 465, 468, 489, 500, 657, 664.
— portrait of, 490.
Talbot, Sir R., 132.
Tasker, D., 392.
Taverner, Capt., 219, 596.
— Jacob, of Trinity, 301.
Taylor and Cooper, 560, 561.
— F., 400.
— Moses, 637.
— portrait of, 638.
— Mr., 529.
Taylour, A., 263.
— Commodore J., 249, 270.
— J. P., 284, 299.
Teesdale, Capt., 488.
TELEGRAPH:—
Atlantic cable first laid, 496, 640.
Anglo-American pre-emption, 497.
arrangement as to railway, 627.
Bishop Mullock's letter, 634.
St. John's and Carbonear line, 635.
Local Act authorizing, 635-6.
Newfoundland Electric Telegraph Company, 636.
New York, Newfoundland, and London Telegraph Company formed, 637.
"Times" declares a cable impracticable, 639.
"Victoria" towing the "S. L. Bryant," picture of, 639.
"Heart's Content" landing the cable, 641.
"cable skit," 643.
modern instruments and duplex, 644.
first message, 659.
Temple Bay, 598.
— Sir R., 148.
Templeman, Mr., 449.
Terra Nova River, 621, 629.
Tessier, C., 529.
— L., 665.
— (Langley &), 460.
— P. G., 508, 615.
— (Thorburn &), 527.
Tetlow, T., 84.
Thirkhill, L., 4, 12.
Thistle family, 137.
— T., 301.
Thomas, Captain, 382, 654, 655.
— A., diary at St. Pierre, 574.
— family, 427.
— H. P., 427.
— portrait of, 427.
— J., 4, 13, 471.
— N., 402.
— title, 337.
— W. B., 427, 429, 431, 432, 433, 434, 437, 457, 463, 664.
— W. and H., 387.
— & Co., 460.
— Wm., 295.
Thoumassey, W., 294.

Thompson, J., 665.
— S., 502.
— v. Williams, 654.
Thorburn and Tessier, 527.
Government build Placentia line, 624.
— Lady, 455.
— Sir R., 495, 508, 514, 529, 614, 615, 665.
— portrait of, 514.
Thomey, A., 690.
— J., 575.
Thorne, R., 30.
— map, 38.
Thorne's, Major, dinner party, 574.
Thornton's map, 1689, 203.
— of S.E. coast of Newfoundland, 192.
Thoroughgood, T., 161.
Three Islands, 48, 185.
Tibbetts, H. B., 636.
Tieldad, J., 262.
Tilt Cove, 279, 496, 658.
— telegraph to, 639.
Tilton Harbour, 378, 683.
Timber. See N., Miscellaneous.
Tinker's Harbour, 610.
Toad's Cove, 271, 301.
— view of, 162.
Tobin (Bland &), 456.
— Hon. J., 457, 467, 497.
— J., & Co., 460.
Tocque, Rev. P., 368.
Tomlinson, Colonel, 167.
Tonge, Capt. W., 382, 654.
Toole, M., 402.
Topsail, 427, 512.
— road, 427.
— railway at, 623.
— Hill, views of, 136, 239.
TORBAY, 270, 271, 272, 288, 297, 301, 305, 308, 341, 412, 415.
— view of, 10.
— road, 427.
Tory, R. and M., 476.
TREATY of—
Aix-la-Chapelle, 290.
American, 400.
Amiens, 377, 543, 544, 575.
Breda, 148.
Ghent, 403.
Paris (1763), 309, 317, 320, 323, 333, 337, 552, 567, 598.
Paris (1814-5), 408.
Ryswick, 225.
St. Germains, 147.
Utrecht, 255, 258, 275, 281, 311, 322, 542, 552, 566.
Versailles, 259, 353, 354, 552, 554.
Washington, 501-3.
Trelawney of Richmond Island, 164.
Tremlett, charges against, 390.
— Chief Justice T., 360, 361, 362, 662.
Trepassey, 48, 111, 174, 182, 210, 246, 262, 286, 297, 301, 348, 416, 542.
Trevanion, Sir N., 254.
— regulations, 272.
Treworgie, John, 161, 163, 199, 205, 427, 542.
— just rule, 163.
— arrest, 164.
— instructions, 167.
— petition, 168.
— services, 169.
Trimingham, —, 382, 655.
TRINITY, 115, 122, 239, 248, 249, 262, 296, 336, 360, 438, 457, 465, 468.
— Whitbourne at, 63.
— plan of, 193.
— view of, 61.
— losses in 1705, 246.
— troops at, 297.
— magistrates, &c. of, 301, 393.

Trinity—cont.
doctors at, 360.
seal fishery, 451.
advantages of railway to, 619.
road to, 628.
telegraph to, 639.
members for, 664.
Trinity Bay, 19, 120, 245, 263, 264, 271, 286.
farming land in, 607.
disaster of 1892, 520.
Tronty, 520.
Trott, S., picking up cables, 546.
— portrait of, 646.
Trout, N., 197.
See game laws, 717.
Trusler, W., 301.
Tub Harbour, 617.
Tucker, Col., 417.
— Hugh, 271.
— Rev. H. W., 444.
— J., 417.
— Lt., 294.
— Chief Justice, R. A., 421, 433, 434, 656, 662.
Tullikin, Lt.-Col., 412.
Tully, W., 361.
Turf, Mr. and Mrs., 271, 272.
Turk's Gut and Cove, 146.
— Island, 345.
Turnavick Islands, 610, 617.
Turner, Wm., 315.
Tweed Island, 477.
Twillingate, 226, 279, 280, 281, 336, 350, 467, 468.
view of, 350.
seal fishery, 451.
settlement at, 542, 552.
trade to Labrador, 597, 602.
advantage of railway to, 619.
telegraph to, 639, 641.
members for, 664.
Tyson in the West Indies, 61.

Udell, J., 616.
Underdown, Capt. John, 247, 253.
Ungava Bay, 587.
— post to, 607, 609.
Uriarte, Don H. de 464.
UNITED STATES OF AMERICA:—
AMERICA, first Act relating to, 33.
confederation, 293.
molasses duty, 299.
revolution, 339.
Continental Congress, 335.
attempts to induce Newfoundland to join the Union, 338.
faction hurt in Newfoundland, 338.
treatment of Royalists, 339.
independence recognised, 349.
capture of Lawrence's despatches, 351.
capture of York Town, 351.
claim fishery rights, 352.
second American war, 397.
Madison's position, 337.
Convention with, 409.
flag hoisted in St. John's, 474.
civil war, 491.
Washington treaty, 501.
fishery award at Halifax, 503.
deep-sea fishing decaying, 533.
tourists to Labrador, 610.
supports Atlantic telegraph, 639.
consumption of fish, 629.

INDEX.

UNITED STATES OF AMERICA—*cont.*
AMERICA—*cont.*
New York, price of fish in, 630.
Newfoundland capable of supplying fresh fish to, 631.
"Fresh fish and Fulton Market," 631.
map of shortest sea route to Europe, 631.
privateers, 340, 350, 388.
sketch of the capture of an American vessel, 346.
privateer in Labrador, 598.
smugglers, 378.
fishermen and traders, 375.
provisions imported, 383.
trade with Newfoundland, 393, 394.
freighters, 454.
St. Pierre, trade at during the war, 570.

AMERICANS:
Amory, J., jun. (Boston), 407.
Barnard, Governor of Mass., 327, 598.
Barnard, Tristram, of Boston, 407.
Benjamin's, S. G. W., description of Bay of Islands, 629.
Bradstreet, Col. John, 284, 290.
Bryant's description of the Grand Falls, 611.
H. G., portrait of, 611.
Carey's, Austin, journey to the Grand Falls, 611.
Cole's, D. M., journey to the Grand Falls, 611.
Cooper, P., 637.
portrait of, 637.
Gardner, Dr., 349, 356.
Field, Cyrus W. *See.*
Franklin, B., 352.
Houston, J., of Boston, 407.
Hubbard's account of Newfoundland fishermen, 153.
Hunt, W. G., 637.
Madison, President, 387.
Mason, Capt. J. *See.*
Maury, Lt., 637.
Morse, Professor, 637.
Nelson, Mr., of Boston, 266.
Packard, Dr., 610.
Perkins, J. (Boston), 407.
Quincy, Josiah, 300.
Rich, B. of Boston, 407.
Roberts, M. O., 638.
portrait of, 638.
Shapleigh, J., 163.
Sluyter, —, 636.
Smith, Capt. J. *See.*
Spencer, Miss, 163.
Taylor, Moses, 638.
portrait of, 638.
Treworgie, J. *See.*
Welch, Capt., 299.
White, Chandler, 637, 638.
Willis, A., 407.
Windthrop, Gov., 152.

MAINE, State of, 21, 153.
Kittery, 163.
Piscadawery, 199.
Eskimo in, 591.
Bowdoin College students reach the Grand Falls, 611.

MASSACHUSETTS, 190, 222.
Cape Ann, 324.
Boston, 152, 266, 284, 316, 380.
Port Bill, 417.
privateer at Labrador, 600.
assistance from, in 1817, 407.
relief from, 529.

UNITED STATES OF AMERICA—*cont.*
MASSACHUSETTS—*cont.*
Charlestown, 152, 239.
Lynne, 154.
Marblehead, 153, 324.
Newberry, 163.
Plymouth Company levy licence fees on English fishermen, 120.
Salem, 199.
York, old, 567.
New Hampshire, 104.
NEW ENGLAND, 155, 159, 162, 211, 288.
settled for fishing, 18.
ship fishermen held Newfoundland, 83.
jealousy of Newfoundland, 88.
Pilgrim Fathers, 89.
settlement, 88, 89, 90.
influence on Newfoundland, 90, 91.
trade with Newfoundland, 145, 151-3, 197, 267, 272, 283, 299, 300, 329.
Captain West's commission, 121.
petitions against cession of Nova Scotia, 148.
passengers to, 153.
coinage, 153.
smuggling fishermen away, 153, 199, 267, 273, 323, 342.
Puritans, 155, 159.
under Cromwell, 164.
agent in Newfoundland, 166, 348.
remission of taxation for consumers of fish, 173.
suffered by surrender of Placentia, 178.
Child's attack on, 189.
fishery in Newfoundland, 191.
Massachusetts bounty for emigrants, 199.
lists of ports and masters trading from, 200.
emigration to, 202.
danger to, from French, 203.
boards, 205.
Downing's account of trade with, 205, 206.
French proposal to destroy, 214.
alarm in, at the destruction of St. John's in 1696, 222.
Royal letter to Governor of Massachusetts Bay, 222.
provisions from, for St. John's, 223.
French propose to attack, 230.
artillerymen, 240.
copy of town meeting in Newfoundland, 254.
exchange on Boston, 264, 266.
power to Custom House officers to search ships, 268.
reason of, fishery in Newfoundland, 268.
aliens forbidden to fish, 273.
"rum and molasses," 273.
trade with the French, 289.
feeling in, 290.
Cape Cod whalers and sealers, 296.

UNITED STATES OF AMERICA—*cont.*
NEW ENGLAND—*cont.*
whalers and sealers, 298.
smugglers, 299, 323, 324.
influence in 1763, 312.
Custom House placed under Boston, 316.
new Custom regulations, 323.
Palliser's treatment of, 325.
whalers in Labrador, 327.
vessels seized, 328.
Custom House severity, 333.
bankers in 1741, 334.
reckless destruction of sea cows at Magdalen Island, 336.
traders at Labrador, 336.
excluded from the Newfoundland fishery, 344.
fish, 346, 347.
agent in St. John's, 348.
"King George" privateer, 415.
at St. Pierre, 568.
smuggling at St. Pierre, 578.
French smuggling into, 579, 580.
in Labrador, 594.
traders to Labrador, 597.
important trade with Labrador, 597, 598.
ships from, 652.
NEW YORK, 151, 415.
view of, in 1673, 152.
Holy Trinity Church, 653.
Sandy Hook, 151.
PENNSYLVANIA, 272.
VIRGINIA, 151, 163, 273.

Vaches, Les, 477.
Vanbrugh, Capt., 280, 284.
Vane, engineer, 269.
Vaughan, Sir W., 110, 137.
colony, boundaries of, 110.
"Golden Fleece," 135.
Veitch, J., 665.
Venison Island, 610.
Tickle, 617.
Cape Islands, 137.
Verd Point, 181.
Verds, Bay de, 178, 232, 246, 262, 286, 296, 301, 468.
members for, 664.
Vergennes, C. de, 352.
Vertes, Isles of, 472.
Verrazano's voyage, 37.
Viegas, G., map, 11.
Viguers, R., 568.
Villala, Capt., 557, 562.
Vincent, Amos, 292.
Virginia Lake, 195.
view of, 470.

Wade at Iron Strand, 602.
Waghorne, Rev. —, 717.
Wakeham, R. R., 411, 428, 436, 439, 441, 455.
Walbank, M. W., 468, 664.
Waldegrave, Admiral, *see* Radstock.
Walker, Admiral Hovenden, 182, 237.
Walker, Sir B., 549.
Wallace, Sir R., 368, 370.
Wallis, John, 174.
Admiral Provo, 390.
Walsh, D., 440.
M., 391.
P., 381.
W., 455.
W. P., 527, 529, 665.

INDEX.

Warde, R., 4, 13.
Warren, Admiral, 289.
   of Rennie, Stuart, & Co., 367.
   Bros., 460.
   J. H., 460, 465, 468, 664, 665.
   M. H. lecture, 341.
   W., 460.
Waterman, R., 301.
Watson, Admiral, 84.
   J. H., 615, 616, 665.
Way, Elizabeth, 427.
Weatherbee, Mr., 502.
Webb, Governor, 285, 304, 567.
Webber, —, 294.
   D. C., 665.
Welch, Capt. M., at Boston, 284, 299.
Welsh colonists, 113.
   M., 375.
   W., 375, 381.
Wescott, Attorney-General, 411.
West and Rendell, 527.
West Coast, French ships on, 354.
   no French on the, 576.
   map of, 558.
Western ships' room, 409.
Weston, Mr. 334.
   P., 305.
   treasurer, 133.
   W., 288, 301.
   Capt., 239.
Whale fishery in Fortune Bay, 298.
Whalers from Cape Cod. 296.
Whaling, 20, 60, 63, 327.
   by Basques, 43, 596.
   picture of, 80.
Wheler, Capt., account of Placentia, 183.
Whetstone, Admiral, 237.
Whitbourne, Sir R., in Newfoundland in 1583, 61.
   account of, 79.
   at Vaughan's colony, 111.
   narrative, 116.

Whitbourne—*cont.*
   petition for employment, 118.
   commission, 267.
   Junction, 513.
   railway to, 623.
White, Capt. Hon. E., 227, 336, 339, 344, 355, 492, 665.
   P. D., 665.
White Bay, 247, 279, 597.
   seals in, 492.
White Bear Bay, Newfoundland, 42.
   Harbour, 610.
White, Chandler, 637, 638.
White Hill plains, 629.
White Island, 278.
Whitely, W. H., 616, 665.
   room, view of, 608.
Whiteway, Sir W. V., 428, 495, 501, 502, 506, 508, 514, 529, 550, 614, 6, 5.
   advocates construction of railway by local government, 623.
   portrait of, 506.
Whittington, Capt., 64.
Whittle, Mr. 529.
Widdicomb, J., 375.
Widdomas, G., of Berry Pomeroy, 157.
Williams, Commodore, 182, 211.
   George, 375, 652, 653.
   Griffith, 296, 427, 652, 653.
   John, 381.
   nurse, 615.
   T., 301, 382, 654, 655.
   Harbour, 617.
   title, 337.
   v. Thompson, 654.
Willis, Ensign, 382, 655.
   A., of Boston, 407.
Willoughbee, Sir P., 137.
Wilson & Co., 460.
   ——, 617.

Winchen, Mr., 269.
Winser, P., 438, 465, 468, 664.
Winser Harbour, 610, 617.
Winsor, 617.
Winter (Perkins and), 410.
   Dr. J., 468, 614.
   Sir J. S., 49, 529, 532, 660, 663, 665.
   portrait of, 531.
Winthrop, Governor, 152.
Winton, F., 665.
   H., 428, 441.
   attack on, 436, 438.
Withers (Ryan &), 441.
Witless Bay, 271.
Wolfenbüttel map, inscription on, about Labrador, 590.
Wollaston, Capt., 103.
Wood (Clift & Co.), 527.
Wood, F. A. 614.
   J. B. 455, 665.
   Samuel, 174.
   W. O., 665.
Woodford, W. J., 665.
Woods, H. J. B., 529, 665.
   J. & Sons, 526.
   S., 527.
   J. & Sons, 527.
Wright, Nathan, 149.
Wrixon, Amy and William, 155.
Wyatt, F. J., 665.
Wyng, Wm., 280.

Yore, Father, 364.
Young, at Calais Roads, in the fire ships, 82.
   A., 345.
   J., 171.

Zealot, fishing at, 576.
Zoar, 595, 618.